International Directory of

COMPANY
HISTORIES

International Directory of

COMPANY

HISTORIES

VOLUME 52

Editor

Jay P. Pederson

ST. JAMES PRESS®

Detroit • New York • San Diego • San Francisco • Cleveland • New Haven, Conn. • Waterville, Maine • London • Munich

International Directory of Company Histories, Volume 52

Jay P. Pederson, Editor

Project Editor
Miranda H. Ferrara

Editorial
Erin Bealmear, Joann Cerrito, Jim Craddock,
Stephen Cusack, Peter M. Gareffa,
Kristin Hart, Melissa Hill,
Margaret Mazurkiewicz, Carol A. Schwartz,
Christine Tomassini, Michael J. Tyrkus

Imaging and Multimedia
Randy Bassett, Dean Dauphinais, Robert
Duncan, Lezlie Light

Manufacturing
Rhonda Williams

LIBRARY OF CONGRESS CATALOG NUMBER 89-190943

ISBN: 1-55862-482-1

BRITISH LIBRARY CATALOGUING IN PUBLICATION DATA

International directory of company histories. Vol. 52
I. Jay P. Pederson
33.87409

Printed in the United States of America
10 9 8 7 6 5 4 3 2 1

CONTENTS _____

Company Histories

PREFACE _____

The St. James Press series *The International Directory of Company Histories (IDCH)* is intended for reference use by students, business people, librarians, historians, economists, investors, job candidates, and others who seek to learn more about the historical development of the world's most important companies. To date, *IDCH* has covered over 5,900 companies in 52 volumes.

Inclusion Criteria

Most companies chosen for inclusion in *IDCH* have achieved a minimum of US$25 million in annual sales and are leading influences in their industries or geographical locations. Companies may be publicly held, private, or nonprofit. State-owned companies that are important in their industries and that may operate much like public or private companies also are included. Wholly owned subsidiaries and divisions are profiled if they meet the requirements for inclusion. Entries on companies that have had major changes since they were last profiled may be selected for updating.

The *IDCH* series highlights 10% private and nonprofit companies, and features updated entries on approximately 45 companies per volume.

Entry Format

Each entry begins with the company's legal name, the address of its headquarters, its telephone, toll-free, and fax numbers, and its web site. A statement of public, private, state, or parent ownership follows. A company with a legal name in both English and the language of its headquarters country is listed by the English name, with the native-language name in parentheses.

The company's founding or earliest incorporation date, the number of employees, and the most recent available sales figures follow. Sales figures are given in local currencies with equivalents in U.S. dollars. For some private companies, sales figures are estimates and indicated by the abbreviation *est.* The entry lists the exchanges on which a company's stock is traded and its ticker symbol, as well as the company's NAIC codes.

Entries generally contain a *Company Perspectives* box which provides a short summary of the company's mission, goals, and ideals, a *Key Dates* box highlighting milestones in the company's history, lists of *Principal Subsidiaries, Principal Divisions, Principal Operating Units, Principal Competitors,* and articles for *Further Reading.*

American spelling is used throughout *IDCH,* and the word ''billion'' is used in its U.S. sense of one thousand million.

Sources

Entries have been compiled from publicly accessible sources both in print and on the Internet such as general and academic periodicals, books, annual reports, and material supplied by the companies themselves.

Cumulative Indexes

IDCH contains three indexes: the **Index to Companies**, which provides an alphabetical index to companies discussed in the text as well as to companies profiled, the **Index to Industries**, which allows researchers to locate companies by their principal industry, and the **Geographic Index**, which lists companies alphabetically by the country of their headquarters. The indexes are cumulative and specific instructions for using them are found immediately preceding each index.

Suggestions Welcome

Comments and suggestions from users of *IDCH* on any aspect of the product as well as suggestions for companies to be included or updated are cordially invited. Please write:

The Editor
International Directory of Company Histories
St. James Press
27500 Drake Rd.
Farmington Hills, Michigan 48331-3535

ABBREVIATIONS FOR FORMS OF COMPANY INCORPORATION

A.B.	Aktiebolaget (Sweden)
A.G.	Aktiengesellschaft (Germany, Switzerland)
A.S.	Aksjeselskap (Denmark, Norway)
A.S.	Atieselskab (Denmark)
A.Ş.	Anomin Şirket (Turkey)
B.V.	Besloten Vennootschap met beperkte, Aansprakelijkheid (The Netherlands)
Co.	Company (United Kingdom, United States)
Corp.	Corporation (United States)
G.I.E.	Groupement d'Intérêt Economique (France)
GmbH	Gesellschaft mit beschränkter Haftung (Germany)
H.B.	Handelsbolaget (Sweden)
Inc.	Incorporated (United States)
KGaA	Kommanditgesellschaft auf Aktien (Germany)
K.K.	Kabushiki Kaisha (Japan)
LLC	Limited Liability Company (Middle East)
Ltd.	Limited (Canada, Japan, United Kingdom, United States)
N.V.	Naamloze Vennootschap (The Netherlands)
OY	Osakeyhtiöt (Finland)
OAO	Otkrytoe Aktsionernoe Obshchestve (Russia)
OOO	Obshchestvo s Ogranichennoi Otvetstvennostiu (Russia)
PLC	Public Limited Company (United Kingdom)
PTY.	Proprietary (Australia, Hong Kong, South Africa)
S.A.	Société Anonyme (Belgium, France, Switzerland)
SpA	Società per Azioni (Italy)
ZAO	Zakrytoe Aktsionernoe Obshchestve (Russia)

ABBREVIATIONS FOR CURRENCY

$	United States dollar	KD	Kuwaiti dinar
£	United Kingdom pound	L	Italian lira
¥	Japanese yen	LuxFr	Luxembourgian franc
A$	Australian dollar	M$	Malaysian ringgit
AED	United Arab Emirates dirham	N	Nigerian naira
B	Thai baht	Nfl	Netherlands florin
B	Venezuelan bolivar	NIS	Israeli new shekel
BFr	Belgian franc	NKr	Norwegian krone
C$	Canadian dollar	NT$	Taiwanese dollar
CHF	Switzerland franc	NZ$	New Zealand dollar
COL	Colombian peso	P	Philippine peso
Cr	Brazilian cruzado	PLN	Polish zloty
CZK	Czech Republic koruny	PkR	Pakistan Rupee
DA	Algerian dinar	Pta	Spanish peseta
Dfl	Netherlands florin	R	Brazilian real
DKr	Danish krone	R	South African rand
DM	German mark	RMB	Chinese renminbi
E£	Egyptian pound	RO	Omani rial
Esc	Portuguese escudo	Rp	Indonesian rupiah
EUR	Euro dollars	Rs	Indian rupee
FFr	French franc	Ru	Russian ruble
Fmk	Finnish markka	S$	Singapore dollar
GRD	Greek drachma	Sch	Austrian schilling
HK$	Hong Kong dollar	SFr	Swiss franc
HUF	Hungarian forint	SKr	Swedish krona
IR£	Irish pound	SRls	Saudi Arabian riyal
ISK	Icelandic króna	TD	Tunisian dinar
K	Zambian kwacha	W	Korean won

International Directory of

COMPANY
HISTORIES

ABC Family Worldwide, Inc.

500 South Buena Vista Street
Burbank, California 91510
U.S.A.
Telephone: (818) 560-1000
Fax: (818) 560-1010
Web site: http://www.abcfamily.com

Wholly Owned Subsidiary of The Walt Disney Company
Incorporated: 1989 as International Family Entertainment
Employees: 1,239
Sales: $724.24 million (2001)
NAIC: 512110 Motion Picture and Video Production;
515120 Television Broadcasting

ABC Family Worldwide, Inc. is one of a slew of cable networks owned by The Walt Disney Company. Operating as a companion channel for broadcaster ABC, ABC Family boasts more than 80 million subscribers in the United States. Programs airing on the network in 2002 included *8 Simple Rules for Dating My Teenage Daughter, Less Than Perfect,* and *That Was Then.*

Origins

When the corporate banner ''ABC Family Worldwide'' was first unfurled, executives at ABC, and their overseers at The Walt Disney Co., found themselves staking a flag on an asset bearing the fingerprints of two previous owners. ABC Family Worldwide, in its new guise, represented the third incarnation of a cable network started by televangelist Marion G. Robertson, more commonly known as Pat Robertson. Although the cable network was frequently tinkered with, rebuilt, reconfigured, and revamped, the three major chapters in its history were engendered by the contrasting philosophies espoused by its owners.

Robertson gave up his job working for W.R. Grace in the late 1950s after becoming ''born again.'' A talk given by a missionary at a New York hotel dramatically changed Robertson's perspective on life, prompting him to rush home, throw away a bottle of Ballantine scotch, take down a print of a Modigliani nude hanging in his living room, and enroll in a seminary school. After receiving a degree in sacred theology in 1959, Robertson bought a UHF station in Virginia, preferring television as his pulpit because the medium ''was a terrifically powerful means of telling people about the Lord,'' according to his March 17, 1997 interview with *Variety.* Before long, Robertson had accumulated a string of UHF stations running from Virginia to Boston, the beginning of what became the Christian Broadcasting Network. In 1977, five years before Robertson sold his UHF stations, he began satellite broadcast of the Christian Broadcasting Network, airing the first show from the Mount of Olives in Israel.

Robertson's network essentially served as the vehicle for the televangelist's signature program, *The 700 Club,* a Christian newsmagazine show and prayer hour. Aside from *The 700 Club* and other Christian programs he produced, Robertson acquired other programming, provided it did not conflict with his strict moral code of conduct. When Robertson announced his candidacy for president in 1987, his son, Tim, began running the network, serving as president and chief executive officer. Among the first changes made by the younger Robertson was a name change, redubbing the channel The Family Channel. ''We became aware we had to have a clear brand identification,'' Tim Robertson said in a March 17, 1997 interview with *Variety.* ''People didn't know what (Christian Broadcasting Network) was and they didn't care. The minute you see 'Family' in all the listings, you know what we are. It really gave us a lift.''

The Family Channel's performance within the Christian Broadcasting Network caused a problem not long after the name change. The channel was generating sufficient amounts of profits to create a tax issue for the nonprofit Christian Broadcasting Network. Consequently, a new company, International Family Entertainment, was created in 1989. The following year, International Family acquired The Family Channel from the Christian Broadcasting Network for $250 million.

After Pat Robertson's failed presidential campaign, Tim Robertson continued serving as president and chief executive officer. During the early 1990s, he focused on increasing The Family Channel's original programming, scoring considerable success in his efforts after acquiring MTM studios from a bankrupt British company in 1993. The acquisition, completed at a bargain price, gave International Family its own production

Company Perspectives:

ABC Family—powered by the ABC brand and the resources of The Walt Disney Company—is the destination for quality, contemporary family entertainment. ABC Family offers a variety of programming appealing to all ages in the household—with an emphasis on adults ages 18–49. Distributed in over 80 million homes via cable and satellite, ABC Family is the only national family channel, providing viewers with the best in original and acquired movies, series, and specials.

arm to make Family Channel movies and programs for syndication. After installing a new production and programming team in early 1995, the network began to display substantial strength, presenting a lineup of syndicated programs such as *The Waltons* and *Rescue: 911* in primetime, *Home & Family* and original game shows during the day, and original movies on Sunday nights. The Family Channel's ratings began to rise, prompting a host of media companies to take notice, including News Corp., run by mogul Rupert Murdoch.

1997 Acquisition by Fox

During the mid-1990s, Murdoch was endeavoring to combat cable stalwart Nickelodeon by creating a channel geared for children. As part of his effort, Murdoch partnered with a production company named Saban Entertainment, run by Haim Saban, whose claim to fame was the hugely popular television program *Mighty Morphin Power Rangers*. In 1995, the combination of Saban's company and Fox Kids Network created Fox Family Worldwide, Inc. (FFW). Murdoch, through News Corp., expressed interest in the network run by the Robertsons in 1996. In 1997, Murdoch and Saban struck a deal, paying between $1.7 billion and $1.9 billion for International Family, thereby gaining ownership of The Family Channel.

The change in ownership led to the second incarnation of The Family Channel. FFW executives, following Murdoch's mandate, sought to attract children and their parents to the newly reconstituted Fox Family Channel, but what they inherited was the legacy of a televangelist. Roughly 60 percent of the viewers were more than 50 years old. The programming geared for children and teens was minimal, prompting new Fox management, led by Rich Cronin, to implement a thorough reconstruction of the network. Management discarded programs such as *Diagnosis Murder* and *Hawaii Five-O,* and in their place built a lineup of acquired television series, movies, and specials tailored for children and teens during the day and family audiences during primetime. The attempt to lure a new stratum of viewers failed. In a May 28, 2001 interview with *Variety,* an FFW executive explained. "We flipped the switch on the programming changes in August 1998," Maureen Smith remarked, "and the 50-plus audience went away in droves, causing our household ratings to take a serious hit." Later in the interview, Smith continued: ". . . viewers perceived the new schedule as designed for kids. And during the day the kids did watch the channel. Unfortunately, their parents didn't show up at night."

In the wake of the August 1998 relaunch of the network, FFW labored to find its balance. Ratings fell, exacerbating the

sting of a financial blow wrought by the acquisition of Robertson's International Family Entertainment. During the first six months of 1998, FFW reported a loss of $53 million after posting a profit of $40 million a year earlier, before the purchase of International Family Entertainment. The network floundered for much of 1999, as the realization sank in that the company had missed its target in the August 1998 re-launch. Cash flow, which had stood at $142.5 million in 1998, fell to $115.2 million in 1999. Primetime ratings for the beleaguered Fox Family Channel dropped 30 percent in 1999. Midway through the year, Saban had to secure a $125 million loan from Fox to pay off FFW's creditors and thwart a technical default on the network's $710 million bank loan.

The enterprise that had flowered during decades of existence under Robertson's leadership quickly soured in the grasp of Murdoch and Saban. Rumors of unrest between the two partners began to surface in 1999, with Murdoch reportedly rankled by Fox Family Channel's performance. Industry insiders speculated that Murdoch was considering exercising an option in his contract that allowed him to acquire Saban's 49.5 percent stake in FFW. Officials from both Murdoch's and Saban's camps denied the rumors, but there was no denying FFW's troubles.

Wholesale changes arrived in 2000, some initiated by executive order and others stemming from internal distress that smacked of a crew abandoning a sinking ship. During the first six months of the year, five high-ranking executives left FFW, including its president, Rich Cronin, who had been hired to spearhead the development of new programming in 1998. Cronin was fired in May 2000, followed by the resignation of Tom Lucas, FFW's senior vice-president of marketing. Several weeks later, Rick Sirvaitis, FFW's president of sales, also resigned, fueling another round of speculation by industry observers. A former Fox executive, wishing to remain anonymous, was quoted in the June 26, 2000 issue of *Electronic Media,* saying, "You've lost Cronin, you've lost Lucas, you've lost Sirvaitis. It's not a happy place right now." With the absence of the executives, FFW scrambled to cover its deficiencies in marketing, sales, and programming supervision. Saban assumed control over the day-to-day activities associated with FFW's sales and distribution.

Amid the turmoil, the business press published reports that Murdoch and Saban were looking to sell FFW, asking for an estimated $4 billion. As opposed to 1999, industry pundits in mid-2000 claimed it was Saban who was considering invoking the buyout clause in his contract with Murdoch's News Corp. A source, speaking on the condition of anonymity, was quoted in the June 26, 2000 issue of *Electronic Media* as saying, "Saban is absolutely over it—he wants out. He's just trying to make sure he gets a premium for it." In the same issue of *Electronic Media,* Saban fired back at the allegations that he was forsaking his turnaround efforts for brokering the largest sum for his stake in FFW. "It's categorically not for sale now—and not for sale ever," he averred. "We are absolutely committed to making this channel work."

In late 2000, Saban activated the clause in his contract with Murdoch that forced the News Corp. chairman to buy out his partner. The business marriage was over, but Murdoch preferred to sell FFW rather than acquire Saban's stake. Murdoch,

Key Dates:

1960s: Pat Robertson begins acquiring television properties, marking the beginning of the Christian Broadcasting Network (CBN).
1988: CBN Cable changes its name to The Family Channel.
1989: International Family Entertainment is formed to acquire The Family Channel.
1993: International Family Entertainment acquires MTM studios.
1997: Rupert Murdoch's News Corp. acquires International Family Entertainment, creating Fox Family Worldwide.
2001: The Walt Disney Company acquires Fox Family Worldwide, creating ABC Family Worldwide.

through News Corp., began searching for an interested party, reportedly engaging in discussions with a list of potential suitors that included AOL Time Warner, Walt Disney, Viacom, Sony, NBC, MGM, and Comcast. Roughly six months after Saban announced his desire to cut his ties to FFW, negotiations stalled, reportedly because Saban refused to back down from $6 billion as the price tag for FFW. Meanwhile, conditions at the network, whose management had fallen to a Fox veteran, Maureen Smith, in June 2000, had not improved. Average household ratings in primetime dropped nearly in half, falling from a 1.3 average in 1998 to a 0.7 average in mid-2001.

2001 Acquisition by Disney

Eventually, a willing buyer for the troubled network was found. Michael D. Eisner, chairman and chief executive officer of Walt Disney Co., decided to acquire FFW, officially announcing the deal in July 2001. Despite the lackluster performance of the network, Eisner was excited about the acquisition, envisioning the strength FFW could add to Disney's property, broadcaster ABC. In a July 24, 2001 interview with the *Rocky Mountain News,* Eisner said, "This is really a unique purchase—a beachfront property which gives us unlimited growth. Combined with our current television assets, we can find ways to cross-utilize and cross-package the networks and their content." The deal closed in October 2001 for $5.2 billion, $100 million less than the price announced during the summer. For the price, the Disney empire eliminated a direct competitor to the Disney Channel in children's and family entertainment, gaining 81 million U.S. subscribers, 24 million subscribers in Europe, and ten million subscribers in Latin America. The acquisition also gave Disney a controlling stake in publicly traded Fox Kids Europe.

Following its purchase by Disney, FFW was put in control of the ABC Television Group and its name changed to ABC Family Worldwide. Plans for the new addition surfaced in late 2001, when ABC announced that it would revive ABC Family's vitality by using it as a secondary outlet for a range of programs, including primetime dramas such as *Alias,* family comedies such as *The Wonder Years,* and possibly repackaged news from ABC. Armed with a sister channel, ABC also was able to join in

a growing trend that saw many in the broadcasting industry "repurpose" programs, that is, rebroadcast a program on cable shortly after it had appeared on network television. "Repurposing" was pioneered by USA Networks, Inc. in 1999, when the cable network aired NBC's *Law & Order: Special Victims Unit* nine days after the program had first appeared on the NBC network.

New ownership of the former FFW also meant new management. Maureen Smith agreed to guide the network through its transitional period as it moved from Fox to ABC, a period that ended in the spring of 2002. Smith was replaced by Angela Shapiro, who had joined ABC in 1995 as senior vice-president of marketing and promotion at ABC Daytime. In 1998, she was appointed president of ABC Daytime, later earning the additional title of president of Buena Vista Productions, a business that also served Disney's programming interests in cable and broadcast syndication. Under Shapiro's rule, which began in April 2002, ABC Family was expected to project a much broader definition of family, as Shapiro targeted the 18- to 34-year-old demographic coveted by advertisers. "The great part of being part of the Walt Disney Co. are synergies," Shapiro remarked in an April 1, 2002 interview with *Variety.* "If you look at the record of what we've done at ABC Daytime and Buena Vista Productions, we've partnered well with news, primetime, theme parks. We will look to do the same in the early stages at ABC Family."

Looking ahead, the future was uncertain for ABC Family. By September 2002, the network was undergoing its third major reconfiguration in four years, yet to shake free from the anemic performance tainting its operation under the management of Cronin and Smith. Under Shapiro, the network was recasting itself, developing a new lineup and a new brand identity. Starting in January 2003, Shapiro planned to air a Monday night schedule of original reality shows anchored by *My Life As a Sitcom.* More immediate plans called for the network to tout itself as "ABC Plus" on Saturday nights beginning in October 2002. Among the programs to be included on Saturday night were *8 Simple Rules for Dating My Teenage Daughter, Less Than Perfect,* and *That Was Then.* Considering the network was in the process of negotiating carriage deals with cable operators such as Time Warner Cable, Cox Communications, and Cablevision Systems late in 2002, the success of the new lineup promised to decide much.

Principal Competitors

Fox Entertainment Group, Inc.; National Broadcasting Company, Inc.; Viacom Inc.

Further Reading

Burgi, Michael, "Extending the Family," *MEDIAWEEK,* July 22, 1996, p. 24.
——, "Find a New Family: Cronin Plans Makeover of Channel in Daytime/Prime Split," *MEDIAWEEK,* November 3, 1997, p. 8.
Dempsey, John, "Fox Family Put Up for Adoption," *Variety,* May 28, 2001, p. 13.
"Fox Family Enters the Mouse House," *Business Week Online,* July 24, 2001, p. 4.
"Fox Family Joins Disney," *Rocky Mountain News,* July 24, 2001, p. 7B.

Goldner, Diane, ''Cabler's 'Club' Has Financial Afterlife,'' *Variety,* March 17, 1997, p. 48.

——, ''Clean, Safe, Successful,'' *Variety,* March 17, 1997, p. 37.

Grego, Melissa, ''ABC Family Divides: Smith Exits, Shapiro In,'' *Daily Variety,* March 27, 2002, p. 5.

Higgins, John M., ''Rupert Stretching Until It Hurts?,'' *Broadcasting & Cable,* January 15, 2001, p. 107.

Katz, Richard, ''Family Way Tough Fit for Fox,'' *Variety,* October 26, 1998, p. 71.

Larson, Megan, ''Fox in a Box on Saban,'' *MEDIAWEEK,* January 1, 2001, p. 5.

McConville, Jim, ''Fox Family on the Block; Saban, News Corp. Believed to Want $4 Billion,'' *Electronic Media,* June 26, 2000, p. 2.

Romano, Allison, ''No Room for Ma, Pa in Family,'' *Broadcasting & Cable,* September 30, 2002, p. 6.

Verrier, Richard, ''ABC Plans Close Ties to Sister Cable Channel,'' *Los Angeles Times,* December 3, 2001, p. C1.

Zoglin, Richard, ''A Devilishly Good Deal for the Family Channel,'' *Time,* May 12, 1997, p. 65.

—Jeffrey L. Covell

Adelphia Communications Corporation

One North Main Street
Coudersport, Pennsylvania 16915
U.S.A.
Telephone: (814) 274-9830
Toll Free: (800) 892-7300
Fax: (814) 274-8631
Web site: http://www.adelphia.com

Public Company
Incorporated: 1972
Employees: 15,735
Sales: $3.58 billion (2001)
Stock Exchanges: NASDAQ
Ticker Symbol: ADELQ
NAIC: 513210 Cable Networks

With more than 5.8 million subscribers in 37 U.S. states and Puerto Rico, Adelphia Communications Corporation is one of the nation's leading cable service providers. Adelphia achieved exponential growth in the 1980s and 1990s through aggressive acquisition strategies. Having made significant investments in fiber optic technology in the 1990s, Adelphia has added digital cable, high-speed Internet access, local and long distance telephone service, voice messaging, and other related services to its repertoire of home and business offerings. The company ran into significant trouble in 2002 when its fraudulent financial dealings and accounting practices were exposed. As a result of the scandal, founder John Rigas and his family ceded control of the company, and Adelphia filed for Chapter 11 bankruptcy protection. The company then entered a period of reorganization.

The Growth of Adelphia and Cable Television: Early 1950s to 1980s

The corporate roots of Adelphia Communications were inseparably linked with the Rigas family, whose experience in the cable television business predated the incorporation of Adelphia Communications by more than three decades. The patriarch of the family, John J. Rigas, first entered the business during its nascence in 1952 when he started his first cable system in Coudersport, Pennsylvania, with his brother Gus Rigas. The name chosen for the company—Adelphia—is the Greek word for "brothers," an apt corporate title for a business that would employ generations of the Rigas family. Then in his early 20s, John Rigas entered an industry in its infancy when he started Adelphia, unwittingly laying the foundation for what would become one of the largest cable television companies in the United States. It would be years, however, before the Rigas family could claim they stood atop a cable empire. Cable television was decades away from enjoying widespread popularity, decades away from the years that would witness the exponential growth in the number of subscribers across the country. Those days arrived during the 1980s, when Rigas, with lengthy experience as a cable television operator, stood poised to reap the rewards from an industry fast on the rise.

Although Adelphia Communications did not officially exist until 1972, the company entered its inaugural year of business with a considerable head start over other fledgling cable operators. The company served as an umbrella organization for the centralization of the various cable properties owned by Rigas, and, consequently, was supported by more than 20 years of experience from its outset. Adelphia Cablevision, Inc., the cable company started by Rigas in 1952, was the oldest of the five cable companies that Rigas reorganized into one company on July 1, 1986. Joining Adelphia Cablevision were Clear Cablevision, Inc., Indiana Cablevision, Inc., Western Reserve Cablevision, Inc., and International Cablevision, Inc., serving a combined total of 200,000 subscribers.

Together these companies formed the new Adelphia Communications, a Coudersport, Pennsylvania-based cable systems operator beginning business with $30 million in annual sales. In less than a decade the company's sales volume would increase more than tenfold and its number of subscribers would rise sixfold, as Rigas moved aggressively to expand his cable television holdings. In the years ahead the five original components of Adelphia Communications would be joined by a host of other established cable systems as Rigas, with his three sons at his side, mounted an aggressive acquisition campaign.

Company Perspectives:

At Adelphia, we recognize that our present and future success depends on each customer's trust in our ability to deliver quality products and service. Our goal is to earn our customers' trust by making sure that every customer is satisfied with the outcome of every contact (s)he has with our people and service we provide. We have not completed our job until we meet this goal 100% of the time.

The company achieved prominence early on in western Pennsylvania and in western New York, where Rigas first established a presence in Niagara Falls in 1972. The addition of International Cablevision—one of the five original companies that formed Adelphia Communications—elevated Rigas's company to the number one position in western New York, giving the company 120,000 subscribers to add to its roster of customers. After taking Adelphia public in August 1986, Rigas completed the acquisition of three cable systems before the end of the year, purchasing the Suburban Buffalo System from Comax Telcom Corp., the South Dade System from Americable Associates, Ltd., and New Castle System from Cablentertainment, Inc.

Expansion Through Acquisitions in the Late 1980s

During the ensuing two years Rigas spearheaded the acquisition of more than ten cable systems, bolstering Adelphia's presence in western New York and extending its area of service into neighboring states. By the end of 1989 the company owned cable television systems throughout an eight-state region comprising Florida, Massachusetts, Michigan, New Jersey, Ohio, Pennsylvania, Vermont, and Virginia. Adelphia lost money each year during its expansion, but perhaps more important to the long-term health of the company was the manner in which it had expanded.

A strategy had emerged during the first few years of the company's existence, one that dictated the direction of its expansion during the late 1980s and continued to describe its physical growth during the 1990s. Instead of purchasing cable systems merely for the sake of increasing the company's magnitude, Adelphia targeted cable systems for acquisition that neighbored existing Adelphia systems, striving to entrench the company's position through acquisition rather than embracing as large a territory of service as possible. The benefits of grouping cable systems together would manifest themselves as Adelphia entered the 1990s, making the company an industry leader and reducing the sting of consecutive money-losing years.

Although the company's profitability had suffered as a result of the ambitious expansion, its revenue-generating capabilities had not. From the $30 million generated in sales during its first year, annual sales shot up to $131 million in 1988, increasing more than fourfold during a three-year span. Further financial growth was expected as the company's physical growth continued unabated, but as before, Rigas made it a practice to set his acquisitive sights on cable systems in proximity to Adelphia systems already in operation. One significant acquisition was the purchase of Jones Intercable in late 1989. Jones Intercable

ranked as the third largest cable system operator in western New York, an area where Adelphia already reigned as the largest cable operator. Further, Jones Intercable in many cases operated in locations near towns that Adelphia already served, making the acquisition a strategic boon to the company's plan to develop an entrenched market position wherever it operated. Noting as much, Michael Rigas (John Rigas's son and Adelphia's vice-president) elaborated on the company's acquisition of Jones Intercable by remarking, "Whenever possible we look for systems that are adjacent to other systems that we own. Generally speaking, we try to cluster our systems together."

Another pivotal transaction completed in 1989 provided Adelphia with a powerful money-making business during the early 1990s. In 1989 the company entered into a partnership with unaffiliated parties to form Olympus Communications L.P., a southeastern Florida cable television joint venture that Adelphia managed for an annual fee. Comprising Adelphia's own South Dade System, which was acquired in late 1986, several neighboring cable systems in West Palm Beach, and several cable systems that were acquired in 1989 from Centel Corporation, Olympus Communications served roughly 250,000 subscribers and epitomized Adelphia's clustering strategy. During the first few years of its operation, Olympus Communications performed admirably, recording double-digit revenue and cash flow growth.

In the wake of the Jones Intercable acquisition and the formation of Olympus Communications, Adelphia began looking to acquire additional cable systems in specific areas, notably in Virginia; West Palm Beach, Florida; Syracuse, New York; and Hilton Head, South Carolina. As the plans for further physical expansion in the 1990s were being formulated, the company was also investing its resources into improving the infrastructure of its various cable systems—something it had been doing since its formation in 1986. In January 1990, the company announced it would start a five-year, $25 million system upgrade. Part of the upgrade consisted of the installation of 2,000 miles of cable, including a fiber-optic network that would double the number of available stations from 36 to 72, give sharper television images, and lessen the chance of interrupted service.

Enjoying National Prominence in the 1990s

Adelphia's continued commitment to improving the quality and technological capabilities of its cable systems stood as one of the hallmarks of its success during the early 1990s, proving to be as instrumental to the company's rise as a national contender as its practice to cluster cable systems together. Another definitive aspect of the company's success was its robust cash flow, which in part was attributable to the economies of scale engendered by the concentration of its cable properties. By 1992 Adelphia had transformed itself through acquisition and internal growth into the tenth largest television cable systems operator in the country—up from the 25th slot the company occupied in 1986—but in terms of cash flow the firm placed second to no one. Adelphia's operating margin of 57 percent of revenues represented the highest percentage in the U.S. cable industry, far higher than the industry average of 35 percent.

Aside from the company's enviable cash flow performance, there were other characteristics of Adelphia's operations that

Key Dates:

1952: John Rigas and his brother, Gus, found Adelphia with the purchase of their first cable franchise in Coudersport, Pennsylvania, for $300.

1972: The Rigas brothers incorporate their company under the name "Adelphia," the Greek word for "brothers."

1986: The Rigas family consolidates several cable properties under the Adelphia name and takes the company public; a period of aggressive expansion through multiple acquisitions is launched.

1989: The company creates Adelphia Media Services to pursue advertising opportunities on local, regional, and national fronts.

1991: The company establishes Adelphia Business Solutions, a subsidiary, to provide a range of communications products to the business community, including high-speed Internet access, long distance phone service, and voice messaging.

1994: Adelphia begins a new period of rapid acquisition.

1998: Adelphia reaches a customer base of over two million subscribers.

2002: Financial fraud scandal erupts at Adelphia; the Rigas family is ousted from the company's board of directors; company files for Chapter 11 bankruptcy protection.

were indicative of its success in the past and pointed to growth in the future. By 1992 the company had invested nearly $350 million since its formation to achieve what one industry analyst referred to as "among the best channel capacities and addressability in the industry." The company's cable systems were state-of-the-art, capable of providing a quality of service that distanced Adelphia from competitors and kept its customers satisfied.

In terms of cash flow and technological capabilities, Adelphia held a decided lead over other competitors in the cable industry as the company operated during the early 1990s. In terms of the demographics of its markets, Adelphia also could boast superiority over many of the country's cable operators. Since its formation the company had targeted mid-sized, suburban markets, carving a presence in communities where incomes were high and populations were expanding. The strategy was paying dividends as Adelphia entrenched its position in these lucrative markets, fueling the company's growth. Historically, the primary regions where the company operated had demonstrated household growth rates that eclipsed the national average. By the early 1990s, after years of consistent growth, Adelphia's markets were recording household growth rates nearly 25 percent above the national average, further bolstering hope that the financial growth of the past would continue into the future.

Sales in 1992 amounted to $267 million, up nearly ninefold from the total collected in 1986. In 1993, sales jumped to $305 million. To sustain this pace of financial growth, Adelphia looked to physical expansion and resumed its acquisition program as it entered the mid-1990s. In 1994 the company agreed to purchase all the cable systems owned by WB Cable Associa-

tion, Clear Channels Cable TV, and those owned by the Benjamin Terry family. In all, Adelphia gained 62,200 subscribers, a figure that paled in comparison to the nearly 1.5 million subscribers the company served at the time, but the acquisitions strengthened the company's position in key markets. The WB Cable system was situated in West Boca Raton, Florida, where Adelphia served 300,000 subscribers. The Terry family cable systems were located in Henderson, North Carolina, and the Clear Channels cable systems were located in the Kittanning, Pennsylvania, area. Further additions to the Adelphia system were made in 1995, when the company agreed to buy cable systems from four small operators that included southeastern Florida cable systems owned by Fairbanks Communications, plus others owned by Eastern Telecom and Robinson Cable TV in the Pittsburgh area, and cable systems in New England owned by First Carolina Cable TV. Together, the acquisitions added 108,000 subscribers to Adelphia's network, and each conformed to the company's strategy of clustering its cable system holdings.

The late 1990s marked a period of feverish consolidation across the cable industry: companies were merging, buying up smaller companies, and even exchanging systems with one another in a race to optimize the efficiency of their customer clusters and maximize economies of scale. During this period Adelphia made a number of key acquisitions that boosted the company into the position of the nation's sixth largest cable operator. In February 1999, Adelphia acquired Frontier Vision Partners L.P., a company with operations in New England, Ohio, Virginia, and Kentucky and a total of 702,000 subscribers. The transaction cost Adelphia $550 million in cash and $431.4 million in stock; further, the company assumed $1.1 billion in debt from Frontier Vision. The following month Adelphia purchased Century Communications Corporation for $3.6 billion plus the assumption of $1.6 billion of Century's debt. The acquisition brought Adelphia 1.6 million new subscribers in California, Colorado, and Puerto Rico. In April 1999, Adelphia made a third billion-dollar acquisition with the agreement to purchase Harron Communications Corporation's cable systems in New England and Philadelphia. This transaction cost Adelphia $1.17 billion in cash and added 300,000 subscribers to its roster. The aggregate gain of these acquisitions pushed Adelphia over the five million customer mark, a significant threshold for maximizing the benefits of an economy of scale.

Scandal Erupts: 2002

Adelphia continued to make other acquisitions and consolidation maneuvers through 1999 and 2000, bringing its subscriber base up to an impressive 5.5 million. Though the company was heavily indebted after the succession of major purchases, analysts were looking favorably on Adelphia as late as January 2002, noting that the company was well positioned for acquisition or merger with another major cable company.

On March 27, 2002, however, Adelphia officials disclosed $2.3 billion in previously unrecorded debt incurred through co-borrowings between Adelphia and other Rigas family entities under the umbrella of the family's private trust, Highland Holdings. Under these loan agreements, the Rigas entities were responsible for repaying the debt, but if they were unable to do so, Adelphia would be liable. The revelations and the investigation that followed sent the company spiraling deeper and deeper into a scandal that the Securities and Exchange Commission (SEC) eventually called, "one of the most extensive financial frauds ever to take place at a public company."

While the accounting omissions caused immediate investor concern, the loans themselves seemed commensurate with company practices dating back to 1997 and thus not necessarily illegitimate. Adelphia moved to delay filing its 2001 annual report and restate its financial results for the past three years in order to clarify and properly account for the debt. Still, within a month of the disclosure, Adelphia faced a 70 percent dive in its stock price, investigations by the SEC and federal prosecutors in Pennsylvania and New York, and possible delisting from the NASDAQ.

The Rigases, it appeared, had used much of the loan money to acquire Adelphia stock; they had also used loan money to finance the purchases of cable properties separate from Adelphia. As the scandal unfolded the litany of questionable dealings between the Rigas family and Adelphia continued to grow: it included, but was not limited to, the purchase of office furniture for Adelphia from a Rigas-owned company at exorbitant prices; the building of a private Rigas family golf course with Adelphia funds; the Rigas family's exploitation of company airplanes and other luxuries; and the maintenance of a chef and other family staff on Adelphia's payroll. While the Rigas family used company funds in numerous inappropriate ways, it also manipulated the accounting of the transactions to create a falsely inflated picture of the company's financial condition. By June 2002 it was revealed that the company had significantly overstated its cash flow as well as the number of its cable subscribers for 2001.

The practical implications of the scandal for Adelphia were devastating. In a move aimed at regaining the confidence of lenders and potential investors, a special committee of independent directors and creditors forced the Rigas family to surrender control of the company, and Erland E. Kailbourne was installed as chairman and interim CEO. The next step was to renegotiate loans and sell off assets in order to stabilize the company's debt. But investing in the future of the tarnished cable company proved to be too risky a venture for any of Adelphia's potential buyers, and after a month of scrambling to find alternatives, the

company filed for Chapter 11 bankruptcy on June 25, 2002, with debts totaling $18.6 billion.

Despite the chaos, figures for June and July 2002 showed a solid performance for Adelphia's base business. With bankruptcy protection alleviating the immediate pressure to liquidate valuable assets, the company hoped to reorganize and regain its footing. Still, at the close of 2002, the forecast for Adelphia's future remained uncertain.

Principal Subsidiaries

Adelphia Cablevisions, Inc.; Clear Cablevision, Inc.; Indiana Cablevision, Inc.; Western Reserve Cablevision, Inc.; International Cablevision, Inc.

Principal Competitors

AT&T Broadband; DIRECTV, Inc.; EchoStar Communications Corporation.

Further Reading

"Adelphia Agreed to Buy," *Television Digest,* June 19, 1995, p. 7.
"Adelphia Said It Had Agreed to Buy All Cable Systems Owned by WB Cable Assoc., Clear Channels Cable TV and Benjamin Terry Family," *Television Digest,* November 7, 1994, p. 8.
"Adelphia to Install Cable As Part of Upgrade," *Business First of Buffalo,* January 29, 1990, p. 10.
Fabrikant, Geraldine, "A Family Affair at Adelphia Communications," *New York Times,* April 4, 2002, p. C1.
Fabrikant, Geraldine, and Andrew Ross Sorkin, "Rigas Family Is Giving Up Voting Control of Adelphia," *New York Times,* May 24, 2002, p. C1.
Fazzi, Raymond, "Adelphia Cable to Expand Channel Offerings in Dover Township," *Knight-Ridder/Tribune Business News,* December 27, 1995, p. 12.
Fink, James, "Adelphia Gets Bigger with Purchase of Jones Cable," *Business First of Buffalo,* August 28, 1989, p. 5.
Lindstrom, Annie, "Adelphia Sparks CATV Paging Industry," *Telephony,* January 16, 1995, p. 18.
Mehlman, William, "Adelphia Cash Flow Margin Paces Cable TV Industry," *Insiders' Chronicle,* August 31, 1992, p. 1.

—Jeffrey L. Covell
—update: Erin Brown

Administaff, Inc.

19001 Crescent Springs Drive
Kingwood, Texas 77339
U.S.A.
Telephone: (281) 358-8986
Toll Free: (800) 237-3170
Fax: (281) 358-3354
Web site: http://www.administaff.com

Public Company
Incorporated: 1986
Employees: 1,200
Sales: $4.4 billion (2001)
Stock Exchanges: New York
Ticker Symbol: ASF
NAIC: 561330 Employee Leasing Services

Administaff, Inc. is one of the top three companies in the professional employer organization (PEO) industry. A PEO contracts with a business to manage its human resources department. Administaff's clients are primarily small and medium-sized businesses with less than 20 employees. Administaff works as co-employer with the client, managing payroll and benefits for the employees, and handling many regulatory issues such as compliance with workplace safety standards. The idea behind Administaff is that small business owners can concentrate on what they do best, while Administaff handles the sometimes burdensome complexity of employee paperwork. Employees can also benefit from the relationship with Administaff because the company takes advantage of economies of scale, offering a range of benefits often not feasible for a small company on its own. Administaff was a pioneer in the professional employer organization industry, starting in Texas in the mid-1980s and expanding to major urban centers across the United States. As of 2002 Administaff had 38 offices serving more than 20 markets, including New York City, San Francisco, Los Angeles, Chicago, Denver, Cleveland, and Atlanta. The company also runs four regional service centers. These are in Houston, Dallas, Atlanta, and Los Angeles. Administaff serves more than 4,400 client companies, and oversees some 70,000 of its clients' employees. Administaff's clients work in a range of industries, including banking, legal services, medical services, insurance, engineering, and light manufacturing.

Birth of an Industry

Administaff, Inc. was founded in 1986 by Paul Sarvadi and Gerald McIntosh. Sarvadi, who remains chief executive of the company, was a charismatic salesman who made the best of his employer's bankruptcy by starting his own business. Sarvadi had a wife and child to support by the time he was 19 and an undergraduate at Houston's Rice University. Consequently, he went to work as an Amway salesman. He worked as a salesman for various multilevel marketing companies for ten years and then was hired at Omnistaff, a company on the cusp of a new industry.

Omnistaff, based in Dallas, was one of the first staff leasing companies. Staff leasing gradually evolved into what is known today as a professional employer organization. Staff leasing varied somewhat from what Administaff does today. Under a company such as Omnistaff, a business owner would fire all of his or her employees; they would be hired by the staff leasing company and then leased back to the original employer. The original employer now had a personnel count of zero. All paychecks and paperwork were taken care of by the staff leasing company. The staff leasing company took a fee based on a percentage of the small business's payroll, usually from 5 to 10 percent. The key savings was in time for the small business owner, who no longer had to worry about keeping track of employee paperwork. Staff leasing also took advantage of a new law, the Tax Equity and Fiscal Responsibility Act of 1982, which allowed business owners a new way to shelter income in a tax-free pension plan. If the staff leasing company put 7.5 percent of employees' wages into a pension plan, then the small business owner was allowed to set up a pension plan for himself or herself, and this could hold up to 25 percent of the business owner's income.

Before the Tax Equity and Fiscal Responsibility Act took effect, there were only a handful of staff leasing firms. By 1985, there were some 275 staff leasing companies in the United States. The leading firm in this burgeoning industry was Omnistaff, which had revenues of about $60 million in 1984,

Company Perspectives:

Administaff's mission is to be the recognized leader in the development, sale and delivery of quality Professional Employer Organization services to our strategically selected market of small to medium-sized businesses. This mission will be accomplished by a highly motivated team of innovative people dedicated to finding, attracting and satisfying clients in a manner that will produce consistent and superior productivity among clients, employees and the Company.

employing some 10,000 workers on behalf of about 1,300 client companies. *Fortune* magazine called Omnistaff the ''kingpin'' of staff leasing, in an overview of the industry published April 1, 1985. Omnistaff was led by James Borgelt, who both bolstered the industry and later tarnished its reputation. Omnistaff declared bankruptcy in late 1985, only months after *Fortune* had lauded the company. Borgelt was later involved with another staff leasing company, American Workforce, Inc., which went bankrupt in 1991. Borgelt eventually was sentenced to three years in prison for stealing from clients.

Sarvadi had apparently just gone to work for Omnistaff when it started to go under. His very first client call was on Gerald McIntosh. McIntosh was impressed with Sarvadi's sales pitch and had no idea that this was the young salesman's first attempt. McIntosh was unable to sign up for Omnistaff's services, however, since he had just sold his company. Instead, he decided to go to work for Omnistaff also. Sarvadi and McIntosh worked together for only a short while before they found themselves unemployed again. They started speculating on what they would do differently if they were to run their own staff leasing firm. Before long they had a detailed business plan, with Sarvadi in charge of sales, and McIntosh in charge of other operations. Although the plan was supposed to be just a ''what if,'' in March 1986 the pair incorporated Administaff and went to work out of a 600-square-foot office. They had no staff and only one phone between the two of them. But they were able to pick up several Omnistaff clients. Once these clients had gotten used to staff leasing, they did not want to go back to their old way of doing business. So Administaff took them on. In the company's first year, it had only three clients, and barely more than 30 leased employees. But the firm brought in $750,000 and quickly went up from there.

Struggle for Legitimacy in the Early 1990s

In 1987, Administaff more than quadrupled its revenue, bringing in $4.2 million. The surge the next year was even more impressive, up to $21 million. The curve continued upward as the company more than tripled its revenue the next year, and more than doubled it in 1990. One reason often cited for the sudden boom in staff leasing in the late 1980s and early 1990s was that costs for employee health plans were skyrocketing at the time. Administaff was able to offer savings to small business owners while costs were going up and up. Administaff executives also noted that the amount of paperwork for which employers were accountable rose at that time, as regulations for insurance and pensions became more detailed. These conditions

helped Administaff build its business and also accounted for the rise of hundreds of other staff leasing firms. The proliferation of companies in the industry helped spread the idea of staff leasing, laying the groundwork for more and more businesses to convert to outsourcing their human resources functions. Yet Administaff's competitors were not always upright, and problems at some staff leasing companies threatened to smear the entire industry. One boon to Administaff was the passage of the Texas Reform Act of 1986, which spelled out more precisely what a staff leasing firm was liable for. Administaff worked closely with a national trade organization, the National Staff Leasing Association, to set standards for the industry. But many staff leasing companies in Texas flouted or evaded the law. By 1991 there were more than 200 staff leasing firms operating in Texas. The Texas Employment Commission and the State Board of Insurance considered only 40 of these companies to be legitimate. Some companies did not offer their employees workers' compensation; others were apparently taking money that was to be set aside for taxes and disappearing. The law was unclear about who was liable if a staff leasing company went bankrupt or closed its doors and an employee had an unpaid insurance or compensation claim. In 1991 a Texas grand jury began looking into fraud charges at eight staff leasing firms, and the Federal Bureau of Investigation and the Department of Labor began investigating the bankruptcy of one of Dallas's biggest staff leasing firms, American Workforce. The many bad apples made conditions difficult for the legitimate companies in the industry. Administaff took out two-page ads in the *Wall Street Journal,* defending the industry and its own reputation. Administaff also vocally supported legislation calling for a hefty annual licensing fee for staff leasing firms and a surety bond from a state-licensed insurance company.

Despite the difficulties of the infant industry, Administaff continued to grow and prosper. By 1992 the company was ranked as the second fastest-growing firm in Houston; it ranked 16th nationwide in a survey done by *Inc.* magazine. The company began to look at markets beyond Texas, too. It opened a Dallas office in 1993, and then set off on a nationwide expansion project. In 1993 Kelly Services, the large temporary help agency, acquired a California staff leasing firm (and by that time the operative phrase had evolved to professional employer organization, or PEO). This seemed to put the spotlight on the industry for financiers, and in 1994 Administaff received substantial capital from two Texas groups, the Texas Growth Fund and Bankers Trust. With some $7 million of new investment, Administaff opened four new offices in 1994, diversifying into the prime urban markets of Atlanta, Phoenix, Chicago, and Washington, D.C. The company also began expanding its headquarters building. Sales for 1995 were more than $716 million. Net income fell from $3.8 million in 1994 to $1.1 million in 1995 because of the many costs associated with the expansion. About half of Administaff's clients were in the Houston area, and only 20 percent were from outside Texas. But the company considered that it had only scratched the surface of the PEO industry.

Public Company in the Late 1990s

Administaff first began making plans to go public in 1995, hoping to raise $40 million to carry out its nationwide expansion. The company delayed its initial public offering (IPO),

Key Dates:

1986: The company is founded.
1994: The company opens offices outside Texas.
1997: Administaff goes public.
1998: The company enters a joint marketing agreement with American Express.

waiting for better market conditions and for some tax issues to be ironed out. By 1996, Administaff had a stable of 1,400 client companies, with a total of 23,000 worksite employees. Administaff itself had about 500 corporate employees. In 1997 the IPO went forward, and the company debuted on the New York Stock Exchange. CEO Sarvadi claimed that the move to go public was as much about public relations as about funding expansion. Sarvadi wanted to raise the profile of Administaff and of the whole PEO industry, and to distinguish his company from the fly-by-night operators that still darkened the industry's reputation. "We wanted to emphasize that we're here to stay," Sarvadi told the *Houston Business Journal* (May 22, 1998). Administaff was at the front of a wave, as four other PEO companies went public that year. But regardless of the public relations aspect, the stock offering raised money for the company, which had plans to open one new sales office every quarter. The firm had 21 offices in 13 different markets by 1998, and it planned to have 90 offices in 40 markets over the next several years.

Administaff made an arrangement with the credit card firm American Express in 1997. American Express bought up 5 percent of Administaff, spending some $17.7 million, and the two companies agreed on a joint marketing plan where American Express would offer Administaff's services to its small business clients. American Express worked with approximately 1.6 million small businesses. The credit company would take on the expense of making the contacts, and Administaff would pay it a commission. Administaff's stock rose quickly when the joint marketing agreement was announced. The firm seemed to have a promising future ahead of it. It was one of the largest companies in the industry, yet it had only 1 percent of the market. The concept of the PEO was catching on, and 16 states now had or were working on licensing laws.

The company pushed into more new markets, moving into Los Angeles in 1998 and later that year opening an office in the San Francisco area. The Bay Area was home to some 40,000 small businesses, many on the cutting edge of the technology industry. This seemed to be ripe ground for Administaff's services. The next year, the company opened two offices in New York City. New York had a huge concentration of businesses that fit Administaff's target client profile. There were more than 97,000 businesses in the small-to-medium range, and this was also an area where Administaff's partner American Express had a large penetration.

By this time Administaff was spread coast to coast, with many stops in between. It had sales offices in Charlotte, North Carolina, in St. Louis and Orlando, as well as four Texas offices, among others. Revenue continued to boom, and after a record-breaking quarter in 2000, the company's stock price shot up. Revenue for 2000 was $3.7 billion, and Administaff found itself on the *Fortune* 500 list of the country's biggest companies. By that year the firm had 35 sales offices, including eight in California. As the technology sector cooled off and the economy nationwide slowed down, Administaff reined in its expansion for 2001. Opening fewer new offices allowed the company to hold down its operating expenses. The company finished 2001 with revenue of $4.4 billion. This represented an increase of almost 18 percent over the year previous, even as client companies laid off or terminated workers. Net income fell sharply, however. Although business conditions across the country were more difficult in 2001 than they had been in the high-flying late 1990s, Administaff was able to continue its growth streak. It moved more solidly into the Midwest in 2002 with a new office in Cleveland. The company was more than halfway to its stated goal of opening offices in 40 markets across the country, as Cleveland was its 21st. Administaff seemed to be focusing on the Midwest, with plans to build a new service center in Chicago by 2004, and hopes for multiple sales offices in some of the region's cities.

Principal Competitors

Paychex, Inc.; Automatic Data Processing, Inc.; Gevity HR Inc.

Further Reading

"Administaff Emerges As Leader in Staff Leasing Industry," *Houston Business Journal,* March 22, 1993, p. 23.
Bieseda, Alexandra, "Administaff," *Texas Monthly,* October 2000, p. 58.
Carroll, Chris, "The Big Business of Small Business," *Houston Business Journal,* May 22, 1998, p. 14.
Fierman, Jaclyn, "Employees Learn to Love Being Leased Out," *Fortune,* April 1, 1985, p. 80.
Fisher, Daniel, "Temp Trouble," *Forbes,* October 5, 1998, p. 196.
Greer, Jim, "Administaff Slows Expansion, Accelerates Expense Control," *Houston Business Journal,* May 11, 2001, p. 18.
Kowalke, Peter, "Full-Service HR Firm Enters Market with Big Plans," *Crain's Cleveland Business,* June 24, 2002, p. 8.
Nowlin, Sanford, "State Pressuring for Regulation of Employee Leasing," *San Antonio Business Journal,* October 18, 1991, p. 13.
Palmeri, Christopher, "We Cure Small-Business Headaches," *Forbes,* October 20, 1997, p. 168.
Preston, Darrell, "Employee Leasing Firms Face Crisis," *Dallas Business Journal,* October 18, 1991, p. 1.
Pybus, Kenneth R., "Expanding Administaff Dusts Off Its Plan for Initial Public Offering," *Houston Business Journal,* November 1, 1996, p. 4.
Sauer, Matthew, "PEO Administaff Loses Business, But Staff Leasing May Be OK," *Sarasota Herald Tribune,* February 2, 1999, p. 1D.
Waldo, Adam, "Administaff, Inc.," *Buyside,* January 2002, p. 44.

—A. Woodward

Alvin Ailey Dance Foundation, Inc.

211 West 61st Street, Floor 3
New York, New York 10023
U.S.A.
Telephone: (212) 767-0590
Fax: (212) 767-0625
Web site: http://www.alvinailey.org

Nonprofit Company
Incorporated: 1958 as the Alvin Ailey American Dance
    Theater
Sales: $15 million (2001 est.)
NAIC: 711120 Dance Companies

Alvin Ailey Dance Foundation, Inc. is the umbrella organization for the Alvin Ailey American Dance Theater, one of the best-known modern dance companies in the United States. Founded by African-American dancer and choreographer Alvin Ailey in 1958, the company was one of the few showcases for black dancers anywhere in the United States. Headquartered in New York, the Alvin Ailey company began touring internationally in 1962. The group has found a devoted following worldwide with its innovative dances, which often explore African-American culture in ways never previously seen. The Alvin Ailey American Dance Theater tours extensively abroad and in the United States. In addition, its junior company, known as Ailey II, tours and performs widely. The Ailey School teaches dance to thousands of students from the age of three through adults. The school's curriculum is based on the dance techniques of Lester Horton and Martha Graham, and includes ballet, West African dance, and other dance techniques. The Alvin Ailey Dance Foundation also runs an extensive arts in education program, bringing dance to schools through performances, workshops, and artist-in-residence programs. The foundation runs Ailey Camps as well, which teach dance and other skills to underserved children. The foundation is currently building a new home in New York City, which will be the largest facility devoted exclusively to dance in the United States.

A Career Shaped by Happenstance: 1931–53

Alvin Ailey, Jr., was born on January 5, 1931, in a wooden cabin in the small southeastern Texas town of Rogers. His mother, Lula Cliff Ailey, and his father, Alvin Ailey, Sr., separated when the boy was just six months old. For years afterward, Lula Ailey subsisted by taking in washing, picking cotton, and doing cooking and cleaning for white families. Ailey and his mother moved frequently, and the child was often left alone while his mother worked. Alvin spent much of his childhood in Navasota, Texas, and then moved with his mother to Los Angeles in 1942. Young Ailey attended Thomas Jefferson High School, a neighborhood public school that served a mostly African-American, Mexican, Chinese, and Japanese population. The school made a point of introducing its students to the arts, taking them on field trips to see performances in downtown Los Angeles. Ailey first saw a professional ballet troupe in 1945, on a school trip to a performance by the touring Ballet Russe. Ailey began attending other dance performances, and soon after he met the charismatic Katherine Dunham, an African-American woman who starred in an eclectic dance performance called the ''Tropical Revue.''

Ailey had friends who were as interested in dance as he was, including Ted Crumb, who was later a member of the Negro Ballet Company, and Carmen de Lavallade, a fellow student at Thomas Jefferson who became a big star on her own and danced with Ailey on Broadway and as a guest with his company. Crumb and de Lavallade steered Ailey to the Lester Horton studios. Lester Horton was a white man who had studied various forms of modern and ethnic dance. He eventually began choreographing his own works, which often dealt with uncomfortable social issues such as police brutality. Horton's works were performed side by side with works of the best known modern dance companies of the time, including those of Martha Graham and Lincoln Kirstein, but headquartered in Los Angeles, he was out of the main current, which flowed from New York. He ran a racially diverse studio at a time when the dance world was extremely segregated. Horton's students learned the gamut of putting on a performance, not only dancing, but making sets and costumes and writing publicity. Ailey began taking dance classes only reluctantly, first watching his friends dance for about six months. His teachers immediately noticed

Company Perspectives:

Promoting the uniqueness of black cultural expression and the preservation and enrichment of the American modern dance heritage.

his talent, but Ailey was shy and unsure whether dance was really for him. After graduating from high school, Ailey attended the University of California at Los Angeles, intending to major in romance languages. He did not do particularly well in college, but he was not sure he was committed to dance, either. He moved briefly to San Francisco, going to San Francisco State College, and then in 1953 found a job as a dancer in a Los Angeles night club. He continued to study and perform with Lester Horton. Horton's company seemed to be achieving a new level of success. The company was invited to perform in New York in 1953, and then invited to the annual summer Jacob's Pillow dance festival in Massachusetts. The company had work lined up when Horton died of a massive heart attack in November 1953. Although Ailey had been ambivalent about his career in dance, with Horton's death he was thrust into a demanding role. He became the group's choreographer, as well as a teacher and one of its star dancers. Within months of Horton's death, Ailey was presenting a show of Horton classics, plus two full-length works of his own. But for Horton's sudden demise, Ailey might never have realized his own gift for choreography.

Beginning a Company of His Own in 1958

In 1954 Ailey went to New York with his friend Carmen de Lavallade to dance in the Broadway show "House of Flowers," starring Pearl Bailey. Ailey and de Lavallade were featured in a duet, and Ailey had a show-stopping solo. But after "House of Flowers" closed, there was little work for Ailey, or for other African-American dancers, no matter how talented. An all-African-American show like "House of Flowers" came around only once every five years or so, and many opportunities for white performers were closed to nonwhite dancers. Ailey taught dance classes and worked sporadically, living hand to mouth. In 1958 he decided to put on a performance at the 92nd Street Y, a popular venue for small theater and dance. The idea, in part, was to show off Ailey's choreography, which had not had much outlet since he left Los Angeles, and also to give underemployed African-American dancers something to do. The show was meant as a one-time performance, and Ailey and 13 other dancers approached it casually, rehearsing where they could in various studios between other jobs. The show premiered Ailey's "Blues Suite," a dance set in a tawdry bar, showing the kind of people the young Ailey had seen in the small Texas towns where he had lived with his mother. This dance in particular got a huge response from the audience and an ecstatic write-up in the major dance journal *Dance Magazine*. Nine months later Ailey put on another show at the 92nd Street Y, this time to a packed house. Other invitations to perform followed, and Ailey and his dancers began to work together as a company. In 1960, Ailey brought out a new dance, "Revelations," set to spirituals and depicting moments of religious joy. The work stunned the audience at the Y, the first to see what became one of the most-performed dance works in the U.S. repertory.

The Ailey company became a recognized force on the U.S. dance scene with the success of "Revelations." But the group had little money, nevertheless, and relied on the charity and volunteer work of friends and well-wishers. The Ailey company's first headquarters was in a donated space at the YWCA on Eighth Avenue and 53rd Street. The company rehearsed, taught classes, and performed in the small space at the Y, known as the Clark Center for the Arts. Ailey's reputation grew in New York, and in 1962 the State Department invited the company to tour Asia. The group spent three months abroad, performing in Australia, Korea, Japan, South Vietnam, the Philippines, Indonesia, Hong Kong, and elsewhere. Afterward, the company performed new dances in New York and traveled through the Midwest and South. In 1964 Alvin Ailey American Dance Theater toured Europe for the first time. The slew of engagements was handled by a booking agent, while the finances of the company were taken care of by a husband-and-wife team of devoted volunteers. Ailey stopped dancing himself during the mid-1960s and spent all his time on choreography and directing his troupe. He repeatedly announced that he would disband the company, even as its fame grew. In 1967 the company became a little more organized when it incorporated as a nonprofit corporation, the Dance Theater Foundation. This way, the group became eligible for government and foundation grants. The dance foundation's first office was in Ailey's small apartment.

Growth in the 1970s

Alvin Ailey American Dance Theater toured abroad so much in the 1960s that it was better known in Europe than in its own country. In 1968 the group began an extended U.S. tour. Ailey continued to produce works that reflected African-American U.S. culture, at a time of great racial strife. His company featured mainly African-American dancers, though he used white and Asian dancers as well. The group's shows brought rave reviews, and the company got support from grants from the National Endowment for the Arts and from the Rockefeller Foundation. The company completed another domestic tour in 1970, and Ailey collaborated with jazz great Duke Ellington on a ballet for American Ballet Theater. Despite the group's growing fame and the influx of grant money, the company was still barely solvent. At the close of the 1970 season Ailey announced that financial problems would force him to disband the dance company. The company recently had moved to new quarters in the Brooklyn Academy of Music, which proved unsatisfactory, and a promised State Department-sponsored tour of the Soviet Union had been canceled. But the group had many supporters, and ultimately it moved back to Manhattan and the Soviet tour was reinstated. The company embarked on another long tour of the United States the next year. The year 1971 also saw the premiere of another Ailey classic, "Cry," which featured the extraordinary six-foot tall dancer Judith Jamison. In new quarters at the American Dance Center on East 59th Street, the company worked relatively comfortably for the next nine years. Ailey established a popular school, and added two student companies. The company reigned over modern dance in the United States in the 1970s, and was lauded on its international tours. By 1978, when the company celebrated its 20th anniversary, the company included 29 dancers, more than twice its original number,

Key Dates:

1953: Alvin Ailey, Jr., premieres his choreography with the Lester Horton group.

1954: Ailey moves to New York for a professional dance career.

1958: The company is founded after the first successful performance of Ailey's original works at the 92nd Street Y.

1962: The company makes its first international tour.

1978: At its 20th anniversary, the company has doubled in size and runs the leading dance school in New York.

1989: Ailey dies; Judith Jamison takes over as artistic director.

1993: The company receives a stabilization grant to straighten out finances.

2001: Several grants allow the company to plan building its own dance center in Manhattan.

and enrollment at the Ailey school was almost 5,000 students. The company's budget had grown to about $3 million annually, and Ailey himself was making a substantial income from choreography commissions and royalties, television appearances, and his salary for directing the company.

Ups and Downs in the 1980s

Alvin Ailey American Dance Theater gave a command performance for President Jimmy Carter at the White House in 1979, and then flew to Morocco for a New Year's performance at the behest of that country's king. Nevertheless, the company was still running a deficit, and when its headquarters building was demolished, it could not afford to build a studio and school to its specifications. Instead it moved into three floors of a midtown building owned by one of its board members. Ailey's health was beginning to fail, and the 1980s were a slower decade for the group than the 1960s and 1970s had been. Ailey was arrested in 1980 for creating a disturbance, apparently while having a mental breakdown. He was released without charge, only to set off a similar incident a few months later. Ailey was apparently increasingly frustrated that his company still had to scrounge for funds and it seemed that he was treated better in Europe than in New York.

Ailey was beset by both mental and physical problems from 1980 on. He was under treatment for manic depression, and he was in pain from arthritis. He continued to choreograph in the 1980s, producing another of his best-loved works in 1984, "For Bird—With Love." Ailey and his company were feted and honored repeatedly in the 1980s, and toured both abroad and domestically. Ailey was made Distinguished Professor of choreography at City University of New York in 1985. In 1986 Philip Morris Companies awarded Ailey's troupe a $300,000 grant, to cover two years of touring. In 1987, Ailey was diagnosed with AIDS. Although he continued to travel and undertake new projects, by that time he was clearly very ill. In 1988, the Ailey company's lease expired on the midtown building it had rented, and yet again the group had to scramble to find a suitable space. Ailey died on December 1, 1989.

Finding Stability in the 1990s

Leadership of the company fell to Judith Jamison, the dancer who had made her mark with Ailey's signature piece, "Cry." She had left the company in 1980 to pursue her own choreography, but she returned after Ailey's death. She became the company's artistic director, dedicated to keeping the vision of Ailey alive. Alvin Ailey American Dance Theater had always made a point of performing work of other choreographers, and during the 1980s, it put on far more non-Ailey works than Ailey originals. So it was not necessarily the loss of its chief choreographer that hurt the company most. But despite the Alvin Ailey group's long prominence, the company was still not on a sound financial footing. The company had amassed a deficit of roughly $1 million during the 1980s, and in the early 1990s, government funding for dance began to dry up. The company could not continue without some restructuring and a plan for future fundraising. Jamison brought in a new director of development and recruited new trustees—generally, corporate CEOs—who could contribute $10,000 and take a seat on the foundation's board of directors. In 1993 the company received a grant from the Lila Wallace-Reader's Digest Fund as part of its Art Stabilization Initiative. The grant gave money to the group not for performing or touring but to let it pay off debts. The grant allowed the company to build capital reserves so that its finances would no longer be so unstable.

By the mid-1990s, the company was in much better shape. It had paid off its debts, increased its revenue from performances, and found other ways to bring in cash. By 1996, the group brought in $3 million through fundraising, about twice the figure from 1992. The Ailey company also got corporations to underwrite some of its domestic shows, while Philip Morris continued to give money for domestic and international touring. The group also increased its marketing efforts, finding new ways to spread the Ailey name, particularly through outreach programs in schools. The company began unusual co-marketing agreements in 1998, trading its name to corporations for major donations. For example Jaguar became the "official car of Alvin Ailey" (Ailey had long dreamed of owning a Jaguar), and a chain of sports medicine clinics used the Ailey name in its advertising, while giving free physical therapy to Ailey dancers. These various stratagems paid off. By 1998, the company had an operating budget of $12 million, and it managed a $1 million surplus. Jamison said in an interview with *Black Enterprise* (December 1991) that for years she had "listened as Alvin struggled with prospective donors on one telephone line and bill collectors on the other." She was determined to ask for and get appropriate funding for her group to avoid that embarrassing struggle, and she was extremely successful.

In the late 1990s, Jamison began to plan for something the company had never been able to afford—a home of its own. Its rented space on West 61st Street was filled to overflowing, and the company had had to move suddenly before when leases expired. So Jamison began working on funding to build a school, studio, and performance space. In 2001 plans were cemented to build a new dance center on 55th Street and Ninth Avenue in Manhattan. New York Mayor Rudolph Giuliani approved a $7.5 million matching grant from the city to the company, surprising many with his generosity. The Dance

Foundation began raising funds needed to complete the building, expected to open in 2004.

Further Reading

Barbieri, Kelly, ''Alvin Ailey Tour Greeted with Increase in Advanced Ticket Sales,'' *Amusement Business,* February 14, 2000, p. 5.

DeNitto, Emily, ''New Steps Bring Alvin Ailey into the Business of Art,'' *Crain's New York Business,* December 7, 1998, p. 4.

Dunning, Jennifer, ''Ailey Troupe Goes in Search of Big Money,'' *New York Times,* November 27, 2001, p. E3.

——, *Alvin Ailey: A Life in Dance,* Reading, Mass.: Addison-Wesley, 1996.

Hruby, Laura, ''$15-Million Promised to Dance Group; Other Gifts,'' *Chronicle of Philanthropy,* December 13, 2001, p. 16.

Moran, Kate Mattingly, ''Giuliani Helps Ailey Get a Home of Its Own,'' *Dance Magazine,* August 2001, p. 30.

Reiss, Alvin H., ''Foundation Support, Board Upgrading Help Top Dance Troupe Achieve Stability,'' *Fund Raising Management,* January 1997, p. 34.

Ross, B., ''Choreographing the Money Dance,'' *Black Enterprise,* December 1991, p. 82.

—A. Woodward

American Gramaphone LLC

9130 Mormon Bridge Road
Omaha, Nebraska 68152-1962
U.S.A.
Telephone: (402) 457-4341
Toll Free: (800) 446-6860
Fax: (402) 457-43322
Web site: http://www.amgram.com

Private Company
Incorporated: 1974
NAIC: 421990 Other Miscellaneous Durable Goods
   Wholesalers; 711130 Musical Groups and Artists

American Gramaphone LLC is one of the most successful independent music labels in the United States. Founded by Louis ''Chip'' Davis to showcase his eclectic music, American Gramaphone reaches millions of fans through its recordings, with distribution mostly outside mainstream music industry channels. The company pioneered what is now known as New Age music. The label's major group is Davis's band Mannheim Steamroller, which is best known for a series of hit Christmas recordings. The group has also put out eight recordings in its ''Fresh Aire'' series, which is classically influenced electronic music on themes of nature and the outdoors. American Gramaphone also produced a series of recordings called ''Day Parts,'' which correspond to different times of the day, as in ''Sunday Morning Coffee'' and ''Dinner.'' Through its catalog, American Gramaphone not only markets its recordings, but also sells a variety of other products, including massage oil, clothing, paintings, coffee and hot chocolate, and other items that tie in to the music. While the recordings are also found in traditional record stores, American Gramaphone distributes much of its music through retailers such as Target, Borders, and Bath & Body Works, and through supermarkets, gift stores, and florist shops. Mannheim Steamroller's music is most often heard on the radio during the Christmas holiday season. The group also plays well-attended live shows across the country.

Country Hit in the 1970s

Chip Davis was born into a musical family in rural Ohio. His father was a high school music teacher, his mother had played trombone in a group called Phil Spitalny's All Girl Orchestra, and his grandmother began teaching him to play the piano when he was four years old. Davis went to music school at the University of Michigan, where he majored in classical bassoon and also played drums in the university's famed marching band. After graduating in 1969, Davis held a variety of jobs in the music industry. He toured with the Norman Luboff Choir and taught music to junior high school students. Davis told *People Magazine* (December 19, 1988) that there were two things he had said he would never do: ''Live in Nebraska and write country and western.'' But he broke his promise to himself, launching his success. In the early 1970s Davis moved to Omaha, Nebraska, where he composed jingles for the advertising agency Bozell Jacobs. Working with partner Bill Fries, Davis came up with a witty series of musical ads for Old Home Bread. The ads featured a fictional truck driver, C.W. McCall, and his girlfriend Mavis, a waitress. Radio listeners began calling stations and requesting the ads, and the Old Home Bread television spots were so popular that *TV Guide* listed them in its regular programming guide. The C.W. McCall campaign won advertising's prestigious Clio award, and MGM Records approached Davis and Fries and asked them to record the jingle as a pop single. This first song, ''Old Home Filler-Up an' Keep On-A-Truckin' Café'' made it to the top 20 on *Billboard* magazine's singles chart in 1974. The next year, Davis and Fries recorded a whole album for MGM Records. This included the song ''Convoy,'' which touched on the craze for citizen's band (CB) radio that was peaking around this time. ''Convoy'' sold a million copies within two months of its release, and was at number one on the *Billboard* country music chart for six weeks. The album sold ten million copies by the time it was done. The duo went on tour as the country group C.W. McCall, with Fries as lead singer. The C.W. McCall group eventually recorded nine albums, selling 20 million records. Davis won the Country Music Writer of the Year award in 1976. The group played what Davis called ''techno-country,'' with a large, lush horn section and lots of backup vocals. But Davis had never

Company Perspectives:

For over 25 years, Chip Davis and American Gramaphone have been innovators in producing music, video, and entertainment products that have touched the lives of millions around the world.

intended to be a successful country music writer, and he soon moved on to a different project.

An Independent Out of Desperation

Davis formed his own record label, American Gramaphone (the misspelling of gramophone was accidental, but it stuck), in 1974, while he was working at an Omaha recording studio. Davis had a part interest in the studio, and bought it outright in 1984. Davis's musical background was quite broad, but despite his immersion in popular music, he never forgot his classical training. He began composing pieces he called "18th-century classical rock," which used both early instruments like harpsichords and recorders as well as modern synthesizers. Davis claimed the structure of the music was classical, though the rhythms were from rock. The music was experimental, and used many cutting-edge recording techniques. When Davis had enough material, he assembled it into an album-length recording, and then endeavored to get a major music company to produce it. The album was called *Fresh Aire by Chip Davis,* and Davis soon made up the name of the mythical musical group who had recorded it, Mannheim Steamroller. (The name is a play on Mannheim roller, a musical term for a particular kind of crescendo favored by some 18th-century composers.) Davis claimed that music executives loved the album, but he could not get a sale. He was told repeatedly that the music was enjoyable, but unmarketable, as it did not fit any preconceived categories. Studio executives would order the album for themselves, directly from Davis, but would not take a risk on putting the compositions on their label.

Though he had had tremendous success with his country songs, Davis was not getting anywhere with his new music. Deciding he would probably never land a contract with a music company, he began selling the album himself under the American Gramaphone imprint. Instead of marketing the albums to music stores, he sold them to dealers in fine audio equipment. Sales people used the album to demonstrate the capabilities of their speakers and turntables, because the record had an unusual range of sounds. Audiophiles began buying the record, and *Fresh Aire* became a cult hit in the United States, Japan, and Germany. Davis went on to put out more Fresh Aire albums based on different thematic material such as summer or winter. The records were lovingly produced, weighing much more than most vinyl records to prevent warping, and with lavish attention to the record sleeve and jacket design. American Gramaphone sold them through audio stores and through mail order as their popularity spread by word-of-mouth. The music got no radio play and only sporadic advertising, but Fresh Aire built a solid fan base around the world.

Building a Niche in the 1980s

After the success of Mannheim Steamroller's first few Fresh Aire albums, Davis decided to try something else a little different. He decided to put out an album of Christmas music. Davis recalls that everyone he talked to about the project was skeptical. Seasonal albums were not selling well in the early 1980s, and there was no reason to think *Mannheim Steamroller Christmas* would break the pattern. But the record, released in 1984, sold 190,000 copies in its first year, surpassing everything else in the American Gramaphone catalog. It was nominated for a Grammy award, and eventually sold over six million copies. Davis followed *Mannheim Steamroller Christmas* with *A Fresh Aire Christmas* in 1988. By two weeks before Christmas, the album had already sold a million copies and was the most popular Christmas record in the country. Mannheim Steamroller toured for several weeks during the Christmas season, playing live shows at large venues. The next Christmas album came out in 1995. *Christmas in the Aire* already had 3.5 million orders placed a month before its release, and it joined the earlier Yule albums as multi-platinum bestsellers. The album was the number-one seller at the Borders Books & Music chain, and one of the bestsellers at the department store chain Target. Mannheim Steamroller's tour for the 1995 album was an immense undertaking. Davis shot a film in England of a Medieval feast. This was projected during the concert in such a way that the live musicians appeared to be sitting among the filmed musicians and playing with them. The high-tech show required three truckloads of equipment and dozens of helpers to set it all up. The idea was to transport the audience back to the time when the traditional Christmas carols were first composed and performed. Davis put an enormous effort into the show, though it only toured domestically and for just a few short weeks.

Mannheim Steamroller took on other projects too. In 1986 the band recorded a soundtrack for the PBS television series *Saving the Wildlife.* In 1989 Davis took the group on a 22-concert tour that benefited rebuilding at Yellowstone Park. The park had been severely damaged by fire a year earlier, and Davis used the musical tour to raise money for restoration. The show featured Davis and the handful of musicians of Mannheim Steamroller accompanied by an 80-piece symphony orchestra. The multimedia show featured slides and film of Yellowstone projected on four huge screens. Turner Broadcasting contacted Davis in the early 1990s, asking him to compose music for the 1994 Goodwill Games in St. Petersburg, Russia. Mannheim Steamroller toured ten cities in the United States with this original music, along with Russian folk songs and classical music by Russian composers, and recorded an album in St. Petersburg called *To Russia With Love.* American Gramaphone also began a series of recordings called "Day Parts," which were dedicated to different times of day or particular moods. "Romance" came out in 1993.

Annual revenue at the music company was estimated at about $5 million by the late 1980s. By the early 1990s, American Gramaphone had carved a decided niche for itself. When Davis first began touting his "Fresh Aire" series, the music was unclassifiable. But the music gradually came under the rubric "New Age." This category encompassed music of a mostly tranquil mood, often with themes of nature, such as the Yellowstone

Key Dates:

1974: Chip Davis founds the company.
1975: First Fresh Aire album is released.
1976: Chip Davis is named "Country Music Writer of the Year."
1984: Mannheim Steamroller issues its first Christmas album.
1998: Mannheim Steamroller Christmas special airs on NBC.

music. Davis himself did not profess to like the New Age label for his compositions, but by the early 1990s there was enough other music of the same general sort that the appellation made sense. Windham Hill was another independent music company founded in the 1970s that sold its records, like American Gramaphone did, outside of traditional music distribution venues. By the late 1980s, some of Windham Hill's music was getting radio play, and Mannheim Steamroller and other similar groups strongly appealed to a growing demographic of the over-30 crowd. American Gramaphone seized on that demographic in a way few other music companies contemplated, adding many items to its quarterly catalog besides records, cassettes, and scores. "In the last seven or eight years, it became evident that I was selling a lifestyle," Davis told *Billboard* (March 30, 1996). "We're selling a wraparound concept," he went on, explaining that 1995 catalog sales included some 30 tons of cinnamon hot chocolate. The catalog's 600,000 subscribers bought hot chocolate, coffee, massage oil, even steak marinade, as accoutrements to American Gramaphone's diverse musical offerings. The company also sold its music and other products through an increasing array of unconventional outlets. American Gramaphone did a lot of business through grocery stores and gift shops, and began selling in flower shops as well in the mid-1990s.

A Successful Brand in the 1990s and After

When "Romance II," another of the Day Parts series, came out in 1998, American Gramaphone distributed it in the soap and lotion chains the Body Shop and Bath & Body Works. The company also hawked its "A Mannheim Massage" release that year on the home shopping channel QVC, along with its own brand of massage oil. By the late 1990s, Mannheim Steamroller had transformed into a complex brand, driven by the music but encompassing everything from collectible artwork to children's books to bags of spices. All this was owned and run by Chip Davis, who had been called the Bill Gates of New Age music by E! Entertainment Television. As Mannheim Steamroller grew in prominence, Davis was able to mastermind bigger live concerts, and also for the first time to broadcast on regular network television. American Gramaphone released a new Christmas recording, *The Christmas Angel,* in 1998, and put together an ice skating show choreographed to the music. This toured in 13 cities, and was also filmed as an hour-long special program on NBC. Davis bought the hour of broadcast time from the network and then sold advertising space. The next year Davis worked on a Mannheim Steamroller album based on tunes from Walt Disney films, in a break from his earlier themes. American Gramaphone entered an exclusive distribution arrangement in 1998 with Navarre Corporation, which then handled all distribution for the company in the United States, Mexico, and Canada.

American Gramaphone released the eighth recording in its Fresh Aire series in 2000. The record company had only 32 titles in its catalog by that year, though almost all the titles were huge sellers. All the Fresh Aire records had gone gold, meaning that they had sold over 500,000 copies, and the Christmas albums were ranked as multi-platinum, selling in the millions. The older titles in the Christmas series continued to sell well seasonally year after year, and the latest release, 2001's *Christmas Extraordinaire* had already sold some four million copies within weeks of its debut. American Gramaphone's catalog reached some 600,000 people, and in the early 2000s Davis had more ambitious projects, such as a performing arts park, a children's music camp, and a video travel series, in the works.

Principal Competitors

Windham Hill Group; Compass Productions.

Further Reading

Allis, Tim, " 'Convoy' Composer Chip Davis Traded in His 18-Wheeler for a Solo Ride on Mannheim Steamroller," *People Weekly*, December 19, 1988, p. 147.

Brown, Steven, "Composer Chip Davis Runs Gamut of Musical Spectrum," *Orlando Sentinel*, December 16, 1993, p. A2.

Cox, Meg, " 'New Age' Music Wins Wider Following As Many People Grow Too Old for Rock," *Wall Street Journal*, April 1, 1987, p. 31.

Flippo, Chris, "Xmas Set Streamrolls Chart for American Gramaphone," *Billboard*, November 25, 1995, pp. 1, 113.

Hackett, Vernell, "Davis, Mannheim Steamroller Tour Pays Tribute to Russian Composers," *Amusement Business*, August 8, 1994, p. 6.

Heckman, Don, "Steamrolling to Success by Keeping to His Game Plan," *Los Angeles Times*, November 23, 1995, p. 1.

Jeffrey, Don, "AG's Mannheim Steamroller Sales Are Anything But Flat," *Billboard*, November 25, 1995, p. 113.

Matzer, Marla, "Davis of Mannheim Steamroller Makes the Most of Holidays," *Los Angeles Times*, December 17, 1998, p. 1.

Morris, Chris, "American Gramaphone Broadens Navarre Distribution Deal," *Billboard*, July 4, 1998, p. 57.

——, "Branding, Catalog & Vertically Integrated Barbecue Sauce: How Four Indies Prosper with or Without Hits," *Billboard*, March 30, 1996, p. 99.

——, "Count American Gramaphone Among the Midliners," *Billboard*, February 24, 2001, p. 64.

Newman, Melinda, "American Gramaphone's 2nd Look at 'Romance'," *Billboard*, January 31, 1998, p. 14.

Zhito, Lisa, "Mutual of Omaha Backs Mannheim Steamroller's 12-City Tour to Benefit Yellowstone Natl. Park," *Amusement Business*, May 7, 1990, p. 6.

—A. Woodward

AMR Corporation

4333 Amon Carter Boulevard
Fort Worth, Texas 86155
U.S.A.
Telephone: (817) 963-1234
Toll Free: (800) 433-7300
Fax: (817) 967-9641
Web site: http://www.amrcorp.com

Public Company
Incorporated: 1934 as American Airlines, Inc.
Employees: 122,820
Sales: $18.96 billion (2001)
Stock Exchanges: New York
Ticker Symbol: AMR
NAIC: 481111 Scheduled Passenger Air Transportation;
   561599 Reservation Services

AMR Corporation is a holding company whose principal subsidiary is American Airlines, Inc., which was founded in 1934. With the acquisition of Trans World Airlines, Inc. (TWA), American became the world's largest airline. It provides scheduled service to 170 destinations throughout North America, the Caribbean, Latin America, Europe, and the Pacific Rim. American's hub cities are Dallas/Fort Worth, Chicago, St. Louis, Miami, and San Juan, Puerto Rico.

In the 20th century, American helped define the full-service airline, pioneering computer reservation systems, frequent-flier miles, coast-to-coast jet flights, the hub-and-spoke system, and advance-purchase discount fares. Under Bob Crandall, the company even learned to thrive during the challenge of deregulation. In the early years of the millennium, however, American was cutting costs and seeking new approaches in the most difficult environment the industry had ever faced.

Early History

American Airlines is a product of the merger of a number of small airline companies. One of these founding enterprises was the Robertson Aircraft Company of Missouri, which employed Charles Lindbergh to pilot its first airmail run in 1926. In April 1927 another of these small companies, Juan Trippe's Colonial Air Transport, made the first scheduled passenger run between Boston and New York City. The nucleus of these and the 82 other companies that eventually merged to form American Airlines was a company called Embry-Riddle, which later evolved into the Aviation Corporation (AVCO), one of the United States' first airline conglomerates. The conglomerate was headed by a Wall Street group, led by Averell Harriman and Robert Lehman, that was not conversant with the new airline business.

In 1930 Charles Coburn formally united the various airlines under the name American Airways Company. American flew a variety of planes, including the Pilgrim 10A. In 1930 the company was granted control of the southern airmail corridor from the East Coast to California. In 1934 the government suspended all private airmail contracts only to reinstate them a few months later under the conditions that previous contract holders were disqualified from bidding and companies could not have the same officers and directors. American Airways thus changed its name to American Airlines and, under the leadership of Lester Seymour, resumed its airmail business, but due to the damage already caused by this interruption, was unable to maintain a profit.

During this period, a Texan named Cyrus Rowlett Smith was becoming a popular figure at American. Smith was originally the vice-president and treasurer of Southern Air Transport, a division later acquired by American. Seymour recognized Smith's ability and made him a vice-president of American in charge of the Southern Division.

In 1934 new American President Smith persuaded Donald Douglas, an aircraft manufacturer, to develop a new airplane to replace the popular DC-2. The company produced a larger 21-passenger airplane, designated the DC-3. Cooperation between the manufacturer and the airline throughout the project set an example for similar joint ventures in the future. American was flying the DC-3s by 1936 and, in large part as a result of the successful new plane, went on to become the number one airline by the close of the decade. The DC-3 proved to be a very popular airplane; its innovative and simple design made it durable and easy to service.

Company Perspectives:

To be the world's leading airline by focusing on industry leadership in the areas of: Safety, Service, Network, Product, Technology, Culture.

During 1937, in reaction to a public scare over airline safety, American ran a printed advertisement that directly asked, "Afraid to Fly?" Citing the statistical improbability of dying in a crash, the copy discussed the problem in a straightforward and reassuring way. "People are afraid of things they do not know about," the advertisement read. "There is only one way to overcome the fear—and that is, to fly." The promotion succeeded in allaying passenger fears and increasing the airline's business.

Aiding the World War II Effort

When World War II started, American Airlines devoted more than half of its resources to the army. American DC-3s shuttled the Signal Corps and supplies to Brazil for the transatlantic ferry. Smith himself volunteered his services to the Air Transport Command. American's president, Ralph Damon, went to the Republic Aircraft Company to supervise the building of fighter airplanes. After the war American returned to its normal operations, and Smith set out to completely retool the company with modern equipment. The modernization went smoothly and quickly. In 1949 American's archrival, United Airlines, was still flying DC-3s, while American had already sold its last DC-3s.

Following World War II, American Airlines purchased American Export Airlines (AEA) from American Export Steamship Lines. The steamship company was forced to sell AEA when the U.S. Congress decreed that transportation companies could not conduct business in more than one mode. It was an attempt to prevent industrial vertical monopolies from forming. American Airlines sold AEA to Pan Am in 1950.

In the late 1940s American suffered another financial crisis, caused mainly by the grounding of the DC-6. The airplanes were experiencing operational problems that led to crashes, and the federal government wanted all of them thoroughly inspected. Six weeks later they were back in service, but the interruption cost American a large amount of money. When banks restricted American's line of credit, Smith joined representatives of TWA and United on Capitol Hill to lobby for fare increases. Subsequently, as part of a compromise, American was awarded an airmail subsidy.

Still facing financial difficulties, company management attempted to raise cash by selling overseas routes served by the Amex (AEA) flying boats. The sale was blocked by the Civil Aeronautics Board (CAB). American needed the cash, and Juan Trippe at Pan Am actually wanted to purchase the overseas routes. As a result, they jointly lobbied the administration of President Harry S. Truman to overturn the CAB decision, but the timing was inauspicious. It was June 1950, and the president was focused on the war in Korea. A few weeks later, after the Korean situation stabilized, Truman did finally rule in favor of

the airlines and American was allowed the sale. Thus the company avoided a debilitating financial crisis.

American made the first scheduled nonstop transcontinental flights in 1953 with the 80-passenger DC-7. In 1955 American ordered its first jetliners, Boeing 707s, which were delivered in 1959. With larger and faster aircraft on the drawing boards, American became interested in, and eventually purchased, jumbo B-747s in the late 1960s. The company also ordered a number of supersonic transports, but was forced to cancel these orders when Congress halted funding to Boeing for their development.

C.R. Smith left American in 1968 for a position in the administration of President Lyndon B. Johnson, serving as secretary of commerce. Smith was succeeded at American by a lawyer named George A. Spater, who changed the company's marketing strategy and attempted to make the airline more attractive to vacationers instead of to the traditional business traveler, a plan that ultimately failed. Spater's presidency lasted only until 1973, when he admitted to making an illegal $55,000 corporate contribution to President Richard Nixon's reelection campaign. Some believe the gift was intended to procure favorable treatment from the Civil Aeronautics Board for American. As a result, American's board of directors decided to fire Spater and draft Smith out of retirement at the age of 74 to head the company again.

Relocating Headquarters to Dallas/Fort Worth in 1979

Smith retired after only seven months when the board of directors persuaded Albert V. Casey to leave the TimesMirror Company in Los Angeles to join American. As the new chief executive officer, Casey reversed the company's fortunes from a deficit of $20 million in 1975 to a record profit of $134 million in 1978. To everyone's surprise Casey moved the airline's headquarters from New York City to Dallas/Fort Worth in 1979. Although some said Casey was unhappy with his inability to gain acceptance in New York's social circles, Casey reasoned that a domestic airline should be based between the coasts. Believing the company needed to be shaken out of its lethargy, he felt that American would benefit from the relocation.

Soon afterward, American introduced "Super Saver" fares during 1977 in an innovative attempt to fill passenger seats on coast-to-coast flights. TWA and United followed suit after they failed to persuade the CAB to intervene.

Also in 1977 American was forced to rehire 300 flight attendants who were fired between 1965 and 1970 because they had become pregnant. The award also included $2.7 million in back pay. Compounding these setbacks, on May 25, 1979, an American DC-10 crashed at Chicago's O'Hare airport. Later blamed on inadequate maintenance procedures, the crash resulted in 273 deaths and a fine of $500,000 by the Federal Aviation Administration (FAA). Although the company collected $24.3 million in insurance benefits, it was forced to pay wrongful death settlements averaging $475,000 per passenger.

The Airline Deregulation Act of 1978 had the effect of making the airline industry suddenly volatile and competitive. American could adjust to deregulation in one of several ways. First, it could sell its jetliners once they were written down, and move into other, more promising businesses. Second, it could

Key Dates:

1930: American Airways Company is formed from a number of smaller airlines and related businesses.
1934: American Airways is renamed American Airlines; the company gains an airmail contract.
1950: American Airlines sells flying boat routes from newly acquired American Export Airlines to Pan Am.
1953: DC-7s allow American to launch nonstop transcontinental flights.
1959: American begins operating its first jets, Boeing 707s.
1978: American posts a record profit of $134 million; American adopts two-tier wage policy.
1979: American relocates its headquarters from New York to Dallas-Fort Worth.
1982: AMR Corporation is formed as the parent company of American Airlines.
1998: American forms oneworld alliance with several world airlines.
2000: The Sabre Group is spun off.
2001: American buys TWA; two jets carrying a full load of passengers and crew are lost in the September 11 terrorist hijackings.
2002: Major restructuring is underway.

scale down only partially, leaving a more efficient operation to compete with new airlines such as New York Air and People Express. A third option was to ask employees to accept salary reductions and other concessions as Frank Borman did at Eastern. In the end, American was not forced to take any of these measures. The company secured a two-tier wage contract with its employees and this new agreement reduced labor costs by as much as $10,000 a year per new employee. In addition, workers were given a profit-sharing interest in the company.

The Creation of AMR Corporation in 1982

Robert Crandall, formerly with Eastman Kodak, Hallmark, TWA, and Bloomingdale's, joined American in 1973 and became its president in 1980. On October 1, 1982, Crandall oversaw the creation of a holding company, the AMR Corporation. According to the company's 1982 annual report, this move would not affect daily business, but would "provide the company with access to sources of financing that otherwise might be unavailable." Known for his impatient and aggressive manner, Crandall may be credited with American's successful, but not completely painless, readjustment to the post-deregulation era. Crandall fired approximately 7,000 employees in an austerity drive, a decision that severely damaged his standing with the unions.

American updated its jetliner fleet to meet the new conditions in the industry during the 1980s by phasing in B-767s and MD-80s. The MD-80s had two major advantages over other aircraft: a two-person cockpit crew and high fuel efficiency. Crandall noted that American was developing a new, inexpensive airline inside the old one.

By the early 1980s, AMR had developed its Sabre computer reservations system into what was widely regarded as the best in

the industry. The Sabre system allowed agents to assign seats, reserve tickets for Broadway plays, book lodgings, and even arrange to send flowers to passengers. Extremely successful in filling space on American flights efficiently and inexpensively, the Sabre system eventually expanded by beginning operations in Europe.

As of 1982, American ran major hubs at Dallas/Fort Worth and O'Hare in Chicago. Secondary hubs in Nashville and Raleigh-Durham were intended to more firmly establish the airline in the Southeast. In addition to a multihub system and the reservations database, American contracted with smaller regional carriers.

American owned a number of subsidiaries when it created the AMR holding company. An airline catering business called Sky Chefs was started in 1942 and served American and several other air carriers. In 1977 American created AA Development Corporation and AA Energy Corporation. These subsidiaries—merged in 1984 to create AMR Energy Corporation—participated in the exploration and development of oil and natural gas resources, many of which were successful. The American Airlines Training Corporation, created in 1979, serviced military and commercial contracts that provided training for pilots and mechanics. All three subsidiaries were sold in 1986.

In 1985 American surpassed United in passenger traffic and regained after 20 years the title of number one airline in the United States. Although the company had dealt reasonably well with disruptions in the industry, and despite its stated intention to grow internally, AMR announced in November 1986 that it would acquire ACI Holdings, Inc., the parent company of AirCal, for $225 million. This move came in response to announcements by American's competitors Delta and Northwest, which had entered into cooperation agreements with western air carriers. The addition of AirCal's western routes significantly increased American's exposure on the West Coast and gave it a base for expanding American services across the Pacific Ocean. The late 1980s also saw AMR delve further into the regional airline business, acquiring Nashville Eagle, establishing American Eagle, and buying additional regional airlines.

Late 1980s Challenges

As the decade of the 1980s ended, the airline industry was challenged by a weakening economy and such costly developments as the fuel price spike caused by the Persian Gulf War, which contributed to industry losses of $2.4 billion in 1990. American pursued a strategy of acquiring key overseas routes from troubled or failed airlines, cutting costs, and using its leading position to harry its opponents in price wars. In 1989 it purchased TWA's Chicago operations and London routes, to which it added, in 1991, six more TWA London routes at a price of $445 million. Also that year, American purchased from failed Eastern Airlines the routes to 20 Latin American sites. By the close of the 1980s American was purchasing planes at a rate of one every five days; its fleet stood among the world's newest. At the same time, Crandall cut executive perks and flight expenses in a general program of internal belt-tightening. The CEO once ordered the removal of olives from all salads served on American planes, saving $100,000 a year.

Throughout the late 1980s and early 1990s, Crandall's ruthless—and effective—competitive strategies were the focus of industry controversy. Smaller airlines, as well as such larger and financially troubled airlines as TWA, accused Crandall of using unfair, "cannibalistic" tactics to create a situation in which a few major carriers, having eliminated their competition, could agree to maintain high prices without fear of being undercut. Crandall countered, however, according to *Business Week,* that American's strategies were perfectly within reason in an "intensely, vigorously, bitterly, savagely competitive" industry. Any shifts within the industry, including the elimination of some weaker companies, he argued, were a necessary if painful part of restructuring an industry with a surplus of carriers. Further, he contended, many of American's ailing competitors brought their woes upon themselves by initiating fare wars, which forced all carriers to sell seats at losses that the smaller carriers ultimately could not afford. The airline industry, Crandall commented in an interview with *Time,* "is always in the grip of its dumbest competitors."

In April 1992 American introduced a new airfare system, designed to simplify rates that had been made complicated over the years by myriad restricted, cut-rate fare specials. The new system included only four fares: first-class, coach, 7-day advance purchase, and 21-day advance purchase. Each price represented a cut in the fare for that category—up to 50 percent for first-class tickets—but the new system also eliminated the promotions that enabled vacation travelers to buy coach tickets at bargain rates. American held that the old discount fares were damaging the industry and that the new rates would be fairer to consumers. Detractors charged that the fares would benefit business travelers far more than tourists, and that the pricing system was designed to drive financially weak carriers out of business by forcing them to make fare cuts they could not afford. American's competitors soon matched its prices, then countered with a new wave of restricted, reduced fares.

After four straight years in the red from 1990 through 1993, AMR finally returned to profitability in 1994. The turnaround was at least in part an industrywide one as the excess capacity and intense fare wars in the U.S. airline industry during the early 1990s disappeared. Lower fuel prices also played a key role. In December 1995 American Airlines suffered its first fatal crash in 16 years when one of its planes crashed near Cali, Colombia. The following year AMR reduced its stake in its Sabre unit by about 20 percent through a public offering.

Alliances and Divestments: 1996–2002

Key developments in the late 1990s included alliances and divestments. One of the most important trends in the airline industry in the 1990s was that of global alliance building. In 1996 American Airlines and British Airways plc announced that they would form an alliance in which the two airlines would virtually operate as a single unit on North Atlantic runs. The plan, however, ran into severe regulatory problems, including a stipulation by the U.S. government that an "open skies" treaty between the United States and Britain precede any granting of antitrust immunity to the British Airways-American link-up. By late 1998 the open skies negotiations had ground to a halt. As it became more likely that the alliance with British Airways might never get off the ground, American Airlines shifted gears and announced in September 1998 the formation of the oneworld alliance. Oneworld initially included American, British Air-

ways, Canadian Airlines, Hong Kong's Cathay Pacific Airways, and Australia's Qantas Airways, with the partners agreeing to link their frequent-flier programs and give each other access to their airport lounge facilities. Finnair and Spain's Iberia were slated to join oneworld in 1999, and Linea Aerea Nacional de Chile (LanChile) agreed to become the eighth member starting in 2000. American also entered into a separate bilateral marketing alliance with US Airways in April 1998, again involving linked frequent-flier programs and reciprocal airport lounge facility access.

In September 1998 AMR announced that it would sell three subsidiaries that had been part of the Management Services Group in order to focus on its core airlines businesses. By the end of the year the company had reached agreements to sell all three, with AMR Combs Inc., an executive aviation services company, going to BBA Group plc of the United Kingdom for $170 million; TeleService Resources, a telemarketing firm, sold to Platinum Equity Holdings; and AMR Services, a ground services and cargo logistics unit, bought by New York merchant bank Castle Harlan. These divestments left AMR with two main lines of business: the Airline Group, which consisted of American Airlines and the American Eagle regional airline operations; and the Sabre Group, in which AMR held an 82.4 percent stake at the end of 1998.

American Airlines continued to be beset by labor troubles throughout the 1990s, including a brief strike by pilots in 1997 which ended after President Bill Clinton intervened, appointing a presidential emergency board to resolve the dispute through imposition of a new contract (under this pressure, the two sides soon reached their own agreement). When Crandall retired in May 1998, it appeared that better relations with labor might be on tap. Crandall's successor as chairman and CEO was Donald J. Carty, who had been president (a title he retained). Around the time of his promotion, Carty was quoted as having told union leaders that he planned to focus on employees because "happy employees make for happy customers, which make for happy shareholders." But trouble erupted following the December 1998 acquisition by AMR of low-cost carrier Reno Air, Inc. for $124 million. Reno Air had 27 planes in its fleet and hub cities in Reno, Nevada, and San Jose, California. Rather than operating it as a low-cost "airline-within-an-airline," AMR aimed to integrate Reno into American Airlines, thereby strengthening American's presence in the western United States. But when American attempted to integrate pilots from Reno Air without immediately giving pay raises to those Reno pilots moving into higher paying positions at American, members of the American Pilots Association (APA) began a sickout in early February 1999 that forced thousands of flight cancellations and crippled the airline. AMR sued the APA, winning a restraining order and an order for a return to work. After the pilots defied this order, a U.S. district judge found the union and its top two leaders in contempt of court for ignoring his order. This ended the sickout, but not before the eight-day action had cost AMR an estimated $150 million in lost business. In late February American and the APA agreed to attempt to resolve their dispute through nonbinding arbitration.

During 1999 American Airlines took delivery of 44 new airplanes, adding the Boeing 737 and 777 to its fleet. It was also in the midst of a $400 million program to overhaul the interiors of its 639-plane fleet, the first such change in 20 years. Sabre, meantime, rode the Internet wave of the late 1990s through Travelocity.com, its travel web site that was one of the leading sites for the purchase of airline tickets. These positive developments were tempered, however, by an antitrust lawsuit filed against American Airlines by the U.S. Department of Justice in May 1999. The Justice Department charged that the airliner in the mid-1990s had slashed fares upon the entry of low-cost rivals into its Dallas/Fort Worth hub, incurring losses in the process until the smaller competitors had been forced out. Following the departure of a rival, American would then raise fares and sometimes reduce service. American Airlines immediately responded with a vigorous denial of the charges, setting the stage for what could be a lengthy, contentious, and precedent-setting lawsuit—a lawsuit that was just one of the many challenges facing AMR at the end of the century.

AMR sold its remaining 82 percent stake in the Sabre computer reservations system group in March 2000. Travelocity, in which Sabre held a 70 percent stake, led all online ticket sales agencies with $1 billion in 1999 bookings. Sabre also provided American's IT services, and had contracts to do so until 2008.

In the summer of 2000, AMR pursued Northwest Airlines with a merger proposal. The company balked at NWA's high asking price, however. In January 2001, American announced a deal to buy ailing TWA and part of US Airways, which was being absorbed by United Airlines. AMR paid $742 million for TWA, which had been the eighth largest airline in the United States. The acquisition made American the world's largest airline, ahead of United. American agreed to hire most of TWA's 20,000 workers in the transaction.

American Airlines and British Airways had applied for anti-trust immunity similar to what allowed KLM and Northwest to cooperate so closely, and effectively. U.S. authorities refused to grant this status to British Airways and American without the two giving up landing slots in London to rivals, and American withdrew its application in February 2002.

A New Environment in the New Millennium

AMR's total operating revenues were $19.7 billion in 2000, resulting in net earnings of $770 million. The year 2001 began poorly for AMR, however, like most U.S. airlines, and continued to get worse. The traditionally strong second quarter— AMR had made a net profit of $285 million a year earlier—saw a loss of $105 million at AMR. A drop in business travel was the main cause.

American lost two aircraft full of passengers and 36 employees in the September 11 hijackings. The FAA banned all civil air operations in the two days following the tragedy, which stranded American planes and passengers at various airports, and delayed the deployment of the company's crisis management team. When thousands of flight crew members felt unable to fly, their unions relaxed their rules and allowed others to give up their own time off to take their place. The crash of American Airlines Flight 587 upon takeoff from JFK Airport in November 2001 added further trauma to a horrific year.

The two-day flying suspension and a drop-off in passenger traffic and ticket prices following the attacks in New York and at the Pentagon hurt most of the major airlines. AMR soon cut its capacity 20 percent, but still lost about $600 million in revenue in the last 20 days of September alone. AMR posted a record quarterly operating loss of $414 million in the third quarter, in spite of $508 million in government aid.

AMR posted a full-year net loss of $1.8 billion on total operating revenues of $19 billion in 2001. The company reduced the workforce by 20 percent, or 20,000 employees. Capital spending for 2002 was reduced 40 percent, from a planned $3.5 billion.

The airline simplified its fleet, retiring its MD-11, MD-90, DC-10, MD-87, and DC airliners in 2001. The fleet numbered 712 planes at the end of the year. In mid-2002, American retired its short-haul Boeing 717 fleet, acquired from the TWA take-over, in favor of the similar-sized Fokker F100s already in its fleet. The carrier aimed to operate only seven types of aircraft by the end of the year, down from 14 in 2000. Soon, the Fokkers also were added to the list of planes to be retired.

American lost $1.1 billion in the first half of 2002—a quarter of the amount lost by all U.S. airlines—and lost another $924 million in the third quarter alone. As business travelers disappeared, management was trying to adopt the budget airline methodology of such carriers as Southwest Airlines Co. It removed magazines from planes and skipped meals on flights of less than four hours. Arrivals and departures schedules were rearranged for efficiency, resulting in longer layovers. American's hub-and-spoke system, large and unionized workforce, and other manifestations of the archetypical full-service airline, however, were deeply entrenched in the company's culture. CEO Donald Carty told the *Wall Street Journal* the airline was looking for a middle ground "neither preoccupied solely with cost nor solely with revenue."

A sweeping overhaul was announced in August 2002. The company was cutting another 7,000 jobs. First-class service was removed on most flights, with the exception of major international routes. Economic instability in Latin America, an American Airlines stronghold, added to the considerable challenges the carrier was facing. The world's largest airline was still among the strongest financially, but AMR was still searching for a way to thrive in a dramatically different industry from the one it dominated for much of the 20th century.

Principal Subsidiaries

American Airlines, Inc.; American Eagle Airlines, Inc.; AMR Investment Services.

Principal Divisions

Passenger-American Airlines; TWA LLC; AMR Eagle; Cargo.

Principal Competitors

Continental Airlines, Inc.; Delta Air Lines, Inc.; Southwest Airlines Co.; UAL Corporation.

Further Reading

"The Airline Mess," *Business Week,* July 6, 1992.

Baumohl, Bernard, Deborah Fowler, and William McWhirter, "Fasten Your Seat Belts for the Fare War," *Time,* April 27, 1992.

Carey, Susan, "TWA's Sale to American Airlines Clears Hurdle, Is to Close Today," *Wall Street Journal,* April 9, 2001, p. B9.

Carey, Susan, and Scott McCartney, "AMR, Northwest Talks to Turn Serious As Pressure Rises for Decision on Merger," *Wall Street Journal,* July 12, 2000, p. C16.

Castro, Janice, " 'This Industry Is Always in the Grip of Its Dumbest Competitors,' " *Time,* May 4, 1992.

Dwyer, Paula, Wendy Zellner, and Stewart Toy, "A Megadeal in the Skies," *Business Week,* June 3, 1996, pp. 50–51.

Elkind, Peter, "Flying for Fun & Profit," *Fortune,* October 25, 1999, pp. 36–37.

Feldman, Joan M., "Adios to Sabre," *Air Transport World,* February 2000, pp. 58–62.

Fisher, Daniel, "The Ghost of Crandall," *Forbes,* November 15, 1999, pp. 52–53.

Goldsmith, Charles, and Julie Wolf, "EU Clears AMR/British Airways Alliance," *Wall Street Journal,* July 9, 1998, pp. A3, A10.

Helyar, John, "A Wing and a Prayer," *Fortune,* Investor's Guide Supp., December 10, 2001, pp. 178–88.

Jackson, Robert, *The Sky Their Frontier: The Story of the World's Pioneer Airlines and Routes, 1920–1940,* Shrewsbury, England: Airlife, 1983.

Jennings, Mead, "If You Can't Beat 'Em," *Airline Business,* January 1995, pp. 22+.

Kindel, Sharen, "(Well) Grounded," *Financial World,* October 12, 1993, pp. 90–91.

Laibioh, Kenneth, "American Takes on the World," *Fortune,* September 24, 1990.

Lieber, Ronald B., "Bob Crandall's Boo-Boos: The Fiery American Airlines Chairman Faces Labor Strife That Could Create Long-Lasting Scars at His Company," *Fortune,* April 28, 1997, pp. 365+.

Mathews, Anna Wilde, and Scott McCartney, "U.S. Sues American Air in Antitrust Case," *Wall Street Journal,* May 14, 1999, pp. A3, A6.

McCartney, Scott, "American Air's Crandall, About to Retire, Is Flying High," *Wall Street Journal,* April 27, 1998, p. B4.

——, "American Turns Its Attention to Performance," *Wall Street Journal,* May 7, 1997, pp. B1, B4.

——, "AMR, Challenging UAL in West, to Buy Reno Air," *Wall Street Journal,* November 20, 1998, pp. A3, A8.

——, "AMR, Forced to Cancel 22% of Flights, Threatens to Sue Pilots Over Sickout," *Wall Street Journal,* February 9, 1999, pp. A3, A11.

——, "AMR Plans to Auction Three of Its Units to Focus on American Airlines Business," *Wall Street Journal,* September 30, 1998, p. A4.

——, "AMR Posts $414 Million Loss Despite Aid from US Government," *Wall Street Journal,* October 25, 2001, p. A4.

——, "AMR Puts Pilot Costs Over $150 Million," *Wall Street Journal,* February 18, 1999, pp. A3, A12.

——, "At American Airlines, Pilots Trace Grievances to Deals in Lean Years," *Wall Street Journal,* February 11, 1999, pp. A1, A10.

——, "Clipped Wings: American Airlines to Retrench in Bid to Beat Discount Carriers," *Wall Street Journal,* August 13, 2002, p. A1.

——, "Tension at AMR Outlasts Fading Sickout," *Wall Street Journal,* February 16, 1999, pp. A3, A14.

Moorman, Robert W., "Eagle Preens Its Plumage," *Air Transport World,* April 1996, pp. 55–56, 59.

O'Donnell, Jane, "4 Airlines Post Loss for Quarter; AMR Exec: 'This Is a Very, Very Difficult Situation for the Industry,' " *USA Today,* July 19, 2001, p. B3.

Phillips, Edward H., "Government Aid Meets the Wolf at the Door; American Airlines: Worst Losses in History," *Aviation Week & Space Technology,* October 29, 2001, p. 68.

Reed, Dan, *The American Eagle: The Ascent of Bob Crandall and American Airlines,* New York: St. Martin's Press, 1993.

Serling, Robert J., *Eagle: The Story of American Airlines,* New York: Dial, 1980.

Tiburzi, Bonnie, *Takeoff! The Story of America's First Woman Pilot for a Major Airline,* New York: Crown, 1984.

Turk, Paul, "American: Skills for Sale," *Airline Business,* March 1993, pp. 60+.

Wong, Edward, "Pass Ideas to Center Aisle. American Needs 'Em," *New York Times,* July 21, 2002, p. 1.

——, "Relying on Business Clients, AMR Posts a Loss," *New York Times,* October 17, 2002, p. 3.

Woodbury, Richard, "How the New No. 1 Got There," *Time,* May 15, 1989.

Zellner, Wendy, "Portrait of a Project As a Total Disaster," *Business Week,* January 17, 1994, p. 36.

Zellner, Wendy, and Nicole Harris, "Where Are All Those Airline Tie-Ups Headed?," *Business Week,* May 11, 1998, pp. 32–33.

Zellner, Wendy, Mike McNamee, and Seth Payne, "Did Clinton Scramble American's Profit Picture?," *Business Week,* December 6, 1993, p. 44.

Zuckerman, Laurence, "At American, the Successor Bets Boldly," *New York Times,* January 13, 2001, p. C1.

—John Simley
—updates: David E. Salamie, Frederick C. Ingram

Anadarko Petroleum Corporation

1201 Lake Robbins Dr.
The Woodlands, Texas 77380-1046
U.S.A.
Telephone: (832) 636-1000
Fax: (281) 874-3385
Web site: http://www.anadarko.com

Public Company
Incorporated: 1959 as Anadarko Production Company
Employees: 3,500
Sales: $8.36 billion (2001)
Stock Exchanges: New York
Ticker Symbol: APC
NAIC: 211111 Crude Petroleum and Natural Gas
    Extraction; 213111 Drilling Oil & Gas Wells

Anadarko Petroleum Corporation is the largest independent oil and natural gas exploration and production company in the United States. The company's North American operations include drilling facilities in the Anadarko Basin; Wyoming; Alberta, Canada; and the Gulf of Mexico. Although 75 percent of the company's reserves are in North America, since the early 1990s it has developed a substantial overseas presence, establishing operations in Algeria, the Red Sea, and Peru. Between its domestic and international holdings, the company owns total proven reserves of more than 2.3 billion barrels of oil and oil equivalent.

Domestic Growth and Expansion: 1959–70

Anadarko was created in 1959 as a wholly owned subsidiary of Panhandle Eastern Pipe Line Company. At that time, Federal Power Commission (FPC) rules placed lower price limits on gas produced from properties owned by pipeline companies than on gas produced from independently owned properties. Panhandle owned a substantial amount of gas-producing property, located primarily in the Anadarko Basin, a gas-rich region covering parts of the Texas and Oklahoma panhandles and southwestern Kansas. Since regulations prevented Panhandle from charging the market price for the gas it produced, the company sought ways to skirt these price ceilings. Efforts in the courtroom failed, leaving the creation of a wholly owned subsidiary for gas exploration and production as the only option. Anadarko Production Company was officially incorporated in June 1959, with Panhandle owning all of its stock. Headquarters for the new company were established in Liberal, Kansas; Frederick Robinson was named chairperson, and Robert Harkins became company president.

Since properties developed by Anadarko were not subject to FPC pipeline pricing regulations, all of Panhandle's undeveloped properties were transferred to its new subsidiary. Although its gas properties that were already developed remained under FPC jurisdiction, Panhandle's oil producing properties were not subject to the same pricing rules. Therefore, they were transferred to Anadarko as well. By the end of 1959, Anadarko had drilled 17 wells in the Anadarko Basin, 14 of which were development wells, all of which were producers. One of the three exploratory wells was also a producer. Before its first full year of operation had ended, Anadarko had spent $2.5 million on exploration and had purchased 27 Texas panhandle producing gas wells.

Anadarko signed its first major long-term contract in 1960, a 20-year agreement with Pioneer Natural Gas Company to provide gas from the Red Cave formation in the Texas panhandle to several communities in the area. The following year, the company built an 84-mile pipeline in Kansas. The pipeline carried gas from the Spivey Grabs Field in Kingman and Harper counties to the Skelly Oil Refinery in El Dorado. Anadarko continued to grow quickly over the next few years, mainly by exploiting its rich properties on its home turf, the Anadarko Basin. Between 1962 and 1964, the company doubled its sales of natural gas, from 27 billion cubic feet to 53 billion. Its oil sales doubled over the same period, from 911,000 to 1.8 million barrels.

By the mid-1960s, Anadarko's future growth clearly depended on expansion outside the Anadarko Basin. Toward this end, in August 1965, the company purchased Ambassador Oil Corporation of Fort Worth, Texas, for $12 million. In purchasing Ambassador, Anadarko acquired assets that included undeveloped leases and proven oil and gas reserves totaling about

Company Perspectives:

At Anadarko, we strive for excellence in all that we do. We hire the best people in the business, then challenge and reward them for their efforts. We provide them training, technology and resources to do the job right. Our very low turnover rate is a true competitive advantage, helping us earn the reputation as a world-class oil and gas exploration and production company.

Everywhere we operate, we manage our assets in a manner that protects the environment and the health and safety of employees, contractors, neighboring communities, customers and partners. And we give back to the communities in which we work.

Our goals are to provide the energy that fuels economic growth and improves lifestyles and, in so doing, to deliver an attractive financial return for Anadarko shareholders.

600,000 acres, located in 19 states and Canada. Most of Ambassador's personnel were retained, and because of its more central location, Ambassador's Fort Worth offices were designated as Anadarko's new headquarters. While this transfer was taking place, Anadarko President Harkins died, and Richard O'Shields was named to replace him.

In 1968, O'Shields was promoted to executive vice-president of parent Panhandle Eastern, and R.C. Dixon succeeded him as Anadarko's top officer. Although the bulk of its operations were still taking place in the Anadarko Basin, the company was quite active in other places, particularly Alberta, Canada, where it was participating in seven oil wells near the Bantry West Field. This Alberta development program also included the acquisition of producing properties with 1.4 million barrels of estimated reserves. By 1969, 12 percent of parent company Panhandle's net income was being generated by Anadarko.

The Search for New Reserves: 1970–80

Anadarko's involvement in offshore exploration began in 1970. That year, the company acquired a one-eighth working interest in drilling rights to nine property blocks in the Gulf of Mexico. In 1971, Robert Stephens succeeded Dixon as Anadarko's president, and under Stephens, the company placed increasing emphasis on offshore operations, developing its own methods for collecting and analyzing geological and geophysical information used to evaluate potential offshore drilling leases. Of the Gulf of Mexico properties in which Anadarko had working interests, 24 blocks showed oil or gas in exploratory drilling between 1971 and 1976, and ten of them proved commercially productive.

In 1972, Panhandle created Pan Eastern Exploration Company, a new wholly owned subsidiary. All of Panhandle's remaining producing properties were transferred to Pan Eastern, which was to be operated by Anadarko. Pan Eastern spent $29 million on leases and drilling in its first year of existence and produced 116 billion cubic feet of gas from its Anadarko Basin reserves. Pan Eastern became part of Anadarko in 1981 and was eventually renamed APX Corporation in 1987. Anadarko's

headquarters were moved from Fort Worth to Houston in 1974. Two years later, when Stephens left the company, his replacement was Robert Allison, Jr., a petroleum engineer whom Stephens had brought on board as vice-president of operations.

Anadarko closed its second decade of operation by breaking the $100 million revenue barrier for the first time in 1978. By 1979, the company was contributing about 30 percent of Panhandle's net income. Around that time, Anadarko sought to expand its activities in the Gulf of Mexico, as higher gas prices resulting from the passage of the Gas Policy Act of 1978 created a major boom in gas exploration. Anadarko joined this boom by entering a farm-in arrangement with Amoco Corporation, in which Anadarko was to operate a project until a discovery was made. After the discovery, Amoco would have the option of re-entering the project as a half-interest partner. Located on Matagorda Island, the block (Matagorda 623) became a producer in early 1980. The group, consisting of Anadarko, Amoco, and Champlin Petroleum Company (to whom Anadarko had sold 25 percent of its deal with Amoco), then bid on a neighboring block that geophysical testing had shown to be promising. In 1982, the first well at Matagorda 622 was completed, and the block was found to have huge gas reserves. The Matagorda 622/623 blocks taken together represented a huge find for Anadarko, and the discovery sparked new interest in the Gulf of Mexico among many wildcat drillers.

The 1980s: Formation of Anadarko Petroleum Company

During this time, the company's onshore projects continued to operate successfully as well. A producing natural gas and oil-like condensate discovery well, 100 percent owned and operated by Anadarko, was completed in San Patricio County, Texas, in 1982. By the mid-1980s, Anadarko was clearly the most important subsidiary of Panhandle, accounting for 37 percent of Panhandle's 1984 profit while contributing only 11 percent of its revenue. Panhandle management recognized that the price of its stock was not reflecting the true value of the company, given the impressive results being turned in by Anadarko. As a result, management decided to spin Anadarko off to Panhandle's stockholders, in order to discourage potential takeover attempts. Anadarko Petroleum Corporation was created in 1985, and all of Anadarko Production Company's oil and gas assets were handed over to the new company.

However, one major obstacle prevented the spinoff from taking place immediately. In 1975, Panhandle had entered a 20-year contract with Sonatrach, Algeria's national energy company, to import liquefied natural gas from that country during the gas shortages of that period. By the time Algeria began shipping the gas in 1982, however, conditions in the United States had changed, and there was no longer a market for the wildly overpriced Algerian gas. Panhandle suspended deliveries, leading to an international squabble between the two companies, during which Panhandle could not spin off any assets, including Anadarko. In 1986, when Panhandle received word that a takeover attempt by a Texas investment group was imminent, attention to the Sonatrach negotiations was heightened and the dispute was settled, with Sonatrach receiving six million shares of Panhandle stock and $300 million in cash. Anadarko then became an independent company, taking APX

Corporation, Anadarko Petroleum of Canada, and other exploration and production subsidiaries with it.

Although the spinoff was essentially a friendly one, it was not entirely without conflict. Late in 1986, Anadarko sued its former parent over contracts the company felt were unfair. Under the terms of the contracts, Anadarko sold gas to Panhandle at below-market prices, an agreement made when Anadarko's board was still dominated by Panhandle officials. The Federal Energy Regulatory Commission eventually freed Anadarko from those agreements. For 1986, its first year as an independent company, Anadarko had net income of $10.1 million on revenue of $205.7 million.

By 1987, Anadarko had natural gas reserves of 1.7 trillion cubic feet, of which only 200 to 250 million cubic feet per day were being produced. In order to make better use of its reserves, in February of that year, the company launched a program of infill drilling at its Hugoton Field property in southwestern Kansas. Infill drilling involved the addition of a second well at an existing unit capable of tapping deeper gas reserves. Infill gas could be sold at a higher price than gas produced by the original well at a site. By early 1989, the company had drilled 146 infill wells. In addition to beefing up its exploration activities, Anadarko grew through acquisition during its first few years on its own. Among its purchases were certain oil producing properties in western Texas from Parker & Parsley Developments Partners, a regional energy company. By 1989, the company's revenue had grown to $361 million.

Global Expansion in the Early 1990s

Ground was broken in Houston in 1991 for Anadarko Towers, the company's new headquarters building and the first major commercial office building started in that city in over five years. Anadarko's revenue slipped to $336.6 million in 1991, but rebounded slightly to $375 million the following year. However, the company's earnings dropped further, sinking to $27 million, half that reported in 1990. In early 1993, Anadarko became the first foreign-owned company to discover oil in Algeria. The company had initially entered that country in 1989, the first year it was opened to foreign investment. Along with two European partners in the venture, Anadarko maintained drilling rights to a 5.1 million-acre area in the Sahara Desert. Anadarko's interest in the venture was 50 percent. Sonatrach, Algeria's national oil and

gas enterprise, in turn retained over 10 percent ownership of Anadarko's common stock.

Later in 1993, Anadarko teamed up with Amoco and Phillips Petroleum in discovering a huge shallow-water oil field in the Gulf of Mexico. The field, called Mahogany, was thought to hold at least 100 million barrels of oil, 37.5 percent of which was owned by Anadarko. For fiscal 1993, Anadarko reported record-high net income of $117 million on revenue of $476 million. For the 12th consecutive year, the company more than matched its production volumes of oil and gas with new proved reserves. Anadarko increased its exploration activities in the Gulf in early 1994. In April, the company paid $98 million for 26 different Gulf properties in a Minerals Management Service lease sale, hoping to repeat the success of Mahogany. Like Mahogany, the properties were nearly all "sub-salt plays," or potential finds located under salt formations. Anadarko also announced further oil discoveries in the deserts of Algeria, and development of those properties was accelerated.

In the short period since its spinoff from Panhandle Eastern, Anadarko's rate of success at wildcat drilling was remarkable. Its wealth of natural gas reserves in the Hugoton Basin also gave the company a great deal of control over its production, a huge advantage in an industry susceptible to market fluctuations. Anadarko was expected to become an even larger force among independent energy companies, if its discoveries of oil and gas in the Gulf of Mexico and Algeria continued into the late 1990s.

New Opportunities at Home and Abroad: 1995–2002

Anadarko's Algerian operations began to reap significant dividends by 1995, when new discoveries increased the company's total reserves in the region to approximately one billion barrels. In addition to these proven reserves, the company's overall success rate in the country, where six of its nine wells had struck oil, made the prospect of future discoveries seem extremely promising. Although the company expected lingering political unrest in Algeria to hamper its operations to some extent, it still hoped to be producing in excess of 30,000 barrels of crude per day within a year after obtaining its exploitation license.

Buoyed by its success in North Africa, Anadarko began exploring other overseas opportunities during the mid-1990s, most notably in the Red Sea. In the fall of 1995 the company entered into a production agreement with the Energy Ministry in Eritrea, in East Africa. With an initial investment of $28.5 million, the company planned to utilize the same computer technology used to analyze salt structures in the Gulf of Mexico to explore similar deposits in the Red Sea, where Eritrea's offshore reserves were still largely untapped. The company expanded its international operations even further the following year, when it entered into an agreement with Perupetro, the state oil company of Peru, to begin preliminary exploration of the country's Ucayali Basin.

However, Anadarko's overseas expansion efforts hit a snag in the late 1990s, when a steep decline in oil and natural gas prices took a significant bite out of Anadarko's revenues. The company's earnings fell by nearly 80 percent for the first quarter of 1998, with overall sales declining by 14 percent. Seeking to salvage something from the drop in prices, Anadarko began to look into expansion opportunities closer to home. In March 1998, the company acquired several new oil fields in Oklahoma from the Occidental Petroleum Corporation. With the cost of reserves down to $6 a barrel, the company was able to make the acquisition for only $120 million, while the addition of these new operations doubled the company's oil reserves in the Anadarko Basin.

The company began to experience a turnaround in July 1998, when it uncovered a reserve of more than 140 million barrels of oil in the Gulf of Mexico. In addition to being Anadarko's largest discovery in nearly two decades, the success also granted some much needed legitimacy to the company's subsalt exploration technology, paving the way for future discoveries in the Gulf and in the Red Sea.

In order to sustain such ambitious expansion, however, the company needed to bolster its operations. To this end, in April 2000 Anadarko announced its intention to acquire the Union Pacific Resources Group. The deal, worth more than $4.4 billion, promised to make the combined entity the largest oil and gas company in North America. In February 2001, the company further increased its presence in the Canadian oil market with the acquisition of Berkley Petroleum in Alberta for $777 million. In July of that year the company also acquired Gulfstream Resources Canada for $137 million. The latter deal gave Anadarko three offshore drilling sites off the coast of Qatar, with proven reserves of more than 70 million barrels of oil. Perhaps most significantly, the deal represented Anadarko's first substantial foray into the Middle East.

Anadarko suffered a setback in January 2002, when an internal accounting error resulted in the announcement of a net loss of $1.35 billion for the third quarter of 2001, substantially higher than the previously expected loss of $270 million. However, the loss did not prevent the company from pursuing further opportunities for growth, and by October 2002, it was able to invest more than $200 million to acquire two substantial oil fields in Wyoming, a state where potential reserves were estimated to exceed 500 million barrels. With this latest acquisition, Anadarko's position as the largest independent oil producer in the United States seemed more secure than ever.

Principal Subsidiaries

RME Petroleum Company; RME Holding Company; Anadarko Canada Energy Ltd.; Anadarko Canada Corporation; RME Land Corp.; Anadarko Algeria Company, LLC.

Principal Competitors

BP p.l.c.; Burlington Resources, Inc.; Exxon Mobile Corporation.

Further Reading

Antosh, Nelson, "Anadarko Ups Estimate of Reserves in Algeria," *Houston Chronicle*, March 9, 1995, Business Section, p. 1.

Burrough, Bryan, "Panhandle Eastern Considering Spinoff or Sale of Unit As Anti-Takeover Move," *Wall Street Journal*, August 19, 1985, p. 5.

Byrne, Harlan S., "Anadarko Petroleum," *Barron's*, December 18, 1989, p. 56.

Davis, Michael, "Anadarko Set to Buy UP Resources; $4.43 Billion Deal Would Unite Firms," *Houston Chronicle*, April 4, 2000, Business Section, p. 1

Durgin, Hillary, "Anadarko Buys More Oklahoma Properties," *Houston Chronicle*, March 12, 1998.

Frazier, Steve, "Anadarko Sues Panhandle Eastern Over Gas Contracts," *Wall Street Journal*, November 25, 1986, p. 18.

Ivanovich, David, "Anadarko Pays $98 Million for Gulf of Mexico Blocks," *Journal of Commerce*, April 4, 1994, p. 5B.

——, "Oil Discovery Is a First for Anadarko in Algeria," *Journal of Commerce*, February 22, 1993, p. 6B.

Mack, Toni, "Elephants, Anyone?," *Forbes*, April 11, 1994, p. 71.

——, "Of Sharks and Albatrosses," *Forbes*, September 23, 1985, pp. 114–15.

Marcial, Gene G., "A Slick Play in Energy," *Business Week*, December 27, 1993, p. 88.

Salpukas, Agis, "Anadarko Planning to Drill in Red Sea Salt Formations," *New York Times*, September 29, 1995, p. D2.

Stuart, Lettice, "New Office Tower Project Is Houston's First in 5 Years," *New York Times*, February 20, 1991, p. D20.

"Thirty Years of History," Houston: Anadarko Petroleum Corporation, 1989.

Thomas, Paulette, "Anadarko to Post Third-Quarter Profit, Faces Choices on Drilling, Acquisitions," *Wall Street Journal*, September 8, 1987, p. 16.

—Robert R. Jacobson
—update: Erin Brown

Asahi Breweries, Ltd.

3-7-1 Kyobashi
Chuo-Ku
Tokyo 104-8323
Japan
Telephone: (03) 5608-5112
Fax: (03) 5608-7111
Web site: http://www.asahibeer.co.jp

Public Company
Incorporated: 1949 as Asahi Beer, Ltd.
Employees: 3,799
Sales: ¥1.43 trillion ($10.86 billion) (2001)
Stock Exchanges: Tokyo Osaka Nagoya Fukuoka
Ticker Symbol: 2502
NAIC: 312120 Breweries; 422810 Beer and Ale
    Wholesalers; 312130 Wineries; 312140 Distilleries;
    422820 Wine and Distilled Alcoholic Beverage
    Wholesalers; 312111 Soft Drink Manufacturing;
    722110 Full-Service Restaurants

Asahi Breweries, Ltd. is the number one brewer in Japan; its 38.7 percent share of the Japanese market in 2001 edged out arch-rival Kirin Brewery Company, Limited, which had held the top spot from 1954 to 2000. Aiding Asahi's surge to the top was the 1987 introduction of Asahi Super Dry, which in a decade became the top-selling beer in Japan, a position it held into the early 21st century; in 2000 Asahi Super Dry was the number four beer brand in the world, with shipments of 20.9 million barrels. Other domestic brands include Kuronama, Fujisan, Super Malt, and Honnama, the latter being Asahi's entrée into the burgeoning *happoshu* (low-malt) category. Asahi is very active overseas and has built a network of alliances with such major brewers as Molson and Miller in North America and Bass and Löwenbräu in Europe, as well as making aggressive moves to capture a major share of the emerging market in China. In addition to its brewery operations, which account for about 75 percent of the company's net sales, Asahi manufactures and markets other alcoholic beverages (including distilled spirits and wines), soft drinks (headed by the flagship Mitsuya Cider), and food products (mainly brewer's yeast extracts and related products); sells pharmaceuticals; and runs restaurants.

Early History

The history of Asahi Breweries is linked with that of virtually every other brewery in Japan. Beer had been introduced to Japan in the mid-1800s. The American in large part responsible for renewing trade relations with Japan, Commodore Matthew Perry, brought several cases of beer to Japan as a gift for the Tokugawa Shogunate. The beverage was so well liked that the Japanese government soon decided to establish a brewing industry. After an extensive search for a suitable area, wild hops were found growing on the island of Hokkaido, the northernmost island in the Japanese archipelago. As a result, in 1876 the Commissioner-General for the development of Hokkaido founded Japan's first brewery in the town of Sapporo. (Coincidentally, the global beer capitols of Munich, Milwaukee, and Sapporo are all located along the 45 degrees north latitude.)

In the late 1880s the government sold its Hokkaido brewery to private interests—and thus the Osaka Beer Brewing Company, Japan Beer Brewery Company, Sapporo Brewery, and Nippon Brewing Company all came into being. In 1888 Hiizu Ikuta was sent to Germany by Osaka Beer Brewing Company to study brewing at the famous School of Weihenstephen in Bavaria. He returned the following year and was appointed manager and technical chief of the Suita Brewery, one of the individual breweries controlled by Osaka. Three years later, in 1892, his creation, Asahi Beer, was released for sale. Osaka was reorganized in 1893 as Osaka Breweries, Ltd.

In 1906 the Osaka Breweries, Sapporo Brewery, and Nippon Brewing Company were amalgamated into the Dai Nippon Brewery Co., Ltd. Asahi, now a separate division of the new company, began a long history of producing nonalcoholic beverages as well as beer. Asahi pioneered the soft drink industry in Japan with both Mitsuya Cider and Wilkinson Tansan, a mineral water. Mitsuya Cider was released for sale in 1907, 17 years after Asahi Beer had first been introduced to the market.

In the years leading up to World War II, particular beer brands tended to dominate local markets. The Asahi brand

Company Perspectives:

The Asahi Breweries Group aims to satisfy customers with the highest levels of quality and integrity, while contributing to the promotion of healthy living and the enrichment of society worldwide.

gained popularity in the Kansai area. The Asahi division expanded in 1921 through the completion of the Hakata brewery and in 1927 with the opening of the Nishinomiya brewery.

Forming Asahi Breweries, Ltd. in 1949

In 1949, as a result of the enactment of the Excessive Economic Power Decentralization Law, Dai Nippon Brewery, which had cornered nearly 70 percent of the beer market in Japan, was divided into two parts—Asahi Beer, Ltd. and Nippon Breweries, Ltd. (the latter later emerged as Sapporo Breweries Limited). In 1951 Asahi introduced Wilkinson Tansan mineral water to the Japanese market. That year also saw the introduction of Japan's first fruit-flavored soft drink, Bireley's Orange. In 1958 the company launched a canned version of Asahi Beer, Japan's first canned beer. Asahi's first plant exclusively devoted to the production of soft drinks was opened in Kashiwa in 1966. Six years later another Asahi soft drink plant began production in Fukushima. By the mid-1970s soft drink sales accounted for 35 percent of the company's total sales.

Asahi also enjoyed other kinds of success. Its Central Research Laboratory, charged primarily with quality control, also developed new products, including "Ebios," a day brewer's yeast renowned in Japan for its medicinal properties; the company introduced Ebios in 1930 and has been manufacturing it ever since. In 1965 laboratory staff invented the world's first outdoor fermentation and lagering tank (the "Asahi Tank"); the West German beer plant construction firm of Ziemann soon negotiated with the company for a license to build the tank.

The early 1970s saw Asahi take its first serious moves outside Japan and in the area of importing. In 1971, in a joint venture with Nikka Whiskey Distilling Company, Asahi established Japan International Liquor to import foreign liquors, primarily Scotch whiskeys (Dewars and King George IV). Also in 1971, Asahi was the first Japanese brewery to have its beer produced overseas under license when it concluded a technical assistance agreement with United Breweries of New Guinea, and a brewery was subsequently constructed at Port Moresby. Two years later Asahi began to import French and German wine. In January 1986 a technology transfer agreement was reached with the San Miguel Corporation of Indonesia for the local production of Asahi beer. Another technical transfer agreement had previously been reached in 1979 with this same company for the use of Asahi's automatic beer gauge system for beer fermentation at other plants under San Miguel control. This system had been jointly developed by Asahi and the Toshiba Corporation.

Asahi entered the restaurant business in the early 1980s. Subsidiary companies—Asahi Kyoei and New Asahi—managed more than 100 restaurants in western and eastern Japan, respectively. The company also entered into a joint venture with the U.S. company Pizza Hut to establish Pizza Hut restaurants in Japan.

Turnaround in Market Share: Mid-1980s

In October 1981 Asahi Chemical Industry (despite their similar names, the companies were not previously related) acquired 22 million shares of Asahi Beer, Ltd. An agreement was concluded between the two companies concerning relations involving personnel, technology, and sales. Asahi Chemical eventually held about 10 percent of Asahi stock, making it one of the brewer's ten largest shareholders.

Another of Asahi's important shareholders at this time was the Sumitomo Group, which held about a 12 percent stake. Over the preceding decades, Asahi's share of the Japanese beer market had declined significantly, from a peak of 36 percent in 1949 to 10 percent in 1981. Among Japanese brewers, Asahi was a distant third, trailing both Kirin and Sapporo Breweries. Executives at Sumitomo Bank had been placed into the president's office starting in the early 1970s, but they were unable to stop the decline. Then in January 1982 another Sumitomo Bank executive, Tsutomu Murai, was sent to Asahi to take over. Murai specialized in turning around troubled companies and had previously helped to rescue Mazda Motor Corporation.

Murai began with a reorganization aimed at improving communication between company departments. He then concluded a series of licensing agreements with foreign companies. In November 1982 the company entered into an agreement with the Löwenbräu Company of West Germany to produce Lowenbrau Beer under license in Japan; production of the German beer began the following April. Asahi also gained needed technical know-how by signing contracts with U.S., British, and German brewers to obtain technology. In 1984 Asahi's soft drink division concluded an agreement with Schweppes, which led to Asahi manufacturing several Schweppes brands in Japan—Tonic Water, Golden French (an apple and ginger drink), Passion Orange, and Grapefruit Dry. Asahi entered into other partnerships, notably to import foreign beers and wines into Japan. Asahi in 1985 formed a partnership with the Australian wine company Lindemann's, after which Asahi sold Australian wine under the "My Cellar" brand.

Perhaps most important, Murai pushed the company to become more attuned to its customers. One byproduct of this was a renewed attention to quality. Asahi abandoned its policy of buying most of its wheat and hops in Japan and began to buy the best raw materials available, regardless of cost or origin. The company also made moves to ensure the freshness of its beer, such as having salespeople visit stores where they would throw out any Asahi beer older than three months.

In 1985 Murai ordered a series of market surveys. Of most significance was that 98 percent of the beer drinkers surveyed advised Asahi to change the taste of its beer; consumers said that they wanted a beer that was rich but left no aftertaste, a combination that the company's technicians said was not chemically possible. Murai insisted that nothing was impossible, and Asahi subsequently developed and introduced in 1986 Asahi Draft, a full-bodied beer with a crisp taste. Then in March 1987 Asahi introduced Japan's first dry beer, Asahi Super Dry, which became

Key Dates:

1889: Japanese government sells its Hokkaido brewery to private interests, simultaneously establishing Osaka Beer Brewing Company and several other brewing companies.

1892: Osaka begins production of Asahi Beer.

1893: Osaka is reorganized as Osaka Breweries, Ltd.

1906: Osaka, Sapporo Brewery, and Nippon Brewing Company are amalgamated into Dai Nippon Brewery Co., Ltd., which includes a separate division called Asahi.

1907: Asahi introduces the Mitsuya Cider soft drink brand.

1949: Dai Nippon is divided into two parts: Asahi Beer, Ltd. and Nippon Breweries, Ltd.

1958: Canned version of Asahi Beer, Japan's first canned beer, is introduced.

1983: Asahi begins producing Lowenbrau Beer under license in Japan.

1987: Asahi Super Dry is introduced and becomes a blockbuster hit.

1989: Asahi Beer, Ltd. is renamed Asahi Breweries, Ltd.

1994: A push into the burgeoning Chinese market begins with the purchase of controlling interests in several breweries.

1995: Wide-ranging alliance with U.S.-based Miller Brewing Company commences.

1996: Super Dry becomes the top-selling beer in Japan.

2001: Asahi enters the *happoshu* segment with the introduction of Honnama; company gains the top spot in the Japanese beer market, edging past longtime rival Kirin.

a blockbuster hit. Super Dry, a cold-filtered draft beer, contained slightly more alcohol than other Japanese beers—5 percent compared with 4.5 percent—but less sugar and was thus lighter; it was also less bitter. The brand became particularly popular among younger drinkers and helped Asahi's market share increase to 17 percent just one year after its introduction.

So successful was Super Dry that Murai had to abandon a planned diversification that aimed to derive half of the company's revenue from nonbeer operations. Instead, beer increased in importance, making up 80 percent of sales in 1988.

Marketing Innovations and Globalization in the Late 1980s and 1990s

By the end of the 1980s Asahi's market share had surpassed the 20 percent mark and the company (which was renamed Asahi Breweries, Ltd. in January 1989) leapfrogged Sapporo into second place among Japanese brewers. In addition to the new brands, Asahi's success in the late 1980s and early 1990s was also attributable to changes in marketing. In Japan, most beer was traditionally sold in small liquor stores by the bottle. Asahi targeted nontraditional customers by producing more of its beer in cans and packaging it in six-packs, and by sending the canned beer into supermarkets and convenience stores. The company

also became much more aggressive in its pitches to retailers who sold beer. Asahi continued to emphasize the freshness of its product and by 1995 was able to deliver beer to stores just ten days after brewing. By 1997 Super Dry had dethroned Kirin's Lager brand from the top spot among Japanese beer brands, and Asahi's overall market share hit 34.4 percent, up from 10 percent in 1985. During the same period, Kirin's market share had plummeted from 60 percent to 43 percent.

From the late 1980s into the mid-1990s, Asahi continued to be active in importing but at the same time stepped up its export activities. A technological agreement was reached with the U.K.-based Bass Brewers Ltd. in 1988, whereby Asahi began to import the Bass Pale Ale brand. In 1996 the two companies entered into a new agreement that called for Bass to produce and market Asahi Super Dry in the United Kingdom and elsewhere in Europe.

In 1990 Asahi gained further access to manufacturing and marketing channels outside Japan by purchasing a significant stake—which stood at 20 percent in 1992—in Foster's Brewing Group Ltd., based in Australia and then the fourth largest beer company in the world. In the succeeding years Asahi expanded its own system of overseas operations so that the purpose of the tie-in with Foster's grew less important. Asahi consequently reduced its stake, then in mid-1997 sold its remaining 14 percent stake back to Foster's.

A 1994 license agreement with Molson Breweries brought Super Dry into the Canadian market. Asahi then targeted the two largest beer markets in the world—the United States and China. In 1995 a wide-ranging alliance with the Miller Brewing Company commenced, which initially featured the introduction of the Miller Special brand in Japan—a brand brewed specifically for the Japanese market—and the Super Dry brand in the United States. In September 1996 Asahi and Miller introduced Asahi First Lady, a beer targeted toward women, in Japan and the United States. In April 1998 Asahi Beer U.S.A., Inc. was established as a U.S. marketing and sales company that would work with the Miller distribution network to increase sales of Super Dry in the world's leading beer market.

On the Chinese front, in 1994 and 1995 Asahi acquired shares in and began managing five Chinese brewing companies in Beijing, Yantai, Hangzhou, Quanzhou, and Jiaxing. Initially four of the companies sold a beer called Asahi Bichu, then in March 1998 Yantai Beer Asahi Co., Ltd. launched the production and sale of Asahi Super Dry. Meanwhile, in December 1997, Asahi entered into a joint venture with the largest beer maker in China, Tsingtao Brewery Co., to construct a state-of-the-art beer plant in Shenzhen. Production of Asahi Super Dry began at this plant in May 1999.

In addition to growing market share in Japan and an increasing presence in Europe, North America, and China, further proof of the brewer's resurgence came in 1996 when Asahi posted record net sales and net income. Asahi repeated the feat in 1997. In mid-1997 the company finished construction of a new research and development center in Ibaraki Prefecture and was confidently building its ninth brewery, the Shikoku brewery, which was subsequently completed in June 1998. In March 1999 Asahi reached an agreement with Bass Brewers whereby

Bass would undertake local production of Asahi Super Dry through an affiliate in the Czech Republic called Prague Breweries, A.S.

Becoming the Number One Japanese Brewer in the Early 21st Century

In the late 1990s and into the early 2000s, the overall beer market in Japan was stagnant (in part because of the shrinking number of young people), but there was a significant shift occurring in the types of beers that Japanese people were consuming. Rapidly growing in popularity were low-malt beers known as *happoshu*. In the mid-1990s, some Japanese brewers decided to take advantage of the fact that beer in Japan is taxed according to its malt content. The tax on low-malt beers was significantly lower, resulting in a retail price about two-thirds that of a regular beer. Budget-conscious consumers snapped up the lower-priced beer in increasing numbers, such that by 2000 the *happoshu* segment accounted for 22 percent of the overall beer market. (To maintain a beer-like taste, producers of *happoshu* used various types of malt substitutes.)

For some time, Asahi had been able to ignore the *happoshu* phenomenon because Asahi Super Dry was defying the trend and continuing to gain market share. As the low-malt interlopers continued to gain market share, however, Asahi felt compelled to launch its own *happoshu* brand. Asahi Honnama launched in February 2001 and captured 22.3 percent of the *happoshu* market for 2001, despite Asahi being the last of the major Japanese brewers to enter the segment. This terrific debut helped Asahi Breweries finally surpass Kirin and claim the top spot in the Japanese beer market for 2001 with a market share of 38.7 percent.

The year 2001 also saw Asahi return to the black after posting a net loss in 2000 that was attributable to large write-offs of unrealized losses from securities holdings and pension-related liabilities. Overall sales for 2001 increased 2.4 percent over the previous year, with the ¥1.43 billion ($10.86 billion) figure being a record for the company. In addition to its successful introduction of Honnama, Asahi also was concentrating on strengthening its nonbeer alcoholic beverage operations in order to develop a more complete lineup of alcoholic products. To that end, Asahi announced in February 2002 that it would acquire the alcoholic beverage businesses of Kyowa Hakko Kogyo Co. for about ¥20 billion ($150.8 million). The deal included production and sales facilities for ready-mixed alcohol drinks, wine, and *shochu*, a distilled liquor comparable to vodka. In April 2002 Asahi reached an agreement with Maxxium Worldwide, a Dutch liquor sales firm, whereby Asahi gained the rights to market in Japan such brands as Remy Martin brandy, Highland Park whiskey, Absolut vodka, Cointreau liqueur, and Maison Louis Latour wine. Also in April 2002 Asahi agreed to purchase the *shochu* and low-alcohol beverage operations of Asahi Kasei Corporation. In August 2002 Asahi declared that it would buy a 10 percent stake in Okinawa-based Orion Beer Co., the fifth largest brewer in Japan with a market share of almost 1 percent. This last was a seemingly minor deal, but it did show that Asahi, having finally gained the top spot in Japanese brewing, was likely to leave no stone unturned in fighting to maintain that long-coveted position.

Principal Subsidiaries

The Nikka Whisky Distilling Co., Ltd.; Asahi Beer Pax Co., Ltd.; Asahi Soft Drinks Co., Ltd. (51.2%); Asahi Beer Food, Ltd.; Asahi Beer Pharmaceutical Co., Ltd. (99.8%); Nippon National Seikan Company, Ltd.; Asahi Beer Malt, Ltd. (91.9%); Asahi Logistics Co., Ltd.; Asahi Food Create, Ltd.; Asahi Beer Garden, Ltd.; Asahi Beer Real Estate, Ltd.; Asahi Beer U.S.A., Inc. (99.2%); Asahi Beer International Finance B.V. (Netherlands); Asahi Beer Europe Limited (U.K.); Buckinghamshire Golf Company Limited (U.K.); Asahi Breweries Itochu (Holdings) Ltd. (China); Hangzhou Xihu Beer Asahi Co., Ltd. (China; 55%); Jiaxing Haiyan Beer Xihu Asahi Co., Ltd. (China; 55%); Quanzhou Qingyuan Beer Asahi Co., Ltd. Fujian (China; 60%); Asahi Breweries Itochu China (Holdings) Ltd.; Beijing Beer Asahi Co., Ltd. (China; 55%); Yantai Beer Asahi Co., Ltd. (China; 53%); Yantai Beer Dong Ying Xinyi Co., Ltd. (China; 60%); Asahi Beer (China) Investment Co., Ltd.; Asahi Beer (Shanghai) Product Services Co., Ltd. (China); Qingdao Tsingtao Beer & Asahi Beverage Co., Ltd. (China; 60%).

Principal Competitors

Kirin Brewery Company, Limited; Sapporo Breweries Limited; Suntory Limited; Takara Holdings Inc.; Mercian Corporation.

Further Reading

"Asahi Flattens Kirin's King of Beers," *Nikkei Weekly,* July 8, 1996, p. 9.

Ellison, Sarah, "Asahi Beer Ads Brew Bewilderment, Taste of Tokyo for Britain's Bass PLC," *Wall Street Journal,* May 15, 2000, p. A9.

Jameson, Sam, "Team Spirit: The Case of Asahi Breweries Illustrates How Bank Rescues of Struggling Firms Help the Japanese Economy. But There Is No Guarantee of Success," *Los Angeles Times,* December 8, 1988, pp. 1, 11.

"Japan's Beer Wars," *Economist,* February 28, 1998, p. 68.

Joyce, Andee, "It's Dry, Dry Again, As Asahi Takes a Super Stab in the US," *Beverage World,* June 30, 1998, p. 8.

Kachi, Hiroyuki, "Asahi Breweries' China Plan Would Leave Rivals in Dust," *Asian Wall Street Journal,* December 15, 1997, p. 14.

——, "Asahi Continues to Catch Up to Kirin in Beer Battle," *Asian Wall Street Journal,* February 20, 1998, p. 7.

Miller, Karen Lowry, "Can Asahi Brew Up Another Blockbuster?," *Business Week,* March 4, 1991, p. 41.

Moffett, Sebastian, "High and Dry: Asahi's Deft Moves Win Over Japan's Beer Drinkers," *Far Eastern Economic Review,* October 3, 1996, pp. 98–99.

Pollack, Andrew, "The Company That Makes Japan's Best-Selling Beer Seeks Inroads into the U.S. Market," *New York Times,* April 20, 1998, p. D8.

"A Right Old Brewhaha in Japan," *Economist* (U.S. edition), February 24, 2001, p. 7.

Smith, Charles, "Satisfying a Dry Thirst: A Japanese Brewery Enjoys Success with a New Type of Beer," *Far Eastern Economic Review,* September 1, 1988, p. 50.

Tomioka, Katsuhiko, "The Secret Behind Asahi's Growth: Interview with Yuzo Seto, President of Asahi Breweries," *Japan 21st,* November 1996, pp. 12–13.

Yamamoto, Yuri, "In Beer Battle, Kirin Goes Flat While Asahi Barrels Ahead," *Nikkei Weekly,* March 3, 1997, pp. 1, 19.

——, "Japan's Brewers Tapping Chinese Market," *Nikkei Weekly,* October 7, 1996, pp. 1, 21.

—update: David E. Salamie

Australia and New Zealand Banking Group Limited

Level 6
100 Queen Street
Melbourne 3000
Victoria
Australia
Telephone: (03) 9273-6141
Fax: (03) 9273-6142
Web site: http://www.anz.com.au

Public Company
Incorporated: 1835 as The Bank of Australasia
Employees: 22,482
Total Assets: A$183.11 billion (US$99.63 billion) (2002)
Stock Exchanges: Australia New Zealand New York
Ticker Symbol: ANZ
NAIC: 522110 Commercial Banking; 522210 Credit Card
Issuing; 522291 Consumer Lending; 522292 Real
Estate Credit; 522293 International Trade Financing;
523110 Investment Banking and Securities Dealing;
523930 Investment Advice; 524113 Direct Life
Insurance Carriers; 525910 Open-End Investment
Funds; 551111 Offices of Bank Holding Companies

Australia and New Zealand Banking Group Limited (ANZ) is the second largest of the "Big Four" banks in Australia, trailing only National Australia Bank Limited. Worldwide, ANZ ranks as one of the top 100 financial services firms. The group offers a full range of retail banking services in its base countries of Australia and New Zealand, serving nearly four million customers through a network of some 900 branches and more than 1,500 ATMs. Additional retail banking operations are located in the Asia-Pacific region, including Indonesia and Hawaii. Other products and services include mortgage financing, consumer financing (ANZ is the number one credit card issuer in Australia), vehicle and equipment financing and rental services, wealth management, corporate banking for small, medium-sized, and large companies, investment banking, and foreign exchange and commodity trading. ANZ and ING Group of The Netherlands run a joint venture in funds management and life insurance called ING Australia Limited. ANZ

was formed when the Australia and New Zealand Bank Limited (ANZ Bank) merged with the English, Scottish and Australian Bank Limited in 1970. ANZ Bank was the result of a merger in 1951 between the Bank of Australasia and the Union Bank of Australia.

19th-Century Origins of the Major Predecessor Banks

The Bank of Australasia (Asia) is believed to have been the idea of Thomas Potter Macqueen, a wealthy colonist who proposed a joint bank and whaling enterprise to some London investors, who liked his idea well enough to become the bank's first provisional directors. Macqueen, however, was caught promoting the rival Commercial Banking Company of Sydney behind the directors' backs, and the Bank of Australasia opened in 1835 without him.

The Union Bank of Australia was founded in a similar fashion. This time a struggling Australian bank, the Tamar Bank in Tasmania, went to London in search of capital and found a group of investors prepared to back a bank in the colony. They founded the Union, which took over the Tamar Bank and opened for business in 1837.

These two groups of investors based their hopes for the Asia and the Union on Australia's potential to meet the large demand for wool by English textile mills. Although some colonial banks already existed, none of these local institutions could match the financial resources of London-based, private trading banks like the Asia or the Union. Moreover, because these colonial banks were unable to tap the British capital market for another 30 years (except for the Commercial Banking Company of Sydney, which did give the British banks some competition), not one of them survived five years. In contrast, the Asia and the Union were immediately successful—the Asia quadrupled its loans between 1836 and the end of the decade.

In 1838 the New Zealand Company, a colonizing enterprise, approached both the Asia and the Union about opening a branch in the firm's new settlement. The Asia hesitated because it had reservations about the New Zealand Company. The Union agreed, however, and became the first bank to do business in New Zealand.

Company Perspectives:

The Bank with a human face. Put our customers first. Perform and grow to create value for our shareholders. Lead and inspire each other. Earn the trust of the community. Breakout, be bold and have the courage to be different.

Between 1838 and 1841 the Australian sheep-farming boom reached new and feverish heights. During this period both the Asia and the Union consolidated their positions and built up businesses secure enough to withstand the severe depression that began in late 1841. Both banks had the financial strength to take advantage of colonial banks decimated by the depression: in 1840 the Union absorbed the Bathurst Bank, in 1841 the Asia acquired the Bank of Western Australia, and, in 1844 at the height of the depression, the Union merged with Archers Gilles & Company.

With the discovery of copper and lead deposits north of Adelaide in 1844, the colonies began moving out of the depression. The discovery of gold near Bathurst, New South Wales, in 1851 soon produced a general boom. In these new economic circumstances, gold and foreign-exchange dealing became significant banking services, and branch-banking programs flourished with the influx of new mining customers eager for mortgages.

During the ''golden decade'' of the 1850s, new banks formed to challenge the foreign-exchange primacy of the Asia and the Union, among them the English, Scottish and Australian Bank (ES&A), which was founded in 1852. Although the ES&A's presence concerned the Asia and the Union, an even greater threat came from the new colonial banks that burgeoned in the country at mid-century. To better compete with English banks, these colonial institutions established London offices of their own, while they also acquired enough colonial investment resources, mainly gold, to provide their own international banking. Thus, from this time on, the Asia and the Union had to share their international role both with new London-controlled banks and with strong colonial competitors.

Surviving the Late 19th-Century Bank Crash

Between 1860 and 1890 Australia saw prolonged and rapid economic development. But the conservative Asia and Union banks began to prepare for the inevitable downturn in the late 1880s; this letter from the secretary of the Asia, Prideaux Selby, to his superintendent, John Sawers, in July 1888 gives the flavor of the time:

> Lower rates. . . . Let really sound customers feel that they do better by borrowing from us than by looking outside. Keep up rates to those we would rather be without and to those who can only give ordinary security. Sell dead securities while the boom lasts. Shake off speculators and doubtful customers. Do not look for immediate results. Give the seed time to germinate before looking to the harvest, and remember that unless the seed be sown and for the time lost to use, there never can be a harvest at all.

Both the Asia and the Union had steadily built cash reserves up to 20 percent of all liabilities to the public and remitted heavily to London rather than permit colonial loans to expand. Moreover, both banks had large floating advances to the money market and extensive and varied holdings of gilt-edged stocks from which they could draw in an emergency. Beyond this, they also had many informal connections with other financial institutions. Thus, during the great bank crash of 1893, both the Asia and the Union had a number of sources to turn to for help, including the Bank of England.

In the 35 years after 1853, 28 colonial banks began operations in Australia. Only six of these colonial banks reached the end of the century without temporary or final failure, and of the eight private trading banks that existed in 1850, only the Asia, the Union, and three others survived.

Many of the post-1850 banks failed because they were governed by over-optimism and an avid search for business without enough concern for security. They opened branch banks in small towns without assessing the costs closely, and they attempted to increase their loan portfolios quickly by minimizing risk factors. The Asia and Union never deviated from their conservative policies, but were cautious about opening new offices and circumspect in approving loans.

With the passing of the banking crisis, both the Asia and the Union attempted to increase their lowered earnings. Salaries were reduced and marginal branch banks were closed, except in western Australia, where gold discoveries promised great opportunities. But, more important than branch policy, both banks tried to restrain the unprofitable accumulation of deposits by cutting interest rates, which they believed would decrease the cost of funds and earn the banks more fees through the marketing of cheaper loans to customers. In 1895 both banks agreed to cut interest rates everywhere in the colonies to 3 percent, even though other banks did not follow.

Despite these measures to preserve profits, the Asia and the Union realized losses in loans to customers who had been devastated in the banking crisis. Although neither bank had missed a dividend payment at any time in its history, stockholders voiced concerns when rates of return fell markedly short of their expectations. Although these dividend results were similar for both banks, the Asia's board maintained confidence in Superintendent John Sawers and his staff, while the Union's board resolved that General Manager David Finlayson should retire.

Expanding in the Early 20th Century

By 1900, the Asia held 12.7 percent of all deposits and 9.3 percent of all advances, and the Union held 12.1 percent of all deposits and 10.6 percent of all advances in Australia, and both were members of Australian banking's Big Four banks (the Bank of New South Wales and the Commercial Banking Company of Sydney were the other two). The other 17 banks in the country were substantially smaller and confined to one or two colonies. Thus, at the beginning of the 20th century the Asia and the Union enjoyed relative strength and prestige throughout the Australian Commonwealth.

In the first decade of the new century, a stable economy prompted both the Asia and the Union to pursue policies of ''complacent growth'' through branch bank expansion. Between 1900 and the outbreak of World War I, the Asia opened

Key Dates:

1835: The Bank of Australasia is founded in London.

1837: Also founded in London is the Union Bank of Australia, which takes over the struggling Tamar Bank in Tasmania.

1838: The Union becomes the first bank to do business in New Zealand.

1852: The English, Scottish and Australian Bank (ES&A) is founded.

1951: Bank of Australasia and the Union merge to form the Australia and New Zealand Bank Limited (ANZ Bank).

1955: ANZ Bank creates a savings bank subsidiary called the Australia and New Zealand Savings Bank Ltd.

1970: ANZ Bank and ES&A merge to form Australia's third largest bank, Australia and New Zealand Banking Group Limited (ANZ).

1976: ANZ changes its domicile from London to Melbourne.

1979: The Bank of Adelaide is acquired.

1984: U.K.-based Grindlays Bank is acquired.

1989: With the acquisition of PostBank of New Zealand, ANZ becomes the largest banking group in that nation.

1992: Deep recession and provisions for bad loans lead to a net loss of A$579 million.

1993: ANZ purchases an 85 percent interest in an Indonesian joint venture bank that is later renamed PT ANZ Panin Bank.

1997: John McFarlane takes over as CEO and launches a thorough restructuring.

2000: Grindlays is sold to Standard Chartered PLC; ANZ is reorganized into 21 highly autonomous units (later reduced to 16).

2002: ANZ and ING Group form ING Australia Limited, a funds management and life insurance joint venture operating in Australia and New Zealand.

73 branches and the Union opened 100. Their competitors, still suffering from the banking crash and the depression, had to worry about reconstruction obligations; their relatively small and weak condition dictated a strategy of mergers and absorption rather than branch banking in the battle for market share.

One major issue for both the Asia and the Union in the early 1900s was their relationship with their head offices in London. Better communications and new personalities in London caused a marked shift in formal executive authority from Australia to Britain. London executives began demanding more intimate details and more informed advice than the general commentaries from Melbourne that they had drawn on for broad policy directives during the 19th century. Understandably, Melbourne executives resented their newly subordinate positions. In the end, the transfer of total executive power to the London offices was facilitated by a new policy of elevating older, more conservative executives to the top ranks in Melbourne.

With the inauguration of Australia as a commonwealth in January 1901, pressure intensified for a government bank. After much debate and discussion, the Commonwealth Bank opened in January 1913. It offered savings accounts, government banking, public debt management, and rural credit, but it could not issue notes and did not have central bank control. Top executives at both the Asia and the Union were highly critical of and hostile to the Commonwealth Bank. But executives in London took a more balanced view, and both boards refused to contribute to campaigns against the government's bank, although several colonial banks had done so. Further, they directed their chief executives to accept the situation and cultivate amicable relations with the Commonwealth's president.

World War I crystallized the banking structures existing in 1914. After the war, however, rivals of the Asia and the Union began to merge to make themselves more competitive. In 1917 the Royal Bank of Queensland and the Bank of New Queensland merged to form the Bank of Queensland; by 1932, when the Bank of New South Wales absorbed the Australian Bank of Commerce, 11 amalgamations had occurred, reducing the number of Australian trading banks from 20 to 9. During this period the ES&A merged with three other banks: the Commercial Bank of Tasmania in 1921, the London Chartered Bank of Australia in 1921, and the Royal Bank of Australia in 1927.

The Asia and the Union continued to expand their branch banking in an attempt to offset their competitors' growing advantages. Between 1918 and 1929 the Asia opened 49 new branches and the Union opened 41. Although both banks could have benefited from mergers with banks in areas such as Tasmania where they were not strong, both kept to the conservative policies that had been in place since the turn of the century until well into the 1920s.

Merger of the Asia and the Union, Forming ANZ Bank, 1951

In London, executives of both the Asia and the Union were aware that their banks had to change strategy if they wanted to rise in rank. Unfortunately, between the Great Depression and World War II, immediate problems took precedence over long-term rebuilding. There was some discussion about a merger between the Asia and the Union during the 1930s, but it was not until 1943 that serious interest in the project revived. At that time, both the Asia and the Union were approached by other Australian banks as possible partners. But each thought of the other as the most natural candidate for a merger.

On its own, each bank was less than half the size of the Bank of New South Wales, the largest bank in the country. They both agreed that a merger would make them more competitive, and also would restore lost stature and prestige. Moreover, if they did not act, it seemed likely that they would be left behind as their smaller competitors did merge.

In addition, both were English corporations, with London head offices and a majority of English shareholders, and their scales and styles of business were quite similar. The Union's strength in pastoral business complemented the commercial and industrial emphasis of the Asia. Only 70 out of 420 branches overlapped. Friendly cooperation within competition had characterized the relationship between the two banks for more than a century.

In 1946 lawyers began work on the details of a merger in which the Asia took over the business of the Union. But while a government threat to nationalize nongovernment banks delayed any action, it was decided that the original merger proposal was too costly. In addition, a group of key Union executives, feeling that the banks were equals and should join accordingly, began to resist being absorbed by the Asia. The solution was to create a new company, the Australia and New Zealand Bank Limited, to subsume both the Asia and the Union. ANZ Bank began business on October 1, 1951.

The merger of the Asia and Union catapulted ANZ Bank to the top tier of banks in Australia and New Zealand. Unfortunately, being bigger failed to make ANZ Bank more profitable. A tight government liquidity requirement forced the bank to cut lending in order to build liquid assets to the prescribed level. To offset the lost loan business, ANZ Bank began looking for new programs to raise profits and reduce expenses. A savings bank subsidiary, which could use existing skills and facilities and be funded within the governments' constraints, was established in 1955. The Australia and New Zealand Savings Bank Ltd. proved very successful.

While ANZ Bank's administrative hierarchy became more efficient in the early 1960s, General Manager Sir Roger Darval decided that emphasizing the bank's domestic business would boost profits. He began an accelerated expansion of branch banking. ANZ Bank opened 127 branches in six years; of these, 112 were in central business districts, signaling ANZ Bank's intent to move away from rural business.

Creation of ANZ Through Merger of ANZ Bank and ES&A, 1970

ANZ Bank had wooed the English, Scottish and Australian Bank four times since 1955. ES&A's conservative controls over lending and liquidity, its highly successful hire-purchase subsidiary, Esanda, and its profit-oriented administration all appealed strongly to the board of ANZ Bank, and ES&A came from the same private trade banking tradition as both the Asia and Union. But most of all, the directors thought that a bigger bank would command more resources than either organization could raise itself. In addition, some feared that foreign banks would move in on ANZ Bank's corporate and international business, possibly by using ES&A as a host for entry.

In 1970 the merger finally took place. The resulting Australia and New Zealand Banking Group Limited became the third largest bank in the commonwealth, double the size of the fourth-place bank. Unfortunately, despite its expanded presence in the marketplace, ANZ saw its profits fall and its expenses rise during its first years, primarily because of a lax administration and unexpectedly high merger costs.

Both ES&A's and ANZ Bank's staffs had opposed the merger, each side fearing it would lose out on the distribution of the higher posts in the new bank. Angered by this situation, the board hired a U.S. management consultant firm in 1973 to help its executives redesign the ANZ Banking Group's organizational structure. A modern formalized planning system specifying long- and short-range goals emerged, creating an effective and efficient environment at last. At the same time, the consultants replaced traditional profit goals with goals tied to rates of return on assets. The group's executives felt that this change

required a large amount of capital immediately. When London objected to the exportation of British capital, the group's board realized it would be in the best interests of the bank to change its domicile. After 141 years, the headquarters of ANZ was transferred from London to Melbourne on February 2, 1976, and two years later ANZ moved into the newly constructed ANZ Tower, a symbol of the total transformation in structure, philosophy, and character the bank had undergone.

International Acquisitions in the 1980s

During the early 1980s monetary authorities in Australia and New Zealand gradually began to relax the controls that had limited banking operations since the 1950s. This, together with a strenuous program of cost-cutting, led to a substantial increase in profits. But deregulation of the industry also opened Australia and New Zealand to foreign banking. In response to this foreign competition, as well as increased domestic competition, ANZ decided to try to buy strength and diversity. In 1979 it merged with the Bank of Adelaide. In 1981 ANZ talked to the Commercial Banking Company of Sydney and then the Commercial Bank of Australia about merging, but neither deal worked out. In 1983 and 1984 the group did succeed in acquiring or buying half equity in the Development Finance Corporation; the Trustees, Executors and Agency Company Ltd.; McCaughan Dyson and Company, a stockbroker; and Grindlays Bank plc, of England.

The 1984 acquisition of Grindlays, with representation in 40 countries, greatly strengthened ANZ's international operations, compelling it to redesign its organizational structure. The bank's hierarchical arrangement of authority was replaced with a horizontal structure of more than 50 business units worldwide. These independent business units brought an entrepreneurial spirit of creativity and ambition as well as increased profits.

Although the bank's 1980s acquisitions, including the 1989 purchase of New Zealand's PostBank, which made ANZ the largest banking group in New Zealand, made it a major international financial player, the group was still, in large part, a regional organization; in 1989, 77 percent of its profits came from operations in Australia and New Zealand.

Failed Mergers and Tough Economic Times in the Early to Mid-1990s

During 1989 ANZ and National Australia Bank, one of the other Big Four Australian banks, entered into serious discussions about a merger, going so far as buying small stakes in each other. But the Labor government, worried about Australians' increasing concern about the power of the big banks in the run-up to a general election to be held in March 1990, blocked the deal. Then almost immediately after Labor's victory in the election, ANZ announced that it planned to purchase majority control of National Mutual Life Association, the number two insurance company in Australia. At A$3.8 billion (US$2.87 billion), it was valued as the largest merger in Australian history, and it promised to rock the nation's banking sector by forming its biggest financial services outfit, which was to be called ANZ-NM Banking and Insurance Group. Once again, however, the Labor government blocked the deal, with Treasurer Paul Keating reasoning that allowing the merger would lead to a series of further mergers within the Australian financial services industries, which as a whole would undermine competition. ANZ was allowed to acquire National Mutual Royal Bank Limited, a joint banking venture between National Mutual and the Royal Bank of Canada that was formed in 1986 and had assets of A$4.5 billion. Also acquired in 1990 were Perth-based Town and Country Building Society, Lloyds Bank PLC's operation in Papua New Guinea, and Bank of Zealand's Fiji unit.

Moving beyond the failed mergers of 1989 and 1990, ANZ struggled through the difficult economic environment of the early 1990s—a deep recession that in Australia included high unemployment (peaking at 11 percent) and high inflation and interest rates as well. The stagnation led to an explosion in nonperforming loans, forcing ANZ and other Australian banks to take huge provisions against bad debts. The nadir for ANZ came in the year ending in September 1992 when provisions of A$1.9 billion (US$1.3 billion) led to a net loss for the year of A$579 million (US$399.3 million). ANZ also made staffing reductions during the recession, announcing the elimination of 5,500 jobs in late 1991. During 1992, a new management team was put in charge of turning around the group's fortunes: John Gough took over as chairman from Milton Bridgland, and Don Mercer succeeded Will Bailey as chief executive. Gough was chairman and former managing director of the Australian conglomerate Pacific Dunlop Limited, while Mercer had joined ANZ in 1984 and had most recently served as head of Australian retail banking.

As the economy slowly recovered and ANZ returned to profitability, ANZ restarted its overseas expansion, concentrating primarily on east Asia. In 1993 the group gained a presence in Indonesia by purchasing an 85 percent interest in a joint venture bank that was later renamed PT ANZ Panin Bank. That year also saw ANZ become the first bank from an English-speaking country to be allowed into the Vietnamese market, opening a branch in Hanoi and a representative office in Ho Chi Minh City. Similarly, the bank entered China by opening a branch in Shanghai and offices in Beijing and Guangzhou. By 1994 ANZ was the largest foreign bank in south Asia, and 10 percent of the bank's total profits were being generated through its Asia-Pacific network. Late in 1995 ANZ expanded into the Philippines by opening a commercial banking branch in Manila. Another change to its overseas network came in 1996 when the domicile of Grindlays Bank was moved from England to Australia, and the subsidiary was renamed ANZ Grindlays Bank Limited. Meanwhile, in August 1995, Gough was replaced as chairman by Charles Goode, who was also chairman of Woodside Petroleum Ltd.

Late 1990s and Beyond: Major Restructuring Under McFarlane

Just after the Asian economic crisis began to unfold in mid-1997, ANZ made another management change. Board dissatisfaction with the slow pace of cost-containment efforts led to Mercer's retirement. Hired as his replacement was an American-trained Scottish banker, John McFarlane. The new CEO had 18 years of experience at Citibank on his resume followed by four years at Standard Chartered PLC, a leading international bank based in the United Kingdom, where he managed much of the bank's overseas operations, including those in south Asia. McFarlane led a thorough restructuring of ANZ's operations.

Under his leadership, the group began reducing its exposure to certain volatile foreign markets that were hit hard by the economic crisis and its aftereffects. In 1998 ANZ closed its London-based capital markets division and emerging markets business following heavy losses on emerging market debt trading. Reflecting a pullback from both international markets and investment banking, the group's investment banking arm was relocated from London to Sydney. McFarlane also worked to strengthen the bank's position domestically by accelerating the cost-cutting program and cutting staff; the workforce was slashed by more than 5,000 from 1997 to 1998. Further changes centered on the mix of domestic operations. Traditionally, ANZ had been more of a commercial/corporate bank, and McFarlane began to bolster the bank's domestic retail banking activities to create more of a retail/commercial bank. By early 1999 conditions in Asian markets had improved enough to permit a cautious return to expansion, and ANZ Panin Bank bought the credit card operations of PT Papan Sejahtera, an Indonesian bank that had fallen into receivership.

During 2000 McFarlane further reduced ANZ's exposure to risky foreign markets by selling ANZ Grindlays and its banking network in the Middle East and south Asia to Standard Chartered for A$3.1 billion. ANZ also began laying the foundation for a takeover of St. George Bank Ltd. by buying a nearly 10 percent stake in the New South Wales–based regional bank. This bid for domestic growth was scuttled in early 2001 after it became clear that it would not be possible to complete a friendly takeover at a reasonable price. ANZ then continued on with an organic growth model, centered around a reorganization that McFarlane announced in July 2000. ANZ divided itself up into 21 highly autonomous units (later reduced to 16), each of which would have to establish its own competitive position and develop its own growth strategy, as well as develop a mix of Internet and branch-based distribution. The units, for example, focused on personal banking in Australia, mortgages, wealth management, small to medium-sized businesses, institutional banking, and global foreign exchange. This decentralized structure ran counter to the prevailing model in the financial services that emphasized cross-selling opportunities through integrated operations. McFarlane felt, however, that the future of financial services lay in specialist players rather than generalists. The new ANZ structure also held the advantage of making it easier to shut down or sell off underperforming operations, as well as take successful units public or set them up within joint ventures with other companies.

ANZ did not completely abandon acquisitions but was now seeking smaller, "in-fill" deals. Late in 2001, for example, the bank bolstered its Asia-Pacific retail banking unit through the purchase of the Bank of Hawaii's operations in Papua New Guinea, Vanuatu, and Fiji for about A$100 million. Then in May 2002 came the first major joint venture deal to follow the new growth formula. That month ANZ combined its Australian and New Zealand funds management operations with ING Group's funds management and life insurance businesses in Australia and New Zealand, forming ING Australia Limited. The new venture was 51 percent owned by Netherlands-based financial services giant ING and 49 percent by ANZ, but the two owners were to have equal say in the management. ING Australia instantly became the fourth largest retail funds manager in Australia, with A$38.4 billion of funds under management, and the number five life insurer. The main point of logic behind the deal was that it would bring together ING's funds management experience with the power of ANZ's bank distribution channels.

Through 2002, McFarlane's thorough if unconventional restructuring efforts were paying off. ANZ reported record net profits that year of A$2.32 billion (US$1.26 billion), a 16 percent increase over the preceding year. Out of the group's 16 specialized units, 14 of them showed an increase in profits for the year. Seeking to continue this growth trend, ANZ was aiming to strengthen its domestic positions in several areas, including personal banking, mortgages, small to medium-sized businesses, and wealth management. The bank was also searching for expansion opportunities in the Pacific region and to a lesser extent in Asia. Maintaining a low risk profile was another key component of McFarlane's formula for success.

Principal Subsidiaries

ANZ Cover Insurance Pty. Ltd.; ANZ Executors & Trustee Company Limited; ANZ Funds Pty. Ltd.; ANZ Lenders Mortgage Insurance Pty. Limited; ANZ Holdings Pty. Ltd.; ANZ Investment Holdings Pty. Ltd.; ANZ Life Assurance Company Limited; ANZ Managed Investments Limited; ANZ Properties (Australia) Pty. Ltd.; ANZ Securities (Holdings) Limited; Australia and New Zealand Banking Group (PNG) Limited (Papua New Guinea); Esanda Finance Corporation Limited; ANZ Capel Court Limited; PT ANZ Panin Bank (Indonesia; 85%); US Distribution Trust I; US Distribution Trust II; Alliance Holdings Limited; NMRSB Pty. Ltd.

Principal Operating Units

Personal Banking Australia; Personal Banking New Zealand; Personal Banking Asia-Pacific; Mortgages; Consumer Finance; Wealth Management; Small to Medium Business; Asset Finance; Corporate Banking; Institutional Banking; Global Capital Markets; Global Foreign Exchange; Global Structured Finance; Global Transaction Services; Corporate Financing and Advisory; Group Treasury.

Principal Competitors

National Australia Bank Limited; Commonwealth Bank of Australia; Westpac Banking Corporation.

Further Reading

Bartholomeusz, Stephen, "ANZ at Last Makes an Idiosyncratic Entrance into Funds Management," *Age* (Melbourne), April 11, 2002, p. 3.
——, "ANZ Beats a Smart Retreat to Follow a Different Drum," *Age* (Melbourne), March 9, 2001, p. 3.
——, "ANZ on Firm Ground with $500 Million Share Buyback," *Age* (Melbourne), November 4, 1999, p. 3.
——, "ANZ Result Shows Banks Have Weathered Storm," *Age* (Melbourne), November 21, 1991, p. 21.
——, "ANZ Result Shows It Is Banking on the Right Lines," *Age* (Melbourne), May 15, 1993, p. 25.
——, "ANZ to Play a Risky Hand," *Age* (Melbourne), April 29, 2000, p. 1.
——, "ANZ Victim of New Element Markets Won't Ignore," *Age* (Melbourne), September 4, 1998, p. 3.
——, "In ANZ's New Game Plan, Expect Less Asia and Less Risk," *Age* (Melbourne), May 6, 1999, p. 3.
——, "McFarlane Has Made ANZ Cleaner, Less Vulnerable," *Age* (Melbourne), November 5, 1998, p. 3.
——, "McFarlane Joins Progressive Values to Prudence at ANZ," *Age* (Melbourne), October 26, 2001, p. 3.
Boreham, Tim, "ANZ Loses the Urge to Merge: Bank Strategy to Divide Not Conquer," *Australian,* July 29, 2000, p. 21.
Butlin, S.J., *Australia and New Zealand Bank,* London: Longmans, 1961.
Deans, Alan, "Not Top of the Pops," *Far Eastern Economic Review,* September 24, 1992, p. 84.
Fraust, Bart, "Australia and New Zealand Group to Acquire Grindlays Holdings: Melbourne Firm to Pay $250 Million for London Company," *American Banker,* June 14, 1984, pp. 2+.
Gottliebsen, Robert, "The ANZ Goes a'Wooing," *Business Review Weekly,* July 20, 1998, pp. 24+.
——, "Why McFarlane Replaced Mercer," *Business Review Weekly,* September 29, 1997, pp. 8+.
Jarrett, Ian, "ANZ Does Better Abroad Than at Home," *Asian Business,* August 1995, p. 55.
Kavanagh, John, "ANZ Lifts Its Game in a Hot Sector," *Business Review Weekly,* February 7, 2002, pp. 34+.
Korporaal, Glenda, "Urge to Merge: Shake-up Expected in Australia's Banking Sector," *Far Eastern Economic Review,* April 12, 1990, p. 58.
Lowenstein, Jack, "The Not-So-Money Deal Downunder," *Euromoney,* August 1990, pp. 35+.
Mayne, Stephen, "ANZ Chief Aims to Be Hands-on," *Age* (Melbourne), July 13, 1992, p. 24.
"McFarlane's Bold Vision for ANZ," *Australian Banking and Finance,* November 28, 1997, pp. 3+.
Merrett, David Tolmie, *ANZ Bank: A History of Australia and New Zealand Banking Group Limited and Its Constituents,* Sydney: Allen & Unwin Australia, 1985.
"The White Men's Burden," *Economist,* June 16, 1984, pp. 69+.
Witcher, S. Karene, "Recovery Seen for Australian Bank Concerns," *Wall Street Journal,* June 22, 1992, p. A7.
Wood, Crispin, "The Odds Shorten for ANZ Takeover," *Business Review Weekly,* February 16, 1998, pp. 48+.

—update: David E. Salamie

BEAR STEARNS

Bear Stearns Companies, Inc.

245 Park Avenue
New York, New York 10167
U.S.A.
Telephone: (212) 272-2000
Fax: (212) 272-8239
Web site: http://www.bearstearns.com

Public Company
Incorporated: 1985
Employees: 10,500
Sales: $8.7 billion (2001)
Stock Exchanges: New York
Ticker Symbol: BSC
NAIC: 523110 Investment Banking and Securities
   Dealing; 523120 Securities Brokerage

Bear Stearns Companies, Inc., the holding company that owns Bear, Stearns & Company, Inc., was created on October 29, 1985, as the successor to Bear Stearns & Company and Subsidiaries, a partnership organized in 1957. The partnership, in turn, was the successor to a company founded in 1923 by Joseph Bear, Robert Stearns, and Harold Mayer as an equity-trading house. Headquartered in New York, Bear Stearns today is a full service brokerage and investment banking firm focused on three core areas: capital markets, wealth management, and global clearing services. The company maintains offices in major cities all over the globe.

Nascent Decade: 1923–33

The original company was founded with $500,000 in capital in response to the thriving investment climate of the early 1920s. World War I, with its heavy demand for capital, had encouraged the public to enter the securities markets in mass, and the young Bear Stearns prospered in the frenzied optimism of those markets. The company began trading in government securities and soon became a leading trader in this area.

Trading fell off sharply, of course, when the New York stock market crashed in 1929. Though Bear Stearns suffered setbacks,

it had accumulated enough capital to survive quite well: during this crisis it not only avoided any employee layoffs but continued to pay bonuses. As the country struggled out of the Depression, Bear Stearns entered into the bond market to promote President Franklin Roosevelt's call for renewed development of the nation's infrastructure through the New Deal.

During the period following Roosevelt's reform measures, the nation's banking system had accumulated a large amount of cash, since demand for loans was very low. At the same time, bonds were very cheap. Bear Stearns made its first substantial profits by selling large volumes of these bonds to cash-rich banks around the country.

By 1933 the firm had grown from its original seven employees to 75, had opened its first regional office in Chicago (after buying out the Chicago-based firm of Stein, Brennan), and had accumulated a capital base of $800,000. That year Salim L. "Cy" Lewis, a former runner for Salomon Brothers, was hired to direct Bear Stearns's new institutional bond trading department. Lewis, who became a partner in 1938, a managing partner in the 1950s, and then chairman, built Bear Stearns into a large, influential firm. An almost legendary character, Lewis's outspokenness and drive were what gave Bear Stearns the style that made it stand out on Wall Street for decades to come.

Lucrative Trendsetting from
the 1930s Through the 1960s:

In 1935, Congress passed the Securities & Exchange Commission's (SEC) Public Utilities Holding Company Act, which precipitated a breakup of utility holding companies. As new securities were being issued for the formerly private companies, Bear Stearns positioned itself to take advantage of the opportunity, trading aggressively at what Lewis later called "the most ridiculous prices you ever saw in your life."

Revolutions in the freight and transportation industries beginning in the 1940s offered other opportunities. As auto transportation became more efficient and civil aviation more feasible, the once booming rail industry began to decline. Bear Stearns was quick to see an opportunity, and as most of the nation's railroads went into bankruptcy, Bear Stearns became

Company Perspectives:

Undoubtedly our greatest strengths are our people and our unique entrepreneurial corporate culture. What sets Bear Stearns apart from the competition is access and teamwork. Clients can access the wealth of experience and depth of knowledge of our senior people while working closely with them to create custom solutions. Our executives have a hands-on approach to running the company, guaranteeing that our most senior people work personally with clients. Our clients enjoy the enduring continuity of personal relationships and the benefits of shared experience over time.

one of the biggest arbitrators of mergers and acquisitions between railroad companies.

In 1948 Bear Stearns opened an international department, although it was not until 1955 that the firm opened its first international office, in Amsterdam. As its international business prospered, the company opened other foreign offices, in Geneva, Paris, London, Hong Kong, and Tokyo.

In the 1950s, Lewis was one of the originators of block trading which, by the 1960s, was the bread and butter of most of Wall Street. Bear Stearns, like other companies, profited nicely from this trading until May 1, 1975, when the SEC's Security Act amendments, which eliminated fixed brokerage commissions, went into effect.

Bear Stearns began expanding its retail business operations in the late 1960s, once again ahead of the trend. It opened an office in San Francisco in 1965, and between 1969 and 1973 opened offices in Los Angeles, Dallas, Atlanta, and Boston. The company was very successful at attracting and managing accounts for wealthy individuals. These accounts also laid the foundation for the company's successful margin operations. In margin trading, brokerage houses loan their clients' securities to short sellers, who match the fund with their own capital and use the entire amount to finance trade, paying interest on the amount loaned.

Risky Business Leads to Profit . . . and Penalty: 1975–99

In 1975, when New York City was near bankruptcy, Bear Stearns proved again that it was a risk taker by investing $10 million in the city's securities. Though it came close to losing millions of dollars, the firm eventually profited greatly from the gamble.

In May 1978, Alan "Ace" Greenberg became chairman of Bear Stearns, following the death of Cy Lewis. Greenberg had joined the firm as a clerk in 1949. He moved up rapidly within the company; by 1953, at age 25, he was running the risk arbitrage desk and by 1957 he was trading for the firm. By the time he became chairman, Greenberg had earned a reputation as one of the most aggressive traders on Wall Street. Like his predecessor, Greenberg shunned long-range planning in favor of immediate returns. It soon became apparent that Greenberg's abilities equaled and perhaps surpassed those of his predecessor. From the time he took over as chairman until Bear Stearns

went public in 1985, the firm's total capital went from $46 million to $517 million; in 1989, it was $1.4 billion.

Bear Stearns's willingness to take risks pushed it into the forefront of corporate takeover activity. The firm was described as a "breeding ground" for corporate takeover attempts, and as masterful at disguising takeover maneuvers. In some instances, however, Bear Stearns's aggressiveness earned it an unsavory reputation. The firm was known to wage proxy battles against its own clients, as it did in 1982 against Global Natural Resources after deciding that Global's management had undervalued its assets and could realize greater profits. In 1986, Bear Stearns developed an option agreement that essentially allowed clients to buy stock under Bear Stearns's name, a tactic that facilitated corporate takeover attempts. The Justice Department and the SEC put an end to such tactics by filing suits against several of Bear Stearns's clients for "parking" stock (all of them settled).

In October 1985, Greenberg and the firm's executive committee announced that Bear Stearns would make a public stock offering in an effort to increase the company's ability to raise capital to finance larger trades. Part of the strategy included the formation of a holding company named Bear Stearns Companies, Inc. Shortly after the initial 20 percent offering, Bear Stearns reorganized from a brokerage house into a full-service investment firm with divisions in investment banking, institutional equities, fixed income securities, individual investor services, and mortgage-related products.

The company was hit hard by the 1987 Wall Street crash, and numerous positions at Bear Stearns were eliminated. This streamlining, however, actually helped the company when the economy fired up once again and revenues from its investment banking division and its brokerage commissions began to increase substantially. By 1991, Bear Stearns had become the top equity underwriter in Latin America. By 1992, the company had successfully included capital industry, biotechnology, and machinery stocks in its ever-expanding analysis of the corporate sector.

In 1992, Bear Stearns saw earnings double to over $295 million. During the same year, the company managed more than $13 billion in initial public offerings (IPOs) for a variety of U.S. and foreign corporations. The company also had become a leader in clearing trades for other brokers and brokerages, and boasted one of the best ratios in the industry of analysts to brokers.

In 1993, James E. Cayne succeeded Alan Greenberg as CEO. As president (a title he would continue to hold), Cayne had helped to guide the company toward new opportunities for profit in investment banking and foreign markets. By contrast to Greenberg, whose executive style was known to be impulsive, even volatile at times, Cayne had found success with a more cautious approach: he was known to avoid taking big risks and often to call upon consultants to enlighten his decision-making process. Together, Cayne and Greenberg were thought to make a powerful and well-balanced team. At the time of Cayne's succession to CEO, Greenberg still retained the title of chairman as well as the final word at Bear Stearns.

In the mid-1990s, Bear Stearns continued its concerted drive to establish itself in emerging foreign markets in Asia and Latin

Key Dates:

1923: The original company is founded by Joseph Bear, Robert Stearns, and Harold Mayer as an equity trading house.

1933: Bear Stearns opens its first regional office in Chicago, and Salim L. "Cy" Lewis—future chairman—is hired to direct Bear Stearns's new institutional bond trading department.

1955: Bear Stearns opens its first international office in Amsterdam.

1965: Bear Stearns begins expanding retail operations in the United States and, over the next eight years, opens offices in San Francisco, Los Angeles, Dallas, Atlanta, and Boston.

1978: Alan "Ace" Greenberg succeeds Lewis as chairman.

1985: Bear Stearns forms a holding company called Bear Stearns Companies, Inc., goes public, and reorganizes from a brokerage house into a full-service investment firm.

1992: Company earnings double to over $295 million for best year in Bear Stearns's history to date.

1993: James E. Cayne succeeds Alan Greenberg as CEO; Greenberg stays on as chairman.

1999: Bear Stearns agrees to pay $42 million to settle civil and criminal fraud charges in connection with its role as clearing broker for A.R. Baron.

2001: James E. Cayne succeeds Alan Greenberg as chairman.

America. Toward this end the company opened a representative office in Beijing in 1994—a diplomatic as well as pragmatic move, as the addition of the Beijing office to Bear Stearns's Hong Kong headquarters was touted as an important demonstration of respect for and commitment to China as a formidable world financial power. Bear Stearns Asia Ltd. was significantly rewarded for this commitment in 1995, when it was chosen by Guangzhou Railway Corporation to be the sole lead underwriter for its public offering, a prime assignment in the eyes of Bear Stearns's competitors in Hong Kong.

Bear Stearns became the focus of negative attention in 1997, however, when it came under investigation by the SEC for its role as a clearing broker for a smaller brokerage named A.R. Baron, which had gone bankrupt in 1996 and defrauded its customers of $75 million. Traditionally, courts had not held clearing firms accountable for losses incurred by the customers of their client firms, but in this case Bear Stearns was accused of overstepping its bounds as a clearinghouse by continuing to process trades, loan money, and extend credit to Baron in the face of mounting evidence that the firm, then in serious financial jeopardy, was manipulating stock prices and conducting unauthorized trading while raiding the accounts of its customers.

By the summer of 1999, after a two-year probe, Bear Stearns settled civil and criminal charges with the SEC and the Manhattan District Attorney, respectively, agreeing to pay a total of $42 million in fines and restitution. In the end, Bear Stearns refused

to accept or deny guilt in the settlements, and made public assurances that the settlements were immaterial to the business and financial well-being of the company. Nevertheless, the scandal tainted the records of Greenberg and Cayne and adversely affected the image of the company; perhaps as a result, shares of its stock generally traded at discounted prices for the next two years.

An Industry Maverick Stays Its Course: 2000–2002

At the beginning of the new century, with the economy weakening, Bear Stearns found itself in a precarious position. By mid-2000, amid a climate of rampant mergers and acquisitions in the securities industry, Bear Stearns's stock price was in a two-year slump; suddenly, it was one of the last independent financial services firms on Wall Street. Though the company seemed to relish its reputation as a maverick, keeping up with competitors, most of whom were merging into global megaforces, was a challenge.

Bear Stearns moved aggressively to expand its London office, adding 100 new employees to the existing 600 in early 2000, and moved to grow its European presence, but analysts criticized Bear Stearns for having moved too late in establishing itself internationally. The company's investment banking revenues languished as a result of this weak international presence.

Speculation was intense that Bear Stearns would itself be bought out by a larger financial institution seeking to secure a position on the international playing field. In the preceding months this had been the case with Donaldson Lufkin and Jenrette, PaineWebber, J.P. Morgan, and Wasserstein Perella. Conveniently, takeover rumors served to drive up the value of Bear Stearns's stock, and by January 2001, the company's earnings reports were proving the company could still continue to prosper on its own. CEO James E. Cayne shrewdly walked the line on this issue, exuding confidence about his company's ability to go it alone, while allowing that he was, nonetheless, willing to consider buyout offers.

In June 2001, at the age of 74, Alan C. Greenberg made the long anticipated announcement that he would step down as Bear Stearns's chairman, handing over his title and the reigns of the company to CEO James E. Cayne.

After the terrorist attacks of September 11, 2001, consumer confidence was critically low, concerns about national security were critically high, and the economy appeared to be headed straight into a recession. Bear Stearns—typically the last in the securities industry to cut jobs—succumbed to the need to reduce expenses by laying off 800 bankers, about 7 percent of its workforce. Ironically, some of the cutbacks included jobs in the London office, the office the company had worked so vigorously to expand a year earlier.

Bear Stearns continued to operate on a different model than the rest of Wall Street, and this worked to the company's advantage in the early 2000s. The company had not been as competitive as some in advising on mergers and acquisitions in the late1990s, and as a result, it was one of the few firms to avoid significant losses from the industrywide downturn in this arena. Further, through maintaining its emphasis on clearing operations, honing in on the housing boom by increasing its focus on packaging and selling mortgages, and selling bonds to investors too skittish to buy stocks, Bear Stearns was the only securities firm to report a first-quarter profit increase in 2002, demonstrating its resilience and its competitive edge once again.

Principal Subsidiaries

Bear Stearns & Company, Inc.; Custodial Trust Co.; Bear Stearns Mortgage Capital Corp.; Bear Stearns Fiduciary Services, Inc.; Bear Stearns International, Ltd.; Bear Stearns Asia Ltd.; Bear Stearns S.A.; Bear Stearns, Ltd. (Japan); Bear Stearns Securities Corp.; Correspondent Clearing; Bear Stearns Home Loans Ltd.

Principal Competitors

Goldman, Sachs & Co.; Lehman Brothers; Merrill Lynch & Co., Inc.

Further Reading

Chaffin, Joshua, ''Bear Stearns to Cut 800 Jobs,'' *Financial Times,* October 19, 2001, p. 34.

Henriques, Diana B., and Peter Truell, ''Should a Clearinghouse Be Its Broker's Keeper?,'' *Business Day,* April 23, 1997, p. D1.

Kruger, Daniel, ''The Card Player,'' *Forbes,* October 14, 2002, p. 91.

McGeehan, Patrick, ''The Bond Business Keeps Bear Stearns on the Upswing, While Morgan Stanley's Earnings Fall,'' *New York Times,* June 20, 2002, p. C8.

Morgenson, Gretchen, ''S.E.C. Fines a Bear Stearns Unit in Fraud Case After Long Inquiry,'' *New York Times,* August 6, 1999, p. A1.

Myerson, Allen R., ''Careful Player Moves Closer to the Top at Bear Stearns,'' *New York Times,* July 14, 1993, p. D1.

''The New Bull Market in Brokerage Stocks,'' *Fortune,* July 15, 1991.

Valdmanis, Thor, ''Lehman, Bear Stearns Report Solid Earnings,'' *USA Today,* January 5, 2001, p. 2B.

Westhoff, Dale, and Bruce Kramer, ''Can Mortgage Refinancings Save the U.S. Economy?,'' *Asset Securitization Report,* October 15, 2001.

—Tony Jeffris
—updates: Thomas Derdak, Erin Brown

BERGDORF GOODMAN

Bergdorf Goodman Inc.

754 5th Avenue
New York, New York 10019
U.S.A.
Telephone: (212) 753-7300
Fax: (212) 872-8677

Wholly Owned Subsidiary of Neiman Marcus Group
Founded: 1901
Employees: 2,000
Sales: $392 million (2000 est.)
NAIC: 448120 Women's Clothing Stores; 448110 Men's
   Clothing Stores

Owned by Dallas-based Neiman Marcus Group, Bergdorf Goodman Inc. is the only premier luxury store situated solely in New York. The legendary establishment is actually two Manhattan stores situated across the street from each other at Fifth Avenue between 57th and 58th Streets. A separate men's operation, established in 1990, is located on the east side of Fifth Avenue. On the west side, Bergdorf Goodman's main store, which opened in 1928, is undergoing long-term remodeling as the store attempts to modernize and regain some lost luster. A trendsetter in the 1970s and 1980s, and responsible for introducing many important designers, Bergdorf Goodman has come under fire from critics who say the store has lost touch with contemporary tastes.

1899: Herman Bergdorf Mentoring Edwin Goodman

The driving personality behind the rise of Bergdorf Goodman as a luxury retailer was without doubt Edwin Goodman. As a six-year-old, Goodman's father, Henry, immigrated to the United States from Germany and settled in Macon, Georgia, where his family ran a dry-goods store. After the Civil War, the Goodmans moved to the North, opening a dry-goods establishment in Lockport, New York. Henry Goodman married Celia Cohn, whose family owned the Superba Cravat Company of Rochester, and was able to give up the drudgery of shopkeeping and go to work for Superba. As a result their son, Edwin, grew up in a middle-class home in Rochester. Early on he decided to become a

tailor and dropped out of high school in order to learn the trade at the Stein-Bloch factory located in Rochester. His talents were quickly noticed and he was encouraged to move to New York City and become involved in making tailored suits for ladies, a rapidly growing and lucrative field. Not all men's tailors were able to make the transition; one who did was a French immigrant named Herman Bergdorf, who owned a Fifth Avenue shop near 19th Street. He was as much interested in living the good life, however, as he was in growing the business, and it was mostly through chance that his work was "discovered." His sister, the social secretary for a prominent woman, Mrs. William Goadby Loew, wore one of his tailored suits to work one day. Mrs. Loew was impressed enough to order one for herself. Once she was seen wearing a Bergdorf suit, his reputation was made and everyone in her fashionable circle besieged Bergdorf with orders. It was in 1899 that Goodman at the age of 23 came to work at Bergdorf's shop to learn ladies' tailoring from the now-acclaimed master. It did not take long before Goodman was not only an accomplished tailor but essentially acting as Bergdorf's partner. With Bergdorf happy to spend more time at his favorite haunt, Brubacker's wine saloon, Goodman ran the shop, displaying an aptitude for business as well as tailoring.

In 1901 Goodman raised money from his family to buy into the business, which was now renamed Bergdorf Goodman. As the retail and theater districts continued their decades-old march up Fifth Avenue, Goodman was eager to join the parade and after some effort convinced Bergdorf to relocate their shop. After they sold their current building, Goodwin used his share of the proceeds to get married and travel to Europe on his honeymoon. While he was away Bergdorf hunted for a new uptown location on the stretch of Manhattan that was known as the "Ladies Miles" because of the abundance of fashionable shops located there. Rather than acquiring a building on Fifth Avenue itself, however, Bergdorf opted for a less expensive side street address, 32 West 32nd Street, a decision that infuriated Goodman. The two men did not remain partners much longer: Goodman bought out Bergdorf, who then retired and enjoyed his remaining years in Paris.

Although he retained the Bergdorf Goodman name, Goodman was now very much on his own, able to trust his own taste and

Company Perspectives:

As the leading fashion specialty store, Bergdorf Goodman is known throughout the world for its elegance, quality and superior service.

follow his own vision without interference from a less committed partner. He wanted to break away from the prevailing notion that shops simply offered their customers a single-breasted or double-breasted version of the same suit, either made out of blue serge or tan covert. He longed to make women beautiful and to this end studied the windows of the more successful shops. Popular at the time were hobble skirts, so named because they severely constricted the ability of the wearer to walk. Goodman designed the ultimate hobble skirt, ultimate in both style and discomfort, which gained him instant success. But despite the demand, he opted to discontinue the item. He decided that discomfort was not style, nor was fad to be confused with fashion. Believing that women should be comfortable in their clothes, he found a way to maintain the elegant lines of the hobble skirt while using a box pleat in the back to provide greater freedom of movement. It was just the first step Goodwin would take in liberating women from the restrictive clothing of the day. He led the way in exposing the neck, abandoning the jabot, a boned article that practically choked the wearer. In an even more daring move, Goodman exposed the ankle.

Moving Bergdorf Goodman in 1914

Goodman began to build an exclusive clientele but by 1914 he was still a ladies' tailor operating out of a cramped salon on a side street. In order to take the next step he decided to move further north on Fifth Avenue to larger accommodations. He found a brownstone at 616 Fifth Avenue, located where Rockefeller Center stands today. After acquiring the property, he razed the brownstone and commissioned a five-story building to replace it. Unsure that his business would be able to support that large a structure, he hedged his bets by renting out much of it.

Goodman's fears turned out to be unwarranted. He outgrew his salon in little more than a decade, the result of a major contribution to the fashion industry—championing high-quality, ready-to-wear garments. He recognized that women's lives were changing and that they simply did not have the necessary time to devote to fittings. He also believed that ready-to-wear clothing did not have to be second-rate merchandise, a point he made repeatedly to manufacturers he visited, browbeating them into producing garments worthy of his fashionable clientele. After taking the initial steps into quality ready-to-wear garments in the early 1920s, Goodman was greatly assisted in expanding the business by his children, Andrew and Ann, and their friend Bernard Newman. All under the age of 25, these *enfants terribles* would have a major impact on the garment industry and the growth of Bergdorf Goodman. In large part their success was the result of Goodman's habit of personally waiting on his customers, despite the growing prestige of his business. His children followed his example and by interacting with customers learned what they wanted. They also participated in Bergdorf Goodman's semiannual sales, visiting the

stock rooms to mark down items and in the process taking note of which items sold well and which ones failed to live up to expectations.

When rumors about the building of Rockefeller Center began to circulate, Goodman's friend and real estate broker Leo Fishel and entrepreneur Fred Brown found a new home for Bergdorf Goodman at its current Fifth Avenue location. It was uncertain whether customers would follow the store uptown, and once again Goodman played it safe by having the new store designed so that it could be broken up into sections that could be sublet if needed. The precaution, as it turned out, was not necessary. With the advent of the Depression Goodman was able to forego his lease and buy the building outright, as well as pick up the mortgages of the surrounding businesses that did not fare as well during the 1930s. The real estate arm of Bergdorf Goodman eventually purchased the entire block. His business was prosperous enough that Goodman could have opened other stores under the Bergdorf Goodman banner, but he firmly believed that by operating in a single location he could better maintain the quality of merchandise and level of service that was instrumental in his success.

Upon Edwin Goodman's death, his son Andrew took charge of Bergdorf Goodman in 1953. The store was already well established with New York society, as well as the merely wealthy, but Andrew was instrumental in enhancing its reputation and expanding its range of merchandise and personalized services. According to *Crain's New York Business,* he ''took the business to new heights as a fashion destination in the 1950s and 1960s.'' In 1972 he sold Bergdorf Goodman to what would become Carter Hawley Hale Stores, and then in 1975 retired.

Bergdorf Goodman in the Vanguard of Fashion in the 1980s

Carter Hawley invested $15 million to renovate Bergdorf Goodman, installing the first escalators and adding about 50 percent more selling space. It also opened a Bergdorf Goodman satellite store in White Plains, New York, but by 1980 the company decided to convert it to a Neiman Marcus store, which management felt was more ''adaptable'' to a suburban location. In the late 1970s there was talk of opening Bergdorf Goodman stores in other cities, such as Boston and Washington, D.C., but these plans never came to fruition. The Fifth Avenue store, in the meantime, continued to thrive. In the 1980s Bergdorf Goodman was in the vanguard of fashion, among the first to recognize new European and American designers and especially important in bringing attention to Milan designers, such as Giorgio Armani, Gianfranco Ferre, and Krizia. Bergdorf Goodman's parent company became the object of takeover bids in the 1980s, and as a way to fend off these advances, Carter Hawley restructured its business. In 1987 Bergdorf Goodman, Neiman Marcus, and Contempo Casuals were spun off as the Neiman Marcus Group, its headquarters located in Dallas, Texas, where the Neiman Marcus department store chain was launched in 1907.

Bergdorf Goodman continued to operate as a single location business with little interference from Dallas. Just before the Carter Hawley restructuring, Bergdorf Goodman introduced ''The Decorative Home on Seven.'' The seventh floor business offered antiques, home furnishings, porcelains, crystals, silver,

Key Dates:

1899: Edwin Goodman goes to work for tailor Herman Bergdorf.
1901: Goodman buys into the business, forming Bergdorf Goodman.
1903: Goodman buys out Bergdorf.
1914: The business moves to the present-day site of Rockefeller Center.
1928: Bergdorf Goodman moves to its current address.
1953: Andrew Goodman takes over the business.
1972: Bergdorf Goodman is sold to Carter Hawley Hale Stores.
1987: Bergdorf Goodman is spun off as part of the Neiman Marcus Group.
1990: Bergdorf Goodman Men opens across the street from the main store.

linens, stationery, and first edition and rare books, as well as delicacies. A more important change was the 1990 addition of Bergdorf Goodman Men, "the ultimate store for gentlemen," located across the street at 745 Fifth Avenue. It offered collections from all the top U.S. and European designers of menswear and sportswear. Services included made-to-measure tailoring, custom shirtmaking, personal shopping, emergency pressing, and spot cleaning. Unfortunately Bergdorf Goodman Men opened during a downturn in the economy and the business did not become profitable until 1995. Bergdorf Goodman redesigned its fifth floor, formerly the Miss Bergdorf department, in 1992. Dubbed "On 5ive," the department added a wide assortment of accessories to complement its eclectic fashions. The floor also offered a shoe department and café.

Guiding Bergdorf Goodman through the recession of the early 1990s was Burton Tansky, a seasoned executive who joined the company in 1990 as vice-chairman and in February 1992 became chairman and chief executive officer. Serving as president was Stanley Elkin, who came to Bergdorf Goodman in 1978 to become chief financial officer, then was named chief operating officer in 1985 and president in 1990. The parent corporation underwent a number of managerial changes in 1994, resulting in Tansky being appointed chairman and CEO of Neiman Marcus Stores. In turn, Elkin became chairman and CEO of Bergdorf Goodman. As the economy improved Neiman Marcus began to formulate big plans for Bergdorf Goodman. The company's CEO, Robert Tarr, told *Women's Wear Daily* in 1996 that the initiative included franchising women's stores in the Far East, establishing men's stores around the United States, and pursuing a private-label business with the Bergdorf Goodman name that also could be sold at Neiman Marcus stores.

With the economy starting to enjoy a long expansion, leading to a bull market for luxury goods, Bergdorf Goodman did not prosper as well as might be expected. Critics charged that the store had become staid and failed to keep up with changing tastes. To reinvigorate and modernize its operation, Bergdorf Goodman initiated a number of changes in the late 1990s. Both the main store and the men's store underwent a sweeping $50 million renovation program. In 1999 the first phase was completed when the cosmetics store was doubled in size, resulting in "A New Level of Beauty" operation that included eight spa rooms for facials, skincare consultations, and special treatments. Bergdorf Goodman also found additional retail space by commandeering office space, with some administrative functions transferred elsewhere in midtown Manhattan.

To help turn around the men's store, veteran retailer Peter Rizzo was brought in as vice-chairman in April 1999 and several months later was named president. In January 2000 Elkin suddenly resigned and Rizzo began openly campaigning for Elkin's position, despite only being on board for eight months and having little experience in the women's market; of the stores' $275 million in annual sales, only $40 million were from the men's side of the business. According to *Women's Wear Daily,* there was speculation that "pressures from the inside and organizational changes may have hastened Elkin's decision to leave. . . . Over the past few years, Bergdorf's operations, with the exception of buying, sales promotion, advertising, and a few other areas visible to the customer, have been centralized into the parent Neiman Marcus Group in Dallas, limiting Elkin's direct control." Moreover, the publication noted reports of friction between Elkin and Rizzo, with sources also suggesting that because of Bergdorf Goodman's relatively small size there was no need for both a CEO and president.

Rizzo's self-promotion, however, did not result in winning the top job at Bergdorf Goodman. Rather, Ronald L. Frasch was named chairman and CEO in April 2000. His appointment was seen as a return to the old guard, and to some a repudiation of Rizzo's aggressiveness. Frasch worked for Bergdorf Goodman in the 1980s and was a colleague of Tansky at Saks. Despite speculation that Rizzo would resign, he stayed on as Bergdorf Goodman pursued the next stages in its turnaround initiatives. According to *Daily News Record,* "Rizzo played a pivotal role in broadening the appeal and modernizing Bergdorf Goodman with younger, more contemporary designer lines and reorganizing the selling floors for a sharper focus to a different audience, in both the men's and women's stores. He also was instrumental in launching new marketing campaigns." Part of those promotional efforts was the creation of a magazine. Rizzo resigned from his position in September 2002, denying rumors that he had been asked to leave and maintaining that he actually had a good relationship with Frasch.

Amid all the changes in the upper ranks of management, as well as extensive remodeling of its store, Bergdorf Goodman found that its attempts to revitalize its business were hampered by a poor economy and the lingering effects of the terrorist attacks of September 11, 2001, which caused a drop in New York tourism. Nonetheless, Bergdorf Goodman retained its reputation and position as one of the world's top specialty retailers.

Principal Subsidiaries

Bergdorf Goodman Men.

Principal Competitors

Barney's, Inc.; Bloomingdale's Inc.; Saks Holdings, Inc.

48   **Bergdorf Goodman Inc.**

Further Reading

Curan, Catherine, ''Leadership Styles Clash at Bergdorf,'' *Crain's New York Business,* May 8, 2000, p. 4.

Diamond, Kerry, ''Bergdorf's Beauty Makeover,'' *Women's Wear Daily,* November 19, 1999, p. 6.

Herndon, Booton, *Bergdorf's on the Plaza,* New York: Alfred A. Knopf, 1956.

Moin, David, ''22-Year Veteran Elkin Leaves Top Spot at Bergdorf Goodman,'' *Women's Wear Daily,* January 18, 2000, p. 1.

Palmieri, Jean E., ''Succeeding Elkin,'' *Women's Wear Daily,* January 21, 2000, p. 1.

—Ed Dinger

Bonnier AB

Torsgatan 21
113 90 Stockholm
Sweden
Telephone: +46-8-736-40-00
Fax: +46-8-728-00-28
Web site: http://www.bonnier.se

Private Company
Incorporated: 1837 as Albert Bonnier Forlag
Employees: 10,342
Sales: $1.59 billion (2001 est.)
NAIC: 323111 Commercial Gravure Printing; 451211
   Book Stores; 511110 Newspaper Publishers; 511120
   Periodical Publishers; 511130 Book Publishers;
   511140 Database and Directory Publishers; 722110
   Full-Service Restaurants

Bonnier AB is one of the Nordic region's leading media groups, losing out the top spot to Finland's SanomaWSOY in 2001. Based in Stockholm, Sweden, the Bonnier family-owned group is active in newspapers, magazines, book publishing, film and television production—notably through subsidiary Svensk Filmindustrie—and other multimedia activities, movie theaters, and retail operations, including book and music clubs. Bonnier's newspaper titles include some of the most prominent in the Scandinavian region, such as *Dagens Nyheter, Dagens Industri,* and *Expressen.* The company also has branched out beyond the region with newspaper titles including *Business AM,* a daily business paper for the Scottish market; *Wirtschaftsblatt,* published in Austria; and *Diena,* which has become the leading daily newspaper in Latvia. Bonnier's Magazine division publishes a huge list of magazine titles in a variety of international markets, and includes titles such as *Amelia,* a women's lifestyle magazine for the Scandinavian markets; gardening magazine *Hagen for alle*; *Veckans Affairer,* a business magazine, and the weekly *Bonniers Veckotidning.* Bonnier's Publishing division represents its historical core, consisting of flagship imprint Albert Bonnier and a number of international publishing houses, including Cappelans in Norway; Piper, Hoppenstedt and Thienemann in Germany;

Tammi in Finland; and comic book publisher SEMIC. Under its Retail division, Bonnier groups its book, music, and video clubs, including Bonnier Bokklubb, the largest in Sweden. The company also owns stakes in broadcasting, including 25 percent of Sweden's TV4 and a controlling stake in Finland's Alma Media. Bonnier is controlled by the Bonnier family and led by Chairman Carl-Johan Bonnier and President and CEO Bengt Braun.

Founding a Swedish Publishing Empire in the 19th Century

The Bonnier publishing dynasty was founded in the early years of the 19th century by a German-Jewish immigrant, Gutkind Hirschel, who had come to Denmark in 1801, settling in Copenhagen. The son of a banking family in Dresden, Hirschel at first supported himself by giving French lessons, then entered the book trade, opening his first bookshop in 1804. By then, Hirschel had married and changed his name to the more neutral (and French-sounding) Gerard Bonnier.

Although book selling remained at the heart of Bonnier's business, he added newspaper publishing in 1816, founding the daily newspaper Dagsposten. Bonnier also had begun to develop business contacts with Sweden, in part to respond to the poor economic climate in Denmark of the period. In the mid-1820s, Bonnier sent his oldest son Adolf, then 21 years old, to Sweden to search for a suitable location for expanding the family bookselling business. In 1827 the family opened their second bookstore, in Gothenburg. Adolf was joined by younger brother David, who took over running the Gothenburg shop while Adolf opened a second Swedish store in Stockholm in 1832. David Bonnier later went on to found a daily newspaper, *Göteborgs-Posten,* in 1859, which was sold off in 1870.

Another Bonnier brother, Albert, expanded the family's growing Swedish interests in 1837 when he opened his own bookstore in Stockholm. By then the family had entered the book publishing business, when Adolf Bonnier had begun publishing art books in 1834. Yet the major force behind the Bonnier family's growth soon became Albert Bonnier, who began his own publishing operations in 1837. Albert Bonnier became a noted literary figure in Sweden, whose titles included *Proof That Napoleon Never Existed.*

Key Dates:

1804:	Gerard Bonnier, a German immigrant who had changed his name from Gutkind Hirschel, establishes a bookstore in Copenhagen.
1816:	Bonnier begins publishing the daily newspaper *Dagsposten.*
1827:	Bonnier's son Adolf opens a bookstore in Göteborg, Sweden.
1832:	Adolf Bonnier opens a second store in Stockholm.
1834:	Bonnier begins publishing operations.
1837:	Brother Albert Bonnier also opens a bookstore in Stockholm and begins a publishing business, Albert Bonnier Forlag.
1859:	AB Forlag begins publishing *Svergie Handelskalender.*
1864:	The *Dagens Nyhets* daily newspaper is founded.
1873:	Albert Bonnier becomes a shareholder in *Dagens Nyhets*; the Bonnier family gains control of the newspaper in 1909.
1923:	AB Bonnier branches out into magazine publishing with *Bonniers Veckotidning.*
1929:	The Bonnier family acquires the Ahlen & Ackerland magazine group.
1944:	The evening daily newspaper *Expressen* is launched.
1952:	The Bonnier family holdings are restructured under Bonnierföretagen AB holding company; the newspaper group remains separate as Dagens Nyheter (later renamed Tidnings AB Marieberg and taken public on Stockholm exchange).
1973:	Svensk Filmindustrie is acquired through Dagens Nyheter.
1977:	The company bundles part of its industrial holdings as public company Grafoprint (later divested).
1987:	The company acquires Cappelans, the third largest book publisher in Norway.
1990:	The Scandinavian Music Club is acquired.
1995:	The weekly magazine *Amelia* is launched.
1997:	Bonnierföretagen acquires Marieberg and delists it.
1998:	Bonnierföretagen AB restructures itself as a holding company, Bonnier AB.
2000:	Bonnier acquires Hoppenstedt, of Germany, and launches a new business daily newspaper in Scotland.
2001:	Bonnier acquires Thienemann.
2002:	The company announces its intention to bid for soon-to-be privatized TV2.

Albert Bonnier's commitment to literature and excellent business skills helped build Albert Bonnier Forlag into a noted Swedish publishing house by the middle of the 19th century, with a reputation for its imported titles, and for launching playwright Strindberg. Bonnier added a number of strong titles, such as the *Sveriges Handelskalendar, Folkkalendern Svea,* the weekly publication *Stockholms Figaro,* and *Hörbergska Tryckas,* acquired in 1856. When brother David fell ill, Albert Bonnier bought up the Göteborg bookstore in 1864.

The year 1864 also marked the founding of a new daily newspaper, *Dagens Nyheter* in Stockholm. Launched by Rudolf Wall, an associate of Albert Bonnier, the newspaper was to grow into one of Sweden's most prominent papers. Bonnier helped finance the newspaper's launch. A restructuring of *Dagens Nyheter* gave Bonnier a minority stake in the company. Under Albert's son Karl Otto, who joined his father in the business in the 1880s before taking over as the head of the Bonnier family's bookstore and publishing group after Albert's death in 1900, Bonnier gradually increased its stake in *Dagens Nyheter,* gaining control in 1909. By then the company had launched another newspaper geared toward children, called *Kamratposten,* in 1892.

The Bonnier publishing operations expanded strongly under Karl Otto's leadership, and by the outbreak of World War II, the Bonnier family had built one of Sweden's most prominent media groups. Karl Otto was joined by his sons, Tor, Ake, and Kaj, who each played an important role in the group's development. Tor Bonnier, Karl Otto's oldest son, played an especially important role in building the family's media interests, particularly in expanding its horizons.

In the first half of the 20th century, the Bonnier group extended its operations beyond its traditional core of book publishing, adding additional newspapers and, in particular, increasing its stake in *Dagens Nyheter.* The Bonnier family also branched out into magazine publishing, launching the weekly title *Bonniers Veckotidning* (*Bonniers Magazine*) in 1923 and *Hemma* (*Housewife*) in 1924, before dramatically boosting its magazine holdings with the purchase of Ahlen & Akerlund, then the largest magazine publisher in Sweden, in 1929.

Postwar Diversification

Although Sweden's neutrality during World War II protected the Bonnier family, the prevailing political climate forced the Bonniers to slow their growth. In 1944, however, the Bonniers moved forward again with the launch of an evening newspaper, *Expressen.* Taking a somewhat radical left-wing position in order to counter the right-leaning (and Nazi sympathizing) tone of the existing evening paper *Aftenbladet, Expressen* quickly took over the evening market, becoming one of the country's most widely read newspapers. The Bonniers launched a number of other successful publications in the immediate postwar era, including the magazine *Aret Runt* in 1946, and the comics group SEMIC in 1950.

The postwar period marked a number of changes for the Bonnier family group. For one, the Bonniers sought to diversify their holdings beyond media publishing, a move that had already been begun, in fact, in the 1930s. In 1946 the group added graphics and printing capacity when it launched the companies Grafisk Färg and Solna Ioffset. In 1949 the family, through its *Dagens Nyheter* holding, bought up the Billingsfors paper mill, which in turn led to the foundation of the Duni group. During the 1950s, the Bonniers continued adding industrial operations, limiting growth primarily to such publishing support areas as magazine paper and ink production. In the 1960s, however, the company began a wider industrial diversification and by the 1970s the group's holdings ranged from manufacturing mattresses and other furniture to recreational equipment and cancer testing equipment.

Until the early 1950s, the Bonnier family's broadened media holdings had been owned and conducted by brothers Tor, Ake, and Kaj. Yet the family's activities had for the most part been operated as three separate businesses, Albert Bonnier Forlag, the book publishing wing; the money-losing Ahlen & Akerlund magazine division, led by Kaj Bonnier; and the *Dagens Nyheter* and *Expressen* newspaper group. With the next generation waiting to join these family operations, the Bonniers moved to consolidate their various holdings into a single entity, Bonnierföretagen AB or Bofo, in 1952. The creation of Bofo, however, soon led to tensions within the family, particularly between Tor's son, Albert, Jr., who had taken over his father's share of the business, and Kaj Bonnier. By the end of 1952, Bofo had bought out Kaj Bonnier's stake in Bofo; as part of that buyout, the family spun off the *Dagens Nyheter* newspaper group into a separate company, in which Kaj Bonnier maintained his ownership stake.

Albert Bonnier was placed in charge of Bofo's magazine division, but quickly took on the role of CEO for the entire group. In 1957, as Bonnier moved to step up the company's industrial diversification, Albert Bonnier turned over management of the magazine division to brother Lukas, while cousin Gerard was given the lead of the company's book publishing operations. Nonetheless, Albert Bonnier emerged as the clear family leader and was credited with transforming Bofo into a major Scandinavian media group.

Facing growing resistance within Sweden because of its dominance of the country's media market, Bonnier began eyeing international expansion, starting with a partnership agreement made with Denmark's Fogtdal newspaper group in 1959. In 1969, Bofo acquired a 49 percent share in Danish publishing group Forlaget Borsen. During the 1970s, Bofo stepped up its foreign operations with the 1976 purchase of France's Editions La Croix, which was subsequently renamed Publications Bonnier.

A more significant move in the expansion of Bonnier's media empire came with its acquisition, through *Dagens Nyheter,* in 1973, of Swedish film and television product leader Svensk Filmindustrie. That acquisition also gave the Bonnier family control of SF Bio, which was to become the leading cinema operator in Sweden. The company's film production division was later boosted by the purchase of the Europe Film production company in 1984. By then, Bofo had taken direct control of Svensk Filmindustrie as well, acquiring that company from the *Dagens Nyheter* group. The newspaper concern, meanwhile, had been expanding as well, launching a new business daily, *Dagens Industri,* in 1976. Yet the *Dagens Nyheter* group found itself struggling during the decade as readership and advertising revenues declined.

Until the mid-1970s, Bofo had been able to raise capital investment through transfers arranged among its various member firms. Changes in Sweden's tax laws, however, forced the private family group to seek outside capital. In 1977, the com-

pany grouped together three of its industrial operations—Duni, Solna, and Billingsfors—and launched them as public company Grafoprint. Nonetheless, Bofo's industrial operations were becoming a drain on the rest of its activities, as Bofo found itself unable to make the capital investments necessary to expand those businesses. By the end of the 1980s, Bofo had sold or closed most of its nonmedia assets. Meanwhile, the *Dagens Nyheter* newspaper group also was taken public, listed as Tidnings AB Marieberg.

Scandinavian Media Powerhouse in the 21st Century

In the mid-1980s, Bofo's operations generated some SKr 4 billion ($520 million). The company's media operations nonetheless represented the largest part of those revenues. With its exit from industrial operations, Bofo focused its efforts on expanding its media holdings. The company began making new acquisitions, including Cappelens, one of Norway's top three book publishers, in 1987. The company had made other book publisher acquisitions, building up a list that included imprints such as Forum, Viva, and Wahlstrom & Widstrand. Other acquisitions followed, including Scandinavian Music Club, the largest in the region, in 1990. In that year, also, the company formed a joint venture with Germany Hoppenstedt to form the business information publishing group Hoppenstedt Bonnier. The following year, the company acquired noted Swedish book publisher Trevi. By then, Bofo revenues had topped SKr 7.5 billion (nearly $1.2 billion).

The Bonnier group continued acquiring scale in the 1990s, buying the daily newspaper *Sydsvenska Dagbladet,* through Mariberg, and adding German publisher Piper in 1994, launching the *Wirtschaftblad* daily financial paper in Austria in 1995. In 1994, also, the company launched its own multimedia wing, Bonnier Multimedia. Two years later the company launched the new magazine *Amelia,* which represented one of the most successful new magazine launches in the Scandinavian region in that decade. The company moved into Finland that same year with the purchase of publishing group Kirjakanava, the country's third largest publisher. Marieberg, meanwhile, had provided the company with an entry into the television market, with a stake in the Swedish pay-television channel TV4. The company continued building up its holding in TV4, raising its stake to 25 percent by the end of the decade.

In 1997, the Bonnier family and Bofo moved to take full control of Marieberg; under the terms of the shareholder buyout, the Bonniers were guaranteed control of the newspaper group up to 2030. Bofo then delisted Marieberg from the Stockholm exchange. The deal, which cost Bofo some SKr 5.4 billion, was financed by bank loans—much of which were paid off through sales of the Bonnier family's extensive portfolio of landmark real estate in Stockholm and elsewhere. Following the absorption of Marieberg, Bofo was restructured into a holding company, under the new name Bonnier AB, in 1998.

By then, Bonnier had begun acquiring a position in the newly formed Alma Media Group, based in Finland, which had been formed through the merger of the Aamulehti newspaper group and the Finnish television group MTV3. Bonnier continued to increase its holding in Alma into the beginning of the new century, raising its stake to 33 percent—just below the automatic "poison pill" trigger point of 33.3 percent that would require the company to make a formal takeover offer. Bonnier, however, maintained its satisfaction with its minority shareholder status.

Bonnier continued its expansion into the 21st century, extending its SF Bio cinema operation into Norway in 1999, then buying up the Hoppenstedt publishing group and fellow German publisher arsEdition, in 2000. In that year, the company moved beyond Scandinavia with the launch of *Business AM,* a daily business newspaper for the Scottish market. In 2001, Bonnier's acquisitions included a 50 percent stake in Forlaget Benjamin, based in Denmark, and the takeover of Verlag Thienemann, of Germany.

The coming deregulation of the European media market—which was expected to loosen foreign ownership restrictions—whetted Bonnier's appetite for acquisitions, as the company announced its intention to play a role in the coming consolidation of the northern European media market. In September 2002, the company announced its intention to bid for the soon-to-be privatized Swedish television station TV2, scheduled to be put up for sale in 2003. The company also continued to expand its newspaper holdings—under pressure with the successful entry of the free daily commuter paper *Metro*—with the launch of its own commuter daily, *Stockholm City,* at the end of October 2002. Bonnier's CEO Bengt Braun also suggested that the company had begun considering opening up its shareholding—whether in a public offering or by selling a stake in the company outright—in order to finance its continued expansion.

Principal Divisions

Bonnier AB; Bonnier Newspapers; Bonnier Books; Bonnier Magazine Group; Bonnier Business Information; Bonnier Entertainment; Bonnier Business Press.

Principal Competitors

Bertelsmann AG; Pearson plc; Reed Elsevier plc; United News & Media plc; Wolters Kluwer NV; Gruner Jahr AG & Co. Druck- und Verlagshaus; Reed International plc; Daily Mail & General Trust plc; Axel Springer Verlag AG; EMAP plc; WH Smith PLC; LOGISTA S.A.; FNAC S.A.; LOGISTA SA; FNAC SA; Reitan Handel ASA; Reitan Narvesen ASA; John Menzies PLC; Ingram Book Group Inc.; Follett Corp.; Sanoma WSOY Group; Timon S.A.; Union INVIVO; Anderson News Co.; Maruzen Company Ltd.; Relais FNAC; Dawson Holdings PLC; Ruch S.A.; Timon SA; Surridge Dawson Ltd.; Ringier AG; Condé Nast and National Magazine Distributors Ltd.; Libro AG.

Further Reading

"Another Free Newspaper Tries for a Share of Swedish Market," *AP Worldstream,* October 21, 2002.
Curtis, Jim, "A Nordic Invasion," *Campaign,* November 24, 2000, p. 38.
Larsson, Mats, *Bonniers – en mediefamilj. Förlag, konglomerat och mediekoncern 1953–1990,* Stockholm: Bonnier AB, 2001.
Lottman, Herbert R., "Growth at Bonnier," *Publishers Weekly,* April 24, 2000, p. 20.
"One of Sweden's Largest and Oldest Newspapers to Cut Staff, Change Format," *AP Worldstream,* June 18, 2002.
Peltola, Anna, "Bonnier Prepares for Onslaught of U.S. Media," *Reuters,* March 8, 2002.

—M.L. Cohen

Building Materials Holding Corporation

4 Embarcadero Center, Suite 3250
San Francisco, California 94111
U.S.A.
Telephone: (415) 627-9100
Fax: (415) 627-9119
Web site: http://www.bmhc.com

Public Company
Incorporated: 1997
Employees: 5,940
Sales: $1.09 billion (2001)
Stock Exchanges: NASDAQ
Ticker Symbol: BMHC
NAIC: 444190 Other Building Material Dealers; 321911
   Wood Window and Door Manufacturing

Building Materials Holding Corporation (BMHC) is a holding company that oversees the operation of its two principal subsidiaries, BMC West Corporation and BMC Framing Inc. With 131 properties in 12 western and southern states, BMHC operates in the building materials and services industry, focusing on satisfying the needs of contractors. The company's retail outlets, operated through BMC West, feature lumberyards outfitted with millwork facilities to fabricate floor and roof trusses, pre-hung doors and windows, and other finished products. Through BMC Framing, the company provides framing services to national and regional homebuilders.

Origins

Upon its formation at the end of 1997, BMHC inherited strategic control over a chain of 55 stores, which generated $725 million in sales during the year. The stores and the revenue represented a decade of growth orchestrated by BMC West Corporation, the corporate entity BMHC was formed to serve. From the end of 1997 forward, BMHC would serve as central command for BMC West and other subsidiaries as they were formed. The establishment of BMHC as a holding company for BMC West represented an important step in a strategic plan developed by

BMC West's management to pursue a future of accelerated growth. With a holding company, BMC West's management theorized, operational management could be centralized, assigning all responsibilities for administering and spurring growth to a single corporate entity. BMHC's duty was to govern the BMC West empire, a duty that encompassed a broad range of responsibilities including targeting and completing acquisitions, taking charge of strategic, financial, and capital planning activities, and handling investor relations. Any understanding of BMHC, however, required an understanding of BMC West, whose corporate birth preceded BMHC's formation by a decade.

BMC West, like BMHC, got a jumpstart of sorts in its corporate life. The company was created after a leveraged buyout (LBO) conducted by executives at the Idaho-based Boise Cascade lumber company. Under Boise Cascade's control there once had been as many as 120 Building Materials Centers (hence the initials "BMC"), but under the bureaucratic management of the giant lumber company the chain suffered, dwindling to 20 stores by 1987 when four managers decided they could do better. Donald S. Hendrickson, Ellis C. Goebel, Steven H. Pearson, and Richard F. Blackwood became the new leaders of the beleaguered chain. Led by Hendrickson, the managers teamed with an investment firm, McCown De Leeuw & Co., to finance the LBO of Boise Cascade's retail arm. George McCown, the general partner of McCown De Leeuw, and Hendrickson were able to secure $40 million in capital from Wells Fargo on a mere $1 million in equity, which proved enough to complete the spinoff of a new, independent company called BMC West Corporation in November 1987. McCown assumed the duties of board chairman, Hendrickson was appointed president and chief executive officer, Pearson became vice-president of human resources, and Blackwood was named vice-president of the company's northern operations.

Although the creation of BMHC signaled a desire for accelerated growth, BMC West, on its own, pursued an aggressive growth plan during its first decade of existence. The company's constant efforts to expand led one trade publication to suggest that "BMC" stood for "Buying More Companies," but acquisitive rampancy did not mean Hendrickson and his team moved blindly forward with their purchasing campaign. The com-

53

pany's acquisition strategy was sharply defined, designed to distinguish its retail concept from ''big box'' competitors such as The Home Depot.

BMC West in the 1990s

BMC West's defining characteristic was its focus on serving professional builders and remodelers, rather than the casual ''do-it-yourself'' customers favored by The Home Depot. Unlike its big box competitors, the company eschewed acquiring properties in major metropolitan areas, preferring to build its presence in markets similar in size to its headquarters city of Boise, Idaho, home to less than 300,000 residents. Given its bias toward contractors, BMC West also preferred to acquire lumberyards with adjoining millwork operations capable of fabricating roof trusses, pre-hung doors and windows, and other finished-wood or ''value-added'' products. Lastly, acquisition candidates had to be making money. BMC West did not intend to be a turnaround specialist. ''When we started out,'' Hendrickson said in a July 1995 interview with *Chilton's Hardware Age,* ''we were so heavily leveraged we had to buy companies that immediately added to our earnings per share. We learned that's a pretty good way to do it.''

As BMC pressed forward with its expansion program in the western United States, it exceeded its own growth projections. The company planned to add as much as $45 million of new business annually throughout much of the 1990s, but the ample number of acquisition candidates meeting its criteria spurred accelerated growth. More often than not, lumberyards wishing to sell approached BMC West rather than the other way around, further facilitating expansion. The company completed its initial public offering (IPO) of stock in August 1991. During its first five years of operation, the company acquired 16 properties and either shuttered or relocated another six units, giving it 32 stores by 1992 when the company was selected as Retailer of the Year by the trade publication *Building Supply Home Centers.*

During the mid-1990s BMC West's rate of growth picked up pace. In 1994 the company acquired ten lumberyards and added $132 million in sales. By mid-1995 when the company was striving to double its annual revenues by 1998, BMC West had added more than $100 million in new business, bolstering its geographic presence to encompass nine western states plus Texas. By 1997, the year of BMHC's formation, BMC West was operating 55 stores, which generated $725 million in sales, more than twice the amount collected five years earlier.

By the time Hendrickson decided it would be in the company's best interest to form a holding company, the format of

BMC West's stores had evolved, underscoring the differences separating BMC West and big box competitors. During the early 1990s the company derived 6 percent of its sales from finished products. As the company entered the late 1990s, it derived approximately 35 percent of its sales from millwork, having greatly expanded its offering of pre-assembled roof and floor trusses, pre-framed walls, and pre-hung doors and windows. The increasing emphasis on selling value-added products was partly responsible for the company's financial growth, particularly its profitability. Expansion through acquisitions added revenue in lumps, but selling more value-added products delivered meaningful growth as well, enabling the company to increase same-store sales by selling higher-price, higher-profit margin products. As value-added product sales increased, commodity lumber sales shrank, accounting for roughly 40 percent of sales during the late 1990s, half the percentage recorded earlier in the decade.

Birth of BMHC and Beyond: 1997–2000s

The announcement that BMC West would separate its strategic, operational, and financial activities into a holding company occurred in February 1997. In a March 1997 interview with *Home Improvement Market,* Goebel explained: ''We feel that with forming the holding company, we'll be able to do the financial things there, we'll be able to work with Wall Street there, and we'll be able to do the acquisition[s] there. Then we can keep the operating management close to our customers and close to the employees.'' Concurrent with the creation of BMHC, headquarters were moved from Boise to San Francisco, where a small office housing no more than a handful of executives was opened. Hendrickson stayed on as president and chief executive officer of BMC West, which led to the appointment of Robert E. Mellor as BMHC's president and chief executive officer. As part of the restructuring that gave birth to BMHC, BMC West was divided into three major operating divisions separated by their geographic differences.

By the time BMHC was formed, the company was attempting to reach $1.2 billion in sales by 2000, double the total recorded in 1995. The time spent creating BMHC did not halt the company's pursuit of its financial goal. In 1997 the company completed five acquisitions, the fifth and largest of which was the $63-million-in-sales Lone Star Plywood & Door Co. purchased in November. The acquisition of Lone Star, a Texas-based operator of millwork and pre-hung door manufacturing facilities in Houston, Dallas, Portland, and Seattle, led to the formation of a fourth BMC West division. Bill Smith, Lone Star's president, was selected to head BMC West's south central division, which included 13 BMC West building centers located throughout Texas.

As BMHC pressed ahead in its inaugural year, steady expansion pushed the company toward its ambitious revenue goal. In June 1998 BMC West signed an agreement to acquire a 19-acre tract of land in Portland. On the land, the company intended to build one of its full-service facilities, featuring a lumberyard, a door facility, and a truss plant. The facility was expected to be fully operational by mid-1999. The company also acquired Rigid Truss Inc., an operator of a truss facility and a wall panel plant in Salem, Oregon, with $6 million in sales. In August 1998 BMHC announced it had acquired two companies, Castleberry

Mill & Lumber Inc. and Heart Truss Co. Based in Dallas, Castleberry generated $53 million in sales from its custom pre-hung door shop and a wood and vinyl window distributorship. Heart Truss, based in Spokane, Washington, operated a truss manufacturing plant generating $51 million in sales in 1997.

In the final year of the decade, BMHC slipped past $1 billion in sales, registering $1.007 billion in revenue and $19.6 million in net income. The financial figures recorded at the end of 1999 were boosted, in part, by the acquisitions completed during the year. BMHC purchased four value-added manufacturing facilities during 1999, including the October purchase of Royal Door, an Oregon-based millwork operation with $25 million in annual sales. The most important development in 1999 occurred when BMHC entered the framing business, leading to the formation of a new subsidiary, BMC Framing Inc. BMHC entered the framing business by acquiring 49 percent of Knipp Brothers Industries, LLC, a framing contractor with operations in Arizona, Nevada, and California. The deal was expected to greatly enhance the portion of sales derived from construction services and manufactured components, one of BMHC's primary goals as it entered the 21st century.

As BMHC progressed toward its fifth anniversary, the company continued to add to its manufacturing and installation capabilities, further distancing itself from the commodity lumber business that had once defined BMC West. When BMHC acquired its stake in Knipp Brothers, it had planned to acquire the remainder of the company in 2004, but instead completed the acquisition three years ahead of schedule. In a move to better align its operations with production homebuilders, BMHC acquired the remaining 51 percent interest in Knipp Brothers, bolstering the stature of BMC Framing and increasing its commitment to the installation side of the residential construction business. The impact on the company's business was measurable. Value-added products and services, which had once accounted for only 6 percent of sales, accounted for 54 percent of the company's sales in the fourth quarter of 2001.

In 2001, BMHC generated $1.09 billion in revenue, coming enticingly close to its goal of $1.2 billion in revenue by 2002.

During 2002 Mellor increased his influence over the company by replacing McCown as chairman, giving Mellor considerable control as president, chief executive officer, and chairman. Shortly after Mellor's ascension to BMHC's chairmanship, the company sealed another deal to increase its framing business. In July, the company announced an agreement to acquire 51 percent of Sanburn Construction, a provider of framing services for more than 15 leading national and regional production homebuilders in the greater Sacramento market and the San Francisco Bay area. The investment led to the creation of KBI Norcal, which was organized as a business unit within BMC Framing. On the heels of this development, BMHC began looking for other investments and acquisitions, endeavoring to march past $1.2 billion in sales. As the company prepared for the future, its maturation from a regional to a national company appeared to be only a matter of time, provided its prudent course of expansion did not stray from past success.

Principal Subsidiaries

BMC West Corporation; BMC Framing Inc.; KBI Norcal (51%).

Principal Competitors

The Home Depot, Inc.; Lowe's Companies, Inc.; Pacific Coast Building Products Incorporated.

Further Reading

Binole, Gina, "Building Material Firm Set to Expand in Portland," *Business Journal-Portland,* June 12, 1998, p. 14.

"BMC Announces Stock Offering, Record Revenues," *Building Supply Home Centers,* November 1992, p. 24.

"BMC West Buys Its Way to the Top," *Building Supply Home Centers,* February 1994, p. 29.

"BMC West Buys Plywood and Door Company," *Do-It-Yourself Retailing,* January 1998, p. 82.

"BMHC Buys Two Value-Added Companies," *Do-It-Yourself Retailing,* August 1998, p. 33.

"BMHC Expands Residential Framing Operations," *Do-It-Yourself Retailing,* August 2002, p. 21.

"BMHC Forms New Business Unit," *Home Channel News NewsFax,* July 1, 2002, p. 1.

"Building Material Firm Set to Expand in Portland," *Business Journal-Portland,* June 12, 1998, p. 14.

Casson, Clarence, "BMC West: Power to Its People," *Building Supply Home Centers,* June 1992, p. 76.

Impellizzeri, Laura, "Boise Cascade Offshoot Nails 4th Buy-Up for Year," *San Francisco Business Times,* October 22, 1999, p. 17.

"Mellor Elected Chairman of BMHC," *Home Channel News NewsFax,* May 6, 2002, p. 2.

Shuster, Laurie, "BMC West on a Buying Spree," *Chilton's Hardware Age,*

Clarks

C&J Clark International Ltd.

40 High Street
Street, Somerset BA16 0YA
United Kingdom
Telephone: (+44) 1458 44 31 31
Fax: (+44) 1458 44 75 47
Web site: http://www.clarks.co.uk

Private Company
Incorporated: 1825
Employees: 15,270
Sales: £937 million ($1.55 billion) (2001)
NAIC: 448210 Shoe Stores; 316212 House Slipper
    Manufacturing; 316213 Men's Footwear (Except
    Athletic) Manufacturing; 316214 Women's Footwear
    (Except Athletic) Manufacturing; 316219 Other
    Footwear Manufacturing; 424340 Footwear Merchant
    Wholesalers

C&J Clark International Ltd. (Clarks) is a world-leading manufacturer and retailer of footwear. The company produces shoes, boots, and other footwear under the renowned Clarks brand name, as well as K Shoes in England and Bostonian in the United States. Clarks is also one of the world's leading manufacturers of children's shoes, which include the Germany-based Elefanten brand, a leading European brand, acquired in 2000. Based in the village of Street, in Somerset, England, Clarks is that country's largest shoe manufacturer, with a particular focus on the ''comfort'' category, and is also the United Kingdom's leading retail shoe specialist, with more than 500 Clarks, Ravel, and K Shops. Formerly committed to manufacturing in the United Kingdom, Clarks has trimmed its manufacturing base in that country from a high of nearly 30 factories in the 1980s to just four remaining sites at the end of the century. As the company has switched its emphasis from manufacturing to design-oriented branded consumer goods, production has shifted to Brazil, China, India, and Portugal. The company also has been working to build its image among consumers, while revitalizing its store formats and marketing campaigns. This restructuring has enabled the company to post renewed profit growth, and rising revenues, which were expected to top £1 billion ($1.6 billion) in 2002. Clarks remains 80 percent owned by the more than 400 members of the founding Clark family. The company has long resisted the temptation to go public; CEO Peter Bollinger, who joined the company in 1994, has reiterated the company's decision to remain a private company.

Founding a Footwear Dynasty in the 1830s

Cyrus Clark, son of Somerset-based farmers, went into business for himself as a wool stapler and tanner, establishing a workshop in the village of Street, in Somerset, England, in 1825. Clark then added the production of sheepskin rugs, before being joined by brother James in 1828, who began looking for a way to make use of the scraps of sheepskin left over from the rug-making business. The younger Clark found his product—slippers—which were launched into production in 1830 and given the name of Brown Petersburgh, which quickly became better known as the Brown Peter. The slippers were a success, and were to remain in production for more than 100 years.

In 1833 James was taken on as a full partner in the business, which was renamed C&J Clark. By then, the company's footwear accounted for more than one-third of its total business. Over the next decade, sales of Brown Peters continued to build, topping 12,000 pairs per year in the early 1840s. The company also had taken advantage of another sheepskin byproduct, adding lamb's wool stockings. The company's growth was aided by the family's Quaker beliefs. As members of the Society of Friends, the Clark family was able to take advantage of personal and business connections throughout the United Kingdom and the British Empire, and the Clarks brand name quickly became a prominent name in British footwear.

The Clarks business nonetheless experienced difficulties during the middle of the 19th century, when demand for the Brown Peter slipped and brought the company to the brink of bankruptcy. When the company again faced bankruptcy in 1863, the decision was made to turn over its operation to James Clark's son William Stephens Clark. The younger Clark became the driving force for the company's growth into the next century. After Cyrus Clark died in 1866, James and William reformed the partnership, while retaining the C&J Clark name.

Under the new generation, Clarks began turning to more industrialized production techniques, including adding Singer sewing machines, which had been invented in the 1850s. The new machines enabled the company to step up its production levels, and also enabled Clarks to begin experimenting with new shoe designs. These were initially sold under a new brand name, Torbrand.

At the beginning of the 1890s, Clarks's design experiments had led to the development of shoes that more closely followed the line of the foot. The company debuted its new "Hygienic" line of shoes in 1893. The success of those shoe styles led the company to specialize in so-called "comfort" shoes.

The next generation of Clarks—William's children John, Roger, and Alice—joined the company in the early years of the 20th century and built it into a modern manufacturing operation, adopting mass production techniques and incorporating new materials and new technologies, including techniques for crafting soles, insoles, and heels to enhance the shoes' comfort. The company also debuted modern warehousing and distribution techniques and began adding vertically integrated operations, giving it control of nearly the entire shoe production process.

By 1920, the company had dropped the Torbrand brand name and placed its own name on its shoes instead. During the 1920s, Clarks responded to the far-reaching changes in fashion, particularly in women's fashion—where shortening hemlines revealed more and more of a woman's footwear—by launching new women's shoe and boot designs.

Booting Up for Success in the 1950s

Not all of the company's expansion came through its own brand name. In 1927, Clarks added a new brand name when it debuted its Wessex line. In the 1930s, the company began looking to expand beyond manufacturing and gain control of its distribution market as well, which resulted in the acquisition of a chain of shoe stores, renamed as Peter Lord, in 1937. The Peter Lord chain grew into a nationally operating retail network of some 180 stores. The company later expanded its retail offerings with the addition of the James Baker chain, which reached 65 stores in England, and the Rayne & Duckett chain, which featured 70 stores in Scotland.

Under the leadership of Bancroft Clark during the post-World War II years, the company enjoyed still more success, as Clarks began building up its international export market. A major factor in the company's success during this period came

with the launch of the Desert Boot. Family member Nathan Clark, who became part of the next generation to take over the company's direction, had served in the British Army in India during World War II and had been inspired by boots brought over from Egypt by a number of British officers. Returning home, Nathan Clark brought the boot design, which featured a suede upper on a crepe sole, to C&J Clark.

The first Desert Boot was produced in 1946, but it was not until the beginning of the 1950s that the company launched full production of the design, which became an instant success. The Desert Boot also expanded the scope of the company's consumer base, traditionally skewed toward the older consumer, to include a growing number of young customers, who adopted the Desert Boot as their own in the 1950s and 1960s. The company had a new hit in the mid-1960s when family member Lance Clark introduced another popular shoe design, the moccasin-styled Wallabee, which went on to become a classic in the comfort shoe category.

Meanwhile, Clarks also began building up a worldwide reputation for its children's shoes, becoming, in the 1960s, one of the first to provide so-called "fitted" shoes that took into consideration the particularities of children's feet. Before long, Clarks had established itself as a world-leading producer of children's shoes; in the United Kingdom alone, the company had captured half of the children's shoe market. Children's shoe manufacture, which required more specialized manufacturing techniques, was also to become the mainstay of the company's U.K. manufacturing base.

Clarks had long invested in developing new technologies, such as a process for vulcanizing rubber soles directly onto leather uppers in the 1950s. In the 1970s, the company began working with the recently developed material polyurethane, adapting the lightweight, resistant material as part of new sole designs, including its polyveldts soles in the 1970s and air-cushioned soles, which formed the basis of the company's Air Comfort line in the 1980s.

At the end of the 1970s, C&J Clark went on an expansion drive. In 1978, the company turned to the United States, acquiring noted shoemaker and retailer Hanover. A year later, the company made a still more significant purchase, buying up Bostonian. Founded in 1899, Bostonian had pioneered the introduction of an extensive range of widths, and then entered the retail market in 1925, building a strong network in the United States. The two acquisitions gave Clarks a manufacturing base with production of some 1.5 million shoes per year, and a retail operation of more than 500 stores throughout the United States.

Clarks followed its U.S. expansion with a boost to its U.K. position in 1981, acquiring K Shoes Ltd. That company had been founded in 1842 by Robert Miller Somervell as an offshoot to his leather merchant business, in the town of Kendal, in Cumbria, England. The company had adopted the K brand for its shoes in 1875, before going on to build up both its manufacturing and a strong U.K.-based retail business, with nearly 240 K Shoe Stores in operation. The K Shoes acquisition complemented Clarks's existing portfolio, with a particular strength in attracting an older consumer segment.

Key Dates:

1825: Cyrus Clark founds a tanning and wool stapling business in the village of Street, in Somerset, England.
1828: Joined by brother James, Clark begins producing sheepskin slippers, called the Brown Peter.
1833: James becomes a full partner; business is renamed C&J Clark Ltd.
1863: William Clark, son of James Clark, takes over the company.
1893: The introduction of the ''Hygienic'' line of shoes begins the company's focus as a ''comfort'' shoemaker.
1937: The company acquires a retail shoe store chain and renames it Peter Lord.
1950: The company launches the successful Desert Boot.
1965: The first Clark Wallabee model is launched.
1978: The company acquires the Hanover shoe manufacturing and retail business in the United States.
1979: The company acquires the Bostonian shoe manufacturing and retail business in the United States.
1981: The company acquires K Shoes Ltd., a U.K.-based shoe manufacturer and retailer.
1988: C&J Clark abandons its plans to go public.
1993: The company puts itself up for sale, then rejects an offer to buy from Berisford.
1996: The company begins restructuring, transforming itself from a manufacturing-oriented business to a consumer-driven, design-oriented branded products group.
2000: The company announces that it has decided not to go public for the near future.
2001: The company acquires Elefanten, a children's shoe manufacturer in Germany.

Private or Public for the New Century?

The K Shoes acquisition had enabled Clarks to boost its market position substantially, becoming the world's second largest family-owned shoe manufacturer, behind Bata, and the United Kingdom's second largest shoe retailer, behind British Shoe Corp. Yet the company's newly expanded U.S. operations lagged behind, in part because of a company decision to emphasize the Bostonian and Hanover brands, instead of the company's own Clarks branded shoes. By the mid-1980s, the company found itself outpaced in the U.S. market by a number of rivals as the comfort category took off in that country. Even in its core British market, the company was losing ground.

After reviewing its operations with McKinsey Consultants, Clarks underwent a thorough restructuring program in 1986, which included encouraging a number of its elderly upper management to take early retirement in order to replace them with younger staff. The company also brought in Lawrence Tindale as chairman, the first time the company turned to someone from outside the Clark family for leadership. The company began repositioning its retail operation, launching a new store concept, Clarks Shop, in an attempt to regain momentum for its core shoe brand. By the end of the decade, the company had streamlined its retail holdings into just three outlets, Clarks Shop, Ravel, and K Shoes.

In 1986, Clarks announced its interest in selling off its U.S. holdings to emphasize the Clarks brand in the United States, but was unable to find a buyer offering the right purchase price. Meanwhile, on the manufacturing side, Clarks introduced new CAD/CAM design and manufacturing technology, placing the company at the leading edge in the shoe industry.

Clarks attempted to broaden its retail operations, targeting the European continent, when in 1987 it signed a deal with Fish Camuto to bring the 9 West retail store concept to Europe. The deal initially called for the opening of nine 9 West stores in London and Paris, with plans to extend into other European countries. By the end of the 1980s, however, the companies dropped their agreement, and Clarks returned its focus to its own operations.

Clarks, which by then counted some 400 family members in its shareholder base, made its first flirtation with a public offering in the late 1980s. In 1988, the family shareholders voted to take the company public. Yet the shareholders' hopes for cashing in on their shares were dashed on the one hand by the collapse of the stock market and the slump into global recession and on the other with the growing threat of competition from cheap shoe imports, as the world's shoe manufacturing increasingly shifted production to lower wage markets. In 1989, the Clark family voted against taking the company public.

In that year, as well, Clarks was forced to begin shutting down its U.K. manufacturing base, moving its own sourcing overseas, which saw it pare down the number of its U.K. production sites to just four by the beginning of the 2000s. Nonetheless, the company's Quaker heritage and its longstanding commitment not only to its workers but to its home base in Street, put the brakes on the restructuring of the company's manufacturing operation. Instead, Clarks attempted to meet the need to cut costs by adopting less expensive materials. The company also attempted to respond to the growing market for athletic shoes, which was draining its shoe sales, by moving into that area as well. In 1989, the company was granted the European marketing license for the United States' Ryka brand; that deal collapsed, however, when it was discovered that Ryka was already a registered trademark in Europe. Instead, Clarks turned to another U.S. sport shoe company, K Swiss, forming a joint venture European distribution company, K Swiss Europe.

In 1990, Clarks brought in a new chairman, Walter Dickson, again from outside the Clark family, to help return the company to growth. Yet the company was hit hard by the recession, which saw both its sales battered and its costs increase. By 1992, the company was forced to slash its dividends, provoking a rebellion from a faction of the Clark family, which demanded Dickson's ouster. Dickson survived, backed by managing director (and Clark family member) John Clothier.

Yet Clarks continued to struggle into 1993. At the beginning of the year, the company decided to sell out, and began taking bids. In 1993, the majority of the board recommended accepting a bid of some £184 million from investment group Berisford. But the Clark family once again divided over the sale—and in the end the family voted not to sell. Dickson left the company, replaced by Roger Pedder, a Clark family member.

The company began restructuring in the mid-1990s toward the goal of going public later in the decade. Clarks began shutting down more of its U.K. manufacturing units, which still numbered 12 sites at mid-decade. The company also began strengthening its design component in an effort to recapture its position, particularly in the fast-moving women's shoe market. Another change was the creation of the new position of chief executive officer. In 1996, the company brought in its first CEO, Tim Parker, who stepped up the company's restructuring efforts.

Under Parker, Clarks began transforming itself from a manufacturing-dominated company to a consumer-oriented, branded products group. Rather than manufacture its products and hope the consumer would buy them, the company now focused on increasing its responsiveness to shifting consumer demands. The company began adopting more modern shoe designs, while revamping its retail store formats and shutting down a number of poorly performing locations. Clarks then began new marketing efforts to broaden the Clarks brand's appeal, which resulted in the highly successful "Act your shoe size, not your age" campaign. Also helping the company was renewed interest in the Desert Boot, which had been made fashionable again by a new generation of British pop stars.

Parker, meanwhile, continued trimming the company's operations, shutting down more factories and selling off the company factory outlet business, which netted a windfall worth some £50 million for the company's shareholders—a move viewed by some as a way to placate family members waiting for a public offering. The company appeared to take a step closer to that goal at the beginning of 2000, when Clarks hired advisors to help evaluate the possibility of a floatation. Yet by the end of 2000, the company announced that it had decided once again to postpone a public offering.

Instead, with its sales swelling—topping £830 million in 2000—C&J Clark once again eyed international expansion. In 2001, the company turned to Germany, paying £23 million to acquire children's shoe specialist Elefanten from industrial conglomerate Freudenberg. That purchase gave Clarks a major position in the German and Benelux markets, as well as boosted its position in the United States. Clarks intended to use the acquisition as a springboard to launch its own Clarks branded children's footwear onto the European continent.

By 2002, Clarks's repositioning was mostly completed. Sales continued to build strongly, topping £930 million by the end of 2001, with expectations to grow past £1 billion by the end of 2002. In that year, Tim Parker left the company and was replaced by Peter Bollinger, who reiterated the company's intention to remain private, at least for the time being. Clarks had successfully weathered a turbulent decade to reemerge as a strongly positioned international brand name for the new century.

Principal Subsidiaries

C and J Clark America Inc. (U.S.A.); C J Clark - Fabrica de Calcado Lda Castelo de Paiva (Portugal).

Principal Competitors

Kesko Oyj Helsinki; Reebok International Ltd.; Industria de Diseno Textil S.A.; Gucci Groep NV; Brown Shoe Company Inc.; Phillips-Van Heusen Corp.; Ssangyong Corp.; Amsteel Corporation Bhd.; Euretco NV; Skechers U.S.A. Inc.; Robert Stephen Holdings PLC; Carolina Shoe Co.; Casual Male Corp.; Esprit Europe AG; Spalding Holdings Corp.; Adidas UK Ltd.; Aerogroup International Inc.; Nimox NV; Euro Shoe Group; Vans Inc.

Further Reading

Bain, Sally, "C&J Clark Steps into the Limelight Over Sell-off Issue," *Marketing,* May 6, 1993, p. 16.

Barker, Sophie, "Clarks Kicks Off the Cosy Slippers and Tries on a Swizzle," *Daily Telegraph,* November 24, 2001.

"Clarks Well Shod As Its Profits Soar," *Birmingham Post,* April 19, 2002, p. 24.

Cope, Nigel, "Clark Family in Sell-off Bonanza," *Independent,* April 16, 1997, p. 24.

Fallon, James, "Restructured Clarks Energizes Global Sales," *Footwear News,* March 14, 1994, p. 30.

Hall, Amanda, "New Spring in Clarks' Step," *Sunday Telegraph,* October 5, 1997.

Sutton, George B., *A History of Shoe Making in Street, Somerset: C&J Clark, 1833–1903,* London: William Sessions, 1979.

—M.L. Cohen

Capital One

Capital One Financial Corporation

2980 Fairview Park Drive
Suite 1300
Falls Church, Virginia 22042-4525
U.S.A.
Telephone: (703) 205-1000
Toll Free: (800) 955-7070
Fax: (703) 205-1755
Web site: http://www.capitalone.com

Public Company
Incorporated: 1995
Employees: 20,000
Total Assets: $28.18 billion (2001)
Stock Exchanges: New York
Ticker Symbol: COF
NAIC: 522210 Credit Card Issuing; 551111 Offices of
    Bank Holding Companies

Capital One Financial Corporation, a holding company, is perhaps best known for its inventive advertising of its credit card products. But it was Capital One's creative use of information technology that helped it rapidly grow to one of the largest providers of MasterCard and Visa in the world. During its short history, the company has expanded not only beyond U.S. boundaries but into a variety of consumer financial products and services.

Credit Where Credit Is Due: 1988–95

Richard D. Fairbank and Nigel W. Morris began building the foundation for Capital One in 1988 under the auspices of Richmond, Virginia-based Signet Bank. In the mid-1980s, Fairbank recognized what he perceived as a missed opportunity by the credit card industry. He called on Morris, a fellow consultant at Strategic Planning Associates (later named Mercer Management Consulting), to help construct a more integrated and scientific approach to marketing bank cards. Fairbank and Morris's plan would allow companies to fine-tune card product and pricing strategies for individual customers through a decision-making structure blending together marketing, credit, risk, op-

erations, and technology functions. The pair pitched the idea to more than 20 national retail banks before Signet signed on and gave Fairbank and Morris the green light to develop the plan. They intended to revolutionize Signet's credit card business, which dated back to the early 1950s and operated in traditional banking fashion.

Citibank had stepped outside the box, when it turned to a direct mail campaign to push its credit cards, a move that was quickly copied by other major commercial banks. Yet, the credit card products themselves remained unremarkable. Interest rates hovered between 18 and 20 percent. In the mid-1980s nonbanking entities offered some new spins to consumer credit. The Discover Card, a Sears, Roebuck and Co. product, introduced the annual rebate. Travel and entertainment card marketer American Express Co. rolled out the Optima card with a 15 percent rate.

Fairbank and Morris envisioned a credit card industry revolution, beginning with Signet's $1 billion credit card operation. "We warned them that this would require virtually starting over, rebuilding a very different company," Fairbank told *American Banker* in September 1998. "We had to create a culture that was very nonhierarchical and challenged everything." But their dreams were almost scuttled by the real estate woes of the late 1980s, when losses forced Signet to seriously consider sinking the endeavor.

The introduction of the balance transfer offer in 1991 saved the day for Fairbank and Morris. Credit card users along with their existing credit card debt were lured to Signet with introductory or "teaser" offers below the 19.8 percent rate typically offered to middle-income customers. "The genius of Morris and Fairbank was to burrow deep into the spending habits and lifestyles of these so-called prime customers to find the better bets, then offer them various rates based on their various risks," remarked Bernard Condon in an article for *Forbes* in April 2001. Other credit card issuers were quick to catch on—Citibank, MBNA Corporation, and First USA, Inc. among them. Consumers' mailboxes were flooded with offers. Fairbank and Morris countered by using their technological know-how to tap into the subprime market, seeking out the best possible risks among customers not typically offered cards, those with no or slightly flawed credit histories.

Company Perspectives:

Our success is directly attributed to our progressive efforts in information technology, customer acquisition, and customer retention. Through our proprietary Information-Based Strategy (IBS), we have the ability to tailor our products to the appropriate customers as well as ensure that each individual customer's needs are being serviced efficiently. We also continue to look at ways in which we can apply our innovative IBS to capitalize on promising markets, including auto finance and patient financing.

Signet's credit card operation quickly became its most profitable enterprise. Citing the need to concentrate on its core businesses, the regional banking operation decided to spin off its credit card portfolio. The new unit was called Oakstone Financial Corporation—so named to reflect "its financial strength and stability," according to Fairbank, who would be chairman and CEO. A $16 per share initial public offering (IPO) in late 1994 led the way to the complete separation of the credit operation in February 1995. Renamed Capital One Financial Corporation, the newly formed company ranked as one of the top ten credit card issuers in the country, with more than five million credit card customers. Since the up and comers in the industry used tactics similar to Capital One to bring in new accounts, keeping customers became a crucial issue. Again relying on its massive information base and on employees trained as retention specialists, Capital One could quickly determine the best possible rate for a customer shopping around for a deal on interest rates. Capital One wanted to keep the customer's credit balance in the fold while maintaining the necessary financial return on that account.

As Capital One grew so did the number of delinquencies in the consumer credit industry. The trend had a negative effect on card issuers' stock value. But, according to *American Banker,* some analysts saw Capital One's Information-Based Strategy (IBS) as a significant advantage. IBS could be used to market a wide array of financial services products beyond credit cards, which gave Capital One a leg up on less technically advanced monoline companies.

Capital One's system for analyzing risk and making marketing decisions, however, came at a price. The building and maintenance of such a detail-rich system required significant capital. Additional output came when it was time to put the system to use and send out those credit card offers. In 1994, Capital One followed just behind Citibank in terms of sheer volume of solicitations. That year the card industry as a whole sent out 2.4 billion solicitations at a cost of nearly $500 million in postage alone, reported *Forbes.*

Raising the Ceiling: 1995–2000

By early 1996, Capital One had shifted away from its dependence on teaser rates to generate new business. According to *American Banker,* new marketing efforts included: cobranded/affinity, secured, and "joint account" cards. The company had been losing customers to competitors offering higher ceilings on loan balances and accounts with no annual fee. Capital One aimed at boosting its revenue in new ways. With secured cards, for example, people with flawed credit histories were required to put down deposits in order to get a line of credit.

In mid-1996, Capital One received federal approval to set up a thrift operation, Capital One FSB. The action allowed, among other things, Capital One to retain and lend out deposits on secured cards. The thrift charter also opened the way for financial activities, such as automobile installment loans. Also in 1996, Capital One expanded internationally, entering the United Kingdom and Canada.

According to a June 1997 article in *Chief Executive,* Capital One served nine million customers and held $12.6 billion in credit card receivables. Capital One's success gained it a position on the Standard & Poor's 500. The company's return on assets exceeded 20 percent each year since going independent. Stock price rose above the $100 mark in 1998.

As envisioned by founders Fairbank and Morris, Capital One moved into new markets. America One Communications Inc., a wireless business subsidiary, was the country's only direct marketer of cellular phone service. With the purchase of Summit Acceptance Corp. in 1998, Capital One entered the automobile finance business. The Dallas-based subprime lending company held $260 million in managed loans. Fairbank told *American Banker,* "We feel we can bring the capability of risk management and more sophisticated marketing methodology into an industry that right now is in a depressed condition, with a lot of companies having run into credit problems."

The hitherto glowing reports by Capital One dimmed somewhat in 1999. America One was smacked with loses related to a wireless communication price war, forcing Capital One to rethink its strategy in that arena. In addition, subprime credit card issuers were being hurt by rising interest rates in mid-1999, but Capital One said that it had already been going after more affluent superprime borrowers, attempting to balance out its loan portfolio. Fairbank and Morris also had turned their attention to the Web. Capital One had held back while other card issuers were eager to log on. But once they decided to make the move, Fairbank and Morris believed, according to *Business Week,* Capital One's culture of innovation would help them catch up and even surpass more established Internet players.

Capital One began a concerted effort to boost brand recognition in 2000. According to the company, brand awareness was just 61 percent in June 1999. Many customers did not even know Capital One was an entity separate from Visa and Mastercard. In an all-out effort to be seen as a national brand, "What's in your wallet?" advertisements began showing up on the airwaves. There were promotions, too. In Chicago, for example, commuters were handed plastic cards alerting them to Capital One's online services and offering a chance to win a free computer.

Since its IPO, Capital One had more than quadrupled its earnings, according to *Forbes,* growing to $470 million in 2000 on credit card receivables of $30 billion. The industry itself had expanded rapidly. U.S. credit card debt hit $3 trillion, nearly twice the amount of four years earlier. Capital One held just 4 percent of total card loans. To keep up its growth rate Capital One needed to keep bringing in new accounts.

Key Dates:

1994: Signet Banking Corporation announces its IPO and creation of a new credit card unit, Oakstone Financial Corporation.

1995: The spinoff is renamed Capital One Financial Corporation.

1996: The company starts doing business in Canada and the United Kingdom.

1998: The company acquires a U.S. auto lending operation.

1999: The company enters the Internet market later than its competitors but ramps up quickly.

2000: Capital One is added to the *Fortune* 500 list.

2001: The company buys online auto finance and elective medical and dental procedures finance businesses.

2002: The credit card industry is under the scrutiny of regulators.

"Getting new customers is crucial not just to goose the company's earnings but to keep the charge-off ratio at a low 4%. An important subtlety about this ratio, not well understood by most investors, is that it mixes chronological apples and oranges," explained Condon in *Forbes*. Bad loans, when compared with current loans outstanding, rather than loans outstanding when the borrower stopped paying, resulted in a different slant on the company's current financial situation.

A key to Capital One's success to this point, and to its credibility among investors, had been its ability to find customers in higher risk segments with the best credit outlook. Were there enough of those good credit risks out there to continue to drive credit card growth? Could Capital One succeed in other financial service niches?

Increased Risks: 2001 and Beyond

Capital One dropped out of the wireless phone service business in 2000 but expanded its financial service offerings in 2001. In May, Capital One acquired AmeriFee Corporation. The Massachusetts-based company made consumer loans for elective medical and dental procedures. Then in October, PeopleFirst Inc., the largest online provider of direct motor vehicle loans, was purchased.

Capital One's marketing blitz, which continued in 2001, included sponsorship of college football's Florida Citrus Bowl. In addition, a "No-Hassle" Platinum Card was launched. Brand recognition reached 92 percent by December.

Overall, Capital One's reputation on Wall Street and within the industry remained solid. During 2001, the company ranked high on a number of "best places to work" lists. The company was also proud of its commitment to community. Following the September 11 attacks on the United States, thousands of Capital One employees volunteered to set up phone systems and then receive calls for the largest telethon in history, helping raise money for disaster relief.

In the midst of all this, some competitors in the credit card industry had begun a downward spiral. Preceding the events of September 11, Capital One's own stock took a beating in reaction to lowered estimates by Providian Financial. Some analysts felt that Providian's troubles were indicative of problems ahead for the industry as a whole. Capital One, like Providian, had a large number of riskier, but higher margin, subprime loans in its portfolio.

The economy soured post-9/11, but Capital One held its own. In 2001, the sixth largest credit card issuer in the United States reached its seventh consecutive year of 20 percent-plus annual earnings growth despite the economic recession, rising unemployment, and fears of more terrorist attacks, observed *American Banker* in January 2002.

Capital One revealed, about mid-July 2002, that the Federal Reserve Board and the Office of Thrift Supervision had taken informal action regarding the company's infrastructure. Capital One agreed to add to its loan-loss reserves and change the way it reported revenue on uncollectible finance charges and fees. Regulators were cracking down on card issuers in an effort to tighten account management standards. In addition, to the dismay of investors, Capital One revealed that the subprime segment of its credit card accounts was larger than previously understood.

To regain the confidence of regulators and investors, Capital One planned to pull back on the subprime while building up the prime and superprime credit card lending segments. A greater emphasis was to be placed, as well, on personal installment and auto loans and the consumer loan business outside the United States. But more negative news came in October 2002, when Capital One announced that it anticipated a drop-off in growth and a jump in the chargeoff rate. Wall Street was not impressed.

Principal Subsidiaries

Capital One Bank; Capital One, F.S.B.; Capital One Bank (Europe) plc (U.K.).

Principal Competitors

MBNA Corporation; Citigroup Inc.; First USA, Inc.; Providian Financial Corporation; Household International, Inc.; Metris Companies Inc.

Further Reading

Bloom, Jennifer Kingson, "Capital One Says It's Riding a Tech Revolution," *American Banker,* September 9, 1998, p. 6A.

Buss, Dale, "Brand Builders: Raising Capital," *Brandweek,* November 19, 2001, pp. 16+.

Cline, Kenneth, "Card Issuer Capital One Sets Up Thrift to Widen Scope," *American Banker,* July 8, 1996, pp. 1+.

Condon, Bernard, "House of Cards," *Forbes,* April 2, 2001, p. 77.

Fickenscher, Lisa, "Capital One Begins to Move Beyond Teaser Rates," *American Banker,* April 9, 1996, p. 14.

"Isn't There More to Life Than Plastic?," *Business Week,* November 22, 1999, p. 173.

Kingson, Jennifer A., "4Q Earnings: Capital One Boasts Banner Year," *American Banker,* January 17, 2002, p. 16.

Kuykendall, Lavonne, and W.A. Lee, "3Q Earnings: Monoline Stocks Drilled," *American Banker,* October 17, 2002, p. 1.

Lee, W.A., "Are None Immune in Card Crackdown?," *American Banker,* July 18, 2002, p. 1.

Leuchter, Miriam, ''Capital One: Fanaticism That Works,'' *US Banker,* August 2001, p. 24.

Martin, Zack, ''Capital One Makes Big Push to Become National Brand,'' *Card Marketing,* December 2000, pp. 1+.

Mathews, Gordon, ''Fear of Delinquency Prompts Jitters About Capital One,'' *American Banker,* August 15, 1995, p. 24.

Millman, Gregory J., ''Plastic Meltdown,'' *Institutional Investor,* December 2001, pp. 105+.

Novack, Janet, ''The Data Edge,'' *Forbes,* September 11, 1995, pp. 148+.

Shook, David, ''A Slower-Growing But Safer Capital One,'' *Business Week Online,* October 4, 2002.

''The Technology Bank,'' *Chief Executive (U.S.),* June 1997, pp. 12+.

Winig, Eric, ''Providian News Sends Capital One Stock South,'' *Washington Business Journal,* September 7, 2001, p. 7.

—Kathleen Peippo

Casual Male Retail Group, Inc.

555 Turnpike Street
Canton, Massachusetts 02021
U.S.A.
Telephone: (781) 828-9300
Fax: (781) 828-6348
Web site: http://www.casualmale.com

Public Company
Incorporated: 1976 as Designs, Inc.
Employees: 1,500
Sales: $195.1 million (2002)
Stock Exchanges: NASDAQ
Ticker Symbol: CMRG
NAIC: 448100 Clothing Stores

Casual Male Retail Group, Inc. is the name assumed by Massachusetts-based apparel retailer Designs, Inc. in 2002. For many years devoted to the selling of Levi Strauss jeans and Dockers casual wear, the company has elected to shift its focus, due in large part to Levi's merchandise falling out of favor with younger consumers. After acquiring Casual Male, which sells clothing for big and tall men, Designs has adopted the Casual Male name to better reflect its new emphasis. Although continuing to operate Levi's and Dockers stores, the company has taken steps to greatly reduce its Levi's business, closing a number of the outlets and combining others. In addition Casual Male has obtained a license to own and operate Candie's outlets and has also entered into a joint venture agreement to open and operate EcKo outlets.

Predecessor Founded in 1976

Designs, Inc. was cofounded in 1976 by Calvin Margolis and Stanley Berger, with the older Margolis serving as chairman and CEO of the company. He originally entered the retail clothing business after a stint in the Army during World War II, and by 1950 he owned his own men's store, called Cal's, in the south end of Boston. In the 1960s he and Berger established a business to cater to young people called the Slak Shak, featuring bell-bottom jeans, tie-dyed pants, and other hippie-era clothing.

As those clothes fell out of fashion in the early 1970s, the partners were approached by Levi's sales reps and decided to focus on Levi's jeans, in 1972 launching a new Levi's-only chain called You & You. Ultimately the company had 34 units, essentially 2,000- to 3,000-square-foot jeans shops, spread across New England. In 1975 Margolis and Berger sold the business to The Gap, a move that allowed The Gap to jumpstart its expansion into the Northeast.

The partners formed a new company, Designs, Inc., in 1976 and after some deliberation concluded that they should continue their relationship with Levi's and take advantage of the vendor's strong brand. After reviewing the Levi's product line they developed a Levi's-only department store concept and obtained permission to incorporate "Exclusively Levi Strauss" in its logo. Although the new stores would be much larger than the You & You units and offer full lines of men's, women's, and children's clothing, Designs would maintain no warehouse or distribution center. Rather, Levi Strauss would ship directly to the stores. The first Designs store, 8,800 square feet in size, opened in Manchester, New Hampshire, in October 1977. Even as the Designs chain grew over the next decade, Manchester would remain the top-selling store for the next decade. In 1986 Designs opened its first outlet store, located in the Potomac Mills Outlet Center in the Washington, D.C. area. Initially this channel was created because Levi's had a surplus of Dockers, its casual line that debuted in 1986. These outlet units, offering Levi's overruns, irregulars, and discontinued lines, proved to be a good complement to Designs' traditional stores. Not only did they broaden the customer base to include tourists and value shoppers, they provided a place for the company to transfer the traditional stores' unsold merchandise at the end of each season.

During its first decade in operation, Designs grew at a modest pace, by 1987 totaling just 29 units, all of which were located east of the Mississippi. Changes in the marketplace, however, provided an opportunity for more rapid expansion. The Gap and other large apparel chains cut back on their Levi's lines, turning instead to private-label jeans manufactured offshore. With Levi Strauss actually growing in popularity at the time, Designs saw a chance to inherit Levi's customers abandoned by the competition. In June 1987 Designs went public at $13 a share to raise funds to fuel expansion, with the goal of growing to 100 units over the next three years. By the end of 1990, the chain reached that threshold, split between its "Designs exclusively Levi Strauss & Co." traditional stores and its "Specials exclusively Levi Strauss & Co." discount units. Although management expected profits to be muted somewhat by expansion, the rollout of new stores proved too fast and each unit required additional time to become profitable. The situation was exacerbated by major competitors such as Sears cutting their prices on Levi Strauss merchandise and forcing Designs to follow suit. As a result the company lost $1.7 million in fiscal 1989 and overall suffered through six consecutive losing quarters.

Considering Selling: 1990

As the U.S. economy slipped into recession, Designs was unable to raise additional expansion money and in November 1990 hired an investment banker to search for a possible buyer. Less than a year, later, however, the company showed enough improvement that it decided to cease all efforts to sell the business. A change in focus from the traditional stores to the outlet operations helped in the turnaround, but of more importance was Levi's expanding its women's product lines and adding the popular Dockers line into the mix. Designs was now better able to compete with its department store competitors. Moreover, The Gap elected to stop selling Levi's merchandise altogether, providing an opening for many Designs' stores to attract loyal Levi's customers. As a joint venture with Levi's, Designs also added two new store concepts: a "Dockers Shop," devoted to casual clothing, and "The Original Levi's Store," which was designed to compete directly with The Gap in major urban areas: Manhattan, Boston, and Washington, D.C.

In January 1993 Margolis retired as Designs' chairman and CEO, replaced by Berger. Margolis died a year later at the age of 69 from complications of heart disease. In December 1994, Joel Reichman was promoted to the CEO position, while Berger stayed on as chair. Reichman had worked closely with Berger since their days together at Slak Shak. Designs was forced to make some adjustments in 1994 when Levi's informed management that it no longer intended to open additional outlet stores through Designs but, rather, would rely on a subsidiary to expand that channel. With a limited supply of overruns and irregulars to stock the outlets, this development did not bode well for Designs. In addition, there were indications that Levi's might open its own domestic retail stores. Designs now sought to diversify its business through the addition of private-label products. In the autumn of 1994 it launched a test program in seven of its stores, adding for the first time non-Levi's apparel. As a result, these units had to remove the "Exclusively Levi's" phrase from their exteriors. The new private-label merchandise was marketed under the name "EFD—Exclusively for De-

signs." To supplement private labels, the company also began offering Timberland brand apparel in 1995, then took a far bolder step by paying $6 million to acquire assets from Boston Trading Co., Ltd., including the Boston Traders brand and 33 Boston Traders outlet stores. Boston Trading, known for its rugbys, knits, and sweaters, bolstered Designs' offerings in men's and women's tops, which management hoped would improve its multiple sales transactions. The mix of the reconfigured Designs' stores would be 70 percent Levi's and 30 percent EFD, Timberland, and Boston Traders.

The move into private labels, however, did not pan out, and by mid-1997 Designs abandoned the effort and elected to return its focus to branded products. It tried offering a number of brands in its Boston Trading Co. and Designs stores. In addition to Levi's and other major brands like Polo Jeans, Tommy Jeans by Tommy Hilfiger, DKNY, and CK Calvin Klein, the stores began to offer emerging brands such as FUBU and Phat Farm that appealed to a younger, hip-hop audience. As part of this restructuring effort, Designs liquidated the Boston Traders brand and closed down 16 Boston Traders outlets and 17 Designs stores. But the shift to multiple brands proved equally disappointing and in 1998 Designs changed gears yet again, deciding to once more focus on Levi's and Dockers product lines, primarily through its outlet stores. In furthering this effort to become more of an outlet-based business, Designs bought 25 outlets from Levi Strauss for $12 million. It also discontinued its joint venture with Levi's, acquiring Levi's interest in 11 outlets in exchange for Designs' interests in Original Levi and Docker stores. Unfortunately for both parties, Levi's was losing touch with its younger consumers, particularly those influenced by hip-hop culture who actively disliked the Levi's brand. In an attempt to appeal to this market Designs converted four old Boston Trader Outlet locations into Buffalo Jeans Factory Stores on a test basis, but this effort also failed to be the cure for the progressively ailing enterprise, which now shed stores at a steady clip. In late 1999 Boston Traders, Boston Traders Outlet stores, and the Buffalo Jeans Outlet stores were all terminated.

At the start of 1996 Designs had 157 stores in operation, but at the end of five years it was down to just 103. Revenues also peaked in fiscal 1996 at more than $300 million, then dipped to $290 million in 1997, $266 million in 1998, and $201.6 million in 1999. With the price of Designs' stock depressed, Seymour Holtzman, president of buyout firm Jewelcor Management, acquired close to a 10 percent stake in the company in 1998. He then led a proxy fight to replace the entire board, with the exception of Berger. The matter grew contentious and raged for more than a year. At one point Holtzman offered $58 million for the company, then withdrew the bid. In the end, however, Holtzman prevailed. In late 1999 Reichman resigned as president and CEO, replaced by board member John Schultz on an interim basis. In April 2000 David A. Levin was hired to replace Schultz, and Holtzman was placed on the company's board. Only days later Holtzman would be named chairman, completing the management turnover.

Levin came to Designs with some 30 years of retail experience, including stints with Revlon's Prestige Fragrance & Cosmetics division, the Camp Coleman division of The Coleman Company, and the Parade of Shoes division of J. Baker, Inc. which became Casual Male. Ironically, Levin started his business career in Iowa in the early 1970s selling painters pants and Army surplus stock, launching a small chain of stores located in college towns in Iowa, Nebraska, and Michigan. Levin's immediate goal at Designs was to make it a pure-play outlet operation. He also looked to cut costs and improve distribution. For years Designs had relied on direct shipping to its stores, but once it opened a 60,000-square-foot distribution center in Orlando, Florida, it was able to cut down on the size of its stores by a fourth. Space dedicated to excess inventory was eliminated, which meant smaller stores and lower rents. To diversify beyond Levi's and tap into a younger demographic, Designs sought new retail partners in 2002. It entered into a licensing agreement to open and operate 75 Candies stores in outlet malls and value centers. Candie's designed, manufactured, and marketed young women's shoes, apparel, and accessories. Only weeks later Designs announced that it entered into a joint venture with hip-hop lifestyle brand EcKo Complex to operate 75 EcKo branded outlet stores.

Designs Has Designs on Casual Male: 2002

All of Designs' plans were soon superceded when Levin recognized an opportunity to buy Casual Male's big-and-tall men's store operation. Having worked for Casual Male when it was known as J. Baker Inc. he was fully aware of the company's strengths and weaknesses. J. Baker was originally a shoe retailer, with the Casual Male business just a sideline, but as shoes became a low-margin business, requiring scale in order to effectively compete, J. Baker began to flounder. Levin was among the executives who advocated that the company abandon the shoe business to focus on Casual Male. They recognized that while most big-and-tall chains catered to women, men were generally served by mom-and-pop retailers. In following this strategy, J. Baker changed its name to Casual Male but assumed too much debt in exiting the shoe business and was ultimately forced into bankruptcy. Levin knew that in fact the Casual Male business had essentially been subsidizing J. Baker's shoe business for years and that unfettered by the parent company's debt it was a very attractive business. In August 2002 he told *Daily News Record,* "It was a hidden jewel. So I approached Seymour and the board of Designs and told them we should buy it."

Designs entered the game late, however. Charlesbank Capital Partners already had a tentative agreement with Casual Male's board for a $137 million purchase. Because of the due diligence phase of Charlesbank's offer, Designs had little more than a month to arrange financing for an offer before its rival's bid was formally accepted. Receiving little help or encouragement from the Casual Male board, Designs managed to place a $145 million bid in time, which then triggered a 14-hour auction that did not conclude until the early morning hours. In the end, Designs won with a bid of $170 million and acquired Casual Male's 473 stores and the Casual Male catalog. Thus, in one stroke Designs increased its annual revenues from around $200 million to $700 million (pro forma).

Although Designs was pleased with Casual Male's merchandising, real estate, and marketing groups, it moved quickly to cut its top-heavy senior management staff. Levin originally planned to lop off $15 million in expenses but soon upped that amount to $25 million. Warehouses and inventory systems of Designs and Casual Male were consolidated, as was administration. Designs moved into the larger Casual Male headquarters located 12 miles away in Canton, Massachusetts. One area of Casual Male that Levin vowed not to change was the chain's emphasis on sportswear, most of which was provided by Casual Male's own private label. Casual Male would also continue to target less expensive shopping strip centers rather than malls. With the Levi Strauss brands continuing to experience erosion, Designs saw its Casual Male business as the future of the company and began to significantly downsize its Levi's and Dockers outlet stores. To acknowledge its major shift in focus, Designs decided in August 2002 to change its name to Casual Male Retail Group, Inc. Management's optimism for the future was reflected in an analysis of Casual Male offered by Levin to *Daily News Record* in August 2002: "The nice part of this business is that it's not sexy. It only turns two times a year, and size management is a huge issue. It's very predictable—the comps are oblivious to the gyrations of other retailers. There's not a lot of fashion leadership, and sales per square foot are not off the charts. But we're 75 percent private label, the margins are good, and we have a very loyal customer who is more concerned about finding his size than getting a bargain."

Principal Competitors

American Retail; J.C. Penney Company, Inc.; Brooks Brothers Inc.; Calvin Klein, Inc.; Eddie Bauer, Inc.; The Men's Warehouse, Inc.; The Gap, Inc.; Wal-Mart Stores, Inc.

Further Reading

Biddle, Frederic M., "With Levi's, Designs Inc. Closes a Gap," January 17, 1993.
Malone, Scott, "Levi Designs a Turnaround," *WWD,* August 3, 2000, p. 12.
Palmieri, Jean E., "Casual Male's New Owners Unveil Big Plans," *Daily News Record,* August 19, 2002, p. 1A.
Palmieri, Jean E., and Evan Clark, "Designs Snags Casual Male for $170 Million," *Daily News Record,* May 6, 2002, p. 1.
Peres, Daniel, "Reichman Has Designs Only on Levi Strauss," *Daily News Record,* June 20, 1994, p. 10.
Reidy, Chris, "Needham, Mass.-Based Apparel Retailer Makes Winning Bid on Clothing Chain," *Boston Globe,* May 3, 2002.
Witt, Louise, "Blue Jeans Meet Red Ink at Designs," *Boston Business Journal,* June 18, 1990, p. 1.

—Ed Dinger

CDW Computer Centers, Inc.

200 N. Milwaukee Avenue
Vernon Hills, Illinois 60061
U.S.A.
Telephone: (847) 465-6000
Toll Free: (800) 797-4239
Fax: (847) 465-6800
Web site: http://www.cdw.com

Public Company
Incorporated: 1984 as Computer Discount Warehouse
Employees: 2,800
Sales: $3.96 billion (2001)
Stock Exchanges: NASDAQ
Ticker Symbol: CDWC
NAIC: 421430 Computer and Computer Peripheral
Equipment and Software Wholesalers

CDW Computer Centers, Inc. is a leading seller of brand name microcomputer hardware and peripheral devices, including desktop and notebook computers, printers, video monitors, data storage devices, multimedia equipment, networking products, and software. CDW markets primarily through direct mail to end users, particularly business customers, in the United States.

Emergence of a New Industry: 1984

CDW was launched in 1984 by former used car salesman and Burger King franchise school dropout Michael Krasny. Krasny, a 1975 graduate of the University of Illinois, had taken a job after college selling used cars at his father's Toyota dealership in Chicago. He did not like the work, but would later attribute much of his success to the simple truths he learned on his father's car lot. Bits of wisdom he would recall included: "Good luck many times comes disguised as hard work," "Pigs get fat, hogs get slaughtered," "Success means never being satisfied," and "People do business with people they like." Among other skills, he learned to negotiate. "Being that I was from the automobile business, I was good at negotiating," he said in the February 12, 1996, *Forbes.* "When I bought the machine [computer], I bought it right."

Krasny disliked the car sales business, but did enjoy trying to computerize the dealership's sales and finance departments. In 1982 he left the dealership, entered and then dropped out of Burger King's franchise school, and then decided to become a freelance computer programmer. The field was relatively young at the time—computers were just beginning to become common in homes and offices—and Krasny had trouble making ends meet. Frustrated and in need of cash, he decided to sell his computer system in 1984. He ran an advertisement in the *Chicago Tribune* classified section that read; "IBM PC 512K Memory—computer, color monitor, software, 2 disc drive, $1,500/best offer. Still in warranty."

To Krasny's surprise, he easily sold the system to the first person that responded to the ad. Furthermore, the second person that called to buy the computer offered to pay Krasny to set up a system for him. Cash-starved Krasny agreed. He bought a computer system, helped the person set it up, and charged a few hundred dollars for his services. Meanwhile, as people continued to call about buying his computer, Krasny developed a sales pitch designed to convince those prospects to let him set up a computer system for them. When some of them agreed, the venture that would become CDW (Computer Discount Warehouse) was born.

Krasny spent the next few years building a business of buying, selling, setting up, and repairing computer systems. Because personal computers were still relatively new, many people were intimidated by the technology. Thus, many of his customers were simply looking for someone who could tell them what to buy, how to set it up and turn it on, and how to keep it running. As computers became more user-friendly and buyers became more comfortable with PC technology, his emphasis shifted to sales. By 1985 Krasny found that he was selling many computer systems to a single buyer, a Chicago entrepreneur who simply resold them by mail at markups of about $300 per machine.

Devising a Formula for Rapid Growth in the Late 1980s

Krasny recognized the potential of the Chicago entrepreneur's mail-order idea, and he knew that he was just as capable of selling his machines by mail. In November 1985 he published his first national advertisement in *PC World* magazine. He hired a salesman to answer the phone, and never looked back. Krasny hired more salespeople and began running more and bigger advertisements in a number of national PC and computer-related publications. Sales shot past $10 million and would head toward $60 million annually by 1989.

While Krasny quickly discovered the power of direct marketing in the computer business, he also learned how to maximize the potential of that vast distribution channel. From the start, he decided to keep prices low and make money by shipping a high volume of units. While his nearby Chicago competitor tagged a $300 markup onto his gear, for example, Krasny charged only $25. He also maintained an intense focus on customer service, which became a hallmark of the CDW organization. The result was that CDW, unlike many of its competitors, managed to develop a loyal base of repeat customers—a valuable asset in the direct marketing business.

Thus, customer service and low prices became the foundation of CDW. "We have the right products at the right price due to our knowledge of what customers want and our close link with our vendors—distributors and manufacturers of computer products," Krasny said in the October 23, 1995, *HFN*. But CDW also prospered as a result of its savvy operational strategy. "Efficiency is the second vital ingredient for our competitive success," said Krasny. "Low overhead, high inventory turnover, and fast delivery to customers are the components of our cost-effective operating model. Third, we are dedicated to continuously improving everything we do."

The combination of a slick operating plan and a savvy marketing strategy helped make CDW one of the top two computer direct marketers by the early 1990s (the leader of the industry was Micro Warehouse). CDW's sales rose to $83 million before surpassing $100 million in 1991, and net income rose to $3.7 million in 1991. CDW's gains in 1991 displayed the value of the company's formula for success. The personal computer business suffered an ugly downturn in that year that squelched sales by most retailers. In contrast, the direct marketing channel continued to grow. As overall personal computer shipments plummeted 14 percent in 1991, traditional retailers watched from the sidelines as direct marketers increased PC sales by a whopping 76 percent. "These guys [direct marketers] are really putting the squeeze on the personal computer dealers," said Owen Linderholm, senior editor of *PC World,* in the April 19, 1993, *Crain's Chicago Business.* "All they [dealers] have left to offer is more service."

New Strategies for the Information Age: The 1990s

More service was exactly what the personal computer market needed less of as the 1990s progressed. Indeed, as computer makers scrambled to develop PCs and peripherals that were more user-friendly and the cost of computer systems dropped, direct marketers like CDW prospered. But CDW remained a step ahead of most of its competitors by continually employing new, shrewd tactics. For example, Krasny realized that many buyers were wary of purchasing expensive computer systems through the mail. To ease their fears, he established a storefront showroom that gave CDW more credibility. It also helped to boost sales, as about 10 percent of CDW's revenue was garnered from its two Chicago stores by the early 1990s.

Krasny also boosted profits by adopting cutting-edge automation technology. For example, Krasny learned from a lawyer friend about the owner of a local company, United Stationers, that had an obsession with automation. Krasny followed that company's lead, automating its billing system and eventually other parts of the company. CDW had been processing 200 orders daily with 12 people in its billing department in the 1980s. By the early 1990s, after implementing new information systems, the same department was churning out 5,000 orders each day with only four workers.

Nevertheless, Krasny continued to value his workers more than his technology, a trait he learned at his father's Toyota dealership. "My father asked people to work very hard, but gave them 150 percent of what they could earn somewhere else," Krasny said in the *Forbes* article. He paid CDW's employees with stock options and vacations, among other perks, and many of the company's salespeople earned well over $100,000 annually.

CDW continued to pursue its proven strategy in 1992 and 1993; it advertised its goods in PC trade publications and sold directly to customers via toll-free phone numbers. CDW targeted medium-size and larger companies, which often purchased large volumes of goods and became important repeat customers (business buyers accounted for roughly 80 percent of sales by the mid-1990s). The company also avoided manufacturing its own systems, a route that many of its competitors chose. Instead, CDW marketed a wide line of brand name computers and peripherals, focusing resources on its key strength of distribution. That simple strategy generated sales of $176 million in 1992 and $271 million in 1992, about $6.3 million and $13.55 million, respectively, of which was netted as income.

As CDW's bank account grew, so did Krasny's. Krasny took the company public in 1993 after changing the name from Computer Discount Warehouse to CDW Computer Centers. The initial public offering of stock brought expansion capital into CDW's war chest and provided Krasny just compensation for his efforts. (His profits from stock sales combined with his 43 percent ownership share gave the 40-plus-year-old entrepreneur a net worth of some $350 million by the mid-1990s.) Investor excitement about CDW's prospects pushed the company's stock price from its offering price of $6.25 to more than $25 within a year. After two years, moreover, the stock was selling at a high of above $60 per share.

CDW benefited in the mid-1990s from numerous industry trends, including a proliferation of multimedia and other peripheral devices, booming computer replacement markets, and an uptick in capital spending by its core business clientele. Important to CDW's success were several big accounts that helped to dump millions of dollars worth of product into its distribution pipeline. CDW had much earlier landed a deal to sell computers for Compaq, the leading computer producer in the United States going into the mid-1990s. Then, in April 1994, computer mammoth IBM granted CDW permission to begin selling its units. Shortly thereafter, CDW also won permission to start selling a new Apple notebook computer.

CDW's success at landing major new vendors reflected the intensifying trend toward direct marketing, particularly to businesses, which was becoming a much more accepted means of saving money on computer purchases. In addition, CDW benefited from an aggressive PC price war that broke out in 1994. Compaq initiated the contest when it slashed prices 11 percent to 22 percent on different models. IBM followed suit with a pugnacious 27 percent price cut. CDW's stock price rose immediately after each of the reductions as investors correctly anticipated big sales. CDW posted an impressive 52 percent gain in revenue in 1994 (to $413 million), and enjoyed record operating profits of $23 million.

Sustained Growth in the Late 1990s

To the surprise of many analysts, CDW maintained rampant growth throughout 1995. With major electronics producers like Hewlett-Packard, Digital Equipment, Sony, Toshiba, and others clambering to get their goods into its distribution system, CDW tallied steady sales and profit gains. By 1995 CDW was marketing 20,000 items through its catalogs, had a 250-member sales force, and boasted a database of nearly one million customers and prospects. About 80 percent of its sales were to repeat customers, which confirmed the wisdom of the company's longtime focus on customer service. Sales for the year hit $629 million, about $20 million of which was netted as income.

CDW broadened its marketing effort in 1995 with the establishment of an "outbound" telemarketing department to contact and sell to prospects. That effort, combined with the 30-plus million catalogs it shipped out every year, was expected to boost 1996 sales. In addition, CDW was planning to diversify its product line to include numerous electronics products of interest to its core business customer base, including personal data assistants, digital cameras, and devices related to video transmission. CDW also planned to launch an Internet marketing program in 1996.

Heightened Competition: Moving Ahead into the 21st Century

Changes in the computer industry in the late 1990s, however, including declining response numbers for catalog mailings, compelled CDW to consider more radical approaches to product marketing. As more and more computer manufacturers, notably Dell and Gateway, began to sell their products to consumers directly, CDW found its position as a major reseller in jeopardy. The company was also dealt a minor blow in November 1997, when Compaq Computers announced its intention to begin marketing its products directly to consumers. Although CDW continued to sell Compaq products, this overall industry shift towards direct sales made it essential that CDW bolster its own brand identity. In addition to redesigning its logo and its web site, CDW launched a television and print ad campaign targeted at small and mid-size businesses in October 1998.

In the mid-1990s, the company also redoubled its emphasis on direct sales, while shifting away from catalogue and Internet marketing. In contrast to major competitors including Dell, which was placing a greater emphasis on web-based sales in the new century, CDW continued to stress continued personal and phone contact with its customers. To this end the company began to build up its sales force, creating management positions for more than 480 sales personnel between 1996 and 1999. In November 1999 CDW installed a 500-member sales team in a new office in downtown Chicago. By the year 2000 the company had plans in place to create an additional 500 positions, with the aim of having a total sales force of 1,100 by the end of 2000. As CDW President Gregory C. Zeman told *Forbes* in November 2000, "It's an old-fashioned, feet-on-the-street model." In addition to establishing new offices in Chicago, the company implemented new incentive programs for its employees and built a 33,512-square-foot fitness and daycare center, nicknamed CDW@Play, at its Vernon Hills headquarters.

Although training such a large workforce put a temporary strain on the company's profits, CDW's revenues did not miss a beat, with sales increasing 43 percent in the third quarter of 1998. Overall, CDW's net profits grew an average of over 40 percent per year between 1995 and 2000. Because of its continued commitment to strong customer service, the company was able to avoid the fate suffered by several of its competitors, and by 1999 it was recording annual sales figures of more than $1.9 billion. Equally significant, the company was able to retain more than 80 percent of its extensive customer base. With 80 to 90 percent of CDW's total revenues coming from repeat customers, the customer service strategy appeared to be sound. For the year 2000, Internet sales only accounted for 12 percent of the company's total earnings.

Even with the economic downturn of the early 21st century, which witnessed a significant decrease in sales of new technology products, CDW continued to maintain its leading position in the computer reselling industry. A major reason for this consistency lay in the company's commitment to customer service. As overall Internet sales declined, and the company's competitors fought for market share, CDW saw its customer base increase by 15 percent in 2001. Although sales figures did dip slightly during this period, CDW's continued emphasis on direct sales, bolstered by a sales team that exceeded 1,200 by

2002, put the company in position to emerge from the economic slump with its profit margins intact.

Principal Subsidiaries

CDW Government, Inc.

Principal Competitors

Dell Computer Corporation; Insight Enterprises, Inc.; Micro Warehouse, Inc.

Further Reading

Croghan, Lore, "Micro Warehouse CDW Computer Centers: The Endless Wave?," *Financial World,* June 20, 1995, p. 18.

Gray, Tom, "CDW Computer Pushes Brand onto National Scene for PCs," *Investor's Business Daily,* December 3, 1998, p. A18.

King, Elliot, "PCs for Sale by Mail," *Target Marketing,* June 1992, p. 17.

Murphy, H. Lee, "Auspicious Beginnings for CDW, Shareholders," *Crain's Chicago Business,* May 2, 1994, p. 10.

Ryan, Ken, "CDW Enjoys Computing Success," *HFN: The Weekly Newspaper,* October 23, 1995, p. 102.

Samuels, Gary, "The Fine Art of Haggling: CDW Computer Centers' Founder Michael Krasny," *Forbes,* February 12, 1996, p. 70.

Tatge, Mark, "Baby Dell," *Forbes,* November 27, 2000.

Veverka, Mark, "Direct Selling Computes for PC Retailer CDW," *Crain's Chicago Business,* April 19, 1993, p. 11.

——, "A Victor in Price Wars: IBM, Compaq Cuts Boost CDW's Sales Picture," *Crain's Chicago Business,* August 29, 1994, p. 70.

Wangensteen, Betsy, "Go-go Tech Issues Swing Like a Yo-yo," *Crain's Chicago Business,* January 1, 1996, p. 4.

Watkins, Steve, "CDW Pushes Direct Stakes Higher By Mixing Tech Clicks with Mortar," *Investor's Business Daily,* June 9, 2000, p. A1.

—Dave Mote
—update: Erin Brown

Century Aluminum Company

2511 Garden Road, Building A, Suite 200
Monterey, California 93940
U.S.A.
Telephone: (831) 642-9300
Toll Free: (888) 642-9300
Fax: (831) 642-9399
Web site: http://www.centuryaluminum.com

Public Company
Incorporated: 1995
Employees: 1,540
Sales: $654.9 million (2001)
Stock Exchanges: NASDAQ
Ticker Symbol: CENX
NAIC: 331312 Primary Aluminum Production

Century Aluminum Company is a holding company based in Monterey, California, but its primary operation is a facility located in Ravenswood, West Virginia. Since the formation of Century in 1995, Ravenswood has moved away from the beverage can aluminum sheet business, as well as the value-added aluminum plate business, to concentrate on the production of primary aluminum. Able to produce 475,000 metric tons of primary aluminum a year, Century is the second largest primary aluminum manufacturer in the United States. In addition to the Ravenswood facility, Century owns an 80 percent stake in a Hawesville, Kentucky, reduction plant and a 49.67 percent share in a Mt. Holly, South Carolina, reduction plant.

Ravenswood, A Postwar Startup

The Ravenswood plant was the main asset of Century when the holding company was formed in 1995 to assume certain aluminum assets of Glencore International AG, a move which helped to distance Ravenswood from the stigma of one of the nation's most notorious whitecollar criminals, Marc Rich. Rich was long believed by many to have exerted control over the business and to have been responsible for a prolonged labor fight that crippled Ravenswood business. The origin of the

Ravenswood plant also was connected to an admired legendary industrialist, Henry Kaiser. He first gained prominence in the 1930s when his construction firm participated in the building of the Hoover Dam and the Grand Coulee Dam. During World War II Kaiser became involved in shipbuilding and later, frustrated with the dominance of U.S. Steel, opened his own steel mill in California. After the war Kaiser turned his attention to the aluminum industry, aided to a large degree by the U.S. government. The Aluminum Company of America, Alcoa, was required to supply the Kaiser Aluminum Company with raw materials as part of an antitrust action. At first Kaiser leased government-owned plants on the West Coast, and then in order to compete against Alcoa in the East he built a plant in Ravenswood, which opened in 1957. The town was advantageously located near major rivers, permitting inexpensive shipping of refined bauxite, Alumina. Nearby coal fields also fueled the power-hungry plant. Moreover, most of the U.S. market for aluminum was located within 500 miles of Ravenswood. The plant itself was an integrated operation, capable of smelting alumina into molten aluminum and turning that product into sheets for soda and beer cans. Ravenswood was a world-class facility when it opened and over the years was well maintained, unlike other aluminum operations that became neglected as the economics of the industry deteriorated.

For many years after World War II aluminum was extremely popular, leading to strong growth in the industry. Demand grew around 10 percent a year, fueled in large part by the aluminum can industry. By 1981, however, there was little room for further growth in cans, the demand of which had increased at an annual 12 percent clip throughout the 1960s and 1970s. With 80 percent of the can market already converted to aluminum, the demand for the metal now fell to just a 3 percent increase per year. Ravenswood, which had been organized by the United Steelworkers of America in 1958, enjoyed good labor relations during prosperous times. But as was the case in many industries, changing economics had an adverse impact. In their book, *Ravenswood,* authors Tom Juravich and Kate Bronfenbrenner comment, ''In the face of a growing economic crisis made largely by its own hand, business turned on workers and unions. While workers had been junior partners in postwar success, they were now asked to become senior partners in failure.'' Shortly after reaching a contract with workers at Ravenswood in 1982, Kaiser asked for concessions, to which the union finally agreed in 1984. According to Juravich and Bronfenbrenner, ''Labor relations had been soured in some fundamental way and Ravenswood would never be quite the same.''

1988 Sale of Kaiser Aluminum Leading to Divestiture of Ravenswood

The empire of Henry Kaiser, who died in 1967, became susceptible to hostile takeovers in the 1980s. First, the steel division was acquired by Joseph Frates III and a group of investors, who quickly flipped the business, earning some $14 million in fees and expenses. Frates then turned his sights on Kaiser Aluminum, which managed to fend him off, but in 1988 the business was targeted by two much larger players, corporate raider Charles Hurwitz and financier Marc Rich, who was already a major influence in the international metals market. When Rich dropped out of the bidding at the 11th hour, Hurwitz and his holding company, Maxxam, Inc., acquired Kaiser Aluminum in a $925 million leveraged buyout. To raise money to pay off the resulting note, Hurwitz sold off a number of assets, including the questionable sale of Ravenswood. Because it produced half of Kaiser's aluminum and had been well maintained, divesting Ravenswood made little business sense. In effect Kaiser Aluminum was being dismantled to raise cash with no regard for the health of the enterprise. In February 1989 Ravenswood was sold to Stanwich Partners, Inc. and began operating under a new corporate entity, Ravenswood Aluminum Company (RAC). A major stake of the business was then sold to Willy Strothotte through Rinoman Investments and another company named Ridgeway, both of which were affiliates of the Clarendon corporation. According to Juravich and Bronfenbrenner, ''Everyone in the industry understood that Marc Rich controlled Clarendon.''

Marc Rich was born Mark Reich but as a child left his native Germany to escape the tide of anti-Semitism. After relocating to Belgium the family eventually made its way to Queens, New York, where the last name was changed to Rich. The son of a trader, Rich dropped out of New York University in 1952 and at the age of 20 went to work for Phillip Brothers, one of the world's top commodity trading companies, where he quickly displayed a genius for trading—and, according to several sources, little concern for scruples. After dealing in metals and other commodities for 20 years, he essentially invented the spot market for oil in the early 1970s. Phillips was uncomfortable dealing in oil, which led to a falling out. Rich and his partner Pinky Green lured away six of Phillips's top traders and established Marc Rich & Co, A.G., in Zug, Switzerland, to take advantage of a local tax loophole. During the 1979 hostage crisis Rich and Green ignored a U.S. embargo on trade with Iran and began buying Iranian oil, paying for it in large part with weapons. According to Juravich and Bronfenbrenner, ''Rich

and Green then got involved in the U.S. domestic oil market. They began selling discounted foreign oil to the major U.S. producers, peddling it as their own.'' When their Texas partners were indicted and convicted for illegal ''daisy-chaining,'' they implicated Rich. In 1983 the U.S. Attorney's office in Manhattan, headed by future mayor Rudolph Guiliani, investigated Rich, who refused to turn over crucial documents from his U.S. operation, Marc Rich, International. Unexpectedly, he announced that the business had been sold to a new company, Clarendon Limited, headed by the indicted Willy Strothotte, a move that a federal judge would later describe as a ''ploy to frustrate the implementation of the court's order.'' Ultimately arrest warrants were issued for Rich and Green, who were charged with 65 counts of racketeering, mail and wire fraud, tax evasion, and trading with the enemy. Rich by now, however, was out of reach of U.S. authorities, operating from Switzerland, where he was confident that he would not face extradition.

In spite of his legal difficulties during the early 1980s, Rich remained very much an active businessman. It was during this time that he decided to become the dominant force in the world aluminum market, from raw materials to finished metal. As he had done with other commodities, Rich owned few assets outright. Rather, according to a 1992 *Institutional Investor* profile, he was at the center of ''a complex network of joint ventures with local partners. Such a strategy allows Rich to exert considerable control over selected commodities at a minimum outlay of capital. It also affords him anonymity.'' In the words of Juravich and Bronfenbrenner, ''It was an arrangement that made proving the connections between a company such as Ravenswood Aluminum and Marc Rich extremely difficult.''

The Rich connection to Ravenswood would become a key factor in the bitter labor negotiations that took place between RAC and the United Steelworkers of America after the two sides were unable to come to terms on a new contract in the fall of 1990. When the old agreement expired at midnight on October 31, 1990, steelworkers were ordered out of the plant, despite their willingness to continue working under the old terms until a settlement was reached. Instead, replacements were brought in and the plant was barricaded with tractor trailers, railcars, and a tall barbed-wire fence. During the many months of the ensuing lockout, the local community became a war zone of sorts, disturbed by numerous acts of violence.

Slipped a copy of an internal audit of RAC by Price Waterhouse, the union learned of the Clarendon connection, and by extension Marc Rich's involvement. Because of Rich's fugitive status and unsavory reputation, the union decided to pressure RAC by portraying him as their true adversary. With help from sympathetic European unions, the Steelworkers picketed Rich in Switzerland and elsewhere. The union also used political influence at home to initiate a congressional investigation of RAC's ownership. It also crippled RAC's business by shaming its customers, such as Anheuser-Busch, Miller Brewing, and Stroh Brewery, who agreed not to buy aluminum sheet for cans from RAC. As a result, after 18 months the company was on what management described in court papers as the ''brink of financial ruin.'' Rich also had other business ventures disrupted by the Steelworkers' public relations campaign. About to sell the Slovakian National Aluminum Company to Rich, the Czechoslovakian government was persuaded to cancel the deal.

Moreover, having a spotlight focused on his affairs prevented Rich from lying low as he attempted to smooth over his legal difficulties and regain the right to return to the United States, where he still had family, while avoiding jail time.

Rich denied having an ownership role in RAC, but his influence over the company was apparent. RAC's contentious CEO and chairman, Emmett Boyle, was forced out by Rich-controlled entities and a new labor contract was subsequently negotiated. According to Boyle in his public proclamations the labor issue was settled because it interfered with Rich's other business ventures and his attempt to return to the United States. (Rich, in fact, would eventually be free of his legal troubles, when he received a controversial presidential pardon in the final hours of the Clinton administration in 2001.) Replacing Boyle was Craig Davis, who had 16 years of experience as an executive with Alumax, a major aluminum producer, as well as a number of years working for the Rich organization in Switzerland. In 1994 Marc Rich and Co. acquired all of RAC. According to Juravich and Bronfenbrenner, Rich "changed his company's name to Glencore International. . . . [M]ost believed the change was part of an effort to insulate the trading company from the negative press generated by Rich's fugitive status and fomented by the Steelworkers' campaign."

After Rich sold his Glencore stock and resigned from the board of directors, RAC management proclaimed the connection to the notorious Rich should finally be put to rest. Juravich and Bronfenbrenner, however, disputed that contention: "Within a year Glencore sold the Ravenswood plant to the Century Aluminum Company, which then went public, apparently releasing the plant from the long reach of Rich and Strothotte. But like its predecessor, Clarendon, Ltd., Glencore continues to own 39.6 percent of Century Aluminum's common stock. It operates under a 'services' agreement whereby Century purchases primary aluminum and alumina from Glencore and Glencore buys back more than one hundred million pounds of Century primary aluminum products each year."

Century Aluminum Going Public in 1996

In addition to the Ravenswood plant, Glencore also included other assets in Century: a 26.7 percent stake in an aluminum reduction plant in Mt. Holly, South Carolina, and an alumina refinery in St. Croix, which was quickly sold off. Glencore postponed Century's initial public offering (IPO) for a number of months, waiting for market conditions to improve. Not only were aluminum prices experiencing volatility, Ravenswood had posted more than $100 million in losses from 1992 to 1994. The company waited until the price of aluminum was trading around 75 cents a pound, a range at which the business could expect to break even. Nonetheless, the 1996 IPO was a disappointment. The company had hoped to place 20 million shares at a price between $15 and $18, with a target of grossing $330 million. In the end, Century was able to sell only 10.5 million shares at $13, a gross of $136.5 million.

Davis stayed on as the CEO and chair of Century, and as a California native he was responsible for the eventual move of corporate headquarters to Monterey. When he first took over, RAC attempted to compete with Alcoa and Alcan in the commodity business, producing aluminum sheets for cans and use in airplanes and automobiles, but was losing money, due in large part to the deterioration of its aluminum can business during Ravenswood's protracted labor problems. Determining that the company was simply too small to compete in the commodity aluminum business, Davis initiated a major shift in strategy even before Century went public. Taking advantage of Ravenswood's under-utilized capabilities, he planned to move Century into value-added products, in particular heat-treated plate. The aerospace industry appeared to be a promising market for future growth. In 1995 Ravenswood became the first North American aluminum plate producer to be certified by Boeing Commercial Airplane Group for plate up to 8.5 inches thick. Previously Boeing had to rely on forged aluminum parts that were greater than six inches. In addition to the aerospace industry, other applications included the manufacture of machine tools and moulds for making plastic parts. Century spent $130 million in upgrading Ravenswood. The company then bolstered its business externally in 1998 by acquiring Alcoa's Vernon, California, cast plate operations.

Despite making inroads in the value-added aluminum market, Century was not doing well enough to justify the investment of another $200 million, which is the amount that Davis believed would be necessary to keep Century competitive. Instead he elected to change strategies once more and return to the commodity side, this time intentionally downsizing to concentrate on the production of primary aluminum, the molten metal itself, as well as premium cast products such as high-purity foundry ingot and billet. As a result, in September 1999 Century sold the rolled products side of the Ravenswood facility and the complementary cast plate business to Pechiney SA, a major French aluminum producer, for $248 million.

Having shed its fabricating businesses, Century began looking to add to its primary aluminum capacity. In April 2000 it increased its stake in the Mt. Holly plant, adding a 23 percent interest. A year later Century acquired an 80 percent interest in a Hawesville, Kentucky, plant capable of smelting 238,000 tons a year. As a result of these transactions, Century became the second largest primary aluminum producer in the country. After guiding Century through a number of changes during his time in charge, Davis, citing personal reasons, announced in February 2002 that he would step down as CEO at the end of the year, although he would remain as chairman of the board through 2004. Replacing him as chief executive was longtime lieutenant Gerald Meyers, the company's president and chief operating officer.

Principal Subsidiaries

Century Aluminum of West Virginia, Inc.; Berkeley Aluminum, Inc.; Virgin Islands Alumina Corporation, L.L.C.; Century Kentucky, Inc.; NSA, Ltd.; Century Aluminum of Kentucky, L.L.C.

Principal Competitors

Alcan Aluminum Limited; Aluminum Company of America; Kaiser Aluminum & Chemical Corporation.

Further Reading

Juravich, Tom, and Kate Bronfenbrenner, *Ravenswood,* Ithaca, N.Y.: ILR Press, 1999.

Koenig, Peter, "Smoking Out Marc Rich," *Institutional Investor,* August 1, 1992, p. 40.

McKay, Jim, "Ravenswood Says Labor Dispute Brought It Near Ruin," *Pittsburgh Post-Gazette,* May 2, 1992, p. 27.

Pinkham, Myra, "Century Invests for Move to Plate," *Aluminum Today,* January/February 1998, p. 36.

Regan, Rob, "Ravenswood Stock Offer May Shed Light on Old Debate," *American Metal Market,* August 10, 1995, p. 1.

Schroeder, Michael, Maria Mallory, and John Templeton, "Making Marc Rich Squirm," *Business Week,* November 11, 1991, p. 120.

Tebbs, Tom, "Monterey, Calif.-Based Aluminum Company Has Global Interests," *Monterey County Herald,* June 7, 2000.

—Ed Dinger

Century Business Services, Inc.

6480 Rockside Boulevard South, Suite 330
Cleveland, Ohio 44121
U.S.A.
Telephone: (216) 447-9000
Fax: (216) 447-9137
Web site: http://www.cbiz.com

Public Company
Incorporated: 1987 as Stout Associates
Employees: 4,900
Sales: $523.6 million (2001)
Stock Exchanges: NASDAQ
Ticker Symbol: CBIZ
NAIC: 541210 Accounting, Tax Preparation,
   Bookkeeping, and Payroll Services

Century Business Services, Inc., with its headquarters located in Cleveland, Ohio, offers a range of outsource business services to small and medium-sized businesses, including accounting and tax preparation, employee benefits, payroll, property and casualty insurance, and consulting. As it rolled up more than 200 local firms in the late 1990s to create a network of service providers, Century allowed its acquisitions to continue to operate under their original names, but the company has since made efforts to use CBIZ as a recognizable brand name. Century has operations spread across 33 states, the District of Columbia, and Toronto, Ontario, Canada.

Canadian Origins: 1940s–80s

Century and its founder, Canadian entrepreneur Michael DeGroote, took a circuitous route to the business of outsourcing backroom operations. DeGroote was born in Belgium in 1933, then immigrated to Canada with his parents in 1948 when they sold their farm and settled in southern Ontario. To help support the family he soon had to drop out of high school and work in the local tobacco fields. When he was 18 he managed to scrape together enough money to buy a surplus army truck and earn a living by delivering manure from dairy farms to the tobacco fields. He further displayed his entrepreneurial spirit a year later when he acquired four gravel trucks and launched a full-fledged trucking business. In 1958 a uranium boom struck northern Ontario when the U.S. government placed a large order for the metal, and DeGroote was able to take advantage of the need for trucks to become a millionaire in his early 20s. A few years later, however, the U.S. government canceled its order and in 1958 DeGroote at the age of 25 was forced to file for bankruptcy. Undaunted, he moved to the city of Hamilton, where he was able to borrow $75,000 from a bank to make a down payment on a small trucking company owned by a man named Laidlaw. DeGroote would transform Laidlaw Transport Ltd. into a major Canadian corporation, transcending any ambitions its founder might have ever held for the business.

DeGroote inherited 21 trucks from Laidlaw and a business that generated $400,000 in annual revenues. A little more than ten years later, Laidlaw owned and operated 200 trucks and boasted $5 million in revenues. As DeGroote grew the business he followed similar goals and employed many of the same techniques he would later put to use in developing Century. He established a target of 25 to 30 percent growth each year, and rather than achieve that number internally he chose to acquire existing operations. He targeted poorly run trucking companies or ones that were inadequately funded and bought them at reasonable prices. In the process, he displayed an uncanny knack for rooting out the best candidates. Following the recession of the early 1980s he also revealed a willingness to adapt to changing conditions and pursue other opportunities. Realizing that trucking was a cyclical business, he moved Laidlaw into areas that he considered recession-proof: schoolbusing and waste disposal. No matter how poor the economy, he reasoned, people would still need to have their children transported to school and garbage hauled to the dump. Again he made the transition through acquisitions, so that in 1985 Laidlaw's school bus operation accounted for nearly half of all revenues, waste disposal another 40 percent, and trucking fell to just 8 percent. In 1985 the company topped $550 million in annual revenues and booked a net profit of $58.7 million. Moreover, Laidlaw was the largest school bus operator in North America and the fourth largest garbage collection company.

Company Perspectives:

Our Mission: To provide an integrated offering of CBIZ's core professional services in each regional market, incorporating the services of CBIZ's national practice areas and utilizing technology to enhance our product offering and streamline service delivery.

DeGroote's Brief Retirement: 1990

In 1988 DeGroote sold his stake in Laidlaw to Canadian Pacific for $499 million in cash and Canadian Pacific stock. Although agreeing to stay on as CEO and chairman of the board, he decided to retire to Bermuda in 1990. He quickly grew bored, however, and soon reentered the waste disposal business. DeGroote was approached by Texas businessman Tom Fatjo, Jr., who was looking for investors for a new company, Republic Waste Industries, and agreed to become involved. Fatjo soon departed and Degroote was installed as chairman, president, and CEO of the business. He brought in a former Laidlaw lieutenant to run the day-to-day affairs while he once again scouted for acquisitions to grow the business. The downturn in the economy of the early 1990s, however, revealed that garbage was not as recession-proof as he had once assumed. The entire industry, including Republic and Laidlaw, was severely hurt. Moreover, the hazardous waste portion of the business was beset by its own troubles. In 1995 DeGroote turned over control to a former competitor, now friend, Wayne Huizenga, who had made Waste Management into the world's largest garbage business. After selling out in 1984 he went on to transform a small chain of video rental stores into the highly successful Blockbuster Video. DeGroote, who through his friendship with Huizenga was able to get involved with Blockbuster at the outset, invested $15 million and made an estimated profit of $350 million to $450 million. After leaving Blockbuster, Huizenga was looking for a shell company for dealmaking and settled on Republic. Both he and DeGroote invested more money into the company, which Huizenga renamed Republic Industries and quickly grew into a multibillion-dollar company.

In preparation of Huizenga taking over Republic, DeGroote spun off the hazardous waste portion of the business as well as a 1992 acquisition, Stout Environmental Inc., which had fared poorly and resulted in a one-time charge of $2.6 million. DeGroote now changed the corporation's name to Republic Environmental Systems Inc. (RESI), which eventually became Century Business Services. He was able to convince Huizenga to invest in RESI, his reputation on Wall Street all but guaranteed to boost the company's stock price, which, in fact, grew from $4 to $36 within the year. A higher price in turn allowed DeGroote to use RESI stock as a way to fund acquisitions. With DeGroote as chair, the company was based in Blue Bell, Pennsylvania, but it only remained involved in the hazardous waste disposal business for a short period of time. In 1996 RESI merged with a Cleveland-based holding company, International Alliance Services, Inc., and its Century Surety Group subsidiary, insurers of hard-to-place lines of insurance and bonds. RESI assumed the International Alliance name and moved its headquarters to Cleveland. The plan at first was to expand, through acquisition, beyond the disposal of hazardous wastes into insuring the risks of transporting both hazardous and non-hazardous wastes, as well as to add other associated businesses. The company also planned to grow nationally, expanding on its base of Cleveland-area customers. One of these acquisitions was SMR & Co., a Cleveland consulting firm that focused on tax-related matters. Its head, Greg Skoda, was hired by International Alliance to become its chief financial officer in December 1996. Through acquisitions he had already turned SMR into one of the fastest growing U.S. companies by creating an outsourcing operation of backroom functions for smaller businesses. During the interview process with International Alliance, a strategy emerged to combine outsourcing with insurance products, so that the company would hold the distinction of being the only firm capable of administering a benefit plan and also insuring it. DeGroote was hesitant at first to embrace the business outsourcing model, but in many ways it fit into his previous experience. The services were widely needed, the industry was ripe for consolidation, with many small companies operating in limited markets, and the economy-of-scale benefits that could be realized were substantial. Not only would International Alliance cut overhead costs by combining smaller firms, it would be able to network their services so that it could provide a one-stop shopping approach for a wide range of backroom operations.

From International Alliance to Century Business Services: 1997

After launching an acquisition binge in 1997 International Alliance sold off the original RESI hazardous waste operation to focus on its growing slate of outsourcing businesses. In November 1997 the company also tacked away from its insurance heritage, as a number of old-guard International Alliance top executives were swept aside in favor of DeGroote and a stable of new vice-presidents and directors. DeGroote now became president and CEO in addition to retaining the chairmanship of the corporation, while Skoda became a point man on acquisitions, relinquishing his CFO role to become executive vice-president. To better reflect its new emphasis, the company changed its name to Century Business Services, Inc. It continued its aggressive program of acquisitions in 1998, snapping up accounting, payroll, and benefits companies. By June of that year it owned more than 100 offices in 28 states. Only 18 months earlier, when RESI and International Alliance merged, it had operated just five Cleveland-area business service firms. Now it was giving giant American Express Co. and its American Express Tax and Business Services unit serious competition in becoming the largest business services provider for small and medium-sized businesses. Not only did American Express Tax and Business Services have the advantage of American Express's deep pockets, it also had the American Express name to trade on. While its rival required acquisitions to adopt the American Express name, Century was at a disadvantage because it permitted new companies to continue operating under their old names. Moreover, Century's growth was very much tied to its high stock price.

In the fall of 1998 the price of Century stock experienced a major drop when the company came under fire from critics, in particular Massachusetts research firm Off Wall Street, which was known as an active short seller. It maintained that Century's acquisitions were too spread out and unable to produce the kind of cross-selling opportunities that its management promised. Off Wall Street also claimed that Century was far from circumspect in its buys, rarely rejecting a possible acquisition. Moreover, the research firm questioned Century's aggressive accounting, such as booking the revenues of an acquisition even before the deals were finalized, which in turn helped to keep Century's stock price artificially high and fuel even further acquisitions. With his company accused of being a house of cards, and watching the price of Century stock steadily decline, DeGroote responded vigorously. He told major shareholders and stock analysts in a conference call that Century was the victim of "deliberate lies" and that some research analysts were "intentionally warping" the company's numbers. More important than his words, perhaps, was his announcement that he was going to purchase "one to two million shares or more" of Century's common stock. DeGroote's actions had the desired effect, and the stock price quickly rebounded.

In 1999 Century's rate of making acquisitions slowed dramatically, characterized by management as a pause for digestion. The company's stock price also sagged, making it difficult to use stock to fund purchases. In order to help build growth internally and better compete against more recognizable American Express and H&R Block's business services subsidiary, Century initiated a branding effort, utilizing its CBIZ ticker symbol used on the NASDAQ. A pair of high-tech subsidiaries were the first to use the name, becoming "CBIZ Technologies." Such an effort, however, was not enough to stem a rising tide of difficulties facing Century. In the fall of 1999 it hired Merrill Lynch to help find a buyer, a search that was called off by the end of the year. In the meantime Century's accounting practices were again called into question, and on December 28, 1999, the company was forced to revise the way it accounted for goodwill, the amount above the book value of an acquisition. Century was amortizing that amount over 40 years, but upon advice from the SEC agreed to shorten it to the more standard 15 years. Because of the change, the company announced at the end of January 2000 that instead of earning profits of 12 cents to 14 cents a share in the fourth quarter of 1999 it might lose as much as two cents. On that same day, President and Chief Operating Officer Fred M. Winkler suddenly retired. It was bad enough for an accounting company to suffer this kind of embarrassment, but a few weeks later the situation would border on disastrous when Century reported that in fact it lost 6 cents a share for the quarter, and 34 cents on the year. After reassuring Wall Street analysts about the validity of its numbers, Century

had suffered severe damage to its credibility, requiring drastic measures. Several members of senior management were immediately terminated and DeGroote stepped down as CEO.

As a result of its accounting missteps, Century also faced lawsuits from some of the former owners of its acquisitions, who had been paid in large part by stock that was now severely devalued. Nevertheless, numerous firms that joined Century remained satisfied with their decision. They maintained that the ability to offer Century's array of services actually brought in more business and attracted larger clients. But of more importance to Century was finding strong leadership that could help repair the breach in trust that now existed with investors. The corporation's lead director, Joseph Plumeri, succeeded DeGroote and Winkler but by September 2000, as Century's stock price fell below $1, he was gone as well. In October, Century hired Steven Gerard to serve as its CEO and charged him with reversing the company's performance and restoring its image. Although not familiar with the accounting industry, he was a well seasoned executive, experienced in turnarounds, boasting strong Wall Street ties. He served as chairman and CEO of Triangle Wire & Cable, Inc., overseeing its restructuring. He also had seven years of experience as vice-president of the securities division of the American Stock Exchange and 16 years with Citibank N.A., where he rose to the position of senior managing director.

Gerard quickly took steps to overhaul Century. Acquisitions were put on hold as he came to grips with the assortment of businesses that had come into the fold in the previous two years. Some were sold off, others closed, and a number were merged with other Century operations. Administrative functions were also consolidated, a significant factor in slashing corporate overhead by 25 percent in 2001. In addition, Gerard took aggressive steps to reduce debt and over the course of 18 months cut it from $147 million to $50 million. He remained committed to expanding the company, establishing three key objectives: improve the growth rate of existing businesses, take advantage of the network to create cross-serving opportunities, and pursue acquisitions. By the spring of 2002 Century was ready to once again grow externally. This time, however, the company focused on filling key gaps, targeting select services—including accounting, business solutions, payroll services, benefits and health, and property and casualty insurance—and targeting select markets, such as Atlanta, Denver, Miami, Minneapolis, New York City, and the Washington, D.C. area. Century also renewed its efforts to extend the CBIZ brand, launching a print and radio advertising campaign in ten key cities, where consolidation of local acquisitions had already begun. Century began this effort without DeGroote as chairman. In October 2002 he resigned, citing health reasons, and was immediately replaced by Gerard, who now served as CEO and chairman of Century.

Principal Divisions

Business Solutions; Benefits and Insurance; National Practices.

Principal Competitors

Automatic Data Processing, Inc.; Ceridian Corporation; ProBusiness Services.

Further Reading

Cornell, Ryan, ''CBiz Out to Shed Its Heavy Load,'' *Crain's Cleveland Business,* August 6, 2001, p. 2.

''Creative Accounting at Century,'' *Business Week,* February 21, 2000, p. 142.

Higgins, Will, ''Who Is Michael DeGroote?,'' *Indianapolis Business Journal,* June 9, 1986, p. 1A.

Mayers, Adam, ''Mike's Midas Touch,'' *Toronto Star,* September 27, 1987, p. F1.

Serres, Christopher, ''Century Rides Express Route for Growth,'' *Crain's Cleveland Business,* June 22, 1998, p. 3.

——, ''CEO Claims Century Stock Victim of Analyst Lies,'' *Crain's Cleveland Business,* November 2, 1998, p. 1.

——, ''Struggling Cbiz Tries Executive Shakeup,'' *Crain's Cleveland Business,* March 6, 2000, p. 1.

Siklos, Richard, ''DeGroote's Third Act,'' *Financial Post,* June 28, 1997, p. 12.

——, ''Wayne's World,'' *Financial Post,* June 15, 1996, p. 16.

—Ed Dinger

China Merchants International Holdings Co., Ltd.

38th Floor East, China Merchants Tower
Shun Tak Centre
168-200 Connaught Road Central
Hong Kong
Telephone: (+852) 2850 8922
Fax: (+852) 2851 2173
Web site: http://www.cmhico.com

Public Company
Incorporated: 1872
Employees: 10,000
Sales: HK$1.21 billion (US$155 million)
Stock Exchanges: Hong Kong
Ticker Symbol: CMI
NAIC: 483111 Deep Sea Freight Transportation; 336611 Ship Building and Repairing; 483113 Coastal and Great Lakes Freight Transportation; 561510 Travel Agencies

China Merchants International Holdings Co., Ltd. (CMIH) is the publicly listed arm of Chinese government-backed China Merchants Holdings Group. CMIH is itself organized as a holding company for interests in shipping, the company's historical activity, including one of the world's largest fleets of Aframax tankers; port operation and related activities; toll road, tunnel, and related infrastructure construction and operation; industrial manufacturing, including container manufacture (the company's China International Marine Containers subsidiary is the world's leading container producer, with a 23 percent share of the global market); paints and paint products, including paints for ships and containers; as well as a vast real estate portfolio. These activities combine to provide more than HK$1.2 billion (US$155 million) in revenues per year. Parent company China Merchants Holdings Group, with approximately HK$50 billion (US$7 billion) in assets, ranks number 26 among Chinese government-owned companies and extends CMIH's range with additional infrastructure, highway, and ports operations; financial holdings including China Merchants Bank, Ping An Insurance, and securities firm China Communi-

cations Securities; travel and tourism through China Merchants International Travel Corp.; and a range of manufacturing, engineering, and telecommunications business. China Merchants is also responsible for the Shekou free-trade mainland development zone across the channel from Hong Kong. Fu Yuning serves as chairman of the board of CMIH and as president of the larger China Merchants. Qin Xiao is chairman of the China Merchants parent company.

Chinese Shipping Pioneer in the 19th Century

China launched its "Westernization" movement under the Qing Dynasty ruled by Emperor Tong Zhi in the mid-19th century. The forced opening of China by the western powers earlier in the century had placed China's shipping industry almost entirely in foreign hands. In 1872, however, then Viceroy Li Hongzhang received permission to set up the country's own shipping company to compete for the shipping routes along the mainland coastline. The company, called China Merchants Bureau and headquartered in Shanghai, started shipping operations in 1873 with the launch of the *Yidun* along the Shanhai-Hong Kong route. By the end of that year, China Merchants had added a second line, this time providing oceangoing shipping between the mainland and the port cities of Kobe and Nagasaki in Japan, then extending its route to the Philippines.

China Merchants grew quickly and by the mid-1870s was able to enter into pricing agreements with the region's dominant shippers, which included British-owned Swire and U.S.-owned Qichang. Then, in 1877, China Merchants took over Qichang, establishing itself as one of the major shippers in the Chinese market. The company then extended its freight pricing agreements to another major shipper, Jardines.

In 1902, China Merchants extended its operations inland, forming the China Merchants River Navigation Company. At the beginning of the next decade, the company linked up with the railroad industry, forming a number of land-sea transportation routes to link Chinese ports with the inland markets. The company also set up the Public School of China Merchants, dedicated to training ship's captains, becoming one of the first bodies to send students to study overseas to gain experience in

Company Perspectives:

Corporate Culture: China Merchants has stridden across two centuries of development and set up many precedents in modern economic history of China. The corporate culture of China Merchants is characterized by "profoundness and innovation," which is unique compared with other enterprises. This culture has enabled China Merchants to survive various major historical changes in modern China, and to seek the opportunities for sustained development. The employees of China Merchants always believe that: vitality lies in innovation.

Western commercial practices. China Merchants also became responsible for drafting China's first body of maritime laws and regulations.

The company continued to gain in prominence, not only in the shipping and transportation industry, but as an important motor for Chinese industrial growth. Indeed, China Merchants provided the financing for much of China's early industrial and commercial development, funding activities such as the Commercial Bank of China, the country's first bank; the Kai-Ping Mine, first machine-operated coal mine in China; the first insurance company, Bureau of China Merchants Insurance; and the country's first steel production operation, Han Yie Ping Corporation. At the same time, China Merchants' own activities diversified to include a wide range of businesses, from shipbuilding and machine manufacturing to animal husbandry and newspaper publishing.

In 1948, China Merchants, which now had head offices in Hong Kong, incorporated as China Merchants Steam Navigation Co. Ltd. By then the company had built up a fleet of more than 490 vessels, including 95 large-scale oceangoing vessels, with total capacity of more than 400,000 tons. The company also had extended its multimodal operations to include air freight, in cooperation with the Central Airline Company. Yet the revolution of 1949 and the Maoist takeover was to change the company.

Mainland Link in the 1950s

During the upheaval surrounding the Communist takeover, China Merchants split in two. A large portion of the company—including 80 of its 95 oceangoing vessels, which represented some 90 percent of the company's total tonnage capacity—fled to Taiwan. Much of China Merchants' top management, however, stayed in Hong Kong and remained loyal to the mainland. In 1950, China Merchants was reopened as a Hong Kong-based company wholly owned by the Chinese government and charged with acting as a commercial and shipping interface between Beijing and the rest of the world.

China Merchants began rebuilding its fleet and resumed its shipping operations in 1956, quickly raising its capacity to more than 180,000 tons by the end of that year. The company also began investing in port operations, rebuilding the Kennedy Town wharf. Other port operation projects included rebuilding new warehousing operations in 1959. Until the beginning of the

1960s, however, China Merchants' shipping operations remained limited to the mainland-Hong Kong trade route. In 1960, the company formed a new shipping company, Yifeng Shipping Enterprise Co., and the following year began rebuilding its oceangoing fleet, launching a second new shipping company, Ocean Tramping. In support of its reinvigorated shipping business, China Merchants launched a new ship repair business, opening the Youlian Shipyard in 1965.

Over the following decade, however, China Merchants' oceangoing business was transferred to the Chinese government's mainland shipping operation, China Ocean Shipping Co. (COSCO). China Merchants, meanwhile, was steering into other directions. In the late 1970s, the Chinese government began initiating new policies that were to open up the country to the outside world. In 1979, China Merchants was given the task of developing and managing the Shekou free trade zone, in Shenzhen, located just across the channel from Hong Kong. That operation, which became China Merchants' single largest operation, was eventually incorporated as China Merchants Shekou Industrial Zone Co. Ltd.

China Merchants had not abandoned shipping, however. In 1980, the company relaunched its oceangoing shipping activities, establishing a new subsidiary, Hong Kong Ming Wah Shipping Co., which started operations with just two 10,000-ton tankers. By the end of the 1990s, Ming Wah's fleet totaled 41 vessels with a total tonnage of 3.8 million tons.

Later in 1980, the company launched subsidiary China Merchants Lighterage Transportation Co., which grew into the Hong Kong region's largest lightering operation with a fleet of 76 vessels. Then, in 1981, China Merchants inaugurated a new shipping line, when it entered a joint venture agreement with Hong Kong Yaumatei Ferry Co. to launch an express passenger ferry service between Hong Kong and Shekou. Meanwhile, China Merchants had become an active participant in the construction and management of a variety of mainland infrastructure projects, including toll roads and tunnels, which led the group into developing its own engineering and construction services.

Public Arm of a Multifaceted Holding Company in the 21st Century

During the 1980s, China Merchants continued expanding its port and port services operations, building the China Merchants Wharf in Hong Kong's Kennedy Town in 1984, and forming shipping services subsidiary China Merchants Shipping and Enterprises Co. that same year. In 1985, the company opened a new port services operation, China Merchants Godown Wharf & Transportation Co. Then, in 1988, the Ming Wah shipping business expanded through the acquisition of the tanker fleet of the Tung Group; the two companies formed a 50–50 joint venture to operate the fleet, which was bought out by Ming Wah in 1997. That acquisition marked the beginning of Ming Wah's growth into China's largest tanker fleet operator.

China Merchants began a drive to diversify its business in the mid-1980s, forming the vehicle China Merchants Holdings Co., Ltd. In 1986, the company bought up Hong Kong-based Union Bank of Hong Kong in a move that marked the first acquisition by a Chinese company of a publicly listed Hong

Key Dates:

1872: The China Merchants Bureau is founded in order to break the Western monopoly on Chinese shipping routes.

1873: China Merchants launches its first vessel, the *Yidun,* on the Shanghai-Hong Kong route, then starts up ocean-going shipping to Japan and the Philippines.

1877: China Merchants takes over U.S.-owned Qichang shipping company.

1902: China Merchants begins inland shipping with the establishment of China Merchants River Navigation Company.

1949: China Merchants is split as most of the fleet flees to Taiwan during the Maoist revolution.

1950: China Merchants reestablishes itself as a Hong Kong-based company owned by the Chinese government.

1956: After rebuilding its fleet, China Merchants resumes shipping operations.

1961: China Merchants returns to oceangoing shipping as it begins to rebuild its fleet, which is later transferred to COSCO.

1979: China Merchants launches the development and management of Shekou, in the newly established Shenzhen free-trade zone.

1980: The subsidiary Ming Wah is formed as China Merchants begins rebuilding its shipping fleet.

1985: The holding company, China Merchants Holdings, is formed.

1986: Union Bank of Hong Kong is purchased.

1987: The company establishes China Merchants Bank, then extends into insurance and securities.

1992: China Merchants International Holdings (CMIH) is launched on the Hong Kong stock exchange, the first Chinese company to seek a public listing.

1998: China Merchants restructures into 12 primary companies and transfers its infrastructure holdings to CMIH; the company acquires Modern Terminals Ltd. (Hong Kong) and Nanshan Development Co. (Shenzhen).

1999: CMIH acquires stakes in Shekou Container Terminal and Asian Aircraft Terminal, both held by China Merchants.

2000: CMIH purchases a 49 percent share of a bulk cargo and container handling terminal in Zhangzhou, in the Fujian province.

2001: CMIH acquires a 33 percent share of another Shenzen port from China Everbright Group.

2002: CMIH announces plan to spend up to HK$9.4 billion on new port acquisitions as it seeks to extend its port operations into other mainland cities.

Kong business. The following year, China Merchants set up its own commercial bank on the mainland, China Merchants Bank—the first to be created since the formation of the People's Republic of China in 1949.

Through China Merchants Bank, the company entered the insurance market, launching subsidiary Ping An Insurance Company of China in 1988. The company also acquired existing insurance businesses in London and Hong Kong. A further extension of China Merchants' financial arm came in 1991, when it set up the securities trade group China Communications Securities. Meanwhile, China Merchants had begun acquiring shareholdings in a number of other businesses and markets, such as a 31 percent stake in a container manufacturer.

In 1992, China Merchants bundled a number of its holdings, including much of its shipping, port, and wharf operations, its ship repair business, various manufacturing operations including container manufacturing and ship and container paint production, into a new business—China Merchants International Holdings Co., Ltd., or CMIH. This company was then listed on the Hong Kong stock exchange, becoming the first Chinese company to seek a public listing in Hong Kong. The offering was an immediate success—rising by 200 percent after its first day of trading, before entering the Hang Sheng China-Affiliated Corporations Index as one of the leading "red chip" stocks of the 21st century.

In a 1995 review of 500 Chinese government-owned businesses, China Merchants was ranked as number 26, with assets

ranging upward to HK$50 billion (US$6 billion). CMIH, with just HK$3 billion (US$400 billion), remained a tiny, yet vital part of the entire group, enabling private investment capital to enter the government-owned group. In 1997, China Merchants moved to boost CMIH, transferring a chunk of its toll road and other infrastructure operations into the public subsidiary. The following year, China Merchants restructured its entire operations—which spanned more than 500 subsidiaries—into 12 primary companies, including CMIH, which was then focused on infrastructure, shipping, port transportation, and container terminals.

CMIH began expanding its port operations at the turn of the century, beginning in 1998 with the acquisition of Hong Kong's Modern Terminals Ltd. and Shenzen's Nanshan Development Co. In 1999, CMIH extended its Shekou-based port operations with acquisitions of stakes in Shekou Container Terminal and Asian Aircraft Terminal, both held by China Merchants. Then, in 2000 with the purchase of a 49 percent share of a bulk cargo and container handling terminal in Zhangzhou, in the Fujian province, the company began a push into other mainland port markets beyond Shekou. In 2001, CMIH acquired a 33 percent share of another Shenzen port from China Everbright Group.

At the beginning of 2002, CMIH announced its intention to spend up to HK$2 billion to upgrade its existing port operations, including plans to expand its Shekou and Chiwan container terminals in Shenzhen. The company also began a drive to extend further into the mainland ports and ports services market by acquiring additional port operations outside of Shenzhen, with plans to spend nearly HK$9.4 billion (US$1.2

billion). In October 2002, the company announced that it was in the process of finalizing the acquisition of ports in Ningbo, in the Zheijang province; Shanghai; Quindao, in the Shandong province; and in Tianjin, which would give the company a presence near Beijing. CMIH expected to remain a major player in the growing Hong Kong and Chinese shipping and ports sector in the new century.

Principal Subsidiaries

Asia Airfreight Terminal Company Limited; China International Marine Containers (Group) Ltd; CMHI Caymans Inc. (Cayman Islands); Cotter International Limited; Fair Oaks Limited; Finstead Shipping Limited (Liberia); Fully Profit Property Limited; Hai Hong Industry (Shenzhen) Co. Ltd.; Hempel-Hai Hong Coatings Company Limited; New Alliance Shipping Inc. (Liberia); New Amity Shipping Inc. (Liberia); Ningbo Changzhen Highway Co. Ltd (People's Republic of China; 60%); Ningbo Zhenluo Highway Co. Ltd (People's Republic of China; 60%); Reed Overseas Development Co. Ltd.; Shenzhen Chiwan Wharf Holdings Ltd; Shenzhen Haixing Harbour Development Co. Ltd.; Universal Sheen Investment Limited; Wharton Overseas Limited; Zhangzhou China Merchants Port Co. Ltd.

Principal Competitors

Sumitomo Corporation; TUI AG; A.P. Moller A/S; FedEx Corporation; Canadian Pacific Ltd.; ThyssenKrupp Materials und Services AG; Tank- og Ruteskibe I/S; Nippon Express Company Ltd.; Exel plc; Danzas Group; Kuhne und Nagel AG und Co; Koninklijke Vopak NV; SCHENKER AG; Kawasaki Kisen Kaisha Ltd; Hyundai Merchant Marine Company Ltd; Dr. August Oetker KG; Hapag-Lloyd AG; John Swire and Sons Ltd.; Transnet Ltd.; Atlantic Container Line Inc.; Bidvest Group Ltd.; Stolt-Nielsen S.A.; Maersk Inc.

Further Reading

"China Merchants to Acquire Ningbo and Tianjin Ports," *Standard,* October 22, 2002.
Flynn, Matthew, "China Ship: Merchants' Class Forges On," *Lloyds List,* December 14, 1998.
Lee, Teresa, "Shake-up at China Merchants," *Hong Kong Standard,* November 10, 1998.
Lin, Ang Bee, "China Merchants to Invest HK$2 Bln on Ports, Logistics," *Reuters,* April 22, 2002.
Zhu, Charlie, "China Merchants Net Up 25 Pct on Ports, Production," *Reuters,* April 19, 2001.

—M.L. Cohen

The Christian Broadcasting Network, Inc.

977 Centerville Turnpike
Virginia Beach, Virginia 23463
U.S.A.
Telephone: (757) 226-7000
Toll Free: (800) 759-0700
Fax: (757) 226-3019
Web site: http://www.cbn.org

Nonprofit Company
Incorporated: 1960
Employees: 1,200
Operating Revenues: $204.9 million (2001)
NAIC: 513120 Television Broadcasting; 513220 Cable
and Other Program Distribution; 512110 Video
Production; 813110 Religious Organizations

The Christian Broadcasting Network, Inc. (CBN) is a nonprofit organization devoted to spreading the Christian Gospel internationally through mass media, education, and humanitarian efforts. Founded by Pat Robertson, the network grew from a single UHF station to a cable and satellite broadcaster with programming seen in 166 countries and broadcast in more than 70 languages. Its flagship program, *The 700 Club,* is seen by more than one million viewers in the United States, and international editions are seen throughout the world.

Establishment of Christian Broadcasting Network: 1960s

The Christian Broadcasting Network, Inc. was established in January 1960 by Pat Robertson. The network began with a single station in Portsmouth, Virginia. At the time Robertson took over the station, it was a defunct UHF station with barely enough power to transmit across Portsmouth's city limits. Robertson renamed the station WYAH-TV after Yahweh, the Hebrew name for God, and began broadcasting on October 1, 1961.

CBN received a modest income from a few local supporters. When it first went on the air, WYAH-TV broadcast half-hour programs from 7 p.m. to 10 p.m. every night. The station gradually expanded its broadcast day from 5 p.m. to midnight. It refused to accept commercial advertisements and was unable to pay for programming.

CBN conducted its first telethon to raise money in the fall of 1963. Its goal was to raise enough money to cover the station's $7,000-a-month operating expenses for 1964. Robertson asked the telethon's viewers to contribute $10 a month, saying that a club of 700 supporters was all that was needed to meet the station's needs. The telethon included guests who sang and shared their religious experiences. During the telethon Robertson asked viewers to pray for the 700 supporters needed to keep CBN on the air. Although CBN continued to struggle financially, the telethon established the basis for a community of supporters.

The 1964 700 Club telethon was more successful and marked a turning point in CBN's financial well-being. As the telethon was broadcast, it generated more funds than the previous year but not enough to cover CBN's growing budget. In the final minutes of the telethon, it appeared that a spiritual revival took hold of the viewing audience, and throughout the next several days CBN received a flood of prayer requests and financial support.

In 1965 Robertson incorporated the telethon's fundraising into a program that he named *The 700 Club.* The program included prayer and ministry along with requests for telephone support. As other stations began to carry the program, its audience grew.

CBN's financial growth in the 1960s enabled it to renovate its broadcast facility in Portsmouth and boost the station's transmission power. CBN began full-color television production and acquired six radio stations in the United States and one in Colombia, South America.

Audience Growth Through Cable Television and International Initiatives: 1970s

CBN began to reach an international audience in 1976 when its first international broadcast was heard in the Philippines. The broadcast included daily transmissions of *The 700 Club.* Around this time CBN was able to purchase 142 acres of land in Virginia Beach, Virginia, and build a new studio headquarters building. In 1977 CBN launched CBN Cable, the first basic TV cable network with satellite transmissions of religious and syndicated family shows. The satellite earth station at the CBN Center in Virginia Beach made possible the first satellite broadcast from Jerusalem. Satellite capability also provided for the live delivery of *The 700 Club,* which allowed CBN to pioneer interactive Christian television through telephone contact with its viewing audience. CBN soon began 24-hour Christian programming via satellite with a mix of religious and syndicated family shows. It also expanded its international broadcasts to the Far East, Canada, South America, Mexico, Africa, and Europe. Within the United States, CBN acquired television stations in Dallas, Atlanta, and Boston.

Another international effort, Operation Blessing International Relief and Development Corporation, was begun in 1978. An affiliate organization of CBN, it was established to help disadvantaged people. The organization matched their needs for clothing, appliances, vehicles, and other items with articles donated by the viewers of *The 700 Club.* CBN's financial commitment to Operation Blessing International reached $1 million by 1982.

Expanding CBN's Audience Through Mass Media: 1980s

By 1981 CBN Cable reached ten million American homes. The cable network prospered during the 1980s and was renamed the CBN Family Channel in 1988. In 1990 the cable network was sold to International Family Entertainment, Inc. IFE was subsequently sold to Fox Kids Worldwide, Inc., which sold the Fox Family Channel to The Walt Disney Company. The cable channel was renamed ABC Family in November 2001.

During the 1980s *The 700 Club* changed its format to become a news magazine program. The show was hosted by Pat Robertson, Terry Meeuwsen, Lisa Ryan, and Gordon Robertson. It opened a news bureau in Washington, D.C. CBN also began producing animation programs with religious themes including *Superbook,* an animated series of Bible stories. When *Don't Ask Me, Ask God* aired, it was the most-watched religious special in television broadcasting history. Another program, *Never Say Goodbye,* was produced for CBS and received an Emmy Award.

Internationally, CBN launched the Middle East Television Network (METV) in 1982. It began broadcasting from South

Lebanon in April 1982 and also had operations in Israel. In the 1990s the station began broadcasting news, sports, family entertainment, and religious programming via satellite. Over the next two decades METV expanded its satellite programming to a potential audience of 200 million people in 15 Middle Eastern nations.

Expanding the Company's International Outreach: 1990s

During the 1990s CBN expanded its international broadcasting efforts, so that by 2000 international editions of *The 700 Club* and other CBN programs could be seen in more than 180 countries. CBN programs were broadcast in more than 70 languages.

In 1990 CBN began targeting the Commonwealth of Independent States (CIS), formerly the Soviet Union. It broadcast primetime specials followed by *The 700 Club* and *Superbook.* Rallies were held throughout the CIS following the broadcasts, and as a result some 190 churches were established there. Similar special projects were conducted in the Philippines and Romania in 1994, the same year that CBN Asia was launched. CBN Asia featured a local version of *The 700 Club* hosted by Gordon Robertson and Filipino cohost Coney Reyes. The program ranked as one of the top Christian programs in the Philippines and was broadcast from CBN Asia's studios in Manila. CBN programs aired via satellite from Manila were also seen in India, Japan, Singapore, Thailand, Malaysia, Myanmar, and Hawaii. In India, a locally produced *700 Club India* began airing in the fall of 1998 and was hosted by Dr. Roy Varghese.

CBN WorldReach was launched in the fall of 1995. Its goal was to reach the world's population of three billion people with messages from the Christian Gospel. To reach a wider audience more effectively, CBN WorldReach employed the technique of media blitzes, which saturated selected regions over concentrated periods of time. Media blitzes used all available forms of media, including television programming, radio shows, videotapes, literature, and other formats. In many cases programs for the media blitzes were produced locally by production teams of CBN International. Blitz television programming typically used a mix of original made-for-TV movies, uplifting docudramas, music and sports specials, and children's animation. Especially successful media blitzes were conducted in Nigeria, Cameroon, and Brazil.

CBN WorldReach typically partnered with local Christian ministries to maximize its impact. During the 1990s and into the early part of the 21st century, CBN WorldReach launched more than 200 WorldReach Centers in nine regions of the world: Latin America, Africa, Europe, Middle East, India, Europe, Southeast Asia, China, and the CIS. Each WorldReach Center spread the Gospel through a combination of media, discipleship, cell church planting, and humanitarian relief efforts. Through 2002 CBN WorldReach claimed to have converted 92 million people to Christianity since its launch in 1995.

Middle East Television (METV) also expanded during the 1990s. In 1997 it began 24-hour satellite broadcasts, and its broadcasts were also seen on all cable systems in Israel. As a result, METV could be seen by a potential audience of 70 million viewers throughout the Middle East. In May 1999 METV began looking for a new broadcast facility, as Israel prepared to with-

Key Dates:

1960: Pat Robertson founds The Christian Broadcasting Network (CBN) with a defunct Portsmouth, Virginia, television station.
1961: CBN begins broadcasting from WYAH-TV in Portsmouth.
1963: CBN conducts its first telethon to raise $7,000, with Pat Robertson requesting 700 supporters give $10 a month.
1965: *The 700 Club* program is added to the end of CBN's broadcast day.
1976: CBN's first international broadcast is heard daily in the Philippines.
1977: CBN launches the first basic TV cable network with satellite transmissions of religious and syndicated family shows.
1978: Operation Blessing International Relief and Development Corporation, an affiliate organization, is established to help disadvantaged people.
1982: CBN launches Middle East Television Network (METV) in Lebanon and Israel.
1988: CBN Cable is renamed the CBN Family Channel.
1990: The CBN Family Channel is sold to International Family Entertainment, Inc.
1994: CBN Asia is launched.
1995: CBN WorldReach is launched.
1997: METV begins satellite broadcasts over the entire Middle East region.
2001: METV is sold to LeSEA Broadcasting.

draw from Southern Lebanon. In May 2000 METV completed construction of a new station and began broadcasting from Cyprus. In April 2001 CBN sold METV to LeSEA Broadcasting, a like-minded organization that was committed to keeping METV on the air to spread the Christian Gospel.

Operation Blessing International (OBI) expanded its humanitarian efforts during the 1990s. In 1992 OBI established the Hunger Strike Force, which included a fleet of refrigerated tractor-trailer trucks that hauled millions of pounds of food and disaster relief across the United States. OBI also purchased and retrofitted an airplane into a flying hospital. The Flying Hospital flew its first mission into El Salvador in 1996. It was sold in 2000 to a charitable nonprofit organization but continued to remain an integral part of OBI's evangelical missions.

Entering New Millennium with 40 Years of Experience

CBN moved aggressively into the 21st century as an experienced television broadcaster and programming producer that enjoyed global distribution. It also had a high level of direct interaction with its viewers through mail, telephone responses, and its web site at www.cbn.com.

CBN's flagship program continued to be *The 700 Club,* hosted by Pat Robertson along with cohosts Terry Meeuwsen, Gordon Robertson, Lisa Ryan, Kristi Watts, and CBN news anchor Lee Webb. The daily program reached an average of one million U.S.

viewers. *700 Club Sundays* was broadcast on weekends and compiled segments from the previous week's programs. International editions of *The 700 Club* were broadcast in many languages and countries, including India, Indonesia, Thailand, the CIS, the Middle East, and in Spanish-speaking regions.

Operation Blessing International continued CBN's international humanitarian efforts. During 2001 it received $51.7 million worth of food, clothing, cleaning supplies, toys, and other items from corporations and product donors. Its Hunger Strike Force delivered 56 million pounds of food in the United States and other countries as well as 11 million pounds of disaster relief supplies to countries such as Mozambique and El Salvador. Other projects conducted by OBI included medical missions that provided eye care abroad; Holiday of Hope outreaches that distributed Bibles, blankets, food, and toys in the United States and abroad; Hope Works programs that expanded job training to the unemployed in the United States and Central and South America; and Bless-A-Child and Back-to-School projects.

CBN Animation continued to produce award-winning features and programs. Through 2001 it had produced 113 original evangelistic specials. In 2001 it won awards for Best Children's Program, Best Animated Program, and Best Use of Computer Animation from Axiem, Telly, and Omni International. CBN Animation also participated in the Daytime Emmy Awards for the first time in 2001.

Like other nonprofit organizations, CBN faced a difficult economic climate in 2001. In March 2001 it laid off 50 workers at its Virginia Beach office, most of them in television production. In addition some network production activities were reassigned to new CBN television studios in Kiev, Ukraine; Manila, Philippines; Jakarta, Indonesia; and Hyderabad, India.

CBN's net assets declined in 2001 by some $40 million from 2000, and its revenue declined from $217.8 million in 2000 to $204.9 million in 2001. Approximately three-fourths of CBN's revenue came from ministry support, with nearly one-quarter from gifts in kind and about $2 million in investment income and other revenue.

Principal Operating Units

CBN Animation; CBN International; CBN WorldReach; Operation Blessing International.

Further Reading

" 'The American Whey' Promo Raises Eyebrows," *Christian Century,* October 13, 1993, p. 972.
"Christian Broadcasting Network to Cut 50 Jobs in Virginia Beach, Va.," *Knight Ridder/Tribune Business News,* March 24, 2001.
Conn, Joseph L., "Render Unto Caesar," *Church & State,* May 1998, p. 4.
Edsall, Thomas B., "Christian Network to Pay IRS Fine," *Washington Post,* March 21, 1998, p. A01.
Garrett, Lynn, "Launching 'The Book,'" *Publishers Weekly,* April 12, 1999, p. 38.
Kustanowitz, Shully, "Christian Network and Israel Ink Pact," *Travel Weekly,* August 8, 1991, p. 36.

—David P. Bianco

Concord EFS, Inc.

2525 Horizon Lake Drive, Suite 120
Memphis, Tennessee 38133
U.S.A.
Telephone: (901) 371-8000
Fax: (901) 371-8050

Public Company
Incorporated: 1970 as Concord Computing Corporation
Employees: 2,628
Sales: $1.7 billion (2001)
Stock Exchanges: NASDAQ
Ticker Symbol: CEFT
NAIC: 522320 Financial Transactions Processing,
    Reserve, and Clearinghouse

Concord EFS, Inc., based in Memphis, Tennessee, provides a full range of electronic payment and deposit services, from authorizing and routing a fund transfer to settlement. The company's Network Services division provides financial institutions with ATM processing, debit card processing, access to a national debit network, and deposit risk management. Concord's Payment Services division processes payments for supermarkets, gas stations, truck stops, convenience stores, and restaurants, as well as major and independent retailers. The company is the leading processor to gas stations and supermarkets, as well as being the United States' largest ATM processor.

Victor Tyler's Establishment of Concord Computing in 1970

The Concord component of Concord EFS dates back to 1970 when Victor M. Tyler established Concord Computing Corporation in the Boston, Massachusetts, area. An electrical engineer who studied at both Yale and MIT, Tyler in 1955 went to work at EG&G Corp., which was primarily involved in the design and testing of weapons systems for the military. In the mid-1960s Tyler was charged with identifying new business ventures for the company, one of which was the new area of electronic credit authorization systems. When EG&G elected not to participate, Tyler, who had been involved in a number of start-ups, decided to take up the idea himself and at age 42 became an entrepreneur,

thinking it would be "fun and easy." He enlisted five colleagues from EG&G and started Concord Computing Corporation, primarily funded by $20,000 invested by a friend and the $30,000 he raised by mortgaging his house. Establishing an electronic credit authorization business, however, proved to be anything but easy. At the end of a year the company was barely established, forcing the partners to take stock of the situation. Because most of their seed money was still available, they could easily cash in, find new jobs, and move on with their lives. Instead, they agreed to press ahead, only to find the second year even more arduous than the first. At one point the employees actually drew lots to see who would quit as a cost-cutting measure. Years later Tyler told the *Boston Globe,* "It was like deciding who is going to get out of the lifeboat because there's not enough food left."

To raise much needed cash to keep the business afloat and operating, Tyler took out another mortgage and borrowed money from his parents. Concord's financial situation then began to stabilize as it landed accounts with major Boston department stores. Although annual revenues grew to $2 million within a few years, the company consistently lost money. "Every month we seemed to lose $20,000 and we couldn't figure out why we couldn't make a profit," Tyler told the *Boston Globe.* In the mid-1970s Concord recruited a new chief financial officer who succeeded in turning around the company, and in 1977, after some internal discord, was able to oust Tyler as CEO. Instead of continuing to provide information services, Concord now began to focus on the less profitable hardware side of the business. As a result the company was once again losing money. Tyler lobbied the board of directors and secured enough support to once again be named the chief executive. He quickly returned Concord's emphasis to service rather than hardware, and within two months the company began posting profits. After years of learning the ropes as an entrepreneur, Tyler finally settled on a successful business formula: "You have to forecast revenue with extreme accuracy and without any optimism. And then you have to be prepared to ruthlessly cut costs."

The Acquisition of EFS in 1985: A Turning Point for Concord

While Concord developed a reputation as thrifty Yankees in the 1980s, the company also began to move beyond simple profitability as a goal and to formulate a broader vision. In

Tyler's words, Concord began to build "payment networks" to take advantage of the new point-of-sale terminals technology and the increasing use of electronic means of funds transfer. The first major step in this direction occurred in 1981 when it acquired a majority interest in Network EFT, a Chicago-based third-party payment processing service for retailers and financial institutions. The Jewel Supermarket chain also owned a major stake in the business. To compete against larger, better financed companies in the industry, Concord sought out niche opportunities, targeting specific customers, then winning their business by offering lower prices and better service. The approach worked so well that in 1984 the company went public to fuel further expansion. A year later Concord used some of those proceeds to acquire EFS, Inc. (Electronic Fleet Systems), a major turning point in the company's history.

EFS, originally involved in the trucking industry, offered fleet management services for trucking companies as well as credit card authorization and settlement services for retailers. It was founded by Dan M. Palmer, who ultimately became Concord's CEO and chair and was responsible for moving the business to Memphis. He graduated from the University of Memphis in 1966 with a degree in business administration. For a number of years he worked as an accountant for Deloitte and Touche in New York, then became the chief financial officer for Bayer Corporation's Arkansas office. Afterward he went to work for Mid Continent, a West Memphis, Arkansas, company that marketed a credit card for truck drivers. Reflecting on how long it took for credit cards with past due accounts to be shut down, Palmer recognized a business opportunity to provide instant verification of credit cards using new point-of-sale technology. He quit his job to start his own business but at first had difficulty convincing banks and investors that the idea was indeed worthwhile. Finally he received help from a former executive of Memphis-based Union Planters Bank, Bill Matthews, who had introduced ATMs to Memphis and was sympathetic to Palmer's vision. In 1982 Palmer created EFS as a subsidiary of Union Planters. EFS fared poorly during its brief existence with Union Planters; the unit was never profitable and unable to establish itself in the marketplace. As part of a restructuring effort, Union Planters decided to unload the business, selling it to Concord at a cut-rate price of $250,000. Palmer stayed on as CEO of EFS and with Concord as a parent corporation he was finally able to make the company prosper, due in large part to actively soliciting mom-and-pop operations, convincing them to start accepting credit cards.

Tyler remained chairman and CEO of Concord through the rest of the 1980s. During that time, the company produced strong results, growing revenues and profits at a steady clip. It exploited numerous niche opportunities, was not overly dependent on any single customer, and was able to leverage superior technology to discount its services and thereby successfully compete against much larger rivals. With EFS accounting for more than 60 percent of all revenues, it was not surprising that

Palmer would succeed Tyler as Concord's CEO in 1990. A year later Palmer also became chairman of the board. The company changed its name to Concord Computing and EFS, and moved its headquarters to centrally located Memphis. It also initiated efforts to become involved in bank card processing in supermarkets and grocery stores, a promising vehicle for future growth. More important, Palmer was transforming Concord from a small electronic funds transfer operation into a major, vertically integrated electronic banking operation.

In September 1991 Concord created a subsidiary, Concord Equipment Sales, Inc., to sell point-of-sale terminal products and other communications equipment. Also in 1991 the company took a more significant step in filling out its business when it filed an application to organize a national bank. In preparation, Concord became a holding company and in February 1992 changed its name to Concord EFS, Inc. A new subsidiary assumed the Concord Computing Corporation name and acquired the operational assets and liabilities of the parent company. After final approval for a bank charter was granted by the Federal Reserve in October 1992, the parent company became a one-bank holding company. Simultaneously, on December 1, 1992, EFS National Bank was formed, issued stock, and acquired the EFS, Inc. subsidiary, which was subsequently dissolved.

The result of all of this shuffling of names and stock swaps was that Concord now had its own bank and was better positioned for future growth on a number of levels. No longer did it have to rely on a sponsor bank to provide settlement services and sponsorship into bankcard associations. In addition to saving money Concord was able to offer new services, such as debit cards, to its existing markets. EFS National Bank limited its activities in order to best support Concord and did not engage in traditional banking activities, such as consumer and commercial lending, deposits, and real estate.

On the same day that its bank charter was approved, Concord also announced a major agreement with the National Grocers Association (NGA) to provide its 65,000 independent member grocers with credit and debit processing services. It was a large and virtually untapped market for Concord. NGA would later contract Concord to provide check authorization services as well.

Another emerging service in the early 1990s was electronic benefit transfer (EBT), which government authorities were beginning to use in order to combat misuse of welfare benefits and food stamps. EBT became the subject of litigation for Concord in February 1993 when it sued Deluxe Data Systems Inc., claiming that Deluxe violated antitrust laws by forcing grocers to agree to use its services exclusively in the state of Maryland. Concord feared that, if unchecked, Deluxe would be able to shut down competition in the potentially lucrative EBT field as other states made the transition to EBT. The matter lingered in the courts for more than two years and jeopardized the future of EBT. Finally in July 1995 the two parties reached a settlement, the terms of which were not disclosed, but at the very least Concord was now better positioned to compete against Deluxe in EBT.

Rapid Expansion in the 1990s

Through the rest of the 1990s Concord grew at an impressive pace. For 1993 the company recorded sales of $75.4 million and

Key Dates:

1970: Concord Computing Corporation is established.
1982: EFS, Inc. is created as a subsidiary of Union Planters Bank.
1984: Concord goes public.
1985: Concord acquires EFS.
1990: Dan M. Palmer becomes CEO; company headquarters moves to Memphis.
1992: The company name is changed to Concord EFS and EFS National Bank is formed.
2001: The $850 million Star Systems acquisition is completed.

net income of $9.9 million. In 1995 sales grew to $127.8 million and net income to $18.3 million. In 1997 sales reached $240 million and net income $42.7 million. Two years later sales topped $830 million and net income exceeded $100 million. Most of this growth was accomplished internally through payment services for retailers, but Concord also began to make acquisitions to move into network services for financial institutions to fuel even further expansion, as well as to better compete in an industry that was undergoing consolidation.

In 1999 Concord acquired Electronic Payment Services (EPS) and its well known MAC brand, the third largest regional ATM network. Not only did it obtain a larger processing platform and bolster the credit card processing part of its business, Concord reached another level in the EFT industry, in league with such heavyweights as First Data Corporation and subsidiaries of National City Corp. and Bank One Corp. In 2000 Concord expanded further into network services when it bought Cash Station, which serviced 645 financial institutions primarily located in Illinois, Indiana, Kansas, Kentucky, Michigan, Missouri, and Wisconsin.

Clearly, regional EFT networks were consolidating and Concord was determined to become a major player. When it acquired Star Systems in an $850 million deal in 2001 it became an industry powerhouse that combined payment and network services, a move that also vaulted Concord into the ranks of the S&P 500 stock index. Now operating in 31 states, Concord was becoming a true national enterprise. By focusing on either its MAC or Star brand it was now in a position to possibly challenge Visa and MasterCard on debit cards and as a point-of-sale brand at retail locations. In April 2001 Concord announced that it had settled on Star as its brand, which would begin to replace MAC and Cash Station logos on ATMs.

Concord also was preparing for the future of electronic payments. It promoted a preauthorized debit card (referred to as ACH) that could be combined with supermarket club cards. Merchants would be able to save on fees charged by Visa and MasterCard, and consumers would be rewarded with bonuses.

The ACH acronym referred to Automated Clearing House, which would be authorized by the consumer to make a bank account transfer. The personal identification number (PIN), however, would be assigned by the supermarket and the card would only be valid at the issuing chain.

Concord also began testing a number of methods to use ATM cards to make Internet purchases, as well as a way to use ATM service to send money to anyone, even people without a bank account. Concord patented a person-to-person service that allowed a sender to visit an ATM and arrange for a specific amount of money to be transferred. A one-time-use PIN would then be assigned. The recipient, informed of the PIN, would then use a special access card to receive the cash from an in-network ATM. Even without such innovations, Concord was looking forward to major growth in its established services. In 2001, for instance, only 20 percent of supermarket payments were made by debit or credit cards. That amount was expected to triple over the next six or seven years.

In 2001 Concord posted revenues of more than $1.7 billion and net income of $216.4 million. After overseeing the company's tremendous growth over the previous decade, Palmer announced in September 2002 that he was stepping down as Concord CEO in May 2003, to be replaced by company President Edward A. Labry III, an executive with Concord since the 1985 merger with EFS. Palmer would, however, remain chairman of both Concord and EFS National Bank.

Principal Subsidiaries

Concord Computing Corporation; EFS National Bank; Star Systems, Inc.

Principal Competitors

First Data Corporation; National City Corp.; Total System Services, Inc.

Further Reading

Clarkson, Amy, "The Ace of the Market," *University of Memphis Magazine,* Winter 2002.

Flaum, David, "Memphis, Tenn.-Based Electronic Transactions Processing Firm Has Room to Grow," *Commercial Appeal,* May 24, 2002.

Gosnell, David, "Debit's Rising Star," *Credit Card Management,* December 2000, p. 16.

"MAC System Owner Agrees to $1 Billion Buyout Pact," *American Banker,* November 25, 1998.

Powell, Gregory, "Concord Adds 50 Employees, Doubles Space," *Memphis Business Journal,* August 20, 1990, p. 1.

Sewell, Tim, "Concord EFS Is No Stranger to Industry," *Memphis Business Journal,* October 6, 1997, p. 44.

Simon, Jane Fitz, "Top Company Concord Computing: A True Comeback Tale," *Boston Globe,* June 13, 1989, p. 35.

—Ed Dinger

Continental Airlines, Inc.

1600 Smith Street
Houston, Texas 77002
U.S.A.
Telephone: (713) 324-5000
Toll Free: (800) 525-0280
Fax: (713) 324-2637
Web site: http://www.continental.com

Public Company
Incorporated: 1934 as Varney Speed Lines
Employees: 42,900
Sales: $8.97 billion (2001)
Stock Exchanges: New York
Ticker Symbol: CAL
NAIC: 481111 Scheduled Passenger Air Transportation;
 481112 Scheduled Freight Air Transportation

Continental Airlines, Inc. is the fifth largest U.S. airline, based on 2001 revenue passenger miles (RPMs). The company carries passengers, cargo, and mail throughout the world. The company serves more than 200 airports worldwide, with the majority of them located in the United States, and has extensive service to Latin America. Domestic flight services are operated mainly through its business hubs in Cleveland, Houston, and Newark, from which the carrier has attained a market leading position in the New York area's transatlantic traffic.

Demoralized by bitter labor relations and a takeover by corporate raider Frank Lorenzo in the 1980s, Continental became a poster child for turnaround management in the 1990s. After almost a decade of financial losses and declining sales, Continental finally turned a profit in 1995. Regional unit Continental Express was spun off in a 2002 initial public offering (IPO) as ExpressJet Airlines, Inc.

The Early Years

The beginnings of Continental Airlines, Inc. can be traced back to 1934, when Walter Varney founded an airline company that he named Varney Speed Lines. Varney Speed Lines was the fourth airline created by its founder; the first had been purchased by Boeing's United Aircraft, and the other two had failed. Varney operated his newest business alone until 1937, at which time a man by the name of Robert Foreman Six used $90,000 to purchase a 40 percent interest in the company.

Six had a background as a pilot and flight school instructor, having dropped out of high school to work odd jobs and take flying lessons in the mid-1920s. In 1929, at the age of 22, Six earned his pilot's license and was running the Valley Flying Service in Stockton, California, which sold scenic air tours of the California countryside to area residents and tourists. When the effects of the Depression halted his flying service, Six worked at a Boeing Air Transport flight school in San Francisco, training airline pilots. He later left the United States and worked for the China National Aviation Company in Shanghai. Upon his return to the United States the following year, Six convinced his new father-in-law to lend him the money that was used to acquire his interest in Varney Speed Lines.

Six's $90,000 investment was used mainly to pay debts that Varney had accrued during the company's first three years. After the company's financial standing was restored, only a small portion of money remained to purchase new or upgraded equipment. Therefore, Six used his negotiation skills to convince the Lockheed Corporation to sell Varney Speed Lines three L-12 planes on credit. Soon thereafter, Six led the company in changing its name from Varney Speed Lines to Continental Airlines, contending that the young airline would never be successful with a name like "Varney." Such efforts soon earned Six a position as the company's president.

Following his appointment to the presidency of Continental Airlines, Six led the company through a period of rapid expansion. First on his agenda was the task of enlarging the airline's fleet of planes. At that time, the DC-3 was the most popular, practical, and durable plane on the market; unfortunately, it was also the most expensive, and Continental could not afford it. Instead, Six decided to purchase a number of L-14 Lodestars from Lockheed, and then hired 12 of the company's first stewardesses to staff the new planes. Meanwhile, the company also was working to expand its flight route network, which had previously consisted of a circuit that ran between Denver, Colo-

Company Perspectives:

Our goals are simple—they are our customers' goals. We continue to deliver a high-quality product each and every day, getting our customers where they want to go, on-time and with their bags, while providing pre-flight and inflight service that is globally recognized for consistency and excellence.

rado, and El Paso, Texas. First to be added were services to Wichita, Kansas, and Tulsa, Oklahoma.

In the midst of his expansion efforts, Six left the company in August 1942 to enlist in the U.S. Army, leaving Continental in the hands of a lawyer named Terrell Drinkwater. The Japanese had attacked Pearl Harbor, and the country was mobilizing for World War II. Six was sworn in as a captain and stationed in New Caledonia. He was later transferred to the Caribbean, where he was able to use his flight knowledge to aid in maintaining a military air conduit between the United States and Brazil. Meanwhile, Continental had earned several government contracts during wartime and was left with $900,000 in cash and a tiny debt of only $60,000.

Postwar Expansion Efforts

Following the war, Six returned to Continental and immediately helped the company acquire a number of DC-3s from military surplus. Although the planes represented an upgrade of the airline company's fleet, DC-3s were no longer the top-of-the-line aircraft that they had been in the 1940s. During the war years, new planes had been developed that were more efficient, many of which had four engines instead of two. These newer planes were designed to carry more passengers greater distances, but were too large for Continental's purposes. Continental was still a small airline when compared with the country's other major airlines, even though its route network had been expanded greatly by the addition of Kansas City and San Antonio, Texas, as flight destinations. But regardless of the company's flight expansion, Continental decided to purchase seven two-engine Convair 340s from Douglas and only two four-engine DC-6Bs, at a total price of $7.6 million. The expenditure represented Continental's gross income for the entire year of 1951, but also made clear Six's commitment to investing in the company's future.

Two years later, as the company continued its push to increase its route network and its flight capacity, Six also engineered the company's first major acquisition. Continental purchased Pioneer Airlines, including its rights to fly into Dallas/Ft. Worth and Austin, Texas. With the purchase came a Pioneer manager by the name of Harding Lawrence, whom Six soon placed in charge of Continental's finances.

Lawrence was an instrumental factor in the success of Continental's next expansion effort, which was the biggest and most ambitious in the company's history to that point in time. In 1955, the Civil Aeronautics Board granted Continental service rights between Denver and Los Angeles, Denver and Chicago, and Chicago and Los Angeles. Operation of the three new cross-country routes put Continental in direct competition with the other major airlines, such as American, United, and TWA—each of which possessed the financial resources to put Continental out of business in a price war.

Continental knew that it would have to purchase several new airplanes once again, including a fleet of the latest jetliners. Therefore, the company invested $60 million in new aircraft: DC-7s, Viscount 810s, and Boeing 707s. The challenge to Continental was then to use its limited jet fleet to cover all of its capacity needs. The problem spurred the creation of Lawrence's "progressive maintenance" program, which routinely called one of the five 707s out of service on a rotational basis. This plan reduced the actual maintenance time spent on the airplanes and allowed the company to identify and correct any problems before they became serious. Thanks to Lawrence's idea, the company was able to use its five 707s for an average of 15 hours a day, which was the longest period of use in the industry at that time. His plan was crucial to Continental's early survival of its entrance into the cross-country flight market.

In 1959, another important player appeared at Continental when Alexander Damm left his job at TWA and was brought aboard by Six. Damm's first contribution was to end Continental's practice of leasing items such as aircraft, trucks, and equipment from other companies. He noted that the country's two most profitable airlines, Delta and Northwest, each used the lowest percentage of leased equipment. He convinced Six to cancel as many leasing arrangements as possible and begin instead to focus the company's resources on purchasing more equipment of its own.

The 1960s: Merger Attempts and Expanded Services

Entering the 1960s, Continental was enjoying a period of relatively good prosperity. In early 1961, a group of bankers in charge of the now financially troubled TWA approached Six with a lucrative offer to become the company's president. When he turned them down, making clear his loyalty to Continental, the group began making offers to merge the two companies. Six still refused, stating that a merger was not in the company's best interest at that time. Therefore, it was somewhat of a surprise later that year when Six and Ted Baker of National Airlines announced a merger of their two companies. The merger, however, was quickly canceled when Six found out that Baker also had secretly negotiated the sale of National to Maytag's Frontier Airlines.

The following year, Continental experienced the first plane crash in the company's 24-year history. The crash occurred on May 22, 1962, and was caused by a bomb that exploded aboard one of the company's 707s. There were no survivors. Continental had already planned on gradually replacing its 707 fleet with new Boeing 720s, a shorter and faster version of the 707. After the bombing, the company increased its original order from four new 720s to five.

In 1963, the Civil Aeronautics Board finally released Continental from its obligation to operate a number of unprofitable rural air services that fed passenger traffic into larger air terminals. Therefore, Continental was able to sell off its smaller aircraft and reassign the pilots and flight staff to its larger and more profitable routes. The following year, the company received a contract from

Key Dates:

1934: Varney Speed Lines is founded.
1937: Robert Foreman Six buys a 40 percent interest in Varney.
1955: Three new cross-country routes are added in an expansion drive.
1967: Continental is first awarded Micronesian routes.
1982: Texas Air Corporation acquires Continental.
1983: Continental files bankruptcy.
1986: Continental emerges from bankruptcy; Continental absorbs other airlines facing bankruptcy, including Eastern, People Express, and Frontier.
1990: Continental declares bankruptcy again.
1993: Continental regains solvency, restructures.
1994: Continental ranks last among majors for on-time performance.
1995: Incentive-led Continental ranks first among majors for on-time performance and earns its first profit in ten years.
1998: Northwest Airlines acquires a majority of voting shares.
2000: Continental buys out Northwest's holding.

the U.S. government to carry out military transportation services in Southeast Asia. A new subsidiary was formed, called Continental Air Services (CAS), and operated alongside Air America, the Central Intelligence Agency's covertly run airline. CAS, however, did not engage in any CIA activity.

Meanwhile, TWA's chairman, Howard Hughes, had fallen out of favor and was offering to sell his controlling interest in TWA to Continental and make Six the newly formed company's president. But Six knew that the deal would require the approval of TWA's new board of directors, who were happy with the company's performance under Charles Tillinghast at that time. Six once again declined the merger proposition, feeling that the management at TWA did not trust Hughes and that they would be unlikely to go along with any of his ideas.

Later that year, Continental suffered a blow to its management team, as Harding Lawrence left the company to accept a position as president of Braniff Airlines. Initially, no attempt was made to replace him. A year later, however, Six brought aboard Pierre Salinger, the late President Kennedy's press secretary, as a member of Continental's board of directors.

In the late 1960s, the Civil Aeronautics Board invited bids for a commercial air service to link the United States to the approximately 2,500 islands in the South Pacific that make up the American Trust Territory. Continental had wanted to operate a trans-Pacific route for years, and it saw this as the perfect opportunity to demonstrate its ability to do so. In November 1967, Continental was awarded routes to various islands in Micronesia and Northern Mariana. A subsidiary called Air Micronesia was created in partnership with Hawaii's Aloha Airlines and an investor group called United Micronesian. A fleet of 727s was obtained, airports along the route were modernized, and a number of hotels were constructed for tourists.

Declining Profitability in the 1970s and 1980s

Unfortunately, Continental faced numerous obstacles as it entered the 1970s, and its financial standing began to suffer. The first blow came just after Richard Nixon took over the presidency of the United States. In one of his very last acts as President, Lyndon Johnson had awarded air traffic rights to Hawaii, Australia, and New Zealand to Continental. To accommodate its increased capacity demands, the company purchased a fleet of four 747s. Barely a month later, Nixon took office and canceled Continental's rights to the three destinations. Later, the routes were awarded again to the company, but then revoked again. Continental was forced to put the four new planes into storage in a hangar in New Mexico, at a cost of $13 million per year. The routes were finally awarded to the company a third time, but three of the 747s had been sold to Iran in 1975.

That year, Continental posted a loss of $9.7 million, marking its first annual loss since 1958 and only the second in the company's 41-year history. The high cost of fuel in the mid-1970s and a poor economic climate in the United States caused the airline industry as a whole to experience a steady decline, and Continental was no exception. The Airline Deregulation Act of 1978 only exacerbated Continental's problems. The Act opened up some of the company's most stable and profitable markets to competition from other airline companies. The final hit came as Continental was obligated to honor a number of different labor agreements that were almost too expensive to maintain, because of the agreements' built-in provisions for inflation.

In 1980, Six stepped down from the day-to-day operations of the company and appointed Alvin L. Feldman as his replacement. Feldman took control of a company that was in serious financial trouble. He immediately attempted to negotiate a merger between Continental and the struggling Los Angeles-based Western Airlines, believing that a combination of forces potentially could lift both airlines back into the black. The merger plans were cut short, however, by the announcement that Texas Air Corporation had decided to increase its stake in Continental from 4.24 percent to more than 50 percent.

Instead of a merger with Western Airlines, Continental's employees made moves to purchase the airline themselves, led by two company pilots named Paul Eckel and Chuck Cheeld. Employees approved the plan by a large margin, and nine different banks agreed to help finance the $185 million employee acquisition. But months later, just before the purchase took place, the banks withdrew their support and Texas Air was able to purchase a 50.84 percent majority stake in Continental. At the company's annual meeting in 1982, Robert Six retired from Continental at the age of 74, after expressing his confidence in Texas Air Chairman Frank Lorenzo to carry Continental back into profitability.

Texas Air completed the full acquisition of Continental Airlines in October 1982. Just a year later, Lorenzo filed Chapter 11 proceedings for the company. Labor contracts were invalidated by the courts, new work rules and pay scales were created, and just 56 hours later, Continental was back in the air. It was the first time that an airline had attempted to continue operations while in bankruptcy. Workers went on strike and formed picket lines.

Management worried that travel agents would stop writing tickets for Continental and that passengers would be lost because of bad publicity surrounding the company's financial situation.

To counter the bad publicity, Continental offered a $49 fare for any nonstop flight that the airline ran. The idea was to bring passengers aboard and let them see that the airline was capable of functioning as usual, with the hope that most would then return again. The promotion was a success; not only did it earn the company return passengers, but labor opposition dissolved and employees elected to return to work. Questionable strike tactics led the pilots to repudiate their union. Soon 4,000 of the original 12,000 employees were rehired at reduced pay with an increased workload. In response, by 1985 Continental's labor costs had been reduced significantly. The following year, the company emerged from bankruptcy as a nonunion airline that sported low fares due to the industry's lowest labor costs.

Lorenzo then began acquiring numerous other airline companies facing bankruptcy, including Eastern Airlines, People Express Airlines, and Frontier Airlines. These new subsidiaries combined with Continental (which had since absorbed Texas International Airlines) to place Texas Air Corporation in more than $4.6 billion of debt. The number of passengers flying Continental had steadily increased since the strikes, however, and Continental was the only division to begin its debt repayment program. As of September 1986, Continental owed its creditors $925 million and was scheduled to break even in a decade.

In 1988, Lorenzo sold Eastern's "Air Shuttle" service to Donald Trump in an effort to keep the airline afloat. But a machinist's strike and an ever declining financial situation forced Eastern into bankruptcy the following year. The bankruptcy court then removed Eastern from Texas Air's control. Texas Air changed its name to Continental Airlines Holdings, Inc. to better reflect the amalgamation of businesses that it represented, and Lorenzo sold his stake in the company before resigning as chairman, CEO, and president. Hollis Harris, the former president of Delta Air Lines, was named as his replacement.

The 1990s and Beyond

In late 1990, fuel prices were at a high point and passenger traffic was at a low point, due to effects of the Persian Gulf War. Continental once again filed for protection under Chapter 11 of the federal bankruptcy code, joining fellow subsidiary Eastern. But Eastern could not recover and was forced to liquidate in 1991. Harris left Continental Holdings in 1991 and was replaced by former CFO Robert Ferguson. That same year, Continental sold its Seattle-Tokyo route to American for $145 million, and the following year, it sold most of its LaGuardia assets and six slots at Washington, D.C.'s National Airport to USAir for $61 million. Continental used the earnings to attempt to wrestle its way out of bankruptcy for a second time.

In 1993, Continental emerged once again from bankruptcy and underwent an extensive reorganization. All of the Continental Airlines Holdings, Inc. subsidiaries and divisions were merged into Continental Airlines, and new stock was issued to replace any previously outstanding publicly held interests in the former parent company. Ferguson remained at the new company's helm and began orchestrating plans to restructure the airline's business focus as well.

Under Ferguson, Continental went ahead with the rapid expansion of its Continental Lite operation, which represented the company's own version of Southwest Airlines' short-haul, no-meal, low-fare flights. In less than a year, the program was expanded from the use of 19 aircraft for 173 daily flights serving 14 cities, to 114 aircraft for 1,000 daily flights among 43 cities. The additional aircraft were made available by eliminating the Denver hub and redeploying planes and equipment to other locations. Unfortunately, Continental Lite proved itself to be unprofitable and contributed greatly to the company's 1994 loss of $613 million.

Going Forward in the Mid-1990s

Meanwhile, Gordon M. Bethune, a former Boeing Co. executive, had joined Continental as president and COO in early 1994. Continental Lite continued to lose money and Ferguson continued to push the program forward until he was ousted late that year. He remained as a director, but was replaced as CEO by Bethune, who immediately set in place a "Go Forward Plan" to turn the ailing company around.

First, Bethune renegotiated Continental's debt, arranged concessions from aircraft lessors, and got Boeing to agree to defer delivery of any new planes on order. He then completely cleaned house, sweeping out almost half of the company's high-ranking executives and replacing them with his own managers from businesses such as Northwest, American, and PepsiCo. He hired Gregory D. Brenneman, a former Bain & Co. consultant with no previous airline experience, as his new COO. He grounded 41 planes, slashed capacity, and cut almost 5,000 jobs in 1995. He abolished most of the company's loss-making Continental Lite services. Then, with a guided focus solely on improving the airline's service to its customers, Bethune saw results. The year 1995 not only saw the company turn a profit for the first time since 1986, but saw it turn a hefty profit of $224 million.

As the 1990s drew to a close, the company focused on the goal of luring more high-paying business travelers back to its flights. To do so, Bethune tied company bonuses to on-time performance, as a means of improving the company's dismal last place standing among major airlines for on-time performance in 1994. By early 1995, the airline had risen to a first place rank for the first time in the company's history. Bethune also brought back the frequent-flier program perks that had been cut during Ferguson's reign and spent $8 million to put food back onto some flights so that Continental would appeal to hurried business travelers.

Although Continental was clearly on the road to recovery as it neared the 21st century, it still faced many obstacles along its path to success. Namely, without a unique attribute to offer customers—aside from convenience in its three hub locations only—the airline was having a difficult time convincing passengers to stray from the other major airlines. Many analysts predicted that it would take a merger to give Continental the marketing capabilities and exposure necessary to pull itself to the top of the heap. But if the turnaround created by Bethune in 1995 and 1996 was any indication of the future, then the company seemed to possess the potential to regain the financial integrity that it had possessed during its early years.

Flying to Win in the Late 1990s

Continental logged a record $319 million in earnings in 1996. "Fly to Win" initiatives were introduced to keep the company moving forward. The airline began standardizing the fleet, mostly around the Boeing 737 for the main line and Embraer EMB 145 regional jets for Continental Express. In 1997, Continental had $4.3 billion worth of orders (127) and options (90) for Boeing 737s.

Although salaries had risen an average of 25 percent since 1994, Continental employees were still paid less than their counterparts at other airlines. Morale and attention to detail were boosted by unique incentives, such as a payment of $65 to each employee every time Continental finished in the top three on-time carriers in the United States. The company reduced absenteeism by raffling off Ford Explorers twice a year to those with perfect attendance. On-time performance and motivated employees were key components in luring demanding (and lucrative) business travelers back to the airline. Part of what made Continental's renewed focus on quality so striking was the cutbacks other airlines were making at the same time.

With major markets in the United States nearly saturated, Continental aimed to increase feeder traffic from abroad through strategic alliances with the likes of Air France, Alitalia, and Virgin Atlantic. By the late 1990s, Continental had accords with 17 airlines. The carrier lobbied the governments of Argentina and Spain for a chance to invest in Aerolineas Argentinas, an opportunity it lost to rival American Airlines. Continental also had considerable operations of its own in Europe, Latin America, and the Pacific. Flying from Newark, Continental was flying more transatlantic flights than anyone in the New York area by 1999.

In 1998 Northwest Airlines acquired a 14 percent equity stake/54 percent voting interest in Continental from President and Chief Operating Officer David Bonderman. The move headed off an attempt by Delta Air Lines to acquire Continental. Northwest paid $519 million for the shares, an investment meant to launch a ten-year strategic alliance. An antitrust lawsuit from the Justice Department two years later pressured Northwest to sell its shares back to Continental. Continental sold its own minority stake in America West in 2000, and two years later ended a code-sharing agreement with the Phoenix-based airline.

Scaling Back in 2001

Continental was the first among major U.S. airlines to cut its staff in the wake of the September 11 terrorist attacks. It let go of 12,000 employees (20 percent of the workforce). Most of these, however, would be called back to work within a year. Bethune soon began lobbying the government for an industry-wide federal bailout.

A fourth quarter loss of $149 million left the airline $95 million in the red for the year, a relatively small setback compared with those of other major airlines. The carrier parked 61 of its jets and 23 turboprops as it waited for traffic to return to normal.

ExpressJet Holdings Inc., the parent company for the regional jet unit Continental Express, was spun off in April 2002 in an IPO that raised $480 million. The IPO had been delayed several months due to the September 11 attacks. Continental owned 53 percent of ExpressJet after the offering.

Continental was reported to have approached Delta Air Lines about a possible merger in 1996. This did not happen, but in August 2002, Continental, Delta, and Northwest proposed a massive ten-year code-share agreement. This would allow the airlines to sell tickets on each other's flights, and to share frequent flier programs and airport lounges. Together the three airlines had a 36 percent share of domestic traffic. The alliance was a response to a pending pairing of United and US Airways.

Principal Subsidiaries

Continental Micronesia, Inc.

Principal Competitors

AMR Corporation; Delta Air Lines Inc.; UAL Corporation.

Further Reading

Antosh, Nelson, "Airlines Will Part Company; Continental to End America West Link," *Houston Chronicle,* March 28, 2002, p. B1.
Armbruster, William, "Rebounding from 9/11: Continental Restores Services, Works to Increase Revenue Yield," *JoC Week,* February 18, 2002, p. 20.
Banks, Howard, "A Sixties Industry in a Nineties Economy," *Forbes,* May 9, 1994, p. 107.
Bethune, Gordon, and Scott Huler, "From Worst to First" (excerpt from *From Worst to First: Behind the Scenes of Continental's Remarkable Comeback), Fortune,* May 25, 1998, pp. 185+.
——, *From Worst to First: Behind the Scenes of Continental's Remarkable Comeback,* New York: Wiley, 1998.
Bond, David, "Recovery, Phase Two: Majors Change Strategy from Super-Sized Alliances to Drinks Over the Atlantic; Carriers Stop Waiting for the Market to Save Them," *Aviation Week & Space Technology,* September 2, 2002, p. 24.
Brenneman, Greg, "Right Away and All at Once: How We Saved Continental," *Harvard Business Review,* September/October 1998, pp. 162+.
Carey, Susan, Scott McCartney, and John Wilke, "Antitrust Suit Could Complicate Future Airline Mergers—Northwest's Controlling Stake in Continental Goes Under Scrutiny in Trial This Week," *Wall Street Journal,* October 23, 2000, p. B10.
Clark, Andrew, "Sex, Scotch and Speed: Gordon Bethune, Chairman and Chief Executive, Continental Airlines," *Guardian* (Manchester, U.K.), September 21, 2002, p. 34.
"Continental Cargo Continues Growth Streak," *Journal of Commerce and Commercial,* September 29, 1997, pp. S18+.
"ExpressJet IPO Proves a Flier," *Airfinance Journal,* May 2002, p. 19.
Flint, Perry, "Speed Racer: Gordon Bethune Has Continental Airlines on the Fast Track to Success," *Air Transport World,* April 1997, pp. 33+.
Flynn, Gillian, "A Flight Plan for Success," *Workforce,* July 1997, pp. 72+.
Goldberg, Laura, "A Woman Who Became a High Flier; Continental Executive Is Still a Pilot," *Houston Chronicle,* February 26, 2000, p. C1.

Hammonds, Keith H., "Continental's Turnaround Pilot," *Fast Company,* December 2001, p. 96.

Harris, Nicole, "Marketing Accord by Three Airlines Raises Questions," *Wall Street Journal,* August 26, 2002, p. A2.

Huey, John, "Outlaw Flyboy CEOs" (interview of Gordon Bethune and Herb Kelleher), *Fortune,* November 13, 2000, pp. 237+.

Josselson, Steven, "Houston, We Have a Problem," *Airfinance Journal,* February 2002, pp. 30–32.

Knez, Marc, and Duncan Simester, "Firm-Wide Incentives and Mutual Monitoring at Continental Airlines," *Journal of Labor Economics,* October 2001, pp. 743–72.

Lipowicz, Alice, "High-Flying Continental Revs Up Newark Plan; While Rivals Trim Growth, Airline to Sharply Expand Foreign Flights," *Crain's New York Business,* March 20, 2000, p. 32.

Moore, Heidi, "ExpressJet Might Fly But Won't Float," *Daily Deal,* September 18, 2001.

Murphy, Michael, *The Airline That Pride Almost Bought,* New York: Watts, 1986.

Oehmke, Ted, "Plane Spoken," *Texas Monthly,* June 1998, pp. 58–65.

O'Reilly, Brian, "The Mechanic Who Fixed Continental: Believe It or Not, CEO Gordon Bethune, a Former Navy Mechanic, Has Made Continental the Best Airline in the U.S.," *Fortune,* December 20, 1989, pp. 176+.

Scippa, Ray, *Point to Point, The Sixty Year History of Continental Airlines,* Houston: Pioneer Publications, Inc., 1994.

Serling, Robert J., *The Story of Robert Six and Continental Airlines,* New York: Doubleday, 1974.

Stevens, Shannon, "Richard Metzner," *Brandweek,* October 20, 1997, pp. 98–101.

Thompson, Richard, "Do the Right Thing," *Corporate Counsel,* December 2001, pp. 54+.

Van der Kraats, Stephan A., "Gaining a Competitive Edge Through Airline Alliances," *Competitiveness Review,* Summer/Fall 2000, pp. 56+.

Whitaker, Richard, "We Win Together," *Airline Business,* July 1997, pp. 34+.

Zellner, Wendy, "Back to 'Coffee, Tea, or Milk?,' " *Business Week,* July 3, 1995, p. 52.

——, "The Right Place, the Right Time," *Business Week,* May 27, 1996, p. 74.

——, "Why Continental's CEO Fell to Earth," *Business Week,* November 7, 1994, p. 32.

—Laura E. Whiteley
—update: Frederick C. Ingram

Cott Corporation

207 Queen's Quay West, Suite 340
Toronto, Ontario M5J 1A7
Canada
Telephone: (416) 203-3898
Fax: (416) 203-8171
Web site: http://www.cott.com

Public Company
Incorporated: 1955 as Cott Beverages Ltd.
Employees: 2,228
Sales: US$1.09 billion (2001)
Stock Exchanges: New York Toronto
Ticker Symbols: COT (NYSE); BCB (Toronto)
NAIC: 312111 Soft Drink Manufacturing

Toronto-based Cott Corporation is the world's top supplier of private label (although the company prefers to call it "retailer brand") carbonated soft drinks. Cott has 15 beverage production facilities located in Canada, the United States, and the United Kingdom, as well as a research facility in Columbus, Georgia. Major customers include Wal-Mart and Safeway in North America and the J. Sainsbury grocery chain in the United Kingdom. The Pencer family, Cott's founders, have in recent years sold their interest in the business to Thomas H. Lee Co., a Boston investment firm, which now runs the company with a 34 percent ownership position.

Harry Pencer Founds Company in 1955

Cott's founder, Harry Pencer, was a clothier in Montreal in the early 1950s and looking for a new business when he became involved in the soft drink industry by happenstance. Supposedly, his three sons—William, Samuel, and Gerald—were attending summer camp on Lake Winnipesaukee in New Hampshire and developed a taste for the regional New England Cott soda brand and its "17 heavenly delicious flavors." Cott Beverage Corporation was established in 1923 by Polish immigrant Solomon Cott and his son Harry Cott, in Port Chester, New York. In 1952 Harry Pencer began to import Cott soda to the province of Quebec, where the fruit flavors such as orange,

grape, black cherry, and raspberry proved popular. In 1955 he acquired Stewart Bottling Company, then licensed the Canadian rights to the Cott label and formed Cott Beverages Ltd. to bottle the Cott line of sodas using the Stewart facility. The Cott family eventually sold the company, and the U.S. rights to the Cott label, to Cadbury Schweppes.

The Canadian business was moderately successful during its first 20 years, establishing a following for its fruit flavors and brand loyalty in the Quebec province. The one area where Cott clearly failed was in producing a good cola, which was essential in achieving a higher level of success in the marketplace. (According to the Pencer sons, their father occasionally attempted taste tests between Cott cola and Coca-Cola or Pepsi—or simply poured Cott cola in the bottles of the major brands without telling them—but they claimed that they were always able to tell the difference.) Cott experienced a setback in 1970 with the recall of cyclamates used as an artificial sweetener in beverages, but by 1976 the company began to extend its reach across Canada. Although it remained a strong brand in Quebec, Cott was struggling when Harry Pencer died in 1983. That year the company lost $367,000.

Harry's sons inherited Cott, and were advised by Coopers & Lybrand to simply liquidate the business. Nevertheless, the eldest son, Bill, along with President Maurice Chouinard, attempted to turn around Cott. The most important step they took was to cut costs by eliminating delivery and the company's 60-truck operation—instead customers picked up the product themselves. As a result Cott was able to dramatically reduce the price of its soda, six bottles now retailing at 99 cents rather than $2.49. To better exploit this low-price niche in the Ontario market, Sam Pencer gave up his job as an insurance broker to work for the company on a full-time basis. The family then took the company public in 1986 under the Quebec Stock Savings Plan. Although shares went out at $7 they soon lost half their value, but other independent bottlers were also struggling at the time. In 1989 Cott bought out its chief competitor in Ontario, Tricopack Beverages. To this point the family business always found a way to survive, but just barely. It had a market capitalization of less than $10 million in 1989 when it began a period of remarkable growth under the guidance of Gerry Cott, the youngest of Harry's three sons.

Company Perspectives:

Our success lies in the production of innovative, high quality retail brand beverages combined with world-class packaging.

Gerry had been the least involved in the family business yet was named chairman of the board at a time when his name was flying high in the financial world. A natural entrepreneur, brash and visionary, he built a financial empire in the 1980s that ultimately crashed and burned. After college in the mid-1960s he ran a gumball machine concession in Montreal for the Steinberg supermarket chain, due in large part to his brother having married Ida Steinberg. He then managed to convince the CEO of the Rolls-Royce Canadian operation to meet with him and asked to run the auto plant's cafeteria. Pencer claimed to run the cafeteria at the Steinberg's headquarters and even escorted Rolls-Royce's head of office services to the cafeteria where he pretended to be in charge, much to the befuddlement of the personnel. The trick worked, he won Rolls-Royce's business and within several years he was running Montreal's largest institutional catering operation. In the 1970s Pencer moved to Calgary to manage a Honda dealership and once again found a way to parlay a small venture into a much larger enterprise—Financial Trustco Capital. In the early years of the 1980s he pursued the dream of creating the first Canadian financial services supermarket. Fueled by junk bonds sold by Michael Milken and Drexel Burnham Lambert, Pencer grew Financial Trustco into a $2 billion insurance, trust, brokerage, and real estate conglomerate. The company was criticized for dubious, although legal, accounting, as well as its reliance on junk bonds. When the stock market crashed in October 1987, the business was overextended and in danger of collapsing. In 1988 Pencer stepped aside and out of the public spotlight, as the main subsidiary, Financial Trust Co., was sold off in a government bailout.

Making a Comeback with Cott: 1989

Chastened and his spirit all but broken, Gerry Pencer returned to the business world in 1989 at the behest of his brother Sam, who convinced him to help run the family soda business. As a result, Chouinard resigned as Cott's president. By now, Sam had already taken the first step in pursuing the private label business, contracted by President's Choice, the Loblaw supermarket chain's well regarded private label business, to supply flavored sodas along with another bottler, HPI Beverages of Edmonton. The Cott plant, capable of producing 15 million cases of soda a year, only had business that totaled three million cases. In order to take advantage of that excess capacity, Gerry approached Coca-Cola and won a five-year contract to bottle Coke, which added credibility to Cott. At the same time, Royal Crown (RC) contacted Sam about taking over the RC franchise in Quebec, due to the recent sale of Canada Dry to Cadbury Schweppes, which was unable to bottle in Canada because of a deal with Coke. Cott assumed the RC license for Quebec in 1989, then added the Ontario franchise the following year.

Pencer saw the Royal Crown connection as a way to realize a longstanding dream of his father's: producing a good tasting cola. In blind taste tests Royal Crown held its own with Coke

and Pepsi but never had the proper marketing to challenge the top two brands. Pencer tried to convince Royal Crown executives to let Cott use their cola concentrate in a modified form for the private label business. While seeking potential supermarket partners, Pencer learned in 1990 that President's Choice was looking for a new cola supplier. He and Sam met with the head, David Nichol, who had also been frustrated in his attempts to produce a cola that could rival Coke and Pepsi in taste. In order to win his business, he told the brothers that Cott would have to meet three conditions: come up with a cola that tasted good, improve the company's packaging, and come in with a price point 30 percent less than Coke and Pepsi. According to Nichol, he never expected to see the Pencers again.

Nichol had become a celebrity by masterminding President's Choice, which transcended the private label category, becoming an upscale in-store brand of some 1,700 products, accounting for close to C$1.5 billion in annual sales. Not only were his taste buds the deciding factor for the addition of new products, his was the face that personally recommended on television that Canadian consumers should try such President's Choice fare as Ancient Damascus Tangy Pomegranate Sauce. In college Nichol had roomed with Galen Weston, whose family owned Loblaw Companies Ltd., Canada's major supermarket and food merchandising group. After Weston took charge of the business he turned to Nichol in early 1972 to help him find an executive to turn around the struggling Loblaw's supermarket chain. Nichol recommended Richard Currie, a colleague at McKinsey & Co., an international management consulting firm where the two men worked. Currie was then instrumental in Weston hiring Nichol to assist him at Loblaw. For several years Nichol was involved in store operations, but product development was clearly his passion. In 1983 he began work on the first products for President's Choice, the brand inspired by the success of the St. Michael's house brand in the United Kingdom. A year later Nichol was made president of Loblaw International Merchants to devote all of his time to building President's Choice, which proved so successful that he was able to extend the brand to a number of major supermarket chains in the United States. Like Pencer, Nichol dreamed big, as well as shared a love of food. He increasingly viewed President's Choice as a revolution, a way to shift the balance of power in the food business from national brand manufacturers to the supermarkets.

After their initial meeting early in 1990, Pencer returned to see Nichol, bringing with him samples of Royal Crown cola. Nichol wanted some changes to the taste of the cola but was very much interested. Pencer then went to Royal Crown offering to add 50 million cases to the company's 150 million cases of annual volume. Moreover, by selling RC cola as a house brand the supermarkets would have an incentive to make shelf space for the product. To seal the deal, however, Pencer had to fly to Florida to meet with Royal Crown's current owner, the elderly, notorious corporate raider Victor Posner. After a week of negotiations with Posner, Pencer emerged with a 25-year private-label rights agreement for North America and a manufacturing agreement throughout the world.

Contract for President's Choice Cola: 1990

Cott took over the President's Choice cola contract and began shipping in March 1990. The soda was an immediate success and Pencer and Nichol became close friends, taking vacations as well as attending trade shows together. Following the house brand strategy Cott grew at a dramatic rate in the early 1990s. From $43 million in sales for fiscal 1989, the company reached the $500 million mark in 1993. Most of the growth took place in the United States where Cott had no bottling facilities. In order to supply the market, the company contracted independent bottlers with excess production capacity, just as Cott had done with Coke. In effect, Cott developed a third soft drink system in North America. The company also expanded through acquisitions, picking up assets of Vess Beverages and Vess Specialty Packaging in the states, and moving into the United Kingdom market with the purchase of Hero Drinks Groups. In addition, Cott signed up the United Kingdom's largest supermarket chain, J. Sainsbury PLC, as well as a number of major chains in other countries, including Spain and Japan. A recession, which made house brands a more attractive option for consumers, also helped to spur Cott's growth. Although Coca-Cola and Pepsi were in no danger of losing significant amounts of market share to the Canadian upstart, both were forced to respond by cutting prices and spending money on promotions to shore up their positions.

In 1991 the company changed its name to Cott Corporation. As time passed Pencer began to view Cott as something more than just a beverage company, his earlier dream of building a financial services giant returning in a new form. If excess production capacity could be harnessed to inexpensively manufacture private label soda, he reasoned, why not copack other products? To help retailers launch their own private-label programs, in 1994 Pencer created a subsidiary, Retail Brands International. To help pursue his vision of building a new age General Mills, he then lured Nichol away from President's Choice, making him chairman and chief executive of another subsidiary, Destination International Inc. (DPI), to develop new private-label products. The initial plan was to target product categories that were similar to the soft drink business at the time Cott entered the private label business. They had to be high-volume, popular brand products that nevertheless did not provide much profit to retailers, such as beer, pet food, and snack foods including ice cream and cookies.

In the end, however, the dream was ill-conceived and short-lived. Although Pencer managed to grow Cott's annual revenues to more than $1 billion by 1997 he was unable to produce

suitable profits. Much of Cott's rapid success was the result not of visionary genius but of taking advantage of Royal Crown's years of development and the soft drink industry's unique excess production capacity. Nichol and his large staff certainly tried their best to produce quality products at DPI's test kitchens, but life without the backing of a college roommate and his giant supermarket chain made business a little more problematic. Nichol may have had a discerning palate, but his taste now seemed to diverge too much from the mainstream. When he headed President's Choice he could simply push a product through the Loblaw system and onto the store's shelves. Now he had a far more difficult time gaining entry, as a result spending an excessive amount of money to secure shelf space.

Early in 1997 Pencer was diagnosed with cancer and underwent brain surgery and chemotherapy. While he struggled to regain his health, the prospects for DPI grew grimmer by the week and before the year was out Cott wrote off the subsidiary and Nichol was out of a job. Several months later, in February 1998, Pencer succumbed to cancer. He left Cott a much larger company but in a perilous condition. Not only debt laden, it had a disparate collection of businesses, from design houses to a mismatched collection of private label products, including pet food and frozen foods. Moreover, its main soft drink business was plagued by inconsistent quality. Near the end Pencer recognized the limitations of copacking and as part of a restructuring effort began to acquire bottling operations to gain better control.

Cott had grown too large too quickly in the 1990s and with the death of Gerry Pencer it was in dire shape. The price of its stock, which reached $35 a share in late 1993, now plummeted to $3. In June 1998 the Thomas H. Lee firm, best known for the money it made in Snapple, paid $70 million for the Pencer family stake in the business and installed a new CEO from the States, Frank Weise. He had many years of experience in the consumer products business, including 24 years with Procter & Gamble and five years at Campbell's Soup. Just prior to taking over Cott he also oversaw the turnaround of a private-label company that specialized in hygiene products, making him an ideal candidate to tackle the problems at Cott. Weise quickly set about cleaning up the books, which were legal but overly aggressive, thereby regaining credibility with investors. He also returned Cott's focus to its core beverage business, selling off the design, frozen-food, and pet food divisions, as well as nonessential soft drink operations in Australia and Norway. Efficiencies at the company's 15 North America and U.K. manufacturing facilities were improved by sharing best practices and a consolidation of seven divisions into just two units. Moreover, he was uninterested in challenging Coke and Pepsi, or pursuing any grand plans beyond exploiting a very lucrative niche in the soft drink industry.

Because Cott still retained the Royal Crown formula, and Coke and Pepsi were once again raising prices, Weise was presented with a chance to quickly restore Cott's beverage business. With revenues improving and the company starting to turn a profit once again, he was soon able to shift from turnaround mode to growth. In late 2000 Cott was in a strong enough position to pay $71.5 million in cash to acquire Concord Beverage and its well-known Vintage brand. A deal of even more importance came in June 2001 when Cott bought out its Royal Crown cola concentrate contract from Cadbury Schweppes and acquired

RC's international division as well as a Columbus, Georgia, plant. It also acquired the U.S. rights to the Cott label, sold decades earlier by the heirs of Harry Cott. Not only did the company fully control its own name, it now owned the RC cola formula and essentially controlled its own destiny.

Principal Divisions

Cott Beverages Canada; Cott Beverages USA; Cott United Kingdom and Europe.

Principal Competitors

Cadbury Schweppes PLC; The Coca-Cola Company; PepsiCo, Inc.

Further Reading

Kelley, Kristine Portno, "Cott to Get You," *Beverage Industry,* April 1995, p. 47.

Macisaac, Merle, "One Flew into the Cuckoo's Nest," *Canadian Business,* June 1996, p. 104.

Millman, J., "Rich Niche," *Forbes,* May 25, 1992, p. 116.

Pencer, Gerry, "You Gotta Potentialize," *Report on Business Magazine,* December 1999, p. 76.

Prince, Greg W., "The Cott's Meow," *Beverage World,* August 15, 2000, p. 24.

Silcoff, Sean, "Goodbye, Galloping Gourmet," *Canadian Business,* October 31, 1997, p. 26.

Stevenson, Mark, "The Hired Hand Waves Goodbye," *Canadian Business,* August 1994.

Wells, Jennifer, "Cheers!," *Globe and Mail,* February 21, 1992, p. 34.

—Ed Dinger

Dogi International Fabrics S.A.

08320 El Masnou
Barcelona
Spain
Telephone: (+34) 93-462-80-00
Fax: (+34) 93-462-80-36
Web site: http://www.dogi.com

Public Company
Incorporated: 1954 as Dogi SA
Employees: 2,010
Sales: EUR 169 million ($149.7 million) (2001)
Stock Exchanges: Madrid
Ticker Symbol: DGI
NAIC: 313312 Textile and Fabric Finishing (Except
   Broadwoven Fabric) Mills; 313311 Broadwoven Fabric
   Finishing Mills; 313230 Nonwoven Fabric Mills

Dogi International Fabrics S.A. is the world's leading manufacturer of elastic textiles for the lingerie, swimwear, and sportswear markets. Based in El Masnou, in Barcelona, Spain, Dogi has achieved its leading position through technological innovation and acquisitions—including the purchase of four plants in Germany, China, the Philippines, and Thailand from Courtaulds Textiles, a Sara Lee subsidiary, in 2001. Following the integration of that acquisition Dogi expects its sales to near EUR 240 million by the end of 2002, up from nearly EUR 170 million in 2001. The acquisition also doubles the company's manufacturing park, which is centered primarily in Spain and includes one plant in France (sold in 2002 but which remains managed by the company until 2005). More than two-thirds of Dogi's sales take place outside of Spain; 56 percent of the company's sales come from the European market, where the company is the number one elastic textiles manufacturer with a market share of more than 18 percent. Dogi has targeted the NAFTA market, particularly the United States, for intensified growth; the NAFTA trade zone accounts for 13 percent of the company's sales, and the company holds a 5 percent share of that market. The Sara Lee/Courtaulds Textiles acquisition also has raised Dogi's profile in the Asian market, a chief source of elastic textile-based clothing. Following

the acquisition, Dogi expects the Asian markets to top 30 percent of its sales; the company's market position in those markets is near 10 percent. Dogi is listed on the Madrid stock exchange and is led by Chairman Josep Domènech Giménez, son of the company's founder.

Family Textiles Manufacturer in the 1950s

Dogi was founded by Josep Domènech Farre, a bricklayer by trade, and his wife Conception as a small, family-owned weaving workshop in El Masnou, in Barcelona. In 1954, however, their son, Josep Domènech Giménez, joined the family business and helped organize a weaving cooperative with other local weaving shops. In addition to manufacturing the broader category of "commodity" textiles, the cooperative also began producing elastic fabrics, which, with the generalization of plastics-based fibers, such as nylon and its derivatives, were in the process of revolutionizing the undergarments industry.

The younger Domènech was quick to recognize the importance of an emerging category in the textiles industry, that of elastic fabrics. Taking control of the cooperative—and renaming it Dogi, using a contraction of his own last names—Domènech also had recognized the need to invest in new technologies in order to claim a place in the elastic fabrics market, unlike more basic textiles. The company's willingness to invest early gave it a long advance over potential competitors as the price of entry rose with the development of new fabric types, such as Dupont's Lycra, first introduced in the late 1950s, and weaving and other technologies. A breakthrough in the elastic fibers market came with the ability to dye elastic textiles and the Domènechs added their first dying and fixing machinery in 1962. Three years later, the company made its mark on the textiles industry, pioneering the blending of elastomer (i.e., elastic) fibers with woven fabrics to create new and more supple textile materials.

Josep Domènech Giménez helped build the company into the leading elastic textiles producer in Spain. In the 1970s, the company expanded rapidly, building up its industrial base with a second factory in Cardedou, Spain. The company's fortunes soared, especially with the beginning of the production of Lycra on an industrial scale. Although Domènech's company contin-

Company Perspectives:

"I have always thought that in the business world, you should have your feet placed firmly in the present, and focus your attention, fully and clearly, on the future. In order to do so, you must be receptive to the needs of the moment, and sensitive enough to foresee the possibilities that may be ahead. I believe this spirit is very much present in DOGI International Fabrics, where a very realistic and demanding sense of what is going on coexists with a very open and adaptable mentality, capable of taking on different situations and challenges. Furthermore, I have always been very aware of the fact that the company is a living entity, in a constant process of movement and renewal; nothing can stand still or come to a stop. We must therefore nourish that life, sharing dreams and enthusiasm with all of those who make up the dynamic and dedicated human team that constitutes the very heart of DOGI International Fabrics. I would like these lines to serve as a tribute to the team that, throughout these years, has made DOGI International Fabrics joint project, possible."

—Josep Domènech Giménez, chairman

ued to produce "commodity" elastic fabrics, it turned its production more and more toward the manufacture of value-added elastics, especially those based on the new Dupont materials.

The successful adaptation of Lycra as a textile material represented another breakthrough in the textiles industry, permitting fabrics that were lightweight, highly elastic, colorful, comfortable to wear, and waterproof. These qualities quickly made Lycra the material of choice for swimsuit fashions, and that industry became an important market for Dogi's elastic products as well. Nonetheless, low-end commodity elastic retained a strong part of the company's sales.

Internationalization in the 1990s

At the beginning of the 1990s, Dogi had captured the leading share in its domestic market, yet remained a minor player on the international scene. Only about one-fourth of Dogi's sales, which reached around 5.5 billion Spanish pesetas (worth approximately EUR 33 million) in the early 1990s, came from outside of Spain. Yet, with the dominant player in the elastics market in Spain, the company found little room for further domestic growth.

A slump in the Spanish textile market in the early 1990s, coupled with the coming end of European trade barriers—which was set to open the Spanish market to outside competition, particularly from Italian elastic fabrics producers—brought the company to a crossroads. The family-owned company also was confronted with Domènech's own approaching retirement and the need to make a decision: whether to maintain a small, family-owned status, or open itself to outside investment capital and a more professional management team.

Domènech chose the latter course. In 1992, the company sold a share of its capital to Spanish investment bank Mercapital, a move that solidified the company's financial posi-

tion as it braced itself for the new internationalization of the European market. The following year, Domènech brought in Richard Rechter as Dogi's managing director. Rechter, whose grandparents had emigrated from Russia to France at the dawn of the 20th century, had come to Spain at the age of four, and had worked for a number of companies before becoming a top executive at Sony Spain.

Rechter, who also was given nearly 8 percent of the company, was given the mandate to transform Dogi into an internationally operating company. Domènech, who remained company chairman, and Rechter set about building a more professionally structured management team, including identifying the most promising members of the company's existing staff. Rechter also helped instill a new corporate culture, transforming the company from a product-driven producer to a service-oriented manufacturing partner.

A major part of the company's new strategy involved heightening its focus on higher-end, added-value fabrics—by the beginning of the next decade, the company's product mix had shifted to the extent that nearly 90 percent of Dogi's sales came from the high-end segment. To achieve this transformation, Dogi began an aggressive investment program, stepping up its in-house research and development capacity.

Dogi quickly began to see the fruits of its transformation, as sales began to rise by some 30 percent per year—already topping 7.4 billion pesetas (approximately EUR 45.5 million) in 1994. By 1995, sales had climbed past 10 billion pesetas (EUR 62 million), more than 40 percent of which now came from outside of Spain. An important breakthrough came when Marks & Spencer tapped Dogi as one of its primary elastic fabrics suppliers—and quickly came to represent some 5 percent of Dogi's total sales. Although the importance of Marks & Spencer to the company's revenues was to come to haunt it at the beginning of the next century—as the British retailer struggled with slipping sales—the contract helped raise Dogi's profile on the international market.

In 1995, Dogi made its first true international expansion move when it acquired Nouvelle Elastelle, based in Le Puy, France. That company had built up a leading position in France, with a 50 percent share of that country's domestic market for elastic fabrics. Yet Elastelle had been hit hard by the recession of the early 1990s and teetered on bankruptcy by mid-decade. Dogi restructured its new French holdings, and succeeded in quickly restoring the operation to profitability. The addition of Elastelle helped boost Dogi's sales past 12.5 billion pesetas by the end of 1996, and also gave the company the leading position in the European market. International sales now represented more than 50 percent of Dogi's total sales. For the time being, however, Dogi's sales remained focused almost entirely on the European market.

Domènech bought back Mercapital's share of the company in 1996, bringing his ownership position past 89 percent, as the company prepared for a public offering. That came at the beginning of 1998, when the company listed on the Spanish stock exchange and became one of the most successful initial public offerings (IPOs) of the year. The IPO enabled the company to begin planning its assault on the global market. Follow-

Key Dates:

1954: Josep Domènech Giménez establishes a textile co-operative based around his family's weaving shop in Barcelona and then takes control of the cooperative, giving it the name Dogi.

1962: Dogi invests in dying and fixing machinery for elastic fabrics.

1970s: The company expands its industrial capacity, including adding Lycra-based fabrics production; Dogi becomes the Spanish leader for elastic fabrics.

1992: Domènech sells a share of the company to Mercapital as a first step in a new internationally oriented growth strategy.

1993: Richard Rechter is hired as managing director to lead the internationalization of the company's sales.

1995: The company acquires Elastelle of France, giving it the leading share in France, which makes Dogi the leading elastic fabrics producer in Europe.

1996: Domènech buys back its shares from Mercapital.

1998: Dogi goes public on the Spanish stock exchange, becoming the most successful IPO of the year.

1999: Dogi acquires 55.5 percent of Textiles ATA of Mexico, giving the company entry into the NAFTA market.

2001: The company buys up the rest of Textiles ATA, and then acquires the Penn Elastics division from Sara Lee's Courtaulds Textiles division, making Dogi the world leader in elastic fabrics.

2002: Dogi announces a EUR 24 million investment and expansion program for Asia; the company sells its Elastelle factory to Fontanille.

ing the IPO, Domènech's share of the company dropped back to slightly more than 50 percent.

Dogi set out to conquer two specific markets: the NAFTA market, especially the United States, which represented one of the world's largest markets, and the Asian markets, which had become the epicenter of the world textiles industry as manufacturers shifted production to lower-cost facilities in China, Malaysia, and elsewhere in the region. Whereas the company managed to establish a foothold in Asia, which represented revenues of some EUR 5 million, its entry into the North American market was hampered by high trade barriers—including a surtax of more than 22 percent on textile goods manufactured outside of the NAFTA zone.

Dogi overcame this obstacle in 1999 when it acquired a majority share of Textiles ATA, based in Tlatleplatl, north of Mexico City, in Mexico. The purchase gave Dogi a 55.5 percent stake in ATA (the company took complete control in January 2001) and access to the North American markets. By then, Dogi had added a new component to its operations, rounding out its core production of fabrics for the lingerie and swimwear markets with the launch of new fabric lines for the sportswear market. Meanwhile, the company's operations were boosted when it reached a cooperation agreement with France's Noyon, one of the European market's leading swimwear producers.

In 2001, Dogi turned its attention more fully to the Asian market. The rising importance of Asian textiles producers in Europe, which had seen its textile production capacity drastically diminished during the 1990s, required Dogi to establish itself in those markets as well. The company's opportunity came in April 2001 when the Sara Lee Corporation, long one of Dogi's major customers, announced its intention to sell off its elastic textiles operations, part of its Courtaulds Textiles division.

For $43 million, Dogi acquired Courtaulds' four elastic fabrics divisions, which included Penn Elastics and its factories in Germany, China, Thailand, and the Philippines. The acquisition also made Dogi the clear worldwide leader in the high-end elastic fabrics sector, and especially boosted its Asian operations, which then accounted for some 31 percent of the company's total sales. The enlarged company, which changed its name to Dogi International Fabrics, was now able to expand its customer targets beyond specialty manufacturers, such as Sara Lee, Victoria's Secret, and others, and target the private labels of major department stores and other retail groups.

As the company integrated its new operations, it was able to forecast a rise in revenues to as high as EUR 240 million by the end of 2002—nearly 45 percent of which was expected to come from outside of the European market. The company also began restructuring its manufacturing operations, refocusing its European production around its Spanish and German facilities. In September 2002 the company announced that it had reached an agreement to sell its Elastelle manufacturing facility to French group Fontanille. Under terms of the sale, Dogi kept the Elastelle brand and commercial organization, as well as use of the Elastelle facility, until 2005. Dogi had completed its transformation from family-owned firm to international leader.

Principal Subsidiaries

Dogi International Fabrics, S.A.; Société Nouvelle Ellastelle; Dogi Holding, B.V. (Netherlands); Dogi Hong-Kong Limited; Textiles Ata, S.A. de C.V. (Mexico); Dogi UK; Seamfree Int (U.K.); Dogi USA Inc.; Courtaulds Textiles Holding GmbH; Penn Elastic GmbH; Penn Italia s.r.L.; Penn Fabrics Jiangsu Co. Ltd. (China); Penn Asia Co. Ltd (Thailand); Jareeporn Pranita Co. Ltd (Thailand; 50%); Laguna Realty Corporation (Philippines; 80%); Penn Philippines Inc.; Penn Philippines Export Inc.

Principal Competitors

Formosa Chemicals and Fibre Corp.; E.I. du Pont de Nemours and Co.; Asia Fiber PCL; Toray Industries Inc; DLH Industries Inc.; Owens Corning; InterTech Group Inc.; Milliken and Co.; Toyobo Company Ltd.; Collins and Aikman Products Co.; Springs Industries Inc.; Formosa Chemicals and Fibre Corp; Nisshinbo Industries Inc; Nam Liong Enterprise Company Ltd.; Beaulieu of America Inc.; Tulsyan NEC Ltd.; Burlington Industries Inc.; Midland Plastics Inc; Interface Inc.; Wellman Inc.; Nitto Boseki Company Ltd.; Pillowtex Corporation; Hexcel Corporation.

Further Reading

"Dogi apuesta por consolidar sus compras para dejar las perdidas," *Expansion,* June 20, 2002.

"Dogi, de compañía local a compañía global," *Textil Expres,* June 2001.

"Dogi se viste con traje de campana," *Actualidad Economica,* December 25, 2000, p. 34.

"Dogi to Invest 28 Mln Eur to 2004 in Factories, Asian Growth," *AFX EUROPE,* August 26, 2002.

Monget, Karyn, "Dogi's Global Plans," *WWD,* May 7, 2001, p. 18.

Sala, Alessandra, "Dogi alla conquista del mercato globale," *PLUS,* July 2001.

Salsa, Carlos, "Una pyme catalana protagoniza la primera salida a Bolsa de 1998," *Expansion,* January 19, 1998.

"Spain's Dogi Buys Sara Lee Companies in Asia," *Reuters,* April 27, 2001.

—M.L. Cohen

ElkCorp

14643 Dallas Parkway, Suite 1000
Dallas, Texas 75254-8890
U.S.A.
Telephone: (972) 851-0500
Fax: (972) 851-0550
Web site: http://www.elcor.com

Public Company
Incorporated: 1965 as Elcor Chemical Corporation
Employees: 1,141
Sales: $506.5 million (2002)
Stock Exchanges: New York
Ticker Symbol: ELK
NAIC: 324122 Asphalt Shingle and Coating Materials
    Manufacturing

Formerly known as Elcor Corporation, Dallas-based ElkCorp chose its current name to more closely identify the company with its Elk brand of shingles, which provides the bulk of the company's revenues. Two business segments comprise ElkCorp: Elk Premium Building Products, and several unrelated ventures lumped under Elk Technologies Group. Building Products accounts for approximately 90 percent of ElkCorp's revenues, and most of that amount is attributed to the sale of premium laminated fiberglass asphalt shingles, manufactured in plants located in Texas, Pennsylvania, California, and Alabama. The company also produces nonwoven fabrics at its Texas plant for use in asphalt shingles as well as other building and construction applications. Elk Technologies Group includes four businesses. The first, Cybershield, applies conductive coatings to plastic components used in cellular phones, PDAs, computers, and other electronics in order to mitigate electrical interference and create circuitry and antennae. The Chromium Corporation subsidiary applies chrome and other finishes to extend the life of major parts used in railroad and marine diesel engines. Elk Technologies is devoted to the development and marketing of a fire retardant coating, VersaShield. Originally intended for use in building products, VersaShield is now being applied to consumer products, such as mattresses, upholstered furniture, curtains, and bed clothing. The final subsidiary, Ortloff Engi-

neers, offers technologies and engineering services to the oil and gas industry and the sulfur recovery industry.

Founding the Company in 1965

The driving force behind the creation of ElkCorp was Roy E. Campbell, an engineer who later in life decided to apply his skills to business. Born in Dallas, he received a degree in civil engineering from Rice University in 1948, then went to work for AMOCO oil. In 1955 he and three colleagues formed a Midland, Texas, engineering consulting firm, Leibrock and Landreth, which soon changed its name to Leibrock, Landreth, Campbell, and Callaway. Deciding they wanted to become entrepreneurs, the partners began launching an assortment of businesses, including chemical and construction firms. In 1965 they formed a holding company to manage these disparate operations, naming it Elcor Chemical Corporation, which was primarily drawn from the initials of the partners. The "L" was for Leibrock and Landreth, the "C" for Campbell and Callaway, and the "O" for another partner named Ortloff. An "E" and "R" were then added to make "Elcor." Although the company offered engineering services to the oil and gas industry, as well as the manufacture of ammonia and fertilizers, the main focus of Elcor at this time was sulfur recovery. Texas was a major source of the world's sulfur supply, the deposits discovered as a byproduct of oil exploration in the state. Elcor's engineers developed methods to extract sulfur from natural gas as well as gypsum deposits. In 1968, backed by two public offerings, the company began construction on a $40 million Texas facility, the Rockhouse Project, to recover sulfur from gypsum using high heat. The changing economics of sulfur, however, proved disastrous. Sulfur from western Canada, recovered inexpensively from sour gas, flooded the market, driving down prices from $40 a ton when Rockhouse was started to as little as $7.50 a ton when the plant came on line. By November 1970 the company was forced to close the operation.

With $50 million in debt and just $2 million in assets, Elcor filed for Chapter 11 bankruptcy protection, in order to convert creditor bonds into shares of stock. By August 1971 Elcor had satisfied its creditors and was ready to continue on as an engineering and construction business. In order to take advantage of a tax loss carry-forward, which was helpful only if the company could produce some offsetting revenues, Campbell looked to buy established, profitable businesses in other industries. His plan was to apply his engineering skills and abilities to develop efficient processes so that increased profits would actually pay for the acquisition.

Acquisition of Elk Roofing Products in 1975

Elcor's first acquisition came in May 1972 when the company bought Chromium Corporation, an American Can Corp. company, which provided chrome plating for industrial diesel engine cylinders. In December of that year, Elcor picked up Elk Roofing Products, a Stephens, Arkansas, company established in 1955 to produce asphalt roofing shingles. Finally in 1975 Elcor acquired Mosley Machinery, a Waco, Texas, business that was the second largest maker of hydraulic scrap-metal processing equipment in the United States.

Also in 1975, Elcor bought a shingle plant in Tuscaloosa, Alabama, marking a greater commitment to the roofing business. Although Elcor came to the field with no experience, Campbell and his colleagues turned that situation to their advantage, taking a fresh look at the roofing business and approaching it with the process orientation they used in the oil and gas industries. They studied a number of technologies used around the world and settled on the Sandy Hill glass mat process for the manufacture of fiberglass-laminated shingles, which would later become the industry standard. Elcor designed a new plant around the method in Ennis, Texas, located 30 miles south of Dallas. The first stage of the Elk facility opened in 1978, becoming the first U.S. plant to apply the Sandy Hill process. A year later productivity was greatly enhanced and costs reduced by the introduction of a high-speed continuous laminating process, another Elk first, as was the 1980 addition of computerized process control. The company was several years ahead of the competition, but by the early 1980s industrywide improvements led to excess capacity, and asphalt shingle prices fell to unacceptable levels. As a result, Elcor decided to drop the asphalt shingle line, which was susceptible to heavy pricing competition, and instead concentrate on the more lucrative premium roofing market. In particular, the company targeted wood shingle customers, emphasizing the potential fire hazard of wood and shorter lifespan than two-ply fiberglass products. Elk's older Arkansas plant, increasingly outmoded and a drain on Elcor's profitability, was closed in 1985. A year later, Elk introduced its Prestique Plus top-of-the-line, extra-thick fiberglass laminated shingle intended for reroofing expensive homes.

Elcor made other changes to its business mix in the 1980s. With the oil and gas industry enduring severe difficulties, Elco closed its Midland oil and gas construction business in 1985 and formed the Ortloff Engineers subsidiary to continue offering engineering and consulting services. With no reason to remain based in Midland, Elcor moved its headquarters to Dallas in

1988. In the meantime, the company opened a new concrete-roof tile plant in Pompano Beach, Florida, but the stock market crash in October 1987 sent shingle prices tumbling, leading to suppressed earnings for Elcor.

For the next couple of years, Elcor and the housing industry were beset with poor economic conditions, which led many homeowners to delay construction or remodeling plans. In 1991 the company was forced to sell its Florida roofing plant, which had been adversely affected by a new housing slump in the state. In addition, Elcor sold off a Chromium plant in Chicago. As a result of asset sales and writedowns, in fiscal 1991 Elcor posted a $15.5 million loss on revenues of nearly $116 million.

With its balance sheet cleaned up, however, the company was poised for a rebound. Later in 1991, with the economy improving and housing starts increasing, the roofing market began to improve. In addition, Elk launched a new product, a fiberglass shingle that looked like wood. The company's recovery also was aided by severe weather that damaged roofs and led to rebuilding. First there was an increase in wet weather caused by the El Niño phenomena, followed by a series of hailstorms in Texas, Kansas, Colorado, and Florida. Elk's shingle manufacturing plants were already pushed to capacity when Hurricane Andrew struck in the late summer of 1992, causing damage in Florida and Louisiana. As a result, Elcor, which changed its name from Elcor Chemical Corporation to Elcor Corporation in 1992, enjoyed profitable years in fiscal 1992 (ending June 30, 1992) and fiscal 1993. Revenues improved to $138.3 million in fiscal 1992 with net income of $8.3 million, followed by sales of $161.4 million and net income of $17.8 million in fiscal 1993.

Wall Street was quick to take notice of Elcor's turnaround: In just nine months the price of Elcor stock quadrupled. Despite having its factories running at full capacity, Elk was actually losing market share in premium shingles, the result of a sharp increase in the product's popularity. To take advantage of this situation and build on its momentum, Elcor in April 1993 announced that it would build a new plant in the Los Angeles area, eventually built in Shafter, California, part of an $80 million capital investment program conducted over the next few years. California, with its large number of wood shingle roofs, was an especially promising market for premium laminated shingles. Not only would the Shafter plant come on line in 1995 at a time when the California economy was expected to be on the upswing, its location cut shipping costs to western states and allowed Elk's Texas plants to better supply the southwestern and midwestern states.

In 1994, Elcor approved the construction of a $30 million plant to produce nonwoven materials for use in making fiberglass shingles as well as other construction products. The new Ennis, Texas, facility opened in 1997. With annual revenues lingering around $160 million, Elcor experienced sharp increases as new capacity came on line. In fiscal 1996, sales topped $196 million, with net profits of $10.7 million, followed a year later by sales of $230.8 million and net profits of $12.3 million.

Enduring the Founder's Death in 1997 and Preparing for the Future

Now 71 years of age, Campbell established a succession plan for Elcor that would allow him to stay on as chairman while Harold K. Work took over as the president and CEO of

Key Dates:

1965: Roy E. Campbell and colleagues form Elcor Chemical Corporation in Midland, Texas.
1970: The company files for bankruptcy protection.
1972: Chromium Corporation and Elk Roofing Products are acquired.
1976: The company changes its name to Elcor Corporation.
1985: The company focuses on the premium shingle market.
1988: Company headquarters moves to Dallas, Texas.
1997: Campbell dies.
2002: The company changes its name to ElkCorp.

the company, taking responsibility for day-to-day operations. The plan was never implemented, however. Campbell became sick, and he died in August 1997 after a lengthy illness. Work subsequently was named Elcor's chairman as well as its president and CEO. He inherited the reins of a healthy and prospering company, and soon spearheaded another $100 million capital investment plan to increase capacity in shingles as well as Elcor's industrial products division.

All aspects of Elcor's business made solid progress in fiscal 1998. Demand for roofing products was strong, especially in the western United States. Excessive wet weather caused by El Niño, ironically, suppressed business because roofing contractors were often prevented from working during long periods of heavy rain. Strong consumer demand for electronics, in particular digital phones, spurred Chromium Corporation's Compushield conductive coatings and conductive gasketing business. In addition, a strong economy resulted in the need for remanufactured diesel engine components, which also benefited Chromium Corporation. The Ortloff Engineers subsidiary saw its revenues double over the previous year, although falling oil prices would soon hurt business, as many customers postponed projects until conditions improved.

As a result of these positive developments, Elcor recorded $268.2 million in revenues in fiscal 1998, a 16 percent increase over the prior year. Net income grew to $18.3 million, a 49 percent improvement. Clearly, the premium shingle business was driving Elcor's balance sheet. In fiscal 1999, the Roofing Products Group enjoyed a 22 percent increase in sales. Overall revenues for Elcor now reached $317.9 million, and net income totaled $21 million.

Despite its lucrative shingle business, the company continued to pursue other revenue streams. In January 1999 Elcor acquired YDK America Inc., a conductive coatings company located in Canton, Georgia. Several months later the business was renamed Cybershield. Although conductive coatings was a small part of Elcor's overall business, the acquisition was an important addition. It gave the company a second location, reassuring major customers that in the event of a natural disaster Elcor would be able to supply their needs, especially because the nine-year-old Canton plant was only operating at a third of its capacity. Moreover, buying YDK brought with it two signifi-

cant new customers, IBM and Compaq Computer, as well as a lion's share of the wireless telephone handset market.

Elcor continued to post strong results in fiscal 2000, as revenues topped $350 million and net income totaled nearly $30 million. When the U.S. economy began to encounter difficulties, however, Elcor experienced the effects in fiscal 2001. Revenues grew at a slower pace, to $379.2 million, and net income fell to $8.8 million. In February 2001 Elcor underwent a change in leadership, with Work stepping down as president and CEO in favor of Thomas D. Karol, who had nearly nine years of experience as the CEO of Pro Group Holdings, a carpet manufacturer and distributor. A year later Karol also would be named chairman of the board.

To help meet demand for its premium shingles, Elcor in June 2001 placed in service a new manufacturing plant located in Myerstown, Pennsylvania. A year later the company announced a two-year $77 million project to add a second shingle manufacturing line in its Tuscaloosa facility, as well as other enhancements to improve productivity. At the same time, management announced that effective September 1, 2002, the company would become known as ElkCorp, an acknowledgment of the importance of the Elk product lines.

Nevertheless, it did not neglect the nonshingle side of the business. Both Cybershield and Chromium faced a challenging future and looked to diversify into new markets. Cybershield consolidated its operations, closing down the Alabama operation, the cost of running two separate plants outweighing the benefits of maintaining separate locations. ElkCorp also formed a new subsidiary, Elk Technologies, to develop and market fabrics using the company VersaShield fire retardant coatings. On balance, however, the future of ElkCorp remained very much dependent on the success of its premium shingle business.

Principal Subsidiaries

Elk Premium Building Products, Inc.; Elk Technologies, Inc.; Cybershield, Inc.; Chromium Corporation; Ortloff Engineers, Ltd.

Principal Competitors

CertainTeed Corporation; G-I Holdings; Owens Corning Corporation.

Further Reading

Golightly, Glen, "Elcor Recovering Along with Leaky Roofing Market," *Dallas Business Journal,* October 4, 1991, p. 31.
Kay, Michele, "Pitching the Roof: Elcor Corp.," *Texas Business,* June 1987, p. 42.
Simnacher, Joe, "Failures Line Elcor's Path to Prosperity," *Dallas Morning News,* February 1, 1987, p. 1H.
——, "A Move in the Right Direction," *Dallas Morning News,* October 4, 1998, p. 1D.
Stouffer, Paul W., "Elcor Profits After Cutting Its Reliance on Oil Business," *Barron's,* March 30, 1987.
Wrolstad, Mark, "Raising the Roof," *Dallas Morning News,* May 4, 1993, p. 1D.

—Ed Dinger

&equant

Equant N.V.

21-23 Gatwickstraat
Sloterdijk
1043 GL Amsterdam
The Netherlands
Telephone: (+31) 20-581-8283
Fax: (+31) 20-688-0388
Web site: http://www.equant.com

Public Company
Incorporated: 1998
Employees: 10,900
Sales: $2.39 billion (2001)
Stock Exchanges: Euronext Paris New York
Ticker Symbols: EQU (Euronext); ENT (NYSE)
NAIC: 334290 Other Communications Equipment Manufacturing; 334111 Electronic Computer Manufacturing; 334220 Radio and Television Broadcasting and Wireless Communications Equipment Manufacturing; 423430 Computer and Computer Peripheral Equipment and Software Merchant Wholesalers; 513390 Other Telecommunications; 541512 Computer Systems Design Services

Equant N.V. is emerging as a leading global telecommunications services provider for the beginning of the 21st century. The Amsterdam-based company provides data and IP network and integration services on a worldwide scale—the company operates in 220 countries, and is capable of providing local support in some 190 countries, giving it the widest reach of any telecommunications provider. Founded as part of the SITA airline network cooperative, Equant still looks to the air transportation sector as one of its primary operating areas, with nearly 730 airlines, reservations systems, airports, aerospace companies, air-freight companies, and government clients accounting for 20 percent of Equant's revenues. Equant has also built up a strong corporate business, counting 600 of the world's top corporations among its clients. Unlike most of its competitors, many of which are facing bankruptcy with the collapse of the telecommunications market in 2001, Equant has avoided costly infrastructure investments, preferring to rent bandwidth according to its needs. This policy

has enabled the company to maintain a solid balance sheet with very little long-term debt. In 2001, Equant merged with France Telecom's Global One—the combination is expected to boost the company's revenues to an estimated $3 billion for 2002. The merger agreement also gave France Telecom a 54 percent ownership stake in Equant, which continues to be listed on the New York and Euronext Paris stock exchanges. Equant is led by Didier Delepine, president and CEO.

Connecting Airlines in the 1950s

In 1949, a consortium of European airlines—including Air France, KLM, Sabena, Swissair, British European Airways and British Overseas Airways, AG Aerotransport of Sweden, Det Danske Luftfartselskab, and Det Norske Luftfartselskap—sought to combine their communications networks. The partners formed Société Internationale de Télécommunications Aéronautiques, or SITA, as a not-for-profit entity to govern deployment of the shared network. SITA's original mission was to provide direct communication linkages among European airports—although U.S. carrier TWA was also a founding member of the alliance—and as such became a pioneer in developing data communications networks.

SITA's first telecommunications center started up operations at the Rome, Italy airport, connecting airports in Paris, Nice, and Frankfurt. Over the next decade, SITA rolled out its network across all of its member companies, which grew to 52 airlines by 1957. By then, the SITA network, which based transmissions around perforated tape and teleprinters, operated communications centers in 75 airports.

By the end of the 1960s, SITA had begun to automate its network, adding computer-based message switching in 1966, before rolling out the world's first worldwide packet switching network—which enabled messages to be broken up into packets, providing for more efficient use of the network's bandwidth—in 1970. By then, SITA's membership ranks had swelled to 136 members.

SITA added interactive capabilities to its network in 1971. The following year, as its membership continued to grow, the company launched subsidiary service International Telecommunications Services, or ITS, charged with offering maintenance services as well as providing SITA members with network integration services. ITS was to become one of the core elements of the later Equant. SITA moved into the United States in 1974, with the launch of its Information Processing Center in Atlanta. The company also debuted a networked passenger reservation system, GABRIEL, that year.

By the beginning of the 1980s, SITA's membership had grown to 340 airlines, which transmitted some two billion messages per year, straining the group's existing capacity. In 1981, the company rolled out its third-generation network, the Data Transport Network, which provided growth overhead for the next decade. SITA debuted a second Information Processing Center in 1983, based in London; the following year, SITA launched its first air-to-ground data transmission system, VHF AIRCOM. In 1984, SITA also debuted its CUTE system, which allowed airlines to pool check-in terminals.

Global Telecommunications Provider in the 1990s

At the end of the 1990s, SITA controlled a vast telecommunications network which reached into more than 190 countries—the organization's not-for-profit status had enabled it to skirt the stringent regulations maintaining domestic monopolies that governed the rest of the global telecommunications industry. SITA was well-positioned to take advantage of the wave of deregulation that swept through the airline and telecommunications industries in the 1980s and early 1990s.

In 1989, SITA extended its membership to the broader air transportation industry, signing on computer reservations systems, tour operators, air freight forwarders, airport authorities, and aerospace manufacturers. By the end of that year, membership grew again, to 385 members. Meanwhile, SITA had also begun exploring means of rolling out its network services to a still broader, corporate market. As the company signed on its first corporate customers—typically globally operating companies attracted by SITA's presence in nearly 200 countries—SITA rolled out its fourth-generation network, the Mega-Transport Network, in 1991. In that year, SITA formed a new subsidiary, Scitor, which became responsible for its non-airline integrated network services operations.

Two years later, SITA boosted its network integration offering with the acquisition of software group Novus, which specialized in transaction processing applications. The acquisition filled out the commercial and technical expertise of SITA's ITS and Scitor subsidiaries, allowing the company to provide a full service network integration package to its corporate clients. Meanwhile, SITA continued to expand its airline-industry operations, deploying the World Tracer baggage tracking system in 1991, rolling out its CUTE 2 terminals system and debuting an air-to-ground telephony system, SATELLITE AIRCOM, in

1992, and, in 1995, launching the AeroNet intranet system for the aerospace and air transport industries. In that year, SITA also extended its network offering to include voice transmission as well as data.

SITA's success in attracting corporate clients—including rising Internet stars America Online and Compuserve, which were in the process of expanding their own networks worldwide—led the consortium to establish a dedicated corporate-oriented subsidiary in 1995. Called SITA Telecommunications Holdings, or STH, the new entity combined the operations of Scitor, ITS, and Novus. SITA then restructured its holding in STH, selling a 30 percent share to investment group Morgan Stanley Capital Partners for $200 million, and transferring a 10 percent stake to an employee shareholding trust. SITA remained STH's majority shareholder—and its largest single client—yet STH now set off to conduct business as an independent company. Meanwhile, SITA and STH formed a joint venture that took control of SITA's global network. Under terms of the joint-venture agreement, STH was given exclusive access to the network for its corporate clients, while SITA retained exclusive rights to employ the network for the airline industry. The partners began rolling out new generation IP (Internet-protocol) network capacity the following year.

STH started to rebrand its operations in 1997 in order to prepare for a future public offering. The company chose the brand name Equant—used to denote the theoretical "center" of space. The company initially applied its new brand only to its Scitor commercial arm, which became Equant Network Services. By the beginning of 1998, however, as STH's three operating divisions began working more closely together, the company decided to rename all of its divisions under the Equant banner—with ITS becoming Equant Integration Services, and Novus becoming Equant Application Services. Lastly, STH itself changed its name, becoming Equant N.V., with Didier Delepine, who had originally joined SITA in 1976, taking over as Equant's CEO.

Telecommunications Survivor in the New Millennium

Equant went public in July 1998, with a simultaneous listing on the New York and Paris stock exchanges, selling 30 million shares and raising $768 million. The company followed up the success of that offering with a secondary offering of another 42 million shares in early 1999. By then, the company's share price had nearly quadrupled, valuing Equant at more than $22 billion.

Equant used some of its new capital base to expand its U.S. presence, buying up Atlanta-based Techforce, a network support specialist founded in 1990, for $73.4 million. Yet the company avoided the frenzy of mergers and acquisitions as the global telecommunications industry raced to consolidate at the end of the century. Equant also departed from the rest of its industry by carefully avoiding committing itself to building its own physical network, which meant the company was able to maintain an extremely low long-term debt portfolio. Nonetheless, Equant launched an infrastructure investment program worth some $100 million in 1999.

Despite the impressive scope of its global network—by the new century, Equant boasted operations in 220 countries, some four times that of its closest competitor—Equant remained a

Key Dates:

1949: SITA (Société Internationale de Télécommunications Aéronautiques) is formed as a partnership consortium among airlines to build a communication network for the European airline industry.

1972: SITA creates International Telecommunications Services (ITS) to provide network integration services to its member companies.

1989: SITA extends its membership to wider airline industry and begins promoting its network services to non-airline industry corporations.

1991: Consortium founds Scitor to oversee its corporate network integration operations.

1993: SITA acquires Novus in order to support ITS and Scitor with network integration software development.

1995: SITA forms STH (SITA Telecommunications Holdings), which takes over as holding company for ITS, Novus, and Scitor.

1997: STH rebrands Scitor as Equant Network Services.

1998: ITS is rebranded as Equant Integration Services and Novus, as Equant Application Services; STH changes its name to Equant N.V. and makes public offering on New York and Paris stock exchanges.

2000: Equant reaches agreement with France Telecom to merge into FT's Global One subsidiary.

2001: Equant and Global One merge, retaining the name Equant.

2002: Equant forecasts revenues of $3 billion for the year.

tiny player in the booming global telecommunications market, with revenues of under $400 million in 1998. This led the company to consider merger overtures from some of its larger competitors, starting with Deutsche Telecom in 1999. Those talks fell through, however. Then in 2000, Equant began talks with France Telecom. Later that year, Equant broached selling itself to California's Global Crossing, but the negotiations failed when Global Crossing balked at Equant's asking price.

Equant continued to go it alone in 2000, adding new successes, such as a joint-venture agreement with Reuters PLC to develop an IP network dedicated to the financial services industry. In another success that year, Equant reached an agreement to help China Netcom build a new national data network for that country. By the end of 2000, Equant had boosted its own revenues to more than $1.6 billion. The company once again entered talks with France Telecom, which was in the process of acquiring complete control of Global One—the data network services provider originally set up as a joint-venture by France Telecom, Deutsche Telecom, and Sprint in 1996.

Equant and SITA now reached an agreement with France Telecom to merge Equant into Global One. Under the merger agreement, France Telecom paid $3.5 billion to acquire SITA's share in Equant—giving France Telecom a 54 percent stake in the newly merged company, which retained the Equant name.

France Telecom also agreed to invest an additional $1.2 billion in the new Equant, which remained headed by Delepine.

Delepine quickly led Equant and Global One through the merger process, establishing the Equant brand across the whole of the operation by mid-2001. By the end of that year, the integration of the two companies was more or less complete— in time for the collapse of the global telecommunications industry. Yet Equant watched from the sidelines as its heavily indebted competitors filed for bankruptcy protection. Despite the collapse in its own share value, Equant remained one of the healthiest in the telecommunications market, with a long-term debt load of just $1 million, a war chest of nearly $500 million, and revenues expected to reach $3 billion in 2002, worth some 10 percent of the global market. The company, which had as its chief handicap a lack of brand recognition, especially in the key U.S. market, looked forward to picking up the pieces of the telecommunications industry—and establishing itself as a new heavyweight in the new century.

Principal Subsidiaries

Equant Application Services; Equant Integration Services; Equant Integration Services, Inc. (U.S.A.); Equant Integration Services, S.A. (Switzerland); Equant Network Operations; Equant Network Services; Equant Network Services International Corp. (U.S.A.); Equant Network Services Ltd. (U.K.); Equant Network Services Pte. Ltd. (Singapore); Equant Network Services, Inc. (U.S.A.); Equant S.A.S. (France); Equant U.S., Inc.; Radianz (U.S.A.; 49%); SITA Equant S.C. (Belgium; 50%).

Principal Competitors

Nippon Telegraph and Telephone Corp; Deutsche Telekom AG; British Telecommunications plc; SuezParis; NTT DoCoMo Inc.; Worldcom Group; Vodafone Group Plc; Suez Lyonnaise des Eaux; Granada PLC; KDDI Corp.; Bouygues S.A.; News Corporation Ltd.; AT&T Broadband L.L.C.; Cable and Wireless PLC; Cox Enterprises Inc.; Teleglobe Inc.; Telefonica Moviles S.A.; Telenor AS; Telia AB; Ameritech Corp.; Portugal Telecom SGPS; BELGACOM.

Further Reading

Delaney, Kevin J., ''WorldCom's Weakness Opens Market to Equant's Strengths,'' *Wall Street Journal*, July 4, 2002.

Gerwig, Joyita and Kate Haldar, ''The 220-Country Niche Player— Despite Its $3.8 Billion Merger, Equant Remains Cautious,'' *Tele.com*, July 9, 2001, p. 15.

''The Global Minnow: Telecoms,'' *Economist*, August 15, 1998, p. 54.

Maiello, Michael,'' Reach Matters,'' *Forbes*, October 14, 2002.

''A Merger That's Working,'' *Global Telecoms Business*, February- March 2002, p. 22.

''The Only Way Is Up, Maybe,'' *Economist*, July 25, 2002.

Secker, Matthew, ''In Search of World Supremacy,'' *Telecommunications Americas*, November 2001, p. 16.

Wilson, Carol, ''In a World of Its Own,'' *Net Economy*, March 18, 2002

—M.L. Cohen

AIGNER

Etienne Aigner AG

Marbachstrasse 9
81369 Munich
Germany
Telephone: +49 (0) 89-7 69 93 0
Fax: +49 (0) 89-7 60 77 85
Web site: http://www.aignermunich.com

Public Company
Incorporated: 1979
Employees: 145
Sales: EUR 44.0 million (2001)
Stock Exchanges: Frankfurt Neuer Markt
NAIC: 316992 Women's Handbag and Purse Manufacturing; 315292 Fur and Leather Apparel Manufacturing; 315992 Glove and Mitten Manufacturing; 315999 Other Apparel Accessories and Other Apparel Manufacturing; 316991 Luggage Manufacturing; 316993 Personal Leather Good (Except Women's Handbag and Purse) Manufacturing; 316999 All Other Leather Good Manufacturing

A horseshoe logo marks the products made by Etienne Aigner AG, a Munich-based manufacturer of quality leather goods such as handbags, belts, and shoes. The company promotes its logo as the symbol of a prestige brand that combines traditional handcrafted quality with innovative Italian-influenced fashion. The firm is named after a Hungarian-born designer and leatherworker who won acclaim in the 1950s for the quality of his products. Two completely independent firms—Etienne Aigner Group in the United States and Etienne Aigner AG in Germany—now carry on the Aigner tradition. The German firm, which markets its products in Europe, Africa, Asia, and Australia, has expanded well beyond the trademark leather goods of its namesake. The company's product lines include "Fashion Accessories" (scarves, neckties, and umbrellas) and "Treasure" (costume jewelry and sterling pieces). In addition, Aigner licenses its name for the manufacture of men's and women's clothing, cosmetics, eyeglasses, and watches. Aigner operates its own retail stores in many key markets, but the franchise system remains a central part of its sales strategy. The company expanded its franchise system and its product lines in the 1970s, and, after weathering difficult years in the mid-1980s, entered a particularly profitable period in 1989. The late 1990s presented challenging economic conditions for luxury consumer goods, but the company is asserting itself in the new millennium with a revamped retail store concept and innovative young designers.

Origins of the Aigner Brand: 1904–65

Etienne Aigner was born to a Hungarian Jewish family in 1904 and grew up in Budapest, the second of three children of a lawyer. While still in school, he began working in the bookbinding trade. His creativity manifested itself as he invented new binding methods and experimented with making his own paper. The bookbinding work brought him his first experience working with leather.

In the 1930s Aigner moved to Paris with his brother Lucien—who later became a well-known photojournalist—and continued his work as a bookbinder until the start of World War II. He learned the latest techniques for treating and working with leather during this period. When the German occupation began, however, Aigner fled Paris and in 1943 headed for the mountains with French Resistance forces. After the war, he returned to Paris, abandoned bookbinding, and embarked on a career in fashion. He applied his leatherworking skills to create fine belts and handbags, selling them to retailers such as Dior, Lanvin, and Rochas.

Aigner moved to New York in 1950, where he joined his brother and sister. In New York he presented a collection of leather goods under his own name, and the Etienne Aigner brand was born. As a logo he adopted a stylized version of his monogram—the letter "A" in the form of a horseshoe. Aigner sold his designs to a local manufacturer, but soon found that his handcrafted approach and "haute couture" style clashed with the mass production mentality of the New York fashion industry. So he set up his own business in his bedroom, making belts in a single color, rich burgundy, because it was the only material he could afford. The belts were well-received and could be found in most leading department stores by the mid-1950s. As

Company Perspectives:

Aigner is the exclusive, international brand for discerning men and women. With its range of leather goods, fashion clothing and accessories, it offers a complete world of carefully blended products from head to toe. Its elegant sporty style has a distinctly Italian feel. The brand's core is a symbiosis of tradition and innovation, combining classical and modern styling. A style which transcends both time and geographical borders. The horseshoe—a symbol of good luck—and the Bordeaux red livery are the brand's distinctive symbols around the world. The Aigner emblem stands for the high quality standard set by the company and its employees; for the customer it represents authenticity, lifestyle and satisfaction.

The Aigner vision: we want those people who attach great importance to superior quality and timeless values to be able to fulfill their wishes perfectly with the Aigner brand.

Once You Have It. You Love It.

his financial situation improved, Aigner was able to expand his offerings to include other colors and also added hemp materials to the product line. The quality of his goods won him the nickname "The Man with the Golden Hands."

Growth of a German Fashion Company: 1965–88

The Etienne Aigner brand made its way back to Europe thanks to a German textile businessman named Heiner H. Rankl. Rankl stumbled upon the Aigner logo at a fashion show in Canada and, after long negotiations, won production and sales rights for the brand in Europe. The Etienne Aigner AG was founded in Munich in 1965. The company developed a leather collection around a trademark look: tortoiseshell leather with open edges. When some aspects of the New York designs, such as metal studs, proved too rustic for European tastes, Rankl adopted a more Italian style for the German company. The U.S. Etienne Aigner, meanwhile, continued on its own track, and was sold to dress manufacturer Jonathan Logan in 1967.

Aigner expanded its product line and its geographical reach during the 1970s. In 1972 a subsidiary company, Etienne Aigner Italy S.r.l., was founded near Florence to be responsible for production of all Aigner leather goods. The leather product line expanded to luggage and shoes. In 1973 the franchise system was started, allowing the brand to go international. A new division, "Fashion Accessories," was introduced in 1974, adding scarves and neckties to the Aigner collection. The following year Aigner entered the cosmetics market with the founding of subsidiary firm Etienne Aigner Cosmetics GmbH near Munich. The firm's debut fragrance was "Etienne Aigner No. 1." Aigner branched out into clothing in 1978 when a fashion collection was presented in a style of "sporty elegance." Finally, the "Treasure" division was founded in 1982 to sell watches and jewelry.

Aigner gradually came under new ownership in the early 1980s. The firm had been incorporated in 1979 under Rankl. A few years later two brothers from Düsseldorf, Wolfgang and

Reinhard Rauball, gradually started taking control of the company. The Rauball brothers took over Aigner in two steps in 1981 and 1983 through their firm Iona Industries. They then took the company public in 1983.

Difficult years followed as Aigner posted losses in the mid-1980s. But the firm continued to develop and hone its product line. In 1987 Aigner granted a license for eyewear. Metzler Optik AG became a long-term partner in the Aigner Eyewear collection. A year later the firm divested itself of its cosmetics subsidiary. Etienne Aigner Cosmetics GmbH was sold to the U.S. Fabergé Group (Elizabeth Arden), but kept producing fragrances and perfumes under a license for the Aigner brand name. The cosmetics firm changed hands several times in subsequent years, first through a sale to Unilever, then a management buyout by Werner Negges, who had headed the cosmetics division since 1981. In 1996 Negges sold full control to Myrurgia S.A., a Barcelona-based cosmetics manufacturer. Throughout the ownership changes, the cosmetics firm continued selling fragrances for men and women at its perfume shops through a license agreement with Etienne Aigner AG.

Prosperity Under New Ownership: 1989–97

The year 1989 marked a turnaround in Aigner's fortunes, as the company paid a DM 5 dividend to shareholders after four years without a dividend. That same year control of the firm passed into new hands, when the Munich-based firm VVB Vermögenstreuhand GmbH took over the Rauball brothers' Iona Industries. It was unclear, however, just who was behind the firm that had taken control. Even the chairman of the executive board, Wolfgang Mueller, said he was not informed about exactly where the trail of ownership led. The matter was not cleared up until five years later.

Aigner's performance improved dramatically in the years after the sale. Dividends increased each year for six years in a row, growing from DM 5 in 1989 to DM 33 plus a DM 25 bonus in 1995. Net income also grew steadily, from DM 6.7 million in 1991 to DM 17 million in 1995, although net sales showed much more modest growth, reaching DM 99 million in 1996 after fluctuating around DM 91 million in the early 1990s. In 1990, the company also gave away its men's and women's fashion lines in licenses.

In 1994, legal proceedings against a Munich businesswoman for tax violations brought to light the actual ownership behind Aigner. Eva Brandl was the CEO of a Munich meat and sausage chain known as Vinzenz Murr. Investigations into her finances revealed that, through indirect holdings, she was the majority stockholder in Aigner. Brandl's tax advisor and relative, Karl Maierhofer, had succeeded Reinhard Rauball in 1989 as chairman of the supervisory board. Now that Brandl's position with respect to Aigner was out in the open, she became a member of the supervisory board.

The proceedings had little affect on Aigner's positive performance. Despite losing three of its Asian stores—one due to the collapse of a warehouse in Seoul and two to an earthquake in Kobe, Japan—Aigner raised its dividends and reported a 25 percent increase in net income in 1995. Analysts praised the company's low debt and substantial cash reserves. Chairman of

Key Dates:

1904: Etienne Aigner is born in Hungary.
1950: Aigner presents a fashion collection of leather goods in New York.
1965: Heiner Rankl obtains rights to the Aigner name and founds Etienne Aigner AG in Munich.
1973: The Aigner brand goes international through the franchise system.
1981: Aigner is sold to the Rauball brothers.
1983: Aigner goes public.
1989: After a period of losses, Aigner is sold to VVB Vermögenstreuhand of Munich.
1996: Dividends go up for the sixth year in a row.
1998: Aigner posts losses amid the Asian economic crisis.
1999: Udo Dengs becomes CEO.
2000: Aigner presents a new store design and takes direct control of some retail shops.

the Executive Board Wilhelm Mueller suggested that Aigner might consider an acquisition.

But operating conditions worsened in the late 1990s. In 1996, changes in the exchange rate pushed up the cost of goods from Italy, where Aigner got three-quarters of its products. Net income dropped slightly that year. In 1997, sales were flat at 99 million DM, and an economic crisis in Asia was beginning to hurt Aigner's performance. The company retained a 33 DM dividend that year, since net income was fairly high at 17.4 million DM, but in 1997 no dividends were paid as Aigner posted its first loss in a decade. About 40 percent of the company's sales came from Asia, and the poor economic climate there contributed to a 3.9 million DM (EUR 0.2 million) loss for the year.

Financial Recovery with a Stronger Retail Presence: 1998–2002

Aigner emerged from the difficulties of the late 1990s under new leadership. Bernd Ehrengart replaced Wilhelm Müller as chairman of the executive board in 1998. But after conflicts with the supervisory board, Ehrengart stepped down and Udo Dengs, an Aigner board member, took his place. Under Dengs, the company's approach was "to find the heart of Aigner, its roots, and to interpret them in a modern age." The company's designers came out with new product lines such as the "Evolution" line of 1999, which was made with distinctive vegetable-tanned leather, and the "Daily Basis Retro" collection of 2002, which replaced the usual homogenized, durable leather with a leather that retained small imperfections and developed a patina with use.

A new design concept for franchise shops was unveiled in 2000. The shops were to have a warm, uncluttered, friendly feel, with panels in deep burgundy to acknowledge that color's central place in Aigner's history and products. The company began playing a larger role in retail operations in order to present the "World of Aigner" in a more uniform way. Although franchise operations remained an important part of the retail strategy, Aigner took direct control of several pilot shops

in premier locations in major German cities and elsewhere. Thirty-six new outlets opened in 2000, followed by 27 new shops the next year. A highlight of the 2001 store openings was a shop in the premium Ginza shopping district in Tokyo. Several shops opened in China and Korea that year as well.

Improved financial results seemed to indicate that Aigner was on the right track. After posting a slight net loss in 1999, the company made a EUR 2.0 million profit in 2000. High prices for leather put pressure on profits, but the company's new product lines, which combined a younger feel with traditional quality, helped boost sales 26 percent over the previous year. Aigner paid a dividend in 2000 for the first time since 1997. In November 2000 the original Etienne Aigner, founder of the prestige brand, died in New York at age 95. He had not played a role in either the U.S. or the European firm for several decades.

Aigner welcomed a new licensee for its line of clothing in April 2001. The Italian fashion company GIC SpA Modyva replaced former partner Gerry Weber International. Aigner also gave a license for timepieces to Peter Eichner Time + Design GmbH in Pforzheim, Germany. Retail expansion that year was particularly concentrated in Asia, with exports increasing to Korea, Indonesia, Taiwan, Malaysia, Thailand, and the Middle East. New locations were also opening in Prague and Moscow. In total, 66 shops were constructed or renovated under the new design concept in 2001, and ten outlets were planned for 2002 in China alone. The investment in construction and renovation kept net profits down, but sales were up 15 percent in 2001.

In 2002 Aigner focused its renovation efforts on the home showroom in Munich. The shop was closed for two months in the summer to be remodeled into the premier showroom for the Aigner collection. At the time, sales in Germany were uncertain, but sales in the broader home market, including Austria and Switzerland, were fairly stable. Those three countries accounted for around 45 percent of Aigner's total sales. But some franchise partners in the home market, as Dengs told the press in August 2002, did not understand "what we mean by prestige." Therefore, Aigner planned to broaden efforts to implement the new shop concept in Germany. With more direct control over stores in key markets, Aigner would be able to ensure its image as a prestige brand for fashion-conscious customers. The company's success depended on winning consumers with the right balance of quality, tradition, and modernity.

Principal Subsidiaries

E.A.-Mode-Vertriebs-Gesellschaft mbH; E.A. Cosmetics Distributions GmbH (50%); Etienne Aigner Italy S.r.l.

Principal Divisions

Leather; Fashion Accessories; Treasure.

Principal Competitors

Coach, Inc.; Guccio Gucci, S.p.A.; LVMH Moët Hennessy Louis Vuitton SA.

Further Reading

"Aigner-Aktionäre Loben Hohe Ausschüttung," *Frankfurter Allgemeine Zeitung*, July 19, 1996, p. 17.

"Die Aigner-Aktionäre Sind Hocherfreut," *Frankfurter Allgemeine Zeitung*, July 21, 1995, p. 17.

"Aigner Erhöht Nochmals die Ausschüttung," *Frankfurter Allgemeine Zeitung*, March 6, 1993, p. 14.

"Aigner Kosmetik Nach Spanien Verkauft," *Frankfurter Allgemeine Zeitung*, March 5, 1996, p. 25.

"Aigner Leidet Unter Konsumflaute in Asien," *Frankfurter Allgemeine Zeitung*, February 28, 1998, p. 21.

"Aigner Präsentiert eine Bemerkenswerte Bilanz," *Frankfurter Allgemeine Zeitung*, May 23, 1995, p. 25.

Dostert, Elisabeth, "Der Konzern Trotzt der Flaute bei Luxusgütern," *Frankfurter Allgemeine Zeitung*, April 11, 2002.

"Eigentumsverhältnisse bei Aigner Aufgedeckt," *Frankfurter Allgemeine Zeitung*, December 9, 1994, p. 24.

"Etienne Aigner," *Frankfurter Allgemeine Zeitung*, November 13, 2000, p. 25.

"Etienne Aigner Mit Überschuss und Dividende," *Frankfurter Allgemeine Zeitung*, March 13, 2001, p. 29.

"Etienne Aigner Wechselt die Führung Aus," *Frankfurter Allgemeine Zeitung*, August 24, 1999, p. 18.

"Obituary of Etienne Aigner, Fashion Designer Known for His Red Leather Handbags," *Daily Telegraph*, December 12, 2000.

—Sarah Ruth Lorenz

European Aeronautic Defence and Space Company

European Aeronautic Defence and Space Company EADS N.V.

Le Carré
Beechavenue 130-132
119 PR Schiphol Rijk
The Netherlands
Telephone: +31 20 655 48 00
Fax: +31 20 655 48 01
Web site: http://www.eads.net

Public Company
Incorporated: 2000 as European Aeronautic Defence and
    Space Company EADS N.V.
Employees: 102,967
Sales: $27.28 billion (2001)
Stock Exchanges: Frankfurt Madrid Paris
Ticker Symbol: EAD
NAIC: 336411 Aircraft Manufacturing; 336413 Other
    Aircraft Parts and Auxiliary Equipment
    Manufacturing; 336414 Guided Missile and Space
    Vehicle Manufacturing; 336415 Guided Missile and
    Space Vehicle Propulsion Unit and Propulsion Unit
    Parts Manufacturing; 336419 Other Guided Missile
    and Space Vehicle Parts and Auxiliary Equipment
    Manufacturing; 541710 Research and Development in
    the Physical, Engineering, and Life Sciences

European Aeronautic Defence and Space Company EADS N.V. is the second largest aerospace company in the world and Europe's leader in several fields, including market helicopters, missile systems, and space launchers. EADS and rival The Boeing Company are the world's only two truly diversified primary manufacturers in the defense industry, yet they are both known primarily for their commercial airliners, notes *Flight International.*

EADS was created through the July 2000 merger of DaimlerChrysler Aerospace AG, Aérospatiale Matra, and Con-strucciones Aeronáuticas SA (CASA). It controls 80 percent of Airbus, which accounts for 60 percent of total revenues. It is also a majority owner (75 percent) of Astrium, Europe's largest space company. EADS has some 100,000 employees at more than 70 facilities located principally in Germany, France, Great Britain, and Spain.

Founders of Flight

The history of EADS reads very much like a general history of European aviation. The companies that were combined over the years to form EADS can trace their origins to the earliest days of flight. CASA, the leading Spanish aerospace firm, was founded in 1923. Blériot, Morane-Saulnier (later Socata) and other French pioneering French firms eventually became part of Aérospatiale Group, created in 1970 from three companies nationalized in the 1950s: Sud-Aviation, Nord-Aviation, and SEREB (Societé d'Etudes et de Réalisation d'Engins Balistiques).

Messerschmitt-Bölkow-Blohm GmbH (MBB)—the result of a merger in 1969—integrated most of the significant German aerospace companies, including Albatros AG, Junkers, Weser Flugzeubau, Hamburger Flugzeugbau, Rohrbach Metallflugzeugbau, Focke-Wulf Flugzeugbau Ernst Heinkel-Flugzeugwerke, Messerschmitt AG, Klemm Flugzeugwerke, and Deutsche Flugzeugwerke. Dornier GmbH, a majority-owned subsidiary of EADS, began as a department of "Zeppelin" in Friedrichshafen in 1914.

Founding of Airbus: 1970

The seeds of pan-Europeanism that ultimately led to the creation of EADS go back at least to 1965, when Germany and France began making plans for what would ultimately become the Airbus series of airliners. By the time Airbus was formed by Deutsche Airbus and Aérospatiale in December 1970, Great Britain had temporarily abandoned the project, though it did participate in that famous symbol of Anglo-French cooperation, the Concorde supersonic airliner. CASA joined the Airbus con-

Company Perspectives:

In EADS we have built a robust platform that naturally draws highly talented people from across Europe and even beyond the continent. Their enthusiasm in this century-old aerospace industry is real, adding a still greater dimension to our undertaking. All our people are committed to a single goal: going further with our successful enterprise by building industry-leading products and offering innovative customer-driven services. We are proud to open this new chapter in aerospace conquest by enabling our talented teams to be still more successful by launching major new programs such as the A380 Superjumbo and the A400M military transport aircraft.

These lines that you are reading have been written for the entire EADS community, inside and outside the enterprise. This community of our corporate stakeholders ranges from those who own our shares to others who work in our ranks, and from those who rely on our products and services to still others who partner with us as suppliers.

sortium in 1971. This grouping of Deutsche Airbus, Aérospatiale, and CASA foreshadowed by 30 years the eventual core lineup for EADS.

Dornier developed a number of successful commuter aircraft in the 1970s and 1980s. In the same time period, CASA was developing a specialty in meeting the commuter aircraft needs of developing nations. CASA focused on collaborative programs as part of its turnaround following massive losses in 1987.

Matra Group had become a $1 billion defense and electronics business. It had a number of joint ventures with U.S.-based technology firms such as Intel and Tandy, and had also developed a satellite business.

The multinational European Fighter Aircraft initiative, begun in the mid-1980s, brought together a few companies that would later become part of EADS: CASA, MBB, and Dornier. Aérospatiale and MBB also began participating in multinational helicopter programs.

Creation of DASA: 1989

Deutsche Aerospace AG (DASA) was created in 1989 from the aerospace holdings of Daimler Benz AG, which had recently acquired Messerschmitt-Bölkow-Blohm (MBB), engines manufacturer MTU München, Dornier GmbH, and Telefunken Systemtechnik (TST). It had about 50,000 employees.

Eurocopter SAS was formed in 1992 from the merger of the helicopter interests of Aérospatiale and DASA. Siemens Sicherungstechnik, the defense electronics unit of Siemens, was added to DASA in 1997.

Aérospatiale and the British firm Marconi Electronic Systems merged their space assets in 1998 to create Matra Marconi Space (MMS). This was merged with the space assets of DASA in October 1999, a few days after the formation of EADS, to create Astrium, Europe's largest space company with 8,000

employees and annual revenues of EUR 2.25 billion. EADS owned 75 percent of the new company.

Prelude to Merger in the Late 1990s

Business Week described the conception behind the creation of EADS as a response to the consolidation in the U.S. aerospace industry that had Boeing becoming even larger through the takeover of McDonnell Douglas Corp. In 1997 Jurgen Schrempp, CEO of DaimlerChrysler, and DASA CEO Manfred Bischoff, initiated the efforts to keep DASA, at $9 billion a year a relatively small player, from being swept into insignificance.

Initially doubting France's new Socialist government would be willing to privatize Aérospatiale, Schrempp began merger talks with British Aerospace PLC (BAe). According to *Business Week*, this spurred the French into action. A deal was worked out to bolster their aerospace holdings by privatizing Aérospatiale and merging it with the Matra High Technology Group, part of the Lagardere Group. This deal, announced in July 1998, created Aérospatiale-Matra in June 1999. The French government retained a major holding in Aérospatiale-Matra.

Even before these two were officially merged, Schrempp had invited the French to join the planned DASA merger with BAe. However, BAe abandoned the idea in January 1999 in favor of a merger with GEC Marconi, maker of avionics, among other things, which created BAe Systems.

Formation of EADS: 1999–2000

In months of secret negotiations, dubbed Project Diamond, the structure of a merger between Aérospatiale-Matra and DASA was hammered out. The French government was limited to a 15 percent minority holding; its influence was further tempered by a put option allowing DaimlerChrysler to sell Lagardere its entire 31 percent holding in the event of a major disagreement with France.

The merger was announced in October 1999. The new Netherlands-registered company, European Aeronautic Defence and Space Company EADS N.V., would have two sets of CEOs and chairmen to represent France and Germany, as well as head offices in Paris, Munich, and Madrid. However, English was the company's official language. Rainer Hertrich, the German CEO, came from a financial management career at DASA. Philippe Camus, his French counterpart, was formerly CEO of Aérospatiale Matra.

EADS had about 90,000 employees at the time of the merger. With pro-forma annual sales of $22 billion (EUR 22.6 billion), EADS was the third largest aerospace company behind Boeing ($58 billion) and Lockheed Martin ($23 billion). The company was a market leader in helicopters, missile systems, and space launchers.

As a whole, the EADS companies lost a collective $940 million (pro forma) in 1999 in spite of Airbus Industrie's $1 billion operating profit. The group was expecting to save EUR 500 million ($471 million) a year by 2004 through combined purchasing and other synergies—though 70 percent of this was to come from the restructuring of Airbus. However, *Forbes* noted that the new company, being "as much a political beast as a commercial enterprise,'' would not go for quick gains from U.S.-style staff cuts.

EADS owned 80 percent of Airbus, with BAe Systems a minor (20 percent) partner. Airbus was challenging traditional U.S. dominance in large military transports and jumbo jets. In the works was a ''superjumbo'' 600- to 800-seat airliner—dubbed the A380—being prepared for a first flight in 2005. The A400M was the military transport under development. Airbus changed from a loose consortium (''Groupement d'Interet Economique'') to an integrated company in January 2001.

Spain's state holding company, SEPI (Sociedad Estatal de Participaciones Industriales), owned all of CASA until it joined EADS on December 2, 1999, as part of its privatization. (DASA, Aérospatiale-Matra, BAe Systems, and Italy's Finmeccanica had been bidding for control of CASA just prior to the formation of EADS). The company had developed considerable expertise in working with composite materials.

EADS shares began trading publicly on July 10, 2000. This also marked the company's first official day of business. The floated shares represented 30 percent of the company. The initial public offering was the first ever offered simultaneously on three exchanges: Paris, Frankfurt, and Madrid.

At least one conflict emerged with all of the international consortia the founding partners were involved in. EADS inherited a 43 percent stake in the Eurofighter venture via CASA and DASA; however, it also held a 45.8 percent interest in Dassault Aviation SA, maker of the competing Rafale fighter, via Aérospatiale Matra. Dassault, known for its business jets and Mirage fighters, rejected an alliance with EADS and was trying to buy back Aérospatiale Matra's shares.

2001 and Beyond

EADS, which had more than a dozen subsidiaries in the United States, opened a corporate office in Washington, D.C., in April 2001. It teamed with Northrop Grumman on a number of defense electronics projects, as well as a maintenance, repair, and overhaul (MRO) facility for large commercial aircraft in Lake Charles, Louisiana. EADS also opened an office in Brussels, home of European Union and NATO headquarters. In June 2001, EADS announced it was buying Hawker Pacific, a defense subsidiary of Australian Aerospace, from Saab of Sweden.

A June 2001 merger agreement provided for the creation of a new European missiles group, dubbed MBDA, from Matra BAe Dynamics (MBD), EADS Aérospatiale Matra Missiles, and Alenia Marconi Systems. This formed the world's second largest missile company after Raytheon Company, with annual sales of EUR 2 billion. The creation of MBDA was part of the restructuring of the Defence and Civil Systems division begun several months earlier.

EADS announced some colossal orders at the Paris Air Show in July 2001. Nine European countries agreed to buy up to $17 billion worth of the A400M military transports in development. International Lease Finance Corp. (ILFC) gave Airbus its largest order ever—$8.7 billion for 111 aircraft. EADS had a total backlog of $160 billion. Still, commercial aircraft sales as a whole were falling, and the missile and defense electronics business had yet to show a profit. Prospects were looking up for the Aeronautics division, driven by orders for military helicopters at the Eurocopter unit.

In 2001, EADS introduced its Competitive Partnership program to develop long-term relationships with suppliers. The program brought suppliers into closer cooperation with EADS in design, development, and procurement processes.

EADS acquired a 26.8 percent stake in Patria, Finland's state-owned defense group, in October 2001. It was also working to bring Italy's Finmeccanica (FNC) into the European Military Aircraft Company (EMAC) transport joint venture.

EADS' revenues rose 27 percent in the company's first full year, reaching EUR 30.8 billion ($27.7 billion). Net income was $842.4 million before a $430 million goodwill writedown that was projected to more than double in 2002.

Shareholders in the company were allowed to exit the company after July 10, 2003. Some analysts perceived the creation of EADS itself as part of DaimlerChrysler's strategy to exit the aerospace business. Others speculated DaimlerChrysler would sell to make up for losses at Chrysler. Similarly, others believed Lagardere dedicated its aerospace and defense resources to the venture to allow it to focus on multimedia projects.

Principal Subsidiaries

EADS CASA (Spain); EADS Deutschland GmbH (Germany); EADS France S.A.S.

Principal Divisions

Aeronautics; Airbus; Defence & Civil Systems; Military Transport Aircraft; Space.

Principal Operating Units

Arianespace (France); Astrium N.V. (75%); ATR (France; 50%); Airbus (France; 80%); Airbus Military Company S.A.S. (France); Bayern Chemie (Germany); Dornier GmbH (Germany); EADS Launch Vehicles (France); EADS Sogerma (France); EADS SOCATA (France); EFW (Germany); Eurocopter (France); Euromissile (France); Eurosam (France); LFK-Lenkflugkörpersysteme GmbH (Germany); Starsem

(France); MBDA (France; 37.5%); EADS Services; EADS Telecom; EADS Systems & Defence Electronics.

Principal Competitors

BAe Systems; The Boeing Company; Lockheed Martin Corporation.

Further Reading

Baker, Colin, "Europe Floats Its New Aerospace Giant," *Airline Business,* August 2000, p. 25.

Banks, Howard, "Walls Around Europe," *Forbes,* May 15, 2000, p. 158.

Baumgardner, Neil, "EADS-MiG Joint Venture's Continuation Dependent on New Orders, Official Says," *Defense Daily International,* June 29, 2001.

"The Big Six; The Survivors," *Economist,* June 1, 1985, p. 7.

Bullock, Chris, "France Opens Door for European Grouping," *Interavia Business & Technology,* May 1999, p. 43.

Burns, Tom, "Deeper Losses Jolt Public Sector Favorite," *Financial Times* (London), Survey: Aerospace, September 1, 1988, p. 15.

"CASA Becomes Part of EADS," *Aviation Daily,* December 3, 1999, p. 4.

"CASA Focusing on Commuter Sales Effort," *Aviation Week & Space Technology,* April 20, 1981, p. 42.

Chuter, Andy, "Airbus Partners to Offer A3XX Following AIC Deal," *Flight International,* June 27, 2000, p. 4.

——, "Transatlantic Defence Tie-Up Planned," *Flight International,* June 19, 2001.

"EADS Acquires Defense Activities of Australia's Hawker Pacific," *Defense Daily International,* June 29, 2001.

"EADS Reorganises Defence and Civil Systems," *Interavia Business & Technology,* January 2001, p. 9.

"Europe Gets a Defence Giant," *Economist* (London), October 16, 1999, pp. 63–64.

Graham, Robert, "CASA Sets Sights on Major Export Deal," *Financial Times* (London), July 6, 1982, p. 21.

Holmes, Stanley, and Carol Matlack, "A Behemoth Lifts Off," *Business Week,* July 2, 2001, p. 24.

Jasper, Chris, "EADS Looks to Resolve Clash with Dassault Over Fighters," *Flight International,* October 17, 2000, p. 28.

——, "European Trio Close on Deal to Launch New Missile House," *Flight International,* October 31, 2000, p. 24.

——, "Ground Zero: Boeing and EADS Are Looking to Diversify Their Interests with Space and Communications Instead of Relying on Airframes for Future Success," *Flight International,* June 21, 2001, p. 49.

Jasper, Chris, and Andy Nativi, "BAe and EADS Enter Final Straight in Race for Alenia," *Flight International,* March 28, 2000, p. 23.

Landers, Michael G., "France Inc.: Can the Economic Miracle Continue?," *Industry Week,* April 5, 1982, p. 40.

Macrae, Duncan, "Cohabitation (French Aerospace Exports)," *Interavia Business & Technology,* March 2001, p. 6.

——, "Profitability Target Raised As Integration Takes Hold," *Interavia Business & Technology,* May 2001, p. 26.

Momberger, Manfred, and Arno L. Schmitz, "Aeronautics in Germany; A Tradition of Aviation Innovation," *Aerospace America,* April 1998, pp. 49+.

Muradian, Vago, "Bischoff: DaimlerChrysler, Lagardere Committed to EADS for the Long Haul," *Defense Daily International,* July 20, 2001.

Nicoll, Alexander, "Essential Guide to Manfred Bischoff; Creating a European Aircraft Industry Will Be the Crowning Achievement of the Former Academic's Career with DASA," *Financial Times* (London), Inside Track, January 3, 2000, p. 11.

——, "Europe's Package Deal," *Financial Times* (London), Comment & Analysis, June 7, 2000, p. 24.

Penney, Stewart, "MBDA Goes Ahead As BAE Systems, EADS and Finmeccanica Sign Up," *Flight International,* May 1, 2001, p. 7.

Ripley, Tim, "Italy's Finmeccanica to Work with EADS Through Summer to Forge EMAC," *Defense Daily International,* June 22, 2001.

Rossant, John, "Birth of a Giant," *Business Week,* July 10, 2000, p. 170.

Sparaco, Pierre, "Restructuring Costs Hit EADS and Thales," *Aviation Week & Space Technology,* March 25, 2002, pp. 35–38.

Szandar, Alexander, "Woes and Worse," *Interavia Business & Technology,* March 2001, p. 4.

Taverna, Michael A., "EADS Sets Groundwork for Long-Term Suppliers," *Aviation Week & Space Technology,* March 18, 2002, p. 62.

Taverna, Michael A., and Jens Flottau, "EADS Counting on Helos, Airlifter to Boost Image," *Aviation Week & Space Technology,* October 29, 2001, pp. 96–97.

Thornton, Chris, "Defence Drive: EADS Is Pushing to Increase Its Military Aircraft Activities to Reduce Its Dependence on Airbus," *Flight International,* June 12, 2001, p. 60.

White, David, "French Aerospace Group Eyes Stake in CASA," *Financial Times* (London), Cos. & Finance: Europe, June 9, 1999, p. 36.

—Frederick C. Ingram

Farmer Bros. Co.

20333 South Normandie Avenue
Torrance, California 90502
U.S.A.
Telephone: (310) 787-5200
Toll Free: (800) 421-6860
Fax: (310) 320-2436

Public Company
Incorporated: 1923
Employees: 1,144
Sales: $215.46 million (2001)
Stock Exchanges: NASDAQ
Ticker Symbol: FARM
NAIC: 311920 Coffee and Tea Manufacturing; 311930
   Flavoring Syrup and Concentrate Manufacturing;
   333294 Food Product Machinery Manufacturing

Farmer Bros. Co. is a manufacturer and distributor of roasted coffee and approximately 300 other items used by the company's restaurant, institution, and office customers. Farmer Bros. operates in 29 western states, serving its clients through roughly 100 branch offices. Roasted coffee accounts for approximately 55 percent of the company's annual sales. The scores of other products packaged and distributed by the company constitute a wide range, including coffee filters, stir sticks, stainless tableware, individual packets of pickle relish, pancake mix, and dozens of other items. A publicly traded, family-run business, Farmer Bros. is controlled by Roy F. Farmer, the son of the company's founder.

Origins

The Californian legacy of the Farmer family's involvement in the coffee business began with Roy E. Farmer. Farmer started the company in 1912, when he began roasting beans and selling them door to door. After establishing his business, Farmer diversified in logical directions. A decade after starting the company, he entered the coffee equipment business. At roughly the same time he incorporated the business, creating Farmer

Bros. as a California corporation in 1923. Much of the company's early success was credited to Farmer's ability to foresee the growth of the western United States. Sensing which areas would experience major rises in population, he established branch offices in important markets such as San Francisco and other fast-growing metropolitan areas.

In the 1930s, Farmer steered the company in an important direction, diversifying into a business area that would account for nearly half of Farmer Bros.' revenue volume at the end of the century. With a growing roasting and equipment business under his control, Farmer realized that he was aptly positioned to operate as a distributor as well. He reasoned that if his company was delivering coffee to customers every week with a truck, he could increase his business substantially by supplying other products needed by his coffee customers. Farmer's epiphany eventually cast Farmer Bros. as a supplier of a range of products, everything from Styrofoam cups to spices. As the company's customer base developed predominantly into restaurants and institutions, the prudence of Farmer's diversifying move increased.

Roy F. Farmer Assuming Control in 1951

After enhancing Farmer Bros.' role as a distributor, Farmer presided over the company's development for the next two decades. Then Farmer died unexpectedly in 1951, passing away at age 59. The sudden death of the company's founder gave control of Farmer Bros. to his son, Roy F. Farmer. The younger Farmer, 35 years old at the time, was ill-prepared for the task at hand. He had little experience, the lack of which was compounded by a minor financial crisis during his first months in charge. His father's death left his family unable to pay for the resultant estate taxes, which forced Farmer to sell a portion of the company's stock to the public. For a company renowned for its love of privacy, Farmer's sale of a portion of the company to the public was seen as the starting point for tensions later in the century. Industry pundits speculated that Farmer rued the day he was forced to let outsiders into the company.

Although Farmer was able to pay his father's estate taxes, his troubles were not over as he took control of the coffee roaster and distributor. His lack of roasting experience became evident when he accepted delivery of several tons of inexpensive Cuban coffee beans. The inferior beans produced coffee that was undrinkable, prompting Farmer to take an intensive, empirical course in coffee roasting. He spent days trying to incorporate the Cuban beans into a drinkable cup of coffee by mixing numerous higher-grade varieties with the Cuban beans. After experimenting with dozens of blends, Farmer succeeded in masking the bad taste produced by the Cuban beans. His success in correcting a mistake engendered Farmer Bros.' strategy for the decades ahead. After the supply of Cuban beans was exhausted, Farmer continued to blend low-grade and higher-grade beans to make an affordable coffee product.

Farmer settled into his role as Farmer Bros.' chairman, chief executive, and president after recovering from his initial mistake. The company's success stemmed in large part from Farmer's ability to keep costs down and his efforts in building an efficient distribution network. As the decades passed, Farmer Bros. flowered into a dominant regional concern, establishing a leading position in a slew of markets dotting the western United States. The passage of time also gradually began to reveal the singular personality of Farmer, which became the focus of attention as Farmer neared the 50th anniversary of his control over the fortunes of Farmer Bros.

By the beginning of the 1990s, Farmer Bros. ranked as the leading supplier of coffee to restaurants, institutions, and offices west of the Mississippi. In the Los Angeles area—a massive market—the company controlled 40 percent of the coffee business. The company's diversification into distributing items other than coffee had matured into a sizable business of its own, accounting for 20 percent of Farmer Bros.' total sales. The company packaged and sold approximately 200 restaurant items by this point in its development, recording operating profit margins that were only slightly below the 10 percent profit margins it reaped from coffee sales. As a whole, the company's operating profit margins were more than double the percentages recorded by major competitors such as Sara Lee Corporation's foodservice operations and Rykoff-Sexton.

Presiding over this success stood Farmer, by then a septuagenarian entering his fifth decade of control over the company. For decades, Farmer's daily routine consisted of performing a coffee-tasting ritual. In Farmer Bros.' ''cupping room,'' Farmer started each day by sampling each of the company's coffee blends. After stirring a sample and inhaling it, Farmer used a silver spoon to taste the blend, spitting each spoonful into a small sink beside him. Those blends that Farmer found offensive received a flag of disapproval, a single coffee bean placed beside it.

Farmer never took a vacation, never willingly talked to the media, and ignored Wall Street analysts. At lunchtime each day, he could be found parked behind the company's roasting plant, sitting inside his 1969 Lincoln Continental, eating lunch alone. His reclusive nature was mirrored by Farmer Bros.: the company did not maintain a corporate relations department or an investor relations department. Although the company was a publicly traded concern, it operated much like a private company, with Farmer exerting tight control over its activities. His firm hold did not slacken for family members, which led to a contentious battle with his sister, Catherine Crowe. During the early 1980s, Crowe launched a proxy battle to gain a seat on the company's board. When Crowe was forced to vacate her seat because of health problems, her son, Steven Crowe, attempted to take her seat. Farmer rejected his nephew's efforts, triggering a family squabble that would endure for decades. As the 1990s progressed, Farmer's rule became increasingly autocratic, drawing not only the ire of family members but of a growing number of shareholders as well.

Shareholder Unrest Continuing into the 21st Century

By the mid-1990s, Farmer Bros. had reached its maturation point. The company's financial totals began to level out, neither increasing nor decreasing by any substantial amount. The stasis was, in part, intentional. Some analysts claimed Farmer could have turned Farmer Bros. into a national concern, but he had chosen not to extend the company's presence into the eastern United States. Farmer Bros. had long since abandoned the posture of an aggressively expanding company. Sales reached a peak of $240 million in 1998, but then began to slip, helping to incite unrest among the company's shareholders. There was nothing glaringly wrong with the way the company was performing—even Farmer's most vocal critics would admit as much. Farmer Bros.' continuous coffee-roasting and packaging system was regarded as one of the most efficient in the industry. Its profit margins were high. Its market position, governed by nearly 100 branch offices in 29 states, was strong. Instead, those shareholders who were troubled by the company's actions focused their complaints on Farmer's secretive rule. Shareholders wanted more information about the company's operations and strategy. They wanted independent directors added to the company's board. They wanted company executives to open up dialogue with Wall Street analysts. Perhaps most important to some of the disgruntled shareholders was for the corporate bylaws to be changed to loosen Farmer's grip on the company. Not surprisingly, Farmer resisted every attempt to make his company more open to the public.

As Farmer Bros. entered the 21st century, the mood among shareholders blackened. From a peak of $240 million in 1998, annual sales had slipped to $206 million by 2001. The company's profits reached a record high of $37.6 million in 2000, but fell 16 percent to $30.6 million the following year. Farmer, in his mid-80s at the time, was suffering from prostate cancer and other ailments, fueling speculation that a succession in power was imminent. His son, Roy E. Farmer, had joined the company in 1976, rising to the post of president in 1993, when he was also appointed as a director of the company. Industry pundits theorized that the younger Farmer would soon gain control over the company, or that Farmer Bros. would be acquired by a rival, but Roy F. Farmer appeared unwilling to let go of the reins of control he had firmly held for more than a half-century.

At Farmer Bros.' 2001 annual meeting, a major stockholder rose from his seat and asked if he could tour the company's coffee operations. According to an article in the November 4, 2002 issue of the *Los Angeles Times,* Farmer never looked up from his seat on the dais, and brusquely responded, "No tours. No tours for unhappy shareholders." Resentment among shareholders was increasing, with Farmer's headstrong behavior the object of their disdain. "His conduct is extraordinary," an investment banker, Gary Lutin, told the *Los Angeles Times* in a November 4, 2002 interview. "This is the only company I have come across where they won't send you an annual report or return your phone call. It is astonishing." Catherine Crowe and her children had joined the fight by this point, calling for the company to divulge more information about its operations and strategy. "We are frustrated," Steven Crowe informed the *Los Angeles Times* in a November 4, 2002 interview. "Our family owns 444,000 shares. That's about $150 million, and it is controlled by people who won't even talk to us."

Farmer Bros.' troubles with its shareholders festered during the summer of 2002. Franklin Mutual Advisors LLC, a mutual fund group that ranked as Farmer Bros.' largest institutional shareholder, holding a 9.7 percent stake in the company, took the lead. Franklin Mutual unsuccessfully opposed the reelection of Farmer Bros.' board of directors in November 2000. In July 2002, the mutual fund petitioned Farmer Bros., asking that the company register with the Securities and Exchange Commission (SEC) as an investment company. The reasoning supporting the request represented another sore point with some shareholders. Farmer Bros. held $282 million in cash and short-term investments, a sum that represented 70 percent of the company's corporate assets. Franklin Mutual and other shareholder groups wanted Farmer Bros. either to use the capital to expand or divvy it up in the form of a dividend. Under the laws regulated by the SEC, investment companies were defined as corporate concerns whose investments represented more than 40 percent of their assets, excluding cash and government securities. By requesting that Farmer Bros. register as an investment company, Franklin Mutual intended to force the company to alter the manner in which it reported its results and to hire investment professionals to oversee its portfolio. Another shareholder group, a Costa Mesa, California, hedge fund named Mitchell Partners L.P., expressed its desires, asking that the

company adopt new bylaws that would require it to place a majority of independent directors on its board.

The pressure on Farmer and his company was intensifying. In August 2002, several weeks after Franklin Mutual submitted its proposal, Farmer Bros. agreed to open its financial books to outside scrutiny. It remained to be seen whether the concession represented the beginning of a less insular attitude at Farmer Bros. The transfer of control from Farmer to whoever took his place was imminent, however. When that moment arrived, a new era would begin, ending the more than 50-year reign of Farmer. The inheritor of his empire, whether it was his son or the management team of a suitor, could look forward to presiding over a company with strong capabilities. Injecting the company with financial vitality and assuaging frustrated shareholders loomed as the primary responsibilities of Farmer Bros.' future leader.

Principal Subsidiaries

Brewmatic Co.

Principal Competitors

Sara Lee Coffee & Tea Worldwide; SYSCO Corporation; U.S. Foodservice.

Further Reading

Brinsley, John, "Several Public Firms Operate Like Private Enterprises," *Los Angeles Business Journal,* April 30, 2001, p. 26.
Cole, Benjamin Mark, "ESOP at Farmer Bros. May Foil Hopes of Speculators," *Los Angeles Business Journal,* December 27, 1999, p. 27.
Dougherty, Conor, "Coffee Company Getting Pushed to Institute Changes," *Los Angeles Business Journal,* July 1, 2002, p. 3.
——, "Farmer Bros. Asked to Open Books," *Los Angeles Business Journal,* August 5, 2002, p. 7.
——, "Farmer Bros. Will Open Its Books," *Los Angeles Business Journal,* August 19, 2002, p. 6.
——, "Investors Pressure Coffee Firm to Act to Lift Stock Price," *Los Angeles Business Journal,* April 8, 2002, p. 1.
Hirsch, Jerry, "Column One: Coffee Chief Stirs Unrest," *Los Angeles Times,* November 4, 2002, p. A1.
King, Ralph, Jr., "Vacations Are for Employees," *Forbes,* June 11, 1990, p. 48.

—Jeffrey L. Covell

Fila Holding S.p.A.

Viale Cesare Battisti, 26
13900 Biella
Italy
Telephone: (015) 350 61
Fax: (015) 350 6399
Web site: http://www.fila.com

Public Company, Majority-Owned by Holding di
Partecipazioni S.p.A.
Founded: 1926 as Societa Anonima Fratelli Fila
Employees: 2,301
Sales: EUR 977.2 million ($842.3 million) (2001)
Stock Exchanges: New York
Ticker Symbol: FLH
NAIC: 316219 Other Footwear Manufacturing; 315220
Men's and Boys' Cut and Sew Apparel
Manufacturing; 315230 Women's and Girls' Cut and
Sew Apparel Manufacturing; 315299 All Other Cut
and Sew Apparel Manufacturing; 448140 Family
Clothing Stores; 533110 Lessors of Nonfinancial
Intangible Assets (Except Copyrighted Works);
551112 Offices of Other Holding Companies

Fila Holding S.p.A. is a major designer and marketer of athletic and casual footwear, activewear, casual wear, and sportswear for men, women, and children. In footwear, the company's best-selling categories are running, cross-training, basketball, and tennis; in apparel, tennis and winter sports are two of Fila's top categories. Other Fila products include sunglasses, watches, underwear, golf clubs, and in-line skates. In addition to the flagship Fila brand, the company also sells a line of leisure apparel and accessories aimed at young people aged 15 to 28 under the Enyce and Lady Enyce brands and markets the CIESSE brand of sports clothing in Italy. Fila does not manufacture any of its products but rather farms production out to independent subcontractors, mainly in the Far East. The company sells its products in more than 50 countries around the world both through directly controlled subsidiaries and via licensing and other distribution deals, reaching about 8,200 unaffiliated retail stores. Fila also directly owns and operates 18 boutiques and 61 outlet stores in several key markets, including Italy, France, the United Kingdom, the United States, Canada, and South Korea.

Although it has been active in the athletic apparel and footwear industry since the mid-1970s, Fila did not truly make its mark in this market until the mid-1990s, when the brand was embraced by trendsetting urbanites. Savvy endorsement contracts with the likes of basketball stars Grant Hill and Jerry Stackhouse helped to push the brand from an eighth place ranking worldwide to number three—behind Nike and Reebok—by 1996. Sales dropped dramatically from the late 1990s into the early 2000s, however, and Fila suffered several years in the red. Although a public company with a listing on the New York Stock Exchange, Fila Holding is controlled by Holding di Partecipazioni Industriali S.p.A. (HdP), an investment group connected with the Agnelli family, the founders of Fiat S.p.A. In June 2001, HdP began seeking a buyer for its 71.9 percent stake in Fila and was still doing so more than a year and a half later.

Early History and Development of Apparel Emphasis in the 1970s

Fila was established in 1923 by eponymous brothers to manufacture knitwear, specifically underwear. The company operated in this field for nearly a half-century, enduring the Great Depression, political upheavals, and high inflation throughout the ensuing decades. It was not until the 1970s and the arrival of managing director Enrico Frachey that the company began to take its present shape. Frachey, who served the company from 1974 to 1979, has been credited with transforming Fila into a manufacturer of athletic apparel. An endorsement contract with tennis star Bjorn Borg proved particularly important to the company's successful penetration of high-end markets for tennis and skiwear. Over the course of the decade, Fila rode a rising tide of popularity into country clubs and onto the ski slopes of Europe and the United States. Although it did not become a runaway hit, Fila and its trademark "F" logo were widely recognized throughout the world of sports apparel and footwear by the end of the 1970s. Frachey left the company late in the decade.

Company Perspectives:

Fila is an authentic sports brand, committed to creating and marketing products that enhance the individual's pursuit of sports as a way to experience greater personal fulfillment.

Fila is committed to building a great company by attracting, developing, exciting and retaining outstanding people.

Fila mirrors the values of a winning sports team: desire for success, team spirit, commitment, enthusiasm, creativity, and fun.

Acquisition by SNIA in the 1980s

During the 1980s, Italian fiber company SNIA BPD S.p.A. acquired an 80.5 percent stake in Fila, while the remaining 19.5 percent was owned by Unione Manifatture S.p.A., a holding company. Fila built a global network of licensees over the course of the decade and concurrently switched from backing athletes to sponsoring athletic events. The most important of the licensees proved to be America's H. Altice Marketing Inc., which was established in 1984 by former Converse executive Homer Altice and was selling 75,000 pairs of Fila shoes annually by its second year in business. Altice targeted his product at Fila's traditional upper-crust constituency, restricting distribution to such high-end retailers as Macy's, Nordstrom, and Neiman-Marcus and such specialty shops as Foot Locker. By 1987, the U.S. licensee's sales totaled 55 million. The brand went into a tailspin in the late 1980s, however, following a serious misstep. According to a 1988 piece in *WWD*, 15 million in Italian overstocks sold to a British liquidator ended up in the United States. The heavily discounted shoes undercut Fila's top-shelf image and flattened U.S. sales.

In the meantime, tennis, ski, and swimwear had continued to be Fila's mainstays; footwear was little more than an afterthought, generating only 7 percent of revenues in 1988. Although the parent company's sales had increased from L 150 billion ($78.5 million) in 1984 to L 180 billion ($138 million) in 1988, Fila suffered several annual losses mid-decade, culminating in a L 7.8 billion ($6 million) shortfall in 1987. SNIA rehired Frachey that year, and the "new" managing director immediately undertook a L 10 billion ($7.6 million) restructuring that included an endorsement contract with tennis luminary Boris Becker, a revamp of the company's design team, and ongoing management shakeups. In 1988, SNIA and Unione Manifatture sold their interests in Fila to Gemina S.p.A., a holding company that was in turn controlled by Italian automaker Fiat S.p.A., for L 62 billion ($47 million).

Finding Success in the Early to Mid-1990s

Fila completed a buyout of its U.S. license in 1991, thereby acquiring that company's $70 million in annual sales. The move signaled a shift in geographic emphasis to the all-important U.S. market and a focus on athletic footwear, particularly basketball shoes. Although Fila had long targeted upper-middle-class whites, the company found that young urban blacks had by the early 1990s become its core constituency. According to apparel industry observers, Fila had become an "aspirational brand," a

label that represented the dreams of inner-city kids whose reality was far removed from the tennis courts and golf courses where the brand had earned its early fame. Like many other of the decade's biggest marketers, Fila embraced its accidental positioning and the tough, gritty image that came with it. Ironically, the strategy was pivotal to helping the brand win over suburban youths increasingly enamored with urban culture. A revival of fashions from Fila's heyday in the 1970s did not hurt the brand's prospects, either.

As they had been in the 1970s, sponsorships were vital to Fila's success 20 years later. In 1994 the company inked an endorsement contract with Grant Hill of the NBA's Detroit Pistons. After he won 1995's Rookie of the Year award, sales of his namesake shoe skyrocketed to more than 1.5 million pairs. The brand continued its youth appeal with the 1995 addition of NBA rookie Jerry Stackhouse to its roster. From 1990 to 1995, U.S. sales as a percentage of overall Fila revenues went from 22 percent to 60 percent. Frachey also turned past growth strategies upside down. In 1990, footwear constituted only 14 percent of annual sales, with the remainder coming from clothing. By 1995 athletic shoes contributed more than 60 percent of revenues.

This combination of strategies helped make Fila America's fastest-growing footwear brand mid-decade, with U.S. sales burgeoning from $70 million in 1991 to almost $386 million, for a 6 percent share of this all-important market in 1995. The brand leapfrogged its second-tier competitors, growing from an eighth place ranking among the world's athletic shoe makers to number three by 1996. Fila's overall revenues mushroomed from L 151 billion in 1990 to L 2.1 trillion in 1996, while net income increased to L 177.7 billion. The parent company's profitability zoomed from 5.8 percent of sales to 8.3 percent over the period. Holders of Fila's American Depository Shares (ADRs) rejoiced as their value shot up from $18 each at issue in 1993 to nearly $66 at the end of 1996. (It was through the May 1993 IPO on the New York Stock Exchange that the holding company, Fila Holding S.p.A., was formed.)

WWD called Fila's 1996 showing "breathtaking," but warned that the future was not free of challenges. For instance, the brand's emphasis on fashion left it vulnerable to competition from designer brands including Tommy Hilfiger, Donna Karan, and Ralph Lauren, all of whom were introducing stylish athletic shoes mid-decade.

Mid-1990s Growth Strategies

Having established itself in the number three spot in the key footwear segment, Fila focused on parlaying its shoe success into continued growth by refocusing on apparel and accessories, diversifying into new sports, targeting women, emphasizing technology, and pursuing geographic expansion. Backed by the L 90 billion ($56 million) raised in a 1995 stock offering, the company invested in a variety of initiatives with a view to achieving L 2 trillion ($1.4 billion) in revenues in 1997.

Fila developed clothing for skiers, snowboarders, skateboarders, and baseball players, and concentrated on building its presence in specialized footwear for basketball, cross-training, running, hiking, volleyball, soccer, and tennis. It also estab-

Key Dates:

1923: Eponymous brothers establish Fila as a manufacturer of knitwear, specifically underwear.
1974: Enrico Frachey becomes managing director and begins the transformation of Fila into a maker of athletic apparel.
Early 1980s: SNIA BPD S.p.A. acquires 80.5 percent stake in Fila, with the remaining 19.5 percent held by Unione Manifatture S.p.A.
1988: Gemina S.p.A. acquires Fila.
1993: In conjunction with an IPO that lists the company on the New York Stock Exchange, Fila Holding S.p.A. is created as a new holding company.
1996: The owners of Gemina create a new holding company called Holding di Partecipazioni Industriali S.p.A. (HdP), and Gemina's stake in Fila is transferred to this new firm.
1997: Falling sales in the United States and Asia lead to the first of several consecutive years in the red.
2001: The first Fila Sport Life flagship stores are opened; HdP announces its intention to sell its stake in Fila.

lished a joint venture with Italian eyewear manufacturer De Rigo S.p.A. to produce a branded line of sunglasses. Fila even created a skin care line including sun lotions and bath products. The company hired a slew of endorsers to support its new sports lines, including beach volleyball player Randy Stoklos, marathon runner German Silva, soccer players Claudio Reyna and Franco Baresi, and tennis player Marc Philippoussis.

The diversification also re-emphasized high-end sportswear and casual footwear with a particular focus on the long-neglected women's market. In 1995 Fila bought market share and expertise in women's and children's clothing via the acquisition of French sportswear manufacturer Dorotennis S.A. The parent company hoped to expand this new subsidiary from its European base into the United States and Asia. New endorsement contracts with top-ranked female athletes, including tennis player Gabriela Sabatini and skier Deborah Compagnoni, supported the drive for the female consumer.

Fila fought the perception that it was a ''fashionable but low-tech'' brand by establishing a research and development center in Portland, Oregon, and staffing it with engineers hired away from Nike. Fila's 1996 annual report stressed the strategic shift, asserting, ''Style is our heritage. Creativity is our strength. Technology is our future.'' The company also established new research and design centers in the key geographic markets of Italy and Korea. Efforts at geographic diversification were so successful that by 1995, Korea had grown to become Fila's second largest market, behind the United States but exceeding Italy. In acknowledgment of the fact that the United States had become its largest and most important market, Fila moved its global operations center to its U.S. headquarters mid-decade.

Having been controlled by Gemina S.p.A. since 1988, Fila's corporate ownership came under question in the mid-1990s.

The stock offerings in 1993 and 1995 had reduced Gemina's stake in Fila to slightly more than 50 percent by 1996. Late in 1996, the owners of Gemina—including the Agnelli family, which also owned Fiat—created a new holding company called Holding di Partecipazioni Industriali S.p.A. (HdP). Placed under HdP were Fila along with designer clothing maker Gruppo Finanziario Tessile S.p.A., publishing and bookselling interests, and several smaller holdings. Rumors soon were circulating about a possible merger between HdP and Italian textile and apparel giant Marzotto S.p.A., which was controlled by the Marzotto family. In March 1997 came the announcement that HdP and Marzotto S.p.A. would merge to create Gruppo Industriale Marzotto, but less than two months later the Marzotta family called off the deal because of concerns that they would not have operating control of the new firm. Fila thus remained a majority-owned, though publicly traded, subsidiary of HdP.

Struggling to Regain Footing in the Late 1990s and Early 2000s

In the late 1990s Fila experienced a dramatic downturn. Problems appeared initially in the U.S. market, where lackluster sales in 1997 led the company to achieve only a small increase in overall revenues and a walloping 71.9 percent drop in profits. In an environment in which athletic footwear as a whole was suffering from declining sales, Fila was hurt further by its failure to penetrate the mainstream U.S. suburban market. The fashion-oriented Fila brand had come to prominence in the urban market, but by the late 1990s urban tastes had shifted to boots and outdoor looks. Fila's diversification drive also had proven to be misguided; the company had expanded into too many product categories and was simply not big enough to compete with an all-sports shoe and apparel giant such as Nike. The company also suffered a significant blow from the Asian financial crisis of 1997–98, which severely reduced sales in Korea and other Asian markets. By 1998, Fila Holding had fallen into the red, posting a net loss of $132.9 million, while its revenues fell 24.8 percent—with U.S. sales dropping an astounding 49 percent.

Restructuring efforts began late in 1997, including workforce reductions (including nearly one-third of U.S. employees), warehouse closures, a reduction in the number of male athletes with Fila endorsement contracts, the closure of all ten U.S. retail outlets, and the elimination of underperforming product lines. There were changes in the top management as well. Jon Epstein took over as head of the main U.S. subsidiary, Fila U.S.A. Inc., in June 1998. Epstein had been national sales manager at adidas America, a unit of adidas-Salomon AG. Late in 1998 Michele Scannavini, who had been sales and marketing director for automaker Ferrari S.p.A., was named CEO of Fila Holding, replacing Frachey, who remained chairman.

The new leaders launched a number of cost-cutting initiatives. In the United States, for example, Fila exited from the distribution business and hired an outside company to distribute its footwear and apparel to retailers; it also replaced its internal sales force with several independent sales agencies. On the product side, there was an important shift back to the company's roots in tennis, skiing, and golf. Fila once again became a sponsor of the U.S. Open and other tennis tournaments and in late 1999 signed Jennifer Capriati to a multiyear endorsement deal. A former teen phenom, Capriati had made a dramatic comeback at age 23 during a series of 1999 tournaments. Revenues fell another 13 percent in 1999, and Fila Holding posted another net loss, although the loss was much smaller than the preceding year. Midyear, Frachey stepped down as chairman and was replaced by Nicolò Nefri, who had been deputy chairman.

Fila's struggles continued in the early 2000s. Net losses were recorded for both 2000 and 2001. During the latter year, the company felt additional negative effects from the global economic downturn, which was exacerbated by the events of September 11. Fila's executives made a continual effort to lay the ground for a comeback. With the U.K. market being one of the company's strongest, Fila in July 2000 acquired the 40 percent stake in subsidiary Fila U.K. Ltd. that it did not already own for EUR 19.5 million. In a further refocusing on core product lines, Fila in November 2000 sold its Dorotennis subsidiary to the French company Phisaco for EUR 13.7 million. To bolster sales, the company launched a five-year, $50 million program to significantly expand its retail operations. The program would include the opening of 40 retail outlets in Europe, including five flagship stores called Fila Sport Life that were about 8,600 square feet in size and 35 smaller, 4,300-square-foot stores. The first two flagships, located in Milan and London, opened during 2001. Fila also began testing the franchising of retail outlets in Italy, with four franchised stores opening in 2001. At the same time, Fila was reducing its retail presence in the U.S. market; it closed 17 of its 38 outlet stores in that country, in part because of reductions in the levels of excess inventory. In addition, Fila closed its subsidiaries in Uruguay, the Philippines, South Africa, and East Africa. In certain markets, the company replaced the subsidiary operations with licensees as a cost-saving measure.

Attempting to reinvigorate the product line and infuse the Fila brand with an Italian aura (for the first time in more than two decades), the company announced in January 2001 a partnership with Italian design company Pininfarina Group to develop a new performance running shoe. Pininfarina was most famous for designing the highly stylish and technically innovative Ferrari automobile. Separately, Fila partnered with Ferrari through a June 2001 agreement whereby Fila would supply the Ferrari Marlboro Formula 1 racing team with apparel and footwear and would also develop a line of Ferrari shoes.

Also in mid-2001, Fila bolstered its financial position through the issuance of 33.3 million new shares of stock to existing shareholders, raising EUR 146.7 million. Through this capital increase, HdP's stake in Fila increased from 54.6 percent to 71.9 percent. Simultaneously, however, HdP announced that it was seeking to sell its stake in Fila and its other fashion units to concentrate on its publishing operations. A U.S. investment group called Continental Partners emerged as a suitor, as did Golden Gate, another investment firm, and VF Corporation, the maker of Lee and Wrangler jeans. By late 2002, however, no deal had been completed.

In the meantime, CEO Scannavini resigned in February 2002 and was succeeded by Marco Isaia, who had served as

Fila's chief operating officer since January 1998. In June 2002 Fila opened a Fila Sport Life flagship store in Tokyo. In September 2002 Fila's shareholders approved a plan to recapitalize the company, which included dipping into company reserves, executing a reverse one-for-two stock split, and completing another capital increase in order to raise a further EUR 146.7 million. With the company headed for another year in the red in 2002 and the sale of the company still pending, Fila faced a very uncertain future.

Principal Subsidiaries

Fila U.S.A. Inc.; Fila Sport S.p.A.; Fila Italia S.p.A.; Fila Sport (Hong Kong) Limited; Fila Korea Ltd.; Fila France S.A. (99.97%); Fila Deutschland GmbH (Germany); Fila U.K. Limited; Fila Argentina S.A.

Principal Competitors

NIKE, Inc.; Reebok International Ltd.; adidas-Salomon AG; K-Swiss Inc.; New Balance Athletic Shoe, Inc.; PUMA AG Rudolf Dassler Sport; Sara Lee Corporation.

Further Reading

Abel, Katie, and Samantha Conti, "Fila Seeks Suitors, Will They Come?," *Footwear News*, June 25, 2001, p. 2.

Bannon, Lisa, "Fila Sees '89 Sales in U.S. Even with '88," *Footwear News*, November 21, 1988, pp. 2–3.

Chirls, Stuart B., "Activewear's Italian-American Exchange," *Daily News Record*, July 10, 1989, pp. 25–26.

Conti, Samantha, "HdP Shopping Fila Around," *WWD*, June 19, 2001, p. 2.

Cunningham, Thomas, "Fila Moves to Regain Roots As an Elite Sports Brand," *Footwear News*, March 15, 1999, p. 2.

De Marco, Donna, "Back to the Future: For New Fila Chief, the Past Is Where It's At," *Baltimore Business Journal*, July 31, 1998, pp. 1+.

Feitelberg, Rosemary, "Fila Details Restructuring, Will Close Outlets," *WWD*, February 6, 2001, p. 11.

——, "Fila: Success, American-Style," *WWD*, July 20, 1995, p. 11.

Feitelberg, Rosemary, and Thomas J. Ryan, "Fila Looks to Regain Its Footing," *WWD*, April 30, 1998, p. 8.

"Fila Forward," *WWD*, May 18, 1995, p. 9.

Forden, Sara Gay, "Fila Planning Expansion in Apparel, Sportswear," *Daily News Record*, January 1, 1996, pp. 12–13.

Forden, Sara Gay, and Samantha Conti, "New Scenario Emerges in the Gemina, Marzotto Talks on GFT," *Daily News Record*, March 3, 1997.

Forden, Sara Gay, Samantha Conti, Stan Gellers, and Miles Socha, "Gemina Said to Ask Marzotto to Take Over GFT, Fila," *Daily News Record*, February 28, 1997, p. 1.

Gelsi, Steve, "Sneaking into Third," *BrandWeek*, December 4, 1995, pp. 24–25.

"Gemina Obtains Control of Fila for $47 Million," *WWD*, November 15, 1988, p. 23.

Hartlein, Robert, "Fila Sports Inc.," *WWD*, February 5, 1992, p. 10.

Lee, Sharon, "Fila: Inner-City Success," *Footwear News*, July 15, 1991, pp. S34+.

Levine, Joshua, "Badass Sells," *Forbes*, April 21, 1997, pp. 142–47.

MacDonald, Laurie, "The Battle for #3 . . . Still Raging," *Footwear News*, July 11, 1994, pp. S18–S20.

Pereira, Joseph, "Nike's Rivals Hope Buyers Want Bargains," *Wall Street Journal*, June 2, 1997, pp. B1, B3.

Rachmansky, Anna, "Fila Strives to Strengthen Brand with New Europe Flagships," *Footwear News*, January 8, 2001, p. 3.

Seckler, Valerie, "Fila Maps Apparel Game," *WWD,* August 10, 1995, p. 8.

Sosnowski, Tom, "Phenomenal Fila," *Footwear News,* December 23, 1996, p. 12.

Thompson, Kelly, "Fila Plans a Fully Loaded Athletic Shoe," *Footwear News,* January 22, 2001, p. 4.

"U.S. Apparel Sales Strong As Fila Earnings Skyrocket," *Daily News Record,* November 9, 1993, p. 4.

Walpert, Bryan, "Fila Gains Foothold in Athletic Shoe Market," *Washington Post,* April 7, 1997, p. WB5.

Waxler, Caroline, "Fleeing Fila," *Forbes,* December 30, 1996, p. 162.

—April Dougal Gasbarre
—update: David E. Salamie

The First American Corporation

The First American Corporation

---

1 First American Way
Santa Ana, California 92707-5913
U.S.A.
Telephone: (714) 800-3000
Toll Free: (800) 854-3643
Fax: (714) 541-6372
Web site: http://www.firstam.com

Public Company
Incorporated: 1968 as The First American Financial
    Corporation
Employees: 22,597
Sales: $3.75 billion (2001)
Stock Exchanges: New York
Ticker Symbol: FAF
NAIC: 524127 Direct Title Insurance Carriers; 541191
    Title Abstract and Settlement Offices

Originally devoted solely to the title insurance business, The First American Corporation, as a result of diversification efforts, now bills itself as a provider of business information and related products and services. The Santa Ana, California, company is divided into three business segments: title insurance and services; real estate information and services, and consumer information and services. Title insurance remains First American's flagship operation, its subsidiary First American Title Insurance Company trailing only Fidelity National Financial Inc. in size. In brief, title insurance provides protection against loss in real estate transactions for purchasers and mortgage lenders in the event that the title to the property has problems, whether they be claims to ownership, liens, encumbrances, or other adverse complications. First American operates in all states and the District of Columbia—with the exception of Iowa where title insurance is not permitted and the company only provides abstracts of titles. Over 70 percent of First American's revenues are generated from the title insurance segment. The real estate information segment offers a number of diverse products and services: tax monitoring, to advise lenders about the status of tax payments on properties securing their loans;

mortgage credit reporting provides credit reports to mortgage lenders; property database services offers mortgage lenders property valuations, title information, tax information, and imaged title documents; the flood determination service tells mortgage lenders the flood zone status of a property, based on government-determined flood hazard areas; and default management services assists mortgage lenders in such areas as foreclosure and claims processing. First American's third business segment is consumer information, much of which represents a recent attempt to diversify beyond the cyclical real estate industry. This segment includes home warranties, one-year protection for homeowners against defects in plumbing, heating, and other household systems and appliances; property and casualty insurance; resident screening, to provide background information on potential tenants for multifamily residences; pre-employment screening to help employers check the backgrounds on job candidates; substance abuse management and testing, offered in conjunction with pre-employment screening services; specialized credit reporting to provide information to non-real estate lenders; automotive insurance tracking and other services, applying First American's real estate title insurance expertise to automobiles; and investment advisory and trust and thrift services, taking advantage of a thrift acquired by a subsidiary in 1988. Although a publicly traded company, First American is in essence a family-run business, headed by the fourth generation of its founder.

Original Company Founded in 1894

First American's growth mirrored that of its home, Orange County, California, which was very much a rural community 100 years ago. In 1889 Orange broke away from the county of Los Angeles, which 20 years before the rise of the film industry in southern California was itself an unassuming, agricultural area. To serve the title abstract needs of Orange County two companies were launched, then in 1894 area businessman Charles Edward Parker combined them to form First American's direct ancestor, Orange County Title Company. He then became president of the Santa Ana firm and remained in charge for many years. Although not displaying spectacular growth, Orange County Title grew at a steady pace. Starting in 1909 it would pay a cash dividend every year for the rest of the century.

By 1924 it began to offer title insurance, one of the first abstract companies in the state permitted to do so.

It was not until Parker's grandson, Donald Parker Kennedy, joined the business in 1948 that Orange County Title began its rise to the top ranks of the title insurance industry, ultimately becoming a company with $3.7 billion in sales. Kennedy was an only child who had never planned to carry on the family legacy with Orange County Title. After earning an undergraduate degree from Stanford University, he received a law degree from the University of Southern California School of Law. He then took his bar exam and while waiting to learn the results began to help out his father and uncle who ran the title insurance company. More than 50 years later he would still be working there. Kennedy was the one who recognized that the business had to expand beyond the boundaries of Orange County if it were to survive. In 1957 the board of directors approved an expansion plan and soon the company's first branch office was established in Ventura, California. In a few short years it was operating in four states. To reflect the company's expansive agenda, Orange County Title changed its name in 1960 to First American Title Insurance. In 1963 Kennedy replaced his uncle, George Parker, as president of the firm, the highest ranking officer because the company had no CEO position. A year later, in order to fund expansion, the firm made its initial public offering, relying on the over-the-counter market.

The business was restructured in 1968 with the formation of The First American Financial Corporation as a holding company. First American Title now operated as a subsidiary, and a trust business was conducted through First American Trust Company. First American Title and other subsidiaries continued to grow the title side of the business, both internally by opening new offices and externally by acquiring existing title and abstract companies. Business was so strong that the company had to expand its Santa Ana headquarters in 1976. By the early 1980s the company was involved in all parts of the country, although it adopted a decentralized approach, in keeping with a belief that the real estate business varies from region to region. As a result, First American granted a great deal of autonomy to its local managers. Not only was the amount of bureaucracy curtailed so that customers enjoyed the advantage of working with a local company, they also knew they had the backing of a major concern.

Fourth Generation Joins Company in 1970s

In the meantime, a fourth generation of the Parker and Kennedy families joined the firm. Parker S. Kennedy was familiar with the title business since childhood, but appeared to be headed in a different direction than his forebears. He went to the University of Southern California on a track scholarship, rather than attending Stanford like his father and grandfather. After earning a law degree from Hastings College of Law in San Francisco he became a member of the California Bar Association then went to practice insurance law for four years with Levinson & Liverman, a Beverly Hills, California, law firm. One of the firm's clients happened to be First American. In 1977 it was the head of the Los Angeles office of First American Title who hired Parker Kennedy, but not before making sure it was acceptable to his father. According to Donald Kennedy, his response was "Absolutely. It saves me from doing it." Not only did the younger Kennedy come to the business with an outside perspective, he also worked at both the Los Angeles and Ventura county offices before teaming up with his father at the Orange County headquarters. Just as his father was instrumental in making a national enterprise out of First American, Parker Kennedy would play a major role in the company's expansion beyond the real estate title business.

Early on, First American did not stray far from its area of expertise. In 1984 it established a home warranties business, followed a year later by a real estate tax service to monitor whether a borrower was paying property taxes. In 1986 the company launched a diversification program which sought to acquire business information companies involved in the real estate transfer business. The tax monitoring service was introduced in 1987, a business that was then greatly enhanced by the 1991 purchase of TRTS Data Services, which made First American the second largest provider of tax monitoring services in the country. In 1988 a subsidiary acquired a southern California thrift. During this period, First American experienced explosive growth, due to a residential real estate boom rather then the company's diversification efforts. Revenues grew from $399.1 million in 1985 to $699.4 million in 1989, a 75 percent increase. When the real estate industry suffered a downturn as a result of poor economic conditions in the early 1990s, First American was adversely impacted. From 1989 to 1991 the company was forced to cut its workforce by 20 percent, but by 1992 First American began to rebound. After posting net income of little more than $3 million in 1991, the company reported $43.3 million in 1992, while revenues ballooned from $757.8 million to more than $1.11 billion over the same period.

First American's diversification efforts continued in the 1990s, but they were seen more and more as a way to provide some protection from future real estate slumps. A credit reporting company was acquired in early 1990, as was a flood certification company, which determined if properties should be required to carry flood insurance. In 1991 these ventures were merged with the tax monitoring service to create a new subsidiary, First American Real Estate Information Services, Inc. It would pursue its own path of aggressive growth through acquisitions, not only to bolster its original businesses but to also move into high-tech areas, such as servicing software systems, and providing database products and services—including property information, appraisal, automated title plans, and document imaging.

Leadership Under Parker Kennedy: 1997–2000s

Parker Kennedy, who had served as president of First American Title since 1989, assumed the presidency of the parent corporation in 1993 and maintained the company's ambitious expansion drive, while his father remained as chairman of the

Key Dates:

1889: Orange County Title Company is formed after merger of two companies.
1924: Company first offers title insurance.
1960: Name is changed to First American Title Insurance.
1968: The First American Financial Corporation is formed as a holding company.
1986: Diversification program is launched.
1993: Stock begins trading on New York Stock Exchange.
2000: Name is changed to The First American Corporation.

board. Also in that year, First American began trading on the New York Stock Exchange. While continuing to build up its core title insurance business, which contributed the lion share of revenues, First American was especially active in building up its mortgage credit reporting business. In 1994 the company acquired Metropolitan Credit Reporting Services, Inc. and Metropolitan Property Reporting Services, Inc.; California Credit Data, Inc.; and Prime Credit Reports, Inc. The following year First American added CREDCO, Inc., making it the largest mortgage credit reporting service in the country, based on the number of reports issued. The flood determination business was bolstered by the 1995 acquisition of Flood Data Services, Inc.

Increasingly, First American turned to technology to gain a competitive edge, despite lacking e-mail capabilities until 1994. In 1995 the company began to construct a wide-area network to connect all of its offices in order to achieve end-to-end connectivity and system integration. Because title insurance was a high volume but low-margin business, the application of technology to speed up processing time had a major impact on the balance sheet by cutting the cost of production. Moreover, First American was then able to leverage its electronic infrastructure and take advantage of the Internet to offer new services, as well as move beyond real estate and better meet the company's goal of diversification. In 1996, to build on its real estate information products business, First American acquired Excelis Mortgage Loan Servicing System and its advanced real-time, online system, capable of being customized to fit user needs. In July 1998 First American added ShadowNet Mortgage Technologies, involved in electronic mortgage preparation, which then began operating under the First American Nationwide Documents brand name. Also in 1998 First American launched the consumer information segment to truly branch out beyond the housing industry, offering such products and services as credit reports to used-car dealers, pre-employment screening to employers, and collateral insurance for commercial loans secured by property other than real estate.

First American was also experiencing growth during the late 1990s in its traditional title business with the emergence of an international market. Although common in the United States, title insurance was essentially nonexistent until recent years. In 1990, in fact, less than 100 policies were written outside the country, despite the fact that for more than 20 years U.S. companies have been licensed to sell title insurance in a number

of countries, including Canada and the United Kingdom. First American Title was in the vanguard of companies who found a way to crack the international market by selling a package of benefits that resulted in a quicker, cheaper way to make real estate transfers, with title insurance serving as an underlying guarantee rather than the marketing focal point. A major innovation by First American Title was the introduction of a standardized policy of title insurance that could be used in almost every country in the world, aimed at U.S. buyers of foreign real estate. In 1998 First American Title sold over 110,000 international title policies, a major improvement over what the entire industry achieved just eight years prior.

To reflect its broader range of business, in 2000 First American changed its name to The First American Corporation. In 2001 First American achieved stellar results, cracking the $3 billion mark in revenues with a total of $3.75 billion, and net income of $167.3 million. Nonetheless, the price of First American Stock failed to show movement, after languishing in the $20 range for many months. Because the title business continued to grow, fueled by low interest rates and heavy refinancing activity, it continued to generate more than 70 percent of the corporation's revenues, despite impressive strides the company had taken in diversifying beyond real estate. First whether American remained truly vulnerable to the vicissitudes of the housing industry or not, the company had to accept that verdict as the reality under which it had to operate. Management would continue to focus on non-real estate ventures, and was particularly excited about the auto market, where the number of transactions each year dwarfed those in real estate. The monetary goal in this area was to post $1 billion in annual revenues by 2006, a number the company hoped to reach by acquisitions as well as internal growth. First American's ability to continue its remarkable growth for a second century was very much dependent on the success of its consumer segment.

Principal Subsidiaries

First American Title Insurance Company; First American Property & Casualty Insurance Company; Data Tree Corporation; First American CMSI; First American Capital Management, Inc.; First American Trust; First American Thrift.

Principal Competitors

Fidelity National Corporation; LandAmerica Financial Group, Inc.; Old Republic International Corporation.

Further Reading

Grifferty, Tom, "Title Insurance for Foreign Investments Is Taking Off," *National Real Estate Investor,* February 15, 1999, p. 52.
Humphreys, Carol, "The Kennedys," *Orange Coast,* October 2001.
Kelleher, James B., "TITLE: First American Diversifies," *Orange County Register,* April 28, 2002.
Silver, Jonathan D., "First American Title Celebrates 100th Anniversary," *Orange County Register,* August 3, 1999, p. C1.
Walker, Theresa, "O.C.'s Kennedy Dynasty," *Orange County Register,* January 19, 2001, p. 1.

—Ed Dinger

Forest City Enterprises, Inc.

Terminal Tower
50 Public Square, Suite 1100
Cleveland, Ohio 44113-2203
U.S.A.
Telephone: (216) 621-6060
Fax: (216) 263-6208
Web site: http://www.fceinc.com

Public Company
Incorporated: 1960
Employees: 4,271
Operating Revenues: $906.57 million (2001)
Stock Exchanges: New York
Ticker Symbol: FCEA
NAIC: 531110 Lessors of Residential Buildings and
    Dwellings; 531120 Lessors of Nonresidential
    Buildings (Except Miniwarehouses)

With properties in 19 states and the District of Columbia worth a total of $4 billion, Forest City Enterprises, Inc. is a developer and manager of commercial and residential real estate. Its extensive portfolio of hotels, apartment communities, and retail and office space is concentrated in large, urban markets. Headquartered in Cleveland, Ohio, the company maintains regional offices in New York, Los Angeles, Boston, Tucson, Denver, San Francisco, and Washington, D.C. In addition to its real estate interests, the company operates one of the nation's largest lumber wholesalers.

Foundation and Development in
the Early 20th Century

The family affair began in 1905, when members of the Ratner clan began to immigrate to the United States from their native Poland. Charles, the eldest and first to arrive in Cleveland, Ohio, founded Forest City Lumberyard in 1922. Upon their arrival, Leonard and younger siblings Max, Fannye, and Dora borrowed money to start a small creamery offering milk, butter, and eggs. Trained as a weaver, Leonard joined his older brother in the lumber business mid-decade, opening Buckeye Lumber in 1924.

Two years later, the Ratners sold their creameries to focus on the lumber and building materials market. In the late 1920s, Leonard and Charles turned the lumberyard over to brother Max, who had just earned a law degree from Case Western Reserve's John Marshall Law School. Fannye's husband, Nathan Shafran, came into the lumber business around this same time. Leonard and Charles then founded B & F Building Co., which constructed single-family homes on Cleveland's east side. Leonard rejoined the family lumber firm in 1934, bringing with him his expertise in residential construction.

Although the company sold construction materials primarily to contractors in the 1920s, 1930s, and 1940s, it had also reached out to the general public during the Great Depression. At this time, Forest City Lumber started a lending program that enabled homeless people to borrow $549 toward the purchase of building materials. By investing their own "sweat equity," these struggling individuals could build a very inexpensive home.

Forest City made its first forays into the real estate business during the 1930s and 1940s by acquiring inexpensive land repossessed by banks and other institutions. Some lots were purchased as cheaply as $10 each. During the interwar period, the company lent land and building materials to local builders with the understanding they would pay for both when the homes were sold. Then Forest City became a pioneer in the construction of prefabricated homes in 1941, but this activity was interrupted by World War II. To help in the war effort, Forest City made wooden munitions boxes for the government.

Sam Miller, who joined the company in 1947, was credited with launching Sunrise Land Co., the land development arm of the business. Miller became a full-fledged member of the family shortly thereafter when he married Leonard's daughter Ruth. Envisioning an opportunity for growth in the postwar housing shortage, the Ratners entered residential construction and were key developers of some of Cleveland's largest suburbs. The group also began to develop its extensive land holdings into apartments and shopping centers. This new focus on consumers may have led the company to begin converting its lumberyards into do-it-yourself home stores in 1955. Forest City's early entry into this important market helped make it Ohio's biggest building materials company by the end of the decade.

Company Perspectives:

Forest City Enterprises is a national owner and developer of real estate, committed to building superior, long-term value for its shareholders and customers. We accomplish this through the operation, acquisition and development of commercial, rental housing, urban entertainment and land development projects. We operate by developing meaningful relationships and leveraging our unparalleled entrepreneurial capabilities with creative talent in a fully integrated real estate organization.

Incorporation Signals Transition: The 1960s and 1970s

Forest City Enterprises was incorporated in 1960 with Leonard Ratner as chairman and Max Ratner as president. In an initial public stock offering that same year, the Ratners sold a 19.5 percent stake of the company at a face value of $4.5 million. Forest City's stock was listed on the American Stock Exchange by 1965. Although the company continued to develop its retail and wholesale lumber businesses during the 1960s and 1970s, this corporate reorganization represented a turning point for Forest City, when real estate came to the fore.

Beginning in 1966, under the direction of Max Ratner's son Charles, Forest City's building materials chain grew from $12 million in annual sales to nearly $200 million over the next two decades. The division added one of the nation's largest lumber distributors, an Oregon company, to its portfolio in 1969. Over the course of the 1960s and 1970s, it opened stores in Detroit, Chicago, and Akron. By the late 1970s the chain boasted 20 do-it-yourself centers.

Forest City's real estate developments took several forms. The company built, owned, and operated shopping centers, malls, office buildings, industrial parks, and hotels. It also acquired Akron-based construction firm Thomas J. Dillon & Co., Inc. in 1968. Under the guidance of Nathan Shafran, Forest City applied its patented method of modular high-rise housing construction to this new subsidiary. The firm's ''Operation Breakthrough'' program erected nearly 60,000 units of low-cost housing for the elderly over the next 30 years. By the end of the 1970s Forest City owned 17 shopping centers and 39 apartment buildings with a combined total of 10,800 housing units. The company had also diversified into mortgage banking, property leasing, and property management, as well as petroleum and natural gas development.

Albert B. Ratner advanced to the presidency in 1973, when Max assumed the chairmanship and Leonard took the title of founder-chairman. Corporate revenues increased from $32 million in 1963 to $235.3 million by 1979, but net income only grew from $1 million to $1.4 million.

The 1980s and 1990s: Major Urban Projects and Foreign Investment

At the dawn of the 1980s, Forest City began to phase out its smaller ventures and concentrate its resources on larger urban developments. The most significant divestment of this transition came in 1987 when the company sold its Forest City Materials chain to Handy Andy Home Improvement Centers, Inc. Forest City had dominated the local home improvement market until the early 1980s, when DIY Home Warehouse and Kmart Corp.'s Builders Square infiltrated Cleveland. Forest City tried to match the competition with deep discounts and a switch to a warehouse format, but soon realized it needed more volume and more buying power to compete with these large, well-financed national chains. This dramatic break with the company's traditional business freed it to focus on the mega-projects for which it would become nationally known in the 1980s and 1990s.

Forest City played a key role in the revitalization of downtown Cleveland, then applied the skills it had gained to urban projects throughout the United States. In 1980 the company bought Cleveland's Terminal Tower, a passenger rail terminal originally built before the Great Depression. Although the $250 million project endured several fits and starts, it would become a cornerstone of the city's rebirth. When completed in 1990, the three million-square-foot, multiuse urban renewal redevelopment featured hotels, a mall, and offices. Renamed Tower City, the project helped push Forest City's real estate portfolio over $2 billion in 1991. Major retail and commercial projects in Boston, Pittsburgh, Brooklyn, Los Angeles, Tucson, San Francisco, Chicago, and elsewhere echoed the scale and impact of Tower City in Cleveland. Forest City also continued to pursue residential developments throughout this period, creating everything from single-family inner city projects to luxury apartments and condominiums.

Although Forest City sailed through the late 1980s and early 1990s credit crunch better than many of its competitors, it was compelled to eliminate its quarterly dividend in 1991 and put the brakes on 17 projects in 1992.

Having specialized in large urban redevelopments for about a decade, a confident Forest City wagered future prosperity on international projects and gambling houses. The company made its first international foray via a 1993 joint venture with Mexico's Grupo Protexa. Ian Bacon, the executive in charge of this endeavor, compared Mexico to the United States of the 1950s and 1960s: a market ripe for the development of regional malls and shopping centers.

Forest City became increasingly involved in the construction and management of casinos—euphemistically dubbed ''urban entertainment'' in the industry—in the mid-1990s. Projects in Pittsburgh, Las Vegas, and Atlantic City either planned for or proposed gambling. Although gambling and its social and economic effects were hotly contested topics in the early 1990s, analyst Sheldon Grodsky wryly told the *Cleveland Plain Dealer*'s Bill Lubinger that, ''This is what they do, whether they do it with gambling-related property or retail or mixed use or apartments—that's real estate development.'' Clearly Forest City and the Ratner family had long been winners at the real estate game, and there was no reason to believe a losing streak was at hand.

Charles A. Ratner, son of Max, became president and chief operating officer, then assumed the role of chief executive officer in 1995 after his father's death. The year also marked the company's 75th anniversary and Forest City's new CEO re-

Key Dates:

1922:   Charles Ratner founds Forest City Lumberyard in Cleveland, Ohio.
1924:   Ratner's brother Leonard founds Buckeye Lumber.
Late 1920s: Charles and Leonard form B & F Building Co. to construct homes in Cleveland.
1930s: Forest City begins acquiring real estate in the Cleveland area.
1941:   Forest City begins building prefabricated homes.
1955:   The Ratners begin converting their lumberyards into do-it-yourself home stores.
1960:   Forest City Enterprises is incorporated and makes an initial public offering.
1968:   The company acquires an Akron, Ohio, construction company.
1970s: Forest City owns 17 shopping centers and 39 apartment buildings.
1980:   The company acquires Cleveland's historic Terminal Tower and launches an extensive renovation project.
1987:   Forest City sells its home store chain.
1990:   The Terminal Tower redevelopment is completed and renamed Tower City.
1991:   Forest City's real estate portfolio reaches $2 billion.
1993:   Forest City partners with a Mexican company to develop commercial properties in Mexico.
1997:   The company moves its headquarters into the new Tower City complex.
2001:   Forest City breaks ground on the redevelopment of Denver's former Stapleton Airport.

vealed a strategic plan outlining financial goals and the strategies necessary to reach them, a mission statement, and a set of core values. Two years later, in 1997, the company moved its stock listing from the American Stock Exchange to the New York Stock Exchange. Also in 1997, Forest City moved its corporate headquarters to Tower City, its recently developed high-profile Cleveland property.

Novel Projects As Company Enters the New Millennium

Forest City closed out the 20th century with a burst of urban development activity. Among the projects the company completed in 1998 and 1999 were a large office building in the Massachusetts Institute of Technology's University Park; a luxury apartment high-rise in Bethesda, Maryland; a mall near San Diego, California; and a shopping center in New Jersey. As these new properties were opening, Forest City had plenty in the pipeline to replace them. In 1998 alone the company launched more than a dozen projects. Two of the most high profile jobs were on opposite coasts: in New York City, the company began construction of a 300,000-square-foot hotel and entertainment complex in Times Square, while in San Francisco it kicked off redevelopment of the city's historic Emporium building near Union Square.

One of its largest and most unusual projects came in 1999 when Forest City was awarded the $4 billion job of redevel-

oping Denver's obsolete Stapleton Airport. The project—which was delayed by numerous obstacles before finally getting underway in early 2001—involved converting some 3,000 acres of former airport land into a community complete with housing, retail, and office space. By the time the company broke ground on the Stapleton project, it was in the midst of planning for a number of other developments including a Times Square headquarters for the venerable New York Times Company; a one million-square-foot mall near Richmond, Virginia; an upscale shopping area in Pasadena, California; and a state-of-the-art facility in Cleveland, designed to house telecommunications and IT companies.

In 2001, as businesses across the United States struggled with a difficult economy, Forest City weathered the storm well. For the year, the company achieved record results in both revenues and earnings and took steps to strengthen its financial liquidity. It also made a secondary public offering of 3.9 million shares (which generated $118 million) and sold seven properties, including a $108 million mall in Tucson. The influx of capital allowed the company to reduce its nonrecourse mortgage debt by almost $96 million.

Forest City stormed into 2002, completing nine property acquisitions and opening five new developments all in the first half of the fiscal year. It also continued to make significant progress in ongoing developments at Denver's Stapleton Airport and MIT's University Park. For the second quarter, the company posted an increase of around 8 percent in both revenues and earnings over the same period in 2001.

Barring unforeseen events, the company appeared likely to continue in an aggressive development mode. In a September 2002 press release, Forest City President Charles Ratner said the company expected to complete at least five more retail projects during the year, as well as reach several milestones at the Stapleton project. In addition, there were 18 projects in construction—eight residential communities, three office developments, and seven retail centers.

Principal Subsidiaries

Forest City Capital Corporation; Forest City Commercial Group, Inc.; Forest City Finance Corporation; Forest City Land Group; Forest City Ratner Companies; Forest City Rental Properties Corporation; Forest City Residential Group, Inc.; Forest City Residential Management, Inc.; Forest City Residential West, Inc.; Forest City Trading Group, Inc.

Principal Competitors

The Inland Group, Inc.; Trammell Crow Company; Trizec Properties, Inc.

Further Reading

Bullard, Stan, ''Forest City Finds Amigo to Build Malls in Mexico,'' *Crain's Cleveland Business,* May 17, 1993, pp. 3, 25.
——, ''Forest City's Miller Likes Privacy, Power,'' *Crain's Cleveland Business,* August 2, 1993, pp. 13, 15.
Chatman, Angela D., ''Ohio Companies Among Tops in Multifamily Units,'' *Cleveland Plain Dealer,* April 1, 1995, p. 9SU.

Clark, Sandra, "Putting Projects on Hold," *Cleveland Plain Dealer,* January 16, 1992, p. 1D.

DeWitt, John, "Halle's Building Splendid Again," *Cleveland Plain Dealer,* December 11, 1985, p. 7D.

Gerdel, Thomas, "Forest City Goes Full Speed on Its Development Course," *Cleveland Plain Dealer,* July 31, 1990, pp. 1D, 8D.

Gleisser, Marcus, "Business Leader Max Ratner Dies," *Cleveland Plain Dealer,* June 2, 1995, pp. 1A, 12A.

——, "Close Family Enterprise," *Cleveland Plain Dealer,* January 15, 1987, p. 2C.

——, "Forest City Named Developer for Project in NYC's Times Square," *Cleveland Plain Dealer,* September 8, 1995.

Hardin, Angela, "A Woman of Influence: Tower City Owes Its Existence to Miller's Determination, Energy," *Crain's Cleveland Business,* April 3, 2000, p. 30.

"Hurting Balance Sheet Helps Firm Build Assets," *Engineering News Record,* October 11, 1979 p. 23.

Karle, Delinda, "Forest City Ends Home Improving," *Cleveland Plain Dealer,* January 15, 1987, pp. 1A, 17A.

Koshar, John Leo, "Ambitious Projects Fill Forest City's Drawing Boards," *Cleveland Plain Dealer,* July 1, 1984, p. 1G.

Lubinger, Bill, "Forest City Forges Gambling Ties," *Cleveland Plain Dealer,* July 10, 1996, pp. 1C, 3C.

Moore, Paula, "Stapleton's Ambitious Developer: Founded As a Lumber Company, Forest City Tackles Monstrous Airport Project," *Denver Business Journal,* January 29, 1999, p. 3B.

Phillips, Stephen, "Forest City Betting on Projects," *Cleveland Plain Dealer,* July 1, 1994, pp. 1C, 2C.

Rudnitsky, Howard, "Survivor," *Forbes,* June 8, 1992, p. 48.

Sabath, Donald, "Forest City to Celebrate Nate Shafran's 50 Years," *Cleveland Plain Dealer,* June 13, 1989, p. 4D.

Sartin, V. David, "Save Tower City, Kucinich Demands," *Cleveland Plain Dealer,* September 1, 1984, pp. 1A, 11A.

——, "Tower City Project Is Scrapped," *Cleveland Plain Dealer,* August 31, 1984, pp. 1A, 10A.

Sullivan, Elizabeth, "Hilton, Forest City Sign Deal on Downtown Hotel," *Cleveland Plain Dealer,* July 27, 1983, pp. 1A, 8A.

—April Dougal Gasbarre
—update: Shawna Brynildssen

Forest Laboratories, Inc.

909 Third Avenue
New York, New York 10022-4731
U.S.A.
Telephone: (212) 421-7850
Toll Free: (800) 947-7850
Fax: (212) 750-9152
Web site: http://www.frx.com

Public Company
Incorporated: 1956
Employees: 3,731
Sales: $1.6 billion (2002)
Stock Exchanges: New York
Ticker Symbol: FRX
NAIC: 325412 Pharmaceutical Preparation Manufacturing

Forest Laboratories, Inc. develops, manufactures, and sells both brand-name and generic prescription and nonprescription drugs in the United States and Europe. The main therapeutic areas that the company concentrates on include depression, Alzheimer's disease/neuropathic pain, hypertension, asthma, and gastrointestinal disease. Since its introduction in 1998, the antidepressant drug Celexa has been Forest's blockbuster, accounting for nearly 70 percent of company revenues by fiscal 2002. Sales of Celexa helped make Forest one of the fastest growing companies in the United States in the late 1990s and early 2000s. Late in 2002 the company stopped promoting Celexa in favor of a second-generation version of the drug called Lexapro. Other key products include Tiazac, used to treat hypertension and angina; Benicar, also a treatment for hypertension; Aerobid, an inhaler for treating asthma; and Infasurf, used to treat respiratory distress in infants. Most of the pharmaceutical products marketed by Forest Laboratories were developed by other companies and then licensed by Forest.

Early Years: Transitioning from Lab Service to Generic Drug Marketer

Forest Laboratories was founded in 1956 as a small laboratory service company. It helped larger pharmaceutical companies, which had hefty research and development funds, to create new drugs. After Forest developed a drug, it would hand the new product off to its client, who would then market, sell, and distribute the offering. Forest achieved a degree of success in its niche and found a steady demand for its services during the late 1950s and early 1960s. In addition, the company swerved slightly from its pharmaceuticals focus by diversifying into other markets: it invested particularly heavily in food businesses—principally candy and ice cream—and also sold branded vitamins. Its foray into other ventures was an attempt to bolster the company's bottom line and to protect it from risks associated with the drug industry.

Forest, which went public in 1967, continued to enjoy the greatest amount of success in its core drug development business. One of its most successful achievements was its creation of a controlled-release technology, called Synchron, that allowed an ingested drug to be slowly released inside the body. It was this penchant for exploiting profitable niches that would later become the base of the company's meteoric rise.

By the mid-1970s accusations had been raised against the company's chairman, Hans Lowey, that he had inflated profits. Howard Solomon, who at the time was serving as outside counsel for Forest, was asked to investigate the charges. He found evidence to support the allegations, Lowey resigned, and Solomon took over as CEO of the company in 1977. Solomon sold off Forest's lagging food businesses and dropped out of the vitamin business to focus on the pharmaceutical market. He then led the company through an important transition from a service firm to a company that actually manufactured and sold its own pharmaceuticals.

Recognizing that the big profits in the drug industry were garnered from the marketing and sale of new drugs, Solomon began looking for a way to break into that side of the business. The company lacked the vast resources, however, that were necessary to fund the development, testing, marketing, and distribution of an entirely new drug. Indeed, it was entirely feasible that, even if Forest could gather enough capital to fund a new drug, the venture could go bust for any number of reasons and force the company into bankruptcy. For example, a newly developed drug could fail to pass federal approval, rendering it commercially useless, or the drug could simply fail to achieve commercial appeal.

Rather than trying to develop and market new drugs, Solomon decided to steer the company toward the drug marketing business through a sort of back door—generics. Generic drugs (drugs that perform the same essential function as the brand-name drugs they mimic, but cost less) were becoming increasingly popular during the late 1970s as an alternative to expensive brand-name pharmaceuticals. Because generics lacked patent protection, however, profits were typically elusive—the first company to introduce the drug could make big profits for a short time, until lower-priced generics from competing companies entered the market.

Solomon was able to successfully exploit the limited opportunities offered in the generics business by focusing on Forest's controlled-release Synchron technology. Forest had already succeeded in applying the technology to drugs for several major pharmaceutical companies. Solomon correctly suspected that a viable market existed for controlled-released versions of several popular drugs. As a result, the company shifted its corporate focus to generics, realizing sound revenue and profit growth during the late 1970s and early 1980s.

Despite its success with generics, Forest Labs' management in the early 1980s was still eager to participate in the potentially lucrative business of marketing brand-name, patented drugs. It had most of the tools necessary to compete in the industry—it maintained a talented research and development arm, which had long been one of its core competencies, and had accrued a degree of manufacturing, sales, and distribution knowledge through its generics business. But Forest still lacked the resources it needed to go toe-to-toe with the industry giants.

Mid-1980s: Shifting Focus from Generics to Licensed Brand-Name Drugs

Forest embarked on a new corporate strategy in the mid-1980s that it hoped would allow it to market and sell proprietary drugs without having to face pharmaceutical industry leaders. It would look for branded drugs that had already been developed and marketed by larger companies, but served very small customer niches. If it found a drug that it felt was undervalued, it would purchase or receive license to the product and increase its value through aggressive marketing. The reasoning behind the strategy was that the big companies tended to ignore their smaller drugs, focusing their resources instead on popular, high-profile, high-profit offerings.

The only weapon needed to carry out the new strategy that was still missing from Forest Labs' armory was a sales force. So, in 1984 Forest purchased the assets of O'Neal, Jones & Feldman Inc., a St. Louis, Missouri-based pharmaceuticals company, for $10 million. O'Neal, Jones & Feldman was put on the block after its president and another executive were convicted and jailed for selling a drug that had not been approved by the Food and Drug Administration (FDA). Tragically, 27 infant deaths were linked to the misbranded drug before the company pleaded guilty to 17 violations.

Forest paid $8.3 million for its new acquisition and assumed an additional $1.5 million in debt. In what turned out to be a savvy purchase, Forest immediately gained an established 71-member sales force. In a carefully plotted stratagem, the company began tagging new drugs on to its existing line of generics and branded drugs, some of which had belonged to O'Neal, Jones & Feldman. For example, the company bought a drug called Esgic, a stress headache remedy, and was able to significantly boost its sales. Forest also purchased other small pharmaceutical companies, continually increasing the size and scope of its sales force and gaining access to new proprietary drugs. In 1989, for instance, Forest acquired UAD Laboratories for $33 million in stock. This deal increased the sales force to 300 and added to the company portfolio a narcotic analgesic product, Lorcet, which within a few years had annual sales of $60 million. All the while, the company's generics business remained strong.

Forest's growth strategy during the late 1980s and early 1990s was relatively simple and straightforward, yet few other firms were successfully implementing the same tactics. Before it purchased an undervalued drug, it would make sure that the product was a good match with the company's existing product line. By emphasizing a small number of therapeutic categories, such as asthma and headache relief, Forest was able to increase the potency of its sales force and achieve a higher number of prescriptions written per sales call. Indeed, whereas many pharmaceutical firms would send salespeople to general practitioners, offering them a range of drug lines, most Forest salespeople focused on a few groups of specialists, particularly allergists, internists, and pulmonary physicians.

Forest's knack for turning an undervalued drug into an industry overachiever was evidenced by its 1986 purchase of Aerobid, an asthma drug, from industry giant Schering-Plough Corporation, for $6 million. Although Aerobid sales totaled only $2.3 million annually at the time of purchase, Forest was able to generate huge returns from the drug. By 1991, in fact, Aerobid revenues had exploded to $30 million annually. Furthermore, bolstered by independent research that recommended increased use of the drug in certain applications, sales of Aerobid eventually rocketed past the $100 million mark by the mid-1990s. Aerobid, along with Forest's other two major drugs (Tessalon, a cough medication, and Propranolol, a generic used to treat high blood pressure), would account for over 40 percent of the company's sales by 1993.

Rapid Revenue Growth in the Early 1990s

By the early 1990s it was clear that Forest Labs' new strategy was a shrewd one. Indeed, the company's annual revenues had ballooned since the mid-1980s to about $133 million by 1990, of which $30 million was profit. Sales increased to $176 million in 1991 as income leapt to approximately $40 million. Importantly, Forest's sales force had swelled to more than 500, including more than 50 salespeople employed by subsidiaries acquired in Europe. "The large sales force is really helping the company pick up drugs that fall through the cracks,'' observed industry analyst Martin Bukoll in a November 1991 issue of *Crain's New York Business.*

The strength of Forest's overall operations was exhibited by a setback that it encountered in 1991. Forest had spent $20 million for a license to market a new drug called Micturin, which had been developed through a joint venture between E.I. du Pont and Merck & Co., Inc. Forest hoped the drug would become one of its primary offerings with over $100 million in annual sales. Unfortunately, the FDA, citing negative side effects, chose not to approve the drug. Although the company's stock price plummeted 30 percent, within a few months it had regained most of its value on expectations of growth from other segments of Forest's operations. Furthermore, growth of Forest's sales, earnings, and equity value continued unabated through 1991 and 1992.

As Forest Labs continued to acquire low-profile underachievers that were being ignored by the major manufacturers, sales mushroomed throughout 1993 and 1994. ''We can do things that large companies can't do,'' explained Solomon in an October 1993 issue of the *St. Louis Post Dispatch.* ''Large companies are not interested unless a product can do $100 million per year in sales.'' Solomon watched his company's sales jump to $239 million in 1992, $285 million in 1993, and to an amazing $348 million in 1994 (fiscal year ending March 31, 1994). Likewise, net income tracked revenue growth, soaring more than 30 percent in 1992 to $50 million, to $64 million during 1993, and then to a whopping $80 million in 1994. The company's workforce had multiplied to about 1,300 worldwide.

To accommodate the company's 100 percent sales growth in less than three years, Forest hurriedly expanded its U.S. and overseas facilities. Its major St. Louis subsidiary, Forest Pharmaceuticals Inc., which accounted for roughly two-thirds of company sales in 1993, was consolidated into a newly renovated 87,000-square-foot facility replete with high-tech manufacturing and distribution systems. The company added 65,000

square feet to a manufacturing operation in Cincinnati, and boosted its New York production facility, which manufactured generics, to 150,000 square feet. Forest was also completing a major new production facility in Ireland in 1994, which would be used to supply its eastern and western European clients.

Although Forest's established brand-name drugs and generics had provided consistent growth for the company since the mid-1980s, it was forced to continue its search for new acquisitions that would supplant its fading superstars. Indeed, many of the brand-name drugs that it had licensed had only a few years of patent protection remaining before generics would diminish their profit margins. As a result, Forest was reliant on new additions to its pharmaceutical arsenal to sustain its rampant growth. Reflecting the company's intent to introduce new products was its growing emphasis on research and development (R&D)—annual R&D expenditures by Forest increased from $10 million in 1990 to nearly $30 million during 1993.

Forest reached a peak in fiscal 1996 when record revenues of $461.8 million were recorded. Leading the way was Aerobid, with sales of $147 million. The very next year, however, the company was hit by several setbacks, leading to a 37 percent decline in revenues and the first loss ($25 million) in company history. During the year, Aerobid began facing stiff competition from a new asthma drug from Glaxo Inc. called Flovent. Sales of Forest's number two drug, the painkiller Lorcet, plunged after its patent expired and generic competitors were quickly introduced into the market. Forest's own generic product business suffered from severe competition from both industry giants and hundreds of smaller players. In addition, while the company's product pipeline remained promising, delays in getting government approvals for several new drugs cost the company additional potential sales.

Explosive Growth in the Late 1990s and Early 2000s Fueled by Celexa

Forest Labs' downturn proved temporary, and the company would soon begin a new period of even more explosive growth. In fact, the foundation had already been laid for the turnaround. Late in 1995 Forest licensed the U.S. rights for Tiazac from Biovail Corporation, a Toronto firm. The 1996 introduction of Tiazac, a once-daily calcium channel blocker used to treat hypertension and angina, marked Forest's entrance into the huge cardiovascular market. After achieving $30 million in sales during its year of introduction, Tiazac generated $158 million in revenues by 2000.

While Tiazac was certainly a success, it and all of Forest Labs' other products were soon far overshadowed by a drug called Celexa. This latest turn in the company's fortunes began in 1994 when CEO Solomon's son Andrew fell into a deep depression. Solomon began researching treatments for his son and discovered a European antidepressant named Cipramil, which had been developed by the Danish company H. Lundbeck A/S. Cipramil had achieved market share in Europe of more than 40 percent mainly because it was considered to have fewer side effects than the U.S. blockbusters Prozac (Eli Lilly and Company) and Zoloft (Pfizer Inc.) The head of Lundbeck had tried to license the drug to several large U.S. drug companies, but each deal fell through—the companies apparently having concluded that Cipramil's sales potential was not large enough for them. For Forest, however, Cipramil was a perfect fit, and so Solomon signed a deal with Lundbeck in early 1996 to license the drug for sale in the United States under the name Celexa.

The FDA approved Celexa in July 1998. To help market the drug, Solomon reached a copromotion deal with Warner-Lambert Company. This alliance ended after only a year, however, because Warner-Lambert agreed in 1999 to be acquired by Pfizer. Rather than pursue another copromotion alliance, Forest elected to go it alone. The company's sales force was substantially beefed up, growing from 850 representatives to 1,425, an increase of 70 percent. The reps touted Celexa's minimal side effects, and to give the product a further edge Forest offered the drug for 20 percent less than the cost of its formidable rivals. The strategy proved brilliant. Celexa quickly grabbed a 9 percent share of the $6 billion antidepressant market. Sales in fiscal 1999—specifically, from launch in September 1998 through March 1999—already amounted to $91 million. Celexa sales then mushroomed to $427 million the following year, with the drug reaching blockbuster status as a $1 billion product by 2002. By that year, Celexa's market share had reached 17 percent.

Overall sales and profits for Forest Labs ballooned thanks to the great success of Celexa. The company posted net income of $77.2 million on sales of $624 million for fiscal 1999, but by 2002 these figures were $338 million and $1.6 billion, respectively. During this same period, the company's stock surged as well, nearly quadrupling in value. In 1999 the stock began trading on the prestigious New York Stock Exchange, having been listed for three decades on the American Stock Exchange. On the down side, Forest was slated to lose patent protection on Celexa in mid-2003, with generic competition expected to be introduced in early 2005, so there was a pressing need to find other winning products—particularly because Celexa was generating more than 60 percent of revenues by fiscal 2001.

A minor success for Forest came in October 1999 when Infasurf was launched. Infasurf was used to treat and prevent respiratory distress syndrome (RDS), an affliction that occurred in tens of thousands of infants annually and could cause death or physical abnormalities. Forest had licensed the drug from ONY, Inc. in 1991. Sales during fiscal 2000 totaled less than $5 million. A much more significant product introduced by Forest was Benicar, an agent used to treat hypertension and therefore a follow-up to the successful Tiazac. Benicar had been developed by Sankyo Pharma Inc., and through an agreement signed in December 2001, it was copromoted by Forest and Sankyo following the receipt of FDA approval in April 2002.

Forest hoped its next blockbuster would be Lexapro. This drug was a new version of Celexa that the company touted as being more pure and powerful than the original. Lexapro was approved by the FDA in August 2002, and Forest launched it the following month. At the same time it stopped promoting Celexa and added an additional 175 sales representatives to further strengthen the sales force. Lexapro got off to a strong start, achieving sales of $21.7 million during its first month on the market. Initial indications were that the level of cannibalizing of Celexa prescriptions were minimal, with most of the Lexapro prescriptions coming either from patients taking an

antidepressant drug for the first time or from patients switching from other antidepressants. To further expand the market potential of the drug, Forest was also working to gain FDA approval for the use of Lexapro in treating other disorders: generalized anxiety, social anxiety, and panic disorders. Some industry analysts believed that Lexapro could grow into a $2 billion-per-year drug by the mid-to-late 2000s.

There were several other promising drugs in the Forest development pipeline, adding to the company's bright prospects for the future. In October 2001 the company submitted a new drug application (NDA) to the FDA for lercanidipine, another hypertension treatment, which was licensed from Recordati S.p.A., a privately held Italian firm. Forest was jointly developing two pharmaceuticals with Merz + Co. of Frankfurt, Germany: memantine, a treatment for Alzheimer's disease, and neramexane, which was being investigated for the treatment of several nervous systems disorders. As a result of a March 1997 ruling by the FDA, Forest was facing the withdrawal of approval for Aerobid because it, like most other asthma inhalers, contained chlorofluorocarbons (CFCs), which were being phased out of use because of the harm they were doing to the environment. Working with the pharmaceuticals division of 3M, Forest was developing a new non-CFC version of Aerobid called Aerospan. An NDA for Aerospan was filed with the FDA in April 2000. Of these and other products in the pipeline, it appeared that memantine was the one most likely to become Forest Labs' next big seller.

Principal Subsidiaries

Forest Pharmaceuticals, Inc.; Inwood Laboratories, Inc.; Forest Laboratories Ireland Limited; Forest Laboratories Europe (U.K.); Tosara Products Limited (U.K.).

Principal Competitors

Merck & Co., Inc.; Pfizer Inc.; GlaxoSmithKline plc; Eli Lilly and Company; Novartis AG; Aventis; Bristol-Myers Squibb Company; Roche Group; Abbot Laboratories; AstraZeneca PLC; Schering-Plough Corporation.

Further Reading

Alson, Amy, "Expansion Sustains Health at Forest," *Crain's New York Business,* February 9, 1987, p. 10.
Barker, Robert, "Unexplored Forest: Probing the Mystery of a Drug Firm's High P-E," *Barron's,* August 27, 1984, pp. 13+.
Benson, Barbara, "Drugmaker Forest Branches Out," *Crain's New York Business,* October 16, 1995, p. 31.
Berfield, Susan, "A CEO and His Son," *Business Week,* May 27, 2002, pp. 72–76+.
Colwell, Carolyn, "Firm Buys Hazeltine Building," *Newsday,* March 18, 1994, Sec. 1, p. 1.
Davison, Robin, "Forest Development Gambit Pays Off," *European Chemical News,* September 20, 1993, pp. 16+.
"Forest Gets Some High Marks for Its Slate of New Products," *Chemical Marketing Reporter,* January 4, 1993, p. 7.
"From a Raw Deal to a Winning Hand," *Business Week,* June 7, 1999, p. 75.
Hovey, Hollister H., "Surging Sales of Antidepressants Have Forest Labs Rolling in Green," *Wall Street Journal,* October 30, 2002, p. B5A.

Hwang, Suein, "Forest Labs Faces Problem As Kabi Withdraws a Drug," *Wall Street Journal,* September 16, 1991.

Kamen, Robin, "Unwanted Drugs a Powerful Elixir," *Crain's New York Business,* November 4, 1991, Sec. 1, p. 3.

Reingold, Jennifer, "Forest Laboratories: Beyond the Trees," *Financial World,* April 11, 1995, p. 16.

Rudinsky, Howard, "Sardines, Not Whales," *Forbes,* December 5, 1994, pp. 47+.

Sonenclar, Robert, "The Credibility of Mr. Solomon," *Financial World,* June 26, 1985, pp. 82+.

Steyer, Robert, "Flu Season: Firm Brings Out Drug for Epidemic," *St. Louis Post Dispatch,* October 18, 1993, p. E3BP.

Temes, Judy, "Local Drug Company Swallows Bitter Pill: First Year of Losses," *Crain's New York Business,* May 26, 1997, p. 3.

—Dave Mote
—update: David E. Salamie

Global Power Equipment Group Inc.

6120 S. Yale, Suite 1480
Tulsa, Oklahoma 74136
U.S.A.
Telephone: (918) 488-0828
Fax: (918) 488-8389
Web site: http://www.globalpower.com

Public Company
Incorporated: 1998
Employees: 1,747
Sales: $723.5 million (2001)
Stock Exchanges: New York
Ticker Symbol: GEG
NAIC: 332410 Power Boiler and Heat Exchanger
   Manufacturing

With its corporate headquarters located in Tulsa, Oklahoma, Global Power Equipment Group Inc. is a leading designer and manufacturer of equipment for gas turbine power plants. The fastest growing segment of the power generation industry, gas turbine power plants use a gas turbine and generator to produce electricity. Until recently most of these plants relied on simple-cycle gas turbine systems, which converted just a third of the fuel energy content into electricity. Combined-cycle plants add a heat recovery steam generator (HRSG), using heat exhaust to produce steam in order to generate additional electricity. Combined-cycle plants convert as much as 57 percent of the fuel's energy content into electricity. Global Power manufactures HRSGs as well as other products needed by both single-cycle and combined-cycle gas turbine power plants, including exhaust systems, filter houses, diverter dampers, inlet systems, specialty boilers and related products, and gas and steam turbine enclosures. The company divides its business into two operating segments: heat recovery equipment and auxiliary power equipment. Marketed under the Braden, Deltak, and Consolidated Fabricators brands, Global Power equipment is used around the world, found in power plants in over 30 countries on six continents.

Corporate Lineage Dating Back to 19th Century

The oldest component of Global Power, as well as the company's Tulsa roots, can be traced to the Braden brand and its founder, Glenn T. Braden. He was born in 1856 in Waterford, Pennsylvania, a state where some of the nation's earliest oil discoveries were made. Fascinated at an early age by the emerging oil industry, Braden by 12 was recovering spilt oil by sopping crude off the surface of puddles with rags. He then proceeded to wring out a large number of oil-soaked rags to produce a barrel of oil, and in this painstaking way was able to earn pocket money. Braden was only 13 when he was hired by the Indian Rock Company to help drill oil wells. After helping his father operate a small refinery for three years, he went to work as a pipe liner for the Union Pipe Line Company, a Standard Oil subsidiary. His association with Standard Oil would last for more than 30 years. An early proponent of natural gas, he invented the Bradenhead, which diverted natural gas from oil wells without disrupting oil production. He was instrumental in Standard forming the Hope Natural Gas Company to transport natural gas from fields in West Virginia to western cities. It was under his supervision that the first natural gasline was laid, stretching from West Virginia to Cleveland, Ohio.

Connection to Tulsa Dates to 1905

Braden's connection to Tulsa, Oklahoma, dates to 1905 when he and T.N. Barnsdall formed the Osage & Oklahoma Company after buying 155,000 acres of land owned by the Osage nation of Native Americans. As part of the land transaction they also picked up a small natural gas plant in Tulsa. A year later Braden created the Oklahoma Natural Gas Company to build a pipeline connecting the Tulsa gas field to a number of Oklahoma communities. Over the next dozen years he built up a collection of gas companies and a pipeline network that was consolidated under the Oklahoma Natural Gas charter in 1917, at which point he resigned from Standard Oil. In 1923 he formed the Braden Steel Company in order to diversify into the steel building business, producing fabricated steel buildings and winches for use in the oil industry. Three years later the steel building operation was incorporated separately as the Braden Steel Corporation. Braden would be well into his 80s when he

---

Company Perspectives:

The company has honed its expertise in the design, manufacturing and delivery of gas turbine equipment with over 30 years of experience in the power generation industry.

---

finally relinquished control, selling the business in 1941 to William Moorer, who headed Braden Steel until 1958 when it was sold to H.G. Lewis and C.W. Flint, Jr., of Clint and Steel. In the mid-1960s the company conducted a study to determine new fields that Braden Steel could enter as a way to diversify its operations. Management settled on the power generation field and began to manufacture air inlet and exhaust silencing systems and enclosures for turbines used in power plants. Over the next few years the company grew this product line so that by 1972 it was the principal supplier to General Electric and Westinghouse.

Braden Steel remained involved in both the metal building and power generation businesses throughout the 1970s, then in 1981 management decided that the metal buildings segment required more manufacturing space. This business was then merged with Metallic Building Company and its operation transferred to a larger Houston, Texas, facility. Braden Steel carried on with its power generation business until March 1984 when it acquired Econotherm Energy Corporation, prompting a reorganization that resulted in Braden operating as a division of Econotherm. Less than two years later the Braden division was sold to AMCA International, and it was at this time that Global Power's current CEO, Larry Edwards, became involved in the business by being named general manager. Although Braden was also involved in non-energy activity, its power generation business began to display exceptional growth during the late 1980s, as sales of gas turbines picked up worldwide. Two former AMCA executives, Vince Martin and Mark Train, then formed Jason Incorporated and in 1989 purchased Braden. Under Jason, Braden expanded its gas turbine business in 1992 by acquiring Metrio Technologies, a Dutch firm. As a result, Braden added diverter dampers, allowing the company to now offer exhaust systems. Two years later Jason acquired DELTAK Corporation and merged it with Braden to form a subsidiary named Jason Power Holdings.

DELTAK was founded by Denis Csathy, a native of Hungary who immigrated to Canada in 1956 in order to escape the turmoil of the Hungarian Revolution. A trained engineer, he went to work for the Minneapolis firm of William Brothers Boiler in 1960 as its chief designer, then in 1963 became the head of its heat transfer division, which was an early pioneer in the design of boilers for use in gas turbine heat recovery. In 1968 the parent company was acquired by American Hoist and Derrick, and the heat transfer business subsequently sold to Riley-Stoker Corporation, based in Worcester, Massachusetts. Rather than accept a transfer, Csathy preferred to stay in Minneapolis and took a position with RayGo, Inc. which had been established several years earlier by Gordon Garis, who had originally hired Csathy at William Brothers. RayGo manufactured road construction equipment but Garis wanted to diversify into waste heat recovery.

As a result, Csathy started a new heat transfer division at RayGo, naming it DELTAK. "Delta" alluded to the name of his patented watertube boiler design, so called because of its shape, while the letter "k" was the engineering symbol for thermal conductivity. DELTAK sold its first heat exchanger units in 1969, but by 1972 RayGo management realized that it was unable to invest the necessary funds in growing the business. Key employees of the division then formed a company to take over the operation. The new DELTAK was headed by Csathy until he was debilitated by a stroke in 1985, leading to his death several years later. The company carried on independently for several years before being acquired by Jason.

In May 1998 the management team of Jason's power generation products division formed GEEG Holdings, L.L.C. in order to acquire the division with backing from affiliates of Saw Mill Capital, a private investment firm that specialized in energy, as well as other financial investments. The acquisition of the Jason assets, resulting in the operational company of Global Energy Equipment Group, L.L.C., was completed in June 1998. Little more than two years later the company was again seeking purchasers, and in August 2000, as part of a $310 million recapitalization transaction, control passed to Harvest Partners, Inc., a New York buyout firm founded in 1981, which acquired an 80 percent stake in the business from Saw Mill Capital. Harvest learned about Global Energy through a member of its advisory board who was involved in the power industry and recognized the potential of the business in light of future growth in gas turbine generating systems. Because Harvest had been studying the energy sector since 1999 it was able to strike quickly when the opportunity arose to acquire Global Energy.

Only a few months after Harvest gained control, Global Energy acquired Consolidated Fabricators Incorporated (CFI) in a $28 million deal. CFI designed and fabricated gas and steam turbine power plant enclosures, a product that was a complement to Global Energy since the two sold different products to the same power plant installation. Based in Auburn, Massachusetts, CFI owned additional manufacturing facilities in South Carolina and Mexico. The company was started in 1971, and in addition to power generation products, it was also involved in the pulp and paper, defense, nuclear, and machine tool industries. Although Harvest maintained that it intended to grow Global Energy both organically and through acquisitions, it was also planning a way to reap a return on its investment. According to Stephen Eisenstein, a general partner of the firm, "We were able to do an acquisition very quickly within three months of closing and the organic growth of the company continued along at a dramatic pace, which led us to the conclusion of an IPO with the sector."

Formation of Global Power As Part of 2001 IPO

With the economy lapsing into recession and the window essentially closed on the IPO market, Global Energy was one of the few companies able to succeed with an initial offering in such an unpromising environment. The company was helped immensely by the California energy crisis, with news reports of rolling blackouts and astronomically high electricity prices. It was an easy message to convey to investors: New power plants had to be constructed and that 90 percent would rely on gas turbine generators, most of which would be combined-cycle plants, an area in which Global Energy was particularly strong. Moreover, Global Energy commanded a 60 percent share of the U.S. market. By all accounts the company was clearly poised for strong growth. A road show for the IPO met with an enthusiastic response, oversubscribed by ten times. Several days before the offering, Global Power Equipment Group was formed to succeed GEEG Holdings. The initial price range of Global Power was $16 to $18, but when the offering, led by Credit Suisse First Boston and Salomon Smith Barney, took place in May 2001 the shares were actually sold at $20, resulting in net proceeds of $131.2 million. The following day, trading commenced on the New York Stock Exchange and shares increased in value some 57 percent, jumping to $31.45. The offering price and initial trading were bolstered somewhat by the announcement of the Bush administration comprehensive energy plan, the conservation part of which promoted fuel cell companies.

Some of the enthusiasm over Global Power began to dissipate later in 2001 in the wake of the terrorist attacks that occurred on September 11, the Enron scandal later in the fall, and a mild winter that hurt the energy sector. Global Power reported excellent results at year-end: revenues grew from $416.5 million in 2000 to $723.5 million in 2001. The company also turned a $7.2 million loss in 2000 into a $138.7 million net profit in 2001. Nonetheless, the company was not without doubters, who pointed to Global Power's dependence on a handful of customers. Roughly three-quarters of all sales came from five companies: General Electric, Mitsubishi Heavy Industries, Siemens-Westinghouse, Bechtel, and Duke Power. Moreover, some questioned if the rush to construct additional power plants was premature and that a stagnant demand for electricity in the United States might lead to customers canceling their orders with Global Power. As a result of these and other concerns, the price of the company's stock dropped significantly, hovering around the $5 mark.

According to Global Power management, however, the key to the company's future lay overseas, especially in China. Statistical evidence also seemed to support the company's prospects, both domestically and internationally. In the United States, over 355 gigawatts of new capacity would have to be found over the next 20 years in order to replace outdated facilities as well as to meet rising consumer demand, and over 80 percent of these new plants were expected to be powered by gas turbines. The situation in the rest of the world looked even more promising for Global Power. As much as a third of the world's population still lacked electricity, and demand for power was expected to rise dramatically in developing Asian nations, with lesser yet significant increases projected for Europe and South America by 2020. To meet this future challenge Global Power planned to pursue strategic acquisitions that would not only broaden the company's product lines but extend its geographic reach. In addition Global Power hoped to improve profitability by taking advantage of its engineering capabilities to launch new products. Although energy remained a cyclical industry, which might temporarily halt Global Power's momentum, there was every reason to believe that the company was likely to prosper into the foreseeable future.

Principal Subsidiaries

Deltak, L.L.C.; CFI Holdings, Inc.; Global Power Equipment Group International.

Principal Operating Units

Heat Recovery Equipment; Auxiliary Power Equipment.

Principal Competitors

Donaldson Company, Inc.; Foster Wheeler Corporation; Spirax Sarco.

Further Reading

Alpert, Bill, "Power to the People," *Barron's,* April 16, 2001, p. 37.
Ray, Russell, "Tulsa-Okla.-Based Power Equipment Firm Focused on Chinese Electricity Growth," *Tulsa World,* June 7, 2002.
——, "Tulsa-Okla.-Based Power Plant Equipment Maker's IPO Raises $147 Million," *Tulsa World,* May 30, 2001.
Robinson, Rick, "IPO for Tulsa, Okla.-Based Power Plant Construction Firm Called Success," *Daily Oklahoman,* May 19, 2001.
Rudakewych, Lesia, "Global Power Makes Strong Wall St. Debut," *Financial Times,* May 19, 2001, p. 8.
Tran, Hung, "Harvest Launches into Acquisition Frenzy," *Buyouts,* August 28, 200, p. 1.

—Ed Dinger

Goodman Fielder Ltd.

75 Talavera Road
North Ryde
New South Wales 2113
Australia
Telephone: (+61) 2-8874-6000
Fax: (+61) 2-8874-6099
Web site: http://www.goodmanfielder.com

Public Company
Incorporated: 1986
Employees: 12,548
Sales: A$2.96 billion ($1.67 billion) (2002)
Stock Exchanges: OTC
Ticker Symbol: GMFIY (ADRs)
NAIC: 311225 Fats and Oils Refining and Blending;
    311211 Flour Milling; 311230 Breakfast Cereal
    Manufacturing; 311423 Dried and Dehydrated Food
    Manufacturing; 311812 Commercial Bakeries; 311821
    Cookie and Cracker Manufacturing; 311822 Flour
    Mixes and Dough Manufacturing from Purchased
    Flour; 311823 Pasta Manufacturing; 311919 Other
    Snack Food Manufacturing; 551112 Offices of Other
    Holding Companies

Goodman Fielder Ltd. is the largest food products producer in Australia and New Zealand. The company holds an extensive portfolio of leading food brands, including Uncle Tobys, Pampas, Meadow Lea, Buttercup, and Bluebird, as well as selected licensed brands, such as Newman's Own, Crisco, and others. Goodman Fielder has structured its operations into five primary divisions. Milling Australia, the leading flour milling company in Australia, produces flours, grains, rice and specialty cereals, cake, bread and other pastry premixes, bread crumbs, dry yeast, and related bakery items. Baking Australia is the number one manufacturer of bread in Australia and includes the Pampas pastry baking products group. GF Consumer Foods contains many of Goodman Fielder's top consumer foods brands; with annual sales of more than A$900 million, this division ranks in the top three in the Australian prepared foods industry. This division also contains the GF Food Services division, which produces edible oils, mayonnaise, and other products for the foodservice market. GF International contains the company's operations in more than 30 countries outside of Australia and New Zealand, with an emphasis on the Asian Pacific and other Asian markets, as well as the Middle East. Last, GF New Zealand represents the merger of much of Goodman Fielder's New Zealand operations, including Bluebird, Quality Bakers, Champion, and Meadow Lea Foods, as the company has begun a drive to redefine itself as a branded products group for the new century. As part of that strategy, Goodman Fielder has been shedding its GF Ingredients division, which included gelatin giant Leiner Davis. Goodman Fielder, which posted revenues of nearly A$3 billion in 2002, is listed on the Australian stock exchange and is led by CEO Tom Park, formerly of Southcorp.

Merging Trans-Tasman Food Groups in the 1980s

Goodman Fielder represented the amalgamation of large portions of the New Zealand and Australian baking and food production industries as a wave of consolidation swept through those industries in the 1970s and 1980s. The resulting flurry of mergers among many small, formerly family-owned businesses produced a small number of large-scale food products groups, with Goodman Fielder itself emerging as the leading player in both countries.

In Australia, Goodman Fielder stretched back to the founding of the Geo. Fielder Co. in 1909. By 1973 that company had taken on the name of Fielders Ltd., before merging with another Australian food group, Gillespie Bros, in 1978. The enlarged group, now named Fielder Gillespie, grew again through a new merger with Davis Consolidated Industries Ltd. in 1983. Fielder Gillespie Davis, as the company then came to be called, became one of Australia's largest food producers, with leading positions in the flour milling and bread baking industries, as well as a significant position in food ingredients, especially food-grade gelatin products. In 1986, Fielder Gillespie Davis looked across the Tasman Sea and proposed a merger with New Zealand's fast-growing flour, baking, and food company, the Goodman Group.

That company had been a small family-owned baking business in Motueka, at the northern end of New Zealand's South

Island, when the owners' son Patrick Goodman, who had trained as an accountant, joined the business in the 1950s. Goodman quickly showed his ambitions for expanding the company and began promoting the bakery's products to area grocers. Taking the approach a step further, Goodman convinced a number of grocers to invest in the bakery, collecting the equivalent of A$2,000 from each investor—by the mid-1990s, these initial investments were each worth more than A$1 million. Goodman also began expanding the business through acquisition, buying up a number of bakeries and expanding into the Nelson area.

The New Zealand baking and milling industry remained highly fragmented and heavily regulated, although by the 1960s the industries had begun to see the beginnings of the later consolidation movement. The looming prospect of deregulation, including the opening of the New Zealand market to foreign competition—and notably Australian foods giant Weston—encouraged bakers and millers to begin seeking partnerships. Goodman led eight other of the Central Region's largest bakers in the formation of a baking cooperative, called Quality Bakers, in 1968.

Quality Bakers gave Goodman and partners a larger sales base from which to launch television advertising and other promotional campaigns, and to begin marketing a single packaged, sliced bread brand, Home Style. The buying strength of the cooperative enabled members to reduce their ingredients' costs; at the same time, members, chosen in part because they operated in different towns, avoided competition among themselves by creating individual sales districts. By 1972, Quality Bakers had extended its membership, reaching 18 member bakeries. Although a number of the cooperative's members, including Goodman, began buying up or merging with other bakeries, Quality Bakers also began purchasing a number of smaller bakeries outright.

Patrick Goodman's ambitions for Quality Bakers went beyond the simple cooperative. Instead, Goodman saw the group as representing a step toward the creation of a larger, vertically integrated baking and foods group that could at once lead the

restructuring of New Zealand's baking industry and head off foreign competition. Yet the structure of Quality Bakers, coupled with the independent-mindedness of most of its members, led Goodman to seek a different vehicle to achieve his aims.

At the beginning of the 1970s, Goodman joined his own company to A.S. Paterson & Co., which at the time was one of New Zealand's top three flour milling companies, and used that company to build a larger milling and bakery group. Goodman and Paterson's Alex Paterson shared the leadership of the new, larger business, AS Paterson. By 1973, five of the original Quality Bakers members agreed to sell out to AS Paterson, forming the nucleus of the company's Goodman bakery division. The owners of the bakeries stayed on as managers, and the bakeries themselves maintained their membership in Quality Bakers. AS Paterson continued to add other Quality Bakers members to its bakery division through the 1970s.

A rift between Patrick Goodman and Alex Paterson led to the latter's ouster in 1976. Goodman took over the company, renaming it the Goodman Group in 1979. The bakery division was then renamed New Zealand Bakeries. The company continued buying up the Quality Bakers members, as well as making a series of acquisitions of nonmember bakeries. Goodman also continued to pursue growth in the milling industry, notably the purchase of a sizable stake in Wattie Industries' Cropper-NRM, then the largest miller in New Zealand (Goodman Group itself ranked second), in 1980. Goodman and Wattie also became partners in a large bakery in Auckland.

By 1982, Goodman had taken over all but five members of the Quality Bakers cooperative and renamed the company's bakery division as Quality Bakers New Zealand. The remaining Quality Bakers members then became franchise holders, with the rights to the Quality Bakers brand name and recipes; two of the company's franchisees eventually sold out to other bakery groups in the mid-1980s.

During that same period, Goodman faced growing competition from foreign firms, including Weston and Allied Foods, which had gained a strong presence in northern New Zealand through its Allied Mills division, and Defiance Mills, a leading Australian food products group. Goodman countered the presence of the foreign groups with its merger with Fielder Gillespie Davis. The newly created Goodman Fielder now spanned two countries, with extensive holdings in baking, milling, and food ingredients. The larger group was quickly joined by Allied Mills, which added its cake mix and margarine operations to the Goodman Fielder group. Allied also added its successful Pampa's pastry division, which it had acquired in 1985.

Overly Ambitious in the 1990s

Led by Patrick Goodman, the Goodman Fielder company began an ambitious expansion program meant not only to solidify its leadership positions in its home markets, but to establish itself internationally as well. In 1986 the company paid A$2.5 billion to acquire 51 percent control of Commercial Products-Fielders Pty. and acquired an initial stake of nearly 15 percent in the Ranks Hovis McDougall group, one of the largest milling and bakery companies in the United Kingdom. The following year, Goodman Fielder took over with Wattie, becoming Goodman Fielder Wattie, as part of its drive to become a leading food products group not only in the Australia-New Zealand market, but in Europe as well. In addition to its own flour and milling operations, which gave the combined group control of more than half of the New Zealand flour and bakery market, Wattie brought Goodman Fielder a diversified food products assortment, including leading positions in New Zealand's frozen, canned, snack, and convenience food segments.

The company made a strong start in its European plans with the purchase, in 1988, of Meneba NV, based in The Netherlands. In that year, also, Goodman Fielder Wattie attempted a hostile takeover of Ranks Hovis McDougall, boosting its holding to nearly 30 percent. That move, however, was blocked by the Australian Monopolies and Mergers Commission. Instead, Ranks Hovis McDougall turned the tables on Goodman Fielder Wattie in 1989, when it launched its own hostile takeover attempt. Yet the company's shareholders rejected the $2.4 billion offer.

Goodman Fielder Wattie had meanwhile continued its acquisition spree, buying up the Australian companies Allflex Holdings, Gelatin Development Corp., Goldstar Bakery, Heidenreich Flour Mills, William Jackett & Son, Moranez, and United Bakeries. The company also extended into Portugal with the purchase of Somone Divergel that year. More acquisitions

followed in 1989, as the company took control of Steggles Holdings, and The Netherlands companies Hocker Holdings, Brood-en-Banketbakkerij Ten Hoopen, and WL Voeders. Another important acquisition came in 1992, when the company acquired Uncle Tobys, one of the most recognized brands in the Australian and New Zealand markets.

By then, however, Goodman Fielder Wattie was beginning to strain under its ambitious expansion effort—which even included a foray into hosiery products. The company's attempt to move beyond bakery and milling and into meats, which came with the purchase of 28 percent of the New Zealand meat processing giant Waitaki, was particularly costly for Goodman Fielder, as Waitaki stumbled at the end of the decade and nearly went bankrupt. Goodman Fielder sold off that holding in 1989.

Meanwhile, the removal of many of the trade barriers designed to protect the New Zealand food industry exposed Wattie's fragility, as the company rapidly lost ground to a new wave of foreign competitors. By 1992, the company was forced to sell off Wattie as well, to the H.J. Heinz Co., and the company's name reverted to Goodman Fielder. Patrick Goodman himself faced the consequences of the company's overly ambitious expansion drive, losing his chief executive's position in 1990, then being forced to resign as chairman in 1992.

Goodman's departure led to a period of management uncertainty in which the company went through three chief executives in as many years, before settling on David Hearn in 1995. Hearn led the company on the first of a series of restructuring drives, cutting out most of the company's noncore operations. In 1996, the company merged its milling and baking operations in Australia and New Zealand into a new unit, Milling and Baking Australasia, and combined its overseas operations into Goodman Fielder International, creating a new Cereal and Snacks division. The company sold off most of its European operations in 1997 and also reduced its presence in the Asian markets as it turned its focus to solidifying its leadership status at home.

In the late 1990s, Goodman Fielder made a new diversification attempt, this time into food ingredients. The company acquired the edible gelatin business form Hormel Foods Corporation in 1998, becoming a world leader in that ingredient segment through subsidiary Leiner Davis. By 2001, however, Goodman Fielder had decided to exit the food ingredients segment, and by 2002 had sold off most of that division.

More successful for the company was its 1999 acquisition of family-owned Ernest Adams Ltd., the leading baked goods company in the New Zealand market. By then, the company also had shored up its position with the addition, in 1997, of the New Zealand milling and baking operations of Australia's Bunge-Defiance. In 1999, as well, the company rolled out a new branded line, Top Nosh, a line of chilled ready meals.

With its losses mounting to A$78 million, Goodman Fielder restructured again in 2001, creating five new key operating divisions: Milling Australia, Baking Australia, GF New Zealand, GF Consumer Products, and GF International. Goodman Fielder also initiated a drive to refocus the company around its high-margin branded products. At the end of 2001, however, the company, confronted with sagging share prices, also brought on a new management team, headed by former Southcorp executive Tom Park.

By the end of its 2002 fiscal year in September 2002, Goodman Fielder's latest restructuring appeared to be a success, as the company's profits soared to A$164 million on sales of nearly A$3 billion. The company then announced its intention to return to external growth, announcing its plans to spend up to A$500 million on a new round of acquisitions to boost the company's new branded foods strategy. From a single family-owned bakery, Goodman Fielder had become Australasia's leading food products group.

Principal Subsidiaries

Fielder Gillespie Davis Finance Pty Limited; GF Australia Limited; Goodman Fielder Mills Limited; GF International (NZ) Limited; Great Southern Roller Flour Mills Ltd; William Jackett & Son Proprietary Limited; Goodman Fielder Superannuation Fund Pty Ltd; Mowbray Industries Limited; Goodman Fielder Food Services Limited; Goodman Fielder International Limited; Goodman Fielder International; Goodman Fielder International Sdn Bhd (Malaysia); Goodman Fielder International (China) Ltd (Hong Kong); NZ Margarine Holdings Limited; Meadow Lea Foods Limited (NZ); Goodman Fielder (Shanghai) Co Ltd (China); M.L. (W.A.) Export Pty Ltd; The Uncle Tobys Company Limited; G Wood Son and Company Pty Ltd; Anchor Foods Pty Ltd; Quality Bakers Australia Limited; Stuart Bakery Pty Ltd; Wakely Bros. Pty Limited; Ernest Adams Australia Pty Ltd; GF Defiance Pty Limited; GFD Australia Pty Limited; GF Albury Mills Limited; GF Narrandera Mills Limited; Sirius Biotechnology Limited; Sirius Biotechnology International Pty.

Principal Divisions

Milling Australia; Baking Australia; GF Consumer Foods; GF International; GF New Zealand.

Principal Competitors

Coca-Cola Amatil Ltd; Foster's Brewing Group Ltd.; BAT Australasia; Philip Morris Companies Inc.; Nestlé Australia; ConAgra Inc.; George Weston Ltd.; Lion Nathan Ltd.; Dairy Farmers Group.

Further Reading

"Australia's Goodman Fielder Told to Wipe Out Restructuring Debts," *AsiaPulse News,* April 23, 2001.
"Goodman Fielder Poised to Deliver Solid Net Profit Growth," *AsiaPulse News,* March 8, 2002.
McNabb, Denise, "Goodman Fielder Review Aims to Cheer Investors," *Dominion,* November 22, 2000, p. 30.
"Nosh Push," *Grocer,* August 21, 1999, p. 15.
Tait, Victoria, "G. Fielder Overhaul Starts to Gel," *Reuters Business Report,* February 14, 2001.

—M.L. Cohen

Group 1 Automotive, Inc.

950 Echo Lane, Suite 100
Houston, Texas 77024
U.S.A.
Telephone: (713) 647-5700
Fax: (713) 647-5800
Web site: http://www.group1auto.com

Public Company
Incorporated: 1995
Employees: 6,000
Sales: $3.99 billion (2001)
Stock Exchanges: New York
Ticker Symbol: GPI
NAIC: 441110 New Car Dealers; 441120 Used Car
    Dealers

Group 1 Automotive, Inc. is a leading consolidator of auto dealerships. The Houston, Texas, *Fortune* 500 company owns more than 70 dealerships that market 29 different brands through 110 franchises spread across nine states: California, Colorado, Florida, Georgia, Louisiana, Massachusetts, New Mexico, Oklahoma, and Texas. Group 1 also sells cars over the Internet and operates 24 collision service centers. It achieves some level of diversity by offering a mix of trucks and cars as well as imports and domestic brands. In 2001, for instance, the bestselling vehicle for the company was Ford's F-series pickup truck followed by the Toyota Camry. All told, 53 percent of sales come from imports. Ever since its initial public offering (IPO) in 1997, Group 1 has aggressively added new dealerships, with a two-pronged acquisition strategy. First, it targets multiple franchise dealerships in attractive markets, businesses that will provide geographic diversity and immediately help to grow the balance sheet. These "platform" acquisitions may then be enhanced by "tuck-in" additions, single-point dealerships in the same area that add brands or services or in some way bring value to the hub operation. Another major facet of Group 1's philosophy is to decentralize the company's operations, retaining local management teams and allowing them to continue running the business in a market they know better than the home office. What Group 1 is able to bring to bear are economies of scale that result in lower advertising and administrative costs, as well as greater buying power and less-expensive credit.

Formation of Group 1 in 1995

Group 1's chairman, president, and chief executive officer, B.B. (Ben) Hollingsworth, Jr., was the one with Wall Street experience among the men who founded the company in 1995. He was accustomed to positions of leadership: After growing up near Dallas, Texas, he attended Rice University on a football scholarship, playing quarterback. Upon graduation he went to work as an auditor at Arthur Young, then in 1967 was hired away by a client, Houston-based Service Corporation International (SCA), a funeral services company. When he joined SCA as a young executive, the business was far from prosperous. According to Hollingsworth, "There was always a question whether we could make payroll." After the business stabilized it went public in 1969 and began to consolidate the funeral services industry, with Hollingsworth serving a key role in the acquisition process. By 1975 he rose to the rank of president in the company and began to travel widely, making valuable contacts. Years later he recalled, "You're on the road talking to analysts, investment bankers, the media." It was under his leadership that SCA went on an acquisition spree that resulted in it becoming the largest funeral services company in North America and a Wall Street darling.

Hollingsworth retired from SCA in 1986, then gained experience in the automotive retailing industry by buying a stake in A.J. Foyt Motors, Inc., a Honda dealership established in 1989 and located in the Houston suburb of Kingwood. In 1995 the seeds of Group 1 were planted when Hollingsworth was invited by Houston automobile dealers Sterling McCall and Charles Smith to meet at The Forest Club, an exclusive country club located in West Houston. The two men wanted to discuss a dealership roll-up and sought advice from Hollingsworth about the implications of taking such a venture public. As Hollingsworth recalled, "They had great dealerships, but they couldn't find Wall Street with a street map." What they did possess was a wealth of experience in the car business. Smith's family, in fact, had been involved in automotive retailing since 1917 and Charles Smith had more than a quarter-century of experience himself. The family's group of Texas dealerships generated revenues of more than $200 million. McCall had a similar level of experience; he was the first to be granted a stand-alone exclusive Toyota dealership in Houston. The three men agreed to go into business together and in December 1995 formed Group 1 Automotive, Inc. to acquire automobile dealerships and their related operations. For the family-owned dealerships, going public had an obvious appeal: it provided an exit strategy as well as security. Instead of having all of their wealth tied up in inventory, they would now have stock and the ability to become liquid if necessary.

October 1997 IPO

Over the course of the next two years Hollingsworth worked to put together an initial public offering (IPO) to launch the new venture, which would be formed around the assets of the founding groups. Hollingsworth joined with John H. Duncan, who operated a Kingwood Isuzu dealership, to form the Kingwood Group. In addition to the McCall Group and Smith Group, another of the founding groups was to be headed by Jimmie Kline whose Washington, D.C.-based Kline Automotive Group operated six Virginia dealerships. Shortly before Group 1 made its initial public offering, however, Kline dropped out, replaced by the Howard Group, headed by Robert E. Howard, who ran one of the largest dealership groups in Oklahoma and boasted nearly 30 years of experience in the car business. Despite a difficult climate for IPOs, Group 1 went forward with its offering in October 1997, pricing its shares at $12 and raising $57.6 million. Just prior to the IPO, backed by Goldman Sachs, the company acquired the assets of the founding groups, so that it started in business with annual revenues in excess of $825 million.

Shortly after completing its initial offering, Group 1 began to roll up dealerships. It completed four acquisitions at the cost of approximately $56 million in cash and stock. Two were platform acquisitions: Carroll Automotive Group, operating Ford dealerships in Miami, Atlanta, and Fort Lauderdale, Florida; and Maxwell Automotive Group, which owned Chrysler Plymouth, Subaru, Jeep, Eagle, and Dodge dealerships in Austin and Taylor, Texas. Both Jim Carroll and Nyle Maxwell signed long-term employment agreements to continue running their respective organizations, along with their management teams. The two other purchases were tuck-ins: Elgin Ford in the Austin area and a Beaumont, Texas, automall, Autoplex 2000, which included Mercedes-Benz, Dodge, Nissan, Volvo, and Buick franchises. These acquisitions were significant to Group 1 for a number of reasons. Not only did they provide the company with its first Ford dealership and supplement its Chrysler representation, they added more than $470 million in annual revenues, taking Group 1 past the $1 billion mark to roughly $1.3 billion. Wall Street, however, was not impressed. After a modest bump following its IPO, Group 1's stock price

began to sag. Other retail auto consolidators were also upstaged by the sexier high-tech sector, which held the potential for spectacular gains, as opposed to the slow, steady growth that Group 1 was able to provide.

Despite the lack of investor enthusiasm, Hollingsworth and Group 1 pressed on with their plans. In March 1998 the company completed its second major purchase, paying $37 million in cash and stock for five dealerships in four separate transactions. Group 1 entered the Albuquerque, New Mexico, market by acquiring Johns Automotive Group, which owned a Chevrolet franchise as well as a Chrysler, Plymouth, and Jeep franchise. Group 1 also entered the Denver area by acquiring Luby Chevrolet, an 80-year-old business that was one of the largest dealerships in Colorado. In addition, Group 1 purchased a pair of tuck-ins: Flamingo Ford in Homestead, Florida, and Austin-area Highland Chrysler, Plymouth, Jeep, and Dodge. Altogether these purchases added some $300 million in annual revenues. Over the course of the entire year Group 1 acquired 33 dealership franchises and also broke ground on a new massive Ford dealership located in Pembroke Pines, Florida. Situated on 23 acres of land the operation would be one of the largest Ford dealerships in the country. It would be run by Carroll Automotive Group, which operated Group 1's platform in the Southeast. As a result of its acquisitions and internal growth, Group 1 topped $1.6 billion in revenues in 1998, with net income of $20.7 million.

In 1999, to fuel further expansion, Group 1 arranged a $500 million credit line, provided by a novel combination of ten commercial banks and the captive finance companies Ford Motor Credit Co. and Toyota Motor Credit Corp. A few months later, the line was doubled to $1 billion with the addition of another commercial bank and BMW Motor Credit Corp., Chrysler Financial, and General Motors Acceptance Corp. Other dealership consolidators soon followed suit, forming similar syndicates. In addition, in March 1999 Group 1 completed a secondary offering of stock, selling two million additional shares, and placed $100 million in ten-year notes, for a gross of $138.9 million. During the course of the year Group 1 was able to take advantage of this financial backing to acquire 11 more dealership franchises. Revenue for the year grew by more than $900 million, reaching nearly $3.6 billion, with net income improving to $40 million. The company's stock, however, continued to languish, which Hollingsworth attributed to the automobile sector being out of favor with investors, due in large part to difficulties of a far more visible consolidator, Wayne Huizenga's AutoNation, which was receiving adverse publicity for failing to live up to expectations.

Entering New Orleans and Boston: 2000

While some of its competitors were forced to slow down their roll-up efforts, Group 1 in early 2000 continued to add dealerships, including two new platforms and a tuck-in. It entered into the New Orleans market by completing the purchase of Bohn Auto Group, which included Buick, Ford Pontiac, and GMC franchises that generated annual revenues in the range of $180 million. A second platform was established in the Boston area with the addition of Ira Motor Group, which boasted annual revenues of $260 million selling Toyota, Lexus, Porsche, Audi, Subaru, Mazda, Isuzu, Buick, and Pontiac. Group 1 also purchased Boston-area dealership Victory Dodge, which it renamed Ira Dodge and added to the new Ira platform.

Key Dates:

1995: Company is formed.
1997: Company acquires founding dealerships and goes public.
1998: Group 1 enters Albuquerque and Denver markets.
2000: Group 1 enters New Orleans and Boston markets.
2002: Group enters southern California market.

Ira Motor Group offered an excellent example of the changes in auto retailing and why consolidation was embraced by many mom-and-pop operations. The business had grown out of a used car lot established in Danvers, Massachusetts, by Ira Rosenberg in 1967. Although it evolved into a nine-dealership enterprise, Ira Motors was very much a family concern, with Ira Rosenberg forging a strong bond with his employees as a way to grow the business. Rosenberg's son, David, started working for his father in the mid-1970s at the age of 12 cleaning cars in the Toyota dealership, then worked in various departments through high school. Intending to work on Wall Street he entered the M.B.A. program at Columbia University only to find that he was more excited about applying what he learned in class to the car business than in pursuing a Wall Street career. He returned home to become general manager of Ira Motors, then took over when his father retired. In the mid-1990s David Rosenberg considered merging with other dealers and going public, but nothing came of the idea. He later came close to going public with Classic Automotive Group of New Jersey but that IPO was called off after the market soured. When he was approached by Group 1 about selling the business he quickly sensed that the two parties shared similar philosophies. Rosenberg told *Automotive News,* "The model that they presented to me was exactly what I was looking for personally and I also thought it was the best thing for my dealerships and for my employees." Devoted to continuing his father's commitment to their employees, the "Ira Family," Rosenberg was now able to reward loyalty with better benefits and stock options, as well as attracting new talent. Rosenberg stayed on to run the new platform, his role with Ira Motors essentially unchanged, but now he had the backing of Group 1 to add more franchises. Rosenberg had other, more personal reasons for teaming with a larger public corporation like Group 1, telling *Automotive News,* "My father, for his whole life, always had everything at risk for the dealership. And it's a lot more security not to have everything on the line all the time. After a while, you learn to live with it, but it's certainly nice not to have it." Moreover, Rosenberg sensed what lay in store for auto retailers: "My crystal ball tells me the people who are going to succeed and thrive are the people with the most resources, (those who) can invest the most in research and development in terms of new technology and strategies of customer retention—and I really think this is the way for us to be ahead of the curve."

For 2000 Group 1 recorded revenues of nearly $3.6 billion and net profits of $40.8 million. As the bubble burst in the tech sector and the economy slipped into recession in 2001, investors began to appreciate the steady growth of Group 1 and car dealers in general. Unlike automakers, they were not saddled with huge fixed costs and during poor times they made money on their high-margin used car operations. As a result, Group 1 stock was finally rewarded by investors with a higher price. Furthermore, the company was able to raise another $100 million in an October 2001 secondary stock offering. Although Group 1 was unable to maintain its record of exceptional increases in 2001, it was still able to grow revenues to almost $4 billion and post a net profit of $55.4 million. Finances continued to improve in 2002, but it was becoming more difficult to find as many dealerships willing to sell, leading some observers to maintain that the best properties had already been acquired. Nonetheless, Group 1 was able to buy four tuck-in acquisitions in Tulsa and Houston at a cost of $85 million. It then completed a major acquisition, buying Miller Automotive Group in a $387 million deal that gave the company a platform in southern California, the largest automotive market in the country. From the start Group 1 had wanted to be in California, and it had long nurtured a relationship with Fred Miller who headed the business. According to Hollingsworth, the Miller family's decision to sell was once again an exit strategy: "Their business has been in the family for almost 60 years. They reached the decision where they needed to get their estate in liquid order and prepare for their eventual retirement. This provided them an outlet." As more family-owned dealerships were rolled up by consolidators, it was likely that the consolidators themselves would eventually start rolling up one another. Whether Group 1 would one day be acquired by a larger concern was very much an open question. When asked by a reporter about that possibility, however, Hollingsworth hinted that he was more interested in being the acquirer rather than the acquired.

Principal Subsidiaries

Bob Howard Automotive—H, Inc.; Luby Chevrolet; Foyt Motors, Inc.; McCall-TL, Ltd.; Mike Smith Automotive—N, Inc.; Ira Automotive Group, LLC.

Principal Competitors

AutoNation USA; Sonic Automotive; United Auto Group, Inc.

Further Reading

Garcia, Shelly, "Miller Automotive Sold to *Fortune* 500 Firm," *San Fernando Valley Business Journal,* August 19, 2002, p. 1.
Greer, Jim, "Driving Force," *Houston Business Journal,* December 3, 1999, p. 14A.
——, "Group 1 Automotive Hits High Gear on Road Trip in the Fast Lane," *Houston Business Journal,* May 25, 2001, p. 16A.
Harris, Donna, "Buyers Wants Stores, But Dealers Aren't Selling," *Automotive News,* October 14, 2002, p. 4.
——, "The Upside of Down," *Automotive News,* January 29, 2001, p. 24I.
——, "Houston-Based Chain Plans IPO," *Automotive News,* June 30, 1997, p. 35.
Sawyers, Arlena, "Group 1 Adds Dealerships As Other Chains Curb Growth," *Automotive News,* February 7, 2000, p. 25.

—Ed Dinger

LLADRÓ

Grupo Lladró S.A.

Ctra de Alboraya s/n, Poligono L
Tavernes Blanques
Valencia E-46016
Spain
Telephone: (+34) 96 318 70 01
Fax: (+34) 96 185 16 30
Web site: http://www.lladro.com

Private Company
Incorporated: 1951
Employees: 2,402
Sales: EUR 220 million ($189 million) (2001 est.)
NAIC: 327112 Vitreous China, Fine Earthenware, and
Other Pottery Product Manufacturing

Grupo Lladró S.A. is known throughout the world for its decorative figurines crafted from porcelain and other materials. The company produces more than 900 different models each year, which are handcrafted by the company's army of more than 2,000 porcelain craftspeople based in the City of Porcelain complex in Tavernes Blancas in Valencia. The company enhances the collectibility of its pieces by limited production runs—whether in quantity or by date—and many of the company's original pieces now fetch prices ranging into the thousands of dollars. Lladró sells its products through a network of some 4,000 retailers worldwide, as well as through the company's own growing retail network of 40 Lladró boutiques worldwide, including a new six-floor, 800-square-meter flagship store opened in Tokyo's Ginza district in October 2002. The company intends to spend $40 million to open up to 50 new Lladró boutiques by 2005. The company also owns the Lladró Museum in Manhattan. As the second generation of Lladrós—the company remains wholly controlled by the founding Lladró family—prepares to take over the company's reins, Lladró has begun an attempt to transition itself into the luxury goods sector, dropping a number of its lower-priced models, ending its distribution relationship with more than 1,500 lower-end retailers, and introducing new figurines and statuettes with price tags ranging up to $35,000. The company also is attempting to

diversify its holdings, acquiring a controlling stake in noted Spanish jewelry designer Carrera y Carrera. Lladró is led by brothers and founders Juan, José, and Vincente, who each own one-third of the company and take turns acting as its chairman. The Lladró brothers have been joined by three of their ten children, Juan, David, and Carmen, who have taken the lead in the company's reorientation for the new century.

From Dirt to Clay in the 1950s

The Lladró family were farmers in Almacera, Valencia, a region of Spain long noted for its ceramics and porcelain production. The Lladró brothers, Juan, the oldest, and José and Vincente, were raised in the difficult economic climate of the 1940s following the Spanish Civil War, and were put to work on the family farm. In the late 1940s, however, Juan Lladró left the farm to take up an apprenticeship with a local ceramics tile factory, where his job consisted of painting the tiles with decorative scenes. With his mother's encouragement, Lladró began taking classes at the local art school. In 1950, the family bought a kiln and Juan began producing his own ceramic designs.

By 1951, younger brothers José and Vincente had joined Juan at the tile factory, and also began taking afternoon classes at the art school. While Juan and José leaned more toward painting and drawing, Vincente's interest quickly turned toward sculpture. The brothers soon began to sell their figures, and in 1953, the Lladrós established their first workshop. Production originally encompassed a wide range of items, including ashtrays, jugs, vases, and ceramic flowers. Yet the brothers quickly added their first sculptural pieces, a series of figurines produced in a style that was to place the Lladró name on sideboards all over the world. The Lladró brothers also turned to working exclusively in porcelain. Yet, as Juan Lladró told *Time International:* "I wanted to make something that once only kings could own accessible to the man in the street."

To achieve this aim, the Lladrós developed their own production techniques, including developing a technique involving pouring liquid porcelain into molds, as well as replacing the traditional coal-fired kilns with gas-drive kilns. The company also brought in a growing number of craftspeople—all of the

Company Perspectives:

Founders Message: "We want our works to be elegant, expressive, to ooze life and have feelings. We want them to reflect the fine side of existence, the positive values of human beings, everything that dignifies life."

Juan, José and Vicente Lladró thus define their artistic manifesto. When the three brothers, several decades ago, began to mould their first, humble, creations in clay, they brought together their personal experiences, turning them into something living with an essentially human meaning. The small workshop became a large company, the sculptures were perfected, gaining artistic importance, but the message nevertheless remained the same. Today, like before, the three founding brothers are present in the day-to-day activities of the company, giving support both to the entrepreneurial management that always followed an innovative line, and to the creation of the sculptures.

companies' pieces remained finished by hand—who received training from the company, which started up its own professional training school in 1962. Lladró also developed its own glazing technique, which enabled the company to produce completed figures after a single firing, while creating what was to become a signature "glow" to its pieces. In this way, Lladró was able to begin to offer series of figurines for as little as $30 each.

Lladró's sales took off by the end of the 1950s, requiring it to move to a larger location in nearby Tavernes Blancqes in 1958. Through the early 1960s the company became the largest producer of porcelain figurines in the Spanish market. The company also had begun exporting its figurines, and by 1965 the first shipments were being sent to the United States, which became one of the company's largest markets, representing some 40 percent of its sales. That same year, Lladró had opened its first retail store, in Valencia.

International Collectors Supplier in the 1980s

The company began construction on its "City of Porcelain" in 1967, opening the workshop and cultural center in 1969. At the end of the 1960s, the company launched two series that were to become synonymous with the Lladró name, the Sad Harlequin and the Group of Horses, both of which proved highly successful. Then, in 1970, the company extended its materials range when it introduced its Gres stoneware series. Another extension of the company's product line came in 1971 when Lladró introduced its first porcelain vases.

Lladró made its first international expansion effort in 1973 when it acquired a 50 percent stake in the United States' Weil Ceramics & Glass, helping the company strengthen its position in North America. Lladró later acquired full control of Weil, which in turn became for a time the holding company for the company's Lladró USA subsidiary.

The launch of the Elite Collection in 1974 provided Lladró with another international success; that range was expanded in 1976 with the Elite Stoneware collection, featuring characters from the Spanish literary tradition. Another hit series debuted in

1978 as the "Pursued Deers," a series of figurines that was later added to the permanent collections of the Brussels Royal Museum of Art and the Modern Art Museum in Santa Domingo. This kind of recognition helped enhance Lladró's appeal among the world's collectors, which had come to include strong sales in Japan as well as through a distribution agreement with Mitsui. Lladró helped stimulate the collection of its figurines through its policy of "retiring" its series—and destroying the molds that created them—in addition to a strict policy of destroying individual pieces with fabrication flaws. In 1985, the company encouraged its collectors again with the creation of the Lladró Collectors Society, which quickly saw its numbers swell to more than 100,000 members.

By then, the Lladró brothers had started to bring in the second generation to the family business, launching three of their children, Rosa, Mari Carment, and Juan Vincenté—one from each brother—on a lengthy apprenticeship. Nonetheless, the Lladró brothers, each of whom owned one-third of the company, continued to share its leadership, following a promise made on their mother's deathbed. Each brother took turns leading the company as its chairman.

In 1986, Lladró stepped up its exports to the fast-rising Japanese market with the creation of a joint venture, controlled by Lladró, with its distributor Mitsui. Two years later the company marked the importance of the North American market, particularly the U.S. market, with the establishment of the Lladró Museum and Gallery in Manhattan, which, in addition to retail facilities, contained one of the most extensive collections of early Lladró pieces. In that year, as well, Lladró formed its U.S. distribution subsidiary, Lladró US, and a new subsidiary for its Australian distribution operations, Ordal Australia.

In the late 1980s, Lladró sought to extend its operations by pursuing two different approaches. On the one hand, the company introduced a new lower-priced line, the Nao collection, targeting a price range from $30 to $60. On the other, Lladró attempted to extend its well-known brand name into other categories, starting with the introduction of a collection of leather goods, including handbags and accessories, in 1989. The company hoped to associate the Lladró name with the international recognition enjoyed by Spain's leather industry. Yet the effort never quite took off with consumers, and by the end of the 1990s the leather line had been closed.

Lladró's porcelain and other figurines, however, continued to build the company's international reputation. The company received new recognition following the success of its exhibit at the Hermitage Museum, in Saint Petersburg, Russia, which added two of the company's pieces into its permanent collection in 1991. By the beginning of the 1990s, the company's sales had topped 1.5 million pieces, sold in more than 140 countries, and accounted for some 60 percent of all Spanish porcelain figures exports—a position that earned the company the Prince Felipe award for internationalization in 1993.

Transitioning to a Luxury Products Group in the 21st Century

Lladró continued to develop through the late 1990s, adding new successful collections, including the Legend Collection

Key Dates:

1950: The Lladró family installs a kiln at their farm in Almecera, Valencia, Spain.

1953: Brothers Juan, José, and Vincenté Lladró launch their own ceramics workshop before beginning production of porcelain figures.

1958: Lladró moves to larger facilities in Tavernes Blanques.

1965: The first Lladró boutique opens in Valencia; Lladró begins exports to the United States, which becomes one of the country's primary markets.

1973: Lladró acquires 50 percent of Weil Ceramics & Glass.

1985: Lladró forms the Lladró Collectors Society, which grows to more than 100,000 members.

1989: The company launches a line of Lladró leather goods, which is later abandoned.

1997: Lladró opens a store on Rodeo Drive in Beverly Hills, California.

1999: Lladró opens a boutique in the Las Vegas Venetian hotel complex.

2001: Lladró acquires 45 percent of jewelry maker Carrera y Carrera; Lladró begins a drive to transition itself as a luxury goods producer; a new prototype boutique opens in Tampa, Florida.

2002: Lladró opens a new 800-square-meter flagship store in Tokyo's Ginza district.

launched in 1999. The company also was building up a strong, internationally operating chain of retail boutiques, including a new store opened on Beverly Hill's Rodeo Drive in 1997. That store was followed by the opening of a two-story, 300-square-meter boutique in Las Vegas's Venetian hotel complex, opened in 1999.

With the youngest of the founding Lladró brothers celebrating his 70th birthday, the company was faced with decisions on how best to prepare its future. The new generation, now represented by David Lladró, began to take on a more decisive role in the company. Lladró, which had developed the not-so-enviable reputation as a maker of kitsch products, now sought to reposition itself as a manufacturer of luxury goods.

To achieve this restructuring, Lladró began cutting out a good portion of its lower-priced items, dropping the number of its products from a high of 1,500 to just 900 per year. The company also moved to eliminate its presence in more down-market venues, such as airport gift shops, eliminating nearly 2,000 of a distributor network that had swelled to some 6,900 worldwide. The company then countered the corresponding drop in sales—estimated to reach as much as 15 percent of sales of some EUR 220 million—with a plan to spend $40 million to expand its company-owned retail boutique by as many as 50 stores by 2005.

As Lladró eliminated its lower-priced items, it began adding higher-priced, and more exclusive, figures, including a porcelain train priced at $35,000. These were placed on display in a newly redesigned boutique featuring modern styling. The success of the company's first prototype shop, opened in Tampa, Florida, in 2001, encouraged the company to roll out the concept worldwide, including a new flagship shop spanning six stories and 800 square meters in the Ginza shopping district of Tokyo.

Lladró also returned to its goal of expanding its holdings beyond its porcelain business. In 2001, the company acquired control of noted Spanish jewelry designer Carrera y Carrera, which was then in the process of seeking to extend itself as a worldwide luxury brand. While risky, the company's push of its brand name into the luxury category, and its drive to expand beyond its core porcelain products, was seen as necessary to maintain the family's fortune—the Lladrós counted among Spain's wealthiest families—into the new century. The success, or failure, of the company's new strategy also was expected to help the company determine the successor or successors for the founding Lladró brothers. As José Lladró told *Forbes* magazine: "I personally haven't yet made up my mind which of the children is the most professional. Time will tell."

Principal Subsidiaries

Lladró Australia Pty. Ltd.; Lladró Canada, Inc; Lladró Comercial, S.A.; Lladró Comercial, S.A. (Belgium); Lladró Deutschland GmbH, Lladró Italia SRL; Lladró (UK) Ltd; Lladró USA, Inc.

Principal Competitors

American Greetings Corporation; Elkem ASA; Waterford Wedgwood plc; Villeroy und Boch AG; Toshiba Ceramics Company Ltd.; Russ Berrie and Company Inc.; AMCOL International Corporation; Doric Products Inc.; Rosenthal AG; Department 56 Inc.; Kyocera Fineceramics GmbH; Josiah Wedgwood and Sons Ltd.; KERAMAG Keramische Werke AG; Guy Degrenne S.A.; Pamesa Ceramica SL; Carbo Ceramics Inc.; W Goebel Porzellanfabrik GmbH und Co KG; VAA - Vista Alegre Atlantis SGPS S.A.; Zschimmer und Schwarz GmbH und Co.; Deroma Holding SpA.

Further Reading

Koehn, Donna, "Porcelain Sculpting Family of Spain Capitalizes on Success of Collection," *Knight Ridder Tribune Business News,* September 13, 2002.

Morais, Richard C., "Breaking the Mold," *Forbes Magazine,* September 2, 2002, p. 197.

Prasso, Sheridan, ed., "Minding the Store: A Kitschmeister Goes Chic," *Business Week,* October 14, 2002, p. 16.

Usher, Rod, "Breaking the Mold," *Time International,* August 20, 2001, p. 61.

—M.L. Cohen

Hall, Kinion & Associates, Inc.

2570 North First Street, Suite 400
San Jose, California 95131
U.S.A.
Telephone: (408) 895-5200
Toll Free: (888) 757-4254
Fax: (408) 383-0902
Web site: http://www.hallkinion.com

Public Company
Incorporated: 1993
Employees: 2,317
Sales: $173.83 million (2001)
Stock Exchanges: NASDAQ
Ticker Symbol: HAKI
NAIC: 561310 Employment Placement Agencies; 561320
   Temporary Help Services

Hall, Kinion & Associates, Inc. (Hall Kinion) touts itself as the talent source, providing world-class contract and direct-hire technology talent. Hall Kinion operates more than 30 offices in 22 markets in the United States, England, and Asia. The sectors served by the company's staffing services include technology, financial services, healthcare services, energy, and government.

Origins

For Brenda Hall, 1981 was filled with tragedy and uncertainty. Her father died that year, and with his passing, Hall lost her only source of income. She had been helping her father run his real estate training service, but his death signaled the end of employment for the 28-year-old Hall. Hall's situation was bleak, her prospects poor. Divorced and bankrupt, Hall was raising two daughters without the assistance of child support from her ex-husband. She had completed only one year of college. She had never earned more than $20,000 a year. Remarkably, a little more than a decade later, Hall was presiding over one of the fastest-growing companies in the United States, in pursuit of reaching a revenue goal of $1 billion.

Hall's pursuit in 1981 was a job, any job. She found employment as a recruiter for a Bay Area franchise of Snelling Personnel Services, a national temporary staffing firm. Hall distinguished herself, earning a promotion to manager within a short time. By 1987, she had remarried and given birth to another daughter. She also had lost her job again. Hall's boss had decided to relocate, but his plans did not involve her. Hall took two months to decide what she should do next. Her plan was bold. Hall decided to borrow $70,000 on her home equity to start a Snelling franchise in San Jose. From that point forward, success followed her as doggedly as misfortune once had.

The San Jose operation managed by Hall proved to be the brightest light in a vast empire of Snelling franchises. Within two months, the San Jose office turned its first profit. By the end of 1987, Hall's operation had generated $464,000 in sales and it had gained the employ of a key individual, Todd Kinion. Hall hired Kinion—her sixth employee—several weeks after setting up shop. She hired Kinion as a high technology recruiting specialist, the specialty of the Hall Kinion operation that would emerge later. From 1987 forward, with Kinion at her side, Hall presided over the dominant franchise in the Snelling chain, which included more than 350 offices nationwide. Hall snatched up one Snelling award after another, earning distinction as Manager of the Year, Office of the Year, and Franchise of the Year on numerous occasions. As the San Jose operation expanded, Hall and Kinion started their own sideline venture, forming Hall Kinion in 1991. Most of their time, however, was devoted to promoting the growth of the Snelling franchise—until a legal dispute entered the frame.

Independence in 1993

In July 1993, a new era in Hall's career began. She filed a breach of contract lawsuit in federal court against Snelling, which was settled in mid-1993. Subsequently, she merged her sidelight venture into the San Jose operation, forming a "new" Hall Kinion, a company "born a $10 million baby," according to Hall, as quoted in the November 8, 1993 issue of the *Business Journal.* By the time of the merger, the San Jose operation had grown to two locations, one in San Jose and the other in Santa Cruz.

At the time of Hall's independence from the Snelling chain, the temporary employment industry was recording robust growth. Nationwide, corporations were downsizing their operations. Increasingly, companies were outsourcing corporate functions to third party contractors and hiring staff on an as-needed basis when particular projects demanded more personnel. As a whole, the temporary employment industry was recording an annual growth rate of 30 percent. Hall's operation was growing at a rate ten times faster than the national average. Given Hall's immediate plans for the company, its strong rate of growth promised to continue. Several weeks after Hall became free of the Snelling chain, Hall Kinion opened its third office, establishing a branch in Provo, Utah. By August 1993, the company had hired the staff for a fourth office, scheduled to open in Fremont, California, in early 1994. A fifth office, slated to open in March 1994, was to be located in Austin, Texas. Beyond these immediate branch openings, Hall had identified 13 suitable locations for the Hall Kinion network of branch offices to be established, in cities that stretched from coast to coast, from Seattle to Boston. Hall predicted the company would generate $20 million in annual revenue by 1995 and $50 million by 1998.

Although the ambitious expansion plans announced by Hall drew notice, much of the attention paid to her growing firm stemmed from the strategy underpinning the expansion. Hall had a vision, one that impressed industry onlookers. Hall sensed a revolution was coming, a sweeping movement whose point of emanation was in Hall Kinion's backyard, in Silicon Valley. Hall planned to shadow, if not lead, the revolution by establishing Hall Kinion branches in important research and development markets. Her company would then use these satellite offices to connect its clients to Hall Kinion's headquarters using sophisticated videoconferencing equipment. In a November 8, 1999 interview with the *Business Journal,* Hall explained: "We see Silicon Valley not as a geographic description, but as a phenomenon that's spreading all over the country, like little fires. Long term, I believe the geographic location will be the heart and brain of high-technology, but the arms and fingers will be all over the United States." Later in the interview, she continued: "The savings of time and money for the company (the Hall Kinion client) and the candidate is enormous. [Videoconferencing] allows a business to see the best talent available in a given specialty, no matter where that talent is located. It opens up the whole hiring spectrum."

As Hall pressed ahead with her strategy and her expansion plan, she marched through fertile soil. By the mid-1990s, the temporary staffing industry was one of the fastest-growing industries in the country. Hall Kinion's industry niche was recording particularly remarkable growth rates. Some high-

technology companies used contract engineers for as much as one-fifth of their workforce. Companies also used temporary staff to fill gaps in their quality-assurance technical teams, adding to demand. In this expanding market, Hall Kinion supplied high-technology companies with contract engineers, temporary administrative and clerical workers, and permanently placed professionals and managers. The company found its candidates by advertising in newspapers, placing postings on Internet bulletin boards, and through a web of business connections. Applicants and employers then were brought together with videoconferencing technology.

In 1994, Hall Kinion's revenues reached $14.3 million. In 1995, by which time the company had added offices in Denver, Seattle, and Portland, Oregon, revenues increased 39 percent to $20 million—the exact figure targeted by Hall two years earlier. The gain was attributable to a substantial increase in the number of applicants placed by the company. Typically, Hall Kinion received a 30 percent commission on the base annual salary of those applicants successfully placed into jobs. In 1995, the company placed more than 700 contract engineers, up markedly from the 290 contract engineers it placed in 1994. During the banner year, the company also placed 900 technical support and administrative applicants, appreciably more than the 550 applicants placed in 1994. The surge in business was enough to make Hall Kinion the largest full-service, high-technology staffing firm in Silicon Valley, and, more impressively, the 44th fastest-growing private company in the United States, as measured by *Inc.* magazine in 1995.

Electric Growth During the Late 1990s

Flush with success, Hall laid out bold plans. She announced that the company would open four branch offices in 1996, selecting Austin, Boston, Phoenix, and Raleigh, North Carolina, as the sites for the next wave of high-technology's "little fires." Hall predicted the company's revenues would double in 1996 and announced her intention to convert to public ownership within two years—an uncommon event in the staffing industry. Hall's next announcement bordered on the outlandish, particularly coming from the chief executive officer of a $20 million-in-sales company. Hall promised a 50-fold increase in sales. "Eventually, we intend to become a $1 billion company," she informed *Knight-Ridder/Tribune Business News* on Christmas Eve, 1995.

Hall Kinion's growth and actions in the years following Hall's stunning pronouncement supported her claim. Revenues more than doubled in 1996, reaching $51 million. In August 1997, within the time frame set by Hall, the company completed is initial public offering (IPO) of stock, raising $35 million. Earlier in 1997, the company had obtained additional capital to finance its expansion, securing $10 million in venture capital and becoming one of the first firms to raise venture capital funds in the staffing industry. Armed with cash, Hall moved forward with her expansion plans, intending to aggressively add to the company's presence in 14 markets, which by the time the company's IPO was completed included an office in London, England. Hall Kinion's new status as a publicly traded company caused her to temper her growth projections, however, lest she disappoint investors. "I will say (we plan) to continue to grow intelligently and strategically," she said in an October 22, 1997 interview with the *Business Journal.* "And to become a major force in uniting the Silicon Valleys of the world," she added.

By the end of the 1990s, Hall Kinion stood as a formidable, rising force in the staffing industry. The company's revenues, which increased 46 percent in 1999, reached $180.8 million for the year. Its net income shot up 74 percent to $7.7 million. The company entered 2000 with 35 offices in 22 markets, not counting an office in Tokyo—the company's third overseas operation—slated to open in February 2000. The pace of growth recorded in 2000 exceeded the record pace established in 1999. In 2000, the company's revenues swelled 64 percent to $296 million, bringing Brenda Rhodes (formerly Brenda Hall) nearly one-third of the way toward reaching her lofty sales goal.

The drive to $1 billion in sales took a hefty blow in 2001. For the year, revenues plummeted by more than $100 million, falling to $173.8 million. Recessive economic conditions were primarily to blame for the devastating loss, but Rhodes remained optimistic about the company's prospects. To create a stronger company, she consolidated and eliminated some of Hall Kinion's branches, which left the company with 31 offices by the end of the year. Hall Kinion also exited three markets during the year and dramatically reduced the size of its workforce.

Looking ahead, the company hoped to rebound from a depressing 2001. Optimism sprang from the company's attempts to diversify its business. For several years, Hall Kinion had been tapping into new markets by providing staffing services to businesses involved in energy services, banking and finance, medical technology, and government services. In the fall of 2001, the company formed a new business segment, Hall Kinion Finance and Accounting, to foster growth in these new markets. By the end of 2001, one-fifth of all the company's placements were in markets governed by Hall Kinion Finance and Accounting. Hoping to receive meaningful growth from its new business activities and to revive its vitality in its traditional area of expertise, Hall Kinion prepared for the future, endeavoring to rekindle the fantastic growth of the late 1990s.

Principal Subsidiaries

TKO; Hall Kinion Associates, UK Ltd.; HK International (Japan).

Principal Divisions

Hall Kinion Finance and Accounting.

Principal Competitors

COMFORCE Corporation; Kforce, Inc.; MPS Group, Inc.

Further Reading

Duan, Mary, "A Fond Farewell to List," *Business Journal,* October 27, 1997, p. S58.
Kaufman, Steve, "Silicon Valley, Calif., Staffing Firm Provides Engineers on Demand," *Knight-Ridder/Tribune Business News,* December 24, 1995, p. 12240082.
Larson, Mark, "Bay Area Tech Recruiter Sets Up Shop in Capital," *Sacramento Business Journal,* November 5, 1999, p. 4.
Semas, Judy, "Hall Kinion's Brenda Hall: Success for Her Seems More Than Temporary," *Business Journal,* November 8, 1993, p. 23.

—Jeffrey L. Covell

HARLEQUIN®

Harlequin Enterprises Limited

225 Duncan Mill Road, Fourth Floor
Toronto, Ontario M3B 3K9
Canada
Telephone: (416) 445-5860
Fax: (416) 448-7191
Web site: http://www.eharlequin.com

Wholly Owned Subsidiary of Torstar Corporation
Incorporated: 1949
Employees: 300
Sales: C$583 million (2001 est.)
NAIC: 511130 Book Publishers

Harlequin Enterprises Limited is the world's largest publisher of romance fiction, a market segment reckoned to account for half of all mass market paperbacks purchased. Harlequin, which works with some 1,000 authors, produced 150 million books in 2001, or one every five seconds. It introduces 80 new titles a month that are translated into 25 languages for sale in 94 international markets. Harlequin's mail-order division sends out one million books a month in North America.

The company redefined the romance category (the company prefers to view itself as "a leading global publisher of women's fiction," of which series romance forms a "major part") by applying branding techniques to paperback novels and distributing them in supermarkets. Women, who spend more time reading than men, have always made up Harlequin's traditional audience. A number have confessed to the influence of these novels on their career choices; many were inspired by the doctor-nurse romances of the 1950s to enter the medical profession; more recently, others, including Harlequin President Donna Hayes, have followed more modern heroines into the field of business.

Intrepid Origins

Richard Bonnycastle, born in 1903, began his career as a lawyer but soon switched to a more intrepid existence as a fur trader for the Hudson Bay Company. After 20 years, he went to work for Winnipeg's Advocate Printers, a branch of Toronto's Bryant Press.

Harlequin was founded in 1949 as a way to keep the presses busy at his new place of employment by entering the burgeoning paperback business. Jack Palmer, head of Canadian operations for the influential Curtis Circulating (distributor for the *Saturday Evening Post* and *Ladies' Home Journal*); Doug Weld of Bryant Press; and Advocate Printers were the owners of the new enterprise. Palmer handled the marketing, Bonnycastle the production.

Harlequin's first book, *The Manatee,* by U.S. author Nancy Bruff, was introduced in 1949 and sold for 50 cents. In the beginning, Harlequin typically acquired rights from other publishers, but a few original books were published as well, including a history of the British monarchy written by future *Globe and Mail* editor Richard J. Doyle. Westerns and mysteries, some quite sensationalistic, made up most of the output, however.

The first few years saw significant sales, but returns and taxes eradicated all profits. Bonnycastle received Palmer's 25 percent interest in the company upon his death in the mid-1950s. With the business apparently facing ruin, Weld also gave his stock to Bonnycastle, who in turn transferred it to his invaluable secretary, Ruth Palmour. Another important woman in the operation was Bonnycastle's wife, Mary, who began proofreading books at home as Harlequin's first editor.

In the 1950s, Harlequin came to be identified with romances set in medical settings in particular. In the late 1950s, Harlequin began a relationship with a leading British publisher identified with the genre, Mills & Boon, Limited. It was romance novels that sold best, and the company began to focus on them exclusively in 1964.

Big Business in the 1970s

Richard Bonnycastle, Jr., son of the founder, is credited with turning the little press into a big business. He relocated Harlequin to Toronto in 1969. Two years later, when sales were C$7.9 million a year, he named Lawrence Heisey as Harlequin's president.

Formerly a marketer for Procter & Gamble, Heisey is considered responsible for bringing paperbacks beyond bookstores and into supermarkets, drugstores, and other unorthodox out-

153

---

lets. Sales boomed as a result. In one promotion, Harlequin bundled free copies of *The Honey Is Bitter* with Ajax cleanser and Kotex feminine napkins. The novels themselves were standardized at 192 pages each—in order to minimize waste of printing paper and shelf space—and branded like commodities.

Harlequin acquired Mills & Boon in 1971. It had been established in London in 1908 by Gerald Mills and Charles Boon. Between the two world wars, the firm began to specialize in romantic fiction. Alan and John Boon, sons of the founder, developed the niche publisher into one of Britain's most successful in the industry.

In late 1975, Toronto Star Ltd. (renamed Torstar Corporation in 1977) acquired a 52.5 percent interest in Harlequin Enterprises Ltd. for $30.6 million. Harlequin itself soon acquired a 50 percent interest in Cora Verlag, the West German publisher that translated its titles.

Harlequin accounted for 10 percent of paperback sales in North America in the late 1970s. Its proposed takeover of Los Angeles-based Pinnacle Books, Inc., another mass market paperback publisher, was blocked by the U.S. Justice Department on antitrust grounds, although Pinnacle specialized in thrillers, not romances.

In 1980, Harlequin Enterprises did acquire the mail-order division of the Miles Kimball Company, a Wisconsin company that had been in business since 1934. Torstar acquired Harlequin's remaining shares in 1981, making it a wholly owned subsidiary.

Booming in the 1980s

Heisey was named chairman of Harlequin in 1982. David Galloway, an executive at Torstar and its future CEO, also held executive positions at Harlequin in the 1980s.

Harlequin did receive Justice Department approval to buy its largest rival, Silhouette Books, from Simon & Schuster Inc. in 1984. The acquisition returned Harlequin to undisputed leadership of the romance novel category in the United States, with a greater than 80 percent share of the $275 million a year market. Harlequin paid $10 million for Silhouette, plus an additional amount based on earnings. As part of the deal, Simon & Schuster again began distributing Harlequin books in the United States, an arrangement that had existed before 1979. Silhouette remained in existence as a separate imprint.

The early 1980s were boom years for the business. Publishers spent heavily to promote their wares, but many withdrew from the market when they failed to find profits. Harlequin's unit sales consisted of 203 million books in 1985. By 1986, Harlequin Enterprises was selling 250 million novels a year. They were translated into 15 languages and sold in 99 countries.

Harlequin had produced an adaptation of *Leopard in the Snow* for television in the late 1970s. It was not considered a success. The company revisited the medium in the mid-1980s, lending its name, but not development capital, to a new production. A film version of *Love with a Perfect Stranger* premiered on Showtime/The Movie Channel in October 1986. It was produced by Yorkshire Television of Britain and Atlantic Video Ventures, a subsidiary of the Atlantic Entertainment Group.

The content of the stories reflected changes in women's roles, and Harlequin introduced new series of books to capture different segments of the evolving female audience. Harlequin launched a new line of U.S.-based romances in 1983. The "Temptation" line, a more explicit series aimed at younger women, was introduced in 1984. A romantic suspense line was also unveiled. More assertive women and more sensitive men were the order of the day. Still, the 1980s were the decade of the (literally) bodice-ripping book covers. Zodiac-laced Starsign Romances came out in April 1991.

In 1989, Harlequin had revenues of C$327 million and an operating profit of C$56 million—a large chunk of parent company Torstar's C$149 million operating profit. Most of the sales—191 million books in all—occurred outside Canada: the books were distributed in more than 100 countries and translated into 19 languages. It published more than 60 titles a month. Harlequin had a stable of 600 authors in North America, and another 350 who reported to the London office; most wrote part-time.

Going Global in the 1990s

Harlequin's operating profit rose to C$64.4 million in 1990 while Torstar's slipped to C$104 million. "Women around the world do not appear to know that we are in a recession," Torstar President David Galloway told the *Financial Post*. Harlequin was then planning to launch a monthly magazine. Heisey retired as chairman in June of that year.

In 1992, Harlequin announced plans to buy Zebra Books, one of its more spirited competitors; however, the deal was not completed. Zebra was a mass market paperback publisher based in New York known for its innovative marketing techniques, such as putting foil and holograms on book covers. Founded in 1974, Zebra had annual sales of more than $40 million and published 400 titles a year in historical romance, true crime, action adventure, and Western lines.

In Britain and Australia, Harlequin titles were published under the Mills & Boon imprint. The company's modus operandi in foreign markets was to team with an established partner, such as Germany's Axel Springer Verlag, France's Hachette, and Italy's Mondadori. As the Iron Curtain began to come down, Eastern Europe was found wanting a romantic escape. Harlequin gave away thousands of books to East Germans visiting West Germany in 1990. It began sales to Czechoslovakia and Bulgaria in 1992; sales to Poland and Hungary soon followed.

Japan, which bought 14 million books in 1992, was its fastest-growing market. Stories set in the Rockies were especially popular there. Harlequin soon worked out a distribution deal with German media giant Bertelsmann A.G. and Denmark's Egmont to create a distribution system in Russia. After Taiwan agreed to international copyright standards in 1992,

Key Dates:

1908: Mills & Boon is founded in London.
1949: Harlequin is founded in Winnipeg.
1972: Harlequin acquires Mills & Boon.
1975: Torstar Corporation acquires majority interest in Harlequin.
1979: Harlequin cancels U.S. distribution deal with Simon & Schuster.
1981: Torstar acquires Harlequin's remaining shares.
1984: Harlequin buys rival Silhouette from Simon & Schuster, restores former U.S. distribution arrangement.
1990: Harlequin gives away thousands of books to East Germans visiting West Germany.
1993: Children's Supplementary Education Publishing (CSEP) division is created.
1994: CBS airs Harlequin's *Treacherous Beauties*.
1996: Harlequin establishes an Internet presence with Romance.net.
2000: eHarlequin.com replaces Romance.net.
2001: Donna Hayes becomes Harlequin's first female president and publisher.

Harlequin was able to tackle the large existing bootleg problem there. The year 1992 was Harlequin's best yet—205 million books were sold, for an operating profit of C$61.8 million on revenues of C$417.9 million.

In 1993, Alliance Communications, a leading Canadian TV production and distribution company, acquired the international TV and video rights to Harlequin's 16,000 titles. CBS was the first to broadcast the resulting productions, beginning with "Treacherous Beauties" in late September 1994. CBS had recently been outbid for NFL football rights by Fox, and was shifting its Sunday afternoon efforts toward a female audience.

Revenue was C$485 million in 1995. Harlequin was selling about 180 million books a year in the mid-1990s. However, romance sales were not meeting expectations in new markets such as China and Eastern Europe. The company had already added an entirely new line of business in what it expected to be a growth market.

The Children's Supplementary Educational Publishing (CSEP) division was created in 1993, inspired by Harlequin CEO Brian Hickey's difficulty in finding materials to help his son at school. Three years later, Harlequin acquired Tom Snyder Productions Inc., a leading producer of educational materials for schools, for $24 million. Other acquisitions in this area included Los Angeles-based Frank Schaffer Publications Inc., Warren Publishing House of Washington state, and New Hampshire's Delta Education. CSEP had revenues of C$55 million in 1996, mostly from teacher's stores, and had 500 employees. Torstar sold this division off in late 1998.

New Lines for the New Millennium

After two years of planning, Harlequin released a new line of "inspirational romances" in September 1998 under the Steeple Hill imprint. These were aimed at the Christian or "traditional values" reader, a fast-growing niche audience. The contents reflected a longing to return to simpler times, said Harlequin Vice-President of Public Relations Katherine Orr. By the end of the 1990s, Harlequin had 13 distinct product lines differentiated by, according to Orr, the "level of sensuality."

Harlequin partnered with Women.com when it first established an online presence with two web sites, Romance.net and eHarlequin.com. However, in late 2000, it broke off its relationship with San Francisco-based Women.com in order to host its web sites at the Toronto offices of Onyx Software Corp. Romance.net, a simple online sales site launched in 1996, was replaced by eHarlequin.com, a community-oriented, membership-based site for women, in the spring of 2000. Local sites based on the eHarlequin concept were launched for Australia, France, Germany, Holland, Italy, Japan, Spain, and the United Kingdom in 2001. In early 2002, eHarlequin.com merged with the Direct Marketing division to form the Direct-to-Consumer Group.

Donna Hayes became Harlequin's first female president and publisher in the spring of 2001. An honors English literature and communications graduate of McGill University with customer service experience at Doubleday Canada, Hayes was also the first Harlequin president to have made publishing the basis for an entire career. Her own entry into business was inspired by a Harlequin romance she read in seventh grade. She first joined Harlequin in 1985, working on the company's book clubs, which account for one-third of sales.

A spinoff of the Temptation series, the Blaze line that debuted in August 2001, stepped up the sensuality factor. In the fall, Harlequin brought out a line of books under the Red Dress Ink imprint. These, inspired by the success of *Bridget Jones's Diary* (Penguin Putnam) and others, followed the adventures of young urban women looking for love. Unlike all the Harlequin books that preceded them, these world-wise dramas left open the possibility of the heroine not finding lasting love at the end. In Japan, a soap opera based on the Harlequin novel *Turning Red* by Erica Spindler was in the works.

Principal Subsidiaries

Harlequin Australia; Harlequin France (50%); Harlequin Germany; Harlequin Greece; Harlequin Holland; Harlequin Hungary; Harlequin Italy; Harlequin Japan; Harlequin Mills & Boon U.K.; Harlequin Poland; Harlequin Scandinavia; Harlequin Spain.

Principal Divisions

Creativity Division; Direct-to-Consumer Group; Overseas; Retail—North America.

Principal Operating Units

Gold Eagle; Harlequin; MIRA; Silhouette; Steeple Hill; Red Dress Ink; Worldwide Mystery.

Principal Competitors

HarperCollins Publishers Ltd.; Kensington Books; Penguin Putnam Inc.; Random House, Inc.

Further Reading

Brand, Rachel, "Harlequin Romances Singles; Authors in Town Modernize, Court Ms. Right Market," *Rocky Mountain News* (Denver), July 19, 2002, p. 2B.

Carter, Bill, "CBS Gives Romance a Chance," *New York Times,* September 26, 1994, p. D1.

"Do You Sincerely Want to Be Seduced?," *Canadian Business,* August 1993, p. 23.

Fulford, Robert, "Romancing the Tome," *Toronto Life,* November 2001, pp. 101–05.

Gerard, Warren, "Patched Up: Harlequin Woos Back Silhouette, While Its Parent Courts a Long-Term Strategy," *Canadian Business,* November 1984, pp. 13+.

Goldman, Lea, "Hungry Heart," *Forbes,* November 11, 2002, p. 151.

Grainger, James, "Harlequin Drops Dispute with Small Press: Ponder Publishing Keeps 'Romance' Name," *Quill & Quire,* April 2000.

Grescoe, Paul, *The Merchants of Venus: Inside Harlequin and the Empire of Romance,* Vancouver: Raincoast Books, 1996.

"Harlequin Reports 15% Profit," *Quill & Quire,* June 1993, p. 12.

"Her Passion Embraced a New Adventure," *Economist,* June 5, 1993.

Hubbard, Jaimie, "Harlequin an International Affair: Eastern Europe Welcomes Romance Novels with Open Arms," *Financial Post* (Toronto), Sec. 1, September 17, 1990, p. 2.

"In Her Arms, He Melted . . ." *Economist,* August 31, 1991.

Isikoff, Michael, "Publishing Hearts Are Aflutter; Harlequin Proposes to Silhouette," *Washington Post,* June 21, 1984, p. E1.

Jenish, D'Arcy, "Love and Lucre," *Maclean's* (Toronto), September 20, 1999, p. 60.

Jennings, Vivien Lee, "The Romance Wars; the Harlequin-Silhouette Deal Ended Years of Increasingly Costly Struggle As Expenses Rose and Tastes Changed," *Publishers Weekly,* August 24, 1984, pp. 50+.

Kershaw, Anne, "New Romantics: They Don't Dabble, They Don't Scribble. They Take Their Writing Very Seriously," *Quill & Quire,* July 1996, pp. 41, 44.

Kramer, Larry, "Unfeeling Government Decides Romance and Thrills Don't Mix," *Washington Post,* February 17, 1979, p. D14.

Lerch, Renate, "Videos Cashing in on Passion for Romance," *Financial Post* (Toronto), Sec. 1, November 17, 1986, p. 1.

Mallet, Gina, "The Greatest Romance on Earth," *Canadian Business,* August 1993, pp. 18+.

McQueen, Rod, "Learning—And Loving It: Children's Supplementary Educational Publishing Is a Subplot in the Romantic World of Harlequin Enterprises. But the Direct-to-Home Educational Market Is About to Explode, Says Harlequin's CEO," *Financial Post* (Toronto), Sec. 2, February 15, 1997, p. 30.

Milliot, Jim, "Harlequin Pushes to Boost Single-Title Sales," *Publishers Weekly,* February 4, 2002, p. 16.

Olive, David, "CEOs of the Century: 25 Greats Who Built Canada," *National Post,* November 1, 1999, p. 142.

Rojo, Oscar, "Harlequin Targets Greater Expansion," *Toronto Star,* October 12, 1992, p. B3.

Siklos, Richard, "Romance Softens Recession's Punch for Torstar," *Financial Post* (Toronto), Sec. 2, May 6, 1991, p. 19.

Simon, Bernard, "Harlequin Sells Novel Romance to TV Group," *Financial Times* (London), Intl. Co. News, April 13, 1993, p. 19.

"Taiwan Has Budding Love Affair with Harlequin Romance Novels," *Financial Post* (Toronto), October 8, 1994, p. S25.

"The Toronto Star Goes on a Multimedia Binge," *Business Week,* February 7, 1977, p. 68.

Van Alphen, Tony, "Harlequin to Buy Zebra Books," *Toronto Star,* April 2, 1992, p. B7.

——, "Lawrence Heisey Retiring As Harlequin Chairman," *Toronto Star,* June 28, 1990, p. C3.

Watson, Thomas, "Harlequin Breaks Off Long-Distance E-Affair: Publisher Plans to Repatriate Web Site for Wired Women," *National Post,* September 8, 2000, p. C1.

Woodard, Joe, "God Starts Cleaning Up the Pulp-Romance: Harlequin Brings Out an "Inspiration" Series to Feed a Growing Hunger for Religion," *Alberta Report,* January 12, 1998, p, 36.

—Frederick C. Ingram

Holley Performance Products Inc.

1801 Russellville Road
Bowling Green, Kentucky 42101
U.S.A.
Telephone: (270) 782-2900
Fax: (270) 780-1858
Web site: http://www.holley.com

Private Company
Incorporated: 1917 as Holley Kerosene Carburetor
    Company
Employees: 909
Sales: $147 million (2001 est.)
NAIC: 336311 Carburetor, Piston, Piston Ring, and
    Valve Manufacturing

Holley Performance Products Inc., based in Bowling Green, Kentucky, is a major manufacturer of aftermarket components used in racing, street, marine, powersports, and industrial high-performance engines. Holley's extensive product lines include performance carburetors, superchargers, intake manifolds, ignition systems, fuel pumps, exhaust systems, internal engine components, and engine kits. The company also produces remanufactured carburetors and fuel injection components. In addition to Holley, brands include NOS, Hooker, Weiand, Flow Tech, General Kinetics, Lunati, Earl's, and Annihilator. Holley Performance products are found at major retailers such as Advance Auto Parts, AutoZone, and O'Reilly.

Holley Brothers As Automotive Pioneers at the Dawn of the 20th Century

The founders of the company that would evolve into today's Holley Performance Products were brothers George and Earl Holley, who grew up in Bradford, Pennsylvania. The eldest, George, was born in 1878, and Earl was born three years later. At a young age George became fascinated with motorcycles and the internal combustion engine. In the 1860s there had been some experimentation in powering a bicycle with a steam engine, but the combination proved far too bulky. Then came the invention of the four-cycle gasoline engine by Nikolaus August

Otto. A German engineer named Gottlieb Daimler, who worked with Otto, began developing engines and a reliable self-firing ignition system in order to propel a vehicle. He and his collaborator, Wilhelm Maybach, first powered a boat with their engine, then in 1885 fitted it to a wooden bicycle frame, producing the world's first motorcycle. Almost 20 years would pass before the motorcycle developed into a truly commercial vehicle. In the meantime, Daimler and Maybach moved on to produce one of the earliest automobiles and form Daimler Motor Company. Daimler's legacy is still recalled in the name of one of today's top automakers, DaimlerChrysler.

George Holley was one of many inventors who followed in Daimler and Maybach's footsteps. As a teenager he built and raced his own motorcycles, and Earl soon began to help him. In 1897 they designed and built a three-wheeled, single-cylinder automobile capable of going 30 miles per hour, which they dubbed The Runabout.

Earl was working as a bank teller, when in 1899 the 18-year-old put his limited business knowledge to work by joining forces with his brother to form Holley Motor Company to manufacture motorcycle engines. Earl, serving as president, handled the administrative end, while George, the chairman of the concern, was in charge of engineering and sales. The demand for motorcycle engines, however, proved to be limited because what customers wanted were complete motorcycles. The brothers began making motorcycles, and George promoted the business with his considerable driving skills. In 1902 he won the first Motorcycle Endurance Contest, and set a number of world speed records for motorcycles at the prestigious Pan American Exposition in Buffalo, New York.

Introducing the Iron Pot Carburetor in 1904

The Holley brothers turned their focus to automobiles after they gained the U.S. rights to a French carburetor. In 1903 they produced their first four-wheel automobile, The Holley Motorette, and although they would sell more than 600 over the next three years, the Holley brothers sensed the need to specialize as the automotive industry began to sort itself out. They were approached by Henry Ford in 1903 to produce carburetors

| **Company Perspectives:** |
| *For over a century, since before the Holley Brothers Company was founded in 1903, the Holley name has been synonymous with high performance.* |

for the Model T, and along with partner George Welch they formed a new corporation, Holley Brothers Company, to produce carburetors as well as ignition-system components.

In 1904 they introduced their first carburetor, the "iron pot," for use in the curved-dash Oldsmobile. When it also began to be used by Ford, the brothers decided to move their operations from Bradford to Detroit, the heart of the rapidly growing U.S. automotive industry. Their first Detroit plant opened in 1907, the same year that their ignition business got a boost when a car using a Holley Magneto won a major 24-hour race.

Over the next ten years the Holley brothers prospered in Detroit, growing in tandem with Ford, and even starting a plant to produce a kerosene carburetor for Ford tractors. In 1917, Henry Ford, who liked to control all aspects of automobile manufacture, decided to acquire the Holleys' car carburetor business. Following the sale, the brothers reorganized around the tractor division, forming Holley Kerosene Carburetor Company, and in addition to Ford they began selling their product to Chevrolet and International Harvester. During World War I, Holley not only sold carburetors and ignition components to the army, but also brass heads for artillery shells. In the final year of the war, because they were no longer limited to the manufacture of kerosene carburetors, the brothers changed their company name to Holley Carburetor Company.

In the 1920s the Holleys branched out into a number of directions. In 1926 they built another Detroit factory, which included an advanced research facility. It was also during this period that the company began to provide carburetors for the airplane industry. Only used at first by Curtiss-Wright, Holley's airplane carburetors were quickly adopted by American Airlines and Pan-American Airlines, as well as the U.S. Coast Guard and armed forces around the world. In 1935 the company introduced a variable venturi carburetor that overcame icing problems. The popular DC-3 airplane adopted the new carburetor, and then during World War II it was adapted for use by bombers and PT boats. Also during the 1930s, Holley expanded its range of automotive parts to include distributors, circuit breakers, heat regulators, and fuel pumps. To help support the growing business, in 1939 Holley opened yet another plant, this one in Portland, Michigan. The extra capacity would soon be vitally needed for the war effort. According to Holley, half of all carburetors used by U.S. troops were made by its factories, whether they were used in cars, trucks, boats, or airplanes.

Because of wartime restrictions, new commercial vehicles were not produced during World War II. With the economy booming after a decade of depression and pent-up consumer demand, the automotive industry was set for a period of explosive growth. Holley, with a second generation getting ready to take charge of the business, also was prepared to prosper in the postwar environment. In 1946 the company opened a new plant

in Clare, Michigan, and two years later a factory in Paris, Tennessee. During this period Holley introduced fuel control devices for gas turbine and jet airplane engines. The company also began to produce a line of side air inlet carburetors for use in trucks and buses. On the automotive side, Holley improved ignition efficiency by developing the first pressure distributor. To accommodate the new robust automobiles that Americans wanted, Holley brought out a four-barrel carburetor. In addition, the company became involved in the aftermarket business, offering genuine Holley parts and carburetor repair kits.

The 1950s saw a number of changes at Holley. In 1951 the main Detroit plant was closed and a new factory was established in Warren, Michigan. Holley then moved into Bowling Green, Kentucky, opening a factory in 1952. The following year, management began to turn over the reins to a new generation. Earl Holley retired from day-to-day responsibilities and George Holley, Jr., became president of the company. Also taking top positions were Danforth Holley, director of Cost Savings, and Jack Holley, vice-president of Sales. Earl Holley stayed on as vice-chairman of the corporation until his death in 1958. Older brother George outlived him, eventually passing away in 1963 at the age of 86. As automobiles changed during the 1950s, becoming ever more powerful, Holley's research and development team kept pace. Today's modular carburetor is the result of work from this time, which resulted in the development of the 4150-four-barrel carburetor used in the 1957 T-Bird. On the other side of the spectrum, compact cars also were becoming popular with the car-buying public. To accommodate the specific needs of this market, Holley designed a single bore carburetor, which was then modified for each compact model.

In 1965 Holley manufactured its 100 millionth carburetor. Although the carburetor remained the company's signature product, Holley had branched into numerous other directions since the introduction of the iron pot. Not only were Holley parts sold around the world, in 1963 a European subsidiary opened a factory in Turin, Italy, to manufacture carburetors, governors, and fuel pumps overseas. To take the next step in growing its business, as well as achieving diversification, Holley chose in 1968 to merge with Colt Industries in a tax-free merger. Colt ultimately changed its name to Coltec Industries, a company with aerospace and industrial operations in addition to automotive parts. Holley merged its Clare, Michigan operation with Colt's Chandlier aircraft division and, renamed as Holley Replacement Parts, the business began a period of expansion. Factories in Water Valley, Mississippi, and Sallisaw, Oklahoma, were acquired in 1973, and the Paris, Tennessee facility built a test laboratory. Holley's popular DOMINATOR racing carburetor, which was launched in 1968, was now modified to produce a consumer line of DOMINATOR intake manifolds. To accommodate fuel-efficient cars, which were becoming increasingly more important, the company developed economy carburetors to fill out their product line. In 1985 Holley also became involved in the fuel injection market.

Around 1980 Holley reached its peak in employment with 2,800 workers. Also at this time the company decided to stop manufacturing original-equipment carburetors and focus on the growing auto-racing market. By the mid-1990s employment dipped below 1,000. Holley Replacement Parts Division was renamed Holley Performance Products in 1994 and subsequently moved its administrative offices to Bowling Green, Kentucky, as well as its warehouse operations, which had been located in Goodlettsville, Tennessee. In addition, a state-of-the-art research and development center was built in the Bowling Green facility. A Detroit sales office, however, was retained to serve automakers and other regional customers.

As a result of these changes, all of Holley's operations were brought closer together, allowing for greater efficiency and better coordination. Centralization was especially helpful in bringing new products to the market, with engineering, research and development, testing, and manufacturing better able to function as a team. Product development also was enhanced by the rise of new technologies, from modeling techniques to automated production equipment and assembly systems.

Management-Led Buyout in 1998

Coltec decided in 1996 to focus its resources on the aerospace and industrial divisions, and it began to divest itself of its automotive components businesses. In 1997 Jeffrey G. King was named president of the Holley Performance Products Division. He came to the company with ten years of experience at Arvin Industries, an automotive systems and components company, and three years at Lincoln Brass Works, where he quickly rose to the rank of executive vice-president and chief operating officer. After only a year with Holley, in 1998, King led a management group in a buyout of the subsidiary, which at the time was generating annual sales of $100 million. Sponsoring the buyout was Kohlberg & Co., a private merchant banking firm operating out of Mount Kisco, New York. Kohlberg invested $51 million in the $100 million deal, gaining a 97 percent stake in Holley. King quickly made it known that the newly independent company would be aggressive about buying into new markets, and was especially interested in moving into the expanding power sports area, which in addition to motorcycles included personal watercraft, snowmobiles, and four wheelers. King's vision, in essence, was to make Holley into a one-stop shop for engines, with the intention of controlling the fuel air from the point it entered an engine to where it exited through the exhaust.

King soon backed up his words with actions, as over the next two years Holley completed a number of acquisitions. On the day the management buyout was completed, in fact, the company announced the acquisition of the fuel injection division of Florida-based Hirel Technologies, which added to Holley's marine product line. Several months later in November 1998, Weiand Automotive Industries of Los Angeles was acquired. Weiand was a highly regarded name in the performance market, manufacturing intake manifolds, water pumps, and supercharger technology for the marine, street performance, and racing markets. Also that month, Holley acquired Lunati Cams and Lunati Pistons of Memphis, Tennessee, adding lines of camshafts, crankshafts, pistons, and connecting rods. In October 1999 Holley bought the Marine and Automotive Supercharger Division of B&M Racing and Performance Products of Chatsworth, California. Holley soon made other important acquisitions, adding Hooker Headers and FlowTech Exhaust Systems of Phoenix, Arizona, followed by the purchase of Nitrous Oxide Systems, Inc. (NOS).

To support its growing stable of subsidiaries and product lines, Holley supplemented its salesforce by forming strategic alliances with several regional sales agencies in 2000. Also in that year, Holley added to its production capacity by striking a deal to move into a 350,000-square-foot facility in Aberdeen, Mississippi. The building, jointly owned by the city of Aberdeen and the county, was formerly used by Walker Manufacturing Co. to produce automobile exhaust systems. Holley personnel originally visited the site to consider buying some of Walker's equipment, but quickly recognized that the plant, which had undergone major renovations, was an attractive site. Moreover, Walker was leaving behind an available trained workforce. With Walker also leaving a vacuum in the local economy, Holley was able to negotiate favorable terms from area officials. Operations at Aberdeen began in January 2001, with 70 percent of the workforce former Walker employees. Holley was then able to close an Arizona facility as well as two Mexican plants, which had been purchased only two years earlier, and transfer those operations to Aberdeen. With a downturn in the economy the level of new business failed to meet Holley's expectations and Aberdeen employed only about 100 instead of the 150 originally projected. As a consequence the Bowling Green distribution center did not hire an additional 100 workers as planned. Although Holley was now generating $160 million in annual revenues, it was not performing at an acceptable level. In August 2002 King resigned and was replaced by the chairman of the board, James Wiggins, who announced his goal of making Holley into "a lean manufacturing operation." Several days later 23 employees were laid off.

Holley approached its centennial as an important player in the aftermarket parts industry. To celebrate its past the company prepared a fleet of ten unique stock vehicles, representing the ten decades of the company's history, each one relying heavily on Holley high-performance parts. One of the two existing Motorettes would be part of the touring show. With 100 years of accomplishments behind it, Holley, despite some bumps in the road, looked forward to many more years of success.

Principal Competitors

Competition Cams Inc.; Edelbrock Corporation; Moroso Performance Products, Inc.

Further Reading

Gaines, Jim, "Holley Lays Off 23," *Bowling Green Daily News,* August 31, 2002.

Gillette, Becky, " 'Reverse NAFTA' Development Creates Jobs in Aberdeen," *Mississippi Business Journal,* February 12, 2001, p. 18.

"Holley Senior Management Wrests Company from Coltec, Inc.," *Aftermarket Business,* August 1, 1998, p. 16.

Paulk, Michael, "Holley Adds 500 New Jobs in Aberdeen," *Memphis Business Journal,* May 5, 2000, p. 1.

Waters, Jim, "Holley to Celebrate Its Golden Anniversary," *Bowling Green Daily News,* March 31, 2002.

—Ed Dinger

HOLMEN

Holmen AB

Strandvägen 1
P.O. Box 5407
SE-114 84 Stockholm
Sweden
Telephone: (8) 666 21 00
Fax: (8) 666 21 30
Web site: http://www.holmen.com

Public Company
Incorporated: 1873 as Mo och Domsjö AB
Employees: 5,097
Sales: SKr 16.66 billion ($1.58 billion) (2001)
Stock Exchanges: Stockholm
Ticker Symbol: HOLMA
NAIC: 322121 Paper (Except Newsprint) Mills; 322122
   Newsprint Mills; 322130 Paperboard Mills

Holmen AB is one of Sweden's largest forestry companies, active in the paper, paperboard, and timber sectors. Its largest operating unit, generating 53 percent of revenues in 2001, is Holmen Paper, which produces newsprint, magazine paper, and telephone directory paper. The unit's four paper mills (three in Sweden and one in Spain) have an annual production capacity of 1.8 million metric tons. Generating 27 percent of revenues in 2001 was Iggesund Paperboard, which produces bleached board and folding boxboard used to package chocolates and other food products, cosmetics, cigarettes, and pharmaceuticals as well as for graphical applications. Annual production capacity for this unit's three mills (two of which are in Sweden and the other in England) is 505,000 metric tons. Holmen also has three smaller units: Iggesund Timber, which produces and sells sawn timber at a single sawmill with production capacity of 200,000 cubic meters per year; Holmen Skog, which manages one million hectares of forestland in Sweden and is responsible for procuring wood for the group's mills; and Holmen Kraft, which has whole or partial interests in 23 hydroelectric power stations in Sweden and is responsible for the provision of electricity for Holmen's mills. Overall, 86 percent of Holmen's revenues in 2001 were generated within the 15 countries of the European Union. L E

Lundbergföretagen AB, a Swedish brokerage firm headed by Fredrik Lundberg, chairman of Holmen, holds 52 percent of the voting rights of Holmen, while the Kempe Foundations, controlled by Holmen's founding family, holds a 16.3 percent stake. Until 2000, Holmen was known as Mo och Domsjö AB (MoDo).

Mid-19th-Century Origins

Holmen's history needs to be seen against the background of the Swedish forestry industry in general. Sweden has long been one of the most heavily wooded countries in Europe, and even now forests cover 68 percent of its territory. Successive Swedish governments have done much to promote the export of forestry products since the middle of the 19th century, when European industrialization increased the demand for timber, and at the same time mass emigration and rising agricultural productivity allowed the release of surplus land for timber harvesting. The legislation that had restricted ownership of forests to the iron industry was repealed, the depletion of the Norwegian forests removed a major source of competition, and the shift in British trade practices toward free trade in the 1840s removed the tariffs and the policy of colonial preference that had kept Swedish products out of what was then the major industrial market.

J.C. Kempe was among the many entrepreneurs who thrived in these circumstances, which, especially in the boom years of the 1850s and 1870s, resembled a gold rush in their impact upon the economy and society. Kempe was a member of a family that had long been settled in Pomerania—then eastern Germany, now western Poland. He went to Sweden to work for his uncle, a sugar refiner, but then entered the forestry industry through a series of accidents. Kempe had a disagreement with his uncle and went to work in a trading office owned by the father of his friend Olof Johan Wikner. Kempe then married Wikner's sister, and in 1823 the two men took over the business after the death of Wikner's father. Their main water sawmill was at Mo, inland from the port of Örnsköldsvik. Kempe became sole owner in 1836 and expanded the business to include iron works, shipbuilding, and manufacturing of wood products. The Swedish sawmill industry started to expand more rapidly around 1850 when steam engines were introduced to replace water sawmills.

Company Perspectives:

Holmen's main product areas are newsprint and magazine paper for newspapers, magazines, directories and advertising; paperboard for consumer packaging and graphical applications. In both these areas Holmen has a strong position on the market, which it intends to develop.

Holmen shall grow at a faster rate than the market. Attractive products and product development provide the prerequisites for growth, both organic and via selective acquisitions.

Holmen focuses on high quality and low production costs within each product area. Cost efficiency is achieved by applying large-scale production and the high competence of the personnel.

Holmen shall have knowledge and control of important raw materials regarding purchasing, price, availability and quality by owning forests, power and recovered paper collection companies.

In 1865 J.C. Kempe built a steam-driven sawmill at Domsjö, near his other mill. By this time he was exporting his timber to Britain, Germany, and France. Mo och Domsjö AB was officially established in 1873.

Expanding into Pulp in the Early 20th Century

Mo och Domsjö, driven by Kempe's wish to make full use of its forest resources, also became one of the leading participants in the pulp industry, which produced the raw material for paper and other products, and which had begun in Sweden in the 1850s. It was in the 1890s that pulp became a leading export. Pulp mills used the lower grades of timber that the sawmills did not want, and much of the waste from the sawmills could also be chemically transformed into pulp in sulfite mills. J.C. Kempe's son Frans built a sulfite mill at Domsjö in 1902–03. The first sulfite pulp mill in the world had been built in Sweden in 1871. Use of sulfite continued to grow, and by 1914 sulfite mill production accounted for more than a third of the company's revenue.

Frans Kempe was also a pioneer in the use of scientific forest management methods. He also worked to provide better housing for the company's workers. Mo och Domsjö continued to innovate and was the first Swedish company to use birchwood, previously used only for fuel, in making paper pulp. Frans continued to expand the company by adding a further sulfite mill.

The Forestry Act of 1903 required regeneration of forests after felling. Even so, new planting could not keep up with demand, and competition developed among the companies as the forests were depleted. By 1906 purchases of land by forestry companies had become a political issue, and the government, fearing the disappearance of peasant landowners, introduced what was virtually a ban on further acquisition of land by Mo och Domsjö and its competitors.

World War I saw a sharp increase in pulp prices, which made sulphite mill production extremely profitable. The company continued to grow under Frans Kempe's son, Carl, who took over the

business in 1916. Mo och Domsjö began production of kraft pulp in 1919, by which time pulp had become MoDo's main product. During the 1920s and 1930s the introduction of new saws, ranging from frame saws to mobile circular saws, decreased production costs in some cases, though their use was limited to certain types of lumber. The means of transporting wood and wood products also changed. River floating had been a cheap and popular method, but the growing use of trucks made the distribution of wood products cheaper and freed the forestry companies from the need to site their mills near rivers.

These interwar years saw a slowdown in the forestry industry. The pulp producers' demand for timber was so great that the forests were seriously depleted and the price of timber rose, while their ability to offer higher wages than other sectors of the industry attracted workers away from those sectors and damaged growth opportunities in other industries. At the same time it was difficult to import extra timber from countries such as Finland because they too had restrictions on their timber trade in an effort to protect their rapidly depleted forests. Firms such as Mo och Domsjö, which combined lumber milling with pulp production and owned their forests, were thus better placed to survive this period than their smaller competitors, and even to expand. By 1939 the company was running two large sulfite mills and one kraft mill. During World War II, production facilities at the sulfite mills had to be used for the production of other types of pulp to replace imports, such as cattle feed stocks. This led to increased production of chemical derivatives, which was to provide a foundation for the development of the chemical industry in Sweden into a profitable unit after World War II, offsetting volatility in the company's core forestry industry.

Launching into and Expanding Production of Fine Paper from the 1950s to the 1970s

The output of pulp greatly increased and the mechanization of the production process intensified in Sweden starting in the 1950s. Within the Swedish pulp and paper industry there were major structural changes between 1953 and 1985. There were 129 production units in Sweden in 1953, but only 57 in 1985, though total production continued to increase. With Erik Kempe as managing director, Mo och Domsjö implemented new techniques for various processes ranging from wood handling to digesting and bleaching. In 1951 it constructed a mill for production of fine paper in Hörnefors. In 1959, after Kempe's death, Bengt Lyberg took over as managing director. The company now became interested in petrochemical production, and a site was chosen on the west coast of Sweden, where a plant was completed in 1963. It acquired other companies in the same field, such as Svenska Oljeslageri AB. Mo och Domsjö's interest in petrochemicals lasted until approximately 1973, when it decided to sell off this side of its business because this diversification was not performing the function originally intended for it.

It was during the second half of the 1960s that the company changed direction under its new chairman, Matts Carlgren, who succeeded Carl Kempe in 1965. In a natural step toward integration, the company began to produce its own paper from its own pulp, building on the success of the Hörnefors mill. Its acquisitions under this strategy included the French fine paper mill Papeterie de Pont Sainte Maxence (PSM) and other fine paper businesses based in Sweden. In 1972 a new plant was opened in

Key Dates:

1836: J.C. Kempe becomes sole owner of a water sawmill at Mo, Sweden.

1865: Kempe builds a stem-driven sawmill at Domsjö, near his other mill.

1873: Kempe establishes Mo och Domsjö AB (MoDo).

Early 1900s: Company builds a sulfite pulp mill at Domsjö.

1919: Production of kraft pulp begins.

1951: MoDo begins producing fine paper at a new mill in Hörnefors.

Late 1960s: Company begins producing its own paper from its own pulp.

1972: A new plant is opened in Husum that integrates production of fine paper and kraft pulp.

1988: MoDo acquires Holmens Bruk, a leading Swedish producer of newsprint; Iggesund Bruk, a leading Swedish paperboard producer; and Thames Board Ltd., a U.K. paperboard manufacturer.

1999: MoDo and SCA merge their fine paper operations into the new 50–50 jointly owned MoDo Paper.

2000: Mo och Domsjö changes its name to Holmen AB; SCA and Holmen sell their 50 percent stakes in MoDo Paper to Metsä-Serla; Holmen acquires Papelera Peninsular, operator of a newsprint mill south of Madrid.

Husum that integrated the production of fine paper and of kraft pulp. As it continued to expand and modernize this fine paper division it established an even stronger position within the European market by acquiring wholesaling companies in the United Kingdom, France, The Netherlands, and Norway. Mo och Domsjö also entered the tissue industry, with several acquisitions of companies in Belgium, the United Kingdom, and in southern Sweden. Integrated as MoDo Consumer Products Ltd., these firms manufactured consumer products including sanitary pads, infant-care products, and other soft paper goods. The group's vertical integration extended into sole ownership of, or partnership in, 30 hydroelectric power stations in the far north of Sweden.

Expanding into Newsprint and Paperboard in the 1980s

During the 1980s MoDo had concentrated on acquiring shares in Iggesund Bruk and Holmens Bruk, and it now decided to gain control of both, doing so in 1988. Holmens Bruk was one of Sweden's leading producers of newsprint. It had originated in the early 19th century, becoming a limited liability company in 1854 and expanding its textile interests alongside its paper production. It bought up forests in southeastern Sweden and established a newsprint mill around 1912. After World War II, the Swedish textile industry gradually ceased to be profitable, and in 1970 Holmens left the industry to concentrate on newsprint.

Iggesund Bruk, by contrast, was a leader in paperboard production. It dated back to the 17th century, when an iron works was founded that went on producing until 1953, while a steelmaking plant continued to operate for a further 30 years. The group's involvement in the forestry industry began early in

the 20th century with the establishment of a sulfite pulp mill and a kraft pulp mill, and the acquisition of a sawmill in Hudiksvall. During the 1960s sulfite pulp production was abandoned, kraft pulp production was expanded, and the production of paperboard began, with a view to supplying the packaging and graphics industries. The group acquired forests and built up interests in steel, engineering, and chemicals through a series of acquisitions. By the late 1980s, however, Iggesund had divested itself of all its nonforestry interests apart from a 50 percent holding in a steel firm. Its main product continued to be paperboard, along with some output of pulp and high-quality wood for the furniture and building industries in Western Europe. Mo och Domsjö's acquisition of the U.K. firm Thames Board Ltd. in 1988 strengthened its position as one of the leading producers of high-quality paperboard in Europe.

MoDo's purpose in taking over Holmens and Iggesund was to create a third giant in the Swedish forest industry, challenging the first- and second-ranking groups, Stora Kopparbergs Bergslag AB and Svenska Cellulosa AB (SCA), by diversifying its output. In the late 1980s the MoDo Group also had interests in 25 companies, which, because the group had only 20 percent to 26 percent of the voting shares, were treated as associated companies.

MoDo showed increased profits in 1987 as the price of pulp rose. In 1988 MoDo decided to sell off its soft paper division to the Finnish company Metsä-Serla Oy. Although this division's domestic market share was significant, the company's leaders felt that its share of the European market as a whole was not sufficiently large to justify its existence as a diversification, and that it would be wiser to concentrate on the profitable fine paper and newsprint divisions. In 1989 MoDo showed a drop in sales, but a rise in profits, owing to the sale of the soft paper division.

MoDo and the Swedish forest industry in general were affected by the general movement in Sweden toward reducing environmental damage. Strict regulation by the Environment Protection Board led the industry to clean up its operations, to such an extent that several lakes "killed" by forest industry effluent became biologically active again. Nevertheless, MoDo's adoption of more environmentally friendly methods such as oxygen bleaching preceded government regulations, and the company was seen as a pioneer in the use of environmentally safe production techniques.

Seesawing Fortunes in the 1990s

The pulp and paper industry suffered through a global recession in the early 1990s, with MoDo consequently posting only a small profit in 1991 and net losses for both 1992 and 1993. The company enacted a number of cost-saving measures during this period, including the closure of a pulp mill and the shutdown of a production line at another mill. MoDo also did not pay a dividend for either 1992 or 1993. MoDo completed one major acquisition during the period, paying FFr 1.46 billion ($250 million) in 1991 to purchase the 83 percent of Alicel/Alipap vid Rouen it did not already own. Alicel/Alipap was a French maker of fine paper.

The early 1990s also saw the formation and abandonment of an alliance between MoDo and SCA. In December 1990 SCA purchased a 32 percent share of the voting rights in MoDo stock. The strategic alliance was forged to promote collaboration in printing, paper production, and joint investments in paper mills. The alliance never really led anywhere, however, as the two companies could not reach agreement on exactly how to collaborate. In September 1992 SCA announced that it was abandoning the alliance, and by early 1995 it had divested itself of all of its MoDo holdings. A large portion of the shares were sold to L E Lundbergföretagen AB, a Swedish brokerage firm headed by Fredrik Lundberg. This company already had a 26 percent voting share in MoDo, and it thus increased its share to a dominant 46 percent.

In August 1994 Bengt Pettersson replaced longtime chief executive Bernt Lof. Pettersson had been the head of Stora Billerud, a packaging unit within Stora. MoDo returned to the black in 1994, bolstered by higher prices and high capacity utilization, and also resumed paying a dividend. Early the following year, MoDo sold its MoDo Packaging unit to Assi-Domän of Sweden for SKr 1.2 billion ($167 million). The unit included a pulp and paper mill in Sweden that produced packaging paper and two paper bag companies in the United Kingdom and Germany. Around this same time, MoDo also sold off stakes in the Swiss packaging group RIG Rentsch and the Slave Lake Pulp Partnership in Canada. The funds generated by these divestments helped finance plant investments, including a SKr 2.1 billion outlay on a new newsprint machine, and reduce the company's extremely high debt burden.

During 1995, the industry enjoyed one of its best years since World War II, and MoDo saw its pretax profits skyrocket to a record SKr 5.22 billion ($761.6 million), nearly triple the figure for the previous year. Price increases were the chief reason for the stellar results, and falling prices were blamed for the declines in profits that were recorded in both 1996 and 1997. MoDo recovered in 1998, posting increases in both revenues and profits, although not to the levels reached in 1995.

Focusing on Newsprint, Magazine Paper, and Paperboard As Holmen in the Early 2000s

In early 1999, MoDo outlined a new company strategy whereby it would concentrate on newsprint and magazine paper, through its Holmen Paper subsidiary, and on paperboard, through the Iggesund Paperboard unit. With a strong balance sheet in place, MoDo also announced that it would pay its shareholders a special dividend totaling SKr 3.11 billion ($402 million), which was equivalent to one-quarter of the firm's market capitalization. The company declared, as well, that it would seek an alliance or merger for its fine paper operations, which had been hit hard by volatile demand in southeast Asia and Russia. In April 1999 MoDo and SCA reached an agreement to merge their fine paper operations into a new 50–50 jointly owned company to be called MoDo Paper. The new firm, which began operation in September 1999, was the third largest fine paper group in Europe. In conjunction with this transaction, MoDo also completed its exit from the pulp market by selling off its sulphite pulp mill in Domsjö in early 2000.

Also in early 2000, Pettersson stepped down as chief executive of MoDo although he remained on the company board. Replacing Pettersson was Per Ericson, who had most recently served as president of Sandvik Steel. To differentiate itself from MoDo Paper, Mo och Domsjö changed its name to Holmen AB, adopting the name of the newsprint and magazine unit, the company's largest operation. Holmen and SCA also announced that they would make MoDo Paper a publicly traded firm, with SCA selling 35 percent of the shares through a public offering and Holmen distributing 35 percent to its shareholders. This plan was called off in March 2000, however, because of adverse conditions in the stock market. Then in May, both companies agreed to sell their 50 percent interests in MoDo Paper to Metsä-Serla, with the transaction completed in August. Metsä-Serla paid Holmen SKr 6.5 billion ($737 million) for its half-interest, resulting in a capital gain for Holmen of about SKr 2 billion. Part of the proceeds were returned to shareholders in the form of a special dividend and part was earmarked for investing in the company's remaining operations. Even prior to the completion of the sale of MoDo Paper, Holmen finalized the acquisition of Papelera Peninsular from the Spanish company Unipapel for about SKr 2 billion ($231 million). Holmen gained a newsprint mill located south of Madrid that was completed in mid-1998 and that had annual capacity of 200,000 metric tons.

Continuing its drive to invest in its core areas, Holmen announced in November 2000 that it would spend SKr 1.85 billion ($183 million) to replace an old machine at its Hallsta mill in Hallstavik, Sweden, with an improved and higher capacity machine for producing high-quality magazine paper. The new machine was brought into production during 2002. In November 2001, meanwhile, Ericson resigned from his position as chief executive, having apparently been a poor choice for the job. Göran Lundin, who had previously headed up Holmen Paper, took over as president and CEO. Lundin was expected to continue to seek ways to bolster Holmen's core activities through both organic growth and acquisitions.

Principal Subsidiaries

Holmen Paper AB; Iggesund Paperboard AB; Iggesund Timber AB; Holmen Skog AB; Holmen Kraft AB; AB Ankarsrums Skogar; Domsjö Klor AB; Fiskeby AB; Haradsskogarna AB; Harrsele Linjeaktiebolag; Holmens Bruk AB; Husum Copy AB; AB Iggesund Bruk; Lägernskog AB; MoDo Holding AB; MoDo-Iggesund CTMP AB; MoDo Forest Management AB; Skärnäs Terminal AB; Ströms Trävaru AB; AB Överums Skogar; Holmen UK Ltd.; Holmen France Finance SAS; Holmen France Holding SAS; Iggesund Paperboard Asia Pte. Ltd. (Singapore); Holmen Suecia Holding SI; Holmen Espana SI.

Principal Competitors

Abitibi-Consolidated Inc.; Norske Skogindustrier ASA; Stora Enso Oyj; Nippon Unipac Holding; UPM-Kymmene Corporation.

Further Reading

Brown-Humes, Christopher, "MoDo Sells Packaging Unit to Assidoman," *Financial Times,* November 4, 1994, p. 21.

Carnegy, Hugh, "SCA Severs Strategic Link-Up with MoDo," *Financial Times,* February 10, 1995, p. 23.

Gårdlund, Torsten, *Mo och Domsjö intill 1940: den ekonomiska utvecklingen,* Uppsala, Sweden: Almqvist & Wiksell, 1951.

Gustavon, Carl G., *The Small Giant: Sweden Enters the Industrial Era,* Athens: Ohio University Press, 1986.

Jewitt, Caroline, "Nordic Deal Reshuffles the European Pack," *Pulp and Paper International,* September 2000, pp. 52, 54–55.

Kenny, Jim, "MoDo Uses Its Assets to Good Effect," *Pulp and Paper International,* June 1999, p. 37.

"Metsa-Serla Buys All of MoDo Paper," *PIMA's North American Papermaker,* July 2000, p. 19.

Montgomery, G.A., *The Rise of Modern Industry in Sweden,* London: P.S. King & Son Ltd., 1939.

Moore, Stephen D., "Sweden's MoDo to Pay $250 Million for Rest of France's Alicel/Alipap," *Asian Wall Street Journal,* June 4, 1991, p. 8.

The New Group: MoDo-Holmen-Iggesund, Örnsköldsvik, Sweden: MoDo, 1988.

O'Brian, Hugh, "New Man Gets on Board As MoDo's Prospects Improve," *Pulp and Paper International,* February 1995, pp. 49 +.

"SCA and MoDo Make a Fine Match," *Pulp and Paper International,* June 1999, p. 7.

"SCA and MoDo to Merge Fine Paper Operations," *PIMA's North American Papermaker,* June 1999, p. 34.

Taylor, Robert, "SCA Abandons Alliance with MoDo," *Financial Times,* September 8, 1992, p. 25.

Wold, David, "The Days of Free Lunches Are Over," *Pulp and Paper International,* June 1993, pp. 73 +.

—Monique Lamontagne
—update: David E. Salamie

Icelandair

Reykjavik Airport
101 Reykjavik
Iceland
Telephone: +354 5050 300
Toll Free: (800) 223-5500
Fax: +354 5888 820
Web site: http://www.icelandair.com

Public Company
Incorporated: 1937 as Flugfélag Akureyrar
Employees: 2,487
Sales: ISK 37.97 billion (2001)
Stock Exchanges: Iceland
Ticker Symbol: IAIR
NAIC: 481111 Scheduled Passenger Air Transportation;
481112 Scheduled Freight Air Transportation; 481212
Nonscheduled Chartered Freight Air Transportation;
481211 Nonscheduled Chartered Passenger Air
Transportation; 488119 Other Airport Operations;
488190 Other Support Activities for Air
Transportation; 532111 Passenger Car Rental; 561520
Tour Operators; 721110 Hotels (Except Casino
Hotels) and Motels

Icelandair (Fluglei'ir hf.), Iceland's largest publicly traded company, has played off its unique mid-Atlantic location to serve as a convenient option for transatlantic air travel. A one-class, backpacker's airline in earlier decades, Icelandair has since made an effort to appeal to business travelers. It still carries a mix of 85 percent leisure to 15 percent business traffic. The company also has been promoting Iceland as a tourist destination in itself. Icelandair carries nearly two million passengers a year; this traffic is highly seasonal. Although Iceland's native population is well-traveled, only a quarter of Icelandair's passengers are natives. In addition to various aviation support operations, Icelandair is the Hertz franchise for Iceland and has interests in hotels and tour operators.

Origins

Iceland's first airline, Flugfélag Akureyrar, was founded on June 3, 1937, at Akureyri on the country's north coast. The services were welcomed by the extremely isolated fishing villages there. Within two years, however, the one-plane operation was grounded due to the capsizing of its Waco YKS seaplane.

The company relaunched in the capital city of Reykjavik in 1940 under the name Flugfélag Islands. Soon, three young Icelandic pilots, fresh from flight training in Canada, formed their own airline, Loftlei'ir ("Skyways"), on March 10, 1944; it began flight operations on April 7.

These two new airlines operated a mixed bag of equipment at first, notes aviation historian R.E.G. Davies. In the mid-1940s, Flugfélag was flying a Waco floatplane, two de Havillan Rapides, a Beechcraft, a Catalina, and in 1946 launched scheduled international service to Scotland and Denmark using Liberators and DC-3s, respectively, chartered from Scottish Airlines. Loftlei'ir began with a Stinson Reliant seaplane. It later took on the name Loftlei'ir Icelandic Airlines.

In February 1952, Flugfélag, then known as Icelandair, took over all of Iceland's domestic routes. By the early 1960s, Icelandair had a mixed fleet of eight aircraft, and Loftlei'ir fielded five Douglas DC-6s.

Loftlei'ir Icelandic took advantage of Iceland's 1946 bilateral agreement with the United States to seriously undercut the fares of IATA (International Air Transport Association) member carriers. From 1952 to 1962, Icelandic shared this concession with Norwegian carrier Braathens SAFE, whose own network stretched east to Hong Kong. The two airlines also cooperated on maintenance at Braathens' base in Stavanger, Norway. At the end of the 1960s, Icelandic had a 2 percent market share of trans-Atlantic traffic; it was a profitable slice of business.

Icelandic's low transatlantic fares helped many young Americans—including future president Bill Clinton—"cross the pond." Some of the traffic was routed directly to Icelandic's base in Luxembourg, which did not have an airline of its own.

Company Perspectives:

Welcome to Icelandair, one of Europe's most progressive and dynamic airlines. Operating from our hub at Keflavik Airport, we offer daily and regular scheduled services to Europe and North America, alone or in conjunction with our code-sharing associates.

With over 60 years aviation experience, Icelandair is in many ways unique among international airlines, in that apart from our role as a passenger and freight carrier, we also provide a one-stop comprehensive travel service to and from our home country, including hotel, car rental and tour facilities.

Discover our world. Welcome aboard.

The low-budget flights, with single-class seating, foreshadowed Freddie Laker's transatlantic travel bargains.

Perceiving a shortage of hotels in the country, the airline got into the hospitality business around 1970. When the main airport was moved to Keflavik, the company turned the Reykjavik terminal into an inn.

1973 Merger

Flugfélag Islands and Loftlei'ir were merged under the new Fluglei'ir holding company on July 20, 1973. Fluglei'ir, which continued to be known as Icelandair in international circles, assumed all operating responsibility for the two airlines on October 1, 1979.

Atlantic crossings accounted for nearly two-thirds of the airline's international traffic in 1974. The airline used DC-8s for transatlantic service and Boeing 727s for European routes.

A worldwide oil crisis in 1979 prompted mass layoffs. An experiment with the widebodied DC-10 aircraft did not help: the type was grounded by the FAA in the peak of the tourist season after an American Airlines crash in Chicago.

Government Investment and Divestment in the 1980s

The government of Iceland acquired 20 percent of Icelandair in a 1981 share issue. Four years later, the government of Iceland sold its 20 percent stake in the carrier, making it privately owned.

About the same time, Sigurdur Helgason, who became CEO in June 1985, began to steer the company into a hub-and-spoke system centered on Iceland, and began developing the country as a tourist destination in itself. This was quite an adjustment, as three-quarters of the company's business had been U.S.-Europe travel. Helgason had earned an M.B.A. degree at the University of North Carolina, Chapel Hill, before joining the company in 1974.

In the mid-1980s, Icelandair was offering trans-Atlantic customers unique island-hopping packages with no extra charge for stopovers in Greenland and Iceland. Weather limited the Green-

land excursions to the summer months. These flights were made with smaller commuter aircraft.

In the fall of 1988, Icelandair canceled money-losing service to Baltimore-Washington and Boston while it awaited delivery of new Boeing 757s to replace its aging, inefficient DC-8s, which first entered service in 1970. The service resumed in 1990. At the same time, Icelandair was instituting a marketing agreement with USAir and launching a new program to attempt to win over lucrative business travelers.

In 1989, reported *Air Transport World*, two-thirds of Icelandair's international traffic was coming from Europe, not the United States, in a reversal of the situation 15 years earlier. Deregulation of U.S. airlines had led to increased price competition from that side of the ocean. Icelandair responded by focusing on Europe, and routing all transatlantic traffic through its hub at Iceland's Keflavik Airport. The historic Reagan-Gorbachev Summit of 1986 helped increase Helsinki's stature as a site for international conferences and conventions.

The company dealt with a seasonal reduction in traffic by directing aircraft to Mediterranean charters in the winter. It was also a rather diversified enterprise. In addition to flying visitors to Iceland, Icelandair owned two hotels, a flight kitchen, a car rental agency, and a travel agency. Cargo—mostly seafood exports—accounted for 10 percent of revenues in 1990.

Soaring in the 1990s

In the early 1990s, Icelandair was carrying more than 750,000 passengers a year—nearly three times Iceland's population. The liberalization (deregulation) of the European air travel market hit the company hard, however. Icelandair posted losses in 1992 and 1993 before managing a net profit of $9.1 million in 1994, when revenues were $215.3 million, up 10.6 percent.

The company spent $336 million to rejuvenate its fleet. Three Boeing 757s replaced the McDonnell Douglas DC-8s the company had been using on long routes. The company leased another 757 to the airline Britannia. Four flexible and efficient Boeing 737s served medium-length routes. Icelandair's domestic Flugleider division replaced its Fokker 27s with five Fokker 50s for the short hops. The planes were named after goddesses from Icelandic folklore—Hafdis, Aldis, Eydis, Vedis, and Fanndis.

In 1991, a devastating year for airlines worldwide, Icelandair managed a $2.3 million profit on turnover of $228 million. In 1992, however, Icelandair posted a net loss of $315,000 on turnover of $227 million. At the time, Icelandair had 1,300 employees and managed two Reykjavik hotels. The relatively new Saga business class accounted for 10 percent of revenue in 1992.

To survive in the liberalized European air market, Icelandair planners believed the airline needed a strong partner. They signed a marketing agreement with The SAS Group in 1993. The airline also signed a code-share deal with small Faeroe Islands operator Atlantic Airways. Passenger count topped one million in 1995.

In late 1996, Southwest Airlines (SWA) began testing its first marketing agreement ever with another carrier, allowing

Key Dates:

1937: Flugfélag Akureyrar is founded on Iceland's north coast.
1939: Loss of its sole aircraft grounds Flugfélag Akureyrar.
1940: Flugfélag Akureyrar is relaunched as Flugfélag Islands.
1943: Flugfélag relocates to capital city of Reykjavik.
1944: Loftlei'ir is founded.
1945: Regular flights to Europe begin.
1949: Direct London route is launched in collaboration with Loftlei'ir.
1952: First North American routes open; newly renamed Icelandair takes over domestic routes.
1973: Flugfélag Islands merges with Loftlei'ir Icelandic Airlines.
1979: Oil crisis triggers mass layoffs.
1985: Icelandair faces brush with bankruptcy.
1989: Restructuring and fleet renewal program begins.
1992: Liberalization of European air market leads to two years of losses.
1993: Icelandair enters marketing agreement with The SAS Group.
1996: Southwest Airlines picks Icelandair for its partner in its first interlining agreement.
1997: Domestic and cargo competition leads to $4 million loss.
1999: After 45 years, the Luxembourg hub is closed.
2001: Code-sharing deal with U.S. railway Amtrak is signed.

Icelandair to bundle a coupon for travel on SWA's Cleveland-Baltimore route with its own transatlantic flights. In August 1998, Trans World Airlines, which had just added Caribbean destinations, linked its frequent flier program with that of Icelandair.

Icelandair posted a net loss of $4.2 million in 1997 due to fierce competition from Islandsflug following deregulation of the domestic market. Cargo competition was also stiff. Icelandair soon recovered, however, logging net earnings of $2.2 million in 1998, thanks to an increase in passenger sales.

The 20 hotels operated by the airline were spun off in 1998 into the Icelandair Hotels Ltd. subsidiary. The airline was also the country's agent for Hertz auto rentals and owned a travel agency. The domestic carrier was called Flugfélag Islands hf., or Air Iceland.

In a 1999 *Air Transport World* article, Icelandair CEO Sigurdur Helgason characterized the airline's decade-long restructuring as emphasizing production in the early to mid-1990s, before shifting to a focus on branding and marketing at the end of the decade. A new aircraft livery was part of the image campaign designed to retire its ''backpacker airline'' label in favor of an emphasis on business travel.

Icelandair had less than a 1 percent share of transatlantic traffic, but was dominant in routes connecting Scandinavia to secondary U.S. markets such as Minneapolis, Boston, and Washington, D.C. On these routes, going through Reykjavik could save travelers up to three hours versus other airlines' hubs. In January 1999, Icelandair dropped its longtime Luxembourg hub from its route network after 45 years.

At the time, the airline continued to update its fleet by phasing out Boeing 737s in favor of larger Boeing 757s. The carrier used the extra space for its expanding cargo business.

New Units, Challenges After 2000

Icelandair brought an intermodal transport concept from Europe to the United States when it inked a code-share deal with Amtrak in 2001. This allowed Icelandair passengers in the United States to buy a single ticket good for both a transatlantic flight and a railway trip to the Baltimore-Washington International Airport.

Icelandair suffered greatly along with the world's other airlines from the downturn in traffic following the September 11, 2001 terrorist attacks on the United States. Falling fares on North Atlantic routes prompted the carrier to refocus on traffic to and from Iceland. Icelandair lost ISK 1.2 billion for the year on revenues of ISK 37.97 billion. It was beginning to recover, however, by the first half of 2002.

The company made a few structural adjustments during this time. Icelandair Ground Services became a subsidiary in the beginning of 2001. A new subsidiary, Fluglei'ir – Leiguflug hf. (Icelandair Charter and Leasing), was launched in early 2002. A new profit center, Shared Services, was later added to provide financial services to group companies.

Principal Subsidiaries

Amadeus Island hf. (Amadeus Iceland; 95%); Bílaleiga Fluglei'a ehf. (Icelandair Hertz Car Rental); Fer'askrifstofa Islands hf. (Iceland Travel; 91%); Fer'asmin'urinn hf. (Destal; 92.5%); Flugfélag Islands hf.; Fluglei'ahótel hf. (Icelandair Hotels); Fluglei'ir – Frakt ehf. (Icelandair Cargo); Fluglei'ir – Leiguflug hf. (Icelandair Charter and Leasing); Flug'jónustan Keflavíkurflugvelli ehf. (Icelandair Ground Services); Iceland Tours Ltd, U.K.; Islandsfer'ir hf.; Kynnisfer'ir fer'askrifstofanna sf. (Reykjavík Excursions; 92.9%).

Principal Operating Units

Customer Club; International Passenger Services; Technical Services; Saga Boutique; Shared Services.

Principal Competitors

Aer Lingus Group plc; Air Atlanta Icelandic; Continental Airlines, Inc.; Islandsflug—Icebird Airlines; KLM Royal Dutch Airlines; Virgin Atlantic.

Further Reading

''Amtrak, Icelandair Enter Service Arrangement,'' *Washington Times,* June 4, 2001.
''Banks Fly at Umbrella Facility and JOL for Icelandair 757,'' *Airfinance Journal,* March 2001, p. 11.

Cameron, Doug, "Start-Ups Avoid an Atlantic Crossing," *European,* July 13, 1998, p. 24.

Coppola, Vincent, "Airline Takes Overland Route," *Adweek* (Southeast edition), October 2, 2000.

Daube, Scott, "Icelandair to Halt Operations at Three Gateways; Will Reopen Them After Delivery of More Efficient Jets," *Travel Weekly,* July 28, 1988, p. 5.

Davies, R.E.G., *A History of the World's Airlines,* London: Oxford University Press, 1967.

Davis, Lou, "The Back Road to Europe; Commuter Level Airlift Promises Revival of Short-Haul Tourist Traffic Along the Original Island-Hopping Air Route Across the North Atlantic," *Air Transport World,* June 1985, pp. 76+.

"Domestic Carrier Finds Fokker 50 Well Suited for Iceland's Challenges," *Aviation Week & Space Technology,* June 29, 1992, p. 37.

Dwyer, Rob, "Smart Geysers," *Airfinance Journal,* February 1999, pp. 38–41.

Friedland, Jennifer, "Jacksonville, Fla. Airport Begins Trans-Atlantic Service with Icelandair," *Florida Times-Union,* September 8, 1994.

Gunning, Gary, "Focus: Icelandair; Celebrating Sixty Years," *Iceland Business,* January 1997, p. 8.

Holyoke, Larry, "TWA Forms Frequent-Flier Alliance with Icelandair," *St. Louis Business Journal,* August 3, 1998, p. 5A.

"Icelandair Speeds Up Promotion," *Travel Trade Gazette UK & Ireland,* March 29, 1999, p. 44.

"Icelandair: The Atlantic Niche Specialist," *Airways,* September/October 1996, pp. 51+.

Jamison, Jane, "Icelandair Weathers the Storm of '91, Predicts Even Stronger '92," *Travel Weekly,* May 4, 1992, pp. 22+.

McDonald, Michele, "Southwest, Icelandair Sign Marketing Agreement," *Travel Weekly,* December 23, 1996, p. 33.

Michels, Jennifer, "National Pride: Icelandair Uses Creative Marketing and Low Fares to Attract Bargain-Hunter Travelers to Its Hot Home Country," *Travel Agent,* September 17, 2001.

Nelms, Douglas W., "Selling the Niche," *Air Transport World,* November 1999, p. 101.

——, "Shifting the Niche," *Air Transport World,* December 1995, p. 71.

Njio, Frits, "Icelandair Strengthens Its Nordic Links," *Interavia/Aerospace World,* July 1993, pp. 47–48.

Odell, Mark, "Fishing for New Markets," *Airline Business,* October 1993, pp. 50+.

Ott, James, "Icelandair Applies U.S. Lessons to Changing European Market," *Aviation Week & Space Technology,* June 29, 1992, pp. 34–36.

Petersen, Othar Orn, "Aviation and Air Transport in Iceland," *Airfinance Journal,* Guide to Aviation Lawyers Supplement 1998, pp. 93–94.

Poling, Bill, "Icelandair to Resume Service at Baltimore/Washington Airport," *Travel Weekly,* April 30, 1990, p. 12.

Proctor, Paul, "Icelandair Sees Opportunity in the North Atlantic," *Aviation Week & Space Technology,* July 20, 1998, p. 48.

Reingold, Lester, "Moving Up-Market: No Longer a Single-Class, Low-Fare Airline, Icelandair Has a New Fleet, New European Services and New Saga Class," *Air Transport World,* September 1990, pp. 118+.

Straszheim, Milton R., *The International Airline Industry,* Washington, D.C.: The Brookings Institution, 1969.

—Frederick C. Ingram

ICN Pharmaceuticals, Inc.

3300 Hyland Avenue
Costa Mesa, California 92626
U.S.A.
Telephone: (714) 545-0100
Toll Free: (800) 548-5100
Fax: (714) 556-0131
Web site: http://www.icnpharm.com

Public Company
Incorporated: 1960
Employees: 11,970
Sales: $858.10 million (2001)
Stock Exchanges: New York
Ticker Symbol: ICN
NAIC: 325412 Pharmaceutical Preparation Manufacturing

ICN Pharmaceuticals, Inc. is a prescription and nonprescription drug developer and manufacturer that distributes its products in more than 100 countries. ICN also operates a biomedical business that accounts for roughly 7 percent of the company's sales volume. ICN is best known in the medical field for its development of ribavirin, an antiviral compound used to treat hepatitis-C, herpes simplex, influenza, and chicken pox, among other viral infections. The company's other products treat bacterial infections, diseases of the skin, neuromuscular disorders, cancer, cardiovascular disease, diabetes, and psychiatric disorders.

Origins

ICN's founder, the controversial Milan Panic, left an indelible imprint on the company he started in a Los Angeles garage. Born in Yugoslavia, Panic participated in the resistance against Nazi occupation of his native country during World War II, fighting the first great fight of his embattled life. After the war, Panic's athletic prowess came to the fore, earning him a place on Yugoslavia's Olympic cycling team. While on tour with the team in 1956, Panic defected, arriving in the United States with $200. After attending the University of Southern California, Panic started ICN in 1960, using his garage to house the company's modest operations. For the 30-year-old Panic, an entrepreneurial dream was set to unfold.

During its formative years, ICN grew by acquiring niche pharmaceuticals such as dermatological drugs, but the company scored its greatest success in the research field. With the help of Dr. Roland Robins, and later, Drs. Weldon Jolley and Roberts Smith, Panic's company developed an extensive collection of nucleoside analogs. Research in this area led, in the late 1970s, to the discovery of the antiviral drug ribavirin, which showed promise in combating the flu as well as other viruses. Panic pinned great hopes on the market opportunities for ribavirin, to the point that the Securities and Exchange Commission (SEC) charged Panic in 1991 with falsely promoting ribavirin as an AIDs cure, which Panic settled without admitting or denying wrongdoing. Before the strengths of ribavirin could be explored, however, the difficult task of clearing regulatory hurdles had to be accomplished.

Because of the differences between viruses and bacteria, shepherding an antiviral drug through the regulatory approval process was decidedly more difficult than bringing an antibacterial to market. Antivirals were charged with a more intricate task than antibacterials, which focused on killing bacteria living outside the cell. Antivirals, on the other hand, were required to eliminate a virus without killing the host cell or harming the host organism. Panic, according to his account, labored arduously to gain a nod of approval from the Food and Drug Administration (FDA). "It was not easy to bring an antiviral drug to market," he reflected in a 2002 company press release, "because no one believed in it. The regulators constantly denied approval and constantly discouraged our research, once even telling me to stop our studies entirely. I refused to stop. ..." Panic eventually prevailed, his success signaled when ribavirin, marketed under the name Virazole, gained approval for the treatment of an often fatal infant respiratory disease called respiratory syncytial virus, or RSV. Eventually, ribavirin was approved in the United States for the treatment of hepatitis-C in combination with another drug, interferon.

International Growth in the Early 1990s

Armed with one of the few antiviral products on the market, a slew of antibacterials, and numerous other ethical (doctor-prescribed) drugs, ICN's fortunes swelled. Prolific growth did not arrive, however, until Panic decided to transform ICN into

Company Perspectives:

ICN is a global pharmaceutical company dedicated to research and innovation in healthcare. ICN Pharmaceuticals is committed to developing, producing and distributing the highest-quality products for the patients, consumers and healthcare partners we serve; attracting and sustaining workers who take pride in themselves, their work and their company; delivering a fair return to our investors; and to improving the communities in which we live and work in the United States and around the world.

an international drug manufacturer and developer. To accomplish this, Panic returned home. In 1991, he acquired a 75 percent interest in Galenika Pharmaceutical, the major drug manufacturer and distributor in Yugoslavia. Renamed ICN Galenika, the acquisition gave ICN new product lines and substantially expanded the company's sales volume, making ICN one of the first Western pharmaceutical companies to establish a direct investment in Eastern Europe following the fall of Communism. At roughly the same time the investment in Galenika was made, Panic also added facilities in several other former Soviet satellite nations and across the globe, etching a presence in Western Europe, Africa, Asia, and Australia. Between 1993 and 1994, Panic also acquired a 41 percent interest in Oktyabr, a Russian drug company. In 1995, Panic increased ICN's investment in Oktyabr to 75 percent, eventually developing ICN into the largest pharmaceutical concern in Russia.

Although the physical and financial growth achieved during the first half of the 1990s were of an unprecedented scale in ICN's history, the achievements were overshadowed by the drama surrounding Panic. In what must have been one of the signal highlights of his career, Panic returned to his Balkan homeland in July 1992 to serve as Prime Minister of Yugoslavia. Once in power, Panic began to grapple with Slobodan Milosevic in an attempt to usurp his power. Panic lost a fraudulent presidential election against Milosevic on December 20, 1992. Before the end of the month, Panic was ousted as Prime Minister, a loss of personal stature that had a reverberative effect on ICN's stature.

Panic Embroiled in Controversy During the 1990s

In opposing Milosevic, Panic had not shied from leveling his criticism loudly and frequently. After Panic's removal from office, the Yugoslav government took its revenge, making ICN pay for Panic's words. The Yugoslav government reneged on payment for pharmaceuticals purchased from ICN, leading to sizable losses for the Costa Mesa-based company, but the losses only represented part of ICN's problems as they related to Panic's conduct. The SEC first began to take extraordinary interest in Panic in 1977, when the regulatory body charged ICN's chairman and chief executive officer with reporting false financial papers. Panic's alleged promotion of ribavirin as an AIDS cure in 1991 again prompted the SEC's intervention. In early 1993, not long after Panic was deposed as Prime Minister of Yugoslavia, a Beverly Hills stockbroker, Rafi M. Kahn, launched a shareholder fight, aiming to oust Panic. Kahn, who

had invested $2 million of his own money, took exception with the considerable salary and bonuses awarded to Panic while ICN's stock languished. In 1992, ICN's stock plummeted from $20.37 per share to $6.50 per share. Meanwhile, Panic had received $619,000 in salary—money received, to Kahn's ire, while Panic was serving as the Prime Minister of Yugoslavia. Further angering Kahn, Panic received a bonus in April 1992 worth an estimated $5.3 million, a sum received while ICN suffered from anemic financial performance and sharply declining stock value. ICN responded by filing a lawsuit against Kahn in April 1993, accusing Kahn of using insider information obtained while he was employed by his brokerage firm as the basis for his shareholder revolt. A week later, Kahn countered, filing a lawsuit against Panic for defamation of character. "I intend to sue him for $50 million," Kahn told the *Los Angeles Business Journal* on April 12, 1993.

Panic withstood the attack to his chairmanship, but his troubles were far from over. In 1994, Panic sold $1.2 million worth of ICN stock, which in 1996 led to the formation of a grand jury to investigate whether Panic had used unfavorable information not shared with shareholders to prompt his disposition of ICN stock. Panic's litigious exposure was ever-widening, rife with shareholder disdain and the increasingly skeptical eye of the SEC. Beyond that, Panic's troubles ran deeper. During the first half of the 1990s, Panic's time spent helping to manage ICN and Yugoslavia was pocked by a flurry of sexual harassment accusations. The tolls for the allegations made against Panic were paid by ICN, ultimately levied against an increasingly restless body of shareholders.

Charges of groping and propositions for sex were lodged one after another during the 1990s. Dating back to at least 1990, female employees began to question Panic's motives. When the concerns were made legally manifest, Panic faced the allegations of at least six ICN employees, between 1993 and 1998, charging that Panic had propositioned them for sex, groped them, or either punished or rewarded them, their promotion or demotion determined by whether they had complied or complained. By 1998, five of the employees had filed discrimination charges with the Department of Fair Employment and Housing of California; four of the accusers sued ICN, costing the company millions of dollars in settlement fees. ICN's general counsel told the *U.S. News & World Report* on July 6, 1998, "The courts are being abused by these silly cases." In the same article, Panic's perception of the events was offered, as quoted from the deposition of ICN's board of directors, "Panic said: 'The complaints are bullshit. They loved me.'"

Aside from the personal notoriety gained by Panic, ICN stood as a solid, mid-sized pharmaceutical company during the mid-1990s. In May 1995, the company paid Becton, Dickinson for its radioimmunoassay product line, which was used for anemia and thyroid diagnostic testing. Under Becton, Dickinson's control, the diagnostic testing product had been distributed primarily in North America and Western Europe, but ICN, able to flex a more comprehensive distribution muscle, intended to extend distribution into Latin America, Asia, Eastern Europe, and the Middle East. In December 1996, the company purchased a 40 percent stake in SeaLite Sciences, Inc., which owned a patented diagnostics technology that could be used to produce extremely sensitive test kits, such as a thyroid test kit.

By the end of 1996, when annual sales exceeded the $500 billion mark, ICN was distributing its prescription and nonprescription products in more than 60 countries. Ribavirin, marketed as Virazole in North America and in most European countries (as Vilona and Virazid in Latin America, and as Virazid in Spain), was approved for commercial sale in more than 40 countries. Although the antiviral agent was approved in the United States only for restricted use in the treatment of RSV, ribavirin was approved for use across the globe for a variety of viral infections, including RSV, herpes simplex, influenza, chicken pox, hepatitis, and HIV. One of fewer than ten antiviral agents marketed worldwide, ribavirin accounted for 10 percent of ICN's sales in 1995. By contrast, the company's numerous antibacterial drugs accounted for roughly one-fifth of 1995's sales volume. The bulk of the company's sales were derived from what the company termed ''other ethical drugs,'' a large collection of prescription analgesics, antirheumatics, hormonals, and psychotropics, among other drugs. These products accounted for 40 percent of sales in 1995. The balance was derived from a collection of ancillary, over-the-counter products that were sold through the company's extensive distribution network.

A Battle for Control in the 21st Century

While the scope of ICN's business expanded, Panic continued to face a host of legal troubles, both in the form of sexual harassment charges and ongoing investigations undertaken by the SEC. The legal problems were costing ICN millions of dollars, exacerbating the animosity felt by a number of agitated shareholders. Proxy battles lodged by shareholders had become an almost annual event, but Panic continued to thwart attempts for his removal. In 2000, royalties from ribavirin, which had become increasingly popular in the treatment of hepatitis-C, were expected to reach $162 million, a fourfold increase since 1998. Despite, or perhaps because of, the exponential gain in ribavirin sales, some shareholders were becoming increasingly frustrated by the company's lackluster stock performance. ''Most shareholders are tired of waiting for value to be created,'' Michael Yellen remarked in the September 4, 2000 issue of *Business Week*. Yellen served as a senior portfolio manager of the AIM Global Health Care fund, which owned two million ICN shares.

In 2000, while the SEC was seeking to bar Panic from ever again running a publicly traded company, the embattled chairman announced in mid-June a restructuring plan for ICN. According to the plan, ICN was to be split into three companies, with Panic slated to control each business. The news caused ICN's stock value to fall further. At roughly the same time the

reorganization was announced, several shareholders pitted forces and began a proxy battle, its aim to remove Panic from his chairmanship. The shareholder revolt persisted for two years, dragging on as the plan to restructure the company never materialized in any action made by Panic. When the company's research and development arm, including the rights to its antiviral franchise, was spun off in April 2002, angry shareholders found another issue to fuel their revolt. The spinoff created Ribapharm, a New York Stock Exchange-traded company whose initial public offering raised nearly $300 million for ICN and netted Panic a $33 million bonus, infuriating already agitated shareholders.

Leading the charge against Panic were two shareholder groups, Franklin Mutual Advisers LLC and Iridian Asset Management LLC, who together owned 10 percent of ICN's stock. In their filing with the SEC, as quoted in the May 6, 2002 issue of the *Los Angeles Business Journal,* the two groups were frank with their assessment: ''We believe (Panic's) presence at the helm of (ICN), his dismissive attitude toward shareholders, and his controversial reputation are among the chief reasons ICN's market valuation lags those of its peers and fails to adequately reflect (ICN's) fundamentals.'' On June 12, 2002, the dissident shareholders prevailed, celebrating Panic's announcement that he was retiring as ICN's chairman and chief executive officer.

The removal of Panic ushered in a new management team. Gone were Panic's personal connections that had been instrumental to ICN's development into an Eastern European powerhouse. Gone too was the stigma of Panic's presence at the company's helm. Into the void created by Panic's departure stepped Robert W. O'Leary, appointed ICN's chairman and chief executive officer on June 20, 2002. The founding chairman and chief executive officer of Premier Inc., a strategic alliance of healthcare and hospital systems, O'Leary took on the difficult task of sparking ICN's turnaround. In a July 29, 2002 interview with the *Los Angeles Business Journal,* O'Leary admitted that ICN's condition was worse than the incoming team had expected. Looking ahead, O'Leary said: ''All options are on the table with one exception—the sale of the company. The challenge for us as board members was— and still is—to instill investor confidence in what is basically a sound business.''

Principal Subsidiaries

ICN Canada, Limited; Alpha Pharmaceutical, Inc. (Panama); ICN Farmaceutica, S.A. de C.V. (Mexico); Laboratorios Grossman, S.A. (Mexico); ICN Pharmaceuticals, Holland, B.V.; ICN Biomedicals, Inc.; ICN Pharmaceuticals Germany GmbH; ICN Pharmaceuticals Australasia Pty Ltd. (Australia); ICN Pharmaceuticals Japan, K.K.; ICN Biomedicals B.V. (Netherlands); ICN Iberica S.A. (Spain); ICN Pharmaceuticals, Ltd. (U.K.); ICN Biomedicals, GmbH (Germany); ICN Pharmaceuticals France S.A.; ICN Biomedicals S.R.L. (Italy); ICN Biomedicals N.V. (Belgium); ICN Oktyabr (Russia; 95%); ICN Polypharm (Russia; 96%); ICN Leksredstva (Russia; 97%); ICN Hungary Company, Ltd. (96%); Fuzio-Pharma Rt. (Hungary; 97%); ICN Polfa Rzeszow (Poland; 98%); AO Tomsk Chemical Pharmaceutical Plant (Russia; 90%); Marbiopharm (Russia; 93%); ICN Dutch Holdings B.V. (Netherlands); ICN Czech Republic; ICN Solco AG (Switzerland); Draig Ltd. (U.K.; 75%).

Principal Competitors

GlaxoSmithKline plc; Merck & Co. Inc.; Novartis AG.

Further Reading

Cecil, Mark, "ICN Is Frozen with Panic Against Heartland," *Mergers & Acquisitions,* July 31, 2000, p. 42.

Cole, Benjamin Mark, "L.A. Cast Gets Swept Up in New Round of ICN Turmoil," *Los Angeles Business Journal,* May 7, 2001, p. 33.

"ICN May Rework Restructuring Plan Again," *Daily Deal,* August 2, 2001, p. 5.

Lubove, Seth, "Panic Attack," *Forbes,* September 30, 2002, p. 52.

Palmeri, Christopher, "The End for ICN's Milan Panic?," *Business Week Online,* May 30, 2002, p. 3.

Reed, Vita, "Investors Gird for Second Attempt to Split Drug Maker," *Los Angeles Business Journal,* May 6, 2002, p. 8.

——, "Panic Gone, New ICN Team Finds Finances in Disarray," *Los Angeles Business Journal,* July 29, 2002, p. 28.

"Ribavarin vs. AIDS," *Fortune,* January 21, 1985, p. 11.

Vrana, Debora, "Shareholder Threatens Defamation Suit in ICN Dispute," *Los Angeles Business Journal,* April 12, 1993, p. 3.

"Will Investors Pull the Plug on Milan Panic?," *Business Week,* September 4, 2000, p. 108.

—Jeffrey L. Covell

Incyte Genomics, Inc.

3160 Porter Drive
Palo Alto, California 94304
U.S.A.
Telephone: (650) 855-0555
Fax: (650) 855-0572
Web site: http://www.incyte.com

Public Company
Incorporated: 1991 as Incyte Pharmaceuticals, Inc.
Employees: 585
Sales: $219.3 million (2001)
Stock Exchanges: NASDAQ
Ticker Symbol: INCY
NAIC: 541710 Research and Development in the
    Physical, Engineering, and Life Sciences

Founded in 1991 and based in Palo Alto, California, Incyte Genomics, Inc. (formerly Incyte Pharmaceuticals, Inc.) provides genomics information to the biotechnology and pharmaceutical industries. Incyte is best known for its original product, LifeSeq, a database which provides a complete and comprehensive view of the human genome. Beyond LifeSeq, Incyte continues to develop and market an integrated platform of genomic databases and technologies, in the service of facilitating the scientific community's understanding of the molecular underpinnings of disease, and the discovery and development of new therapeutic drugs. Incyte also holds an extensive commercial portfolio of U.S.-issued patents for full-length human genes and the proteins they encode.

Born to Lead: 1991–93

Incyte Genomics, Inc. was incorporated in April 1991 under the name Incyte Pharmaceuticals. The company was created by Schroder Venture Advisers, Inc., a New York venture capital firm, in order to buy assets and technology from a then-liquidating St. Louis biotechnology company called Invitron Corporation. Roy A. Whitfield, formerly the president of Invitron's subsidiary, Ideon, became CEO of Incyte; Randall W. Scott, one of Invitron's founding scientists, became Incyte's president and chief scientific officer.

From its inception, Incyte was a pioneer in the emerging science of genomics, the study of the structure and function of the genetic material that makes up an organism. Incyte's vision—and the scientific and business promise of genomics—was that new genomic technologies, especially the development of high-throughput computer-aided gene sequencing, would assist researchers and pharmaceutical companies in their quest to understand and define the molecular underpinnings of disease; greater understanding of the relationship between genetic material and disease would in turn lead to innovative therapeutic applications, especially the discovery and development of new, more effective—and highly lucrative—drugs.

Incyte was the first of the genome science companies to go public. The company made its initial public offering on November 4, 1993, selling 2.3 million common shares at $7.50 on the American Stock Exchange under the ticker symbol IPI. The company would later trade on the NASDAQ under the ticker symbol INCY. The net proceeds of the offering were funneled back into research and development, particularly for the expansion of Incyte's high-throughput gene sequencing and analysis program.

Building and Marketing a Computerized Genetic Encyclopedia in the Mid-1990s

Incyte's first major project was to use its high-throughput gene sequencing and analysis technology to create the world's most extensive and comprehensive "genetic encyclopedia"—a database called LifeSeq, which the company billed as the *Gray's Anatomy* of the 21st century, a tool that promised to revolutionize the pharmaceutical industry's research, drug development, and the whole spectrum of processes involved in the diagnosis and treatment of disease. LifeSeq featured two primary tools: a DNA Sequence database and a Gene Expression database. The sequence database mapped the sequences or arrangement of DNA structures, and the expression database analyzed and annotated these sequences, classifying them according to probable function and the cells and tissues in which they were found or "expressed."

During the mid-1990s, Incyte successfully marketed its ever growing database and analytic tools to many of the top pharmaceutical companies. Sales took the form of yearly subscriptions that allowed companies access to LifeSeq. Payments were made by funding further Incyte research and development or by purchasing shares of Incyte common stock. The LifeSeq database proved valuable to subscribers for a wide range of pharmaceutical and diagnostic purposes: for example, subscribers used Incyte's product to study the processes, pathways, and resistance patterns of particular diseases on human tissue; study the effect of a new drug on human tissue; and search for human analogs to promising animal tissues.

Incyte's first major subscriber was New York-based pharmaceutical giant Pfizer. The agreement, valued at $24.8 million, was forged in June 1994. Incyte sold subscriptions on a non-exclusive basis, with the goal of making LifeSeq available to as many companies as possible. By January 1996, Incyte's roster of subscribers included Johnson and Johnson, Abbott Laboratories, Hoechst AG, Novo Nordisk A/S, Pfizer, and Pharmacia & Upjohn, Inc. These subscribers, representing 12 percent of the top 50 pharmaceutical companies (as measured by research and development spending) supplied Incyte with an aggregate of at least $100 million for further development of its database technologies. In turn, Incyte worked closely with these pharmaceutical partners to continue to upgrade the design and features of its products to best meet the needs of the scientists who used it.

Initially, the Incyte database contained only the company's own proprietary data. In May 1996, a new version of the database was released. It included public-domain gene sequence data that had been processed through Incyte's bioanalysis software. With this valuable addition, scientists could, for the first time, study publicly available sequence data alongside the proprietary sequences.

As Incyte continued to gather information about thousands of genes—using sophisticated instruments to extract DNA from cells and then decipher its chemical code—it applied for patents on the genes that it discovered. Eventually, Incyte offered LifeSeq Public as a free database with unrestricted access to information about genes within the public domain. Incyte's proprietary human gene sequence database, to which it sold subscriptions, was then called LifeSeq Gold. This database

featured transcripts of 120,000 genes, more than half of which were proprietary to Incyte, such that scientists could not access information about these genes from any other commercial source. By 2000, Incyte's subscribers would include more than 20 of the top pharmaceutical companies in the world.

Acquisitions and Strategic Partnerships in the Late 1990s

In the late 1990s, the race to complete the map, or sequencing, of the human genome was coming to a close. A company called Celera Genomics Group was in tight competition with the U.S. Department of Energy's publicly funded Human Genome Project, based out of the Washington University medical center in St. Louis, Missouri. Analysts speculated that, as human genome data became more readily available to the scientific community over the next few years, Incyte would have increasing difficulty finding and keeping subscribers to its LifeSeq database. In order to maintain its position as an industry leader, Incyte needed to further diversify and specialize its products and expertise and continually expand its network of partnerships in order to leverage the power of its technology and intellectual property assets.

In 1996, in an effort to generate new revenues, Incyte acquired a St. Louis company called Genome Systems for about $8 million in stock. Genome Systems was founded in 1992, the brainchild of two Washington University scientists who recognized the growing need to industrialize the process of finding, storing, and shipping gene fragments to thousands of scientists and researchers worldwide. Referred to as a "gene depot" or "clone warehouse," the facility in St. Louis contained 100 industrial freezers, each housing half a million DNA clones stored in their own individual test tubes. The warehouse supplied the genetic material of all kinds of organisms, including mice, fish, rats, dogs, soy plants, and bacteria—as well as humans. Scientists at universities, government institutions, or private companies could purchase individual DNA clones for as little as $22 for a common gene fragment or up to several thousand dollars for a critical, full-length gene. Incyte had only one real competitor in the business of large-scale custom genomics, a company called Invitrogen. The Genome Systems subsidiary brought in significant revenues for several years, but its other real value to Incyte was in giving the company the means to clone its own genes for research, thereby freeing the company of its dependence on other commercially available products. Incyte officials believed that this self-reliance was critical to staying ahead of the competition.

In September 1997, Incyte joined forces with SmithKline Beecham to launch a new company called Diadexus, based in Santa Clara, California. Through a joint, $25 million investment in Diadexus, the two companies collaborated on the development and production of new, gene-based diagnostic products. The alliance was indicative of the desire of both companies to stake out competitive territory in the fast-growing field of pharmacogenomics. In this specialized area, research focused on using a patient's personal genetic information to tailor both diagnosis and treatment to the individual for maximum effectiveness of prescribed drugs with minimum adverse side effects.

Indeed, as the field of genomics continued to mature, increasing attention became focused on genetic variations, minute differences between similar genes, known as single nucleotide polymorphisms (or SNPs), which were thought to be significant factors in identifying individual disease susceptibility and response to drug treatment.

In August 1998, in response to increasing industry enthusiasm to create a database of SNPs, Incyte purchased a privately owned British biotechnology company called Hexagen for $41 million to form the cornerstone of a new subsidiary division called Incyte Genetics, which would market software and data for the specialized area of genetic variations. Incyte acquired Hexagen primarily for the company's signature technology, which provided for the rapid identification of differences in DNA sequences from one individual to the next. Incyte predicted that its new division would not generate a profit until 2002, so it made the prudent decision to issue separate common stock for Incyte Genetics, so as not to cause preexisting investors any anxiety about earnings.

For eight quarters in 1997 and 1998, Incyte had distinguished itself as one of the very few genomics companies to generate a profit. Annual fees for subscriptions to its database accounted for most of Incyte's revenue during this time, with sales from its custom genomics business totaling nearly a quarter of yearly earnings. Profits fell off after 1998, though, as Incyte invested heavily in gene-discovery equipment to enhance its proprietary database, and generally began to shift the focus of its business.

Mining the Proteome for Profit: 2000–2002

In March 2000, Incyte Pharmaceuticals changed its name and the name of its subsidiaries to Incyte Genomics, Inc., a move designed to more accurately communicate the company's commitment to providing genomic information on a non-exclusive basis to biotechnology, pharmaceutical, and academic researchers worldwide.

At the same time, as part of a yearlong effort to greatly expand its customer base, Incyte launched its web site, Incyte.com, and with it, the beginning of its e-commerce geno-

mics program, known as LifeSeq GENE-BY-GENE. Whereas the price of a full subscription to the Incyte database was prohibitively expensive for smaller companies and individual researchers, with this new offering, information about every gene in Incyte's database became equally accessible and affordable to institutions, companies, and researchers of every caliber. With the new web site, any scientist with Internet access could submit a confidential query about a specific gene of interest: the initial "best view" of the gene sequence was available for free; additional gene sequence information about that gene, as well as a physical copy of the gene, could be purchased via e-mail.

In the spring of 2000, Celera Genomics and the Human Genome Project announced their respective triumphs in completing the map of the human genome, and the first race of the genomics revolution was over. But while sequencing the genome represented a monumental accomplishment, scientists acknowledged that this was only the tip of the iceberg—for scientific understanding as well as business success. The next step was to determine the function—and dysfunction—of genes, to attribute to specific genes and gene variations a role in the onset and development of disease, and/or a role in responding to drug treatments. To do this, scientists turned their attention to proteins. Most genes act as instruction manuals for the production of proteins, and it is the proteins that do the work within living cells, and change when a normal cell becomes diseased.

The new frontier—mining the proteome, the set of human proteins—was called proteomics. Proteomics required new, more sophisticated technologies for analyzing proteins, as well as for handling the massive quantities of data that such analysis yielded. The real rewards of proteomics, however, were greater, as progress in this area greatly improved the accuracy and efficiency of the drug development process and in so doing opened the door to mega-profits.

Once again, the nimble and innovative Incyte managed to keep itself at the forefront of the industry. In December 2000, it acquired a privately held, Beverly, Massachusetts company called Proteome, Inc. Proteome had developed its own database, called the BioKnowledge Library, to provide researchers with information about gene and protein function. The two companies attested that with their combined technologies, they would be peerless in their ability to provide the scientific community with cutting edge protein annotation for the genome.

In 2001, Incyte forged another strategic alliance with a company called Lexicon Genetics Incorporated, whose own database, LexVision specialized in gene function information. The two companies agreed offer access to each other's databases, as well as to collaborate in the arena of therapeutic protein drug discovery. Here again, Incyte had found a way to extract new utility from its existing database and locate new revenue opportunities.

By the end of the third quarter of 2001, Incyte announced plans to undergo a major restructuring. The company discontinued its custom genomics business, laying off 400 workers due to flagging profits and the perception that these non-core product lines were no longer contributing to the company's overall competitive advantage. The elimination of this niche endeavor allowed the company to concentrate its resources more fully on its core database, intellectual property, and partnership businesses, toward an aggressive shift into the most lucrative area of the industry: drug making. To this end, Incyte signed key agreements with two pharmaceutical companies, Genentech and Medarex, to collaborate on drug development.

Also in 2001 Incyte named a new CEO, Paul A. Friedman, and a new president and chief scientific officer, Robert Stein, both former top executives at Dupont. Roy A. Whitfield stayed on as chairman of Incyte's board of directors. On the heels of these appointments, Incyte also recruited a number of other experienced pharmaceutical executives to its senior scientific staff, as well as 30 scientists with extensive experience in drug discovery. These measures were all aimed at bolstering Incyte's internal capabilities in the arena of therapeutic discovery and development.

Early in 2002, Incyte and partner Iconix Pharmaceuticals released a new commercial research tool, DrugMatrix. Heralded as a significant advance in chemogenomics—an emerging field that examined the interactions between chemicals and the genome—DrugMatrix brought together the previously discrete fields of genomics, chemistry, toxicology, and pharmacology in a new, highly integrated environment to aid in the acceleration of drug discovery. Once again, Incyte was finding new ways to leverage and profit from its existing information business assets, and at once to harness other companies' assets to further its own internal projects.

While Incyte reported a decrease in total revenues for the second quarter of 2002 (largely associated with the loss of revenues from its discontinued custom genomics business), the company was holding fast to its strategy to manage its information product line to be cash-positive, and to devote these revenues as much as possible to its drug discovery and development initiatives.

Principal Subsidiaries

Incyte Microarray Systems.

Principal Competitors

Abgenix, Inc.; Applera Corporation; Human Genome Sciences, Inc.

Further Reading

Barrett, Amy, John Carey, and Ellen Licking, "Biotech's Next Holy Grail," *Business Week,* April 10, 2000, p. 136

Dennis, Carina, and Richard Gallagher, editors, *The Human Genome,* New York: Palgrave, 2001.

"Incyte Pharmaceuticals, Inc., Goes Public on the AMEX," *PR Newswire,* November 4, 1993.

"Incyte to Lead Revolution in Healthcare with Next-Generation Genomic Information Network," *PR Newswire,* January 10, 2000.

Pollack, Andrew, "Finding Gold in Scientific Pay Dirt," *New York Times,* June 28, 2000, p. C1.

Zweiger, Gary, *Traducing the Human Genome: Information, Anarchy, and Revolution in the Biomedical Sciences,* New York: McGraw-Hill, 2001.

—Erin Brown

Ingram Micro Inc.

1600 East St. Andrews Place
Santa Ana, California 92705
U.S.A.
Telephone: (714) 566-1000
Toll Free: (800) 456-8000
Fax: (714) 566-7900
Web site: http://www.ingrammicro.com

Public Company
Incorporated: 1989 as Ingram Micro D, Inc.
Employees: 13,500
Sales: $25.19 billion (2001)
Stock Exchanges: New York
Ticker Symbol: IM
NAIC: 421430 Computer and Computer Peripheral
    Equipment and Software Wholesalers

As the largest global wholesale distributor of computer and electronics products, Ingram Micro Inc. acts as the middleman between manufacturers and a wide range of retail outlets, value-added resellers (VARs), small businesses, large enterprises, and other customers. Originally a business unit of Ingram Industries, Inc., Ingram Micro grew through a series of mergers and acquisitions. It is a publicly traded company with annual sales in excess of $25 billion. The Ingram family retains control of Ingram Micro by owning 75 percent of its voting stock.

Mergers Leading to Creation of Ingram Micro Inc.: 1982–89

Ingram Micro Inc. was created through a series of mergers among software distributors. In the first half of 1985 Software Distribution Services was acquired by the Ingram Distribution Group. Software Distribution Services was founded in 1982 in Buffalo, New York, and had become one of the top four software distributors in the United States by 1985. Ingram Distribution Group was a unit of Ingram Industries Inc., which *PC Week* described as ''a small conglomerate with operations in marine transportation, energy, distribution, and insurance.'' Ingram

Distribution Group began distributing entertainment and educational software in 1983. It started by distributing programs for the Commodore computer and later expanded into software for Apple and IBM PCs.

Once Ingram Distribution Group acquired Software Distribution Services, the company was renamed Ingram Software. Ingram Software expanded later in 1985 by purchasing Softeam, a software distributor based in Compton, California. The acquisition of Software Distribution Services included a 50 percent interest in Aviva Software of Toronto, Canada. In December 1986 Ingram Software purchased the remaining half of the Canadian operation and renamed it Ingram Software Ltd. Ingram purchased another Canadian distributor, Frantek Computer Products, Inc., in March 1988 and renamed its Canadian operations Ingram Micro Canada with headquarters in Toronto.

In February 1988 Ingram Software was renamed Ingram Computer. Ingram Computer was headed by CEO and Chairman David Blumstein, who joined the company in January 1988. While Ingram Computer was not profitable in 1987 and had a growth rate of about 10 percent, Blumstein was able to lead the company into profitability in 1988 with a growth rate of more than 30 percent. Blumstein was also responsible for reducing the company's workforce by about 10 percent.

By January 1989 Ingram Industries had acquired nearly 59 percent of the stock of Micro D, the leading software distributor in the United States. Ingram then launched a public tender offer to buy the remaining shares of Micro D at $12.50 a share. By March Micro D agreed to accept a tender offer from Ingram of $14.75 a share, or about $44 million, for the remaining 41 percent of the company's outstanding stock.

The new company was called Ingram Micro D. Micro D's CEO Chip Lacy became its chairman and CEO, while Blumstein became the company's vice-chairman. The merger was seen to be a complementary one, with Micro D specializing in large retail computer chain stores and Ingram servicing value-added resellers (VARs) and smaller retail stores. Micro D had sales of $553 million in 1988, and the combined firm was expected to have about $1 billion in revenue for 1989, with a 35 percent share of the U.S. software distribution market and 14 percent of the hardware market. The company consolidated Micro D's seven stocking locations with Ingram's four locations into a remaining total of eight shipping locations in the United States. The company also had two shipping locations in Canada. Ingram Micro D's headquarters were located in Santa Ana, California, the site of Micro D's old headquarters. The company also maintained an East Coast operations center in Buffalo, New York.

Ingram Micro D quickly established VAR programs for second-tier vendors, which enabled it to sell systems by the largest computer manufacturers such as IBM Corp., Hewlett-Packard Co., and Compaq Computer Corp. Ingram Micro D subsequently established segmented business units to focus on the sale and service of specific products. The company also created the Alliance, a division focused on high-volume system sales.

Growing into a Multibillion-Dollar Company: 1990–96

Ingram Micro expanded into Europe in 1989 with the purchase of Softeurop, a software wholesaler based in Brussels, Belgium, that had subsidiaries in France and The Netherlands. Ingram expanded its European presence in 1991 with acquisitions in the United Kingdom and a start-up operation in Italy. A European Coordination Center was established in Brussels in 1992 to coordinate the activities of the company's five European subsidiaries. Additional European acquisitions took place in 1993 and 1994, including House of Computers in Germany; Datateam in the Scandinavian countries of Denmark, Norway, and Sweden; and Keylan in Spain.

Ingram Micro entered the Asia-Pacific region in 1992 by establishing operations in Malaysia and Singapore. In January 1993 Ingram acquired a majority interest in Mexico's largest wholesale distributor and began operations in Central America as Ingram Dicom. By 1993 Ingram Micro had expanded into global distribution through a series of strategic acquisitions.

In 1991 sales topped $2 billion for the first time and registered a 41 percent increase over the previous year. For the first quarter of 1992 sales grew another 40 percent to a record $606 million, with international sales accounting for about 15 percent of revenue. Ingram Micro was the leading wholesaler of personal computer products.

With the prices of individual workstations falling from $50,000 to less than $10,000, computer manufacturers began to consider outsourcing their sales efforts and refocusing their direct sales forces on higher-priced merchandise. As part of this trend, in 1992 Ingram Micro became the wholesale partner of choice for Hewlett-Packard, which authorized Ingram to distribute its HP Apollo 9000 Series 700 workstations and X stations to VARs. At the time the HP workstation was the only one Ingram was offering to the VAR market.

Ingram also began to expand its original equipment manufacturer (OEM) base in the mid-1990s. In 1994 the company became an authorized reseller to VARs for Compaq Computer Corp. In mid-1995 Netscape Communications Corp. selected Ingram Micro to be its North American distributor. Ingram also distributed products for about 30 OEM vendors who made products such as disk drives and other equipment, which Ingram sold to VARs and systems integrators who were building at least 100 systems a month.

Ingram was the leader of a fast-growing trend in computer distribution. For 1993 distributors accounted for about 40 percent of the estimated $6.5 billion in sales of PC-related products. Ingram developed programs to distribute to electronics chain stores who were becoming interested in selling personal computers, offering them in-store training and merchandising programs. Ingram's business model was to be a one-stop shop that could accurately process orders in a timely fashion. As the middleman between computer manufacturers and retailers, Ingram and other distributors had to offer services to both. Ingram claimed to have an order-fill rate of 97 percent, and all orders received by 5 p.m. were shipped the same day. Ingram also offered retail customers a 150-day returns policy on most of its products. Ingram's principal markets were warehouse clubs, office product stores, and mass merchants. It signed agreements with Staples and Office Max as well as Wal-Mart and Target. It also made inroads into alternate channels such as video stores and music outlets.

For 1994 Ingram reported domestic sales of $4.1 billion and overall sales of $5.8 billion. Significant growth was reported in the networking market, with Ingram's Technical Products Division reporting sales of $1.02 billion. The Technical Products Division sold a mix of routers, hubs, interface cards, servers, and database products for networks from manufacturers such as 3Com, Compaq, Intel, Bay Networks, and Novell.

Although the company had a $300 million line of credit and sufficient financial resources, it was planning to go public in 1996 as part of the restructuring of parent company Ingram Industries. In 1995 the conglomerate announced it would form three independent companies: Ingram Industries, Ingram Entertainment, and Ingram Micro, with Ingram Micro the only one going public. Ingram Industries was to be headed by company founder Bronson Ingram's widow, Martha Ingram, who became president and CEO. Ingram Industries' subsidiaries included Ingram Book Company and Ingram Merchandising Services, as well as Ingram Barge Co., Ingram Materials Co., Ingram Cactus Co., and Permanent General Cos. Ingram Entertainment was focused on distributing videocassettes and was headed by David Ingram, son of company founder Bronson Ingram, who died in the summer of 1995. Bronson Ingram's other sons, John and Orrin, remained president of Ingram Book Co. and senior vice-president of Ingram Barge Co., respectively.

The reorganization divided up the Ingram Distribution Group. As a result Chairman Philip Pfeffer resigned but remained on the board of directors of both Ingram Industries and Ingram Micro. During 1995 Chip Lacy was promoted to co-chairman and CEO of Ingram Micro, and Jeff Rodek joined the company as president and chief operating officer (COO). Under Rodek numerous management changes were made at the senior executive level of Ingram Micro as the result of a new business model that was more focused on customer segments. Two top sales vice-presidents were promoted to senior vice-presidents, with one focused on VARs, enterprise systems, and OEM functions. The other was responsible for the dealer channel, major accounts, field sales, and government and education resellers. Ingram's Consumer Market Division, which had grown to account for 20 percent of sales, was broken out as a separate business unit.

For 1995 Ingram Micro had revenue of $8.6 billion and a profit of $84.3 million. That compared to net income of $63.3 million on sales of $5.83 billion in 1994.

Prospering Despite Management Changes: 1996–2002

Ingram's preparations for its initial public offering were complicated by the reorganization of Ingram Industries. As the company awaited a favorable ruling from the Internal Revenue Service (IRS) for a tax-free split-up, disagreements arose among top executives over corporate governance issues. Ingram Micro CEO Chip Lacy was dismissed effective May 31, 1996, over ''irreconcilable differences regarding corporate governance during Ingram's final period as a private company,'' according to Martha Ingram's public statement. Lacy was a respected veteran in the distribution industry who was credited not only with driving Micro D's growth, but also with leading Ingram Micro from a company with less than $1 billion in annual revenue to a company that would reach $12 billion in 1996 revenue. In August 1996 Ingram named Jerre Stead, former CEO of AT&T Global Information Solutions and Legent Corp., as CEO of Ingram Micro.

Ingram Micro's IPO took place on November 1, 1996. The company sold 20 million shares at $18 per share, with proceeds of approximately $392 million. The company's stock price rose about 15 percent by the end of the year, giving Ingram Micro a market capitalization of more than $3.5 billion. The company used $366 million from its IPO to pay back debt owed to its former parent company, Ingram Industries. Although Ingram Micro was now a publicly traded company, the Ingram family retained control of 75 percent of the firm's voting shares.

Ingram Micro posted strong growth in 1996 and 1997. The company reported 1996 revenue of $12 billion and net income of $110.7 million. In 1997 revenue increased to $16.6 billion,

and net income reached $193.6 million. Much of the growth was attributed to strong sales in Europe, where quarterly sales grew by 38 percent in the first quarter of 1998. Ingram Micro expanded its European operations in 1997 with the acquisition of TT Microtrading in Finland and J&W Computer GmbH in Frankfurt, Germany. In 1998 Ingram Micro made its largest European acquisition to date with the purchase of Macrotron AG of Munich, Germany, for $100 million from its parent, Tech Data Corp. of Clearwater, Florida. The acquisition of Macrotron AG added more than 1,000 employees and increased Ingram Micro's presence in Germany, Austria, and Switzerland. Macrotron had about $1.2 billion in annual sales.

Ingram Micro also continued to expand in Latin America. In October 1997 it acquired Computek, one of the largest regional computer wholesale distributors in Latin America with offices in Brazil, Chile, Peru, and Miami, Florida. In 1998 Ingram Micro acquired Nordemaq Ltda. in Brazil and in 1999 opened subsidiaries in Argentina, Panama, and Costa Rica. The company also established a Latin America Export Division in 1998 in Miami to serve international markets where it did not have a stand-alone, local operation.

Ingram Micro gained entry to ten Asia-Pacific countries with a minority investment in Electronic Resources Ltd. (ERL) in November 1997. ERL was a leading Asian computer and electronic products distributor based in Singapore. In October 1998 Ingram allied with Softbank Corp. to provide coverage of Japan, and in 1999 Ingram Micro acquired 100 percent of ERL and renamed it Ingram Micro Asia Ltd.

In the United States Ingram Micro agreed to pay as much as $78 million to acquire Intelligent Electronics Inc.'s $3 billion distribution business, with the exact amount dependent on IE's Reseller Network Division balance sheet at the time the deal closed. The acquisition boosted Ingram Micro's projected annual revenue to $15 billion for 1997 and $20 billion for 1998. As it turned out, Ingram Micro's sales for 1997 reached $16.58 billion and $22.03 billion for 1998. Strong sales were posted for telecommunications and networking products, while European sales climbed 70 percent in 1998 and U.S. sales grew by about 16 percent.

Ingram Micro began to experience revenue shortfalls in 1999. In the first quarter the company laid off about 10 percent of its workforce, or 1,400 employees. Its stock fell by 50 percent, or $3 billion in market capitalization. Later in the year CEO Jerre Stead stepped down as Ingram Micro's CEO, although he remained as chairman. In October President and COO Jeff Rodek left the company. For 1999 Ingram Micro reported sales of $28.07 billion. Net income was $183.4 million, down from $245.2 million in 1998.

The years 2000 and 2001 were characterized by new executive leaders and a focus on cost cutting. In March 2000 Ingram Micro named Kent Foster as CEO and president. Foster was formerly president of GTE Corp. At the beginning of 2001 Ingram Micro Chief Financial Officer (CFO) Mike Grainger was named the company's president and COO. As CFO Grainger had led the company through its IPO and was now in charge of its global operations. In November 2001 Ingram Micro consolidated its U.S. and Canadian operations into a single

North American unit. Other cost-cutting measures taken in 2001 included layoffs, consolidating distribution centers, and reorganizing several internal departments. For 2001 Ingram Micro reported revenue of $25.19 billion and net income of just $6.7 million, compared to 2000 revenue of $30.72 billion and net income of $226.2 million.

Ingram Micro continued cutting costs in 2002 as it prepared for an economic recovery. In the first half of the year it cut about 500 jobs, with further layoffs reducing its workforce to about 13,500 employees later in the year. As Ingram Micro sought to improve its bottom line, it remained focused on providing a high level of service to its customers.

Principal Competitors

Arrow Electronics, Inc.; Avnet, Inc.; Daisytek International Corp.; Synnex Information Technologies, Inc.; Tech Data Corp.

Further Reading

Anastasi, Robert, "Ingram Micro IPO Was Financial Highlight of the Year," *Computer Reseller News,* December 16, 1996, p. 39.

April, Carolyn A., "Appointments: Ingram Micro Looks for a New CEO," *InfoWorld,* September 13, 1999, p. 20.

Campbell, Scott, "HP, Razorfish, Ingram Micro, Cambridge Technology, Inacom, Compucom Report Results," *Computer Reseller News,* February 21, 2000, p. 110.

——, "Ingram Micro, CHS Beat 4Q Estimates," *Computer Reseller News,* February 23, 1998, p. 250.

——, "Ingram Micro's Future Lies in New CEO's Hands—Foster Care," *Computer Reseller News,* March 13, 2000, p. 116.

——, "Ingram to Tighten Belt Again," *Computer Reseller News,* September 23, 2002, p. 12.

Cruz, Mike, "Ingram Micro Consolidates," *Computer Reseller News,* November 5, 2001, p. 30.

——, "New COO Grainger: Big Plans Ahead for Ingram Micro," *Computer Reseller News,* January 22, 2001, p. 81.

DeMarzo, Bob, "Don't Dare Go to Sleep," *Computer Reseller News,* May 27, 1996, p. 19.

DeMarzo, Bob, et al., "Dukes: IPO Still on Track," *Computer Reseller News,* June 3, 1996, p. 197.

Doler, Kathleen, "Ingram-Micro D Merger Already Affecting Distribution Channel," *PC Week,* March 13, 1989, p. 78.

Doler, Kathleen, and Madeline Epstein, "Micro D Directors Endorse Latest Merger Offer from Ingram Industries," *PC Week,* January 23, 1989, p. 58.

Duffy, R., "Ingram, Software Distribution to Merge," *PC Week,* May 7, 1985, p. 189.

Ferguson, Bob, "Micro D-Ingram Tie Near; Spurs Management Shift," *Electronic News,* March 13, 1989, p. 35.

Hausman, Eric, "The Road to $20B," *Computer Reseller News,* May 5, 1997, p. 1.

Hausman, Eric, and John Longwell, "Ingram's IPO: Is It a Family Affair?," *Computer Reseller News,* October 9, 1995, p. 37.

"Ingram Files IPO," *Computer Reseller News,* July 22, 1996, p. 5.

Longwell, John, "Ingram: Management Moves, New VAR Focus," *Computer Reseller News,* October 16, 1995, p. 39.

——, "Ingram to Widen OEM Base," *Computer Reseller News,* March 6, 1995, p. 147.

McGee, Marianne Kolbasuk, "Networking Products Boost Ingram Micro," *Information Week,* February 15, 1999, p. 179.

Milliot, Jim, "Ingram to Form Three Separate Companies," *Publishers Weekly,* October 2, 1995, p. 10.

Moltzen, Edward F., "Proxy Reveals Ingrams Hold the Reins," *Computer Reseller News,* April 14, 1997, p. 42.

Morrissey, Jane, "High-End Sales to VARs Boost Ingram's Q1 Results," *PC Week,* May 18, 1992, p. 201.

O'Heir, Jeff, "Chip Lacy," *Computer Reseller News,* November 16, 1997, p. 67.

——, "High Drama Around Ingram IPO," *Computer Reseller News,* December 9, 1996, p. 189.

——, "Ingram Micro in J&W Acquisition," *Computer Reseller News,* August 25, 1997, p. 149.

Pereira, Pedro, "Ingram Micro to Buy Tech Data Subsidiary, Macrotron," *Computer Reseller News,* June 15, 1998, p. 10.

——, "Ingram Sales Soar," *Computer Reseller News,* March 6, 1995, p. 139.

Ryan, Ken, "Ingram Micro's True Value Approach," *HFD-The Weekly Home Furnishings Newspaper,* August 23, 1994, p. S6.

"Second Source," *PC Week,* December 27, 1993, p. 107.

Sharp, Bill, "Dance of the Dirigibles," *HP Professional,* April 1992, p. 10.

White, Todd, "Merisel Merrily Ignores PC Biz Bad Times," *Los Angeles Business Journal,* February 24, 1992, p. 3.

Wolf, Marty, "Ingram Micro News Could Portend Further Consolidation," *Computer Reseller News,* March 22, 1999, p. 58.

Yamada, Ken, and Charlotte Dunlap, "Netscape Signs Ingram Amid IPO," *Computer Reseller News,* August 14, 1995, p. 26.

—David P. Bianco

Invitrogen Corporation

1600 Faraday Avenue
Carlsbad, California 92008
U.S.A.
Telephone: (760) 603-7200
Toll Free: (800) 955-6288
Fax: (760) 602-6500
Web site: http://www.invitrogen.com

Public Company
Incorporated: 1989
Employees: 2,726
Sales: $629.29 million (2001)
Stock Exchanges: NASDAQ
Ticker Symbol: IVGN
NAIC: 325413 In-Vitro Diagnostic Substance
    Manufacturing; 325414 Biological Product (Except
    Diagnostic) Manufacturing

Invitrogen Corporation develops, manufactures, and markets more than 10,000 products for customers involved in life sciences research and the commercial manufacture of genetically engineered products. The company's research kits are used to simplify and improve gene cloning, gene expression, and gene analysis. Invitrogen also is involved in cell structure activities, which provides customers with the material to grow cells in the laboratory and to produce pharmaceutical and other materials made by cultured cells.

Origins

Although Invitrogen occupied a dominant position in the biotechnology industry at the end of the 1990s, its rise to the industry's elite started fitfully. The company began as a partnership formed in California in 1987, before incorporating in 1989. The company's founders included researchers from the San Diego area, members of the scientific community who worked for local companies such as Syntro Corp., Mycogen Corp., and Scripps Clinic. One member of the founding group rose to the fore, a graduate of the University of California at San Diego's chemistry department named Lyle C. Turner. Turner was attempting to shape Invitrogen into a developer of biomedical research kits used for genetic research. His efforts were hampered early on, however, during the initial, critical phase of the company's development.

In late 1989, founding partner Bill McConnell left the organization to form his own company, called McConnell Research. McConnell's departure forced Turner to use most of Invitrogen's capital to purchase the departing founder's interest in the company. The leveraged buyout left the fledgling company in a precarious position. Without the collateral required to secure a bank loan, Turner searched for another source of financing and found aid from the California Export Finance Office (CEFO). CEFO was a division of the World Trade Commission, an organization chartered to help small and mid-sized California businesses who needed capital to expand into foreign markets. The aid provided by CEFO resolved Invitrogen's financial crisis, enabling the young company to gain its footing and expand internationally. By 1990, the company's distributors were located in eight countries: Canada, the United Kingdom, Germany, Switzerland, Italy, The Netherlands, Sweden, and Japan. Sales, which had totaled $2 million in 1989, were expected to reach $4 million in 1990. The company's payroll, which began with three employees in 1987, had swelled to 42 employees by 1990.

The encouraging growth recorded by Invitrogen as it entered the 1990s provided a stable foundation for the company's progress throughout the decade. As Invitrogen developed, it targeted two main markets, the life sciences research market and the commercial production market. Invitrogen's customers in the life sciences research market included laboratories, medical research centers, government institutions such as the National Institutes of Health, and companies involved in biotechnology, pharmaceutical, energy, chemical, and agricultural activities. Within the life sciences market, Invitrogen positioned itself to address the needs of two disciplines, cellular biochemistry and molecular biology. Cellular biochemistry included the study of genetic functioning and the biochemical composition of cells, yielding information that was used in developmental biology. Molecular biology involved the study of deoxyribonu-

Company Perspectives:

To thousands of customers worldwide, Invitrogen is an innovative partner in life science research and the commercial production of biomolecules. Through our products and services, we strive to accelerate biological discovery and understanding so scientists can accomplish experiments faster, easier, and more reliably.

cleic acid (DNA) and ribonucleic acid (RNA)—the genetic information systems of living organisms. Invitrogen's involvement in the commercial production market centered on serving industries engaged in the commercial production of rare or difficult to obtain substances through genetic engineering. A broad collection of industries was involved in such activity, ranging from the biotechnical industry to the food processing and agricultural industries.

Invitrogen's essence was its development, manufacture, and marketing of research tools in kit form that simplified and improved gene cloning, gene expression, and gene analysis techniques. These techniques were used to promote gene-based drug discovery, the success of which was expected to be greatly aided by the Human Genome Project. A multiyear, global effort, the Human Genome Project sought to identify the three billion building blocks of the human genetic code. The project, which was nearing completion at the dawn of the 21st century, was endeavoring to provide the blueprint of humanity. With such a blueprint, scientists were expected to develop new medicines that would be safer and more effective than any pharmaceutical products on the market.

Although Invitrogen marketed scores of products, one stood out among the rest. The company's patented TOPO Cloning technology dramatically accelerated the cloning process, reducing the time it took for one step in the process from 12 hours to five minutes. With the success of its patented cloning technology and the litany of other Invitrogen products, the company was able to record respectable growth throughout the 1990s, moving well beyond the $4 million recorded at the beginning of the decade. By the company's tenth anniversary, it had eclipsed the $50 million-in-sales mark, generating $55.3 million in revenues. Much of Invitrogen's financial growth arrived later in its development, coming via acquisition. Invitrogen's acquisition spree exponentially increased its revenue volume and its product portfolio, engendering a company that within a few short years was fast in pursuit of the $1 billion-in-sales mark.

Acquisitions in the Late 1990s

The launch of Invitrogen's acquisition campaign coincided with its conversion to public ownership. In 1999, the company completed its initial public offering (IPO) of stock, debuting on the NASDAQ. In August 1999, the company completed its first pivotal transaction, merging with San Diego-based NOVEX, a developer of products used for gene and protein analysis, in a $52 million deal. NOVEX developed and manufactured precast electrophoresis gels, which was a technique used to visualize the results of many different types of molecular biology experi-

ments. Next, in December 1999, the company signed a letter of intent to acquire Huntsville, Alabama-based Research Genetics, Inc., a leading supplier of products and services for gene-based drug discovery research. (At roughly the same time, the Human Genome Project celebrated a major breakthrough, when scientists succeeded in mapping the entire genetic pattern of a human chromosome.) In anticipation of Research Genetics' inclusion within the Invitrogen fold, Turner explained the impact of the acquisition in a December 13, 1999 interview with the *San Diego Business Journal.* "We will now be able to serve customers from the earliest phases of gene identification and target validation," he said, "and continuing through the various stages of cloning, protein expression, and analysis." The acquisition was completed on February 2, 2000, making Research Genetics, a $23 million-in-sales company prior to the acquisition, an Invitrogen subsidiary.

Financial growth, which had occurred at a measured pace throughout much of the 1990s, exploded as Invitrogen exited the decade and entered the 21st century. Acquisitions fueled the increase in the company's revenue volume, lending worldwide recognition to the Carlsbad, California-based company. While the final details of the Research Genetics deal were being hashed out, the company centered its sights on its next target, an Israeli company named Ethrog Biotechnologies Ltd. Ethrog had developed and patented a system for the electrophoretic separation of macromolecules. Invitrogen spent $15.1 million to acquire Ethrog, completing the deal in June 2000. The purchase of Ethrog was followed by an acquisition of astounding scale for a company of Invitrogen's size, its inclusion vaulting Turner's company toward market dominance.

Acquisition of Life Technologies in 2000

On the heels of the $15 million Ethrog acquisition, Invitrogen announced a cash and stock merger valued at $1.9 billion. In July 2000, Invitrogen neared the end of negotiations to acquire Dexter Corporation. Under the terms of the agreement, Dexter was to be dissolved, marking the end of the oldest company listed on the New York Stock Exchange. Dexter traced its roots back to a decade before the American Revolution, to Seth Dexter II, who began operating a sawmill along the Connecticut River in 1767. Dexter's business had evolved far beyond sawmill operations in the intervening years, growing to include the molecular biology operations of Life Technologies, Inc., the object of Invitrogen's desire. Founded in 1983, Life Technologies developed, manufactured, and supplied products used in life sciences research and the commercial manufacture of genetically engineered products. Invitrogen's merger with Life Technologies promised to add to the Carlsbad company's already powerful presence in the gene cloning, expression, and analysis market.

The life sciences community applauded the merger, which was expected to create the largest competitor in the molecular biology reagent business. One analyst, in a July 17, 2000 interview with *Chemical Market Reporter,* assessed the impact of the business combination, saying, "This will enable Invitrogen to become the leader in supplying researchers in all aspects of molecular biology from basic bench labwork to cutting-edge genomic and protemics." Another analyst, in the same article, added, "We view the proposed transaction as confirmation of

Key Dates:

1987: Invitrogen is formed as a partnership.
1989: Invitrogen is incorporated.
1999: Invitrogen completes its initial public offering of stock.
2000: Invitrogen acquires Life Technologies, Inc.

Invitrogen's continued emerging role as the industry's leading consolidator of enabling research tools and technologies.'' The effect of the merger on Invitrogen's stature was immense, adding Life Technologies' $409 million in 1999 sales to create a company with more than $500 million in sales and operating income ranging between $80 million and $100 million annually. Upon completion of the merger, the company's product portfolio would swell to more than 5,500 products, its employee ranks would increase by 2,300 workers, and it would control about 40 percent of the market for kits and products used in gene cloning, gene expression, and gene analysis.

The merger was completed in September 2000. The following month, Invitrogen reorganized its business into two divisions as part of the formidable task of integrating Life Technologies within the company's operations. The molecular biology division was formed to spearhead the company's involvement in gene cloning, gene expression, and gene analysis. Invitrogen's chief operating officer, Lewis Shuster, was tapped to head the new division. At the same time, Invitrogen's cell culture division was formed to focus on the markets for cell culture media and serum production. Stark Thompson, Life Technologies' president and chief executive officer, was selected to lead the cell culture division, which was expected to generate one-third of Invitrogen's annual revenues. The bulk of the company's revenue-generating capabilities fell to the molecular biology division, which was expected to contribute three-quarters of Invitrogen's total sales. In the years ahead, the molecular biology division was expected to record 21 percent annual growth, while the cell culture division was expected to record more modest annual growth of 4 percent.

Invitrogen's sales increased to roughly $630 million in 2001, the first full year of Life Technologies' inclusion within Invitrogen. The total represented a more than sixfold increase over that recorded before the company's IPO sparked its acquisition campaign. In 2002, the process of dealing with the merger was still underway, as the company endeavored to consolidate its operations. In May, Invitrogen announced that it planned to close the Huntsville, Alabama, facility it gained from the Research Genetics acquisition. Production was to be shifted to several of the company's other facilities, a move that was expected to save as much as $10 million annually. The company also was in the process of shuttering both Invitrogen and Life Technologies facilities in The Netherlands as part of a general restructuring of European operations. Additional integration efforts included the elimination of product lines that Invitrogen's management determined were not compatible with the company's strategic goals. The company expected to discontinue product lines representing as much as $55 million in annual

sales, most of which were obtained from the merger with Life Technologies.

As Invitrogen celebrated its 15th anniversary and planned for the future, it was expected to continue playing the role of industry consolidator. An indication of its commitment to growth via acquisition occurred in October 2002, when the company announced a $42 million agreement to acquire Informax, which developed software that helped to design, manage, and interpret research kits for gene identification and cloning. Whatever the company's future development engendered, Invitrogen's management could take pride in its achievements during the first 15 years of existence. The company, as it pressed ahead with future plans, enjoyed widespread esteem within the biotechnology industry. In April 2002, a market research firm, BioInformatics LLC, conducted a survey of 1,799 pharmaceutical researchers. The scientists were asked to name the first company they thought of for products and services in drug discovery. The answer supplied by the majority of the pharmaceutical researchers was Invitrogen.

Principal Subsidiaries

Research Genetics, Inc.; Life Technologies, Inc.

Principal Divisions

Molecular Biology; Cell Culture.

Principal Competitors

Affymetrix, Inc.; Applied Biosystems Group; Clontech Laboratories, Inc.

Further Reading

Beel, Susan, ''Biomed Firm Has Doubled Exports,'' *San Diego Business Journal,* October 22, 1990, p. 8.

Chang, Joseph, ''Invitrogen to Acquire Dexter and Life Tech. in $1.8 Bn Deal,'' *Chemical Market Reporter,* July 17, 2000, p. 1.

Edgecliffe-Johnson, Andrew, ''International: Invitrogen Makes Bid for Life Technologies,'' *Financial Times,* July 19, 2000, p. 33.

''Invitrogen Builds $500 Million War Chest,'' *GenomiKa,* December 19, 2001, p. 9.

''Invitrogen Consolidates Assets,'' *Chemical Week,* May 8, 2002, p. 30.

''Invitrogen Cuts Revenue Forecast for First Quarter,'' *GenomiKa,* March 13, 2002, p. 7.

''Invitrogen Most Recognised Life Science Company,'' *GenomiKa,* July 3, 2002, p. 7.

''Invitrogen Splits to Form Two Divisions,'' *GenomiKa,* October 11, 2000, p. 3.

''Move Over Dot-Coms, Biotech Is Back,'' *Business Week,* March 6, 2000, p. 116.

Van Arnum, Patricia, ''Invitrogen's Purchase of Life Tech Creates Leader in Molecular Biology,'' *Chemical Market Reporter,* July 17, 2000, p. 18.

Webb, Marion, ''Invitrogen Plans More Expansion with Buyout,'' *San Diego Business Journal,* December 13, 1999, p. 4.

Westervelt, Robert, ''Invitrogen Purchase of Dexter Clears Antitrust Review,'' *Chemical Week,* September 6, 2000, p. 10.

White, Suzanne, ''Human Genome Sciences,'' *Washington Business Journal,* March 16, 2001, p. 19.

—Jeffrey L. Covell

Invivo Corporation

4900 Hopyard Road, Suite 210
Pleasanton, California 94588
U.S.A.
Telephone: (925) 468-7600
Fax: (925) 468-7610
Web site: http://www.invivo-corp.com

Public Company
Incorporated: 1964 as Gentran
Employees: 213
Sales: $54.27 million (2001)
Stock Exchanges: NASDAQ
Ticker Symbol: SAFE
NAIC: 334510 Electromedical and Electrotherapeutic
Apparatus Manufacturing; 334513 Instruments and
Related Product Manufacturing for Measuring,
Displaying, and Controlling Industrial Process
Variables; 334519 Other Measuring and Controlling
Device Manufacturing; 423450 Medical, Dental, and
Hospital Equipment and Supplies Merchant
Wholesalers

Invivo Corporation touts itself as the leading producer of vital signs monitoring devices used during magnetic resonance imaging (MRI) procedures. Invivo designs, manufactures, and markets monitoring systems that measure the vital signs of patients, selling its product in the United States, Europe, and Asia. Invivo sells monitoring systems for patients outside the MRI environment as well. The company also designs, manufactures, and markets a line of safety and industrial instrumentation products that measure and detect toxic gases and low levels of oxygen. The company has established relationships with most of the world's largest MRI equipment manufacturers, including Siemens A.G. Medical Engineering Group, Philips Medical Systems, Hitachi Medical Corporation, and GE Medical Systems.

Origins

Invivo evolved in both name and business orientation during the 20th century, shedding both its original name and its origi-

nal business by the time the company entered the 21st century. The company commenced business in 1964 as Gentran, a supplier of melt pressure instrumentation to manufacturers in the plastics, rubber, food, and medical industries. It would take years before Invivo's predecessor gained any recognition of note, its anonymity preserved by its diminutive financial stature and its failure to contribute meaningfully to its markets. After its formation, Gentran next appeared on the media radar in December 1985, when the company was acquired by Milwaukee, Wisconsin-based Pillar Corp., a company best known later for developing business planning software. Less than a year after its acquisition by Pillar, Gentran embarked on a new era in its development, an era whose arrival was signaled by the adoption of a new corporate title.

Gentran was spun off from Pillar in October 1986, when the company was reincorporated as Sensor Control Corp. Several months later, in February 1987, Sensor Control completed its initial public offering (IPO) of stock, but it did not emerge as a company completely free from Pillar's control. Pillar controlled 44.3 percent of Sensor Control after the IPO, with its chairman and president, Ernest Goggio, who served as Sensor Control's chairman, owning 46.9 percent of the company. Goggio, in his mid-60s at the time, selected James Hawkins as Sensor Control's president and chief executive officer. Hawkins, in his early 30s at the time, would preside over Sensor Control's development until its maturation into Invivo and continue to lead the company as it entered the 21st century.

At this juncture in the company's history, its financial totals remained low, particularly for a concern that was approaching its 25th anniversary. In 1986, Sensor Control generated a little more than $2.5 million in revenue, from which the company earned $268,000 in profit. Proceeds from the IPO enabled Sensor Control to complete several acquisitions, which helped to increase the company's financial stature marginally. In 1987, the company acquired Gamma Instruments Inc. and Tactile Robotic Systems Inc. The following year, Sensor Control failed in a bid to acquire Boonton Electronics Corp., but the company succeeded in purchasing Linear Laboratories Corp. By the end of 1988, Sensor Control also succeeded in reaching the $5 million-in-sales mark, posting $528,000 in profit for the year.

MRI Monitoring Device Unveiled in the Late 1980s

The arrival of Sensor Control's 25th anniversary roughly coincided with the debut of its first notable product. By 1989, the company manufactured measurement and sensing systems for industrial markets. Sensor Control's product line included melt pressure systems, noncontact infrared temperature measurement systems, noncontact metal thickness gauges, and tactile sensing systems with custom software packages. Sensor Control's product line also included one signal product, the commercial success of which eventually would steer the company in a new business direction. The late 1980s marked the debut of the OMNI-TRAK 3100.

The OMNI-TRAK 3100 represented Sensor Control's pioneering development of vital signs monitoring during magnetic resonance imaging (MRI). An MRI was a noninvasive diagnostic tool that used magnetic fields and radio frequencies to produce images of internal organs and structures of the body. With the OMNI-TRAK 3100, physicians were able to monitor vital signs while the patient was undergoing an MRI procedure, a remarkable achievement because of the complexities of a monitor device and MRI equipment working together. For both to work well in concert, a monitor could not degrade the image produced by the MRI, while, at the same time, the monitor signal had to be protected from the MRI's magnetic field and radio frequencies, thereby ensuring the information gleaned by the monitor remained accurate. Sensor Control overcame the challenges inherent in producing a successful vital signs monitor. The OMNI-TRAK 3100 provided continuous monitoring of all key aspects of a patient's vitality, including electrocardiograph (ECG), respiration, heart rate, blood oxygen levels, invasive and noninvasive blood pressure, and expired carbon dioxide levels.

Thanks to the debut of the OMNI-TRAK 3100, Sensor Control entered the 1990s operating in two business segments. Part of the company's attention was devoted to patient safety monitoring, while part of the company's attention was devoted to safety and industrial instrumentation, which included gas detection and monitoring devices. The Occupational Safety and Health Administration (OSHA) and other regulatory agencies required the use of such devices in confined settings where toxic gases or low levels of oxygen were suspected. As the company progressed through the decade, it would concentrate on both sectors, but by the decade's end Invivo's management, led by Hawkins, would demonstrate a decided bias toward building the company's patient monitoring business.

Expansion of Medical Business During the Latter Half of the 1990s

The shift in concentration toward the patient monitoring side of Invivo's business occurred during the mid-1990s. Not long after the company's 30th anniversary, Invivo's management

decided to develop a full-featured monitor for general medical applications, a decision that moved the company beyond the MRI environment for the first time. In anticipation of the development of a new medical product, the company significantly increased its sales force and stepped up its marketing efforts between 1995 and 1997, attempting to ease its entry into a new market. The development program culminated in the introduction of the Millennia monitor in the latter half of 1996, marking the company's entry into the general patient monitoring market. The Millennia, a portable, 15-pound vital signs monitor, included a module for anesthetic agent identification and analysis, allowing an anesthesiologist to confirm the type and amount of anesthetic gas being administered to a patient.

By the time the Millennia made its debut on the market, the financial stature of Invivo had increased from its days as Sensor Control. The $5 million-in-sales company that exited the 1980s stood as a nearly $36 million-in-sales company by the end of the company's fiscal year in June 1997. For the remainder of the 1990s, sales increased steadily, although not robustly, as the company expanded, particularly its medical device subsidiary, Invivo Research—the essence of the modern Invivo Corporation.

On the heels of Invivo's entry into the general patient monitoring market, the company strengthened its presence in the MRI arena. In April 1998, the company unveiled its next-generation MRI monitor, the OMNI-TRAK 3150. A smaller, portable version of the OMNI-TRAK 3100, the company's new MRI monitor was capable of communicating with the Millennia remote display controller, using state-of-the-art radio transmission to send data to physicians and technicians in both the MRI room and the control room. Providing a boost to business, the OMNI-TRAK 3150, in conjunction with the company's other medical device products, led to record financial totals for fiscal 1999. In June 1999, the company reported a 20 percent increase in total sales, posting $48.8 million in revenue. The increase was attributable to the company's patient safety monitoring segment, where revenues at Invivo Research leaped 30 percent. For the year, the company's patient safety monitoring segment generated $30.1 million in revenues and $4 million in net income. Invivo's safety and industrial instrumentation segment generated $18.6 million in revenues and $3.2 million in net income.

Divestitures Beginning in 2001

As Invivo exited the 20th century and entered the 21st century, the attractions of the $2 billion worldwide market for patient monitoring products began to pull the company decidedly in one direction. Safety and industrial instrumentation devices, once the exclusive business of Invivo's predecessors, increasingly lost their importance within the Invivo organization during the first years of the 21st century. An exodus of Invivo's assets in the safety and industrial instrumentation segment began in 2001, as a series of divestitures left the company almost entirely dependent on medical markets. In March 2001, the company announced that it had sold its subsidiary G.C. Industries to Santa Clara, California-based Vici Metronics Inc. Invivo had purchased G.C. Industries in 1991, when the company was an $850,000-in-sales manufacturer of gas detection instruments, calibration equipment, and sensors. The divestiture represented a loss of 1 percent of Invivo's total annual sales. Hawkins, in a March 6, 2001 press release issued by the com-

Key Dates:

1964: Invivo's predecessor, Gentran, is founded.
1985: Pillar Corp. acquires Gentran.
1986: Gentran is reincorporated as Sensor Control Corp.
1987: Sensor Control completes its initial public offering of stock.
1996: The Millennia, a general patient monitoring device, is introduced.
1998: Invivo's next-generation MRI monitor, the OMNITRAK 3150, is introduced.
2001: Divestitures increase the importance of Invivo Research.

pany, explained the reasoning behind the disposition. "We acquired G.C. Industries 10 years ago," he wrote, "when we had a different focus than we have today, and we have now determined that G.C. Industries no longer fits well strategically with our medical and safety and industrial businesses."

As Invivo began to weed out parts of its safety and industrial instrumentation device business, it recorded positive advances with its medical business. The company increased its sales and marketing efforts in 2001, establishing a subsidiary in England to foster growth in the United Kingdom. In August, Invivo received approval from the Japanese Ministry of Health & Labor to market its MRI monitors in Japan, the second largest market behind the United States in terms of installed MRIs.

In 2001, Invivo's safety and industrial sales dropped 16 percent, triggering another round of divestitures. In May 2002, the company completed the sale of Sierra Precision, a manufacturer of pressure gauges and hoses, to 3D Instruments LLC, which stripped Invivo of 11 percent of its sales volume. Hawkins, in a May 20, 2002 press release, wrote, "With the divestiture of Sierra Precision, we expect the gross profit margin for Invivo Corporation will show a substantial increase as Sierra

Precision's gross profit margin was substantially lower than our gross profit margin for Invivo Corporation." Next, in June 2002, the company sold Lumidor Safety Products, a manufacturer of portable and fixed gas detection instrumentation, to Zellweger Analytics, Inc. Lumidor accounted for 15 percent of Invivo's sales. After the disposition of Sierra Precision and Lumidor, Invivo Research was responsible for 96 percent of Invivo's annual revenues.

Against the backdrop of the divestitures, Invivo's medical monitoring business was recording encouraging growth. During the first and second fiscal quarters of 2002, Invivo Research posted sales gains of 13 percent and 17 percent, respectively. As the company plotted its future course, much of its success depended on the growth of its patient monitoring equipment. In this area, particularly the MRI niche, the company stood well positioned. The inherent challenges of producing an effective MRI monitor limited the number of competitors Invivo faced. According to the company's calculations, it was one of only three MRI monitor producers in existence. In this small pool of competitors, Invivo considered itself to be the market leader, a position the company hoped to maintain in the future.

Principal Subsidiaries

Linear Laboratories Corp.; Gentran; Invivo Research, Inc.

Principal Competitors

Mine Safety Appliances Company; Spacelabs Medical, Inc.; Welch Allyn Protocol, Inc.

Further Reading

"Gentran," *Rubber World,* October 1995, p. 16.
"Sensor Control Corp.," *Business Journal,* November 12, 1990, p. 41.
"Sensor Control Corporation," *Business Journal,* January 30, 1989, p. 27.

—Jeffrey L. Covell

Ionics, Incorporated

65 Grove Street
Watertown, Massachusetts 02472-28821
U.S.A.
Telephone: (617) 926-2500
Fax: (617) 926-4304
Web site: http://www.ionics.com

Public Company
Founded: 1948
Employees: 2,100
Sales: $466.7 million (2001)
Stock Exchanges: New York
Ticker Symbol: ION
NAIC: 333319 Other Commercial and Service Industry
Machinery

Ionics, Incorporated is a leading water purification company active throughout the world in the supply of water and water treatment. The company purifies water using desalination membranes, which it invented and patented in the 1950s. Its products are used by customers and the company itself to desalt brackish water and seawater. Ionics is organized into four business groups: the Equipment Business Group, the Ultrapure Water Group, the Consumer Water Group, and the Instrument Business Group. The Equipment Business Group makes up 44 percent of the company's sales and designs, engineers, and constructs advanced membrane-based, conventional, and thermal-based water- and wastewater-treatment systems for municipalities and industrial customers. These customers include the beverage, automotive, and chemical processing industries. The Consumer Water Group accounts for about 27 percent of the company's business. It sells home water-purification systems and also markets consumer bleach-based products. The Ultrapure Water Group, which constitutes 23 percent of sales, provides water needed to rinse silicon wafers, microchips, and discs for hard drives. The Instrument Business Group accounts for the remaining sales and produces analyzers to measure water contamination. Ionics' revenues spiked in 2001 when it sold its Aqua Cool Pure Bottled Water subsidiary to Perrier Vittel S.A.

for $200 million. During the same year, the company also entered into a partnership to provide 79 million gallons of purified water per day to Kuwait.

A Vision in 1948

Ionics grew out of fear that the fresh water supply on Earth was diminishing to the point that there might not be enough to sustain life in the future. The company was founded in 1948 by a group of scientists and engineers from the Massachusetts Institute of Technology (MIT) and Harvard. They invented the ion-exchange membrane, which they used to desalinate, or remove salt from, water. The membrane could also be used to remove other chemicals from water and clean brackish (somewhat salty) water. The group received a patent for its membrane in 1950 and was featured on the front page of the *New York Times* in 1952.

While the world did not run out of fresh water, there was certainly a shortage of clean water in certain areas, especially in the Middle East. The first membrane was installed for commercial purposes in Saudi Arabia in 1954.

The success of the desalination techniques led the company to develop a broad range of processes utilizing different separation methods. These methods removed various contaminants from water and could be used in different parts of the United States where fresh water had become contaminated. In 1957, Ionics installed its first water-treatment system in the United States. This system desalted a portion of the water supply in Coalinga, California. A few years later, a system was installed in Buckeye, Arizona, to clean the entire water supply there. The company continued to expand overseas while growing in the United States. In 1969, the world's largest brackish-water treatment plant was installed in Siesta Key, Florida. By this time, Ionics had sold hundreds of desalination systems to clean the water in the Middle East.

ED and EDR in the Early 1970s

Ionics invented ion-exchanged membranes for use in water treatment along with electrodialysis (ED), a process that uses these membranes to desalt concentrated solutions. With ED, salts in the water became either positively or negatively charged ions. ED created a semipermeable barrier that allowed the passage of either the positively charged ions or the negatively charged ions. It then excluded the ions with the opposite charge. Eliminating one type of ion helped rid water of salts.

Ionics invented the electrodialysis reversal (EDR) process to deal with the problem of membranes becoming dirtied or scaled over time. By reversing the electrical current, this buildup was removed. Both ED and EDR were significant developments in the water-processing industry and were still used as of 2002. Ionics opened its first commercial ED plant in Malaga, Spain, in 1972.

Cloromat and Aqua Cool Pure Bottled Water

The company unveiled its award-winning Cloromat system in 1973. Cloromat manufactured sodium hypochlorite, a chemical used to disinfect drinking water. The first Cloromat system was used to sterilize water and wastewater in Manchester, New Hampshire. Cloromat systems were sold worldwide for about 13 years. Around this time, the company entered the consumer bleach market in Brisbane, Australia, with subsidiary Elite PTY Ltd. This was the first of many successful company endeavors in Australia.

Ionics entered the bottled-water market in 1984 when it introduced its Aqua Cool Pure Bottled Water. The bottled water was eventually sold in 33 locations in the United States. Ionics was commended for the ten million gallons of Aqua Cool it donated to American and British troops during Operation Desert Storm and Operation Desert Shield.

Despite Aqua Cool's annual $70 million in sales, Ionics sold the business in 2001 to Perrier-Vittel S.A., a subsidiary of Nestlé, S.A., for $220 million. Explained Arthur L. Goldstein, chairman and chief executive officer of Ionics: ''Ionics is selling its Aqua Cool Pure Bottled Water business, primarily to enable greater corporate focus on its activities in water desalination, water reuse, surface-water purification, ultrapure water and water-quality instrumentation. These growing businesses, in which Ionics is a world leader, are based on Ionics' core technologies in membrane-based water treatment and are expected to require substantial resources and capital commitments in the future.''

Pure Thoughts for the New Millennium

In 1998, Ionics celebrated its 50th anniversary. In 1999, as it headed into the millennium, Ionics began construction on a water-desalinization plant in Barbados using reverse osmosis technology. Barbados was one of the most water-scarce countries in the world, and RO technology would help alleviate present and future drought. The plant was built in Spring Garden, St. Michael. One year later, it produced fresh drinking water for 20 percent of Barbados' 264,000 residents.

Reverse osmosis (RO) technology was an energy-efficient method of filtering salts from brackish water and seawater to meet EPA requirements for surface water treatment and safe drinking water. It cleared away natural organic and mineral substances, as well as pollutants, and greatly reduced the occurrence of bacteria, viruses, salts, nitrates, pesticides, color, and hardness in water. Ionics' RO technology was used all over the United States, as well as in Italy, the Caribbean, the Canary Islands, and Malaysia to produce high-quality process and drinking water. Many nuclear and fossil-power producers, pharmaceutical and petrochemical manufacturers, and public-water suppliers throughout the world used this technology.

Patent Troubles and a Profitable Consortium in 2001

On April 23, 2001, Ionics announced that three lawsuits brought against the company by United States Filter Corporation (U.S. Filter) had been settled. The lawsuits had alleged infringement of certain patents relating to electrodeionization (EDI) and one patent related to an application utilizing RO technology.

EDI technology was used by water purification companies to consistently remove impurities in water without using hazardous chemicals. It was cheaper for the consumer than other technologies and was highly efficient. When RO was used as a pretreatment method, EDI removed over 99.9 percent of feedwater ions. EDI technology was used to purify water for semiconductor chip manufacturing and hard disc drives, and to generate power in the United States, France, Northern Ireland, Italy, China, Japan, Taiwan, and Canada. Ionics opted to settle the lawsuits, agreeing to make payments to U.S. Filter. Under the terms of the settlement, Ionics did not have to give up any of its rights with respect to its existing EDI technology.

Arthur L. Goldstein, Ionics' chairman and CEO, stated: ''We are pleased to have resolved this litigation in such a satisfactory manner, bringing to an end a process that had become both expensive and a burden on management time. The settlement gave no future adverse financial impact on the company, and we remain free to continue all of our current activities in the EDI and RO fields.'' Goldstein also noted: ''We have been very pleased by the commercial success of our EDI products in the microelectronics, power and other markets, and we fully intend to continue our long-term commitment to the development of this technology.''

Also in 2001, Ionics became part of a consortium with Mohammed Abdulmihsin Al-Kharafi & Sons Co. The consortium was awarded a $380 million contract to supply Kuwait with 79 million gallons of water a day. The contract was the largest ever for a membrane system used for water reuse. The Kuwaiti plant converted wastewater into water usable for agriculture and irrigation. Ionics' role in the venture was to supply the membrane systems and operate the membrane facility.

In 2002, Ionics started the largest seawater RO desalting plant in the Western Hemisphere, located in Trinidad, West

Key Dates:

1948: Ionics, Incorporated is founded by a group of scientists and engineers.
1949: First desalination membrane is made.
1950: First patent is received on membrane.
1952: Ionics' membrane is featured on the front page of the *New York Times*.
1957: First U.S. municipality installs membrane desalting plant.
1969: World's largest brackish water-treatment plant is installed at Siesta Key, Florida.
1971: Ionics installs largest brackish-water desalting plant in Europe in Brindisi, Italy.
1972: Company opens first commercial Electrodialysis (ED) power plant in Malaga, Spain; first ED plant in petrochemical industry opens in North Africa.
1984: Ionics introduces Aqua Cool Pure Bottled Water.
1990: Motorola selects Ionics to design and build two advanced water systems for major new semiconductor processing facilities in Texas and Arizona.
2001: Company is part of consortium awarded $380 million contract for a water reclamation facility in Kuwait; Aqua Cool business is sold to Perrier Vittel S.A. for $200 million.
2002: Ionics starts the largest seawater RO desalting plant in the Western Hemisphere in Trinidad, West Indies.

Indies. During the same year, the company began an ultrafiltration (UF) system in Minneapolis that supplied the city's population of 500,000 with 70 million gallons of filtered water a day. A completion date was set for 2004.

Ionics' vision for the future was to preserve and enhance the environment and the overall quality of life around the globe. As of 2002, with the ever increasing population, as well as the constant need for clean water, Ionics implemented a strong and necessary focus on pollution prevention and education. CEO Arthur Goldstein stated, "I believe that if responsible progress is to be made we need to create some type of real or virtual partnership among the parties with an interest in or an obligation to our water resources." He then went on to add, "State and federal governments are beginning to show signs of realizing that the long-held concept of fixing blame is not the way to solve pollution-related problems."

Ionics was also working on a new technology called "Ionics EDR 2020." It removed more minerals and salt (50 to 90 percent) than older technologies, and was surprisingly more affordable because it had an increased membrane area, allowing use of fewer membranes. It was mainly used to purify brackish water for drinking and for demineralization of waters used for industrial

processes. Ionics was at the forefront of the industry and would most likely continue to climb as it developed more innovative technologies to make the earth a cleaner place to live.

Principal Subsidiaries

Ionics Pure Solutions; Ionics Apollo Ultrapure Water; Ionics Fidelity Purewater; Ionics Sievers Instruments; Ionics Aqua Design Incorporated; Aqua Cool Pure Bottled Water; Elite Consumer Products; Ionics Life Sciences, Incorporated; Ionics Ahlfinger Water; Ionics Resources Conservation.

Principal Operating Units

Equipment Business Group; Ultrapure Water Group; Consumer Water Group; Instrument Business Group.

Principal Competitors

Osmonics, Inc.; United States Filter Corporation; ZENON Environmental, Incorporated.

Further Reading

"Global Water Industry Needs United Effort," *Water and Environment*, January 1999.
Howe, Peter J., "Ionics Wins $320M Kuwaiti Contract," *Boston Globe,* June 25, 2002, p. D2.
"Ionics Agrees to Sell Operations," *Wall Street Journal,* December 4, 2001, p. 1.
"Ionics Gets Nigerian Contract," *Wall Street Journal,* December 30, 1993, p. B7.
"Ionics Gets $20 Million Contract," *Wall Street Journal,* March 30, 2000, p. 1.
"Ionics, Inc. Looking for Next Wave in Water Purification," *Boston Globe,* June 8, 1993, p. 52.
"Ionics, Inc.: Swing to a Loss Is Blamed on Patent Fight, Axed Plan," *Wall Street Journal*, February 28, 2001, p. B15.
"Ionics, Inc. Wins a Contract," *Wall Street Journal,* September 22, 1999, p. 1.
"Ionics: Pure Play in Pure Water," *New York Times,* March 10, 1992, p. D10.
"Ionics Sells Water Company to Nestlé for $220 Million," *New York Times,* January 1, 2002, p. C3.
"Nestlé to Buy Ionics' Bottled Water Business," *New York Times,* December 4, 2002, p. C4.
Orme, William A., Jr., "Water, Water Everywhere Just Waiting for Price to Drop," *New York Times,* June 23, 2001.
Yocum, Keith R., "Ionics: Atop the Clean Water Wave," *Boston Globe,* March 10, 1991, p. 42.
"Zero Liquid Discharge System Helps Power Plant Take Heat off River," *Industrial Wastewater Magazine,* July/August 2001.

—Tracey Vasil Biscontini

JAKKS Pacific, Inc.

22619 Pacific Coast Highway, Suite 2
Malibu, California 90265
U.S.A.
Telephone: (310) 455-6200
Fax: (310) 317-8527
Web site: http://www.jakkspacific.com

Public Company
Incorporated: 1995
Employees: 310
Sales: $284.31 million (2001)
Stock Exchanges: NASDAQ
Ticker Symbol: JAKK
NAIC: 339932 Game, Toy, and Children's Vehicle
    Manufacturing; 339931 Doll and Stuffed Toy
    Manufacturing

JAKKS Pacific, Inc. is a multi-brand toy company managed by industry veterans Jack Friedman and Stephen Berman. Typically, JAKKS Pacific adds to the marketability of its products by taking generic items and enhancing their value by securing licensing agreements. Foremost among its products is a line of action figures based on World Wrestling Federation (WWF) personalities. The company's brands include "Flying Colors," "Road Champs," "Remco," "Child Guidance," and "Pentech." The branded items include action figures, dolls, writing instruments, art and crafts products, and miniature die-cast cars.

Origins

When Jack Friedman cofounded JAKKS Pacific in 1995, it was his third entrepreneurial creation, each a start-up toy company. A native of Queens, New York, Friedman began his professional career during the 1960s when he started working as a sales representative for a toy company named Norman J. Lewis Associates. Not one to relish the vagaries of a traditional employer-employee relationship, Friedman began drumming up his own concepts for toy products. In 1970, his ideas came to fruition with the formation of LJN Toys, a company started with the financial backing of his employer, Norman J. Lewis. Lewis later sold his interest in the company to a Chinese investor, but Friedman remained committed to promoting the company's growth. By 1983, LJN Toys was a $51 million-in-sales company, exuding sufficient financial vitality to attract the attention of a much larger suitor on the other side of the country. MCA Inc., at the time the parent company of Universal Studios, was on an acquisition spree during the mid-1980s, displaying particular interest in toy companies. In 1985, MCA acquired a 63 percent interest in LJN Toys, completing a $32 million stock deal that required Friedman to pack his bags and move to Los Angeles.

Friedman signed a long-term employment agreement with MCA and began running LJN Toys from southern California. The relationship did not last. Preferring to be on his own in the business world, Friedman broke free from MCA's grasp two years after his move from New York. His next business venture was THQ Inc., a southern California video game company that Friedman founded in 1990. During THQ's formative years, Friedman acquired licenses to Hollywood productions and based the development of the company's video games on popular films. The company flourished at first. Friedman sold his 46 percent stake in the company on its initial public offering of stock, netting himself $13 million. In 1992, THQ's sales exploded, jumping more than 70 percent, but then the dynamics of the video game industry began to change. In an August 26, 2002 interview with the *Los Angeles Business Journal*, JAKKS Pacific's chief financial officer, Joel Bennett, explained the turn of events. "Then," Bennett said, referring to the early 1990s, "games were more like toys than technology." When the development of gaming software evolved toward the technological side, "it became beyond Jack's comfort zone," Bennett explained. "He's kind of a low-tech guy."

Frustrated, trapped in a business for which he had no natural affinity, Friedman struggled to remain content at THQ. After the company reported a staggering $18 million loss for 1994, Friedman left to start another company. To assist in the venture's start-up, Friedman enlisted the help of his longtime friend Stephen G. Berman. Between 1988 and 1991, Berman had served as president of Balanced Approach, Inc., a distributor of

Company Perspectives:

JAKKS Pacific engages children in creative play, in the true spirit of the phrase. Our products encourage learning and interaction. They inspire fun and spark creativity among children of all ages, interests, backgrounds and abilities. While our core business is toys, our offerings have grown to include writing instruments, back-to-school items, slumber bags, kites, pool floats and other leisure products. This is absolutely by design. We counter the fragmented, seasonal and fiercely competitive nature of our industry by executing a business strategy centered on growth through diversity and operational excellence. This means developing new core products. Growing and consolidating existing product lines. Pursuing strategic acquisitions. Expanding international sales. And capitalizing on operating efficiencies achieved through disciplined management and a lean, flexible infrastructure. Since our founding in 1995, JAKKS Pacific has executed this strategy aggressively, faithfully and successfully, achieving year-over-year growth and an exceptional balance sheet.

personal fitness products and services. Berman left Balanced Approach in 1991 to join Friedman at THQ, where he served a four-year stint as vice-president and managing director of THQ International, Inc., a subsidiary of THQ, Inc.

Together, Friedman and Berman started JAKKS Pacific in 1995. Friedman was appointed chairman and chief executive officer. Berman, after leaving THQ International in August 1995, was named executive vice-president, secretary, and chief operating officer. From the start, Friedman's objective was to use JAKKS Pacific to consolidate the fragmented toy industry. The industry was dominated by the "Big Two," Hasbro, Inc. and Mattel, Inc., who together controlled one-third of the approximately $15-billion-at-wholesale U.S. toy industry. After the Big Two, as Friedman perceived it, there was ample room for growth. Friedman hoped to cut a swath through the hundreds of small competitors and the handful of medium-sized toy companies by acquiring its rivals and by forging licensing agreements with other companies. Eventually, if the company's strategic course proved sound, JAKKS Pacific could one day join the industry's upper echelon and sit side-by-side with Hasbro and Mattel.

Signing an Agreement with WWF in 1995

JAKKS Pacific's survival as a fledgling toy company was guaranteed during the company's first year of existence. In 1995, Friedman signed a pivotal licensing agreement with Titan Sports, Inc. that secured an invaluable revenue stream for the young company. Titan Sports was the parent company of the World Wrestling Federation (WWF), whose popularity exploded during the 1990s. Friedman signed an exclusive, ten-year deal that gave JAKKS Pacific the rights to develop and market a line of action figures based on the WWF's wrestling personalities, such as Stone Cold Steve Austin and the Undertaker. From the licensing agreement and the thousands of WWF action figures to follow, JAKKS Pacific derived much of its growth for the next several years. Berman, in an August 18,

1998 interview with the *Los Angeles Times*, explained the importance of the licensing agreement to JAKKS Pacific's fortunes. "The WWF has been to us what GI Joe was to Hasbro," he remarked. "That's how Hasbro started their growth; GI Joe allowed them to acquire other brands and other companies. Our WWF is allowing JAKKS to do the same."

Not long after the signal WWF deal was put into action, Friedman gained the financial resources to begin his quest for accelerated growth. By the end of 1996, the company's first full year of operation, it generated roughly $10 million in sales, a pittance compared to the sales totals supporting Hasbro and Mattel, who counted their revenue in the billions of dollars. There was a long way to go, and Friedman got underway in 1997. The company purchased Road Champs Inc., a manufacturer of miniature die-cast cars. In the fall of 1997, the company purchased the Remco brand, identified with a line of die-cast cars. At the same time, the company purchased a brand of toddler development toys marketed under the name Child Guidance, acquiring both brands from Azrak-Hamway International Inc. The acquisition of Road Champs and Child Guidance drew another comparison by Berman to JAKKS Pacific's much larger rivals. He pointed out that both Mattel and Hasbro owned brands geared toward preschoolers, Fisher-Price and Playskool, respectively, and, like JAKKS Pacific's Road Champ line of miniature cars, Mattel owned the Hot Wheels brand.

As Friedman orchestrated JAKKS Pacific's acquisition campaign, he did so without incurring any appreciable debt, using stock and cash to pay for assets. Another favorable aspect of the company's acquisition strategy was its ability to stay lean as it grew. The company manufactured and stored its products in Asia, employing only a dozen or so warehouse personnel in the United States and keeping the size of its corporate staff to a minimum. As acquisitions were completed, the company kept its overhead costs down and remained nimble. Once companies were acquired, JAKKS Pacific discarded the property's administrative and distribution departments and shed any products that had not proved to be consistently profitable before absorbing the business into its pared-down corporate structure.

Late 1990s Expansion

In 1998, JAKKS Pacific's expansion program continued to diversify the company's product line beyond its mainstay line of WWF action figures. Analysts applauded the move to lessen the company's dependence on a single product line. During the year, the company signed a licensing agreement with Bass Anglers Sportsman Society Inc. to create a line of fishing-themed toys. The company also signed an agreement with Petersen Cos. to develop a line of Road Champs cars based on the classic roadsters featured in Petersen's automotive magazines.

At this point in its development, the company was beginning to catch the attention of the national business press. As the deals with Bass Anglers and Petersen were being forged, the company could proudly point to triple-digit sales growth for the previous two years. In 1997, the company generated $41.9 million in sales, a 250 percent increase from the total recorded in 1996. Roughly half of the company's financial growth was attributable to its popular line of WWF action figures, which ranked among the top five best-selling action figures sold by retailer Toys 'R' Us, Inc. at its 700 stores. The growth was enough to vault the company into the ranks of the 15 fastest-growing companies in California in 1997.

In 1999, Friedman continued to expand JAKKS Pacific's product line. In June, the company announced the acquisition of privately held Berk Corp. A manufacturer of educational foam puzzles, mats, and blocks, Berk was organized as a division within JAKKS Pacific's preschool unit, Child Guidance. The addition of Berk gave the company more than 100 products bearing licenses from Walt Disney, Nickelodeon, Warner Bros., and Children's Television Workshop. In October, the company acquired Flying Colors Toys Inc. for $36 million in stock. Flying Colors produced activity sets, modeling compound playsets, and lunch boxes bearing licenses from popular television shows such as Nickelodeon's *Blue's Clues* and Warner Bros.' *Looney Tunes.* Roughly a year after the acquisition, Flying Colors produced arts and crafts products that were released in concert with the film based on the popular Harry Potter character.

As JAKKS exited the 1990s, its place within the national landscape of toy companies was secured. In 1999, the company was selected as one of the 100 fastest-growing companies in the country by *Fortune* magazine, a distinction it would earn for the next two years. Diversification had reduced the company's reliance on WWF action figures, as the sale of education foam puzzles, lunch boxes, and a bevy of other products created a more well-rounded company. By 2000, WWF action figures accounted for approximately 35 percent of the company's sales, down from the more than 60 percent recorded just several years earlier. "Our business isn't based on home runs," Berman explained in a December 18, 2000 interview with the *Los Angeles Business Journal.* "Our business is based on singles and doubles, and if we get a triple or a home run, that's great. But we're looking for evergreens," he added, referring to perennial, money-making products coveted by toy companies.

The arrival of JAKKS Pacific's fifth anniversary could be justifiably celebrated. When the company acquired Pentech International Inc., a New Jersey-based maker of pens, pencils, and markers, in 2000, it became the fourth largest toy company in the country. Acquisitions had fueled much of the growth that had vaulted the company from a dead start into the industry's elite. Between 1997 and 2001, when the company completed eight acquisitions, JAKKS Pacific's annual sales increased from $41.9 million to $284.3 million. During the same period, the company's net income increased by a factor of 10, mushrooming from $2.8 million to $28.2 million. The company's

stock value soared, increasing from $5.33 per share to $18.95 per share. As recessive economic conditions began to emerge, some analysts continued to remain optimistic about JAKKS Pacific's prospects. "JAKKS has positioned themselves to be less vulnerable to economic downturns because the vast majority of their products retail for less than $10," remarked one analyst in the July 15, 2001 issue of the *Daily News.* Or, as another analyst expressed in the same article, "People don't stop buying toys for their kids in a soft economy, but they may stop buying more expensive ones."

Despite the optimism, the bleak economic times caught up with JAKKS Pacific. In 2002, several of the company's largest customers, retailers such as Wal-Mart, Toys 'R' Us, and Target, began reducing their inventory levels. Other customers, including Kmart and Ames Department Stores, were operating under Chapter 11 bankruptcy protection. Consequently, JAKKS Pacific's inventory levels swelled, increasing from $32 million to nearly $50 million during the first six months of 2002. Investors, sensing the wariness of the massive retail chains, grew wary themselves, driving JAKKS Pacific's stock down 41 percent during the first half of 2002.

Amid the slowdown, Friedman pressed ahead with expansion. In February 2002, the company agreed to a two-step arrangement to acquire New York-based Toymax International Inc., a designer and marketer of product lines such as "Go Fly a Kite," "Funnoodle," "Laser Challenge," "Creepy Crawlers," karaoke machines, and radio-controlled vehicles. The $55 million transaction was expected to be completed by the end of 2002, at which point Toymax would become a wholly owned JAKKS Pacific subsidiary.

As JAKKS Pacific prepared for the future and a return to more salubrious economic conditions, its strengths were manifold. Looking ahead, the company could expect meaningful growth from its international operations, which were beginning to mature as it completed its first decade of existence. Kidz Biz Ltd., which began distributing the company's products in the United Kingdom in 1999, was acquired by JAKKS Pacific in 2001, becoming the company's European sales headquarters. In addition, the company forged an agreement with Funtastic Limited in 2001 to distribute JAKKS Pacific products in Australia and New Zealand. As the company pressed ahead with its domestic expansion, its pursuit of international business promised to deliver growth as well, inching JAKKS Pacific toward its goal of catching Mattel and Hasbro.

Principal Subsidiaries

Berk Corp.; Flying Colors Toys Inc.; Kidz Biz Ltd. (U.K.).

Principal Competitors

Hasbro, Inc.; Marvel Enterprises, Inc.; Mattel, Inc.

Further Reading

Brinsley, John, "Investors Have Hard Time Taking Toy Firm Seriously," *Los Angeles Business Journal,* December 18, 2000, p. 35.
Bronstad, Amanda, "Focus on Lower-End Helps Shares of Toy Maker Climb," *Los Angeles Business Journal,* November 26, 2001, p. 25.

194   **JAKKS Pacific, Inc.**

Finnigan, David, ''JAKKS Figures Big in WWF Strategy,'' *Brand-week*, March 4, 2002, p. 16.

Gregory, Stephen, ''Hot Wrestling Toys Turn JAKKS Pacific into a Winner,'' *Los Angeles Times*, August 18, 1998, p. 4.

——, ''JAKKS Pacific Acquires Berk, Maker of Oversize Foam Toys,'' *Los Angeles Times*, June 29, 1999, p. 2.

''JAKKS Expanding with Purchase,'' *Los Angeles Business Journal*, May 29, 2000, p. 49.

''Marriage Matters,'' *Playthings*, August 1999, p. 6.

Morgan, Richard, ''JAKKS to Buy Toymax,'' *Daily Deal*, February 10, 2002, p. 3.

Palazzo, Anthony, ''Case Study: Toy Company Is Tested in Changing Climate,'' *Los Angeles Business Journal*, August 26, 2002, p. 1.

—Jeffrey L. Covell

JLG Industries, Inc.

1 JLG Drive
McConnellsburg, Pennsylvania 17233
U.S.A.
Telephone: (717) 485-6523
Fax: (717) 485-6417
Web site: http://www.jlg.com

Public Company
Incorporated: 1969 as Fulton Industries, Inc.
Employees: 2,801
Sales: $770.1 million (2002)
Stock Exchanges: New York
Ticker Symbol: JLG
NAIC: 333120 Construction Machinery Manufacturing

JLG Industries, Inc. is the world's leading producer of mobile aerial work platforms and a leading manufacturer of telescopic material handlers and telescopic hydraulic excavators. The company sells primarily to businesses that rent or sell the products to industrial, commercial, institutional, and construction customers. JLG manufactures boom lifts, scissor lifts, vertical mast lifts, telescopic excavators, and telehandlers. Boom lifts have a horizontal work platform and can extend up to 50 feet. Scissor lifts, for which the company is especially well-known, are machines featuring platforms mounted on scissor-like devices that can extend the platforms vertically up to about 40 feet. Vertical mast lifts, to provide another example, are aerial work platforms that can fit through standard door openings when retracted. More than 63 percent of the company's sales stem from its aerial work platforms. About 15 percent of its sales come from after-sales service and support. While the company sells most of its products domestically, 27 percent of product sales are to international customers. Headquartered in McConnellsburg, Pennsylvania, the company also has production facilities in Bedford, Pennsylvania, and operations in Scotland and Australia. In 2000, JLG's sales peaked at over $1 billion but then declined due to a difficult economy.

Fulton Industries, Inc. in 1969

JLG began as Fulton Industries, Inc., a small metal fabrication shop in McConnellsburg, Pennsylvania. Shortly after its inception in 1969, the company was purchased to develop a prototype for high-reach equipment, which would be welcomed by workers frustrated with cumbersome scaffolding and ladders. The company's name was changed to JLG Industries, Inc.

A crew of 20 workers completed the original JLG boom lift in 1970. The boom could be raised up to 27 feet. When raised, its platform remained stable and horizontal. The boom lift had innovative design concepts, such as an ability to hold tools to reduce clutter at work sites. Some of these design concepts are still used today. JLG boom lifts sold well in the United States. They were sold primarily to equipment rental companies, which then rented them to construction companies. These companies used the lifts to enter hard-to-reach areas not accessible by traditional scaffolding and platforms. JLG established a European presence in 1977 with the opening of a headquarters in Scotland.

Scissor Lifts in 1979

In 1979, the company opened a facility in Bedford, Pennsylvania, to produce and assemble scissor lifts. The first scissor lifts had a platform mounted on a scissor-like mechanism and could extend up to 30 feet. In 1981, the company introduced oscillating axles for boom- and scissor-lift operators.

The company's scissor lifts were enormously successful throughout the United States. Around this time, JLG sought to further expand internationally. In 1983, the company opened a production facility in Port MacQuarie, Australia. JLG's Australian operations serviced customers throughout Asia and the Pacific Rim.

JLG's rapid growth continued into the mid-1980s. During this time, its 10,000th boom lift was rolled off assembly lines in McConnellsburg and it patented an "Extend-A-Reach" feature that offered customers "greater flexibility for platform placement." This feature allowed customers to use JLG products in hard-to-reach areas with many obstacles. Extend-a-Reach pushed JLG a step ahead of its competitors.

A Second Scissor-Lift Facility in the 1990s

The early 1990s were tough years for JLG. The company suffered two years of heavy losses. To cut expenses, it redesigned its production process and switched to continuous-flow manufacturing. With this type of manufacturing, parts moved continuously on the factory floor until the product was assembled. Employees were also cross-trained to operate more than one machine, so they could move to different places along the assembly line.

"JLG, along with companies like Danaher, Black & Decker, and Teleflex have gotten religion about lean production and continuous improvement techniques," said James C. Lucas, an analyst for the *Central Penn Business Journal*. "They continue to benefit as a major player in what we call 'the revolution occurring on the factory floor in America.'"

JLG predicted that the new manufacturing process would save the company $10 million by 1994. The company's decisions proved to be good ones. By 1997, JLG boasted net revenues of over $500 million. These revenues jumped to $720 million by 1999. In 2000, JLG's revenues surpassed $1 billion with a net income of $60.5 million.

To try and meet the demand for its scissor lifts, the company opened a second facility in Bedford in 1997. The following year, its 50,000th scissor lift came off assembly lines.

Gradall Industries in 1999

JLG acquired Gradall Industries, Inc., based in Orrville, Ohio, in 1999. Gradall had originally manufactured hydraulic excavators, but by 1982 it had expanded its product line to include rough-terrain material handlers. Commercial, industrial, and residential customers used Gradall products for excavation and demolition work. Gradall machines were designed for specialized excavation tasks such as waste removal.

Gradall had changed hands seven times since its inception in 1946, but the company was especially excited about becoming a subsidiary of JLG. "Without any hesitation this is the best owner we've ever had and could ever hope to have. JLG is a very successful company," said James Cahill, vice-president of manufacturing, in the *Orrville Bureau Editor*. Cahill added that he considered JLG a front-runner in new product development. He

believed that JLG purchased Gradall, at least in part, for its attractive facilities. Gradall owned a 430,000-square-foot facility in New Philadelphia, Ohio, and had just purchased a 300,000-square-foot former Volvo GM Heavy Truck facility. The Volvo facility cost Gradall $3.7 million. JLG purchased Gradall for $20 per share—a total purchase of about $200 million.

Forming JLG University

To educate its employees and provide a forum for its customers, JLG entered into a partnership with Penn State University to form JLG University. "Just as JLG is known for quality products and services, Penn State University is known for the quality of education it provides," said L. David Black, JLG president, chairman, and chief executive officer. "As JLG approaches the $1 billion sales mark, we are faced with challenges and opportunities to make it equally important to develop our people along with our markets. Through JLG University, we will facilitate continuous development of a global high performance team, ongoing improvement of our suppliers and the uncompromising commitment to meeting the needs of our customers, all of which is expected to ultimately enhance shareholder value. Our people are our greatest asset, and being able to give them the tools to meet the challenges of a changing and growing marketplace is of key importance. The establishment of JLG University demonstrates the magnitude of our commitment." JLG University was organized into five colleges: professional development, leadership development, skilled trades, customer support, and supply chain. The colleges offered workshops and seminars, credit and non-credit courses, certificate programs and undergraduate and graduate degree programs.

A Drop in Sales

After surpassing $1 billion in sales, the company received a prestigious Telly Award for excellence in business-to-business marketing. JLG was recognized in the "Non-Broadcast Business Promotional Video" category for a company video on its 450 Series of telescopic boom lifts.

It suffered a drop in sales shortly after this, however. In 2001, revenues slipped to $964 million, and in 2002 sales plunged over 20 percent with a net-income drop of about 84 percent. JLG attributed the abrupt downturn to a struggling economy, however, and remained optimistic about its future.

In an effort to boost sales, the company concentrated on international expansion. It focused on increasing sales in Europe as well as in developing markets in Latin America. It also introduced two new scissor lifts, one with a platform height of 33 feet and another with a platform height of 43 feet. Both new scissor lifts featured the largest standard deck in their size class—over 7 feet wide and 16 feet long. The company also unveiled its "Workstation in the Sky" series of tools to complement the aerial platforms.

Bill Lasky, chairman of the board, president, and chief executive officer, said the following in a company press release: "During fiscal year 2002, we enhanced our competitive position and strengthened our balance sheet. There were numerous economic events this year such as terrorist attacks, high-profile

Key Dates:

1969: Company is founded as Fulton Industries, then purchased, reoriented, and renamed JLG.
1970: First JLG aerial work platforms are manufactured.
1977: JLG breaks into European market, opens oversees headquarters in United Kingdom.
1979: Plant in Bedford, Pennsylvania, is opened to manufacture scissor lifts.
1981: Company introduces oscillating axles.
1986: Ten thousandth boom lift comes off assembly line in McConnellsburg.
1997: Company opens second scissor lift plant in Bedford.
1999: Company opens JLG University in cooperation with Pennsylvania State University to better serve both its employees and customers.

bankruptcies, and accounting scandals, all of which contributed to mixed economic signals and a resulting conservative approach by our major customers to fleet expansion or replacement. We continue to focus on what is within our control in the short-term while keeping an eye to the future.'' Lasky went on to state that, although the company could not precisely predict when a turnaround in business would occur, several positive factors, including fewer competitors and the possibility of bargain acquisitions, boded well for the future of JLG.

Principal Subsidiaries

Gradall Industries, Inc.

Principal Competitors

Caterpillar Inc.; Terex Corporation; W.R. Carpenter North America, Inc.

Further Reading

Adams, Chris, ''Industrial Lift Makers Ratchet Down As Boom Eases Overcapacity,'' *Wall Street Journal,* August 21, 1997, p. B4.
Burns, Eileen Barrett, ''JLG Industries Re-engineers to Increase Profits,'' *Central Penn Business Journal,* June 16, 1995, p. 5.
Cochran, Thomas N., ''JLG Industries: Seeking New Heights,'' *Barron's,* November 21, 1988, p. 55.
''JLG Calls Friendly Takeover Bid Lacking in Substance,'' *Wall Street Journal,* October 10, 1992, p. C18.
''JLG Industries, Inc.,'' *Wall Street Journal,* September 22, 1994, p. B12.
''JLG Industries, Inc. Fiscal Fourth-Quarter Net Expected to Meet Estimates,'' *Wall Street Journal,* September 4, 1996, p. C.
''JLG Industries, Inc., Investor Group Renews Bid for Firm at Reduced Price,'' *Wall Street Journal,* July 22, 1992, p. A6.
''JLG Industries, Inc. Material Handling Division Will Be Sold by Company,'' *Wall Street Journal,* September 19, 1995, p. B.
''JLG Industries, Inc. Work Force to Be Cut 30%; Net Seen Below Estimates,'' *Wall Street Journal,* July 31, 1997, p. A4.
''JLG Lowers Its Earnings Forecast,'' *New York Times,* May 5, 2001, p. C3.
''JLG Maker of Aerial Work Platforms Will Buy Gradall,'' *New York Times,* May 12, 1999, p. C4.
''JLG, Ousted Chairman Agree to End Dispute; Stock Set for Offering,'' *Wall Street Journal,* September 20, 1993, p. B10.
''JLG Secondary Stock Offering,'' *Wall Street Journal,* November 12, 1993, p. C17.
''JLG Shares Surge After Earnings Double,'' *New York Times,* May 24, 1996.
Stern, Gabriella, ''JLG Fires Grove As Chairman After Co-Founder Sought to Oust Board,'' *Wall Street Journal,* May 3, 1993, p. B2.

—Tracey Vasil Biscontini

JOFFREY
BALLET OF CHICAGO

The Joffrey Ballet of Chicago

70 East Lake Street, Suite 1300
Chicago, Illinois 60601
U.S.A.
Telephone: (312) 739-0120
Fax: (312) 739-0119
Web site: http://www.joffrey.com

Nonprofit Company
Incorporated: 1954 as Robert Joffrey Ballet
Operating Revenues: $9 million (2001 est.)
NAIC: 711120 Dance Companies

The Joffrey Ballet of Chicago is one of the premiere dance companies in the United States. The Joffrey made a truly American art out of ballet, which had been an almost exclusively European province, by presenting classic 19th- and 20th-century dances along with new American works. The Joffrey is renowned both for its preservation of bygone masterpieces such as Nijinsky's *Le Sacre du printemps* and Kurt Jooss's *The Green Table* and for its development of modern ballet choreography. Founder Robert Joffrey's well-known ballets include *Pas de Déesses, Astarte, Remembrances,* and *Postcards.* Cofounder and current artistic director Gerald Arpino is one of America's best-loved and most prolific choreographers, whose works include *Sea Shadow, Incubus, Ropes, Light Rain,* and *Billboards.* The company's repertoire also includes works by George Balanchine, Frederick Ashton, Laura Dean, Mark Morris, and many more contemporary choreographers. The Joffrey Ballet began as a touring company based in New York, and later had a bicoastal presence with a longstanding residency in Los Angeles. The company moved to Chicago in 1995. The Joffrey tours nationally and internationally, and offers workshops at schools and universities across the country. The Joffrey Ballet is supported through grants and donations, which account for about 60 percent of its budget. Ticket sales and other earned income provide the other 40 percent of its needs. Altogether the company brings in approximately $9 million annually.

Founders Joffrey and Arpino: The 1940s Through the Mid-1950s

Robert Joffrey was born in Seattle in 1928, the son of immigrants from very different backgrounds. His father, Joseph Joffrey, had come to Seattle from Afghanistan in 1916. Joseph's name before it was anglicized was Dollha Anver Bey Jaffa Khan. Joseph and a brother came to this country together, first working in sawmills to support themselves. Later they sold chili from a stand, and Joseph then opened a restaurant, the Rainbow Chili Parlor. Joseph Joffrey was a devout Muslim, yet he married a Catholic woman, Marie Gallette, a violinist from Italy who ended up a cashier in his restaurant. The two did not have much in common, and they did not get on easily. Robert Joffrey was their only child.

Young Robert was both bowlegged and asthmatic, and his pediatrician may have advised his parents to enroll him in some sort of physical activity to bolster his health. At eight years old Robert began boxing lessons, but he loved the dancing he had seen in movies, and he soon convinced his parents to switch him to dance lessons. His teacher immediately noticed his flair. When he was only 12 Joffrey appeared as a supernumerary in Michel Fokine's ballet *Petrouchka.* At 15, he began studying ballet with Mary Ann Wells, a respected local teacher who had a lasting influence on him. Wells put him in her most advanced classes, and had him teach beginning students. Although he was still bowlegged and, at five foot four, considered too short to be a professional dancer, he was extremely talented and completely devoted to ballet.

In 1945, when Joffrey was 16, he met Gerald Arpino. Arpino's mother had known Joffrey's mother in Italy. Arpino was six years older than Joffrey and in the Coast Guard. When his ship stopped in Seattle, he looked up his mother's friend. Mary Joffrey sent the young man to find Robert at the dance studio where he was rehearsing. Arpino knew nothing of ballet, but when he walked in the door, the instructor liked his lean physique and dragged him into class. Arpino, too, had a natural gift for dance, and after this he frequently went AWOL from his ship in order to take more classes. He also fell in love with Robert Joffrey. The two were romantically involved for several

Company Perspectives:

The Joffrey Ballet of Chicago is a world-class American ballet company committed to artistic excellence and innovation. Performing in Chicago and throughout the world, this classically trained company expresses the artistic vision and creativity of founders Robert Joffrey and Gerald Arpino. The company presents a unique repertoire from masterpieces of the past to cutting edge works of the 21st century.

years and remained close friends and artistic collaborators until Joffrey's death in 1988. The pair pretended to be cousins, but apparently Joffrey's family understood and accepted the nature of their liaison. The couple lived together in the Joffrey family home, then moved to New York in 1948.

In New York Joffrey and Arpino had numerous dance opportunities. Joffrey danced with Roland Petit's Ballets de Paris, while Arpino danced in several Broadway shows. By 1950 Joffrey also was teaching at New York's High School for the Performing Arts. In 1953, Joffrey suffered a terrible injury onstage, tearing a calf ligament so badly that his doctor advised him to give up dancing. So Joffrey began focusing on teaching, with the idea of forming his own ballet company. He founded the American Ballet Center (better known as The Joffrey Ballet School) in 1953 on Sixth Avenue in Greenwich Village, and that summer he presented several of his works at the annual Jacob's Pillow Dance Festival in Massachusetts.

In 1954 the newly created Robert Joffrey Ballet debuted a program of Joffrey's original works at the 92nd Street Y. The 92nd Street Y was an acclaimed venue for modern dance in New York, where the most esteemed choreographers, including Martha Graham and Agnes de Mille, premiered their works. It was unusual for a ballet company to be granted the space, but Joffrey's from the beginning was an unusual company that bridged the gap between classical and modern styles. Joffrey wrote *Pas de Déesses (Dance of the Goddesses)* for the 92nd Street Y recital, which proved to be one of his most enduring works.

Joffrey premiered another set of ballets the next year, and began making an impression on notable dance critics. In 1955 Joffrey was invited to teach several of his dances to the English company Ballet Rambert. He returned to the United States to choreograph for theater, including a televised production of a fairy tale opera called *Griffelkin*. Joffrey received plenty of attention for *Griffelkin* and his other works, and he caught the eye of an agent at Columbia Artists Management, Inc. Columbia Artists wanted a small ballet company that could tour the country, something portable, classical, but accessible to audiences who had not seen much dance. Joffrey and Columbia Artists worked out an arrangement to fill this niche, and thus created the Robert Joffrey Theatre Dancers, Joffrey's first real company.

On Tour in the 1950s

Gerald Arpino was the principal dancer in the small troupe. There were only five other dancers, both because Columbia Artists would pay for six only and because no more could fit in a station wagon. Joffrey's idea for the company was that it would have a teenage image, although most of the members were actually in their late 20s and Arpino was 33. European ballet companies had typically presented a frosty veneer of enviable sophistication. By contrast, the Joffrey dancers were to project a front of youthful enthusiasm, of kids next door who just happened to be fantastic dancers. They performed four ballets a night in college and high school auditoriums, almost entirely in small towns. Most of the audiences had never seen ballet or, presumably, a live dance performance of any kind, and The Joffrey made a big impression.

Columbia Artists renewed The Joffrey's contract the next year, and in 1958 the company gave 69 performances. These were almost all one-night stands, with hundreds of miles of driving in between. But the company had exchanged the station wagon for a more comfortable bus. They played in larger cities this time as well, including San Francisco and Seattle. The company continued to tour through 1961, adding dances by other choreographers. The troupe was welcomed and admired, with some dancers, particularly Arpino and ballerina Lisa Bradley, garnering warm reputations of their own.

The company had expanded to 17 dancers by 1961. That year Arpino showed his choreography for the first time, presenting *Ropes* and *Partita for 4*. He blossomed into a prolific and beloved choreographer, whose engaging modern works became the cornerstone of The Joffrey repertory.

Under the Influence of Rebekah Harkness Kean in the 1960s

The Robert Joffrey Theatre Dancers had begun life as a portable troupe, geared for traveling. But by the early 1960s, the company had matured and grown. Joffrey afforded new dancers for the touring company by paying them lower wages than his established dancers—only $65 to $75 a week. There were many other expenses, as well, such as sets and costumes and labor to haul and organize equipment and set up the stage. In addition, the touring company did not make money when it was not performing. Joffrey's school brought in a steady income, but by 1962 it was clear that it could not support the company as well. Joffrey had been given at least one significant anonymous donation that allowed the company time to rehearse and learn new works. But in order to keep going, the company (which changed its name to the Robert Joffrey Ballet in 1961) needed to attract a new source of funding. At that time, there was little government support for the arts. The National Endowment for the Arts (NEA) was not established until 1965, and many artists and organizations depended on private patronage.

Joffrey considered disbanding the company in 1962, but he managed to keep it going with help from friends and family. Then he met Rebekah Harkness Kean at a New York party. Kean was the widow of William Hale Harkness, heir to the Standard Oil fortune, and was reputed to have inherited $60 million when Harkness died. She had since been married again, to Dr. Benjamin Kean, and she used her wealth to support dancers and musicians through her Rebekah W. Harkness Foundation. She was a composer herself, and had written music for several professional dance pieces. Joffrey agreed to audition his company for her, giving her a private showing.

In the summer of 1962 Harkness invited Joffrey and his whole company to her estate, Watch Hill, to spend 12 weeks choreographing and rehearsing. But there were strings attached. Through an intermediary, she gave a musical score to Arpino, asking him to use it for a new dance piece. Arpino, not realizing the work was Harkness's, turned it down. Joffrey managed to get another choreographer to use the music, for a dance called *Dreams of Glory,* which The Joffrey would perform.

Partially because The Joffrey now had Harkness's deep pockets (so part of its costs were subsidized), the U.S. State Department sponsored the company to go on a world tour. The dancers would show audiences around the globe a piece of exciting American culture. In the winter of 1962 The Joffrey Ballet set off for its first international tour, with stops in Europe, the Middle East, India, and Afghanistan, Joffrey's ancestral homeland. The tour was in most ways a rousing success, with a command performance for the Shah of Iran. But the company had trouble with *Dreams of Glory,* the piece set to Rebekah Harkness's music. The ballet, about children in a museum imagining growing up to be president, was by all accounts a failure, and Harkness was irritated and upset.

Yet the tour led to an invitation to travel to the Soviet Union the next year. When the company returned to New York, Joffrey began choreographing new works to take to Russia. He again worked at Watch Hill, and this time Arpino agreed to write a dance to some new Harkness music. Harkness began having thoughts of starting her own ballet company and hiring Arpino as artistic director. Harkness also made her authority felt at Watch Hill. She objected to a piece choreographer Anna Sokolow was working on for The Joffrey, and eventually she told the dancers to stop rehearsing it. It was evident that Harkness wanted to do much more than write checks to The Joffrey Ballet. While she was instrumental in getting the com-

pany its first international tour and then its Manhattan debut in 1963, she hindered the group by meddling with artistic decisions. The Joffrey performed for President Kennedy in October 1963, then left for its tour of the Soviet Union. Harkness underwrote the tour, along with the U.S. State Department and another private donor. Again, the tour was a fantastic success, as Russian audiences had never seen this kind of ballet before.

In January 1964, The Joffrey set off on its last domestic tour for Columbia Artists, playing in major cities as well as many smaller towns. Relations between Harkness and Joffrey had grown chilly, though Harkness was still pumping money into the group, to the tune of possibly $40,000 to $50,000 a week. While the group was traveling, Rebekah Harkness announced that she was starting her own company, the Harkness Ballet. She had asked Arpino to direct the new group, but he refused. Then she offered Joffrey the job, and he, too, turned her down. But Harkness asserted her rights to works Joffrey and others had created under her patronage, and to sets and costumes for which she had paid. Joffrey was unsure what to tell his dancers. Harkness was offering them steady pay in her new company, and he did not know if he would be able to continue. Eventually, some Joffrey dancers joined Harkness's company, and Joffrey was forced to regroup.

In New York and Los Angeles: 1970s–80s

After the bitter break with Rebekah Harkness, Joffrey was forced to start almost from the beginning. The school was still running, and it gave him a pool of new young dancers from which to choose. But the company had grown so large and sophisticated with the injection of Harkness's money that it was difficult to go back to a leaner organization. The company applied to The Ford Foundation for grant money. Unfortunately, The Joffrey was not eligible, because it did not have nonprofit status. Normally, applying for nonprofit status was arduous and expensive, and could take a year of filing legal papers. But the company had a lucky strike in its choice of lawyer, Howard Squadron. Squadron had been working on filing for nonprofit status for a Boston arts group that had folded before the process was completed. The Joffrey was able to use this almost finished application, and it became the nonprofit Foundation for American Dance almost overnight. The company's business director, Alex Ewing, twisted the arms of many of his Yale classmates, who became Joffrey board members and contributors. In November 1964, the Robert Joffrey Ballet received an initial grant of $35,000 from The Ford Foundation, with the promise of more for the next year. The newly reorganized company made its debut in August 1965 at the Jacob's Pillow Dance Festival.

In 1966, The Joffrey was appointed the resident dance company of New York's City Center. The company's official name then became the City Center Joffrey Ballet. The company would have an annual season at the Center with all expenses paid and approximately $17,500 a week. This initiated a fruitful period for The Joffrey. Robert Joffrey choreographed one of his most famous and popular ballets, *Astarte,* in 1967. The multimedia show seemed to capture the mood of the era like no other ballet, and it was featured on the cover of *Time* magazine. Joffrey also began reviving classic ballets, something he had always longed to do. He began putting on the works of ballet greats Léonide Massine and Frederick Ashton in the late 1960s.

The company also expanded, with the addition of an apprentice corps of young dancers who were being groomed for the main Joffrey. This began in 1968 as The Joffrey Apprentice Company, and it changed its name in 1971 to The Joffrey II Dancers. Arpino created some of his most popular works in the early 1970s, including most notably *Trinity.*

The Joffrey was in the highest echelons of American dance. Yet it was far from financially stable. In 1973 City Center management announced that it was reducing its funding for The Joffrey. The dance company was running a deficit of $1.3 million, and apparently the Center's management thought the group was fiscally irresponsible. The company was rescued by another large grant from The Ford Foundation. But funding for the arts in New York began to dry up. The dance audience had grown enormously in the years since The Joffrey began touring, and now it was reaching a plateau. City government was faced with budget problems, too. In 1976 the City Center stopped supporting The Joffrey, which then changed its name back to simply The Joffrey Ballet. The company struggled to keep going. By 1979, the company was forced to lay off many of its dancers and cancel both its New York season and a planned international tour. Costs had risen enormously, and even with a severe escalation in ticket prices, the company could not pay its own way.

It looked like The Joffrey would have to fold, and the company's business director began planning the company's bankruptcy filing. Then at the close of 1979, the National Endowment for the Arts stepped in with a special grant of $250,000 to keep The Joffrey going. It was an unusual move by the arts organization, and The Joffrey was put on a strict schedule of financial audits. But the company was saved. In 1980 Joffrey hired a crop of new young dancers, mainly from Joffrey II, as he had had to let many of his mature stars go.

In 1981 the Music Center of Los Angeles asked The Joffrey if it would consider becoming its resident dance company. The Joffrey then became a bicoastal company, with homes in both New York and Los Angeles. Some of the machinations behind the move to Los Angeles were apparently due to Nancy Reagan, wife of then-president Ronald Reagan. Their son Ron had been a scholarship student at The Joffrey school, and then was inducted into Joffrey II. Reagan was evidently an accomplished dancer who succeeded on his own merits. Yet his parents had influential friends, and it pleased Nancy Reagan to have her son closer to her in California. Ron Reagan was a full member of The Joffrey Ballet for only a short time before resigning. But his presence seemed to attract many new donors with ties to the Republican party. The Joffrey also began attracting corporate donations, something that was new at the time. Tobacco giant Philip Morris Companies Inc. began sponsoring The Joffrey in its 1981–82 season.

Los Angeles underwriters raised $2 million for the company's first two seasons in Los Angeles, and The Joffrey was able to pay off its debts. The relationship with the Music Center provided much needed financial stability in the early 1980s. Yet there were still problems. The Music Center wanted The Joffrey to move all of its operations to Los Angeles by late 1984, but the Center had not provided adequate rehearsal space or offices. So this did not happen. The company maintained separate marketing departments for its New York and California shows, and The Joffrey had something of a split identity.

Robert Joffrey began bold plans for putting on major classic ballets over the next five years, but by 1985 a few of his intimates knew that he was ill with AIDS. The Joffrey put on Nijinsky's *Le Sacre du Printemps,* a groundbreaking 1913 ballet, in Los Angeles in October 1987. Shortly afterward, Joffrey had to be hospitalized. He was very ill over the next year, though he would not admit publicly that he had AIDS, and his plans for the future of the company were laid out only as wishes, not as legally binding contracts. Joffrey died on March 25, 1988, at the age of 59.

The Joffrey After Joffrey: The 1990s and Beyond

Robert Joffrey had recommended that the company's board appoint Gerald Arpino as artistic director. This was done, but Arpino was a very different character from Robert Joffrey, and not everyone on the board believed he was capable of the responsibility. Arpino had tended to stay in the background while Joffrey was alive, and he put most of his energy into choreography. Joffrey on the other hand had ended up with little time for choreography while he was consumed with keeping the company afloat. In 1989 The Joffrey's annual budget was more than $12 million, yet it still had a deficit of approximately $3 million. A member of the board of directors accused Arpino of having gone over budget on a ballet he was presenting at a gala in Washington, D.C., to honor President George Bush. Arpino proved that he had actually come in under budget for the dance, but that bookkeeping errors had made it seem like the opposite. Arpino found other financial errors, too, including the company's failure to pay $868,000 in payroll taxes to the Internal Revenue Service. One of the company's chief backers in Los Angeles, businessman David H. Murdock, offered to cover the deficit, but only if Arpino was removed. This set off a struggle between The Joffrey's patrons and its artistic director. The Joffrey dancers warmly supported Arpino. In May 1990, several Joffrey directors resigned from the board, effectively leaving the company to Arpino. "I have regained the company," Arpino said in an interview with *Dance Magazine* (July 1990). "I did what I had to do—not just for myself, but for the arts and artists. We have to stand up for ourselves." Arpino swiftly raised money from new sources. But in 1991 the company ended its relationship with the Music Center of Los Angeles, where David Murdock was a powerful patron.

The company went on a national tour in 1992, but it abruptly canceled its annual season in New York, citing the expense and lack of support from the city. The Joffrey kept going with an anonymous donation of $1.25 million that year. It was operating in the black, but it had to be cautious about expenditures, and its future was not certain. The company had a major hit in 1993 with Arpino's *Billboards,* danced to the music of pop singer Prince. It was the kind of broadly appealing show that had sustained Arpino's popular reputation.

But by early 1995, The Joffrey was in serious financial trouble, owing back pay to many dancers. The company laid off its 43 dancers in January while a dispute with the dancers' union was hashed out. Later that year the company announced that it was moving to Chicago. There had been plans from at least

1991 to move the company to the Windy City, where it had many patrons and a long history of successful performances. The company considered merging with Ballet Chicago, but instead moved wholesale on its own, occupying new quarters downtown at 185 North Wabash Avenue. The Joffrey had the ecstatic support of Maggie Daley, wife of Chicago Mayor Richard Daley, and of Lois Weisberg, the Chicago commissioner of cultural affairs. The move was seen as a coup for the city, while The Joffrey was released from supporting an ever-more-expensive presence in Manhattan. The Joffrey played a fall and summer season in Chicago, plus a holiday season of *The Nutcracker.* Ticket sales increased year after year in Chicago. By 2000, the company was raising some 40 percent of its budget from ticket sales and other earned income. It had a number of corporate donors, including Philip Morris, AT&T, and American Airlines. The Joffrey's new chairman of the board was the president and CEO of Chicago-based Sara Lee Corporation. Corporate and other donations made up 60 percent of The Joffrey's income. Once firmly settled in Chicago, the company finally began building cash reserves to keep it from the ups and downs that had made its past so difficult. The Joffrey Ballet of Chicago began planning to move into new facilities downtown in time for its 50th anniversary in 2006.

Further Reading

Anawalt, Sasha, "Arpino Returns," *Dance Magazine,* July 1990, p. 17.

——, *The Joffrey Ballet: Robert Joffrey and the Making of an American Dance Company,* New York: Scribner, 1996.

——, "Joffrey Perseveres," *Dance Magazine,* August 1990, p. 13.

Barzel, Ann, "The Joffrey Comes Home: Joffrey Ballet of Chicago," *Dance Magazine,* May 1996, p. 66.

Bauman, Risa, "Bi-Coastal Dance Troupe Adopts Single Marketing Strategy," *Direct,* March 1991, p. 26.

"Joffrey Cancels New York Season," *Dance Magazine,* February 1992, p. 12.

Reiss, Alvin H., "Arts Groups Come Back from Financial Precipice to Reach New Heights," *Fund Raising Management,* June 2000, p. 40.

Troester, Maura, "Joffrey Back in Action," *Dance Magazine,* December 1995, p. 28.

Wernick, Ilana, "Joffrey Ballet Announces It Will Move to Chicago," *Back Stage,* September 15, 1995, p. 1.

——, "Joffrey Spinoff and Arpino Draw Ire from AGMA," *Back Stage,* May 19, 1995, p. 1.

—A. Woodward

Julius Baer Holding AG

Bahnhofstrasse 36
CH-8010 Zurich
Switzerland
Telephone: (+41) 1-58-888-1111
Fax: (+41) 1-58-888-1122
Web site: http://www.juliusbaer.com

Public Company
Incorporated: 1890
Employees: 2,399
Total Assets: SFr 14.05 billion ($8.89 billion) (2001)
Stock Exchanges: Zurich
Ticker Symbol: BAER
NAIC: 522110 Commercial Banking

The leading independent private bank in Switzerland, Julius Baer Holding AG has come to epitomize the Swiss banking tradition after more than 100 years of providing exclusive services to its wealthy customers. Private Banking remains the group's largest area of operation, accounting for one-third of the group's annual net operating income, which reached SFr 1.4 billion in 2001, and more than 50 percent of the total assets under the group's management, which topped SFr 126 billion in 2001. Baer (alternatively spelled as Bär) services its clientele—the company targets private customers worth at least $25 million and willing to invest a minimum of $2 million with the group—through its army of personal bankers, offering an industry-leading ratio of 100 customers per banker, compared with more than 700 per banker for Baer's larger competitors. Baer private banking customers can expect a range of services, including portfolio management, investment advice, estate planning and related services, financial planning and tax services, and a variety of other amenities, including concierge services. While the company's largest business comes through its private customers, Baer also services institutional investors. The company has recently broadened its target market beyond its traditional Switzerland and New York base, with offices and branches opening in other areas of the United States and in Europe. Baer's other areas of operations include Trading Services; Asset Management, with an emphasis on Euro-

pean market investments; and Brokerage Services, with offices in Amsterdam, Frankfurt, Madrid, Milan, New York, Paris, Stockholm, and Zurich (the company owns seats on each local exchange). A public company listed on the Swiss stock exchange, Baer remains controlled and led by the founding Baer family, now in its third and fourth generation at the head of the company.

Swiss Private Banking Pioneer in the 1890s

The Julius Baer banking group had its start at the end of the 19th century. In 1890, the general partnership Hirschhorn & Grob was established to provide banking services in Zurich, Switzerland. In 1896, Julius Baer, then 39 years old, was taken into the partnership, which then reformed itself under the name Hirschhorn, Uhl & Baer. With the death of principal partner Louis Hirschhorn in 1901, the partnership was dissolved once again and reformed under the sole leadership of Julius Baer. Renamed Julius Baer & Co., the firm was granted a seat on the Zurich stock exchange that same year.

Baer's firm soon became a family business—in 1913, Baer was joined by son Walter, who was to take over as head of the bank after his father's death in 1922. Walter Baer was joined by one of his brothers that same year. The Baer family had by then become among the most influential members of the Zurich—and Swiss—private financial industry. Julius Baer had previously served as vice-chairman of the Zurich Stock Exchange Association, and son Walter was named chairman of that body in 1931. Three years later, Walter Baer led the formation of the Association of Swiss Private Bankers, established in response to legislation passed that year that narrowed the scope of activities of Switzerland's banks.

With the rise of the Nazis to power in Germany, especially after the outbreak of World War II, the Baer family, who were Jewish, took steps to preserve their business in the event of a German invasion of Switzerland. In 1940, part of the family traveled to the United States and set up a business office, Baer Custodian Corporation, in New York City. That office, though only temporary, nonetheless introduced the Baer bank to the New York financial market—which was to become a focus for the company in the years following the war. Part of the Baer

Company Perspectives:

Julius Baer Group's Mission: We believe private property is an essential feature of an open society and of a future worth aspiring to. We support social and cultural activities. We recognize and respect the ethical principles of a humane society and structure our operations in such a way as to preserve natural resources. Clients: We offer our clients professional service and individual expert advice with a view to increasing their security, independence and affluence. Our two main objectives are asset preservation and capital growth. Employees: Our employees are our greatest asset and we encourage them to maximize their potential through ongoing further training. We support initiative, personal commitment and the acceptance of responsibility. We aim to be a socially responsible employer and attach great importance to the welfare of our staff. Shareholders: We maintain and strengthen shareholders' confidence by setting clear goals, providing regular, transparent reporting, and generating above-average returns combined with excellent performance.

family that went to New York was later Chairman Hans J. Baer, who, after studying at Horace Mann University, Lehigh University, and New York University, returned to Switzerland in 1947 to join the private banking firm.

International Growth in the 1960s

Like many of Switzerland's private banks, Baer expanded its operations into the securities trading and stock market as assets management grew to become an important area of the firm's operations. In 1962, the group extended its securities activities to its New York office, setting up Baer Securities Corporation, which was later reformed as Julius Baer Securities Inc. In 1966, Baer turned toward Mexico, setting up its first company in that country, Baer Mexicana. Two years later, Baer entered the U.K. market, opening Julius Baer International Ltd. to tap into the London financial community.

In addition to its international expansion, Baer also began diversifying its products, launching its first Swiss Investment Fund, called Baerbond, in 1970. The death of Walter J. Baer that year (brother Werner had died in 1960) marked the end of the second generation of Baers at the head of the by then prestigious bank. Yet the Baer family remained firmly in control as the third generation, particularly Nicolas J. Baer, who went on to serve as president of the Association of Swiss Private Bankers, took over the leadership of the group. In 1974, the company formed a new offshore operation, Baerbank (Overseas) Ltd. in the Cayman Islands, which changed its name to Julius Baer Bank and Trust Company the following year. Baer also incorporated a new company, Bank Julius Baer & Co. Ltd., which took over the assets of the founding company. Baer then moved to restructure its growing number of companies under a single entity, Julius Baer & Co. (Holding) Ltd.

Hans J. Baer was appointed the company's chairman in 1975, a position he was to hold through the end of the century. Baer continued the group's selective international expansion, opening an office in San Francisco in 1978, then launching

Julius Baer Investments as a separate office in London in 1980. Baer went public that year, listing on the Zurich stock exchange—an unusual move for the highly discrete world of Swiss private bankers. Nonetheless, the Baer family remained strongly in control of the family business.

Baer, which had established its international presence primarily through its securities operations, opened its first foreign bank branch office in London in 1982. That year the company added a new product, an offshore investment fund called Liquibaer. In 1983, the company turned its attention to New York, establishing Julius Baer Investment Management, which offered international pension fund products to the U.S. market. The following year, Baer opened its first full-service bank branch in New York—which received fiduciary powers from the Comptroller of the Currency, the first foreign bank to be accorded that status. It also allowed the company to combine banking and securities trading services under the same roof—something not available to U.S. banks.

Baer next turned to Hong Kong, establishing a representative office in that city in 1985. The company also expanded in Switzerland itself, acquiring a 51 percent share of a branch in Geneva in 1986. By then, Baer had firmly established itself as one of the most respected names in the worldwide financial community—yet the group itself remained relatively tiny. With just $1.5 billion in assets under the group's management, Baer was not even large enough to take a place in the top 20 of Swiss banks.

Into the early 1990s, however, Baer underwent a significant growth spurt, particularly in North America, setting up new offices in Los Angeles in 1989 and in Palm Beach, Florida, in 1991, and launching a joint venture, BJB Global Investment Management Ltd., to enter the Canadian market in 1993. The banking group also began acting as a securities agent in the United States for a growing number of smaller overseas banks. Another factor in Baer's growth was its decision to boost its private banking activity in the United States, where securities had long been the company's primary source of revenues. The company began targeting what it labeled as ''Europhile'' Americans, that is, wealthy individuals attracted by the highly personal approach of Swiss-styled private banking. As a result, Baer's asset management portfolio grew strongly, reaching $23 billion in 1992, then climbing to $32 billion the following year.

Baer continued to expand elsewhere, launching a subsidiary in Frankfurt, Germany, Bank Julius Bär (Deutschland) AG, and a Guernsey subsidiary, Julius Baer Trust Company (Channel Islands), both in 1989. In 1990 the company launched a new Luxembourg-based investment fund. In 1994, the company added a branch of Bank Julius Baer in Guernsey and also entered Monaco with the establishment of Société de Gestion Julius Baer (Monaco). The following year, the company launched a new Zurich-based subsidiary, Julius Baer Asset Management Ltd.

Private Banking Leader at the Dawn of the 21st Century

In 1996, Baer surprised the Swiss private banking community when it announced that it had acquired a 51 percent controlling stake in family-owned Swiss private bank Bank Falck & Co., based in Lucerne. By 1998, Baer had completed the take-

Key Dates:

1890: A banking partnership is founded as Hirschhorn & Grob, in Zurich, Switzerland.

1896: Julius Baer joins the Hirschhorn partnership, which is reincorporated as Hirschhorn, Uhl & Baer.

1901: Julius Baer takes control of the partnership, which is renamed Julius Baer & Co. and granted a seat on the Zurich stock exchange.

1940: The Baer family sets up its first office in New York, Baer Custodian Corporation.

1962: Baer launches Baer Securities Corporation in New York.

1966: A subsidiary opens in Mexico.

1968: The company sets up its first subsidiary in the United Kingdom, Julius Baer International Ltd.

1974: Company holdings are restructured under Julius Baer (Holding) Ltd.

1980: Baer lists shares on the Zurich stock exchange.

1986: Baer acquires a majority stake in the branch office in Geneva.

1989: A subsidiary is formed in Germany.

1996: The company acquires 51 percent of Bank Falck & Co. in Lausanne (100 percent in 1998).

1999: The company opens branch offices in Milan and Amsterdam.

2000: The company opens a branch office in Madrid and branch offices in Berne and Basel.

2001: The company opens a branch office in Stockholm.

2002: Raymond J. Baer is named chairman.

over of Falck and converted it as a branch of Bank Julius Baer. By then, the company had added a new bank branch in Lausanne, a new Paris-based subsidiary, and a representative office in Vienna. As the decade drew to a close, Baer continued to build up its international network, adding branch offices in Milan and Amsterdam in 1999, offices in Berne, Basel, and Madrid in 2000, and an office in Stockholm in 2001.

With the global economy booming at the dawn of the 21st century, Baer's own fortunes grew strongly, as the group topped total assets under management of SFr 126 billion ($80 billion) and total corporate assets of $8.89 billion by 2001. Part of the company's growth came through the establishment of a dedicated Brokerage division to tap into the charging stock market—the company had even attempted to join the online brokering rush. The move into brokering, however, was to turn against the group, with a collapse of the markets in 2001, and the group was forced to shut down its online operation, losing its investment.

In 2002, Baer placed the next generation of the family at its head, in the form of Raymond J. Baer, who led the company on a drive to refocus its efforts on its core private banking business. Baer also set out to revive that division as well. During the late 1990s, the company also had attempted to open itself to a broader customer group, dropping its preferred minimum investments to as low as $150,000. At the beginning of the new century, however, Baer revised its customer profile, setting a preferred minimum investment target of $2 million from clients with a personal worth of at least $25 million.

As the Swiss private banking industry appeared to be edging toward a consolidation phase—led by the merger of venerable banks Lombard Odier and Darier Hentsch in 2002—Baer preferred to bank on its independence. As Raymond J. Baer told *Forbes:* "A lot of banks are consolidated to achieve critical mass. This means that there is usually a lack of vision about what their challenges are. We don't believe that critical mass is the issue." Instead, Baer turned toward the new century with its own vision, based on a heritage as one of the world's most prestigious banking groups.

Principal Subsidiaries

Bank Julius Bär (Deutschland) AG; Infidar Investment Advisory Ltd. (72%); Julius Baer Asset Management Ltd.; Julius Baer Bank and Trust Company Ltd. (Cayman Islands); Julius Baer Family Office Ltd.; Julius Baer France SA; Julius Baer International Limited (U.K.); Julius Baer Investline Ltd.; Julius Baer Investment Advisory (Asia) Ltd. (Hong Kong); Julius Baer Investment Advisory (Canada) Ltd.; Julius Baer Investment Management Inc. (U.S.A.); Julius Baer Investment Funds Services Ltd.; Julius Baer Investments Limited (U.K.); Julius Baer Italia Investment Funds Services Srl; Julius Bär Kapitalanlage Aktiengesellschaft (Germany); Julius Baer (Luxembourg) SA; Julius Baer Securities Inc. (U.S.A.); Julius Baer Trust Company (Cayman) Ltd.; Société De Gestion Julius Baer (Monaco) S.A.M.

Principal Divisions

Private Banking; Trading Services; Asset Management; Brokerage Services.

Principal Competitors

UBS AG; Lavoro Bank AG; Schweizerische Nationalbank; EFG Bank European Financial Group; HSBC Republic Bank Suisse S.A; Graubundner Kantonalbank Chur; Valiant Holding; Coutts Bank Schweiz AG; Banque Privée Edmond de Rothschild S.A.; Banca Unione di Credito; BDL Banco di Lugano; Luzerner Regiobank; Bank Sarasin und Co.; Clariden Bank Group; Bank Linth; Corner Banca S.A; Gewerbekasse in Bern; Bank Hofmann AG; Bank Hapoalim Switzerland Ltd.; WIR Bank.

Further Reading

"Julius Baer Offers Global Opportunities," *Global Fund News,* September 2002, p. 8.

"Julius Baer Sights on West Coast," *Fund Marketing Alert,* May 20, 2002, p. 9.

Kitchens, Susan, "Private Banking Middlemen," *Forbes,* October 14, 2002.

Krauss, James R., "Baer Looks Beyond Trading to Widen U.S. Base," *American Banker,* April 26, 1994, p. 4.

——, "Switzerland's Bank Julius Baer Predicts Another Boom Year for U.S. Operations," *American Banker,* January 21, 1999.

Kutler, Jeffrey, " 'Small' Swiss Banker Hans Baer Hits the Big Time in US," *American Banker,* February 14, 1986, p. 29.

Rieker, Matthias, "European Style for Baer's U.S. Unit," *American Banker,* December 3, 2001, p. 1.

—M.L. Cohen

K'Nex Industries, Inc.

P.O. Box 700
Hatfield, Pennsylvania, 19440-0700
U.S.A.
Telephone: (215) 996-7722
Toll Free: (800) 543-5639
Fax: (215) 996-4222
Web site: http://www.knex.com

Wholly Owned Subsidiary of The Rodon Group
Incorporated: 1992 as Connector Set Toy Company
Employees: 105
Sales: $100 million (1998 est.)
NAIC: 339932 Games, Toys, and Children's Vehicle
  Manufacturing

K'Nex Industries, Inc. manufactures the second-ranked children's construction toy in the world, K'Nex. K'Nex building sets comprise various sizes of rods that snap into connectors. Children can make a variety of things from them, such as cars, space ships, and ferris wheels. Some K'Nex kits are retailed as building sets for specific projects, such as the 1,280-piece Screamin' Serpent Roller Coaster. Others are starter sets or for more open-ended projects. The company manufactures K'Nex at one 223,000-square-foot plant in Hatfield, Pennsylvania. The K'Nex brand is particularly strong in Europe, where the company makes about two-thirds of its sales. Fifty percent of its K'Nex International division is owned by giant toymaker Hasbro. Hasbro also owns 10 percent of K'Nex Industries' domestic operations.

Plastics Manufacturer Gets a New Idea: 1992

K'Nex Industries was founded in 1992 by Joel I. Glickman. Glickman had a background in industrial engineering and worked for his family's business, The Rodon Group, which made specialty plastic injection molded products. Rodon had been founded in 1956, and its products ran the gamut from eyeglass cases to the table-shaped plastic devices which pizza deliverers stand on pizzas to keep the boxes from collapsing. Glickman was nearing 50 when he got the idea for a high-quality plastic building toy. Apparently a shy man, Glickman found himself at a wedding unwilling to mingle with the guests. Instead, he was fooling

around with the plastic drinking straws at the buffet table. Then it occurred to him that he could design a construction set using straw-like rods and connectors. Glickman went to work using Rodon's injection molding machinery, and soon had designed a prototype for K'Nex. The toy was made out of a proprietary brand of acetyl copolymer, a strong, flexible material. This plastic was about four times the price of the polypropylene that most plastic toys were made of. But K'Nex needed the specific characteristics of the high-quality plastic. The pieces had to be rigid enough to stay together, but not so rigid that children's hands would have difficulty snapping and unsnapping them. Consequently, the early K'Nex sets had a relatively high retail price, and this was an initial barrier to marketing.

Glickman tried to sell his new construction set to the two major U.S. toy companies, Hasbro and Mattel. Neither were interested. Glickman also approached Lego A/S, the Danish company that produces the world's best-selling construction toy. Lego refused to even look at Glickman's prototype. Undeterred, Glickman started producing K'Nex building sets at Rodon's facility. He sold them directly to toy shops, with most of his business going to smaller stores which could handle the high sticker price—from $25 to $100 a set. But Glickman also caught the eye of marketers at Toys 'R' Us, the huge nationwide toy retailer. The toy chain test-marketed K'Nex in Philadelphia and Detroit in 1992, and sales were spectacular. The toy had the makings of a hit, and Toys 'R' Us Chairman Charles Lazarus singled out the new construction kit at the next industry toy fair. By the Christmas season of 1993, K'Nex was selling at several other major retailers, including Target Stores and Kmart. Glickman also did his own promotion of K'Nex, especially stressing that the set was an educational toy. He made a 2,000-square-foot portable exhibit of K'Nex, and brought it to children's and science museums in 13 cities in 1993. By 1994, sales of K'Nex reached $44 million in the United States. The company inked a deal with Pizza Hut to give away small K'Nex sets in its kids meals in 1994. That same year K'Nex won *Family Fun* magazine's toy of the year award. The sudden success of K'Nex attracted the attention of Mattel and Hasbro, though they had passed on K'Nex the first time around. After negotiating with both companies, Glickman sold 10 percent of the U.S. operations of Connector Set Toy Company (renamed K'Nex Industries in 1996) to Hasbro.

Company Perspectives:

Founded in 1992 and 1956, respectively, K'Nex and its parent company, The Rodon Group, operate as an extended family. Over the years they have internalized and embodied a system of principles, procedures and values that serve to enhance the success of both companies and to encourage the personal and professional growth of the people in their employ. This is what we believe: We believe that the company can be financially successful while behaving in a socially and environmentally responsible manner. We believe that our product, K'Nex, is unique and worthwhile; that it is capable of enriching the lives of those who use it, both through pure enjoyment and through its educational impact; and that these genuine qualities must be sustained with all the innovation and creativity we can muster. We believe that K'Nex is as safe as human ingenuity can make it, and we must make this intrinsic in every design we devise and publish. We believe that the company has a responsibility to provide a safe and fulfilling work environment, and an opportunity to grow and learn.

Sales Picking up in Europe: Mid-1990s

The toy industry was notoriously fickle, with fad toys experiencing phenomenal sales one year, only to fade to oblivion by the next Christmas. The industry was also increasingly taken up with high-tech computer toys and games. The early 1990s saw something of a backlash, and K'Nex debuted at a time when interest in construction toys was making a comeback. The French company Meccano S.A. reintroduced the classic construction toy Erector Set in the United States in 1991. Erector Sets had not been sold in this country for ten years. Sales of construction toys jumped almost 14 percent in 1992, making the whole market worth some $267 million. The dominant player in the market, Lego, seized on the trend by bringing out over 70 new products in 1993. K'Nex came out just when interest in construction toys was heating up, and in its first two years it did extremely well. But then sales started to fall, and the company struggled to market itself successfully against better-known and more lavishly funded competitors.

Despite renewed interest in construction toys, the category made up only about 3 percent of the overall U.S. toy market. K'Nex stood out from many of its competitors by being relatively high-priced. Wal-Mart stores declined to carry K'Nex, claiming that its customers would not be interested in paying so much for the construction sets. Wal-Mart and other discount merchandisers accounted for over one-third of U.S. toy sales. After its fine start, K'Nex found it difficult to keep building its domestic sales because it was not in discount stores. To keep up its presence in the United States, K'Nex Industries needed to advertise directly to children through television commercials. The firm changed its advertising agency several times in the mid-1990s. It spent an estimated $10 million in 1995 with a series of television spots designed by the California agency Ground Zero. The next year the company spent about the same amount, using the New York agency Kirshenbaum Bond & Partners. The Kirshenbaum ads featured a motorized K'Nex

construction, with a monster movie theme. But domestic sales stayed flat.

In the meantime, the company began to have great success in Europe. K'Nex Industries had sold 50 percent of its international division to Hasbro in order to use the bigger company's overseas distribution network. K'Nex found that not only did construction toys have a much bigger share of the European toy market—from 8 to 12 percent, versus 3 percent in the United States—but marketing was much easier. Television advertising was far less important to European toy sales, because parents typically chose toys for their children based on displays they had seen in toy stores. Glickman had shown a huge K'Nex display called Big Ball Factory to buyers at Wal-Mart, who were unimpressed. While Wal-Mart declined to carry K'Nex, the British toy store chain Entertainer Ltd. made a hit out of K'Nex. The K'Nex Big Ball Factory display "stopped pedestrians in their tracks," Entertainer's marketing director told the *Wall Street Journal* (May 21, 1998). K'Nex also promoted its construction sets in England by working with Tetley Group Ltd. to give away K'Nex pieces in Tetley tea boxes. Children could collect the small sets, apparently fueling the desire for more. Within a few years, K'Nex claimed 40 percent of the British construction toy market, setting it on par with the world-dominating Lego.

K'Nex tried similar cross-promotions in other countries abroad. In Belgium, gas stations owned by Shell Petroleum Ltd. gave away K'Nex pieces, reaching at least 1.5 million consumers. The company made a similar arrangement with one of Turkey's largest newspapers, Meydan. The paper gave away some 82 million K'Nex pieces as part of a circulation drive, which resulted in a doubling of circulation for Meydan and vast market penetration for the toy company. European sales moved ahead in double digits, hitting $70 million by 1997. The brand held the number two market spot in the region, behind Lego. Sales in the United States were just over half what the company was making in Europe, standing at about $39 million.

A New Assault on the Domestic Market in the Late 1990s

For K'Nex, almost all the good news was overseas. The U.S. trend in construction toys had not lasted long. Meccano S.A. sold its U.S. division to a Canadian company in 1997, having failed to bring back the moribund Erector Set brand. Mattel, too, had its own construction line, Construx, which it took off the U.S. market in 1998. But that year K'Nex Industries hoped to revitalize its domestic marketing and add sales growth at home. Overall sales stood at an estimated $100 million by 1998. The company hoped to capture a bigger slice of the U.S. market by introducing a line of Star Wars K'Nex kits through a licensing deal with LucasFilm. But negotiations with the film company were unsuccessful, and Lego brought out the Star Wars character line instead. Though it trailed Lego, K'Nex had grown to become a prominent brand. Lego still claimed a 65 percent share of the U.S. construction toy market, and K'Nex claimed between 11 and 12 percent. In order to penetrate Wal-Mart and other discount toy marketers, K'Nex began bringing out small construction sets of only a few pieces. These retailed for as little as $1.99. In 1999 K'Nex announced it had hired another agency to handle its television advertising, with the account now going

Key Dates:

1992: Connector Set Toy Company introduces K'Nex toys.
1993: K'Nex enjoys its first nationwide Christmas season.
1994: Portions of domestic and international business are sold to Hasbro.
1996: Company is renamed K'Nex Industries, Inc.
1998: Sales of K'Nex toys thrive in Europe.
2001: K'Nex Roller Coaster set ranks as bestseller in construction toy segment.

to Griffin Bacal. The spot showed boys building various things with K'Nex, and then animation brought the creations to life.

K'Nex made another bold move in 1999, beginning to market and distribute another venerable construction toy, Lincoln Logs. Lincoln Logs was created in 1916 by John Lloyd Wright, son of famed architect Frank Lloyd Wright. The wooden interlocking blocks had enchanted countless children, but the brand had not been selling well for many years by the time K'Nex became interested. The brand was owned by Playskool, which in turn was owned by K'Nex' partner Hasbro. K'Nex marketers thought they could bring back the brand, which was geared to kids aged from three to five. Hasbro initially rejected K'Nex' offer, but in 1999 the two companies signed a three-year licensing agreement giving K'Nex broad leeway to reposition the brand. K'Nex soon brought out television advertising for Lincoln Logs, which had made no attempt to advertise since 1993. The company also made changes to the product, though it continued to be made out of wood. The company brought out Lincoln Logs activity sets, which included railroad tracks, plastic figures of people and horses, and preconstructed buildings. This centered the building set within what the company called a "themed play land," hopefully extending the time children spent with the sets.

Domestic sales seemed to be picking up for K'Nex as the millennium turned. The company was named Vendor of the Year by Toys 'R' Us in 2000, for its general excellence in sales and in service. By the Christmas season of 2001, the construction toy industry looked like it was turning around. While overall toy sales were flat that season, construction toys were expected to grow by about 8 percent. When the dust settled, construction toys in general had had a great year in 2001, growing by 14 percent, and K'Nex managed to outperform the market considerably. Its

Screamin' Serpent Roller Coaster was the top-selling item in the building sets category for that year, meaning many thousands of parents had shelled out roughly $90 for the set, which was supposed to take at least five hours to assemble. Buoyed by this leading item, K'Nex Industries' sales grew over 30 percent for 2001. The company entered the 2002 season with an array of products, from small sets for younger children to the more advanced motorized Cyber Swarm of robotic insect models to the huge and elaborate K'Nex Electronic Arcade, a working pinball game. That year K'Nex toys were sold at Toys 'R' Us, Wal-Mart, Target, Zany Brainy, and FAO Schwarz stores in the United States, and in 44 countries abroad.

Principal Divisions

K'Nex International.

Principal Competitors

Lego A/S; Learning Curve International, Inc.; Ritvik Holdings Inc.

Further Reading

Benezra, Karen, "Pizza Hut K'Nex the Dots," *Brandweek*, July 4, 1994, p. 4.
"Eighty-Five Holiday Seasons of Log Cabin Dreams," *M2 Presswire*, November 29, 2001.
"Kirshenbaum Meets K'Nex," *Adweek*, January 15, 1996, p. 42.
"K'Nex Industries," *DSN Retailing Today*, March 11, 2002, p. 13.
"K'Nex Scores a Big Hit," *Playthings*, October 1995, p. 24.
"K'Nex to Build Lincoln Logs' Future," *Playthings*, March 1999, p. 52.
Lauzon, Michael, "Construction Toys Build Sales," *Plastics News*, December 23, 1996, p. 1.
Lenihan, Rob, and Kim Hank, "New Campaigns," *Adweek*, February 2, 1998, p. 42.
Pereira, Joseph, "Slighted in U.S., Whimsical Toy Is a Wow in Europe," *Wall Street Journal*, May 21, 1998, pp. B1–B2.
Reed, Danielle, "Toy Trouble," *Wall Street Journal*, December 14, 2001, pp. W1, W4.
Stanley, T.L., "K'Nex Logs Link to Lincoln Logs," *Brandweek*, February 1, 1999, p. 12.
"Toys Hold Lessons for Plastics Designers," *Design News*, April 8, 1996, p. 37.
Tyrer, Kathy, "Toy Company's Promotion Gets Off the Ground," *Adweek*, October 16, 1995, p. 4.
Weber, Joseph, et al., "The K'Nex Thing for the Lego Set," *Business Week*, December 6, 1993, p. 54.

—A. Woodward

Kiehl's Since 1851, Inc.

112 Madison Avenue
New York, New York 10016
U.S.A.
Telephone: (212) 901-1100
Toll Free: (800) 543-4571
Fax: (212) 901-1200
Web site: http://www.kiehls.com

Private Company
Founded: 1851
Sales: $40 million (2001 est.)
NAIC: 446120 Cosmetics, Beauty Supplies, and Perfume
    Stores

Based in New York City, Kiehl's Since 1851, Inc. is a natural hair and skin care products subsidiary of French cosmetics giant L'Oréal. Kiehl's has been built up by three generations of the Morse family, and since 2000 L'Oréal has continued to follow the formula that made Kiehl's products chic and the original store a tourist attraction. The company's East Village address is the site of a 19th-century apothecary, which is crammed with all manner of curiosities, from family photographs to pictures of Olympic skiers and fighter airplanes, as well as a collection of vintage motorcycles. Despite little spending on marketing and no overt attempts to woo journalists, Kiehl's has garnered an untold amount of favorable press, mostly the result of unsolicited testimonials from New York's celebrity makeup artists and hairdressers. Kiehl's is also known for the amount of time its staff is willing to lavish upon individual customers, as well as its eagerness to give out free samples. Although quite expensive, Kiehl's products are simply packaged, another enduring tradition of the business rather than a current affectation of minimalism. Long before its present-day rivals, Kiehl's was producing its several hundred natural products without the use of animal testing and applying such idiosyncratic names as Tea Tree Oil Body Cleanser, Pineapple Papaya Facial Scrub, and French Rosewater Facial Toner. Under L'Oréal, Kiehl's has opened a second store in San Francisco and is planning for future openings in other major markets.

Kiehl's Since 1851

Many years before the Morse family created a line of hair and skin care products, its East Village location was home to John Kiehl. In 1851 he established a small neighborhood apothecary, yesteryear's version of a drugstore where common compounds as well as more exotic nostrums were prepared onsite. Kiehl sold virility creams, baldness cures, and even a product called Money Drawing Oil. The Morse family connection to Kiehl's began in the years before World War I, when a Russian Jewish family named Moskovitz immigrated to the United States and adopted the surname Morse. A young son named Irving then found work as an apprentice at Kiehl's. He would serve in the U.S. Army during World War I and earn a pharmacology degree from Columbia University. In 1921 he bought Kiehl's, transforming it into a modern, full-scale pharmacy while also adding homeopathic cures and herbal remedies from the old country.

In 1923 a son named Aaron Morse was born. He would also study pharmacology at the Columbia School of Pharmacy, leaving early to join the army as a pilot during World War II. Following the war and the completion of his degree, he started a Hoboken, New Jersey business, Morse Laboratories Inc., to produce a fluoride therapy product called Ostrocal; later in the decade he began making antibiotics. During the 1950s he became active in helping his father run Kiehl's and by 1961, the same year his daughter Jami was born, he decided to concentrate on Kiehl's and took over control of the family business. In 1964 he sold Morse Laboratories, which was moved to Paterson, New Jersey, and renamed Biocraft Laboratories.

Kiehl's soon took on the personality of Aaron Morse. During the 1960s he phased out the pharmacy and the homeopathic products, turning his attention instead to developing and selling the natural care products that would make Kiehl's famous. In 1964 he introduced the company's popular acne-fighting Blue Astringent, and in 1969 Musk Oil. A wide array of products were formulated, then mixed by hand and packaged on the premises. Aaron Morse eschewed fancy and expensive packaging, favoring generic containers, to which he affixed simple handwritten labels, crammed with as much information as possible. He assigned imaginative names to his products, such as Castille Grapefruit Bath and Shower Soapy Liquid Cleanser.

Company Perspectives:

We at Kiehl's are committed to upholding the standards that our founding family originally initiated and that have been espoused and preserved over the years. The fundamental philosophies, product standards and core values that have always distinguished Kiehl's remain unchanged: Science, Education, Giving, Service, Respect, and Quality.

It was Aaron Morse who created the Kiehl's policy of giving out large amounts of free samples. It was less of a business policy than it was a reflection of the man. He was simply more interested in making a friend than a sale, in pursuing a personal ethic than a profit. Years before corporations made a point of instituting "visions and values" programs and formulating mission statements, Aaron Morse took time to produce "The Mission of Kiehl," writing: "A worthwhile firm must have a purpose for its existence. Not only the everyday work-a-day purpose to earn a just profit, but beyond that, to improve in some way the quality of the community to which it is committed. Each firm—as should each person—contributes to those around it; and by dint of its day-to-day efforts, the message it thereby imparts is a revelation of the quality standard at which its life's work is conducted."

In 1983 Aaron Morse told *Women's Wear Daily,* "Beauty, quality, health and education are what Kiehl's is about." In addition to being idealistic, Aaron Morse was endearingly eccentric. He believed that his customers should be influenced by a visit to Kiehl's, which allowed him an opportunity to educate by sharing his enthusiasm for pet interests. He provided a small library with books that included a copy of *Gray's Anatomy* (and kept a skeleton handy for ready reference) as well as a book on World War II bombers. He expanded the store in order to create a makeshift museum where, among other objects, he would display part of his motorcycle and car collection. He brought in a xylophone and timpani, for use by himself as well as customers. He might have the public address system play an opera or Ella Fitzgerald or patriotic music. His staunch patriotism was evident in the large number of American flags spread throughout the store, which was also decorated with the old-fashioned apothecary bottles of his essential oil collection, photographs of airplanes and Olympic skiers, and other knick-knacks, all of which aroused the curiosity of customers and provided an opening for Aaron Morse to engage in conversation. He claimed to be an expert on any number of subjects, and was equally eager to discuss the workings of the human body as he was the engine of a car. Kiehl's exotic furnishings, especially its cars and planes, had the added benefit of keeping men amused while women shopped. Aaron Morse also branched into unisex products, adding items for men. As with his store's hodgepodge décor, he was less ahead of his time than he was simply true to his own personality. Even as Kiehl's began to gain a reputation for being cool during the antiwar 1960s, he continued to play his martial music and lead his employees waving American flags on impromptu parades through the East Village. According to a *New York Times* profile, "few will forget the Veterans Day that he turned off the music ... and started reading the Emma Lazarus poem inscribed on the bottom of the Statue of Liberty ('Give me your tired, your poor, your huddled masses ...') in front of incredulous customers." Indeed, his behavior sometimes bordered on the bizarre: during one phase his constant companion was a chimp.

First Department Store Account: Nieman Marcus, 1975

Aaron Morse was simply not interested in growing Kiehl's as large as possible, valuing instead the ties between his products and his customers. For years he declined offers to sell to major department stores, finally relenting in 1975 when Nieman Marcus in Beverly Hills became the first account. Even then, it was more personal than business, the result of his playing tennis with the department store's chief executive. Another department store account, New York's upscale Barney's, was due to his friendship with owner Barney Pressman.

After his father died in 1980 and he was later diagnosed with cancer, Aaron Morse convinced his daughter Jami, his only child, to begin the process of taking over the business. Jami's parents had separated before she was born, but because her elementary school was close to Kiehl's she often stopped by on her way home and became fascinated with the operation. At the age of 11 she moved to Los Angeles with her mother, and later attended Harvard University before dropping out. Like her father she was an avid skier, and combined that interest with teaching exercise to become a trainer for racecar drivers and the Austrian ski team, ultimately marrying one of the racers, Klaus Heidegger. She was living in Austria in 1985 when her father convinced her to return to New York and help run the business.

While Jami and her father were in agreement on many aspects of Kiehl's, she found it difficult to make changes. Recalling the early years in an interview with the *Los Angeles Times,* she said, "Coming into it, I didn't imagine that it would be as challenging as it was. It was hard to get my decisions accepted and respected. I wanted to make a brochure of all the products. My father thought it was a waste of money. Any little decision like that could become a power struggle. We're screamers, and we used to have notorious shouting sessions." She eventually produced the brochure as well as a quarterly newsletter. She also started a mail-order business and began to supply select foreign accounts. She even hired a public relations expert, but the $1 million marketing budget was essentially limited to samples, which were gaining additional distribution in charity gift bags, a practice in keeping with her father's commitment to giving back to the community. In 1987 Klaus Heidegger retired from competitive skiing and joined his wife in New York to help run Kiehl's. As Aaron Morse's health continued to deteriorate, the couple took over complete control in 1988.

Klaus was instrumental in computerizing the mail-order business and essentially modernizing the company. Products were no longer produced onsite, and although manufacturing was moved to a facility in Hackensack, New Jersey, products continued to be mixed by hand in the traditional way, albeit in larger quantities. Even lipstick, Kiehl's only cosmetic, was hand poured and flamed. Jami expanded the company's mail-order business and added department store accounts: Bergdorf Goodman, Saks Fifth Avenue, as well as Harvey Nichols in England. She did not have to solicit these accounts and, in fact, turned down a number of opportunities. Despite her fights with her father over expansion, she very much shared his vision for Kiehl's. She was perhaps even more adamant about giving away samples, going so far as to periodically check on Kiehl's department store accounts to make sure that sales personnel were giving away enough products and spending enough time with customers. She retained the simple packaging and the East Village storefront, devoting individual attention to customers in much the same way her father had. Six feet tall with long dark hair, and often wearing ankle weights to work in order to stay in shape, she developed her own reputation for eccentricity. Like her father she relied on instinct over formal business planning, and believed in personal attention to detail. She wrote all of the company newsletters and dealt with every piece of mail.

Jami Morse, despite lacking the training of her father and grandfather, was also very much involved in product development, often drawing on her family life to find inspiration. With the birth of her first child, Nicoletta, she began to develop baby products for personal use. Her pediatrician was so impressed with her diaper rash cream that it led to requests from his patients and resulted in a Kiehl's line of baby products, introduced in 1991. By the end of the decade major cosmetic companies would begin to realize the potential for upscale baby care products. Jami and her husband's interest in sports also led to a line of shampoos, muscle rubs, and skin protectors for athletes. As Nicoletta grew older and took up horseback riding, Kiehl's even developed some equine products.

After Nicoletta's birth, Jami and Klaus moved to Los Angeles in order to raise their family in the same outdoor lifestyle that Jami cherished as a child. They continued to run Kiehl's despite the need for one or the other to fly back to New York in order to address even the smallest issues. Nevertheless, the company thrived, with earnings improving at a steady rate and products spreading to exclusive hair salons and department stores throughout the world. While little had really changed with the Kiehl's approach to business, the rest of the world seemed to catch up to it in the 1990s. The East Village location was more in vogue than ever. The unusual interior of the store, the natural products, the lack of advertising, even the refusal to cater to the beauty press, made Kiehl's all but irresistible to the trendy set. While its popularity grew by word of mouth, Kiehl's gained further recognition from a broad range of celebrities—

models, actresses, singers, and stylists—who influenced the press from around the world to write glowingly about the company. The exclusivity and mystique of Kiehl's was a marketer's dream. For Jami Morse and Klaus Heidegger, however, it would begin to seem like a nightmare.

During the holiday season of 1999 Kiehl's received a great deal of press attention, resulting in an overwhelming demand for its products. The mail-order division had particular trouble in dealing with the increased volume and Kiehl's, which prided itself on the personal touch, now found itself unable to ship its products in a timely fashion or even to match the right note cards with the right recipients. Moreover, new products that were due to be introduced simply could not find room on the factory's production schedule. Jami and Klaus had already discussed the possibility of cutting back, but now discovered that they could not terminate department store contracts, nor could they control the demand for their products. Jami had wanted to pass the business onto her daughter as it had been passed on to her, but now she came to the conclusion that Kiehl's could not survive in its present condition. The business either had to grow to the next level or it would simply begin to fall apart under the weight of demand, and the relationship with customers that set it apart from competitors would soon erode. Logistical resources, far more so than money, would resolve the mounting problems with Kiehl's.

L'Oréal's Purchase of Kiehl's: 2000

For years, a number of large companies coveted Kiehl's, but all offers were rejected. In February 2000, Jami Morse approached Philip Shearer, president of Cosmair Inc., the U.S. luxury products subsidiary of L'Oréal. While its competitors were acquiring a number of other specialty companies, Cosmair targeted just one, Kiehl's, and quietly wooed Jami Morse for over two years before she called. According to a *Fortune* interview, she said that Shearer "seemed to be genuinely interested in Kiehl's. He knew what we were doing; he'd read my newsletters; he knew the ingredients in particular products. I thought he understood who I was and what I was trying to do with Kiehl's."

The reported purchase price for Kiehl's ranged from $80 million to $150 million. No matter how much L'Oréal paid, however, it insisted that it would allow Kiehl's to conduct business as it always had, with the clear intent of reassuring customers, many of whom expressed concern about the future of the company. Jami Morse and Klaus Heidegger were retained as co-presidents of Kiehl's, and Michele Taylor, a marketing executive from Lancôme, a L'Oréal make-up and skin care products company, was hired to serve as general manager. At the end of January 2001, Taylor took over as president after Jami Morse and her husband resigned, although they remained as advisors. Satisfied that a transition to new ownership was accomplished, Jami Morse now expressed a desire to step away from day-to-day involvement with Kiehl's in order spend more time with her husband and children.

Under Taylor's leadership, Kiehl's functioned much the same as before. Taylor even took over the desk used by Irving and Aaron Morse in order to derive inspiration. Most of the changes involved the beefing up of the company's infrastructure, which allowed Kiehl's to not only meet demand but to enable the introduction of products that Jami Morse had been unable to launch. Taylor did look to expand into cosmetics, but in a cautious manner, likely focusing on items with skin care benefits. Kiehl's flagship store in Manhattan, however, appeared sacrosanct. Not only did L'Oréal intend to maintain the store in its current condition, it pledged not to reproduce it as the company began to open new outlets around the world. Many years earlier, Jami Morse and her father had discussed the opening of another store in Los Angeles. In 2001 a second Kiehl's location opened in San Francisco, housed in a Victorian townhouse that management felt was in keeping with the Kiehl's sensibility. Other store openings followed, including the company's first L.A. area store, in Santa Monica, in August 2002. Clearly, the Kiehl's mystique was a very valuable property for L'Oréal, and the parent company appeared very much committed to maintaining it.

Principal Competitors

Estée Lauder Inc.; Revlon Inc.; Shiseido Company, Limited.

Further Reading

Chaplin, Heather, "Selling Out," *Fortune Small Business,* July-August 2000, p. 97.

Hawn, Carleen, "A Company with Attitude," *Forbes,* October 7, 1996, p. 73.

Hays, Constance L., "Kiehl's Cosmetics Company Bought by France's L'Oréal," *New York Times,* April 18, 2000, p. C2.

Robins, Cynthia, "Selling the Family Secret: Founder's Granddaughter Guides Kiehl's into New Era," *San Francisco Chronicle,* July 29, 2001, p. B10.

Sexton, Norma, "A Unique Morse's Code at Kiehl's," *Women's Wear Daily,* July 29, 1983, p. C12.

Stout, Hillary, "Ad Budget Zero; Buzz Deafening," *Wall Street Journal,* December 29, 1999, p. B1.

Williams, Monte, "Farewell to the Man Behind Kiehl's," *New York Times,* May 7, 1995, p. CY8.

Witchel, Alex, "New Owners Let Kiehl's Be Kiehl's," *New York Times,* August 12, 2001, p. 6.

—Ed Dinger

KOMATSU

Komatsu Ltd.

2-3-6, Akasaka
Minato-ku
Tokyo 107-8414
Japan
Telephone: (03) 5561-2687
Fax: (03) 3505-9662
Web site: http://www.komatsu.com

Public Company
Incorporated: 1921
Employees: 30,760
Sales: ¥1.04 trillion ($7.79 billion) (2002)
Stock Exchanges: Tokyo Osaka Nagoya Sapporo
    Fukuoka Luxembourg Frankfurt
Ticker Symbol: KMTUY
NAIC: 333120 Construction Machinery Manufacturing;
    333131 Mining Machinery and Equipment
    Manufacturing; 334413 Semiconductor and Related
    Device Manufacturing

Komatsu Ltd. is the world's second largest manufacturer of construction and mining equipment, after Caterpillar Inc. More than 70 percent of the company's revenues are generated from the sale of construction and mining equipment, including bulldozers, dump trucks, hydraulic excavators, mobile debris crushers, motor graders, rough-terrain cranes, tunnel-boring machines, and wheel loaders. Komatsu also has a major division devoted to the production of electronics. This business, responsible for about 7 percent of revenues, is involved in the production of electronic materials, including silicon wafers and polycrystalline silicon, both of which are used to make semiconductors; semiconductor manufacturing equipment; factory and office automation equipment; and local area network–related peripheral equipment. Komatsu divisions produce a wide variety of other products, including metal forging and stamping presses, sheet metal machinery, machine tools, forklift trucks, armored personnel carriers and other defense equipment, recycling plants, prefabricated office structures, and outdoor power equipment.

Although its main manufacturing operations are in Japan, Komatsu owns production plants and sales and service units in other countries, mainly the United States, Canada, Mexico, Brazil, the United Kingdom, Germany, Italy, Indonesia, China, Thailand, India, and Taiwan. Komatsu is involved in a number of joint ventures with various domestic and foreign partners, including Cummins Inc. of the United States, Bangkok Motor Works Co., Ltd. of Thailand, Larsen & Toubro Ltd. of India, and Ushio Inc. of Japan. About 54 percent of the company's net sales are generated outside of Japan, with 25 percent stemming from North and South America, about 12 percent each from Europe and from Asia (excluding Japan) and Oceania, and 4 percent from the Middle East and Africa.

19th-Century Origins

Komatsu had its origins in 1894 when the Takeuchi Mining Company was founded. A major expansion occurred in 1917, during World War I, when the Komatsu ironworks was established to manufacture mining equipment and machine tools to expand the mining operations. The name Komatsu came into existence in 1921 when the ironworks separated from the mining company to become Komatsu Ltd. Tashiro Shiraishi, an engineer, was the founder and first president, serving until 1925. In the 1920s and 1930s the firm grew as a major manufacturer of machine tools and pumps, including development of a metal press in 1924 and the firm's first farm tractor in 1931. Production of steel materials began in 1935.

By 1929 the number of employees had risen to 742, from its original 1921 workforce of 121 employees, but during the depth of the Great Depression in 1933 it dropped to 505 workers. The firm soon increased production and by 1936 increased its staff to 601. Mitsugi Nakemura served as president during the depression and war years, from 1934 to 1946.

During World War II the firm expanded by supplying the navy with antiaircraft artillery shells and bulldozers. Komatsu's first major product after the war was a redesigned bulldozer, which came off the assembly line in 1947. One year later diesel engines were produced. From 1947 to 1964 President Yoshinari Kawai provided key leadership in rebuilding the company and making it a global multinational corporation.

Company Perspectives:

The mission of our business, centering on construction, mining and utility (compact) equipment, is to contribute to the prosperity of our customers through safe, innovative products and services and globalized operations while working to ensure the stable growth of the Komatsu Group by establishing a solid position in each market. We are working to become an international leader in the quality and reliability of our products produced around the world, the quality and speed of customer support, and safety and environment concerns.

The Korean War gave the Japanese economy a boost with orders from the United States to supply its troops in Korea. At that time the firm had plants in Awazu, Osaka, Kaweasaki, Himi, and Komatsu, Japan. Forklift trucks, dump trucks, and armored cars were added to the line in 1953, with shell mold castings introduced the following year. By 1959 defense production included armored personnel carriers and self-propelled cannons.

International activities increased in 1955 when both construction equipment and presses were shipped outside the country. In 1958 operations began in India with an agreement between the firm and the Indian government to manufacture tractors. Three years later, another license agreement was signed with a U.S. manufacturer, Cummins Engine Company, to make and sell diesel engines.

1960s: Sights on Caterpillar

By the early 1960s the firm had grown to the point where a new headquarters was needed, and the Komatsu Building was constructed in Tokyo. In 1964 the firm received the Deming Prize for quality, named after William Edwards Deming, the American quality guru whose writings on quality control between 1950 and 1952 became the bible of Japanese manufacturing.

Ryoichi Kawai became president in 1964. The 1960s saw an economic buildup for Japan as a result of the Vietnam War, and Komatsu's expansion continued at a rapid pace. In the latter part of the decade a new engine plant began production in Japan, a radio-controlled bulldozer was introduced, and a technical research center was established. In 1967 the company established its first overseas subsidiary, N.V. Komatsu Europe S.A., which was based in Belgium. President Kawai articulated the company's goal was to "surpass Caterpillar." Each year, Kawai presented his managers with a clear set of priorities modeled after Caterpillar's performance. The yearly priorities were then worked into detailed plans of action, known as Plan, Do, Check, Act (PDCA). Kawai's growth strategy was clearly successful. Over the next 20 years, Komatsu grew from a small local manufacturer to a serious competitor in the global construction market. As a result, Komatsu's management style became widely studied and emulated.

Global Expansion: 1970s–80s

In 1970 the firm began its first direct investment in the United States, with the establishment of Komatsu America Cor-

poration. Other foreign operations soon followed, in Singapore, Australia, Mexico, Brazil, and China. Komatsu began producing bulldozers in Brazil in 1975, marking the company's first production of construction equipment outside of Japan.

In 1981 Komatsu was awarded the Japan Quality Control Prize, to honor the company's outstanding production quality. The following year Shoji Nogawa became president. The 1980s brought expansion of global operations. In 1985, after a number of incentives from the state of Tennessee, Komatsu purchased a 55-acre empty plant in Chattanooga, a purchase that reflected a decision by the firm to challenge its principal rival, Caterpillar, in its home market. This move gained Komatsu its first U.S. manufacturing facility. Canadian operations expanded as well, as two plants were built in Quebec and Ontario. European operations included an interest in the West German construction firm of Hamomag AG, a licensing agreement with FAI S.p.A. of Italy, and a plant in the United Kingdom.

The year 1987 marked expansion in other areas, such as the establishment of two financial subsidiaries in Europe, the marketing of plastics injection molding machinery, and the development of a telephone with a data terminal. At the same time, the construction market was changing, and Komatsu's sales began to slump. From 1985 to 1987, construction equipment sales dropped each year. As a result, the company president, Shoji Nogawa, was dismissed by Chairman Ryoichi Kawai, and changes were instituted. In 1988 an international business division was set up in the Tokyo headquarters. The division had three regional groups that were the main focus of the firm's international business operations: the Americas, Europe, and Japan. The goals of the division included development of joint ventures around the world and overseas purchase of parts.

In 1988 the company established a new subsidiary, Komatsu Trading International, to increase imports to Japan, in response to the Japanese government's commitment to reduce its trade surplus by importing more foreign products. As a result, logging machinery from Canada, backhoe loaders from Italy, and high-powered motor boats from Norway were brought into Japan for sale in the domestic market under importer agreements between Komatsu and companies in the respective countries.

Also in 1988, Komatsu sharpened its competitive edge in the U.S. market by forming a joint venture with Dresser Industries, Inc., Komatsu Dresser Company. Included within the venture were Komatsu's two U.S. subsidiaries and Dresser's construction machinery division, thereby forming the second largest maker of construction machinery in the United States. The combination enabled Komatsu to move assembly of its construction equipment to the United States, using Dresser plants that were running at 50 percent capacity while Komatsu was unable to fill all of its orders.

New Targets: Early to Mid–1990s

A new president, Tetsuya Katada, took over in 1989. Katada decided that Komatsu's management had been hampered to some extent by the company's goal of catching Caterpillar. Whereas this strategy had worked remarkably well in expanding the company while the global market was growing, now that worldwide demand for construction equipment was down,

Key Dates:

1894: The Takeuchi Mining Company is founded.

1917: The company creates the Komatsu ironworks to manufacture mining equipment and machine tools.

1921: The ironworks are separated from the mining company to form Komatsu Ltd.

World War II: The company supplies the Japanese navy with antiaircraft artillery shells and bulldozers.

1947: Komatsu begins manufacturing a redesigned bulldozer, marking the expansion into construction equipment.

1953: Production of forklift trucks and dump trucks begins.

1955: The company begins shipping construction equipment and presses outside Japan.

1961: A joint venture to make and sell diesel engines is created with Cummins Engine Company of the United States.

1964: Komatsu is awarded the Deming Prize for quality.

1967: The first overseas subsidiary, Komatsu Europe, is established in Belgium.

1970: The first U.S. subsidiary, Komatsu America Corporation, is created.

1975: The first production of construction equipment outside of Japan begins, at a plant in Brazil.

1985: U.S. manufacturing activities begin with the purchase of a plant in Tennessee.

1988: Komatsu and Dresser Industries, Inc. form Komatsu Dresser Company, a U.S.-based construction equipment joint venture.

1994: Komatsu purchases full control of Komatsu Dresser.

1996: Komatsu Dresser is renamed Komatsu America International Company.

1997: Expansion into mining equipment leads to the establishment of Komatsu Mining Systems, Inc. as the global mining equipment headquarters.

1999: Komatsu reports a net loss for the fiscal year—its first ever.

Komatsu did not have the flexibility to adapt. Katada believed that the creativity of Komatsu's middle managers had been sacrificed while everyone was concentrating on Caterpillar, and that managers had grown afraid to question the direction of the company. Katada's solution was to stop comparing Komatsu to Caterpillar. He encouraged managers to think of Komatsu as a "total technology enterprise," and to find new products and markets that fit the wider definition of the company. Komatsu's new goal became the somewhat broader "Growth, Global, Groupwide," with a more concrete aim to double sales by the mid-1990s.

Katada's success became clear quickly. Sales had been declining since 1982, but after Katada initiated the new business strategy, sales began to climb again. Komatsu's nonconstruction business grew by 40 percent between 1989 and 1992. Nevertheless, the Komatsu Dresser Company lost money, because of deteriorating markets for heavy equipment and problems with the merger. The Dresser and Komatsu product lines were to remain distinct under the merged company, but this resulted in dealers within the company directly competing with each other. Dresser managers also reported problems communicating with their Komatsu counterparts. This was to some extent remedied when Komatsu began bringing its American employees to Japan to learn more about Japanese culture and work. Steep appreciation of the Japanese yen also ate into Komatsu's profits. In 1993 Komatsu introduced cost-cutting measures, including some cuts in its workforce and streamlining of its manufacturing facilities in Japan.

The firm had shown a quick response to the 1992 integration of Europe by the European Common Market. British operations included purchase agreements with the British firm of Perkins Engines Ltd. for diesel engines to power Komatsu excavators. The U.K. plant in Birtley was the main production facility for European construction equipment. Other parts came from Spain, France, Belgium, and Germany. An additional agreement with the Italian firm of FAI to manufacture under license mini-hydraulic excavators added to a strong European presence. Komatsu also began expanding its production of large trucks in the United States and Brazil in 1993, and increased its imports of parts from Brazil, South Korea, Indonesia, and China.

Komatsu also continued its longstanding relationship with Cummins Engine Company. In 1993 the companies formed two joint ventures to manufacture and sell diesel engines. A Japan-based unit was created to make Cummins' small engines, and a unit based in the United States was formed to produce Komatsu's large engines.

There were a number of ownership changes that affected the Komatsu Dresser venture in the early to mid-1990s. In August 1992 Dresser Industries spun off its industrial businesses, including its 50 percent stake in Komatsu Dresser, to its shareholders, forming Indresco, Inc. Then in September 1993 Komatsu increased its stake in the venture to 81 percent by buying out part of Indresco's interest. Finally, in 1994 Komatsu purchased Indresco's remaining stake, taking full control of Komatsu Dresser. In January 1996 the U.S. subsidiary was renamed Komatsu America International Company.

A key to Komatsu's continued growth was its diversification into new markets, including nonconstruction businesses. Electronics became Komatsu's second most important business area. To increase its presence in this area, Komatsu made a strategic alliance with Applied Materials, Inc., a U.S. manufacturer of computer display panels, in 1993. Komatsu invested tens of millions of dollars in a 50 percent share of a new joint venture with the U.S. company. By 1995 the venture, called Applied Komatsu Technology Inc., had become a competitive force in the Japanese market for computer liquid crystal displays. Meanwhile, in 1994 Komatsu expanded into the local area network (LAN) equipment market by beginning production of two types of hubs and a print server.

Komatsu also began to focus more on business ventures related to recycling. In 1994 the company began a joint venture with Japan Samtech Co. Ltd., a leading Japanese maker of incinerators. In 1995 Komatsu entered an agreement with a leading plastics recycler in the United States, Pure Tech International, to begin building and marketing recycling plants in Japan. Komatsu also continued to press for an expansion of its core construction business worldwide in the mid-1990s. Construction in Komatsu's domestic market boomed in 1995 and 1996, sadly because of the massive Kobe earthquake in January 1995. Around the world, Komatsu had 15 plants in ten countries outside Japan as of 1995, and the company entered new joint ventures in Thailand, Vietnam, and China in that year. In June 1995 Satoru Anzaki became the new president of Komatsu, and former president Kataka became chairman.

From fiscal 1995 to fiscal 1998 Komatsu enjoyed four consecutive years of increasing net profit and sales. The company was aided by the booming U.S. economy and a surge in spending on infrastructure projects in the burgeoning market of east Asia. This period was highlighted by a continued drive into new markets and the formation of several more joint ventures.

In January 1996 Komatsu joined with Mannesmann Demag AG to form the German venture Demag Komatsu GmbH, which was charged with developing and producing super-large hydraulic excavators for the global mining industry. Komatsu had already entered the mining market through its former joint venture with Dresser, which brought to the company the Haulpak line of mining trucks. Further involvement in this sector came through the March 1996 acquisition of controlling interest in Modular Mining Systems, Inc., maker of electronic mine management systems. Then in April 1997 Komatsu created Vernon Hills, Illinois–based Komatsu Mining Systems, Inc. as the international headquarters for its rapidly growing mining equipment business. Also created in 1997 and also based in Vernon Hills was Komatsu Utility Corporation, which took over the manufacturing of backhoe loaders, compact excavators, compact wheel loaders, and compact bulldozers and the marketing of these products to the utility, construction, and rental markets.

The desire to capture a greater share of the increasing market for construction machinery in southeast Asia led Komatsu in mid-1996 to create Komatsu Asia & Pacific Pte. Ltd. in Singapore to coordinate and expand its operations in the region. That year the company also began manufacturing construction equipment in Thailand, giving it two production bases in Asia, the other being in Indonesia. In early 1998 Komatsu joined with Larsen & Toubro Ltd. of India to form Bangalore-based L&T-Komatsu Limited, which would make Komatsu hydraulic excavators and sell them in India and bordering countries. Around this same time, Cummins Engine and Komatsu formed a third joint venture, a Japan-based firm called Industrial Power Alliance, Ltd. This venture was an extension of the previous ones and was formed to research and develop next-generation industrial diesel engines. (Cummins Engine shortened its name to Cummins Inc. in 2001.)

Late 1990s and Beyond: Declining Fortunes and Restructuring Efforts

The late 1990s and early 2000s brought a sharp decline in Komatsu's fortunes. One factor was fallout from the Asian economic crisis that erupted in mid-1997 and that brought a halt to the rapid growth in southeast Asia. At the same time, the already struggling Japanese economy went into its steepest postwar recession, prompting Komatsu customers to slash their orders for construction equipment. In addition, Komatsu's electronics business was hit hard by the deterioration in the price of and the demand for silicon wafers. Record results from the still buoyant U.S. and European economies were not enough to keep Komatsu from falling into the red for the fiscal year ending in March 1999—the first full-year loss in the company's history. Net sales declined that year by 3.8 percent.

Komatsu responded by launching a restructuring of its domestic construction equipment manufacturing operations in November 1998. Three factories were closed over the course of the next two years, resulting in a 20 percent reduction in production floor space. Komatsu also halted production at its semiconductor plant in Hillsboro, Oregon, announcing that it would concentrate its production in Japan and Taiwan. In a further pullback in its electronics business, Komatsu in November 1999 sold its stake in Applied Komatsu Technology, the flat panel display joint venture, to its partner, Applied Materials. Komatsu also reorganized its management structure during 1999 by slashing the number of board members from 26 to 8 and appointing a person from outside the company to the board. These moves were designed to speed up the decision-making process and enhance the objectivity and transparency of management. Katada and Anzaki remained chairman and president, respectively.

Although Komatsu returned to profitability in fiscal 2000 and 2001, the recovery would prove short-lived. During these two years, the company established additional joint ventures. In February 2000 an agreement was reached with Linde AG of Germany on global collaboration in the production and marketing of forklift truck and related products. Komatsu joined with Ushio Inc. of Japan in August 2000 to form a joint venture called Gigaphoton Inc. to develop, manufacture, and sell excimer lasers used as lithography tools in the production of semiconductors. In December 2000 Komatsu acquired Hensley Industries, Inc., a U.S. maker of construction and mining equipment components.

Also in 2000, Anzaki hired Keith Sheldon, a retired General Motors Corporation, for the new position of global financial officer. Sheldon's task was to overhaul Komatsu's system of financial management, prepare the company for an eventual listing on the New York Stock Exchange, and lay the foundation for revamping the company through takeovers and spin-offs of noncore operations. For a Japanese company to hire a foreigner for such a high-level position was quite bold, and it was indicative of Anzaki's desire to transform Komatsu into a more American- or European-style company. In a similar vein, Anzaki a few years earlier had begun trying to boost the company's return on equity in clear imitation of U.S. and European multinationals. And during fiscal 2001 Komatsu announced that it planned to introduce a stock option scheme for 47 top employees. In June 2001 Masahiro Sakane, an executive vice-president, was appointed president, succeeding Anzaki, who became chairman.

Construction machinery orders in Japan declined precipitously in fiscal 2002 as the government greatly reduced its spending on public works projects. Demand also was falling in the now struggling U.S. and European economies. The main bright spot was China, which continued to grow. Komatsu was hit further by a drastic decline in the semiconductor market. Revenues for the year declined 5.5 percent, and the company fell back into the red, posting a net loss of ¥80.6 billion ($606 million).

Responding to this dismal performance, Komatsu announced a major restructuring in October 2001. Aiming to reduce annual fixed costs by ¥30 billion ($250 million) by 2004, the company said it would reduce its workforce by 2,200 workers, or about 10 percent. Komatsu also took a ¥26 billion write-off to shut down its Oregon semiconductor plant. In an attempt to reignite sales growth in its core construction machinery operations, the company said it would attempt to capture a larger share of the rental equipment, used equipment, and machinery repair markets. Further restructuring efforts came in 2002. The firm's U.S. construction, mining, and utility operations were merged within the Komatsu America Corp. subsidiary; included were Komatsu America International, Komatsu Mining Systems, and Komatsu Utility. The move was intended to cut costs and improve efficiency. It was clear that Komatsu was taking aggressive action in an attempt to spark a turnaround.

Principal Subsidiaries

Komatsu Zenoah Co.; Komatsu Hokkaido Ltd.; Komatsu Aomori Ltd. (98.1%); Komatsu Miyagi Ltd.; Komatsu Niigata Ltd. (70%); Komatsu Tokyo Ltd.; Komatsu Tokai Ltd.; Komatsu Gifu Ltd. (70%); Komatsu Kinki Ltd.; Komatsu Kyoto Co., Ltd.; Komatsu Minami Kinki Ltd.; Komatsu Nara Ltd.; Komatsu Hyogo Ltd. (89.7%); Komatsu Kagawa Ltd.; Komatsu Okayama Ltd.; Komatsu Hiroshima Ltd.; Komatsu Yamaguchi Ltd.; Komatsu Oita Ltd.; Komatsu Nishi Nihon Ltd.; Komatsu Kagoshima Ltd. (91.9%); Komatsu Okinawa Ltd.; Komatsu Parts Ltd.; Komatsu Used Equipment Corp.; Komatsu Trading, Inc.; Komatsu Diesel Co., Ltd.; Komatsu Safety Training Center Ltd.; Komatsu Castex Ltd.; Komatsu Metal Ltd.; Komatsu Electronic Metals Co., Ltd. (63.2%); Komatsu Semiconductors Corporation; Komatsu Electronics, Inc.; Komatsu Forklift Co., Ltd.; Komatsu House Co., Ltd. (88.5%); Komatsu Building Co., Ltd.; Komatsu Industries Corporation; Komatsu Machinery Corporation; Komatsu Artec Ltd.; Komatsu General Services Ltd.; Komatsu Business Support Ltd.; Komatsu Engineering Corp.; Komatsu Information Providing Ltd.; Komatsu Logistics Corp. (97.1%); Komatsu America Corp. (U.S.A.); Komatsu America International Company (U.S.A.); Komatsu Mining Systems, Inc. (U.S.A.); Komatsu Latin-America Corp. (U.S.A.); Komatsu Reman North America, Inc. (U.S.A.); Modular Mining Systems, Inc. (U.S.A.; 66.1%); Hensley Industries, Inc. (U.S.A.); Komatsu Cummins Chile Ltda. (81.8%); Komatsu do Brasil Ltda. (Brazil); Komatsu Mexicana S.A. de C.V. (Mexico); Komatsu Europe International N.V. (Belgium); Komatsu Mining Germany GmbH; Komatsu UK Ltd.; Komatsu Hanomag AG (Germany; 98.4%); Komatsu Utility Europe S.p.A. (Italy); Komatsu France S.A.; Komatsu Europe Coordination Center N.V. (Belgium); Komatsu Southern Africa (Pty) Ltd. (South Africa; 80%); Komatsu Asia & Pacific Pte. Ltd. (Singapore); PT Komatsu Indonesia Tbk (55.1%); Bangkok Komatsu Co., Ltd. (Thailand; 74.8%); Komatsu (Changzhou) Construction Machinery Corp. (China; 85%); Komatsu (Changzhou) Foundry Corp. (China; 95%); Komatsu (China) Ltd.; Komatsu (Shanghai) Ltd. (China); Komatsu Australia Holdings Pty. Ltd.; Komatsu Australia Pty. Ltd. (60%); Komatsu Silicon America, Inc. (U.S.A.); Advanced Silicon Materials LLC (U.S.A.); Komatsu Silicon Europe N.V. (Belgium); Formosa Komatsu Silicon Corporation (Taiwan; 50.9%); Komatsu America Industries LLC (U.S.A.); Komatsu Finance America Inc. (U.S.A.); Komatsu Finance (Netherlands) B.V.

Principal Competitors

Caterpillar Inc.; CNH Global N.V.; Terex Corporation; Ingersoll-Rand Company Limited.

Further Reading

Flint, Jerry, "The Enemy of My Enemy," *Forbes,* November 14, 1988, pp. 42+.

Gabb, Annabella, "Komatsu Makes the Earth Move," *Management Today,* April 1988, pp. 77+.

Gross, Lisa, "Bargained Birthright?," *Forbes,* June 6, 1983, pp. 46+.

Kelley, Bill, "Komatsu in a Cat Fight: Komatsu's Taking the Fight for Dominance in the Construction Equipment Industry to Caterpillar's Own Back Yard," *Sales and Marketing Management,* April 1986, pp. 50+.

Kelly, Kevin, "A Dream Marriage Turns Nightmarish," *Business Week,* April 29, 1991, pp. 94–95.

Kelly, Kevin, Neil Gross, and Kathleen Deveny, "A Weakened Komatsu Tries to Come Back Swinging," *Business Week,* February 22, 1988, p. 48.

"Komatsu: Catching Caterpillar," *Economist,* August 14, 1982, pp. 54+.

"Komatsu Digs Deeper into the U.S.," *Business Week,* October 1, 1984, p. 53.

"Komatsu Plans to Trim Jobs in Revamping," *Wall Street Journal,* September 17, 1993, p. A7.

Krisher, Bernard, "Komatsu on the Track of a Cat," *Fortune,* April 20, 1981, pp. 164+.

Kruger, David, and Ichiko Fuyuno, "Komatsu Heads for the Trenches," *Far Eastern Economic Review,* November 22, 2001, pp. 58–61.

Marsh, Peter, "Digging for Ideas in the West," *Financial Times,* May 2, 2000, p. 14.

Pollack, Andrew, "Applied Materials Plans Venture with Komatsu," *New York Times,* June 18, 1993, p. D3.

Rahman, Bayan, "Komatsu Weighs Up the Situation," *Financial Times,* December 6, 2001, p. 3.

Tharp, Mike, "Komatsu Tries to Emulate Caterpillar," *New York Times,* November 29, 1980, p. 29.

Williams, Michael, and Douglas Appell, "Komatsu Hopes Overhaul Can Lift It Out of Slump," *Asian Wall Street Journal,* September 18, 2000, p. 13.

—Joseph A. LeMay
—updates: Angela Woodward, David E. Salamie

Lend Lease Corporation Limited

Level 46
Tower Building
Australia Square
Sydney NSW 2000
Australia
Telephone: (02) 9236-6111
Fax: (02) 9252-2192
Web site: http://www.lendlease.com.au

Public Company
Incorporated: 1958
Employees: 10,484
Operating Revenues: A$12.48 billion (US$6.87 billion)
   (2002)
Stock Exchanges: Australia
Ticker Symbol: LLC
NAIC: 233110 Land Subdivision and Land Development;
   233220 Multifamily Housing Construction; 233310
   Manufacturing and Industrial Building Construction;
   233320 Commercial and Institutional Building
   Construction; 522292 Real Estate Credit; 525930 Real
   Estate Investment Trusts; 525990 Other Financial
   Vehicles; 531120 Lessors of Nonresidential Buildings
   (Except Miniwarehouses)

Lend Lease Corporation Limited, one of Australia's top public companies, is a leading integrated global real estate group, with operations in 41 countries on six continents and a major presence in the Asia-Pacific region, the United States, Europe, and South America. From its inception the company has been an integrated property service, engaged in property development, management, and investment, as well as construction of residential, commercial, and industrial facilities (the latter conducted through a key subsidiary called Bovis Lend Lease); in more recent years, Lend Lease added funds management to its roster of services.

Post–World War II Foundations

In the late 1940s, Australia was basically a nation of sheep farmers. The country, with a population of 8.3 million, was undeveloped and maintained a colonial dependence upon Europe and other nations for many of the basic necessities of life, in exchange for wool. World War II showed the danger of such an existence, and the nation was very much in favor of developing its own natural resources and skills.

Australia's dry climate made a source for a plentiful supply of water necessary to the development of the nation. The solution lay in a project called the Snowy Mountains Scheme, which entailed the taming of a snow-fed alpine river by the interruption of its seaward course. The river would then be sent through 130 kilometers of tunnels through a mountain range and a system of holding reservoirs to join rivers on the other side, 900 meters below. This design, however, was beyond the resources of this relatively small nation. What became known as the Snowy Mountains Hydro-Electric Authority (SMHA) was the trigger that implemented Australia's most ambitious immigration program. A government mission traveled worldwide, recruiting tradesmen, engineers, and laborers.

In Amsterdam the call was answered by Bredero's Bouwbedrijf of Utrecht (Bredero's) and The Royal Dutch Harbour Company. In 1950 Bredero's sent a 30-year-old engineer, Gerard J. (Dick) Dusseldorp, to Australia on a fact-finding tour for the Dutch construction firm. What he discovered was a country ripe for development and about to enter a period of great growth and prosperity. His report convinced the two firms to embark on a joint venture. In 1951 they formed a company called Civil & Civic Contractors and put Dusseldorp in charge. Its first assignment was to supply and erect 200 prefabricated houses for the Snowy Mountains project. The 35 workers for the job were recruited in Holland by Dusseldorp and brought to Australia under the liberalized immigration laws.

Civil & Civic completed its first assignment within 15 months, but out of the SMHA came further jobs for the fledgling company. Bridges, houses, flats, and hospital extensions were added to the projects the company was to complete in the area of Cooma and

Canberra. As a result, a locally engaged workforce was soon growing around the nucleus of the original 35 Dutch workers.

At all times, however, G.J. Dusseldorp, who was by then Civil & Civic's managing director, was looking for a way to expand the company's operations. He focused on Sydney, Australia's largest city, which was about to experience the largest building boom in its history.

Evolution of a Full-Service Contractor in the 1950s

Dusseldorp, as a developer, was continually seeking a better way to do things, not only to boost company profits, but also to set standards of excellence within the industry. For him, the traditional system of tendering (or subcontracting) was, in his words, "a gushing stream of waste." When other firms were unreliable, the contractor had to shoulder the burden of their mistakes. He wanted to establish a system that was to remain the foundation of the company's philosophy—undivided responsibility for any project from start to finish.

Civil & Civic had a chance to try out the new system when a small project in Sydney in 1953 was presented to the company. Dusseldorp was determined to prove that there was a better way to handle a construction project. An oil refinery needed a gatehouse to be added to a new plant currently under construction. Civil & Civic designed and built it within six weeks. It was the firm's first design and construction project.

In 1954 Dusseldorp's chance had come to put Civil & Civic on the map by building Sydney's first concrete skyscraper. He was determined, however, to become the sole entrepreneur, thus ensuring complete control over the project. He wanted to take over the option, the council-approved plans, and the services of the architect and engineer. All that Dusseldorp now lacked was the money.

He approached Bredero's in Holland for a £100,000 loan, which he was refused, but the president of the Reconstruction Bank of Holland was present at Dusseldorp's presentation. He was impressed with Dusseldorp's style, determination, and confidence, and backed the loan.

When building work began Dusseldorp was faced with yet another problem besetting the construction industry—industrial action by the workers' unions. He therefore proposed to the unions an agreement that among other things would include a productivity bonus. Although viewed at first with skepticism, it proved a great success as building workers began to feel like valued employees.

Caltex House was finished months ahead of the original schedule and established Civil & Civic as a leading contractor. Now the company could sell itself as a new composite building service that operated in conjunction with leading architects and engineers. Such a service was designed to eliminate delays and reduce costs.

Creation of Lend Lease in the Late 1950s

Yet Dusseldorp was not satisfied. He was still searching for a better package to present to prospective buyers or leasers. During the building boom of the early 1960s there was a great need for new construction of all kinds. Many companies, as a result of their own success, were being forced to build larger premises. The buying of larger premises inevitably meant tying up capital that was needed for business operations. Dusseldorp concluded that what most businesses were looking for were premises that they could lease.

He also saw a need for cooperative projects that would bring together people with a common interest, such as doctors who needed professional consulting rooms. Such professionals would not be able to finance such projects independently. Dusseldorp had the solution.

He decided to float a finance and investment company and go to the Australian public for funds to finance Civil & Civic projects on completion, thus gaining entrepreneurial control over their projects. In April 1958, Lend Lease Corporation Limited was established and floated on the stock exchange with Civil & Civic holding 40 percent of the shares.

This original share issue was floated to finance the construction of a seven-story building containing professional consulting rooms. The deal was that North Shore Medical Centre Pty. Ltd., which owned the land, had the right to occupy or nominate the occupant of specified areas in the building. Lend Lease was to take up the whole of the issued capital of the company on completion of the building and would then sell the professional suites on term contracts over varying periods, while retaining part of the space in the building as an investment—in other words, lending and leasing.

It was not long before Lend Lease began to acquire its own sites, plan the development, and construct buildings in cooperation with Civil & Civic. They were set to provide and complete development of large-scale projects of real estate.

Both Civil & Civic and Lend Lease were out to gain prestige and publicity. They began to tender for projects that would put them in the public eye. Buildings such as the Academy of Science in Canberra would win them the Sulman prize for architecture. It was not until February 1959, however, that Lend Lease became a household name. It was at that time that the company contracted to build stage one of the Sydney Opera House.

Civil & Civic and Lend Lease were not ordinary construction outfits. The management of both organizations had an interest in urban planning and renewal. Plans for new building sites would always include open areas with fountains and plazas so that beauty as well as commerce might be enjoyed.

As the organization grew, it also had to change. Between 1959 and 1962 Lend Lease acquired its original sponsor, Civil & Civic, as well as six companies whose manufactured products were useful to its construction business. These companies supplied Lend Lease with elevators, windows, and building materials. The company also bought a ski resort and a motel chain. It

was set to change from the role of financier of other people's projects to that of developing and managing real capital assets for long-term property investors.

In June 1960 a subsidiary company was formed to take control of Lend Lease's joint operations with Civil & Civic. The parent company formulated policy and provided specialist advisory skills. It also developed new projects and raised the money to carry out these projects. The subsidiary, Lend Lease Development Pty. Ltd., selected and purchased the sites, dealt with the authorities, and managed the design and construction of the site, as well as the sale or lease of projects.

Lend Lease was now involved in a multitude of projects from commercial buildings to suburban housing to recreational sites. The group was expanded to include 14 operating companies. Their presence was virtually ubiquitous in Australia, especially in the cities of Sydney, Canberra, Melbourne, Launceston, Brisbane, and Perth.

In May 1968 one of Lend Lease's largest projects, Australia Square, was officially opened by the Duke of Edinburgh. It won the Sulman Award for Architectural Merit, as well as the Civic Design Award of the New South Wales chapter of the Royal Australian Institute of Architects for a work of outstanding design.

By 1971 property values in Australia were peaking. Dusseldorp could see that the bottom was soon going to drop out of the office development market and it was decided that Lend Lease would end its work in this field. It would instead turn its attention toward shopping centers. The shift in activities was not unusual for this corporation. The key to its success was its ability to keep its finger always on the pulse of change.

Lend Lease continued to retain a long-term interest in properties developed without long-term capital investment, and to be free of fluctuations in the property market through public subscription and independent property trusts. Lend Lease was the first developer to go public and to form in 1971 General Property Trust, a publicly owned real estate trust to hold its properties.

International Growth in the 1970s

On June 30, 1971, Dusseldorp's contract with Bredero's, which made him available as principal executive of the group, expired. Dusseldorp agreed to be retained until June 30, 1975, with a renewable clause thereafter. The new agreement allowed Dusseldorp to have interests outside Australia. Dusseldorp wanted to try his style of business in the United States. Through its subsidiary, U.S. Lend Lease, established in 1972, formed International Income Property (IIP).

Despite the multitude of activities in which Dusseldorp and his team were involved, he was nonetheless paving the way toward his own retirement by grooming his executives for future management. His contributions to the success of Lend Lease were considerable. Although he surrounded himself with a team of some of the best people in the business, there is no doubt that the inspiration for the projects, as well as the new ways of handling development and finance, all sprang from the mind of Dusseldorp. His aversion to borrowing kept the firm's debts below 50 percent of its total capital, a low figure compared with those of rival developers. Year after year, despite an adverse financial climate and lows in the property market, Lend Lease was to produce profits for its shareholders. The firm did not retain its own publicity department, but worked quietly and expertly at all its projects, so much so that it prompted the *Financial Times* to comment, "Unlike many prominent Australian companies, it [Lend Lease] attracts little publicity and even less adverse comment from analysts."

In 1971 Bredero's sold its shareholding in Lend Lease, and J. DeVries, a founding director of Lend Lease, retired from the board. W.M. Leavey, managing director of Lend Lease, replaced him. Stuart G. Hornery became managing director of Civil & Civic, with R.G. Robinson as chairman.

In 1978 Dusseldorp commented in the annual report, "In the conditions which have prevailed, to have obtained one million dollars worth of business every working day represented an extraordinary effort by everyone in the group." It was also the year in which employees became the largest shareholding block, holding 26 percent of the shares.

Lend Lease's success—during one of the greatest slumps in the property market—lay in its concentration on earnings and cash flow rather than ownership of assets. It acted as a service corporation. It also stuck to a policy of refusing to undertake construction unless an end-buyer was in place.

New Chairman Leading the Group Through the 1980s and 1990s, Creating a Global Power

In 1988 Dusseldorp retired as chairman and was succeeded by Hornery, who had served as managing director since 1978. Dusseldorp left a corporation in which 30 percent of all projects were planned, designed, built, fitted, financed, managed, and refurbished for their economic life. It was a company with novel staff ownership schemes, well-tended links with investors, and numerous corporate sponsorships. Dusseldorp cultivated good relations with employees, shareholders, and local communities alike.

Hornery also made a mark on the firm bringing in insurance and related financial services to the group by acquiring MLC in a two-step maneuver: taking a 50 percent interest in 1982 and then making MLC a wholly owned subsidiary in 1985. Lend Lease was able to provide, through MLC, savings, mortgage investment, and superannuation as well as life and general insurance products that would cover its clients from cradle to grave. The financial services division proved a shrewd diversification for the early 1990s, contributing nearly half of Lend Lease's after-tax profit by 1991. The conglomerate's 1993 acquisition of a minority stake in Australia's oldest bank, Westpac Banking Corp., was interpreted by some analysts as a step toward its goal of becoming that country's largest financial services company. Lend Lease, however, began phasing out its stake in Westpac in 1996.

During the 1990s, Hornery's objective for the group of companies was steady and continuous growth through extending MLC's offshore investments and developing global property investment capability. The company's property investment funds focused on emerging markets, especially in Asia. By 1995, it had funds targeting Thailand, Indonesia, and other Asian nations. International expansion of Lend Lease's con-

struction interests continued as well. The corporation acquired U.S.-based Yarmouth Group, Inc., a firm specializing in real estate investment management, in 1993 and purchased a minority stake in Hoyts Theaters cinema chain with locations in the United States, Australia, and New Zealand, in 1994. In addition to his company's new business interests, Chairman Hornery also remained committed to continuing the company policy of enhancing the urban environment and playing a leading role in changing Australia's cities for the better.

While Lend Lease's sales declined from A$1.7 billion in fiscal 1990 to A$1.5 billion in 1995, the company continued to add to its 20-year record of increasing after-tax profit, which grew from A$160.5 million to A$260 million during the first five years of the decade. The company reported revenues of A$2.05 billion in 1996 as well as another increase in profits despite a declining Australian property market.

Continuing its drive to become a truly global concern, Lend Lease acquired Equitable Real Estate Management Inc. from the Equitable Cos., a subsidiary of the AXA group, for US$400 million. Equitable Real Estate was the largest pension fund adviser in the United States and a major player in real estate investment management. The acquired unit was merged with Yarmouth to form ERE Yarmouth, which was renamed Lend Lease Real Estate Investments, Inc. in 1998. By late in 1998, this subsidiary had more than US$30 billion in assets under management, making it the largest pension fund adviser in the world and one of the world's largest real estate investment managers. Of this asset total, US$25 billion came from the United States. Meanwhile, back home, Lend Lease won several high-profile construction projects, including several for the 2000 Olympics scheduled for Sydney. The most notable perhaps was one for the Olympic Village, and ground was broken for that project during 1997.

In early 1998 Lend Lease announced that it was cutting back on its push into Asian markets in the wake of the financial crisis that erupted in that region in the middle of the previous year. In late 1997 and early 1998, the company entered into advanced discussions with National Mutual Holdings Ltd. about forming joint ventures that would combine the two companies' funds management and insurance operations in Australia and New Zealand. The two sides, however, were unable to work out details concerning who would control the joint ventures and how they might be terminated after a proposed three-year trial period, and the deal collapsed.

In early 1999, in a move to beef up the firm's infrastructure operations, Lend Lease purchased a 25 percent stake in Morrison & Co. Ltd., an infrastructure advisory house based in New Zealand that managed the publicly listed infrastructure fund Infratil Australia. The company also gained an option to buy out all of Morrison within five years. In late 1999 and early 2000 the U.S.-based Lend Lease Real Estate Investments unit was bolstered through two acquisitions together costing nearly half a billion dollars: the Boston Financial Group, a limited partnership specializing in multifamily housing investment management; and five commercial mortgage businesses, including Holliday Fenoglio Fowler, LP, purchased from Dallas-based Amresco Inc.

Lend Lease's blockbuster deal for 1999, however, and in fact the firm's largest acquisition yet, eclipsing the 1997 deal for Equitable Real Estate, was that of Bovis Construction Group, which was purchased from the U.K.-based Peninsular and Oriental Steam Navigation Company (P&O) for £285 million (A$710 million). Bovis was P&O's global project management and construction services arm and provided Lend Lease with significant presences in two key markets—the United States and the United Kingdom—as well as operations in the Asia-Pacific region and Australia. Bovis was merged with Lend Lease Projects (the former Civil & Civic unit) to form Bovis Lend Lease, which was headquartered in London.

To further intensify its focus on integrated global real estate operations, Lend Lease sold its MLC funds management and life insurance business to National Australia Bank Ltd. for A$4.56 billion (US$2.74 billion). This mid-2000 transaction proved to be the last major deal of Hornery's tenure as chairman, which ended with his retirement in November 2000. Under Hornery's leadership, Lend Lease had become a truly global player—in fact one of the most powerful global property companies in the world. Jill Ker Conway took over as chairwoman of Lend Lease, with David H. Higgins continuing to serve as managing director, a position he had held since 1995.

Critical Juncture in the Early 2000s

The post-Hornery era got off to a very rocky start, with the company taking write-downs connected with Fox Studios in Sydney, a joint venture with News Corporation Limited, and with Internet-related investments, and also issuing a series of profit warnings that were tied in large part to the sale of the steadily profitable MLC. In addition, the U.S.-based Lend Lease Real Estate Investments was not performing as well as expected. As a result, Lend Lease's string of 25 straight years of growth in after-tax profits came to an end. For the fiscal year ending in June 2001, the company reported after-tax profits of A$151 million (down from A$432 million) on operating revenues of A$11.54 billion (down from $13 billion). The company's stock price fell from $22.30 per share in mid-December 2000 to nearly $11 per share in June 2001. Later in 2001 Bovis Lend Lease was selected as lead manager of the cleanup of the World Trade Center site in New York City following the devastation of September 11.

In May 2002, with the company continuing to struggle to replace the steady profits that had been derived from MLC, Higgins announced that he planned to resign but would stay on until a replacement was found. The move came despite the improvement in the company's performance during 2002 when after-tax profits increased to A$226 million. In early August 2002 Lend Lease spent £294 million (US$461.3 million) to acquire Akeler Holdings SA, a real estate and investment company that specialized in U.K. business park developments and had additional operations in Portugal and Germany. Later in August rumors began to circulate that Lend Lease was contemplating a breakup, splitting the Real Estate Investment business off from the Real Estate Solutions business that included Bovis Lend Lease and its development unit. The possibility of such a move—which would return the company to its beginnings as a pure construction company—coupled with the uncertainty surrounding a successor to Higgins, seemed to indicate that Lend Lease had reached a crucial juncture in its history.

Principal Subsidiaries

PROJECT AND CONSTRUCTION MANAGEMENT: Bovis Lend Lease Pty. Limited; Bovis Lend Lease Holdings, Inc. (U.S.A.); Bovis Lend Lease, Inc. (U.S.A.); Bovis Lend Lease LMB, Inc. (U.S.A.); Bovis Lend Lease Holdings Limited (U.K.); Bovis Lend Lease Limited (U.K.); Bovis Lend Lease International Limited (U.K.); Bovis Lend Lease Europe (U.K.); Bovis Lend Lease Overseas Holdings Limited (U.K.); Bovis Lend Lease Project Consulting (Shanghai) Co. Limited (China); Schal Bovis, Inc. (U.S.A.); Bovis Lend Lease Projects Pte. Limited (Singapore); Bovis International Inc.—New York (U.S.A.); Bovis Lend Lease Microelectronics (U.S.A.); Bovis Lend Lease S.A. (Argentina; 90%); Bovis Lend Lease Inc. (Brazil). INTEGRATED DEVELOPMENT BUSINESS: Lend Lease Development Pty. Limited; LLD Precinct 2 Pty. Limited; Lend Lease Moore Park Pty. Limited; Lend Lease Moore Park Management Pty. Limited; Lend Lease Europe Holdings Limited (U.K.); Lend Lease Europe Limited (U.K.); Blueco Limited (U.K.); Lend Lease Continental Holdings Limited (U.K.). REAL ESTATE INVESTMENTS: Lend Lease Real Estate Investment Limited; GPT Management Limited; European Retail Services Limited (U.K.); Lend Lease Europe Retail Investments Limited (U.K.); Lend Lease (US), Inc.; Lend Lease (US) Finance, Inc.; Yarmouth Lend Lease King of Prussia, Inc. (U.S.A.); Lend Lease Investments Holdings, Inc. (U.S.A.); Lend Lease Real Estate Investments, Inc. (U.S.A.); Lend Lease Agri Business, Inc. (U.S.A.); CapMark Service LP (U.S.A.); Holliday Fenoglio Fowler, LP (U.S.A.); Lend Lease Asset Management LP (U.S.A.). EQUITY INVESTMENTS: Lend Lease Custodian Pty. Limited. GROUP SERVICES: Lend Lease Finance Limited; Lend Lease International Pty. Limited; Lend Lease Securities and Investments Pty. Limited; Lend Lease Management Services Limited.

Principal Competitors

AMP Limited; New World Development Company Limited; Sun Hung Kai Properties Limited; Skanska AB; Peter Kiewit Sons', Inc.; Parsons Corporation; Taylor Woodrow plc; Equity Residential; Lincoln Property Company.

Further Reading

Bagwell, Sheryle, "No Worries?," *Business Review Weekly,* May 16, 2002, pp. 60+.

Clark, Lindie, *Finding a Common Interest: The Story of Dick Dusseldorp and Lend Lease,* New York: Cambridge University Press, 2002.

Condon, Turi, "Frustrated Investors Turn on Lend Lease," *Business Review Weekly,* June 22, 2001.

——, "The Risks for Lend Lease," *Business Review Weekly,* March 2, 2001.

Cummins, Carolyn, "Lend Lease Chief Makes Surprise Exit," *Sydney Morning Herald,* May 21, 2002, p. 19.

Featherstone, Tony, "Lend Lease Infrastructure Surprise," *Business Review Weekly,* March 15, 1999.

Forde, Kevin, "Lend Lease Aims for As Much Class in Finance As Property," *Rydge's,* October 1985, pp. 54+.

Fraser, Andrew, "Local Stumble Interrupts Lend Lease Long March," *Australian,* November 11, 2000, p. 43.

Frith, Bryan, "National Mutual, Lend Lease Deal Made in Heaven," *Australian,* January 21, 1998, p. 24.

——, "Who Wore the Trousers Was What It's About," *Australian,* May 14, 1998, p. 24.

Harris, Mike, "Oz's Hoyts Breaking Chains: Firm Selling Cinema Franchises to Frisco Bank, Aussie Investor," *Variety,* September 12, 1994, p. 29.

Hughes, Anthony, "Lend Lease Confident It Can Construct a New World at Low Risk," *Sydney Morning Herald,* August 18, 1997, p. 37.

——, "L[end]Lease $710m Bet on UK Play," *Sydney Morning Herald,* October 5, 1999, p. 33.

Jimenez, Cathryn, "Higgins Defends Global Grand Plan," *Australian,* February 16, 2001, p. 39.

——, "How Lend Lease Chief Realised a Vision," *Australian,* October 20, 2000, p. 37.

Jimenez, Cathryn, and Maurice Dunlevy, "Lend Lease Vulnerable After Loss," *Australian,* May 21, 2002, p. 21.

"Lend Lease Seeks Exploration Revival Through Eromanga Oil," *Rydge's,* February 1985, pp. 34+.

"Lend Lease's Morschel Resigns As Top Officer," *Wall Street Journal,* March 8, 1995, p. 4B.

Lynch, Damien, "NAB Will Acquire MLC in a Cash Transaction: Bank to Pay $2.4 Billion for Lend Lease Arm," *Asian Wall Street Journal,* April 11, 2000, p. 2.

Martinez, Barbara, "As If Lend Lease Wasn't Big Enough Already: Property Investment Giant Swiftly Builds Its Lineup to Become a Powerhouse," *Wall Street Journal,* December 22, 1999, p. B14.

Murdoch, Blake, "Hoyts Confirms Theaters Sale," *Hollywood-Reporter,* September 13, 1994.

Murphy, Mary, *Challenges of Change: The Lend Lease Story,* Sydney: The Pot Still Press, 1984.

Rennie, Philip, "Lend Lease's Losing Gamble," *Business Review Weekly,* March 2, 2001.

Rudnitsky, Howard, "A Hand from the Grave," *Forbes,* May 11, 1981, pp. 83–84.

Ubels, Helen, "Lend Lease Buys Properties Unit from GE," *Asian Wall Street Journal,* August 6, 2002, p. M3.

Vitorovich, Lilly, "Lend Lease Plans to Replace Chief Executive," *Asian Wall Street Journal,* May 21, 2002, p. M3.

Witcher, S. Karene, "Australian Sells Westpac Stake to Lend Lease," *Wall Street Journal,* May 12, 1993, p. B3B.

—Anastasia N. Hackett
—updates: April Dougal Gasbarre, David E. Salamie

Leupold & Stevens, Inc.

14400 NW Greenbrier Parkway
Beaverton, Oregon 97006
U.S.A.
Telephone: (503) 646-9171
Fax: (503) 526-1455
Web site: http://www.leupold.com

Private Company
Incorporated: 1949
Employees: 520
Sales: $110 million (2001 est.)
NAIC: 333314 Optical Instruments & Lens
Manufacturing; 339920 Sporting and Athletic Goods
Manufacturing; 421460 Ophthalmic Goods
Wholesalers; 421490 Other Professional Equipment
and Supplies Wholesalers; 421910 Sporting and
Recreational Goods and Supplies Wholesalers

Leupold & Stevens, Inc., a fourth generation family-owned company, is one of the oldest and best-known manufacturers of top-of-the-line riflescopes and binoculars. The Leupold line, designed primarily for hunters and shooters, includes rifle, handgun, and spotting scopes; mounting systems; and optical tools and accessories. All of the company's scopes are known for their decorative gold ring. Leupold & Stevens also sells products for a variety of military and law enforcement applications. Its customers include the Federal Bureau of Investigation (FBI), the U.S. Navy Seals, and various police special weapons and tactics teams. The company also manufactured water-measuring devices used in irrigation, flood forecasting, and water supply and wastewater engineering until 1998.

A Manufacturer of Surveying and Water Recorder Products: 1907–39

Markus Frederich Leupold began a one-man operation for the repair of surveying equipment in Portland, Oregon, in 1907 with financial backing from his friend and brother-in-law, Adam Voelpel. "Fred" Leupold was born in Ravensburg,

Germany, in 1875, and immigrated to the United States from Germany at the age of 16 in 1891. After a number of jobs, he worked as a precision machinist for C.L. Berger & Sons, a Boston surveying instrument manufacturer. Leupold and Voelpel named their new business after themselves.

Leupold & Voelpel grew slowly in answer to the need for skillful repair of surveying and drafting equipment, and the business soon employed three others. In 1911, after a fire occurred in their building one floor below them and street vibrations interfered with the accuracy of their machinery, Leupold & Voelpel moved to a building adjacent to the Leupold residence. The firm had successfully established its credentials among surveyors, and the brothers-in-law made the decision to begin manufacturing surveying equipment.

Very shortly thereafter, two events occurred that changed the course of the young company. Competition from bigger and better financed companies forced Leupold & Voelpel to investigate other markets, and Leupold and Voelpel met John Cyprian Stevens, an inventor and consulting engineer and hydrologist. Stevens was born in 1876 in Kansas and had earned a civil engineering degree from the University of Nebraska. From 1902 until 1910, Stevens had worked for the U.S. Geological Survey in water studies. He soon afterward patented a device to record the flow of water that dramatically outperformed the competitive devices of the day. Stevens's device, which Leupold & Voelpel agreed to market in 1911, needing checking only several times a year as opposed to every eight days. By 1914, the demand for the new water level recorder had increased considerably. That year Stevens joined the company as a third partner, and the company renamed itself Leupold, Volpel & Co. (Voelpel had changed the spelling of his name earlier to avoid anti-German sentiment in the United States.)

Business for Leupold, Volpel & Co. grew slowly but steadily during World War I as the Stevens product line expanded into other models. Twice the company had to enlarge its quarters. Then, in the 1920s, the firm's water recorders and surveying products made their way around the world to India, Russia, Scandinavia, Canada, Japan, and Central and South America. By the 1930s, Leupold, Volpel & Co. had grown to number 40 full-time employees, and although, occasionally, working hours were cut during the Depression, no employee was let go.

In 1939, J.C. Stevens's son, Robert, joined the company, and took over responsibility for sales, marketing, and advertising. By then, production had increased dramatically. This growth was due largely to the introduction of another Stevens invention in 1938, the Telemark, a water level recorder that transmitted data over telephone lines. By 1942, the company had outgrown its production space and moved to larger quarters. Volpel had died in 1940, and the company now became Leupold and Stevens Instruments Company, reflecting both the new management and the direction in which the company was heading.

Growth Following Introduction of New Type of Riflescope: 1940s–70s

Three events combined in the 1940s to produce the company's next big break, the production of a more precise riflescope. As industrial America began to gear up to meet the manufacturing needs of World War II, Leupold & Stevens turned to manufacturing sextants and peloruses—navigational devices that take bearings based on observed objects—for the U.S. Navy and the U.S. Merchant Marine. It also began to repair the Merchant Marine's telescopic gun sights. In the course of these repairs, the company's engineers made the discovery that replacing the oxygen inside a telescopic sight with pure, bone-dry nitrogen meant the sight no longer fogged. Fred Leupold died in 1944, and management of Leupold & Stevens passed on to the next generation: Leupold's sons, Norbert and Marcus, and Stevens's son, Robert. After Marcus Leupold missed shooting a buck on the rainy west side of Oregon's Cascade Range because his scope fogged with interior moisture, the new leaders, all avid outdoorsmen, turned their attention to producing a better riflescope.

The firm drew on its experience gained repairing gunsights during the war and combined that with its expertise in designing sophisticated optics for surveying equipment. The result was the first Leupold riflescope, called the Plainsman, in 1947, a new generation of riflescopes less likely to draw moisture and more easily adjusted for accuracy. The Plainsman instantly became popular among hunters and shooters as the most water-resistant scope of its era. It featured internal adjustments and a permanently sealed main tube.

The continued success of Stevens water recorders and the emerging popularity of the Leupold riflescope led to incorporation of the company in 1949. Marcus Leupold became president of the newly incorporated entity. In 1953, Stevens suffered a stroke and withdrew from business activity for the remainder of his life. He died in 1970. Under Marcus Leupold's leadership,

the company began to realize the potential for growth that lay with its riflescope business. By 1960, Leupold scopes were on their way to establishing themselves as the premier scopes on the market. The firm also continued to advance its water flow meters, and, in 1961, introduced a new line that measured sewage flow. The company's staff of 150 moved shop to a new 66,000-square-foot plant in Beaverton, Oregon, in the Portland Metro area in 1968. In 1969, Norbert Leupold, who was graduated from Oregon State University with a degree in civil engineering in 1929, became president of the company.

The 1980s: Unsuccessful Experimentation with Acquisitions

Throughout the remainder of the next two decades, the demand for Leupold & Stevens' hydrographic and sporting products accelerated. The company continued to grow and to expand its production facilities, evolving new manufacturing technologies and products that enabled hunters and shooters to take ever more precise aim. In 1970, Leupold & Stevens closed down its instrument repair and rental department, the last remaining vestige of the firm's origins. Then, in the 1980s, the hunting gear market began to shrink. In response, in 1984 Leupold & Stevens formed a special division for corporate ventures and acquisitions designed to broaden the company's mix of business. It purchased Fabmark Inc., a Hillsboro, Oregon, manufacturer of highly refined sheet metal for the electronics industry with customers such as Tektronix and Hewlett-Packard in 1984. Biamp Systems Inc., a sound equipment manufacturer, followed in 1985.

By 1986, however, the company was rethinking its diversification strategy. Inventories started climbing, and the company did not seem to be growing. In addition, in the face of an unfavorable exchange rate between the United States and Japan, where Leupold & Stevens purchased its optical glass, the company took measures to conserve resources, shutting down much of production capacity between November 1986 and mid-January 1987, laying off 60 workers temporarily and another eight permanently. Leupold & Stevens embarked on an employee "cross-training" program that allowed workers to shift back and forth between making parts and assembling finished products in an effort to eliminate excess inventories.

Management decided to return Leupold & Stevens to its core business. It sold off Biamp 15 months after purchasing it, at considerable loss, in 1986. In 1988, it sold off Nosler Bullets Inc., a Bend ammunition maker that it had owned since 1969. Two years later, it divested itself of Fabmark. According to Werner K. Wildauer, who had become president in 1983, the company would continue to hunt for acquisitions, but only in optics and closely related industries. Leupold & Stevens also stepped up its research and development spending, looking to create a stream of new products and to expand its presence in the water measurement and instrumentation business, thereby turning the tide on its flat revenues and falling profits.

New Technology and the Resurgence of Demand: Late 1980s–90s

By mid-1987, demand for hunting and shooting products had resumed, and the company had expanded its offerings to

Key Dates:

1907: Markus Frederich (Fred) Leupold founds a business for the repair of surveying equipment.

1911: Leupold & Voelpel (the latter name is eventually changed to Volpel) moves to a building adjacent to the Leupold residence

1914: The company becomes Leupold, Volpel & Co. after J.C. Stevens joins the company as a third partner.

1938: The company introduces the Telemark, invented by J.C. Stevens.

1939: Robert Stevens joins the company.

1942: The company moves to larger production space; company changes its name to Leupold & Stevens Instruments Company after Volpel's death.

1944: Norbert Leupold joins the firm.

1947: The company introduces the Plainsman.

1949: Leupold & Stevens incorporates.

1953: Stevens retires after a stroke.

1968: The company moves to new facilities in Beaverton, Oregon.

1969: The company buys Nosler Bullets Inc.

1984: Leupold & Stevens opens a new division to head up acquisitions; the company acquires Fabmark Inc.

1985: The company acquires Biamp Systems Inc.

1986: The company sells Biamp Systems Inc.

1988: The company sells Nosler Bullets Inc.

1990: The company sells Fabmark Inc.

1998: Leupold & Stevens sells Stevens Water Monitoring Systems.

more than 100 scope products, including non-firearm telescopes. Leupold & Stevens added two to four new scopes a year between 1990 and 1995. By 1992, the company claimed 35 percent of the U.S. market in high quality optics, and, by the mid-1990s, with the nation looking to move to stricter gun control, business was once again booming. Worried that the purchase of sporting firearms might be curtailed by legislation, hunters and shooters put $14.5 billion into guns and ammunition in 1994. For Leupold & Stevens, this meant that production shot up as much as 40 percent over 1993. In 1994, the company had to expand its plant by 15,000 square feet in order to keep up with demand. In 1995, it was running three shifts a day, employing 525 workers, and had begun another expansion of 30,000 square feet. In 1998, it sold off Stevens Water Monitoring Systems to concentrate on its other business.

By the mid-1990s, newer, different technologies led to a plethora of new products for hunters and shooters. In fact, according to the *Oregonian* in 1996, these new products, which included special hearing devices designed to amplify natural sounds, night-vision binoculars, automatically timed feeding devices, computerized global positioning systems, and motion sensor devices, were coming on line as quickly as the state came up with regulations to delimit their use. A spokesperson from the Oregon Department of Fish and Wildlife, quoted in the *Oregonian* in 1996, said that "We've just about pushed technology to the limits of acceptance. ... We're going to need some help from the hunter sorting it all out." Leupold & Stevens insisted that it remained concerned with the issues surrounding hunting; however, it needed to stay on the cutting edge because companies unwilling to change to new technologies could "go by the wayside."

The company was among the earliest supporters of the Heritage Foundation, pledging 1 percent of its total sales to this organization, founded, in 1999, upon the belief that companies that make their profits from the shooting sports industries should work to preserve hunting and shooting rights. Under the direction of President and CEO Tom Fruechtel, who assumed leadership of the company in 1998, Leupold & Stevens maintained its commitment in the early years of the new millennium to keeping the company closely held, to promoting positive messages about hunting and shooting sports, and to lobbying against gun control.

Principal Competitors

Bausch & Lomb Inc.; Burris; Bushnell; Nikon Corporation; Swarovski International Holding AG.

Further Reading

Anderson, Michael A., "Leupold & Stevens Retreats, Refocuses After Sale," *Business Journal* (Portland), November 3, 1986, p. 9.

Colby, Richard, "Leupold & Stevens Consolidates, Returns to Optical Roots, Success," *Oregonian*, November 16, 1990, p. D8.

A History of Leupold & Stevens, Inc., 1907–1971, Beaverton, Oreg.: Leupold & Stevens, Inc., 1971.

Kirkland, John, "Focused on the Target," *Oregon Business*, October 1992, p. 30.

"Manufacturer Sets Layoffs," *Oregonian*, November 4, 1986, p. D14.

Marks, Anita, "Leupold & Stevens Has Expansion in Its Sights," *Oregonian*, April 7, 1995, p. 1.

Monroe, Bill, "Hunting Goes High Tech," *Oregonian*, September 12, 1996, p. C1.

—Carrie Rothburd

Luxottica SpA

Localita Valcozzena
32021 Agordo, Belluno
Italy
Telephone: (+39) 0437-6441
Fax: (+39) 0437-63223
Web site: http://www.luxottica.it

Public Company
Incorporated: 1961
Employees: 24,636
Sales: EUR 3.06 billion ($2.73 billion) (2001)
Stock Exchanges: New York Milan
Ticker Symbol: LUX
NAIC: 339115 Ophthalmic Goods Manufacturing

Luxottica SpA is the world's largest manufacturer of eyeglass frames and sunglasses, and is also one of the world's leading optical retailers through subsidiaries LensCrafters and Sunglass Hut. Based in the remote village of Agordo, Italy, Luxottica produces more than 130,000 eyeglass frames each day from six factory sites. The company's frames and sunglasses are sold under a variety of company brand names, including Luxottica, Ray Ban, Vogue, Persol, Arnette, Killer Loop, Revo, Sferoflex, and T3. Luxottica also manufactures eyeglasses and sunglasses under license for such brands as Armani, Chanel, Ferragamo, Bulgari, Byblos, Genny, Ungaro, Tacchini, Moschino, Web, Anne Klein, and Brooks Brothers. In addition to its retail distribution network, Luxottica has built up an internationally operating wholesale distribution network of 29 company-owned branches, as well as 90 independently operated branches, which supply the company's products to more than 115 countries. Luxottica's quest for vertical integration has even extended to its customer's eyes—the company controls the EyeMed Vision Care group, one of North America's leading vision care providers with more than 30 million members. Luxottica is controlled by founder and Chairman Leonardo Del Vecchio, who owns more than 70 percent of the company's stock. Luxottica is quoted on both the New York and Milan stock exchanges. In 2001, the company posted more than EUR 3 billion ($2.75 billion) in sales.

Eyewear Craftsmanship: 1960s

One overriding theme has distinguished Luxottica's history: eliminate the middleman. In the 1950s and 1960s, Del Vecchio honed his own skills, meticulously learning every facet of the ophthalmic frame manufacturing process. In the 1970s, he worked to automate the process with machinery of his own design, then linked every stage of production, from design to inventory, via computers. In the 1980s, Del Vecchio began acquiring Luxottica's formerly independent international distributors. The 1990s have seen what may be the culmination of Luxottica's drive for vertical integration, the acquisition of retail outlets. Each of these steps has resulted in increased efficiency, paving the company's route to profitable, rapid growth.

Born in 1935 in Milan, Luxottica founder Leonardo Del Vecchio has been called "Italy's version of Horatio Alger." His father, a street merchant who hawked vegetables, died five months before Leonardo was born, leaving the family so destitute that the youngster spent seven years of his childhood in an orphanage. As a youth, Del Vecchio apprenticed as a designer in a tool and die factory specializing in small metal components. After studying drawing and engraving at the Brera Academy of Art, the young designer struck out on his own in 1958, manufacturing molded plastic eyeglass components in Milan. With financial backing from two key customers, he moved his 14-man shop in 1961 to Agordo, a picturesque mountain town in a region of northern Italy known for its handcrafted jewelry.

Although he had no formal training in economics, the young entrepreneur soon realized that he could retain more profits through vertical integration. Del Vecchio renamed the business Luxottica and set out to expand its capacity to include the full range of eyeglass components. Over the course of the decade, he added metalworking capabilities, plastic milling, and other processes to his company. In a 1991 interview, Del Vecchio told *Financial World*'s Stephen Kindel that "by mastering all the technologies, we [became] very competitive on price, without having to compromise our quality." This process culminated in the 1969 launch of Luxottica's first complete set of optical frames.

Luxottica had a brush with oblivion in 1971, when the company's two outside investors called in their L 190 million in loans

Company Perspectives:

Mission: We at Luxottica aim at protecting the eyes and enhancing the faces of men and women all over the world, by manufacturing and selling ophthalmic eyewear and sunwear characterized by their high technical and stylistic quality, in order to maximize our customers' wellbeing and satisfaction.

Our eyewear and our collections are the result of a continuous research and development process, aiming at anticipating and interpreting the needs, wishes and aspirations of people around the world.

Our technical and manufacturing expertise, a result of 40 years of experience and our commitment, allow us to reach high quality standards.

Our business is based on a continuous innovation of our manufacturing technologies, the research of style and design, the analysis of the evolution of people's lifestyles, and the interpretation of fashion trends.

Our widespread distribution network and our sales chains have been organized to offer a high-quality before and after-sales service, at all times and anywhere. A service that is homogeneous, yet nonstandardized, because it is designed and suited to meet the specific local needs.

That's why millions of consumers in 115 countries in all five continents have chosen, and keep choosing us.

to Del Vecchio. But Del Vecchio's fortunes quickly reversed when the entrepreneur brought in a new partner, Scarrone; he then bought out this former competitor within the year.

Drive for Integrated Production in the 1970s

Del Vecchio continued to systematically integrate his eyeglass business, focusing on technological advances throughout the 1970s. Noting that it was not materials, but retooling to accommodate fashion changes, that drove cost increases, Del Vecchio began to tackle that side of his business. Having taken courses in advanced machine design in 1969, he began to devise automated molding and milling equipment. He also adopted techniques from allied industries, borrowing specialized electroplating procedures from local jewelers, for example. Ample funding for research and development in plastics compounding, metallurgy, and basic chemistry ensured the quality of future products.

Perhaps most important, Del Vecchio guided Luxottica's implementation of computerization. By the end of the decade, the company had integrated all facets of its process, from design to manufacturing and inventory control. This early application of computer technology not only gave Luxottica a significant cost advantage over its competitors, but also helped make small production runs more efficient. This factor would become increasingly important as the influence of ever-changing fashion trends impacted the eyewear industry.

Geographic Consolidation Through Acquisition in the 1980s

Luxottica concentrated on consolidating its international distribution network in the 1980s. International sales have al-

ways been vital to Luxottica's success. In fact, the very first sets of the company's frames were not sold in Italy, as one might expect, but in the United States. In 1970, the company assigned exclusive rights to distribute its eyewear in the United States to Avant Garde. The Luxottica line was not offered in Italy until 1975. After taking control of Avant Garde in the early 1980s, Luxottica increased its U.S. market share from less than 2 percent to more than 7 percent, enough to lead this highly fragmented industry.

Under the direction of Leonardo Del Vecchio's son and expected successor, Claudio, revenues from the American division—which constituted more than half of the Italian firm's total sales—increased from $28 million in 1982 to $143 million by 1990. Over the course of the decade, Luxottica acquired nine of its 12 international distributors and took significant equity positions in the remainder with an eye toward full ownership. The company applied its own finely honed standards to its new affiliates, winning opticians' and retailers' loyalty by offering computerized ordering, inventory services, and just-in-time delivery. In the early 1990s, Luxottica found itself in the unusual position of increasing brand awareness and penetration in Europe, where it only had about 5 percent of the market.

Fueled by acquisitions and continual economizing, Luxottica's revenues increased from L 16 billion in 1979 to L 194 billion in 1985. But in spite of this spectacular financial and geographic expansion, Leonardo Del Vecchio remained "Signor Nessuno" (Mr. Nobody) among Italy's leading businessmen.

Designer Lines Spark Late 1980s Growth Spurts

Three principal trends converged in the late 1980s to jump start Luxottica's sales and earnings growth. Prescription eyeglasses evolved from a fashion liability into an important accessory, to the point that even those who did not need to correct their vision might wear frames with noncorrective lenses just to complete a particular "look." Luxottica capitalized on this trend by amassing a collection of designer labels in the late 1980s and early 1990s. To its own Luxottica and Sferoflex ophthalmic frames and Sfersol sunglasses, the company added Giorgio Armani, Genny, Byblos, Giugiaro, Valentino, and Yves Saint Laurent. Del Vecchio correctly reasoned that people who might not be able to afford a Giorgio Armani suit might opt instead for the designer's eyewear.

As the share of company sales generated by designer glasses increased from nil to more than 38 percent, Luxottica's revenues and earnings mounted. Sales increased from L 194 billion in 1985 to more than L 460 billion in 1991, by which time net income exceeded L 60 billion. By the early 1990s, designer eyewear drove the company's gross margins to an astonishing 70 percent.

Luxottica went public on the New York Stock Exchange with a January 1990 floatation of 23 percent of the company's equity in the form of American Depositary Receipts (ADRs). Luxottica was the first Italian company ever to bypass the Milan Stock Exchange to list on the New York Stock Exchange. Company executives treated financial analysts to their stylish sunglasses to help promote the initial public offering (IPO). Luxottica Chairman Roberto Chemello told Lisa Bannon of

Key Dates:

1958: Leonardo Del Vecchio starts up a business making tools and parts for eyeglasses in Milan.
1961: Del Vecchio and two financial partners launch Luxottica in Agordo.
1967: The company begins production of its own Luxottica branded eyeglass frames.
1971: Luxottica ends its contract manufacturing operations to concentrate on its eyeglass manufacturing wing.
1974: The company buys up Scarrone, its Italian distributor, in the first move to become a vertically integrated operation.
1981: The company launches a German sales subsidiary.
1982: The company acquires a U.S. distributor to begin sales operations in the United States.
1984: The company launches subsidiaries in England, France, and Canada.
1988: The company starts to produce Armani-branded eyewear under a licensing agreement.
1990: Luxottica goes public on the New York Stock Exchange.
1995: Luxottica acquires Lensmasters, formerly part of United States Shoe Corporation, and becomes a retail optical leader.
1999: Luxottica acquires the sunglasses division of Bausch & Lomb, including Ray Ban and other brands; the company launches the managed vision care subsidiary EyeMed Vision Care.
2001: Luxottica acquires Sunglass Hut International and becomes the world's leading eyewear retailer.

WWD, "We want to show the financial world our image is international, not just Italian, which is in line with the international nature of our business." Del Vecchio elaborated in a 1991 interview with Forbes's Katherine Weisman: "If we listed [on the Milan Exchange], we would have been a piccolissima cosa [teeny thing]. On the NYSE, c'e rispetto [there's respect] for everybody, piccolo e grande." The founder retained the $80 million proceeds of the IPO for himself. Debt-free Luxottica did not need the money, and he had certainly earned the reward. By 1994, the shares had quadrupled in value.

Acquisitions Bringing Integration Full-Circle in the Early 1990s

In 1995, Del Vecchio and Luxottica took its largest single step toward vertical integration with the hostile $1.4 billion takeover of United States Shoe Corporation. This initially surprising development was precipitated by heightened competition in the frame industry and reduced reimbursements from third-party payers such as insurers and health maintenance organizations. Luxottica had traditionally sold to individual opticians, and had more than 28,000 clients in the United States by the early 1990s. But at that time, the company increasingly found itself squeezed between shrinking insurance allowances for frames and its competitors' price cuts to match those limits. Del Vecchio knew he could not rely on the designer market alone for continued profitable growth, but he also did not want

to start chasing the industry's lowest common denominator. He found an oblique solution to the dilemma in United States Shoe Corporation.

Luxottica was not interested in the target's shoe manufacturing business or its retail apparel subsidiaries. Instead, Del Vecchio was eager to capitalize on its chain of nearly 700 LensCrafters optical stores and that operation's $767 million in annual sales. Established in 1983, LensCrafters was one of the first businesses to combine vision professionals, eyeglass frames, and prescription lens processing in one easily accessed mall location. The company's "about an hour" turnaround time completed the convenient package. Anticipating the immense potential of this new concept, United States Shoe acquired the budding three-store chain barely a year after it was founded. The financial backing of this billion-dollar conglomerate helped LensCrafters become the largest retail eyewear chain in the United States by 1988. It achieved global sales leadership in 1992.

As part of the 1995 transaction with Luxottica, United States Shoe sold its footwear group to Nine West Group Inc. for $600 million prior to its own acquisition. But Luxottica was unable to find a buyer for United States Shoe's 1,300 money-losing apparel retailers, which included Casual Corner, Petite Sophisticate, August Max, Casual & Co., and Capezio chains. As a result, the parent transferred this division to La Leonarda Finanziaria Srl, a separate Del Vecchio interest. The addition of LensCrafters more than doubled Luxottica's annual revenues from L 812.7 billion in 1994 to L 1.8 trillion in 1995.

Global Eyewear Leader in the 21st Century

Luxottica faced the end of the 20th century with an array of growth strategies in its arsenal. The company hoped to further increase sales of designer eyewear, which had already topped 50 percent of annual revenues, by placing stronger emphasis on these more expensive lines in LensCrafter stores. At the same time the company sought to boost its sales of its own brands in the U.S. market. Previously, Luxottica's brands had represented only a tiny portion of LensCrafters' business. Taking control of that company enabled Luxottica to step up its presence in the retail chain, eventually increasing its share of LensCrafters' stock to some 70 percent.

Luxottica continued its diversification into sunglasses and sports eyewear with the 1995 acquisition of Italian sunglass manufacturer Persol SpA. By that time, sunglasses constituted more than one-third of annual sales. In addition, in a radical shift from its traditional trade-only promotions, Luxottica planned to boost its consumer advertising with an image-oriented campaign.

Through the late 1990s, Luxottica continued to build up its strong brand portfolio, adding licenses from such designers as Bulgari in 1996, Ferragamo and Ungaro in 1998, and Chanel in 1999. Meanwhile, Luxottica's revenues were growing strongly, jumping from EUR 419 million in 1994, nearing EUR 1.25 billion in 1996, and climbing to EUR 1.9 billion in 1999.

The year 1999 marked a new milestone for Luxottica. In that year the company reached an agreement to acquire the sunglasses division of optical maker Bausch & Lomb for $640 million. That purchase brought the company one of the world's strongest stables of sunglasses brands, notably, the famed Ray Ban brand, and others, including Killer Loop, Revo, and Arnette. By then, Luxottica had taken its quest for vertical integration into another direction, setting up EyeMed Vision Care to group managed vision care provider operations in the United States, with a network of some 19 million members and 8,000 practitioners.

Luxottica finally listed on the Milan stock exchange in 2000. The company then sought new expansion opportunities, including planning a move into Poland, as a first point of entry into the Eastern European market. Luxottica struck again in 2001 when it announced that it had succeeded in acquiring Sunglass Hut International, the world's leading sunglasses retailer with nearly 2,000 shops worldwide. The purchase price, hammered out after a year of negotiations, reached $690 million, including nearly $200 million in debt. Following the Sunglass Hut acquisition, Luxottica merged its two North American retail businesses headquarters, helping to cut costs. The company also convinced its largest suppliers to cut their prices—in part by replacing a strong percentage of Sunglass Hut's stock with the company's own sunglasses brands. With sales topping EUR 3 billion at the end of 2001, Luxottica global leadership in the eyewear market stood on a solid, vertically integrated foundation.

Principal Subsidiaries

Luxottica S.R.L.; Avant Garde Optics Inc. (U.S.A.); Luxottica Sun Corporation (U.S.A.); Luxottica Fashion Brillen (Germany); Luxottica Portugal Sa (Portugal); Mirari Japan Co., Ltd.; Luxottica Hellas Ae (Greece); Luxottica France S.A.R.L.; Luxottica Iberica Sa (Spain); Luxottica U.K. Ltd.; Luxottica Canada Inc.; Luxottica Belgium N.V.; Luxottica Do Brasil Ltda; Luxottica México S.A. De C.V.; Luxottica Sweden A.B.; Luxottica (Switzerland) Ag; Luxottica Nederland B.V.; Oy Luxottica Finland Ab; Luxottica Vertriebs G.M.B.H. (Austria); Luxottica Australia Pty Ltd.; Luxottica Argentina S.R.L.; Luxottica South Africa (Pty) Ltd.; Luxottica Optics Ltd. (Israel); Luxottica Gozluk Tic. A.S. (Turkey); Luxottica Norge As (Norway); Luxottica Gulf L.L.C. (U.A.E.); Luxottica Malaysia Sdn Bhd (Malaysia); Mirarian Marketing Pte. Ltd. (Singapore); Luxottica Poland Sp.Zo.O.; Rayban Sun Optics India Ltd.

Principal Competitors

B Braun Melsungen AG; Essilor International S.A.; Bausch and Lomb Inc.; Allergan Inc.; Cristaleria Espanola SA; Cole National Corporation; Instrumentarium Corporation; Lantis Eyewear Corporation; NCH Corporation; SAFILO SpA; Sola International Inc.; Fielmann AG; Oakley Inc.; Halma p.l.c.; Optische Werke G Rodenstock; Krys Vision Originale Vision Plus; OPSM Protector Ltd.; Bacou USA Inc.; EganaGoldpfeil Holdings Ltd.; Marchon Eyewear Inc.

Further Reading

Costin, Glynnis, ''Luxottica's Designing Eyes,'' *WWD,* September 14, 1990, pp. 6–7.

D'Angelo, Luca, ''Luxottica Group—A Transition from a Workshop to a Global Firm'' (Master's thesis), Cambridge, Mass.: Massachusetts Institute of Technology, 1994.

Goldoni, Luca, *A Far-Sighted Man,* Verona, Italy: Luxottica SpA, 1991.

Hessen, Wendy, ''Customers Eye Luxottica's Big Move,'' *WWD,* May 1, 1995, pp. 20–21.

Kroll, Luisa, ''Lens Master,'' *Forbes,* February 4, 2002, p. 60.

''Leonardo Del Vecchio; Chairman and Chief Executive, Luxottica,'' *Business Week,* June 17, 2002, p. 76.

Lyons, David, ''Persistence Paid Off for Suitor of Sunglass Hut,'' *Daily Business Review,* March 7, 2001, p. A1.

Morais, Richard, C., ''Luxottica's Golden Spectacles,'' *Forbes,* May 20, 1996, p. 98.

Saporito, Bill, ''Luxottica Group Cutting Out the Middleman,'' *Fortune,* April 6, 1992, p. 96.

Sullivan, Ruth, ''One Man's Vision Which Put Luxottica in the Frame,'' *European,* October 14, 1994, p. 32.

Weisman, Katherine, ''Piccolissima cosa No More,'' *Forbes,* April 29, 1991, p. 70.

Willan, Philip, ''Leonardo Looks Good in Glasses,'' *European,* September 7, 1995, p. 32.

—April Dougal Gasbarre
—update: M.L. Cohen

Madden's on Gull Lake

11266 Pine Beach Peninsula
Brainerd, Minnesota 56401
U.S.A.
Telephone: (218) 829-2811
Toll Free: (800) 247-1040
Fax: (218) 829-6583
Web site: http://www.maddens.com

Private Company
Incorporated: 1934
Employees: 714
Sales: $20 million (2001 est.)
NAIC: 721110 Hotels (Except Casino Hotels) and
   Motels; 713910 Golf Courses (Except Miniature,
   Pitch-n-Putt)

Minnesota-based Madden's on Gull Lake is a premier family and golf resort that has served guests for over 60 years and has remained one of the longest family-owned, independent resorts in the region. The resort features comfortable and contemporary conference facilities amid the relaxing atmosphere of towering pine trees and miles of shoreline. Situated on over a thousand acres in the heart of Minnesota's resort country, Madden's owns and operates three golf courses, including its championship course known as The Classic. The three main lodging facilities, Madden Inn and Golf Club, Madden Lodge, and Madden's Pine Portage, together accommodate up to 575 people daily. The resort features both fine and casual dining, tennis, boating, waterskiing, massage and fitness opportunities, shopping, croquet, swimming, volleyball, basketball, lawn bowling, badminton, shuffleboard, horseshoes, and numerous children's activities through the resort's supervised kids program.

Lumber and Railroad Dominance: 1800s and Beyond

In the mid- and late 1800s much of the central lakes territory of the newly incorporated state of Minnesota with its towering white pine trees was devoted to the timber industry. Lumber was harvested and floated through various rivers and stream beds or carted off by wagon load to population centers for building the nation. With increasing industrialization railroads were added to move people and freight more efficiently, and towns and cities grew up along the rail lines. Lumber camps and railroad ports were Brainerd's mainstay, and the community of settlers in this north central Minnesota town were generally connected in some manner to either the lumber or railroad industries. With the passage of time and the rapid change industrialization brought, tourism would become the region's other great commodity. The pristine landscape, with miles of lakes and forests, became a refuge for people escaping city life.

The history of Madden's, located north of Brainerd on Gull Lake, is similarly tied to both logging ventures and the railroad. The land that would become part of Madden's had been originally claimed from Native Americans, taken over through treaty for development purposes by the U.S. government. Throughout Minnesota's early years the peninsula and surrounding lakeshore passed through several hands. The government initially gave the land to the Northern Pacific Railroad who eventually sold it off to various logging interests.

Short of developing logging roads through the peninsula next to Gull Lake, the territory did not see notable change until 1909 when a businessman named T.H. Harrison bought the land with plans for its residential use. Harrison purchased the real estate, planning to sell off parcels of prime shoreline to residents of Minneapolis for vacation property.

Harrison believed that streetcars would soon be moving city dwellers to the central lakes region. Harrison dreamed of a stream of vacationers leaving the city by streetcar traveling up past Lake Mille Lacs to their final destination on Gull Lake. Unfortunately for Harrison, the streetcar line was never extended very far north of the city and he passed away before he could see the acreage surrounding Gull Lake transformed.

It was his son John Harrison who would continue his father's legacy and begin in earnest to bring change to the peninsula. After T.H. Harrison's death in 1914, his estate including his property holdings were left to his wife, with his son John appointed as trustee.

Company Perspectives:

Spend the day on the water. Or any way you like. There's a reason we're Minnesota's Classic Resort. One visit and you'll know why. No two rooms are alike here. Some say that's part of our charm. But no matter where you lay your head at the end of a busy day, we'll make you feel special.

John, eager to pick up where his father had failed, created a partnership in 1926 with a Kansas City real estate developer by the name of Chester Start. Start and Harrison formed the Pine Beach Golf Course Corporation and the Pine Beach Corporation in 1926. The developers wasted little time, and a new golf course was opened for business the following July.

While the predicted streetcar line was never built, the mass production of the motor car aided the developers to a far greater degree than the two could ever have imagined. Affordable automobiles allowed the general population a freedom of travel never before experienced. For the urban population of the Twin Cities heading "up north" instantly became a favorite and frequent jaunt among the prosperous city dwellers in the late 1920s and early 1930s.

Anticipating the need for hotel accommodations at lakeside, Harrison and Start formed another corporation in partnership with several other investors known as the Pine Beach Hotel Corporation in 1928. Among the other partners were several local Brainerd area businessmen and Arthur Roberts, a moderately successful hotel operator from Rochester, Minnesota. The Pine Beach Corporation deeded some land to the Hotel Corporation and plans were drawn up and completed by 1929. The hotel opened for business the following year. Arthur Roberts became the sole owner and operator of the hotel in 1930 when he bought out the other partners and renamed the enterprise Roberts Pine Beach Hotel.

In 1931 a young vacationer named Jack Madden summered at the Pine Beach Hotel on Gull Lake. Upon his college graduation, Madden made plans to return to the area and manage the clubhouse and golf course. Madden and his uncle Tom Madden leased the property for $500, hiring Jack's younger brother Jim to assist them in the club and caddy for the golfers. Unfortunately, the timing of the Maddens' lease at Gull Lake could not have been worse. The economy had just begun its tailspin into what became the Great Depression.

The hard economic times during the 1930s took a toll on the development plans at Gull Lake. Many of the affluent city dwellers were ruined or close to ruined financially and vacations and luxury junkets were the first of many cutbacks that they would make.

The first year the Maddens took over the clubhouse the family actually lost money on the lease but the Maddens continued to believe that the clubhouse could be profitable and made plans to buy the property from Start and Harrison. Start and Harrison were willing to negotiate terms for the sale of the golf course with no money down. The new owners incorporated the business in 1934, though Start maintained a stake in the company for a few years.

The early years of the Maddens' work on Gull Lake were characterized by small-scale additions to the property. In 1936, Jack Madden and Chester Start built Mission Point, a simple vacation resort featuring three small cabins, several garages, and a maids' quarters. Madden was intent on greatly expanding the vacation site, planning subsequent stages of development as he went along.

In 1937 Jim Madden became a full equity partner in the business at Pine Beach when Tom Madden turned over his interest in the business to Jim. Operations continued to expand despite a wartime shortage of building materials and, in 1941, the Maddens, convinced of their ability to manage things on their own, bought out Chester Start's share of Mission Point.

Growing the Resort: 1941–60s

With full ownership in the Madden family, development at Pine Beach began in earnest. In 1942 the brothers added on to the existing cabins at Mission Point and renamed the residential spot The Lodge. Shortly after becoming a partner, Jim Madden was called to serve in World War II and had to put his contribution to the business on hold. During Jim's absence, Jack and Peg Madden continued to run The Lodge and golf course.

In 1946, Jim Madden returned from military service and the brothers continued the expansion and remodeling of the facilities on Gull Lake. The Maddens bought out the Malcolm Hotel, a facility that was originally built in 1923 and that had been used throughout its years for a variety of purposes. The Malcolm Hotel had been a hotel and boarding house, an Elks Club, and a private residence. The Maddens renamed the hotel the Pine Edge Inn.

The 1946 remodeling included the old golf clubhouse which was turned into guest rooms. A new wing with a coffee shop, dining room, and kitchen was also added. The project was completed for the following summer season with guest quarters expanded by an additional 20 rooms.

In 1948 and 1949 the Maddens built two new dining rooms known as the Prime Rib Room and the Garden Room. The economy had bounced back solidly from the Depression and wartime and the Maddens, having managed to keep the business afloat, were now poised to further expand and grow their small resort.

In 1954 the Maddens opened the 20 rooms known as the Voyageurs Resort. This area included an office and VIP suite for special guests of the resort. In 1957 a former desk clerk, John Arnold, returned to Madden's as a partner in the resort. Arnold had developed crucial experience related to the hospitality industry in his years at both the St. Paul Athletic Club and Northwest Airlines. Arnold had worked at the Athletic Club as assistant manager and was the director of foodservice at Northwest Airlines, two areas of expertise that would help make Madden's all the more comfortable for its guests.

Paying tribute to the history of the region Peg Madden, returning inspired from a trip to Knott's Berry Farm in California, lent her creative hand to the family business by opening Lumbertown, USA at Madden's in 1959. Peg Madden recreated a replica of early life in the region with a model village made up of storefronts and decorated with antique artifacts. Madden's contribution of Lumbertown USA served to illustrate for Mad-

Key Dates:

1931: Jack Madden graduates from college and summers at Pine Beach, a golf course and resort established in 1926.

1932: Jack Madden and his uncle Tom Madden lease the Pine Beach Golf Clubhouse for the summer; two years later they purchase and incorporate the resort under the family name.

1936: Jack Madden and Chester Start build Mission Point.

1937: Jack's brother, Jim Madden, takes over Tom Madden's interest in the enterprise; Jack Madden buys out Chester Start's share of Mission Point.

1946: The Madden brothers buy the Malcolm Hotel and rename it the Pine Edge Inn.

1957: John Arnold becomes a co-owner.

1969: Madden's, as the business becomes known, buys out Rutger's Pine Beach Lodge and renames it Pine Portage Inn; company also buys The Green Hill resort and 80 acres of adjoining property.

1989: Brian Thuringer becomes a partner.

1991: Tennis and Croquet Club opens.

1997: The Classic, a new championship golf course, opens.

2001: Jim Madden dies after a long illness.

den's guests and visitors the colorful life in the logging camps and primitive towns that the lumber barons set up for their workers. The area also provided an educational component to the recreation and leisure the resort already furnished.

The Maddens also opened their first convention facility in 1959, known as Town Hall. The resort had hoped to attract large groups of businessmen by offering an environment where work could be mixed with the leisure of golfing and boating.

A par 3, nine-hole golf course was opened in the early 1960s but the single most historic event of the decade took place in 1964. On July 4th with the grand opening of O'Madden's Pub scheduled to take place, a fire broke out and burned the original Madden's Inn and all of the additions to the building.

The Madden family, Arnold, and the resort staff worked through the night and, remarkably, were able to open for business the following day with a few minor room changes. Jack Madden later commented that although the fire seemed a disaster at first, in retrospect it was probably a good thing for the business overall. Madden vindicated the event by admitting that the old Inn was a horrible building from the start and the resort took the opportunity to build a much nicer facility in its place.

A new golf course was also built in the 1960s and the partners bought the Roberts Pine Beach Hotel and renamed it the Madden Inn. Another 18-hole golf course was begun during the same period called Pine Beach West and was developed in sections. The first nine holes of the course, known as the Sylvan, opened in 1968. The golf course was accompanied by a new clubhouse with four apartment-type suites and a pool.

In another attempt to expand Madden's Resort, the owners bought the old Ruttgers Pine Beach Lodge and renamed it the

Pine Portage Resort in 1969. The family and John Arnold also purchased the Green Hill resort and 80 acres of property owned by Les and Ruth Goetting that same year.

The 1970s brought a few additions to resort life including a renovation and addition to the Town Hall Convention complex and a new restaurant name, the Lumber Baron Steak House. In 1973 the second nine holes of Pine Beach West opened, though the course was not completed until 1975. A cookout area and tennis course rounded out the amenities later in the decade.

In early January 1978 Jack Madden suffered a heart attack while vacationing in Florida. Madden died on January 6th, leaving behind a lifetime of work dedicated to the recreation and rejuvenation of others.

The Next Generation: Renovation and Luxury in the 1980s

The 1980s were a decade known for the demand for personal luxury. The societal demand for indulgence had an impact on the resort industry as well. Throughout the 1980s Madden's redecorated and renovated the vast majority of its buildings. Over 90 percent of the facilities were upgraded in some manner. The grounds at Madden's stayed competitive by offering more features consistent with a luxurious lifestyle. Croquet lawns, health spa features, and shopping opportunities were all added to the facilities at Madden's. The resort also became a venue for championship croquet matches within the United States. In 1986 a new Town Hall Conference Center opened for business with over 42,000 square feet of indoor meeting space and the resources to host large business conventions.

The corporation added a new family partner in 1989. C. Brian Thuringer, Jim Madden's son-in-law, was made a part-owner. Thuringer had managed the Pine Edge Inn for eight years before his partnership became official.

In 1991 a new tennis and croquet club was built which served as the recreational hub for activities at the resort. A pizza and sub shop was also opened for Madden's guests. In 1997, Madden's opened its crown jewel of golf opportunities, The Classic. Madden's championship course was ranked by *Golf Digest* as the third best new upscale course in North America, and *Golf and Travel* picked The Classic as its 27th of the best top 40 resort courses in the nation.

Madden's was known for its golf clinics and schools as well. The Chris Foley Golf School at Madden's offered a variety of classes and clinics throughout the season. Men, women, and children were scheduled for classes and weekends devoted to helping improve their game.

In March 2001, the last of the original Madden's owners passed away. Jim Madden died at his home after suffering from a long illness. His business legacy was a premier Minnesota resort which during that year would host 75,000 guests, all of whom would likely identify with the company's musings on what, in the final analysis, constituted a "Classic" resort: "Maybe it's the tradition that families have made this their getaway for over 50 years. Maybe it's the memory of your first time on water skis. Or the crackling fires on Mission Point.

Whatever it is, you'll find it here. Ready and waiting for you to create your own classic memories.''

Principal Competitors

Premier Resorts Ltd.; Izatys Golf & Yacht Club; Breezy Point Resort.

Further Reading

Merrill, Ann, ''James Madden Dies; Ran Resort on Gull Lake,'' *Star Tribune* (Minneapolis), March 12, 2001 p. 5B.
Rahn, Mike ''Madden's Mirrors the Growth of Our Area's Resort Industry,'' *Lake Country Journal,* n.d.

—Susan B. Culligan

Metropolitan Life Insurance Company

1 Madison Avenue
New York, New York 10010-3690
U.S.A.
Telephone: (212) 578-2211
Toll Free: (800) 638-5433
Fax: (212) 578-3320
Web site: http://www.metlife.com

Public Company
Incorporated: 1866 as National Travelers' Insurance
Company
Employees: 46,000
Total Assets: $256.89 billion (2001)
Stock Exchanges: New York
Ticker Symbol: MET
NAIC: 524113 Direct Life Insurance Carriers

Metropolitan Life Insurance Company (MetLife) has a long history of leadership in the financial services market. MetLife is the largest life insurer in the United States with more than $2 trillion of life insurance in force. A leader in savings and retirement products and services for individuals, small business, and large institutions, MetLife serves 88 of the *Fortune* 100 largest companies. The company operates in more than a dozen countries and continues to expand its global markets, an important part of meeting its goal to serve 100 million customers by 2010.

Roots Dating Back to the Civil War: 1860s–70s

Metropolitan's origins can be traced to the National Union Life and Limb Insurance Company, a firm originally chartered in 1863 to underwrite the lives and limbs of Union soldiers during the Civil War. The company had trouble getting started. Simeon Draper, the company's chief promoter, found it difficult to raise the necessary $100,000 capital. A company insuring only servicemen during the bloodiest war in U.S. history did not seem to be a very promising business proposal. Frustrated, Draper stepped down and a group of businessmen from Brooklyn petitioned the New York legislature to revise the company's charter to allow life insurance for civilians as well. National Union Life and Limb's president, Major General Daniel E. Sickles, a war hero, resigned shortly before the company actually began writing policies. Sickles was replaced by Orison Blount, a respected member of the business community. Blount, though multitalented, had no experience in the insurance business, and the company struggled to gain a foothold.

In 1865 the company changed its name to National Life and Travelers' Insurance Company and underwent two reorganizations within a period of two years, in 1866 splitting its life and casualty lines into separate companies, National Life Insurance Company and National Travelers' Insurance Company. The latter company initially offered only casualty lines, selling its first policy in 1867, and adding life insurance to its casualty lines later that year. National ultimately evolved into one of the premiere life insurance companies in the United States, Metropolitan.

On March 24, 1868, National Travelers' Insurance Company was reorganized as Metropolitan Life Insurance Company. The company's president, James R. Dow, had led the National Travelers' Insurance Company for several years. Originally, Dow had applied for the position of medical examiner for the casualty insurer, but because of his pleasant disposition, and a $15,000 investment, he was appointed a director and elected president. Dow and another director of the company, Joseph F. Knapp, had lobbied for the reorganization—in order to head the company in a single direction. When the company changed its name to Metropolitan Life Insurance Company it also dropped its casualty insurance business.

Metropolitan's early years saw the rapid growth of the life insurance industry. The Industrial Revolution had introduced more hazards to everyday life, creating a widespread demand for insurance of all kinds. The Civil War had been a particular boom for the life insurance trade, and the industry grew at a frenzied pace in the war's wake. Whole life insurance was the preferred type of policy. Endowments were somewhat popular, term insurance was less common, and annuities were rare. In 1869, $614 million worth of life insurance had been written in the United States, of which Metropolitan had written 2,930 policies valued at $4.86 million.

235

The industry's growth was somewhat reckless in these early years. Many companies had trouble attracting agents without paying outrageous commissions. To get business, many agents insured questionable risks. Although Metropolitan had a successful first year, it was still small compared with other life insurers. It had just $594,000 in assets, compared with the $30 million of Mutual Life of New York—the largest life insurance company at that time.

A significant portion of Metropolitan's business in the early years came from New York City's population of German immigrants. The company had two outstanding German-speaking agents, Abraham Kaufmann and Moritz Reno. A German division was soon set up, headed by Kaufmann. In 1869 Kaufmann initiated a relationship with a German fraternal society called the Hildise Bund. Metropolitan sold small life insurance policies to members of the society, with the bund collecting the premiums on a weekly basis. The organization required life insurance—with Metropolitan—as a condition of membership from each of its applicants. As German settlers migrated west, so too did the bund's relationship with the company. Metropolitan's agreement with the Hildise Bund was the company's first excursion into the field that would turn it into a giant—workingman's, or industrial, life insurance.

In 1871 Dow died and was succeeded as president by Joseph F. Knapp. In 1873 a severe depression gripped the nation. Metropolitan's business dropped from 8,280 new policies in 1874 to 510 in 1879. Many life insurance companies were unable to meet their obligations and failed. As a result, popular confidence in life insurance hit an all-time low.

Revitalizing the Company Through Industrial Insurance: 1880s to Mid-1890s

In 1879 Knapp traveled to London to observe the success of the Prudential Assurance Company of London, a company that had become successful writing industrial insurance. Knapp's interest in insurance for the masses was longstanding. He returned to New York more determined than ever to push Metropolitan into industrial insurance.

Knapp imported hundreds of British insurance agents familiar with industrial insurance to spearhead Metropolitan's efforts. These recruits trained local agents in the art of writing life insurance for small amounts, collecting the premiums weekly, and accounting to the home office. Metropolitan's success was stunning: $9 million in industrial insurance was written the first year; $18 million the second; and by 1886, just six years after the policy was officially introduced, Metropolitan had more than $100 million of industrial life insurance in force. The company expanded its agency force rapidly during the 1880s.

Hundreds of new agents ventured west and south to sell insurance to the country's working class. The cost of this expansion was great, and Knapp risked at least $650,000 of his own money to keep Metropolitan going during difficult years. By the time of Knapp's death in 1891, Metropolitan had established itself as the leader in industrial insurance, with more policies in force than Prudential and John Hancock combined.

In October 1891, following the death of Knapp, Vice-President John Rogers Hegeman became president, but it was the company's new vice-president, Haley Fiske, who was in charge of the company's day-to-day operations and policymaking. Although Metropolitan was a leader in industrial insurance, its ordinary life business had dwindled. Fiske initiated an effort to recover it.

For the most part, life insurance companies were offering so-called tontine insurance. Named after its Neapolitan inventor, Lorenzo Tonti, these policies paid dividends to their subscribers. Tontine policies were basically annuities, but their values increased based on one's longevity. As subscribers died, their portion of the fund was ceded to surviving policyholders. The last survivor took all. Although Metropolitan had written such policies in its early days, in the 1890s it was critical of them. The company's rate book of 1892 stated, "The Metropolitan believes the time has come when the plain common sense men who make up the bulk of life insurance policyholders are looking for a plain business contract . . . which leaves nothing to the imagination; which borrows nothing from hope; requires definite conditions and makes definite promises in dollars and sense" (as quoted in Marquis James's *The Metropolitan Life: A Study in Business Growth*). Metropolitan began to make inroads into the ordinary life business, writing no-frills nonparticipating policies like whole life, term life, single-premium life, limited-payment life, and endowments.

Scrutiny of Industry's Practices: Late 1890s–Early 1900s

The late 1890s and early 1900s were a time of journalistic muckraking, and insurance companies, like big business in general, became targets for the pens of journalistic zealots. Particularly unpleasant for Metropolitan were accusations that industrial insurance, which covered even a family's youngest children, encouraged infanticide for the collection of benefits. Metropolitan spearheaded the defense of industrial insurance, and after several years the controversy died down. Life insurance companies, however, were not out of the investigative woods. In a few years the most comprehensive probe yet would bring about reform in the industry.

In 1905 a New York State legislative committee headed by Senator William W. Armstrong launched an investigation of the major life insurance companies, hoping to do away with any abusive practices. The chief counsel for the investigation was Charles Evans Hughes, later governor of New York and chief justice of the Supreme Court. Hughes called top executives of all the major life insurance companies to testify before the committee, including several officers—Hegeman among them—of Metropolitan, the fourth largest life insurer at the time.

Although acknowledging that there were certain deficiencies in industrial insurance, the committee made no recommendations

Key Dates:

1863: A group of New York businessmen form National Union Life and Limb Insurance Company.
1865: The company is renamed National Life and Traveler's Insurance Company.
1866: Life and casualty lines split into two separate companies.
1868: National Traveler's Insurance Company is reorganized as Metropolitan Life Insurance Company.
1879: The addition of industrial life insurance helps to revive the company following nearly a decade of economic depression.
1893: Metropolitan Tower, which would become a New York landmark, is commissioned.
1909: Metropolitan has more life insurance in force than any other company.
1915: The company is transformed into a mutually held company.
1939: A federal investigation of life insurance companies is launched, but the industry ultimately is left to police itself.
1946: By March, Metropolitan has paid out $42.1 million on World War II deaths.
1966: Metropolitan is replaced by Prudential as the number one life insurer in terms of assets.
1975: The company begins writing individual retirement annuities.
1980: The company completes the largest single building purchase (Pan Am Building) in history.
1998: The board of directors authorizes demutualization.
2000: Metropolitan Life Insurance Company (MetLife) launches the seventh largest IPO ever held in the United States.

for change to the life insurance market. Tontine insurance, which Metropolitan had decided years before not to write, was outlawed altogether. Limits were placed on the amount of ordinary insurance that companies could write each year. Huge companies such as New York Life Insurance Company and Equitable were forced to change drastically their business practices, but Metropolitan was given merely what amounted to a slap on the wrist—abuses were cited but no remedies proposed nor penalties imposed. It gave the company a degree of public confidence not enjoyed by other companies, which helped its sales surge past its competitors' in the next few years. By 1909 Metropolitan had more life insurance in force than any other company.

The Armstrong Committee hearings did bring to light some questionable practices conducted by Metropolitan, however, and resulted in charges of third-degree forgery and perjury being brought against Hegeman. The actual impropriety of certain transactions was questionable, and in time all of the charges were dismissed.

Restructuring Business: 1910s–20s

While this controversy shook the halls of justice, Metropolitan agents continued the business of writing life insurance. The company had grown considerably over the years. As 1905 dawned the company had $1.47 billion of insurance in force. In 1909 the headquarters at 1 Madison Avenue was expanded. The company commissioned the architectural firm Le Brun and Sons, the same firm that had created its original edifice at the same address in 1893, to design a new building. The well-known Metropolitan Tower was the result. The 50-story tower was the world's tallest building until 1913 and was considered one of the wonders of the modern world.

In 1913 Metropolitan was authorized to write accident and health insurance. In 1914 it wrote its first group accident and health policy on its own employees. A year later annual medical and dental checkups were given to employees.

In January 1915 Metropolitan transformed from a stock company to a mutual company, in effect becoming owned by its policyholders. The change was intended to thwart future attempts by unscrupulous stockowners to manipulate the insurance company's millions for personal gain. From this point on, the company's profits were redistributed to its policyholders in the form of dividends.

U.S. participation in World War I resulted in about 18,000 claims by the survivors of U.S. servicemen on life insurance policies at Metropolitan and 7,500 claims from Canadian servicemen. By the end of the war $8.25 million was paid in death benefits. After the war, a worldwide flu outbreak took a far greater toll, claiming 83,000 Metropolitan policyholders by June 30, 1919. Met paid $27.6 million as a result of that epidemic.

In April 1919 President John R. Hegeman died, after 28 years at the Metropolitan helm. He had spent a total of 49 years as an officer of the company, having seen its assets increase by a factor of 55, and insurance in force by a factor of 17. His close associate over those years, Haley Fiske, assumed the presidency.

For the next ten years, Fiske continued to introduce new forms of coverage and improve old forms. In 1921 industrial policies were liberalized to pay full benefits beginning with the date of issue rather than half benefits for the first six months. In 1928 a double-indemnity clause provided for the payment of double the face value of an industrial insurance policy in the case of accidental death. These improvements were made without additional premiums.

During the prosperous early 1920s, all forms of life insurance sold extremely well. Group policies added considerably to Metropolitan's success during the decade. Assets topped $2 billion in 1926. The company's group life insurance in force grew from $60 million in 1919 to $2.25 billion a decade later. In 1928 the company wrote the largest group policy to date, for the General Motors Corporation for $400 million.

Great Depression and World War II: 1930s–40s

In March 1929 Frederick H. Ecker became president of Metropolitan upon Haley Fiske's death. Several months later the stock market crashed and the Great Depression started. Metropolitan's conservative investment policies helped it to weather the hard times. The company had stayed out of the speculative equities markets and had focused instead on real estate and bonds. The stock market crash initially had a positive impact on life insurance sales. Investors who had lost heavily tried to supplement the losses to their estates by increasing their life insurance. Ordinary insurance sold at record volume in 1930 and 1931. As the Great Depression deepened, however, and unemployment reached massive proportions, new policies stagnated and many policyholders were forced to discontinue their premium payments and allow their policies to lapse. In addition, many borrowed money against their policies or surrendered them for the cash value. Metropolitan was in sound financial condition and had no trouble meeting its obligations. Adjustments in the company's investment portfolio were necessary as rents fell and farm commodity prices dropped; Metropolitan reduced its investments in city mortgage and farm lending.

The Great Depression of the 1930s and the New Deal philosophy that accompanied it focused a great deal of attention on the nation's financial industries. In the late 1930s U.S. President Franklin D. Roosevelt urged Congress to look into malpractice of big business. The lawmakers responded by establishing the Temporary National Economic Committee for the Investigation of Concentration of Economic Power. The TNEC, as the committee became known, spent a year, beginning in 1939, interviewing officers of life insurance companies. The first witness called was Metropolitan's Frederick Ecker, chairman of Metropolitan's board of directors since 1936, when Leroy A. Lincoln had become president. After much testimony, the TNEC issued its report in 1941. Government officials were hoping for federal regulation of ordinary life insurance, and the addition of industrial insurance to the new Social Security program. The TNEC, however, in a mere three pages, suggested only that the states beef up their existing regulatory mechanisms. The committee's most forceful recommendation affected a large segment of Metropolitan Life's business, asking for a change in the operation of the industrial insurance business, and stating that in the alternative the elimination of such coverage might be required. Without proposing any new means of federal regulation, however, the life insurance industry was, for the most part, left to police itself.

World War II resulted in a number of policy changes for Metropolitan customers. While existing policies were continued under the same terms, new policies were written as war risks with special premiums and stipulated conditions. For the most part, the business of life insurance remained the same, except for the extraordinary numbers of claims due to combat. By March 1946 Metropolitan paid out $42.1 million on 51,956 lives lost as a direct result of the war.

Increased Investment: 1950s–60s

After the war, Metropolitan continued to grow rapidly and its investment dollars went into real estate projects all over the country, including landmark middle-income complexes in the Stuyvesant Town and Riverton districts in New York City. The rents on these properties were kept low in exchange for tax breaks from the city.

In 1951 Leroy A. Lincoln became chairman of the board at Metropolitan. Charles G. Taylor took over the duties of president but soon was replaced by Frederick W. Ecker, whose father had held the office years before and was now elevated to honorary chairman. Throughout the 1950s, Metropolitan was

the leading life insurer in the United States, having enjoyed that position steadily since 1909. Metropolitan held to a conservative investment posture and continued to offer low-cost insurance. In 1954, the company was the first in life insurance to install a major computer system. Metropolitan continued to support health and safety practices. In 1956 the company was behind a push to set up poison control centers.

In 1957 Frederick W. Ecker became CEO of Metropolitan and in 1959, chairman of the board. The younger Ecker's leadership stressed conservatism. Metropolitan was the largest private capital pool in the country, and the company managed it so tightly that some thought the company old-fashioned. Equities investments were avoided in the 1960s as they were in the 1920s. Other insurance companies implemented more aggressive investment and marketing strategies.

In 1963 Gilbert Fitzhugh became president of Metropolitan. In 1966 he moved up to chairman of the board and the presidency was filled by Charles A. Siegfried. In 1966 Metropolitan was replaced by Prudential as the number one life insurer in terms of assets. Prudential surpassed it in number of policies in force in 1974.

In 1968, a year after race riots rocked U.S. cities, the life insurance companies made a commitment to invest in inner cities. Metropolitan Life invested $322 million for rebuilding or new building of housing. Chairman Fitzhugh recognized the need of the company to respond to recent changes in the business, and Metropolitan, for the first time, purchased common stocks for its portfolio. Equities investments reached $1 billion in 1972. In addition to loosening up the company's investment strategy, Fitzhugh looked for new areas of insurance to market. Metropolitan began offering aviation reinsurance after 1971, and formed a subsidiary, Metropolitan Property and Liability Insurance, in 1972.

Policy Changes: 1970s

Metropolitan also made changes in its life insurance business. New products were offered, including individual variable annuities, in 1969, and after 1972 the company abandoned the debit insurance business upon which it had been built. Agents would no longer collect premiums weekly or monthly on low-cost policies.

Beginning in 1970, Metropolitan began to decentralize its operations by setting up a number of regional service centers across the country. By the end of the decade, Metropolitan had head offices at Tampa, Florida; Tulsa, Oklahoma; Providence, Rhode Island; Dayton, Ohio; Pittsburgh, Pennsylvania; Aurora, Illinois; and New York City. Regional computing centers for record keeping were set up at Greenville, South Carolina; Wichita, Kansas; and Scranton, Pennsylvania.

In October 1973 Richard R. Shinn became chairman of Metropolitan Life. Like his predecessor, Shinn had spent his entire career at Metropolitan, becoming president in 1969. Shinn continued Metropolitan's course of diversification. In 1975 the company began writing individual retirement annuities. In 1976 a subsidiary to reinsure health insurance, Metropolitan Insurance and Annuity Company, was established. In

1978 a subsidiary to reinsure property and casualty business, Metropolitan Reinsurance, began operations.

Metropolitan focused also on group policy coverage. In 1974 its group life broke an industry record with $118.68 billion in force. In 1976 Metropolitan introduced Multiple Employer Trust group policies, which provided insurance under employee benefit programs. In 1978 group plans covering 50 to 200 employees were introduced. By 1979 Metropolitan had more than $200 billion of group insurance in force. Total life insurance in force topped $300 billion.

By the end of the decade, the flaws of Metropolitan's decentralization program, begun in 1970, became apparent. Spreading out the company's bureaucracy had caused frustration among employees, and the sales staff was defecting at a rate of 40 percent per year—high turnover for Metropolitan. Although agents were encouraged to solicit middle- and upper-income customers, few big policies were written. The corporate initiative to push bigger policies was simply being ignored. One frustrated Met salesman commented, as reported in the November 21, 1977, issue of *Business Week,* "This metamorphosis has not been thought out as thoroughly as executives at the top might lead you to believe. Just go out and try to sell a policy over $10,000. You'll find the underwriters in the home office using a fine-tooth comb. They think anybody who wants a big policy is trying to cheat the company. It takes seven to eight weeks to get the big cases through."

Revitalizing the company's personal insurance sales mechanism became a priority in 1979. The number of managers between the chief marketing officer and the sales representative was reduced from six to three over the next five years. An open-door policy was instituted in order to eliminate the memo-writing mentality at Met. Executive Vice-President Pierre Maurer, in charge of the reorganization, told employees in 1983, "Always wage war against paper—it's the greatest waster of management time and energy," (as reported by *Best's Review,* July 1984). By the mid-1980s, Metropolitan was a leaner company, having eliminated 60 percent of its redundant middle management.

Diversification: 1980s

In 1980 Metropolitan purchased the Pan Am Building in New York City for $400 million. The sale was the largest single building purchase in history. The company also established a joint venture with Metropolitan Structures of Chicago, resulting in one of the largest commercial real estate development companies, with a net worth of $500 million. In the whirlwind financial climate of the 1980s, Metropolitan entered risky investment areas. It dabbled in leveraged buyouts and in venture-capital investments for high-technology research and development.

Deregulation of financial services throughout the 1980s gave impetus to a number of new subsidiaries. In 1982 Metropolitan Tower Life was formed to write specialty lines. In 1983 MetLife Marketing Corporation was set up to supplement the agency distribution system; MetLife General Insurance Agency was formed to sell products, through agents, that Metropolitan Life Insurance Company did not offer; and MetLife Capital Corporation was established as an equipment leasing company.

In 1984 the company began using the name Metropolitan Life and Affiliated Companies, better to reflect its diverse nature. Also in 1984, a highly successful advertising campaign featuring the well-known Peanuts comic strip characters kicked off with the slogan, "Get Met. It Pays."

A new management team, with John J. Creedon as CEO and president and Robert Schwartz as chairman, took over in 1983. Both were career Metropolitan men. Metropolitan continued to expand its product mix in an effort to regain lost ground from its rival, Prudential. In 1984 Metropolitan's "whole life plus" policy, offering up to one-third more coverage with no increase in premium, introduced just three years prior, became the company's best-selling policy.

In 1985 Metropolitan acquired Charter Security Life Insurance Companies and in so doing took over its line of Single Premium Deferred Annuities. A number of other acquisitions were completed that year: the Century 21 Real Estate franchise organization; the fifth largest full-service mortgage banker in the United States, Crossland Capital Corporation, which was renamed MetMor Financial, Inc.; Albany Assurance Company, Ltd., of the United Kingdom, a major marketer of variable life insurance and pension products; and Litton Industries Credit Corporation, a leasing company, renamed MetLife Capital Credit Corporation.

While looking for new markets for its products overseas, Metropolitan found some untapped markets in the United States. The company discovered that recent immigrants make good insurance customers. In 1983 Metropolitan began a marketing program geared to selling insurance to the 15 million Spanish-speaking people permanently residing in the United States. By 1985 Met was number one in the seven top Hispanic markets nationwide. In 1986 the company began to develop an Asian-American marketing strategy.

In 1986 Metropolitan introduced two new individual life insurance products, single premium life and universal variable life. It continued to add companies to enhance its mix of financial services in the later 1980s. In 1987 the assets of insolvent annuity-writer Baldwin-United Corporation and the Texas Life Insurance Company were acquired. In 1989 the group life and health business of the Allstate Insurance Company was purchased.

The trend in the late 1980s was toward globalization of financial markets. In keeping with the trend, Metropolitan initiated operations in Tokyo in January 1987. Six months later, the company entered into an agreement with Spain's Banco Santander to sell insurance and pension products in that country. Metropolitan began selling insurance in Taiwan in 1989.

MetLife HealthCare Management Corporation was established in 1988 to set up health maintenance organizations. During the 1980s, health insurers were faced with rising healthcare costs. Metropolitan, long in the business of promoting healthful habits, in 1987 sponsored a two-hour television program as part of its assault on the fastest growing problem for health insurers—acquired immune deficiency syndrome (AIDS). By 1989 it had committed $6.5 million for AIDS education.

In 1989 Robert G. Schwartz took over the duties of president and CEO upon John J. Creedon's retirement. Schwartz stated that the company's first priority for the future was to ''build upon the inherent strength in our traditional lines of business— personal insurance, group insurance, and investments.'' Schwartz also identified the goals of increased productivity, development of the company's people, accurate assessment of demographic changes, and strengthening Metropolitan's ability to respond to market changes.

Metropolitan Life Insurance Company's sheer size and long tradition made it something of an institution in itself. While the company was for a time the victim of its own success—content to follow market changes rather than anticipate them—the Metropolitan that emerged from the 1980s appeared to be positioned for success in the years ahead.

Traversing Rocky Terrain: 1990s

Harry P. Kamen, a longtime MetLifer, was named chairman and CEO in April 1993. He quickly faced a major problem: the discovery that agents in Tampa, Florida, were using deceptive sales practices. The resulting fallout was damaging not only to Metropolitan but to the entire life insurance industry.

Metropolitan agents had been selling nurses life insurance policies under the guise of retirement savings plans. The company had to pay out millions in rebates to affected customers as well as fines leveled by regulators. The distrust created had negative impact on earnings and, consequently, the company's financial ratings.

In response to the scandal, Metropolitan charged senior executives with overseeing changes designed to prevent a repeat performance. According to a March 1994 *Sales & Marketing Management* article, a business standards committee was created, the customer relations department was centralized, and ethics and compliance committees were established. The sales training and promotion programs, which had been under local control, also were centralized.

The word compliance took on new meaning throughout the industry. ''Before Metropolitan Life Insurance Co. came under fire when its agents were caught misrepresenting life insurance policies, the compliance department was thought of as a group of lawyers who filed policies with insurance departments or handled consumer complaints. A recent cartoon summed it up: It shows one executive telling another that 'running it by legal' meant sprinting past the company's lawyers with document in hand,' '' wrote Sean Armstrong for *Best's Review* in March 1995.

Not only had the Florida incident sparked investigations of MetLife's sales practices and materials in more than a dozen states, it triggered probes of other large insurers as well. The inquiries brought about changes in laws and regulations. For example, top executives and board members of insurers faced a greater degree of accountability for actions of their sales force. Insurers moved to clean house and the industry's professional organizations attempted to rebuild their tarnished reputation.

Beginning in October 1994 at its New York headquarters, Metropolitan Life began a massive re-engineering program. Increased earnings and improved customer service to policy holders topped its list of goals. An outside consulting firm helped Metropolitan examine all areas of operation. Plans for updating technologies, trimming costs, and improving return on investment were put in place. The company's operating earnings, total revenues, and net investment income all had declined from 1993 to 1994.

Metropolitan Life's re-engineering program came with a big price tag—and not just in consulting fees. The company reported a net loss of $672 million in 1995. According to an April 1996 *National Underwriter Life & Health* article, the year's results were hurt by large capital losses, including write-offs related to the sale of three business units: Century 21 Real Estate Corp., MetMor Financial, and Metropolitan Trust Company of Canada. Additional capital loss came from the sale of real estate holdings: the company had been trying to reduce its percent of total investment assets in properties from about 10 percent to between 5 and 6 percent.

Metropolitan Life's numbers improved in 1996 thanks to improvements in operations and due to its merger with New England Mutual Life: both net income and assets under management increased. The level of life insurance in force also climbed, to $1.6 trillion from $1.4 trillion the previous year.

''MetLife is an extremely sound company financially,'' A.M. Best's Larry Mayewski, told *National Underwriter* in April 1997. ''They are conscious of earnings and return on capital, and have taken significant steps in recent years to get to a level of earnings for a company their size. There is really nothing striking that jumps out as a major problem.'' Robert H. Benmosche had been instrumental in ironing out some of the company's most pressing problems.

Benmosche's marketing and operations skills led Kamen to bring him on board in 1995 to direct the integration of New England Mutual. Put in charge of the retail sales force in 1996, Benmosche focused on retention, compliance, and productivity. He also upgraded technology.

Benmosche had been flung into the world of business at a tender age, when his father died leaving his mother a hotel and restaurant to run and a load of debt to pay off. Following high school and college, he served in the Army and developed strong technical skills, setting up field communication networks overseas. Once back in civilian life he worked as a communications consultant and then with Chase Manhattan Bank's systems group. From 1982 to 1995, Benmosche built a solid reputation at PaineWebber in the operations end of the brokerage business.

Benmosche was no less successful at Metropolitan: he rose to chairman, president, and CEO in January 1998. As head of Metropolitan, Benmosche faced a rapidly changing financial services industry. Megamergers were in the works putting increased pressure on mutual insurers such as MetLife. MetLife itself was seen as a possible buyout target by some. The company's core business of whole life insurance for the middle class had been in decline for much of the decade.

In November 1998 the board of directors approved the demutualization of the insurance company, and Benmosche began to prepare for entry into the public sector. Top management was streamlined; cost-cutting measures, including layoffs,

were implemented; bonuses were more tightly tied to performance; new products, such as long-term care insurance, were
introduced; a program to train agents in selling investment
products was established—consumers increasingly put money
once used for insurance premiums into stocks and mutual funds.

In the Public Eye: 2000 and Beyond

The barriers separating financial services businesses of insurance, banking, and brokerage were broken down by the
Gramm-Leach-Bliley Act in 1999. The Glass-Steagall Act of
1934 had kept these various sectors from crossing over into
each other's territory. Repealed, the drive to build multiproduct
organizations was off and running and going public could help
Metropolitan compete more effectively in the new environment.
Among other things, it would increase the company's ability to
raise capital.

The insurance company's 12 million policyholders were
given the option to take stock, cash, or policy credits as part of
the demutualization. MetLife would raise $2.5 billion through
its April 2000 initial public offering (IPO).

Stock price soared during its first nine months on the
market, but analysts began downgrading their ratings when
MetLife's performance proved to be lackluster. The newly
public company had made no large acquisitions, earnings per
share remained flat, and net income slumped despite increased
revenues.

According to a January 2001 *American Banker* article,
Benmosche planned to boost earnings through aggressively
restructuring the company and drawing more revenues out of its
core institutional and individual insurance areas, which produced 91 percent of 1999's $25 billion in revenue.

MetLife also began redefining its brand identity in 2001.
Since the mid-1980s, advertising had featured Snoopy. A new
slogan, "Have you met life today?," was introduced as part of a
campaign emphasizing the financial services aspects of the
company. On a related note, MetLife entered the retail banking
business, providing another layer of services for its customers.

The September 11th attack on the United States resulted in a
major blow to MetLife's 2001 net income: it fell 50 percent, in
part due to related payouts and investment losses. On the other
hand, revenues had climbed 18 percent since Benmosche took
command. Return on equity—helped by a $1 billion stock
buyback in 2001—was also on the upswing. Consequently,
Forbes declared in April 2002 that MetLife was "in far better
shape" thanks to Benmosche's efforts but also noted the turnaround effort was "still a work in progress."

Principal Subsidiaries

Reinsurance Group of America, Incorporated; GenAmerica Fi-
nancial Corporation; Texas Life Insurance Company; Nathan &
Lewis Securities, Inc.; State Street Research & Management
Company; Walnut Street Securities, Inc.; MetLife Bank, N.A.;
MetLife Securities, Inc.

Principal Competitors

Prudential Insurance Company of America; American International Group; Aetna Life Insurance Company of America.

Further Reading

Armstrong, Sean, "The Sales Police," *Best's Review—Life-Health Insurance Edition,* March 1995, pp. 34+.

Birger, Jon, "Not Same Old Life," *Crain's New York Business,* March 1, 1999, p. 1.

Brewer, Geoffrey, and Nancy Arnott, "Can MetLife Insure Honest Selling?," *Sales & Marketing Management,* March 1994, p. 13.

Connolly, Jim, "Met Life Incurs Costs As Revamping Continues," *National Underwriter Life & Health—Financial Services Edition,* April 22, 1996, p. 31.

Coolidge, Carrie, "Snoopy's New Tricks," *Forbes,* April 15, 2002, p. 100.

Cox, Brian, "Met Life in Midst of Huge Re-engineering Program," *National Underwriter Life & Health—Financial Services Edition,* September 18, 1995, pp. 40+.

Dublin, Louis I., *A Family of Thirty Million: The Story of the Metropoli-tan Life Insurance Company,* New York: Metropolitan Life Insur-ance Company, 1943.

Gjertsen, Lee Ann, "Does Bob Benmosche's New MetLife Have What It Takes to Break Out?," *American Banker,* January 8, 2001, p. 1.

James, Marquis, *The Metropolitan Life: A Study in Business Growth,* New York: Viking Press, 1947.

Levinsohn, Alan, "Insurers Go Public," *Strategic Finance,* July 2000, p. 68.

Mannino, Barbara, "Staying the Course," *Best's Review—Life-Health Insurance Edition,* May 1998, pp. 40+.

"MetLife Reinvents Its Identity with Launch of Ad Campaign," *Best's Review,* June 2001, p. 95.

"Metropolitan Life: Citadel of Safety," *Forbes,* September 1, 1962.

Nathans, Leah, "Fighter Pilot," *Business Week,* December 14, 1998, p. 124.

Schmitt, Frederick, "Met Life's 1996 Earnings Well Received by Analysts," *National Underwriter Life & Health—Financial Ser-vices Edition,* April 14, 1997, pp. 3+.

Van Aartrijk, Peter, Jr., "Meet the New Metropolitan Life," *Best's Review,* July 1984.

Wipperfurth, Heike, "Breaking Tradition, Remaking MetLife," *Crain's New York Business,* April 9, 2001, p. 27.

—Thomas M. Tucker
—update: Kathleen Peippo

MGIC Investment Corp.

270 E. Kilbourn Avenue
Milwaukee, Wisconsin 53202
U.S.A.
Telephone: (414) 347-6480
Toll Free: (800) 558-9900
Fax: (414) 347-6696
Web site: http://www.mgic.com

Public Company
Incorporated: 1985
Employees: 1,149
Total Assets: $4.56 billion (2001)
Stock Exchanges: New York
Ticker Symbol: MTG
NAIC: 524130 Reinsurance Carriers, 524126 Direct
Property and Casualty Insurance Carriers, 551112
Offices of Other Holding Companies

MGIC Investment Corp. (MGIC) is a holding company whose chief subsidiary is Mortgage Guaranty Insurance Corp., a provider of private mortgage insurance coverage to the home mortgage lending industry in the United States and Puerto Rico. Most of MGIC's sales come from insurance premiums, although the company also offers its in-house payment and default predictive tools to other lenders. MGIC also invests in troubled mortgages through its interest in Credit-Based Asset Servicing and Securization (C-BASS) and provides property valuation services.

Birth of a New Industry: 1957–69

In 1957 Max Karl, a 47-year-old former real estate attorney and the son of Jewish Russian immigrants, scraped together $250,000 from investors and founded MGIC (Mortgage Guaranty Insurance Corp.), a company that insured low down payment mortgages against foreclosure. With the formation of MGIC, Karl also created a new industry, the private mortgage insurance industry, which took on the Federal Housing Administration (FHA) in providing loans to low-income homebuyers. Private mortgage insurance was a financial guaranty business in which an insurer assumed a portion of a lender's risk in making a mortgage loan. The "risk" was that a borrower would default on a loan and the insurer would have to pay a claim. For this risk, the insurer collected a premium from the lender, which typically recovered the cost of the premium from the borrower. Until the formation of MGIC, the FHA had been the only mortgage insurer to work with homebuyers who put up less than 20 percent of the down payment on their purchase.

As a real estate lawyer in Milwaukee, Karl was familiar with the private mortgage insurance fiascos of the pre-Depression years and the expanded role of the FHA afterward in providing mortgage insurance. By 1956 Karl had come up with the idea for his company, in response to the increasing red tape involved in closing loans with 100 percent government guarantees and FHA-imposed ceilings—which were often below the yield from conventional mortgages—on mortgage interest rates.

Karl believed a private company that insured only the top portion—25 to 30 percent after the homebuyer's 5 percent down payment—presented lenders with a less costly and easier way to provide low down payment financing to borrowers unable to provide a 20 percent or larger down payment. Regardless of his backers' lack of enthusiasm, Karl persevered. "Almost everyone who knew much about stocks thought [the] company would never make it," he commented in a 1973 *Wall Street Journal* article. "They thought we were too big a risk."

Karl, however, felt confident his idea was sound. "[The] only thing that would hurt us would be a depression, which seemed remote." Putting his trust in the low rate of foreclosures since World War II, Karl got MGIC's license to operate in Wisconsin in February 1957, and the next month, the company insured four home mortgages. MGIC, which went public in 1961, provided speedy service using the information collected by the lending institution and approved insurance applications within a day or two of filing. This compared to the FHA's four- to six-week waiting period on approval. It also insured low down payment mortgages at about half the cost to the homebuyer of FHA insurance. Karl's idea caught on, and beginning in 1958, the company's profits increased every year. In 1961, he took his company public.

From 1967 to 1973 profits for MGIC more than quadrupled every year. This explosive growth was, in part, the result of changes in federal regulations. In 1971 regulatory authorities expanded lending limits, to permit savings and loan associations to make mortgages up to 95 percent of appraised value (compared to 90 percent before) as long as loans were insured. Limits on the dollar value of mortgages were also raised. MGIC more than doubled the volume of its home loan insurance from $2.8 billion in 1971 to $7.5 billion in 1972 to top the FHA's loan volume; about 40 percent of this increase occurred in the 95 percent loan category. Karl was quoted in the *Wall Street Journal* in 1973 as saying, "I've always felt the proper role for the government was helping lower income groups acquire housing which would be unsound for us to insure anyway. . . . Most of the business, it seems to me, would be better served by private companies."

Diversification in the 1970s

Having succeeded in the home mortgage field, MGIC moved to diversify its business by making more services available to lenders. In 1967 the company's first move had been to form a unit to insure mortgages on commercial buildings, which it marketed as a tool to enable builders and developers to get financing on more liberal terms. "It made sense to me that if mortgage insurance improved the ability of buyers to finance homes, it could do the same thing for owners of factories, warehouses, apartments and other commercial buildings," Karl said in the 1973 *Wall Street Journal* article. Soon thereafter, MGIC extended the concept of private insurance to mobile homes.

Another move toward diversification occurred in 1970 when MGIC acquired two homebuilding and land development companies in Florida, Janis Properties Inc. and LaMonte-Shimberg Corp., and added a unit to provide temporary construction financing to builders whose projects were a potential source of home mortgage insurance. In a more radical move in 1971, the company introduced American Municipal Bond Insurance Corp. (AMBAC) to insure the principal and interest of municipal bonds against default. MGIC formed another unit in 1972 to provide the first nonfederal secondary market for buying and selling conventional mortgages, allowing lenders to free funds tied up in mortgages for further lending. This unit augmented activities of the Federal National Mortgage Association (Fannie Mae) and the Federal Home Loan Mortgage Corp. (Freddie Mac). In 1973 the company introduced a program to insure the principal and interest of subordinated debentures issued by savings and loan associations, and began to offer directors' and officers' liability insurance.

With growth came competition, and there were ten rivals by 1973. Yet MGIC remained at the forefront of its field. Of approximately $11 billion in private residential mortgage insur-

ance written in 1972, MGIC wrote $7.5 billion, and the number of claims it had to pay annually—foreclosure on losses—remained a negligible $2 million or less annually. Then suddenly in 1974, problems began to surface. First, its mobile home mortgage and commercial property mortgage ventures began to sour. MGIC also found itself borrowing short-term to finance its secondary mortgage market inventory. After a $1.9 million net loss in 1974, MGIC engaged in a major reorganization. Karl became chairman and Gerald Friedman, his nephew, assumed charge of operations as president. The company stopped writing insurance on mobile homes and closed down its secondary market operation.

The private mortgage insurance industry continued to grow. By 1977 private mortgage insurers were responsible for 12 percent of all new mortgages—up from 3.7 percent in 1970—and were writing some $21 billion in new coverage. Mortgage-backed pass-throughs or certificates—a security built on pools of mortgages with monthly payments passed on to investors—were gaining ground in the industry, and Bank of America turned to MGIC for insurance when it became the first private lender to package such a certificate. This move as well as MGIC's longstanding position at the head of its industry attracted much positive attention to the company and made it ripe for a takeover.

In 1981, Baldwin-United Corp., a multibillion-dollar asset holding company with subsidiaries in life, property, and casualty insurance, and savings and loans, bought MGIC for $1.2 billion. Baldwin-United had been in the business of manufacturing pianos until 1968, when a series of acquisitions built it into a financial services conglomerate specializing in insurance with 250 subsidiaries. In addition to insurance, the company was best known for annuities and S&H Green Stamps. Friedman resigned his presidency in opposition to the merger. Baldwin-United took MGIC off the New York Stock Exchange.

On the Rebound: 1980s and 1990s

Although MGIC continued to perform well, its acquisition contributed to the downfall of Baldwin-United because Baldwin became unable to service the debt it took on to purchase MGIC. In May 1983 corporate turnaround expert Victor H. Palmieri took over the beleaguered Baldwin-United and put MGIC and its major subsidiaries—Mortgage Guaranty Insurance Corporation, American Municipal Bond Assurance Corporation, and MGIC Indemnity Corporation—on the auction block, forced to do so by the state insurance commissions of Arkansas, Indiana, and Wisconsin. The next year, Baldwin-United filed for bankruptcy.

MGIC operated under the supervision of the Wisconsin Office of the Commissioner of Insurance from 1983 to 1985. In 1985 the Northwestern Mutual Life Insurance Company (NML) and Management Financing Corp., an acquisition vehicle created by MGIC's management, bought MGIC Investment Corp. for $255 million. The "new MGIC" served as an autonomous subsidiary of NML with John J. McCormack as chief executive officer.

The 1980s were a tumultuous period in the home mortgage finance industry, a period marked by home price stagnation and depreciation. During the housing boom of the 1970s and early

1980s, MGIC had slashed prices and slacked off on standards in an effort to retain market dominance. By the mid-1980s these practices had come back to haunt it as economic troubles and deflated property values in the oil-producing regions of the country in the early 1980s led to increased mortgage loan defaults by late 1986. Losses piled up and the number of private mortgage insurers dwindled from 14 to seven in the late 1980s. In 1987, the year William Lacy took over as president and chief executive officer of MGIC, the company had a net loss of $32 million. Although MGIC remained the market leader (followed closely by General Electric Mortgage Insurance Company), it was worth little more than its value when NML acquired it.

Earnings grew at a very slow pace throughout 1988. Then, in 1989, the year Karl retired, the company began to show signs of rebounding. Once again in the 1990s, industry growth was rapid as more people used mortgage insurance to buy a home. In 1991, increased demand for insurance, lower house prices, changes in regulations, financial support, and tax relief led to a marked increase in the number of transactions for private mortgage insurers. Mortgage bankers who had historically used government programs became more comfortable working with private insurers in the wake of rules that limited the amount of closing costs homeowners could finance and required a higher up-front payment for mortgage insurance than had been standard on conventional mortgages. For its part, MGIC stepped up marketing efforts in hopes of improving its 29 percent market share. NML's confidence in MGIC prompted them to take the company public in 1991; so many investors wanted MGIC stock that underwriters added 1.5 million shares to the initial public offering. Four years later, NML put half of its 20 percent stake up for sale.

By 1996, MGIC had grown 25 percent since going public. Earnings for 1991 had been $75 million, increased to $102.3 million the following year, and up to $207 million in 1995. The driving force behind MGIC's growth was a sizable increase in new business. Low interest rates had helped create an environment conducive to MGIC's continued growth, and the company had invested heavily in technology—for electronic underwriting, processing of insurance certificates, and renewal billing.

As part of MGIC's ongoing move to diversification, it joined with Enhance Financial Services Group to form C-BASS, short for Credit-Based Asset Servicing and Securitization LLC, to provide reinsurance for municipal bond insurers in 1997. The company also joined with Freddie Mac to create a new default management system for mortgage insurers, Early Indicator. Later MGIC began to offer home warranty contracts to lenders in a move to attract business and to package a group of support products, called CRM Strategies. These included a direct mail program to customers; "Defender," an interactive voice-response telephone program to take information from customers and calculate the likelihood of refinancing; and "Customers Forever," an Internet program to apply for a loan jointly owned with M&I Data Services. In 2000, MGIC formed eMagic.com, a subsidiary to incorporate the company's web site.

During 2001, MGIC enjoyed a record volume of new insurance which resulted in high earnings of $639 million. Premiums exceeded $1 billion for the first time. Amid signs that loans were starting to perform poorly in a deteriorating economy, MGIC raised its loss reserves. Looking ahead, Curt Culver, who had replaced Lacy as chief executive and president of MGIC Investment in 2000, expected the company's growth prospects to be strong. Favorable demographic trends, an increasing homeownership rate among immigrants and minorities (who represented a disproportionately large segment of the nation's population growth), and high housing affordability, all boded well for the future of MGIC.

Principal Subsidiaries

Mortgage Guaranty Insurance Corp.; eMagic.com, LLC; Credit-Based Asset Servicing and Securization, LLC; Customers Forever, LLC.

Principal Competitors

CMI; GC Capital Mortgage Insurance Corp.; PMI Mortgage Insurance Co.; Radian Group; Ticor; Triad Guaranty Insurance; United Guaranty Residential Insurance Corp.

Further Reading

Bergquist, Erick, "Mortgage Insurer Woes a Bad Omen?," *American Banker*, October 29, 2001, p. 1.
Byrne, Harlan S., "Magic Max: How Mr. Karl Created a Booming Industry from a Little Company," *Wall Street Journal*, March 14, 1973.
——, "Not Running Scared," *Barron's*, March 28, 1994, p. 16.
Cooper, Geoff, "Big Investment, Big Headache, Big Offering," *Business Journal—Milwaukee*, June 24, 1991, p. 1.
——, " 'New' MGIC, a Different Kind of Magic," *Business Journal—Milwaukee*, May 9, 1992, p. 1.
"The Magic Returns for Mortgage Insurers," *Business Week*, December 5, 1977, p. 104.
"MGIC," *Business Journal—Milwaukee*, May 25, 1996, p. 21.
Mullins, Robert, "Culver Dishes Up Consistency for MGIC," *Business Journal—Milwaukee*, February 19, 1999, p. 25.
Weiner, Lisabeth, and Lynn Bremer, "Northwestern Mutual Purchases 90 Percent of MGIC, Largest U.S. Mortgage Insurer," *American Banker*, March 7, 1985, p. 2.

—Carrie Rothburd

MICHAEL C. FINA
FIFTH AVENUE • NEW YORK

Michael C. Fina Co., Inc.

545 Fifth Avenue
New York, New York 10017-3609
U.S.A.
Telephone: (212) 557-2500
Toll Free: (800) 289-3462
Web site: http://www.michaelcfina.com

Private Company
Founded: 1935
Employees: 150
Sales: $75 million (2001 est.)
NAIC: 452110 Department Stores

Michael C. Fina Co., Inc. is a family-run New York City single-store Fifth Avenue retailer specializing in jewelry and giftware. Since the mid-1930s the store has catered to discriminating New Yorkers, selling high-quality merchandise at discounted prices while also offering solid customer service. Michael C. Fina is especially successful in its bridal registry business, as well as its corporate gift program. The company is headed by the second generation of the Fina family, brothers Charles and George, with a third generation also actively involved.

Entering the Silver Business: 1920s

The company's namesake and one of its three founders, Michael C. Fina, was born in Brooklyn in 1907, the son of a barber. At the age of 15 he dropped out of high school to enter the silver business as a salesman. For the next dozen years he learned his trade in Manhattan. He was working for a silver wholesaler, J.W. Johnson, when he and two colleagues decided in 1935 to create their own silverware retail and wholesale business. His partners were Rose Rosenblatt and fellow salesman Lou Ellmore. They established their business at a fourth floor location at 580 Fifth Avenue on the corner of 47th Street, the heart of New York's diamond district. With Rose handling the company's finances, Fina and Ellmore focused on sales. In the early years the company specialized in silver plate and sterling silver hollowware, such as trays, tea sets, and candelabras. Ellmore remained with the business for only a short time; by 1942, Rosenblatt and Fina had married.

From the outset, the business made its mark by offering top merchandise at reasonable prices and adding a personal touch, with the store owners always willing to personally address the needs of their customers. As a result, Michael C. Fina enjoyed steady, continuous growth over the years. By the early 1950s the store expanded its product lines to include flatware, which soon led to the store moving from the fourth floor at 580 Fifth Avenue to larger accommodations on the second floor. The company also started printing catalogs to support all the merchandise it now carried. In the early 1960s Michael C. Fina moved beyond silver and began to sell fine and casual china and crystal. It was also in the 1960s that the store became an early entrant in New York's bridal registry business, a move that proved key to Michael C. Fina's continued growth. The store's reputation for quality merchandise, low prices, and excellent customer service made for a natural fit with the bridal business. Moreover, it introduced more New Yorkers to Michael C. Fina, and business from one wedding often led to that for another. By the late 1960s, a second generation of the Fina family became involved in the business as two of Michael and Rose's seven children, sons George and Charles, joined their parents at the store.

Death of Michael Fina: 1975

In the 1970s Michael C. Fina added jewelry to its offerings. Also during that decade, in February 1975, Michael Fina died under tragic circumstances at the age of 67. After driving Charles and his family home following a Sunday night visit, he returned to his own house in Forest Hills around 9:30 when according to the police he parked his Cadillac in the garage, located directly beneath the master bedroom, and neglected to turn off the engine. The next morning Charles became concerned when his father failed to follow his customary practice of telephoning before leaving to pick him up on their routine commute into Manhattan. When he called the house and no one answered, Charles became concerned and drove to his parents' house. He found his mother still in her bedclothes lying unconscious in the foyer, presumably having fled the carbon monoxide that had seeped into the bedroom. Michael Fina, on the other hand, was a heavier sleeper than his wife and never managed to attempt an escape. Charles found his father in his bed, killed by the fumes. Rose was rushed to St. John's Hospital, treated in the intensive care unit, and recovered from the episode. A subsequent investigation by the police uncovered a hole in the garage ceiling caused by a water leak, which allowed the carbon monoxide direct access to the bedroom.

Rose Fina remained actively involved in the business for another 20 years, but the running of Michael C. Fina now fell on the shoulders of Charles and George. The store continued to thrive, however, its family touch more than able to hold its own against its main competition, the much larger and better known area department stores such as Fortunoff, Bloomingdale's, Macy's, and A&S. Michael C. Fina was also able to remain in the sterling and estate silver businesses, which many of its rivals decided to drop. By the late 1980s, the company initiated a number of changes to ensure continued growth. It opened a street level space at 580 Fifth Avenue to augment its second floor location and invested to upgrade its already strong bridal registry, installing new computer equipment and creating its own database program in order to include as much information as possible about a bride and her selections. Moreover, the company began to advertise the registry in the *New York Times* and such national magazines as *Brides* and *Your New Home*. As a result the registry business experienced a major growth spurt. Brides from around the country, not just the New York City area, began to register with Michael C. Fina. An 800 phone number for customers and a price quote service helped to facilitate out-of-town purchases. To support the growing registry business, the company relied heavily on a 65,000-square-foot Queens warehouse, which featured strong computerized inventory control systems that allowed for the timely filling of orders.

In 1992 Michael C. Fina added 2,000 square feet to its store, much of which was used to accommodate its growing crystal and china collection, as well as for the expansion of the bridal business, which was moved to a separate, designated area on the ground floor. By now the store was registering 10,000 brides a year, but in reality was doing even more bridal sales because its low prices siphoned off business from other registries. With the economy suffering a downturn, the bridal business was a strong suit for Michael C. Fina, because it was essentially recession proof. The enlarged store also allowed the company to move into housewares, an important bridal segment that it was unable to previously support. To accommodate customer requests for everyday products, Michael C. Fina now added casual crystal and dinnerware, cookware, cutlery, and a limited number of small appliances suitable for the bridal business. Locating housewares as well as tabletop products on the ground level, enhanced by upgraded lighting and fixturing, also played into a strategy of improving in-store traffic and attracting walk-in business with more modestly priced merchandise.

A similarly profitable area for Michael C. Fina was the baby business, which featured silverplated baby cups and other gifts. Michael C. Fina's bridal database proved useful in growing this

segment as well. The store offered bridal customers a $25 certificate towards the purchase of its wedding rings in order to keep the registrant's name in its database for three years, allowing the store to touch base with customers on special family occasions, such as anniversaries and birthdays. Also in the early 1990s Michael C. Fina established a corporate division, which served corporate customers who awarded recognition gifts to longtime, valuable employees. This business was greatly enhanced by the Michael C. Fina catalog and developed into an elaborate program, which included personalized communications and a presentation video. As a result of its enlarged store and product lines, Michael C. Fina by 1992 boasted annual sales of $30 million.

After expanding its tabletop business as much as possible, the natural progression for Michael C. Fina was to begin offering distinctive table linens as part of a cross-merchandising strategy. In the fall of 1995 the store introduced Waterford Linens by WC Designs, which could be coordinated with popular patterns of Waterford Crystal as well as Wedgwood, a sister line of dinnerware. The store also sold merchandise from Sybaritic, then several months later added the linens of Christofle, an upscale tabletop manufacturer. Early results from table linens were so encouraging that management was eager to become a complete tabletop resource, with a particular emphasis on coordination with its dinnerware. Textiles in general looked promising. Merchandise Manager Hillary Donohue was asked about the store moving into other textile categories by *HFN* in 1996, and she commented, ''I would love to expand into decorative pillows and bed linens but right now, we just don't have the space.'' Not only was the store limited in size, it was further hindered by a massive staircase that ran down the center.

New Flagship Store Opens in 1998

Although Michael C. Fina had outgrown its home of 60 years, Manhattan real estate values escalated so much in the 1990s that even the traditionally less upscale stretch of Fifth Avenue between 34th and 50th streets became extremely expensive, making it unlikely that Michael C. Fina would opt to move from its diamond district location. In 1997, however, the store's landlord decided to double the rent. With added expense already a given, management elected to move to a new location with more Fifth Avenue frontage and larger show windows, signing a 15-year, $8 million lease. The new address was 545 Fifth Avenue, on the corner of 45th street, the site of an old Horn & Hardart automat cafeteria, but now located closer to more upper-end retailers. The new flagship store, which opened in April 1998, featured 20,000 square feet of retail space spread over three floors, and instead of the eight feet of window display on Fifth Avenue at the old location, it boasted 20 feet, as well as an additional 60 feet of display windows on 45th Street. Designed by the Fitzpatrick Group, the new store featured an oval shape, which was conducive to a shop-within-a-shop concept, offering each of its vendors an excellent location and allowing such major lines as Ralph Lauren, Calvin Klein, Lynn Chas, Versace by Rosenthal, and Christofle the room necessary to make appropriate presentations. Michael C. Fina also looked to grow its already successful bridal registry business, expanding the space devoted to the department to 750 square feet and also adding three new full-time consultants to its staff of five. Other departments enjoyed the benefits of added space as well. Table-

Key Dates:

1935: Original store opens at 580 Fifth Avenue.
1975: Michael C. Fina dies.
1992: Original store is expanded by 2,000 square feet.
1998: New flagship store opens at 545 Fifth Avenue.
1999: Rose Fina dies.

top, for instance, was now able to feature a 45-foot wall of sterling and silverplated flatware. A new gourmet housewares department was doubled in size, and the store was now able to expand its china offerings, and add woodenware as well as high-end electrics. The recent addition of table linens would also have its own shop and for the first time Michael C. Fina was able to open a baby shop to support the company's strong effort with baby goods.

Michael C. Fina's new home offered greater visibility in the New York market, but the Fina family also began to view the flagship location as a springboard for gaining a national presence, serving as a prototype for a suburban New York site, or perhaps southeastern cities such as Miami and Atlanta. A *Crain's New York Business* article of 1998, however, expressed some skepticism about the company's prospects: "Industry insiders say Fina may have a tough time adjusting to its Fifth Avenue address. At the same time that the retailer rushes to court a new broader customer base, it will have to work to keep its current following mollified with its trademark discounted prices. 'People may think the fancy address means Fina is no longer price-sensitive,' says Faith Hope Consolo, senior managing Director of Garrick-Aug Associates.'' Nevertheless, the Fina family expressed confidence that it would be able to retain its traditional clientele while reaching out to new customers.

Michael C. Fina turned to the Internet in late 1999 to help in its effort to expand its customer base, as well as keep pace with

its major competitors. The store's web site focused on tabletop items, jewelry, and gifts, and once again the bridal business was given special emphasis. Careful preparation for the venture included surveying brides at the Manhattan store to determine how many had Internet access at home, their online purchasing histories, and their comfort level with an online registry. Given sufficient support from its bridal customers, Fina elected to proceed with the new registry. In addition to selling the company's wares, the site also provided product care and bridal tips. Furthermore, in 1999 Michael C. Fina lost its ties to the original founders when Rose Fina passed away at the age of 87 after a lengthy illness. Nevertheless, the business continued to be very much family owned and operated and appeared well positioned for the future.

Principal Divisions

Baby; Bridal; Corporate.

Principal Competitors

Bloomingdale's Inc.; Fortunoff Fine Jewelry and Silverware Inc.; Saks Inc.

Further Reading

Gault, Ylonda, "Brand-New Setting for Michael C. Fina," *Crain's New York Business,* May 25, 1998, p. 15.
Johnson, Sarah, "A Table Linen Thrust," *HFN,* June 3, 1996, p. 23.
Kehoe, Ann-Margaret, "Fina Bets on Brands," *HFN,* May 19, 1997, p. 45.
Ratliff, Duke, "Michael C. Fina Gives Housewares a Home," *HFD,* January 11, 1992, p. 90.
Wendlinger, Lisa, "Fina Intensifies Bridal Push," *HFD,* July 6, 1992, p. 57.
——, "Fina's Bridal Finesse," *HFD,* February 10, 1992, p. 42.
Zisko, Allison, "Michael C. Fina Opens Internet Shop," *HFN,* December 20, 1999, p. 20.

—Ed Dinger

Minerals Technologies Inc.

The Chrysler Building
405 Lexington Avenue
New York, New York 10174-1901
U.S.A.
Telephone: (212) 878-1800
Fax: (212) 878-1801
Web site: http://www.mineralstech.com

Public Company
Incorporated: 1992
Employees: 2,305
Sales: $684.4 million (2001)
Stock Exchanges: New York
Ticker Symbol: MTX
NAIC: 212325 Refractory Minerals Mining and/or
    Beneficiating; 325188 All Other Basic Inorganic
    Chemical Manufacturing

Minerals Technologies Inc. is a leading force in the international papermaking industry, responsible in large part for transforming the process by which paper was produced in North America and creating a market niche, which it quickly dominated. The company is known for designing and implementing an innovative system to produce precipitated calcium carbonate (PCC), a filler and pigment used in the production of paper, as well as for manufacturing mineral-based monolithic refractory products, which are used primarily by the steel industry to resist the effects of high temperatures.

1968: Originating As a Division of Pfizer, Inc.

The company traces its history to 1968, when pharmaceutical giant Pfizer Inc. formed and incorporated its special minerals division, which comprised an amalgamation of companies involved in the excavation of minerals—particularly limestone—that Pfizer had acquired earlier in its history. While some of the acquisitions dated back to the 1940s, a majority arrived during the 1960s, when the company began purchasing in earnest the properties that would eventually form its specialty

minerals division. With these minerals excavation companies and minerals reserves, Pfizer produced various minerals—limestone, lime, talc, and calcium—for the building materials, steel, paints and coatings, and chemical industries, as well as other manufacturing industries, which together, composed one of three product lines that would fuel the division's growth throughout its existence under Pfizer's corporate umbrella.

The division's second product line was established seven months after its incorporation through the acquisition in September 1968 of New York City-based Quigley Company, Inc., a manufacturer of mineral-based refractory products used to resist the effects of high temperatures in manufacturing processes utilized by the steel, cement, and glass industries. With the addition of Quigley, Pfizer's specialty minerals division now offered two product lines—both sold chiefly to the steel industry—that provided a foundation for the division's growth and supported its existence for roughly the next two decades. Although refractory products and mineral mining and processing were integral contributors to Pfizer's mineral-related operations, the specialty minerals division's third product line, precipitated calcium carbonate (PCC), was the key to its success, vaulting first Pfizer then its spinoff, Minerals Technologies Inc., into a dominant position in the papermaking industry.

Developing the PCC Satellite Plant Concept in the 1980s

Produced from a mixture of lime, carbon dioxide, and water, PCC was used primarily as a filler in alkaline process, wood-free paper and, to a lesser extent, as a specialty pigment to make coated and uncoated paper. Its use as an alternative to more expensive wood pulp and to other fillers, such as kaolin clay and titanium dioxide, had been known for years. Historically, however, North American manufacturers of wood-free paper utilized acid technologies, rather than alkaline technologies, significantly limiting the demand for PCC. Although manufacturing costs associated with producing PCC were low, both drying and transporting the product were expensive processes, adding more than $100 per ton of filler and giving Canadian and American wood-free paper producers little incentive to convert to an alkaline-based process.

Pfizer's specialty minerals division would provide these manufacturers with the incentive to switch to an alkaline process, but not until roughly 20 years after its incorporation and not until a lengthy research and development program produced a solution to the prohibitive cost of PCC. As Pfizer's researchers perceived it, the problem with PCC was not how it was produced as much as where it was produced, so the specialty minerals division began developing a plan to manufacture PCC in proximity to the pulp and paper mills that would use the product. The concept, under development by 1982 at the company's research center in Easton, Pennsylvania, and its lime and limestone plant in Adams, Massachusetts, changed the way a majority of the paper was produced in North America and positioned Pfizer's specialty minerals division as a burgeoning force in the paper industry.

By producing PCC in plants adjacent to pulp and paper mills, the specialty minerals division eliminated both the need to dry PCC and the costs incurred from shipping it, yielding a delivered product that was substantially cheaper than purchasing PCC from an independent, "merchant" plant. Adjacent, or satellite plants, as designed by Pfizer's specialty minerals division, used carbon dioxide produced by the host paper mill, combined it with dissolved lime, then delivered the product in slurry form, saving the mill more than 50 percent in its PCC costs and creating a new niche in the paper filler market. Although innovative, the satellite PCC plant concept was suitable only for producers of alkaline-based paper, not for the vast majority of manufacturers who produced paper under acid conditions, but, while the satellite program was being refined during the early and mid-1980s, the price of fillers used in acid technologies, particularly the price of titanium dioxide, began to climb. Coupled with the innovative and relatively inexpensive satellite PCC plant concept developed by Pfizer's specialty minerals division, the rising cost of wood pulp, titanium dioxide, and other fillers provided sufficient incentive for papermakers employing acid technologies to seriously consider adopting the division's PCC system. The decision these producers made quickly transformed their industry, and along with it, the future of Pfizer's specialty minerals division.

The first satellite PCC plant, the first of many to follow, was dedicated in 1986, four years after the development program was initiated, marking the beginning of a new era for the specialty minerals division, then in its 18th year of operation. Before the first plant was completed, a $10 million facility constructed near Consolidated Papers, Inc.'s paper mill at Wisconsin Rapids, Wisconsin, plans were announced for another, this time in Ticonderoga, New York, adjoining International Paper Company's pulp and paper mill. Both of these facilities were owned and operated by Pfizer's specialty minerals division, an arrangement that was typical of the onsite facilities to follow, and each produced approximately 30,000 tons of PCC a year, affording paper mill

operators substantial savings. Over the course of the next two years, from the end of 1986 to the end of 1988, three additional plants were constructed, then another 12 during the next two years, giving Pfizer 17 satellite PCC plants by the conclusion of 1990. By the end of the following year, the specialty minerals division's last full year as a subsidiary of Pfizer, the number of onsite PCC plants had swelled to 21, while conversely, Pfizer had begun to do the opposite, shedding itself of assets deemed inconsistent with its future plans.

Eight additional satellite PCC plants were put into operation in 1992, the greatest increase in one year since the specialty minerals division's onsite project had begun six years earlier. Against the backdrop of this prodigious expansion—which brought the total number of facilities in operation to 29 and cast Pfizer as the central agent of change in the papermaking industry—larger, more defining issues were being discussed that led to the creation of a new company and ended Pfizer's long history of involvement in the specialty minerals business.

Like other U.S. healthcare companies, Pfizer Inc. spent the early 1990s reexamining its future role in an industry that appeared destined for dramatic, sweeping change. As the 1992 U.S. presidential election neared and the debate concerning national healthcare reform intensified, many healthcare executives maneuvered to anticipate the effects of widespread federal legislation, pinning the future success of their companies on decisions made in uncertain times. Among the larger, more diversified healthcare companies, a pattern emerged, as several multinational concerns began to shed assets unrelated to the healthcare market. One of these large, diversified healthcare companies was Pfizer Inc., a $7 billion corporation with wide-ranging interests in pharmaceuticals, hospital products, consumer healthcare products, chemicals, and minerals, among others.

During the early 1990s, Pfizer began divesting properties deemed inconsistent with the company's plans for its future, which, as Pfizer's Chairman William C. Steere, Jr., related to the *New York Times,* consisted of pursuing a "strategy of focusing on [Pfizer's] strengths as a research-based, diversified health care company." Toward this objective, Pfizer sold its citric-acid business in 1990, touching off a series of strategic divestitures over the course of the next two years that represented a loss of more than $1 billion in total sales and led to the divestiture of the company's specialty minerals division, a $359 million contributor to the company's 1991 annual sales.

1992: Becoming an Independent Company

In August 1992, Pfizer announced plans to sell the bulk of the company's interest in specialty minerals through the public offering of stock in a newly created company, Minerals Technologies Inc. (MTI). Approximately 60 percent of Pfizer's interest in its specialty minerals division was sold by the end of October, and the remaining 40 percent was sold six months later, in April 1993, completing the full divestiture of Pfizer's specialty minerals division and beginning Minerals Technologies' first year of business as a manufacturer and marketer of PCC, refractory products, and other minerals.

Concurrent with Pfizer's initial announcement to spin off its specialty minerals division in August 1992 was the selection of

MTI's chair and chief executive officer, Jean-Paul Vallés, who had joined Pfizer in 1967, one year before the specialty minerals division was incorporated. In the three years leading up to Pfizer's divestiture of its specialty minerals division, Vallés had been responsible for several of Pfizer's businesses, including the specialty minerals division that now represented Minerals Technologies. Vallés left his position as vice-chairman of Pfizer and assumed stewardship of Minerals Technologies' three business lines, the most promising of which continued to be its design and operation of satellite PCC plants.

Although Minerals Technologies' two other product lines figured less prominently in the company's future than its involvement in onsite PCC production, they nevertheless were essential contributors to the company's annual sales volume, providing diversity and stability to predicate the company's further expansion in its PCC business. Minerals Technologies' refractory product business, which generated $147.6 million in sales in 1993 compared to the $171.1 million derived from PCC sales, was operated through the company's subsidiary, Minteq International Inc. Minteq sold refractory products in North America, Europe, and Asia, giving the company the geographic breadth to help mitigate the product line's dependence on the historically capricious steel market. This involvement overseas was particularly important in Minerals Technologies' first year of existence, when sluggish steel markets in the United States and Japan were offset by Minteq's production facilities in South Korea, where steel production was robust, and in China, which, for the first time, produced more steel than the United States.

In addition to its presence in strong steel-producing regions, Minerals Technologies also owned minerals reserves in the eastern, midwestern, and western areas of the United States. From these reserves, estimated to last between 40 and 70 years, the company mined and processed limestone and talc as well as manufactured mineral-based and technology-based products which, combined, constituted Minerals Technologies' other mineral products line, a contributor of $109.6 million to the company's sales volume in 1993.

Strategic Expansion in the 1990s

While refractory products and other mineral products together generated more than 50 percent of Minerals Technolo-

gies' total sales in 1993, the company's greatest expectations were invested in the expansion of its satellite PCC concept, the essence of the company's future. By the end of 1993, Minerals Technologies was operating 34 onsite PCC plants, which accounted for more than 90 percent of all satellite PCC production. Expansion had extended the company's presence into Europe, where Minerals Technologies operated an onsite plant in Saillat Sur Vienne, France, and three more plants in Finland. In Europe, where for years paper producers had manufactured their product under alkaline conditions, the company's focus was not on converting from acid to alkaline papermaking as it was in North America, but on convincing European manufacturers to use PCC, rather than ground chalk or ground calcium carbonate. Toward this objective, Minerals Technologies announced a joint venture in August 1993 with Partek Corporation, an international industrial group based in Finland and Scandinavia's largest producer of lime, to produce PCC in the Nordic countries and in Eastern Europe.

With this European expansion bolstering the company's position in the global paper industry, Minerals Technologies entered 1994 looking to translate its success in the wood-free segment of the paper industry into success in the wood-containing segment. By this time, the company's development of satellite PCC plants had dramatically altered the wood-free segment of the paper industry, converting an industry that predominantly had utilized acid-based technology to an industry in which 80 percent of the paper produced was made with alkaline technology. Efforts to effect a commensurate transformation of the wood-containing industry had been stalled by the tendency of wood-containing paper to darken in an alkaline environment. However, in 1993 Minerals Technologies successfully commercialized an acid-tolerant PCC, opening up a vast new market for the company's expertise in PCC production. As Minerals Technologies entered its first full year as a separate, independent company, expectations ran high, with plans to further solidify its position in the wood-free paper industry and to begin its involvement in the wood-containing paper industry, both of which promised to sustain the company's growth throughout the 1990s.

Indeed, MTI grew at an impressive rate throughout the remainder of the 1990s, maintaining its focus on the international expansion of its satellite PCC concept. Having found the Japanese market, then the second largest paper market in the world, particularly difficult to penetrate, in 1997 MTI launched a joint venture with Japanese companies Fimatec Ltd. and Mitsubishi to manufacture and market PCC in that country. By the terms of the agreement, MTI would provide its technical expertise in building and running PCC plants, while the Japanese corporations would focus on marketing the idea. By 1998, MTI had established 55 plants worldwide, including locations in Brazil, Israel, southeast Asia, South Africa, and China.

Alongside expansion in the PCC market for paper products, MTI also pursued opportunities for increased production of specialized PCC, including Ultrafine, Super-pflex, and U.S. Pharmacopeia grades, commonly used in plastics, sealants, and food industries. To this end, in 1993 the company invested $18 million in its Adams, Massachusetts, facility, giving it the capacity to produce calcium crystals of various grades. In 1998, the company acquired a facility with similar capabilities in Lifford, England. The following year, MTI established a third site for the production of specialty grade PCC, investing $20 million to construct a manufacturing facility in Brookhaven, Mississippi. These new operations were seen as critical for continued growth across the diverse range of markets for specialty PCC.

Through continued emphasis on research and development, MTI was able to introduce a new product, CalEssence, to the specialized PCC market in 1997. Responding to a flurry of publicity, particularly in California, over the lead content in some calcium supplements and calcium-based antacids, MTI had developed CalEssence PCC, a grade of calcium carbonate containing only trace levels of lead. By using CalEssence PCC, manufacturers could meet the heightened restrictions for lead content. The introduction of CalEssence was a reflection of MTI's belief that its ability to provide value-added products to its customers was a critical component of the company's long-term success.

During the mid- to late 1990s, MTI also enjoyed increased demand for its patented Acid-Tolerant PCC technology. A breakthrough deal in the wood-containing paper industry was reached in 1997 when MTI and Myllykoski Paper Oy of Finland agreed to implement this technology in its production of super-calendered groundwood papers, the high-shine quality of paper used for magazines and catalogues. With the agreement, Myllykoski established itself as the world's first manufacturer of PCC-based supercalendered paper, and Minerals Technologies made its first major stride toward penetration of the groundwood paper market, which accounted for approximately half of the overall paper market worldwide.

Responding to Weakened Economic Conditions in the Early 21st Century

The first years of the 21st century brought weakened conditions to the paper, steel, and construction industries—the main sectors MTI served—particularly in North America. Fortunately, one of the critical benefits of the satellite PCC business to MTI was that these operations were typically established with ten-year contracts, effectively insulating MTI from the ups and downs of the normal business cycle.

Still, MTI took further steps to shore up its financial performance. In June 2001, the company announced that it would cut 120 full-time employees—about 5 percent of its total workforce—from its worldwide operations. Making its first significant staff reduction since the company's formation in 1992 was a difficult decision, but MTI officials maintained that it was necessary to reduce operations costs and improve efficiency.

MTI saw another opportunity to improve its overall financial strength by bolstering the sales and profitability of its Minteq subsidiary, mainly through the 2000–2001 acquisitions of Ferrotron Elektronik GmbH, the refractory business of Martin Marietta Magnesia Specialties, and Rijnstall, NV. These acquisitions enabled MTI to keep pace with the changing nature of the refractory business, especially the increasing demand for new, high-tech products and services.

With the company's demonstrated agility and the seemingly unlimited growth potential of PCC markets, Minerals Technologies appeared well positioned to continue the consistent growth it had achieved in the 1990s.

Principal Subsidiaries

Specialty Minerals Inc.; MINTEQ International, Inc.

Principal Competitors

Engelhard Corporation; J.M. Huber Corporation; Martin Marietta Materials, Inc.

Further Reading

"Another Pfizer Lime Plant," *Chemical Week*, February 11, 1987, p. 20.

Freudenheim, Milt, "Pfizer Selling Off Control of Specialty Minerals Unit," *New York Times*, August 18, 1992, p. C4.

"Joint Venture Is Formed with Company in Finland," *Wall Street Journal*, August 13, 1993, p. B5.

Jones, John A., "Minerals Technologies Brings Cost Savings to Paper Mills," *Investor's Business Daily*, April 28, 1993, p. 28.

"Minerals Technologies Announces Restructuring to Reduce Costs," *Business Wire*, June 12, 2001.

"Minerals Technologies Inc.," *Wall Street Journal*, March 1, 1993, p. B5.

"Minerals Technologies Inc. Acquires Ferrotron Elektronik, a German Maker of Advanced Laser Scanning Devices for the Steel Industry," *Business Wire*, April 3, 2000.

"Minerals Technologies Inc. to Acquire Refractories Business of Martin Marietta Materials, Inc.," *Business Wire*, February 23, 2001.

"Minerals Technologies Introduces CalEssence Precipitated Calcium Carbonate with Low Lead Levels," *Business Wire*, February 13, 1997.

"Minerals Technologies' Shares," *Wall Street Journal*, April 7, 1993, p. B10.

"Pfizer Board Clears Sale of Stake in Unit, Repurchase of Shares," *Wall Street Journal*, August 18, 1992, p. A12.

"Pfizer on Line," *Chemical Marketing Reporter*, July 21, 1986, p. 9.

"Pfizer Plans PCC Unit," *Chemical Marketing Reporter*, October 19, 1987, p. 9.

"Pfizer Takes Its Satellite Plants Overseas," *Chemical Week*, June 4, 1986, p. 5.

"Pfizer to Build Plant," *Chemical Marketing Reporter*, November 13, 1989, p. 9.

"Pfizer to Construct Calcium Carbonate Plant," *Chemical Marketing Reporter*, April 21, 1986, p. 3.

Plishner, Emily S., "Satellites Launch Minerals Technologies on Growth Trajectory," *Chemical Week*, June 9, 1993, p. 26.

Shapiro, Lynn, "Chemical Stocks Seen As Bargain," *Chemical Marketing Reporter*, December 14, 1992, p. 3.

—Jeffrey L. Covell
—update: Erin Brown

MOONEY AEROSPACE GROUP, LTD.

Mooney Aerospace Group Ltd.

3205 Lakewood Boulevard
Long Beach, California 90808
U.S.A.
Telephone: (562) 938-8618
Fax: (562) 938-8620
Web site: http://www.mooneyltd.com

Public Company
Incorporated: 1989 as Advanced Aerodynamics &
    Structures, Inc.
Employees: 150
Sales: $11 million (2002 est.)
Stock Exchanges: OTC BB
Ticker Symbol: MASG.OB
NAIC: 336411 Aircraft Manufacturing; 541710 Research
    and Development in the Physical, Engineering, and
    Life Sciences

Mooney Aerospace Group Ltd. (MAG) is the holding company for the Mooney Airplane Company, maker of high performance single engine aircraft. Before 2002, when MAG was called Advanced Aerodynamics & Structures Inc. (AASI), the company had spent ten years attempting to bring an advanced business aircraft to market. The innovative but ill-fated Jetcruzer project was a textbook example of the technical and regulatory challenges inherent in such an undertaking.

AASI acquired Mooney in 2002, and soon renamed itself after the venerable manufacturer. Mooney had been making planes, with distinctive swept-forward tails their trademark, since the 1950s. Their efficiency and high performance earned them a reputation as the sports cars of the general aviation industry. In 2002, Mooney had three lines of aircraft, Eagle, Ovation 2, and Bravo, which sold for up to $500,000 each. The company had produced more than 10,500 aircraft since starting production in 1953.

Origins

Albert W. Mooney and his brother Arthur both learned drafting skills from their father, who built railroad trestles in the West. Al, a self-taught aircraft designer, began working at Colorado's Alexander Aircraft in the mid-1920s. In 1929, he formed Mooney Aircraft Co., but it foundered in the Great Depression, selling just one plane, called the M-5.

Al then worked with a number of pioneering designers in the nascent aviation industry, including Giuseppe Bellanca and Knight Culver. The Mooney brothers founded Mooney Aircraft Company in Wichita, Kansas, on July 5, 1946, with financial backing from Charles "Pappy" Yankey and W.L. McMahon.

The new Mooney Aircraft's first product, the Mooney Mite or M18, first flew in 1947. It was a one-place aircraft with wooden wings and tail. Like the designs to follow, the Mite featured Mooney's trademark swept-forward tail.

In 1953, Mooney moved to Kerrville, in the Texas Hill Country, drawn by good flying weather and the Mooney family's own dairy farm. There was also a good supply of skilled workers in the German immigrant population. The four-person Mooney M20 first flew on August 10, 1953, and was certified in 1955. The M20C, rolled out in 1962, was Mooney's first all-metal plane.

After the death of Charles Yankey, Hal Rachal and Norm Hoffman took over the company in September 1955. Both Al and Art Mooney left the company to work for Lockheed.

The Kerrville plant was producing 760 planes a year at its peak in the 1960s. However, it would soon come to a halt. Mooney underwent a bankruptcy filing in early 1969, and was soon acquired by American Electronics Labs. Later in the year, it was sold to Butler Aviation. It was renamed Aerostar Aircraft Corp. in 1970. The company ended production in 1971. A few years later, Republic Steel acquired the company's tooling and rights to the Mooney name and designs, and production soon recommenced.

The Mooney 201, based on the previous Executive model, was introduced in 1977. Its aerodynamic refinements raised its top speed to 201 mph, hence the name. It was considered the most efficient non-turbocharged piston engine aircraft in general aviation. The Mooney 201 had a reputation for efficiency,

Company Perspectives:

Mooney Airplane Company (MAC) has a long and rich history of producing the highest performance single engine aircraft available and pioneering the Performance/Value equation. Its ubiquitous brand, the forward swept tail, is instantly recognizable at airports all over the world and helps to create its speed advantage.

Every great aviator or aviation pioneer—man, woman or company, has a story to tell. It started with the Wright Brothers, moved to Charles Lindbergh, through Glenn Curtis, Amelia Earhart, Wiley Post, Chuck Yeager and includes the legendary designer, Al Mooney.

Al Mooney created a basic aircraft design that has been market tested for over 50 years and still upholds the tradition and legacy of the highest Performance/Value *equation offered in General Aviation.*

achieving up to 20 miles per gallon. It sold for an average equipped price of about $124,000.

The number of derivatives of Al Mooney's basic design continued to multiply. The fuselage was extended to produce the company's mid-length, or "Renaissance" models of the 1970s. The mid-length 201 was further refined to produce the 205. The 252, later renamed M20K, was a turbocharged variant.

Mooney in the 1980s

As the general aviation market slowed, Mooney introduced a couple of creative financing options. In 1980, Mooney brought out its Retail Interest Assistance Program (RIAP), a way of knocking a few points off interest charges at a time when the prime rate was 20 percent. The Rapid Equity Accumulation Plan (REAP), introduced two years later, was a fixed payment plan whose number of payments was determined by changes in interest rates.

In June 1984 Mooney Aircraft, which had been controlled by Republic Steel Corporation since 1973, was subsumed by LTV Corporation, which had just merged with Republic. Mooney Aircraft President Roy Lopresti soon led a management buyout. LTV sold the Mooney Aircraft Corporation to newly created Mooney Holding Corporation in August 1984. Euralair, a French air charter operator, soon acquired Mooney, which was renamed Mooney International.

In the mid-1980s, Mooney introduced three new high-performance, four-place models: the 201LM, the 252 (four-seat), and the 205. While other manufacturers were scaling back or suspending production of piston engine aircraft, Mooney's 1986 deliveries were up 55 percent to 140.

Mooneys have been called the sports cars of the general aviation industry, and the M20L, brought out in 1988, helped strengthen that association. This was the first "long body" Mooney, and it used an engine derived from the Porsche 911. In early 1991, Mooney introduced its bid for a two-seat aerobatic Air Force trainer. Only one of the planes, dubbed the M20T, was ever built.

Mooney International entered a partnership to build a new $1 million high-performance business aircraft with Socata, an affiliate of Aérospatiale, in the late 1980s. The TBM 700 was powered by a single turboprop engine. Mooney held a 30 percent share of TBM S.A., the company set up to manage the program and market the planes, and would be responsible for constructing the plane's wings and portions of the fuselage. Final assembly lines were being set up in France and in the United States, which was expected to account for two-thirds of the plane's sales. The TBM's start-up costs were an estimated FFr 300 million ($54 million). Mooney bailed out of the TBM program after two years, citing a lack of financial resources. Mooney employed 300 people and was producing 12 planes a month in the late 1980s.

Mooney in the 1990s

Mooney began performing subcontracting work for other manufacturers in 1990. The work quickly grew from a sideline to account for a quarter of the company's 1994 revenues of $26 million. By then, Mooney was making 5,500 different parts for Boeing, Lockheed Martin, Fairchild, and McDonnell Douglas. Mooney also delivered 71 of its light aircraft in 1994.

Mooney was shipping about 100 planes a year in the late 1990s, with annual revenues approaching $40 million. However, a number of factors would bring the company to bankruptcy. In December 1999, Mooney discovered that a new drilling/riveting machine had been drilling holes slightly larger than called for in aircraft specifications. This necessitated extensive inspections and reworking, costing the company up to $1 million.

Further, an economic downturn in 2001 affected sales of small aircraft manufacturers; Mooney's high-end models, which sold for up to $450,000 each, were more expensive than other small planes, and more susceptible to such downturns than larger aircraft used by corporations.

AVAQ Group Inc., an investor group led by Paul Dopp, had acquired Mooney in 1997. Chris Dopp, son of Mooney Chairman Paul Dopp, resigned from the company in July 2001 after two years as the company's president and CEO. A couple of weeks later, Mooney Aircraft filed for Chapter 11 bankruptcy protection. The company had furloughed half of its 230 workers. For the next few months, the Kerrville plant made only spare parts for the existing world fleet of 10,000 Mooney aircraft.

AASI: 1992–2001

While Mooney International was trying its hand at subcontracting, its future owner, a newly formed California company, was attempting to bring a new jet business aircraft to market. Darius Sharifzadeh, an aeronautical engineer and pilot, formed Advanced Aerodynamics & Structures Inc. (AASI) in Burbank, California, in 1989 to develop a plane of his own design, the Jetcruzer 450.

Taiwanese industrialist Song Gen Yeh provided $20 million to start the company. Carl Chen, former space scientist with Hughes, was picked as AASI's president.

The Jetcruzer 450 was canceled when company officials calculated its odds of commercial success were low. AASI then went to work developing the Jetcruzer 500, a larger, higher performance plane.

Key Dates:

1946: Al and Art Mooney establish Mooney Aircraft Company in Kansas.
1953: Mooney relocates to Kerrville, Texas, and begins production.
1962: All-metal M20C debuts.
1966: Mooney produces a record 767 planes.
1973: Republic Steel acquires Mooney Aircraft.
1984: LTV Corporation purchases Republic and becomes the new owner of Mooney in June; management-led buyout headed by Mooney President Roy Lopresti liberates Mooney from LTV in August.
1989: Advanced Aerodynamics & Structures Inc. (AASI) is founded in Long Beach, California.
1996: AASI goes public.
2001: Mooney Aircraft files for Chapter 11 bankruptcy.
2002: AASI acquires Mooney Aircraft, which becomes Mooney Aerospace Group.

Like its four-place predecessor, the six-place Jetcruzer 500 featured a novel canard design, with a small wing in the front of the plane, and a rear-mounted engine. The fuselage was constructed of graphite composites, while the wings were made of conventional aluminum. AASI started out aiming for a sales price of $900,000 each, versus the $1.4 million that Socata was then asking for the TBM 700—another single engine turboprop.

The Stratocruzer, a twin-engine, 13-passenger version, was also in the works with a projected price of $3 million. A large cargo aircraft, the Freedom DS-888, was also on the drawing board, priced at just $1.3 million.

AASI went public in December 1996. The company used $35 million gained to build a factory in Long Beach and to develop the Jetcruzer 500. The company produced its own tooling to build the plane. According to Chen, the design tools and materials needed to build planes had come down significantly in price in the previous 20 years.

AASI claimed a backlog of 188 Jetcruzer aircraft worth $226 million in 2000. The company employed a hundred workers, most formerly employed with Northrop Grumman, Lockheed Martin, or Boeing.

Then priced at $1.6 million, the Jetcruzer was to undercut comparable aircraft by one-half. It would be capable of speeds up to 345 mph and cruise as high as 30,000 feet. However, one of the Jetcruzer 500's main advantages was also its main problem. Mounting the engine at the rear of the fuselage produced less drag. However, it also made it more difficult to cool the engine oil.

An abortive takeover deal was announced in December 2000. Los Angeles-based Tiwenz Group, a media firm, was acquiring a 71 percent holding in AASI in a stock swap. However, AASI called off the deal within a couple of months.

Chen left the company in January 2001. Roy H. Norris, former president of Raytheon Aircraft Co., led the new manage-

ment. The Jetcruzer program, which had consumed $70 million, would soon be canceled. The company's shares were delisted from the NASDAQ in April 2001.

Purchase of Mooney by AASI: 2002

AASI CEO Roy Norris decided the time was right for consolidation in the general aviation industry, and he thought that demand would pick up due to the hassles that had come to be associated with commercial airlines. Thus, in February 2002, AASI announced the acquisition of Mooney Aircraft in a cash and stock deal worth $11 million. LH Financial, a New York investment group, controlled about 70 percent of Mooney Aerospace Group's stock.

After acquiring Mooney Aircraft, AASI was renamed Mooney Aerospace Group, Ltd. The AASI plant in Long Beach was being turned into a service center for Mooney planes. The computerized production system was disposed of, being deemed inefficient in the production of single engine aircraft. Norris rolled back prices on Mooneys 20 percent to stimulate sales. To keep costs low, the company sidestepped its dealer network, selling direct from a handful of small offices.

Norris first stated the company was taking at least another 18 months to prepare the Jetcruzer 500 for certification. However, this program was soon cancelled altogether over significant technical problems, such as an excessive noise level and a center-of-gravity problem. Mooney announced plans to return $1.6 million worth of $10,000 deposits that had been placed on the Jetcruzer.

In May 2002, Raytheon Aircraft Co. was reported to be expressing some interest in selling Mooney its Baron and Bonanza line of piston engine planes. This would extend Mooney's product line into six-place aircraft. However, this deal apparently fizzled.

Peter Larson, formerly chief financial officer at Cessna, became Mooney Aerospace's CEO in August 2002 upon the resignation of Roy Norris, who had stepped down after the completion of the Mooney Aircraft acquisition.

After fabricating 100 planes a year in the late 1990s, Mooney production fell to just 28 aircraft in 2001. The company was aiming to produce around the same number in 2002 but up to 100 in 2003.

Mooney was reported to be pursuing Raytheon for sale of its Beechcraft propeller plane business, which would give the company a line of larger, six-place aircraft. It was also discussing the acquisition of rights to produce CA-100 light business jets from Century Aerospace. Norris had said he was expecting to spend $70 million through 2004 to expand Mooney.

Principal Subsidiaries

Mooney Airplane Company, Inc.

Principal Competitors

Cessna Aircraft Co.; Cirrus Design Corporation; The New Piper Aircraft, Inc.; Raytheon Aircraft Co.

Further Reading

"Chocks Away," *Economist,* October 1, 1994, p. 84.

Collogan, David, "Jetcruzer 500 Going Back to the Drawing Board; AASI Wins Approval to Take Over Mooney Aircraft," *Weekly of Business Aviation,* February 11, 2002, p. 69.

——, "Jetcruzer Is Dead, But Norris Has Big Plans for Mooney," *Weekly of Business Aviation,* June 24, 2002, p. 295.

——, "Management Changes at Mooney in Wake of Roy Norris' Departure," *Weekly of Business Aviation,* August 26, 2002, p. 91.

DeMeis, Richard, "Designing a Personal Aircraft—the Mooney 201," *Aerospace America,* November 1984, p. 70.

George, Fred, "Mooney 205 Replaces 201 for 1987," *Business & Commercial Aviation,* October 1986, pp. 94+.

Hanigan, Ian, "Long Beach, Calif.-Based Aerospace Firm Delisted from Nasdaq," *Press-Telegram,* April 20, 2001.

——, "Long Beach, Calif.-Based Jet Developer Cancels Deal with Los Angeles Firm," *Press-Telegram,* February 16, 2001.

——, "Los Angeles Multimedia Firm Acquires Long Beach, Calif. Aerospace Firm," *Press-Telegram,* December 15, 2000.

Higdon, Dave, "Fast and Furious," *Flight International,* May 20, 1998, p. 36.

——, "Sociable Climber," *Flight International,* March 11, 1998, p. 30.

Higginbotham, Keith, "Long Beach, Calif. Aircraft Builder Moves to Acquire Airplane Company," *Press-Telegram,* February 6, 2002.

Hirsch, Jerry, "New Jet Having Trouble Getting Off the Ground," *Los Angeles Times,* August 23, 2000, p. C1.

——, "Region's Know-How Pilots New Plane," *Los Angeles Times,* May 21, 2000, p. C1.

Kiefer, Francine, "Makers of Small Planes Trying to Regain Sales Altitude," *Christian Science Monitor,* Bus. Sec., October 26, 1982, p. 11.

Knap, Chris, "FAA Certification for California Aircraft Makers Plane Is Two Years Late," *Orange County Register,* September 27, 2000.

Kotkin, Joel, "Rising Upstarts Breathe New Life into Battered Aerospace Industry," *New York Times,* Sec. 3, January 23, 2000, p. 7.

Lee, Don, "Getting New Plane Off the Ground; Advanced Aerodynamics' Jetcruzer Is a Long Shot for Quick FAA Approval and Market Success," *Los Angeles Times,* Bus. Sec., October 13, 1992, p. 3.

Lenorovitz, Jeffrey M., "Mooney Leaves TBM-700 Turboprop's Team, Socata to Continue Single-Engine Program," *Aviation Week & Space Technology,* May 13, 1991, p. 99.

——, "Socata, Mooney Proceed with TBM 700 Production," *Aviation Week & Space Technology,* June 26, 1989, p. 53.

McKenna, James T., "Mooney Aircraft Expands Role As Subcontractor," *Aviation Week & Space Technology,* June 12, 1995, p. 155.

McMillin, Molly, "Raytheon May Sell Lines to Aerospace Group," *Wichita Eagle,* May 30, 2002.

Mooney, Al, and Gordon Baxter, *The Al Mooney Store: They All Fly Through the Same Air,* Fredericksburg, Tex.: 1985.

"Mooney Aircraft Files for Bankruptcy Protection, Makes Management Changes," *Weekly of Business Aviation,* July 30, 2001, p. 45.

"Mooney Rolls Out New Aerobatic Plane; Gives Go-Ahead for Civil Version," *Weekly of Business Aviation,* February 18, 1991, p. 69.

Nelson, Brett, "Space Cowboys," *Forbes,* October 28, 2002, pp. 141, 144.

Nowlin, Sanford, "California Firm Buys San Antonio, Texas-Area Aircraft Maker," *San Antonio Express-News,* March 20, 2002.

——, "New California-Based Parent Wants to Remake Mooney Aircraft As Industry Leader," *San Antonio Express-News,* June 26, 2002.

——, "Once-Ailing Aircraft Maker Catches Tail Wind," *San Antonio Union-Tribune,* July 13, 2002, p. C3.

——, "San Antonio, Texas-Area Aircraft Maker Looks for Buyer," *San Antonio Express-News,* September 6, 2001.

Olcott, John W., "The Mooney Lean Machine," *Business & Commercial Aviation,* December 1985, pp. 100+.

Proctor, Paul, "General Aviation Manufacturers Focus on Technology Advances to Spur Sales," *Aviation Week & Space Technology,* May 18, 1987, p. 108.

Roberts, Raequel, "Texas-Built Airplane Sky 'Sports Car' That's Developing Pilots Cult," *Houston Post,* June 4, 1989, p. D4.

"Roy Lopresti Looks Toward Future," *Air Progress,* October 1984, pp. 50+.

Sanchez, Felix, "Chief Resigns from Advanced Aerodynamics & Structures in Long Beach, Calif.," *Press-Telegram,* January 11, 2002.

Sarsfield, Kate, "Rescuer Norris Leaves Mooney," *Flight International,* August 27, 2002, p. 22.

Wilson, Janet, "Aircraft Plant Wants to Share the Secrets of Aviation," *Austin American Statesman,* September 3, 1989, p. E17.

—Frederick C. Ingram

Mueller Industries, Inc.

8285 Tournament Drive, Suite 150
Memphis, Tennessee 38125-1743
U.S.A.
Telephone: (901) 753-3200
Fax: (901) 753-3250
Web site: http://www.muellerindustries.com

Public Company
Incorporated: 1893 as H. Mueller Manufacturing
    Company
Employees: 3,750
Sales: $1.04 billion (2001)
Stock Exchanges: New York
Ticker Symbol: MLI
NAIC: 331421 Copper Rolling, Drawing, and Extruding;
    332913 Plumbing Fixture Fitting and Trim
    Manufacturing; 332996 Fabricated Pipe and Pipe
    Fitting Manufacturing; 326191 Plastics Plumbing
    Fixtures Manufacturing

Mueller Industries, Inc. is a leading U.S.-based manufacturer of copper, brass, plastic, and aluminum products. The company's Standard Products Division, which generates about three-quarters of overall revenues, produces copper tube, holding a leading position in air-conditioning and refrigeration tubes; both copper and plastic fittings for plumbing and heating applications; and valves. The products of this division are mainly sold to wholesalers in the heating, air-conditioning, plumbing, and refrigeration markets. The Industrial Products Division, which primarily serves original equipment manufacturers, produces brass and copper alloy rod, bar, and shapes; aluminum and brass forgings; aluminum and copper impact extrusions; refrigeration valves and fittings; fabricated tubular products; and gas valves and assemblies. The company operates 22 factories—20 in the United States and a single plant each in France and the United Kingdom. Only about 13 percent of Mueller's sales originate outside the United States.

Early History of Innovation

Mueller Industries traces its history back to 1852 when 20-year-old Hieronymous Mueller migrated to the United States. Mueller was an inventor with an interest in plumbing—particularly plumbing using copper. In 1872 he patented an improved water tapping machine. In 1877 he became the first to pour castings using brass, an alloy of copper and zinc. Mueller parlayed these inventions into manufacturing facilities, and in 1893, with $68,000 in capital, he incorporated his business in Michigan as the H. Mueller Manufacturing Company.

The firm prospered throughout the next two decades. In 1913, as Great Britain entered World War I, Mueller completed its first Canadian plant. With the United States' entrance into the war, Mueller, like many industrial companies, participated in a general increase in manufacturing. In order to produce munitions, the company began construction, in Port Huron, Michigan, of the first commercial forging facility in the United States. When that plant opened on December 17, 1917, the business was reincorporated as Mueller Metals Company.

After the war, Mueller continued to make technological advances, key to the growth of significant industries. For the nascent mechanical refrigeration industry, the company provided brass forging that did not leak refrigeration gas like the porous castings previously in use. In addition, the Port Huron plant pioneered high-strength brass forging for gears, bearings, and pumps used by manufacturers of mechanical devices.

Mueller was still directing its primary efforts at the plumbing supply business, however. In 1923 the company introduced soft copper tube for underground water supplies and, in 1924, hard copper tube for indoor water supplies. By 1927, Mueller Brass Company (the new name having been adopted in 1925) was firmly established in the plumbing business and was producing a full line of fittings and valves produced in its own foundry.

Perhaps the company's most important innovation came in 1930 when the company introduced the revolutionary Streamline solder-type fitting. Previously, fittings—which joined pieces of tube—had been the weakest sections of pipes. The new solder-joined fittings, however, were actually stronger than the tubes they connected. It was because of this development that all-copper plumbing and heating systems were established as industry standards.

After the stock market crashed in 1929, Mueller fell victim to the same types of pressures other industrial companies were experiencing. Moreover, as a company that provided supplies to industrial firms, especially in the area of housing construction, Mueller experienced sales that generally reflected the low level of economic activity in the country. This being the case, Mueller canceled dividends and tightened its belt during the first half of the 1930s.

Surprisingly, Mueller returned to profitability by the mid-1930s, reinstating dividends in 1935. Toward the end of the decade, the war in Europe and a reviving economy at home spurred production. Mueller became highly profitable, a fact borne out by generally increasing dividends, including the record $2.25 dividend the company paid in 1941.

Postwar Expansion

After the war, Mueller remained profitable, especially during the 1950s when earnings fluctuated between $2.50 and $5.50 per share, and sales averaged around $59 million. Given positive economic conditions, President and CEO F.L. Riggin decided to expand the company. In December 1951 he paid $1.25 million for Valley Metal Products Co. of Plainwell, Michigan. He bought, and later sold, Sheet Aluminum Corporation, of Jackson, Mississippi, and in March 1958, he acquired American Sinteel Corporation, a Yonkers, New York, manufacturer of powder metal parts.

Along with acquisitions, Riggin upgraded existing facilities and built new ones. In 1954 he launched an eight-year program to expand and diversify the production of fabricated goods. In this effort, he placed particular emphasis on specially engineered, copper-based alloys. In addition, Riggin opened an impact extrusion facility in Marysville, Michigan, in 1958. The plant, which shaped aluminum and copper by forcing it through a die, adapted the inherent strength and minimal weight of extrusions to specialized needs of customers who ranged from aerospace manufacturers to home appliance suppliers.

During the early 1960s, Mueller continued to do well, adding a larger proportion of defense subcontracting to its mix of customers. At this time the company was producing rods, forgings, tubes, and castings made from aluminum, copper, brass, bronze, and other alloys. Among the many semi-finished and fabricated items the company produced were powdered metal, screw machine parts, machined castings, forgings and impact

extrusions, refrigeration valves and fittings, chromium- and nickel-plated fabricated items, electrotinned and hot-dipped fabricated items, and copper pipes, tubes, and fittings used in plumbing, heating, and air conditioning.

Mueller continued to grow, reporting profits of $2.35 million on sales of $80.8 million in 1963. The company also acquired the assets of the Bay Engineering Company of Bridgeport, Michigan, the following year. Management, however, did not cling to the idea of a large, independent Mueller with an indefinite future.

1965–79: The USSRAM Era

For some time, U.S. Smelting Refining and Mining (USSRAM) had been acquiring Mueller stock and by 1965 had amassed a 72 percent share of the company. That year USSRAM made an offer to acquire the remainder of Mueller through a stock swap—a proposal that was approved overwhelmingly by both companies. Technically, Mueller Brass and USSRAM merged to become a new Mueller subsidiary called Mueller Brass Corp. Upon completion of the consolidation, however, the subsidiary's name was changed to U.S. Smelting, Refining, & Mining Company and USSRAM's management took over the new company, in effect absorbing Mueller.

USSRAM was a mining company whose primary products were gold, silver, lead, and zinc. Founded in 1906, the company was relatively stable until the early 1960s when a proxy fight led to the ascension of Martin Horwitz to the offices of president and chief executive officer in 1964. Under Horwitz, USSRAM had followed an aggressive path of acquisitions and had begun to develop the Continental Copper Mine in New Mexico. In acquiring Mueller, Horwitz was looking to join copper mining and smelting with the production of copper products.

The merger proved to be profitable from the start. In 1969, after Horwitz invested $17 million in Mueller's interests and $16 million in the copper mine, USSRAM's sales reached an all-time high of $170 million, while income hit a record $12 million.

In fact, the merger provided Mueller with the capital to introduce new products, modernize old facilities, and build new plants. In 1967 the company began to offer plastic pipe and fittings. The Port Huron rod mill was modernized in 1971—doubling its copper alloys capacity. That same year construction of a Fulton, Mississippi, tube mill—including a 6,300-ton automated extrusion press—was completed. In a speech reprinted by the *Wall Street Transcript,* Horwitz called the Fulton plant "possibly the most efficient tube mill in the United States." He concluded that given the plant's low cost operation, it had "enabled Mueller to report profits when other mills were reporting losses and still others were closing down."

In the early 1970s, USSRAM changed its name to UV Industries, Inc. to better represent an increasingly diverse product mix that, by then, also included electrical equipment. Mueller, in the meantime, continued to expand, though not quite at the pace it did in the late 1960s. In 1973 the company purchased plants in Hartsville, Tennessee, to produce refrigerator and air conditioning components. By 1976, however, slow housing

Key Dates:

1893: Hieronymous Mueller incorporates his copper and brass plumbing products business in Michigan as H. Mueller Manufacturing Company.

1917: The business is reincorporated as Mueller Metals Company.

1925: Company changes its name to Mueller Brass Company.

1930: Mueller Brass introduces the revolutionary Streamline solder-type pipe fitting.

1958: Company opens an impact extrusion facility in Marysville, Michigan.

1965: Having previously amassed a 72 percent share of Mueller, U.S. Smelting Refining and Mining (USSRAM) acquires the remaining shares and takes full control.

1967: Mueller begins producing plastic pipe and fittings.

1970: USSRAM changes its name to UV Industries, Inc.

1979: Sharon Steel Corporation acquires UV Industries.

1987: Sharon Steel files for bankruptcy; Mueller remains a viable enterprise and does not file for Chapter 11.

1990: Mueller acquires U-Brand Corporation, maker of plastic valves and pipe fittings and other products; Mueller emerges from the Sharon Steel bankruptcy proceedings as an independent company called Mueller Industries, Inc.

1991: Mueller moves its headquarters from Port Huron, Michigan, to Wichita, Kansas.

1996: The headquarters are moved to Memphis, Tennessee.

1997: European beachhead is established through the purchases of U.K. firm Wednesday Tube Company and French company Desnoyers S.A.

1998: Copper tube maker Halstead Industries, Inc. is acquired.

2002: Company completes the divestment of its noncore natural resources assets by selling Utah Railway.

starts had led to a performance that, while acceptable, was nowhere near what it might be in a boom economy.

1980s: The Sharon Steel Era

In 1977 Victor Posner, chairman of Sharon Steel Corporation, offered to buy UV Industries. Posner was a Miami Beach businessman who had dropped out of high school and made a fortune in real estate by the time he was 30. He got involved in mergers and acquisitions and eventually used his NVF Company to gain control of Sharon, then the 12th largest steel company in the United States. One of Posner's tactics was to use subordinate debentures—bonds subordinate to other claims and backed by the general credit of the issuer—rather than a specific lien on particular assets in order to fund his activities.

This was the means of payment he proposed in the acquisition of UV Industries. UV, however, was wary of Posner and the two sides went back and forth with extensive negotiations. Finally, on November 26, 1979, it was agreed that Sharon would acquire UV for an interim note worth $517 million and the assumption of UV's liabilities. However, Sharon could not sell any UV assets until the interim note was exchanged for cash. This particular clause was important because it was widely assumed that Posner would pay for the deal by selling UV's large portfolio of investments and marketable securities. According to the *Wall Street Journal*, some analysts thought that cash would be hard to come by and that Posner had "erred badly in trying to swallow UV."

Under the Posner regime, Mueller remained profitable, and in 1983 the company's Canadian subsidiary in Strathroy, Ontario, began manufacturing metric fittings. Sharon, however, had difficulties. The company's debts were too high, and in 1985, Sharon defaulted on $33 million in interest payments. Bondholders could have forced the business into bankruptcy immediately; instead, they negotiated with Posner, who wanted them to swap their subordinated debentures for a package of common shares and low-interest and zero-coupon notes.

The largest bondholder was Quantum Overseas N.V., an investment fund based in Curacao that was headed by high-stakes investor George Soros. Quantum and the other holders allowed payments on the debentures to be extended more than 20 times while they tried to negotiate a settlement. In 1986 it was rumored that Sharon would sell Mueller to Quantum for $55 million, but that exchange never took place.

Finally in 1987, Quantum called in the $96.9 million in Sharon securities it held and in April of that year, Sharon filed for Chapter 11 bankruptcy. Over the next two years, Quantum officials and Sharon's other creditors worked to hammer out a plan to divide Sharon's assets and help the company emerge from bankruptcy.

During this time, Mueller was not static. The company had never filed for Chapter 11 and remained a viable enterprise. In 1990 Mueller acquired U-Brand Corporation, an Ashland, Ohio, company whose plants in Ashland and Upper Sandusky, Ohio, manufactured plastic valves, pipe couplings, steel pipe nipples, malleable iron pipe fittings, iron castings, and plastic pipe fittings for wholesalers and hardware stores. In addition, Mueller continued to innovate, bringing out—coincident with new strict EPA regulations—the SRD-1 which allowed customers in the refrigeration and climate control industries to capture and recover fluorocarbons during repair operations.

Early 1990s: Regaining Independence As Mueller Industries

The issues surrounding Sharon were finally resolved on December 28, 1990, when negotiators, headed by Raymond Wechsler, an advisor to the Quantum Fund, hammered out a plan to divide up the company. After 25 years as a subsidiary, Mueller reemerged as an independent company called Mueller Industries, Inc. The new Mueller was an industrial concern that held its traditional plumbing and flow control equipment operation as well as natural resource holdings centered around a division called Arava Natural Resources Company, Inc. This new sector of the business included the Utah Railway Company—a short-line that carried coal to Provo, Utah, for transshipment by major rail carriers—Alaskan gold mining operations, and a variety of mining interests in Canada and the West. (Sharon's steel assets were spun off into a new firm called Sharon Specialty Steel, Inc.) During 1991 Mueller moved its headquarters from Port Huron, Michigan, to Wichita, Kansas.

In its first year as an independent company, Mueller announced a loss of $43.7 million on sales of $441 million. Almost all of the 1991 loss was due to a revaluation of assets, coupled with costs related to the bankruptcy proceeding and restructuring of the business following the reorganization. Harvey L. Karp, who became chairman and CEO on October 8, 1991, moved quickly to shape up the company. He enhanced the balance sheet by selling $25 million worth of investment grade notes and negotiated for expanded borrowing capabilities that provided $40 million. In an effort to focus on the company's core manufacturing business, the sale of the malleable iron business—which had not been profitable for Mueller—was arranged in 1992. To help upgrade operations neglected for many years, Karp made a commitment to allocate more capital and undertake improvement projects. He also negotiated settlements of litigation that asserted a $16.5 million guarantee obligation for the Sharon Steel business. This settlement turned out to be very favorable when Sharon filed Chapter 9 in the fourth quarter of 1992. Finally, among other key executives, Karp recruited William D. O'Hagan, who had 32 years experience in the industry, to be Mueller's chief operating officer and president. Karp's efforts paid off handsomely—for the year ended 1992, earnings were up significantly, reaching $16.6 million on sales of $517.3 million.

After Mueller emerged from Sharon Steel's shadow, the Quantum Fund held about 46 percent of the common stock, with the remainder owned by Sharon Steel's creditors. The stock initially traded on the NASDAQ exchange, but the company gained a listing on the New York Stock Exchange in February 1991. During 1993 the Quantum Fund sold the bulk of its stake to the public through a secondary offering. Then in 1994 Mueller bought Quantum's remaining 9.6 percent stake for $25.9 million. Also in 1994, O'Hagan was promoted to president and CEO, with Karp remaining chairman.

The steadily expanding economy in the mid-1990s fueled growth in housing starts, which was the key economic indicator for Mueller given the large portion of sales that were generated from the construction industry. Both revenues and earnings advanced steadily during this period, culminating in the 1996 figures of $61.2 million in net income on net sales of $729.9 million. During 1995 the company declared a two-for-one stock split and also announced that the headquarters would be moved from Wichita to Memphis, Tennessee. The move, completed in May 1996, was taken in order to place the head office closer to Mueller's core manufacturing operations in Tennessee and Mississippi. The mid-1990s were also marked by major capital outlays in which Mueller invested about $100 million in plant improvements that increased production capacity and improved efficiency in the company's manufacturing operations.

Turning Acquisitive in the Late 1990s

During the late 1990s, as Mueller continued to enjoy annual increases in revenues and profits, the company stepped up its growth efforts by completing a string of significant acquisitions.

The first came in late December 1996 when Precision Tube Company, Inc. of North Wales, Pennsylvania, was purchased for $6.6 million. Founded in 1948, Precision Tube produced copper, copper alloy, and aluminum tubing and fabricated tubular products, with its main product line being copper tubing for the baseboard heating industry. These products were produced at the company's mill in North Wales, while a second plant in Salisbury, Maryland, manufactured semirigid and flexible coaxial cables and assemblies used in the defense industry and in microwave technology. The company achieved sales of about $20 million in 1996.

In the first half of 1997, Mueller established its first significant European beachhead through the acquisition of two copper tube manufacturers. In February the company spent $21.3 million for Wednesday Tube Company, based in Bilston, West Midlands, England. Then, three months later, a French firm, Desnoyers S.A., was acquired for $13.5 million. Desnoyers operated two plants near Paris, in Laigneville and Longueville, and during 1996 produced 60 million pounds of tube, resulting in net sales of $100 million. The Laigneville mill was later shut down and its operations consolidated into those of the other two European plants.

With the company's streak of record results continuing, another two-for-one stock split was declared in early 1998. Three acquisitions were completed later in the year. In August Mueller acquired B&K Industries, Inc., an Elk Grove Village, Illinois–based importer and distributor of residential and commercial plumbing products with sales in 1997 of about $50 million. A key in this deal was that B&K distributed its products to all major distribution channels, including the retail market—hardware stores and home centers—which Mueller had not previously penetrated to any great extent. Next, Mueller bought Lincoln Brass Works, Inc., a metal fabrication firm with plants in Jacksboro and Waynesboro, Tennessee, and annual sales of $35 million. Lincoln's product line complemented Mueller's brass forging operations and included custom control valve assemblies, custom metal assemblies, gas delivery systems, and tubular products, mainly for the gas appliance market. Finally, in November 1998 Mueller completed the acquisition of Halstead Industries, Inc. for about $92 million in stock. The privately held Halstead, which was founded in Pittsburgh in 1936 and which had sales in 1997 of approximately $250 million, produced copper tubing for plumbing, air conditioning, and refrigeration applications at plants in Wynne, Arkansas, and Clinton, Tennessee. Following the acquisition, Halstead was renamed Mueller Copper Tube Products, Inc.

In addition to its series of acquisitions and its continued investment of tens of millions of dollars to modernize and update existing plants, Mueller during the late 1990s also divested a number of its natural resources operations as these businesses were increasingly viewed as noncore. At the end of 1997 the company sold off a coal mining business whose operations had been shut down earlier in the decade. Alaska Gold Company, a subsidiary that operated an open pit gold mine in Alaska, was sold to Novagold Resources, Inc. for $5.5 million in April 1999. This left Mueller with one main natural resources operation, that of Utah Railway, the short-line coal-carrying railroad. Mueller recorded its sixth straight year of revenue growth and its eighth consecutive year of earnings growth in 1999. Net sales surpassed the $1 billion mark for the first time, totaling $1.2 billion, while net income increased 31.7 percent, reaching $99.3 million.

Maintaining Profitability in the Uncertain Environment of the Early 2000s

The economic downturn that coincided with the beginning of the 21st century halted Mueller's string of record results, although the company was able to stay in the black. For 2001, sales fell 15 percent while net income declined 28 percent. To minimize the effects of the downturn, Mueller instituted a number of cost saving measures, including a wage freeze, and streamlined its sales and manufacturing operations. The company's plant in Clinton, Tennessee, was closed down, and Mueller also exited from the metric copper fittings sector, closing its Canadian plant in the process. In August 2002 the company completed the divestment of its noncore assets with the sale of Utah Railway to Genessee & Wyoming, Inc. for $55.4 million. As it surveyed the future, Mueller's outlook was clouded somewhat by the continued economic weakness and by the prospect of a larger downturn in the housing market, a sector that had remained relatively buoyant thanks to historically low interest rates.

Principal Subsidiaries

Mueller Brass Co.; Itawamba Industrial Gas Company, Inc.; Streamline Copper & Brass Ltd. (Canada); Mueller Plastics Corporation, Inc.; Mueller Brass Forging Company, Inc.; Mueller Copper Fittings Company, Inc.; Mueller Copper Tube Company, Inc.; Mueller Formed Tube Company, Inc.; Mueller Impacts Company, Inc.; Mueller Line Set Inc.; Mueller Press Company, Inc.; Mueller Refrigeration Products Company, Inc.; Lincoln Brass Works, Inc.; Precision Tube Company, Inc.; Mueller Tool and Machine, Inc.; Mueller Casting Company, Inc.; Micro Gauge, Inc.; Microgauge Machining, Inc.; Propipe Technologies, Inc.; Mueller Europe, Ltd. (U.K.); Mueller de Mexico; Mueller Europe, S.A. (France); B&K Industries, Inc.; Mueller Copper Tube Products, Inc.; Mueller Streamline FSC Ltd. (Virgin Islands); Arava Natural Resources Company, Inc.; United States Fuel Company; King Coal Company; Canco Oil & Gas Ltd. (Canada); Aegis Oil & Gas Leasing Ltd. (Canada); Bayard Mining Corporation; Washington Mining Company.

Principal Divisions

Standard Products Division; Industrial Products Division.

Principal Competitors

Wolverine Tube, Inc.; NIBCO, Inc.; Cerro Copper Products Co., Inc.; Chase Industries, Inc.; Charlotte Pipe & Foundry Company; Cambridge-Lee Industries Inc.; Amcast Industrial Corporation; Cerro Metal Products Company, Inc.; Extruded Metals Inc.

Further Reading

Barton, Christopher, ''Mueller Industries Gears to Take Advantage of Economic Rebound,'' *Memphis (Tenn.) Commercial Appeal,* May 10, 2002, p. C2.

Brannigan, Martha, ''Sharon Steel Is in Talks to Sell Its Mueller Unit,'' *Wall Street Journal,* December 2, 1986.

Daniel, Fran, ''Mueller Industries Agrees to Buy Halstead,'' *Winston-Salem (N.C.) Journal,* August 11, 1998, p. D1.

Harrigan, Susan, ''Victor Posner Faces Hair-Raising Month As Exchange for UV Note Is Postponed,'' *Wall Street Journal,* July 21, 1980, p. 2.

Mari, Albert, ''Chase, Mueller Reduce Their Brass Rod Prices Initiating New Decline,'' *American Metal Market,* September 30, 1976.

''Mueller Brass Co. Lowers Copper Water Tube Price,'' *Wall Street Journal,* April 15, 1963.

''Mueller Brass Expects Record Fiscal '63 Sales Above $75 Million Mark,'' *Wall Street Journal,* September 30, 1963.

''Mueller Tube Mill Nears Completion,'' *American Metal Market,* June 25, 1970.

Norman, James R., ''Pulling Sharon Steel off the Scrap Heap,'' *Forbes,* August 20, 1990.

Overstreet, James, ''Mueller Moving Manufacturer to Lease New Headquarters,'' *Memphis (Tenn.) Business Journal,* June 19, 1998, pp. 1+.

Paulk, Michael, ''Mueller Plant Upgrade Long Time Coming,'' *Memphis (Tenn.) Business Journal,* July 21, 2000, p. 3.

''Plan for Sharon Steel to Leave Chapter 11 Is Set by Co-Sponsors,'' *Wall Street Journal,* October, 26, 1989.

Sacco, John E., ''Mueller Acquires Precision Tube,'' *American Metal Market,* January 9, 1997, p. 2.

Scott, Jonathan, ''Mueller Quietly Approaches $1 Billion in Sales Mark,'' *Memphis (Tenn.) Business Journal,* October 1, 1999, p. 32.

Shearer, Brent, ''Mueller Completes One Deal, Planning Another,'' *American Metal Market,* September 10, 1998, p. 1.

''UV Industries, Inc.,'' *Wall Street Transcript,* December 13, 1976.

VanValkenburgh, Jaan, ''Mueller Acquires Precision Tube,'' *Memphis (Tenn.) Commercial Appeal,* January 8, 1997, p. B8.

——, ''Mueller to Relocate Main Office to Memphis, Offer Transfer to 60,'' *Memphis (Tenn.) Commercial Appeal,* August 29, 1995, p. B5.

Watson, Mark, ''Mueller to Sell Railroad Company,'' *Memphis (Tenn.) Commercial Appeal,* August 21, 2002, p. C2.

—Jordan Wankoff
—update: David E. Salamie

Newell Rubbermaid Inc.

Newell Center
29 East Stephenson Street
Freeport, Illinois 61032-0943
U.S.A.
Telephone: (815) 235-4171
Toll Free: (800) 421-1941
Fax: (815) 381-8155
Web site: http://www.newellrubbermaid.com

Public Company
Incorporated: 1902 as W.F. Linton Company
Employees: 49,425
Sales: $6.91 billion (2001)
Stock Exchanges: New York Midwest
Ticker Symbol: NWL
NAIC: 321999 All Other Miscellaneous Wood Product
   Manufacturing; 323118 Blankbook, Looseleaf Binders,
   and Devices Manufacturing; 326199 All Other Plastics
   Product Manufacturing; 326299 All Other Rubber Prod-
   uct Manufacturing; 327212 Other Pressed and Blown
   Glass and Glassware Manufacturing; 332116 Metal
   Stamping; 332211 Cutlery and Flatware (Except
   Precious) Manufacturing; 332212 Hand Edge Tool
   Manufacturing; 332213 Saw Blade and Handsaw
   Manufacturing; 332214 Kitchen Utensil, Pot, and Pan
   Manufacturing; 332510 Hardware Manufacturing;
   333992 Welding and Soldering Equipment Manufactur-
   ing; 332999 All Other Miscellaneous Fabricated Metal
   Product Manufacturing; 337125 Household Furniture
   (Except Wood and Metal) Manufacturing; 337215
   Showcase, Partition, Shelving, and Locker Manufactur-
   ing; 337920 Blind and Shade Manufacturing; 339931
   Doll and Stuffed Toy Manufacturing; 339932 Game,
   Toy, and Children's Vehicle Manufacturing; 339941
   Pen and Mechanical Pencil Manufacturing; 339942
   Lead Pencil and Art Good Manufacturing; 339943
   Marking Device Manufacturing; 339994 Broom, Brush,
   and Mop Manufacturing; 339999 All Other Miscella-
   neous Manufacturing

Newell Rubbermaid Inc. is a diversified manufacturer and marketer of a variety of high-volume brand-name consumer products. The firm is organized into four business groups. The Rubbermaid group makes such products as storage containers, waste and recycling containers, closet organization systems, cleaning products, outdoor play systems, high chairs, infant seats, strollers, play yards, and children's toys and furniture; key brands include Rubbermaid, Curver, Little Tikes, Graco, and Century. The Sharpie group produces writing instruments, highlighters, art supplies, office accessories, and hair care accessories; brands include Sanford, Sharpie, Paper Mate, Parker, Waterman, Uni-Ball, Liquid Paper, Eldon, and Goody. The Levolor/Hardware group makes drapery hardware, window blinds and other window treatments, paint applicator products, hand torches, cabinet hardware, hand tools, and power tool accessories; among the brands of this group are Levolor, Kirsch, Newell, Amerock, BernzOmatic, and Vise-Grip. The Calphalon Home group produces cookware, bakeware, glassware, dinnerware, kitchen tools and utensils, ready-made picture frames, and photo albums; brands include Calphalon, WearEver, Regal, Anchor Hocking, Pyrex, and Burnes of Boston. The company's products are sold primarily through mass merchandisers, including discount, variety, chain, and hardware stores, as well as warehouse clubs, hardware and houseware distributors, home improvement centers, office product superstores, and grocery and drugstores. Nearly 75 percent of the company's revenues are generated in the United States, with 18 percent originating in Europe and 4 percent each in Canada and in Central and South America. Wal-Mart Stores, Inc. is by far the largest of Newell Rubbermaid's customers, accounting for about 15 percent of total sales.

The two main strands of Newell Rubbermaid's history came together in March 1999 when Newell Co. acquired Rubbermaid Incorporated. Originally founded soon after the dawn of the 20th century to make brass curtain rods, Newell evolved into a maker of a wide range of brand-name consumer products. The low-profile company grew mainly through acquisition, buying dozens of firms in the late 20th century and then improving their profitability through an integration process known as "Newellization." Rubbermaid was a much better known company when it was acquired by Newell, which subsequently changed its name to Newell Rubbermaid. Originally known as the

---

Company Perspectives:

Each and every day, our products touch millions of people where they work, where they live and where they play. Our portfolio of power brands provides a compelling platform for growth that we are leveraging with breakthrough product innovation, high-impact marketing and attention-grabbing presentation at the point of sale. At the same time, we are aggressively pursuing the type of operating efficiency that characterizes the world's best companies.

Our vision is to create a global powerhouse in consumer and commercial products and to provide a superior return to our shareholders. Frankly, we can't think of a more exciting opportunity.

Wooster Rubber Company (which was founded in 1920) and initially specializing in rubber products, Rubbermaid developed into a top maker of consumer brand-name products—primarily plastic products.

Newell's Curtain Rod Roots

Newell Co. traces its roots to the short-lived W.F. Linton Company, an Ogdensburg, New York, firm incorporated in 1902 to make brass curtain rods. The Linton Company received $1,000 to move the company from Providence, Rhode Island, to Ogdensburg from the Ogdensburg Board of Trade, with the board's president, Edgar A. Newell, signing off on the loan. In 1903 the company went bankrupt and Newell took control of its operations, renaming the firm Newell Manufacturing Company, Inc.

Although he was familiar with sales, Newell had no understanding of manufacturing and, as a result, hired and subsequently fired several general managers between 1903 and 1907. Edgar Newell then hired his son Allan to run Newell Manufacturing and started a new company, Newell Manufacturing Company Ltd. (Newell Ltd.), in Prescott, Canada. Established to capitalize on Ogdensburg's location, which made shipments south costly and left Canadian distribution channels more financially attractive, Newell Ltd. purchased a small dockside building in Prescott.

Newell Manufacturing's initial product line was composed exclusively of brass curtain rods, created through a method of tube making that utilized a waterwheel; Newell's was powered by the nearby Oswegatchie River. In 1908 Newell began producing a greater variety of curtain rod shapes after adopting a new, faster, and more adaptable manufacturing process that used roll forming machines. By the end of the decade the Newell companies were employing about 20 people and generating annual sales of about $50,000.

Throughout Newell Manufacturing's second decade, increasing managerial authority was given to Allan Newell, although Edgar Newell retained all voting shares of both Newell companies. In 1912 the domestic company began construction of a new factory, which was completed a year later.

Although Ogdensburg operations were sailing smoothly, by 1912 Newell Ltd. found that curtain rods were not enough to keep its operations afloat. A new manager, Lawrence "Ben" Ferguson Cuthbert, was given a chance to bail out the Canadian plant in return for a 20 percent cut of its gross profits. Between 1912 and 1913 Newell Ltd. acquired the factory it had been leasing and expanded its plating department to produce a variety of products, including towel racks, stair nosings, ice picks, and other items requiring a finish of brass, zinc, or nickel. The expanded product line spurred additional sales, and Newell Ltd. soon became profitable.

As war spread across the globe, the cost of brass rose, and Newell hired the Baker Varnish Company to devise a new metal-coating method tailored to Newell's roll forming manufacturing process. By 1917 Newell's curtain rods were being coated with a nontarnishable lacquer. Not only were the new rods cheaper to produce than brass rods, but because they would not tarnish, they were better suited to lace and ruffle curtains.

With its new curtain rod Newell courted and won the business of Woolworth stores, after agreeing to buy out Woolworth's on-hand stock of curtain rods. Newell's first buyback deal soon paid dividends, boosting sales and helping to establish the company's first long-term relationship with a major national retailer.

In 1920 Edgar A. Newell died and, for the first time, stockholder changes were made at the company. Cuthbert called in his profit-stake from running Newell Ltd., and, after some subsequent legal jousting, the company's stock ownership was resolved. Allan Newell received a 64 percent share in Newell Ltd., and Cuthbert received 33 percent of Newell Manufacturing and 20 percent of Newell Ltd. Albert Newell, Edgar's other son, who had been helping with sales, received 66 percent of Newell Manufacturing and 16 percent of Newell Ltd. Allan Newell was named chairman and president of Newell Manufacturing but bowed out of active affairs with the company, opting for a political life that eventually led him to the New York State Assembly. Albert Newell was also reluctant to be involved with the family business, and management of both companies passed to Cuthbert, who moved to Ogdensburg.

Formation of Western Newell in 1921

In 1921 Cuthbert, the Newell brothers, and a former Ogdensburg employee named Harry Barnwell each put up $5,000 to start a new curtain rod factory in Freeport, Illinois. The new business, Western Newell Manufacturing Company, was designed to take advantage of local railroad transportation and serve as a western branch of Newell Manufacturing. Barnwell served a brief stint as Western Newell's president before selling his 25 percent stake in the operations to Cuthbert's cousin, Leonard Ferguson, who was recruited to manage the fledgling company. Like Newell Manufacturing, Western Newell began operations with ten employees and initially produced curtain rods in a red brick factory it rented. The company quickly became profitable, and in 1925 a new factory was erected. By 1928 Western Newell's sales had grown to $485,000, more than twice that of Newell Ltd. and about half that of Newell Manufacturing. At the time of the stock market crash in October 1929, Western Newell was producing a wide variety of drapery hardware, including extension curtain rods, ornamental drapery rods, and pinless curtain stretchers.

Key Dates:

1902: Ogdensburg, New York–based W.F. Linton Company is incorporated to make brass curtain rods.

1903: Linton goes bankrupt; Edgar A. Newell takes control of the firm, renaming it Newell Manufacturing Company, Inc.

c. 1910: Newell forms an affiliated company in Prescott, Canada, called Newell Manufacturing Company Ltd.

1920: The Wooster Rubber Company is formed in Wooster, Ohio, to make toy balloons.

1921: Another Newell-affiliated company, Western Newell Manufacturing Company, is formed to run a curtain rod factory in Freeport, Illinois.

1933: James R. Caldwell forms an enterprise called Rubbermaid, whose first product is a red rubber dustpan.

1934: Wooster Rubber and Rubbermaid merge, retaining the former's corporate name and headquarters and the latter's brand name.

1955: Wooster Rubber goes public.

1956: Wooster branches into plastic products, introducing a plastic dishpan.

1957: Wooster Rubber changes its name to Rubbermaid Inc.

1966: The Newell companies are consolidated into Newell Manufacturing Company, which is based in Freeport.

1970: Newell Manufacturing is reincorporated in Delaware as Newell Companies, Inc.

1972: Newell goes public.

1983: Cookware maker Mirro Corporation is acquired by Newell.

1984: Rubbermaid acquires the Little Tikes Company, maker of plastic toys.

1985: Newell Companies is renamed Newell Co.

1986: Rubbermaid acquires MicroComputer Accessories.

1987: Glassware maker Anchor Hocking Corporation is acquired by Newell.

1993: Newell acquires Levolor Corp., Lee/Rowan Co., and Goody Products Inc.

1994: Newell acquires Home Fashions Inc., Faber-Castell Corporation, and Corning Incorporated's European consumer products operation.

1996: Rubbermaid acquires Graco Children's Products Inc.

1997: Newell acquires the Kirsch decorative window hardware brand and Rubbermaid's office products unit.

1998: Newell acquires Calphalon Corporation and two German firms: the Gardinia Group and Rotring Group; Rubbermaid acquires the Curver Group and Century Products Company.

1999: Newell acquires Rubbermaid for $6 billion; Newell changes its name to Newell Rubbermaid Inc.

2000: Newell Rubbermaid acquires the stationery products division of Gillette Company, gaining the Paper Mate, Parker, Waterman, and Liquid Paper brands.

2001: Joseph Galli, Jr., comes onboard as president and CEO and launches a thorough restructuring.

2002: The company acquires American Tool Companies, Inc., maker of hand tools and power tool accessories.

Despite a dramatic slide in sales that forced the companies to lay off workers and reduce workdays, the Newell companies made it through the Great Depression without dipping into red ink. The bottom of the Depression's well for Newell Manufacturing came in 1933 when that company logged only about one-half of its 1929 level of sales, or $425,000. With a small operational base and modest salaries, Western Newell fared the best of the two American companies during the Depression, and by 1933 the 12-year-old Western Newell, with sales figures 25 percent lower than Newell Manufacturing, had a net income 30 percent greater than the original company. In 1933 Western Newell earned $61,000 on sales of $320,000, whereas Newell Manufacturing earned $47,000 on sales of $425,000. By 1937 Western Newell, under the leadership of Ferguson, had surpassed Newell Manufacturing in both revenues and income, earning $126,000 on sales of $553,000, whereas Newell Manufacturing earned $70,000 on sales of $511,000. At Cuthbert's suggestion, in the late 1930s the Newell brothers agreed to give Ferguson a small stake in Newell Manufacturing, effectively taking the founding company out of the hands of the Newell family, although the brothers retained rights to voting control through the late 1940s.

Between 1938 and 1939 Newell Manufacturing established a third domestic factory, this one in Los Angeles, and made its first acquisition—Drapery Hardware Ltd. of Monrovia, California (DRACO), a maker of wooden and heavy iron drapery fixtures that eventually was sold to S.H. Kress and other smaller customers. Before the 1930s drew to a close a number of officer changes were made: Cuthbert was named to succeed Allan Newell as president of Newell Manufacturing and Ferguson was named president of Western Newell, although Allan Newell remained president of Newell Ltd. and chairman of all three companies.

During World War II the Freeport factory won a coveted Army/Navy "E" Award for excellence in wartime production, churning out more than 230 million metallic belt links for machine guns within a two-year period. During the postwar decade the Newell companies enjoyed steady growth, although no new manufacturing plants were started or acquired. In 1954 the Newell family ceded further power over its namesake companies as complete operational control was given to Leonard Ferguson, who became president of all three Newell companies.

1960s and 1970s: Consolidating the Newell Companies and Going Public

During the early 1960s Newell acquired the rights to additional drapery hardware brands and names, including Angevine and Silent Gliss. In 1963 Ferguson was named chairman and chief executive of the three Newell companies and two years later his son, Daniel C. Ferguson, became president of the companies. Under the leadership of the father-and-son team, in

1966 all Newell companies were consolidated into one Illinois corporation, Newell Manufacturing Company, with headquarters in Freeport. Under the guidance of Daniel Ferguson, the $14 million family business turned its focus from its products to its customers and initiated a multiproduct strategy designed to boost sales to its existing buyers.

During the 1970s Newell continued to acquire other companies, greatly expanding its product line in the process. In 1968 Newell purchased a majority interest in Mirra-Cote Industries, a manufacturer of plastic bath accessories. In 1969 Newell acquired Dorfile Manufacturing Company, a maker of household shelving, and E.H. Tate Company, which brought the ''Bulldog'' line of picture hanging hardware into the Newell line of products. During the late 1960s DRACO began phasing out of manufacturing operations and finally closed its doors in the early 1970s. In 1970 the company was reincorporated in Delaware as Newell Companies, Inc. The following year Newell added sewing and knitting accessories to its product line when it acquired The Boye Needle Company, a Chicago-based world leader in knitting needles and crochet hooks, and Novel Ideas, Inc., another maker of do-it-yourself sewing materials.

In April 1972 Newell went public as an over-the-counter stock and that same year initiated an acquisition strategy that would later be replayed in various forms. Newell made an offer to buy EZ Paintr Corporation, a paint and sundries company in which Newell already had a 25 percent stake, and EZ Paintr in turn filed a pair of lawsuits to fight back against a possible takeover. But in February 1973 Newell gained majority control of EZ Paintr after its president and cofounder agreed to sell his family's interest in the paint supply company, a move opposed by EZ Paintr's management. By March 1973 Newell had ousted the EZ Paintr board and Daniel Ferguson had become president of the company, which yielded complete control of its stock to Newell six months later. In 1974 Newell completed another drawn-out acquisition and purchased complete control of Mirra-Cote.

In 1975 Leonard Ferguson died and a descendant of Ben Cuthbert, William R. Cuthbert, was later named chairman. Between 1976 and 1978 Newell expanded its shelving, paint, and sundries offerings and acquired Royal Oak Industries, Inc., Baker Brush Company, and Dixon Red Devil Ltd. (later renamed Dixon Applicators). During the same period the company sold some of its knitting products businesses, including Novel Ideas. In May 1978 Newell acquired 24 percent of the financially troubled BernzOmatic Corporation, a manufacturer of propane torches and other do-it-yourself hand tools. In February 1979 Newell gained operational control over Bernz-Omatic after its president, who had earlier sold convertible debentures to Newell, yielded his position to Ferguson and Newell had taken control of the smaller firm's board.

In June 1979, after coming off of its first $100 million sales year, Newell began trading on the New York Stock Exchange. About the same time Newell began targeting a new customer base—the emerging mass merchandisers such as Kmart—in order to piggyback on the increasing popularity of such stores.

1980s: Accelerating the Pace of Acquisition and the Newellization Process

Newell entered the 1980s riding on the growth of mass merchandisers while continuing to expand and complement its product line through acquisitions. Between 1980 and 1981 Newell acquired the drapery hardware division of The Stanley Works and Brearley Co., a manufacturer of bathroom scales. In April 1982 Newell acquired complete control of BernzOmatic and in December of that year entered into a $60 million financing and stock purchase agreement with Western Savings & Loan Association, with the S&L paying $18.4 million for a 20 percent stake in Newell, which it gradually sold off to private investors during the next five years.

Through two separate stock deals worth more than $42 million, in 1983 Newell acquired Mirro Corporation, a maker of aluminum cookware and baking dishes. In May 1984 Newell increased its number of common stock shares from 14 million to 50 million and later that year through a stock swap acquired Foley-ASC, Inc., a maker of cookware and kitchen accessories. In May 1985 the company changed its name to Newell Co. In June 1985 Newell acquired a 20 percent stake in William E. Wright Company from a group dissenting from the majority, including three board members and the grandson of Wright Company's founder. A few months later Newell raised its stake in Wright, a maker of sewing notions, and by the end of the year Newell had obtained majority control of the company and ousted Wright's board and top officers.

In January 1986 William P. Sovey, former president of conglomerate AMF Inc., was named president and chief operating officer. Ferguson remained chief executive and was named to the new position of vice-chairman. In October 1986 Newell acquired the assets of Enterprise Aluminum, the aluminum cookware division of Lancaster Colony Corporation.

By 1987 Newell had acquired complete control of Wright, which was added to a list of about 30 acquisitions the company had logged since Ferguson had become president. In July 1987 Newell—true to its acquisition formula—paid $330 million to acquire control of Anchor Hocking Corporation and its targeted glassware operations. At the time of the acquisition Anchor, with $758 million in sales, had nearly double the annual revenues of Newell and provided its new parent with brand-name tabletop glassware, decorative cabinet hardware, and microwave cookware, with each product line holding a number one or two position in its respective market. Within a week after the takeover Newell began employing its usual post-acquisition strategy on a large scale, dismissing 110 Anchor employees and closing its West Virginia plant. Through this strategy, which became known as ''Newellization,'' Newell aimed to boost the profitability of acquired companies by improving customer service and partnerships, reducing overhead costs by centralizing administrative functions, abandoning underperforming product lines, and reducing inventory. Acquired companies continued to be ''Newellized'' into the early 21st century.

Between 1988 and 1989 Newell acquired several small companies that made bakeware, paint sundries, metal closures, cabinet hardware, and aluminum cookware, and sold its Carr-Lowrey specialty glass container business and its William E.

Wright/Boye Needle home-sewing business. In 1989 Newell unsuccessfully tried to buy a 20-plus percent investment in Vermont American, a maker of consumer and industrial tools that turned to another suitor after suggesting Newell would be a disruptive force in its operations.

Newell closed its books on the 1980s having achieved a number of significant financial accomplishments. Between 1987 and 1989 the company's income rose more than $48 million, while during the course of the entire decade sales spiraled from $138 million to $1.12 billion as income ballooned from $7.8 million to $85.3 million. Newell also was listed number 22 on the *Forbes* list of the best stocks of the 1980s, having provided a total return to stockholders that averaged 39.5 percent per year.

Early 1990s: Expanding into Office Products and Picture Frames

Newell entered the 1990s as a market leader in electronic data interchange, a computer-to-computer system that allowed Newell customers to place orders electronically. Attempting to once again piggyback on a growing mass merchandiser market—namely the trend to sell office supplies through mass retailers—in 1991 Newell entered the office products business by acquiring two small firms, Keene Manufacturing, Inc., and W.T. Rogers Company.

In 1991 Newell also increased its interests in hardware firms and agreed to invest $150 million in the Black & Decker Corporation in a stock deal giving Newell a 15 percent stake in the hardware company. (The following year Newell backed away from a move to purchase a 15 percent interest in another hardware manufacturer, Stanley Works, which had filed an antitrust suit against Newell.) In 1991 Newell also acquired a 6 percent stake in the Ekco Group Inc., a maker of houseware products, kitchen tools, and bakeware, which was later sold.

In 1992 Newell became a major force in the office products market. It acquired both Sanford Corporation, a leading producer of felt-tipped pens, plastic desk accessories, storage boxes, and other office and school supplies, and Stuart Hall Company, Inc., a well-known stationery and school supply business, in two stock swaps totaling more than $600 million. The two businesses combined brought Newell's annual office products sales to $350 million. The year 1992 also saw Newell—in what some perceived as a return to its roots—acquire Intercraft Industries, Inc., the largest supplier of picture frames in the United States. That year Newell sold its closures business for $210 million, and the company's books for the year reflected a record $119 million in earnings on a record $1.45 billion in sales.

In a 1992 changing-of-the-guard, Daniel Ferguson bowed out of active management to move up to chairman, replacing the retiring William Cuthbert, and Thomas A. Ferguson (no relation to Daniel and Leonard Ferguson) was named president. Sovey was named to succeed Daniel Ferguson as vice-chairman and chief executive. Although the company had another Ferguson in line to run Newell, by 1992 stock dilution had reduced insider control of the company to 15 percent. Nevertheless, four members of the 11-person board were members of the Ferguson, Cuthbert, or Newell families.

1993–98: Acquisition Spree of Nearly $2 Billion

Having already completed more than 50 acquisitions from the late 1960s through 1992, Newell completed a dizzying series of deals from 1993 through 1998. The company spent about $1.9 billion on acquisitions during this period, completing 18 major acquisitions that added about $2.6 billion in annual revenues to Newell's coffers.

Three key deals were consummated in 1993. In April, Sunnyvale, California–based Levolor Corp. was acquired for $72.5 million, giving Newell a leading maker of window blinds that had 1992 sales of $180 million. Then in September Newell bought Lee/Rowan Co., based in St. Louis, Missouri, for $73.5 million, gaining a leading manufacturer of wire storage and organization products with $100 million in 1992 revenues; Lee/Rowan fit in quite well alongside Newell's Dorfile hardware and shelving brand. Two months later Newell spent $147.1 million for Goody Products Inc., which was based in Kearny, New Jersey. With sales in 1992 of about $218 million, Goody produced hair care accessories, such as brushes, barrettes, and ponytail holders, as well as Ace combs; Goody also produced OptiRay sunglasses, but Newell sold that business to Benson Eyecare Corporation in January 1994.

Rounding out its window treatments portfolio, Newell in August 1994 acquired Home Fashions Inc., based in Westminster, California. Achieving revenues of $140 million in 1993, Home Fashions produced window coverings, including vertical blinds and pleated shades, under the Del Mar and LouverDrape brand names. In a similar move, the office products operations were bolstered through the October 1994 purchase of Faber-Castell Corporation, which specialized in pencils and rolling-ball pens under the Eberhard Faber and Uni-Ball names. One month later, Newell spent $86 million to acquire Corning Incorporated's European consumer products business, which had 1993 revenues of $130 million. This deal included manufacturing facilities in England, France, and Germany; the trademark rights and product lines for Corning's Pyrex, Pyroflam, and Visions cookware brands in Europe, the Middle East, and Africa; and Corning's consumer distribution network in these areas. Newell also became the distributor of Corning's U.S.-made cookware and dinnerware products, including the Revere Ware and Corelle brands, in these same regions. This acquisition gave Newell its first major overseas foothold.

Newell gained a virtual stranglehold on the picture frame market with the acquisitions of Decorel Incorporated in October 1995 and Holson Burnes Group, Inc. in January 1996. Decorel, which had sales of more than $100 million in 1994, was the third largest U.S. maker of picture frames but also gave Newell entry into the framed-art business. North Smithfield, Rhode Island–based Holson Burnes was acquired for $33.5 million and was the number two frame supplier in the country, behind Newell itself. Its brands included Burnes of Boston photo frames, sold mainly to department stores and specialty stores, and Holson photo albums, which were distributed through mass merchandisers and discounters. Revenues in 1994 for Holson Burnes totaled $130 million. Newell also gained a stronger position in writing instruments by purchasing Berol Corporation in November 1995. Among Berol's products were graphite and coloring pencils, and its 1994 sales exceeded $200 million.

Concluding its heaviest one-year spending spree yet, Newell spent $563.5 million to complete four major deals during 1997. Office products were the subject of two of the acquisitions, the March purchase of the Rolodex brand from Insilco Corporation and the June buyout of the office products business of Rubbermaid. Under the Rolodex brand, which generated about $68 million in 1996 revenues, were such products as card files, personal organizers, and paper punches. With 1996 sales of $162 million, the Rubbermaid unit produced desk and computer accessories, chairmats, resin-based office furniture, and storage and organization products under the Eldon and MicroComputer Accessories brands. In May 1997 Newell bought the Kirsch brand from Cooper Industries, Inc., thereby gaining the leading producer of decorative window hardware in the country, with annual sales in excess of $250 million. Then in August 1997 Newell acquired two subsidiaries of American Greetings Corporation: Acme Frame Products, Inc., producer of picture frames, and Wilhold Inc., maker of hair care accessory products. At the end of 1997 Sovey retired from active management, and he became Newell's chairman, replacing Daniel Ferguson. Taking over Sovey's former position of vice-chairman and CEO was John J. McDonough, who had been a senior vice-president of finance at Newell in the early 1980s and had served on the board of directors since 1992. Continuing as president and COO was Thomas Ferguson.

With the exception of the May acquisition of gourmet cookware maker Calphalon Corporation, all of the major 1998 acquisitions served to strengthen Newell's position outside the United States. In March Newell acquired Swish Track & Pole from Newmond plc. With 1997 sales of $65 million, Swish was a producer and marketer of decorative and functional window furnishings in the United Kingdom, France, Belgium, and Italy. Another European window treatment maker was brought onboard in August through the purchase of the Gardinia Group, which was based in Isny, Germany, and had 1997 revenues of $160 million. Newell acquired a Brazilian maker of aluminum cookware, Panex S.A. Industria e Comercio, in June. In September the company purchased another German firm, Hamburg-based Rotring Group, which had 1997 sales of $280 million. Rotring produced writing instruments, drawing instruments, and art materials under the Rotring, Koh-I-Noor, Grumbacher, and Accent brands; it also owned a subsidiary called Cosmolab Inc. that specialized in color cosmetic pencils. Newell spent $413.3 million on its 1998 acquisitions; the company also sold off its Stuart Hall business and the plastics division of Anchor Hocking that year.

The steady stream of acquisitions paid off for Newell in the form of record earnings of $396.2 million and record revenues of $3.72 billion for 1998. The earnings figure was more than four and a half times the level of 1989, while sales had more than tripled during the same period. For the ten-year period ending in 1998, Newell's compound annual growth rates for sales and earnings per share were 13 percent and 16 percent, respectively. Starting with the 1994 purchase of the European consumer products unit of Corning, Newell had made a concerted overseas push; as a result, sales outside the United States increased from 8 percent of total sales in 1992 to 22 percent in 1998. It was from this position of strength that Newell announced in October 1998 by far its largest acquisition ever: the $6 billion purchase of Rubbermaid that would be consummated in March 1999.

Rubbermaid Beginnings: Toy Balloons and a Better Dustpan

The Wooster Rubber Company got its start in May 1920, when nine Wooster, Ohio, investors pooled $26,800 to form a company to manufacture toy balloons, sold under the Sunshine brand name. Wooster Rubber, contained in one building in Wooster (a small town about 50 miles south of Cleveland), was sold to Horatio B. Ebert and Errett M. Grable, two Aluminum Company of America executives, in 1927. Grable and Ebert retained the firm's management. By the late 1920s, a new factory and office building had been constructed to house the prosperous business, but the fortunes of Wooster Rubber fell during the Great Depression. In 1934 Ebert spotted Rubbermaid products in a New England department store, and worked out a merger between the two firms.

Rubbermaid got its start in 1933, when a New England man named James R. Caldwell, who had first entered the rubber business as an employee of the Seamless Rubber Company in New Haven, Connecticut, looked around his kitchen during the depths of the Great Depression to see what he could improve. Caldwell and his wife conceived 29 products, among them a red rubber dustpan. Although the rubber dustpan, designed and manufactured by Caldwell and his wife, cost $1.00—much more than the 39-cent metal pans then available in stores— Caldwell "rang ten doorbells and sold nine dustpans," as he recalled in an interview published in the *New York Times* on May 19, 1974. Convinced there was a market for his products, Caldwell gave his enterprise a name—Rubbermaid—and expanded his line to include a soap dish, a sink plug, and a drainboard mat, selling these products in department stores throughout New England.

In July 1934 Caldwell's fledgling enterprise merged with Wooster Rubber. Still called The Wooster Rubber Company, the new group began to produce rubber household goods under the Rubbermaid brand name. With the merger, under Caldwell's leadership, Wooster Rubber had a happy reversal in fortunes, and sales rose from $80,000 in 1935 to $450,000 in 1941. Of the 29 new products Caldwell and his wife had thought up in their kitchen in 1933, the company had marketed 27 of them by 1941.

In 1942, however, U.S. involvement in World War II caused the government to cut back civilian use of rubber, so that raw materials would be available for products necessary to the war effort. This eliminated Rubbermaid's housewares business, but the company was able to convert to military manufacturing. Beginning with rubber parts for a self-sealing fuel tank for warplanes, and moving on to other products such as life jackets and rubber tourniquets, the company manufactured military goods through the end of the war, in 1945. In 1944 Wooster Rubber introduced an employee profit-sharing plan.

Following the advent of peace, Wooster Rubber picked up its prewar activities where it had left off, and resumed production of rubber housewares. Because wartime shortages had not yet been completely redressed, however, no coloring agents were available, and all Rubbermaid products were manufactured in black for several months. In 1947 the company introduced a line of rubber automotive accessories, including rubber floormats and cupholders.

The company's first international operations commenced in 1950, when Wooster Rubber began producing vinyl-coated wire goods at a plant in Ontario, Canada. By 1956 the plant was producing a complete line of Rubbermaid products.

Mid-1950s: Branching into Plastic Products

In 1955 Wooster Rubber went public, offering stock on the over-the-counter market. This capital infusion allowed the company to branch into plastic products, and in 1956 a plastic dishpan was introduced. This switch required significant re-tooling from the manufacture of exclusively rubber goods.

In 1957 Wooster Rubber changed its name to Rubbermaid Incorporated to increase its association with its well-known brand name. The following year, the company began its first expansion beyond its traditional focus on household goods by broadening its targeted market to include restaurants, hotels, and other institutions. Rubbermaid initially produced bathtub mats and doormats for these customers. By 1974 industrial and commercial products provided 25 percent of the company's sales.

After James Caldwell's retirement and a one-year stint as president by Forrest B. Shaw, the company presidency was taken over by Donald E. Noble in 1959. Noble had joined Wooster Rubber as a "temporary" associate in 1941. Also during 1959, Rubbermaid stock was sold for the first time on the New York Stock Exchange. The following year, Rubbermaid's management set a goal of doubling the company's earnings every six years, a goal that was consistently met throughout Noble's tenure. Noble also placed a heavy emphasis on new product development, evidenced by the objective he set in 1968 that aimed to have 30 percent of total annual sales come from products introduced over the preceding five years.

In 1965 Rubbermaid made its first move outside North America, purchasing Dupol, a West German manufacturer of plastic housewares, whose products and operations were similar to Rubbermaid's U.S. operations. "Our plan is to grow from within except when an acquisition can lead us into a market we already have an interest in," Noble told the *Wall Street Journal* on August 2, 1965, explaining the company's growth policy during this period.

In 1969 Rubbermaid added the sales party to its traditional marketing efforts, a sales technique first popularized by Tupperware. The party division had its own line of slightly more elaborate merchandise, accounting for around 10 percent of Rubbermaid's sales within five years. Nevertheless, the party plan was not profitable until 1976.

Difficult Years in the 1970s

In the early 1970s Rubbermaid marketed a line of recreational goods such as motorboats and snow sleds, but the company lacked the necessary distribution to support the products and abandoned the effort. "We bombed," the company's vice-president of marketing told a *Wall Street Journal* reporter on June 9, 1982.

Rubbermaid continued to grow in the early 1970s, but the combination of government controls on prices and the shortage of petrochemical raw materials caused by the energy crisis of the early 1970s kept a lid on earnings. In 1971 Rubbermaid began to market its products through direct supermarket retail distribution. Although initially profitable, this practice resulted in the company running afoul of the Federal Trade Commission (FTC) in 1973. The FTC challenged the company's pricing policies in connection with its role as distributor, charging Rubbermaid with illegal price-fixing and violations of antitrust laws. The complaint alleged that Rubbermaid engaged in price-fixing between wholesalers because it sold its products directly to some retailers—acting as its own wholesaler—and also allowed other wholesalers to sell its products, while stipulating the price for the products. Rubbermaid discontinued its minimum price agreements with wholesalers and retailers in 1975, citing pending legislation and negative public opinion. In 1976 the FTC ruled unanimously that Rubbermaid had violated antitrust laws and issued a cease-and-desist order to prevent the company from renewing these practices.

As part of its continued growth, Rubbermaid opened a new plant in La Grange, Georgia, in 1974, to relieve demand on its main Ohio plant and to supply the automotive products division. Despite rising earnings since 1968, a sharp increase in the price of raw materials, combined with a change in accounting practices, caused a large drop in Rubbermaid profits in 1974. By this time, Rubbermaid was selling 240 different items, of which about one-tenth were products introduced that year. The company continued to place strong emphasis on innovation and the introduction of new products, generated by a research-and-development staff of designers, engineers, and craftsmen. This staff built prototypes to be used and critiqued by thousands of consumers, resulting in an eight-month process from drawing board to store.

The company experienced labor unrest in 1976, when 1,100 members of the United Rubber Workers called a strike at Rubbermaid's only unionized plant, in Wooster, Ohio, after rejecting a proposed contract. Although the strike eventually was settled amicably, traditionally the company had sought to minimize union activity by building plants outside union strongholds, in places such as Arizona, where it began construction of a plant near Phoenix in 1987 to serve its western markets. In 1985 the company successfully negotiated a contract with its Ohio workers, providing a three-year wage freeze in return for guarantees against massive layoffs.

1980s: Streamlining and Acquisitions

Noble retired in 1980, and Stanley C. Gault took over as chairman. Gault, a former General Electric Company (GE) executive and a son of one of Wooster Rubber's founders, had grown up in Wooster and worked his way through college in a Rubbermaid plant. Despite the company's record of steady growth throughout the 1970s, caused in part by Rubbermaid's expansion from old-line department stores into discount and grocery stores, Gault felt that the company had become somewhat stodgy and complacent. In 1980 he set out to quadruple its sales (about $350 million in 1981) and earnings (about $25.6 million in 1982) by 1990. Anticipating a recession, Gault streamlined operations and introduced bold new products, such as the "Fun Functional" line of brightly colored containers. Gault's stress on growth through the introduction of new products was exemplified by his continuance of the company's campaign to reap 30 percent of each year's sales from products introduced during the last five years.

By 1983 Gault had eliminated four of Rubbermaid's eight divisions: the unstable party-plan business and the automotive division were each sold at a loss, and the European industrial operations centered in The Netherlands and the manufacture of containers for large-scale garbage hauling also were eliminated.

The remaining divisions were combined into two areas: home products (accounting for about 70 percent of the company's sales) and commercial products. The home products division was further restructured into seven product groups: bathware, food preparation and "gadgets," containers, organizers, sinkware, shelf coverings, and bird feeders and home horticulture. Rubbermaid continued to advertise heavily in both magazines and on television, emphasizing consumer promotions to get customers into the store and offering rebates and coupons for its products for the first time.

In tandem with the product reorganization, about half of Rubbermaid's middle management was eliminated, and 11 percent of the company's management was fired. Many top spots were filled by former GE employees.

In 1981 Rubbermaid had made its first outright acquisition, buying privately held Carlan, owner of the Con-Tact plastic coverings brand name. In the 1980s Rubbermaid was able to move successfully beyond housewares and institutional customers, entering new industries through the strategic purchase of other companies. The company entered the toy industry in 1984 by buying the Little Tikes Company; went into the booming computer field in 1986, with MicroComputer Accessories; into floor care products with Seco Industries in the same year; and into the brush industry with a Canadian company, Viking Brush, in 1987.

Following these and other acquisitions, Rubbermaid created additional divisions to accommodate its new product lines. In 1987 a seasonal products division was formed to produce and sell lawn and garden products, sporting goods, and automotive accessories. A year later the company created an office products division, which included MicroComputer Accessories and—eventually—Eldon Industries, acquired in 1990. Little Tikes became the core of a juvenile products division. The three new divisions gave the company five divisions, with the preexisting home products and commercial products divisions.

Rubbermaid formed a joint venture with a French company, Allibert, to manufacture plastic outdoor furniture in North Carolina in 1989. In addition, the company expanded its capacity in plastic and rubber products in 1985 with its purchase of the Gott Corporation, maker of insulated coolers and beverage holders. Rubbermaid formed a second joint venture—with the Curver Group, owned by Dutch chemical maker DSM N.V.—in 1990 to make and sell housewares and resin furniture in European, Middle Eastern, and north African markets through Curver-Rubbermaid. This diversification resulted in continued growth throughout the 1980s, despite the rising price of petrochemical resins, the raw materials for plastics. Rubbermaid ended the 1980s with 1989 sales of $1.45 billion.

1990–98: Major Acquisitions, Two Restructurings, Declining Fortunes

Throughout the early and mid-1990s Rubbermaid continued to pump out new products at an amazing rate—about 400 annually—which along with several major acquisitions pushed sales higher every year. Net earnings grew as well, until a major restructuring in 1995–97 cut company profits. Management changes marked the early years of this period as Gault retired in 1991 and was succeeded by Walter W. Williams, who soon retired at the end of 1992. After a brief transition period during which Gault was brought back to the company, Wolfgang R. Schmitt, who had joined Rubbermaid in 1966 as a product manager, became chairman in 1993 after having attained the CEO spot the previous year and having served as cochairman with Gault during the transition period.

In 1992 the company acquired Iron Mountain Forge Corporation, an American maker of commercial playground systems. Two years later Ausplay, the leader in commercial play structures in Australia, was purchased. Both Iron Mountain and Ausplay became part of the juvenile products division. Also brought into the Rubbermaid fold in 1994 were Empire Brushes, a leading U.S. maker of brooms, mops, and brushes; and Carex Inc., which made products for the burgeoning home healthcare market. Carex was placed in the company's commercial products division.

As of 1993, Rubbermaid generated only 11 percent of its sales outside the United States, and almost all of that went to Canada. Schmitt aimed to increase nondomestic sales to 25 percent by 2000 (later, this goal was boosted to 30 percent) and began to seek out acquisition and joint venture opportunities to help reach this goal. In 1994 the company entered into a joint venture with Richell Corporation, a leader of housewares in Japan, to form Rubbermaid Japan Inc. After abandoning its stake in Curver-Rubbermaid, a partnership that ended up being noncompatible, Rubbermaid reentered the European housewares market in 1995 when it bought Injectaplastic S.A., a French plastics manufacturer of such items as home and food storage products, camping articles, bathroom accessories, and garden products. Also in 1995 the company bought 75 percent of Dom-Plast S.A., the leading maker of plastic household products in Poland. By 1996 foreign sales were up to 16 percent of overall sales, a rate of increase that, if continued, would mean the company would fall well short of its 30 percent goal. Nevertheless, in early 1997 Rubbermaid announced that it had entered into a strategic alliance with Amway Corporation to develop and market in Japan a line of cobranded premium Rubbermaid products.

In addition to slow overseas growth, a number of other factors forced Rubbermaid to embark in the mid-1990s on its first major restructuring. In the spring of 1994 the prices of resins, used in nearly all of the company's products, began to rise and eventually doubled, increasing manufacturing costs. Rubbermaid also faced increasing competition in the 1990s as other housewares makers improved their products but kept their prices lower than Rubbermaid's premium prices, leading to customer defections and retailer dissatisfaction with the company's pricing policies.

In response to these difficulties, Rubbermaid began a two-year restructuring effort in late 1995. A charge of $158 million was taken in 1995 to cover such cost-cutting moves as closing nine factories and eliminating 1,170 jobs (the charge was the company's first ever). An earlier effort to achieve $335 million in productivity savings reached fruition in 1996. That year also saw Rubbermaid streamline its product lines, by eliminating 45 percent of its stock-keeping units (SKUs), which when combined generated only 10 percent of overall sales. The company also added a new infant product division to its organizational chart with its 1996 acquisition of Graco Children's Products Inc., maker of strollers, play yards, and infant swings, for $320 million. But Rubbermaid also divested its office products division by selling it to Newell for $246.5 million in May 1997. At the same time the company merged its seasonal products division into its home products division, combining these operations because they had similar distribution channels. As a result of these moves, Rubbermaid was left with four divisions: home products, commercial products, juvenile products, and infant products.

The company significantly increased its overseas sales in January 1998 when it acquired its onetime partner, the Curver Group, for $143 million. Curver was the leading maker of plastic housewares in Europe, with 1996 sales of about $222 million. Meantime, despite the major restructuring launched in late 1995, Rubbermaid was still struggling. As a result, yet another restructuring was announced in January 1998. The company aimed to achieve $200 million in annual cost savings by shutting down inefficient plants, shifting production to lower-cost locations, centralizing purchasing, and cutting the workforce. By the fall of 1998 Rubbermaid also had divested three of its businesses, including its decorative coverings unit, which included the Con-Tact brand, and had launched the largest consumer advertising campaign in company history. Rubbermaid also completed one more acquisition in 1998—its last as an independent company—purchasing Century Products Company from Wingate Partners for $77.5 million. Fitting in nicely alongside the Graco line, Century produced car seats, strollers, and infant carriers. For the year, Rubbermaid achieved revenues of $2.55 billion, a slight increase over the preceding year, while net income declined 42 percent, standing at $82.9 million.

Millennial Formation of Newell Rubbermaid Inc.

Newell and Rubbermaid had discussed a merger in mid-1997, but the talks broke down when the two sides could not agree on who would run the company and where it would be headquartered. By late 1998, however, Rubbermaid's position had deteriorated to the point where it gave in on these points and agreed to be bought by Newell for $6 billion in stock. To the credit of the Rubbermaid managers, the price represented a hefty 49 percent premium over the company's stock price. John McDonough, Newell's vice-chairman and CEO, continued in these same positions for the newly named Newell Rubbermaid Inc. Upon completion of the deal in March 1999, Rubbermaid Chairman and CEO Schmitt became vice-chairman of the company, and William Sovey remained chairman. McDonough was hoping that the usual Newellization process could revitalize Rubbermaid, and he also anticipated that Rubbermaid's renowned ability to develop new products might be spread to the Newell product lines. One of the biggest challenges for Mc-

Donough was in improving Rubbermaid's abysmal customer service and its troubled distribution system. Restructuring costs totaled $241.6 million in 1999, dragging profits down to $95.4 million; revenues for the first year of the new Newell Rubbermaid amounted to $6.41 billion.

While the Rubbermaid operations were being overhauled—a process that proved more difficult than anticipated—Newell Rubbermaid continued making acquisitions, with a particular emphasis on Europe. In April 1999 the company bought Ateliers 28, a French maker of drapery hardware. In October of that same year the company acquired Reynolds S.A., a manufacturer of writing instruments based in Valence, France. That same month, Newell Rubbermaid purchased McKechnie plc's consumer products division, which included Harrison Drape (maker of drapery hardware and window furnishings), Spur Shelving (shelving and storage products), Douglas Kane (cabinet hardware), and Nenplas/Homelux (functional trims). From December 1999 through May 2000, Newell Rubbermaid completed the acquisitions of three European picture frame businesses: Ceanothe Holding, based in France; Mersch, which operated in both Germany and France; and France-based Brio. The largest acquisition during this period, however, was of a U.S. business: the stationery products division of Gillette Company, acquired in December 2000. Newell Rubbermaid gained a rich stable of brands, including Paper Mate, Parker, and Waterman writing instruments and Liquid Paper correction products. The Gillette division had posted revenues of $743 million in 1999.

The painful integration of Rubbermaid into the company led to inconsistent earnings and a slumping stock price. Late in 2000 the stock fell to its lowest level since 1994. Soon after, at the beginning of November 2000, McDonough resigned from the company. Sovey, his predecessor, temporarily took the reins as CEO, before Joseph Galli, Jr., was brought onboard as president and CEO in January 2001, with Sovey returning to the chairman's post. Galli had previously spent 19 years at Black & Decker, where he rose to the number two position before leaving in 1999. He then had short stints with "New Economy" firms amazon.com, Inc. and VerticalNet Inc. before accepting the Newell Rubbermaid post.

Galli launched a thorough restructuring in a turnaround attempt. In May 2001 the company announced that it would eliminate 3,000 positions from its workforce over a three-year period, a reduction of 6 percent. The plan also involved the consolidation of manufacturing facilities as the company aimed to cut operating costs by $100 million per year. During 2001 alone, 14 facilities were shuttered. The company also sought to shift some manufacturing to lower-cost locations in Mexico, China, Poland, and Hungary. Galli also overhauled senior management, bringing in a slew of outside executives, including 15 from Black & Decker. To solidify the company's position with its major customers, Newell Rubbermaid established the Key Account Program, whereby separate sales organizations were created for three of the largest customers, Wal-Mart, The Home Depot, Inc., and Lowe's Companies, Inc. Cost savings from the restructuring were to be plowed back into new product development and marketing initiatives. The latter included the first television advertising campaign for the Rubbermaid brand in three years and a $20 million sports marketing campaign involving the sponsorship of Nascar drivers and races. Another key objective was to pare back the company's heavy debt load, which had been incurred during its 1990s acquisition spree. One method to do this was to divest underperforming operations. In June 2001 Newell Rubbermaid announced that it would sell its Anchor Hocking glassware division to Libbey Inc. for $332 million. The deal was blocked, however, on antitrust grounds.

As he attempted to turn around Newell Rubbermaid, Galli stayed away from acquisitions, and no major deals were completed in 2001. In April 2002, however, the company took full control of American Tool Companies, Inc., a Hoffman Estates, Illinois, firm in which Newell Rubbermaid had already held a 49.5 percent stake. The deal was valued at $419 million and brought into the company fold a line of branded hand tools, including Vise-Grip pliers and Quik-Grip clamps, and a line of power tool accessories, such as Irwin wood-boring bits and Hanson drill bits. For Galli, the addition of American Tool was a return to his Black & Decker power tool roots. The American Tool brands, which generated $444 million in sales in 2001, were placed within Newell Rubbermaid's Levolor/Hardware group.

The acquisition of American Tool perhaps signaled a return to the Newell tradition of growth through acquisition, and the optimistic Galli told *Forbes* in October 2001 that he was aiming to grow the company into a $50-billion-in-sales behemoth. Nevertheless, Newell Rubbermaid's restructuring efforts had not yet been completed, and sales and profits were being hampered by the difficult economic environment of the early 21st century. Perhaps the most compelling reason for optimism was that, through the renewed focus on product development, more new products were introduced during 2002 than had debuted in the three previous years combined.

Principal Subsidiaries

Berol Corporation; Newell Investments, Inc.; Newell Operating Company; Rubbermaid Incorporated; Rubbermaid Texas Limited; Sanford Investment Company; Sanford, L.P.

Principal Operating Units

Rubbermaid; Sharpie; Levolor/Hardware; Calphalon Home.

Principal Competitors

Sterlite Corporation; Tupperware Corporation; Avery Dennison Corporation; Société BIC; Hunter Douglas N.V.; Springs Industries, Inc.; Lancaster Colony Corporation; The Coleman Company, Inc.; Dorel Industries Inc.; Mattel, Inc.; Hasbro, Inc.; WKI Holding Company, Inc.; The Stanley Works; The Black & Decker Corporation; Cooper Industries, Ltd.; Myers Industries, Inc.; Libbey Inc.

Further Reading

Aeppel, Timothy, "Rubbermaid Is on a Tear, Sweeping Away the Cobwebs," *Wall Street Journal*, September 8, 1998, p. B4.
——, "Rubbermaid Plans New Restructuring, Predicts Charges of at Least $200 Million," *Wall Street Journal*, January 22, 1998, p. B6.
Benmour, Eric, "Vermont American Suitor Proves Tenacious," *Business First-Louisville*, August 28, 1989, Sec. 1, p. 1.

Borden, Jeff, "Newell Makes Its Move," *Crain's Chicago Business*, November 25, 1991, p. 46.
Braham, James, "The Billion-Dollar Dustpan," *Industry Week*, August 1, 1988, p. 46.
Byrne, Harlan S., "Newell Co.," *Barron's*, April 12, 1993, p. 52.
Cahill, Joseph B., and Timothy Aeppel, "Newell Faces a Big Challenge in Rubbermaid Takeover," *Wall Street Journal*, November 3, 1998, p. B4.
Campanella, Frank W., "Wide and Growing Line Spurs Rubbermaid Gains," *Barron's*, October 3, 1977.
Christensen, Jean, "How Rubbermaid Invites Profits," *New York Times*, May 19, 1974.
Cimperman, Jennifer Scott, "Rubbermaid Endures Newellization," *Cleveland Plain Dealer*, June 29, 2000, p. 1C.
Coleman, Calemetta Y., "Newell Builds Success from Diamonds in the Rough," *Wall Street Journal*, April 14, 1995, p. B4.
Conley, Thomas P., "The NHMA Report: Electronic Partnerships Provide Bottom-Line Payoffs," *Discount Merchandiser*, January 1993, pp. 45–46.
Cuthbert, William R., *Newell Companies—A Corporate History—The First 40 Years*, Freeport, Ill.: Newell Co., 1983.
David, Gregory E., "Let Us Prey: Having Swallowed 31 Companies in 25 Years, Ruthless Newell Remains on the Prowl," *Financial World*, June 21, 1994, pp. 29–30.
Defotis, Dimitra, "Household Help: Rubbermaid Stock Cooks with a New CEO," *Barron's*, February 5, 2001, p. 40.
Deutsch, Claudia H., "A Giant Awakens, to Yawns: Is Rubbermaid Reacting Too Late?," *New York Times*, December 22, 1996, pp. F1, F13.
Farnham, Alan, "America's Most Admired Company," *Fortune*, February 7, 1994, pp. 50–54.
Gallun, Alby, "Newell Confronts Its Next Hard Sell," *Crain's Chicago Business*, June 10, 2002, p. 4.
——, "Newell's Galli Must Cook Up a Turnaround," *Crain's Chicago Business*, January 15, 2001, p. 4.
——, "Newell's New Colors: Ends Acquisition Binge to Focus on Boosting Existing Brands," *Crain's Chicago Business*, June 4, 2001, p. 3.
Hackney, Holt, "Strategic Alliances," *Financial World*, October 29, 1991.
Hallinan, Joseph T., "Newell CEO Tries to Shake Up Concern with Little Success," *Wall Street Journal*, January 14, 2002, p. B3.
"How Rubbermaid Managed to Fail," *Fortune*, November 23, 1998, p. 32.
Kelly, Kevin, "Newell Isn't Bagging Big Game Anymore," *Business Week*, July 8, 1991, pp. 83–84.
Lipin, Steven, and Timothy Aeppel, "Newell to Buy Rubbermaid for $5.8 Billion," *Wall Street Journal*, October 21, 1998, p. A3.
Magnet, Myron, "Meet the New Revolutionaries," *Fortune*, February 24, 1992, pp. 94–101.
Murphy, H. Lee, "Newell Dresses Up Its Image with a Shade-y Acquisition," *Crain's Chicago Business*, April 12, 1993, Sec. 1, p. 7.
Narisetti, Raju, "Can Rubbermaid Crack Foreign Markets?," *Wall Street Journal*, June 20, 1996, pp. B1, B4.
Neiman, Janet, "New Structure Poured for Rubbermaid Push," *Advertising Age*, November 9, 1981.
Noble, Donald E., *Like Only Yesterday: The Memoirs of Donald E. Noble*, Wooster, Ohio: Wooster Book Co., 1996.
Nulty, Peter, "You Can Go Home Again," *Fortune*, June 15, 1981, p. 180.
O'Connor, Matt, "Simple Secret of Newell's Success: Basic Strategy Pays Off for Consumer Firm," *Chicago Tribune*, July 27, 1987, Sec. 1, pp. 1, 5.
Osterland, Andrew, "Fixing Rubbermaid Is No Snap," *Business Week*, September 20, 1999, pp. 108, 110.

Ozanian, Michael K., and Alexandra Ourusoff, ''Never Let Them See You Sweat: Just Because Rubbermaid Is One of the Most Admired Companies in the Country Doesn't Mean Life Is Easy,'' *Financial World,* February 1, 1994, pp. 34–35, 38.

Pellet, Jennifer, ''No Paint, No Gain,'' *Discount Merchandiser,* March 1992, pp. 74–75.

Pouschine, Tatiana, ''The Old-Fashioned Way,'' *Forbes,* January 6, 1992, pp. 66–68.

Schiller, Zachary, ''The Revolving Door at Rubbermaid: Is CEO Schmitt's Tough Style Driving Executives Away?,'' *Business Week,* September 18, 1995, p. 80.

Scott, Carlee R., ''Newell Plans to Acquire Sanford Corp. in Stepped-Up Move into Office Products,'' *Wall Street Journal,* November 25, 1991, p. A5.

Smith, Lee, ''Rubbermaid Goes Thump,'' *Fortune,* October 2, 1995, pp. 90–92, 96, 100, 104.

Stevens, Tim, ''Where the Rubber Meets the Road,'' *Industry Week,* March 20, 1995, pp. 14–18.

Stouffer, Paul W., ''Heading for a Billion: Major Acquisition Bringing Newell Toward a Record Sales Mark,'' *Barron's,* August 24, 1987.

Taylor, Alex III, ''Why the Bounce at Rubbermaid?,'' *Fortune,* April 13, 1987, p. 77.

Tisch, Carol, and Lisa Vincenti, ''Rubbermaid Bounces Back,'' *HFN— The Weekly Newspaper for the Home Furnishing Network,* January 17, 2000, p. 90.

Upbin, Bruce, ''Rebirth of a Sales Man,'' *Forbes,* October 1, 2001, pp. 94–96+.

White, Joseph B., ''Workers' Revenge: Factory Towns Start to Fight Back Angrily When Firms Pull Out,'' *Wall Street Journal,* March 8, 1988, pp. 1, 24.

Yao, Margaret, ''Rubbermaid Reaches for Greater Glamour in World Beyond Dustpans and Drainers,'' *Wall Street Journal,* June 9, 1982.

—Roger W. Rouland and Elizabeth Rourke
—update: David E. Salamie

PDI, Inc.

10 Mountainview Road, Suite C-200
Upper Saddle River, New Jersey 07458-1937
U.S.A.
Telephone: (201) 258-8450
Fax: (201) 258-8582
Web site: http://www.pdi-inc.com

Public Company
Incorporated: 1987 as Professional Detailing, Inc.
Employees: 4,963
Sales: $696.6 million (2001)
Stock Exchanges: NASDAQ
Ticker Symbol: PDII
NAIC: 541613 Marketing Consulting Services

PDI, Inc., formerly Professional Detailing, Inc., was the first company to offer product detailing services to the pharmaceutical industry on a fee-for-service basis. Founded by Pat Dugan in 1987, PDI first established itself as a leader in the Contract Sales Organization (CSO) business by designing customized, dedicated sales teams to represent individual products. While the new industry took off, PDI maintained its leadership position by continually innovating to diversify and specialize the range of services it provided, from product marketing and brand management to marketing research and medical education. PDI has represented such pharmaceutical giants as Pfizer, GlaxoSmithKline, AstraZeneca, Bayer, Eli Lilly, and Johnson & Johnson.

Developing the Industry's First
Part-Time Contract Sales Model: 1986–95

PDI, Inc. was founded in 1987 by pharmaceutical marketing entrepreneur John P. Dugan under the name Professional Detailing. PDI was originally a division of Dugan/Farley Communications, a medical advertising agency that Dugan had founded in 1972. With PDI, Dugan wanted to create a high-quality outsourcing service for the pharmaceutical industry. The service, called product detailing, comprised all facets of customized representation for both prescription and over-the-counter drugs to the medical community: sales representatives met face-to-face with doctors and other healthcare decision makers to present technical reviews of the products they promoted; these reviews outlined everything from the legal issues surrounding the drug, to its role in disease treatment, to dosages, side effects, and cost.

With drug companies expanding their product portfolios at a rapid rate and an increasing number of new pharmaceutical products awaiting FDA approval, Dugan foresaw a growing need for these companies to develop new marketing strategies. By outsourcing their marketing needs to PDI, pharmaceutical companies could reap the benefits of customized, industry standard sales teams without having to build the teams themselves, or invest in that sales force as permanent employees. If PDI could deliver premium quality marketing services while enabling pharmaceutical companies to cut costs and conserve in-house resources, the company could attract some of the biggest names in the pharmaceutical industry.

In 1990, Professional Detailing broke off from Dugan/Farley Communications to become the first contract sales organization (CSO) in the business. Later that year, Charles T. Saldarini was promoted from general manager to president and chief operating officer of PDI. Saldarini had come on board at PDI in 1987. He had begun as a sales manager but rose quickly to leadership positions, first as director of marketing services and then as general manager. With the 1990 transition, Pat Dugan retained the title of chief executive officer, but Saldarini assumed full responsibility for the daily operations of the company.

A couple of early innovations to the business model were critical to PDI's success. First, in 1991, the company converted to vertically dedicated program management. This meant that PDI designed and implemented a product's marketing program to account for every phase of that product's lifecycle, from prelaunch to FDA approval and through patent expiration. Further, PDI developed a dedicated sales team for each client. Customized to fit the individual client's needs, the team did not represent the products of any other drug manufacturers. So identified was the team with their particular client that they often carried that client's business cards.

In another visionary move, PDI revolutionized the medical sales industry during 1992 and 1993 by converting its sales people from contract employees who received compensation on a per-call basis to salaried employees. In part by offering this kind of security and commitment to its salespeople, PDI managed to grow its team of full- and part-time sales representatives from 130 to 930 people in four years.

Building Infrastructure for the Transition to Full-Time Contract Sales: 1995–2000

In 1995, PDI entered into a relationship with Pfizer, Inc., a leading pharmaceutical company with broad global reach. Pfizer signed PDI to provide product detailing for two drugs: Glucotrol XL, a diabetes medication, and Cardura, a heart disease medication. This agreement gave PDI a pivotal boost in credibility by distinguishing it as a CSO qualified to represent the top tier pharmaceutical companies in the world.

The year 1995 also marked the beginning of a deluge of FDA approvals for new drugs. PDI recognized that many of its clients now wanted and needed full-time representation to launch and maximize the profitability of their new products, so the company entered a new period of transition to accommodate this need. In 1996, PDI built its first large scale, full-time sales force for pharmaceutical giant GlaxoWellcome (later renamed GlaxoSmithKline). The 300-representative team was deployed to support Ceftin, an antibiotic; Wellbutrin, an antidepressant; and Imitrex, a migraine medication.

In 1997, PDI's revenues leaped 65 percent to $54.5 million, and it seemed clear that the company was becoming a dominant force in contract sales. In April 1998, PDI made its initial public offering of 2.8 million shares on the NASDAQ stock exchange under the symbol PDII, with proceeds designated for investments in growth, infrastructure, and future acquisitions. Later that year, the company launched a web site. The site was designed to be a ''one-stop-shopping'' destination where visitors (potential clients, employees, and investors) could research information about the current state of the pharmaceutical industry, as well as the nature of the contract sales service that PDI offered.

In 1999, PDI made two key acquisitions. In the second quarter they acquired TVG, Inc. Based in Fort Washington, Pennsylvania, TVG had grossed $18.4 million in revenue in the preceding year. TVG was a provider of communications programs and sophisticated marketing research and consulting services whose client base included 18 of the top 20 pharmaceuti-

cal companies in the world. The Education/Communications division of TVG focused on facilitating contact with and providing product education to doctors via every avenue from dinner meetings to teleconferencing. Meanwhile, the marketing research and consulting division of TVG worked on brand profiling and positioning, as well as marketing and message development strategies. Like PDI, TVG worked with a product over the span of its lifecycle, though TVG specialized in the important prelaunch phase. PDI acquired all of TVG's outstanding stock in exchange for over a million shares of its own common stock. The transaction was estimated to be worth about $31 million, given the price of PDI stock at the time. The acquisition of TVG enabled PDI to greatly diversify the range of vertically integrated services it could provide for its clients.

In the third quarter of 1999, PDI acquired ProtoCall, LLC. Based in Cincinnati, Ohio, and having recorded more than $8 million in revenue in the preceding year, ProtoCall provided syndicated contract sales services to the pharmaceutical industry. PDI purchased ProtoCall for $4.5 million in cash, with the agreement to make contingent payments up to $3 million in 2000, depending upon whether its new subsidiary performed up to projected levels. The acquisition of ProtoCall, which later became known as the PDI Shared Sales Team, enabled PDI to offer their services as a face-to-face selling resource for companies that could not afford to contract a full, dedicated sales team. Shared teams sold multiple, non-competitive brands from a variety of pharmaceutical companies within targeted geographic areas. The benefit of this acquisition was to make PDI's services accessible and attractive to a wider range of clients.

From Contract Sales to Commercial Partner: 2000–2002

As PDI entered the 21st century, the company was poised again for major transition. Preliminarily, the company experienced a shift in its senior management: Steven K. Budd succeeded Charles T. Saldarini as president. Budd had been hired as PDI's vice-president in 1995 and later promoted to executive vice-president and chief operating officer. Saldarini retained the position of CEO, in addition to assuming the position of vice-chairman of the board of directors.

At a more fundamental level, the company was seeking to modify its business model. There were many limitations inherent in the fee-for-service model PDI had long embraced. The optimum outcome of any discrete contract relationship was renewal of the contract; conversely, the CSO was faced with the ever present risk of contract termination. Moreover, PDI's leadership believed that even the consistent achievement of renewed contracts would not, in and of itself, provide PDI with the stability or profits necessary to maximize the value of the company. Having succeeded in becoming a dominant contract sales force, then, PDI was now turning its ambition toward developing fuller commercial partnerships with the companies it represented. Though commercial partnership would bring increased risk to PDI, as the company would be investing its own capital in the brands it promoted, it would also bring greater rewards, including longer-term relationships, increased profits as a result of revenue sharing, greater visibility within the industry, and a critical level of control over its brand commercialization strategies. All of these outcomes would translate to greater stability

---

Key Dates:

1987: Professional Detailing, Inc. is founded by Pat Dugan as a division of Dugan/Farley Communications.

1990: Professional Detailing, Inc. (PDI) becomes independent of Dugan/Farley Communications, under the sole ownership of Pat Dugan; Charles T. "Chuck" Saldarini assumes leadership of PDI.

1991: PDI converts to "vertically dedicated" program management with a dedicated sales team for each client.

1998: PDI goes public, trading on the NASDAQ under the symbol PDII.

2000: PDI forms LifeCycle Ventures and enters into a strategic relationship with iPhysician.net.

2001: Professional Detailing, Inc. officially changes its name to PDI, Inc.

---

for PDI, whose ultimate goal was to become the sales and marketing partner of choice to the U.S. pharmaceutical industry.

In order to persuade its clients to enter into more substantial partnerships, PDI needed to target its new business model at an unmet need within the industry. In 2000, the pharmaceutical market was still being flooded with new FDA approvals. It was imperative for drug manufacturers to devote the bulk of their marketing resources to the launch and promotion of their new blockbuster drugs in order to achieve maximum exposure and sales of these products in the critical early stages of their lifecycles. However, as a result, these companies often lacked the additional marketing resources to continue pushing the sales of products in the more mature phases of their lifecycles. PDI recognized that with the proper promotion, the older, more established drugs in a company's portfolio could continue to bring in substantial revenues. As a solution to the problem of funding these sales efforts, PDI established a wholly owned subsidiary called LifeCycle Ventures. When contracted, LifeCycle Ventures (LCV) would assume completely, or in conjunction with the client, the burden of financing and overseeing the marketing program for these more established drugs, in exchange for a percentage of that drug's sales revenue. By adding LCV to its repertoire of contract service options, PDI created the infrastructure to support its desired role as a commercial partner and increased the depth of its value to drug manufacturers.

PDI experienced the first major endorsement of its LCV innovation in the third quarter of 2000, when GlaxoWellcome signed a five-year LifeCycle Extension agreement giving PDI the exclusive U.S. rights to market, sell, and distribute Ceftin, the top-selling antibiotic for respiratory infections. Ceftin had already been on the market for 12 years but was considered one of the core brands in GlaxoWellcome's portfolio, delivering more than $332 million in U.S. sales in 1999. PDI had been providing product detailing services to GlaxoWellcome for seven years and promoting Ceftin specifically for three. By the terms of the new agreement, LCV would actually buy certain minimum quantities of Ceftin every quarter and commence marketing, sales, and distribution efforts from there. This agreement represented a significant breakthrough for PDI as the company's first true at-risk venture.

In the fourth quarter of 2000, PDI got its first big opportunity to prove that the marketing capabilities of LifeCycle Ventures could be as successful in bringing a product to market as they had been in fostering a product's growth and maximizing its lifecycle. PDI signed a five-year agreement with United Therapeutics Corporation, a pharmaceutical company with operations in Maryland, North Carolina, and Illinois, to handle the commercialization of beraprost, a drug for peripheral cardiovascular disease that was still under development and pending FDA approval. PDI was contracted on a regular fee-for-service basis to handle the prelaunch and launch phases of beraprost's lifecycle, with the possibility of developing a revenue sharing relationship with United Therapeutics in the future.

Even while PDI was engaged in modifying its business model with the strategic mission of transitioning from a service-based to a product-driven company, PDI continued to expand its operations in other ways. A key development of 2000 was the signing of an exclusive three-year agreement between PDI and iPhysician.net, a company that had pioneered an Internet-based product detailing service application called e-Detailing to facilitate communication between doctors and the sales representatives of pharmaceutical companies. Using a computer-based videoconferencing system, sales representatives could gain "entrance" to the private offices of physicians and interact with them in real time. iPhysician.net also offered an e-Meeting application whereby doctors could meet electronically with their colleagues as well as salespeople to participate in educational symposia, focus groups, and other marketing research. Thus, an important strategic partnership was formed when PDI invested $2.5 million in i.Physician.net to become the company's only CSO affiliate in the United States. Herewith, PDI secured a $1 million service agreement whereby i.Physician.net would tap PDI's ProtoCall sales force to recruit video sales representatives for its e-Detailing network. In addition to supplying them with personnel, PDI would become the sole provider of video call center facilities to i.Physician.net. Further, PDI gained the right to extend iPhysician.net's e-Detailing technology to all of its current and future clients. The agreement solidified an exclusive partnership through which PDI would harness the latest technology to maintain its position at the forefront of the CSO business.

Not only did PDI extend its technological reach, it extended its geographic reach in the fourth quarter of 2000 as well when it invested about $760,000 in a United Kingdom CSO called In2Focus Sales Development Services, Limited. This was PDI's first step toward a strategic alliance that would expand PDI's capabilities into Europe.

Having moved shrewdly to increase market penetration for pharmaceutical products, PDI decided in 2001 to expand the range of products it marketed as well. That year, PDI established a new business unit to begin to exploit opportunities in the Medical Devices and Diagnostics (MD&D) market. PDI brought on a new team of experienced MD&D managers, intending to combine their expertise with the solid foundation and proven sales and marketing strategies it had already applied to pharmaceuticals. In September 2001, PDI solidified its commitment to entering the MD&D market when it acquired InServe Support Solutions, a company that provided clinical education, after-sales support, and in-hospital sales efforts for medical device and diagnostic products. In purchasing InServe, PDI paid $8.5 million in cash to former stockholders, with the agreement to make contingent payments up to $3 million in 2002, depending upon whether its new subsidiary performed up to projected levels.

Also in 2001, PDI officially changed its name from Product Detailing, Inc. to PDI, Inc. By this time it was offering four different partnership options to its clients: PDI Copromotion, whereby PDI shared the risks and rewards of the sales and marketing effort based on prearranged percentages; PDI LifeCycle Extension, whereby PDI assumed brand responsibility for products nearing patent expiration; PDI Product Commercialization Services, available on a fee-for-service or partnership basis, for products in the prelaunch phase of their lifecycle; and PDI Contract Sales.

PDI leveraged these specialized applications to forge a number of important deals in 2001. In the second quarter, PDI signed a long-term copromotion agreement with Santen Pharmaceuticals Co., Ltd. for the marketing, sales, and distribution rights to Quixin, a topical treatment for bacterial conjunctivitis. Also in the second quarter, PDI signed a key agreement with Novartis Pharmaceuticals Corporation: PDI gained the U.S. rights to market, sell, and distribute Lotensin and Lotensin HCT through its LifeCycle Extension application, as well as co-promotion rights to Lotrel, one of Novartis's fastest-growing brands. Finally, in the fourth quarter of 2001, PDI signed a deal with Eli Lilly and Company to copromote Evista, a high-profile drug for the prevention and treatment of osteoporosis.

PDI suffered some disappointments at the beginning of 2002, including Bayer's termination without cause of its con-tract with PDI, disappointing sales figures for Evista, and, most notably, the early termination of the Ceftin agreement with GlaxoSmithKline (GSK, formerly GlaxoWellcome). Despite year-end assurances of stronger than expected Ceftin sales in 2001, PDI's sales were not strong enough to meet sufficient earnings benchmarks relative to the minimum purchase requirements of Ceftin put forth in the GSK contract. The Ceftin termination, less than two years into the five-year term, resulted in losses of tens of millions of dollars for the fourth quarter of 2001 and a significant earnings void at the outset of 2002. Still, despite these setbacks, PDI persisted with aggressive moves to position itself as a commercial partner to pharmaceutical companies. The company's revision of its business model was proving to be visionary, as FDA approvals had slowed considerably, and the contract sales market had begun to falter.

Principal Subsidiaries

LifeCycle Ventures, Inc.; TVG, Inc.; ProtoCall, Inc.; InServe Support Solutions, Inc.; PDI Investment Company, Inc.

Principal Competitors

Boron, LePore & Associates, Inc.; Nelson Communications Inc.; Ventiv Health, Inc.

Further Reading

Lacey, Stephen, "Professional Detailing: 'Initial' Public Offering," *IPO Reporter,* April 20, 1998.
"PDI's LifeCycle Ventures Selected by GlaxoWellcome Inc. for Exclusive U.S. Marketing, Sales and Distribution Rights for Ceftin," *Business Wire,* October 2, 2000.

—Erin Brown

PERDIGÃO

Perdigao SA

Avenida Escola Politécnica, 760
05350-901 Sao Paulo
Brazil
Telephone: (+55) 11-3718-5300
Fax: (+55) 11-3718-5287
Web site: http://www.perdigao.com

Public Company
Incorporated: 1934 as Brandalise, Ponzoni & Cie
Employees: 19,291
Sales: R 2.79 billion ($1.4 billion) (2001)
Stock Exchanges: Sao Paulo
Ticker Symbol: PRGA
NAIC: 311615 Poultry Processing; 311611 Animal
(Except Poultry) Slaughtering; 311612 Meat
Processed From Carcasses; 424440 Poultry and
Poultry Product Merchant Wholesalers

Brazil's Perdigao SA is the second largest producer of pork and poultry products, behind Sadia, with vertical operations including pork and poultry and grain farms, plants for producing animal feed, incubation and genetic research facilities, slaughterhouses and poultry processing facilities, and cold storage warehousing and distribution operations. Although some 63 percent of Perdigao's sales, which neared R 2.8 billion ($1.4 billion) in 2001, come from Brazil itself, Perdigao has built up a growing international business, with exports, through subsidiary Brazilian Fine Foods, to more than 70 countries in the United States, Europe, Asia, and the Middle East. In the late 1990s, Perdigao, which was taken over by a consortium of pension funds in 1994, has begun to diversify into processed foods, with lines of frozen vegetables, ready meals, frozen pizza, and other food items. The company also has extended its meat operations to include turkeys. Perdigao is listed on the Brazilian stock exchange and is also traded on the New York Stock Exchange—the first Brazilian food products company to do so—through Level II ADRs. The company is led by Chairman Eggon J. da Silva and CEO Nildemar Secches.

Corner Store Operator in the 1930s

Two Italian immigrants, Saul Brandalise and Angelo Ponzoni, opened a grocery store in Vila das Perdizes in the state of Santa Catarina, Brazil, in 1934. Brandalise, Ponzoni & Cie quickly sought to expand the business. At first the partners attempted to expand by adding other stores, merging their company with Floriani, Bonato & Cie, which operated a store in nearby Bom Retino, in 1937. The merger lasted only a year, however. Instead, Brandalise and Ponzoni turned toward food production, and in 1939 formed an association with another company that operated a slaughterhouse and processing plant for pork meats and byproducts. By 1941, Brandalise, Ponzoni & Cie were ready to launch their own line of pork products. For this, the company launched a new brand name, Perdigao (partridge), using the bird as its logo.

Brandalise and Ponzoni expanded the business again in 1943 when they acquired Sociedade Curtume Catarinense, which gave the company tanning facilities for the pork skin byproducts of its main meat processing facility. The tannery, later known as Curtume Perdigao, also began processing skins acquired from other pork processors. Renamed Brandalise, Ponzoni SA Comércio e Industria in 1945, the company continued to diversify its interests, adding flour milling, with the opening of a wheat mill in 1946, and lumber, with the purchase of a sawmill in 1947.

The company's expansion dovetailed with its drive toward vertical integration in the 1950s. In 1954, the company opened its own farm, Granja Santa Gema, in the town of Videira, where the group began developing and raising high-quality pig breeds. The farm also marked the company's expansion into poultry production—by 1955, the company had begun to slaughter chickens as well. To support its growing industrial operation, Brandalise and Ponzoni launched the company into two new directions, opening a feed plant for its own animals, and starting up a distribution subsidiary, Expresso Perdigao. In 1957, the company added air transport with the purchase of two Douglas DC-3s, which allowed it to begin distribution to the important Sao Paulo market.

Brandalise and Ponzoni formally changed the name of their company to Perdigao in 1958. Over the next decade, Perdigao made steady improvements in the quality of its livestock. The company also introduced microbiological controls as it stepped up its research and development investments. In 1968, Perdigao added automated processing equipment for its chicken production, allowing it to raise production from 500 birds per day to more than 1,500 per day.

Diversification and National Expansion in the 1970s

Perdigao expanded its tanning business in 1970, acquiring Empório Courus, which was merged into the existing tannery subsidiary to form Perdigao Courus SA. The company also formalized its animal feed production operation, which began supplying third parties, forming subsidiary Perdigao Raçoes SA, later known as Perdigao Alimentos, in 1974.

Until the mid-1970s, Perdigao's poultry processing was performed in the same facilities as its pork processing business. The growth of the company's own poultry production—as poultry production expanded to become one of Brazil's major food industries—led Perdigao to construct a dedicated poultry slaughtering facility in Videira in 1975. That same year, Perdigao pioneered another area of the Brazilian poultry market, as it became the first in the country to export its products, with a shipment to Saudi Arabia. The following year, Perdigao became one of the founders of UNEF, the Brazilian union of chicken exporters, which helped raise Brazil into one of the world's leading poultry-producing countries.

In 1976, Perdigao used its feed production operations to launch itself into the larger area of industrial soy products manufacturing, building a facility to provide oil refining and other processing operations. The following year, the company added a new subsidiary, Perdigao Veloso, located in Salto Veloso, and began producing pork chicken and beef products, such as hamburger and salami. The company continued adding to its industrial park through the end of the decade, building a new plant in Catanduvas in 1979, then launching two new farm and industrial processing complexes in Herval D'Oeste and Capinzal in 1980.

Perdigao S/A Comércio, along with its two main operating companies, Perdigao Alimentos S/A and Perdigao Agroindustrial S/A, went public in 1980, listing on the Brazil stock exchange. The following year, Perdigao began marketing a new poultry brand, Chester, after the company's research and development team had succeeded in breeding a chicken that concentrated 70 percent of its meat in its breast and thigh portions. The Chester brand was then expanded in 1982 to include low-fat products.

Perdigao's industrial development continued into the 1980s, with the launch of a new chicken farm, feed, and slaughtering

facility in Orleans, in Jaguaruna, in 1983, then opened another integrated chicken production complex, Borella SA, in Marau, in 1985. The following year, Perdigao attempted to enter the beef market as well, acquiring Frigoplan Ltda, located in Lages—that facility was later transformed into a processing center for frozen processed foods. At that time, Perdigao exited a number of noncore operations, including its sawmill and its supermarket business. Soon after, Flavio Brandalise, son of Saul Brandalise, took over the company's leadership as president.

Perdigao's industrial growth enabled it to expand throughout much of Brazil during the 1980s. The company moved into Serafina Correa with the creation of two new farm and slaughterhouse complexes, Sulina Alimentos S/A and Ideal Avícola S/A, the former for pork production, the latter dedicated to poultry in 1988. That year, the company also launched a soy processing subsidiary in Cuiaba, Amazonia SA, and formed a chicken breeding joint venture with the United States' Cobb-Vantress. Other partnerships followed, such as an agreement with Japan's Mitsubishi Corporation to step up Perdigao's international exports. The company also debuted a new brand, Turma de Monica, and a line of processed meat products.

Professional Management for the New Century

Perdigao moved into canned vegetable production in 1989 with the acquisition of Swift, based in Santo André. The company added a new cold storage facility with Mococa SA. The opening of the Brazilian market, which enabled Brazilian companies to expand internationally for the first time, led Perdigao to take the leap in 1990 with the launch of a joint venture in Portugal with Persuinos, for the production of sausages. That partnership was disbanded the following year, however. Nonetheless, Perdigao achieved some success overseas, particularly with an award for its sausage products at the Paris food fair of 1991. The company's Capinzal and Marau facilities also gained EC permission to begin poultry imports into Europe that year.

By the mid-1990s, however, Perdigao's expansion, coupled with the disastrous economic climate of the early years of the decade, had nearly forced the company into bankruptcy. In 1993, the company brought in minority shareholder Egon Joao da Silva as the group's president. In 1994, the Brandalise and Ponzoni families sold their controlling stake in the company to a consortium of Brazilian pension funds, which appointed Da Silva as chairman and brought in Nildemar Secches as president.

The new management team led Perdigao on an extensive restructuring drive, shutting down or selling off its noncore operations, which now included animal feed proteins and concentrates production, among others. Perdigao then embarked on a long-term investment program designed to boost its production efficiency and to achieve a higher-quality product. Through the end of the 1990s, the company spent more than $260 million on upgrading and modernizing its industrial facilities. Meanwhile, Perdigao, under threat from the flood of cheap Asian imported meats into Brazil starting in the mid-1990s, also began repositioning itself into higher-margin meat and poultry categories.

In 1996, Perdigao added a new production facility in Rio Verde, with a total production capacity of 280,000 chickens and 3,500 pigs per day. The following year, the company opened a

Key Dates:

1934: Saul Brandalise and Antonio Ponzoni open a grocery store in Vila das Perdizes, Brazil, forming Brandalise, Ponzoni & Cie.

1939: The company acquires slaughtering facilities and enters pork meat production.

1941: The company launches the Perdigao (Partridge) brand and logo.

1943: The company acquires Sociedade Curtume Catarinense and begins tannery operations.

1954: The company begins vertical integration with the opening of a pig and poultry farm, feed, slaughtering, and processing facility, Granja Santa Gema.

1955: The company begins a chicken slaughtering and processing operation; the company forms a distribution subsidiary, acquiring two airplanes to deliver products to the Sao Paulo market.

1958: The company changes its name to Perdigao SA.

1968: The company adds automated processing equipment to triple the volume of chicken processed per day.

1970: The company acquires Empório Courus to expand its tannery operations.

1975: Perdigao opens a dedicated poultry slaughtering and processing facility; the company begins poultry exports.

1980: The company goes public with a listing on the Sao Paulo stock exchange.

1989: The company diversifies into canned vegetable production.

1994: A consortium of Brazilian pension funds acquires Perdigao and restructures operations.

1996: The company opens a new production facility with a total production capacity of 280,000 chickens and 3,500 pigs per day in Rio Verde.

1997: The company opens a new feed plant, in Marau, which becomes the largest in Latin America; the company launches the Healthful Choice brand of frozen vegetables as part of a diversification drive into new high-margin processed food products.

1998: The company launches the Healthful Choice of the Sea frozen fish products brand.

2001: Perdigao forms BRF Trading, an export joint venture with Sadia.

2002: The company takes over full control of BRF; announces plans to extend its processed food operations into cheese production.

new feed plant, in Marau, with a production capacity of 33,000 tons per month. That year, Perdigao completed its restructuring drive, which included merging its operating companies into a single, publicly listed entity, Perdigao SA.

As part of its drive into higher-margin food production, Perdigao began investing in other food categories in the late 1990s. One of the first of these was a move into frozen vegetable production, importing from Belgium for distribution in the Brazilian market under the Healthful Choice brand, beginning in 1997. In 1998, the company extended the Healthful Choice brand to include processed, frozen fish products as well. Then, in 1999, Perdigao turned to the fast-growing market for ready-made meals, launching its own branded line, Toque de Sabor (Touch of Flavor). That product line was then expanded in 2000 to include a range of frozen pizzas under the brand name Apreciatta. In that year, the company acquired Frigorífico Batávia, which enabled it to enter the market for turkey meats under the Batavia brand name. In 2001 the company was ready with the launch of a new brand, Light & Elegant, featuring a range of low-sodium turkey products.

Perdigao continued to increase its industrial park as it moved into the new century, expanding its feed plant in Catanduvas in 1999. That plant became the largest animal feed production facility in all of Latin America. In 2001, the company announced the beginning of a new investment phase, with plans to spend some $250 million to build the largest pig and poultry breeding and slaughtering facility in Latin America. That year, in addition, Perdigao joined with Sadia—the largest pork and poultry producer in Brazil—to form an export joint venture, BRF Trading, to bring the partners' products to such emerging markets as Russia, Africa, and the Caribbean, with plans to boost sales to more than $500 million per year. The partners ended the joint venture in 2002, however, with Perdigao retaining control of BRF, which posted sales of more than $190 million in the first nine months of that year.

Meanwhile, Perdigao continued its drive to reinvent itself as a diversified food products company. The company continued to boost its frozen foods line, which already accounted for some 12 percent of the company's sales. Perdigao also continued to expand its ready-made meal lines, adding two new products in 2002. In September of that year, Perdigao announced its intention to add another product category, cheeses, with production to begin in Sao Paulo and Parana by the end of the year. With sales of nearly R 2.8 billion ($1.4 billion), Perdigao had transformed itself from a single grocery store to a major international food products group.

Principal Subsidiaries

Perdigao Agroindustria SA; BRF International SA.

Principal Competitors

Vitarich Corporation; Cargill Inc.; ConAgra Foods Inc.; Tyson Foods Inc.; Smithfield Foods Inc.; Orkla ASA; Alfa S.A. de CV; ContiGroup Companies Inc.; Nutreco Holding NV; QP Corp.; Maple Leaf Foods Inc.; Perdue Farms Inc.; Keystone Foods L.L.C.; Sadia SA; Hillsdown Holdings Ltd.; Pilgrim's Pride Corporation; Gold Kist Inc.; Seaboard Corporation; NFZ Norddeutsche Fleischzentrale GmbH; Doux S.A; Grampian Country Food Group Ltd.; Lambert-Dodard-Chancereul; UNICOPA.

Further Reading

''All Clucked Up: Brazilian Chickens,'' *Economist,* April 4, 1998.

''Perdigao Bets on Frozen Food,'' *South American Business Information,* September 26, 2002.

''Perdigao Expanding in Europe,'' *South American Business Information,* November 9, 2001.

''Perdigao Investing $250 Million in New Complex,'' *Feedstuffs,* September 24, 2001, p. 31.

''Perdigao, Sadia Form Export Company,'' *Feedstuffs,* October 1, 2001, p. 9.

''Perdigao Sees Market Share Grow,'' *Eurofood,* August 31, 2000, p. 9.

''Sadia and Perdigao End Partnership,'' *South American Business Information,* October 30, 2002.

—M.L. Cohen

Prime Hospitality Corporation

700 Route 46 East
Fairfield, New Jersey 07004
U.S.A.
Telephone: (973) 882-1010
Fax: (973) 882-8577
Web site: http://www.primehospitality.com

Public Company
Incorporated: 1969 as Prime Motor Inns Inc.
Employees: 6,903
Sales: $485.4 million (2001)
Stock Exchanges: New York
Ticker Symbol: PDQ
NAIC: 721110 Hotels (Except Casino Hotels) and Motels

Prime Hospitality Corporation is a major owner, operator, and franchiser of hotels. The company owns or franchises more than 240 hotels in 32 states. Prime has two main brands, AmeriSuites and Wellesley Inn & Suites. AmeriSuites caters primarily to business travelers on long-term stays, and accommodations include kitchenettes, work space, complimentary breakfasts, and other amenities. Wellesley Inns are mid-priced hotels. The Wellesley Inn & Suites hotels offer a mix of suites similar to the AmeriSuites rooms, designed for stays of a week or more, along with more traditional hotel rooms for the business or leisure traveler. Prime Hospitality also operates hotels under contract to other chains. These are mostly upscale hotels owned by chains including Hilton, Radisson, and Sheraton. In addition, the company operates budget hotels under contract in four states. These belong primarily to national chains such as Days Inn, Howard Johnson, and Comfort Inn & Suites. Prime was a high-growth company in the 1980s, at one point one of the top three lodging chains in the country. The company went into and out of bankruptcy in the early 1990s, and has since concentrated on expanding its two core brands.

A Sleeper Going National in the 1980s

Prime Hospitality Corporation started out as the entrepreneurial dream of four New Jersey builders. Peter E. Simon, Melvin Taub, Samuel Brodie, and Herbert Kay began building and developing properties together in the 1950s. Their company specialized in building low-cost motels. They took the company public in 1969 as Prime Motor Inns, Inc. Prime Motor Inns was able to keep its costs down, building for less than its competitors. The company began to grow rapidly by the mid-1970s, with revenue increasing by 25 percent a year on average. By the early 1980s, Prime had built more than 70 motels for big national chains such as Sheraton, Holiday Inn, Ramada, and Howard Johnson. Although the company was publicly owned, its founders and their families controlled about 30 percent of the shares, and Prime was tightly run by its centralized management team. Prime began branching into hotel and motel management, and also grew through acquisition. In 1984 Prime bought American Motor Inns, Inc., a company that owned some 50 motels. Sales grew more than tenfold from the mid-1970s to the mid-1980s, with revenue of more than $300 million by 1985. Although Prime had grown rapidly and made millionaires of its founders, it was still little known in the hospitality industry. Then in 1985 Prime suddenly found itself one of the largest hotel chains in the country when it acquired the venerable chain Howard Johnson.

The Howard Johnson chain of motels and restaurants was an American classic, well known for the distinctive orange roofs on its buildings. But by the early 1980s the brand seemed hopelessly dated, and the company's latest owner, British firm Imperial Group PLC, could do little to shake the chain back to life. Imperial had paid $630 million for Howard Johnson in 1980. In 1985 Prime Motor Inns picked up the chain for only $235 million. Prime took possession of the Howard Johnson name, 470 hotels, both company-owned and franchised, and 174 HoJo restaurants. Prime seemed to have come from nowhere to become a major player on the hospitality scene, set to rival Holiday Inn in the mid-priced market. The company invested some $70 million in refurbishing its company-owned Howard Johnsons and dropped franchisees who failed to make similar significant improvements. Prime began advertising the chain heavily to business travelers, and sold off some properties. The company was known as one of the most profitable hotel owners and operators in the mid-1980s, at a time when many of its competitors were seeing softening business conditions.

Company Perspectives:

Prime Hospitality Corporation, one of the nation's premiere lodging companies, owns, manages, develops and franchises 243 hotels throughout the United States. The Company owns and operates two proprietary brands, AmeriSuites (all-suites) and Wellesley Inns & Suites (limited service). Also within Prime's portfolio are owned and/or managed hotels operated under franchise agreements with national hotel chains including Hilton, Radisson, Sheraton and Holiday Inn.

By 1988 revenue had surpassed $400 million, and income had quadrupled from five years earlier, to $77 million. The company was still basically run by its founders. Peter Simon had become chairman of the company, while his son David Simon became president and chief executive. Peter Simon's nephew Joel Simon ran the firm's hotel operating subsidiary, Prime Management Company. The company still had a staff of only about 200, and it had continued tight cost controls. Prime had built a reputation for smart moves by its successful handling of the moribund Howard Johnson chain. It also had picked up some small regional hotel chains in the late 1980s, including the Texas-based AmeriSuites, and the East Coast chain of 24 Wellesley Inns. In 1989 the company announced that it was buying the franchising operations of the Ramada Inn chain, which had close to 500 hotels. Ramada was restructuring in order to concentrate on its gaming and resort properties, and Prime picked up the domestic Ramada franchises for $180 million. The deal also gave Prime Ramada's chain of budget hotels, called Rodeway, with 150 properties. After the deal went through, Prime was left with about 1,100 hotels and motels in its portfolio, making it either the second or third largest hotel franchiser in the United States. Aside from Howard Johnson and Ramada, Prime operated some 130 hotels under franchise to other top hoteliers including Hilton, Sheraton, Holiday Inn, and Marriott.

Reversals in the Early 1990s

After it took on the large Ramada chain, Prime also announced ambitious plans to begin building more new Howard Johnsons, hoping to open 50 hotels a year over the next five years. Everything seemed rosy for the company, which aimed to dominate the medium-priced hotel market soon, knocking off market leader Holiday Inn. The company's stock had risen over the 1980s as Wall Street took note of its formidable profit picture. Its stock price climbed from $1 a share in 1980 to a high of $45 in 1987, and at the beginning of 1990 leveling off at around $23. Revenue had rocketed to more than $1.5 billion after the Ramada deal closed, and Prime seemed prepared to build on its success by adding on significantly to the Howard Johnson chain. Yet Prime's foundation was not as solid as it looked. A downturn in the economy, particularly in the Northeast where Prime was strongest, and a loss of confidence by investors, combined to send the company into a quick spiral to bankruptcy.

One problem was that Prime was booking an increasing proportion of revenue from one-time property sales, construction fees, and from mortgages and notes receivable it held, and less from its core business. The company was involved in many complicated deals where it sold property by financing the seller, taking the bulk of the sale price in notes. The hospitality industry started to suffer in 1990, partially because of overbuilding, partially because of an overall weakening economy. This hit mid-priced hotels harder than others. Consumers were extremely sensitive to changes in room rates at the mid-price level, where an increase of two dollars was apparently enough to send travelers away in search of a better deal. So these hotels could not easily raise prices to cover rising costs. This meant that not only did Prime's business suffer, but the franchisees and others in this segment of the industry to whom it had loaned money had trouble keeping up payments. Prime tried to raise money on Wall Street early in 1990, and was hit by tough questions about its loans and accounting. Within a matter of months, Prime's long upward trend reversed. By May 1990 Prime was no longer talking about building more Howard Johnsons, but was instead selling 65 percent of the Howard Johnson and Ramada Inn franchise to a New York investment group for $140 million. For the quarter ending that March, the company reported a 98 percent drop in profit. The company had debt of at least $550 million, and it began to have trouble making payments. In September, Prime filed for Chapter 11 bankruptcy.

Under Chapter 11, the company could continue to operate as it worked out ways to pay its creditors. At this point it became clear that Prime needed to make drastic changes, and almost all of its top executives, including the founders, left or retired. David Simon stayed on, and hired a turnaround specialist, John Elwood, to get the company back on its feet. Elwood made financial changes that transformed the company into more of a traditional hotel operator and less of a real estate developer. Prime collected money owed it relating to its purchase of the Ramada franchise, and also bought back its own debt on the open market. By 1992, Prime, now renamed Prime Hospitality Corporation, had debt of only $270 million, and it was able to come out of bankruptcy. It booked four profitable quarters in 1993, and by 1994 the company was beginning to make expansion plans again. The company's management grew less centralized during the bankruptcy, giving regional executives more independence and creative leeway. Prime worked on shoring up its restaurant operations, which it had previously run at a loss. The proximity of a restaurant was a big draw for a hotel, and Prime had run restaurants in spite of the difficulty of making them pay. But under the new management system, Prime's restaurants were expected to at least break even. By 1994 the worst was behind Prime, and it began planning to bring its two remaining hotel chains, AmeriSuites and Wellesley, into national prominence.

Chain Growth in the Late 1990s

The postbankruptcy Prime Hospitality was a much smaller company than it had been. Whereas it had been one of the largest hotel companies in terms of number of rooms, now it owned only the small Wellesley chain and the even smaller AmeriSuites. The suite hotel was a growing and profitable sector of the hospitality industry, pioneered by the Residence Inn chain in the 1970s and soon copied by a host of competitors in the late 1980s. Suite hotels catered to business travelers staying a week or more, and were a cross between a traditional

Key Dates:

1969: Four New Jersey builders incorporate Prime Motor Inns.
1985: Prime acquires the Howard Johnson chain.
1989: Prime acquires the domestic franchise business of Ramada Inn.
1990: Prime files for Chapter 11 bankruptcy.
1992: Prime emerges from bankruptcy.
1997: Prime buys the HomeGate extended-stay chain.
1999: HomeGate is merged into the Wellesley Inn chain.

hotel and an apartment complex. Suites came with kitchens or kitchenettes so that guests could cook and eat in their rooms, and in some cases were cheaper to run than ordinary hotels because long-term guests required less service. Prime considered selling its Wellesley chain in 1995 so that it could put all of its resources into expanding the AmeriSuites chain. But in 1996 Prime instead bought up the remaining Wellesley Inns it did not directly own. The chain at that time consisted of 30 hotels located in New Jersey, New York, Virginia, Maryland, Pennsylvania, and Florida. The next year, Prime bought a chain of extended-stay hotels called HomeGate in a stock deal worth about $134 million. HomeGate had only eight hotels open, but it had an additional 34 under development, with plans to build 20 or so more. The company ran out of funds to expand on its own and accepted the merger with Prime. Prime built and ran the HomeGate chain until 1999, when the hotels were converted to the Wellesley brand.

Meanwhile, the company was rapidly building new hotels. Although in the mid-1990s Prime had preferred to own its hotels, it began a push to recruit franchisees in 1998. By that time it had nearly 120 AmeriSuites open or due to open, and it looked for seasoned hoteliers to sign on to build more. Prime also owned 21 HomeGate hotels, with more than 40 more in the pipeline, and it also hoped to find franchisees for these and its Wellesley chain. But apparently the rate of growth was too much for Prime to sustain. For the third quarter of 1998, the company announced that earnings would be about 30 percent less than expected, and it expected much less new hotel development over 1999. The company had built some 90 hotels over the past two years. In an interview with *National Real Estate Investor* (October 1998), CEO David Simon called the frantic building spree "a pretty herculean task." Simon resigned after the announcement of lowered profits, and he was followed a month later by John Elwood.

The company's new chairman was A.F. Petrocelli. Petrocelli admitted that part of the problem with David Simon's leadership was the perception that he had paid too much for the HomeGate chain. Hence Prime changed course in 1999, deciding to merge the HomeGate brand into the Wellesley Inns chain, now known as Wellesley Inns & Suites. The extended-stay category had become extremely competitive, and Prime seemed to have better results with running traditional hotels for transient travelers. In addition, this gave the company just two brands to focus on. Prime had received only one application for a HomeGate franchise since beginning its drive to recruit new

hoteliers a year earlier. In 2000 the company again began heavy recruiting for franchisees, offering large financial incentives. The Wellesley chain had almost 70 hotels, many in Florida, Arizona, and Texas, and the company hoped to build up its presence in the Northeast.

Prime also moved to expand the AmeriSuites chain. In July 2000 the company closed a deal with ShoLodge to take over the leases of 27 of that firm's Sumner Suites chain and convert them to AmeriSuites. Prime had almost 200 AmeriSuites either open or in development in late 2000, including the Sumner Suites conversions. Many new AmeriSuites were in urban areas. The chain hoped to pick up business travelers in Chicago, San Diego, Washington, D.C., and other thriving commercial centers. AmeriSuites featured large rooms with special amenities such as microwaves, refrigerators, silverware and dishes, and irons and ironing boards. Roughly 40 percent of AmeriSuites customers were women, many on business, and the chain made a special effort to please women travelers by boasting heightened security. The chain also tried to up its appeal to business travelers with Internet reservations and billing, reducing paperwork. Rooms also were equipped with high-speed Internet access.

The company spent an estimated $1 billion on building and converting AmeriSuites in the late 1990s into the new millennium. Some of this growth had been financed by selling off properties. In 2001 Prime hired a new vice-president for franchise sales in order to divest more of its own properties and bring in some 25 to 50 new franchisees a year. The company hoped to sell off more than 100 corporate-owned hotels over the next five years, to finance further growth and retire debt. By this time the company had cash reserves of $1.2 billion and seemed in good shape to expand its two brands and perhaps to acquire another. By mid-2002, Prime had 143 AmeriSuites in operation, with six more under construction and almost 60 franchise agreements hammered out for new properties. The company also had more than 75 hotels up and running in the Wellesley chain. Prime continued to offer incentives to attract new franchisees, as its growth strategy depended on attracting more to its chains.

Principal Divisions

AmeriSuites; Wellesley Inns & Suites.

Principal Competitors

Six Continents Hotels, Inc.; Marriott International, Inc.; Interstate Hotels & Resorts, Inc.

Further Reading

Aikman, Rebecca, "A Big Innkeeper That Nobody's Heard of—Yet," *Business Week,* October 28, 1985, p. 87.
Amster, Robin, "Prime, Citing Losses and Debts, Files for Chapter 11 Bankruptcy," *Travel Weekly,* September 27, 1990, p. 73.
——, "Prime to Sell a 65% Interest in Two Chains," *Travel Weekly,* May 21, 1990, p. 1.
——, "Ramada to Sell Its Hotel Division to New World for $540 Million," *Travel Weekly,* April 27, 1989, p. 1.
Andorka, Frank H., "Franchising Hits Prime's Time," *Hotel & Motel Management,* June 15, 1998, p. 1.
Ballon, Marc, "Hotel Chain Bags Wealthy Acquirer," *Inc.,* November 1997, p. 17.

"Deal of $132 Million Set for HomeGate Hospitality," *Wall Street Journal,* July 28, 1997, p. B4.

Frabotta, David, "Prime Targets Middle-Class Market," *Hotel & Motel Management,* January 10, 2000, p. 6.

——, "Prime to Grow Franchise, Management Divisions," *Hotel & Motel Management,* September 3, 2001, p. 3.

Molnar, Linda, "Prime Motor Inns Inc.," *Business Journal of New Jersey,* July 1990, p. 52.

"Prime Hospitality CEO Resigns As Earnings Drop to $1 a Share," *National Real Estate Investor,* October 1998, p. 10.

"Prime Hospitality Net to Trail Estimates, Chief to Step Down," *Wall Street Journal,* September 16, 1998, p. A6.

"Prime Selling One Chain to Help Expand Another," *Hotel & Motel Management,* September 18, 1995, p. 1.

Rowe, Megan, "Prime Motor Inns: Lean, Mean and Hungry," *Lodging Hospitality,* November 1989, p. 28.

——, "Prime Time," *Lodging Hospitality,* February 1994, p. 32.

"A Sleeper of a Hotel Stock?," *Fortune,* October 27, 1986, pp. 132–33.

Watkins, Edward, "Prime Hospitality Gets Aggressive," *Lodging Hospitality,* June 1, 2002, p. 16.

——, "Wall Street: Lodging's Friend and Foe," *Lodging Hospitality,* October 1998, p. 6.

Wechsler, D., "Lend Now, Worry Later," *Forbes,* January 22, 1990, p. 99.

Whitford, Marty, "Prime Cans HomeGate Brand," *Hotel & Motel Management,* May 17, 1999, p. 1.

Wolff, Carlo, "Priming a Franchise Powerhouse," *Lodging Hospitality,* November 2000, p. 46.

—A. Woodward

PROVIDIAN

Providian Financial Corporation

201 Mission Street
San Francisco, California 94105-1831
U.S.A.
Telephone: (415) 543-0404
Fax: (415) 278-6028
Web site: http://www.providian.com

Public Company
Incorporated: 1984 as First Deposit Corporation
Employees: 7,000
Total Assets: $37.66 billion (2001)
Stock Exchanges: New York Pacific
Ticker Symbol: PVN
NAIC: 522210 Credit Card Issuing; 522310 Mortgage
and Nonmortgage Loan Brokers

Providian Financial Corporation is one of the leading issuers of credit cards in the United States. As of late 2002, the company had more than 13 million customer accounts and $20 billion in managed receivables. During the 1990s, the company grew rapidly by aggressively targeting the subprime segment of the credit market (which includes higher risk customers with prior credit problems or limited credit history), while charging higher interest rates and imposing higher service charges. This strategy proved to be fatally flawed, and in the early 21st century, Providian launched a turnaround effort that included a new focus on the middle market and prime credit sectors.

Commonwealth Life Roots

The earliest roots of Providian Financial can be traced back to Commonwealth Life Insurance Company. When founded in 1904, Commonwealth Life was intended to serve as a catalyst to economic development in Kentucky and as a means to keep both business and capital within state borders. To emphasize this connection, the firm was named after the Commonwealth of Kentucky. It also adopted the state's motto, "United We Stand, Divided We Fall," and its seal. Two of the company's founders figured prominently in its early years. Colonel Joshua D. Pow-

ers, the firm's first president, was a lawyer, a state legislator, and founder of several corporations. Darwin W. Johnson joined the company as secretary-treasurer after working for several years in the tobacco business.

Initially, Commonwealth sold insurance only in Kentucky, specializing in ordinary life insurance and also inexpensive coverage for low-income workers. This latter type of insurance policy was called industrial, or weekly premium debit, insurance because the insurance agent collected the premiums in person, every week. Although these premiums were often paid in the form of chickens, eggs, or produce, the company's fortunes grew rapidly, leading to expansion into other states, including Alabama. Because of the concentration of blue-collar workers, urban areas offered the most lucrative marketing opportunities.

Over the next 20 years, Commonwealth's business experienced both peaks and valleys. Between 1914 and 1918, its life insurance sales increased, although death losses from World War I and an influenza epidemic depressed overall financial results. The postwar recession of 1921 did not affect the company's growing prosperity, which continued during the rest of the decade. The company sustained major losses due to the Great Depression, but rebounded by 1935 as a result of the intensified efforts of its field sales force.

During this period, the company was led by Darwin Johnson, who had succeeded an ailing Joshua Powers as president in 1922. Johnson's death in 1936 touched off a power struggle on the board of directors that ended in the election of Homer Ward Batson as the company's next president. When Batson took over, the company was experiencing serious financial problems. Although it appeared on the surface that the company was doing well, many of its loans were not guaranteed with sufficient collateral and others had little chance of ever being repaid. In addition, the company's practice of paying liberal dividends to shareholders, even during the Depression years, resulted in a critical shortage of funds. Batson immediately implemented a series of measures intended to increase the company's capital and place it on stronger financial footing. All officers were required to take a salary reduction; unnecessary lights were to be turned off, and clerks were expected to use pencils until they

284

were too short to be held comfortably. The consolidation of several field offices, elimination of problem policies, and suspension of dividend payments for 1938 contributed to the company's economic recovery.

Not all of Batson's initiatives proceeded as smoothly. In 1936, he sent form letters to the recipients of several small loans to request full payment. One of these borrowers was James E. Dunne, the publisher of *Dunne's Insurance Reports*. In response, Dunne proceeded to circulate a scathing assessment of Commonwealth's financial condition among the subscribers of *Dunne's Insurance Reports*. He subsequently attempted to oust Batson as president and ruin the company. Commonwealth's management eventually ran a series of advertisements in local newspapers to restore public confidence in the company.

Dunne's allegations of mismanagement and insolvency later were brought before a Jefferson County grand jury, but the company successfully defended itself against the charges. To provide stronger control over Commonwealth's future financial operations, however, the state's insurance commissioner required the company to submit all loan applications for more than $20,000 to both the insurance commission of Kentucky and that of the state in which the loan was to be made.

With this incident behind it, Commonwealth turned its attention to the marketplace. It found that its existing industrial insurance benefits were no longer competitive and the methods by which premiums had been calculated were out of date. A revitalized product line introduced in 1941 boosted sales force morale and increased insurance sales. That same year, the board of directors elected Morton Boyd as president and Batson became honorary chairman. Boyd focused on expanding Commonwealth's insurance business through the agency sales force.

The onset of World War II restricted the availability of many goods and provided few alternatives for consumer spending. High employment levels increased the demand for life insurance, spending considered helpful to the war effort because of its anti-inflationary effects. With customer demand higher than ever, Commonwealth's sales force had difficulty covering the market because it competed with the military for manpower and supplies such as gasoline. The war also affected the nature of the company's insurance policies. New issues written by Commonwealth

and other insurers excluded members of the military from receiving death benefits. Policyholders who had purchased insurance prior to entering the military were allowed to retain their coverage. This procedure cost the company a significant amount of money in wartime mortality claims. When the war ended, the company concentrated on improving sales efficiency and quality through better recruitment and training of agents. Blue collar unemployment drove the weekly premium insurance business down, but sales of ordinary insurance picked up the slack.

The company continued to grow during the rest of the 1940s. The insurance business was becoming increasingly competitive, with many firms using the success of a particular product in one state as a springboard to marketing in another location. Commonwealth watched with more than a casual interest as one of its competitors in Alabama, Liberty National Life Insurance Company, successfully marketed burial insurance policies that also provided for the funeral service to be handled by a funeral home owned by the company. To counteract a likely expansion of this program into Kentucky, Commonwealth designed a similar product based on a standard weekly premium policy. The Kentucky Funeral Directors' Association was contracted to handle the funeral arrangements so that Commonwealth did not have to directly enter the funeral business. The product was an instant success, with some agents writing as many as 100 policies in the first week.

Growth continued in the 1950s with only a minor disruption caused by the Korean War. Commonwealth embarked upon a program of aggressive expansion beyond Kentucky. In 1952, it developed a new concept in life insurance that enabled policyholders to pay their premiums through regular automatic withdrawals from their checking accounts. Although the company met with some initial resistance from bankers, other insurers became enamored with the simplicity of the concept. Their decisions to introduce similar versions of Commonwealth's Bank-O-Matic program eventually persuaded reluctant bank executives to lend their support.

By 1954, the Korean War had given way to a recession that forced Commonwealth to curtail its ambitious expansion plans and focus instead on maintaining its field sales force. When agent turnover started to increase in response to a drop in sales, the company invested heavily in recruitment and training of new sales personnel. As the economy recovered, competition in the life insurance market intensified and Commonwealth introduced a new family coverage policy.

In 1958, Boyd became chairman and was succeeded as president and chief executive by William H. Abell, who had previously served the company as general counsel and a member of the board. Under his leadership, the branch-agency system was restructured into a more efficient and unified organization, improvements were made in agents' retirement benefits, and several product innovations were launched.

Diversifying in the 1960s

As Commonwealth entered the 1960s, it became evident that weekly premium insurance was no longer a viable product. Social Security and increased wages for middle-class workers decreased need for the burial insurance benefits that had made

Key Dates:

1904: The Commonwealth Life Insurance Company is founded in Kentucky.

1940s: The company begins selling burial insurance.

1962: A wider attempt at expansion begins with a pilot program selling residential fire and homeowners insurance and individual auto policies.

1963: Indiana-based Empire Life and Accident Insurance Company is acquired.

1969: The company is reorganized under a holding company called Capital Holding Corporation.

1981: National Liberty Corporation is acquired by Capital Holding; Parker Pen Corporation acquires Tilton, New Hampshire-based Citizens National Bank, later known as First Deposit National Bank; Parker Pen also acquires Redding Savings & Loan Association of California, later known as First Deposit Savings Bank.

1984: Capital Holding acquires First Deposit Corporation, parent of First Deposit National Bank and First Deposit Savings Bank—thereby entering the credit card market.

1988: Shailesh J. Mehta is named president of First Deposit Corp.

Early 1990s: First Deposit branches out into home-equity loans and secured credit cards.

1994: Capital Holding changes its name to Providian Corporation; First Deposit Corp. is renamed Providian Bancorp, Inc.

1997: Providian Corp. sells its insurance operations to AEGON N.V.; Providian Bancorp is spun off to shareholders as Providian Financial Corporation, with Mehta serving as chairman and CEO.

2000: Providian Financial agrees to repay consumers $300 million to settle allegations of deceptive business practices.

2001: Credit losses lead to plunging earnings and Mehta's resignation; new CEO Joseph W. Saunders launches a turnaround effort.

the weekly premium concept so popular. The gradual loss of business in this area compelled Commonwealth to investigate new avenues of growth. In addition, competing life insurance companies that offered health and accident coverage were able to offer customers a more complete selection of insurance products, enabling them to attract sales personnel. Commonwealth initially considered entering the health and accident field, but, when it appeared that the federal government would be heavily guiding the nation's healthcare system, the company shifted its focus to automobile, fire, and casualty insurance.

The company originally intended to enter this market via acquisition, but ultimately developed the business internally as a subsidiary. By mid-1962, a pilot operation based in Louisville, Kentucky, began selling residential fire and homeowners insurance and individual automobile policies. Problems arose, ranging from computer billing errors to underwriting mistakes, and the new operation barely broke even. Nevertheless, Common-

wealth gradually expanded its new products market beyond Kentucky.

Aggressive expansion into other states proved to be more difficult than originally anticipated because the company's contacts, particularly among local bankers, were not as strong as in its home state. It was at this time, however, that Commonwealth was offered the opportunity to acquire the Indiana-based Empire Life and Accident Insurance Company. Empire's chairman sought the merger to resolve an ongoing conflict between two of its executives who were also his sons-in-law. The companies joined forces on October 31, 1963, under the Commonwealth banner. This development gave Commonwealth a stronger position in Indiana, and added a significant number of black customers to its rolls. Since its early years, when advertising stressed that Commonwealth wrote "white lives only," Commonwealth had served only the white market. Kentucky funeral parlors were still segregated at this time, so with the Empire merger, the company was forced to begin handling black burial business in Kentucky, resulting in the formation of the Kentucky Bonded Funeral Company.

The state of Florida was identified as the company's next site for expansion. Commonwealth management believed that by targeting a southern state, the company would meet with less sales resistance than it had faced in Indiana. Florida was also especially attractive because of its projected growth in population and economy.

Commonwealth continued to experience problems in hiring additional general agents because of a lack of attractive sales incentives and a narrow product line. By the late 1960s, the Vietnam War had made this situation even worse. Despite a healthy economy, which enhanced the market potential for insurance, the lack of available staff to cover sales territories placed the company's expansion strategy on indefinite hold. This situation became more critical as the war intensified and the costs of developing the Florida market increased. Attempts to acquire other companies proved fruitless, because most candidates were reluctant to be part of Commonwealth.

Emergence of Capital Holding in 1969

After much consideration, the company embarked upon a plan to form a holding company. At first, this holding company would consist of the existing Commonwealth organization but, in time, would serve as an umbrella for acquired subsidiaries that would be permitted to operate autonomously. The new organization was incorporated in Delaware in 1969 as Capital Holding Corporation, a name considered appropriate regardless of the type of business the company purchased. William Abell, Commonwealth's president since 1958, assumed the same position in the holding company and became chairman after the 1969 acquisitions of National Trust Life Insurance Company and Peoples Life Insurance Company. The following year, Capital purchased First National Life Insurance Company. The operations and sales force of this New Orleans, Louisiana-based organization were later integrated with those of Commonwealth, paving the way for the company's entry into the Louisiana market.

Capital's gradual growth through acquisition created opportunities and provided the necessary resources to expand its product line and improve its competitive standing. It also benefited from such socioeconomic factors as the baby boom of the 1970s, a growing young adult market, and the increasing availability of disposable income. The company suffered, however, from weak management and a conservative board of directors that remained fixated on the outmoded method of selling life insurance door-to-door. By the latter half of the decade, Commonwealth instituted a training program to help its agents increase their return on collection calls by converting these customers into buyers of new insurance products.

Several new products were also introduced. One of these policies, the Capitalizer, represented a major departure from the company's traditional philosophy. Until this point, Commonwealth had sold policies with set premiums and had assumed the risk of changing interest and mortality rates and expenses. In contrast, the Capitalizer offered an adjustable premium that would vary according to future profits or losses in the company's investments or changes in its mortality experience. This feature enhanced the company's ability to compete with mutual funds, which had recently become popular.

Thomas C. Simons, who was hired away from another insurance company to become the company's chief executive officer in 1978, set out to make major changes in Commonwealth's marketing strategy. He believed that the company's strength was its ability to sell products to the middle-income bracket of the market. His goal was to find new ways to reach this market before larger insurers did.

Pursuing the Middle Class and Entering the Credit Card Market in the 1980s

In 1981, Capital acquired National Liberty Corporation, a holding company that sold health insurance to middle-class consumers by direct mail, telephone solicitation, and television commercials. In addition to providing Capital with a business that fit its existing operations, National Liberty offered an efficient marketing system with the capability to improve both sales productivity and customer service. One year later, Capital began selling insurance and other financial products at service centers within Kroger's retail food stores, capitalizing on a growing consumer trend toward one-stop shopping, and setting the stage for similar future strategies.

In 1984, Capital purchased San Francisco-based First Deposit Corporation from Parker Pen Corporation for $10 million. Parker's entry into financial services was similar to that of other nonbanking companies who had discovered that they could move into the banking business by buying a bank and then stripping it of its commercial loans or demand deposits—in the process forming what was known as a nonbank bank. In October 1981 Parker bought Tilton, New Hampshire-based Citizens National Bank, which had been founded in 1853 and chartered in 1865. The bank was stripped of its commercial lending operations and later renamed First Deposit National Bank. In November 1981 Parker purchased Redding Savings & Loan Association of California, which was renamed First Deposit Savings Bank. The two units were set up as subsidiaries of a San Francisco-based holding company called First Deposit Corporation. Leading Parker's drive into banking was Andrew S. Kahr, a financial entrepreneur who was most famous for creat-

ing the Cash Management Account, an innovative integrated-investment vehicle aimed at individuals that was introduced by Merrill Lynch & Co. in 1977. Kahr was president and CEO of First Deposit and continued in that role under the new ownership by Capital Holding. Among First Deposit's activities was the development of a credit card issuing operation. Kahr's first credit card was a Visa card that had no annual fee (which was unusual at the time) but that carried a high interest rate of 21.9 percent and that also required a person to borrow at least $1,000 as a cash advance in order to receive the card. Another unusual feature at the time was that only 2 percent of the balance had to be paid off each month. Given these various features the card was clearly aimed at the lower ends of the credit spectrum, and First Deposit continued to pursue the subprime market under Capital Holding.

In another 1984 development, Bank of America agreed to allow Capital to sell automobile, homeowners, and life insurance from specific bank branches in return for an office rental fee. By 1986, however, this venture still had not shown a profit and Capital terminated the project. Despite this setback, 1986 ended on a high note with the successful acquisition of Worldwide Underwriters Insurance Company, a direct-response marketer of automobile and homeowners insurance. In 1987, as it strengthened its hold on the moderate-income segment of the marketplace, the company sold its Georgia International Life Insurance Company subsidiary, which focused primarily on higher-income households.

Capital joined with four other insurance companies in 1988 to settle previous complaints lodged by Delaware's insurance commissioner. The companies were accused of collecting higher life insurance premiums from blacks, reflecting differences in life expectancy between the black and white populations. Although the insurers claimed that they had not sold such policies in more than 20 years and were unaware that race-based premiums were still being paid, they agreed to increase the death benefits for black beneficiaries who had overpaid on their policies.

Simons died in August 1988 and was succeeded as chairman and CEO of Capital Holding by Irving W. Bailey II. He had been with the company for ten years and had most recently served as president and chief operating officer. Bailey continued his predecessor's strategy of developing niche businesses, which, unlike life insurance, faced little price competition. Under Simons, the company had introduced such products as burial policies for people with annual incomes under $15,000, life insurance policies for people making between $15,000 and $25,000, and insurance policies specifically developed for veterans.

Soon after Bailey took over, Capital Holding launched a new "living payout" policy that supplemented other life insurance plans. Capital would pay insured people with terminal illnesses one-half of the total face value of their primary policies while they were still living. Upon their deaths, Capital Holding would recoup this amount from the primary insurance company. In 1989, Capital spent $156 million to purchase Southlife Holding Company, a Nashville, Tennessee-based insurer, to increase its market share in the home-service field.

Meanwhile, on the credit card front, Kahr had grown tired of managing a company, and in 1988 he sold his interest in First

Deposit Corp. and turned over the reins to Shailesh J. Mehta (Kahr helped guide the company as a consultant through the year 2000). Born in Bombay, India, Mehta was a mathematical genius who had been hired away from Cleveland Trust Company. When he joined the company in 1986 at the age of 37, First Deposit had just $414 million in card balances. By the end of 1989, that figure was approaching $2 billion, and First Deposit had more than 600,000 credit card customers. Already, First Deposit was generating 10.6 percent of Capital Holding's pretax profits. Mehta and other executives at First Deposit, most of whom also had math and engineering backgrounds, developed sophisticated algorithms and databases to find particular types of potential customers for credit card solicitations. In particular, Mehta and his colleagues sought out heavy borrowers who were willing to make minimum monthly payments and who would tolerate high interest rates and fees—a formula for maximizing income and profits from a credit card operation. Although First Deposit became a leader in targeting the riskier subprime portion of the credit market, the reliance on mathematical models helped the firm identify people who might have had prior credit problems but who were still likely to repay their debts, thereby keeping the customer default level to a manageable level (though higher than the industry average).

Fast Credit Card Growth; Becoming Providian: Early to Mid-1990s

Capital Holding and its subsidiaries continued to grow in the early 1990s. In 1991 Durham Corp., a life insurer based in Raleigh, North Carolina, was acquired for $257 million. The fastest growth, however, continued to come from First Deposit, which by late 1993 ranked as the 14th largest bank credit card lender, with 1.5 million customer accounts and $4 billion in card balances. But First Deposit ranked first in profitability and had seen its profits balloon from $17 million in 1988 to $53 million in 1990 to $118 million in 1993. As a subsidiary of an insurance holding company, First Deposit was able to keep a relatively low profile despite its stunning growth and obvious ability to generate profits, but already criticism about its business practices was beginning to surface. Consumer advocates were critical, for example, of credit insurance products that First Deposit offered to its customers, contending that such insurance was either unnecessary or inferior to cheap life insurance policies or disability insurance. The company's credit cards were also chastised for their high interest rates and poorly disclosed fees. Meanwhile, First Deposit expanded into other areas of consumer lending, such as home-equity loans and secured credit cards. The latter, which required the posting of cash collateral in the form of a savings deposit (typically $200 to $300), were clearly aimed at the subprime sector of the credit market— consumers with no credit history or with credit problems. By 1994, the company had already become the nation's second largest issuer of secured cards, trailing only Citibank, with more than 250,000 such accounts.

In 1994 Capital Holding changed its name to Providian Corporation, and First Deposit was renamed Providian Bancorp, Inc. This was part of a drive to create a more integrated company. During 1994 the increasing importance of the banking unit became even clearer, as Providian Bancorp generated 40 percent of the overall operating profits of the corporation.

Further evidence came in December of that year when Mehta was named president and COO of the holding company.

Jettisoning Insurance to Focus on Credit Cards in the Late 1990s

With the banking unit seeing its profits increase each year by more than 20 percent, while the insurance operations were experiencing little if any growth, Providian decided to stake its future on the former. In December 1996 the firm announced that it would sell its insurance operations to AEGON N.V., a Dutch financial services giant, in a $3.5 billion deal and spinoff to shareholders of the Providian Bancorp banking unit. In June 1997 the transaction was completed with Providian Bancorp emerging as a publicly traded, San Francisco-based company with the new name of Providian Financial Corporation. Mehta was named chairman and CEO of the company, while Bailey became vice-chairman of AEGON. Providian Financial began as the 12th largest U.S. credit card issuer, with about $8 billion in card balances, and the number one issuer of secured credit cards, with 750,000 cardholders.

Having severed its insurance roots, Providian moved quickly to expand its credit card holdings through acquisitions. During 1998 the company bought from First Union Corporation two separate blocks of credit card loans, each worth about $1.1 billion. Providian also bought another $350 million of receivables from Morgan Stanley Dean Witter & Company in 1998. In early 1999, as part of a drive into electronic commerce, Providian purchased GetSmart for $33 million. Based in Burlingame, California, GetSmart was an Internet service that matched consumers with loan products, including credit cards, mortgages, auto and student loans, debt consolidation, and business financing. By the end of 1999 Providian had grown its loan portfolio to $21 billion, making it the number eight credit card issuer in the country. There were now 12 million Providian cardholders.

Millennial Downfall and Attempt at Turnaround

The meteorically rising Providian Financial began to falter in mid-1999 when charges of unfair business practices started to proliferate. In conjunction with the San Francisco district attorney's office, the Office of the Comptroller of the Currency (OCC) launched an investigation of Providian. In June 2000 the OCC issued a report concluding that the company had ''engaged in a pattern of misconduct in which it misled and deceived consumers in order to increase profits.'' The allegations against Providian included misleading consumers about the interest rates on their credit cards and promoting a ''no annual fee'' credit card that carried a mandatory $156 annual ''credit protection fee.'' Providian agreed to repay consumers at least $300 million to settle the allegations in the largest ever OCC enforcement action. Providian, which admitted no wrongdoing, also agreed to pay the city and county of San Francisco a $5.5 million fine and was ordered to halt some of its marketing campaigns that had been deemed deceptive. Around this same time, the company, in response to mounting complaints from customers who claimed they had been charged late fees for payments that had been made on time, added a two-day grace period beyond the due date in which customers could pay a bill without incurring a late charge. Then in December 2000 Providian agreed to pay another $105 million to settle a number of consumer class-action lawsuits alleging deceptive marketing and sales practices.

Despite these setbacks, Providian remained a Wall Street darling, with its market capitalization skyrocketing 453 percent from 1997 to 2000. Late in 2000, the stock hit its all-time high of $66.72 per share. By that time, the company ranked as the number five credit card issuer in the nation, with $30 billion in card balances—one-third of which was attributable to subprime customers.

To maintain the company's spectacular growth, which had been fueled in large part by the interest and fee income garnered from Providian's subprime customers, Mehta began seeking out more and more subprime customers. The company lowered its standards, giving cards to customers who would previously have been rejected by Providian's sophisticated mathematical models. With the economy faltering and subprime customers among the first to feel the effects, consumer bankruptcies and subprime default rates began to rise. Charge-offs for uncollectable loans began to rise quickly, increasing from 7.6 percent in the fall of 2000 to 12.1 percent one year later. In August 2001 Providian revealed about $30 million in credit losses for the second quarter. During the third quarter, credit losses helped spark a 71 percent decline in net income from the previous year. During the second half of 2001, Wall Street finally discovered the extent of the company's problems and punished the stock price, which fell 92 percent from July to October—to less than $5.

On the day that the third-quarter earnings were announced, Mehta declared that he would resign from the company as soon as a replacement was brought on board. In November 2001 Joseph W. Saunders was named president and CEO, having most recently served as chairman and CEO of FleetBoston Financial Corporation's credit card business. Over the next year, Saunders led a wide-ranging turnaround effort. Part of the impetus for change came from federal regulators, who prohibited Providian from accepting new accounts from subprime customers and who limited that company's asset growth to 2.5 percent per quarter. Saunders subsequently announced that Providian planned to focus on the middle market and prime credit sectors. Instead of growing, Providian moved to slim down its loan portfolio, selling off its credit card businesses in the United Kingdom and Argentina, $8.2 billion of its best-quality credit card loans, and $2.4 billion of its high-risk subprime credit card accounts. The company also sold or shut down several call centers and offices. The cutbacks reduced the workforce from 13,000 to fewer than 7,000 by late 2002. In March 2002 Providian offered to pay $38 million to settle a securities fraud class-action lawsuit, but a slew of other suits had been filed charging that executives had misled investors about changes in its accounting for credit losses that were said to have taken place in 2001. These suits clouded the company's future, but the turnaround seemed to be proceeding apace, particularly given that there had been much speculation in late 2001 that the company would be sold or would be forced into bankruptcy. After posting a $481 million loss for the fourth quarter of 2001—as a result of more than $1 billion in special restructuring charges—Providian posted profits in both the first and second quarters of 2002. Nevertheless, the company was unlikely to return to the levels of growth and profitability attained in the late 1990s given the new focus on less risky—but also less profitable—customers.

Principal Subsidiaries

Providian National Bank; Providian Bank; Providian Bancorp Services.

Principal Competitors

Citigroup Inc.; Bank One Corporation; MBNA Corporation; J.P. Morgan Chase & Co.; Household International, Inc.; Bank of America Corporation; Capital One Financial Corporation.

Further Reading

Andresky, Jill, "Thank You, Tom Simons," *Forbes,* March 23, 1987, p. 99.

Armstrong, David, "Insurer's Takeover to Create New S.F. Company," *San Francisco Examiner,* December 31, 1996, p. D1.

Bennett, Robert A., "Providian Simply Wants to Make Money," *U.S. Banker,* May 2000, p. 42.

Berthelsen, Christian, "Providian Sells Some High-Risk Accounts," *San Francisco Chronicle,* April 16, 2002, p. B1.

Bloom, Jennifer Kingson, "Providian to Buy Internet Loan Firm for $33M," *American Banker,* February 19, 1999, p. 10.

Breitkopf, David, and Lavonne Kuykendall, "Which Way for Card Giant After Mehta?," *American Banker,* October 22, 2001, p. 1.

Brenner, Lynn, "Capital Holding to Keep Bank Unit, Sell Receivables," *American Banker,* February 9, 1989, p. 10.

Byrne, Harlan S., "Capital Holding Corp.," *Barron's,* April 23, 1990, pp. 55–56.

Campanella, Frank W., "Direct Response: It Provides New Life for Insurer Capital Holding," *Barron's,* June 27, 1983, pp. 54+.

Coleman, Calmetta, "Providian, Regulators Strive to Keep Firm Under Control: New Chief Is Appointed, Curbs Are Placed on Lending, and Sale of Units Planned," *Wall Street Journal,* November 30, 2001, p. B4.

——, "Providian Taps Fleet's Saunders As New CEO," *Wall Street Journal,* November 27, 2001, p. C15.

Drummond, James, "Sharp Marketing," *Forbes,* February 5, 1990, p. 118.

Fickenscher, Lisa, "Providian Faces Slew of Lawsuits Over Its Imposition of Late Fees," *American Banker,* June 14, 1999, p. 1.

——, "Providian Spinoff Going Public," *American Banker,* February 27, 1997, p. 1.

——, "Providian, Under Pressure, Works on Image Repair," *American Banker,* March 16, 2000, p. 1.

Fraust, Bart, "Parker Pen Co. Won't Take a Banking Refill: Will Sell Its 80% Interest in First Deposit Corp.," *American Banker,* March 9, 1984, pp. 1+.

Gerard, Victor B., *Commonwealth Life Insurance Company: A History of the Development Years,* Louisville, Ky.: Commonwealth Life Insurance Company, 1984.

Gorham, John, "Card Player," *Forbes,* December 10, 2001, pp. 80–81.

——, "Customer Rage," *Forbes,* July 5, 1999, pp. 65–66.

Hansell, Saul, "Merchants of Debt," *New York Times,* July 2, 1995, Sec. 3, p. 1.

Koudsi, Suzanne, "Sleazy Credit," *Fortune,* March 4, 2002, pp. 143–44, 146–47.

Kutler, Jeffrey, "First Deposit Shuns Mass Marketing for Profitability," *American Banker,* October 21, 1993, pp. 16+.

Lee, W.A., "Reinvented Providian Sees Rebirth," *American Banker,* March 28, 2002, p. 1.

Maher, Thomas M., "Capital Holding and National Liberty: New Directions," *National Underwriter,* March 13, 1981, p. 22.

McGough, Robert, "The Short Meets the CEO," *Financial World,* April 2, 1991, pp. 80–83.

Niedzielski, Joe, "Aegon Buys Providian Units for $3.5B," *National Underwriter Life and Health/Financial Services,* January 6, 1997, p. 1.

"Parker Pen Slips into Financial Services," *Business Week,* April 5, 1982, pp. 95+.

Punch, Linda, "The Pure-Play Meltdown," *Credit Card Management,* January 2002, pp. 14, 16–17.

Shaw, Whitney R., "Profitable Policies," *Barron's,* January 12, 1981, pp. 46+.

Simons, Thomas C., "An Update on a Low-Profile Giant," *National Underwriter Life and Health/Financial Services,* May 28, 1983, pp. 12+.

Stillwell, Newcomb, "Made for Each Other," *Forbes,* February 16, 1981, p. 94.

Trager, Louis, "Bank's Low Profile Belies High Profitability," *San Francisco Examiner,* September 19, 1994, p. D1.

Zuckerman, Sam, "Credit Giant Accused of Piling on Charges: Employees Say Providian Urged Them to Mislead," *San Francisco Chronicle,* June 1, 1999, p. A1.

——, "How Providian Misled Card Holders," *San Francisco Chronicle,* May 5, 2002, p. A1.

——, "Providian Loss a Whopping $481.2 Million," *San Francisco Chronicle,* February 8, 2002, p. B1.

——, "S.F. Credit Card Firm Admits Billing Errors," *San Francisco Chronicle,* July 23, 1999, p. A1.

—Sandy Schusteff
—update: David E. Salamie

Public Storage, Inc.

701 Western Avenue, Suite 200
Glendale, California 91201
U.S.A.
Telephone: (818) 244-8080
Fax: (818) 553-2388
Web site: http://www.publicstorage.com

Public Company
Incorporated: 1980
Employees: 4,400
Sales: $834.64 million (2001)
Stock Exchanges: New York
Ticker Symbol: PSA
NAIC: 531130 Lessors of Miniwarehouses and Self-
    Storage Units; 531311 Residential Property Managers

Public Storage, Inc. is the largest operator of self-storage centers in the United States. The company maintains direct or indirect equity investments in 1,384 self-storage facilities in 80 U.S. and Canadian cities, preferring to locate its miniwarehouses in large metropolitan areas. Public Storage also has an investment in an affiliate organization, PS Business Parks, Inc., which owns or manages 16.1 million square feet of industrial, office, and retail properties located in 11 states. Public Storage is led by its founder, Bradley Wayne Hughes, who serves as chairman and chief executive officer.

Origins

A native of Oklahoma, Bradley Wayne Hughes built a career around real estate. After receiving his undergraduate degree from the University of Southern California, Hughes worked as a real estate developer in southern California, but his rise to the top of the business world did not begin until he was in his 40s, and not until he took a road trip to Texas. During the early 1970s, Hughes was driving in Texas when he passed a self-storage warehouse erected by the side of the road. Self-storage facilities were rare at the time, prompting Hughes to park his car and pretend to be a customer. Hughes was told he could put his name on a waiting list; all the available space was already occupied. Hughes needed no further incentive to enter the business himself when he returned home.

Hughes was spurred to enter the self-storage business for two reasons. First, he believed there was a potentially large demand for self-storage space in southern California, home to a particularly itinerant population. If the self-storage business foundered, Hughes reasoned, he could always raze the miniwarehouses and build apartments or office buildings in their place. The important asset was the land; building self-storage centers, at the least, offered the chance to collect a return on the real estate investment until it could be developed into a more lucrative property.

With $50,000 and a partner, Kenneth Volk, Jr., Hughes entered the self-storage fray. It took roughly one year for the two partners to build their facility, due to time spent researching, buying land, obtaining zoning approval, and ultimately constructing the facility. When the first self-storage center was completed, built alongside a busy freeway in El Cajon, California, in 1972, Hughes hoped to experience the success he had witnessed in Texas. He hung up a sign that read, "Private Storage Spaces," and was quickly disappointed. For a frustratingly long time, no customers showed up, until finally one person arrived and asked if storage was available to the general public. Hughes realized his error and changed the sign to read: "Public Storage."

Any fears Hughes had that the self-storage business might not deliver the most profitable results for the land were quickly assuaged. Bulldozers would not be needed. The first miniwarehouse broke even with only a 35 percent occupancy rate, achieved within three months. Further, construction costs for the facilities in the early 1970s were 35 percent to 40 percent lower than the construction costs for apartment buildings, yet storage rates per square foot were the same as for apartments. The financial opportunities excited Hughes and Volk, prompting the pair to open 20 miniwarehouses within the next two years. More expansion followed, occurring at an especially frenetic pace during the 1980s. The company's early and aggressive entry into the market determined its success to a large extent, but of equal importance was the manner in which the physical expansion was financed.

Company Perspectives:

Our primary business is storage. We provide storage solutions to a diverse America. We focus on storage and our moving service has emerged as a key complementary enterprise. Recent tax law changes relating to real estate investment trusts have enabled us to acquire and expand ancillary business activities connected to our storage business, namely reinsurance covering tenant goods, moving services, consumer truck rentals, storage containers and selling moving and storage supplies from retail stores at our properties. Our seasoned property management system, in conjunction with our national reservation center, enables our ancillary businesses to generate additional consumer contact and to cross-market goods and services in greater volume. We believe our ancillary businesses help us rent more space at higher rates.

Triggering Growth Through First Real Estate Limited Partnership in 1977

Hughes loathed debt. He refused to borrow to fuel Public Storage's expansion, preferring instead to solicit investors to pay for real estate and construction. In return, the investors received a percentage of Public Storage's business. Hughes turned to the rapidly growing real estate limited partnership market for his supply of cash, forming his first partnership in 1977. It took approximately a year for the partnership to raise $3 million, but, not long afterward, the money came pouring in, willingly offered by investors who had heard of the fortunes to be made in allying with Hughes.

Like Hughes, investors perceived great value in the land occupied by Public Storage's miniwarehouses. During the late 1970s and early 1980s, the southern California land purchased by Hughes exploded in value, which greatly enriched Public Storage's investors. They saw their investments quadruple in value, creating a stir within the investment community that enabled Hughes to raise cash for expansion nearly at will. During the mid-1980s, Hughes was collecting between $200 million and $300 million a year from institutional and individual investors, providing sufficient resources for him to launch a national expansion campaign. Hughes targeted the 39 largest cities in the nation and began opening up as many as 100 new self-storage centers a year. Between 1978 and 1989, more than 200,000 investors heeded Hughes's calls for cash, enabling him to raise an estimated $3 billion for expansion. With the investments, Hughes was able to thoroughly dominate the self-storage industry by building an empire of 1,000 miniwarehouses. His preeminence was impressive. "We're bigger than our nine next-largest competitors put together," Hughes remarked in a February 5, 1990 interview with the *Los Angeles Business Journal.* "Consider them the McDonald's of the ministorage business," an analyst said in the November 28, 1989 issue of *Financial World.*

Although Hughes held a commanding lead in the industry, Public Storage was not alone in its bid to populate the landscape with self-storage units. In 1979, there were 3,500 miniwarehouses in operation in the United States. By the late 1980s, there were 18,000 self-storage outlets in the country, offering more than 900 million square feet of storage space and generating estimated annual revenues of $4 billion. In one four-year period during the 1980s, capacity in the industry doubled, threatening to glut the market. Hughes's facilities, though far outnumbering the properties operated by his rivals, felt the sting of a crowded market. Occupancy rates at many Public Storage facilities stalled at 85 percent, and rental rates stopped rising. Further, as more developers jumped into the self-storage business, the cost of land increased, taking some of the financial luster off Hughes's deals. The effect of these external factors was compounded by internal pressures and several tactical errors.

Developing into a national chain was proving more difficult than expected, causing expansion to slow. The company was growing at such a frenetic pace that finding skilled managers was becoming difficult, as was contending with weather conditions and labor markets that differed from southern California's. "What once took us seven months was now taking us 11, 12, and 13 months," recalled Harvey Lenkin, Public Storage's president, in a November 28, 1989 interview with *Financial World.* Adding to the difficulties were several mistakes made by Hughes. He began including office parks into the deals forged in his numerous partnership agreements. Office parks, which Public Storage had difficulty in managing, suffered from severe overcapacity problems, leading to sizable losses. The financial drag of the office parks, which sometimes accounted for as much as 35 percent of the deal brokered by Hughes, dramatically affected the return earned by investors, who were dismayed to learn that they had not earned nearly as much as Public Storage's early investors had earned. Two other glaring miscues by Hughes stood out: In 1985, he purchased a broker-dealer network called Christopher Weil & Co. to orchestrate Public Storage's partnership deals; in 1986, he and a group of executives purchased a pizza chain. By 1988, both businesses had collapsed after recording substantial losses.

The problems were there, but as Robert Wrubel, a *Financial World* reporter, noted in the magazine's November 28, 1989 issue, "that Hughes is still around to tell the tale reflects well on him." Indeed, it was Hughes's own strengths that enabled him to overcome his foibles, particularly his criteria and method for expansion. Hughes's refusal to take on debt as a means to finance expansion enabled Public Storage to withstand economic cycles that halted the expansion of his rivals. In turn, his ability to raise vast sums of capital allowed Public Storage to grow quickly and decisively outdistance competitors before they had an opportunity to mount a serious challenge. Hughes further disabled competitors by adhering to his strategy of targeting the 39 largest cities and then saturating the markets within the city by opening four to six self-storage centers at a time. By employing his saturation strategy, Hughes could rely on a single development office for each city, which reduced construction and operating costs and, of particular importance, allowed Hughes to justify the expense of advertising on television, something few of his rivals could afford. "There are a lot of benefits that come from concentrating properties in the major markets where we could have 15, 20, 60, 70, 90, 100 properties in a metropolitan area as opposed to having three," Lenkin explained in a November 1998 interview with *National Real Estate Investor.*

In mid-April 2000, Public Storage representatives flew to Seattle and initiated talks with Shurgard officials about combining the two companies. Shurgard management rejected the offer, to the chagrin of some of the company's shareholders, and withstood the unsolicited advances of its larger rival. Public Storage decided against a hostile takeover, and several weeks later reduced its stake in Shurgard.

Key Dates:

1972: The first Public Storage miniwarehouse opens in El Cajon, California.
1977: Bradley Wayne Hughes forms his first real estate limited partnership.
1986: PS Business Parks is organized as a division.
1995: Public Storage merges with Storage Equities, Inc.
1998: Storage Trust Realty is acquired.
2000: The company fails in its bid to acquire Shurgard Storage Centers.

Consolidation in the 1990s

Hughes exited the 1980s pursuing a goal of reaching 2,000 self-storage centers by 1994, an objective that called for the company to double in size. Economic conditions during the early 1990s, however, proved more conducive to consolidation than expansion. The primary source of Public Storage's cash for the previous two decades, the real estate limited partnership market, had nearly disappeared as Hughes celebrated his 20th year in the self-storage industry. In response, Hughes began organizing his properties into real estate investment trusts (REITs), an enticing financial arrangement for investors. Under the terms of a REIT, investors started collecting a 10 percent yield within the first year of the REIT's operation, rather than having to wait three years as was often the case in a limited partnership. Further, a REIT was forced to distribute at least 90 percent of its income to shareholders, thereby freeing itself from having to pay corporate taxes.

By 1995, Hughes's self-storage empire was organized into 17 REITs, including 21.3 percent of Storage Equities, Inc., the largest portion that was publicly traded. In the final move of the consolidation process, Public Storage acquired Storage Equities in 1995, creating the fourth largest publicly traded REIT in the United States, with $1.4 billion in market capitalization. Prior to the merger, Public Storage, as a private company, had served as a property manager and tenant adviser for Storage Equities. The merger doubled Public Storage's size, putting all of Hughes's private real estate assets into a public company, the new Public Storage.

By the end of the 1990s, Public Storage consisted of 1,200 self-storage centers with 635,000 spaces. Aside from expanding through internal means, Hughes expanded through acquisition, targeting several of his largest rivals. In 1998, Public Storage acquired a stake in Storage Trust Realty, then offered to buy the company. Storage Trust rejected the offer, but later agreed to the deal, forced to concede after relenting to shareholder pressure. In February 2000, Public Storage began investing heavily in Shurgard Storage Centers, the third largest self-storage operator, spending roughly $50 million to become the company's largest shareholder by early April. Shurgard's leader, Chuck Barbo, presumably anticipated Public Storage's intent—"We knew somebody was buying our stock and assumed it was

As Hughes approached his 70s and Public Storage celebrated its 30th anniversary, both the man and the company maintained a firm hold on the industry. Public Storage towered over its rivals, operating nearly 1,400 self-storage sites. As the company prepared for the future, with continued expansion on the agenda, it promised to maintain its impressive lead for years to come.

Principal Subsidiaries

PS Business Parks, Inc. (24%); Connecticut Storage Fund; Diversified Storage Venture Fund; PS Co-Investment Partners; PS Insurance Company, Ltd. (Bermuda); PS Orangeco Holdings, Inc.; PS Orangeco, Inc.; PS Partners IV, Ltd.; PS Partners V, Ltd.; PS Partners VI, Ltd.; PS Partners VIII, Ltd.; PS Partners, Ltd.; PSA Institutional Partners, L.P.; PSAC Development Partners, L.P.; Public Storage Institutional Fund; Public Storage Institutional Fund II; Public Storage Institutional Fund III; Public Storage Institutional Fund IV; Public Storage Pickup & Delivery, L.P.; Storage Trust Properties, L.P.

Principal Competitors

AMERCO; Shurgard Storage Centers, Inc.; Storage USA, Inc.

Further Reading

Heath, Tracy, "Public Storage Inc. Cashes in on Storing Your Stash," *National Real Estate Investor,* November 1998, p. 48.

Newman, Morris, "Public Storage: Mini-Storage Turns Landscape Orange," *Los Angeles Business Journal,* February 5, 1990, p. S40.

Paris, Ellen, "Rent-A-Closet," *Forbes,* June 15, 1987, p. 136.

Paulk, Michael, "Self-Storage Space Near Saturation," *Memphis Business Journal,* December 24, 1999, p. 3.

Proctor, Lisa Steen, "$800 Million Man Who Still Commutes," *Los Angeles Business Journal,* May 19, 1997, p. 25.

Rudnitsky, Howard, "The King of Self-Storage," *Forbes,* October 23, 1995, p. 126.

——, "Packing It In," *Institutional Investor,* September 2000, p. 211.

Sartor, Alexandra, "Dailey Thinking Inside the Box," *ADWEEK Western Edition,* July 17, 2000, p. 6.

"Shurgard Rebuffs Public Storage," *Puget Sound Business Journal,* May 5, 2000, p. 3.

Wilkinson, Stephanie, "Winning the War in the Mini-Storage Business," *PC Week,* December 1, 1987, p. 64.

Woolard, John, "Public Storage Locking into Business Due to Downturn," *Los Angeles Business Journal,* July 2, 2001, p. 27.

Wrubel, Robert, "California Cold Storage," *Financial World,* November 28, 1989, p. 76.

—Jeffrey L. Covell

Red Wing Pottery Sales, Inc.

1920 West Main St.
Red Wing, Minnesota 55066
U.S.A.
Telephone: (651) 388-3562
Toll Free: (800) 228-0174
Fax: (651) 388-8421
Web site: http://www.redwingpottery.com

Private Company
Incorporated: 1877 as Red Wing Stoneware Co.
Employees: 24
Sales: $1.5 million (2001 est.)
NAIC: 327112 Vitreous China, Fine Earthenware and
   Other Pottery Product Manufacturing; 442299 All
   Other Home Furnishings Stores

Red Wing Pottery Sales, Inc. is a retailer of dinnerware and art pottery located in a small Minnesota town along the Mississippi River. The store sells imported wares in a large showroom as well as two locally produced lines of pottery that replicate the stoneware produced in the town in the late 19th and early 20th centuries. The store also serves as a tourist attraction for collectors of the pottery that was produced in Red Wing before the factory closed in 1967.

The Red Wing name is best known for the stoneware industry that flourished in the town in the late 19th and early 20th centuries. At that time, the factories in Red Wing were among the largest producers of stoneware in the United States. The stoneware, dinnerware, and art pottery produced from 1877 to 1967 is now sought after by collectors across the nation. The Red Wing Collectors Society, formed in 1977, meets annually in Red Wing to support collection and research on the historic stoneware. Items in good condition can fetch high prices. The Red Wing Pottery Sales web site lists the value of a 10 to 20 gallon crock at $50 to $90, while a 50 to 60 gallon crock is worth as much as $1,500.

The 19th-Century Birth of a Prosperous Industry

Stoneware was first produced in Red Wing in 1861, when a German immigrant named John Paul moved to a farm near Red Wing. Paul had been a potter in Germany and was familiar with the processes needed to produce durable stoneware, including how to build a kiln, how to cool the stoneware carefully, and how to glaze the product in order to seal porous clay. Paul made stoneware for himself using the natural red clay along the Mississippi River, and later established a small pottery business in an old schoolhouse. However, Paul's production method, using only a potter's wheel and a wood-fired kiln, was not efficient enough to support a larger endeavor. Paul left the area soon after the Civil War.

William M. Philleo continued the pottery industry with a plant that operated from 1863 to 1880. Philleo improved on Paul's technique by mixing red clay with silica to produce tougher stoneware. However, the chemical makeup of the clay made it unfit for the usual glazing processes. Philleo was most successful with unglazed earthenware and architectural terra cotta. The factory burned down in 1870, but Philleo rebuilt and produced pickle jars, crocks, and churns under the name Red Wing Terra Cotta Works until 1880, when he moved the business to St. Paul.

Philleo's one-time foreman, David Hallum, had used his tenure at the Terra Cotta Works to experiment with various mixes of clay and firing techniques. In 1874 he started the Minnesota Pottery Co., using an improved production method. The new method made use of white clay, which was found under the layer of red clay and was able to withstand very high temperatures. Hallum would fire pots in a giant kiln for four days, and, when the temperature peaked, throw rock salt into the kiln. The chloride in the salt vaporized and the pure sodium adhered to the surface of the stoneware. The resulting product was hard, waterproof, and acidproof. The salt-glaze technique, with its characteristic "orange peel" finish, was used in Red Wing until the end of the century. However, Hallum was driven out of business when an Akron, Ohio competitor deliberately undersold him at half price over the course of two years.

The pottery industry gained its first solid footing in Red Wing in 1877. A group of local investors gathered enough capital to buy Hallum's assets and hired him to run the Red Wing Stoneware Co., which was the first of three large pottery factories to be founded in Red Wing in the late 1800s. The company, headed by businessman E.T. Howard, built a sizeable

Company Perspectives:

We are in business to provide pottery, dinnerware and gifts to our retail customers, and to provide one of the best visitor attractions in southeast Minnesota with our large retail salesroom and our pottery manufacturing operation.

factory making use of large up-draft kilns fired with wood and coal. Numerous fire holes in the bottom of the kiln allowed for control of the conditions inside, and a central chimney produced an immense draft. Many technological changes later adopted by other local companies originated at the Red Wing Stoneware Co., including colored markings on pots and the eventual replacement of the salt glaze with white zinc glaze.

The pottery industry prospered, taking advantage of the distribution system already in place for Red Wing's grain exporting business. Major products in the early days of production were crocks, jugs, churns, and water coolers. But the industry soon diversified into producing items such as mixing bowls, canning jars, baking pans, and chicken feeders. Because stoneware was the only viable option for storage in the 19th century, there was great demand for stoneware of all types.

In 1883 a second group of investors founded the Minnesota Stoneware Co. The two pottery companies maintained good relations, sharing some of the same stockholders and producing similar wares. The market was big enough for both factories to be successful, since the pottery industry had no large competitors in all of the Dakota territory and northern Wisconsin. After the first few months of operation, Minnesota Stoneware was producing 18,000 gallons of stoneware a week from 44 employees. The company was more efficient than its competition and made use of new down-draft kilns. When the Red Wing Stoneware factory burned down in 1884, it was rebuilt with the new type of kiln.

The third of the three early factories, North Star Stoneware Co., was incorporated in 1892. The company built a modern factory notable for its efficient production techniques and the use of molds, rather than the hand-turning technique, for almost all of its products. Unfortunately, an economic downturn in the early 1890s forced all three companies to reduce production and close down for extended periods. To cope with the situation, the companies in 1894 formed a marketing and sales cooperative, the Union Stoneware Co. North Star was the weakest link in the cooperative and was absorbed by the other two companies in 1896.

By 1900, the pottery industry was once again prosperous. The two existing companies had added more kilns and modernized their methods. The white "Bristol" glaze, making use of a chemical recipe that included large amounts of zinc oxide, replaced the salt-glaze method. The new glaze produced more uniform results and reduced the amount of stoneware that was destroyed during the firing process. Another innovation was in the area of stoneware decoration, as stamps were increasingly used in place of hand-painted designs. Efficiency was also improved by a growing reliance on molds rather than the hand-turning method. Molds could be used in several different ways. In the "jiggering" method, clay is placed in a plaster mold and a paddle comes down into the center of the mold, forcing the

clay into the desired shape. Another possibility was the slip-casting method, in which clay, reduced to a runny consistency, is poured into a mold and congeals on the inside surface. The excess clay is poured out once the deposit has reached the desired thickness.

Both pottery factories burned down in 1900 but were soon rebuilt and back in operation. After the fire, the affiliation between Minnesota Stoneware and Red Wing Stoneware increased and the division between their individual product lines, employees, and equipment blurred. In 1906 the companies merged completely and reincorporated as the Red Wing Union Stoneware Co. Around 1909 the distinctive red wing trademark and stamped oval company identification replaced the blue or black birch leaves and other markings found on earlier stoneware.

Changing Focus in the 20th Century

The 20th century saw the development of new, convenient household products, challenging the prosperity of the stoneware industry. After 1910 the industry lost market share due to the increasing use of glass and metal for canning and cooking. In the 1940s, the proliferation of plastic made stoneware storage a quaint relic of the past. A new direction was required if the industry was to survive.

Dinnerware and art pottery provided this new direction as the 20th century advanced. In the early 1930s the company discontinued the production of the traditional crocks, jars, and churns and began experimenting with new products. Rumrill art pottery, marketed by George Rumrill and designed by his wife, was sold from 1933 to 1938. In 1935 a line of dinnerware patterns, solid color place settings, and serving pieces known as Gypsy Trail was introduced. The next year the company dropped the old-fashioned reference to "stoneware" in its title and renamed itself Red Wing Potteries, Inc. Brightly colored, hand-painted products such as tea cups, relish trays, vases, pitchers, and ashtrays appeared in company catalogs. Fiesta Ware and Nokomis Ware became well-known product lines. The company developed a reputation for high-quality, hand-painted dinnerware. In 1967 it was the only producer of hand-painted dinnerware in the United States.

Foreign imports, using cheaper production methods, provided stiff competition, however. Postwar Japan became a major producer of dinnerware and pottery in the mid-1950s. Plastics were also becoming more widespread. Wage concessions kept the company alive for a time, but by 1967 the company had been in marginal operation for several years. The stage was set for the confrontation that would finally close the Red Wing factory.

In June 1967 the firm's production workers called a strike. They demanded higher pay, better benefits, and a pension plan. The firm's president, R.A. Gillmer, countered that such concessions would force the factory to close. The strike dragged on through the summer without a resolution. On August 24, after unsuccessful attempts at reaching an agreement, the firm's stockholders met and voted to close the factory.

The shutdown was a blow to the city of Red Wing. The pottery factory was the county's top taxpaying industry and one of the city's largest employers with more than 100 workers. But the impact was more than economic. Red Wing lost the industry

Key Dates:

1861: German immigrant John Paul makes the first pottery in Red Wing.
1877: Red Wing Stoneware Co. is incorporated.
1883: Minnesota Stoneware Co. is founded.
1892: North Star Stoneware Co. is founded.
1896: North Star is absorbed by the other two companies.
1906: The two remaining companies merge completely as the Red Wing Union Stoneware Co.
1936: Name change to Red Wing Potteries, Inc. reflects a shift in focus.
1967: Pottery factory closes after a strike.
1996: Replica salt-glazed pottery begins to be produced for the retail store.
2001: Firm now employs its own potters to produce salt-glazed pottery.

that had spread the city's name across the Midwest and formed its identity for 90 years.

Retail and Rebirth After 1967

Traces of the pottery industry managed to survive the shutdown of the factory. Company President R.A. Gillmer bought the significant assets of the Red Wing factory for $76,000, while the warehouse in St. Paul went to Tri-Investments Co. for $68,500. Gillmer formed the corporation Remnicha, Inc., named after a Dakota word for the Red Wing area. Remnicha continued to operate the factory outlet that had opened a year earlier. The store sold the remaining inventory of locally manufactured pottery and gradually introduced imported dinnerware, pottery, and gifts. Once liquidation of the Red Wing Pottery, Inc. assets was complete in 1970, Gillmer changed the firm's name from Remnicha to Red Wing Pottery Sales, Inc. By the mid-1970s, only a few items from the old factory, mostly remnants of unmatched sets, remained on the store's shelves. Instead the showroom was filled with pottery from around the world, including the brand names Pfaltzgraff, Fiesta, Noritake, and Johnson Bros.

But pottery production in Red Wing never died out completely. By the late 1990s, the showroom carried two locally produced lines of pottery. The first was made by Red Wing Stoneware Co., a firm founded in 1984 by potter John Falconer. Falconer bought the rights to the Red Wing name and technical records and began making replicas of the bristol-glazed Red Wing stoneware that was produced after about 1900. In 2001 the firm employed two potters who made hand-turned stoneware with a potter's wheel, as well as about ten other workers involved in making pottery from molds using the slip-casting method. The firm's products were sold locally to wholesale customers and could be purchased at the retail store adjoining the pottery factory on the edge of town. Red Wing Pottery Sales, Inc. added the locally produced stoneware to the imports on its shelves.

In 1996 Red Wing Pottery Sales, Inc. introduced its own line of locally manufactured pottery. Scott Gillmer, grandson of R.A. Gillmer, announced that the firm would produce salt-glazed stoneware, replicating the method used in the Red Wing factories up until about 1900. The company expressed its hope that the pottery would be both functional and valuable as a collector's item. In 2001 the firm employed two potters who hand-turned each piece on a potter's wheel and stamped it with the firm's logo, the date, and the potter's initials. The chance to once again see locally produced pottery in Red Wing added to the attractions of the town for tourists and collectors. Both pottery firms offered tours of the production facilities. Although overshadowed by the ghost of the industry that died in 1967, new locally manufactured pottery was once again gaining a foothold in Red Wing.

Further Reading

Gillmer, Sue, "A Brief History of the Pottery Industry in Red Wing," http://www.redwingcollectors.org/History.htm.

Johnson, Frederick L., *Goodhue County, Minnesota: A Narrative History*, Red Wing: Goodhue County Historical Society Press, 2000, pp. 99–101, 295–96.

"Potteries Salesroom Is Sold to Remnicha," *Red Wing Daily Republican Eagle*, February 9, 1968.

Tefft, Gary, and Bonnie Tefft, *Red Wing Potters & Their Wares*, Menomonee Falls, Wis.: Locust Enterprises, 1996, 200 p.

Viel, Lyndon C., *The Clay Giants*, Des Moines: Wallace-Homestead Book Co., 1977, 128 p.

"What Is Red Wing Stoneware?," http://www.msr.net/gsrw/page2.html.

—Sarah Ruth Lorenz

Royal Olympic Cruises
The intelligent way to see the world.

Royal Olympic Cruise Lines Inc.

Akti Miaouli 87
18538 Piraeus
Greece
Telephone: (+30) 1-429-1000
Fax: (+30) 1-429-0862
Web site: http://www.royalolympiccruises.com

Public Company
Incorporated: 1995
Sales: $128.8 million (2001)
Stock Exchanges: NASDAQ
Ticker Symbol: ROCLF
NAIC: 483112 Deep Sea Passenger Transportation;
    483114 Coastal and Great Lakes Passenger
    Transportation

Royal Olympic Cruise Lines Inc. (ROC) is a leading operator of cruise ships and tours in the Mediterranean Sea—the Greek company is the number one cruise ship operator in the eastern Mediterranean market with a market share of about 55 percent, and the second largest in the entire Mediterranean market with more than 9 percent of the total market. The company owns and operates a fleet of eight cruise ships for overnight cruises, and an additional ship used for one-day cruises. Most of the company's business takes place during the months of March through November, during which time the company concentrates on the Eastern Mediterranean, particularly destinations to the Greek islands and neighboring countries. During the December to April off-season, ROC turns to the North and South American markets, operating two cruise ships to such destinations as the Amazon and Orinoco Rivers. ROC also charters out one of its ships to another tour operator during the winter season. Although most of the company's fleet is made up of secondhand vessels, some of which date back to the late 1950s and early 1960s, ROC has begun a fleet expansion at the dawn of the 21st century, taking delivery of two high-speed cruise ships, capable of top speeds up to 33 knots, in 2000 and 2002. Like the rest of the company's fleet, the new vessels are relatively small, offering space for up to 800 passen-

gers. All of the company's vessels sail under the Greek flag. The company is traded on the NASDAQ stock exchange, but is majority held by ROC Holdings, which itself is jointly owned by the founding Potamianos family and Cyprus tour and cruise operator Louis Tourist Agency.

Cruising into the 1950s

Royal Olympic Cruise Lines was created in 1995 following the merger of two well-established, family-owned cruise ship operators, Epirotiki and Sun Line. Both companies had begun cruise operations in the Greek islands during the 1950s, at a time when Greece began developing itself as a modern tourist destination in the postwar era. Epirotiki's operations stretched back to 1830, when it was founded as a shipping company by George Potamianos, making it one of the world's oldest continuously operating shipping lines. Epirotiki went on to develop a leading position in the Greek cargo and passenger transportation trade, and began operating cruises among the Greek islands in the 1930s. In the 1950s, Potamianos's grandson, Anastassios, took over the direction of the company and focused it entirely on the cruise ship market, which was then undergoing a transformation from being a privilege of the wealthy to becoming a common vacation option affordable to the larger, middle-class traveling public.

Epirotiki partnered with the Hellenic National Tourist Office to launch the first Aegean Sea cruises in 1954. In the 1960s, Epirotiki began expanding its offerings, adding a number of Caribbean destinations, enabling the company to complement the off-season in Greece with winter itineraries elsewhere. The company tapped into the growing American tourism market, serving ports in Florida, Texas, and elsewhere. Epirotiki also became one of the first cruise ship companies to begin cruise services to Alaska.

By the end of the 1980s, Epirotiki, now headed by the great-grandsons of the company's founder, brothers Andreas and George Potamianos, was operating a fleet of 12 vessels, most of which were relatively small-sized, with its largest ship offering passenger capacity of only some 800 passengers. As competitors, including fast-rising Carnival Cruise Lines, began adding

Company Perspectives:

Welcome Aboard: From classical treasures to exotic grandeur, Royal Olympic presents innovative itineraries to the Greek Isles, Eastern and Western Europe, Central and South America, and the Caribbean. We invite you to take a look at why Royal Olympic is different from the rest and why you should sail with us on your next vacation.

larger and larger ships, Epirotiki remained committed to its smaller-size format, emphasizing more personalized service than that available on the larger cruise liners.

The end of the 1980s and the beginning of the 1990s brought choppy waters for Epirotiki, however. Fears of terrorism cut deeply into the tourist market, and particularly scared passengers off of cruise ships in the late 1980s. In 1988, one of the company's cruise ships, the *Jupiter,* was hit by a freighter near the company's Piraeus home port, sinking the *Jupiter* and causing the drowning deaths of two passengers. The following year, a passenger was killed by an unsecured hatch on another cruise ship, the *Neptune*; that year, as well, another boat, the *Odysseus,* was forced to harbor in Portugal after it began taking on water. In 1991, two more ships in Epirotiki's fleet were out of commission, after an explosion on the company's flagship, the *Pegasus,* in the Venice harbor, and the sinking of another ship, the *Oceanos,* off the South African coast. The latter disaster was followed by severe criticism of the company, specifically complaints that the ship's captain and crew had abandoned the ship ahead of its passengers. Nonetheless, all of the passengers aboard were safely rescued.

Epirotiki fought back by rebuilding its fleet, debuting four newly acquired ships for the 1992 season, including two vessels with capacity of more than 700 vessels. By 1993, however, the company seemed unable to resist the prevailing mood of consolidation sweeping the cruise ship industry—which was hard hit again by the global recession and by the collapse of the tourist industry following the outbreak of the Persian Gulf War. While rumors suggested that Epirotiki would pursue a marriage with domestic rival Sun Line, the company instead turned toward a partnership with industry heavyweight Carnival Cruise Lines.

Merging to Mediterranean Leadership in the 1990s

In 1993, Carnival agreed to sell one of its ships to Epirotiki in exchange for a 17 percent stake in the Greek company. That agreement was meant as the first phase of a multistep transaction that would eventually give control of Epirotiki to Carnival. In 1994, the two companies carried out the second phase of the deal, transferring a second Carnival vessel to Epirotiki, and bringing Carnival's shareholder's position up to 43 percent. At that point, Epirotiki restructured its management, appointing the Potamianos brothers cochairmen, and bringing in a new CEO, Pam Conover, who had formerly headed up Citicorp's shipping operations. But Conover's management style quickly clashed with that of the Potamianos family. Conover was briefly removed from her position at Epirotiki, but at the beginning of 1995, Carnival stepped up its position, increasing its holding to 49

percent. Although 51 percent remained with Epirotiki, a significant part of that stake was in fact held by Carnival ally Paris Katsoufis, a Greek-born American citizen, who now took on the position as chairman of the board—relegating the Potamianos brothers to the honorary positions of chairman emeriti.

By mid-1995, however, the Carnival-Epirotiki construction had collapsed in the face of Greek cabotage rules. These stated that only ships flying the Greek flags were allowed to provide full-scale operations among the Greek islands. Moreover, in order to qualify to fly the Greek flag, cruise ships must be significantly owned by Greek citizens and staffed by Greek sailors. When the government refused to recognize Katsoufis's Greek citizenship, the Potamianos family once again regained control of their company.

Instead, in August 1995, Epirotiki agreed to merge its operations with its chief rival, Sun Line, creating a new company, Royal Olympic Cruise Lines, or ROC. Sun Line was another family-owned company, founded in 1958 by Charalambos and Isabella Keusseoglou as a luxury cruise operator on the Aegean Sea. Like Epirotiki, Sun Line had expanded beyond Greece in the 1960s, adding Caribbean destinations. In 1975, Sun Line added the South American continent, with trips to Mayan sites, then added cruises up the Amazon River in the 1980s. Sun Line remained a far smaller operation than Epirotiki, with just three cruise ships in operation at the time of the ROC merger.

Operated as a joint venture between the two families, ROC initially maintained its two brand names, with Sun Line oriented toward a more affluent, older, and primarily American customer base, and Epirotiki attracting a younger, more diversified passenger list. In 1997, ROC began planning a public offering in part to prepare the company for the expected end of cabotage rules in 1999. The company restructured its holdings, creating a new entity, Royal Olympic Cruise Lines, and listed on the NASDAQ stock exchange in 1998, raising some $91 million. The founding families nonetheless retained a controlling share of more than 51 percent in the company through their privately held ROC Holdings vehicle. The company then launched a new drive to add to its fleet, acquiring two former North Atlantic ocean lines. The company also announced that it had ordered—for the first time—two "newbuild" cruise ships from Germany's Blohn & Voss shipyards. The new ships were designed as fast cruise ships, with cruising speeds of 27 knots and top speeds up to 33 knots.

By 1999, however, ROC was once again in trouble, as the war in nearby Kosovo caused a collapse in the Greek tourism market. The floundering company, which saw its stock price drop from a high of $15 per share to just $2 per share, was once again the center of takeover interest by other cruise operators eager to break into the Greek cruise market. By the end of the year, ROC had found its suitor, in the form of Cyprus-based Louis Cruise Lines, which acquired 70 percent of ROC Holdings—including the Keusseoglou family's 50 percent stake—which gave it a 40 percent share of the ROC cruise line operation. Louis immediately injected some $5 million in cash to shore up ROC's operation.

Things started looking up for ROC again at the beginning of the 21st century, as it took delivery on the first of its new cruise

<table>
<tr><td colspan="2">Key Dates:</td></tr>
</table>

Key Dates:

1830: Epirotiki is founded by George Potamianos as a cargo and passenger shipping company in Greece.

1930s: Epirotiki begins operating a cruise liner service.

1954: Epirotiki focuses operations on cruise services and begins cruise liner operations on the Aegean Sea.

1958: Sun Lines is founded as a luxury cruise operator on the Aegean Sea by Charalambos and Isabella Keusseoglou.

1994: Carnival Cruise Lines gains a controlling share of Epirotiki.

1995: The Potamianos family regains control of Epirotiki and forms the Royal Olympic Cruise (ROC) joint venture with Sun Line.

1998: Royal Olympic Cruise Lines goes public with a listing on the NASDAQ stock exchange.

1999: Louis Cruise Lines of Cyprus acquires a controlling stake in ROC.

2000: ROC takes delivery of its first high-speed cruise ship, *Olympic Voyager.*

2002: ROC takes delivery of its second high-speed cruise ship, *Olympic Explorer*; the Potamianos family rebuilds its stake in the company to 50 percent.

ships in 2000. The *Olympic Voyager* gave the company a new, four-star brand. The vessel's industry-leading speed also allowed ROC to offer more extensive itineraries, enabling the company to pack in additional port stops to please the traveling public. ROC looked forward to expanding its Olympic brand with the delivery of the *Voyager*'s sister ship, to be named *Explorer* and scheduled to set sail in May 2001. Delivery of that ship, however, was delayed, as ROC and Blohn & Voss began a dispute over possible defects in the *Explorer*'s construction. The *Explorer* at last set sail in June 2002 and was greeted enthusiastically by the tourist industry. The new vessels were featured at the center of the company's itinerary plans for the 2002–03 season. The company was especially eager to introduce the new, faster ships to the American markets, where the greater distances between port destinations had long been a stumbling block for expanded cruise itineraries.

The Potamianos family, which had retained a 15 percent share of the company indirectly through a holding in Louis, returned to a more prominent position in ROC's shareholding in 2002, when it bought back a stake in ROC from Louis. That transaction gave both the Potamianos family and their Cyprus-based partner a 50 percent stake in the company. With more than 170 years of shipping history, Royal Olympic Cruise Lines remained a force in its Mediterranean base, and a growing presence in the worldwide cruise industry.

Principal Subsidiaries

Athena 2004 S.A. (Liberia; 80%); Bare Boat Chartering Company; Caroline Shipping Inc. (Liberia); East Ocean Shipping Corporation (Liberia; 80%); Eurocroisieres Sarl (France); Freewind Shipping Company (Liberia; 80%); Gallery Navigation Ltd. (Liberia); Grammon S.A.; Icarus Travel Limited (U.K.); Ocean Quest Sea Carriers Ltd. (Liberia; 80%); Olympic World Cruises Inc. (Liberia; 80%); ROC Lines Limited (U.K.); RO Cruises, Inc. (U.S.A.); Royal Olympic Cruises Ltd. (Liberia; 80%); Royal World Cruises Inc. (Liberia; 80%); Simpson Navigation Ltd. (Liberia; 80%); Solar Navigation Corporation (Liberia; 80%); Valentine Oceanic Trading Inc. (Liberia).

Principal Competitors

TUI AG; Carlson Companies Inc.; My Travel Group PLC; Carnival Corporation; Hapag-Lloyd AG; Royal Caribbean Cruises Ltd.; P and O Australia Ltd.; Societe Louis-Dreyfus et Cie; Seabourn Cruise Line; Norwegian Cruise Line Ltd.; NCL Holding ASA; Wan Hai Lines Company Inc.; Stena Line Scandinavia AB; Bakri Trading Co.; Shipping Corporation of India Ltd.; Holland America Line Westours Inc.; Korea Line Corp.; Sovkomflot Joint Stock Shipping Co.; China Shipping Development Company Ltd.; Scandlines Deutschland GmbH; Viking Line Ab; Andrew Weir and Co. Ltd.

Further Reading

Blum, Ernest, "High-Speed Olympic Voyager to Chart New Waters," *Travel Weekly,* August 3, 2000, p. C4.

"Cyprus' Louis Cruise Buys Stake in Royal Olympic," *Reuters,* October 29, 1999.

Lincoln, Lori, "Sun Line, Epirotiki Merge with Eye to Growth," *Travel Weekly,* October 16, 1995, p. 15.

Lowry, Nigel, "Cruise: Louis Snares Royal Olympic," *Lloyd's List,* October 22, 1999.

——, "Lifeline for Royal Olympic," *Lloyd's List,* November 11, 1999.

"Royal Olympic Charts Course with New Voyages: Aboard Olympia Explorer, Olympia Voyager," *Travel Weekly,* December 3, 2001, p. C6.

"Royal Olympic Expands," *Travel Trade Gazette UK & Ireland,* February 26, 2001, p. 26.

Savvides, Nick, "Greek Shipping Falls to US Methods," *European,* February 10, 1995, p. 32.

Tobin, Rebecca, "After Delays, Olympia Explorer Makes Debut," *Travel Weekly,* June 3, 2002, p. C8.

—M.L. Cohen

Schweitzer-Mauduit International, Inc.

100 North Point Center East, Suite 600
Alpharetta, Georgia 30022
U.S.A.
Telephone: (770) 569-4200
Toll Free: (800) 514-0186
Fax: (770) 569-4209
Web site: http://www.schweitzer-mauduit.com

Public Company
Incorporated: 1995
Employees: 3,359
Sales: $499.50 million (2001)
Stock Exchanges: New York
Ticker Symbol: SWM
NAIC: 322121 Paper (Except Newsprint) Mills; 339944
Carbon Paper and Inked Ribbon Manufacturing

Schweitzer-Mauduit International, Inc. is the world's largest producer of the various types of paper used in the manufacture of cigarettes. Roughly 10 percent of Schweitzer-Mauduit's business is derived from the manufacture of specialty paper products, including lightweight printing and writing papers, coated papers for packaging and labeling applications, and paper used for a variety of applications, ranging from business forms to drinking straw wrap. The company operates eight mills located in the United States, France, and Brazil. Sales and administrative offices are maintained in the United States, France, Hong Kong, Brazil, and Spain. Schweitzer-Mauduit's cigarette, plug wrap, and tipping paper is used in approximately 25 percent of all the cigarettes produced in the world. The company serves roughly 200 customers in more than 90 countries.

Origins As a Family Business

Schweitzer-Mauduit began not as a manufacturer but as an importer. The Georgia-based company, which ranked as the preeminent cigarette paper producer at the end of the 20th century, was founded at the beginning of the century in New Jersey. In 1908, a family-run business named Peter J. Schweit-

zer first started importing cigarette paper from France to the United States, marking the firm's entry into an industry it would later dominate. The Schweitzer family business did not assume the role of manufacturer until 14 years after its founding, but once it did the company slipped into its role as a specialty paper producer with the precision required for the demands of the job.

As the company aggrandized its manufacturing operations through acquisitions and plant expansions, it focused its efforts on creating superior grades of cigarette paper. There were three principal types of paper used in cigarettes—plug wrap paper, cigarette paper, and tipping paper—each serving a distinct purpose in the function of a cigarette. Plug wrap formed the outer layer of the cigarette filter, functioning as a restrainer that held the filter materials in a cylindrical form. Cigarette paper constituted the body of the cigarette, wrapping the column of tobacco in the cigarette. The manufacture of cigarette paper represented an engineering feat, requiring highly specific tolerances be met in regard to a host of factors, including weight, porosity (a measure of air flow permeability), opacity, tensile strength, texture, and burn rate. Tipping paper joined the filter to the tobacco column, its careful production critical to the distinctive finished appearance of a cigarette. To engender a proper finished appearance, tipping paper had to be printable and glueable at high speeds.

Schweitzer-Mauduit's development during the 20th century was fueled through acquisitions. The company's manufacturing activities commenced in 1922, when the Schweitzer family acquired a French manufacturer named Papeteries de Malaucene. The acquisition gave the company what would become its major source of tipping paper and cigarette paper. Located near Avignon, Papeteries de Malaucene began manufacturing paper in the mid-16th century, adding considerable experience to the 14-year-old Schweitzer family business. Next, the Schweitzers developed a manufacturing presence in the United States, acquiring a mill in New Jersey in 1940. Located in Spotswood, the mill became a chief source of cigarette paper for Schweitzer-Mauduit.

Post-World War II Expansion

A decade after the Spotswood acquisition, the Schweitzer family completed a series of acquisitions in what would be its

Company Perspectives:

Schweitzer-Mauduit International, Inc. is a diversified producer of premium specialty papers and the world's largest supplier of fine papers to the tobacco industry. Schweitzer-Mauduit conducts business in over 90 countries and employs approximately 3,500 people worldwide, with operations in the United States, France, Brazil and Canada.

last years of ownership. In 1950, the company acquired three mills in western Massachusetts. The following year, the Schweitzers acquired half its namesake, purchasing Papeteries de Mauduit. Located in Quimperle, in western France, the manufacturing facility eventually became the largest cigarette paper mill in the world. In 1955, the company acquired a piece of American history when it purchased the Ancram mill in northern New York. Originally an iron works established in 1743, the facility was used to make a chain-link blockade of the Hudson River during the Revolutionary War. The site, later in Schweitzer-Mauduit's development, became the center of the company's reconstituted tobacco wrapper and binder business.

Reconstituted tobacco represented Schweitzer-Mauduit's other facet of tobacco-related business. By the end of the 20th century, the company manufactured reconstituted tobacco in two forms: leaf, and wrapper and binder. Reconstituted leaf was used by cigarette manufacturers as a filler to blend with virgin tobacco to achieve particular taste characteristics and other attributes. Wrapper and binder were used in the manufacture of machine-made cigars. Binder, like cigarette paper, functioned as a restrainer, holding the tobacco leaves in a cylindrical shape during the production process. Wrapper was used to cover the outside of the cigar, giving it a uniform, finished appearance. Schweitzer-Mauduit conducted its reconstituted wrapper and binder production in the United States and its reconstituted leaf production in France.

After a half-century of control, the Schweitzer family relinquished ownership of its business in the late 1950s. The specialty paper-making assets built up over decades had become attractive enough to draw the interest of a much larger suitor, Kimberly-Clark Corporation, the giant paper products company that marketed Kleenex. The Irving, Texas-based corporation acquired the Schweitzers' business in 1957. Under the control of Kimberly-Clark, expansion continued, resuming in 1963 when the company established Le Tabac Reconstitue, later to become LTR Industries. Located in Spay, in north-central France, LTR Industries became Schweitzer-Mauduit's chief source of reconstituted leaf products, eventually developing into the world's largest independent producer of such products. Three years after establishing LTR Industries, Kimberly-Clark strengthened its tipping paper capabilities by constructing the Greylock Mill, located in Lee, Massachusetts, near the three mills acquired in 1950.

1995 Spinoff

Independence returned to Schweitzer-Mauduit after a nearly 40-year absence. For strategic reasons, Kimberly-Clark's man-agement decided to divest Kimberly-Clark Specialty Products, its U.S., Canadian, and French assets that manufactured tobacco-related papers and other specialty paper products. The decision led to the August 1995 incorporation of Schweitzer-Mauduit as a wholly owned subsidiary of Kimberly-Clark. Wayne H. Deitrich, a Kimberly-Clark senior executive for seven years, was appointed the subsidiary's chief executive officer. At the end of November, Kimberly-Clark distributed to its stockholders all of the common stock of the Schweitzer-Mauduit subsidiary. The distribution of stock constituted the Schweitzer-Mauduit spinoff as an independent, publicly traded company. Immediately after the spinoff, Deitrich was elected chairman of Schweitzer-Mauduit.

Deitrich and his fellow executives embraced independence. From their perspective, Schweitzer-Mauduit, as a separate entity, could react more nimbly to customer demands than it could have when the company was part of a much larger concern with many nontobacco interests. What Schweitzer-Mauduit's management took charge of in the last weeks of 1995 was a $463 million concern with its U.S. and corporate headquarters based in Alpharetta, Georgia. Physically, the company controlled the manufacturing facilities acquired during the Schweitzer family's ownership. Schweitzer-Mauduit operated three manufacturing centers in the United States, including facilities in Lee, Massachusetts; Ancram, New York; and Spotswood, New Jersey. The company also owned a Canadian subsidiary in Winkler, Manitoba. Schweitzer-Mauduit's French properties included Papeteries de Mauduit, Papeteries de Malaucene, and LTR Industries. With these properties as its foundation, the company prepared for growth, promising to complete acquisitions. A company executive, in a March 1996 interview with *World Tobacco,* explained: "We plan to use our strong cash flow to make new investments and develop our existing capabilities, both in terms of product development and service enhancements, and in the area of increasing our capacity."

The company delivered on its promise of aggressive expansion. During its first two years of independence, Schweitzer-Mauduit invested $87.3 million in production capacity and quality improvements, including a new long-fiber-paper machine that began operating in March 1997 and the replacement of Kimberly-Clark's computer systems with its own state-of-the-art integrated computer system. By the end of 1997, the company controlled 21 percent of the global market for cigarette paper, possessing the capability of producing one-quarter million metric tons of cigarette paper, plug wrap paper, tipping paper, and reconstituted tobacco annually.

Schweitzer-Mauduit celebrated its 100th anniversary by completing two important acquisitions, one of which marked the company's entrance into a new, massive market. In February 1998, the company completed the $62 million acquisition of Companhia Industrial de Papel Pirahy (Pirahy), the only cigarette paper producer in Brazil. With revenues of $75 million in 1997, Pirahy controlled roughly half of the South American market for cigarette paper, boasting an annual paper capacity of 63,000 metric tons. Deitrich planned to use Pirahy as a manufacturing springboard to facilitate Schweitzer-Mauduit's expansion throughout South America and into Latin America. During the year, the company also bolstered its manufacturing operations in France by purchasing Ingefico, S.A., including its pulp

---

Key Dates:

1908: Cigarette paper importer Peter J. Schweitzer is founded in New Jersey.
1922: Papeteries de Malaucene is acquired.
1940: Spotswood, New Jersey, mill is acquired.
1950: Several mills in western Massachusetts are acquired.
1957: Schweitzer family business is acquired by Kimberly-Clark Corp.
1963: LTR Industries is established.
1995: Kimberly-Clark spins off its tobacco-related specialty papers business, creating Schweitzer-Mauduit International Inc.
1998: Brazilian manufacturer Companhia Industrial de Papel Pirahy is acquired.
2002: Expansion project at LTR Industries begins.

---

and specialty paper subsidiaries Groupe SAPAM and Papeteries de la Moulasse. Ingefico's mills in Saint Girons had been active in the tobacco-related papers industry since 1900, marketing its products under the Job Cigarette Paper brand. Ingefico, which was organized as a Schweitzer-Mauduit subsidiary named Papeteries de Saint-Girons, possessed an annual production capacity of 14,000 metric tons of paper and 6,000 metric tons of pulp. Together, the two acquisitions appreciably affected Schweitzer-Mauduit's global stature. By the time the acquisitions were completed, the company controlled an estimated 27 percent of the world cigarette paper market, compared with its 21 percent share prior to the French and Brazilian acquisitions.

Before and immediately after the acquisitions, Schweitzer-Mauduit suffered financially, a prelude to more serious problems that would surface at the decade's end. Slower sales, higher taxes in France, and the costly process of installing its own integrated computer system contributed to lackluster financial performance. Between November 1997 and July 1998, the company's stock value depreciated by more than 40 percent, falling to its lowest point since the spinoff from Kimberly-Clark.

By the beginning of the 21st century, the problems had become more serious, as Schweitzer-Mauduit found itself combating a global oversupply of tobacco-related papers. Supply exceeded demand, inhibiting the company's ability to offset rising production costs by raising its prices. Aside from battling with a glutted global market, Schweitzer-Mauduit also faced localized problems. Brazil's economy was in ruins during the early years of the 21st century, forcing a response from Schweitzer-Mauduit's management. In mid-2001, the company announced a plan to restructure its Brazilian operations primarily because of energy problems. After the Brazilian government ordered a 25 percent reduction in electricity consumption by the paper industry, Schweitzer-Mauduit announced that it was ceasing production of uncoated printing and writing papers in Brazil. The business, which generated $25 million in sales in 2000, represented Schweitzer-Mauduit's least profitable product line in Brazil. The manufacture of the specialty papers also used the largest amount of electricity.

As Schweitzer-Mauduit prepared for the future, some comfort could be taken from indications that market conditions were improving. By the end of 2001, the company's quarter-to-quarter profitability began to show signs of vitality, returning to a pattern of consecutive increases. Entering 2002, the company's management was confident enough to announce plans for expansion. Deitrich and his team announced in April 2002 that they were adding a third reconstituted tobacco leaf production line at LTR Industries. The $59.2 million project, scheduled to be completed in early 2004, was expected to add additional annual capacity of 33,000 metric tons to its operations in Spay, France, giving it a total annual capacity of 80,000 metric tons. While construction progressed with the expansion project, Deitrich pressed ahead, confident that Schweitzer-Mauduit would remain the dominant player in the industry for years to come.

Principal Subsidiaries

Schweitzer-Mauduit Canada, Inc.; Schweitzer-Mauduit Spain, S.L.; Schweitzer-Mauduit France S.A.R.L.; LTR Industries S.A. (France; 72%); Papeteries de Mauduit S.A.S. (France); Papeteries de Malaucene S.A.S. (France); Papeteries de Saint-Girons S.A.S. (France); Schweitzer-Mauduit do Brasil S.A. (99%).

Principal Competitors

Wattens; Miquel y Costas; Julius Glatz GmbH; Cartieira Del Maglio S.p.A.

Further Reading

Bicker, Rachel, "Kings of the Mill," *World Tobacco,* March 1998, p. 15.
"New Type of Tobacco Introduced," *Pulp & Paper,* March 2000, p. 22.
"Quest for Quality As Group Goes It Alone," *World Tobacco,* March 1996, p. 19.
"Schweitzer-Mauduit Announces Fourth Quarter and 2000 Results and Quarterly Dividend," *123Jump,* April 27, 2001.
"Schweitzer-Mauduit International Inc.," *Market News Publishing,* July 26, 2001.
"Schweitzer-Mauduit International Inc.," *Market News Publishing,* April 26, 2002.
"Schweitzer-Mauduit Makes Investment," *Pulp & Paper,* February 1998, p. 25.
Walmac, Amanda, "Despite the Tobacco Firms' Woes, These Three May Return Up to 41%," *Money,* July 1996, p. 60.

—Jeffrey L. Covell

Sensient Technologies Corporation

777 East Wisconsin Avenue
Milwaukee, Wisconsin 53202-5304
U.S.A.
Telephone: (414) 271-6755
Toll Free: (800) 558-9892
Fax: (414) 347-3785
Web site: http://www.sensient-tech.com

Public Company
Incorporated: 1882 as Meadow Springs Distillery Co.
Employees: 3,454
Sales: $816.9 million (2001)
Stock Exchanges: New York
Ticker Symbol: SXT
NAIC: 311423 Dried and Dehydrated Food
    Manufacturing; 311942 Spice and Extract
    Manufacturing; 325131 Inorganic Dye and Pigment
    Manufacturing; 325132 Synthetic Organic Dye and
    Pigment Manufacturing; 325199 All Other Basic
    Organic Chemical Manufacturing

Sensient Technologies Corporation is a major international manufacturer and supplier of colors, flavors, fragrances, and other specialty ingredients used in the production of foods and beverages, cosmetics, pharmaceuticals, and personal care and household products. The company also produces ink-jet inks, chemicals for laser printing, and dehydrated vegetables as ingredients for food processors. Sensient's Flavors & Fragrances Group operates principally through two subsidiaries, Sensient Flavors Inc. and Rogers Foods, Inc., while a subsidiary called Warner-Jenkinson Company, Inc. heads up the Color Group. The company operates in more than 60 countries and generates more than half of its revenues outside the United States.

Sensient's history is marked by a series of shifts in focus. The firm was founded in the late 19th century as a distillery and then began concentrating on yeast—a byproduct of the distilling process—during Prohibition. Beginning in the early 1960s the company—by then known as Universal Foods Corpora-

tion—expanded into a variety of other food businesses, including soft-drink bottling, cheese, snack foods, and frozen foods. In the mid-1980s Universal entered the food color and flavor business. During the next decade, most of the food businesses were jettisoned, while the company put increasing emphasis on its ingredients operations. After the latter business was built up further through a string of acquisitions in the mid- to late 1990s, the firm's latest transformation came to a climax in the early 21st century when the yeast business was sold off and the Sensient Technologies name was adopted.

Distillery Beginnings

Meadow Springs Distillery Co., the earliest incarnation of Sensient Technologies, was founded in December 1882 by three Milwaukeans: Leopold Wirth, Gustav Niemeier, and Henry Koch, Jr. At the company's first stockholders' meeting the following month, Wirth was elected to the company's presidency, Niemeier became vice-president, and Koch secretary-treasurer. Wirth was a well-known merchant in Milwaukee, dealing in horses, furs, and a variety of other items. His entry into the distillery business probably came about as a result of one of his sideline business ventures. Wirth would purchase spent grain from area distillers, use it to fatten up thin, cheaply bought cattle, then sell the cattle at a sizeable profit. Opening a distillery was a way of compacting this operation, while at the same time tapping into the growing whiskey market. The major financial backer of Meadow Springs was Adolph C. Zinn, a local financier. William Bergenthal, the owner of a distillery and a successful outlet—the Wm. Bergenthal Wholesale Liquor Company—was named to manage day-to-day operations at the distillery.

Meadow Springs sold its first barrel of whiskey on July 5, 1883. The whiskey was produced at Bergenthal's distillery. A month later, the company bought its first piece of property, a choice plot at the bottom of a hill in the Menomonee Valley. To the one building that already stood on the property, Wirth added a grain elevator, a railroad siding, and a pipeline for the spent grain. In September, Koch resigned, and Bergenthal became the company's secretary, retaining his duties as general manager. About a week later, Wirth was forced to resign as president, when a number of surprise billings and overdue claims arrived from out of town, including writs of attachment for $2,000 from the Chicago Distilling Company, and debt notices from Philip D. Armour & Co., the Chicago packing firm. A stockholder and local cattle dealer named Henry Heilbronner was elected president.

In 1886, August Bergenthal, William's brother, replaced Niemeier as vice-president of Meadow Springs. A year later, both brothers were elected to the board of directors. At the same meeting, Levi Tabor was named president. In March of that year, however, both Tabor and William Bergenthal resigned during a dispute over a company purchase. Tabor was succeeded as president by August Grau, vice-president of the Bergenthal company and a recently elected director of Meadow Springs. August Bergenthal became secretary and treasurer. Grau would remain president of the company for 35 years. In May 1887, the name of the company was changed to National Distilling Company. Among the changes that accompanied the renaming of the firm was the addition of a filtering press for squeezing yeast. The primary line of yeast the company produced was called Red Star.

National Distilling began to expand in the 1890s. The company opened yeast distribution branches in several cities during this period, including Duluth, Chicago, Detroit, and Cleveland. National's net earnings for 1894 were over $112,000. In 1903 the company established a second manufacturing plant on the site of the recently purchased local DuPont Chemical Company facility.

Prohibition Era Shift to Yeast As Main Product

By 1917, National was operating over 30 yeast branches throughout the region, with major outlets in Louisville, Kansas City, and Detroit. In 1917 the government passed a measure outlawing the use of grains to make liquor, meaning that liquor could be sold but not manufactured. Two years later, the 18th Amendment to the Constitution created Prohibition. National responded by changing its name once again, this time to the name of its most important nonalcoholic product. It became Red Star Yeast and Products Company.

During Prohibition, Red Star focused increasingly on yeast production and distribution. John Wiedring, the company's laboratory chief, introduced a new process for making yeast by aeration in 1918. By 1921, Red Star was operating 50 branches throughout the eastern half of the United States. The company's yeast was marketed as a health food, and sales were brisk. In July 1922, new leadership was needed when Grau and Bergenthal died suddenly within a few weeks of each other. The presidency was

assumed by Bruno Bergenthal, August's son. The company grew rapidly through the remainder of the 1920s. Its 27th Street and Cudahy manufacturing facilities were expanded and a higher quality drier was purchased during that time.

The repeal of Prohibition in 1933 created a dilemma for Red Star. The company needed to decide whether to reenter the liquor distilling business or to continue to concentrate on yeast production. Beer and gin were once again brought into production in 1933. By 1937, however, Red Star had pretty much committed to yeast and vinegar as its main products. Factors leading to this shift in direction included the bottoming out of the gin market in 1935, and a legal quarrel over the use of the National Distilling name waged against the National Distillers Products Corporation of New York. With its gin department already shut down, Red Star gave up its right to the National brand name for a settlement of about $20,000.

In 1938, a policy disagreement led to Bergenthal's resignation. He was replaced as president by Charles Wirth, Jr., grandson of Leopold Wirth, one of the company's founders. Bergenthal stayed on as chairman of the board until his retirement in 1940. During World War II, the government became interested in the nutritional qualities of yeast. Because active dry yeast was less perishable than earlier forms, it was considered an excellent food item for a mobilized Army. Therefore, huge amounts of the yeast were ordered from Red Star and other companies by the government to meet the baking needs of the growing military. When the war ended, Red Star began looking for ways to diversify its product line with related baking items. The company experimented for a short time with a frozen egg department, but this venture proved to be too risky and was quickly aborted.

Charles Wirth, Jr., died of a heart attack in 1950. He was succeeded as Red Star president by his cousin, Russell Wirth. Under Russell Wirth, Red Star diversified quite a bit within the realm of yeast products. During the 1950s, the variety of products the company was marketing included packaged yeast for rolls and mixes, consumer yeast, feed yeast for livestock, nutritional yeast for cereal and baby food, and, of course, compressed and dry yeast cakes for bakers. Pillsbury, using millions of packages of yeast supplied by Red Star, was the leader among companies marketing hot roll mixes, which enjoyed a period of great popularity during the 1950s. Because of its ability to anticipate the needs of the yeast market, and to tailor its products accordingly, Red Star was one of only five to emerge among major yeast producers in the country, from a group of about 24 that existed in the 1930s.

In 1951, Red Star opened a plant in New Orleans, enabling the company to better serve the southern market, as well as reduce the cost of transporting molasses from that region. Several acquisitions in the mid-1950s elevated Red Star to the status of nationwide yeast distributors. These included the purchases of Food Industry Corporation in Dallas, San Francisco's Consumer's Yeast Corporation, and the Peerless Yeast Company, also located in California. The company went international in the 1950s as well. A yeast production plant was opened in Cuba. Red Star had interests of up to 25 percent in yeast operations in Peru, the Philippines, Iran, Korea, and elsewhere. Agreements for technical services were entered in Guatemala and Colombia. Later in the 1950s, Red Star's Cudahy plant was

Key Dates:

1882: Meadow Springs Distillery Co. is founded by three Milwaukeans.

1887: Company's name is changed to National Distilling Company; firm begins producing yeast, with the major line called Red Star.

1919: With the beginning of Prohibition, company begins focusing more on yeast; name is changed again, to Red Star Yeast and Products Company.

1933: Following repeal of Prohibition, the firm begins producing beer and gin once again.

1937: Red Star exits from the distilling business; yeast and vinegar are now the main products.

1961: Universal Foods Company, a maker of institutional food products, is acquired; Red Star goes public.

1962: Red Star changes its name to Universal Foods Corporation.

1963: Stella Cheese Corporation is acquired.

Early 1970s: Company expands into soft-drink bottling.

1979: Rogers Foods, Inc., producer of dehydrated onion and garlic, is acquired.

1984: Universal swaps its soft-drink bottling business for Warner-Jenkinson Company, Inc., thereby gaining entry into the food color and flavor business.

1985: Company enters the frozen potato business with the purchase of Idaho Frozen Foods.

1990: Universal exits from the cheese business; British flavoring producer Felton International is acquired.

1991: The food, drug, and cosmetic color business of Morton International, Inc. is acquired.

1994: Universal's frozen food unit is sold to ConAgra, Inc.

1999: Pointing Holdings Limited, a major food color producer based in the United Kingdom, is acquired.

2000: Universal Foods changes its name to Sensient Technologies Corporation.

2001: Sensient sells its Red Star Yeast & Products division to Lesaffre et Compagnie; the industrial dye business of Crompton Corporation is acquired.

reflect the wider spectrum of its activities. The new name was Universal Foods Corporation. Universal made a major acquisition with the 1963 purchase of Stella Cheese Corporation. By 1965, the company's sales had grown to $31 million.

In 1965, Robert Foote became Universal's president, and Wirth became its chairperson. Around that time, the company began marketing an active dry yeast for use in wine production. By 1967, most of the major food companies in the United States were Universal customers, including General Mills, Kraft, Hormel, Gerber, and Ralston Purina. Universal purchased the National Yeast Company, a New Jersey firm, in 1968. By that time, the company, mainly by virtue of its acquisition of Stella, controlled about 20 percent of the nation's aged Italian cheese market. It also controlled 12 percent of the market for industrial yeast, and 30 percent of the chili powder and paprika production. In September 1968 Universal was stunned by the murder of Russell Wirth. August K. Bergenthal, Bruno's son, was convicted of the crime and sentenced to life imprisonment (he was paroled in 1981). It seemed that the younger Bergenthal harbored longstanding resentment regarding the events that led to his father's exit from the company's presidency.

Universal continued to grow steadily in the 1970s. Sales in the first half of the decade grew from $61 million in 1970 to $151 million in 1975. Two areas the company moved into heavily during the 1970s were soft-drink bottling and gourmet foods. Universal acquired the bottling franchises for 7-Up and other beverages in a number of states, starting with Michigan. The company entered the gourmet foods market with the 1972 acquisition of Lankor International Inc., and followed this up with the acquisitions of Rema Foods Inc. and Ramsey Imports, giving Universal a substantial foothold in the fancy processed foods market. In 1976, John Murray was elected president of Universal Foods. Foote, like his predecessor Wirth, stayed on as chairperson. In 1977, production began on a line of imitation cheeses. The cheese product was made from vegetable oil at costs that were 30 to 40 percent lower than those of the real item. That year, Universal common stock was first traded on the New York Stock Exchange.

In 1979, Universal purchased Rogers Foods, Inc., a California company engaged in the dehydration of onion and garlic. The early 1980s brought the expansion of the company's bottling operations, including the addition of the St. Louis franchises for Royal Crown Cola and Canada Dry. In 1981, the company bought out one of its longstanding competitors, the Federal Yeast Company, solidifying its position as a major player in the yeast business. By 1983, three of Universal's five divisions—cheese, beverages, and fermentation—were together accounting for about three-fourths of the company's sales, each providing about a quarter of the total. Over the next couple years, Universal chose to narrow its focus somewhat. In 1983, the company dismantled its snack food division, selling off its cookie and pretzel business. The following year, Universal left the bottling business, essentially trading it for entry into the food color and flavor business. This was accomplished by dealing four 7-Up bottling plants to Philip Morris in exchange for Warner-Jenkinson Co. plus about $10 million cash.

Universal moved into the frozen potato business in 1985 and 1986, with the purchases of Idaho Frozen Foods from Sara Lee Corporation, and of Rogers Walla Walla Inc. The two compa-

closed when it was discovered that Lake Michigan had eroded much of the 140-foot cliffs on which the facility rested, leaving the complex in danger of toppling into the lake. The vinegar works that operated there were sold to the Richter Vinegar Company, and, in 1957, the ten-acre plot of land on which it was built was sold to Milwaukee County.

Diversifying and Emerging As Universal Foods in the 1960s

Red Star began to diversify outside of the yeast business in the early 1960s. In 1961 and 1962, the company purchased Universal Foods Company of Chicago, a maker of institutional food products, and Chili Products Corporation of Los Angeles, a company that produced paprika and chili peppers. The company went public in 1961, making stock available for the first time to people outside the small circle of founding families and their friends. Red Star's sales that year were $12.1 million. The following year, the company's name was once again changed to nies taken together had sold about $100 million worth of frozen potatoes to the food service industry the previous year. As the 1990s approached, Universal removed itself from a couple of the markets in which it had been operating. In 1988, the company divested its import division, which consisted of Rema Foods and Gourmet Products. In 1990 Universal got out of the cheese business, selling that division to INVUS Group, Ltd., a subsidiary of the Belgian firm R.T. Holding S.A. By that year, under chair and chief executive Guy Osborn, sales had reached over $873 million. Frozen potato products accounted for nearly 30 percent of the company's revenue for that year; the explosion in sales followed the 1987 introduction of a new curly-shaped, coated fry that proved very successful.

Meanwhile, the late 1980s also saw Universal fend off a hostile takeover bid. High Voltage Engineering Corp., a Burlington, Massachusetts, maker of industrial instruments and electrical parts, made several takeover offers, but the Universal board rejected the advances each time. High Voltage was controlled by New York investors, and the takeover attempts were made in partnership with S. & W. Berisford PLC, a U.K. food, beverage, and financial services company that had agreed to manage Universal Foods following a takeover. The hostile pursuit of Universal ended up in federal court, where High Voltage contended that Wisconsin's takeover law, which included statutes that protected the targeted party in a hostile takeover offer, was unconstitutional. In May 1989 a federal appeals court ruled that the law was in fact constitutional, and several months later the U.S. Supreme Court refused to take up the case, prompting High Voltage to abandon its bid.

Shifting Focus to Ingredients in the 1990s

In April 1990, Universal became a major force in the flavor market with the acquisition of the British flavoring producer Felton International. Another flavor company, Fantasy Flavors, an Illinois dairy flavoring company, was acquired the following year. Also in 1991, Universal purchased the food, drug, and cosmetic color business of Morton International, Inc. Universal reported record sales in 1992, in spite of an off year for the frozen potato business as a potato glut led to depressed pricing. The color division made a particularly strong showing in 1992, emerging as the market leader among North American companies in that field. That division was enlarged in 1993 through the purchase of Spectrum S.A. de C.V., a major Mexican food color distributor. In January 1994 Universal boosted its aroma chemicals business with the purchase of Destilaciones Garcia de la Fuente, S.A., based in Granada, Spain. This acquisition gave Universal entry into new areas of the aroma sector, such as fragrances used in personal care products and detergents.

Continuing its shift in emphasis to food ingredients and other specialty chemicals, Universal sold its frozen food unit in August 1994 to ConAgra, Inc. for $220 million in cash, leaving the company with just one food products business—yeast. The proceeds were used in part to fund an acquisition spree that further expanded the firm's ingredients operations. During 1994 Universal acquired the Biolux Group of Belgium, maker of flavor enhancers, nutritional ingredients, and other products derived from brewer's yeast; and Champlain Industries Limited, which was based in Mississauga, Ontario, Canada, and produced flavorings and flavor enhancers. Universal became the

largest vegetable dehydrator in Europe by purchasing three European dehydrated vegetable processors in 1994 and 1995: Mallow Foods of Ireland, Silva Laon of France, and the Dutch firm Top Foods. Universal thereby gained a European counterpart to its U.S. dehydrated product business, Rogers Foods. The emphasis on international growth resulted in a sharp increase in overseas sales: by fiscal 1995, when the company reported sales of $792.9 million, 40 percent of the revenues came from outside the United States—in contrast to the 6 percent figure of eight years earlier.

By 1996 Universal Foods had elbowed its way onto the list of the top ten flavor and fragrance firms in the world. In October of that year, Kenneth P. Manning was promoted to president and CEO of the company, having served as president and COO since 1992. Osborn continued as chairman only until April 1997 when Manning assumed that position as well. Under Manning's leadership, Universal continued its aggressive buying spree, entering new sectors—particularly nonfood areas—and new countries in the process. In early 1997 the company moved into the ink-jet ink market with the purchase of Tricon Colors, Inc., based in Elmwood Park, New Jersey. Universal's Latin American food color operations were strengthened with the September 1997 acquisition of Pyosa, S.A. de C.V., a Mexican firm. On the flavor side, Universal acquired another Mexico company, Arancia Ingredients Especiales, S.A. de C.V., in January 1998. Arancia, which had annual sales of $16 million, produced savory flavors and other food ingredients.

Three European firms were also acquired in 1998, continuing Universal's rapid expansion on that continent. In April DC Flavours Ltd., a U.K. producer of savory and seasonings flavors, was acquired. DC Flavours provided Universal with access to the rapidly growing European snack food sector, as the firm was one of the United Kingdom's leading flavor suppliers to that industry. Universal gained an all-important foothold in Germany, the largest flavor market in Europe, through the May purchase of Sundi GmbH, a firm that specialized in all-natural flavor ingredients. Then in September, Reggiana Antociani S.R.L., a natural color producer based near Parma, Italy, was acquired. Reggiana specialized in producing anthocyanin, an extract from grape skins used in fruit juices, flavored teas, wine coolers, and fruit fillings. To complete its six 1997 and 1998 acquisitions, Universal spent a total of $121.5 million.

Also during 1998, Universal sued two former employees for allegedly posting defamatory comments about the company on Internet message boards. In late 1999 the company settled one of the suits out of court, while the other was dismissed by the judge in the case. When Universal learned that the *Milwaukee Business Journal* was planning to run a story about the lawsuits, and that the story would include information from one of the defendants about a U.S. Department of Justice investigation of price-fixing in the yeast industry, the company asked a judge to block distribution of the business newspaper. The judge refused. These incidents garnered Universal a great deal of unwanted publicity.

Universal Foods spent $93.2 million on four acquisitions during 1999. Two companies were purchased in February: Les Colorants Wackherr and Quimica Universal. Wackherr, based in Paris, France, supplied colors for the cosmetics industry, while Quimica specialized in the production of carminic acid and annatto, natural colors used in food and other applications. In April, Universal significantly expanded its global color operations through the acquisition of Pointing Holdings Limited, a U.K. firm that ranked among the world's top five producers of food colors. Pointing, which also produced flavors and specialty chemicals for cosmetics and household products, had annual revenues of nearly $43 million, with 60 percent of that occurring in Europe and the remainder stemming from North America, South America, and Australia. Rounding out the 1999 deals was the August purchase of Nino Fornaciari fu Riccardo SNC, a natural food color company based in Reggio Emilio, Italy. Like Reggiana Antociani, Fornaciari was also a producer of anthocyanin. Universal Foods recorded net income of $80.1 million on revenue of $920.2 million for the 1999 fiscal year. Out of the revenue total, the flavors business was responsible for nearly $400 million; the colors division, nearly $250 million; and the fragrances unit, about $28 million. Universal's yeast business posted revenue of $140 million in 1999, with the remaining revenues coming from the firm's dehydrated products and Asia Pacific divisions.

Early 2000s: Jettisoning Yeast, Repositioning As Sensient Technologies

In the first month of 2000, Universal spent $49.4 million to complete two more acquisitions of color companies. Purchased first was Dr. Marcus GmbH, a leading maker of natural colors based in Hamburg, Germany. In addition to gaining new technologies, this buyout also gave Universal access to several new markets, including Hungary, Poland, the Czech Republic, and Romania. The second acquired company was High Ridge, Missouri–based Monarch Food Colors Inc., a producer of colors for the food, pharmaceutical, and cosmetics industries.

In August 2000 Universal Foods announced that it had reached an agreement to sell its Red Star Yeast & Products division to Lesaffre et Compagnie, a French yeast manufacturer. To highlight the shift in focus away from food products and toward colors, flavors, fragrances, and other ingredients for both food and nonfood products, the company changed its name to Sensient Technologies Corporation later in 2000. The name "Sensient" came from a combination of the words *sensory, science,* and *ingredients.* The sale of Red Star appeared to have fallen through in late 2000, however, after the U.S. Justice Department raised antitrust concerns. But in February 2001 a deal was reached whereby the government approved the takeover with the stipulation that Universal retain its 20 percent stake in Minn-Dak Yeast Company, Inc., a small yeast producer based in Wahpeton, North Dakota. Cash proceeds from the sale totaled $113 million. In conjunction with the divestment of the yeast business, Sensient reorganized itself into two main operating groups: flavors and fragrances, which now also included the dehydrated products business, and colors. The Asia Pacific division continued to operate separately, marketing the company's products in the Pacific Rim.

With the sale of the last of its food products businesses, Sensient could now devote its full attention to its faster growing specialty chemicals operations. Following the dozen acquisitions the company had completed since the beginning of 1997, there was a need for some consolidation of operations, so Sensient

announced in December 2000 a restructuring involving the closure of plants in Missouri and the Netherlands and the elimination of 200 jobs from the workforce. In a further cost-saving move, an additional 200 positions were cut in April 2001.

Sensient began a new string of acquisitions in November 2001 with the purchases of Kimberly-Clark Printing Technology, Inc. from Kimberly-Clark Corporation. Through the acquired business, which was renamed Formulabs, Inc., Sensient expanded into several new areas, including wide-format graphic inks, textile inks, and other industrial inks. In December 2001 the company paid $32 million to acquire Crompton Corporation's industrial dye business, which was known as Crompton Colors. This business generated annual sales of about $40 million from the production of dyes used in paper and printing applications, plastics, and ink-jet printing ink. Sensient next purchased SynTec GmbH in January 2002. Based in Wolfen, Germany, SynTec produced electrophotography chemicals and dyes used in laser printers and copiers as well as specialty chemicals used in organic light emitting diode applications, such as cellular telephone screens and flat screen televisions. In March 2002 Sensient acquired the flavors and essential oil businesses of C. Melchers GmbH & Company, a supplier of flavors for coffees and teas as well as a wide range of essential oils, aroma chemicals, and other formulations for flavor, cosmetic, and fragrance applications. One month later, ECS Specialty Ink and Dyes of Morges, Switzerland, was acquired. ECS made inks for specialty printing. In September 2002 Sensient announced the acquisition of Cardre, Inc., a Plainfield, New Jersey, producer of specialty ingredients used in cosmetics applications and sunscreen products. The newly focused Sensient Technologies was likely to continue its expansion into new markets, new technologies, and new territories through further acquisitions.

Principal Subsidiaries

Flavor Burst, Inc.; Inter-Agro, USA, Inc.; Rogers Foods, Inc.; Sensient Technical Colors, LLC; Sensient Flavors Inc.; Sensient Flavors International, Inc.; Universal Holding Co., Inc.; Warner-Jenkinson Company, Inc.; Formulabs, Inc.; Monarch Food Colors L.P.; Cardre, Inc.; Promavil N.V. (Belgium); Freshfield Foods Limited (Ireland); DC Flavors Limited (U.K.); Ratina Participations, S.A. (Luxembourg); Reggiana Antociani Italia S.R.L. (Italy); Les Colorants Wackherr SA (France); Pointing Holdings Limited (U.K.); Dr. Marcus GmbH & Co. KG; Sensient India Private Limited; Reggiana-Warner Jenkinson S.R.L. (Italy); SynTec GmbH (Germany); C. Melchers GmbH & Company (Germany); ECS Specialty Inks and Dyes (Switzerland).

Principal Divisions

Asia Pacific Division.

Principal Operating Units

Flavors & Fragrances Group; Color Group.

Principal Competitors

International Flavors & Fragrances Inc.; McCormick & Company, Incorporated; Dragoco Gerberding and Co. AG; Kerry

Group plc; BASF Aktiengesellschaft; Givauden S.A.; Firmenich S.A.; Northwestern Flavors, Inc.; Burns, Philp and Company Ltd.; Quest International Fragrance.

Further Reading

Bergquist, Lee, "Universal Nets Cash for Acquisitions," *Milwaukee Sentinel,* April 19, 1994, p. 1D.

Brown, Paul B., "Solid, or Merely Stolid?" *Forbes,* December 5, 1983, p. 194.

Byrne, Harlan S., "Universal Foods Corp.," *Barron's,* August 27, 1990, pp. 38 +.

Campanella, Frank W., "Big Cheese," *Barron's,* October 20, 1986, pp. 59 +.

——, "Changing the Mix," *Barron's,* August 26, 1985, pp. 35 +.

Daykin, Tom, "Sensient Is Sued by Ex-Workers over Pay," *Milwaukee Journal Sentinel,* July 29, 2002, p. 1D.

——, "Sensient Targets Internet Critic," *Milwaukee Journal Sentinel,* March 5, 2002, p. 1D.

——, "Universal Foods Beats Its Drum," *Milwaukee Journal Sentinel,* January 24, 2000, p. 1D.

——, "Universal Foods Changes Its Name," *Milwaukee Journal Sentinel,* November 6, 2000, p. 1D.

Daykin, Tom, and Joel Dresang, "Attacking Critics Can Backfire, Firm Finds: Suing Former Workers Has Brought Unwanted Press for Universal Foods Corp.," *Milwaukee Journal Sentinel,* September 25, 1999.

Floreno, Anthony, "Universal Foods Intends to Take a Global Approach," *Chemical Market Reporter,* October 21, 1996, p. 29.

Gallagher, Kathleen, "Bright Future Seen for Color Division of Universal Foods," *Milwaukee Journal Sentinel,* March 14, 1999.

Gordon, Mitchell, "Yeasty Prospects," *Barron's,* November 7, 1983, pp. 51 +.

Hajewski, Doris, "French Firm Buys Red Star," *Milwaukee Journal Sentinel,* August 10, 2000, p. 15D.

Holley, Paul, "Universal Hopes Wall Street Finds Makeover Attractive," *Milwaukee Business Journal,* April 13, 1996, pp. 1 +.

Kirchen, Rich, "In Aftermath of Attempted Takeover, Universal Foods Prospers," *Milwaukee Business Journal,* April 30, 1990, p. 13.

——, "Is Competition Taking the Curl Out of the Curley Q?," *Milwaukee Business Journal,* January 13, 1992, p. 9.

Laderman, Jeffrey M., "Hungry Eyes on Universal Foods?," *Business Week,* October 10, 1988, p. 126.

Landau, Peter, "Universal Foods Acquires Global Food Color Maker," *Chemical Market Reporter,* April 26, 1999, p. 13.

——, "Universal Foods Corporation Expands Its Colors Offering," *Chemical Market Reporter,* March 20, 2000, p. 24.

Manning, Joe, "At the Helm of Universal: Manning Charts Course for Growth, Future," *Milwaukee Journal Sentinel,* March 1, 1999.

"On the Rise," *Barron's,* April 20, 1981, pp. 45 +.

"Pizza to Go, Heavy on the Soybeans," *Forbes,* March 1, 1977.

Sauer, Pamela, "Universal Foods Launches New Identity As Sensient Technologies," *Chemical Market Reporter,* November 13, 2000, p. 21.

Schmitt, Bill, "Sensient Acquires German Flavors and Essential Oils Business," *Chemical Week,* April 3, 2002, p. 29.

Torres, Craig, "Some Find Universal Foods a Tasty Morsel, Though Its French-Fry Business Now Is Soggy," *Wall Street Journal,* October 20, 1992, p. C2.

"Universal Foods Adopting Unique Management Structure That Works," *Milling and Baking News,* August 29, 1989, pp. 16 +

"Universal Foods Enjoys Yeasty Record of Growth," *Barron's,* February 20, 1978.

Universal Foods: The First 100 Years, Milwaukee: Universal Foods Corporation, 1982.

"Universal Foods to Purchase Felton's International Flavors," *Chemical Marketing Reporter,* April 9, 1990.

Walsh, Kerri, "Sensient Acquires Crompton's Industrial Colors Business," *Chemical Week,* December 12, 2002, p. 17.

——, "Sensient Takes on a New Color," *Chemical Week,* April 18, 2001, pp. 49, 51.

—Robert R. Jacobson
—update: David E. Salamie

Shurgard Storage Centers, Inc.

1155 Valley Street, Suite 400
Seattle, Washington 98109
U.S.A.
Telephone: (206) 624-8100
Fax: (206) 624-1645
Web site: http://www.shurgard.com

Public Company
Incorporated: 1993
Employees: 1,000
Sales: $210.27 million (2001)
Stock Exchanges: New York
Ticker Symbol: SHU
NAIC: 322212 Folding Paperboard Box Manufacturing

Shurgard Storage Centers, Inc. is one of the largest self-storage companies in the United States. Operating as a real estate investment trust, Shurgard manages a network of 477 storage centers in the United States and Europe, 30 of which are managed for third parties. The company's facilities are spread throughout 20 states. In Europe, the company operates in 72 locations in France, Belgium, Sweden, The Netherlands, and the United Kingdom. In addition to purchasing a storage unit via telephone, Shurgard customers can also purchase storage space on the company's web site or through commercial account representatives. Shurgard also provides portable containerized storage units which can be delivered to customers and then picked up for the return to a Shurgard warehouse.

Origins: The 1960s to 1980s

An industry pioneer, Shurgard began operating roughly a decade after the self-storage industry was created. Self-storage properties first appeared in the southwestern United States during the early 1960s, their development sparked by a growing need for low-cost, accessible storage. A number of factors contributed to the initial demand for self-storage properties, the same factors that would later fuel the industry's growth in the years leading up to the formation of Shurgard's predecessor company. The demand for self-storage sprang from the charac-

teristics of post-World War II society: an increasingly mobile population requiring short-term storage as individuals relocated residences; the increasing cost of housing, which led to smaller houses and less available storage space; the increasing popularity of apartments and condominiums; and more discretionary income, which enabled individuals to purchase boats, recreational vehicles, and other large items which required sizable storage space. Adding to the surge in demand was the proliferation of small businesses during the latter half of the 20th century, which meant cramped offices required offsite storage space for sundry needs.

Chuck Barbo, Shurgard's founder and longtime leader, devoted his career to fulfilling the demand for self-storage. His family, led by his great-grandfather Lars Barbo, emigrated from Norway in 1871 and settled in the Pacific Northwest. Chuck's grandfather, Christoffer Barbo, was ten years old when the family arrived in the United States and later teamed with one of his brothers to start a logging and construction company in Bellingham, Washington, near the U.S.-Canada border. Like his grandfather and great-uncle, Chuck Barbo also pursued a career as an entrepreneur, but not at first. He enrolled at the University of Washington in Seattle intending to earn a business degree, a goal Barbo shelved after only one quarter of studies, his passion lost after suffering through introductory accounting classes. Barbo then switched his field of concentration, opting to major in history and education. He earned his teaching credentials and taught history at a junior high school in Seattle, but the lure of the business world soon pulled him away from teaching.

During a summer break from teaching in 1966, Barbo entered the real estate business by selling property on Whidbey Island, one of the San Juan Islands located north of Seattle. "I earned more money in two months of selling real estate than I'd have made in four years of teaching," Barbo recalled in Shurgard's 2001 annual report. "Even though I'm a miserable accountant," he continued, "I figured that one out in a hurry." His teaching days numbered, Barbo moved south, making an hour's drive to Olympia, Washington, the birthplace of Shurgard.

Once in Olympia, Barbo opened his own business, a real estate investment company that served as the connection for

Company Perspectives:

If you're shopping for storage space, it's time to Expect More. And that's precisely what you'll get at Shurgard. We'll give you more in the way of extra services, like a guarantee to always have a cart available, or our promise that you can talk to a real human being 24 hours a day. So if you're interested in reserving a storage space, buying packing supplies, renting a truck, or learning more about packing your stuff or showing your home, you've definitely come to the right place. After all, why expect less?

meeting a local developer named Don Daniels. In 1971 the pair formed the Barbo-Daniels Group, which acquired and developed various commercial properties. Among the properties developed by the firm was a tilt-up concrete mini-warehouse called B-D Mini-Storage, located just south of Olympia, in Tumwater. Although Barbo envisioned business opportunities in the self-storage industry, others, particularly bankers, were skeptical. "Back in the early 1970s," Barbo wrote in the Shurgard's 2001 annual report, "no one had any idea whether self-storage was a legitimate business or not. Imagine trying to convince some tight-fisted bankers that a junior high school teacher turned real estate developer was on to the next great thing."

Barbo succeeded in obtaining the capital to develop B-D Mini-Storage, sparking his interest in developing further storage centers. He launched a bid to develop a national chain of storage centers. As he progressed toward achieving his lofty goal during the 1970s and 1980s, difficulties in securing capital emerged again, forcing Barbo to develop a solution that would determine the way Shurgard was later structured. When interest rates escalated, the bankers Barbo earlier characterized as "tight-fisted" entirely closed their hands, shutting off Shurgard's capital. To overcome the problem and to continue Shurgard's expansion, Barbo formed the first of a series of public partnerships to fund the construction of new storage centers. Eventually, Barbo formed two dozen such limited partnerships, raising nearly $700 million for his expansion coffers, enough to provide capital for nearly 20 years of growth.

Reorganization in the Early 1990s

In the early 1990s Barbo began developing a plan to consolidate his numerous public partnerships, which were sponsored by a separate property management company, Shurgard, Inc., into a single corporate entity. As one of the steps taken to create a unified force, Shurgard Storage Centers, Inc. was incorporated in July 1993. Barbo's nearly two-year effort to consolidate $442 million of real estate partnerships culminated in early 1994, when 17 of the 24 limited partnerships were merged into one body. At the end of March 1994, 17 million shares, held by roughly 55,000 limited partners, debuted on the NASDAQ exchange. At the time of the offering, Shurgard was organized as a real estate investment trust (REIT) which operated 139 storage centers and two business parks in 17 states, the result of Barbo's 22-year effort to build a national chain. One year after the company's debut on the NASDAQ, the outside property management company, Shurgard, Inc., was merged into Shurgard

Storage Centers, Inc., creating a self-administered and self-managed REIT.

Following the massive effort to create a single corporate entity, Barbo was ready to expand. Short-term plans called for the acquisition of 20 storage centers and the development of eight others in 1994. Expansion during the year was targeted for markets in Seattle, Portland, Phoenix, Atlanta, Dallas, Nashville, Richmond, and northern Virginia. In 1994 Barbo also made a bold and unprecedented move for a self-storage company when he established an office in Brussels to explore the feasibility of opening storage centers in Europe. The investigation revealed potential, leading to the formation of a Belgian subsidiary, SSC Benelux & Co., in 1995, making Shurgard the first U.S. storage company to establish operations in Europe.

By 1996 Shurgard was touting itself as the second largest operator of storage facilities in the United States. The company operated storage facilities in 275 locations in the United States and Europe, which generated $110 million in revenue for the year. A new subsidiary, Storage To Go, was also formed in 1996 and given the responsibility of introducing a new containerized storage format. The venture, restricted to markets in Seattle, Portland, and San Francisco at first, featured portable storage containers delivered to customers for packing and then picked up for storage in a Shurgard warehouse.

Late 1990s Expansion

Barbo's 25th year in the self-storage industry was celebrated by growth both at home and abroad. Expansion in 1997 included the acquisition of seven sites in Washington and three locations in Michigan, for which the company paid $20 million. Shurgard, through SSC Benelux, also increased its presence in Europe, acquiring three warehouses in France for $5.4 million. Sales for the year reached $140 million, more than twice the total recorded five years earlier, and net income hit $42 million, up considerably from the $22 million posted in 1992.

To ensure Shurgard's financial growth maintained its pace, Barbo looked for inventive ways to fund the company's expansion. His strategy appeared to be sound, but in order to continue as the dominant competitor in its key markets—the greater Seattle, Portland, and San Francisco areas, as well as markets in Arizona, Texas, Florida, Georgia, and Michigan—Barbo needed more capital. Barbo formed a joint venture with a San Francisco-based REIT named Fremont Realty Capital in 1998 to acquire up to 18 properties. He joined forces with Fremont Realty Capital again in May 1999, forming a second joint venture to acquire up to 16 storage centers. By expanding through joint ventures—something he would continue to do in the future—Barbo was able to lessen the cost of development. Capital losses associated with fledgling properties developed or acquired through joint venture arrangements were taken off Shurgard's financial books, enabling Barbo to expand without the capital drain he would otherwise have incurred.

In his bid to become the industry's leading storage center operator, Barbo chased behemoth competitor Public Storage, Inc. Based in Glendale, California, Public Storage towered over its rivals, owning or holding a stake in nearly 1,400 storage properties spread throughout 37 states. Although Shurgard

chains, a tactic once tried by Public Storage and later abandoned. According to the trade group Self Storage Association, there were estimated to be between 25,000 and 30,000 self-storage locations in the United States, with as many as 70 percent belonging to independent owners. Barbo hoped to bring as many as 3,000 such locations in as Shurgard partners, telling the *Puget Sound Business Journal* on July 28, 2000, "I want to be able to meet customer needs all over the United States, and we're not going to be able to build enough (new storage centers) to do that." Through the licensing program, Barbo intended to sign up storage center operators who were located in markets where Shurgard did not already maintain a presence. In its failed program, Public Storage had used its partnership program in markets where it already maintained a presence.

By 2002 Shurgard controlled approximately 450 storage centers in the United States and Europe. The company's actions in its 30th anniversary year promised further expansion in the years ahead, although the celebratory year was pocked by one regressive move. In February the company announced it was closing two of its five Shurgard Storage To Go warehouses and discontinuing service in Atlanta and Orange County, California. The company's delivery service of storage containers in Seattle, Portland, and Oakland was unaffected by the closures. On a brighter note, the company acquired a 74 percent interest in Morningstar Storage Centers LLC, the largest self-storage operator in the Carolinas with 40 properties in North and South Carolina. Completed in July 2002 for $64 million, the deal augured continued growth for the company as it entered its fourth decade of existence.

trailed far behind, controlling roughly 1,000 fewer properties, Barbo looked to one area for growth that Public Storage did not—Europe. Shurgard owned 19 European properties (with ten more under development), and Barbo was determined to push forward. In October 1999, Barbo raised $249 million to finance Shurgard's second leg of expansion in Europe. Investors included the familiar Fremont Realty Capital, as well as Deutsche Bank, AIG Global Real Estate Investment, and Credit Suisse First Boston, which received a 43 percent stake in Shurgard's European division. With the capital gained through the arrangement, Shurgard opened 19 new storage centers overseas in 2000, giving the company a presence in Belgium, France, the United Kingdom, The Netherlands, and Sweden.

As Shurgard pressed its case abroad in 2000, the battle with Public Storage took on a new twist. In February, Public Storage began investing heavily in Shurgard, spending roughly $50 million to become the company's largest shareholder by early April. Barbo seemed to have anticipated Public Storage's intent—"We knew somebody was buying our stock and assumed it was them," he said in a March 3, 2000 interview with the *Seattle Times*"—particularly if he was aware of Public Storage's recent history. Public Storage had acquired a stake in Storage Trust Realty in 1998, then offered to buy the company. Storage Trust rejected the offer but later agreed to the deal, forced to concede after relenting to shareholder pressure. In mid-April 2000, Public Storage representatives flew to Seattle and initiated talks with Shurgard officials about combining the two companies. Shurgard's management declined the offer, to the chagrin of some of the company's shareholders, and withstood the unsolicited advances of its larger rival. Public Storage decided against a hostile takeover and several weeks later reduced its stake in Shurgard.

On the heels of Public Storage's advances, Barbo formed another joint venture. In May 2000 he announced a $160 million deal with Chase Capital Partners to acquire and operate an unspecified number of storage centers that were to be developed by Shurgard. Barbo's efforts to accelerate expansion went further in July when he announced a new program to forge partnerships with smaller, independent self-storage chains throughout the United States. Called "Shurgard Preferred Partners," the program involved the licensing of the Shurgard brand name and the provision of services by Shurgard to independent

Principal Subsidiaries

Morningstar Storage Centers LLC (74%); SSC Benelux & Co.; Storage To Go.

Principal Competitors

Storage USA, Inc.; Public Storage, Inc.; AMERCO.

Further Reading

Bishop, Todd, "Shurgard Allies for Growth," *Puget Sound Business Journal,* July 28, 2000, p. 1.
DeSilver, Drew, "Shurgard Spurns California Suitor," *Seattle Times,* May 3, 2000, p. E1.
Epes, James, "Shurgard REIT Will Open to Uncertainty in Market," *Puget Sound Business Journal,* March 25, 1994, p. 4.
Ferrendelli, Betta, "Shurgard Sees Plenty of Room Left in Self-Storage Biz," *Puget Sound Business Journal,* June 15, 2001, p. 23.
"Rival Buys Shurgard Stake, Eyes Possible Combination," *Seattle Times,* March 3, 2000, p. C1.
"Shurgard Buys 74% Stake in Morningstar Storage," *Winston-Salem Journal,* July 3, 2002, p. D1.
"Shurgard Closing Two Warehouses As Way to Cut Costs," *New York Times,* February 5, 2002, p. C12.
"Shurgard Founds JV with Chase Capital Partners," *Real Estate Finance and Investment,* May 29, 2000, p. 9.
"Shurgard Raises $249 Million for Expansion in Europe," *Seattle Times,* October 13, 1999, p. C2.

—Jeffrey L. Covell

Solutia Inc.

575 Maryville Centre Drive
St. Louis, Missouri 63166-6760
U.S.A.
Telephone: (314) 674-1000
Fax: (314) 694-8686
Web site: http://www.solutia.com

Public Company
Incorporated: 1997
Employees: 9,170
Sales: $2.8 billion (2001)
Stock Exchanges: New York
Ticker Symbol: SOI
NAIC: 325211 Plastics Material and Resin Manufacturing

Solutia Inc. is the former applied chemical and fiber operations of Monsanto Corporation, spun off as an independent company in 1997. After some changes to its business mix, the St. Louis-based company is focused on three strategic platforms: performance films, integrated nylon, and specialty products. The performance films platform is centered around polyvinyl butyral, a plastic interlayer used in laminated glass, which because of its increased strength has a number of applications, from windows made to withstand hurricanes to automobile windows reinforced to prevent break-ins. Integrated nylon is comprised of five business segments: carpet fibers (Solutia is North America's largest manufacturer of nylon staple fiber to the carpet industry); nylon plastics and polymers, used to enhance such qualities as strength and fire resistance in critical components used in the auto industry and elsewhere; industrial nylon fibers, which are extremely robust with a wide range of applications, from cargo slings to dental floss; acrilan acrylic fiber, widely used in apparel, craft yarns, upholstery fabrics, as well as brake fibers; and intermediate, "building block" chemicals essential to the manufacture of pigments, herbicides, solvents, resins, detergents, fertilizers, and animal feed supplements. Specialty products is Solutia's final business platform and includes three diverse segments: resins and additives, used in thermoset paints and coatings; industrial products, which

includes high performance industrial fluids and lubricants; and pharmaceutical services, which help drug companies to develop manufacturing processes for new drug candidates.

Formation of Monsanto: 1901

Monsanto's founder, John Francisco Queeny, worked as a purchaser for wholesale drug house Meyer Brothers Drug Co. for 30 years before establishing his own business in St. Louis, Missouri, in 1901. Alluding to his wife's maiden name, Olga Mendez Monsanto, he formed Monsanto Chemical Works and began to manufacture the artificial sweetener saccharin, soon followed by caffeine and vanillin. Because of World War I, Monsanto became more heavily involved in the chemical industry, which had long been dominated by Germany and other European combatants, who could no longer supply U.S. needs. The company was able to successfully find a way to produce the antiseptic phenol as well as the vital ingredient in aspirin, acetylsalicyclic acid. In the years after the war, Monsanto changed its name to Monsanto Chemical Company and went public to fuel expansion, then in 1928 Queeny's son Edgar took over the business and by way of acquisitions moved the company into the manufacture of phosphorus and plastics. Nonetheless, it became the largest aspirin manufacturer in the country, a distinction held until the 1980s. In the 1930s Monsanto bought into detergent manufacturing as well as resin production. Monsanto's ability to make further gains on European competitors was again aided by another world war. In addition to producing such important wartime materials as phosphates and inorganic chemicals, Monsanto made a vital contribution to the war effort by developing styrene monomer, used to produce a synthetic form of rubber.

Expansion After World War II

In the post-World War II economic boom, Monsanto became involved in grass fertilizer, helping to maintain the rising number of suburban lawns, then in the 1950s it began to produce urethane foam, used in the interiors of the automobiles so eagerly bought by American consumers. Monsanto also produced its first herbicide, Randox. Edgar Queeny retired in 1960, and under new leadership the company established an agricultural chemicals division. By the time it shortened its name to Monsanto Company in 1964 the company encompassed eight divisions. With the rise of environmental concerns in the 1960s, Monsanto and its chemical products began to come under fire. The legacy of one of the company's oldest products, polychlorinated biphenyls, better known as PCBs, would one day haunt Solutia.

Monsanto had a 40-year monopoly on PCBs, which had a number of applications, found in such products as paints and adhesives, and used to lubricate machinery as well as insulate transformers, capacitors, and electrical equipment. Monsanto began manufacturing PCBs in 1935 in an Anniston, Alabama plant. Although later scientific studies would reveal that high concentrations of PCBs might cause cancer, birth defects, and nerve disorders, by 1951, according to court documents, the company was aware that PCBs were a toxic substance. Later in the decade the U.S. Navy rejected the use of PCBs in hydraulic fluids in submarines because government tests using rabbits indicated toxicity. The fact that in 1955 Monsanto took steps to protect the workers at the Anniston plant was a tacit admission that PCBs were dangerous. Nevertheless, no one communicated that threat to the people who lived nearby. Other company memos indicated that Monsanto executives appeared more concerned with the potential of lost sales than the health of its neighbors. In 1966 a company researcher deposited 25 healthy fish into a local Anniston creek. within 10 seconds none could swim, and after four minutes all were dead, many absent their skins. Nonetheless, it would be another six years before the Anniston plant was closed, and more than ten years before Monsanto halted PCB production entirely—two years before a national ban took effect in 1979. While General Electric would be forced to dredge the Hudson River in a $500 million effort to clean up PCBs in New York, Monsanto managed to avoid a major cleanup of Anniston, due to Alabama's minimal environmental protection laws.

Monsanto was caught up in other controversies in the 1970s and 1980s. Along with other companies it was sued over its manufacture of agent orange, a defoliant used in the Vietnam War, which allegedly caused permanent damage to a high number of soldiers. The matter was settled out of court in 1984 when Monsanto and seven other defendants agreed to pay $180 million. Although Congress had created a Superfund during the Carter administration to clean up polluted sites in the United States, several years passed before President Reagan was pressured into signing an $8.5 billion reauthorization act, funded by a surcharge on the chemical industry. Monsanto now began to shift its focus to biotechnology, a far less regulated industry in which the company had already scored some positive research results. In 1982, for instance, Monsanto scientists were the first to genetically modify a plant cell. The company then demonstrated its commitment to the development of biotech products by investing $150 million to construct a genetic engineering lab in Chesterfield, Missouri. By 1990 Monsanto was very much committed to biotechnology, but it was the Monsanto Chemical Co., a $4 billion business, that was generating the cash needed to support the research & development required in the life sciences, as much as 8 percent of the company's operating budget.

Spinoff of Chemical Business: 1997

Monsanto's chief executive, Richard J. Mahoney, was instrumental in shifting the company's focus to the life sciences, but his successor, Robert B. Shapiro, who took charge in March 1995, was even more committed to the biotech side of the business. In 1996 Monsanto acquired interests in biotech companies Calgene, Ecogen, and DeKalb Genetics, as well as a pair of biotech research firms. Also, in early 1996 Monsanto began to market its first biotech products, a herbicide-tolerant soybean and insect resistant cotton. Several months later, as the first crops were ready to be harvested, it was clear that the genetically engineered strains had outperformed expectations. It was in October 1996 that Shapiro surprised employees as well as outside observers when he announced that Monsanto might sell off its core business, the chemical operations, in order to refashion itself as a pure life-sciences company. By the end of the year, he indicated that Monsanto would spin off the chemical side as a separate public company. According to trade publication *Chemistry and Industry,* "The rationale for the split was familiar: chemical margins are too low and they depress the share price. Life sciences deliver higher returns and increase shareholder value. Monsanto wanted to become a global leader in agricultural biotechnology and healthcare."

Named to head the spinoff was the longtime executive vice-president in charge of chemicals at Monsanto, Robert Potter. To name the new company he formed an employee team, which also canvassed input from customers and investors. The word "Solutia" was coined in order to convey that the company was committed to "transforming the ordinary into the indispensable through chemistry." While Potter assembled his management team he was also involved in the process of determining the makeup of the spinoff. In order to maximize value for Monsanto shareholders, the composition of Solutia was skewed in favor of the parent corporation. The spinoff inherited ten business units, with annual revenues in the $3 billion range, instantly ranking Solutia among the nation's top 25 chemical companies. Excluding joint ventures, it would operate 24 manufacturing facilities in five countries, with a worldwide workforce of 8,800. But Solutia also assumed more than $1 billion in debt, another $900 million by taking on 70 percent of Monsanto's retirement liabilities, and another $200 million in environmental liability. As a result, Solutia was slated to open with a $300 million negative book value. Because it was imperative that Potter and his team take charge on day one, they prepared a 30-month plan. Although they were given a challenging balance sheet to manage, they hoped to take advantage of a friendly rivalry with the parent corporation and encourage their workers to show their ex-colleagues that the wrong part of Monsanto had been spun off. Moreover, after many years of watching their profits used to support the life science operations, veterans of the chemical division were pleased to see that the profits they earned were finally reinvested in their businesses.

In September 1997 Solutia was spun off from Monsanto, with Monsanto shareholders receiving one share of Solutia for every five shares of Monsanto. Potter immediately initiated a cost-cutting program, including the elimination of some 600 jobs, and took steps to shed some of the company's heavy debt load. He also instituted a research and development strategy that differed from the biotech-oriented Monsanto: All resources would target specific customer needs. In general his 30-month plan proceeded smoothly and ahead of schedule, but by June 1998 Potter was frustrated by the company's lagging stock price. In early 1999 he considered a merger with Eastman Chemical and Cytec Industries, but Solutia's low-priced stock made it a poor currency and the deals were ultimately scuttled. In April 1999 Potter stepped down as CEO, replaced by John Hunter, the 30-month plan essentially completed a year ahead of schedule. Debt was reduced by nearly $500 million, employment trimmed by 1,000, and the company was able to buy back 7 percent of its outstanding stock. Although revenues in 1998 declined by 4 percent over 1997, net income improved by 57 percent, or nearly $250 million, the result of cost-cutting measures. Despite the strong results, investors remained skeptical about Solutia, questioning how long it could sustain earnings by merely controlling expenses. The company needed to generate organic growth, but it was clear to management that external expansion would also be necessary in order to achieve a goal of becoming a $5 billion company within five years.

After operating within Monsanto, which in recent years had been selling off chemical interests rather than buying them, Solutia's management had to reacquaint itself with the merger and acquisitions process. In April 1999 it made its first deal, the $200 million purchase of CPFilms, Inc. a leading maker of window film and other high-tech film products used in the automotive and construction industries. Solutia then lost out on acquiring NSC Technologies, Monsanto's fine chemical unit. Later in the year Solutia acquired Vianova Resins, makers of coating ingredients for the automotive and industrial sectors, paying $640 million. Although eager to grow the company, Solutia's management also demonstrated that it was not willing to overpay and lapse into a high debt position. Ideally the company was looking for a "fourth leg," a new area of business to complement its existing operations. At the same time, it was taking steps to move some of its lower-growth businesses, such as rubber chemicals and phosphorus, into joint ventures.

As Solutia entered 2000, its management team was becoming increasingly frustrated with the performance of its stock, which was selling at just seven times earnings. On the heels of the Vianova Resins acquisition, in fact, the price of Solutia shares dropped 15 percent. Partially explaining investor skepticism was the uncertainty caused by Potter unexpectedly stepping aside as chairman in September 1999, Hunter assum-

ing that role as well as chief executive. Whatever the reasons for the lack of investor confidence, Hunter made it clear that he was more than willing to sell the company or take it private in order to increase shareholder value. In the meantime, Solutia continued to divest itself of non-core assets and looked to add new businesses. In February 2000 it established a Pharmaceutical Services Division by acquiring CarboGen Laboratories, followed by the March purchase of AMCIS AG. While Solutia was able to increase net sales in 2000 to nearly $3.2 billion, net income fell to $49 million. The following year saw revenues drop to $2.8 billion and the company posted a $59 million loss.

Despite poor results in 2001, Solutia's stock price maintained its value in the second half of the year. In early 2002, however, litigation involving the decades-old manufacture of PCBs in Anniston, Alabama, would have a debilitating effect on the company's stock. Even before the trial began, the price fell by 28 percent on the strength of a *Washington Post* article that summarized the case, despite management's insistence that it had reserves in place to deal with the matter, but the situation would grow even worse. With the law firm of high-profile attorney Johnnie Cochran, famous from the O.J. Simpson murder case, representing the mostly poor black plaintiffs, the upcoming trial was sure to attract media attention. In February an Alabama jury found Monsanto and Solutia guilty of property damage for 17 plaintiffs, which opened the door to the next phase of litigation, which would take at least a year to complete. The price of Solutia stock continued to drop, so that by the autumn of 2002 the company had shed $800 million in its market capitalization. Although Solutia's fundamental strengths did not appear to warrant such a valuation, the market was clearly uncomfortable with uncertainty surrounding the company. With litigation continuing indefinitely, Solutia faced many more months of challenges and was unlikely to regain investor confidence in the near term.

Principal Subsidiaries

Monchem, Inc.; Solutia Europe S.A./N.A.; Solutia Systems, Inc.

Principal Divisions

Pharmaceutical Services.

Principal Operating Units

Performance Films; Specialty Products; Integrated Nylon.

Principal Competitors

Akzo Nobel N.V.; Dow Chemical Co.; E.I. du Pont de Nemours & Company.

Further Reading

Byrne, Harlan S., "Good Chemistry," *Barron's,* June 29, 1998, p. 24.

Forrestal, Dan J., *Faith, Hope, and $5,000: The Story of Monsanto: The Trials and Triumphs of the First 75 Years,* New York: Simon and Schuster, 1977.

Gilbert, Virginia Baldwin, "Monsanto Celebrates 100 Years amid Praise and Blame," *St. Louis Post-Dispatch,* December 1, 2001, p. C8.

Hudson, Repps, "Shareholders OK Spinoff by Monsanto," *St. Louis Post-Dispatch,* August 19, 1997, p. 1A.

Hunter, David, "Solutia Targets Costs, Capacity," *Chemical Week,* August 27, 1997, p. 76.

Lambrecht, Bill, "Monsanto Knew PCBs Would Be Problem," *St. Louis Post-Dispatch,* January 6, 2002, p. A1.

Melcer, Rachel, "Chemical Company Solutia Tries to Focus on Current Business, Not Lawsuits," *St. Louis Post-Dispatch,* September 15, 2002.

Walker, William, "Monsanto's PCB Scandal," *Toronto Star,* February 17, 2002.

Westervelt, Robert, "Solutia's Second Act Targeting the Top Line," Chemical Week, June 30, 1999, p. 18.

—Ed Dinger

Spherion Corporation

2050 Spectrum Boulevard
Fort Lauderdale, Florida 33309
U.S.A.
Telephone: (954) 938-7600
Toll Free: (800) 900-4686
Fax: (954) 938-7666
Web site: http://www.spherion.com

Public Company
Incorporated: 1992 as Interim Services Inc.
Employees: 370,000
Sales: $2.71 billion (2001)
Stock Exchanges: New York
Ticker Symbol: SFN
NAIC: 561320 Temporary Help Services

Spherion Corporation, formerly Interim Services Inc., is a temporary staffing and consulting firm serving more than 33,000 clients, including a substantial number of *Fortune* 100 corporations. Spherion operates 940 branch offices in eight countries, maintaining a presence in the United States, Australia, Canada, The Netherlands, New Zealand, the United Kingdom, Hong Kong, and Singapore. The company's business is divided into three operating segments: recruitment, technology, and outsourcing. These business segments provide blue-collar and white-collar staff on a temporary and permanent basis. Spherion's outsourcing business provides recruiting, customer support, and administrative support on a long-term basis.

Origins

Spherion, a name adopted at the dawn of the 21st century, was the corporate title for a staffing services business whose roots stretched back to 1946. Throughout the course of the 20th century, the company underwent numerous name changes as the range of the services it provided expanded. Originally, however, the company was formed to provide temporary help to businesses involved in industrial and light industrial activities, giving the firm blue-collar roots that would be still evident a half-century later. Service expansion ensued in the decades to follow, highlighted by a signal diversification during the mid-1960s. In 1966, the company began providing temporary workers to nursing and home care clients, marking the beginning of the company's involvement in the healthcare industry. The next defining moment in the company's development occurred roughly 20 years later, its arrival engendered by the intervention of accounting firm H & R Block, Inc.

In August 1978, H & R Block acquired the company, which at the time was operating as Personnel Pool of America, Inc. A little more than a decade later, in January 1991, H & R Block acquired another temporary service business named Interim Systems Corporation. Interim Systems operated in essentially the same business areas as Personnel Pool, providing clerical, secretarial, light industrial, and healthcare personnel. Interim Systems maintained 178 branch offices—a significant measure of a staffing services firm's size—operating its offices in 20 states and three Canadian provinces. On the last day of 1991, H & R Block combined the two companies, creating a large, North American staffing services firm with considerable expertise in supplying blue-collar workers on a contract basis. On June 15, 1992, the new combined company changed its name to Interim Services Inc., the direct predecessor to Spherion.

Acquisition Spree Triggered by Independence in 1994

H & R Block held on to Interim Services for roughly two years before spinning the company off. On January 27, 1994, Interim Services completed its initial public offering (IPO) of stock, debuting at $20 per share. At the time of the IPO, the company operated 373 offices in the United States and Canada, but that figure soon would change. Interim Services' IPO marked the beginning of an aggressive expansion campaign whose intensity carried on throughout the 1990s. During the first two years of the buying spree, the company acquired 14 staffing services companies whose aggregate revenues amounted to $265 million.

During the first year of the acquisition campaign, Interim Services acquired five companies, adding $41.4 million to its sales volume. The first of the five acquisitions was the June 1994 purchase of Community Home Health Professionals, which operated four offices and generated $3 million in annual revenue. The acquisition provided a boost to Interim Services' involvement in the healthcare industry, as did the next acquisition, completed in August, the $1.2 million-in-sales, one-office Med South Health Care. The largest acquisition of the year followed next, the September purchase of Hospital Staffing Services. Hospital Staffing operated 18 offices, generating $23.5 million in annual sales. After acquiring Therapy Staff Services/Gulf Rehabilitation in October, which added another $12 million in annual revenue, the company completed its only acquisition outside the healthcare sector. In December, Interim Services purchased ICS Temporary Services, which was grouped within the company's commercial staffing division. With one office, ICS generated a $1.6 million a year in revenue.

As Interim Services proceeded with its ambitious expansion plan, the acquisitions completed were grouped within two divisions: commercial, which included two units, commercial staffing and professional services; and healthcare. The commercial staffing segment served clients who needed temporary personnel with clerical and light industrial skills. The segment also aided in the management of temporary and permanent personnel. Interim Services' professional services segment offered consulting and staffing services tailored for clients whose needs fell into information technology (IT), legal, accounting, and human resource areas. The company's healthcare division provided physicians, nurses, therapists, home healthcare aids, and home companions.

After spending nearly all of its attention in 1994 on bolstering its healthcare segment, Interim Services turned its attention to its other business areas in 1995. In June, the company completed two acquisitions, both of which were organized into its professional services division. OCS Services & Group and Career Associates each operated five offices, together generating $21.7 million in annual revenue. In September, the company acquired Juntunen, adding two offices and $13.6 million in sales, and in November, the company acquired Hernand & Partners, an operator of three offices with $2.7 million in revenue. The largest acquisition of the year joined Interim Services' fold in December and, like all the acquisitions completed in 1995, was absorbed by the company's professional services

segment. The company acquired in December was Computer Power Group, an $81 million-in-sales company with 17 offices.

In 1996 Interim Services added $105 million to its revenue base through acquisitions, completing a two-year expansion plan that left the company with 998 offices. The largest purchase of the year occurred in May, when the company acquired Brandon Systems Corp., a professional services concern with 32 offices and $89 million in annual revenue. During the year, Interim Services also purchased Allround/Interplan, a commercial staffing company based in The Netherlands, part of the Interim Services' ongoing efforts to establish a presence overseas. By the end of the year, the company was providing staffing services in the United States, Puerto Rico, Canada, The Netherlands, and the United Kingdom. Revenues for the year eclipsed $1 billion, making Interim Services, according to its calculations, the fourth largest provider of staffing services in the United States and the seventh largest in the world. At this point in its development, Interim Services derived 53 percent of its sales from commercial staffing services, 27 percent from professional services, and 20 percent from healthcare.

During the latter half of the 1990s, Interim Services completed roughly 20 acquisitions. Some of the acquisitions were quite small, similar in size to the more diminutive of the companies acquired between 1994 and 1996. Several of the companies represented massive acquisitions for Interim Services, beginning with the April 1997 acquisition of Michael Page Group PLC, a London-based staffing services company. The transaction was valued at $578 million, roughly four times the value of Michael Page in 1993, giving Interim Services ownership of a specialist in providing job placements for junior and senior management. Under the terms of the acquisition, Michael Page was allowed to retain its identity and operate as a complementary business to Interim Services, rather than being absorbed by the Ft. Lauderdale, Florida-based concern.

The rapidly growing economy during the late 1990s created fertile soil for most companies, but for temporary staffing firms the halcyon years presented their own challenges. Unemployment rates fell to historic lows, making it difficult for Interim Services to find applicants for its temporary and permanent placement services. To adjust to the problems presented by a robust economy, Interim Services began marketing itself as a recruiter for its clients instead of broadcasting itself as a temporary employment agency. As this shift in market orientation was underway, the company completed a strategically significant acquisition.

In March 1999, Interim Services announced that it was acquiring one of its rivals, Norrell Corp. The merger, a $553 million stock deal, gave Interim Services nearly 400 new offices, making it the third largest temporary staffing company in the United States, trailing only Manpower Inc. and Kelly Services. Norrell Corp., founded by Guy Millner, who twice entered Georgia's gubernatorial race, operated as a temporary employment company, serving some of the largest companies in the country, including Coca-Cola, United Parcel Service, and IBM. The merger, hailed as a good strategic fit by industry observers, gave Interim Services a $300 million outsourcing unit and call center service, two businesses the Ft. Lauderdale company did not previously own. The transaction also significantly strengthened Interim Services' technology, accounting, and commercial staffing operations.

Key Dates:

1946: Spherion's predecessor is founded.
1966: The healthcare market is entered for the first time.
1978: H & R Block, Inc. acquires Personnel Pool of America.
1991: H & R Block acquires Interim Systems Corporation and merges it with Personnel Pool of America.
1992: Interim Services Inc. is adopted as the new corporate title for the combined companies.
1994: H & R Block sells Interim Services to the public through an initial offering of stock.
1997: Michael Page Group is acquired.
1999: Norrell Corp. is acquired.
2000: Spherion Corporation is adopted as the new name for Interim Services.
2001: Michael Page Group is sold; Cinda Hallman is appointed president and chief executive officer.

Signs of Problems Emerging in 2000

Problems surfaced at Interim Services at roughly the same time the company adopted Spherion as its new corporate title. In March 2000, Spherion fell short of its earnings estimates for the first time, leading to internal and external scrutiny that sparked dramatic changes. An economic downturn exacerbated the financial burdens wrought by the company's near decade-long acquisition campaign. Between 1989 and 2000, the company's revenues had increased from $593 million to $2.1 billion in large part through acquisitions. The period framed the tenure of Raymond Marcy, who as chief executive officer had orchestrated the acquisition spree. Industry pundits charged that Marcy and his management team had underestimated the costs incurred from absorbing the 35 acquisitions completed during the period, leaving the company hobbled by debt as the economic climate soured.

The search for a solution to Spherion's problems led to divestitures, substantial layoffs, and new management. By the fall of 2000, the company had retained Credit Suisse Boston as an advisor to determine what should be done with the Michael Page division. In the spring of 2001, the company decided to sell Michael Page to the public through an IPO, netting $186 million when the offering was completed. In April 2001, Marcy resigned as chairman, chief executive officer, and president, ushering in a new era for the company, one led by Cinda A. Hallman.

Hallman left her post as vice-president of global systems and processes at Du Pont Co. to join Spherion as its new president and chief executive officer. During Hallman's first months of stewardship, Spherion implemented a series of cost-cutting measures, including laying off 700 employees, reducing administrative expenses, and shuttering 100 of its branch offices. The company divested several consulting companies it had acquired in recent years and, of significance, it exited the healthcare market. In addition, the company officially terminated its acquisition campaign in 2001. Spherion announced that it had no intention to complete any sizable acquisitions in the coming years, except for small purchases in the company's new areas of emphasis, recruitment and outsourcing.

Hallman espoused an altered vision of Spherion's future. To cure the company's ills, she intended to exploit the economic downturn by focusing on outsourcing, that is, handling recruiting, customer support, and administrative tasks, such as secretarial work, for companies. Aside from providing a new source of growth for the company, outsourcing was expected to impart greater financial stability to Spherion, creating long-term customers. Outsourcing contracts typically ran for five years, making Spherion's ability to predict its financial future more acute. Looking ahead, Hallman was attempting to double Spherion's revenues from outsourcing contracts by 2004, hoping to reach the $1 billion mark. "We've got our timing right," Hallman said in a November 26, 2001 interview with *Forbes.* "We just have to get off our butts and move."

Principal Subsidiaries

Spherion Financial Corporation; Spherion (Europe) Inc.; Spherion Technology (UK) Limited; Spherion Assessment Inc.; Norrell Corporation; Spherion (Europe) Staffing Limited (U.K.); Spherion Limited (Ireland); Spherion Recruitment Group B.V. (Netherlands); Spherion Australia Pty. Ltd.; Spherion (S) Pte. Ltd. (Singapore); Spherion Limited (Hong Kong).

Principal Operating Units

Recruitment; Technology; Outsourcing.

Principal Competitors

Adecco S.A.; Manpower, Inc.; Kelly Services, Inc.

Further Reading

Aneiros, Fabian, "Spherion Rides Cyclical Market, Adds Online Services," *South Florida Business Journal,* June 15, 2001, p. 44.
Coppola, Vincent, "HDC Shows Businesses Spherion Is the 'Better Way,' " *ADWEEK Southwest,* September 16, 2002, p. 4.
Davis, Katy Eckmann, "Interim Services' Help Wanted TV Recruits College Grads, Not Temps," *ADWEEK Southwest,* June 1, 1998, p. 5.
Fakler, John T., "Analyst Cuts Outlook As Spherion's September Slides," *South Florida Business Journal,* November 9, 2001, p. 20.
German, Clifford, "Interim Buys Page in Pounds 346M Cash Deal," *Independent,* March 4, 1997, p. 15.
Gordon, Joanne, "Desperate Times," *Forbes,* November 26, 2001, p. 89.
Joyner, Tammy, "Florida-Based Rival Purchases Norrell," *Atlanta Journal-Constitution,* March 26, 1999, p. E1.
Martinson, Jane, "US Recruitment Group Buys Michael Page for Pounds 346M," *Financial Times,* March 4, 1997, p. 19.
Roberts, Ricardo, "Spherion Speaks of Spinning Off Its Michael Page Unit," *Mergers & Acquisitions Report,* October 23, 2000.
"Staffing Services Company Spherion Reports $8.6 Million Loss for Second Quarter," *Daily Business Review,* August 2, 2002, p. A5.
Weiss, Todd R., "Du Pont IT Exec Quits to Be CEO," *Computerworld,* April 16, 2001, p. 20.

—Jeffrey L. Covell

Standard Pacific Corporation

15326 Alton Parkway
Irvine, California 92618
U.S.A.
Telephone: (949) 789-1600
Fax: (949) 789-1609
Web site: http://www.standardpacifichomes.com

Public Company
Incorporated: 1992
Employees: 1,026
Sales: $1.38 billion (2001)
Stock Exchanges: New York
Ticker Symbol: SPF
NAIC: 233210 Single Family Housing Construction

Standard Pacific Corporation is one of the largest home-builders in the United States, operating in California, Texas, Arizona, Florida, and Colorado. Standard Pacific primarily constructs single-family detached dwellings, focusing on large projects such as planned communities. The company also operates a mortgage banking subsidiary named Family Lending Services, Inc. that offers mortgage loans to its customers in California. Through a joint venture company, SPH Mortgage, Standard Pacific provides mortgage loans to customers in Arizona and Texas. Standard Pacific's founder, Arthur E. Svendsen, serves as the company's chairman, assisted by Stephen J. Scarborough as president and chief executive officer.

Origins: 1960s–80s

Founded by Arthur E. Svendsen, Standard Pacific started its homebuilding operations in 1966, commencing business with a single tract of land in Orange County, California. For roughly the first 15 years of its development, the company's building activities were restricted to markets in southern California. Serving as Standard Pacific's chairman and chief executive officer from the start, Svendsen focused on constructing mid-priced and more expensive houses, attempting to position the company for second-time homebuyers wishing to move up the price scale. Throughout its history, the company's development was buffeted and aggrandized by the conditions prevalent in its industry. The housing market was an exceptionally capricious business, characterized by a volatility that could inflate or drain a builder's fortunes with great speed. Svendsen's challenge was to take advantage of the boom years and to withstand the bust years, to survive and thrive during the decades of constant change.

The recessive conditions of the early 1970s proved to be Svendsen's first great challenge. He withstood the test, expanding geographically beyond the company's base in Orange County. Svendsen developed houses in neighboring counties during the decade, expanding into Los Angeles, Riverside, San Bernardino, San Diego, and Ventura counties.

The next deep trough in the housing market occurred during the early 1980s, when rising interest rates resulted in only 1.07 million housing starts, described as a "disastrous" year by the February 6, 1984 issue of *Fortune* magazine. Although Svendsen's company, operating as the hyphenated Standard-Pacific, shared in the misery experienced by nearly all homebuilders, the company did not flinch in the face of anemic conditions. Unlike other homebuilders, Standard-Pacific retained possession of large tracts of land during the market downturn. In several instances, particularly in the Los Angeles and San Diego areas, the investments were made at favorable financial terms and situated in prime locations. By holding on to the land, Svendsen positioned himself to increase Standard-Pacific's market share. When the housing market began to recover, evinced by housing starts creeping up to 1.7 million in 1983, Svendsen was able to underprice his competitors.

The improving conditions following the disastrous early 1980s led to a surge in housing starts later in the decade. As market conditions improved, Svendsen made a strategic decision aimed at relieving Standard-Pacific's tax burden. In December 1986 the company converted to a master limited partnership, freeing it from paying taxes twice, once on its profits and again on its dividends. Under this structure, Standard-Pacific distributed between 60 percent and 70 percent of its earnings to holders of partnership units. The partners then paid taxes, the sum determined by prorating their share of company's income that was subject to taxation.

Standard-Pacific basked in the surge of business sparked by the upswing in housing construction. The greatest market

---

Company Perspectives:

Standard Pacific is one of the nation's largest and most successful homebuilding companies with shares traded on the New York Stock Exchange. We take pride in having created more than 49,000 homes in California, Texas, Arizona, Colorado, and Florida over the past four decades. This pride comes from knowing that home ownership is a cherished American tradition. A new home is also the largest single financial commitment most families ever make. All of us at Standard Pacific are dedicated to offering the utmost in new home choice, quality, and value. New home developments that bear the name Standard Pacific carry a signature of our longstanding commitment to excellence in design and craftsmanship that has earned the trust and respect of homeowners year after year. When you are looking for a place in which to build your future, look for the signature of excellence that comes with a Standard Pacific home.

---

growth occurred in the company's primary area of activity— "California is the hottest market in the country," a building analyst at Salomon Brothers exclaimed in the April 27, 1987 issue of *Fortune* magazine—but Standard-Pacific also benefited from its expansion into markets in Texas, made several years earlier. By this point in the company's development, it also had diversified into financial services, operating a savings and loan named Standard Pacific Savings & Loan, which served as the financing arm for Svendsen's growing business.

Growth and Change in the 1990s

The boom years of the late 1980s gave way to the bust years of the early 1990s as recessive conditions again delivered a blow to the homebuilding industry. During the bleak economic times, Standard-Pacific dropped the hyphen from its name and, in 1992, reorganized into a traditional corporate structure, which was expected to improve the company's ability to raise funds.

Market conditions improved for Standard Pacific as the company exited the early 1990s. By 1995, the company ranked as one of the nation's 50 largest homebuilders and the fifth largest homebuilder in California, but the distinctions were not enough to mask the stain on Standard Pacific's balance sheet for the year. The company generated $346 million in revenue for 1995, but reported a net loss of $27.4 million. In the first quarter of 1996, the company posted $573,000 in net income, down substantially from the $1.1 million recorded for the same period in 1995. The downward trend extended to the company's sales as well, which dropped 8.3 percent from $77.3 million to $70.9 million during the first quarter of 1995 and 1996, respectively.

Near the end of the summer in 1999, two changes were made in the company's senior management. In August, the company announced the resignation of its 65-year-old president, Ronald R. Foell, who had occupied the post for 27 years. At the same time, Standard Pacific announced the resignation of April J. Morris, the company's chief financial officer. The business press expressed little surprise at the resignation of Foell, given his age, but the resignation of Morris, one of the few female

senior executives in the industry, caused a stir. "This is not good news," explained an analyst in an August 1, 1996 interview with the *Los Angeles Times*. "Any time a chief financial officer resigns without any clear reason, it raises questions," he stated. "They (Standard Pacific) still have some problems and I'm concerned."

Other analysts were worried as well. One analyst at Prudential Securities reacted to the Morris resignation without concern, but he did express some reservations about Svendsen's role as chief executive officer. "They are losing a very capable CFO, but that doesn't mean she can't be replaced," Larry Horan remarked in an August 1, 1996 interview with the *Los Angeles Times*. "The more important thing is who will replace their [chief executive]," Horan said, referring to 72-year-old Svendsen. "This company really needs some new strategy and vision that will help it resume growth." Other analysts were troubled by the company's beleaguered thrift, Standard Pacific Savings & Loan. The savings and loan had once held more than $420 million in loans and assets, but by the mid-1990s its vitality had been drained. Between 1993 and 1995 Standard Pacific Savings & Loan racked up $5 million in losses, adding further to its parent company's woes. In 1995 Standard Pacific suspended the thrift's operations, taking time out to decide whether to liquidate the troubled subsidiary.

As would be revealed in the late 1990s, the concern about the management shake-up was misplaced. Standard Pacific's treasurer, Andrew H. Parnes, was promoted to chief financial officer, replacing Morris. Ronald Foell's replacement came from within Standard Pacific's ranks as well, a promotion that drew little attention from the business press. Steven J. Scarborough, a Standard Pacific employee since 1981, was tapped as the company's new president to Svendsen's continuing role as chief executive. Scarborough had headed the company's Orange County building division before earning promotion to executive vice-president. To Scarborough went much of the credit for Standard Pacific's revival, the source of the "vision" that one of the company's critics had said was lacking. Scarborough's arrival in 1996 served as a marker in Standard Pacific's history, representing the starting point of robust growth that would carry on throughout the remainder of the decade and into the 21st century.

The growth of the housing market fueled Standard Pacific during the late 1990s, particularly as the company evolved more into a builder of planned communities, rather than single homes. The nagging issue of what to do with Standard Pacific Savings & Loan, however, remained. In May 1997 the company laid out plans for the disposition of the thrift, but completing the deal proved to be troublesome. In June 1997 an Irvine, California-based mortgage banking company, First Alliance Corp., made an $11 million bid for the savings and loan. In February 1998 the deal collapsed after federal regulators failed to give their approval. Similar frustration was felt following Standard Pacific's announcement in February 1998 that it was acquiring Olson Co., a southern California builder of small new home projects in older cities. Yet the acquisition was scuttled in May 1998, with no reason for the collapse provided to the public.

If Svendsen and Scarborough were discouraged by the abandoned deals, the release of the company's annual financial totals

Key Dates:

1966: Standard-Pacific commences operations on land in Orange County, California.
1986: The company converts to a master limited partnership.
1992: Standard Pacific drops the hyphen from its company name.
1996: Stephen J. Scarborough is appointed president.
1998: Standard Pacific enters Arizona's homebuilding market.
1999: The company tops $1 billion in sales for the first time.
2000: The first foray into Colorado is completed through the acquisition of Writer Corporation.
2002: Standard Pacific enters Florida's homebuilding market.

in the spring of 1998 must have provided much relief. The company announced the best financial results of its 37-year history in 1997. Profits tripled to $27.3 million and sales swelled 46 percent, reaching $584 million. Standard Pacific shareholders shared in the growth, watching the company's stock price increase a remarkable 160 percent in 1997. One year later, when the financial totals for 1998 were released, there was cause for further celebration. An expanding California housing market lifted construction activity to record levels, leading to another record year for the company. Sales jumped 30 percent during the year, rising to $759 million, and profits increased 68 percent, reaching $46 million.

Against the backdrop of strident financial growth, Standard Pacific succeeded in its efforts to expand. In 1998, for the first time in more than 20 years, the company crossed a state boundary. By acquiring a building operation in Phoenix, Standard Pacific entered the homebuilding market in Arizona, adding to its presence throughout California and in Texas, where it operated in Dallas, Houston, and Austin. An additional diversification occurred in 1998, when the company began offering various types of mortgage loans through a new mortgage banking subsidiary, Family Lending Services, Inc. After the company's foray into Arizona, it began providing similar loans to its Arizona customers through a joint venture company, SPH Mortgage, formed with Wells Fargo. In 1999, SPH Mortgage began supporting the company's homebuilding operations in Texas at roughly the same time Standard Pacific succeeded in severing its ties to Standard Pacific Savings & Loan. American General Corp., a Houston-based financial services company, announced in April 1999 it had been granted approval to acquire the thrift.

The year 1999 marked the end of an era. In December, Svendsen announced he was passing the duties of chief executive officer to Scarborough, ending the 76-year-old's nearly 40-year tenure as Standard Pacific's chief executive officer. Svendsen remained chairman, but in Scarborough's dual capacity as president and chief executive officer, he wielded much control, presiding over the company's homebuilding operations in California, Texas, and Arizona. The succession plan had been discussed for a number of months, ensuring a smooth transition. Under Scarborough's leadership, sales had increased 70 percent

from 1997's total, while new home construction had reached 3,400, an increase of 75 percent from the construction completed in 1997. The company ended the decade by eclipsing $1 billion in sales with $1.19 billion, up substantially from the $759 million generated the previous year.

Full Speed Ahead in the New Century

Not long after taking the helm, Scarborough's responsibilities increased as Standard Pacific continued its geographic march. In January 2000, after two years of casual discussions and six months of detailed discussions, Writer Corporation agreed to be acquired by Standard Pacific in a deal that provided for the latter's entry into Colorado's homebuilding market. With $82 million in sales, Writer Corp. ranked as the 11th largest homebuilder in the metropolitan Denver area. Under the terms of the acquisition, which was completed in August 2000 for $65.4 million, Writer Corp. continued to operate under its existing name and with essentially the same management, including the company's founder, George Writer, Jr. By the time the deal was concluded, Standard Pacific could count itself as one of the 12 largest homebuilders in the United States.

As Standard Pacific prepared for the future, the growth achieved between 1996 and 2001 provided encouragement for further expansion. During the five-year period, the company's revenues tripled and its net income soared at an average annual rate of 70 percent. In 2002 the company pressed ahead boldly, completing a series of acquisitions that significantly expanded the scope of its operations. In the spring, the company entered the Florida homebuilding market through the acquisition of a Miami-based builder, Westbrooke Homes, and an Orlando-based homebuilder, Colony Homes. Standard Pacific struck again in June 2002, when the company announced it had agreed to purchase Westfield Homes USA for $59 million. With operations in Tampa Bay and southwestern Florida, Westfield Homes helped flesh out Standard Pacific's geographic presence, adding another piece to the expanding homebuilding empire constructed by Scarborough.

Principal Subsidiaries

Westfield Homes USA Inc.; Writer Corp.; Family Lending Services, Inc.

Principal Competitors

Centex Corporation; KB Home; D.R. Horton, Inc.

Further Reading

Buggs, Shannon, "American General Gets Thrift-Deal OK," *Houston Chronicle,* April 29, 1999, p. 2.
"California Builder to Buy Writer," *Denver Post,* February 1, 2000, p. C1.
Granelli, James S., "Deadline, Deal Expire for First Alliance," *Los Angeles Times,* February 3, 1998, p. 4.
Labich, Kenneth, "Optimism on Housing Stocks," *Fortune,* February 6, 1984, p. 127.
Mendes, Joshua, "No Bust in Sight for These Builders," *Fortune,* April 27, 1987, p. 302.
"Standard Pacific Buys Another Home Builder," *New York Times,* June 6, 2002, p. C4.

"Standard Pacific Buys Writer Corp. for $65.4 Million," *Denver Post,* August 26, 2000, p. C2.

Stanton, Russ, "Standard Pacific's Top Guns Get Big Bonuses in Strong Year," *Los Angeles Times,* March 26, 1998, p. 4.

Strickland, Daryl, "Housing: Arthur Svendsen, Who Founded the Firm, Will Remain Chairman," *Los Angeles Times,* December 17, 1999, p. C3.

Vrana, Debora, "Management: Standard Pacific of Costa Mesa, After Big Yearly Loss, Names New President and Chief Financial Officer," *Los Angeles Times,* August 1, 1996, p. 4.

"West Coast Builder to Acquire Colony," *Origination News,* May 24, 2002, p. 44.

—Jeffrey L. Covell

Starkey Laboratories, Inc.

6700 Washington Avenue South
Eden Prairie, Minnesota 55344
U.S.A.
Telephone: (952) 941-6401
Toll Free: (800) 328-8602
Fax: (952) 828-9262
Web site: http://www.starkey.com

Private Company
Incorporated: 1967 as Professional Hearing Aid Service
Employees: 3,550
Sales: $350 million (2001 est.)
NAIC: 334510 Electromedical and Electrotherapeutic
    Apparatus Manufacturing; 541710 Biotechnology
    Research and Development Laboratories or Services

Starkey Laboratories, Inc. is the world's leader in manufacturing custom hearing instruments. The company operates 33 facilities in 18 countries around the globe. In addition to building some of the world's most highly regarded hearing aids (endorsed by numerous celebrities, including guitar legend Les Paul; country recording artist George Strait; NFL coach Dan Reeves; Hollywood stars Rod Steiger, Jane Russell, and Ernest Borgnine; and professional wrestler Vern Gagne), Starkey produces other technological devices designed to test, protect, and enhance the auditory health of people everywhere. The company markets its products under the Starkey Lab's name and also sells hearing devices through three wholly owned subsidiaries, Omni, Qualitone, and Nu-Ear.

Through the company's Starkey Hearing Foundation, Starkey Labs and its founder and owner William Austin provide hearing testing and hearing aids to people around the world who cannot afford to buy the products themselves. Begun in 1978, the Hearing Foundation has provided over 20,000 hearing aids to needy patients each year.

Building a Better Hearing Aid: 1961–80

In 1961 William Austin began working in his uncle's company, The Minnesota Hearing Aid Center. Austin had been pursuing a career in medicine and was enrolled at the University of Minnesota Medical School. Austin's work at The Minnesota Hearing Aid Center fitting patients for hearing devices helped him recognize that he was better suited for a career in business than medicine, and more importantly that the hearing aid business would help bridge his scientific interests and his broader interest in treating patients.

In 1962 Austin opened a retail hearing aid storefront in Sioux Falls, South Dakota. The store operated for a short while, but Austin found his first true success in 1967 when he opened a hearing aid repair service in a suburb of Minneapolis, St. Louis Park, Minnesota. What began as Professional Hearing Aid Service in 1967 led to a lifelong commitment on the part of Austin to help the hearing impaired throughout the world.

Professional Hearing Aid Service both fitted and repaired hearing aids but the newly founded company experienced its first pivotal growth when it began offering a flat service rate for equipment repairs. In a broader move, the company struck deals with hearing aid dispensers offering to service their products at a set rate, a practice that was new to the industry, and one that was very well received.

Within a very short time Austin's business was flourishing and he had to hire additional repair technicians. In two years, Professional Hearing Aid Service had over 30 employees and controlled the largest market share in the Twin Cities.

Austin did not stay satisfied with the repair end of the business for long and soon had his eye out for new industry innovations. Within a short time he located a small three-employee laboratory named Starkey. The laboratory had successfully cast inner ear molds, and Austin believed that the technology to make ear canal impressions would substantially impact the hearing aid industry. It had been widely accepted within the trade that the primary reason the hearing impaired refused to wear hearing aids was the stigma attached to wearing them. The cosmetic or vanity factor affected hearing aid manufacturers' sales more than any other issue. Austin invested in the notion that the more inconspicuous the device the greater the market share, and he bought Starkey labs and its technology in 1971. Austin merged his two companies, retaining the name Starkey Laboratories, Inc. for his new enterprise.

Starkey Labs issued its first CE model custom fitted in-the-ear amplification device in 1975. The company coupled the hearing aid with a warranty and satisfaction guaranteed trial period that later became an industry benchmark. Over the next few years Austin built Starkey into the world's leader in custom designed hearing aids.

By 1975 Starkey had outgrown its St. Louis Park facility and moved its operations to a spacious 13-acre campus in Eden Prairie, Minnesota. Austin's belief that the more unobtrusive a hearing device, the more likely the hard of hearing public was to wear it, was paying off and the company continued to grow, reaching revenue of $6 million by 1975.

In 1977 a campaign named the CARE program was begun to educate consumers. The program made use of booklets and videos showing the benefits restorative technology could provide. Starkey's campaign was developed to convince the average person that by amplifying sounds a person with hearing loss could lead a much better quality of life.

While improving the image of hearing aid users, Starkey Labs also began a fund in 1978 to make hearing aids affordable to the needy. The Starkey Fund was originally begun when hearing aid dispensers recycled their used batteries though Starkey. The dispensers then received credit that was donated to those who needed financial assistance in purchasing a hearing aid. The Starkey Fund later evolved into the Starkey Hearing Foundation, serving the world's poorest population in need of hearing technology.

By the late 1970s Diagnostic equipment was targeted by the laboratories. Austin and his staff developed several key research tools including the CHAT hearing aid tester, the Tinnitus Research Audiometer, and the Digital Dram Meter. All three inventions helped make testing patients a much more sophisticated and patient-specific process that led to further specialized development of hearing aid models.

The Reagan Years and Enormous Growth

The 1980s brought a good deal of international and national expansion to the company. Starkey Labs opened offices in Toronto, Canada; Glencoe, Minnesota; Hamburg, Germany; and Paris, France, between 1980 and 1982.

In 1983, the company brought to market the very first inter-ear canal hearing aid, known as the CE-5 Series. It was when a CE-5 series hearing aid was fitted for then President of the United States Ronald Reagan that the demand for hearing instruments took a dramatic upturn.

Reagan had suffered significant hearing loss when a blank gun cartridge had been shot off close to his ear on the set of a movie he was making. In the capacity of president, Reagan found that his hearing loss was making his interaction with dignitaries and the press extremely difficult. He thus called on Starkey Labs to remedy the situation. The new hearing device fitted by Bill Austin himself was hardly noticeable to the public and helped break down the stereotype of a hearing aid wearer. Moreover the public was educated by the press coverage on many aspects of hearing loss and the technology available to fix most hearing problems. Overnight demand for the model became so great that the publicity boosted sales exponentially and actually for a time had an adverse effect on the company. Though sales were at an all time high the company was not equipped to meet the demand and the volume took its toll on the employees of the firm. Too much growth, too quickly with the consequential supply and distribution problems were almost too much for the company. Fortunately over time things stabilized and Starkey Labs managed to stay competitive within the industry.

Like many other worldwide businesses in the 1980s a growing trend was consolidation through mergers and acquisitions. Large more established firms were taking over or squeezing out their competitors in many fields. Starkey Labs had managed to become one of the biggest names in hearing technology by this time and in addition to buying out several competitors the company continued its expansion by opening new manufacturing and retail units throughout the world. According to an article in *Minnesota Business* referring to the hearing aid industry, ''to obtain more resources manufacturers began consolidating. Worldwide there were roughly 70 manufacturers in 1990 but that number had fallen to just 32 by the end of the decade.''

In 1984 through 1985 Starkey opened facilities in Sydney, Australia; Atlanta, Georgia; Mt. Laurel, New Jersey; Portland, Oregon; Austin, Texas; and Marin, Switzerland. In 1988 Starkey opened new facilities in Miami, Florida, and Budapest, Hungary. A year later, Starkey Labs helped keep the industry consolidation going by acquiring Omni Hearing Systems and Nu-Ear Electronics. The companies became subsidiaries of Starkey while retaining their own names and markets.

By 1990 Starkey was ranked number one in the world in its ability to service all makes and models of hearing aids and was also cited for its inventory of replacement parts for a vast variety of models of hearing aids.

The 1990s continued Starkey's quest to become a leader in the hearing aid business worldwide. In the early 1990s Starkey opened a laboratory in Tokyo, Japan. It was at this point that the company felt pressured to compete with other companies that had already offered digital technology. The company placed a great deal of its resources towards research and development in digital and computer embedded technology and released the Digibot, S-AMP, Discovery CE-9 Series, Resolution programmable, Tympanette CIC, and Video Otoscope units during this period.

In 1995 Starkey Labs opened operations in Suzhou, China, and Auckland, New Zealand, and introduced a series of new products and services including its Euroline, Aura Care, Hear Net Online, and Interra BTE. The trend toward expansion continued the following year with new businesses in Warsaw, Seoul, Oslo, Stockholm, Prague, and Matamoros, Mexico.

Key Dates:

1967: William Austin opens Professional Hearing Aid Service in St. Louis Park, Minnesota.
1971: Austin buys out Starkey Labs to secure ear molding technology and renames his hearing aid business Starkey Laboratories, Inc.
1973: Starkey markets the CE-1 custom hearing aid with in-the-ear technology.
1975: Starkey builds 15-acre campus facility in Eden Prairie, Minnesota, to accommodate the company's growth.
1976: Starkey opens a subsidiary business in Manchester, England.
1977: Starkey launches the CARE program to promote the use of hearing enhancement technology.
1978: The Starkey Fund (later the Starkey Hearing Foundation) was begun to help provide hearing assistance to the needy.
1983: President Ronald Regan is fitted for hearing device; sales soar.
1989: Starkey buys Omni Hearing Systems and Nu Ear Electronics.
1993: The Tympanette (the first entirely in-the-ear aid) is marketed.
1995: Starkey headquarters and several international sites receive ISO 9001 Certification.
1996: Sequel Custom Programmable Instruments and Professional Fitting System are released.
1999: Starkey brings out digital hearing aid models.

Starkey Labs acquired a competitor, Qualitone, in 1996. In the late 1990s, Starkey further expanded by developing business in southeast Asia and continuing to grow its Latin American business.

Although the company had at times experienced supply problems with its digital aids, the management at Starkey Labs was convinced it had overcome the problems and was secure in its place as a leader in hearing technology. Austin and Starkey were featured in the December 2001 issue of *Minnesota Business* and the founder confidently declared, "we're properly positioned to move forward." Austin also shared his estate plans and his intention to will the stock in his company to his Hearing Foundation, with the option for employees to buy the company from the Foundation.

By the new millennium, Starkey Labs had become a $350 million company, with operations spanning the globe. The company's philanthropy through the Starkey Foundation and the work of Bill Austin provided great visibility and genuine goodwill to the business and all those involved with the Foundation. Starkey Labs held over 200 patents and had proved to be and innovator throughout its years. The business had moved towards digital and PC technology, and was attempting to gain a critical foothold in the digital marketplace. With many of the world's population aging and suffering from age-related hearing loss. Starkey appeared ready to capture its share of the multibillion-dollar biotech market.

Principal Subsidiaries

Omni Hearing Systems; Nu-Ear Electronics; Qualitone.

Principal Divisions

Prohear; Hearing Health Care Card; North American Commercial Leasing, Inc.; Star Travel.

Principal Competitors

Great Nordic; Oticon Holding AS; Widex APS; Siemens AG; Philips NV; Micro-Tech Inc.; Bernafaon-Maico; Dahlberg Inc.

Further Reading

Anderson, Dennis, "Hearing Loss Affects Hunters, Shooter; Hearing-Protection Devices Offers Relief From Loud Blasts," *Star Tribune,* (Minneapolis, Minnesota) September12, 1999, p. 22C.
Bonillas, Paula, "Return to Peru," *Hearing Health,* p. 38.
——, "Who is Bill Austin?" *Hearing Health,* p. 50.
"Boom; Reagan-Roused Reverberations," *Fortune,* January 23, 1984, p. 8.
"Danish Company to Buy Beltone Maker of Hearing-Aids," *New York Times,* April, 27, 2000.
Druskoff, Mark, "Medical Mogul," *Minnesota Business,* December 2001, p. 26.
"Ear We Go, Ear We Go, Ear . . . ," *Herald* (Glasgow) May 16, 2000.
Goetzl, David, "Beltone Sees Big Market in Graying Baby Boomer," *Advertising Age,* April 5, 1999, p. 3.
Leary, Warren E., "U.S. Warns Hearing-Aid Manufacturer Against False Claims," *New York Times,* April 27,1993, p. A8.
"New Hearing Aid Could Be Music to Your Ears," *Time,* April 13, 1998, p. 41.
Parris, Matthew, "Bright Minds Scrambled in the House of Fun," *Times* (London) July 27, 1999.
Sellinger, Margie Bonnett, "Thanks to Modern Electronics, the President's Hearing Seems to Be Right on the Button," *People Weekly,* August 20, 1984, p. 36.
" 'Surround Sound' in a Hearing Aid," *Business Week,* April 20, 1998, p. 142.
Wallis, Claudia, "Help for Reagan's Hearing; The First Citizen Gets a Tiny Hi-Fi Set for His Right Ear," *Time,* September 19, 1983, p. 59.
Whitestone, Heather, *Listening with My Heart,* Doubleday: New York, 1997.

—Susan B. Culligan

Steel Dynamics, Inc.

6714 Pointe Inverness Way
Fort Wayne, Indiana 46804
U.S.A.
Telephone: (260) 459-3553
Fax: (260) 969-3590
Web site: http://www.steeldynamics.com

Public Company
Incorporated: 1993
Employees: 676
Sales: $606.98 million (2001)
Stock Exchanges: NASDAQ
Ticker Symbol: STLD
NAIC: 331111 Iron and Steel Mills; 331221 Cold-Rolled
   Steel Shape Manufacturing

Steel Dynamics, Inc. is a rising, vibrant force in the U.S. steel industry. Using scrap steel melted in electric arc furnaces, the company casts steel products used in buildings, automobiles, and other manufactured items. Hot-rolled, cold-rolled, and coated steel sheet products are produced by the company's flat roll division in Butler, Indiana, which uses a revolutionary thin-slab casting technology. The company's structural and rail division, located in Columbia City, Indiana, produces structural shapes and beams, as well as standard and premium rail used by North American railways. Its thin-slab technology is patterned after a process developed by a German equipment manufacturer, first utilized by U.S. steelmaker Nucor Corporation, where Steel Dynamics' three founders were employed prior to venturing out on their own.

Origins: The Early 1990s

"In 1993," wrote Keith Busse for the corporate web site, "my colleagues and I set out to do something that had not been done in the United States for many years." What he and his cofounders, Mark Millet and Richard Teets, Jr., were attempting to accomplish had not been achieved in a century. The three innovators, with Busse taking the lead, were attempting to start a new U.S. steel company without corporate backing, en-

deavoring to independently finance a start-up venture without preexisting financial credentials. Lacking the traditional means of support, the three founders parlayed their reputations and vision into a substantial amount of cash. By September 1993 Busse had raised $370 million. Busse succeeded in raising the capital because steel-savvy investors were well aware of what he, Millet, and Teets had achieved in Crawfordsville, Indiana, with a division of Nucor. Busse promised investors he would improve upon the revolutionary success achieved in Crawfordsville and better it with Steel Dynamics in Butler, Indiana.

Investors were more than willing to hand over millions of dollars to Busse because of his accomplishments at the Charlotte, North Carolina-based Nucor Corporation. Busse spent 21 years working for the celebrated steelmaker rising from division controller to general manager, eventually becoming vice-president and general manager of the Nucor Steel Division in Crawfordsville. Busse's leadership of the Crawfordsville operations occurred at an exciting time for Nucor and the steel industry's onlookers. A German equipment manufacturer, SMS, had developed a revolutionary steelmaking technique that turned melted steel into a continuous ribbon measuring roughly two inches thick. These ribbons, or "thin slabs," could be rolled into sheet steel faster and with substantially less machinery than the conventional 10-inch-thick slabs used by integrated steelmakers. In 1987 Nucor forged an agreement with SMS to build the world's first thin-slab minimill, a project to be headed by Busse and located in Crawfordsville.

As Busse took charge of the project, he gathered the team that would make steelmaking history. One of the first managers hired by Busse was Richard Teets, who joined Nucor in 1987 as engineering manager at Crawfordsville. Teets managed the design and construction of the new thin-cast slab facility, paying particular attention to ensuring that environmental and other standards were met during the design and construction processes. Mark Millet, who earned a degree in metallurgy from the University of Surrey, England, joined Nucor in 1981 when he began serving as the chief metallurgist for the company's division in Darlington, South Carolina. When Nucor entered its agreement with SMS, Millet was tapped to oversee the design, construction, staffing, and operation of the melting and casting facility.

Company Perspectives:

We helped pioneer the continuous thin-slab casting technique of steel production that has been embraced by minimills the world over. Our innovative technical team continues to develop and refine our processes and equipment. We continually monitor operating results and make needed improvements. Our design/build management team is well respected in the American steel industry, having completed multiple mill projects on time and on budget. Our philosophy in designing production facilities is to hire the people early who are going to operate the plant and get them deeply involved in the design of plant layout and equipment.

The continuous thin-slab casting process proved to be a commercial success. The accolades drawn by the Crawfordsville operation spawned a host of emulators during the 1990s as many new minimill operations started up, hoping to ape the success achieved by Nucor. (Minimills, which operated at a lower cost than integrated steelmakers, used scrap metal to produce steel, whereas integrated steelmakers produced virgin metal from iron ore). Among the entrants was Steel Dynamics, led by Busse and his Nucor colleagues, which convincingly promised to improve upon the success at Crawfordsville. In a September 3, 2001 interview with *Fortune* magazine, Millet commented, "We had an acute and intimate knowledge of what worked and what the shortcomings were."

After securing the capital to finance the construction of a thin-slab minimill, a formidable task in itself, the next great challenge facing Busse was site selection for the Steel Dynamics plant. Profitability, the foremost aim of the company—"We are in the business to make money; we are not in the business to make steel," Millet remarked in the September 2001 *Fortune* article—depended greatly on keeping raw material, electricity, and labor costs low. Busse elected to establish the Steel Dynamics plant in the northwestern Indiana community of Butler, close to both automotive and other steel scrap supplies, which accounted for roughly half of the company's total production costs. One of the earliest investors, OmniSource, was a scrap merchant with whom Busse signed a long-term purchase agreement at favorable terms. Once the Butler plant was equipped with furnaces, securing inexpensive electricity became intrinsic to achieving profitability—one of the company's 190-ton electric arc furnaces consumed 100 megawatts of electricity in a single firing, enough to light up a small city. Again Busse secured a beneficial deal, signing an agreement with American Electric Power for 2.8 cents per kilowatt-hour, considered to be at the low end of the price scale paid by minimills. Steel Dynamics achieved perhaps its greatest success in its relationship with labor, but before agreements with production personnel took precedence, the company needed to build its plant.

The Butler Plant: 1994–96

With an initial capital cost of $275 million, the Butler plant began construction in the fall of 1994. On November 10, 1995, construction was completed and commercial operation began in January 1996. Both the cost and the 14-month construction

period were record lows, providing evidence that Busse's dual roles as chief executive officer and president were being executed with skill. Financial losses were expected as the fledgling Steel Dynamics started out, but the speed at which the company became profitable greatly impressed analysts. During its first six months of operation, the company reported $14 million in operating losses, but the streak stopped there; by July 1996 Steel Dynamics broke even for the first time. In August, the company posted $1.75 million in net income, followed by the $2.45 million in September, beginning a pattern of escalating profitability that earned the esteem of many within the steel industry.

Company officials credited much of Steel Dynamics' initial and later success to its workforce. The company's employees were a motivated group, spurred to keep costs down and efficiency high by a number of incentive programs. Production workers were able to double their hourly rate if weekly production goals were met, which was not an uncommon management tactic employed by minimills, but Steel Dynamics went further to guarantee its employees performed at the highest standard. The company offered what it referred to as a "conversion bonus," which was a pay incentive for keeping costs down. "Everyone looks at cost and tries to find ways to keep it down," Barry Schneider, manager of engineering and services at Steel Dynamics, explained in the September 2001 profile in *Fortune*. "For instance," Schneider continued, "the guy who sticks the probe into the furnace to take its temperature knows each probe costs about $10. He's going to want to do that only once, not four times. If somebody sees oil dripping from something, they're not going to let it drip forever, because that's coming out of their pay." Aside from production bonuses and cost-containment bonuses, all employees also were given stock options twice a year and annual profit-sharing awards. "Steel Dynamics has a unique workforce that really busts its rump," remarked an analyst at Morgan Stanley Dean Witter in the same issue of *Fortune*.

By the end of 1996, once Steel Dynamics had begun to demonstrate consistent profitability, Busse was ready to sell the company on Wall Street. By December the company's losses had grown to $50.7 million since its September 1993 inception, and Busse wanted to clear the company from some of its debt. Busse hoped to raise $140 million from an initial public offering (IPO) of stock, earmarking $75 million for capital expansion and the remainder for refinancing the company's debt. Upon completion of the IPO, Steel Dynamics investors would still retain approximately 80 percent of the company's stock.

After the preparations for the company's IPO, Steel Dynamics began to hit its stride and recorded impressive financial and production increases. In 1997, shipments increased more than 50 percent, eclipsing 1.2 million tons. Sales for the year jumped as well, swelling by 66 percent to reach $420 million. Most impressive, the company's net income reached $43.9 million, obliterating the $9.8 million loss posted in 1996. In 1998, amid plant expansions in Butler, the company recorded another banner financial year. Shipments increased 18 percent to more than 1.4 million tons and sales grew by 23 percent, reaching $515 million.

Expansion in the 21st Century

Robust growth continued to characterize its progress as Steel Dynamics entered a new century. At a time when many steel-

---

Key Dates:

1993: Three Nucor Corporation executives form Steel Dynamics.
1996: The thin-slab minimill in Butler, Indiana, begins commercial operation.
1997: Steel Dynamics reports its first annual profit.
2001: Construction of a structural steel and rail plant begins in Columbia City, Indiana.
2002: The Columbia City plant begins operation.

---

makers were suffering, Steel Dynamics reported glowing financial figures for 2000, with profits up 36 percent to $54 million and sales up 12 percent to $693 million. Recessive economic conditions entangled the company the following year—but compared to the injuries suffered by many of its rivals—the problems were minor. Between 1998 and 2001, 19 steelmakers filed for bankruptcy, a figure representing 25 percent of U.S. capacity. For further relief, Busse and his management team could compare their company's performance against that of Nucor. According to analysts at Morgan Stanley Dean Witter, Steel Dynamics was recording an operating profit per ton of $55 compared to Nucor's average of $43 per ton.

Management pressed boldly ahead in 2001, even as the company's growth abated. In May 2001 the company began constructing a $315 million structural steel and rail mill in Columbia City, Indiana. Construction of the plant progressed "well ahead of schedule," according to Busse in the April 22, 2002 issue of *American Metal Market*. Completed in May 2002, the new facility was expected to produce approximately 200,000 tons of structural products by the end of the year. Construction and equipment installation for the rail portion of the mill were slated for late 2002, with rail production scheduled for early 2003.

The completion of the new mill in Columbia City represented only one of the highlights enjoyed by Steel Dynamics in 2002. Financial vitality returned, resuming the prolific pace of growth that had characterized the late 1990s. In the second quarter of 2002, the company's net income reached $17.7 million. For the first six months of 2002, Steel Dynamics' net income more than tripled on a 22 percent increase in sales, providing strong indications that robust growth lay in the company's future. As Busse prepared for the company's second decade of existence, he began to contemplate growing Steel Dynamics through acquisitions. "We are looking at other good companies," he informed *American Metal Market* on February 4, 2002. "We've talked to a number of people and looked at a lot of things. That [acquiring companies] may be the way to grow in the future."

Principal Subsidiaries

Iron Dynamics, Inc.

Principal Competitors

Commercial Metals Company; Nucor Corporation; United States Steel Corporation.

Further Reading

Balcerek, Tom, "Despite Late Slump, SDI Stays Profitable," *American Metal Market,* February 6, 2002, p. 3.
Creswell, Julie, "America's Elite Factories," *Fortune,* September 3, 2001, p. 206.
Petry, Corinna C., "Wall Street: Grist for the Mill?," *American Metal Market,* November 20, 1996, p. 2.
Robertson, Scott, "SDI Lays Out Plans: Open, Restart, Expand," *American Metal Market,* April 22, 2002, p. 4.
——, "Seven Years Later, SDI's Keith Busse Still Itches to Grow," *American Metal Market,* February 4, 2002, p. 10.
"Steel Dynamics Boosts Income, Sales," *American Metal Market,* February 2, 2000, p. 2.
"Steel Dynamics Logs Record Sales, Shipments," *American Metal Market,* July 12, 2002, p. 3.
Teaff, Rick, "Steel Dynamics Money Set; Finishing Mill Project's Cost Climbs to $190 Million," *American Metal Market,* August 18, 1995, p. 2.

—Jeffrey L. Covell

Stelmar Shipping Ltd.

Status Center
2A Areos Street
Vouliagmeni 16671 Athens
Greece
Telephone: 011-30-10-9670001
Fax: 011-30-10-9670150
Web site: http://www.stelmar.com

Public Company
Incorporated: 1992 as Blue Weave Tankers
Employees: 750
Sales: $111.2 million (2001)
Stock Exchanges: New York
Ticker Symbol: SJH
NAIC: 483111 Deep Sea Freight Transportation; 484110
    General Freight Trucking, Local

Stelmar Shipping Ltd. is a holding company for a fleet of oceangoing tankers involved in transporting crude and refined grades of petroleum products. Stelmar Shipping operates 31 vessels that trade worldwide, operating primarily under the terms of time charter contracts. The company's charterers are oil companies, state-owned oil companies, and international oil trading houses. Relative to its competitors, Stelmar Shipping maintains a young fleet, with contracts ranging between one and seven years' duration for a majority of its fleet.

Origins

Stelmar Shipping was founded by a 24-year-old taking his first steps as an entrepreneur. At first blush, the prospect of a neophyte using a tanker company as his first start-up venture appeared odd, but Stelios Hagi-Ioannou was no ordinary 24-year-old. The second son of an immensely wealthy Greek shipping family, Hagi-Ioannou made his start in the business world with vast financial resources at his disposal, the fruits cultivated by his father, Loucas Hagi-Ioannou, and his maritime group, Troodos Shipping. Stelmar Shipping represented the first business venture started by the younger Hagi-Ioannou—Stelios, as

he preferred to be called—the first venture in his career as a "serial entrepreneur," another epithet favored by Stelios.

After graduating from the London School of Economics in 1989, Stelios worked for his father's company, Troodos Shipping. Loucas Hagi-Ioannou bankrolled Stelios's start as an entrepreneur, staking his son with £30 million to follow in his footsteps. Stelios used the capital to start his own tanker company, Blue Weave Tankers, in September 1992. (Blue Weave changed its name to Stelmar Tankers (Management) Ltd. in February 1993, the new name a combination of "Stelios" and "maritime.") At the company's inception, Stelios recruited a management team that would remain intact during the company's formative decade. Key executives included Peter Goodfellow, Stamatic Molaris, Bruce Ogilvy, and Nick Hartley.

Stelios's petroleum transportation company, as it existed at the beginning of the 21st century, was cobbled from a patchwork of what would become subsidiary companies. The collection of companies were brought together under the corporate umbrella of Stelmar Shipping Ltd., a holding company formed in January 1997. In the five years separating Stelios's entry into the tanker business and the formation of Stelmar Shipping as a holding company, roughly a dozen shipowning companies were formed, each created to govern the operation of a single ocean-going vessel. These shipowning companies were controlled by several companies, the primary entities, along with several management companies brought together under the Stelmar Shipping corporate umbrella. These key components included: Stelmar Tankers (Management) Ltd., which provided a wide range of shipping services, including maintenance, technical support, and financial and accounting services; Martank Shipping Holdings Ltd., a holding company of shipowning concerns, which was formed in March 1993; and Marship Tankers (Holdings) Ltd., another holding company of shipowning concerns, formed in August 1993.

Stelios's tanker business became operational roughly six months after the formation of the shipping-services provider, Stelmar Tankers. The first vessel, controlled by Martank Shipping, was the *Fulmar,* acquired in April 1993. A second vessel, controlled by Marship Tankers, the *Primar,* was acquired in July 1993. Both vessels were acquired from Teekay Shipping

Company Perspectives:

Since the founding of the Company in 1992, management has maintained a commitment to locking in its modern product ships on profitable time charters. Our philosophy has always been to utilize the time charter strategy in order to smooth out the tanker cycles. Since inception, our time charter strategy has enabled us to reduce earnings volatility and achieve consistent profitable growth.

Corporation. Before the end of the year, Stelios added two more vessels, both acquired from Amoco Corporation. In September, the *Colmar* was acquired, followed by the purchase of the *City University* in October. With the acquisition of his first four vessels, Stelios positioned himself in the two segments of the petroleum-shipping trade that would direct Stelmar Shipping's expansion strategy.

From the outset, Stelios shaped his shipping business to compete in the transportation of crude and refined petroleum products, commonly referred to as "dirty" and "clean" products, respectively. The National Petroleum Association (NPA) scale of color determined the classification of an oil product as either a clean or dirty grade, with the number one representing the cleanest grade and the number nine representing the dirtiest grade. The dividing point between clean and dirty products was typically defined as 2.5. Customers wishing to transport clean petroleum products nearly always demanded a vessel with an immediate history of carrying only clean products to avoid contamination of their clean products. Consequently, vessel owners, such as Stelios, eschewed switching the status of their vessels from clean to dirty. With the vessel acquisitions completed in 1993, Stelios positioned himself to transport both grades of petroleum products. *Fulmar* and *Primar* traded in clean products, and *Colmar* and *City University* traded in dirty products. Clean products commonly carried by Stelios's vessels included naphtha, gasoline, jet fuel, diesel, and gasoil. Dirty products carried by his company included fuel oil, low sulfur waxy residue, and carbon black feedstock.

As Stelios expanded his fleet, he did so by primarily acquiring vessels of two classes, which were defined by deadweight, the standard unit of measurement by which tankers were known. Deadweight represented the cargo carrying capacity of a vessel in metric tonnes, in addition to the weight of bunkers, stores, and fresh water. Stelios focused on two classes of vessels, Handymax tankers and Panamax tankers. Handymax tankers, such as *Fulmar, Primar, Colmar,* and *City University,* ranged between 30,000 deadweight and 50,000 deadweight. Panamax tankers were larger, measuring between 60,000 deadweight and 70,000 deadweight, the greatest dimensions able to transit the Panama Canal. To a lesser extent, the Stelmar Shipping fleet would include Aframax tankers, which measured between 80,000 deadweight and 120,000 deadweight.

Once equipped with vessels, Stelios espoused an operating philosophy that focused on time charter contracts. There were three main types of charter contracts: spot charter, bareboat charter, and time charter. Under the terms of a spot charter

contract, the charterer hired the vessel for a single voyage. A bareboat charter contract provided the vessel for a set period of time—typically several years—with the contractor taking responsibility for all operational matters, including maintenance, insurance, and crewing. Under the terms of a time charter contract, charterers hired the vessel for a set period of time, ranging between several days and several years. Unlike bareboat charter contracts, time charter contracts stipulated that the owner of the vessel, rather than the charterer, assumed responsibility for operational matters, for which the owner charged a daily hire rate. As Stelios's shipping business expanded, nearly all of the vessels would be hired under time charter contracts.

Fleet expansion continued in 1994, when the company ordered the construction of its first new vessel. A South Korean shipyard constructed a 46,000-deadweight Handymax tanker christened *Nedimar,* which Martank Shipping took delivery of in January 1996.

By the time Stelios ordered the construction of *Nedimar,* his attention already had begun to stray into different business pursuits. The serial entrepreneur was about to proliferate. Stelios met Richard Branson, the founder of Virgin Airlines, in 1994 and became entranced with launching his own airline, whose inspiration was drawn from Branson's highly publicized venture and from the success of U.S.-based, regional carrier Southwest Airlines. Aping the flamboyant, media-savvy behavior of the Virgin Airlines founder, Stelios flowered into a highly public figure—"Since very early on in my shipping days, I've immersed myself in the media world," he said in a September 13, 2002 interview with *PR Week.* Before the end of 1994, with his sights set on launching his own airline, Stelios relinquished day-to-day management of his shipping business, although he remained the company's chairman. In 1995, after receiving $7.5 million from his father, Stelios launched easyJet Airline Co., a short-haul, low-cost carrier relying, like Southwest, on the Boeing 737. The successful start of easyJet gave birth to Stelios's "easy" empire, leading to the formation of easyGroup in 1998, easyEverything (later rebranded as easyInternetCafe) in 1999, and a slew of other "easy" business ventures that combated competitors by offering discount prices.

Fleet Expansion During the Late 1990s

Although Stelios's other business ventures stole the headlines, Stelmar Shipping continued to expand, operating beneath the media radar. In 1997, after Stelmar Shipping was formed in January, three more vessels were acquired, increasing the company's Panamax and Aframax tonnage. In June, the company purchased the *Loucas,* an Aframax tanker, followed by the October acquisition of the *Kliomar,* an Aframax tanker, and the December acquisition of the *Polys,* a Panamax tanker. By the end of 1997, Stelmar Shipping was generating $33.6 million in revenue from its fleet of nine vessels, from which the company earned $5.1 million in net income.

In the last two years of the 1990s, Stelmar Shipping continued to emphasize increasing the number of its larger vessels. In 1998, the company acquired three Panamax tankers, the *Keymar,* the *P. Alliance,* and the *Takamar.* In 1999, another Panamax tanker, *Jacamar,* was acquired, bringing Stelmar

<table>
<tr><td colspan="2" align="center">**Key Dates:**</td></tr>
<tr><td>**1992:**</td><td>Stelios Hagi-Ioannou starts his own tanker company.</td></tr>
<tr><td>**1993:**</td><td>Stelmar Shipping's first four vessels are acquired.</td></tr>
<tr><td>**1994:**</td><td>Stelmar Shipping commissions the construction of its first new vessel.</td></tr>
<tr><td>**2000:**</td><td>The company's expansion program accelerates.</td></tr>
<tr><td>**2001:**</td><td>The initial public offering of stock is completed.</td></tr>
</table>

Shipping's fleet to 12 vessels and doubling revenue volume from 1997's total to $68.5 million by the end of 1999.

2001 Debut on the New York Stock Exchange

As Stelmar shipping entered the 21st century, it embarked on a period of rapid expansion. The company divested its first vessel, *Loucas,* in 2000, but compensated for the loss by renewing its new-building activity. In July 2000, Stelmar Shipping signed an agreement with Korea-based Daewoo Shipbuilding to build four Panamax tankers, which were scheduled for delivery during the first half of 2002. Less than a year after signing the agreement with Daewoo, Stelmar Shipping positioned itself for further expansion by completing its initial public offering (IPO) of stock. In March 2001, Stelmar Shipping began trading on the New York Stock Exchange, netting $89 million in proceeds from the IPO. The company used the proceeds to finance the purchase of ten Handymax tankers, a $128 million deal that increased the size of its fleet to 21 vessels. By the end of the year, the company recorded its seventh year of profitability, posting an impressive $34 million in net income—nearly a sevenfold increase from 1997's total—on $111.2 million in revenue.

Stelmar Shipping celebrated its tenth anniversary year by continuing to exhibit encouraging financial performance and physical growth. Stelios stepped aside as chairman at the end of 2001 to devote more time to his ever expanding business interests, paving the way for the ascension of Nick Hartley as Stelmar Shipping's chairman. Peter Goodfellow served as the company's chief executive officer. In the wake of Stelios's departure, the company completed a secondary offering of stock in April 2002,

raising roughly $69 million in gross proceeds. With the capital gained from the 4.9 million shares sold, Stelmar Shipping financed the acquisition of two Handymax vessels and ordered the construction of two Panamax vessels, which were delivered in July 2002. The additions increased the size of the company's fleet to 31 vessels. Before the end of the year, the company pressed ahead further with expansion, commissioning the construction of four new Panamax tankers, which were scheduled to be delivered by mid-2004. With existing expansion plans slated to increase Stelmar Shipping's fleet to 36 vessels, company management celebrated their 10th anniversary in September in Athens with a fireworks display and cake-cutting ceremony, confident that the years ahead would solidify Stelmar Shipping's position as a leading tanker company.

Principal Subsidiaries

Stelmar Tankers (Management) Ltd. (Liberia); Stelmar Tankers (UK) Ltd. (U.K.); Marship Tankers (Holdings) Ltd. (British Virgin Islands); Martank Shipping Holdings Ltd. (British Virgin Islands).

Principal Competitors

Frontline Ltd.; OMI Corporation; Teekay Shipping Corporation.

Further Reading

"Easy Does It," *Time International,* September 18, 2000, p. 54.

Einhorn, Cheryl Strauss, "Shipshape: Honing Its Competitive Edge, Stelmar Shipping Delivers in Rough Seas for Oil Tankers," *Barron's,* September 9, 2002, p. 32.

"Full Speed Ahead at Stelmar," *Business Week,* June 17, 2002, p. 103.

Gwin, Peter, "Greek Entrepreneur Building Easy Empire," *Europe,* September 2001, p. 5.

"Jumping Ships," *Financial Times,* February 1, 2002, p. 13.

Qassim, Ali, "The Man Behind EasyJet's Success," *Campaign,* October 10, 1997, p. 29.

"Stelios Haji-Ioannou," *Business Week,* January 14, 2002, p. 74.

"Stelmar Shipping Ltd.," *Oil and Gas Journal,* July 8, 2002, p. 9.

"View from the Top," *PR Week,* September 13, 2002, p. 11.

—Jeffrey L. Covell

STMicroelectronics NV

20 Route de Pré-Bois
ICC Bloc A
1215 Geneva 15
Switzerland
Telephone: (+41) 22-929-29-29
Fax: (+41) 22-929-29-00
Web site: http://www.st.com

Public Company
Incorporated: 1987 as SGS Thomson
Employees: 40,300
Sales: $6.36 billion (2001)
Stock Exchanges: Euronext Paris New York Milan
Ticker Symbol: STM
NAIC: 334415 Electronic Resistor Manufacturing;
    334412 Printed Circuit Board Manufacturing; 334413
    Semiconductor and Related Device Manufacturing;
    334414 Electronic Capacitor Manufacturing; 551112
    Offices of Other Holding Companies

STMicroelectronics NV is one of the world's leading semiconductor manufacturing companies. The company holds the top spot among European chip makers and as high as the number three position (according to Gartner Dataquest in 2001) among the global top ten. ST manufactures a broad range of semiconductor products, with an emphasis on a variety of niche categories. ST is the world's leading manufacturer of analog ICs (integrated circuits) and MPEG-2 decoder chips, used to provide video decompression for DVD players and digital television set-top boxes. ST is also the world's second-leading maker of nonvolatile memories, and the number four producer of Flash memory. These specialties have given the company leading positions in a variety of product markets: the global leader for set-top boxes and hard drives; number two maker of chips for DVDs and smart cards; the number three maker of ICs for the automotive industry; and the number four position as a chip supplier to the mobile telephone and other telecommunications applications. The Franco-Italian company, based in Geneva, Switzerland, is listed on the New York, Euronext Paris,

and Borsa Italiana (Milan) stock exchanges. The French and Italian governments remain major shareholders in the company, formed by the merger of the formerly state-owned SGS Microelettronica and Thomson-CSF semiconductor business in 1987. ST continues to be led by Pasquale Pistorio, who has overseen the company's development from a money-losing, debt-ridden lightweight to a solidly profitable industry heavyweight.

The Pride of the European Semiconductor Industry in the 1980s

The merger of Italy's SGS Microelettronica and France's Thomson-CSF's semiconductor operations was greeted with ridicule by many industry observers. Neither company had succeeded in imposing itself on the global semiconductor market, by then dominated by the United States and Japan. SGS Microelettronica, although profitable, was crippled by a heavy debt load, while the Thomson-CSF business had long been losing money. Meanwhile, neither company had been able to keep apace with the rapid technological developments of the era, as semiconductor manufacturers began investing heavily in new DRAM (random-access memory chip) technologies. Yet both companies were strongly backed by their respective governments, which were eager to maintain their own—and Europe's—presence among the world's semiconductor industry.

SGS Microelettronica had been started up in the 1950s, when then-Olivetti subsidiary Telectro began its own semiconductor manufacturing operations to supply its parent company, then undergoing its own transformation as an electronics company, and others. Telectro established a new subsidiary, Société Generale Semiconductor, in 1957 and acquired a license to produce chips from Fairfield Semiconductor. SGS Microelettronica, helped along by Olivetti's own expansion, became a major European chip maker, yet remained dwarfed by such industry giants as Intel and Texas Instruments.

By the end of the 1970s, SGS, like the rest of its European counterparts, was losing money—with losses reaching as high as 25 percent of the company's revenues. After Telectro had been acquired by France's Alcatel, ownership of SGS was transferred to the Italian government, becoming part of Finmec-

Company Perspectives:

Star Power: A fusion of key strengths driving our growth.

Our future growth will be driven by our ongoing execution against the same four fundamental strategies that have produced our great track record. While our people will continue to be very creative in how we execute those strategies, we will remain highly disciplined to their strategic intent. Those four strategies are clear to us. We have a very different view of globalization, and we will continue to expand thoughtfully in a way that benefits both our business and our society. Our marketplace results are the direct offspring of pragmatic innovation, and because that innovation is integrated at every level of our business, strategic advantage comes from strong emphasis on manufacturing science. And because we understand the power of truly allying with other great enterprises, our business exceeds our Company because of our strategic partnerships.

canica, itself a subsidiary of the Italian government industrial holdings vehicle IRI. In 1980, SGS's new owners brought in Pasquale Pistorio, who had served as a vice-president at Motorola, to try to resurrect the sagging semiconductor business. Pistorio pushed through a number of reforms, including convincing workers to allow the company to go to a seven-day-per-week schedule, as well as allowing its female workers to join the night shift. These and other reforms soon bore fruit; by 1983, SGS Microelettronica had turned a profit, achieving the distinction of becoming the only profitable European semiconductor company.

To compete on a global level, however, Pistorio recognized that SGS would have to grow much larger. By the mid-1980s, Pistorio had set a target of achieving a 5 percent share of the world semiconductor market, a target that necessitated a tripling of SGS's revenues, which stood at just $400 million in 1983. SGS began to look about for suitable acquisition targets to help it gain scale. The company also at this time began its first moves toward the specialization of its semiconductor production—unable to compete on the so-called "commodity" market, dominated by Asian manufacturers, and lagging far behind DRAM production, then the fastest-growing segment with the arrival of the personal computer, Pistorio began to lead SGS into newer niche categories, such as SOCs (system on a chip) and EPROM (electronically programmable read-only memory) and the erasable EEPROM variant. Pistorio wagered that the future of the semiconductor industry resided beyond the personal computer in a broader range of consumer appliances and applications.

The last category brought it into contact with the semiconductor manufacturing wing of France's Thomson-CSF, as the two companies formed an EPROM development partnership. SGS and Thomson-CSF had already gained experience working together at the beginning of the 1980s. As the two sides met to work on the EPROM project in 1987, their government parents began to discuss a marriage between the two companies.

By then, the Thomson-CSF semiconductor operation had been losing money for years. Yet that company had long been at the forefront of France's technological efforts, particularly since the merger of Thomson-Brandt and Compagnie Generale de Telegraphie San Fils in 1968, which formed the high-technology group Thomson-CSF. That company emerged as a leading European semiconductor maker, but, like SGS, suffered from its relatively small size. Government-ownership, which had led to a highly inefficient management organization in parent Thomson-Brandt, also crippled the company's ability to achieve scale. Nonetheless, Thomson-CSF attempted to build up its semiconductor division in the mid-1980s, especially through the acquisition of Mostek, based in the United States. The Thomson–CSF company also played a pioneering role in a number of future technologies, including smart card technologies that were to take off in the next decade.

In 1987, the French and Italian governments decided to merge the Thomson-CSF and SGS Microelettronica semiconductor businesses, creating SGS Thomson, with Pasquale Pistorio placed as its CEO. The newly enlarged group was created with a great deal of skepticism, and even ridicule, particularly as its combined losses topped $200 million on revenues of just $850 million. A strong proportion of SGS Thomson's losses were due to its debt load of some $630 million. The company also suffered from overcapacity, with some 22 manufacturing facilities in operation, the majority of which were woefully out of date. Over the next two years following the merger, SGS Thomson continued to lose money.

Yet Pistorio began restructuring SGS Thomson's operations, shutting down seven of its manufacturing facilities. The company also began construction of a new, state-of-the-art production plant in Grenoble, France, which brought the company up-to-date in the early 1990s. Meanwhile, SGS Thomson continued emphasizing its specialized product development, particularly its SOC technology. Among the company's first products were new smart power products, which became essential ingredients in new electronic ignition systems for the automotive industry, among others.

SGS Thomson achieved a new breakthrough in 1989 when it produced a new chip for Finland's Nokia, then in the process of reinventing itself as a major telecommunications player. SGS Thomson's chip combined power supply and power management features on a single chip, enabling Nokia's phones to achieve standby battery life cycles of more than 60 hours. Nokia remained a major SGS Thomson customer, accounting for as much as 11 percent of the company's sales.

Developing World Dominance in the 1990s

Another area in which SGS Thomson became an early player was its development of MPEG decompression chips. The company's dedication to MPEG technology was risky, as a number of other digital video decompression schemes were competing for what promised to be a huge market in the future. SGS Thomson gained an early lead in the MPEG market, however, releasing its first Motion Estimation Processor in 1990. By 1993, the company had debuted its "multimedia" chip, capable of decompressing digital video files for display on a television set. This chip helped the company take a major position in the new set-top box market, starting with supplying the chip for the Hughes digital satellite television set-top box.

Meanwhile, the company's history of developing EPROMs and EEPROMs had given it the outright lead in both categories as these chips took on increasing importance.

In 1993, SGS Thomson's plants adopted 0.5 micron technology, placing it on the same level as its major competitors. The company, which until then remained more or less focused on the European market—which accounted for more than half of the company's sales—began making moves to balance its geographic mix. In that year the company expanded its U.S. operations with the purchase of TAG Semiconductors. At the same time, SGS Thomson government owners provided the company with some $1 billion, enabling the company to pay down its debt.

Both the Italian and French governments were by then undergoing a privatization drive, and in 1994, SGS Thomson was taken public, listing on both the New York and Paris stock exchanges. While both governments remained major shareholders, the newly privatized SGS Thomson set out to achieve Pistorio's long-held goal of building a 5 percent share of the world's semiconductor market. That goal still appeared far off, however, as the company's 2.8 percent of the market left it below the industry top ten.

SGS Thomson's investments in its specialized technologies began to pay off by the mid-1990s. Smart cards, that is, credit-like cards with embedded microchips, were gaining wide acceptance in a variety of areas, including telephone cards and the pay television market—by 1996, SGS Thomson had shipped more than one billion of its EEPROM-based smart card devices. The company launched another innovative product, the so-called PC-on-a-chip, which presented a single chip design combining memory, processing, graphics, and sound capability. At the same time, the company extended its interest in the telecommunications sector as it began developing chips for ADSL and

DSL broadband devices. In 1996, also, the company launched its latest EEPROM development, superflash memory, which combined flash memory technology with the flexibility of EEPROM technology.

The company also had continued to make progress on improving its geographic spread, beginning construction on a new production facility in China, which was completed in 1998. Meanwhile, despite a downturn in the semiconductor market, the company pressed on with an aggressive investment drive, adding new facilities in Italy, France, and Singapore before the end of the decade. The company's investment program topped $1 billion per year at the end of the 1990s, and reached $2 billion for 2000 alone.

Thomson sold off its shares in SGS Thomson in 1998, and the company then changed its name to STMicroelectronics. In that year, also, the company listed its shares on the Borsa Italiana stock exchange in Milan as well. By then, ST had gained a solid financial base, with revenues climbing past $4 billion and profits topping $400 million in 1997. The company's investments, particularly the growing importance of its specialized technologies, saw it make rapid gains in the industry at the end of the decade, climbing to eighth place by 1999 and jumping to fourth place in 2001.

In addition to its in-house technology development, ST made a series of add-on acquisitions at the end of the 20th century, including purchasing the United States' Metaflow Technologies Inc., in 1997, in an effort to enter the computer processor market. In 1999, the company added the hard drive division of Adaptec, enabling the company to become a market leader in that sector, as well as Arithmos, which designed chips for digital display terminals. The company took over the Canadian semiconductor business of Nortel Networks in 2000, but shut down that operation a year later because of overcapacity.

By the end of 2001, ST had climbed into the top five—with some analysts granting the company the number three spot among semiconductor companies worldwide. As the rest of the industry faced a dramatic slump in semiconductor sales, ST remained one of a very few in the industry to enjoy strong profits. The company was praised for achieving not only geographic balance—Europe accounted for only 37 percent of sales, the United States for 18 percent, and Asia for 33 percent, with another 6 percent in Japan—but also for its balanced product mix. While ST's competitors suffered from their overexposure to the sluggish DRAM market, ST had instead focused on developing its diversified IC business, which accounted for some 60 percent of its revenues, backed by strong sales in memory and logic products.

ST continued to build onto its holdings, scoring a coup with the announcement in June 2002 of its agreement to acquire the microelectronics operations of France's Alcatel. That deal, worth some $345 million, gave ST the undisputed leadership of the DSL market. The company also had boosted its share of the DSL market with the purchase of Tioga Technologies Ltd. that same year. The formation of ST had been greeted by skepticism by observers who doubted Europe would be able to play a major role in the worldwide semiconductor industry. Still led by Pasquale Pistorio, ST had proven the skeptics wrong, and turned toward the new century and the future as a driving force in its industry.

Principal Subsidiaries

Australia STMicroelectronics PTY LTD (Australia); STMicroelectronics Ltda (Brazil); STMicroelectronics (Canada), Inc. (Canada); Shenzhen STS Microelectronics Co. LTD (China; 60%); STMicroelectronics (Shanghai) Co. LTD (China); STMicroelectronics Design and Application s.r.o. (Czech Republic); STMicroelectronics OY (Finland); STMicroelectronics S.A. (France); STMicroelectronics (Rousset) S.A.S. (France); Waferscale Integration Sarl (France); STMicroelectronics GmbH (Germany); STMicroelectronics LTD (Hong Kong); STMicroelectronics Pvt Ltd. (India); STMicroelectronics Ltd. (Israel); Accent S.r.l. (Italy; 51%); CO.RI.M.ME. (Italy); STMicroelectronics S.r.l. (Italy); STMicroelectronics KK (Japan); STMicroelectronics (Malaysia) SDN BHD (Malaysia); STMicroelectronics SDN BHD (Malaysia); STMicroelectronics LTD (Malta); Electronic Holding S.A. (Morocco); STMicroelectronics S.A. (Morocco); STMicroelectronics ASIA PACIFIC Pte Ltd. (Singapore); STMicroelectronics Pte Ltd. (Singapore); STMicroelectronics S.A. (Spain); STMicroelectronics A.B. (Sweden); STMicroelectronics S.A. (Switzerland); STMicroelectronics E.E.I.G. (U.K.); STMicroelectronics Ltd (U.K.); Inmos Ltd. (U.K.); Thomson Components Ltd. (U.K.); Metaflow Technologics Inc. (U.S.A.); STMicroelectronics (RB), Inc. (U.S.A.); STMicroelectronics Inc. (U.S.A.); STMicroelectronics Leasing Co. Inc. (U.S.A.); The Portland Group, Incorporated (U.S.A.).

Principal Competitors

Intel Corporation; Toshiba Corporation; NEC Corporation; Samsung Electronics Co. Ltd.; Texas Instruments Inc.; Motorola, Inc.; Hitachi Ltd.; Infineon Technologies AG; Micron Technology, Inc.

Further Reading

Dunn, Darrell, "STMicro Moves Toward the Penthouse," *Electronic Buyers' News,* June 12, 2000, p. 1.

Hutheesing, Nikhil, "Me Too," *Forbes,* August 29, 1994, p. 88.

Morrison, Gale, and Romanelli, Alex, "STMicro's DSL Power Play," *Electronic News,* April 22, 2002, p. 1.

"PASQUALE PISTORIO; Chief Executive, STMicroelectronics," *Business Week,* June 17, 2002, p. 44.

Scouras, Ismini, "STMicro Rising Through the Ranks—Projected to Vault to Fifth Place in Worldwide Semiconductor Market," *EBN,* December 17, 2001, p. 54.

"STMicroelectronics Buy of Alcatel Unit Clears EU," *Daily Deal,* June 25, 2002.

Walker, Sophie, "STMicroelectronics to Outpace Market in 2000," *Reuters,* March 28, 2000.

Wilson, Drew, "Dodging Bullets: How STMicroelectronics Holds Up Under Fire," *Electronic Business Asia,* November 2001, p. 30.

—M.L. Cohen

Synovus Financial Corp.

One Arsenal Place
901 Front Avenue, Suite 301
Columbus, Georgia 31901
U.S.A.
Telephone: (706) 649-2311
Fax: (706) 649-2342
Web site: http://www.synovus.com

Public Company
Incorporated: 1972 as CB&T Bancshares, Inc.
Employees: 10,166
Total Assets: $18.51 billion (2002)
Stock Exchanges: New York
Ticker Symbol: SNV
NAIC: 551111 Offices of Bank Holding Companies;
    522110 Commercial Banking; 522210 Credit Card
    Issuing; 522220 Sales Financing; 522291 Consumer
    Lending; 522292 Real Estate Credit; 522320 Financial
    Transactions Processing, Reserve, and Clearinghouse
    Activities; 523120 Securities Brokerage; 523920
    Portfolio Management; 523991 Trust, Fiduciary, and
    Custody Activities; 524126 Direct Property and
    Casualty Insurance Carriers

Synovus Financial Corp. is a major bank holding company with banking operations in Georgia, Alabama, South Carolina, Florida, and Tennessee. Through its 39 community banks in those states (25 of which are in Georgia) and the more than 250 branches and offices of the banks and their subsidiaries, Synovus offers a range of financial services, including commercial and retail banking, trust services, mortgage banking, leasing services, financial management, securities brokering, and automobile and homeowner's insurance. In addition to these financial services operations, the company also holds an 81.1 percent stake in Total System Services, Inc. (TSYS), the second largest processor of credit card transactions in the United States (trailing only First Data Corporation). Largely through an aggressive acquisition program, Synovus achieved stellar growth throughout the 1980s and early 1990s, increasing its assets more than sevenfold to $7.3

billion. Its assets were more than doubled again by the early 21st century thanks to a new wave of buyouts that began in 1998.

Developing from One Bank to a Regional Multibank Player

Synovus's earliest forerunner, Columbus Bank and Trust, was formed in 1930 from the merger of two Columbus, Georgia, banks, Third National Bank and The Columbus Savings Bank, both of which had been founded in 1888. The first turning point in the bank's history came in 1958 when James W. Blanchard began an 11-year stint at the helm. Blanchard was highly regarded by his fellow managers and employees. Under his guidance, Columbus's assets nearly tripled, growing from $32 million to $93 million. Also, in a move that would eventually lead to the formation of TSYS, Columbus in 1959 became one of the first banks in the nation to offer its customers a charge card. To handle the increasing load of credit card transactions, Columbus computerized its card processing operations in 1966.

Blanchard, unfortunately, died of lung cancer in 1969, leaving the bank without a chief executive. Columbus had a seasoned banking staff from which it could have drawn Blanchard's successor, but the bank's board hired Blanchard's son, James H. (Jimmy) Blanchard. The board's decision was startling because the younger Blanchard was only 28 years old and a practicing attorney with no banking experience. "We already had executives who knew banking, but what we needed was dynamic leadership," said Columbus Chairman William B. Turner in *Georgia Trend*. "We had watched Jimmy grow up; we had seen his success at school. He was a very, very capable, involved person who we felt would make a good choice."

Doubting his ability to lead Columbus, Blanchard rejected the bank's offer. But three months later, realizing that it was a tremendous opportunity, he changed his mind. "I wouldn't have been asked to do it if my last name had not been Blanchard," he told *Georgia Trend*. "It was a radical decision. I wasn't really equipped to do it. But I decided to do it, and I'm glad I did." Blanchard took Columbus's helm in 1970 and spent several years getting acclimated to the industry and environment at Columbus.

Company Perspectives:

Achieving our vision to be the finest financial services company in the world begins with an unwavering commitment to our corporate values. Integrity. Service. Putting people first. Treating folks right and doing the right things. This is not corporate rhetoric, this is our character. We won't compromise these values under any circumstances.

In an important move early in Blanchard's tenure, Columbus Bank and Trust changed its structure to a bank holding company to take advantage of new state and federal laws related to the banking industry. CB&T Bancshares, Inc. was created in 1972 to be a one-bank holding company for Columbus Bank and Trust. Through CB&T, Columbus could expand its operations more easily within the state of Georgia. It could also begin participating in a number of non-banking-related financial markets.

Although Blanchard lacked banking experience, he later considered that deficiency an advantage because his mind was more open to emerging opportunities. "I think not being a banker was a real plus," he said in *Forbes.* An example of Blanchard's enlightened opportunism was his interest in fee-based financial services. Blanchard's intrigue with fee-based financial services was piqued in 1974 when a Florida banker told him about the huge fees he was having to pay for credit card processing. Blanchard thought CB&T could combine its computerized operations with the advancements in telecommunications that were occurring at the time, to provide credit card processing services. Moreover, because CB&T had access to inexpensive labor, Blanchard thought that the bank could undercut the competition and still enjoy large profit margins. In 1974, therefore, CB&T began offering bankcard processing services to banks in Georgia, Alabama, Kentucky, and Washington. These services were based on the bank's processing software, called the Total System, which had been completed the previous year.

Blanchard also played a key role in lobbying for passage of the multibank holding company bill, which the General Assembly of Georgia approved in 1976. The bill enabled banks in the state to acquire banks in counties outside their own county. CB&T became the first bank to act on this law when it acquired Commercial Bank (of Thomasville, Georgia) at the beginning of 1977. Several more Georgia community banks were acquired over the next few years: Security Bank and Trust (Albany), Commercial Bank and Trust of Troup County (LaGrange), Sumter Bank and Trust (Americus), People Bank (Boston), Coastal Bank (Brunswick), and First State Bank (Valdosta).

1980s: Banking Beyond Georgia and Forming TSYS

By the late 1970s CB&T had become a regional bank holding company with more than $500 million in assets and annual income of about $5 million. Although CB&T had established itself as a major player in its core regional markets, during the next decade the holding company would far exceed the pace of growth it had achieved in any previous period. The expansion would result largely from continued state and federal deregulation, most notably the legislation the U.S. Congress passed in

the mid-1980s that allowed bank holding companies to begin expanding their operations across state lines. More importantly, though, CB&T's keen and aggressive management would help it to overcome many of its peers, making it one of the fastest growing banks and financial service providers in the nation.

CB&T launched an ambitious growth program in 1983 when it acquired three banking systems in Georgia: Buena Vista Loan and Savings Bank, Bank of Hazlehurst, and Citizens Bank and Trust of West Georgia, a relatively large banking chain based in Carrollton. In 1984 CB&T added just one institution, Citizens Bank of Colquitt, Georgia. That acquisition boosted CB&T's asset base to nearly $1 billion and its annual net income to nearly $12 million.

Augmenting the company's profits during this period was its subsidiary, Total System Services, Inc. CB&T had spun off its growing transaction processing operations in 1983, creating TSYS (pronounced tee-sis), which was publicly traded but majority owned by CB&T through Columbus Bank and Trust. As a division of Columbus, TSYS had generated fees of about $15 million in 1982, but by 1985 and as a subsidiary TSYS had sales of $28 million, of which $4.3 million was netted as profit.

Blanchard increased CB&T's expansion effort in 1985, acquiring three Georgia-based banks. Also that year CB&T entered the securities sector by buying a full-service brokerage company (which would later be renamed Synovus Securities, Inc.). During 1986 and 1987 the company acquired six more institutions, bringing its total asset base going into 1988 to nearly $2 billion. Furthermore, following interstate banking deregulation, CB&T bought two Florida banks and one Alabama bank in 1988, and one bank each in Alabama, Georgia, and Florida in 1989. As a result of an aggressive acquisition strategy and keen management, CB&T saw its assets grow to $2.4 billion by the end of the 1980s as its net income rose to a record $31.4 million. CB&T had boosted both its holdings and profits more than fourfold since the start of the decade.

Though CB&T grew rapidly during the 1980s, its growth reflected a dominant banking industry trend toward consolidation that had been occurring since the late 1970s. Banks had increasingly been under pressure since the late 1970s from less-regulated financial sectors that were quickly stealing market share. In an effort to compete in the difficult environment, bank holding companies had been purchasing smaller rivals. The owners and managers of those holding companies typically benefited from economies of scale. In addition, the better managed banks were able to improve the performance of the acquisitions by restructuring their operations and improving their margins. CB&T was one of more than 1,300 bank holding companies that emerged by the end of the 1980s. It was also among the most successful.

Although CB&T's general growth strategy was reflective of overall trends, its specific tactics represented a departure from industry norms. Most bank holding companies completely integrated the banks that they acquired into the parent organization. Integrating acquisitions usually entailed changing the name of the bank and its branches to reflect the parent's name, making the bank look and feel like the other banks throughout the holding company's chain, and sometimes installing an entirely

Key Dates:

1888: Third National Bank and The Columbus Savings Bank are both founded in Columbus, Georgia.

1930: The two Columbus banks merge to form Columbus Bank and Trust.

1958: James W. Blanchard begins an 11-year stint as head of the bank.

1959: Columbus Bank and Trust becomes one of the first U.S. banks to offer charge cards.

1970: Blanchard's son, James H. Blanchard, takes the helm.

1972: CB&T Bancshares, Inc. is created as a one-bank holding company for Columbus Bank and Trust.

1974: CB&T begins offering third-party credit card transaction processing to banks in Georgia and other states using processing software called the Total System.

1977: Following passage of the multibank holding company bill, CB&T makes its first acquisition, Commercial Bank of Thomasville, Georgia.

1983: The bank's third-party transaction processing business is spun off as Total System Services, Inc. (TSYS), which becomes a publicly traded firm majority owned by CB&T.

1988: CB&T's banking operations cross state lines for the first time through the acquisitions of banks in Florida and Alabama.

1989: CB&T changes its name to Synovus Financial Corp.

1993: Synovus acquires Birmingham Federal Savings Bank of Birmingham, Alabama.

1995: Synovus acquires its first South Carolina bank, National Bank of South Carolina.

2002: Community banking operations are expanded into Tennessee with the purchase of the Bank of Nashville.

new management team. The general idea was to reduce costs, such as those related to advertising and administration, by creating an integrated chain of similar banks.

CB&T adopted a unique, decentralized approach. It allowed the banks that it purchased to retain their name and management. One result was that CB&T had higher operating costs. But Blanchard believed that the strategy resulted in overall greater returns because the banks retained their local image and appeal. To the surprise of some critics, CB&T significantly outperformed industry averages with the strategy throughout the 1980s.

As CB&T swelled its asset base through merger and acquisition during the 1980s, it also continued to post solid gains with its TSYS subsidiary. In fact, TSYS benefitted greatly from banking industry trends during the decade. Indeed, when bank holding companies acquired new banks they were often faced with the task of processing as many as twice the number of credit card accounts that they had previously managed. Rather than scramble to expand their own processing facilities, they turned to companies like TSYS, paying them a fee to service the accounts for them. At the same time, several non-banking entities sought TSYS's services.

TSYS's competitive advantage over similar service companies was a technical orientation. Indeed, CB&T had invested heavily in top-notch technology to make its subsidiary one of the most efficient, low-cost credit card account processors in the nation. As a result of its efforts, TSYS had quickly become one of the largest contenders in that industry, second only to American Express. By 1990, TSYS was processing 16 million accounts, generating fees of about $84 million annually, and capturing annual profits of nearly $12 million. It was the processor of choice for several major creditors, including General Electric Capital Corp. and Prudential. In 1990, moreover, the company scored a major victory when it landed a five-year contract to service the newly created AT&T Universal Card. Within three years that huge client added ten million new accounts and was contributing nearly 30 percent of TSYS's entire revenue base.

In the meantime, CB&T rounded out the decade of the 1980s by adopting a new name: Synovus Financial Corp. The name Synovus was a combination of the words *synergy* and *novus*. According to the company, the latter word means "usually of superior quality and different from the others listed in the same category."

Steady Growth Throughout the 1990s

After achieving growth during the 1980s, Synovus aggressively increased its expansion efforts during the early 1990s. After a depression in real estate and construction markets in the late 1980s, a string of bank and savings and loans failed. As banks failed at a rate unparalleled since the Great Depression, still-healthy banks were selling at an apparent discount. Synovus took advantage of the bargains. During the first three years of the 1990s, it bought 20 new banks that were scattered throughout Georgia, Alabama, and north Florida. By 1992, Synovus's asset base had risen to $5.2 billion as its net income had increased to $61 million.

Synovus tempered its acquisition activity during 1993, choosing instead to focus on streamlining its existing operations. The company added one new bank to its fold— Birmingham Federal Savings Bank of Birmingham, Alabama, its largest acquisition to date. Synovus's 1993 gains, however, were largely attributable to Synovus's fast-growing TSYS subsidiary. In 1993, the transaction processor announced a string of successes, including a new seven-year contract with its biggest customer, AT&T, and negotiations to acquire the card-processing business of Bank of America, one of the largest credit card issuers in the nation. Most importantly, TSYS a year later implemented a new $33 million proprietary software system (dubbed TS2) designed to place it at the forefront of the industry in terms of service and cost. "It is the single biggest event in the history of this company," Blanchard said about the new system in the *Atlanta Constitution*. "This is like a rocket ship to the moon in terms of technology."

During 1994 Synovus acquired two more banks, including Peachtree National Bank of Peachtree City, Georgia, which had $78 million in assets. The following year Synovus acquired Riverdale, Georgia-based Peach State Bank, which had assets of $41 million. Peach State Bank was located in a county adjacent to that of Peachtree National, and so the former was merged into the latter. The firm also formed Synovus Mortgage Corp. in 1994 in order to provide mortgage services throughout the Southeast. Seeking to bolster the amount of non-interest income generated outside of TSYS, Synovus expanded the trust department of Columbus Bank and Trust into Synovus Trust Company in 1995. Through the new subsidiary, Synovus began expanding its trust, risk management, and related services into more of the community banks that were within its umbrella. Back on the acquisition front, Synovus increased its roster of community banks to 34 with the early 1995 purchases of NBSC Corporation and Citizens and Merchants Corporation. While the latter was a relatively small addition of a bank based in Douglasville, Georgia, with assets of $47 million, the former amounted to the largest purchase in Synovus's history and its first buyout of a South Carolina bank. NBSC was a holding company for the National Bank of South Carolina, which had 43 branches and $1 billion in assets. Synovus purchased NBSC for $153 million in stock. These latest additions increased Synovus's asset total to $7.9 billion by the end of 1995, while net income for the year increased 28.1 percent, to $114.6 million.

For the next two years, Synovus acquired no banks, adding only two NationsBank Corporation branches in Rome, Georgia, in late 1996. Because the NBSC acquisition was such a large one, the overall balance at Synovus between the banking side and TSYS had tilted too far in favor of the former—at least in the eyes of shareholders. To maintain his firm's stock price, Blanchard sought to return TSYS's contribution to the overall net income back to the 30 percent figure that had prevailed in the late 1980s and early 1990s. As Blanchard told *Georgia Trend* in May 1997, "Essentially, the investment community wants more Total System Services and less bank." One component of the effort to boost the TSYS contribution was the formation in 1996 of a joint venture with Visa U.S.A. Inc. called Vital Processing Services L.L.C. Vital was created to offer merchants electronic payment processing and related services.

During 1998 TSYS gained a major new client when it inked a deal with Sears, Roebuck and Co. to handle transactions related to more than 60 million Sears credit card accounts. That year also saw Synovus launch another string of acquisitions with the purchase of three banks in north Georgia. In August, Synovus purchased Community Bank Capital Corporation, the parent company of the Bank of North Georgia, which was based in Alpharetta and had assets of $348 million. Synovus bought Watkinsville-based Bank of Georgia in November. Then in December the $161 million-asset Georgia Bank and Trust Co., based in Calhoun, was acquired. Bank of Georgia, which had $55 million in assets, was subsequently merged into Athens First Bank & Trust Company, but the other two banks retained their names and management.

Several more deals were completed in 1999. The largest one, consummated in September, was a $115 million stock swap for Merit Holding Corporation, parent of two Georgia community banks, Mountain National Bank in Tucker and Charter Bank & Trust Co. of Marietta. The two banks had combined assets of $306 million. Two Florida banks were also acquired in 1999: $65 million-asset Ready Bank of West Florida, which was merged into Vanguard Bank & Trust Company, based in Valparaiso; and $60 million-asset Horizon Bank of Florida, which

was merged into another Synovus affiliate, Bank of Pensacola. Synovus also acquired Wallace & de Mayo in 1999. The firm, based in Norcross, Georgia, specialized in debt collection and bankruptcy management services, and Synovus planned to offer these services to TSYS clients. Wallace & de Mayo was renamed TSYS Debt Management, Inc. following the purchase. Net income leaped another 14.7 percent for the year, reaching $225.3 million, and the latest acquisitions pushed the asset total to $12.5 billion. During the 1990s, Synovus saw its profits grow an average of 17 percent per year.

Increased Emphasis on Assets: Early 2000s and Beyond

A depressed stock price—fueled in part by TSYS's loss of the AT&T Universal Card account when AT&T sold that card portfolio to Citigroup—kept Synovus on the acquisition sidelines during the final months of 1999 and most of 2000. The company did acquire ProCard, Inc. in May 2000. Based in Golden, Colorado, ProCard provided organizations with software and Internet applications to help them manage purchasing, travel, and fleet card programs. During that year TSYS bolstered its overseas operations through two major deals. The Royal Bank of Scotland Group plc, the second largest issuer of credit cards in the United Kingdom, selected TSYS to process its card transactions. In addition, TSYS purchased a 51.5 percent stake in GP Network Corporation, a provider of merchant processing services to financial institutions and retailers in Japan.

In February 2001 Synovus's South Carolina affiliate, the National Bank of South Carolina, got a major boost through the acquisition of Spartanburg-based Carolina Southern Bank, which had assets of $200 million. Likewise, Bank of Pensacola was enlarged through the December 2001 purchase of $304 million-asset FABP Bancshares, Inc., parent of First American Bank of Pensacola. In August 2002 Synovus expanded its community banking operations into a fifth state through the purchase of $490 million-asset Community Financial Group, Inc., parent of the five-branch Bank of Nashville. Later in 2002, Synovus announced its intention to acquire two more banks. It would gain its first presence in the rapidly growing central west coast region of Florida by purchasing $408 million-asset United Financial Holdings, Inc., parent of United Bank of St. Petersburg and United Bank of the Gulf Coast, based in Sarasota. The other acquisition target was $340.7 million-asset FNB Newton Bankshares, Inc., parent of Covington, Georgia-based First Nation Bank. The latter deal further entrenched Synovus in the booming metropolitan Atlanta market. As Synovus increasingly targeted higher growth markets for expansion, it also began identifying lower growth areas for divestment. For example, the company was in the process in late 2002 of selling two banks in rural Georgia, Citizens Bank of Cochran and Bank of Hazlehurst.

Meantime, seeking to increase its asset management unit, Synovus acquired the Atlanta firm Creative Financial Group, Ltd. in February 2001. Creative Financial and its operating unit, Robert Andrew Securities, Inc., focused on financial planning for the wealthy and had $546 million in assets under management. In a further expansion in the asset management arena, the company launched Synovus Funds, a new family of mutual funds, in 2001. In May 2002 Synovus acquired GLOBALT, Inc., an Atlanta-based provider of investment advisory services managing $1.21 billion in assets for its clients. These latest moves were intended to provide Synovus with a third major leg on which to prosper in the early 21st century, namely financial management services, which included brokerage, trust, and insurance services (the other two legs being community banking and TSYS). Blanchard, who continued his solid leadership of the company, was aiming to have Synovus's revenue split about equally between the three business areas within ten years. This appeared to be a daunting task given that financial services management generated only about 1 percent of revenues in 2002, but the dramatic growth potential of the newly targeted market made it much more realizable.

Principal Subsidiaries

GEORGIA CORPORATIONS: Columbus Bank and Trust Company; Total System Services, Inc. (81.1%); Synovus Trust Company; Commercial Bank; Commercial Bank & Trust Company of Troup County; Security Bank and Trust Company of Albany; Sumter Bank and Trust Company; The Coastal Bank of Georgia; First State Bank and Trust Company of Valdosta; Bank of Hazlehurst; The Cohutta Banking Company; Bank of Coweta; Citizens Bank and Trust of West Georgia; First Community Bank of Tifton; CB&T Bank of Middle Georgia; Sea Island Bank; Citizens First Bank; The Citizens Bank; The Citizens Bank of Cochran; Athens First Bank & Trust Company; Citizens & Merchants State Bank; Bank of North Georgia; Georgia Bank & Trust; Charter Bank & Trust Co.; Total Technology Ventures, LLC (60%); Creative Financial Group, LTD; Synovus Securities, Inc. ALABAMA CORPORATIONS: Synovus Financial Corp. of Alabama; Community Bank & Trust of Southeast Alabama; First Commercial Bank of Huntsville; The Bank of Tuscaloosa; Sterling Bank; First Commercial Bank; CB&T Bank of Russell County; Synovus Trust Corp. FLORIDA CORPORATIONS: Quincy State Bank; The Tallahassee State Bank; Bank of Pensacola; Vanguard Bank & Trust Company; First Coast Community Bank. TENNESSEE CORPORATIONS: The Bank of Nashville. NATIONAL BANKING ASSOCIATIONS: The National Bank of Walton County (GA); Peachtree National Bank (GA); The First National Bank of Jasper (AL); The National Bank of South Carolina (SC); Mountain National Bank (GA); pointpathbank, N.A. (GA). DELAWARE CORPORATIONS: ProCard, Inc.

Principal Competitors

SunTrust Banks, Inc.; Wachovia Corporation; BB&T Corporation; SouthTrust Corporation; Regions Financial Corporation; AmSouth Bancorporation; Union Planters Corporation; First Data Corporation.

Further Reading

Bach, Deborah, "Newlyweds Bank Abandoned: Pure-Play Virtual Blues Give Synovus Cold Feet," *American Banker,* March 1, 2001, p. 1.

Billips, Mike, "Dot-Coms Investing Lone Cloud in Synovus Financial's Blue Sky," *Georgia Trend,* April 2000, p. 107.

Boraks, David, "Synovus Pins Its Profit Hopes on Growth-Market Strategy," *American Banker,* October 9, 2002, p. 1.

Brannigan, Martha, "Synovus, Like a Southern Belle, Goes Courting Quietly: Georgia Concern Prospers by Buying Small Banks, and Leaving Them Alone," *Wall Street Journal,* February 6, 1995, p. B3.

Crockett, Barton, "Synovus at Crossroads After Decade of Growth," *American Banker,* February 16, 1993, p. 1A.

Fleming, John, "James Blanchard: Is It Time to Deregulate Banking?," *Georgia Trend,* February 1991, sec. 1, p. 72.

Gillam, Carey, "More Than Plastic in the Cards for Synovus: Company Aims to Turn Its Sleepy Banks into Sleek Automated Sales Centers," *American Banker,* August 6, 1997, p. 4.

Grimes, Millard, and Tom Barry, "The Georgia Trend Most Respected CEO of 1997: James H. Blanchard," *Georgia Trend,* May 1997, pp. 20+.

Homa, Lynn, "Georgia Bank Firm Seeks High-Tech Image via New Name—Synovus," *American Banker,* August 22, 1989, p. 5.

King, Jim, "Synovus CEO Putting Hope on 'Rocket Ship,'" *Atlanta Constitution,* October 3, 1993, sec. H, p. 1.

Lindsey, Kelly, "Big Profits from Small Banks: Like Other Regional Banks, Synovus Has Been on a Buying Spree," *Georgia Trend,* October 1993, sec. 1, p. 28.

Novack, Janet, "Backwater Bliss," *Forbes,* August 20, 1990.

Rhoads, Christopher, "Ga. Bank Thrives Under Synovus Umbrella," *American Banker,* July 24, 1995, p. 8.

Salwen, Kevin G., "CB&T Bancshares, in Growth Strategy, Faces Problem of Keeping Unusual Sidekick Robust," *Wall Street Journal,* January 18, 1989, p. C2.

Seward, Christopher, "Synovus to Merge with Bank in S.C.," *Atlanta Constitution,* October 6, 1994, sec. E, p. 1.

Sisk, Michael, "Power to Its People," *U.S. Banker,* September 2002, pp. 32–34, 40.

"Synovus Builds a 'New Bank' Around Wealth Management," *ABA Banking Journal,* September 2001, p. 70.

"Synovus Financial: Does Its Price Fully Reflect Its Performance?," *Better Investing,* May 1994, p. 58.

"Synovus Financial Plans to Bank on Marriage," *Community Banker,* May 2000, pp. 46–47.

Watkins, Steve, "Synovus' Jim Blanchard: Chief Executive's Winning Attitude Keeps His Company Expanding," *Investor's Business Daily,* July 17, 2001.

—Dave Mote
—update: David E. Salamie

Systemax, Inc.

22 Harbor Park Drive
Port Washington, New York 11050
U.S.A.
Telephone: (516) 608-7000
Fax: (516) 608-7111
Web site: http://www.systemax.com

Public Company
Incorporated: 1999
Employees: 3,778
Sales: $1.6 billion (2001)
Stock Exchanges: New York
Ticker Symbol: SYX
NAIC: 334111 Electronic Computer Manufacturing;
   454113 Mail Order Houses

Systemax, Inc. is a direct market retailer of custom configured and preconfigured personal computers, computer peripherals, such as data communications and networking equipment, and computer supplies. Systemax manufactures and distributes ISO 9001-certified personal computers under its private-label brands, Systemax, Tiger, and Ultra, offering state-of-the-art specifications and using name brand components. National brands available through Systemax include Hewlett-Packard, IBM, Compaq, Sony, Toshiba, and Macintosh. Systemax uses three direct to consumer methods of marketing: mail-order catalogs, Internet web sites, and account relationship marketing to business users. More than 40,000 products are available from 20 Internet sites and about 40 different mail-order catalogs, with more than 125 million copies distributed annually to North America and Europe. The company also sells office furniture and materials handling products, such as equipment for moving and lifting stock, protective clothing, and storage equipment.

Expansion of Family Business: Late 1970s

Systemax started as a materials handling business in Long Island, serving customers in the New York area. Founded by two brothers in 1949, the company supplied materials handling equipment, such as hand trucks and carts, and industrial supplies, such as cables, metal shelving and bins, and safety equipment. The company issued its first mail-order catalog in 1972 under the name Global Industrial Products.

In the late 1970s Richard Leeds and twins Bruce and Robert Leeds joined their father's business after completing college. The three had worked in the family business from a young age, on the factory floor and in clerical and sales positions, and understood its inner workings. They joined Global as young adults with the intention of expanding company operations. Robert and Bruce joined the company in 1977, when revenues were at $3 million; Richard joined in 1981. The brothers brought complementary areas of interest and knowledge, Richard with finance, Robert with computer science, and Bruce with acquisitions and expansion. They developed an efficient business model through a process of consensus with the management team and division heads; the model provided a foundation for calculated risks in growing the business.

The first steps in expansion involved obtaining new business outside of the New York area and adding new products. The company began to offer office furniture along with industrial products and, in 1985, the company issued its first catalog offering computer products, distributed under the name *Global DirectMail*. The acquisition of Dartek Corporation in 1986 extended Global's base of operations. Located in Chicago, Dartek offered computers and computer supplies by mail-order catalog, including Mac computers wholesale. Further geographic expansion occurred through implementation of an outbound telemarketing program to national customers. The national accounts program offered specialized ordering, custom billing, bulk discounts, and special stock requests. In 1990 the company entered the European market through the acquisition of Heathrow Computer Supplies based in London. Distributing 65 million copies of ten different catalogs, Global reached 1990 revenues of $178.6 million and garnered a net income of $2.3 million.

The biggest risk the Leeds took involved the 1992 purchase of Misco, a supplier of computer products in the United States, Canada, and Europe. Global purchased Misco from a much larger company for $16 million when Misco was losing money. In 1991 Misco reported revenues of $113 million, more than double Global's own revenues, with 26 percent of revenues originating in the United Kingdom, Germany, Italy, and Spain. Global retained existing management but implemented its own model of distribution and marketing to reduce overhead expenses and increase efficiency. The company also redesigned the catalog and expanded the product line with lower-priced goods. Through Misco, Global began to offer brand name computer-related products, including data communications and networking equipment, software, and general supplies.

By 1994 Global published 24 full-line and specialty catalogs, distributing 114 million copies, 27 million in Europe. With a prospect list of more than 35 million potential customers, Global sold computer products to 1.2 million active customers through eight distribution centers in the United States and Canada and six sales and distribution centers in Europe. In 1994 the company recorded revenues of $484.2 million and net income of $17.1 million.

1995 IPO Funding Continued Growth and Development

In June 1995 Global went public, offering 8.3 million shares of stock at $17.50 per share. Global used the funds from the initial public offering (IPO) for company debt and continued expansion and development. Global's expansion strategy involved increased distribution in Europe, the addition of brand name computer products and custom configured computers, and operational support. By the end of 1995 Global expanded its market presence in the United Kingdom, Germany, France, Italy, and Spain and issued catalogs in Austria, Switzerland, Belgium, Ireland, and Portugal for the first time.

In November Global acquired TigerDirect, Inc., a mail-order retailer of computer hardware, software, and accessories to consumer and corporate users. TigerDirect contributed a prospect list of 3.5 million names and 400,000 active customers to Global's resources. Global reorganized TigerDirect for profitability by reducing overhead expenses, reorganizing purchasing methods to reduce risk of excess inventory, and eliminating unprofitable catalogs. Global continued the *Tiger* and *Power Up!* catalogs as well as the Tiger brand of personal computers.

In early 1996 Global expanded operations in Chicago by consolidating two distribution centers into one larger facility. The 241,000-square-foot distribution center more than doubled existing capacity. Global used the additional space to initiate a personal computer configuring operation, building network-ready personal computers and servers and preconfigured personal computer networks. In addition, the facility accommodated service for the company's growing business in national brand name computers. New products included IBM desktop and laptop computers as well as servers, and Hewlett-Packard printers, scanners, drives, and networking equipment. Global received authorization to offer Compaq computers via direct mail and to distribute Compaq's Presario line through retail stores (then in development).

The company reported a 44 percent increase in revenues in 1996, to $911.9 million, garnering a net income of $43.7 million. The increases were attributed to successful business-to-business marketing to mid-sized corporations and growth in TigerDirect's small office/home office sales market.

In early 1997 Global issued three new catalogs directed to niche computer supply markets. *Global Ergo Answers* offered ergonomically correct products and office furniture that reduced the strain and injury from working long hours at a computer. The catalog was directed to human resource managers and their concern for employee productivity and well-being. Capitalizing on Global's position as one of the top five suppliers of wire shelving, *Global Wire Products* offered wire shelving for the foodservice, healthcare, computer, and industrial markets. The third catalog, *Global Traveler,* offered portable computer hardware, software, and peripherals to business travelers. US Air Shuttle provided catalogs to its customers in the seat-back pockets of planes along the heavily traveled routes between Boston, New York, and Washington, D.C. Global opened retail Business Centers at Logan International Airport in Boston, LaGuardia Airport in New York City, and National Airport in Washington, D.C.

International expansion at this time involved a joint venture with 06-Software Centre Europe, the largest catalog retailer in The Netherlands to offer brand name personal computer software, supplies, and services. The joint venture, Global Computer Products B.V., acquired the assets and liabilities of 06. Formed in June 1997, the venture allowed Global to expand into a new market at a lower cost than a new start-up.

Late 1990s: Emphasis on Build-to-Order Computers and Internet Marketing Initiatives

As part of the company's plan to enter the build-to-order segment of the personal computer industry, Global added two new executive positions. The chief information officer and the vice-president of operations oversaw the streamlining of supply chain management, sales, inventory, and warehouse procedures and systems to accommodate build-to-order operations. Global integrated its three-point marketing system for effective organization. The marketing system involved sales through direct market catalogs, online catalogs, and the development of business-to-business account relationships.

Global entered the private-label build-to-order personal computer business with the September 1997 acquisition of Infotel, Inc. Purchased for $40 million in cash and $8.3 million in stock, Infotel would add $235 million to Global's annual revenues. Founded in 1982, Infotel originated as a dealer of computer

Key Dates:

1972: The company distributes its first mail-order catalog as Global Industrial Products.
1985: A computer products catalog is distributed for the first time.
1990: Global enters the European market through acquisition.
1994: The acquisition of Misco expands the company's reach in North America and Europe.
1997: The build-to-order computer market is accessed through the acquisition of Infotel, Inc.
1998: Sales exceed $1 billion, earning Global a place on the *Fortune* 1000 list.
1999: The company takes a new name, Systemax, and ships its 500 thousandth personal computer in August.
2002: In-store kiosks allow customers to custom configure personal computers.

printers and eventually added a line of private-label products. In 1991 Infotel began to offer its own line of personal computers. Global purchased Infotel for its popular *MidWest Micro* catalog of computer products for the small office/home office market. The *Infotel Distributing* catalog offered the Ultra brand of value-added resellers (personal computers). Global wanted Infotel for its production capacity for build-to-order personal computers; the Fletcher, Ohio-based company's factory accommodated production for up to $1 billion in computers per year.

Global planned to use Infotel's production capacity to supply units for online sales of Tiger brand build-to-order personal computers through TigerDirect. The web site, launched in late 1997, offered computer-generated price quotes with specialists available to review quotes as well as to review compatibility and functionality of hardware and software requested by the customer. The online store sold Tiger brand systems as well as national brand names, including Toshiba, Sony, Compaq, and Hewlett-Packard.

Global reached two major milestones in 1997 and 1998. The company surpassed $1 billion in revenues in 1997, earning a place on the *Fortune* 1000 list of largest corporations in the United States in 1998. The company had grown at an average annual compound rate of 27 percent from 1988 to 1997. In 1997 Global distributed 40 color catalogs, many directed to unique market categories, and sold goods via more than six Internet sites. With a sales force of 1,300, Global distributed more than 40,000 in-stock or build-to-order products through 16 sales and distribution centers in the United States, Canada, and Europe. The company reported a same-day shipping record for 90 percent of new orders.

Global continued its successful strategy of international and online sales growth through acquisition. In August 1998 Global acquired Dabus Data Produkter AB of Sweden for $10 million. Dabus offered computers and computer supplies through direct market catalogs or the Internet to 12 European countries. Global hoped that the acquisition would facilitate entry into other Scandinavian markets. In February 1999 Global purchased

Simply Computers Limited, a computer retailer based in London, contributing $100 million to annual revenues, with $20 million from Internet sales.

In September 1998 Global had launched an online auction house for personal computers and accessories, Ezbid.com. The site offered 65 to 80 products daily, including new and refurbished desktop computers, accessories, software, data communications products and overstock items, as well as digital cameras, and, later, consumer products such as electronics and small appliances. The bids started as low as one dollar, with bidding taking place over the course of one to four days. An e-mail system notified customers when someone had placed a higher bid on an item, so that the customer could bid again. The following spring Global promoted EZbid through televisions commercials on cable stations such as Bravo and The History Channel.

The Internet became a more important outlet for Global, prompting the company to seek new opportunities online. In early 1999 Global reported that its web sites averaged more than $1.5 million in sales weekly. The company sought high-profile links online, such as on the Yahoo search engine. A partnership agreement with Digital River provided more than 100,000 digital products, electronically downloadable via Global online stores in the United States and the United Kingdom.

Positioning the Systemax Brand for the National Stage: 1999

To reflect the prominence of the company's integrated marketing system and the development of its Systemax brand of build-to-order personal computers, Global changed its name to Systemax, Inc. in May 1999. The company planned to consolidate all private-label merchandise to the Systemax brand, except for the Ultra brand for value-added resellers. Billed as "The Perfect PC," Systemax personal computers represented quality, state-of-the-art systems at a lower cost than national name brands. Lower overhead costs allowed the company to price computer products 10 to 15 percent lower, even though Systemax used the same third-party component and warranty vendors, including the recognized brands Intel, Microsoft, AMD, and others. In its business-to-business relationship marketing, Systemax offered personalized sales and configured product specifications according to individual company needs in small and large quantities. Thus Systemax offered a single source for personal computers, computer supplies, office furniture, and industrial equipment. The company planned for growth, with the aim to sell one million personal computers per year and to make Systemax a national name brand. Toward this end the company began construction on a 112,000-square-foot addition to the Fletcher, Ohio facility.

The acquisition of the Proteva personal computers business provided Systemax access to consumer electronics store chains and national and regional mass merchandisers, including Sears, Value America, and The Wiz chain of consumer electronics stores. Assets acquired included customer lists, the Proteva brand name and trademarks, and in-store kiosks where customers could configure and purchase build-to-order computers. Systemax viewed the acquisition of Proteva as a consolidation of the "white box" market of off-brand personal computers. The acquisition gave Systemax a production facility capable of producing 200,000 computers per year. The company closed a Wisconsin facility and added 300,000 square feet to the acquired facility.

Systemax increased its marketing activities to promote the Systemax brand. The company initiated its first national campaign with advertisements on cable stations ESPN, SNN, and MSNBC, and in major computer magazines. New distribution outlets included the Home Shopping Network and ValueVision. The company hired 300 new sales people in 1999, expanding its relationship marketing concept, for a total of 1,000 account executives.

Systemax reported sales of $1.75 billion in 1999, a 22 percent increase over 1998. North American sales accounted for 72 percent of revenues, at $1.3 billion, while European sales accounted for 28 percent, at $491 million. The company attributed the growth to increased sales through relationship marketing, up 53 percent and accounting for 41 percent of sales. From its 19 web sites, Systemax reported $83 million in sales, an increase of 197 percent over 1998. The company counted 1.8 million active customers from a prospect database of 48 million potential customers.

Net income declined to $36 million in 1999, from $41.3 million in 1998, prompting Systemax to streamline operations in 2000. The company sold EZbid and reduced its U.S. workforce by 8 percent through attrition and elimination of redundant positions. The company closed ZAC Software, its software direct marketing subsidiary, and implemented a new manufacturing system for increased efficiency on the assembly line. Inventory problems, which came to light in late 2000, prompted Systemax to install a TradeStream logistics technology that provided real-time warehouse and inventory management and reduced the number of employees necessary for these operations.

The Internet continued to play an important role in Systemax's strategy to become a nationally recognized brand. High standards of service gained TigerDirect the Gold Star Status on BizRate.com, a web site that evaluated online businesses based on consumer opinion. America Online placed TigerDirect on Shop@AOL as a "gold tenant." In February 2001, Systemax entered into an alliance with Elgin Financial Savings Bank to give Systemax computer users instant access to that company's real-time online banking products and services through custom computer configuration. Systemax offered Elgin customers a discount on personal computers.

Systemax struggled with a slow economy and slower sales of personal computers. The company reported sales of $1.6 billion in 2001, a decline due to lower sales to business customers, though national advertising stimulated consumer sales. North American sales declined for the second year in a row to $982.6 million, while sales in Europe increased slightly to $564.4 million. Internet sales more than doubled, accounting for $218 million of revenues, with traffic growing rapidly at TigerDirect, the company's star web site. Systemax recovered from a loss of $40.8 million in 2000, due to liquidation of excess inventory, reporting net income of $700,000 in 2001.

Systemax initiated new strategies to improve efficiency in 2002. These included implementation of a new web-automation technology in Systemax's European operations to provide faster connection to vendor systems for immediate response to customer inquiries of product availability and pricing. In May Systemax began to test the "Six Sigma Breakthrough Strategies" at the Fletcher facility. Six Sigma provided techniques to spot defects in operational and administrative processes and to change them for improved effectiveness and cost savings. The project included training for managers and executives. In related actions the company sold a facility near its Port Washington headquarters and reduced the staff by 50 jobs.

A new marketing initiative involved the installation of build-to-order kiosks in all 42 units of The Wiz chain of consumer electronics stores in the New York City area. The kiosks featured easy-to-use, point-and-click interface to allow customers to easily custom configure a Systemax Venture desktop computer or Systemax Pursuit laptop computer. The product would then be shipped directly to the customer's home.

Principal Subsidiaries

Global Computer Supplies, Inc.; Dartek Corporations; Misco America Inc.; TigerDirect, Inc.; Midwest Micro Corporation; Misco Germany, Inc.; Misco Italy Computer Supplies S.P.A.; HCS Global S.A.; Systemax Europe Ltd.

Principal Competitors

CompUSA, Inc.; CDW Computer Centers, Inc.; Insight Enterprises, Inc.; PC Connection Inc.; Micro Warehouse, Inc.

Further Reading

"Global DirectMail Expands into PC Sales with $48M Acquisition of Infotel," *Computergram International,* September 16, 1997.

"Global Turnaround Begins in Europe," *Long Island Business News,* November 24, 1997, p. 37.

Lanctot, Roger C., "Richard Leeds," *Computer Retail Week,* November 17, 1997, p. 78.

Martorana, Jamie, "Global Introduces Internet Auction Site," *Long Island Business News,* October 9, 1998, p. 5A.

"Systemax Forms Strategic Alliance with Elgin," *Long Island Business News,* February 2, 2001, p. 13A.

Walzer, Robert, "Systemax to Dump Net Biz, Beef PC Sales," *Long Island Business News,* March 24, 2000, p. 5A.

—Mary Tradii

TECHNE Corporation

614 McKinley Place NE
Minneapolis, Minnesota 55413
U.S.A.
Telephone: (612) 379-8854
Fax: (612) 379-6580
Web site: http://www.techne-corp.com

Public Company
Incorporated: 1981
Employees: 494
Sales: $130.9 million (2002)
Stock Exchanges: NASDAQ
Ticker Symbol: TECH
NAIC: 334516 Hematology Instruments Manufacturing;
541380 Testing Laboratories

TECHNE Corporation is a holding company whose main operating subsidiary is R&D Systems, located in Minneapolis, Minnesota. Since 1976, R&D Systems has been making hematology controls, which are used to verify the accuracy of blood analysis instruments. Starting in the late 1980s, however, the company's developing Biotechnology Division began to eclipse the Hematology Division as the centerpiece of TECHNE's operations. The Biotechnology division manufactures specialized proteins, including antibodies and cytokines, that are used by scientists in research laboratories. TECHNE's products are used to investigate possible therapies for multiple sclerosis, wound healing, AIDS, and tumor growth. TECHNE is the world's leading manufacturer of cytokines, which are purified proteins that act as communicators between cells, stimulating or halting growth, or changing a cell's function. The company also sells assay kits, which are prepackaged kits used to test for the presence of a particular molecule. The Biotechnology Division now accounts for approximately 85 percent of TECHNE's revenues. The company has a subsidiary in England, R&D Systems Europe Ltd., that distributes TECHNE's products in Europe. R&D Systems Europe has a sales subsidiary in Germany known as R&D Systems GmbH. TECHNE's president, chairman, CEO, and treasurer is Thomas Oland, who first came to the company as a consultant in

1980. Oland's work ethic and stable, frugal management style are often cited as the basis for TECHNE's record of steadily increasing revenues for more than a decade.

A Rough Start: 1977–85

David Mundschenk founded Research and Diagnostics Systems in Minneapolis in 1976. The company specialized in hematology controls—precisely measured blood samples that could be used to calibrate laboratory instruments and act as controls in blood tests. R&D Systems' first product, a Platelet-Rich-Plasma control, was introduced in 1977.

The company performed poorly in its early years. By 1980 R&D Systems was faltering, directionless, and deep in debt. Late that year Roger Lucas, a company executive and former professor of biochemistry at the State University of New York, met an accountant named Thomas Oland. Lucas hired Oland to liquidate the company. Oland, however, saw potential in R&D Systems' hematology products and negotiated with creditors to give the company time to introduce its newest blood product. In 1981 R&D Systems became only the second manufacturer in the world to introduce a Whole Blood Control with Platelets. The product was well-received and bought time for the company to get back on its feet. Oland continued working with R&D Systems as a consultant.

In 1983, however, a misstep by the company founder plunged the company back into an unfavorable situation. Mundschenk bought control of Hycel, a French maker of hematology products, for only $50,000, unaware that the company had an oversized debt load. Oland examined the company's finances and found that Hycel owed a corporate client $800,000. When R&D Systems' board of directors found out about the ill-advised acquisition, they threatened to shut the company down unless Oland took control. As a result, Oland became CEO, and biochemist Roger Lucas headed up a division as chief scientific officer.

The competent leadership now in charge at R&D Systems attracted the attention of two venture capitalists. Investors George Kline and Peter Peterson owned a shell company known as TECHNE Corporation. They had founded the company in

1981 to pursue profitable acquisitions, and took it public in 1983. In 1985, acting on faith in Oland's management ability, TECHNE bought R&D Systems for about $1.9 million. R&D Systems was subsumed into the corporate shell.

Development of Growth Factors: 1986–90

That year R&D Systems also began development of a new product line. The new products were specialized proteins known as human cytokines. Cytokines are produced naturally by the body and control the growth, development, and functioning of cells. Researchers saw great therapeutic potential in the molecules, including making wounds heal faster, stimulating bone growth, and stopping the growth of certain cancer cells. A full understanding of cytokines would allow researchers to determine exactly how a protein would act on a cell and give them the ability to target specific health problems with few side effects. As a result, cytokines were in demand at government and university laboratories.

TECHNE's investment in the development of cytokine growth factors contributed to a $487,000 loss in 1985. The next year, TECHNE spent $675,000 on research in the new field. Research focused on a protein known as TGF-beta, short for "transforming growth factor." At the time, TGF-beta was the second of only three proteins that were able to stimulate or suppress the growth of cell tissue. R&D Systems was the only commercial supplier of the product, and was able to sell it for the equivalent of $9 billion an ounce, mainly to researchers for laboratory applications.

The development of growth factors followed naturally from TECHNE's hematology operations. The company's hematology controls were produced largely from pig blood. TGF-beta was found in the blood's platelets, so TECHNE was able to use its ready blood supply to isolate the protein using a proprietary method. Oland saw great potential for TECHNE's protein growth factors. He told the *Minneapolis Star and Tribune* in 1986, "We think that our long-range future will be in growth factors. We think it's the hottest new field in science, and we just hope we can keep pace with it." His optimistic view seemed to be corroborated when, in October of that year, the scientists who had discovered growth factors 30 years earlier received a Nobel Prize for medicine.

TECHNE's research operations took another step forward in 1988, when the company hired several molecular biologists who had been laid off by another Twin Cities company, Molecular Genetics. The biologists helped TECHNE reduce its production costs by developing a way to grow materials in bacteria rather than buying blood and tissue for processing from vendors. That year the company officially formed its Biotechnology Division.

Steady Growth in the 1990s

The production of growth factors became a central aspect of TECHNE's operations. By the early 1990s the company was positioned to make acquisitions that would confirm its reputation as a leading producer of cytokines. In August 1991 TECHNE bought the research reagent and diagnostic assay kit business of Amgen Inc., a California-based biotechnology firm. The acquisition went smoothly because it involved a transfer mainly of inventory and property, rather than personnel. The sale gave TECHNE the right to sell Quantikine diagnostic kits.

Later that fall, TECHNE sold its French subsidiary Hycel, the company that had aroused such dismay when Mundschenk first bought it in 1983. Although the sale of Hycel resulted in some lost revenue at TECHNE, growth in the company's main subsidiary, R&D Systems, made up for the loss. Revenues for 1991 were $22.3 million, and net income reached $1.96 million, a 17 percent increase over the previous year. Under Oland's leadership, similar growth rates continued through the end of the decade.

Several factors accounted for TECHNE's steady increase in revenues. Because the company's products were developed for use in biotechnology research rather than for the therapeutic market, TECHNE did not have to contend with stringent product approval guidelines at the U.S. Food and Drug Administration. The company was able to cultivate long-term relationships with university and government research centers, which ensured reliable demand for its products.

Industry insiders also gave Oland much of the credit for TECHNE's success. When he took over the leadership position in 1983, he applied his personal habits of careful money management to the company. *Corporate Report* said he ran the company with a "miser's touch" in a 1999 article in which Oland was profiled as one of the top underpaid CEOs in Minnesota. In the article, analysts praised Oland's work ethic, noting that he left the office at 9 p.m. most nights. Coworkers agreed that he worked incredibly hard, and said he had few interests outside of the company. George Kline, one of the founders of TECHNE, was quoted as saying, "He is one of the rare people who puts shareholders and employees first and his own financial well-being second." The Minneapolis business periodical *CityBusiness* also took note of Oland's low-key, effective management style. A 2000 article said he was hard-working and media-shy, preferring to let the company's performance speak for itself. "Tom is absolutely dedicated to the company. It's his baby, so to speak, and he likes to be very much involved in all aspects," research analyst Chad Simmer told *CityBusiness*.

TECHNE's steady growth continued through the 1990s. The company bought British Biotechnology Products (BBP) Limited in 1993 for $2.3 million. The firm had maintained a distribution agreement with R&D Systems for several years before the sale. BBP eventually became the headquarters for TECHNE's European research and development unit. The company was renamed R&D Systems Europe, Ltd., and continued to distribute products from R&D Systems in Minneapolis. The acquisition of BBP pushed TECHNE's revenue to $40.3 million for 1994, up from $28.7 million the year before.

Overseas expansion continued in 1995, when TECHNE established a sales subsidiary in Germany with an office near

Key Dates:

1976: David Mundschenk founds Research and Diagnostics Systems.

1980: Thomas Oland comes to R&D Systems as a consultant.

1981: George Kline and Peter Peterson found TECHNE.

1983: Oland becomes head of R&D Systems following an ill-advised decision by Mundschenk.

1985: The shell company TECHNE buys R&D Systems.

1988: TECHNE forms a Biotechnology Division to produce specialized proteins.

1991: TECHNE buys Amgen's research reagent and diagnostic assay kit business.

1993: TECHNE buys a British biotechnology company, founds a European division.

1995: TECHNE establishes a sales subsidiary in Germany.

1999: TECHNE buys Cistron's reagent business and immunoassay patents.

2002: TECHNE's sales reach $130.0 million after more than a decade of steady growth.

Frankfurt. Germany was TECHNE's largest European market. Expansion at home also continued apace. TECHNE added 80,000 square feet to its offices in 1993 and planned another 90,000-square-foot expansion in 1996.

In 1997 TECHNE carried out a restructuring of its European operations. The company decided to focus on its core cytokine-related products and pulled some underperforming molecular biology products from the market. In the summer of 1998 TECHNE managed to remove its chief competitor from the market, acquiring Genzyme Corporation's research products business for about $65.5 million. The Genzyme unit had reported sales of about $15 million in 1997. The acquisition added approximately 4,000 customers and 350 products, including antibodies, proteins, and research kits, to TECHNE's existing base of 8,000 customers and 1,900 products. TECHNE was now the world's leading source for cytokines and related products.

The Genzyme unit's sales were lower than expected after the acquisition, but only because former Genzyme customers rapidly converted to R&D Systems products. Overall sales for 1998 once again showed steady growth. Net income for 1998 reached $15.2 million on sales of $67.3 million, compared to net income of $6.7 million on sales of $47.7 million three years earlier.

Rise and Fall of Biotechnology: 1998–2002

The biotechnology market as a whole experienced substantial growth in the late 1990s, and TECHNE blazed ahead with a series of acquisitions. TECHNE bought the reagent business and immunoassay patents of Cistron in 1999. Cistron had worked with TECHNE as a partner for many years, but decided that it wanted to withdraw from the production of research reagents and concentrate on the research and development of therapeutic applications instead. TECHNE paid $750,000 for Cistron's unit. The following year TECHNE increased its ownership in the drug developer

ChemoCentryx and acquired research and diagnostic market rights to all products developed by the firm.

For the past decade, TECHNE had been a well-kept secret on the stock market. Oland avoided media attention and expected the company's performance to speak for itself. In late 1999, however, investors discovered TECHNE and pushed the company's share price from $30 to $160 a share in the ten-month period ending July 2000.

In the fall of 2000 TECHNE filed a lawsuit against Amgen, from whom it had bought two units in 1991. Since the sale, Amgen had been supplying TECHNE with a product known as Erythropoietin in a cooperative agreement. Amgen said that they had mistakenly failed to invoice for the product and demanded $27 million in back payments. Oland countered that it was unreasonable to demand payment after failing to notify TECHNE for nine years that payment was due, especially since TECHNE had only made $2.7 million in sales related to Amgen's product. The companies went to court, and in January 2002 the court judged in Amgen's favor. TECHNE settled the litigation in May 2002 with a $17.5 million cash payment to Amgen.

The lawsuit had little effect on TECHNE's ever increasing revenues. Net income was up 60 percent in 2000 to $26.6 million on revenues of $103.8 million. In the fall of 2001 TECHNE invested in Discovery Genomics, a company located in Minneapolis that worked on determining the function of individual genes. In an arrangement similar to the ChemoCentryx deal, TECHNE acquired about 40 percent of Discovery Genomics and won the right to develop antibodies and immunoassays for proteins discovered by the company, and sell them on the research market free of royalties.

The terrorist attacks in New York and Washington, D.C., on September 11, 2001, as well as the litigation settlement with Amgen and a general cutback in the biotechnology industry, hurt TECHNE's stock price in 2002. Nevertheless, the company continued to perform well in the area of operations. Sales in 2002 were $130.9 million, compared to $115.4 million in 2001. Due to the Amgen settlement, net income fell slightly from $34.0 million to $27.1 million in 2002.

TECHNE continued introducing hundreds of new products each year, thus bolstering revenue from older products whose sales had leveled off. The company's products were frequently mentioned in scientific journals. In 2002 the company appeared poised to continue its long-lasting upward trajectory.

Principal Subsidiaries

R&D Systems Europe, Ltd. (U.K.); R&D Systems GmbH (Germany); R&D Systems, Inc.

Principal Divisions

Biotechnology Division; Hematology Division.

Principal Competitors

Amersham Biosciences; Baxter International Inc.; Endogen, Inc.

Further Reading

"Completion of Acquisition by TECHNE," *PR Newswire*, July 30, 1993.

Fiedler, Terry, "Building Blocks of the Biotech Boom," *Star Tribune*, September 4, 2000, p. 1D.

Griffith, Jessica, "Oland Is Quiet, Hands-On," *CityBusiness (Minneapolis, MN)*, September 7, 2001, p. 12.

Gross, Steve, "Local Firm Has a Sizable Interest in Growth Factors," *Minneapolis Star and Tribune*, October 23, 1986, p. 1M.

Haeg, Andrew, "Oland Drives TECHNE with a Miser's Touch," *Corporate Report-Minnesota*, July 1999, p. 24.

Levy, Melissa, "TECHNE to Acquire Research Products Unit from Genzyme," *Star Tribune*, June 24, 1998, p. 1D.

Niemela, Jennifer, "TECHNE's Low-Key CEO Gets High-Impact Results," *CityBusiness (Minneapolis, MN)*, July 7, 2000, p. S25.

"TECHNE Announces Judgement and Appeal," *PR Newswire*, January 8, 2002.

"TECHNE Corporation Announces Stock Buy-Back Program and Expansion Plans," *PR Newswire*, May 4, 1995.

"TECHNE Files Lawsuit," *PR Newswire*, September 19, 2000.

"TECHNE Releases Unaudited Fourth Quarter and Annual Operating Results for Fiscal Year 1992," *PR Newswire*, August 17, 1992.

—Sarah Ruth Lorenz

Tredegar Corporation

1100 Boulders Parkway
Richmond, Virginia 23225
U.S.A.
Telephone: (804) 330-1000
Fax: (804) 330-1177
Web site: http://www.tredegar.com

Public Company
Incorporated: 1988 as Tredegar Industries Inc.
Employees: 3,200
Sales: $767.6 million (2001)
Stock Exchanges: New York
Ticker Symbol: TG
NAIC: 322221 Coated and Laminated Packaging Paper and Plastics Film Manufacturing; 331316 Aluminum Extruded Product Manufacturing

Tredegar Corporation, based in Richmond, Virginia, is primarily involved, through subsidiaries, in two unrelated businesses: plastic films and aluminum extrusions. The company's film products are used as liners and backsheets in diapers, feminine-hygiene products, surgical masks, industrial packaging, permeable groundcovers, and cheesecloth. Procter & Gamble is responsible for some 30 percent of all film product revenues. Tredegar's Aluminum businesses rely on the extrusion process, in which large sections of aluminum are forced through forms to make various shapes. Aluminum extrusions are used in such products as curtain walls, window components, tub and shower doors, ladders, running boards, boat windshields, and furniture. The Tredegar Investments subsidiary is a venture capital operation that targets technology start-up companies. Recently Tredegar has decided to cease activities in the biotech arena, where subsidiaries Therics and Molecumetics were involved in the development of bone replacement products, soft-tissue products, drug delivery products, and chemistry-based drug discovery technology. Chairman John D. Gottwald and his family own nearly a third of Tredegar.

Lineage Dating to 19th-Century Paper Manufacturer

Tredegar was spun off in 1989 from Ethyl Corporation, which 30 years earlier had been acquired by Albemarle Paper Manufacturing Company, owned by the Gottwald family. Albemarle was established in Richmond in 1887 by area businessmen, taking advantage of the James River to power a paper mill that produced blotter and kraft paper. It was in 1918 that Floyd Dewey Gottwald, Sr., a native of Richmond, left his job as an assistant paymaster for the Richmond, Fredericksburg and Potomac Railways to take a position at Albemarle. Over the next 20 years he worked his way up in the organization and in 1941 became president. Two years later his son, Floyd Gottwald, Jr., joined the company, which was in the process of becoming 70 percent owned by the Gottwald family. Ablemarle's primary product was blotting paper, but with the introduction of the ballpoint pen in 1945, the popularity of the fountain pen began to fade and with it the market for blotting paper. Albemarle also felt pressure on the kraft paper segment during the 1950s when dry cleaners began using polyethylene bags for garments instead of the paper bags that Albemarle supplied. It was clear that the Gottwalds were tied to declining products and that drastic measures were in order.

In 1962 the elder Gottwald learned that General Motors and Standard Oil were interested in selling Ethyl Corporation, which the two companies had formed in 1924 to manufacture tetra ethyl, a lead additive that eliminated knocking in car engines. Because of its patent on the substance, Ethyl established a strong foothold in the gasoline additive market. When the patent expired, the company was able to maintain an edge in the market through the 1950s. Large chemical companies such as Du Pont or Dow Chemical might have been interested in acquiring Ethyl once its corporate parents decided to put the business on the block but, because of strict enforcement of antitrust laws at the time, both Dow and Du Pont shied away, leaving an opening for Gottwald, who recognized a chance to manufacture polyethylene bags through Ethyl. Turning to a variety of sources, including Prudential and three other insurance companies, a number of investment houses, and Chase Manhattan Bank, he was able to cobble together $200 million.

The investors received notes in exchange for their cash, and in this way tiny Albemarle was able to buy Ethyl in an early example of the leveraged buyout, prompting a memorable headline in the *Wall Street Journal*: "Jonah Swallows the Whale." The company was then restructured so that Albemarle became a subsidiary of Ethyl, and the blotter paper business was subsequently sold to help pare down the considerable debt that Gottwald had taken on. In addition, Ethyl's headquarters was moved to Richmond.

Ethyl's 1960s Diversification Efforts Leading to Tredegar Product Lines

Although most of Ethyl's revenues would continue to come from the sale of tetra ethyl, the company was also diversifying into product lines that would one day become part of Tredegar. In 1963 Ethyl acquired VisQueen, which made polyethylene film for food packaging. In 1966 the company bought William Bonnel Company, makers of shaped aluminum. After Floyd Gottwald, Jr., took over for his father in 1968, diversification took on even greater importance, as growing environmental concerns led to the elimination of leaded gasoline. Scientists attempting to learn more about the formation of the Earth traced lead isotopes in the Arctic and Pacific and inadvertently discovered that airborne lead was actually poisoning people, especially in cities, where subsequent research showed that the urban population had 50 percent more lead in their blood than their counterparts in rural areas. The cause, according to numerous studies, was leaded gasoline, which prompted Congressional action. Ethyl contested these findings and fought back with a public relations campaign that claimed eliminating lead would exacerbate the situation because inefficient knocking engines would end up releasing even more noxious fumes into the atmosphere. The company's arguments fell on deaf ears, however, as Congress eventually passed the Clean Air Act, which banned lead in gasoline. Ethyl, at the very least, was able to buy time. Further, because the ban was then gradually phased in, the company took steps to lessen its dependence on the tetra ethyl business, which continued on in European markets, focusing instead on chemicals, plastics, and aluminum. The development of disposable diapers was of particular help, since Ethyl provided the plastic lining for the Procter & Gamble Pampers line. In 1981 Ethyl became involved in the insurance business when it acquired First Colony Life Insurance. Along the way the company also picked up an assortment of coal mines and gas and oil properties.

Because of strong management from the Gottwald family, which was now reinforced by a third generation entering the ranks, Ethyl, despite its disparate businesses, was a successful enterprise. In late 1988, however, the company announced that it was consolidating its plastics, aluminum, and energy groups into a new subsidiary, Tredegar Industries Inc., all of the assets

of which management had considered selling off. Ethyl then spun off this hodgepodge assortment of assets to shareholders as an independent, publicly traded business, its shares distributed in July 1989. The Tredegar name was an allusion to the Civil War-era Tredegar Iron Works, a famous Richmond facility that supplied cannon and other armaments to the South. Floyd Gottwald's son, John D. Gottwald, who was only in his early 30s, was named president and CEO. As an undergraduate college student he studied Geology at Washington and Lee University before earning a master's in business administration from the University of Richmond. His obvious task at Tredegar was to weed out the company's weak businesses and strengthen the ones with the greatest long-term potential.

Adjusting its business mix, Tredegar struggled at first, hindered by the effects of a poor economy, which especially impacted the company's aluminum extrusion business. With housing starts down, the demand for many of Tredegar's products slumped. But it was due primarily to the unloading of unprofitable assets that the company saw its sales decline from $637 million in 1989 to $547 million in 1990. In 1990 Tredegar sold its U.S. oil and gas properties, as well as an automotive plastics operation and a division that made windows and doors. Because it was unable to sell Capitol Products, which also manufactured windows and doors in addition to other consumer goods, Tredegar opted to simply close down the business. At the same time, management was also searching out new opportunities. It formed a venture capital firm, Tredegar Investments, in 1990 to invest in communications, life sciences, and information technology companies.

Although revenues fell to $474 million in 1991, Tredegar stopped losing money and posted a profit on the year. Nonetheless, management continued to buy and sell assets. In 1991 Tredegar acquired Swing-Shift Burdi, a forklift parts maker, then later in the year sold a beverage closure business. Tredegar in 1992 moved into the computer software business, buying APPX Software, a Richmond developer of business applications software. Tredegar also became involved in the pharmaceutical industry through its Seattle Molecumetics subsidiary, a biotech drug and vaccine discovery and development business.

Divesting Energy Interests: 1994

Tredegar decided to divest its energy businesses in 1994. The company's remaining oil and gas properties, located in western Canada, were sold for $8 million. Elk Horn, with mineral rights in eastern Kentucky coal, was sold to Pen Holdings, Inc. for an aggregate consideration of $72 million. A coal trading business, Elk Horn Coal Sales Corporation, was sold separately. Although Elk Horn contributed $30 million in annual revenues, Gottwald made it clear at an annual meeting that "Energy is not where Tredegar wants to invest." Instead, he preferred to channel the cash realized from the Elk Horn sale into a stock buyback effort or to make strategic acquisitions in the company's core plastics and metals businesses. They showed such improvement in 1995 that the company posted net income of $24.1 million, or $1.80 per share. Moreover, in September of that year the board of directors declared a three for two stock split. Despite the overall success of the plastics and aluminum products segments, management remained diligent about fine tuning Tredegar's assets. The company began

Key Dates:

1962: Gottwald family-owned paper company acquires Ethyl Corporation.
1988: Tredegar Industries subsidiary is formed to consolidate Ethyl's plastics, aluminum, and energy assets.
1989: Tredegar is spun off as independent company.
1990: U.S. oil and gas interests are sold off.
1992: Tredegar becomes involved in biotechnology through Molecumetics.
1994: Last of energy assets is sold.
2001: Norman Scher replaces John Gottwald as president and CEO.
2002: Tredegar decides to exit biotechnology.

plans to sell off Molded Products and Brudi, and in March 1996 Tredegar sold the former to Precise Technology for $57.5 million. Later in the year the company sold off Brudi for $18.1 million. To bolster plastics and aluminum products, Tredegar made a number of other moves. In 1997 it acquired an aluminum extrusion and fabrication plant located in El Campo, Texas, from Reynolds Metals Company. On the film side, Tredegar also announced in 1997 that it planned to open a manufacturing facility in China to supply permeable film for use in diapers, feminine pads, and other disposable personal products to China and throughout Asia where such items were little used and offered great potential for future growth. Until the plant came on line, Tredegar operated out of a Procter & Gamble factory located in Guangzhou, China. Tredegar also announced in 1997 that it would build a plant in Eastern Europe (eventually built in Hungary) in order to supply embossed and permeable films for disposable personal products to supply emerging markets on that continent. Since 1989 the company's Dutch plant had been able to supply European markets but was now unable to meet the growing demand for Tredegar products in Europe and Russia, markets similar to China and Asia where the sale of disposable personal products held great promise for the future. Moreover, the addition of facilities in China and Hungary contributed to the company's efforts at globalization, which included existing manufacturing facilities in Brazil and Argentina. In 1998 Tredegar expanded its aluminum operations to Canada, acquiring the assets of Exal Aluminum Inc. and its two aluminum extrusion plants with annual sales of more than $90 million. Tredegar also expanded its presence in biotechnology with the 1999 acquisition of Therics, a Princeton, New Jersey, company involved in the development of bone and tissue replacement.

In 1999 Tredegar's film products business struggled while the aluminum extrusions business continued to flourish. As a result, revenues for the year topped $820 million, a significant increase over 1998's $700 million, but net earnings fell from $69.8 million in 1998 to $52.65 million in 1999. Tredegar took steps in 2000 to revitalize the film products business by acquiring ADMA and Promea, both operating in Italy, a move that also furthered its globalization strategy. ADMA manufactured films for personal hygiene products, while Promea manufactured the equipment used in making films and laminates. Although the two companies' combined annual sales totaled less than $10 million, they added valuable sales contacts, not only in Europe but in China and the Middle East. Also in 2000 Tredegar focused on its technology group, which was comprised of Tredegar Investments and the Therics and Molecumetics biotech operations. Management considered spinning off the group as an independent company, but in the end decided to make a greater financial commitment to Therics and Molecumetics. In addition to seeking external financing for both subsidiaries, Tredegar planned to provide some $60 million in funding for Therics from Tredegar Investments, which would no longer make new venture investments although it planned continued support for its portfolio companies.

With a weakening economy in 2001, Tredegar was forced to make adjustments. Demand in both plastics and aluminum were down, forcing the closure of two manufacturing facilities, an aluminum extrusion plant in El Campo, Texas; and a Tacoma, Washington, plant that made film for disposable diapers. Tredegar's venture capital investments in the hard-hit technology market also suffered. In September 2001 Tredegar made a managerial change, as Gottwald ascended to the chairmanship, a new position in the corporation. Until that time he served as part of a three-member executive committee. He now turned over day-to-day operations to Norman A. Scher, who took over as president and chief executive officer. Scher had previously served as chief financial officer. Several months later at Tredegar's annual meeting he announced that the company had decided to drop out of biotechnology and put Molecumetics and Therics up for sale. He maintained that the businesses had a better chance of reaching their potential as part of a larger biotech company that was able to provide the necessary resources. Tredegar would now focus all of its attention on its two remaining businesses, film and aluminum, which were likely to regain their strength as the economy improved.

Principal Subsidiaries

The William L. Bonnell Company, Inc.; Tredegar Film Products Corporation; Tredegar Investments Inc.

Principal Competitors

Alcan Inc.; BP p.l.c.; Mitsubishi Chemical Corporation; Mitsui Chemicals, Inc.; AEP Industries Inc.; Pliant Corporation; Minnesota Mining & Manufacturing Company; Alcoa; Griffon Corporation; Kaiser Aluminum & Chemical Corporation.

Further Reading

Baum, Laurie, "Ethyl's Gottwald Delivers the Most for His Money," *Business Week,* May 5, 1986, p. 50.
Hannon, Kerry, "Life After Lead," *Forbes,* May 18, 1987, p. 65.
Lamb, Bobby, "Ethyl Consolidates Groups," *Baton Rouge Morning Advocate,* December 17, 1988, p. 7B.
Lemons, Teresa, "Tredegar's Quiet Growth, Dull Products, Exciting Profits," *Richmond Times-Dispatch,* January 26, 1997, p. F1.
Swain, Tom, "The Long Run," *Saturday State Times,* March 28, 1992, p. 2C.

—Ed Dinger

UBS AG

Bahnhofstrasse 45
CH-8098 Zurich
Switzerland
Telephone: (01) 234 11 11
Fax: (01) 234 34 15
Web site: http://www.ubs.com

Public Company
Incorporated: 1912 as Union Bank of Switzerland
Employees: 69,684
Total Assets: SFr 1.24 trillion ($838.2 billion) (2002)
Stock Exchanges: Swiss New York Tokyo
Ticker Symbol: UBS
NAIC: 522110 Commercial Banking; 522210 Credit Card
   Issuing; 522291 Consumer Lending; 522292 Real
   Estate Credit; 522293 International Trade Financing;
   523110 Investment Banking and Securities Dealing;
   523120 Securities Brokerage; 523920 Portfolio
   Management; 523930 Investment Advice; 523991
   Trust, Fiduciary, and Custody Services; 524113 Direct
   Life Insurance Carriers; 525910 Open-End Investment
   Funds; 551111 Offices of Bank Holding Companies

UBS AG was formed from the 1998 megamerger of Swiss Bank Corporation and Union Bank of Switzerland. The resulting giant ranked as the second largest bank in Europe (trailing Deutsche Bank AG) and one of the ten largest financial institutions in the world, with assets approaching $900 billion in the early 2000s. The corporation has four main units. UBS Wealth Management & Business Banking includes the leading retail banking operation in Switzerland, with 317 branches and 1,250 ATMs serving about four million individual and corporate clients, along with the world's leading private banking business, with the latter offering wealthy clients a wide range of individually designed products and services. UBS Global Asset Management ranks as one of the world's leading institutional asset managers and providers of mutual fund products. UBS Warburg operates globally as the group's investment banking and securities business. UBS PaineWebber is one of the leading wealth

management firms in the United States, with a network of more than 8,300 financial advisors managing $436 billion of invested assets for 1.9 million, mainly affluent, individuals. Overall, UBS has 1,500 offices in 50 countries, and it manages $1.49 trillion of invested assets for its clients around the world.

19th-Century Founding of Swiss Bank

Of the two 1998 merger partners, Swiss Bank Corporation was the first to be established, though by only a few years. In 1854 a group of six private bankers in Basel started the "Bankverein" in response to the growing credit needs of Switzerland's railroad and manufacturing industries. The bank's founders initially resisted joint stock ownership because they wanted to keep the bank small and manageable, but they gradually yielded this position in the early 1870s as a number of new competitors entered the market and as colleagues in Germany and Austria increased pressure to have a large bank headquartered in Basel. Thus in 1872 the Basler Bankverein was established as a joint stock company.

In its first year of operation the Basler Bankverein was nominated as the official Swiss bank of issue for the French national loan, for financing the growing textile and metal industries in France. Beginning in 1873, however, the bank encountered several major setbacks. The Vienna stock exchange collapse, falling prices, and many bad loans forced the bank to forego issuing dividends to shareholders in favor of establishing a loss reserve. With this reserve, it was able to withstand an economic slowdown and problems in the domestic railway industry that occurred later that decade.

Over the next 20 years, the bank experienced a series of ups and downs that paralleled fluctuations in the Swiss industry and trade. Nevertheless, the bank played a significant, although restrained, role in establishing new industrial companies within Switzerland as well as new banks in Italy and Belgium.

After merging with the Zürcher Bankverein in 1895, the bank changed its name to the Basler and Zürcher Bankverein. Upon acquiring the Schweizerische Unionbank in St. Gall and the Basler Depositen-Bank in 1897, the bank began operating under its present name, Schweizerischer Bankverein, with of-

Company Perspectives:

Our vision is to be the pre-eminent global integrated invest-ment services firm and the leading bank in Switzerland. We are the world's leading provider of private banking services and one of the largest asset managers globally. In the invest-ment banking and securities businesses, we are among the select bracket of major global houses. In Switzerland, we are the clear market leader in corporate and retail banking. As an integrated group, not merely a holding company, we create added value for our clients by drawing on the com-bined resources and expertise of all our businesses.

fices in St. Gall and Zurich in addition to the headquarters in Basel. (The English name of the bank was initially Swiss Bank-verein; in 1917 the name was changed to Swiss Bank Corpora-tion.) Although a new internal structure was set up to offer autonomy to each office through three local board committees managed by one central group, this system proved too difficult to manage on a uniform basis and was later revised so that the central committee was involved more directly in the daily affairs of each office.

As the bank attempted to resolve these operational issues, it continued to grow both through its participation in Switzer-land's industrial growth and foreign trade, and through the acquisition of smaller, weaker financial institutions. It also sup-ported the government's efforts to buy back the country's major railroads from foreign investors during the early 1900s.

This activity came to an abrupt halt in 1914 with the advent of World War I as the bank supported neutral Switzerland's wartime economy and aided the country's war effort. Unlike other banks, which incurred major losses abroad during this period, Swiss Bank Corporation survived the war's financial pressures in spite of restricted access to its assets held outside the country. One noticeable effect of the war on the bank, however, was the collapse of several industrial firms in which the bank had held a major interest.

Beginning in 1924, the bank took an active role in rebuilding the international economic system by extending loans to other countries. It also served as a depository of foreign funds for investors threatened by inflation and political instability in their own countries. In 1929 the bank assisted in locating the newly formed Bank for International Settlements in Basel. This body was formed to mediate the payment of war-related reparations.

As the country struggled to overcome the Depression in the aftermath of the stock market crash in New York and the devaluation of the Swiss franc in 1936, the bank was forced to draw upon its already strained resources to help other institu-tions stay afloat. When it became apparent that the world was about to fall victim to another major war, the bank received a large influx of foreign funds for safekeeping and also rallied its own resources in preparation for the conflict by opening an agency in New York in 1939 to store assets in case of an invasion. As traditional business fell off once the war began, the Swiss government became the bank's largest customer as funds were directed toward the country's defense. This war had a predictable effect on dividend payments and earnings, but Swiss Bank endured as best it could.

Postwar Growth at Home and Abroad

Dr. Rudolf Speich became chairman in 1944, soon to face the problems and opportunities of the postwar period. At the end of World War II, Swiss Bank's assets were nearly SFr 2 billion. Once postwar finances had been sorted out, the bank turned its attention to financing private rather than state industry and to rebuilding the shattered economies of Europe. By 1947 Swiss Bank was lending money abroad again, and between 1945 and 1948 it contributed some SFr 2.5 billion to Switzer-land's efforts to help its neighbors rebuild. Meantime, the bank in 1945 completed the acquisition of the Basler Handelsbank (Commercial Bank of Basel), a major though financially trou-bled bank that had been founded in 1862.

By 1958 the bank's assets had doubled, to SFr 4 billion, and under Samuel Schweizer, who became chairman in 1961, they had doubled again by 1964. Fueling this growth was a growing number of branches, both domestic and international. In addi-tion to the London banking office, which had opened in 1898, and the New York operation that began in 1939, the bank opened offices all over the world. In the United States, offices were opened in San Francisco in 1965 and Los Angeles in 1968. In 1965 it became one of the first European financial institutions in Tokyo.

During the 1970s, because of heavy competition within Switzerland, the bank focused on the business of multinational corporations based in the United States and Canada, expanding its offices to several other North American cities. In 1972, it formed the Swiss Bank and Trust Corporation Ltd. on Grand Cayman Island, followed by financial services subsidiaries in Hong Kong in 1973, in London in 1974, and in Luxembourg a year later.

A notable exception to this global focus was Swiss Bank's participation in a major restructuring of the Swiss watchmaking industry, which was suffering from competition from techno-logically superior Japanese companies. Swiss Bank and some of its competitors extended new credit to the nation's watch-makers, enabling them to use quartz technology in watches rather than obsolete mechanical designs. Also at home, Swiss Bank in 1978 acquired a majority interest in Geneva-based Ferrier Lullin & Cie, SA, cementing its position in the private banking sector.

That same year, the bank appointed a new chairman, Hans Strasser, to lead it into a new decade. Strasser was the first high-ranking Swiss banking official to come from the working class; he had been an employee of the bank for more than 30 years. Strasser was instrumental in shifting some of the overall deci-sion-making responsibility from the bank's central management to its head branches and their respective subsidiaries. At the same time, management worked to establish a better balance between domestic and international banking activity, temporar-ily restraining the development of new business opportunities by the foreign offices, and, in particular, decreasing the number of less profitable interbank loans until business with private and commercial customers increased at home.

Key Dates:

1854: Six private bankers in Basel form the "Bankverein."
1862: Bank of Winterthur is founded.
1863: Toggenburger Bank opens for business.
1872: The "Bankverein" becomes a joint stock company under the name Basler Bankverein.
1895: Basler Bankverein merges with the Zürcher Bankverein, forming the Basler and Zürcher Bankverein (BZB).
1897: Following two more mergers, BZB changes its name to Schweizerischer Bankverein (initially translated into English as Swiss Bankverein).
1912: Bank of Winterthur and Toggenburger Bank merge to form Schweizerische Bankgesellschaft (with the initial English name being Swiss Banking Association).
1917: Swiss Bankverein changes its English name to Swiss Bank Corporation (SBC).
1921: Swiss Banking Association changes its English name to Union Bank of Switzerland (UBS).
1945: SBC acquires Basler Handelsbank; UBS acquires Eidgenössische Bank; the headquarters of UBS is moved to Bahnhofstrasse 45 in Zurich.

1967: UBS acquires Interhandel, a Swiss financial company.
1986: Phillips & Drew, a London brokerage and asset management house, is acquired by UBS; UBS also acquires the West German bank Deutsche Länderbank, which is renamed Schweizerische Bankgesellschaft (Deutschland) AG.
1991: Martin Ebner, through an investment trust called BK Vision AG, takes an 18 percent stake in UBS and questions management decisions for the next several years.
1992: Chicago-based derivatives specialist O'Connor & Associates is acquired by SBC.
1995: SBC acquires Brinson Partners Inc. of Chicago, an institutional asset management firm, and S.G. Warburg Group PLC, a leading European investment bank.
1997: SBC acquires U.S. investment bank Dillon Read & Co.
1998: Swiss Bank and Union Bank merge to form UBS AG.
2000: The U.S. brokerage firm PaineWebber Group Inc. is acquired.

Internationally Active in the 1980s

During the 1980s, the bank also played a significant part in protecting Swiss interests in its existing international business affairs. In 1982 the bank formed SBC Portfolio Management International, Inc. in New York. In addition, as one of the world's largest private gold dealers, it joined with the country's two other leading banks, the Union Bank of Switzerland and the Credit Suisse, to form Premex A.G., a brokerage house designed to strengthen Swiss involvement in the international precious metals market, and in particular to reinforce gold bullion trading activity in Zurich, which had recently begun to falter.

Three years later, the three banks were allies once again in refusing to participate in Swiss franc note issues lead-managed by the Swiss subsidiaries of two Japanese banks, the Long-Term Credit Bank of Japan and Industrial Bank of Japan. Basing their protest on claims of unequal treatment of foreign banks by the Japanese government, the Swiss banks argued that since they were not permitted to underwrite securities or join the bond underwriting syndicate in Japan, Japanese banks should face similar restrictions in Switzerland.

Toward the end of 1985, in another minor incident, but one with political ramifications, the Supreme Court of Switzerland ordered the bank to release information to Scotland Yard about an account that had allegedly been used to deposit a $2.9 million ransom paid in an Irish Republican Army blackmail scheme two years earlier. The bank claimed that providing this information would endanger the customers involved, but the court held that it was in the country's best interests for the bank to cooperate with the British government, although it required that the information supplied by the bank be used only in prosecuting the IRA.

In 1986, the growing problem of international debt facing the world's financial institutions reached a critical juncture. In an attempt to keep Mexico from defaulting on its foreign loans, an international group of bank creditors attempted to negotiate a bridge loan to Mexico that would allow the country to fulfill its interest obligations on existing debt until a longer-term financing package was arranged. Alone in its resistance to this plan, Swiss Bank proposed instead that Mexico be permitted to miss upcoming interest payments, which would then be added on to the amount of the present loan. Under pressure from the International Monetary Fund and the other banks involved, Swiss Bank eventually agreed to participate in the original lending plan. Two years later, a more satisfactory agreement enabled the banks to exchange their existing Mexican loans for $10 billion in new higher-yield 20-year bonds issued by the Mexican government.

At the end of 1986 the bank's investment banking operation added a branch in The Netherlands to its existing network of offices in London, Tokyo, New York, Frankfurt, Melbourne, and Zurich, providing more direct Swiss access to Dutch equities and bonds in the guilder market. This expansion was followed in 1987 by the acquisition of Savory Milln, a London-based securities broker, and Banque Stern, a French investment bank, as well as a controlling interest in the Paris brokerage house of Ducatel-Duval. These takeovers were in Swiss Bank Corporation's tradition of international expansion, necessary in a small country with a limited—and crowded—domestic banking market.

Worldwide competition was inevitable and in 1988 the Swiss banking community as a whole attempted to make up ground lost to more aggressive American, Japanese, and British financial rivals. No longer able to remain cautious and grow solely by offering foreign investors the stability of the Swiss economic system and the tax advantages of a Swiss account as it had in the first half of the century, Swiss Bank attempted to further strengthen its international portfolio and solidify its U.S. presence with the purchase of a multiple-story office tower in New York for its North American headquarters.

In 1988 in the midst of these attempts to redefine its business strategy, the bank, along with the Union Bank of Switzerland and Credit Suisse, found itself embroiled in a $1 billion money-laundering scheme operated by a Lebanese-Turkish drug syndicate. Although the bank did hold accounts for some of the people involved, it denied that it had acted in violation of Swiss banking laws. In addition, in early 1989, Swiss Bank was excluded from participating in a C$500 million issue of Eurobonds because the Canadian government suspected it of conducting business with South African authorities.

The bank went on the offensive beginning in February 1989 when, as one of the underwriters of Swiss franc bonds issued by RJR Nabisco, Inc., it attempted to force the company to redeem these notes because of an impending buyout by Kohlberg Kravis Roberts & Co. According to the provisions of the original bond issue, the bondholders were entitled to the return of their investment in the event of a corporate reorganization. The lawsuits filed by the bank on behalf of its bondholders were settled over the next two months before the eventual sale of the company.

Building a Global Trading and Investment Bank: 1990–97

Swiss Bank began the 1990s as the weakest of the "Big Three" Swiss banks. Its international operations were particularly weak and had been hit hard by a series of bad loans that had been made to global real estate developers and takeover firms. But under the leadership of Marcel Ospel, who was head of international operations at the beginning of the decade, and Georges Blum, who was named president of the bank in 1993, Swiss Bank adopted a new international strategy. The conservative, lending-oriented approach was to give way to a riskier but potentially more rewarding goal: rapidly develop a strong global trading and investment banking operation. At the same time, the bank's traditional domestic retail, corporate, and private banking activities were to be maintained.

The first major departure from the traditional Swiss conservatism that had marked most of the bank's history came in 1992 with the acquisition of O'Connor & Associates, a Chicago-based options trader specializing in the burgeoning derivatives sector. Founded in 1977, the highly successful O'Connor had had a strategic partnership with Swiss Bank since 1988. To shake up Swiss Bank's sleepy international operations, executives from the American firm were placed in top management posts at Swiss Bank.

Next, Swiss Bank acquired another Chicago firm, Brinson Partners Inc., to bolster its international asset management operations. Purchased for $750 million in stock in early 1995, Brinson had $36 billion under management and was one of the largest managers of U.S. institutional funds in global securities markets. Later in 1995, Swiss Bank's international ambitions took a major step forward through the purchase of S.G. Warburg Group PLC, a leading European investment banking firm based in London, for £860 million ($1.34 billion). Not included in the deal was Mercury Asset Management PLC, a funds management outfit 75 percent owned by Warburg. The merging of Warburg and Swiss Bank's existing investment banking operations created SBC Warburg, one of the top players in global investment banking. In a 1996 reorganization, SBC

Warburg became one of four Swiss Bank divisions, the others being the Domestic Division (renamed SBC Switzerland in 1997), SBC Private Banking, and SBC Brinson (the asset management unit).

In mid-1996 Ospel was promoted to president of Swiss Bank, with Blum taking over the chairmanship. While building up its international operations, Swiss Bank was struggling to turn around its domestic business, which was beset by loan losses in real estate and other sectors as the Swiss economy had been mired in recession the entire decade. To address the problems in its domestic loan portfolio, the bank took a special provision of SFr 2.8 billion, which led to a loss for the year of SFr 1.96 billion. Swiss Bank also had to deal with inefficiencies in its domestic retail banking unit, which was the smallest of the Big Three Swiss banks but had the largest network of branches. The bank announced, therefore, that it would close about 80 of its 325 branches and cut its Swiss-based workforce by about 13 percent, representing about 1,700 employees.

In addition to celebrating its 125th anniversary in 1997, Swiss Bank took the important step of buying a U.S. investment bank, Dillon Read & Co. The U.S. house was bought for $600 million in stock and bolstered SBC Warburg's U.S. mergers-advisory business. With this latest acquisition, SBC Warburg was renamed SBC Warburg Dillon Read. In July 1997 Swiss Bank reached an agreement with Long-Term Credit Bank of Japan, Ltd. to enter into a series of joint ventures in Japan, including an investment bank, an asset management firm, and the first-ever private banking enterprise in Japan. The two companies also said that they would each buy 3 percent stakes in the other. The year 1997 concluded with the historic announcement in December of the merger of Swiss Bank Corporation and Union Bank of Switzerland.

Early History of Union Bank of Switzerland

Union Bank of Switzerland (UBS) was formed in 1912 when Bank of Winterthur and Toggenburger Bank merged. Bank of Winterthur was founded in 1862 and established itself as a business lender with strong international connections. (In 1872 the Bank of Winterthur participated in the founding of the Basler Bankverein, the forerunner of Swiss Bank Corporation.) Initially based in Lichtensteig, a small town in eastern Switzerland, Toggenburger Bank was founded in 1863 and became a general-service regional bank. In addition to its savings and mortgage banking businesses, it also engaged in securities trading. In 1882 Toggenburger Bank opened a branch in St. Gall, after which the bank gradually shifted its operations to that city, which is also in eastern Switzerland.

When the two banks amalgamated to form Schweizerische Bankgesellschaft, the resulting institution possessed nine branch offices and SFr 202 million in assets. But although the two banks seemed like complementary partners—one with an international reputation, the other with a strong domestic base—UBS confined its operations at first to its regional strongholds in the east and northeast of the country. (The English form of the bank's name was initially Swiss Banking Association, but it was changed to Union Bank of Switzerland in 1921 in imitation of the French form of the name: Union de Banques Suisses.)

During its initial decades of existence, UBS operated from dual headquarters in the cities of Winterthur and St. Gall. Operations in Zurich gradually increased, however, to the point where the bank constructed an important new building at Bahnhofstrasse 45, where the headquarters would eventually be relocated (Bahnhofstrasse being the Wall Street of Zurich). In the years following World War I, the bank expanded its operations into the cantons of Aaragau, Bern, and Ticino through the opening of new branches and the acquisition of local banks. It continued to prosper through the 1920s, and by the end of the decade it possessed assets worth SFr 992 million.

UBS struggled along with the rest of the world during the Great Depression, suffering a decline in its assets. It did not really recover, in fact, until after World War II. Despite Switzerland's famed neutrality, the war hurt the bank by virtually shutting down its international businesses. While banks in major countries like the United States and Germany began to recover from the Depression because of wartime economic expansion and their governments' need for emergency financing, UBS's performance continued to lag.

Concentrating on Domestic Growth in Postwar Era

Once the war ended, however, so did the bank's slump. Only a few months after Germany's defeat in 1945, it acquired Eidgenössische Bank, a prominent Zurich financial institution that had become insolvent during the war. This acquisition pushed UBS's assets to SFr 1 billion and established it as one of Switzerland's largest banks. That same year, UBS shifted its headquarters from Winterthur and St. Gall to Zurich, specifically Bahnhofstrasse 45—a site that still houses the headquarters of UBS AG. In 1946 UBS established a presence in the United States for the first time when it opened a representative office in New York in 1946. But the bank's strategy during the postwar years concentrated on developing its domestic business. It continued to open branches and acquire smaller institutions within Swiss borders throughout the 1950s. By 1962, UBS had 81 branch offices and its assets had reached SFr 7 billion, making it, for the first time, the biggest bank in Switzerland.

In 1965 UBS and other major Swiss banks found themselves unwillingly embroiled in an international controversy when nervous investors sparked a run on the British pound. Swiss banks, through their reputation as the world's safest money havens, had accumulated substantial deposits in pounds sterling, and it was from them that unwanted pounds were withdrawn for sale on the currency markets. The banks themselves sank $80 million into stopping the panic, but the British were not impressed—Labor Party politicians derisively labeled them "the gnomes of Zurich." In response, UBS Chairman Alfred Schaefer complained to *Time,* "These campaigns really wound us. At times it makes one melancholy."

UBS underwent a burst of expansion in the late 1960s funded in large part by the 1967 acquisition of Interhandel, a Swiss financial company possessing substantial cash holdings from the sale of its majority stake in GAF, the American chemical concern. In 1968 UBS acquired four small domestic savings-and-mortgage banks, strengthening its mortgage banking operations. In 1969 it diversified into consumer lending, leasing, and factoring through the acquisition of four more

domestic financial companies: Banque Orca, Abri Bank Bern, Aufina Bank, and AKO Bank.

UBS opened its first foreign branch office in 1967 in London. It continued to expand its overseas business in the 1970s, establishing Union Bank of Switzerland Securities Limited in London in 1975 and UBS Securities Incorporated in New York in 1979. Both of these subsidiaries were devoted to gaining a share of foreign underwriting markets.

But UBS lagged behind its competitors in expanding its foreign operations during a period when internationalization became the watchword of the financial industry all over the world. UBS was the last of the three largest Swiss banks to establish a branch office in the United States, which it finally did in 1970, in New York. Its foreign securities subsidiaries also remained small compared with those of Swiss Bank Corporation and Credit Suisse. UBS's caution in testing international waters, however, was a longstanding matter of policy. The bank's directors still remembered how the sudden termination of foreign business during World War II had delayed its recovery from the Depression, and concentrated instead on building up its domestic business long after its competitors had begun to internationalize.

Internationalizing in the 1980s

As a result, UBS began losing what international business it had in the 1980s because its operations were relatively unsophisticated. It also was faced with the fact that it had just about reached the limits of expansion in the domestic banking arena. Thus in the middle of the decade, under the leadership of Robert Holzach and Nikolaus Senn, who had become chairman and president, respectively, in 1980, the bank made a fresh assault on the Eurobond market in an attempt to become a leading European underwriter. In February 1985, UBS surprised Eurobond underwriters when it brought major bond issues worth a total of $850 million for Nestlé, Rockwell, IBM, and Mobil to market at unusually low yields. The low yields were meant to attract corporate customers who liked the prospect of paying lower interest rates on their issues, but left competing underwriters astonished by UBS's aggressiveness and the high prices that it charged for the bonds. The general manager of a rival bank attributed its approach to the Eurobond market to the influence of the preponderance of Swiss army officers in UBS's hierarchy. "They make immensely careful preparations before making a move, and then they throw all their power into an advance," he told *Euromoney* in 1984.

UBS did not stop there in its late drive to internationalize. Anticipating the 1986 deregulation of Britain's financial markets, it acquired the London brokerage and asset management house Phillips & Drew early that year. Also in 1986 it bought the West German bank Deutsche Länderbank, which it renamed Schweizerische Bankgesellschaft (Deutschland) AG, and established a Phillips & Drew office in Tokyo. In 1987, it opened an Australian merchant banking subsidiary, UBS Australia Limited.

During the summer of 1987, UBS sought to solidify its position in the London markets with a bid to take over the British merchant banker Hill Samuel Group PLC. The deal fell through, however, when UBS refused to accept Hill Samuel's ship-broking and insurance services in the deal along with its core merchant banking businesses. Rumors circulated that UBS might then go after Kleinwort Benson, a British merchant bank that was reeling at the time from a slump in the bond market and a series of unfortunate acquisitions. As it turned out, however, UBS was having enough trouble digesting Phillips & Drew. The brokerage subsidiary lost £48 million as a result of the October 1987 stock market crash, but even before then an inadequate settlement system had cost it £15 million when a rush of bull market—inspired orders proved overwhelming. Between April 1987 and February 1988, UBS spent a total of £115 million on Phillips & Drew. Also in 1988 Senn took over the chairmanship of UBS; succeeding Senn in the presidency was Robert Studer, an investment banker who had previously served as director of the bank's finance department.

A Period of Weakening: 1990–97

During the early 1990s, as the Swiss economy fell into a prolonged recession, UBS outperformed its main rivals, benefiting from its position as the most conservative of the Big Three. Because of its conservative strategy, UBS managed to avoid involvement in any number of infamous corporate collapses. The bank was able to continue its overseas expansion, acquiring Chase Investors, the U.S. money management unit of Chase Manhattan, in 1991. The unit was subsequently renamed UBS Asset Management (New York) Inc. Asia was the object of a number of expansionary moves, including the opening of offices in Taipei, Taiwan; Seoul, South Korea; Bangkok, Thailand; and Labuan, Malaysia, from 1991 to 1995. Furthermore, in 1992, UBS Securities (Hong Kong) Ltd. was established. In the United Kingdom, the Phillips & Drew unit returned to profitability in 1992 after years of red ink; the unit was renamed UBS Ltd. in 1993. Back home, UBS ventured into the life insurance market for the first time through the establishment of UBS Life, which opened for business in 1993. That year CS Holding, parent of Credit Suisse, outbid UBS in a battle for Switzerland's fifth largest bank, the troubled Swiss Volksbank. Undeterred, UBS succeeded in expanding its domestic branch network the following year through the acquisition of five smaller banks. In September 1995 UBS entered into a partnership with Swiss Life, the country's largest life insurer, to cooperate on the sale of insurance products; as part of the deal, UBS took a 25 percent stake in Swiss Life, and the latter gained a 50 percent share of UBS Life, which was renamed UBS Swiss Life. In its last major acquisition before the merger with Swiss Bank, UBS acquired the Cantonal Bank of Appenzell-Ausserrhoden in 1996.

During the mid-1990s, UBS came under fire from dissident shareholders, critical of the conservative way the bank was being managed. The main opposition voice was that of Martin Ebner, a maverick financier who founded BK Vision AG in 1991. Through this investment trust, Ebner purchased shares of Swiss banks, including an 18 percent share in UBS—a holding that comprised nearly two-thirds of the overall holdings of the trust. BK Vision thus became the largest shareholder in UBS. Ebner attempted to leverage this holding into forcing changes at the bank, with his main argument being that UBS should reduce its exposure to retail banking and slash its bloated domestic branch network while at the same time ratcheting up its more lucrative operations, particularly asset management. After Ebner attempted to gain control of UBS in mid-1994, the bank responded with a shareholder proposal to unify what had been a two-class share structure, a move that would reduce Ebner's power. The plan won narrow approval in late 1994, but subsequent lawsuits filed by Ebner—including charging Studer with criminal fraud—delayed the implementation of the share changeover. In 1996 Ebner opposed the election of Studer as chairman of UBS, an effort that failed but that garnered 31 percent of the shareholder votes, an indication of the level of investor dissatisfaction. Mathis Cabiallavetta was appointed president of the bank at this time.

By being such a constant distraction, Ebner's battles with UBS management, though mostly unsuccessful, weakened the bank. The managers of CS Holding thought that UBS's travails might present the opportunity for a merger of the two Swiss bank giants. They approached UBS about a merger in early 1996, only to be quickly rebuffed. Later in 1996, the prolonged Swiss recession having wreaked havoc on the bank's loan portfolio, UBS announced that it would take a one-time charge of SFr 3 billion ($2.3 billion) to deal with problem loans. As a result, the bank reported a net loss for the year of SFr 348 million ($267 million), its first loss since World War II.

The embattled Studer compounded the bank's difficulties by mishandling the sensitive issue of dormant bank accounts that had been held by Holocaust victims. Swiss banks had come under heavy criticism for their actions during World War II. Reports of the banks' financial dealings with Nazi Germany were published, and Jewish groups pushed for reclamation of money that had been placed into Swiss bank accounts before World War II by victims of the Holocaust. The Swiss banks were initially reluctant to cooperate with these efforts—in part because of their traditional secrecy—but the resulting worldwide outcry forced the banks to publish lists of people who owned dormant accounts that had been opened before 1945, accounts that contained a total of SFr 61.2 million ($41.3 million) in them. Although UBS actually had far fewer dormant accounts than the other two members of the Swiss Big Three, the bank's handling of the affair was a public relations disaster. In one of the two most infamous incidents, Studer declared on television that the Jewish money lost in the Swiss accounts amounted to "peanuts." In the other, a security guard at the bank uncovered wartime records that were headed for the shredder, was subsequently fired, and was accused by Studer of violating secrecy laws. One consequence was that certain customers in the United States, including New York City, began boycotting UBS. In early 1997, the Big Three banks agreed to set up a SFr 100 million ($70 million) humanitarian fund for the victims of the Holocaust.

The Birth of UBS AG: 1998

By late 1997 it was readily apparent that Swiss Bank Corporation and Union Bank of Switzerland were two banks moving in opposite directions. Swiss Bank had well positioned itself to compete in the globalized financial services world through its 1990s acquisition spree that garnered it O'Connor & Associates, Brinson Partners, S.G. Warburg, and Dillon Read. By contrast, UBS was clearly reeling and had failed, unlike its two Swiss rivals, to complete any significant acquisitions in recent years (the newly named Credit Suisse Group had acquired Winterthur Insurance in a $9.51 billion deal in mid-1997). Thus, despite the combination of Swiss Bank and UBS announced in December 1997 being touted as a "merger of equals," it quickly became clear that Swiss Bank was taking over UBS, even though the former (with assets of SFr 439 billion) was smaller than the latter (with assets of SFr 578 billion). About four-fifths of the top jobs at the new institution, which would adopt the new name UBS AG, went to executives from Swiss Bank. Ebner's nemesis Studer was to have no role in the new bank. Finally, although Swiss Bank Chairman Blum would not continue on with UBS AG either, and Cabiallavetta was named chairman, it was Swiss Bank President Ospel who was certainly in charge of the new bank as its CEO.

Beyond the management details, the merger, which was consummated in late June 1998, created the second largest commercial bank in the world, with assets approaching $600 billion. It also ranked as the world's largest private banking and asset management group, with assets under management of SFr 1.32 trillion. After uniting, the two banks began integrating their extensive domestic retail networks, slashing nearly a quarter of the overall workforce of 56,000. With these reductions, the engineers of the merger were seeking to create a much more profitable company, through annual cost savings of SFr 3 billion to SFr 4 billion within a period of three to four years. The merger got off to a rocky start, however, as the bank announced in the fall of 1998 that it was taking a SFr 950 million ($697 million) charge related to exposure to Long-Term Capital Management, a U.S. hedge fund that had nearly collapsed. The exposure stemmed from the activities of the old UBS, and Cabiallavetta resigned as part of the fallout from the affair. Alex Krauer, who had been a vice-chairman, took over as the new chairman. Also in 1998, UBS AG and Credit Suisse reached an agreement with the parties that had filed Holocaust-related class-action lawsuits in the United States. The two banks agreed to pay $1.25 billion into an escrow account to settle all claims.

During 1999 UBS AG began to pare back noncore operations and holdings, including selling about $2 billion in real estate. In February the bank terminated the 1995 agreement that had been signed by the old UBS and Swiss Life. UBS AG sold its stake in Swiss Life, and Swiss Life took full control of the UBS Swiss Life joint venture. On the acquisition side, the bank beefed up its private banking operations through two purchases: the European and Asian private banking activities of Bank of America and the Bermuda-based firm Global Asset Management. In February 2000 UBS AG announced a major reorganization of the bank's activities into three main businesses: UBS Switzerland, which included retail and private banking within Switzerland; UBS Warburg, which included not only investment banking but also private banking outside of Switzerland; and UBS Asset Management, which took responsibility for institutional asset management and mutual funds. A fourth leg was gained in November 2000 through the acquisition of Paine-Webber Group Inc. for $11.8 billion. The purchase filled in a key gap in UBS AG's global wealth management operations, namely North America. Founded in 1879, PaineWebber was the fourth largest brokerage firm in the United States, with client assets of $452 billion. Early in 2001 the Wall Street firm was renamed UBS PaineWebber. Also in 2001 Ospel moved up to

become chairman, and in December Peter Wuffli became president after a short stint in that post by Luqman Arnold.

Following the purchase of PaineWebber, it appeared that UBS AG had settled into a period of consolidation and organic growth—large, headline-making acquisitions were no longer on the agenda. Smaller deals would continue to be made. In early 2002 the bank completed a well-publicized purchase of a 51 percent stake in the main trading business of Enron Corporation, the energy trading giant that had collapsed late in the previous year. It was expected that acquisitions to fill holes in the investment banking operations would be pursued. On the consolidation front, the UBS Asset Management unit was renamed UBS Global Asset Management in February 2002, and that name was to replace various regional brands that had been in use, including Brinson in North America and Phillips & Drew in the United Kingdom. In July of the same year, the UBS Switzerland unit was renamed UBS Wealth Management & Business Banking. Although the new UBS AG had not gotten off to a stellar start, a little more than four years after the megamerger its prospects for the future had brightened considerably.

Principal Subsidiaries

Armand von Ernst & Cie AG; Aventic AG; Banco UBS Warburg SA (Brazil); Bank Ehinger & Cie AG; BDL Banco di Lugano; Brinson Advisors Inc. (U.S.A.); Brinson Canada Co.; Brinson Partners (New York) Inc. (U.S.A.); Brinson Partners Inc. (U.S.A.); Cantrade Privatbank AG; Cantrade Private Bank Switzerland (CI) Limited (Jersey); EIBA "Eidgenössische Bank" Beteiligungs- und Finazgesellschaft; Factors AG; Ferrier Lullin & Cie SA; Fondvest AG; Global Asset Management Limited (Bermuda); IL Immobilien-Leasing AG; Paine-Webber Capital Inc. (U.S.A.); PT UBS Warburg Indonesia (85%); PW Trust Company (U.S.A.; 99.6%); SG Warburg & Co. International BV (Netherlands); SG Warburg Securities SA; Thesaurus Continental Effekten-Gesellschaft Zürich; UBS (Bahamas) Ltd.; UBS (Cayman Islands) Ltd.; UBS (France) SA; UBS (Italia) SpA (Italy); UBS (Luxembourg) SA; UBS (Monaco) SA; UBS (Sydney) Limited (Australia); UBS (Trust and Banking) Ltd. (Japan); UBS (USA) Inc.; UBS Americas Inc. (U.S.A.); UBS Asset Management (Australia) Ltd.; UBS Asset Management (France) SA; UBS Asset Management (Italia) SIM SpA (Italy); UBS Asset Management (Japan) Ltd.; UBS Asset Management (Singapore) Ltd.; UBS Asset Management (Taiwan) Ltd. (84.1%); UBS Asset Management Holding Limited (U.K.); UBS Australia Limited; UBS Bank (Canada); UBS Beteiligungs-GmbH & Co. KG (Germany); UBS Capital (Jersey) Ltd.; UBS Capital AG; UBS Capital Americas Investments II LLC (U.S.A.); UBS Capital Asia Pacific Limited (Cayman Islands; 92.9%); UBS Capital BV (Netherlands); UBS Capital II LLC (U.S.A.); UBS Capital Latin America LDC (Cayman Islands); UBS Capital LLC (U.S.A.); UBS Capital Partners Limited (U.K.); UBS Capital SpA (Italy); UBS Card Center AG; UBS España SA (Spain); UBS Finance (Cayman Islands) Limited; UBS Finance (Curaçao) NV (Netherlands Antilles); UBS Finance (Delaware) LLC (U.S.A.); UBS Finanzholding AG; UBS Fund Holding (Luxembourg) SA; UBS Fund Holding (Switzerland) AG; UBS Fund Management (Switzerland) AG; UBS Fund Services (Luxembourg) SA; UBS Global Trust Corporation (Canada); UBS Immoleasing AG;

UBS International Holdings BV (Netherlands); UBS Invest Kapitalanlagegesellschaft mbH (Germany); UBS Leasing AG; UBS Life AG; UBS Limited (U.K.); UBS O'Connor LLC (U.S.A.); UBS PaineWebber Inc. (U.S.A.); UBS PaineWebber Incorporated of Puerto Rico; UBS PaineWebber Inc. (U.S.A.); UBS Portfolio LLC (U.S.A.); UBS Principal Finance LLC (U.S.A.); UBS Private Banking Deutschland AG (Germany); UBS Realty Investors LLC (U.S.A.); UBS Securities Limited (U.K.); UBS Trust (Canada); UBS Trustees (Bahamas) Ltd.; UBS Trustees (Cayman) Ltd.; UBS Trustees (Jersey) Ltd.; UBS Trustees (Singapore) Ltd.; UBS UK Holding Limited; UBS UK Limited; UBS Warburg Asia Limited (China); UBS Warburg (France) SA; UBS Warburg (Italia) SpA (Italy); UBS Warburg (Japan) Limited (Cayman Islands); UBS Warburg (Malaysia) Sdn Bhd (70%); UBS Warburg (Nederland) BV (Netherlands); UBS Warburg AG; UBS Warburg Australia Corporate Finance Ltd.; UBS Warburg Australia Corporation Pty Limited; UBS Warburg Australia Equities Ltd.; UBS Warburg Australia Limited; UBS Warburg Derivatives Limited (China); UBS Warburg Hong Kong Limited; UBS Warburg International Ltd. (U.K.); UBS Warburg LLC (U.S.A.); UBS Warburg Ltd. (U.K.); UBS Warburg New Zealand Equities Ltd.; UBS Warburg Private Clients Ltd. (Australia); UBS Warburg Pte Limited (Singapore); UBS Warburg Real Estate Securities Inc. (U.S.A.); UBS Warburg Securities (España) SV SA (Spain); UBS Warburg Securities (South Africa) (Pty) Limited; UBS Warburg Securities Co. Ltd. (Thailand); UBS Warburg Securities India Private Limited (75%); UBS Warburg Securities Ltd. (U.K.); UBS Warburg Securities Philippines Inc.

Principal Operating Units

UBS Wealth Management & Business Banking; UBS Global Asset Management; UBS Warburg; UBS PaineWebber.

Principal Competitors

Credit Suisse Group; Citigroup Inc.; Deutsche Bank AG; HSBC Holdings plc; The Royal Bank of Scotland Group plc; Barclays PLC; Merrill Lynch & Co., Inc.; Goldman Sachs Group Inc.

Further Reading

"Battle of Trafalgar," *Economist*, January 21, 1995, pp. 74+.

Bauer, Hans, *The Eventful Hundred Years of the Swiss Bank Corporation*, Basel, Switzerland: Swiss Bank Corporation, 1972.

Bennett, Neil, "Extrovert Giant Among the Gnomes," *Times* (London), June 5, 1993.

Bray, Nicholas, and Margaret Studer, "UBS Banks on Conservative Strategies," *Wall Street Journal*, June 1, 1993.

Cameron, Doug, Charles Piggott, and John Parry, "No Bank Is Safe," *European*, December 11, 1997, pp. 8+.

Celarier, Michelle, "UBS to Investors (Except Ebner): There's Lots to Like," *Global Finance*, February 1995, pp. 60–64.

"A Cultural Revolution," *Economist*, August 6, 1994, p. 61.

Evans, Garry, "The Ospel Interview," *Euromoney*, April 1997, pp. 36–44.

Ewing, Jack, "Has UBS Found Its Way Out of the Woods?," *Business Week*, March 29, 1999, p. 101.

Fairlamb, David, "UBS's Mr. Fix-It," *Business Week*, April 15, 2002, p. 44.

Faith, Nicholas, "Switzerland's Big Three Have a Fight on Their Hands," *Euromoney*, December 1980, p. 93.

Gasparino, Charles, "PaineWebber Agrees to Be Bought by Swiss Bank UBS for $12 Billion," *Wall Street Journal*, July 12, 2000, p. C1.

Gilardoni, Diego, *La Svizzera è bella: un paese in crisi fra la vicenda dei beni ebraici e dell'oro nazista e la fusione UBS-SBS*, Bellinzona, Switzerland: Edizioni Casagrande, 1999.

Hall, William, and Norma Cohen, "Swiss Banks to Aid Nazi Victims," *Financial Times*, February 6, 1997, p. 2.

Javetski, Bill, and William Glasgall, "An Audacious Alpine Assault: Can Once Stodgy Swiss Bank Corp. Turn Itself into a Global Finance Powerhouse?," *Business Week*, March 6, 1995, pp. 86+.

Kinkead, Gwen, "Gnomes at Home," *Forbes*, August 22, 1983, p. 158.

Koenig, Peter, "Can the UBS Colonels Win the Overseas Battle?," *Euromoney*, July 1989, pp. 34+.

Kraus, James R., "Shaking Up Swiss Bank Corp.," *American Banker*, July 26, 1994, pp. 4+.

Lewis, Julian, "Busting the Big Banks' Closed Shop," *Euromoney*, August 1989, pp. 73+.

——, "Swiss Sluggard Strives to Catch Up," *Euromoney*, October 1991, pp. 26+.

Marshall, Julian, "UBS Gets a Facelift," *Euromoney*, March 2002, pp. 58–60.

Parry, John, "Bottom Line for Bungling Banker," *European*, November 6, 1997, p. 34.

Peterson, Thane, Kerry Capell, William Echikson, and Stanley Reed, "How the Big One Changes Banking," *Business Week*, December 22, 1997, pp. 52, 56.

Pretzlik, Charles, "Lost Battle Left Ospel Determined to Win War," *Financial Times*, February 14, 2002, p. 29.

Sesit, Michael R., "Swiss Bank Corp. Plans to Purchase Brinson Partners," *Wall Street Journal*, September 1, 1994, p. C1.

Shirreff, David, "Another Fine Mess at UBS," *Euromoney*, November 1998, pp. 41–43.

——, "The Plunder of UBS," *Euromoney*, March 1998, pp. 28+.

"A Smooth Run for Switzerland's Big Banks," *Economist*, June 17, 1989, pp. 87+.

Spiro, Leah Nathans, "Why Swiss Bank Lured a Minnow," *Business Week*, June 2, 1997, p. 128.

Steinmetz, Greg, Patrick McGeehan, and Matt Murray, "Swiss Merger Stirs Up Financial Industry," *Wall Street Journal*, December 9, 1997, p. A3.

Strehle, Res, Gian Trepp, and Barbara Weyermann, *Ganz oben: 125 Jahre Schweizerische Bankgesellschaft*, Zurich: Limmat, 1987.

Studer, Margaret, and Nicholas Bray, "Swiss Banks Face Obstacles As Role Shifts," *Wall Street Journal Europe*, February 25, 1992, p. 13.

Templeman, John, Mark Maremont, and William Glasgall, "The Big Cheese in London Banking Could Be Swiss," *Business Week*, July 27, 1987, p. 37.

"The Travails of UBS," *Economist*, March 11, 2000, p. 76.

"Trouble in the Chocolate Box," *Economist*, April 29, 1995, pp. 86+.

Walker, Marcus, and Suzanne McGee, "Swiss Bank Fills Gap with PaineWebber," *Wall Street Journal*, July 13, 2000, p. A18.

Whitney, Glenn, "Swiss Bank Agrees to Buy Warburg Group," *Wall Street Journal*, May 11, 1995, p. A4.

—update: David E. Salamie

Union Financière de France Banque SA

32 avenue d'Iéna
75783 Paris
France
Telephone: (+33) 1-40-69-65-17
Fax: (+33) 1-47-20-09-20
Web site: http://www.uffbanque.fr

Public Company
Incorporated: 1968 as Diffusion Immobilier
Employees: 1,200
Sales: EUR 167.2 million ($160 million) (2001)
Stock Exchanges: Euronext Paris
Ticker Symbol: UFF
NAIC: 523930 Investment Advice; 523110 Investment Banking and Securities Dealing

Union Financière de France Banque SA (UFF Banque) is an asset manager with a difference. The company has developed an innovative approach toward investment and wealth creation, targeting individuals—and particularly those with small- and medium-sized portfolios, rather than the wealthy—with two core investment products: the Personal Investment Plan (PIP), which enables a client to build up his portfolio through regular installments; and the Investment Account, which provides for the management of existing assets. Each product group offers a variety of collective investment vehicles, ranging from securities-based unit trusts to mutual funds and life insurance, to real estate portfolios and the management of a portfolio of rental properties. UFF Banque boasts more than 140,000 clients, some 89 percent of which are private individuals. Of these, nearly 50 percent have an average age of 54, with average assets of EUR 34,000; another 41 percent are in their mid-40s with assets of EUR 11,000; and the remainder are in their 60s with an average asset portfolio of EUR 214,000.

The majority of UFF Banque's customers are from the French provinces outside of Paris, served by a network of more than 30 branch offices and a commercially oriented network of nearly 1,000 advisors. In addition to its individual clients, UFF Banque has also attracted a number of corporate clients, particularly for its pension fund and similar products. The company has also been actively seeking wealthier clients, by rolling out new investment products and through a tongue-in-cheek advertising campaign launched in 2000 featuring such anticapitalists as Mao Tse-tung and Karl Marx. The successful campaign helped the company average some 11,000 new clients per year at the turn of the millennium, with total assets managed rising to EUR 5.5 billion, generating EUR 167 million in commissions and profits of more than EUR 33 million in 2001. UFF Banque is listed on the Paris Stock Exchange, trading on the secondary market; the majority of the company's shares are held, however, by French insurer Abeille Vie, itself a subsidiary of Aviva (formerly CGU).

Assets Management with a Difference in the 1960s

The French social upheaval of 1968 had a lasting impact on that country—touching its traditionally conservative banking industry and particularly the sector devoted to assets management, long the exclusive domain of the wealthy. At the end of the 1960s a number of people began to challenge the notion that only the rich should have access to assets management professionals. One of these was Guy Charloux, who in 1968 set up Diffusion Immobilier. Backed by the powerful French financial institutions Union des Mines and especially Banque de Suez, which was to remain a majority shareholder of the company into the 1990s, Diffusion Immobilier set out to offer assets management services to individuals—even those with modest portfolios.

Charloux's idea was to create a new type of savings bank, specializing in "wealth creation." Rather than offering individual portfolio management, the company sought to establish collective products using the assets of its customers as deposits. A primary difference offered by Diffusion Immobilier was its commercial nature, as the company began building up a network of "conseillers en gestion de patrimoine" (assets management advisors), whose roles were to act as salespeople for the company's products while building a personal relationship with the customer, including visits to the customer in his or her own home. In this way, Charloux sought to lower the entry barrier for the individual customer.

Diffusion Immobilier launched its first product, the Progressive Investment Plan (PIP), in 1968. Presented as an entirely

360

Our activity: Giving everyone access to wealth. Union Financière de France has loyally followed its calling for the last 34 years: to provide as many people as possible with the service normally reserved to the wealthiest people. To achieve success in this, we rely on our highly trained and experienced team of financial advisors who provide customised advice to our prospective clients in the comfort of their own homes. And so begins a long relationship of trust between our clients and their advisors: from the definition of the client's wealth objectives, deciding on a medium or long term strategy, to regular advice throughout the creation and management of the client's wealth. Our investment recommendations are based on collective products, which include both access to the financial skills of the very best asset managers and diversification of risk. We have created our own range of collective products under the exclusive brand name "Union Financière de France" and we entrust the management of these financial products to asset managers selected by tender. Our financial advisors are at the full disposal of their clients: meeting them at least twice a year and at any other time the client may wish it. We believe that if our clients have placed their money with Union Financière de France, then they have also placed their trust.

new type of long-term savings plan, PIP enabled customers to build up assets in regular installments. At the same time, PIP gave clients access to the French stock market—which had long remained all but closed to the small-scale investor—by enabling them to buy into a collective stock market product. As its clients began to build their portfolios and the firm attracted new clients, Diffusion Immobilier launched a second product, the Compte d'Investissement (Investment Account, or CI), in 1969. The CI permitted clients to place their existing assets into a management account with access to the firm's products.

Transitions in the 1970s and 1980s

Diffusion Immobilier also began developing new investment products. Real estate and rental property holdings were added in 1973, while the company also added mutual fund investments to its securities portfolio. In 1976 the firm added its Life Assurance Plan with Variable Capital, through a partnership with French insurance company Abeille Vie, which also provided management of the plan.

In 1978 Diffusion Mobilier changed its name to Union Financière de France (UFF), and redefined itself as a financial institution. The firm was not yet officially allowed to call itself a bank, a status acquired only in the late 1980s. Nonetheless, UFF continued to attract new clients for its investment products. In order to generate new business, UFF took a two-pronged approach: the first was to develop a strong commercial staff—by 1980, 164 of the firm's 200 employees were salespeople; the second was a rapid expansion beyond the highly competitive Paris region. Instead UFF targeted the French provinces, largely under-served by the financial investment community. UFF

quickly set up a network of branch offices and by 1980 had 13 agencies across France.

In the 1980s, UFF continued to innovate with its product range. The firm introduced two new product groups in 1983, the Real Estate Investment Fund and a life insurance policy offering lump sum payments. Until the mid-1980s, meanwhile, the company's securities investment activity had been as UCITS (Undertakings for Collective Investment in Transferable Securities), a category defined by the European Union to facilitate cross-border investments. In 1985, however, UFF began instituting its first unit trusts, which eventually replaced its UCITS products. By then UFF had seen strong growth, more than tripling its employees and boasting a sales force of over 500. The company moved into new Paris headquarters in 1986.

The UFF sales force highlighted the company's aggressive approach to attracting new clients. Sales personnel were trained by UFF itself in a program lasting several months and featuring both theoretical and practical training, including stints in branch offices. Graduates of the program received the title of Assets Management Advisors. In this way UFF developed a sales force with a variety of personal backgrounds, in what was described as a "melting pot" of personnel.

Creating Wealth in the 1990s

The year 1987 represented a new phase in UFF Banque's evolution as its shareholder base changed. Banque Indosuez, the former Banque de Suez, acquired a majority position in UFF. At the same time, insurance partner Abeille Vie acquired a 10 percent share in the company, while UFF began allowing its employees to acquire shares in the firm for the first time. By the end of the year UFF had gone public, with a listing on the Paris Stock Exchange's Unlisted Securities Market. This listing led the way to UFF's being granted formal bank status. The group changed its name to Union Financière de France Banque (UFF Banque) to highlight its new status in the French financial community. Until then, UFF Banque had focused on developing a client base among individuals, the majority of which maintained small- to mid-sized assets portfolios. In 1987, however, UFF Banque began developing a new range of group retirement savings plans in order to move into the corporate market as well. Meanwhile the investment bank's sales force had continued to grow, topping 1,000 among a network of 18 agencies. An increasing proportion of UFF Banque's operations became dedicated to developing its corporate accounts; nonetheless, UFF Banque maintained its strong service commitment to its individual customers.

In 1988 the 20-year-old UFF Banque launched a number of new innovative products. Newton Avenir Capital Retraite and Newton Avenir Epargne Retraite were assets- and savings-based life insurance policies featuring units of account, making UFF Banque one of the first French investment banks to offer this type of product. The company then debuted its real estate investment fund, UFIFrance Immobilier, which specialized in office building investments in the Paris region.

UFF Banque extended its Newton product range with Newton Avenir Patrimoine in 1991, a multiunit life insurance plan featuring lump sum payments; and Newton Luxembourg, the company's first international product offering, which enabled

Key Dates:

1968: Guy Barloux sets up Diffusion Immobilier with the backing of Banque de Suez and Union des Mines in order to provide assets management services to individuals.

1973: Diffusion Immobilier launches its first life insurance products through Abeille Vie.

1978: The company changes its name to Union Financière de France (UFF) in order to emphasize its role as a financial services company.

1987: UFF acquires bank status and makes a public offering on Paris Stock Exchange's Unlisted Securities Market; Banque Indosuez (formerly Banque de Suez) acquires a majority share of UFF Banque; UFF Banque begins offering corporate investment services.

1988: UFF launches its first of range of Newton investment products.

1991: Newton Luxembourg, the company's first international investment product, is created.

1993: UFF Banque listing is switched to the Paris Bourse's secondary market.

1997: Abeille Vie acquires majority shareholding in UFF Banque.

2000: UFF Banque rolls out a new advertising campaign to boost its client base, attracting 20,000 new clients over two years.

2001: The UFF Banque web site is launched and a new IT infrastructure is rolled out, along with the creation of two new business units, UFF Sports Advice and UFF Wealth Engineering.

2002: Two new savings products and a corporate investment product are launched.

the development of multiple currency assets while benefiting from Luxembourg's favorable tax climate.

The company continued its growth despite the harsh economic climate of the early 1990s. By 1992, UFF Banque boasted more than FFr 20 billion (worth approximately EUR 3 billion) in managed assets. The bank also featured a new product line, called the Personal Equity Savings Plan. UFF Banque's growth enabled it to place its share on the Paris Bourse's secondary market in 1993. The following year, 1994, UFF Banque targeted another largely under-served market, setting up a special pension product for France's freelance workers under the so-called "Loi Madelin," which was enacted in 1994 to recognize the professional basis of freelance workers' retirement plans and insurance policies. Two years later, UFF Banque expanded its corporate product range with the establishment of a number of cash management vehicles for corporations.

In 1997 UFF Banque found itself with a new majority shareholder when Banque Indosuez sold its holding to Abeille Vie, by then a subsidiary of the United Kingdom's Commercial Union (renamed Aviva in 2002). The change in ownership also brought in Abeille Vie executive Philippe Tizzoni, who took over as UFF Banque's chairman and chief executive. By 1999

the bank's managed assets topped EUR 4.5 billion and it launched another new product, UFF Horizon, an investment account. The company also began preparing to boost its position in the investment market, with a particular interest in attracting a wealthier segment of the investing population. The company hired polling group SOFRES to conduct a survey of its client base. The results heartened UFF Banque, as many of its clients declared themselves highly satisfied with the bank's service. The SOFRES survey was the first step toward a reevaluation of UFF Banque's brand image.

Banking and Investing in the New Century

The company rolled out a new advertising campaign in 2000. Featuring the images of such famed anticapitalists as Karl Marx and Mao Tse-tung, the ad campaign helped the company attract more than 20,000 new clients by the end of 2001. UFF Banque also installed a new IT system in 2001, which included supplying its entire network of advisors with laptop computers to provide them with full access to the company's infrastructure. At the end of the year UFF Banque debuted a new web site as part of its service and promotion effort. The company also planned to roll out another new advertising campaign to continue boosting its clientele—which numbered more than 140,000 clients, including some 16,000 corporate clients.

UFF Banque had remained committed to its record of innovation as it entered the 21st century. By the end of 2001, UFF Banque had created two new business units: UFF Wealth Engineering, and, in order to tap into the growing pool of wealthy professional athletes, UFF Sport Advice. In 2002 the company launched two new savings products and an investment vehicle, UFF Innovation 2, enabling clients to take part in the equity of nonlisted companies. Philippe Tizzoni announced his retirement in 2002 and was replaced by François Lesieur as UFF Banque's chief executive.

Principal Subsidiaries

UFIFrance Patrimoine; UFIFrance Gestion; Segesfi; SNC UFIFrance; UFF International SA (Luxembourg); Newton Gestion Luxembourg SA.

Principal Competitors

Agence Francaise de Developpement; SFCE Sevres Cedex; ISIS SA; Borzo-Bel; Etablissements Maurel et Prom; SEAE; Siparex; Societe Immobiliere d'Epone; Francarep; IPBM; Paris Orleans SA; Societe de Tayninh; Carpinienne de Participations; Societe Centrale d' Investissements; COFISMED; Fauvet Girel Etablissements SA; Group IDI; Initiative et Finance Investissement SA; GIEFCA.

Further Reading

German, Clifford, "CU Takes Stake in French Insurer," *Independent*, July 23, 1997, p. 18.

"Le 'melting pot' de l'Union Financière de France banque (UFF)," *Le Monde*, February 11, 2001.

Livre d'Or, Union Financière de France, Paris: 1998.

—M.L. Cohen

United Business Media

United Business Media plc

Ludgate House
245 Blackfriars Road
London SE1 9UY
United Kingdom
Telephone: (020) 7921-5000
Fax: (020) 7928-2728
Web site: http://www.unitedbusinessmedia.com

Public Company
Incorporated: 1918 as United Newspapers Ltd.
Employees: 7,566
Sales: £932.5 million ($1.36 billion) (2001)
Stock Exchanges: London
Ticker Symbol: UBM
NAIC: 511110 Newspaper Publishers; 511120 Periodical
    Publishers; 514110 News Syndicates; 514191 On-Line
    Information Services; 541613 Marketing Consulting
    Services; 541910 Marketing Research and Public
    Opinion Polling; 561920 Convention and Trade Show
    Organizers

United Business Media plc (UBM) is a leading U.K.-based international business publishing and services firm. The company's largest division, generating 59 percent of overall revenues, is the professional media unit, which is led by CMP Media, the leading U.S. high-tech professional media firm. Among CMP Media's offerings are newspaper and magazine publications (including *Information Week*), Internet versions of the print products as well as portals, direct marketing services, trade shows and conferences, research and consulting, and custom publishing. CMP Healthcare Group provides education and information to healthcare professionals, while the U.K.-based CMP Information provides an array of integrated media services in specific market sectors, such as agriculture, entertainment, and travel. The unit also includes two branches: CMP Europe and CMP Asia. Accounting for about 21 percent of revenues is the market research division, which is led by NOP Research Group, the number two market research company in the United Kingdom. Other operations of this division include Mediamark Research, the leading U.S. syndicated magazine research company; and RoperASW, a major U.S.-based consumer research firm. UBM's third leg is involved in news distribution and contributes about 14 percent of sales. This division is headed by PR Newswire, a distributor of corporate press releases via wire, fax, and e-mail. Two-thirds of UBM's revenues originate in North America, one-quarter in the United Kingdom, about 5 percent in the Asia-Pacific region, and 3 percent in continental Europe and the Middle East.

UBM's earliest roots are in the newspaper field, and it was known for most of its history as United Newspapers. The company changed its name to United News & Media plc in 1995 to reflect widening interests, and one year later gained a number of broadcasting and entertainment properties through a merger with MAI PLC. In 2000, after the sale of its newspaper unit and most of its consumer-related media properties, the company adopted its current name. UBM retained a few consumer media assets: a 35 percent stake in the United Kingdom's Channel 5, a 20 percent interest in Independent Television News, and two U.K. classified advertising periodicals, *Dalton's Weekly* and *Exchange & Mart*.

Early History of United Newspapers

From the middle of the 19th century the newspaper industry had grown faster in the United Kingdom than in any other country in the world. Educational reform provided a literate readership interested in foreign affairs and domestic politics, and rapidly improving road and rail links facilitated distribution throughout the country. The industrial revolution had created towns and cities that were able to provide a local newspaper with readers and advertisers. Advances in technology—linotype and rotary presses, typewriters, telephones, and telegraphs—enabled local and national newspapers to operate profitably.

Politicians were quick to realize the great influence that newspaper editors had over the electorate, and from the 1850s onward there was a considerable interchange between the Parliament and Fleet Street, the traditional home of U.K. journalism. David Lloyd George, prime minister in the United Kingdom during World War I, was an adept user of the press and was not afraid to exercise his influence to negate the effects of a political crisis. When the *Daily Chronicle* employed as a military correspondent a stern critic of his policies, Lloyd George responded by calling together a group of Liberals to buy out the owners of the paper.

United Newspapers Ltd. was formed in 1918 by these supporters of the prime minister. The company bought two papers in the deal, of which the *Daily Chronicle* was the most important. The other paper, *Lloyd's Weekly News,* had been founded in 1842 and held the distinction of being the first newspaper with a circulation of one million readers. The board of United Newspapers soon began to publish a northern edition of the *Daily Chronicle* as a rival to the Conservative Lord Northcliffe's *Daily Mail* and also acquired the *Edinburgh Evening News* and the *Doncaster Gazette,* papers that carried on the strong Liberal tradition of Lloyd George and his politically minded associates. In 1925 the company went public as United Newspapers plc.

In 1927 the company was sold for £2.9 million to the Daily Chronicle Investment Group, a joint venture of Liberal interests led by the Marquis of Reading, Sir David Yule, and Sir Thomas Catto. A covenant in the sales document restricted the owners to running the paper "in accordance with the policy of Progressive Liberalism" to further social and industrial reform, free trade, and "other programmes of Liberal and Radical measures adopted by the Liberal party."

Within a year United Newspapers was again in the hands of a new owner, William Harrison, a Yorkshireman who had trained as a solicitor in London. Although Harrison was a Conservative, he proclaimed that the group would continue to support Lloyd George and the Liberal cause. As chairman of the Inveresk Paper Company, Harrison bought a controlling interest in United Newspapers. The latter was then amalgamated in 1929 with Provincial Newspapers Ltd., an umbrella organization taking in some 17 local newspapers that Harrison had acquired in the early and mid-1920s.

Harrison's belief in the regional market molded United's acquisition strategy for the next 50 years, but this strategy was also responsible for his downfall. In the autumn of 1929, 80 percent of the value of the shares in the Inveresk Paper Company was written off because of the Great Depression. In December Harrison resigned as chairman when it was revealed that Inveresk had debts of £2.5 million and that United Newspapers had no immediate means to pay for a £500,000 modernization

program for the *Daily Chronicle.* Both companies were highly leveraged at a time when investment capital in all sectors of the economy was nearly impossible to secure.

The board of United Newspapers—led by Sir Bernhard Binder, founder of the chartered accountants Binder Hamlyn, and managing director Jack Akerman—was now facing a major crisis. Its solution was to merge the *Daily Chronicle* with the *Daily News* to produce a new title, the *Daily News and Chronicle.* In a move to provide finance for United's provincial press, 50 percent of the ownership of the new paper was sold to News and Westminster Ltd.

The mid-1930s were difficult for United Newspapers. It was a time of depression and mass unemployment, especially in United's marketplace, the north of England. Fears for the company's survival increased when Lord Rothermere announced his venture, Northcliffe Newspapers, with a stated aim of producing an evening paper in every city and metropolitan area served by United Newspapers. But in a move executed by Jack Akerman and Sir Herbert Grotrian, who had replaced Binder as chairman, United Newspapers sold its 50 percent share in what—in June 1930—had become the *News Chronicle* for £500,000 and was instantly freed from its debt. The reaction from the City was ecstatic, and United's preference shares rose from one shilling sixpence to 25 shillings, as final proof that the crisis had been averted.

The war years were less difficult for United than they were for those newspaper groups that were based in heavily bombed Fleet Street. An increase in news was cruelly matched by newsprint rationing, distribution and communication problems, and government censorship. Although Sheffield and Hull suffered damage from Luftwaffe bombing comparable to that inflicted on London, presses in Scotland, Leeds, and the west country fared better, and United Newspapers was able to consolidate its success in these areas.

Late 1940s: Beginning of the Drayton Era

The next event of importance for the directors of United Newspapers occurred in the winter of 1946 with an invitation to dinner at the Hyde Park Hotel from Harold Charles Drayton. Drayton—always known as "Harley"—was the epitome of the self-made man; born in rural Lincolnshire, he started his working life as a £1-a-week office boy and rose through the ranks of the City, eventually controlling the 117 Old Broad Street Group, a large and diverse empire of companies with worldwide interests.

Although Drayton described himself as almost uneducated, he was in truth an erudite and imaginative businessman. He realized that United Newspapers was holding assets of immense value, in the shape of offices and printing houses in the center of major towns and cities throughout the United Kingdom. Within a few weeks of the Hyde Park dinner, Drayton began negotiating with United Newspapers and eventually bought 500,000 shares, representing approximately one-third of the equity of the company. After several months as an ordinary board member, Drayton became chairman on New Year's Day 1948.

Years of steady but unspectacular profits for United followed, enlivened by a number of small and cautious acquisitions. Drayton realized that the directors of the company, three

Key Dates:

1918: Supporters of the U.K. prime minister, David Lloyd George, buy two newspapers, the *Daily Chronicle* and *Lloyd's Weekly News,* forming United Newspapers Ltd.

1925: Company goes public as United Newspapers plc.

1929: After William Harrison buys a controlling interest, United Newspapers is merged with Provincial Newspapers Ltd., publisher of about 17 local newspapers.

1930: Under financial pressure, the company merges the *Daily Chronicle* with the *Daily News* to form the *Daily News and Chronicle*—later the *News Chronicle;* a 50 percent stake in this paper is sold.

1936: To resolve another financial crisis, the remaining stake in the *News Chronicle* is divested; the company now concentrates on regional newspapers.

1946: Harold Charles Drayton purchases one-third of the company.

1948: Drayton becomes chairman.

1981: David Stevens takes over as chairman, leading the company through a period of diversification and expansion abroad.

Early 1980s: United Newspapers makes its first major U.S. acquisitions: Gralla, trade magazine publisher and trade show promoter; Miller Freeman, medical and computer trade magazine publisher; and PR Newswire.

1985: Company gains control of Fleet Holdings, owner of the *Daily Express,* the *Sunday Express,* and the *Star.*

1987: Extel, provider of financial and sporting information, is acquired.

1995: United Newspapers changes its name to United News & Media plc (UNM).

1996: UNM merges with MAI PLC, gaining various television assets; NOP Research Group, a market research company; and a number of financial services operations. Blenheim Exhibitions and Conferences is acquired.

1998: The regional newspaper business is divested; MAI's financial services unit is spun off into a separate company called Garban plc.

1999: UNM acquires Audits & Surveys Worldwide Inc., Continuing Medical Education, Inc., and CMP Media Inc.

2000: Divestments totaling £3.2 billion are completed; United News & Media is renamed United Business Media plc to highlight the new focus on business publishing and business services.

2001: Market research firms Allison-Fisher International, Inc. and Roper Starch Worldwide LLC are acquired; the latter is merged with Audits & Surveys Worldwide to form RoperASW.

of whom were in their 70s, would soon have to be replaced. Two important additions were made to the board; significantly, they were both men who had risen through the ranks of Provincial Newspapers, a company associated with United that had been formed in 1930.

Ken Whitworth had been advertising manager of a group of local newspapers based in south London before joining the Royal Air Force in 1939. He returned from four years as a prisoner of war in Japan to prove his business worth as a member of several of Provincial's boards. William Barnetson had started as an editorial writer on the *Edinburgh Evening News* and swiftly rose to become editor. He demonstrated his management skills on the board of the Edinburgh paper and later on the board of Provincial. After the quiet years of the 1950s, when the United Kingdom struggled to recover from the ravages of World War II, United Newspapers entered the 1960s with the commercially minded Whitworth and the editorially gifted Barnetson as joint managing directors. With Harley Drayton as chairman it was to be the first golden age of United Newspapers.

United Newspapers entered the 1960s as a wealthy company with an established stable of widely read regional newspapers. It was to Barnetson's credit that he did not rush headlong into reckless expansion but instead formulated a cautious acquisition strategy that relied as much on the goodwill of competitors as on his own undoubted capacity for striking deals. United's move in 1963 to larger premises in Tudor Street was indicative of United's imminent emergence as a major player in the U.K. newspaper industry.

In 1963 the *Nelson Leader* and the *Colne Times,* both struggling Lancashire papers, were bought by United, which rationalized operations by transferring printing to its own under-utilized plant at Burnley. Later in the same year United sold the 49 percent stake in the *Hull Daily News,* held by Provincial, for £1.7 million to Associated Newspapers. In November, United gave the *Edinburgh Evening News* to the Thomson group in exchange for two Sheffield papers, the *Telegraph* and the *Star.* For Thomson it meant the end of competition for its *Evening Dispatch* in Edinburgh and for United the loss of a fine paper was offset by the strengthening of its position in Yorkshire. This deal was followed by an agreement to sell United's *Yorkshire Evening News* for 20 percent of the equity of the far stronger Yorkshire Post Newspapers. Drayton adroitly realized that it was necessary to lose a battle, or at least to appear to lose a battle, to win the war. The purchase of the group of newspapers centered on the Blackpool office of the *West Lancashire Evening Gazette* and further consolidated United's position in the north of England.

Harley Drayton was succeeded as chairman by William Barnetson in April 1966. Barnetson followed Drayton's strategy and tactics when he sold the *Doncaster Gazette* to Yorkshire Post Newspapers in exchange for 49 percent of a new joint venture company, Doncaster Newspapers Ltd., which was set up to publish the *Doncaster Evening Post.* With Ken Whitworth's help as managing director, United introduced new economies in preparation for the company's greatest years of expansion.

The year 1969 started quietly with the acquisition of a group of weekly papers in north London. United then took the brave step of entering the periodicals market when Bradbury Agnew and Co., fearing hostile predators, offered its flagship *Punch,* the *Countryman,* and a number of printing houses to the company. During the tail end of the 1960s *Punch* had been suffering from a problem that was to recur with some regularity over the next 20 years. Seen as a magazine for dentist's waiting rooms, it found itself out of step with contemporary humor, but United worked closely with then editor William Davis to counter this problem.

While the deal with Bradbury Agnew was being finalized, United had begun to increase its shareholding in Yorkshire Post Newspapers. In October 1969 United acquired the total equity of the group in a transaction that was more of a mutually beneficial merger than a hostile takeover. In just one year United Newspapers had more than doubled in size.

1980s Through Early 1990s: Diversifying and Expanding Geographically Under Stevens

The 1970s saw a further period of deliberate consolidation for United Newspapers. Under Lord Barnetson the company had become firmly established as one of the Big Four of the U.K. regional press, and acquisitions were designed to increase further its share of the local market. When Barnetson died in 1981 his successor David Stevens, later Lord Stevens of Ludgate, knew that if the group was to survive it would have to venture beyond traditional areas of interest and concluded that expansion abroad was vital. He instigated a process of rationalization that saw the closure of unprofitable papers in Sheffield, Doncaster, and Wigan and the sell-off of the group's printing interests.

Stevens's leadership of United coincided with the rise of the 1980s media magnates. Rupert Murdoch and Robert Maxwell did more than simply buy out the interests of the Astors, the Beaverbrooks, and the Rothermeres; they replaced the old-fashioned newspaper proprietor with an aggressive, profit-driven businessman who was prepared almost continually to buy and sell media interests. Stevens, with a public profile deceptively lower than that of his major competitors, ensured that United Newspapers did not lag behind.

In January 1985 United Newspapers bought a 15 percent stake in Fleet Holdings, owner of the *Daily Express,* the *Sunday Express,* the *Star,* and the Morgan Grampian Group, from Robert Maxwell's Pergamon Press. When Lord Matthews, chairman of Fleet, refused to elect him to the board, Stevens initially launched a £223 million takeover offer in August 1985. This was well below the price of the company's shares at the time and was accepted by less than 1 percent of Fleet shareholders. The bid was subsequently raised to £317 million, significantly larger than the market value of United Newspapers itself. The skills Stevens had learned as a fund manager in the City enabled him to gain complete control of Fleet Holdings by October.

Express Newspapers gave United Newspapers its first national newspaper in 50 years, but the return to Fleet Street was to be far from easy. The *Daily Express* had been losing readers in the middle market and was further hit by the launch of *Today* in 1986. Numerous changes in editorial staff led to a confused editorial style, and the paper's image problem was not helped by a steady turnover of advertising agencies.

Stevens initially reduced the number of regular employees from 6,800 to 4,700 and forced through new agreements with the national printing unions and the paper's own chapels. In the ensuing years to 1990, the number was further reduced to 1,700. Electronic production and direct input of copy to computers meant that the labor-intensive process of hot metal composition could be bypassed. A ban on secondary picketing, enforced by the Employment Acts of 1980 and 1982, further weakened the hold of the traditional printing unions, which had already been shaken by protracted strikes and violent demonstrations in Warrington and Wapping. These measures returned the newly acquired national papers to profitability, enabling Express Newspapers to embark on a program of investment to ensure the future viability of its newspapers. This strategy involved the utilization of the new print technology, investment in color presses, increased paginations, and reduced advertising proportions, with the clear aim of improving the papers' appeal to their target audiences. By 1990 there were strong indications of the success of this strategy, with all Express titles showing stable circulation and strong shares of their respective advertising markets. By the end of the 1980s the *Daily Express* and the *Daily Star* were, respectively, the fourth and sixth most popular daily titles in the United Kingdom. The *Sunday Express* was by far the biggest selling Sunday broadsheet paper and the fifth most popular of all national Sunday newspapers.

Stevens's first major overseas acquisitions took place in the United States. Gralla, a family-run publisher of trade magazines and promoter of trade shows, was bought in 1983 for $44 million. Miller Freeman, publisher of a number of medical and computer trade magazines, was the next U.S. acquisition, followed by PR Newswire, a corporate and financial news agency. In the domestic market, United took control of Link House Publications in 1989 in a move that added the classified advertising paper *Exchange and Mart* to United's increasingly impressive list of titles.

Stevens also was determined to diversify into different markets. In 1987 Extel, a provider of financial and sporting information, was bought for £250 million. Benn Brothers plc, producer of directories and tax guides, was bought in 1987. In 1989 the *Daily Express* was the last national newspaper to leave Fleet Street, moving to the other side of the Thames River to new offices at Blackfriars Bridge.

The UNM Era: 1995–2000

By the beginning of the 1990s Lord Stevens had transformed United Newspapers from a publisher of regional U.K. newspapers to a diversified media group whose additional interests included the national U.K. papers *Express* and *Daily Star,* trade magazines, advertising publications, news services, and trade show activities. Geographically, the company had gained a considerable presence in the United States and was expanding certain businesses—most notably Miller Freeman and PR Newswire—into Asia. In 1995 this diversification was highlighted through the company changing its name to United News & Media plc.

Even more dramatic changes were in the cards for UNM during the remainder of the decade, under the continued direction of Stevens. In February 1996 a £2.9 billion ($4.5 billion) merger joined the operations of UNM with those of MAI PLC—with the combined entity retaining the United News & Media name. MAI's interests included two television licenses in the United Kingdom for the Independent Television Network (ITV); a 29 percent stake in Channel 5, a national commercial broadcasting service in the United Kingdom that made its on-air debut in 1997; NOP Research Group, a market research company; and various financial services firms. MAI too had an agreement, also concluded in February 1996, with Time Warner to partner on a £225 million ($344 million) Movie World theme park and film studio complex to be built just west of London. But it was the extension into television broadcasting, production, and distribution that made the MAI merger most attractive to UNM. Following the merger, the head of MAI, Clive Hollick, became chief executive of UNM, while Stevens remained chairman.

Within just a few years of this blockbuster deal, United News & Media made a series of acquisitions and divestments that further transformed the company. In late 1996 UNM bolstered its trade show operations through the £592.5 million ($905 million) purchase of U.K.-based Blenheim Exhibitions and Conferences Ltd., which was soon integrated into Miller Freeman. This acquisition made UNM into the largest exhibitions group in the world. During 1997 United News acquired HTV, a Welsh independent television broadcaster; Telecom Library, a magazine publisher and trade show organizer in the United States; and Lemos Britto, a Brazilian trade show organizer.

In early 1998 UNM made a dramatic break from its past with the divestment of its regional newspaper business through three separate sales, totaling £450 million ($700 million). In November of that same year, the company demerged the financial services businesses inherited from MAI into a separate public company called Garban plc. These moves left a more focused UNM, with three main business segments: business services, which included Miller Freeman, PR Newswire, and market research operations NOP and Mediamark Research; broadcasting and entertainment, which included the independent television licenses, the Channel 5 stake, and television show production and distribution activities; and consumer publishing, which included the *Express* and the *Daily Star* national U.K. newspapers and advertising periodicals in the United States and the United Kingdom. In the late 1990s more than half of the company's revenues were generated by business services, which was also UNM's most profitable sector.

During 1999 Ronald Hampel, former CEO and chairman of Imperial Chemical Industries plc, succeeded Stevens as chairman. That year, UNM made several more acquisitions, with the deals bolstering core operations and highlighting an ongoing interest in U.S. growth and an increasing interest in Internet-based opportunities. In January, United News & Media—through PR Newswire—acquired NEWSdesk International, a leading European Internet distributor of corporate news for the high-tech industry. Two months later UNM spent $42.5 million for Audits & Surveys Worldwide Inc., a leading U.S. market research firm, and $111 million for Continuing Medical Education, Inc., a provider of continuing medical education resources for U.S. physicians, including conferences and seminars, trade magazines, home study products, and web sites. Then in June, United News purchased CMP Media Inc. for $920 million. The Manhassat, New York-based CMP's operations included the

publication of such high-tech trade magazines as *Information Week, Computer Reseller News,* and *Electronic Engineering Times,* and the maintenance of 40 online web sites, including TechWeb and ChannelWeb. CMP became a part of Miller Freeman but maintained a separate identity.

The company's transformation into a focused business publisher and provider of business services reached its culmination in 2000, with the process being launched in the final months of the preceding year. In November 1999 UNM announced its intention to divest a number of businesses in order to create a more focused group. In March 2000 Visual Communications Group, a stock photo library acquired in 1994, was sold to Getty Images, Inc. for $220 million. UNM's U.S. advertising periodicals business, UAP, Inc., was sold in May to Trader Publishing Company for $520 million; United Advertising Publications plc, the U.K. advertising periodicals unit, was retained. Two months later, the U.S. side of Miller Freeman—minus CMP Media—was sold to the Dutch publisher VNU N.V. for $650 million, and Miller Freeman Europe was sold to Reed Elsevier for £360 million.

As these disposals were being made, there were also significant developments with the company's television assets. In November 1999 UNM reached an agreement with Carlton Communications plc, another ITV licensee, on an £8 billion ($12.6 billion) merger. U.K. regulators gave conditional approval to the merger, requiring that the combined company divest one of its ITV licenses. This led to the collapse of the merger. UNM also discussed a merger with Granada Media plc, a third ITV licensee. In the end, however, United News & Media elected to sell off its three ITV licenses and related assets to Granada for £1.75 billion, in a deal completed in December 2000. UNM retained stakes in several television and related businesses, including its stake in Channel 5, which had been increased to 35 percent in January 2000; a 20 percent stake in Independent Television News Limited, a news provider; and a 33 percent interest in SDN Limited, a digital multiplex operator.

Soon after deciding to sell the ITV licenses, UNM made another important decision: It would sell off its remaining newspaper interests in order to focus fully on business publishing and services. In November 2000 the Express Newspapers unit was sold to the Northern & Shell Group for £125 million. This brought the total for the year's disposals to £3.2 billion. To emphasize the change in focus the company changed its name to United Business Media plc. Of the proceeds, portions were earmarked for debt reduction and future acquisitions, with £1.25 billion returned to shareholders in April 2001.

Emergence of United Business Media in the Early 2000s

UBM emerged from the whirlwind of activities in 2000 as a major player in professional media, news distribution, and market research. The balance of operations had shifted significantly toward the United States, with 75 percent of operating profit now originating in North America. The U.S. focus was enhanced with the completion of two major acquisitions in 2001: the June purchase of Allison-Fisher International, Inc. for $45 million and the August buyout of Roper Starch Worldwide LLC for $88 million. Based in Detroit, Michigan, Allison-Fisher was the leading supplier of syndicated market research for the automotive industry. Roper Starch, based in New York City, was a leading U.S. consumer market research firm. It was merged with Audit & Surveys Worldwide to form RoperASW. UBM also offered to acquire MediaLink Worldwide Inc., a New York company specializing in video news releases, but was rebuffed.

Unfortunately, the UBM era got off to a rough start thanks to the economic downturn that began in 2001. Magazine publishers were hit hard as companies sharply cut back on their advertising, and the high-tech oriented CMP Media suffered a stiffer blow than most—because of the tech stock implosion—and had to endure a 26 percent drop in ad pages during 2001. To stem losses and cut operating costs, the workforce was slashed, with 1,400 jobs shed during the year. Operating profits on continuing businesses fell 50 percent over the previous year and stood at £81.1 million. Including restructuring and other charges that totaled £448.9 million, UBM reported a pretax loss of £541.2 million. The operating environment continued to be a rough one in 2002, leading the company to announce the elimination of a further 500 positions, with large reductions at CMP Media and PR Newswire. The latter was suffering from a serious downturn in the volume of press releases because of the economic sluggishness; the severe drop in mergers, acquisitions, and IPOs; and the fallout from the wave of corporate scandals, which led companies to be more publicity adverse than usual. As UBM awaited a turnaround in the advertising market that might mark a return to profitability, Hampel retired as chairman in October 2002, with longtime board member Geoff Unwin assuming his position.

Principal Subsidiaries

BUSINESS TO BUSINESS MEDIA: CMP Media, LLC (U.S.A.); CMP Europe Ltd.; CMP Information Ltd.; CMP Asia Ltd. (Hong Kong); United Entertainment Media, Inc. (U.S.A.); Expoconsult B.V. (Netherlands); PR Newswire Association, Inc. (U.S.A.); PR Newswire Europe Ltd.; Audits & Surveys Worldwide, Inc. (U.S.A.); MMI Holdings, Inc. (U.S.A.); Mediamark Research, Inc. (U.S.A.); NOP Research Group Ltd.; RoperASW LLC (U.S.A.). CONSUMER MEDIA: United Advertising Publications plc. HEAD OFFICE: United Finance Ltd.; United Finance (Jersey) Ltd.; United Business Media Finance, Inc. (U.S.A.); United Business Media (Jersey) Ltd.

Principal Divisions

Market Research; News Distribution; Professional Media.

Principal Competitors

VNU N.V.; International Data Group; Reed Elsevier Group plc; ACNielsen Corporation; Taylor Nelson Sofres plc; Information Resources, Inc.; NFO WorldGroup, Inc.; Ziff Davis Media Inc.; Advanstar Communications Inc.; CNET Networks, Inc.; Key3Media Group, Inc.; Business Wire.

Further Reading

Davidson, Andrew, "Lord Stevens," *Management Today,* March 1995, pp. 53–54, 56.

Gapper, John, "Arculus Chooses a Tricky Moment to Go," *Financial Times,* February 14, 1998, p. 21.

——, "United News Shares Slip on Demerger Plans," *Financial Times,* July 24, 1998, p. 24.

Great Britain, Monopolies and Mergers Commission, *EMAP plc and United Newspapers plc: A Report on the Proposed Transfers of Controlling Interests As Defined in Section 57(4) of the Fair Trading Act 1973 and of the Business of Publishing and Distributing Three Newspapers Owned by EMAP plc to United Newspapers plc,* London: HMSO, 1992, 82 p.

Harding, James, and Ashling O'Connor, "Failed Merger Leads to a Scattering of the Assets," *Financial Times,* July 22, 2000, p. 14.

Harverson, Patrick, and Raymond Snoddy, "Express in £3Bn Merger Deal with TV Group MAI," *Financial Times,* February 9, 1996, p. 1.

Isaac, Debra, "The News at United," *Management Today,* July 1985, pp. 42 + .

Jenkins, Simon, *The Market for Glory: Fleet Street Ownership in the Twentieth Century,* London: Faber and Faber, 1986.

Koss, Stephen, *The Rise and Fall of the Political Press in Britain,* 2 vols., London: Hamish Hamilton, 1991–1994.

Newman, Cathy, "Southnews Pays £47.5m for United Southern Arm," *Financial Times,* February 19, 1998, p. 21.

——, "Three-Way Split for United Media Sale," *Financial Times,* January 8, 1998, p. 23.

——, "United Sells Regional Titles for £450m," *Financial Times,* February 28, 1998, p. 18.

O'Connor, Ashling, "The Barclays Could Receive an Express Delivery," *Financial Times,* October 7, 2000, p. 16.

——, "Desmond Wants It All 'OK!' at the Express," *Financial Times,* November 23, 2000, p. 28.

——, "United Business Ready for U.S. Buying Spree," *Financial Times,* February 28, 2001, p. 25.

——, "United News Sells Unit to Reed Elsevier," *Financial Times,* July 26, 2000, p. 24.

Parker-Pope, Tara, and Sara Calian, "Joie de Screamer: Time Warner Plans More U.S.-Style Thrills for Europe," *Wall Street Journal,* February 14, 1996, p. B8.

Price, Christopher, "Lord Stevens Prepares to Wind Down," *Financial Times,* November 13, 1996, p. 22.

——, "United News Agreed Bid Values HTV at £371m," *Financial Times,* June 28, 1997, p. 20.

Rich, Motoko, "United's Swift Move Wins Battle of Blenheim," *Financial Times,* October 16, 1996, p. 30.

Saatchi & Saatchi, *Top Fifty European Media Owners,* London: Saatchi & Saatchi Communications, 1989.

Schofield, Guy, *The Men That Carry the News: A History of United Newspapers Limited,* London: Cranford Press, 1975, 201 p.

Snoddy, Raymond, "Battle for Channel 5 Won by MAI and Pearson," *Financial Times,* October 28, 1995, p. 1.

——, "Lord Stevens Looks to a Richer Future," *Financial Times,* April 10, 1995, p. 10.

——, "TV Contestants on Their Marks," *Financial Times,* February 9, 1996, p. 15.

Snoddy, Raymond, Scheherazade Daneshkhu, and Alice Rawsthorn, "MAI to Join Time Warner in £225m Film Theme Park," *Financial Times,* February 13, 1996, p. 1.

Taylor, A.J.P., "Lloyd George: Rise and Fall," in *Essays in English History,* London: Hamish Hamilton, 1976.

Wheatcroft, Patience, "The Human Factor," *Management Today,* October 2000, p. 33.

—Andreas Loizou
—update: David E. Salamie

United Dominion Realty Trust, Inc.

400 East Carey Street
Richmond, Virginia 23219
U.S.A.
Telephone: (804) 780-2691
Toll Free: (800) 800-2691
Fax: (804) 343-1912
Web site: http://www.udrt.com

Public Company
Incorporated: 1972
Employees: 2,400
Sales: $623.18 million (2001)
Stock Exchanges: New York
Ticker Symbol: UDR
NAIC: 525930 Real Estate Investment Trusts

United Dominion Realty Trust, Inc. (UDRT) is the fourth largest public apartment real estate investment trust in the United States. UDRT owns and operates more than 77,000 apartment units housed within 274 communities spread across 21 states. The company manages, develops, and renovates middle-market apartment communities, owning a portfolio including "B" to "A" quality properties, having evolved from its roots in Virginia as an owner of "C" grade properties. The company's biggest market is in Houston, followed by Dallas.

Origins

UDRT was founded as a Virginia corporation in 1972, beginning its business life as a real estate investment trust (REIT), then a relatively new corporate breed. REITs were authorized by the passage of the Real Estate Investment Act of 1960, whose purpose was to stimulate investment in real estate. As a general rule, REITs were exempt from federal income taxation provided they distributed nearly all of their taxable income as dividends to shareholders. The exemption from taxation opened the doors to investors who otherwise would have been precluded from engaging in real estate ownership and professional real estate management. For the first time, small inves-

tors, encouraged by the provisions of the Real Estate Investment Act, could pool their investments and participate in an industry previously restricted to the wealthy elite. In the wake of the democratization that followed the passage of the Real Estate Investment Act, REITs—companies dedicated to owning and, in most cases, operating income-producing real estate—began to appear. REITs focused their investment activities on a variety of property types, including apartments, offices, warehouses, and shopping centers. For its part, UDRT focused primarily on acquiring and managing apartment complexes, although during its first decades in business the company invested in shopping centers, office buildings, and industrial buildings.

By the time UDRT celebrated its 30th anniversary, it could count itself among the five largest publicly held apartment REITs in the nation, but the company's first years in business hardly suggested the stature it would later attain. The company did not gain its second employee until its third year of business, in 1974, when it owned only five apartment properties and a shopping center. UDRT's second employee, John P. McCann, was an important addition, marking the arrival of the single most influential individual in the company's first 30 years of business. McCann, who eventually was named chairman emeritus of the company after 27 years of service, joined the firm when it was no more than a locally oriented concern. Under McCann's stewardship, UDRT evolved from a local into a regional company, before maturing into a nationally operating concern.

As UDRT began its gradual evolution into one of the country's largest apartment REITs, it did so by building a portfolio of older B and C grade properties, that is, lower-grade apartment complexes. Although the company would later shy from acquiring lower-grade properties, particularly apartment properties classified as C grade, the strategy enabled the firm to gain its footing in a burgeoning industry. The two acquisition strategies defined the two eras of the company's development during the 20th century, each philosophy adopted because of extant economic conditions and because of UDRT's own economic strength. During the company's first era of development, which spanned nearly 20 years, it was forced, in large part, by a limited supply of capital to acquire only C grade apartments, relegated to targeting properties deemed underleased, undermanaged, and

Company Perspectives:

The middle market apartments that comprise United Dominion's portfolio are generally affordable to approximately 75 percent of all renters in the country. This large base of prospective residents creates a high degree of earnings predictability for the Company. Another degree of predictability and safety is created by our resident profile. Our residents tend to be renters-by-necessity that are attracted to our apartments because of their proximity to employment centers, their price point, and, to a lesser extent, their services and amenities. Given our average rent of $703 per month, we have less exposure to the higher rental rates that new development apartments command.

undermaintained. In this market segment, the company excelled, exhibiting great talent for exploiting the resale market. Success in this area was determined predominantly by renovation and assiduous scrutiny of property management costs. By demonstrating skills in these two disciplines, UDRT was able to succeed financially where other property management companies had failed.

Underpinned by a sound operating strategy, UDRT gained momentum and flowered into a regional concern. The company expanded in the southeastern United States initially, acquiring properties in North Carolina, Tennessee, Florida, and Georgia, as well as properties located closer to home in Virginia and Maryland. As the company expanded during the 1980s, it added significantly to its shopping center assets, the last decade UDRT would seek to embellish its mall holdings. The company acquired 12 shopping centers during the decade, purchasing properties located predominantly in Virginia, but on the whole UDRT was interested in apartment complexes. During the late 1980s, 70 percent of UDRT's portfolio consisted of apartment holdings, an unusually high percentage in the industry. The company's bias toward apartment properties held it in good stead as rising interest rates slowed the migration of apartment dwellers into homes of their own, proving to be a countercyclical boon to business during the latter years of the decade.

Expansion Beginning in Earnest in 1991

A turning point in UDRT's development occurred as the company's 20th anniversary neared. In 1991, economic conditions, notably a real estate credit crisis, created unique opportunities that UDRT was able to take advantage of because of its financial strength. The changes enabled UDRT's management to distance itself from the acquisition mantra of "underleased, undermanaged, and undermaintained" and to begin to pursue more attractive real estate properties. For the first time in its history, the company started to acquire more stable properties, specifically apartment complexes with high occupancy levels that required little substantial renovation. Economic conditions also allowed the company to embark on a major expansion of its apartment portfolio, triggering growth that inevitably led to UDRT's geographic expansion. The company entered new markets in the Washington, D.C., and Baltimore area, central and south Florida, and Nashville and Memphis, Tennessee, fleshing out its presence in the Southeast.

UDRT's buying opportunities—the fuel for its expansion—came from several types of sellers. During the early 1990s, insurance companies were interested in reducing their real estate exposure, many real estate limited partnerships were financially distressed, the RTC and FDIC were inclined to dispose real estate assets, and numerous lenders had foreclosed on properties. With scores of attractive acquisition candidates on offer, McCann and his management team pressed ahead aggressively, beginning the gradual transformation of UDRT's portfolio. Between 1991 and 1993, the company spent $250 million to acquire 36 apartment communities, which represented the addition of 9,237 units. The following year, the company eclipsed the efforts of the previous two years, spending $404 million to acquire 11,433 units grouped within 47 apartment complexes. The year's purchases moved UDRT into Alabama and Delaware for the first time. Midway through this initial expansion phase of the 1990s, management strengthened its commitment to apartment investments, resolving, near the end of 1992, to concentrate exclusively on its apartment business. Toward this end, the company began divesting its interests in shopping centers and commercial and industrial buildings. One shopping center was sold in 1994 and another four malls were divested the following year, as well as an industrial park.

As UDRT entered the latter half of the 1990s, the transformation sweeping through the company's portfolio became more readily discernible. The company's actions in 1991 represented a turning point, but the definitive moment of change did not occur until 1997, its arrival engendered by a signal acquisition. In December 1996, UDRT acquired Southwest Property Trust Inc., a publicly traded REIT that owned 44 apartment complexes with 14,320 units. The significance of the acquisition was not in its size—although the addition of more than 14,000 units represented a sizable boost to UDRT's portfolio. Rather, the significance was geographic: Southwest Property's apartments were located primarily in Texas, moving UDRT out of its traditional markets in the Southeast and the Mid-Atlantic for the first time. The former local concern, turned regional, was now chasing recognition as a national REIT.

Following the purchase of Southwest Property, UDRT continued its geographic march across the country. In March 1998, the company purchased ASR Investments Corporation, another publicly traded REIT. ASR owned 7,550 apartment homes grouped within 39 communities in Arizona, Texas, New Mexico, and Washington, further broadening UDRT's coverage in the Southwest and providing entry into the Pacific Northwest. Before the end of the year, in December, UDRT completed another acquisition, acquiring American Apartment Communities II, Inc. American Apartment owned 53 apartment communities with 14,001 units located in California, the Pacific Northwest, the Midwest, and Florida. Once integrated into the company's fold, the acquisition provided UDRT with entry into markets in Portland, San Francisco, Sacramento, San Jose, Monterey, Los Angeles, Denver, Indianapolis, and Detroit. By the end of 1998, with its presence stretching across the country, UDRT owned 86,893 apartment homes.

Restructuring in the Late 1990s

UDRT was moving in both directions during the last years of the 1990s. As the company added to its portfolio in sizable

Key Dates:

1972:	United Dominion Realty Trust (UDRT) is founded in Virginia.
1974:	John P. McCann joins UDRT.
1991:	An accelerated expansion program begins.
1996:	Southwest Property Trust Inc. is acquired.
1998:	ASR Investments Corporation and American Apartment Communities are acquired.
2001:	McCann retires and is replaced by Thomas Toomey.

chunks, it also disposed of properties that were experiencing slow growth and no longer reflected the company's emphasis on higher-grade apartments. Between 1998 and 2001, the company sold more than 15,000 apartment homes as part of its restructuring effort. In a December 1999 interview with *National Mortgage News,* McCann explained the transformation: "Prior to 1997, the company was really a regional company operating in the Southeast. At that point in time, we owned about 35,000 apartments from Baltimore to Florida. Over the last three years, we have been growing our target markets, getting to what we would define as a more efficient size. We have been upgrading our portfolio." By the end of the decade, UDRT could accurately describe its portfolio as primarily B to A quality, which meant that the average UDRT tenant paid rent equivalent to $.75 per square foot per month. In his interview with *National Mortgage News,* McCann drew a comparison: "If someone were to define our portfolio back in 1996, they would have said that on the quality scale, it is B to C grade. That means the resident is a middle- to lower-income household. Our average rent would have been more in the range of $.60 per square foot per month."

As UDRT entered the 21st century, its pace of physical growth shuddered to a halt. Dispositions exceeded acquisitions between 1998 and 2001, as the restructuring process ensued. The changes were not limited to weeding out lower-quality apartment homes; sweeping management changes also occurred. McCann ended his service as president and chief executive officer as UDRT's 30th anniversary approached. In February 2001, Thomas Toomey was selected as president and chief executive officer. Previously chief operating officer for Apart-

ment Investment Management Company, Toomey was one of seven new additions to UDRT's executive ranks as the new decade began.

During UDRT's 30th anniversary, the company continued to expand, promising further acquisitions in the future. In January 2002, the company purchased the remaining stake it did not own in three apartment communities located in Euless and Carrollton, Texas, and in Phoenix. UDRT paid Credit Suisse First Boston roughly $46 million for its 75 percent interest in the nearly 800 units housed within the three communities. In May 2002, the company acquired a 416-unit apartment complex in suburban Denver, paying $34 million for the A graded units. With further acquisitions expected, UDRT, ranked as the fourth largest concern of its kind in the nation, threatened to catch its large rivals. The company's new management team, led by Toomey, was energized for the task at hand.

Principal Subsidiaries

United Dominion Realty, L.P.; Heritage Communities L.P.

Principal Competitors

Archstone-Smith Trust; Equity Residential; Gables Residential Trust.

Further Reading

Curran, John J., "The Bright Jewels in Real Estate," *Fortune,* Fall 1987, p. 24.

Hackney, Holt, "United Dominion Realty: The REIT Stuff," *Financial World,* March 14, 1995, p. 22.

"Richmond, Va., Realty Trust Cuts 200 Jobs, Assembles New Management," *Knight-Ridder/Tribune Business News,* March 29, 2001.

"United Dominion Building a National Presence," *National Mortgage News,* December 13, 1999, p. 13.

"United Dominion Buys Washington-Area Apartment Complex," *Real Estate Finance and Investment,* May 27, 2002, p. 5.

"United Dominion Realty Buys Atlanta Apartments," *Atlanta Business Chronicle,* June 18, 1990, p. 31A.

"United Dominion Realty Trust in Richmond, Va., Acquires Three Complexes," *Knight-Ridder/Tribune Business News,* January 5, 2002.

—Jeffrey L. Covell

United Utilities PLC

Dawson House
Great Sankey
Warrington, Cheshire
WA5 3LW
United Kingdom
Telephone: (+44) 1925-237-000
Fax: (+44) 1925-237-073
Web site: http://www.unitedutilities.com

Public Company
Incorporated: 1989 as North West Water Group PLC
Employees: 15,052
Sales: £1.21 billion ($2.55 billion) (2001)
Stock Exchanges: London New York
Ticker Symbol: UU
NAIC: 221310 Water Supply and Irrigation Systems;
    221320 Sewage Treatment Facilities; 221122 Electric
    Power Distribution; 221310 Water Supply and
    Irrigation Systems; 237110 Water and Sewer Line and
    Related Structures Construction

United Utilities PLC is a pioneering ''multi-utility'' group combining operations in water supply and electric power distribution, as well as diversified—and nonregulated—operations including call center and customer management services, infrastructure management and maintenance services, as well as telecommunications services. United Utilities has reorganized its operations to highlight its diversified structure, forming five divisions to oversee its primary business areas. United Utilities Service Delivery combines the company's water supply and waste treatment operations, built around its North West Water subsidiary, and its electrical power distribution network, formerly known as Norweb (the company sold off the electricity supply operations of that business in 2000). Both operations focus around the group's home base in northwestern England. United Utilities Contract Solutions operates internationally in the three main areas of utilities operations management, network connections and metering services, and renewable energy generation installations. Contract Solutions operates throughout

the United Kingdom and is also active, especially in partnership with U.S. construction group Bechtel, in Asia, Australia, and Central and Eastern Europe. United Utilities Customer Sales was created to take over the management of the parent group's customer services operations, as well as to provide services to third-party businesses. Vertex, slated for a public offering as early as 2003, provides call center management and other business process services for third-party groups, with a focus on utilities and municipalities. Last, Your Communications, which has grown out of the former Norweb Telecom, has positioned itself as a diversified telecommunications provider for the corporate market, offering voice, data, wireless, and wireless broadband capacity. These activities give United Utilities combined revenues topping £1.2 billion. The company anticipates further diversification, with plans to acquire gas distribution facilities in its Northwest region.

Privatizing Program in the 1980s

By the end of the 1980s, the conservative-dominated British government, led by Margaret Thatcher, had completed, in large part, a vast effort to privatize many formerly government-run industries, including launching the privatization of the country's gas and electricity utilities. Privatizing the United Kingdom's water supply, however, proved a more delicate task, given that people need water to survive. Yet the government looked toward the private sector to rebuild the mostly antiquated—and often dilapidated—water supply system in the United Kingdom.

Operating water supply systems had originally been open to private enterprise in the United Kingdom; as early as the 18th century, construction of the water supply networks in the country's towns and cities was often shared among private companies and the municipalities themselves. As the towns and cities grew during the early years of the Industrial Revolution, municipal governments took on a greater share of the responsibility for laying water piping systems and for the supply and quality of the water itself. Improvements in manufacturing techniques enabled the new local utilities to replace their early piping systems—which often featured stone and wood piping—with new iron and lead pipes. By the middle of the century, responsibility for water supply had increasingly become the sole province of the local government, a situation that was structured under law by a series of legislation, beginning with the Health Act of 1848 and continuing through a series of Water Acts promulgated in the 1870s. In addition to supply water, the local water utility also took on the disposal and treatment of wastewater.

Water supply remained, however, a local endeavor, as each town and city developed its own water supply and wastewater treatment infrastructure, leading to the development of a large number of nonstandardized water utilities. In 1924, the government created a new system of local water authorities, which became responsible for water supply throughout England and Wales. Oversight for the country's water resources was taken over by a growing number of river authorities. Although a degree of consolidation occurred, at the beginning of the 1970s, the United Kingdom's water supply industry remained highly fragmented, counting nearly 30 river authorities, some 160 water supplies, and more than 1,300 water and sewage treatment authorities. None of these bodies, however, were of sufficient size to invest in modernized equipment and facilities, and the country's water system as a result had become badly antiquated, with high levels of water leakage, a growing pollution problem among the country's waterways and coastline, and mounting concern over the contamination of the water supply itself, particularly by the presence of high levels of lead in certain parts of the country.

The British government took its first steps toward improving the country's water supply sector when new legislation was passed under the Water Act of 1973, providing for a consolidation of the country's local water authorities into just ten regional water authorities. These authorities then took over complete control of a region's water supply, wastewater, and sewage treatment needs, as well as responsibility for protection of its water resources, and the environmental protection of the region's rivers and coastlines. North West Water Authority was created in that year to take over the northwestern region of England, becoming one of the largest of the new authorities. Yet North West also faced improving one of the most antiquated and dilapidated systems in the country.

By the mid-1970s, North West Water, along with the other regional water authorities, faced increasing environmental awareness, including growing concerns over health issues involving the nation's water supply, coupled with a number of new European Community-led directives, which established more stringent drinking water and sewage disposal standards. Already barely able to keep up with the massive investments needed to update the nation's water supply system, the regional authorities quickly found themselves generating massive debts. By the mid-1980s, as the Thatcher government scored a number of successes in its privatization drive, North West and the other water authorities found themselves confronted with growing government impatience at the sector's continuing losses.

The British government announced its intention to privatize the water sector in 1989. As part of the preparations for the public offering of the country's ten newly created water companies, the government agreed to write off some £5 billion of combined debt—North West Water's share of that debt was worth some £1 billion—and disburse an additional £1.6 billion in cash. Meanwhile, to ensure the success of the privatization, the government set deliberately low opening share prices for the utilities.

Growth Through Diversification in the 1990s

North West Water, led by Chairman Dennis Grove, while the second largest of the newly private water companies, was also considered one of the weakest in the industry, in part because of the former authority's past inefficiencies. Yet North West Water began life as a private company with an ambitious capital investment program, representing the largest commitment of any of the ten water companies. The company's investment program quickly topped £200 million in its first year, and by 1990 the company had earmarked some £400 million in investment. At the same time, North West Water announced long-term environmental investments of more than £1 billion over the decade to come as the company sought to wipe out one of its primary sources of criticism leveled at the former water authority. The company ended its first full year of operations with revenues of more than £511 million, and pretax profits of £75 million.

From the start, however, North West Water's ambitions went beyond its position as a regional water company. The creation of the regional water authorities in the 1970s had given North West Water, and the British water supply industry in general, a great deal of experience in bringing together and operating large-scale and cross-community utility systems, a position that gave the company an advantage in the worldwide market. North West Water began to leverage its experience in the late 1980s, marketing its expertise in the design and operation of large-scale water supply and sewage treatment systems on the global scale. North West Water targeted in particular the developing markets in Asia and South America, where strengthening economies were leading governments to invest in improving meager and even nonexistent public utility systems.

In 1988, North West Water scored its first success in this area, when it led a consortium to win the 20-year contract to modernize, expand, and operate the water supply system in Ipoh, in Malaysia. Other contracts followed, including an entry into Thailand with a contract to design, build, and operate a waste treatment plant, as well as a 50-kilometer sewer network, in Bangkok. The company also was called in as an advisor by the Indonesian government as it began plans to privatize that country's water system at the beginning of the 1990s.

North West Water faced limits in its growth in the United Kingdom—the water supply business remained heavily regulated, and the possibility of geographic expansion remained limited. Instead, North West Water began seeking other, nonregulated avenues for growth. In 1990, the company spent more than £50 million on acquisitions, buying up Water Engineering and Jones Environmental from Jones Group Holdings, for a total price of nearly £13 million, giving it operations in the design, manufacture, and installation of water and wastewater treatment facilities in England and Ireland. Those purchases were joined by the $75 million acquisition of the United States' Envirex from Banner Industries, a manufacturer of wastewater and industrial sludge treatment plants and systems. The Envirex acquisition, which boosted North West Water's total turnover by more than £60 million, also brought the subsidiary General Filters, which specialized in drinking water systems for the municipal market.

In 1991, North West Water boosted its U.S. presence with a new acquisition, paying $130 million to acquire the Wallace & Tiernan Group, based in New Jersey. Founded in 1911, Wallace & Tiernan had pioneered the use of chlorine for disinfecting water; by the beginning of the 1990s, Wallace & Tiernan was the world's top designer and manufacturer of chemical-based systems for water and wastewater disinfection and treatment. Although North West Water sold off most of that operation to Vivendi in 1997, the acquisition expanded the company's expertise in what the company later called Contract Solutions. North West Water also gained Wallace & Tiernan's strong internationally operating network.

North West Water's international operations scored new successes in the early 1990s. In 1993, the company joined the Indah Water Konsortium, which was awarded the contract to modernize and operate the sewer system in Kuala Lumpur. By 1994, Indah had gained the sewerage concessions for much of Malaysia, including Petaling Jaya, Seremban, Port Dickson, Langkawi, and Labuan. This success came on top of other recent solo successes, as the company won contracts in Mexico City, and in Sydney and Melbourne in Australia.

Multi-Utility Operator for the New Century

The arrival of a new management team, led by Chairman Desmond Pitcher and CEO Brian Staples, marked the beginning of a new era for North West Water. Staples and Pitcher stepped up the company's U.S. operations with a partnership agreement with the U.S. construction group Bechtel, combining North West Water's design and operations expertise with Bechtel's construction clout in order to bid for water supply contracts in the United States. The joint venture, called US Water, enabled North West Water to avoid having to make costly investments in building up its own construction operation, while providing a more solid basis for its worldwide expansion. Two years later, the two companies expanded their cooperation agreement on a worldwide scale with the creation of a new joint venture subsidiary, International Water Limited.

By then, North West Water had taken on a new name—United Utilities—after beating out rival bidders, including the United States' TXU, and paying £1.8 billion to take over Norweb, which held the electric power concession in England's northwestern region, and which had also begun branching out into the telecommunications sector, forming Norweb Telecom. Met initially with skepticism—and a bit of government resistance—the merger created one of the United Kingdom's first and largest ''multi-utility'' groups. United Utilities quickly took advantage of similarities in the two companies' operations, not least of which was their focus on the same geographic area. In 1997, the company merged both companies' operations in customer service and call center management to form a new subsidiary, Vertex, which then went on to compete for and win third-party contracts.

The approaching deregulation of the British electricity market at the close of the 20th century led United Utilities to attempt to expand its own electric power supply business, which had been renamed Norweb Energi in 1998. In 1999, United Utilities entered merger talks with National Power, in a proposed deal worth some £11 million. Those talks fell through at the last minute, however. Instead, United Utilities turned around and sold off Norweb Energi to TXU in 2000. United Utilities maintained control of Norweb's electricity distribution network, however.

In 2001, United Utilities, now led by CEO John Roberts, restructured its operations, redefining itself around five core divisions, including Your Communications, the renamed Norweb Telecom unit. The company had hoped to spin off Your Communications in a public offering, but was forced to abandon that move, at least temporarily, as the telecommunications market floundered at the beginning of the 21st century. Instead, the company pinned its hopes on services subsidiary Vertex, in a public offering scheduled to take place as early as 2003.

United Utilities continued to grow as the new century began, acquiring assets of Welsh utility operator Hyder, including its metering, network services, and "green" energy divisions in 2001. The company also won a four-year, £450 million outsourcing contract from Welsh Water, followed by a contract in 2002 to install and replace meters for Welsh Water customers. The company's Vertex subsidiary also was making strong gains, including winning a contract with the Westminster City Council to handle its call center and customer service operations, and a ten-year contract to provide customer management services for Canada's Hydro One. Meanwhile, the company began planning its future, including an extension into the gas distribution market and an interest in buying up utilities in its neighboring regions. United Utilities had successfully recreated itself as one of the most diversified, and most profitable, of the United Kingdom's former water authorities.

Principal Subsidiaries

AS Tallinna Vesi (Estonia; 25%); Inversora Electrica de Buenos Aires SA (Argentina; 45%); Mcarthur Water Pty Limited (Australia; 50%); Riverland Water Pty Limited (Australia; 50%); Sofijska Voda A.D. (Bulgaria; 40%); United Utilities Australia Pty Limited; United Utilities Contract Solutions; United Utilities Green Energy Limited; United Utilities Industrial Limited; United Utilities International Limited; United Utilities Operational Services Limited; United Utilities Properti Limited; Vertex Data Science Limited; United Utilities Customer Sales; United Utilities Service Delivery; United Utilities Electricity PLC; United Utilities Water PLC; Yabulu Water Pty Limited (Australia); Yan Yean Water Pty Limited (Australia; 50%); Your Communications Limited.

Principal Competitors

Electricite de France; Centrica plc; British Gas Trading Ltd; RWE Energie AG; N.V. Nederlands Gasunie; Bayernwerk AG; National Power plc; Scottish Power U.K. plc; Powergen U.K. plc.

Further Reading

Garrett, Paul, "United Hits Targets to Sound of City Cheers," *Utility Week,* December 7, 2001, p. 10.

Harrison, Michael, "United Utilities Wins Westminster Contract," *Independent,* July 17, 2002, p. 19.

Sastri, Sumi, "United Has Designs on Neighbours' Networks," *Utility Week,* May 31, 2002, p. 3.

Shepherd, Nick, "United Scores Another Win at Welsh Water," *Utility Week,* April 26, 2002, p. 9.

"United Utilities Planning Now for Enhanced Future Profits," *Institutional Investor,* February 1998, p. 100.

"United Well Supported," *Birmingham Post,* November 30, 2001, p. 22.

Wilsher, Paul, "British Water Makes Waves Overseas," *Management Today,* October 1993, p. 86.

—M.L. Cohen

UnumProvident Corporation

One Fountain Square
Chattanooga, Tennessee 37402-1307
U.S.A.
Telephone: (423) 755-1011
Fax: (423) 755-3962
Web site: http://www.unumprovident.com

Public Company
Incorporated: 1887 as Mutual Medical Aid and Accident
    Insurance Company
Employees: 13,100
Total Assets: $42.44 billion (2001)
Stock Exchanges: New York
Ticker Symbol: UNM
NAIC: 524113 Direct Life Insurance Carriers; 524114
    Direct Health and Medical Insurance Carriers; 551112
    Offices of Other Holding Companies

UnumProvident Corporation is a holding company for a group of companies that collectively are the leading disability insurers in both North America and the United Kingdom. The company also operates in Japan, France, The Netherlands, and Argentina as well. Through its key brands—Unum, Provident, Paul Revere, and Colonial—the firm offers both group and individual disability insurance in addition to such complementary offerings as long-term care insurance, life insurance, and employer- and employee-paid group benefits. UnumProvident is the result of the 1999 union of UNUM Corporation, which had been the leading group disability insurer in North America, and Provident Companies Inc., which had been the leader in individual disability insurance.

Provident's Late 19th-Century Origins in Accident Insurance

Provident Companies traced its origins back to that of the Mutual Medical Aid and Accident Insurance Company, which was founded in Chattanooga, Tennessee, in May 1887. Founders included lawyers, an architect, and a real estate sales-

man, none of whom had any real knowledge of insurance. Chattanooga was enjoying a boom at this time, as mineral hunters had discovered coal and iron ore nearby in the 1870s. There was an industrial explosion in the South in the 1880s. Chattanooga's future seemed limitless in 1887, as steel went into production south of the Mason-Dixon Line for the first time, and the mineral wealth ignited development. The insurance industry was dominated by the eastern old-line companies who would not cover high-risk workers. Mutual Medical chose these "uninsurables"—workers at coal mines, blast furnaces, coke ovens, and certain railroad occupations—for its market niche. The employing company would withhold 2.5¢ a day from laborer's wages in return for $7.50 coverage a week for lost time, and compensation for death or lost limbs. For workers whose only other recourse had been passing the hat, the policies were attractive.

The founders were forced to reverse their medical-aid policies almost immediately, after realizing that a single yellow fever epidemic—like the one in 1878—could wipe out the company. They bought back some 100 medical policies and resolved to sell only accident insurance. The company changed its name and incorporated as Provident Accident Insurance Company in December 1887. When local iron ores proved unsuitable for steelmaking, Chattanooga's development stalled. Companies withdrew, businesses defaulted, and seven banks collapsed. In five years of business, Provident had moved five times. It had 850 accident policies and no life policies. By 1892 Provident also had moved through 15 directors, and two Scotsmen offered to pay $1,000 for a one-half interest in the directionless company. Thomas Maclellan and John McMaster bought out the other owners by 1895.

In those days the insurance industry was regarded with deep suspicion, as many unsound insurance companies had soured public confidence. Maclellan and McMaster applied themselves foremost to reversing this mistrust, even choosing to go without salaries when necessary in order to pay claims promptly. By 1893 the number of policyholders had doubled. The following year saw premiums coming in from out of state. As full owners in 1895, McMaster became president and Maclellan became secretary and treasurer. Their partnership ended in 1900 because of differences, and, by prior agreement, the company went to the higher bidder. Maclellan then took over the company and became its president.

Maclellan added two lines to Provident's coverage: sickness insurance and industrial insurance. Sales—which had been McMaster's strength—suffered with McMaster's departure. In 1905, the Armstrong Committee's investigation of New York State's insurance industry sparked more public mistrust, and state legislatures moved to enact reforms, including requirements of larger reserves. In 1909 Provident was forced to withdraw from Alabama and West Virginia after legislative reforms. It remained, however, in Tennessee, Kentucky, and Virginia, collecting premiums of $108,000 in those three states in 1909. While its field of operations was shrinking, Provident was hit with increased competition when insurance companies flocked to the South, where regulatory laws were less severe than elsewhere. Maclellan reorganized the company in 1910 with added capital, changing it from a mutual to a stock company. In 1911 Provident's previously shrunken territory doubled when it entered North Carolina, Georgia, and Alabama.

Expanding into Life Insurance and Completing Acquisitions: 1910s–30s

When World War I started in 1914, domestic fears affected financial markets, and Provident's policy lapses were more than 20 percent. To combat this, the company slashed operating expenses and entered new sales regions. At the end of 1915, Provident had increased its premium income by $100,000 over the previous year. The war-revived economy combined with the coal boom of 1916, and Provident prospered as well. By the end of 1916, the company had a more than 65 percent increase in premium income. The year 1916 saw the sudden death of Thomas Maclellan, who was then succeeded by his son, Robert J. Maclellan, as president. Two new departments, railroad and life,

were formed. The company, which was soon renamed Provident Life and Accident Insurance Company of America, sold its first life insurance policy to its new president, Robert J. Maclellan.

Provident was hard hit by the influenza epidemic in 1918–19 that killed nearly ten times the number of Americans lost in World War I. The disaster proved a good advertisement for insurance, however, and Provident's premium income increased as a consequence in 1919 by more than 50 percent, exceeding $1 million.

Provident thrived along with the U.S. economy in the 1920s. It moved into a new 12-story building in 1924. That same year, the company wrote its first group plan, for the Tennessee Electric Power Company. Because the company maintained a policy of fair, prompt payment, only three of the 48,000 claims Provident processed in 1926 ended up in court. Most of its 100,000 policyholders were still working in the mines, lumber camps, steel mills, and railroad yards. An automobile liability department was formed as that industry blossomed in the 1920s, but losses closed the department in 1924. In 1925 the company's operations were still concentrated in the Southeast, but they spread north and west in 1926, with the purchase of the Standard Accident Company of Detroit. Within two years, Provident had extended to 34 of the then-48 states. With the Standard purchase came $500,000 annually in premiums. The 1929 acquisition of the Meridian Insurance Company, of West Virginia, added another $300,000 in premiums.

After the stock market crash of 1929, Provident's premium income declined. In 1931 Provident purchased the accident insurance business of the Southern Surety Company. The Des Moines, Iowa-based company's accident premiums totaled $1 million annually. The acquisition of Southern also provided an experienced staff. Provident managed not to borrow during the difficult years of the early 1930s, and by 1934, sales were picking up slightly. By its 50th anniversary, in 1937, Provident's assets were nearly $10 million, and it had an annual premium income of $7.5 million.

Postwar Development into Multiline Insurer

More industry changes came at the close of World War II as labor unions gained power and group insurance policies came into focus as an ordinary, and thus deductible, employer business expense. In 1946 Provident's accident and health income had grown by 25 percent over the year before. This growth rate was more than double the national average for the industry. The company's first subsidiary was formed in 1951, the Provident Life and Casualty Insurance Company. The subsidiary sold no casualty insurance; it was formed to allow Provident to do business in New York according to its state insurance laws, without subjecting the rest of the company to those same regulations. New York was the last frontier left for the company, as it had entered Canada in 1948. In 1952 R.L. Maclellan succeeded his father, Robert J. Maclellan, as president. The company moved into yet larger quarters. In 1955 it wrote the largest single group hospital and surgical policy in history, with premiums exceeding $5 million annually. Of 250 companies writing group life in 1954, Provident ranked 11th. Meanwhile, Provident's insurance pension business had grown in just six years to a $2 million operation in 1954. The following year it

Key Dates:

1848: Elisha B. Pratt founds the Maine-chartered but Boston-headquartered Union Mutual Life Insurance Company.

1881: As president, John E. DeWitt engineers the shifting of Union Mutual's headquarters to Portland, Maine.

1887: Mutual Medical Aid and Accident Insurance Company is founded in Chattanooga, Tennessee; medical aid policies are dropped and the company changes its name to Provident Accident Insurance Company.

1910: Provident is reorganized—changed from a mutual to a stock company.

1917: Provident begins offering life insurance and eventually changes its name to Provident Life and Accident Insurance Company of America.

1940: Union Mutual expands into accident and health insurance.

1960s: Union Mutual develops a group long-term disability business.

1970s: Provident develops an increasingly diverse product line, with particular growth in group health insurance.

1986: Union Mutual converts from a mutual firm to a public company and adopts the new name UNUM Corporation; in the aftermath, UNUM begins focusing on disability insurance, primarily the group variety.

1990: UNUM acquires National Employers Life Assurance Co. Ltd., the largest disability provider in the United Kingdom.

1992: UNUM acquires Duncanson & Holt, Inc., a leading accident and health reinsurance underwriting company.

1993: UNUM acquires Colonial Companies Inc., parent of Colonial Life & Accident Insurance Company, which offers payroll-deducted nonmedical insurance.

1994: Unum Japan Accident Insurance Company Limited is established.

1995: Provident divests its group health insurance business.

1996: A new holding company called Provident Companies Inc. is formed.

1997: Provident acquires Paul Revere Corporation, one of the leading individual disability insurers in the United States, and GENEX Services, Inc.

1999: Provident and UNUM merge to form UnumProvident Corporation, based in Chattanooga.

---

was $5 million. Robert J. Maclellan died in 1956, not long after celebrating his 50th year with the company.

In 1960 Provident made another move into larger quarters. Growth also was reflected in its premium income, which nearly doubled between 1959 and 1965. Asset growth was fueled in large part by increasing individual life products sales. In 1964 Provident reported $5 billion worth of life insurance in force. It closed the decade with triple the assets and premium income of 1959.

The accident department signed one of its largest accounts in 1970, with the American Medical Association. R.L. Maclellan died in 1971, and Hugh Maclellan, another grandson of the company's first Maclellan, assumed the presidency. Two subsidiaries were formed in 1974 to stimulate the company's flexibility: the Provident General Insurance Company, which sold automobile and homeowners' insurance; and the Provident National Assurance Company, which sold variable annuities. This last grew out of the purchase of the American Republic Assurance Company. Especially strong was Provident's group department, whose premium income in the 1970s placed it among the top ten writers of group health insurance—ahead of established giants such as John Hancock and New York Life. Self-insurance flourished after the Employee Retirement Income Security Act was passed by Congress, sending ripples throughout the industry by the mid-1970s. In 1976 *Forbes* ranked Provident first in sales growth and in earnings per share among the top investor-owned life insurance companies. In 1977 Hugh Maclellan left the presidency to chair the finance committee, and H. Carey Hanlin took his place.

Struggles in the 1980s

The 1980s dealt Provident and the insurance industry a series of hard blows. By 1980 Provident ranked seventh among the nation's stockholder-owned life insurers for insurance in force. Its primary business was group life, group accident, and health insurance, with the group business concentrated among groups of 500 or more. Between 1969 and 1979, sales of individual life insurance increased 73 percent, with the emphasis on tax-favored insurance plans. Then the mid-1980s brought a rash of regulations for the taxation of life insurance companies, starting with the stop-gap Tax Equity and Fiscal Responsibility Act (TEFRA) in 1982. Whereas TEFRA reduced company taxes, the 1984 Deficit Reduction Act increased them considerably. Then the 1986 Tax Reform Act, by redefining the nature of life insurance policies, restricted certain promising Provident tax-favored products, such as corporate-owned life insurance.

While adjusting to these changes, Provident also was contending with healthcare cost inflation, which rocketed in 1986 and 1987, with claims costs rising by 20 percent to 25 percent a year. The company suffered low earnings during these years. To right itself, Provident responded with large-loss-case management, preferred-provider organizations (PPO), and flexible benefit plans. Unlike most of its competitors, Provident decided not to invest in company-owned health maintenance organizations (HMOs). This decision proved sage when other companies with massive capital investments in HMOs were hit doubly hard by that industry's problems. The combination of healthcare cost inflation; government regulation; AIDS; new high-tech, high-cost medical treatments; and stock market volatility proved significant hurdles for Provident and others in the industry. As the company celebrated its centennial in 1987, it also reached the trough in its down cycle, when declining earnings and the purchase of the group business of Transamerica Occidental further reduced company profits. Provident continued to experience low earnings in 1988 but rebounded with record earnings the following year, after addressing inadequate pricing and focusing on core business. The company's after-tax net income increased 65 percent in 1989 over 1988, with an especially strong recovery in the employee benefits portion of its business. Meantime, in 1988, the presidency passed from Hanlin to Winston W. Walker.

Refocusing on Individual Disability Insurance in the Early to Mid-1990s

Although Provident's earnings in the early 1990s were an improvement over those of the late 1980s, the company was still struggling because of a number of underperforming operations. In November 1993 J. Harold Chandler, a senior executive with NationsBank Corporation, was brought on board as president and chief executive. Chandler initiated a thorough restructuring that laid the foundation for the merger with UNUM.

One of the key moves of the restructuring involved the sale during the first half of 1995 of the firm's group health insurance business to Healthsource Inc. for $231 million (the price was cut from the $310 million figure that was initially announced in December 1994). Provident also began winding down its guaranteed investment contract business and sold off the bulk of its commercial mortgage loan portfolio. To fund future growth, the company reduced its annual dividend on its common stock. During 1996 the parent holding company, Provident Life and Accident Insurance Company of America, was dissolved and replaced by a new holding company called Provident Companies Inc. In addition to simplifying the corporate structure through the elimination of a subsidiary holding company, this move also was coupled with the elimination of the company's dual-class stock structure through which the Maclellan family had held super-voting rights. The latter step diminished the family's control over the company, although the clan still retained more than 50 percent of the common stock and three slots on the 11-person board of directors. A final piece of Chandler's turnaround program was a change in the types of individual disability insurance being sold, with the new policies generally offering less generous terms in a move designed to rein in soaring claims.

In carrying out these various maneuvers, Chandler made it clear that the future focus of the company was in the area of individual lines—not group insurance—particularly individual disability and life products. Provident then substantially bolstered its position in the individual disability sector by acquiring the Paul Revere Corporation from Textron Inc. in a cash and stock deal worth nearly $1.2 billion. This acquisition, completed in early 1997, combined the two biggest U.S. players in individual disability insurance, increasing Provident's annual revenues to more than $4 billion and making it the clear number two disability insurer in the United States, trailing only UNUM. The merger also enabled Provident to expand its channels of distribution and provided opportunities to cut costs through economies of scale. To help fund the purchase of the Worcester, Massachusetts-based Paul Revere, Swiss insurance giant "Zürich" Versicherungs-Gesellschaft (later known as Zurich Financial Services) agreed to invest $300 million in Provident, gaining a 15 percent stake in the company and two seats on the company board.

Also in early 1997 Provident acquired GENEX Services, Inc. of Wayne, Pennsylvania. GENEX was a provider of case management, vocational rehabilitation, and related services used in the handling of disability and workers' compensation claims. GENEX also had a dental insurance arm, but this unit was sold later in 1997 to Ameritas Life Insurance. In a further divestment of noncore lines, Provident sold its individual and tax-sheltered annuity business to American General Corporation during 1998. Then in November 1998 Provident reached an agreement to merge with UNUM Corporation.

UNUM's Union Mutual Origins

UNUM Corporation traced its beginnings to the formation of the Union Mutual Life Insurance Company. Elisha B. Pratt had been one of the founders of Connecticut Mutual Life Insurance Company in 1848, but after a falling out with the management of that firm, Pratt obtained a charter in Maine to form Union Mutual, which was launched on July 17, 1848. Despite the location of the charter, Pratt ran the company out of his Boston home. Union Mutual soon expanded operations to the South and then to Oregon, Nevada, and Puerto Rico following the Civil War.

In 1876 John E. DeWitt was named president of Union Mutual. Five years later, DeWitt began plotting to move the company to Maine in response to a new law that required one-third of the company profits to be shared with Massachusetts General Hospital. DeWitt persuaded the Maine legislature to enact a law requiring Maine-chartered companies to be headquartered in that state. Then DeWitt and one other director held a board meeting in Portland, Maine, at which they elected a new board. The following day, DeWitt packed up the Boston office and moved it to Maine.

Union Mutual continued to grow during the next several decades. Then in 1940 the company took over the bulk of the business of Massachusetts Accident Company, an accident and health insurer that had gone into receivership. This marked the company's first significant move outside of its traditional individual life and endowment lines, and the accident and health business gradually became Union Mutual's most important line of business in the years that followed.

During the 1960s, under the leadership of Carleton G. Lane, Union Mutual began computerizing its operations and established a holding company to aid the company's expansion and diversification. An equally important development during the decade was the company's establishment of a group long-term disability business, an effort headed by Alfred J. Perkins, a company vice-president. Group disability insurance would later become the company's flagship product.

Colin C. Hampton was named president of Union Mutual in 1969, becoming chief executive as well the following year. Also in 1969, the Maine legislature enacted a law permitting the conversion of mutual insurance companies to stock form. Responding quickly to this opening, Hampton formally proposed demutualizing the company—that is, converting it from ownership by policyholders to ownership by stockholders—in 1970. Hampton believed that going public would bring much needed expansion capital into the company. He also felt that Union Mutual would benefit from the accountability imposed by a corporate structure. But the support did not exist for what at the time was considered a radical move.

Demutualizing in 1986

By the early 1980s Union Mutual was managing assets of approximately $2.3 billion and employing a workforce of about 1,900. Although it was a leader in the long-term disability insurance segment of the industry, the company was not viewed as a competitor with major national or international prospects. Moreover, it was gradually being overshadowed by much larger insurance companies with national marketing programs and increasingly automated operations.

In recognition of the encroaching threat to the company, Hampton in 1982 took measures to shift Union Mutual's focus away from market segments that were becoming dominated by the major national insurers. In addition, at the end of 1984 he formally began the process of converting the company from a mutual to a public firm, an effort that took nearly two years to come to fruition. In September 1986, company directors hired James F. Orr III to help Hampton oversee the demutualization. The 43-year-old Orr was an executive at Connecticut Bank and Trust Co. before joining Union Mutual. He recently had helped to complete the merger of that bank and The Bank of New England, and Union Mutual directors felt that his background complemented their situation. Orr, who had been a track star at Villanova University in the 1960s, was recognized as an intelligent, frank, even-tempered achiever. He welcomed the move to Maine for both personal and professional reasons. "The company was in a very, very exciting period of transition—demutualization. It was the first, if not only, major demutualization in insurance that's ever taken place," Orr recalled of the move in the October 1990 issue of *Business Digest of Southern Maine*. "The lifestyle in Maine was also appealing. My family and I had been coming to the Maine coast for 25 or 30 years, so putting it all together was just a tremendous opportunity."

In 1986 Union Mutual changed its name to UNUM Corporation, *unum* being the Latin word for the numeral one. In November of that year, UNUM distributed its entire net worth of $700 million to its policyholders. The company simultaneously sold new shares to new shareholders, a move that brought $700 million into the corporation's coffers. Although demutualization eventually proved to be a wise move, the transition was sometimes turbulent. Policyholders and employees were not accustomed to having the company's business scrutinized by the general public. As a result, Orr was deluged with complaints at times. "Looking back on it, I think we all underestimated how difficult it would be to get the people in the company oriented to having a new stakeholder group out there, namely, our shareholders," Orr noted in the *Business Digest of Southern Maine*. Orr helped smooth the transition by increasing the size of performance-based incentives for employees, a program that Hampton started.

Focusing on Group Disability Insurance in the Late 1980s

In addition to his efforts to engineer the transition to a public company, Orr began to aggressively reorganize and reposition UNUM to compete and grow. Within a year of his arrival—Orr officially assumed the chief executive slot in 1987—he slashed $25 million from UNUM's annual expenses by trimming back the workforce and dumping some of the organization's slumping divisions.

Union Mutual had been trying to exit various nonperforming businesses since the early 1980s. Orr intensified that effort in 1986, and UNUM eventually bailed out of several of its core businesses, including life insurance, general investment contracts, and individual annuities and pensions. Most important, Orr and fellow executives decided to eliminate the company's involvement in the medical insurance business. Orr poured the resources saved from that business segment into sales and marketing programs for its remaining products.

With its diversified lines of insurance and financial products eliminated for the most part, UNUM had become primarily a provider of long-term disability insurance. UNUM sold most of its policies to groups—a company's employees, for example—but also registered sales to individuals and small businesses such as medical practices. These agreements stipulated that, when a policyholder was out of work for an extended period because of a disability, UNUM would pay a percentage of the person's salary for a predetermined time period until the individual could return to work. In 1988 nondisability businesses still accounted for roughly two-thirds of UNUM's $1.5 billion in annual premiums. But nearly all of its $129 million in after-tax income came from disability premiums. Cognizant of this state of affairs, Orr continued to reduce UNUM's large pension and individual life businesses.

Orr's decision to concentrate on the long-term disability market was influenced in part by UNUM's established leadership position in the relatively small industry. In addition, the long-term disability market was growing quickly in comparison with most other types of insurance. Between 1962 and 1986, in fact, the number of Americans prevented from working because of a disability more than doubled to 9.3 million, a rate of growth that outstripped population growth more than fourfold. Some industry observers noted that, although sales of disability policies were increasing at a rapid rate of about 15 percent annually, the potential U.S. market of 117 million (by one estimate) was only 36 percent saturated by the late 1980s.

Between 1985 and 1988 UNUM significantly bolstered its lead in the U.S. disability insurance market. By early 1989, UNUM's portfolio held a heady 30 percent of all U.S. disability policies and had captured about 17 percent of industry revenues. UNUM's market share was a whopping four times larger than that of its four largest competitors combined. It achieved those gains by underpricing the competition. One reason for the company's impressive performance was its $13 million annual investment in what it called "benefits management," which cut UNUM's claim payouts through investigation and reduction of false claims. The program also helped clients to secure Social Security payments owed to them. UNUM's competition scrambled to match the company's efficiency. Allstate Insurance Co., for example, cut its policy prices by 15 percent in the mid-1980s in an effort to lure away UNUM policyholders. It was unable to post profits, though, and Allstate dropped out of the business in 1988.

Continued Restructuring Efforts and Acquisitions in the Early to Mid-1990s

As UNUM's disability business surged, so did its revenues and profits. Between 1987 and 1990 sales rose from about $1.6 billion to roughly $2.2 billion. Profits, moreover, jumped from just under $100 million in 1987 to $160 million in 1989 and then to nearly $220 million in 1990. Orr was confident about UNUM's future prospects for the early and mid-1990s: "When we go into a marketplace, we want to stake out a leadership position," he asserted in *Forbes*. That confidence was reflected in Orr's vision of the company's standing in the latter part of the 1990s. Aside from dominance of the U.S. disability market, that vision included charitable efforts in the local community, a healthy corporate culture and workforce, and international expansion. One key action meant to help the company meet the latter goal was the 1990 purchase of National Employers Life Assurance Co. Ltd., the largest disability provider in the United Kingdom.

UNUM's most powerful competitive advantage during the late 1980s and early 1990s was its coveted database. First established in the early 1970s, by the beginning of the 1990s the UNUM database consisted of information on 26,000 clients and 2.8 million insured individuals. Using the detailed information base, UNUM was able to precisely measure risks of disability stemming from numerous occupational, social, economic, and geographic factors. Such data gave UNUM an edge over its competitors in valuing risks, pricing policies, and creating specialized products for small niche markets. During the early 1990s, UNUM's database advantage was reflected by a 15 percent return on equity from its long-term disability business, a rate of return significantly higher than the industry average.

As a result of increased operational efficiency and intense market focus, UNUM's sales and profits continued to surge during the early 1990s. Annual revenues bolted to more than $3 billion in 1992 and then to $3.4 billion in 1993 as net income jumped to $300 million. By 1993, moreover, UNUM's asset base had grown to nearly $12.5 billion. Part of the growth was attributable to various acquisitions and joint ventures. In December 1992, for example, UNUM finalized an agreement with Equitable, a leading U.S. insurance company, to have Equitable's 8,300-member sales force sell only disability products designed by UNUM. The same year, UNUM purchased Duncanson & Holt, Inc., a leading accident and health reinsurance underwriting manager. That acquisition increased UNUM's reach in the United States, Great Britain, Canada, and Singapore. Similarly, in 1994 UNUM established UNUM Japan Accident Insurance Company Limited, a Japanese subsidiary. Back home, UNUM acquired Columbia, South Carolina-based Colonial Companies Inc., parent company of Colonial Life & Accident Insurance Company. Colonial Life specialized in payroll-deducted voluntary benefits, including disability, accident, and life insurance.

After posting successive and impressive gains throughout the late 1980s and early 1990s, UNUM stumbled in 1994. Assets and sales increased, but net income dropped to $154 million and the company experienced its first stock price drop (of 14 percent) since it had gone public in 1986. The slide was primarily the result of setbacks related to UNUM's individual disability business. The company suffered serious losses from that segment during 1994, prompting executives to announce late in 1994 that UNUM would no longer market individual, noncancelable disability products in the United States. The losses occurred, in part, because of significantly increased claims by UNUM-insured doctors, which accounted for about 15 percent of the company's business. UNUM believed that changes in the profession gave doctors more reasons to claim disability payments—which were often $20,000 to $30,000 per month—rather than recover and return to work. UNUM lost $61.7 million from the segment in the third quarter of 1994 alone, a figure that prompted it to lay off 350 workers.

UNUM continued its drive to divest noncore product lines by selling off its dental insurance and group tax-sheltered annuity businesses. The former was sold to Ameritas Life Insurance in 1995, while the latter was purchased by Lincoln National Corporation for $72 million the following year. Also in 1995, UNUM began selling individual disability policies once again, after creating a more flexible product line that recognized different degrees of disability and that offered policyholders incentives to return to work. In 1996, the company launched its first national television advertising campaign, which was mainly intended to build awareness of UNUM among the general public. By early 1997 the turnaround of the company's financial performance was evidenced by the more than doubling of its stock price since the low that it hit in November 1994. UNUM responded by declaring a two-for-one stock split and increasing the quarterly dividend by a penny. Also in 1997 UNUM acquired Boston Compañía Argentina de Seguros S.A., a Buenos Aires-based insurer involved in the property/casualty, workers' compensation, and life sectors.

Forming UnumProvident in 1999

Leading up to the late 1990s, Provident and UNUM had separately pursued similar strategies of divesting noncore operations and concentrating on the disability insurance sector, with Provident focusing on the individual market and UNUM the group market. UNUM's Orr and Provident's Chandler began discussing a possible merger of the two firms in April 1998, and in November of that year came the announcement that an agreement had been reached.

The merger, which was completed on June 30, 1999, and which was valued at about $5 billion, involved Provident shareholders receiving 0.73 shares of the new entity's stock for each of their shares, while UNUM shareholders exchanged their shares on a one-for-one basis. Technically, Provident was the surviving entity and adopted the new name UnumProvident Corporation. Headquarters for the company remained in Chattanooga, but significant operations were kept in Portland, Maine, as well. The merger created the largest disability insurer in the world, with about $8.4 billion in combined revenue and total assets of $38.2 billion; in the United States, UnumProvident held about 35 percent of the overall disability market. Orr was named chairman and CEO of the new company, a position he was slated to hold until July 2001, and Chandler assumed the presidency.

Just prior to completion of the merger, UNUM announced that it intended to exit from the reinsurance business, selling Duncanson & Holt in the process, and through a series of transactions the successor company succeeded, for the most part, in this effort by the end of 2001. Provident and UNUM also announced that they planned to eliminate about 1,575 jobs, or about 11 percent of their combined workforce, following completion of the merger, through early retirement packages, layoffs, and job elimination. This was part of the companies' effort to cut operating expenses by $130 million to $140 million by eliminating overlapping operations.

Postmerger Struggles at the Dawn of the New Century

Despite the logic that lay behind the combining of two leading disability insurers, UnumProvident got off to a very rough start. Difficulties integrating the sales forces led to a decline in policy sales. During the second and third quarters of 1999, the company took hundreds of millions in charges for merger-related activities, including severance packages and the elimination of duplicate facilities, and to the winding down of the reinsurance operations, as well as charges meant to bolster reserves. These charges resulted in net losses for the quarters and for the year overall. The losses sent the company stock plummeting, down a staggering 70 percent from June 1999 to February 2000. Five class-action lawsuits were subsequently filed on behalf of investors, charging that company management misled investors and failed to properly conduct due diligence prior to the merger (in October 2001 the parties reached a tentative agreement that would involve UnumProvident paying $45 million to settle all the claims). In November 1999 came the surprise announcement that Orr was resigning immediately and that Chandler would take on the additional titles of chairman and CEO. Orr's departure highlighted for many of the former UNUM employees in Portland that power at the new company clearly resided in Tennessee and with Provident executives. The old UNUM culture—the firm was affectionately called "Mother UNUM" and known for having a worker-friendly environment—appeared to be vanishing, and morale in Portland was wilting.

The return to profitability in 2000 and 2001 appeared to indicate that UnumProvident had weathered the difficult integration and was operating more smoothly. Net income totaled $564.2 million in 2000 and $579.2 million in 2001. During 2001 UnumProvident acquired the assets of EmployeeLife .com, an Internet services company offering employers help with the management and administration of employee benefits. The operation was transferred to a new subsidiary called Benefits Technologies, Inc., which did business under the name BenefitsAmerica. Also during 2001, the company sold Provident National Assurance Company, an inactive subsidiary licensed to sell annuities in most states, to Allstate Life Insurance Company.

Despite the improving financial performance, UnumProvident's stock continued to languish well into 2002. Investors were apparently concerned that the company's performance and future prospects were being hampered by a number of factors, including low interest rates (which negatively affected the strength of the firm's $28 billion in investments), the weak U.S. economy, and rising claims; the latter two factors typically work together, as workers in a weak economy are more likely to file claims. Adding to the company's headaches

was a series of revelations of investment losses related to a string of high-profile financially troubled firms, including Enron Corporation, WorldCom, Inc., TeleGlobe Inc., and Adelphia Communications Corp. Furthering the uncertainty surrounding UnumProvident was a lawsuit filed in June 2002 by a former medical director at the company's headquarters in Chattanooga. According to an article in the *Portland (Maine) Press Herald,* the suit claimed that UnumProvident had a "policy of summarily denying disability claims and using its medical staff to back up the denial." The company vigorously denied the allegations. For the first six months of 2002, UnumProvident recorded net income of $163.5 million, less than half the $329.1 million figure for the previous year.

Principal Subsidiaries

Provident Life and Accident Insurance Company; Unum Life Insurance Company of America; The Paul Revere Life Insurance Company; Colonial Life & Accident Insurance Company; First Unum Life Insurance Company; Provident Life and Casualty Insurance Company; GENEX Services, Inc.; Unum Limited (U.K.); Unum Japan Accident Insurance Company Limited; Benefits Technologies, Inc.; Provident Investment Management, LLC.

Principal Competitors

The Hartford Financial Services Group, Inc.; Metropolitan Life Insurance Company; Prudential Financial, Inc.; CIGNA Corporation; Aetna Inc.; AFLAC Incorporated; Aon Corporation.

Further Reading

Cox, Brian, "Provident Sells Group Medical Business," *National Underwriter Life and Health/Financial Services,* January 2, 1995, p. 42.

——, "UNUM to Leave Individual Non-Cancelable DI Market," *National Underwriter Life and Health/Financial Services,* November 14, 1994, p. 3.

Drury, Allan, "Underachieving, But Confident of Strategy," *Portland (Maine) Press Herald,* May 21, 2002, p. 1C.

Frandzel, Steve, "Provident Reverses Earnings Free Fall," *Business Atlanta,* June 1990, pp. 126+.

French, Dorry, "Unum's Long Term Orr-Ganizer," *Business Digest of Southern Maine,* October 1990, p. 2.

Horgan, Sean, "Here for the Long Term: Life Is Good at UNUM, Firmly Ensconced in Portland and Ever a Darling of Insurance Analysts," *Portland (Maine) Press Herald,* September 16, 1997, p. 1C.

Jereski, Laura, "We Understand Risk," *Forbes,* March 20, 1989, pp. 127–28.

Jorden, James F., Michael T. Greif, and Perry Ian Cone, "The Day Union Mutual Went Public," *Best's Review—Life-Health Insurance Edition,* April 1987, pp. 19+.

Kerr, Peter, "Less Is Key to an Insurer's Success," *New York Times,* February 10, 1993, p. D1.

Knowles, Robert G., "Savoring the Turnaround at Provident L&A," *National Underwriter Life and Health/Financial Services,* March 18, 1991, pp. 3, 8.

Lipin, Steven, and Leslie Scism, "Provident Reaches Accord with Textron to Buy Paul Revere Unit for $1.2 Billion," *Wall Street Journal,* April 29, 1996, p. A3.

Lohse, Deborah, "Provident Cos. and UNUM Agree to Merge," *Wall Street Journal,* November 24, 1998, p. A3.

Longwith, John, *Provident: A Centennial History,* Chattanooga, Tenn.: Provident Life and Accident Insurance Company, 1986.

Lunt, Dean, "Out of the Shadows: UNUM Has Never Focused Its Efforts on Its Individual Insurance Lines, But That's About to Change," *Portland (Maine) Press Herald,* December 23, 1997, p. 1C.

——, "UNUM Merger Gets Shareholders' OK," *Portland (Maine) Press Herald,* July 1, 1999, p. 1A.

——, "UnumProvident: A Merger Made in Heaven?," *Portland (Maine) Press Herald,* December 6, 1998, p. 1F.

——, "UnumProvident 'Moving Again,'" *Portland (Maine) Press Herald,* May 20, 2000, p. 6D.

——, "UnumProvident: Time to Deliver," *Portland (Maine) Press Herald,* December 12, 1999, p. 1F.

——, "UNUM, Provident Will Merge," *Portland (Maine) Press Herald,* November 24, 1998, p. 1A.

——, "Winds of Change Coming to UNUM in Person of New Boss," *Portland (Maine) Press Herald,* April 18, 1999, p. 1A.

Lunt, Dean, and Edward D. Murphy, "UnumProvident CEO Orr Exits Early," *Portland (Maine) Press Herald,* November 2, 1999, p. 1A.

McGough, Robert, "Yankee Clipper: UNUM Sails the Fast Track from Its Home Port in Maine," *Financial World,* June 11, 1991, p. 38.

Murphy, Edward D., "Doctor: UNUM Denies Claims," *Portland (Maine) Press Herald,* September 25, 2002, p. 1A.

——, "Insurer Tells Employees Suits Won't Affect Them," *Portland (Maine) Press Herald,* September 27, 2002, p. 1A.

Niedzielski, Joe, "Merger of Provident, Revere Creates Indiv. DI Behemoth," *National Underwriter Life and Health/Financial Services,* May 6, 1996, pp. 1+.

Panko, Ron, "Sharpening the Focus," *Best's Review,* August 2002, pp. 74–76, 80–82.

"Reducing Risk: Provident Life's Managed Benefits Are Surging," *Barron's,* October 27, 1980.

Scism, Leslie, and Steven Lipin, "Provident's Purchase of Paul Revere Signals Recovery," *Wall Street Journal,* April 30, 1996, p. B4.

Strosnider, Kim, "Fraud with Peril: UNUM Is Stepping Up Efforts to Insure That, When It Comes to Making Fraudulent Claims, It Doesn't Pay," *Portland (Maine) Press Herald,* April 28, 1996, p. 1F.

——, "UNUM Selling Annuities Business," *Portland (Maine) Press Herald,* January 25, 1996, p. 8B.

——, "UNUM Takes to the Air," *Portland (Maine) Press Herald,* August 27, 1996, p. 1C.

Treaster, Joseph B., "Two Leading U.S. Disability Insurers Plan Merger," *New York Times,* November 24, 1998, p. C25.

West, Diane, "Provident Exits Commercial Mortgage Loan Market," *National Underwriter Life and Health/Financial Services,* November 6, 1995, p. 55.

—Carol I. Keeley and Dave Mote
—update: David E. Salamie

US Airways Group, Inc.

2345 Crystal Drive
Arlington, Virginia 22227
U.S.A.
Telephone: (703) 872-5100
Toll Free: (800) 428-4322
Fax: (703) 872-5307
Web site: http://www.usairways.com

Public Company
Incorporated: 1937 as All American Aviation, Inc.
Employees: 40,900
Sales: $8.29 billion (2001)
Stock Exchanges: New York
Ticker Symbol: U
NAIC: 481111 Scheduled Passenger Air Transportation

US Airways Group, Inc. (formerly USAir Group, Inc.) is a holding company for several commercial airlines, of which US Airways (formerly USAir) is the largest. Through its fleet of about 300 jets, US Airways provides service to 95 destinations. In addition to its flagship carrier, which generated 87 percent of the parent company's operating revenues in 2001, other subsidiaries operate a regional feeder network under the US Airways Express name. US Airways is strongest in the Northeast, and has had international success with transatlantic and Caribbean routes.

Mail Delivery Origins

The company was originally incorporated in Delaware in 1937 as All American Aviation, Inc. by a glider pilot named Richard C. du Pont, of the Delaware du Ponts. On May 12, 1939, the airline began to deliver mail around the mountains of Pennsylvania and West Virginia. Since many communities did not have airstrips, the company devised a system employing hooks and ropes that enabled the mail plane to drop off one mailbag and pick up another without landing. Du Pont's method brought regular mail service to a number of once-isolated communities and was widely imitated. Later, All American began transporting passengers on its limited network. Despite the addition of more destinations the airline remained a small operation, serving many remote communities throughout the Alleghenies.

When the United States became involved in World War II, du Pont went to work on the Army's glider program in California. The mailbag snare he developed was adapted by the Army's Air Corps and used to rescue downed pilots behind enemy lines. Du Pont also helped to develop a glider that could be picked up by an already airborne airplane, a system that was used in the evacuation of Allied troops from the Remagen beachhead in Germany. Du Pont was killed in a glider crash in 1943.

After the war, All American Aviation changed its name to All American Airways; in 1953 the name was changed again to Allegheny Airlines. That same year the government chose Allegheny to operate shuttle services between smaller eastern cities and major destinations served by larger airline companies. Allegheny was provided a subsidy to operate these services to communities that otherwise would have had no air service.

The company experienced a period of healthy growth for several years in the 1950s and 1960s. The old DC-3s it was flying were replaced with new Convair 440s, Convair 540s, and Martin 202s. The operations and maintenance base was also relocated from Washington, D.C., to a modern complex in Pittsburgh. Allegheny began buying jets in 1966. In 1968 the company acquired Lake Central Airlines and in 1972 purchased Mohawk Airlines.

Concurrent with this steady growth, Allegheny was obliged to operate the government-assigned "feeder" services, but starting in 1967 Allegheny began subcontracting these routes to smaller independent carriers. The independents were able to make a profit on the routes because they had lower costs, they were not unionized, and their equipment was better suited for the rural "puddle jumper" routes, while the government was happy to release Allegheny from its obligations and discontinue the subsidies. Since the independents fed passengers mostly to Allegheny, the company itself had become a large regional airline.

Despite Allegheny's growth, passengers had a low opinion of the airline, which had acquired the nickname "Agony Air."

Company Perspectives:

US Airways Group, Inc. is the parent corporation for US Airways mainline jet and express divisions as well as several related companies, all in the air transportation industry. From the company's beginnings in 1939 as All-American Aviation, Inc., the present-day US Airways is the inheritor of a number of famous names in U.S. aviation. US Airways has been an aviation innovator, particularly in the building of alliances through code-sharing.

The company's on-time record was poor, its customer service was described as unpleasant, and flight cancellations were common. In many cities the airline had a monopoly on air service, so there was little incentive to improve customer relations.

Emerging As USAir in 1979

Fortunately for Allegheny its chairman and president, Edwin Colodny, had previously served with the Civil Aeronautics Board (CAB). This experience provided him with the knowledge to acquire and protect the company's right to fly to certain destinations, and to successfully raise fares. Before any of his policies could be put into effect, however, the Airline Deregulation Act of 1978 was passed. Vigorously opposed to the passing of this act, Colodny argued that permitting all airlines to freely enter into any market would allow the larger airlines, with their vast resources, to raid markets served by smaller companies with the intention of driving them out of business. This did not happen. Instead, the larger airlines used their new freedom under deregulation to contend with each other, while regional operators such as Allegheny were virtually unaffected. Deregulation also provided new opportunities for regional airlines. For the first time, Allegheny was allowed to operate long-haul routes to Texas and the West Coast. With such an opportunity, the company clearly required an improvement upon its "Agony Air" reputation. Colodny decided to begin with a new name. He chose "USAir" over several other names, including "Republic Airlines" (which was later used by the old Minneapolis-based North Central Airlines). Allegheny officially became USAir on October 28, 1979.

Under the name USAir the company launched an advertising campaign in which it claimed to "carry more passengers than Pan Am, fly to more cities than American, and have more flights than TWA." This coincided with the inauguration of new routes to the Southwest, which were originally intended to prevent company jets from remaining idle during the traditional winter slump in the northeastern markets. In addition, USAir planned to implement a Pittsburgh-London route, but withdrew the application due to fears of "overambition." According to Colodny, "overexpansion is the most tempting of all possible sins of airline managements under deregulation. And, if overdone, it can result in a serious bellyache. In designing a route system, a carrier must limit its ego." As a result, the airline concentrated on consolidating its markets and strengthening its central Pittsburgh hub.

Colodny maintained that two-thirds of U.S. air travel was in markets of less than 1,000 miles, and USAir made it a point to concentrate on developing these local markets. The short duration of these flights, however, meant that the airplanes had to make more takeoffs and landings, which in turn increased maintenance costs. In the late 1980s the company flew DC-9s, B-727s, 737s, 757s, 767s, as well as several smaller aircraft for its express fleet subsidiaries. The average age of its 446 planes was nine years, one of the lowest averages in the industry.

The airline's ontime record significantly improved as a result of strict attention to scheduling and the "first flight of the day" standard, which prevented late starts from pushing back the whole day's schedule. The airline also perfected a system of efficient bad-weather maintenance. These measures contributed to what company officials claimed was the second lowest number of complaints to the CAB (Delta was first) based on passenger volume.

In order to remain competitive with other airline companies that were merging to form even larger companies, the USAir Group announced in December 1986 that it would be acquiring Pacific Southwest Airlines (PSA) for $400 million. The announcement surprised many industry analysts because USAir's predominantly East Coast airline network had few integration points with PSA, which was concentrated along the West Coast. First operated as a subsidiary of the USAir Group, PSA was later absorbed by USAir. The merger increased the amount of traffic on USAir by 40 percent and gave USAir landing rights in a number of cities on the West Coast.

Early 1990s Downturn

Nevertheless, USAir entered 1992 battered by a poor economy, as well as the fallout from a trouble-ridden merger with North Carolina-based Piedmont in 1987. The company had suffered three consecutive years of net losses (the largest in 1990, at $454 million), the forfeiture of many domestic routes, fierce price wars, and a series of staff reductions and wage freezes. Agis Salpukas, writing for the *New York Times,* declared: "USAir continues to bleed, but at a much slower rate. Costs have been cut, through a mix of layoffs, deferred orders of new planes and the closing of overlapping facilities." According to Salpukas, the company, if not yet sound financially, had nonetheless succeeded in refurbishing its public image. "No longer—or, at least, not so often—is the carrier referred to as Useless Air because of problems with flight delays, lost luggage and surly employees." Meanwhile Colodny retired in 1991, with Seth Schofield taking over as CEO.

On March 22, 1992, USAir suffered a tragedy when Flight 405, bound from LaGuardia to Cleveland, crashed into Flushing Bay within minutes after takeoff. Twenty-seven people, more than half of the flight's passengers, were killed. The crash, under investigation by the National Transportation Safety Board, was precipitated by a blustery snowstorm and problems involved in deicing planes at LaGuardia once they had been cleared for takeoff.

Following encouraging news from market analysts that USAir would bolster its East Coast presence with the acquisition of a minority stake in the Trump Shuttle (renamed USAir Shuttle) and major slot expansions at LaGuardia and Washington National, British Airways PLC (BA) announced in July

1992 that it had arranged to form a strong alliance with USAir and would purchase a 44 percent stake in USAir for $750 million. Colin Marshall, chief executive of the profitable BA, intended to create a dependable feeder market of overseas routes through the U.S. carrier. But American, United, and Delta Air Lines (the U.S. "Big Three") vigorously lobbied against the deal and demanded enhanced access to the British market if the deal was to be approved by the U.S. government. In December 1992 the purchase was blocked. In early 1993 BA and USAir restructured their agreement into a $400 million BA purchase of 25 percent of USAir. This investment/alliance, under which USAir gave up its London routes, received U.S. government approval. The government also approved a code-sharing arrangement that enabled the partners to offer their customers a seamless operation when they used both airlines to reach their destination.

USAir continued to be beset by its high-cost operating structure, and posted losses in 1993 and 1994, marking six straight years in the red. It was also the subject of bankruptcy speculation in the press. Under Schofield's plan to cut expenses by $1 billion a year and helped by a resurgent U.S. economy, USAir returned to profitability in 1995, posting net income of $119 million. In late 1995 Schofield, frustrated in his efforts to secure concessions from the company's pilots, suddenly announced his resignation. In January 1996 Stephen M. Wolf, former chief executive of United Airlines, came out of semiretirement to become chairman and CEO of USAir. Wolf quickly brought in a former colleague of his at United, Rakesh Gangwal, as president and chief operating officer.

Renamed US Airways in 1997

Wolf and Gangwal made the attainment of union concessions a key to the company's future. While negotiations continued, the company announced in November 1996 that the parent company would change its name to US Airways Group, Inc. and

USAir would become US Airways, changes that took effect in February 1997. Around this same time, the company's alliance with BA fell apart after BA announced an alliance with American Airlines, with lawsuits following. The US Airways-BA code-sharing deal expired in March 1997. In late 1997 US Airways finally reached an agreement with the pilots' union on a five-year deal that established pay parity with the four largest U.S. carriers. With this concession in hand, the company was able to proceed with an order for 400 Airbus A320s, scheduled for delivery from 1998 through 2009. The new airplanes would enable US Airways to continue as a major airline, rather than being forced to shrink into a regional one.

A newly revitalized US Airways made a host of strategic maneuvers during 1998. The company purchased full control of US Airways Shuttle, in which it had held a minority stake since 1992; launched the low-cost, low-fare MetroJet carrier to help it compete against Delta Express and Southwest Airlines, which had encroached into US Airways' core markets; reached an agreement with Airbus to purchase up to 30 widebody A330-300 aircraft for international flights; added to its transatlantic service with the debut of Philadelphia-London, Philadelphia-Amsterdam, and Pittsburgh-Paris runs; and, finally, entered into a marketing alliance with American Airlines involving linked frequent-flier programs and reciprocal airport lounge facility access. In May 1998 Gangwal became president and CEO of US Airways Group, with Wolf remaining chairman.

US Airways Group reported net income of $538 million in 1998, a reflection of its renewed strength. While the carrier had succeeded in cutting its high-cost structure and returned to the black, it faced severe challenges in an era of industry consolidation. Other major carriers were rapidly linking up through global alliances, and it seemed likely that US Airways would have to become more aggressive in this area if it wanted to remain a major carrier itself. By the late 1990s American Airlines had linked with both US Airways and BA, so it seemed possible that US Airways and BA would resurrect their partnership, perhaps creating an American-US Airways-BA trilateral alliance, which would certainly be a global airline power.

In December 1998, US Airways contracted with Sabre Group Holdings to provide the airline's IT services for 25 years. The $4.3 billion deal gave US Airways the same computer reservation system as American Airlines.

US Airways' home markets continued to be assailed by low-cost carriers Southwest Airlines Co. and start-up JetBlue Airways Corp. The MetroJet unit was growing, though the company would not say whether it was profitable. By the summer of 1999, MetroJet was connecting 23 cities with 40 aircraft. US Airways was also expanding its transatlantic flights, flying to London's Gatwick Airport from Philadelphia and Charlotte. The Caribbean was probably the most promising area of growth.

United Merger Proposal: 2000

Its influence concentrated in the Northeast, US Airways was not truly a national airline. Chairman Stephen Wolf stated it needed a larger partner to avoid the fate of other mid-sized airlines like Eastern and Pan Am. United Airlines, then the world's largest carrier, announced plans to buy US Airways for $4.3 billion in May 2000. The deal would have created an airline with 145,000 employees and 500,000 passengers a day. US Airways' strengths along the East Coast would mesh nicely with United's cross-country routes. To fend off antitrust criticism, the companies planned to sell off most of US Airways' Reagan Airport (Washington, D.C.) operations to a newly formed, minority-owned airline, DC Air. Led by Black Entertainment Television founder Robert L. Johnson, DC Air would be operationally dependent upon United for at least its first few years.

However, the proposal was not enough to get past a Justice Department that was already moving to undo Northwest Airlines Corp.'s purchase of a controlling interest in Continental Airlines Inc. Opponents of the deal feared the merger would set in motion a major consolidation of the industry, reducing the number of dominant carriers from six to three. Further, United's powerful pilots' union opposed the deal over pay and seniority issues.

Although United invited American Airlines to take 49 percent of DC Air and 50 percent of the US Airways Shuttle—with the odd provision that it give its half of the Shuttle back should American's national market share pass United's by more than 7.5 percent. With opposition from lawmakers, the Justice Department, labor unions, Wall Street, and consumer advocates, the deal was called off in July 2001.

US Airways laid off 11,000 employees after the September 11, 2001 terrorist attacks and trimmed its fleet 25 percent to 310 aircraft. The MetroJet unit was abandoned. In the next year, the carrier would receive $320 million in federal aid to keep it afloat, as well as a $900 million loan guarantee, conditional upon the airline cutting costs $1.2 billion a year through 2008. US Airways lost $2.1 billion in 2001; business traffic, on which the airline depended, had begun a serious downturn early in the year.

Rakesh Gangwal resigned as US Airways CEO in November 2001. His role was taken over for a while by Chairman Stephen Wolf. Formerly head of Avis Rent A Car, David N. Siegel became the company's CEO in March 2002. He soon presented the "first draft" of a recovery plan that sought to make US Airways a lower cost carrier. The number of 50-seat regional jets (RJs) in the fleet was to be doubled to 140, and operated by MidAtlantic Airways, Inc., formerly Potomac Air, a subsidiary formed during the United merger discussions.

US Airways and its would-be merger partner, United, announced the two carriers were cooperating in a code-share deal in July 2002. This marketing arrangement allowed each to sell tickets on each other's flights, and to honor each other's frequent flyer programs. US Airways also had code-share arrangements with smaller operations Trans States, Chautauqua Airlines, and Mesa Air Group, which had invested in US Airways stock after 9/11. A new GoCaribbean alliance was also soon worked out with Caribbean Star Airlines, Nevis Express, and Winair.

Restructuring in 2002

US Airways filed for Chapter 11 bankruptcy protection on August 11, 2002. Soon, David Bonderman's Texas Pacific Group (TPG), which had bailed out Continental Airlines (while US Airways CEO David Siegel was employed there) and America West, provided $200 million to keep US Airways flying. If the reorganization were successful, TPG would own 38 percent of the carrier.

However, TPG was edged out at the last minute by Retirement Systems of Alabama, which acquired 37.5 percent of US Airways Group for $240 million. Retirement Systems, which had assets of $25 billion, also provided $400 million in debtor-in-possession financing. The airline continued to cut back staff and flights. The unions, concerned that US Airways successfully emerge from its bankruptcy, agreed to $900 million in labor cuts. The industry as a whole was dealt another massive blow in December, when UAL Corporation, parent of United Airlines, declared bankruptcy as well.

Principal Subsidiaries

Allegheny Airlines, Inc.; Material Services Company, Inc.; MidAtlantic Airways, Inc.; Piedmont Airlines, Inc.; Potomac Air, Inc.; PSA Airlines, Inc.; US Airways Leasing and Sales, Inc.; US Airways, Inc.

Principal Operating Units

US Airways Express; US Airways Shuttle.

Principal Competitors

AMR Corporation; Delta Air Lines, Inc.; JetBlue Airways Corp.; Southwest Airlines Co.; UAL Corporation.

Further Reading

Alexander, Keith L., and Seth Payne, "USAir: This 'Dog' May Be Having Its Day," *Business Week,* June 21, 1993, pp. 74, 76.
Antonelli, Cesca, "US Airways Must Snare an Overseas Partner to Continue Profitable Path," *Pittsburgh Business Times,* April 17, 1998, p. 5.
Arndt, Michael, and Lorraine Woellert, "Unfriendly Skies for an Airline Merger," *Business Week,* June 5, 2000, p. 50.
Banks, Howard, "Canceled Flight," *Forbes,* April 16, 2001, pp. 54–55.
Bond, David, "United, US Airways Cash in Merger Chips," *Aviation Week & Space Technology,* July 9, 2001, pp. 45–48.
——, "United, US Airways Try Again to Link Up," *Aviation Week & Space Technology,* July 29, 2002, p. 50.
"Bronner Airways," *Pensions & Investments,* October 14, 2002, p. 10.
"Champagne on Ice," *Airfinance Journal,* Business Yearbook 1999, pp. 4–6.
Del Valle, Christina, "Brawl in the Cockpit at USAir," *Business Week,* September 25, 1995, p. 59.
Del Valle, Christina, Wendy Zellner, and Susan Chandler, "USAir's European Squeeze Play," *Business Week,* September 2, 1996, pp. 62–63.
Dwyer, Paula, et al., "Air Raid: British Air's Bold Global Push," *Business Week,* August 24, 1992.
Feldman, Joan M., "Unfinished Business," *Air Transport World,* September 1999, pp. 24–34.
Foust, Dean, Keith L. Alexander, and Aaron Bernstein, "USAir's Frightening Loss of Attitude," *Business Week,* June 6, 1994, p. 34.
Fulman, Ricki, "Bronner Says US Air Deal Will Pay Off When Industry, Now 'In a Dither,' Turns Around," *Pensions & Investments,* September 30, 2002, pp. 1, 41.
Jennings, Mead, "Snowed Under: Growth of the British Airways-USAir Alliance Has Been Put on Hold As USAir Attempts to Put Its Own House in Order," *Airline Business,* April 1994, pp. 26+.

Kleinfeld, N.R., "The Ordinary Turned to Instant Horror for All Aboard USAir's Flight 405," *New York Times,* March 29, 1992.

McDonald, Michele, "Flying Solo," *Air Transport World,* September 2001, pp. 44–47.

Miller, James P., "US Air's Wolf Gives Gangwal the CEO's Job," *Wall Street Journal,* November 19, 1998, pp. A3, A14.

Noonan, David, "Turbulence Ahead," *Newsweek,* June 5, 2000, p. 40.

Odell, Mark, "US Airways Chief Is Latest Casualty of Crisis," *Ft.Com* (London), November 27, 2001.

Ott, James, "Executive Pay Clouds US Airways Recovery," *Aviation Week & Space Technology,* September 3, 2001, p. 82.

—— "US Airways' Restructuring Has to Sway Skeptics," *Aviation Week & Space Technology,* May 20, 2002, p. 156.

Reeves, Frank, and Jim McKay, "US Airways to Lay Off 471 Pilots, 915 Attendants; Daily Flights Also Facing Cutbacks," *Pittsburgh Post-Gazette,* October 26, 2002, p. A1.

Salpukis, Agis, "USAir Discovers There Is Life After a Messy Merger," *New York Times,* January 19, 1992.

Shives, Robert, and William Thompson, *Airlines of North America,* Sarasota, Fla.: Crestline, 1984, 240 p.

Spiegel, Peter, "Can Heroes Work Miracles?" *Forbes,* April 6, 1998, pp. 53+.

Thomas, Cathy Booth, "Is There a Doctor on Board?" *Time,* August 26, 2002, pp. 28–29.

"US Airways Forms RJ Subsidiary," *Air Transport World,* July 2002, p. 22.

"USAir's Seth Schofield Is Named Chairman," *Wall Street Journal,* May 14, 1992.

Velocci, Anthony L., Jr., "MetroJet's Expansion Tests Rivals' Mettle," *Aviation Week & Space Technology,* April 12, 1998, p. 57.

——, "US Airways Accord Sets Stage for Growth," *Aviation Week and Space Technology,* October 6, 1997, pp. 35, 38–39.

Walker, Karen, "US Airways Cry Wolf!," *Airline Business,* August 1997, pp. 24+.

Whitaker, Richard, and Mead Jennings, "BA and USAir Forge a New Deal," *Airlines Business,* February 1993, pp. 20+.

Woellert, Lorraine, "US Airways: Into the Next Cloud," *Business Week,* April 10, 2000, p. 44.

Woellert, Lorraine, and David Leonhardt, "Pulling US Airways Out of a Dive," *Business Week,* September 14, 1998, pp. 131–32.

Woellert, Lorraine, and Michael Arndt, "Somebody Still Likes US Airways," *Business Week,* September 2, 2002, p. 37.

—John Simley
—updates: David E. Salamie, Frederick C. Ingram

VIASYS Healthcare, Inc.

227 Washington Street
Suite 200
Conshohocken, Pennsylvania 19428
U.S.A.
Telephone: (610) 862-0800
Fax: (610) 862-0836
Web site: http://www.viasyshealthcare.com

Public Company
Incorporated: 2001
Employees: 1,850
Sales: $358.4 million (2001)
Stock Exchanges: New York
Ticker Symbol: VAS
NAIC: 339112 Surgical and Medical Instrument
   Manufacturing

VIASYS Healthcare, Inc. is a global market leader in health-care technology. The company is a spinoff of Thermo Electron Corporation, a scientific instrument business, and was created from the acquisition of some dozen biomedical companies. VIASYS reorganized these companies into three business segments or groups: Respiratory Care, Neuro-Science, and Medical and Surgical Care. VIASYS went public shortly after its inception in 2001 and had sales of over $358 million in its first year. VIASYS markets its products to hospitals, laboratories, physicians, and equipment manufacturers in over 100 countries.

A String of Acquisitions in the 1990s

In the 1990s, Thermo Electron Corporation, a leading supplier of laboratory, analytical, and process-control equipment, acquired a string of well-known biomedical companies. These companies provided equipment used for either respiratory care, medical and surgical care, or neuro-care. Among those in respiratory care were Bear Medical Systems, Inc., Bird Products Corporation, Erich Jaeger GmbH, SensorMedics Corporation, and Stackhouse, Inc. Companies in medical and surgical care included CORPAK MedSystems, Medical Data Electronics,

Inc., Thermedics Polymer Products, and Tecomet. Grason-Stadler, Inc., Nicolet Biomedical, and Nicolet Vascular provided neuro-care. Together, these companies generated about $350 million in sales a year.

VIASYS Healthcare, Inc. in 2001

On November 15, 2001, Thermo Electron spun out these biomedical companies as a separate business—VIASYS Healthcare, Inc. The companies were now subsidiaries of VIASYS. "We are excited to make our debut as an independent public company with market-leading products, a terrific team of dedicated employees, and strong momentum integrating the company," said Randy H. Thurman, president and chief executive officer of VIASYS in a company press release.

The following day, VIASYS went public on the New York Stock Exchange. The company sold 26 million shares valued at $14 per share. The offering generated approximately $370 million.

VIASYS immediately organized its operations into three groups: Respiratory Technology, Neuro-Care, and Medical and Surgical. With its combined Thermo Electron companies, the Respiratory Technology segment was the world leader in respiratory diagnostics, holding about a 60 percent market share. The primary products produced by this segment were instruments used to test pulmonary system and lung function. The Respiratory Technology segment also introduced sleep therapeutic products.

The Neuro-Care segment produced instruments used to diagnose neurological, audio, and cardiovascular disorders. The Medical and Surgical segment designed, manufactured, and marketed critical-care disposable devices and wireless patient monitoring systems.

New Products and Structural Changes in 2002

As a new company, VIASYS planned to establish itself as a market-leader by launching new, innovative products and modifying the structure of its subsidiaries. In June, the company unveiled SNAP, a handheld EEG monitor that was the first of its kind. According to a company press release, SNAP, which was

Company Perspectives:

VIASYS Healthcare Inc. is committed to becoming a world-class healthcare company focused on respiratory, neuro-care and medical/surgical technologies. Our stakeholders include the care providers and patients who rely on the quality of our products; our investors who deserve long-term return on shareholder equity; and our employees to whom we are committed to providing an entrepreneurial environment that stimulates and rewards their creativity and innovation.

As a leading healthcare technology company, VIASYS Healthcare, Inc. is committed to a long-term, sustained investment in research and development. In order to build upon our existing product leadership, we must invest in technologies that anticipate and continually meet the needs of our customers and the patients we serve. Our commitment to excellence for life underscores everything we do: industry leadership in R&D, the highest quality products, an outstanding company-wide environment for our employees, and a commitment to creating shareholder value.

manufactured by VIASYS subsidiary Nicolet Biomedical, enabled anesthesia professionals to reliably measure the effects of anesthesia and monitor patients' brain activity levels. SNAP was approved by the FDA in June and went on the market in July.

Gerald Brew, president of VIASYS' Neuro-Care Group commented on the importance of the company's new product: "SNAP is a clear extension into new anesthesia monitoring markets which leverages our EEG market leadership and three decades of neuro-related expertise. SNAP is the first of several unique VIASYS anesthesia products and the first handheld product approved for use in the space-constrained Operating Room Theater."

In July, the company announced that one of its subsidiaries, SensorMedics, formed an alliance with CONSORTA, Inc. CONSORTA was itself a national healthcare alliance made up of more than 400 acute-care facilities and 1,700 alternate care sites. Under the terms of its agreement with CONSORTA, SensorMedics was the preferred source to supply high-frequency oscillatory ventilators, pulmonary and metabolic analyzers, and sleep diagnostic systems to CONSORTA's members.

In September, VIASYS' Critical Care Group began shipping its new AVEA ventilator to customers. AVEA was an integrated life-support system designed to meet the needs of neonatal, pediatric, and adult patients, especially those in intensive care. The ventilator differed from competitors' products and previous models in that it had compressor technology that allowed it to perform with or without an external air source. It incorporated respiratory diagnostics to assist in decreasing the time a patient spent on a ventilator.

During the same month, VIASYS announced plans to divest its subsidiary Medical Data Electronics (MDE). By letting go of MDE, VIASYS had exited the patient-monitoring business. Thurman explained the move in a company press release: "The decision to divest MDE is consistent with our strategy of

focusing on and investing in our Critical Care, Respiratory, Neuro-Care, and Med Systems businesses." The company suffered a pretax charge of $15 million in the third quarter because of the decision.

VIASYS announced the acquisition of E.M.E. (Electro Medical Equipment) located in Brighton, United Kingdom, and its related U.S. subsidiaries in October. The deal cost VIASYS $22.5 million in cash and stock. E.M.E. was a prominent supplier of devices and disposables used to non-invasively treat newborns with respiratory problems. The company was well-known for its Infant Flow, a product based on a form of nasal CPAP (Continuous Positive Airway Pressure). Thurman believed that the acquisition of EME was a great strategic move for VIASYS for several reasons. "Its products provide an extension to our global critical care business and are complementary to the many products we offer for the care of the neonate," he explained in a company press release. EME had revenues of nearly $17 million in 2002.

During the same month, VIASYS received the prestigious Zenith Award from the American Association for Respiratory Care (AARC) for excellence in product service and quality.

VIASYS received an additional honor in November when the *New England Journal of Medicine* published the results of a large, independent, multi-center trial using the company's 3100A High Frequency Oscillatory Ventilator. During the trial, the ventilator was used to treat respiratory distress in very premature infants. The trial found that infants on the VIASYS ventilator suffered fewer deaths and less chronic lung disease compared to those on conventional ventilators. The study stated that for every 11 infants treated with the ventilator, one death or case of chronic lung disease was prevented. Deniese LeBlanc, SensorMedics' product manager, commented on the study in a company press release: "We are very pleased that these new results in a large number of infants, and in the current times of better prenatal care and newer therapeutics, demonstrated the same benefits of the 3100A ventilator previously published in eight smaller trials. Considering that these infants were smaller than in any of our earlier trials, the study provides additional support for the use of 3100A HFOV as the standard of care for ventilating premature infants."

Around the same time, the company launched Oxycon Mobile, a portable cardiopulmonary exercise system. It measured a patient's oxygen consumption, carbon dioxide production, and minute ventilation. While other systems also offered these measurements, this system was portable; it did not require the patient to be connected to a large stationary machine. The free movement offered by the system allowed physicians to better monitor patients in different and additional settings. They could even monitor patients during typical day-to-day activities.

A Challenging-but-Bright Future

VIASYS did well in its first year: the company posted a net income of $16.3 million on revenues of $358.4 million. Its sales and income in 2002 looked to be about the same, despite a slip in net income in the quarter ending in September. The company attributed the drop in profits to restructuring charges and costs related to the consolidation of facilities. Thurman summed up

Key Dates:

1990s: Thermo Electron Corporation embarks on acquisition spree, purchasing a number of biomedical companies.

2001: Thermo Electron spins off VIASYS Healthcare, Inc.; VIASYS goes public on the New York Stock Exchange.

2002: Company unveils SNAP, a handheld EEG monitor; acquires U.K.-based E.M.E. (Electro Medical Equipment); receives Zenith Award for excellence in product service and quality; and launches Oxycon Mobile, a portable cardiovascular system.

the company's progress in 2002: "As we approach the completion of our first full year as a publicly traded company, VIASYS Healthcare has made significant progress in integrating businesses, capturing synergies, introducing new products and restructuring our operations to position our company for the future. The consolidation of 14 companies into one VIASYS organization is 11 months in the making and we have made significant strides against all of our strategic imperatives."

VIASYS' plans for the future included developing new lines to complement existing products. These lines included an inhaled drug delivery system and products used in stroke therapy and biofeedback. It also planned to better manage its service operations by consolidating its service operations into one worldwide service division. The company also hoped to acquire and integrate new businesses with products that would enhance its own. Finally, VIASYS aimed to cut costs and better streamline its many operations.

Principal Subsidiaries

Bear Medical Systems, Incorporated; Bird Products Corporation; CORPAK MedSystems; E.M.E. (Electro Medical Equipment); Grason-Stadler, Inc.; Jaeger Toennies; Nicolet Biomedical; Nicolet Vascular; SensorMedics Corporation; Spirotech; Stackhouse Incorporated; Tecomet; Thermedics Polymer Products.

Principal Operating Units

Respiratory Care; Neuro-Science; Medical and Surgical Care.

Principal Competitors

GE Medical Systems; Siemens Medical Solutions; Tyco Healthcare Group.

Further Reading

"VIASYS Healthcare's SensorMedics Subsidiary Signs with CONSORTA Inc.," *BW Health Wire*, July 9, 2002.

—Tracey Vasil Biscontini

Vulcan Materials Company

1200 Urban Center Drive
Birmingham, Alabama 35242
U.S.A.
Telephone: (205) 298-3000
Fax: (205) 298-2963
Web site: http://www.vulcanmaterials.com

Public Company
Incorporated: 1956
Employees: 10,000
Sales: $3.02 billion (2001)
Stock Exchanges: New York
Ticker Symbol: VMC
NAIC: 212319 Other Crushed and Broken Stone Mining
   and Quarrying (pt); 212321 Construction Sand and
   Gravel Mining; 324121 Asphalt Paving Mixture and
   Block Manufacturing; 325181 Alkalies and Chlorine
   Manufacturing

Vulcan Materials Company, with headquarters in Birmingham, Alabama, is the largest producer of construction aggregates in the United States and a leader in the world market. Construction aggregates include crushed stone, sand, gravel, and slag, which are used in the construction of highways, commercial buildings, and houses. The company operates quarries serving 22 states as well as Washington D.C., Mexico, Aruba, Chile, and the Cayman Islands. Revenue from crushed stone excavated in Vulcan quarries accounts for the vast majority of the company's total sales, though its two chemical business units are also leaders within their industry for industrial and commercial use of caustics and chlorine-based solvents.

Vulcan produces a variety of chemicals, including chlorine, caustic soda (sodium hydroxide), caustic potash (potassium hydroxide), and chlorinated solvents. The primary market for chlorine is in the treatment of water and sewage, manufacturing pulp and paper, and as a major ingredient in many other manufacturing processes. Caustic soda is used mainly in the production of aluminum, soap and detergent products, and wood pulp. Caustic potash is utilized in the production of other potassium chemicals

as well as in fine soaps and lotions. Lastly, chlorinated solvents are employed for cleaning metals and textiles and as an intermediate chemical in the manufacture of other materials.

Background: Birmingham Slag Company, 1909–56

Vulcan Materials was created in 1956 when the Birmingham Slag Company of Birmingham, Alabama, merged with the Vulcan Detinning Company of New Jersey. Birmingham Slag had been founded in 1909 by Solon Jacob and Henry Badham, two entrepreneurs who decided to turn a waste product of the steel industry, slag, into a commodity they could sell. Slag is the nonmetallic residue left behind in the process of smelting iron ore. The city of Birmingham had long been a center for steelmaking, and the industry had been stockpiling huge amounts of slag by the time Vulcan Detinning came along.

Jacob and Badham built a processing plant next to the Tennessee Coal, Iron, and Railroad Company's slag pile in nearby Ensley, Alabama, and began selling the material as ballast for railroad tracks. Fortuitously, the founding of Birmingham slag occurred one year after the Ford Motor Company introduced its famous Model T automobile. When the country began demanding more paved roads, Birmingham Slag discovered that it possessed the perfect construction material.

Despite its early success, Birmingham Slag was for sale by 1916. Charles Lincoln Ireland, an Ohio banker whose family was operating stone quarries in Ohio, Kentucky, and West Virginia, purchased a controlling interest in the company. He sent his three sons—Glenn, Eugene, and Barney—to Alabama to run Birmingham Slag. Charles, in the meantime, went off to Central America to buy surplus equipment being sold after the completion of the Panama Canal. He returned with two steam shovels, a steam hoist, a star drill, and other equipment purchased at the bargain-basement price of $6,590.

The Irelands opened a new slag processing plant in Ensley in 1918. They also opened plants in the central Alabama towns of Fairfield and Wylam and in northern Alabama near Muscle Shoals. In 1919 and 1920 the company secured contracts to process slag at three more Alabama steel mills—Republic Steel in Thomas, Central Iron and Steel Company in Holt, and Gulf States Steel Company in Alabama City. Despite plenty of business after World War I, finances were tight. Records indicate that during this period the Ireland family often had to guarantee loans at the First National Bank of Birmingham personally to meet the company's payroll. Nevertheless, Birmingham Slag was ready when state legislators passed the 1922 Alabama Bond Issue for Good Roads, setting off a boom in road construction.

In 1923 Birmingham Slag formed the Montgomery Gravel Company and began providing sand and gravel for a dam being built in Cherokee Bluffs, Alabama. It expanded this business the next year by creating the Atlanta Aggregate Company to market sand and gravel in Georgia. By the 1930s Birmingham Slag also owned several ready-mix concrete plants and was producing asphalt and concrete blocks.

In 1939 Birmingham Slag signed a contract with the newly formed Tennessee Valley Authority (TVA) to dredge part of the Tennessee River so a dam and power plant could be built at Watts Bar, thus marking yet another business expansion for the company. Birmingham Slag continued to prosper during World War II, providing aggregates and concrete for such wartime efforts as the Manhattan Project in Oak Ridge, Tennessee; the Huntsville, Alabama, Redstone Arsenal; and a major munitions depot at Fort McClellan in Anniston, Alabama.

After the war, construction of the new federal interstate highway system proposed in the early 1950s presented a potential bonanza for Birmingham Slag. The company, however, needed more capital than a family-owned business could muster in order to take advantage of the opportunity. In addition, Charles W. Ireland, the grandson of the Ohio banker, had become president of Birmingham Slag in 1951 and was looking for ways to lessen the inheritance taxes family members faced. The answer presented itself in the form of a merger with the publicly traded Vulcan Detinning Company of Sewaren, New Jersey.

Vulcan Detinning Company: 1902–56

Vulcan Detinning had been formed in 1902 by Adolph Kern, who owned the Vulcan Metal Refining Company in Sewaren and the Vulcan Western Company of Chicago. The new company, Vulcan Detinning, used a process developed in Germany to recover pure tin from tin-plated scrap. Kern subsequently helped establish a rival company in Pennsylvania, the Republic Chemical Company. In 1912 he left Vulcan Detinning to join Republic Chemical, taking the company's trade secrets with him and setting off a series of lawsuits. Vulcan Detinning and Republic Chemical merged in 1920, after Kern was no longer associated with either company.

William J. Buttfield—who had joined Vulcan Detinning as a director in 1912, when Kern left for Republic Chemical—guided Vulcan Detinning through the early part of the 20th century. During the Depression of the 1930s he used his commodities brokerage background to shift the company's resources into importing coffee and rubber. Vulcan Detinning continued to pay dividends even though the Sewaren detinning plant was closed from 1932 until 1937. Employees were kept on the payroll and were occupied with the repairing and reconditioning of plant facilities. By 1940 Vulcan Detinning was again flourishing although the Sewaren plant, reopened in 1937, was closed permanently in 1938. Buttfield was also credited with being one of the industrialists who in the months preceding the Japanese attack on Pearl Harbor, finally convinced the United States to begin stockpiling critical materials such as tin.

The merger between Birmingham Slag and Vulcan Detinning was completed in 1956. At the time, Alfred Buttfield, the son of William J. Buttfield, was president of Vulcan Detinning. He became chairman of the board of the newly named Vulcan Materials Company.

A New Era: 1957–66

Until the merger, Birmingham Slag, although successful, had been a modestly sized regional company. Vulcan Materials Company was traded on the New York Stock Exchange and quickly became a company of national importance. The merger allowed Vulcan to diversify and create a business less dependent on the construction industry, as well as raise capital for expansion. From 1956 to 1960 Vulcan's net worth increased almost sevenfold to $72 million from $11 million. It also became the largest producer of construction aggregates material in the country.

Although Charles W. Ireland was credited with providing the vision for Vulcan's rapid growth, Bernard A. Monaghan was considered its architect. Monaghan, a Rhodes Scholar and graduate of Harvard University Law School, was the Ireland family's corporate attorney. He negotiated the merger with Vulcan Detinning and later orchestrated the acquisition of a dozen construction aggregate companies through the 1950s and into the early 1960s. He joined Vulcan in 1958 as executive vice-president and, soon after, became president and chief executive officer.

One of the companies with which Monaghan negotiated a merger was Lambert Brothers, Inc., an Appalachian quarrying company with a storied history. The nine Lambert brothers, from a family of 15, were low-income Smoky Mountain residents who, according to company lore, started with a mule and a wheelbarrow and built a $9 million business in one generation. During the 1930s they moved their portable rock crushing equipment throughout the Appalachian states and as far west as Oklahoma to work on road construction. The story of their success is peppered with tales of bare-knuckled fights and high stakes poker. By the mid-1950s Lambert Brothers was the largest rock-quarrying firm in the United States.

It was during this period of rapid expansion that Vulcan also became a chemicals manufacturer. In 1957 it bought the Union Chemical and Materials Corporation of Chicago, a construction aggregate company in the booming Midwest market that had merged with the Frontier Chemical Company. Frontier pro-

Key Dates:

1902: Adolf Kern creates Vulcan Detinning Company in Sewaren, New Jersey.
1909: Solon Jacob and Henry Badham found Birmingham Slag Company in Birmingham, Alabama.
1956: Birmingham Slag Company and Vulcan Detinning Company merge to form Vulcan Materials Company.
1957: Vulcan Materials buys and merges with several companies, including Lambert Brothers and Union Chemical and Materials Corporation.
1960: Vulcan Materials is ranked as the nation's largest producer of construction aggregates material.
1967: Vulcan acquires Ohio-based Aluminum and Magnesium, Inc.
1975: The company begins natural gas and oil exploration through a joint venture with Oklahoma's Southport Exploration, Inc.
1981: Vulcan buys Southport Exploration.
1985: Vulcan sells Southport Exploration and exits the natural gas and oil business.
1987: Vulcan begins its ambitious Crescent Market Project, a $170 million joint venture in Mexico.
1990: First stone from Mexican quarry begins shipping.
1992: Sales top the billion-dollar mark for the first time.
1994: Chemicals division splits into two separate units: Chloralkali Business and Performance Systems Business.
1998: Vulcan buys CalMat and is buoyed by the passage of TEA-21 for federal highway construction.
1999: Sales top $2 billion for the first time.
2001: Vulcan buys out Grupo ICA's half of the Crescent Market joint venture.
2002: Twenty-five of Vulcan's quarries in the United States and Mexico win prestigious environmental awards.

duced sodium hydroxide (caustic soda), chlorine, and hydrochloric acid for the oil industry at plants in Texas and Kansas.

The mergers with Union Chemical, Lambert Brothers, and seven other companies owned by the Lamberts were approved by Vulcan's stockholders in one fell swoop in 1957. At the time, *Fortune* magazine called it one of the most complex corporate acquisitions ever arranged. Vulcan continued its strategy of buying family-owned aggregate businesses over the next 30 years. In 1982 in a story entitled "Cinderella," a *Forbes* correspondent observed that Vulcan had created a "quasi-monopoly in the crushed stone business" by buying more than 90 quarries in the 1950s and 1960s "when quarries were a dime a dozen."

Expansion and Refocusing: Late 1960s to Early 1990s

In 1967 Vulcan purchased Aluminum and Magnesium, Inc., an Ohio-based aluminum recycler. Until 1988 when Vulcan sold its metals division, detinning and aluminum recycling had formed the nucleus of the metals processing business. Vulcan also spent ten years in oil and natural gas exploration, forming a joint venture in 1975 with Oklahoma-based Southport Explora-

tion, Inc. Vulcan acquired Southport Exploration in 1981 but sold the business in 1985.

In July 1987 Vulcan formally announced its Crescent Market Project, a $170 million joint venture with one of Latin America's largest construction conglomerates, Ingenieros Civiles Asociados, S.C. (Grupo ICA), to quarry limestone from the wilds of the Yucatan Peninsula. Vulcan had first looked to Mexico as a potential quarry site to serve the Gulf Coast area of the United States in 1973. The idea had been abandoned and then revived in 1978. In 1981 the company began a concentrated effort to locate quarry sites in the Mexican state of Quintana Roo. Afterwards, Pete Wiese, the Vulcan geologist who headed the exploration, described the effort in the company's annual magazine, *Profile:* "Quintana Roo was pretty unsettled. I had a machete and I would just get out of the car and cut through the jungle to the coast and see what I could see."

The joint venture eventually settled on a site about 45 miles south of Cancun and only a few hundred yards from ancient Mayan ruins that had been built out of the same tan limestone. An agreement was made with the Mexican National Institute of Archeology and History to underwrite the cost of locating, mapping, and conserving the ruins. The Crescent Market Project also included construction of a deep water port, which required dredging more than three million tons of stone from the harbor at Playa del Carmen.

Overcoming technological and logistical challenges, including Hurricane Gilbert—which battered the Yucatan coast in 1988 and caused more than $400,000 damage to the stone processing plant then under construction—Vulcan and Grupo ICA began shipping stone from Mexico to the United States in 1990. Most of the Mexican limestone was destined to become construction material aggregates, but because of a high calcium content was also being used in products as diverse as fertilizer and toothpaste. The Mexican quarry won the National Stone Association Showplace Award in 1990, its first year of operation.

In 1991 the quarry shipped 2.5 million tons of limestone, about a third of the estimated annual capacity. By late 1992 Vulcan, looking ahead to a recovering economy and refocused attention on the nation's infrastructure, was estimating that the Crescent Market Project would become profitable in 1993.

The *W.H. Blount,* a refitted Panamax-class vessel named for a former chief executive officer and then chairman emeritus of Vulcan Materials, was put into operation in March 1991 to carry limestone from the Mexican quarry. More than 700 feet long and 100 feet wide, the *W.H. Blount* was one of the largest self-unloading ships in service. It could carry more than 64,000 tons of limestone, or about 2,667 truckloads. A second, similar ship was put into service in late 1992.

Aside from the Crescent Market Project (which had begun in 1987), Vulcan continued with other acquisitions, taking on Texas-based White's Mines, Inc. and two affiliated companies for $89 million that year. At the time, it was the largest acquisition in the company's long history. The purchase gave Vulcan control of five more quarries, including the Uvalde limestone quarry west of San Antonio. The quarry produced rock asphalt, a stone naturally impregnated with asphalt, making it a natural paving material.

Three years later, in 1990, Vulcan surpassed the White's Mines acquisition by paying more than $110 million for the Reed Crushed Stone Company, Inc. and two related companies. Included in the purchase was the Reed quarry near Paducah, Kentucky, the largest single crushed stone quarry in the country. The purchase also included a fleet of barges and a coal transshipping and blending business, putting Vulcan Materials in the coal-handling business for the first time.

Environmental Concerns: Early 1990s

Vulcan's chemical business was heavily regulated and often prompted public concerns about environmental health and safety. In 1990 Vulcan committed to reducing hazardous emissions at its chemical plants by 90 percent over the next five years, primarily by turning hydrochloric acid into calcium chloride, which could be used as a dust stabilizer and deicer. Vulcan had been disposing of excess hydrochloric acid, a waste product of other chemical production processes, by pumping the acid into limestone deposits a mile below ground in a deep-well injection process permitted and approved by the Environmental Protection Agency (EPA). The limestone neutralized the acid; however, it was still considered a hazardous emission for reporting purposes under Title III of the Federal Superfund Amendment and Reauthorization Act. This resulted in Vulcan being listed among the worst polluters in the United States.

In order to change its status as a major polluter, Vulcan completed construction of a new calcium chloride facility at its Wichita, Kansas, chemical manufacturing complex early in 1993. Even before it opened, the plant received a Certificate for Environmental Achievement from Renew America, a national environmental organization based in Washington, D.C. The processing facility, with a capacity of 18 million pounds per year, was designed by Tetra Technologies, which also distributed the calcium chloride. Used primarily to purify drinking water, calcium chloride also served as a biocide in the fruit-processing industry and as a cleaning material in electronics.

In addition to its construction of the calcium chloride facility, Vulcan's chemicals division was phasing out production of chlorofluorocarbons (CFCs) and assisting in the development of nonozone depleting CFC replacements. Vulcan was a member of two major trade associations—the National Stone Association and the Chemical Manufacturers Association—which were active in addressing environmental health and safety concerns. The company also participated in the Wildlife Habitat Enhancement Council, a nonprofit organization that encouraged the development of wildlife sanctuaries on corporate owned lands. In 1990 the Vulcan quarry in Warrenton, Virginia, was the first site in the nation to be certified by the Wildlife Habitat Enhancement Council; Vulcan also received the Virginia Conservationist of the Year Award for its efforts at the quarry. As of 1992, 15 Vulcan quarries had been certified by the organization.

Historically, Vulcan Material's two principal businesses provided economic stability; construction aggregates did well when the chemical market was depressed and vice-versa. Construction spending in the United States, however, when adjusted for inflation, decreased every year between 1986 and 1991, the longest continual decline since the Great Depression. With the economy in recession, the company recorded three straight years of lower

net income from a high of $136 million on net sales of $1.05 billion in 1988 to $52.6 million on net sales of $1.01 billion in 1991. In 1992 net sales increased by 7 percent to $1.07 billion, while net earnings rose by 79 percent to $93.98 million.

Entering 1993 the company was encouraged by a recovering economy and by the renewed focus on upgrading and expanding the nation's highways. Though the U.S. Congress had passed the Intermodal Surface Transportation Efficiency Act in December 1991, its effects were not fully in play until 1993. Vulcan benefited from the increased federal spending on highway construction, especially in crushed stone—shipments rose to 117 million tons, eight tons higher than the previous year—and prices went up for the first time in five years. Real estate, also part of Vulcan's construction division, recovered slightly for the year but remained relatively soft. Vulcan's chemicals division, however, suffered during 1993 with both lower sales and earnings. Despite the construction of a new sodium chlorine plant in Wichita, Kansas, a sharp decline in caustic soda prices caused an imbalance in chlorine products. Luckily for Vulcan, its construction division's strong results offset the chemical unit's woes and year-end net sales climbed slightly to $1.13 billion for 1993.

Acquisitions and Growth: Mid- to Late 1990s

To shore up its difficulties with its chemicals division, Vulcan invested heavily in acquisitions and the construction of new facilities to increase the unit's scope and the breadth of its involvement in new and emerging technologies. Three 1994 acquisitions fit this trend: the first was the Tucson-based Peroxidation Systems, Inc., an established municipal, industrial, and environmental water treatment firm (renamed Vulcan Peroxidation Systems, Inc.); the second and third were both part of Exxon Corporation and became wholly owned subsidiaries of Vulcan as Callaway Chemical Company (based in Georgia) and Callaway Chemical Limited (based in Vancouver, British Columbia). The latter buys marked Vulcan's serious entrance into the production of chemicals used in the paper, textile, and water treatment industries. The disparate focuses of these acquisitions from Vulcan's core chemical operations led to the formation of two separate business units—the Chloralkali unit (consisting of its traditional operations of caustics and chlorine-based products) and the Performance Systems unit (covering the newer operations in paper, pulp, textile, and environmental water treatment).

Despite its efforts to expand the chemical division and prevent its complete reliance on the frequently unstable caustic and chlorine market—the chemicals unit posted its first loss in 24 years. Vulcan's management was not, however, overly concerned since they believed in its long-term outlook and knew it would take time to recoup acquisition costs. Another reason was the performance of its construction division, which experienced record growth. Sales of stone and related construction materials were way up, and even the real estate market had rebounded. A jump in both the construction of residential homes and federal highways pushed the division's earnings up 39 percent to $162 million, offsetting the chemical unit's loss of $7.3 million and bringing Vulcan's overall earnings to $98 million on net sales just shy of $1.3 billion for 1994.

By 1995 Vulcan's long-term vision for its chemicals division paid off handsomely—the unit enjoyed a robust market in caustics and chlorine, and turned its previous year's loss into earnings of more than $87 million. The construction division maintained its record-breaking growth, too, shipping more than 136 million tons of crushed stone and other aggregates to bring earnings to $182 million on sales of $885 million. Vulcan reached overall net sales of just under $1.5 billion for 1995 as a new company president took the reins. Donald M. James, who had joined Vulcan in 1992 as a senior vice-president and general counsel, took on the added responsibilities of chief executive in 1996 as Howard Sklenar ended his nearly 25 years of service with Vulcan by retiring from daily operations. Sklenar was named chairman emeritus in 1997 when James assumed the title of chairman.

In the last years of the century, Vulcan grew steadily until a phenomenal leap in 1999 took the company well over the $2 billion net sales mark. Sales for 1997 and 1998 posted respectable single-digit gains of 6 and 7 percent, respectively, while earnings from 1996 to 1997 climbed 11 percent and from 1997 to 1998, doubled to 22 percent. Yet 1999 took Vulcan into a vastly different arena, with net sales soaring by 33 percent from 1998's $1.8 billion to 1999's $2.4 billion. This growth was due in part to several acquisitions and joint ventures, including the 1998 purchase of CalMat Company, California's leading aggregates producer, and Vulcan's ongoing joint venture with Grupo ICA, which was shipping millions of tons of limestone throughout Mexico and the United States. Another joint venture was with Mitsui & Co., Ltd., which teamed with Vulcan to build a new plant and substantially increase production of various caustic chemicals. Additionally, Vulcan's construction division began to reap the benefits of the federal government's TEA-21, a new highway rebuilding and construction bill passed in 1998, which provided $157 billion over the next six years for the refurbishment and new construction of national highways.

An Eye to the Future: The 2000s

By the year 2000, Vulcan had expanded its construction aggregates empire to have facilities in 21 states, the District of Columbia, and Mexico, with 236 operational quarries. The following year, Vulcan bought Grupo ICA's portion of their Mexican joint venture, the Crescent Market Companies, paying over $121 million for sole ownership of the Playa del Carmen operations. Despite the size and scope of its businesses, Vulcan was an enormous yet rather quiet conglomerate. Many Americans did not know the Vulcan name (except perhaps in the *Star Trek* sense), but the company was satisfied with what it termed its "boring" image. In its 2001 annual report, Vulcan poked fun at itself while admitting the aggregates industry might not be exciting to the average person, stating, "Sexy? No. But very profitable." Yet to Vulcan, its shareholders, and Wall Street, being profitable was all that mattered. By the numbers, Vulcan Materials hit overall revenues of $3.02 billion for 2001 with net sales at $2.5 billion and earnings climbing to nearly $381 million.

Though more than once in its long history Vulcan Materials had been on the EPA's hit list, Vulcan had instead become a poster company for environmental concerns and even a leader in the beautification of quarries. Twenty-four Vulcan quarries in the United States and its Crescent quarry in Mexico won top honors from the National Stone, Sand & Gravel Association's About Face Awards in early 2002. Vulcan Materials Company continued to be the country's leading aggregates producer, as well as a major force in the production of chloralkali compounds and derivatives for industrial and commercial use.

Principal Subsidiaries

Vulcan Chemical Technologies, Inc.; Vulcan Gulf Coast Materials, Inc.; Vulcan Materials Company; Vulcan Performance Chemicals, Inc.; Wanatah Trucking Company Inc.

Principal Competitors

The Dow Chemical Company; Lafarge North America Inc.; Martin Marietta Materials, Inc.; Florida Rock Industries, Inc.; CRH plc.

Further Reading

Archibald, Robert, and Robert Beard, "Making Waves in Gulf Coast Markets," *Pit & Quarry,* June 1991.

Blevins, Dallas R., and Jessie L. Forbes, *Vulcan Materials: Alabama's Share of the Fortune* (unpublished), University of Montevallo, Alabama, 1984.

Blount, W. Houston, "The Past As a Challenge to the Future," speech delivered to The Newcomen Society in North America, Birmingham, Alabama, October 13, 1982.

Bonnie, Fred, "The Low Cost of a High Public Relations Profile," *Skillings' Mining Review,* January 2, 1993.

Carmichael, Jane, "Cinderella," *Forbes,* March 15, 1982.

Connel, Greg, "Rolling with the Changes," *Pit & Quarry,* January 1990.

Pierce, Frank, "Vulcan Materials Company: Alabama's Share of the Fortune," *Journal of the Birmingham Historical Society,* December 1985.

"Vulcan Quarries Recognized for Outstanding Beautification Efforts," *Pit & Quarry,* March 2002, p 17.

"Vulcan to Acquire CalMat," *Pit & Quarry,* December 1998, p 9.

"Vulcan to Purchase 50 Percent Share of Vulcan/ICA Joint Venture," *Birmingham Business Journal,* January 19, 2001, p 9.

"Vulcan Ranked Among World's Best-Managed Companies," *Pit & Quarry,* October 2000, p 16.

Weaver, Bronwyn, "Community Involvement Rewrites Familiar Story," *Pit & Quarry,* June 1990.

Wolf, Terry, "eRocks: If You're Not Serving Customers Online Maybe It's Time to Start Thinking About It," *Pit & Quarry,* October 2000, p S2.

—Dean Boyer
—update: Nelson Rhodes

Watsco Inc.

2665 South Bayshore Drive, Suite 901
Coconut Grove, Florida 33133
U.S.A.
Telephone: (305) 714-4100
Fax: (305) 858-4492
Web site: http://www.watsco.com

Public Company
Incorporated: 1956
Employees: 2,700
Sales: $1.24 billion (2001)
Stock Exchanges: New York
Ticker Symbol: WSO
NAIC: 421730 Warm Air Heating and Air-Conditioning
   Equipment and Supplies Wholesalers; 561320
   Temporary Help Services

Watsco Inc. is the nation's leading distributor of air conditioning, heating, and refrigeration equipment, the largest player in a fragmented industry. The company wholesales various brands of heating and cooling equipment to more than 35,000 contractors across the country and in Puerto Rico. Watsco also sells parts and equipment to the refrigeration market, including compressors, evaporators, valves, coolers, and ice machines. Watsco's subsidiary Dunhill Staffing operates in an entirely different business segment, providing temporary personnel placement. Watsco expanded enormously through acquisitions, especially in the 1980s, when it grew from a Florida supplier into a dominant force in the Sunbelt region. Its three largest markets are Florida, California, and Texas, where air conditioning is standard for most housing. Much of the company's growth came not from new housing but from replacement service as air conditioning units installed during housing booms in the 1970s and early 1980s reached obsolescence ten or 20 years later. Albert Nahmad has run Watsco since 1973. He and Director David Fleeman own approximately 50 percent of the company.

A Small Player Through the 1970s

Watsco Inc. was incorporated in Florida in 1956 and began selling shares to the public in 1962. In 1968 it was first listed on the American Stock Exchange, and the company began making acquisitions. Watsco's prime business was manufacturing heating and cooling equipment and door and window parts, with headquarters in Hialeah. After 1969, Watsco bought up a slew of smaller companies in different industries and scattered locations. Watsco merged with Sun Engineering in 1969, and in 1971 spent $217,000 to pick up Chicago-based Wabash Corp. and Kesco Products of New York. The company acquired another manufacturing plant in 1973, Allin Manufacturing, and the next year snapped up Mumma Tool & Die Company. In 1977 Watsco paid Clairol, Inc. $275,000 for its Sybil Ives line of hair care products. Watsco ran a Professional Hair Care division, consisting of Sybil Ives and another manufacturing unit, until 1982. Annual revenues through the early 1970s were from $3 million to $4 million. In a profile on Watsco in *Florida Trend* magazine (October 1992), the company's sales and earnings throughout the 1970s were characterized as "unspectacular." The company in many ways fit the model of the corporate conglomerate that dominated that era, with operations spread across several market segments—hair care and air conditioning could hardly be more different—with disparate plants from Florida to Los Angeles.

The company came under the control of a new leader in 1973, Albert H. Nahmad. He became chairman, president, and chief executive officer in December of that year, and eventually he took the company in a new direction. Nahmad had a background both in business and in engineering. He earned a bachelor of science degree in mechanical engineering from the University of New Mexico, followed by a master's degree in industrial management from Purdue University. He then worked for several years for the chemical and packaging conglomerate W.R. Grace, and for the accounting firm Arthur Young & Co. (later Ernst & Young). For several years after Nahmad's ascendancy at Watsco, things did not look too different. The company continued to pick up smaller firms, including Del Mar Engineering Co. in 1977 and Cam-Stat Inc. of Los Angeles in 1981. The company divested its Professional Hair Care division in 1982. It made $540,000 on the sale, nearly twice what it had paid for the Clairol division five years earlier. In addition, Nahmad made several moves to somewhat consolidate Watsco. In 1982 Watsco's Los Angeles-based subsidiary Del Mar moved its base to Hialeah, where it became part of

Watsco's Production Enterprises division. The next year another California subsidiary, Cam-Stat, also moved to Hialeah, so that Watsco's operations were not so far-flung. The company also made a significant investment in 1982, buying up an 8.5 percent interest in Florida Commercial Banks, Inc. for slightly more than $3 million. Two years later Watsco sold its interest in the bank for more than $8.5 million.

Beginning to Move in the 1980s

By the mid-1980s, Watsco's revenue had grown to about $15 million. Watsco's air conditioning business was apparently doing well. Florida had seen a boom in housing in the 1970s as many people migrated to the state, and Watsco continued to thrive even as the boom flattened because it sold replacement parts. Air conditioners, used almost year-round in Florida, usually wore out after about ten years, so the replacement cycle was in full swing in the 1980s even as new home construction slowed. By 1986, Chairman Nahmad was anxious to expand Watsco, which was flush with cash. Nahmad made it known that he was looking for acquisitions, and even took out an advertisement in the *Wall Street Journal* asking people with companies to sell to contact him. The company soon settled on its Sun Belt strategy, growing by acquisition of heating and cooling distribution companies in southern California, Arizona, Nevada, and other warm-weather areas. But first Watsco took an unexpected step. Its first major acquisition of the mid-1980s was not related to its core business any more than hair care had been. In 1988 Watsco put down approximately $2.5 million for a temporary staffing firm called Dunhill Staffing Systems, Inc. Dunhill had revenue of roughly $21 million annually, and temporary employment was expected to be a high-growth business. Nahmad first announced that he would spin off the division for a profit within a few years, but Dunhill continued to be a part of Watsco through late 2002.

The real key to Watsco's growth came the next year, when Watsco greatly increased its market share in the air conditioning distribution business with two other acquisitions. By 1988, Watsco's revenue had risen to about $22 million, and it was still focused mainly on manufacturing parts for the heating and cooling industry in Florida. Watsco bought 80 percent of one of Florida's largest residential air conditioning distributors, Gemaire Distributors, Inc., for $17 million. The other 20 percent of the company was held by Rheem, an air conditioner manufacturer that occupied the number two spot in the industry. Three months after picking up the majority of Gemaire, Watsco bought 80 percent of another distributor, the Harry Alter Co. Watsco had held slightly more than 10 percent of the air conditioning distribution market in Florida in 1988. With the

addition of its new subsidiaries, Watsco soon had about 16 percent of the Florida market. In 1990, Watsco followed this up by buying a 50 percent interest in the largest residential air conditioner distribution company in California and Arizona. This was Heating and Cooling Supply, Inc., a privately held firm. Watsco had planned to buy 80 percent of Heating and Cooling, raising money through a special stock offering. Iraq's invasion of Kuwait and the possibility of war in the Persian Gulf flattened the stock market, making Watsco's stock offering a bad bet, and the company withdrew it. Instead Watsco settled for a smaller piece of Heating and Cooling, paying $31.4 million. Rheem again bought the other half. But the acquisition allowed Watsco to double its share of the distribution market in southern California and Arizona, and company revenues shot up. By 1991 Watsco was bringing in $169 million, up from $22 million just three years earlier.

Steady Growth in the 1990s

An interesting fact in Watsco's surge of growth was that the country was in recession and housing was in a downswing in Florida and California. New building starts were down, and yet Watsco thrived by selling parts and distributing equipment to contractors for replacement jobs. In Florida, air conditioners lasted about ten years, and in California, where the machines were generally on only half the year, they typically lasted 20. The early 1990s coincided with peak need for air conditioner replacement in both states, following earlier growth in housing. Watsco also grew by moving into new markets. It opened a branch of Heating and Cooling Supply in Las Vegas in 1991, expecting vigorous housing growth there. Watsco also began exploring the distribution business in Latin America. The company got a surge of business in the wake of Hurricane Andrew as well. The hurricane devastated southern Florida in August 1992, and some 90,000 homes were damaged or destroyed. The rebuilding effort required tens of thousands of new air conditioners.

As Watsco's distribution business took off, its manufacturing business also prospered. By 1993 about three quarters of the company's revenue came from distribution. The manufacturing side of the business had not kept up, and yet it remained strong and profitable. Besides making replacement parts, Watsco began manufacturing electronic temperature controls, which it sold to other heating and cooling manufacturers. These had a profit margin of nearly 40 percent, about twice the margin of the distribution business. Watsco also began making a new product in 1992, which it called the Flash. The Flash was a machine that captured and filtered chlorofluorocarbons (CFCs), the coolant commonly used in air conditioners and refrigerators. The Flash was manufactured by a Watsco subsidiary in Hialeah, and it was important because the Clean Air Act enacted in July 1992 prohibited the release of CFCs into the air. The Flash made it possible for air conditioning repairers to recycle CFCs, in compliance with the law. With this new product, Watsco hoped that its manufacturing business would equal the distribution side by the end of the decade.

But it was the distribution business that continued to lead the way through the 1990s. The industry was still fairly fragmented, made up of many small players, and Watsco had many opportunities to expand by acquisition. "There's no one out there consolidating in the industry except us," CEO Nahmad told the

Key Dates:

1956: Watsco is founded in Hialeah, Florida.
1962: The company goes public.
1968: The company moves to the American Stock Exchange.
1973: Albert Nahmad becomes chairman, president, and CEO.
1988: Watsco acquires Dunhill Staffing.
1989: The company acquires a majority interest in Gemaire.
1994: Watsco moves to the New York Stock Exchange.
1998: The company sells its manufacturing division.

Wall Street Journal (June 20, 1994). In that interview Nahmad also announced that Watsco's profit for 1994 was expected to go up by about 20 percent. The company moved to the more prestigious New York Stock Exchange that year. In 1996 Watsco bought out Rheem's minority interest in the subsidiaries they had controlled together, Gemaire, Heating & Cooling Supply, and Comfort Supply, a 1993 acquisition that they had split 80/20. These all became wholly owned subsidiaries of Watsco. The company also bought Three States Supply Company that year, as well as a North Carolina distributor called Central Air Conditioning Distributors, Inc. Then in early 1997 Watsco paid approximately $22 million for Coastline Distribution, Inc. and four manufacturing plants, all owned by Inter-City Products Corporation. Inter-City was one of the nation's largest manufacturers of heating and cooling equipment, with several major brands, including Comfortmaker and Arcoaire. It had 25 branches of its Coastline Distribution business, spread through Florida, Georgia, Alabama, the Carolinas, the Washington, D.C. area, and parts of southern California. The addition of Coastline brought the number of Watsco distribution outlets up to 116. Within a few months, Watsco announced that it was buying two distribution operations from the air conditioner maker Carrier Corporation. This was the company's 15th acquisition in the heating and cooling equipment distribution business since 1989, and it brought the number of Watsco's distribution branches up to 133.

With the distribution business growing so quickly, Watsco decided to sell off most of its manufacturing business in 1998. Its nondistribution business by that time contributed less than 8 percent of Watsco's total revenue. It sold its manufacturing subsidiary Watsco Components Inc. that year to International Comfort Products Corporation. Watsco continued to snap up smaller distributors, in 1998 buying a Georgia firm that distributed heaters and air conditioners to the mobile home industry. Kaufman Supply had annual revenue of more than $100 million, and looked to have a lucrative niche in the thriving mobile home market in the Southeast.

By the late 1990s, Watsco had become a billion-dollar company. It had made significant inroads into the heating and cooling distribution markets in key Sunbelt states. In 1999, the company announced that it was ready to move into New England, which was new territory for Watsco. New England was served by some 40 different distributors, and the total market

for heating and cooling, including parts and supplies, was estimated to be worth more than $400 million. Watsco bought up two major Northeast distributors, Homans Associates, Inc. and Heat, Inc. in 1999, and declared that it was actively looking for more acquisitions in the area. Watsco had more than 300 distribution outlets after it added Homan and Heat. The company finished 1999 with record growth. Revenue grew 17 percent, to $1.25 billion. Watsco was by now the largest independent distributor of residential heating and cooling equipment in the country. It continued its push into the Northeast in 2000 with the purchase of Anderson Sales Corporation, based in Farmingdale, New York. Anderson had annual revenues of around $40 million, with five distribution branches in New York and New Jersey.

By 2000, Watsco seemed to be entering another mode, concentrating on increasing efficiency and profitability in its existing operations instead of focusing on growth through acquisition. The company reported sales of $1.3 billion, up slightly from the previous year. Watsco began closing several dozen branches in 2000, and it closed more in 2001. It also announced that it would eliminate some product lines that were not selling well or had poor profit margins. The company looked for other ways to cut costs, too. It restructured the unit it had bought from Kaufman Supply, which sold heating and cooling to mobile homes and other manufactured housing. This market had declined more than 20 percent in 2000, and Watsco laid off workers and revamped the business in anticipation of a recovery some time later. Watsco also invested in new technology in the early 2000s, introducing an online service providing heating and cooling contractors 24-hour access to Watsco's distribution network. Revenue for 2001 shrank slightly. Yet Watsco still seemed to see opportunities for future growth in the distribution market. Company analysts perceived the distribution industry as undercapitalized and fragmented, suggesting there was still a place for a well-heeled consolidator.

Principal Subsidiaries

A&C Distributors, Inc.; ACDoctor.com Inc.; Air Supply, Inc.; Air Systems Distributors, Inc.; Atlantic Service & Supply, Inc.; CAD Watsco, Inc.; Baker Distributing Co.; Central Air Conditioning Distributors, Inc.; Coastline Distribution, Inc.; Cooling Holding, Inc.; Comfort Supply, Inc.; CP Distributors, Inc.; Gemaire Distributors, Inc.; GMC Distributors, Inc.; H.B. Adams Distributors, Inc.; Heat Incorporated; Heating & Cooling Supply, Inc.; Homans Associates, Inc.; NSI Supply, Inc.; Three States Supply Co. Inc.; Weathertrol Supply Co.; William Wurzbach Co., Inc.; Dunhill Staffing Systems, Inc.; Dunhill Temporary Systems, Inc.

Principal Competitors

United Technologies Corporation; York International Corporation; American Standard Companies Inc.

Further Reading

Fakler, John T., ''Watsco Inc. Stock Downgraded,'' *South Florida Business Journal,* February 18, 2000, p. 19.
Faloon, Kelly, ''Watsco to Close Locations in 2001,'' *Supply House Times,* February 2001, p. 19.

Hersch, Valerie, ''Right Place, Right Time,'' *Florida Trend,* October 1992, p. 47.

Irvine, Martha, ''Watsco Expects Its Net Income to Jump About 20% in '94, CEO Nahmad Says,'' *Wall Street Journal,* June 20, 1994, p. A9.

Kirsch, Sandra L., ''Watsco,'' *Fortune,* December 4, 1989, p. 134.

Lamm, Marcy, ''Nothing Chilly About Sales,'' *Atlanta Business Chronicle,* June 12, 1998, p. 1A.

Ozemhoya, Carol U., ''Clean Air Hot Ticket for Watsco,'' *South Florida Business Journal,* June 22, 1992, p. 1.

Solo, Sally, ''Watsco,'' *Fortune,* April 19, 1993, p. 93.

''Two Distribution Operations of Carrier to Be Acquired,'' *Wall Street Journal,* December 4, 1996, p. B4.

''Watsco Announces Actions to Improve Profitability,'' *Air Conditioning, Heating & Refrigeration News,* January 29, 2001, p. 11.

''Watsco to Explore Sale of Assets,'' *Wall Street Journal,* January 7, 1998, p. C18.

—A. Woodward

The Weather Channel Companies

300 Interstate North Parkway
Atlanta, Georgia 30339
U.S.A.
Telephone: (770) 226-0000
Web site: http://www.weather.com

Wholly Owned Subsidiary of Landmark Communications, Inc.
Incorporated: 1981
Employees: 900
Sales: $302 million (2000 est.)
NAIC: 513210 Cable Networks

Through cable TV, radio, and Internet operations, The Weather Channel Companies provide around-the-clock weather information. The Weather Channel, Inc., the U.S. network, reaches more than 95 percent of cable homes in the United States, or more than 84 million subscribers among cable and satellite dish users. Led by *USA Today,* more than 60 newspapers with a combined circulation of eight million carry weather news from The Weather Channel. The channel gets high ratings in the early mornings and in times of severe weather.

With 350 million page views a month, weather.com is the Web's leading weather provider. The company broadcasts to nine million subscribers in Latin America and offers global weather information through language-specific sites there and in Europe. Through a joint venture, The Weather Channel owns half of Canada's The Weather Network.

Origins

John Coleman had a dream. A meteorologist for ABC's *Good Morning America,* he believed in the public's appetite for weather information. The market existed, he knew, for an around-the-clock weather channel. He had a difficult time, however, finding other believers. TV weather was at that time limited to three-minute spots on local news—something ACNielsen had never even measured.

After unsuccessfully shopping his idea to many major media companies, Coleman eventually caught the ear of Frank Batten, Sr., chairman of Landmark Communications, a privately held media conglomerate based in Norfolk, Virginia, that owned newspapers, and TV and radio stations. Batten liked to sail and was perhaps more attuned to the weather than most people. He also knew that cable operators were eager for content, and that their local weather information was primitive.

In his 2002 chronicle, *The Weather Channel: The Improbable Rise of a Media Phenomenon,* Batten recalled the July 1981 press conference where he announced his exciting new concept: just weather, 24 hours a day. Few of the unimpressed journalists in the room would have predicted that in 20 years their colleagues would be referring to the company as a "cash cow" or "media phenomenon."

About $40 million was raised to launch the network. The start-up costs were considerable. John O. "Dubby" Wynne, former corporate counsel and head of broadcasting at Landmark, engineered many of the deals that brought the company into existence. The Weather Channel (TWC) acquired a lease for a scarce transponder on the dominant Satcom I satellite at a cost of $10.5 million. The company also had to convince the National Weather Service to standardize its forecasts at its 500 local stations. In addition, the company needed to develop equipment to allow cable operators to pull the appropriate local weather information from the satellite signal.

TWC was headquartered in the Cumberland Mall area northwest of Atlanta. The city was chosen for a number of reasons, including a reliable ABC satellite uplink allowing Coleman to fulfill his contract with *Good Morning America.* The city's temperate weather was another factor.

The Weather Channel first went on the air on May 2, 1982—a date that coincided with the beginning of the National Cable Television Association's annual conference in Las Vegas. The first studio, dubbed the "Weather Closet," measured just 15 feet by 15 feet. A lightning bolt zapped the channel's transformer in 1983, keeping it off the air for five hours.

Company Perspectives:

TWC Mission: We will be the indispensable source of weather and related information that helps consumers prepare for and understand the weather and how it affects their lives. TWC Vision: To make a difference in people's lives one forecast at a time.

In the same year, a financial crisis almost kept the channel off the air for good. It was resolved by having cable operators pay a fee to carry the programming. Although TWC became one of the most visited (if briefly viewed) cable channels, advertising revenues were simply not paying all the bills. In January 1984, TWC began charging cable systems a monthly fee of five cents per basic subscriber.

Advertisers were slowly warming up to the TWC concept, especially those with a weather-related angle to their products. Makers of batteries, hot beverages, and cold medicines adored the channel during the winter. Michelin's famous baby-in-a-tire ads got plenty of airing during rainy weather.

During episodes of severe weather, such as during the blizzard of March 1993, TWC could momentarily best its giant Atlanta neighbor, CNN, in the ratings. TWC also helped popularize hurricane tracking as something of a national pastime, broadcasting coordinates every ten minutes. By this time, TWC was carried on 5,000 cable systems to 54 million subscribers. It had 400 employees, including 52 meteorologists and 32 news anchors.

Storming the Internet in 1995

TWC got onto the Internet early. It became CompuServe's weather provider in February 1995. The first version of weather.com, TWC's own web site, launched a couple of months later. Company President Michael Eckert reckoned, however, that TWC had a thousand competing sites, mostly poor quality ones. As most of TWC's weather data, being obtained from the National Weather Service, was public domain, Eckert aimed to differentiate The Weather Channel's web site with good visual design and constantly updated, detailed information. This required a considerable outlay in technology. Soon, the site was presenting this info via 3-D weather maps and animation. By mid-1996, the web site was logging four million hits a week.

The company's cable TV programming also was evolving. In 1995, TWC began featuring live reports from the field. The audience was growing at more than 25 percent a year. Ad revenues topped $40 million, while subscriber fees were estimated at $48 million. The company also was rolling out weather-related CD-ROMs, videos, and books.

In the United States, the channel rolled out a series of witty ads aimed at appealing to weather fanatics. The ads portrayed patrons of a sports bar watching The Weather Channel, cheering "Warm Front" vs. "Cold Front."

European versions of The Weather Channel debuted in mid-1996. As part of its international expansion, The Weather

Channel acquired a 50 percent stake in Toronto-based Pelmorex, which operated a Canadian cable weather network, in September 1996. Pelmorex CEO Pierre Morrisette retained voting control.

Growing fast, TWC by mid-1997 had 400 employees at its metro Atlanta headquarters. The company moved its sprawling operations into one eight-story building. It also upgraded to digital production and broadcast technology.

The company faced new competition from MSNBC Weather, a satellite dish service that did not last very long. Competition in Europe was tougher. The Weather Channel also had to deal with meddlesome governments, often with media interests of their own. Although The Weather Channel's four European channels attained more than 20 million subscribers, they were shut down in January 1998.

Michael J. Eckert, one of the company's cofounders and its CEO since 1985, stepped down in March 1999. He told the *Atlanta Journal and Constitution* that for the channel to succeed in the new millennium, it needed to be five things: "Personalized, customized, convenient, fast and portable."

Decker Anstrom, previously head of the National Cable Television Association, became The Weather Channel's next CEO. Just two years later, he was named president and chief operating officer of parent company Landmark Communications, while retaining the CEO spot at The Weather Channel, which was Landmark's fastest-growing and most profitable business, according to the *Atlanta Journal and Constitution.*

The company's 1999 revenues were estimated by one source at $185 million, with operating profits of $70 million. *The Weather Channel: The Improbable Rise of a Media Phenomenon,* however, put TWC's share of Landmark's $790 million in 2000 revenues at $302 million.

In the fall of 1999, The Weather Channel became the preferred weather provider for America Online. About the same time, it began transmitting its Weatherscan Local service to a Time Warner cable system in Memphis via the Internet. Weatherscan Local, which provided all-local, all-the-time weather info on digital cable systems, was rolled out nationally in March 2002. It had 3.5 million subscribers within a few months.

The Weather Channel's parent company, Landmark Communications, acquired Weather Services International (WSI) in February 2000 for $120 million. WSI, based in Massachussetts, provided weather information and graphics for TV stations. The Weather Channel had long used WSI to handle National Weather Service data.

Weather.com, which began with "one meteorologist, one IT person and one marketing person, all working part time," had a staff of 140 in 2000. It had expanded beyond simple weather statistics into travel and even vacation information.

The Weather Channel, which was unchallenged for 20 years, began to get some direct competition in late 2000, when WeatherPlus arrived on the scene. WeatherPlus started with broadcasts in The Netherlands, but was headquartered near Philadelphia and had its operations center in The Weather

---

Key Dates:

1982: The Weather Channel is launched.
1985: Revenues from cable operators exceed those from advertisers.
1986: TWC switches to an anchor format.
1995: Weather.com is launched.
1997: TWC moves to a new facility.
1998: TWC enters the top dozen cable networks, reaching more than 70 million subscribers.
2001: The "Live by It" campaign promotes viewers' emotional connection to TWC.

Channel's Atlanta backyard. AccuWeather, a long dominant forecasting service for radio stations and local broadcast television stations, also competed with The Weather Channel on the Internet, via hundreds of sites, including CNN.com and MSNBC.com. The Weather Channel resumed efforts to expand overseas, but began using an Internet-only strategy.

Getting Emotional in 2001

In 2001, TWC began a "Live by It" advertising campaign emphasizing the "emotional connection" its broad audience felt toward it, hoping to encourage them to use it more frequently by seeing the channel as a "trusted and caring friend instead of just a box of meteorological data," wrote the *Atlanta Journal and Constitution*. The emphasis switched from the-weather-as-the-star to the connection between weather and the viewer's life, said the company's marketing people. The anchors were being groomed for personality and energy; more video of people active outdoors was being incorporated into the programs.

The company quadrupled its promotional budget to more than $20 million for 2001. New programs such as "Your Weather Today," a morning show for working women, began airing. Another, "Storm Series," aired in prime time and profiled encounters with dangerous weather.

As its online unit struggled to attain profitability, The Weather Channel cut 18 jobs there and in the Latin American operations. The company employed 900, including 120 meteorologists.

Bill Burke, a former executive at the Turner Broadcasting System, became The Weather Channel's next president in February 2002. In the spring of 2002, The Weather Channel cross-promoted its five-part "StormWeek" series with the A&E network, which was airing a two-part movie called *Shackleton* about a 1914 expedition to the South Pole. The two channels reached a similar audience; both were strong in the age 25 to 54 demographic.

TWC's ratings continued to be most affected by the weather itself. Tropical storms Isidore and Lili led a record 2.9 million users to weather.com in late September 2002, while the Latin American site and The Weather Channel cable network both doubled their usual audience.

Principal Subsidiaries

Pelmorex, Inc. (Canada; 50%); The Weather Channel, Inc.; Weather Services International.

Principal Divisions

The Weather Channel, Inc.; The Weather Channel Radio Network; Newspaper Services; The Weather Channel International; weather.com; The Weather Channel New Media and Interactive TV.

Principal Competitors

AccuWeather; WeatherPlus.

Further Reading

Albright, Mark, "Ill Wind Blows to This Channel's Good," *St. Petersburg Times,* August 2, 1995, p. 1E.

Batten, Frank, and Jeffrey L. Cruikshank, *The Weather Channel: The Improbable Rise of a Media Phenomenon,* Boston: Harvard Business School Press, 2002.

Fass, Allison, "Two Cable Networks Cooperate in a Bid to Cut Through Clutter," *New York Times,* April 4, 2002, p. C5.

Gatlin, Greg, "Weather Channel Owner Acquires WSI for $120M," *Boston Herald,* Finance Sec., February 9, 2000, p. 32.

Gunther, Marc, "The Weather Channel: Hot Enough for Ya?," *Fortune,* October 25, 1999, pp. 46+.

Haddad, Charles, "On the Digital Weather Front," *Atlanta Journal and Constitution,* May 25, 1997, p. 1P.

——, "Weather Channel Adds to Holdings Away from US; Cable Telecaster Buys Stake in Canadian Counterpart," *Atlanta Journal and Constitution,* September 19, 1996.

——, "Weather Channel Forecast Hangs on Technology," *Atlanta Journal and Constitution,* July 14, 1996, p. 7P.

——, "Weather Channel Transmitting Via Internet," *Atlanta Journal and Constitution,* October 2, 1999, p. 1C.

——, "The Weather Channel Yields to Poor Climate in European TV," *Atlanta Journal and Constitution,* January 30, 1998, p. 1G.

Haddad, Charles, and Doug Cress, "Tuning In: Rain or Shine, Atlanta Channel a Clear Success," *Atlanta Journal and Constitution,* July 15, 1993, p. F1.

Haley, Kathy, "Aiming High: New Long Form Programming Is Just the Beginning of TWC's Strategy to Become One of TV's Most Important Networks," *Broadcasting & Cable,* April 29, 2002, pp. 3A+.

Hall, Lee, "Give Anstrom the Business: Exec 'Enjoying' Changes from NCTA to the Weather Channel," *Electronic Media,* August 23, 1999, p. 2.

Husted, Bill, "Computers Help Forecasters Track Weather, Warn of Severe Storms," *Atlanta Journal and Constitution,* May 5, 2002.

"Innovating on Screen: New Features Are Proliferating in Both National and Local Programming," *Broadcasting & Cable,* April 29, 2002, pp. 6A+.

"Integrity First: One Thing Hasn't Changed Throughout TWC's Entrepreneurial History—Its Culture," *Broadcasting & Cable,* April 29, 2002, pp. 13A+.

Katz, Frances, "Weather Channel CEO Resigning for Sunny Days with Family," *Atlanta Journal and Constitution,* March 24, 1999, p. 6D.

——, "Weather.com Well Past Its TV Origins," *Atlanta Journal and Constitution,* May 17, 2000, p. 10E.

Kempner, Matt, "Change in the Air at the Weather Channel," *Atlanta Journal and Constitution,* April 28, 2002, p. 1Q.

——, "Newcomer Seeks to Invade Atlanta-Based Weather Channel's Turf," *Atlanta Journal and Constitution,* October 21, 2000.

——, "Weather Channel CEO Promoted; Anstrom Taking Helm at Parent Company," *Atlanta Journal and Constitution,* May 23, 2001, p. 3D.

——, "Weather Channel Names New President," *Atlanta Journal and Constitution,* December 15, 2001.

——, "Weather Channel Pinning Hopes for International Growth on Net," *Atlanta Journal and Constitution,* November 2, 2000, p. 3E.

Meeks, Fleming, "What Brand Is Your Weather?," *Forbes,* October 23, 1995, pp. 320+.

Morris, Chris, "They're Jokes No More: After 10 Years, Weather Channel Winning Respect," *Atlanta Business Chronicle,* April 3, 1992, pp. 3A+.

"The Road to Ubiquity: New Media Play a Growing Role in Bringing People Access to TWC 'Anytime, Anywhere,' " *Broadcasting & Cable,* April 29, 2002, pp. 10A+.

Stamler, Bernard, "The Weather Channel's New Campaign Aims for Viewers Who Aren't Climate 'Fanatics,' " *New York Times,* May 15, 2001, p. C15.

Vogelstein, Fred, "You Can't Change the Weather Channel," *US News & World Report,* September 27, 1999, p. 47.

"Weather Networks Storm into Europe," *Cable & Satellite Europe,* June 1996, p. 7.

—Frederick C. Ingram

Weeres Industries Corporation

1045 33rd Street S.
P.O. Box 98
St. Cloud, Minnesota 56302-0098
U.S.A.
Telephone: (320) 251-3551
Toll Free: (800) 397-6686
Fax: (320) 654-9188
Web site: http://www.weeres.com

Private Company
Founded: 1952
Employees: 175
Sales: $30 million (2001 est.)
NAIC: 336612 Boat Building

Weeres Industries Corporation is the oldest manufacturer of pontoon boats in the United States. The company's founder, Ambrose Weeres, constructed the first pontoon boat in 1951. Since that time Weeres Industries, located in central Minnesota, has built and sold more than 30,000 pontoon boats. Although Weeres is primarily an American company, its pontoons are afloat across the Atlantic on the Nile and Thames rivers, and in Sweden's Stockholm harbor. The company sells high quality pontoons exclusively through dealers in 20 states. Weeres pontoons range in size from the simple four-person, 16-foot fishing model to a 28-foot, luxury tri-toon that can accommodate 30 people.

Weeres Industries also manufactures fiberglass offshore fishing boats through its subsidiary brands Palm Beach and Key Largo. In addition to the St. Cloud headquarters, Weeres operates Palm Beach Marinecraft in New Ulm, Minnesota, and Marine Manufacturing Corporation in Douglas, Georgia. Weeres also builds and sells swimming rafts and paddleboats, which account for about 5 percent of the company's business.

Keeping Business Afloat: 1950s

As the ''Land of 10,000 Lakes,'' Minnesota has often been the source of innovations related to water recreation. Lake City,

Minnesota, located along Lake Pepin and the Mississippi River, was the birthplace of waterskiing, and a number of boat manufacturers, fishing-oriented businesses, as well as perhaps the most prominent name in life preservers and related gear, Stearns, have their home base in Minnesota. Not surprisingly, pontoon boats originated in the state, in the small Stearns County town of Richmond, where innovator Ambrose Weeres created the first pontoon in 1951. His initial boat was basically a plywood sheet strapped to 55-gallon steel drums. Weeres and acquaintance Edwin Torborg tested their pontoon on Horseshoe Lake, near Richmond. (Some sources credit Torborg as the designer of the pontoon, but the historical account is unclear. Weeres has been recognized several times as the sole inventor of the pontoon.)

The prototype pontoon even included a steering device and a mount for an outboard motor. After storing the boat for the winter, Weeres learned the hard way that the steel pontoons collapsed when the air contracted due to cold temperatures. He redesigned the boats slightly, including small breathing tubes in each pontoon to allow for fluctuations in air temperature.

That first year Ambrose Weeres constructed four boats. In 1952 he founded Weeres Industries and took orders for 40 more boats. The inventor displayed his pontoons at a boat show in Chicago, inducing another 100 orders for pontoon boats.

In 1956, company founder Ambrose Weeres was pursuing new innovations, and created the paddleboat. Weeres Industries soon added paddleboats to its product line.

Business Ups and Downs: 1960s–70s

Knese built a large production facility near St. Cloud, Minnesota, and worked to forge business relationships with area boat dealers. A company marketing highlight occurred when Knese arranged for Weeres pontoons to be used in the water events of the Minneapolis Aquatennial celebration, a weeklong summer community festival attended by thousands of Minnesotans. More potential buyers saw the boats in use and were intrigued. Business increased enough that Knese added two more production facilities in 1964. The number of employees grew to 22.

Sometime between 1964 and 1976, Dick Anderson purchased the business, which by this stage was also producing swimming rafts. But pontoon boats remained its manufacturing focus. In 1976, Weeres Industries produced more than 900 pontoons. For a short time Weeres also produced trailers for pontoons, water bikes, and snowmobiles. The newer pontoons at this time could accommodate larger motors, making it easier for users to pull waterskiers.

During the years Anderson owned the company, sales ranged from $1 million to $1.5 million per year, and production varied greatly from year to year. Weeres produced low, mid-range, and luxury pontoons from 16 feet to 28 feet in length. By this time the competition in the field had grown, and the marine industry overall was beginning to weaken.

1982: New Owners with a Commitment to Growth

By the early 1980s, the company was near declaring bankruptcy, according to Clint Lee, one of the two business investors who purchased the company in 1982. Lee said the financing for his purchase included assumption of the company's debt. At that time the company had just 16 employees, and annual sales were under $1 million. According to Lee, the company had faltered for several years because the owners failed to reinvest the profits in the business.

Neither Lee nor partner Gordon Brown had a background in the boating industry. Lee had experience running small businesses, and he was looking for a business opportunity in manufacturing that produced a tangible product. So he looked at Weeres. His decision to purchase Weeres Industries was facilitated by reading a commentary in *Kiplinger's* that forecasted great growth in the boating industry, particularly in the pontoon boat area. The previous five years had been slow for marine manufacturing.

One thing that attracted Lee and Brown to Weeres specifically was that the company had some of the most expertly skilled aluminum welders in the industry. Aluminum welders were hard to find and difficult to train. In large part because of that exceptional craftsmanship, Weeres had a reputation for superb quality. Weeres pontoons were built like tanks, according to Lee, but they lagged behind the competition in the area of styling.

Lee and Brown focused on improving quality and lowering costs. They were committed to reinvesting the profits into the business. Early on in their ownership tenure they invited Ambrose Weeres and his family for an outing on a large luxury Weeres pontoon with an inboard/outboard motor. They wanted Mr. Weeres to see how far his invention had come. A few years later Lee and Brown contemplated moving the company to South Dakota because the cost of doing business was so much lower there. The fact that South Dakota was further away from their primary market factored into their decision to stay put. In

1985 Weeres Industries purchased Palm Beach Boats, in Douglas, Georgia, which manufactured both salt-water and freshwater pontoons.

Company Growth, International Expansion: Late 1980s–90s

When Lee visited Sweden in the late 1980s, he noticed there were no pontoons in the Stockholm harbor. Seeing an opportunity, Lee made a business deal with the best yacht builder there, Storebor Brux Company, to assemble and sell Weeres pontoons. Weeres sent the pontoons disassembled in containers, and assigned an assembler from Minnesota to work in Sweden. Unfortunately, shipping costs greatly increased the pontoon prices. The arrangement with Storebor led to the sale of about 15-20 pontoons, but faltered when the country's economy took a turn for the worse.

In the late 1980s, pontoon manufacturers noticed a dramatic change in the demographics of pontoon owners. No longer were pontoons just for retired couples with lakeshore property. Because the newer pontoon craft were easy to trailer, and were safe and versatile, young families started buying them as well. To appeal to more buyers, Lee, the chief executive officer and president, and Brown, chairman and sales manager, spent quite a bit of time and money redesigning the boat and furniture, to improve the visual appeal and comfort while lowering costs. They found they could hold the cost down and improve the product.

Weeres Industries secured its place in the Minnesota history books in 1991 when Ambrose Weeres was among the first four people to be inducted into the Minnesota Marine Hall of Fame. Not only known for its original creation that hatched the industry, Weeres Industries had a continuing record of innovation. The company was most likely the first pontoon manufacturer to use pressure treated plywood so the preservative would penetrate deeply into the wood. Weeres was also one of the first companies to use aluminum pontoons, making the boats lighter, faster, and more buoyant.

The company's most rapid growth came between 1992 and 2002. One contributing factor may have been that Weeres began selling boats, trailers, and motors in a "package deal." Lee believed bundling the boats, motors, and trailers helped increase sales because consumers were able to spend less time and energy putting the pieces together. No doubt the booming American economy was also a factor, as consumers found more disposable income available to spend on recreational pursuits. In the late 1990s, Weeres saw 30 to 35 percent annual growth, and the staff grew to 60 employees.

In the mid-1990s Weeres started Marine Manufacturing Corporation in Douglas, Georgia, to produce fiberglass offshore fishing boats under the brand name Key Largo. The company soon ranked as the top producer of offshore fishing boats for the Florida market.

The company received national recognition in 2000 when *Pontoon and Deck Boat* magazine named Weeres the "Best-Built Luxury Pontoon." In the early 2000s, Weeres focused on marketing its various lines primarily east of the Mississippi. The company worked exclusively through dealers in 20 states and Canada.

Key Dates:

1951: Ambrose Weeres builds the first pontoon boat.
1952: Weeres Industries is founded by Ambrose Weeres.
1954: Weeres sells business to Ray Knese.
1955: Weeres Pontoon is named "Boat of the Year" by the *Winona Daily News*.
1956: Ambrose Weeres invents the paddleboat.
c. 1970: Dick Anderson purchases Weeres Industries from Ray Knese.
1982: Clint Lee and Gordon Brown purchase Weeres Industries.
1988: Weeres partners with Storebor to manufacture pontoons in Sweden.
1990: Minnesota state legislature recognizes Ambrose Weeres as "Mr. Pontoon."
1991: Founder Ambrose Weeres is inducted into the Minnesota Marine Hall of Fame; he dies at age 84.
2000: Weeres is recognized for the "Best-Built Luxury Pontoon" by *Pontoon and Deck Boat* magazine.

Expansion to the western United States had been hindered by the smaller number of recreational water spaces there. Weeres pontoons could also be seen on the Blue Nile River in Africa; on the Thames near Windsor Castle, where they were offered for rent; and also in Sweden, Switzerland, and Italy.

Weeres Pontoons were designed for a variety of uses—fishing, swimming, waterskiing, or just for cruising lakes and streams. The specialty models helped to attract new users. Weeres offered several different selections in its pontoon series—including the Sundeck, Fisherman, Suntanner, Sportsman, and Flightdeck. Pontoon boat sizes ranged from 16 feet to 28 feet in length, with the largest boasting a 30-person capacity. Most were within the eight-foot width legal limit so they could be transported by trailer.

Beyond the Creator's Vision

Pontoon extras in the new century went far beyond what Ambrose Weeres ever dreamed of. Accessory selections included portable toilets, changing rooms, electronic fish finders, radios, tape and CD players, roof enclosures, swivel seats, wheelchair gates, aerated livewells for keeping fish or storing cold beverages, and mini-kitchens with microwaves and refrigerators.

President Lee credited the company's success to continually trying to improve the product and working closely with and improving the dealer network. He and Brown were committed to onsite management and to "plowing money back into the company." Lee asserted that Weeres still employed the best welders in the industry. "We picked an exceptional employee base and added to and improved on that." Weeres pontoons had a reputation for lasting forever. Although that did not help repeat business, buyers often tended to upgrade to larger or more luxurious pontoons.

Weeres Industries also stressed point-of-sale advertising. If dealers had shows, Weeres sent their salespeople to provide all the necessary answers for prospective buyers. The same was true for boat shows, where dealers set up booths and Weeres sales representatives were available to field questions.

The 50th anniversary of the company in 2002 passed with minimal celebration. Weeres management and employees remained focused on their core objective: producing high-quality boats and satisfying their customers. Looking to the future, Lee did not expect any dramatic changes in the pontoon boat industry, but he believed the company's fiberglass offshore business would see growth. Company owners Lee and Brown, both well past the average age of retirement, remained at the helm of Weeres, prepared for expansion and continued success.

Principal Subsidiaries

Palm Beach Marinecraft; Marine Manufacturing Corporation.

Principal Competitors

Godfrey Sweetwater; Premier Marine, Inc.; Genmar Industries, Inc.

Further Reading

Anderson, Dennis, "Riding a Wave: Pontoon Boats, You Can't Call 'Em Barges Anymore," *Minneapolis Star Tribune,* January 22, 1995, p. 16C.

Chanen, David, "Obituaries: Ambrose Weeres," *Minneapolis Star Tribune,* October 1, 1991, p. 4B.

"Mr. Pontoon' Alias Ambrose Weeres," *Crossings,* Stearns [County, Minnesota] History Museum, March 2001.

Ratnayake, Hiran, "Fifty Years of Pontoons," *St. Cloud Times,* May 5, 2002, p. 10D.

—Mary Heer-Forsberg

Wellman, Inc.

595 Shrewsbury Avenue
Shrewsbury, New Jersey 07702
U.S.A.
Telephone: (732) 212-3300
Toll Free: (800) 639-7956
Fax: (732) 212-3344
Web site: http://www.wellmaninc.com

Public Company
Incorporated: 1969
Employees: 2,500
Sales: $1.1 billion (2001)
Stock Exchanges: New York
Ticker Symbol: WLM
NAIC: 314999 All Other Miscellaneous Textile Product
    Mills; 325211 Plastics Material and Resin
    Manufacturing

Founded as a small, family-owned wool company, Wellman, Inc. has grown into a multinational *Fortune* 500 company involved in the recycling and manufacture of fibers and plastic resins. Through its two business units, the Packaging Products Group and the Fibers and Recycled Products Group, Wellman is a leader in packaging resins and synthetic fabrics around the world. Many of its proprietary products—Fortrel, Sensura, PermaClear, EcoClear, and the HP 800 series resins—are trademarked for their innovative qualities. In the 21st century Wellman was the world's largest PET (polyethylene terephthalate) plastic recycler and intended to maintain this rank through ongoing research and development projects.

In the Beginning: Late 1920s to 1960s

Wellman traces its history to the Massachusetts wool combing company Hill & Nichols (later renamed Nichols & Company), established in 1927. Almost three decades later, in 1954, Nichols & Company organized Wellman Combing Company in Johnsonville, South Carolina, marking the first plant of its kind in that state. Ten years later, seeing an opportunity to move into the burgeoning synthetics market, Wellman began to produce nylon fibers, mainly for use by the carpet industry. This was soon followed by the manufacture of polyester staple fibers, which were usually made into fiberfill to be used in such products as cushions, quilts, pillows, and parkas, as well as nonwoven and industrial applications. The fibers were produced from recycled raw materials converted from fiber and film waste.

Due to the steady growth of the plastics business, it was decided that the fiber operations should be separated from other activities at the Johnsonville facility, and the Engineering Resins Division was established in 1968. Using recycled nylon fiber and virgin polymers, the division specifically manufactured nylon engineering resins, which were marketed to a variety of industries including automotive, consumer products, and even electrical parts for use in such products as fans, headlight housings, aerosol valves, and lawn and garden equipment.

In order to reflect the changing nature of the firm's business, the Wellman Combing Company was renamed Wellman Industries, Inc. in 1969, while Nichols & Company became Wellman, Inc. Three years later Wellman International Limited was established in Mullagh, Ireland, as a wholly owned subsidiary in order to produce polyester and nylon staple fibers for European markets. These fibers were manufactured from recycled raw materials, in part supplied by, ironically, other European fiber producers with which Wellman International was competing. The fibers were then exported, mainly to the United Kingdom and Europe.

Expansion and Growth: 1970s–80s

During the 1970s Wellman's growth was relatively slow since its main business was tied to the inconsistent supply of waste materials picked up from major chemical companies. By 1979, however, the company had begun its steady progression toward becoming a major company with the establishment of a PET (polyethylene terephthalate) soft drink bottle recycling operation in Johnsonville. The opening of the facility came at a time when consumers were becoming much more environmentally aware, which in turn led to a steady supply of waste materials to be recycled by the company. Wellman rightly forecasted that manufacturers would soon advertise the use of recycled materials in the packaging of their products.

By developing the proprietary technology to recycle PET bottles, the company quickly became a frontrunner in the recycling industry and eventually the nation's leading recycler. Using empty soda bottles collected from states with bottle deposit laws, collection increased markedly from 1983 to 1990 when 30 states enacted laws either granting tax breaks and/or loans to postconsumer recycling programs, or had mandated separate collection of recyclable materials.

Sacks Industries, a Clark, New Jersey-based fiber broker and manufacturer of nonwovens purchased a 50 percent stake in Wellman in 1983. Operations of the two companies were subsequently merged and Tom Duff of Sacks Industries was appointed vice-president and chief operating officer. Wellman's nonwoven business grew out of two Sacks plants located in Charlotte, North Carolina, and Commerce, California. The Charlotte facility used polyester fiber for the home furnishings industry to serve as cushioning and insulation in such products as bedspreads, comforters, and furniture cushions. Production at the Commerce plant utilized green polyester fiber, made from recycled green PET soft drink bottles by the Fibers Division, to make geotextiles used for soil reinforcement and filtration in various civil engineering applications, including landfill and pond linings, and the stabilization of roads and railroads.

Two years after Wellman and Sacks Industries merged, the two companies were purchased by a group of investors and company managers in a leveraged buyout. Tom Duff became president and CEO of the newly renamed Wellman, Inc. In June 1987 the company went public when its stock began trading on the NASDAQ exchange at a price of $10.25 per share. Wellman stock was offered on the New York Stock Exchange the following year at an initial share price of $17.50.

In 1989 Wellman entered into two arrangements that would not only ensure the company of a steady supply of recyclable materials, but a market for the resulting products as well. The first agreement, with Browning-Ferris Industries (BFI), a large waste collector, allowed Wellman to buy all the household plastic the company picked up in curbside programs. The second arrangement was with Constar International Inc., one of the largest PET bottle makers in the nation. Constar bought vast amounts of used PET bottles for recycling and agreed to purchase much of Wellman's recycled plastic for use in its manufacturing.

Constar hoped to avoid complaints from environmentalists by using an estimated 25 percent recycled plastic in each of its bottles. In addition, through a 1989 joint venture Wellman and Constar (as Wellstar) began acquiring European bottle manufacturers with facilities in The Netherlands, France, and the United Kingdom. Wellstar, said to be the largest PET plastic bottle maker in Europe, sold the bottles and then bought them back for recycling.

Also in 1989 Wellman acquired Fiber Industries Inc. from Hoechst Celanese Corp. Fiber Industries was a leading manufacturer of premium polyester textile fibers sold under the brand name, Fortrel. The company became part of Wellman's Fibers Division, doubling Wellman's asset and revenue base, and positioning the company as a leading producer of polyester fiber.

Bigger and Better in 1990s

In 1990 construction of Wellman's first international PET bottle recycling plant was completed by its European subsidiary in Spijk, Netherlands, to manufacture polyester fiber. Later that year Wellman acquired New England CRInc, another move meant to facilitate its use of recyclable plastics. New England CRInc was the leader in the design, construction, and operation of advanced materials recovery facilities (MRF). The company built the first highly-mechanized MRF plant in the United States and had exclusive North American rights to a patented German recyclable sorting technology, the Bezner automated materials sorting system. New England CRInc separated and processed commingled recyclables, such as plastic, aluminum, and glass containers as well as paper collected from curbside recycling programs. By 1992 there were ten full service MRFs in operation and the company accounted for about 2 percent of Wellman's total sales.

By 1992 activities from the Fiber Industries acquisition had reached an estimated 82 percent of the company's total net sales. Wellman also had fiber producing facilities located in Fayetteville, North Carolina, and Darlington, South Carolina. Wellman also made two more acquisitions that furthered the company's manufacturing and marketing capabilities. A newly completed polyester fiber plant located in Marion was purchased, in addition to Creative Forming, Inc. (CFI), the largest user of recycled PET in the thermoforming market. CFI custom designed, manufactured, and marketed thermoformed plastic packaging products from virgin and recycled PET and other materials. The purchase of CFI enabled Wellman to enter the high growth PET packaging market, while providing another means of using the company's virgin and recycled PET materials. By the end of 1992, with net sales topping $828 million, Wellman manufactured more than a quarter of the nation's staple fiber and 13 percent of its partially-oriented yarn (POY) fibers.

By the mid-1990s Wellman aggressively continued to expand, with plans to triple its PET output and operations both domestically and abroad. One step in this direction was the 1995 purchase of Akzo Nobel, a Netherlands-based PET manufacturer; another was Wellman's $400-million plan for a new polyester production plant in Pearl River, Mississippi, with an annual capacity of over 450 million pounds of PET products and over 225 million pounds of polyester fiber. Next came a major coup: Wellman beat out DuPont for a lucrative recycling contract with Ford Motor Company in 1996, to supply the automotive giant with nylon fibers for use in Windstar minivan engine fans. As Wellman was busy with construction plans for its Mississippi plant and began supplying recycled nylon to Ford, it was hit by spiraling prices for polyester and a strike in its Ireland manufacturing facility. Despite sales over the $1

Key Dates:

1927: Hill & Nichols (later Nichols & Company) wool combing company is established.
1954: Wellman Combing Company is created, opening its first plant in South Carolina.
1964: The company begins manufacturing nylon fibers, mostly for use in carpeting.
1969: Wellman Combing Company is renamed Wellman Industries, Inc. and parent Nichols & Company becomes Wellman, Inc.
1983: Half interest in Wellman is bought by New Jersey's Sack Industries, then the companies merge.
1985: A leveraged buyout creates a new Wellman, Inc., with Thomas Duff as chief executive.
1987: Wellman goes public on the NASDAQ market.
1989: Wellman moves its stock to the New York Stock Exchange and begins several strategic joint ventures.
1990: First international recycling plant is completed in Spijk, The Netherlands.
1992: The company buys a new polyester fiber plant in Marion, South Carolina.
1995: Wellman buys Akzo Nobel of The Netherlands.
2000: Sensura fabric is introduced for use in apparel.
2002: Holofiber tests well as an ability-enhancing fabric for athletic apparel.

billion mark, Wellman faced a loss in the third quarter and was forced to refinance its debt on the new Pearl River plant.

The last year of the century brought both highs and lows for Wellman. The long-awaited Pearl River plant finally commenced operations, after several construction delays, in the second quarter. Wellman's elation was replaced by woe when electrical problems forced its Palmetto, South Carolina, PET facility to close. The effects of power outages and surges not only caused equipment damage and failure but a significant decrease in PET production—around 50 million pounds—and a third quarter loss for the company of nearly $9 million. Luckily, the Pearl River plant took up some of the manufacturing slack and allowed Wellman to meet most of its commitments. At year-end, Wellman posted net sales of $935.4 million, down from the previous year's $968 million.

Wellman in the 21st Century

While the Pearl River operation was strong with its PET recyclables, its stable fibers, used in clothing and textiles, did not fare so well. In late 2000 Wellman announced it was suspending stable fiber production at Pearl River and consolidating operations with its Palmetto plant in South Carolina. The cessation of this part of its business, however, had no affect on PET production, which continued to grow both domestically and abroad. Yet with this growth came fierce competition, and Wellman was forced to raise prices several times to keep ahead of high costs and a fluctuating market. While net sales for 2000 topped $1.1 billion and income had climbed to just shy of $63 million (up from 1999's loss of $6.1 million), Wellman was faced with several hurdles in the coming year.

A probe by the U.S. Department of Justice (DOJ) into price fixing put Wellman and most of its competitors on edge in 2001 and 2002. Wellman, as well as DuPont, KoSa, and Nan Ya Plastics, cooperated with government officials investigating pricing practices from September 1999 to January 2001. Concerned only with polyester stable fibers used in the clothing and textiles industries, it was true that Wellman and its rivals had each raised prices to offset rising manufacturing costs and raw materials. It was in Nan Ya Plastic's case, however, that the DOJ believed there was a criminal conspiracy to fix prices and consequently indicted a former manager in September 2002.

With the DOJ investigation behind it, Wellman concentrated on the future. The company had decided to exit the POY (partially-oriented yarn) business and also sold its two polyester staple plants in Fayetteville, North Carolina, and Marion, South Carolina. The Pearl River plant had operated at limited capacity for a time and its staple fiber output sat idle for much of 2001, though Wellman planned on renovating the facility for PET resin use. On the positive side, both of Wellman's business units—the Packaging Products Group and the Fibers and Recycled Products Group—had exciting new products either already in use or in the testing stages. The HC 800 series packaging resins were both innovative and well received by plastic bottle manufacturers for soda pop, juice, and water; while EcoClear, for environmentally conscious customers, continued to be a bestseller. Over in the Fibers division, Wellman's new cotton-like fabric, Sensura, was already a hit with such apparel companies as Champion, Levi Strauss, and Eastern Mountain Sports.

Another fiber innovation, called "Holofiber," also had company officials and industry insiders excited in late 2002. For use in activewear, these specially designed hollow fibers were injected with a polymer that when touching the skin allowed capillaries to relax and expand, which in turn gave athletes more strength and endurance. Though Holofiber was only in the earliest stages of testing, the results were promising. If Holofiber maintained its success in subsequent testing, Wellman could indeed revolutionize the activewear and athletic apparel markets.

Through the years, Wellman had its share of ups and downs but far more success than the reverse. By the end of 2002 the company not only had new proprietary products coming to national attention, but a stable of existing products used throughout the world for packaging and textile needs.

Principal Subsidiaries

Wellman International Limited.

Principal Operating Units

Packaging Products Group; Fibers and Recycled Products Group.

Principal Competitors

DuPont-Akra Americas (DAK Americas); The Dow Chemical Company; Eastman Chemical Company; Nan Ya Plastics Corporation.

Further Reading

"America's Fastest Growing Companies," *Fortune,* April 22, 1991, pp. 67–76.

Breskin, Ira, "Wellman Expands Its Polyester Portfolio; New Investments Target Growing PET Market," *Chemical Week,* February 1, 1995, p. 46.

Cook, James, "A Perfect LBO Candidate," *Forbes,* October 31, 1988, pp. 74–76.

Feder, Barnaby J., "Profits, and Problems, for Recycler," *New York Times,* January 8, 1991, pp. D1, D5.

The History and Operations of Wellman, Inc., Shrewsbury, N.J.: Wellman, Inc., 1993.

Kemezis, Paul, "Eastern Gulf States Build Momentum," *Chemical Week,* May 15, 1996, p. 30.

Koselka, Rita, "Casey at the Bottling Plant," *Forbes,* August 6, 1990, pp. 88–89.

Leicham, Sharon, "New Wellman Fiber Could Help Boost Endurance of Athletes," *Outdoor Retailer,* August 2002, p. 82.

Malone, Scott, "Justice Dept. Probing Polyester Price Fixing," *Women's Wear Daily,* September 17, 2002, p. 2.

"Merger to Beef Up Recycling," *Packaging,* January 1993, p. 18.

Nulty, Peter, "Recycling Becomes a Big Business," *Fortune,* August 13, 1990, pp. 81–86.

"PET Industry Reveals Its Changing Face," *Chemical Marketing Reporter,* February 1, 1993, pp. 5, 25.

"Rising Costs Prompt Polyester Price Increases," *Chemical Week,* April 17, 2002, p. 39.

"Wellman Links with Eastman for PET Expansion," *Chemical Week,* July 3, 2002, p. 9.

"Wellman Sets Bottle Resin PET Expansion," *Chemical Marketing Reporter,* January 16, 1993, p. 9.

Westervelt, Robert, "Electrical Failure Hits Wellman Profits," *Chemical Week,* September 15, 1999, p. 12.

——, "Wellman Idles Staple Fiber Unit," *Chemical Week,* December 13, 2000, p. 8.

Young, Ian, "Wellman Enters European PET Business with Akzo Deal," *Chemical Week,* June 7, 1995, p. 9.

—Dorothy Kroll
—update: Nelson Rhodes

Whitbread PLC

CityPoint
One Ropemaker Street
London EC2Y 9HX
United Kingdom
Telephone: (020) 7606-4455
Fax: (020) 7806-5444
Web site: http://www.whitbread.co.uk

Public Company
Incorporated: 1889 as Whitbread and Company PLC
Employees: 61,470
Sales: £1.82 billion ($2.86 billion) (2002)
Stock Exchanges: London
Ticker Symbol: WTB
NAIC: 722110 Full-Service Restaurants; 722213 Snack
     and Nonalcoholic Beverage Bars; 721110 Hotels
     (Except Casino Hotels) and Motels; 713940 Fitness
     and Recreational Sports Centers

Whitbread PLC is one of the leading players in the U.K. leisure industry, concentrating in the early 21st century on restaurants and coffee shops, hotels, and health and fitness clubs. Whitbread's roots, however, were in brewing. Founded as a single brewery, the company grew to become one of the most prestigious of London's older breweries, with its history closely paralleling that of the Whitbread family, which retained continuous control of the company from 1742 to 1992. Whitbread began to diversify in the early 1960s. Its long involvement in the pub industry led to a deeper delving into the restaurant sector, with a key development being the 1974 launch of the Beefeater casual dining chain. The company later began opening outlets of two U.S.-based chains—Pizza Hut and T.G.I. Friday's—in the United Kingdom and acquired the Costa Coffee chain in 1995. During this same period, Whitbread developed into the number two hotelier in the United Kingdom by creating the Travel Inn chain in 1987 and gaining the U.K. rights to the Marriott brand in 1995. The company entered the health and fitness sector in 1995 through the purchase of the David Lloyd Leisure brand. In the early 21st century, Whitbread

has shifted its focus to these newer areas of operations, breaking with its history by selling off first its brewery operations in 2000 and then its pubs in 2001.

Samuel Whitbread Established Brewery in 1742

Samuel Whitbread, at the age of 14, was sent to London by his mother in 1734 to become an apprentice to a brewer. Whitbread, raised as a Puritan, proved to be an extremely hard worker. In 1742, eight years after coming to London, he established his own brewery with a £2,000 inheritance and additional underwriting from John Howard, the renowned prison reformer. As the brewery became successful, Howard's investment became more lucrative—it even led to a reciprocation of financial support by Whitbread for Howard's reform movement.

By 1750 Whitbread had acquired an additional brewery located on Chiswell Street. At this time there were more than 50 breweries in London, but, despite intense competition, the Whitbread brewery expanded rapidly. By 1760 its annual output had reached 64,000 barrels, second only to Calvert and Company.

Whitbread was enthusiastic about new brewing methods. He employed several well-known engineers who helped to improve the quality and increase the production volume of the company's stout and porter (a sweeter, weaker stout).

The Whitbread family had a long history of involvement in English politics. Samuel Whitbread's forefathers fought with Oliver Cromwell's Roundheads during the English Civil War and later developed a connection with the Bedfordshire preacher and author John Bunyan. Samuel Whitbread himself was elected to Parliament in 1768 as a representative of Bedford. His son, Samuel II, succeeded him in Parliament in 1790, and Whitbread descendants served in Parliament almost continuously until 1910.

Samuel Whitbread died in 1796. Samuel II assumed control of the brewery, but was so preoccupied with Parliament that by 1799 he was compelled to take on a partner. The partnership, however, was short-lived. The brewery entered into seven more partnerships over the next 70 years, only two of which were successful. Most notably, Whitbread's 1812 partnership with

Company Perspectives:

Our business is focused on growth sectors of the UK leisure market—lodging, eating out and active leisure.

Our priorities, on behalf of our shareholders, are to grow our business and to achieve annual improvements in the return on their capital.

We are doing this by:

Growing the profitability, scale and market share of our leading brands; Seeking new brands that have the potential to reach significant scale; Managing our business so that shareholder value is added by each of our activities; Ensuring that each of our brands is a leader in its field for customer service; Becoming the employer of choice in the UK leisure industry; Working to meet our responsibilities to the wider stakeholders in our business, including commercial partners and the communities in which our brands operate.

the Martineau and Bland brewery resulted in a full merger of the two companies' brewing operations. The Martineau and Bland facility at Lambeth, however, was later closed down and its equipment was moved to Chiswell Street.

During the early 19th century the bulk of Whitbread's business was conducted with "free houses," public houses—or pubs—neither owned by, nor bound to sell only the products of one brewer. These pubs numbered several hundred, and their business remained fairly stable. But when the Drury Lane Theatre burned down in 1809, Samuel II saw an opportunity to profit from its renovation. He led a committee to restore the theater, invested heavily in the project, and persuaded several friends to join him. The venture yielded only a small dividend when the theater was reopened, and cost Whitbread the friendship of many of his fellow investors. In Parliament, Whitbread opposed the resumption of war with Napoleon, a position that made him even more unpopular. In July 1815, shortly after the battle of Waterloo, Samuel Whitbread II committed suicide.

Whitbread's sons, William Henry and Samuel Charles, inherited their father's interest in the brewery. Whitbread family control, however, had been greatly diminished by the company's nine partners. It was not until 1819 that the Whitbread brothers were able to reestablish direct family control over the operation. The number of partners was reduced, and the brewery remained under Whitbread control for many years.

In 1834 Whitbread introduced ale to its product line. The ale gained immediate popularity and resulted in a substantial increase in turnover for the brewery. Whitbread expanded even more dramatically after 1869, when the family established its last partnership. One year earlier, the company had begun producing bottled beer.

Going Public in 1889

During the 1880s, a sudden and significant decline in demand for beer caused many "free houses" to sell their leases to breweries (and thereby become "tied houses"). Breweries such as Whitbread, which had established numerous tied houses, were forced to extend loans to public house operators so that they could remain in business. The capital required to purchase free house leases and to extend loans could be satisfied only by the public through share flotations. Therefore, when Whitbread's partnership agreement expired in 1889, the partners decided to transform the brewery into a public company.

An attempt by brewers to raise the profitability of tied houses by reducing beer prices backfired; their tenants competed on price and went even further into debt. A recession in 1900 forced Whitbread to write down the value of its tied house properties—a move that may have saved the company. Demand for beer recovered steadily and permitted Whitbread to increase its production every year from 1899 to 1912. Accordingly, the value of tied houses recovered as they became profitable. Just prior to World War I, however, the government raised its license duty on tied houses, rendering many of them financial liabilities. Whitbread stopped buying tied houses, and instead concentrated on expanding its bottled beer trade.

Although Whitbread weathered this difficult period virtually intact, many competitors were forced to close. Whitbread's ability to survive was attributed to three factors: the maintenance of a harmonious relationship between the brewer and the publican (public house operator), sustaining a good public image of the brand, and keeping influence in government.

Francis Pelham Whitbread, the director of the brewery at the time, devoted his energies to maintaining a stable atmosphere for profitable brewing; as chairman of the Brewers Society, he promoted better brewer-vendor relations. Later, as chairman and treasurer of the politically active National Trade Defence Association, he lobbied against the temperance movement in Parliament. After World War I he played a major role in the formation of policies within the brewing industry and was particularly opposed to the proliferation of tied houses.

During the interwar period Whitbread took over the Jude Hanbury brewery. As its situation with vendors remained unsettled, Whitbread concentrated further on the expansion of bottled beer sales. Whitbread beer had become available throughout the world. Francis Whitbread, however, became increasingly divorced from the everyday operation of the brewery; his position as a spokesman for the industry and his dedication to philanthropic activities occupied most of his time.

On December 29, 1940, German incendiary bombs landed in five separate areas of the brewery. Each of the fires was put out by the company fire brigade, with the exception of a malt fire, which, like burning coal dust, is very difficult to extinguish. It was finally doused a week later. Damage to the brewery and the surrounding area was great. Nevertheless, Whitbread resumed brewing almost immediately.

Francis Pelham Whitbread died in 1941. His leadership of the brewery was highly conservative—especially when compared with the policies of his successors. Francis was in many ways a popular figurehead for the company. Much of the actual burden of management fell on the shoulders of Samuel Howard Whitbread, who served with the company from 1915 until his death in 1944. William Henry Whitbread assumed leadership of the company that year but was forced to postpone his plans for the rehabilitation of the brewery until after the war.

Key Dates:

1742: After working as an apprentice, Samuel Whitbread establishes his own brewery in London.
1750: Whitbread opens a second brewery on Chiswell Street.
1760: The annual output of the company's stout and porter has reached 64,000 barrels.
1834: Ale is added to the product line.
1868: Production of bottled beer begins.
1889: The company goes public.
1955: Whitbread begins expanding through the acquisition of smaller brewers, eventually by 1971 taking over 26 regional breweries.
1968: The company gains the right to brew Heineken lager under license.
1974: The first Beefeater restaurant opens.
1982: Whitbread enters a joint venture with PepsiCo, Inc. to open Pizza Hut restaurants in the United Kingdom.
1985: The company signs a franchise agreement to develop U.K.-based outlets of the T.G.I. Friday's casual dining chain.
1987: The Travel Inn budget hotel chain is launched.

1989: Boddingtons brewery is acquired; a decision to focus principally on hotels and restaurants, while retaining brewery operations, leads to the sale of the wine and spirits division to Allied-Lyons.
1990: The Monopolies and Mergers Commission issues an order related to its investigation of the U.K. system of tied houses, leading Whitbread to sell 1,300 of its pubs and lease another 1,000 by 1992.
1995: Whitbread purchases 16 Marriott hotels and signs an agreement with Marriott International to develop the brand in the United Kingdom; the company acquires the David Lloyd Leisure chain of sports and fitness clubs; the Costa Coffee chain of coffee shops is acquired.
1999: Whitbread's bid to acquire the U.K. retailing operations of Allied Domecq—including 3,500 pubs—fails.
2000: Swallow Group, operator of 36 upscale hotels, is acquired; Whitbread Beer Company is sold to Interbrew S.A.
2001: The company's pub operations are sold to Morgan Grenfell Private Equity.

Wave of Amalgamations in the Postwar Era

Although the war ended less than a year later, the British economy continued to suffer from aftereffects for many years. Conditions were so grave that Whitbread was unable to begin its modernization until 1950. At that time Whitbread undertook a sweeping rationalization program, which included the concentration of human resources and retooling of machinery.

Other smaller breweries were in less stable condition, and many were threatened with bankruptcy. Whitbread, however, offered an amalgamation scheme to these breweries. Under this formula, called the "Whitbread Umbrella," failing breweries agreed to coordinate their operations and distribution networks with Whitbread. Many of these arrangements resulted in Whitbread's eventual acquisition of the smaller brewers. In the period from 1955 to 1971 Whitbread took over 26 breweries and expanded its number of tied houses from less than 100 to 10,000.

Some of the breweries acquired by Whitbread were large well-established companies. Beginning with the Dutton brewery in 1964, Whitbread took over Rhymney in 1966, Threlfall and Fremlin in 1967, Strong in 1968, and Brickwood in 1971. These additions to Whitbread also gave the company greater geographical coverage—Threlfall's was located in the northwest port of Liverpool, and Brickwood's was in Portsmouth, on the south coast.

Streamlining and Beginnings of Diversification in the 1970s

The 1970s were characterized as a period of streamlining for Whitbread and also saw the beginning of a move toward diversification. The company disposed of many of its marginally profitable or outdated operations—even the Chiswell Street

brewery was closed in 1976. Still, Whitbread suffered from the aftereffects of a serious economic recession during the mid-1970s, and the company came close to bankruptcy. A gradual economic recovery led to improvements in the market that greatly strengthened Whitbread's financial position.

Meanwhile, however, as popular demand shifted from ale to lager, total beer consumption began to fall. Whitbread started to deemphasize certain brewing assets and began to diversify outside brewing. The company had already gained a chain of wine retail outlets when it acquired Thresher in 1962. Along the way, Whitbread built up a wines and spirits division that included Beefeater Gin, Long John Scotch Whiskey, and Cutty Sark Scotch Whiskey. Food was added in 1974 with the opening of the first Beefeater Restaurant & Pub, which was in the casual dining sector, and with the 1979 debut of Brewers Fayre, a chain of pub food outlets.

Notwithstanding these nonbeer ventures, Whitbread did not abandon the brewing industry but in fact became more active in licensing non-U.K. brewer's brands. In 1968 the company gained the right to brew Heineken lager under a license agreement and in 1976 the Stella Artois brand began to be brewed by Whitbread under a similar agreement. The Belgian beer soon became the best-selling premium lager in the United Kingdom.

Further Diversification in the 1980s

Whitbread continued to diversify in the 1980s under the guidance of new leadership. William Henry Whitbread had given up day-to-day control of the company during the 1970s, whereupon Samuel Whitbread (a fifth-generation descendant of the company's founder) became chief executive and, eventually, chairman in 1984. He initially sought to bolster his company's restaurant holdings. In 1982 a 50–50 joint venture with

PepsiCo Inc. began, which went on to build a significant chain of Pizza Hut restaurants in the United Kingdom. T.G.I. Friday's joined the company's restaurant fold three years later, when Whitbread signed a franchise agreement to develop U.K.-based outlets of this chain, also in the casual dining sector. By the 1995–96 fiscal year, beer operations accounted for only 43 percent of profits, with wine and spirits accounting for 20 percent and retail operations 37 percent.

Next, Whitbread entered the hotel industry. The year 1987 marked the debut of the Travel Inn chain, budget hotels that were usually located next to another Whitbread property such as a Brewers Fayre, Beefeater, or T.G.I. Friday's. Whitbread's diversification program gained further momentum in 1989 when management announced that the company would focus on the leisure retailing industries in general, with a particular emphasis on areas, such as travel and eating out, that were projected to grow rapidly through the end of the century. Brewing was still to be included in the mix but would continue to account for smaller percentages of company profits, notwithstanding the 1989 acquisition of Boddingtons brewery. Another sector to be retained was the Thresher unit, which specialized in retail outlets for alcoholic beverages; Thresher was subsequently bolstered with the opening of the first Wine Rack in 1989 and the 1991 acquisition of Bottoms Up, a chain of wine superstores. On the divestment side was the company's wine and spirits division, which included a distiller of such brands as Beefeater Gin and a U.S.-based importer and distributor of wines and spirits. The division was sold late in 1989 to Allied-Lyons PLC for £545 million ($880.2 million).

Compliance with MMC Orders Dominating the Early 1990s

The year 1989 was also important because it was the year that Whitbread began to plan for its compliance with new rules on tied houses set down by the British government's Monopolies and Mergers Commission (MMC). After an investigation into the system of tied houses that had been created from the numerous mergers in the brewing industry in the 1960s and 1970s, in early 1990 the MMC ordered brewers with more than 2,000 pubs to sell or lease half of the number greater than 2,000, meaning that Whitbread would have to do so with about 2,300 pubs. The MMC gave brewers a November 1, 1992, deadline to comply. Meanwhile, Peter Jarvis, who had joined Whitbread from Unilever in 1976, took over as chief executive in 1990. Later, in August 1992, Michael Angus, chairman of The Boots Company PLC and former chairman of Unilever, became chairman of Whitbread as well, taking over from Samuel Whitbread, who remained on the board as a nonexecutive director. This management team—noticeably minus a Whitbread for the first time in the company's 250-year history—led the company through the MMC compliance process.

Following the issue of the MMC orders, Whitbread first pulled its pubs out of its brewery division. It then sold about 1,300 of them by the deadline, and leased the remaining 1,000 on a short-term basis. At the time the United Kingdom had too many pubs, and property values had fallen sharply since the boom years of the early 1980s. Consequently, Whitbread's profits took a large hit from the forced sales and squeezed its plans to expand its retail activities. A plan for Whitbread to take the Pizza Hut chain into

continental Europe fell apart when the company could not afford to commit the initial £100 million needed.

A further consequence of the MMC orders was that Whitbread had to untangle itself from its complicated system of cross-holdings in regional brewers—held through Whitbread Investment Company—that it had developed during its acquisition spree. In November 1993 Whitbread acquired Whitbread Investment Company, then in March 1994 sold nearly all its regional brewery stakes, raising about £300 million in the process.

Renewed Spending Spree in the Mid-1990s

Whitbread thus emerged from the MMC orders with some cash to spend on its retailing sectors. A new wave of activity began in 1994 with the acquisition of the Maredo steak restaurant chain located in Germany. In August 1995 Whitbread paid Canada-based Scott's Hospitality Inc. £180 million ($288.2 million) for 16 Marriott hotels and also signed an agreement with Marriott International, Inc. to develop the brand name in the United Kingdom. That same month, the company acquired David Lloyd Leisure (DLL) for £200.7 million ($321.3 million). DLL, named after tennis champion David Lloyd, operated 20 private sports and fitness clubs as well as 24 nursery schools through its Gatehouse Nursery Services subsidiary. In March 1997 DLL bought Curzon Management Associates and its five London gym sites.

Whitbread's restaurant holdings received further boosts in 1995 and 1996. The Costa Coffee chain of coffee shops was acquired in October 1995. In July of the following year, £133 million ($208.8 million) was spent to purchase Pelican Group and its 110 restaurants spread throughout several chains, most notably Café Rouge, a French bistro/café; Dôme, a bar/café emphasizing beer, drinks, coffee, and café-style food; and Mamma Amalfi, a family-style Italian restaurant. In November 1996 Whitbread bought the BrightReasons group for £46 million ($72.2 million). The key chain acquired therein was Bella Pasta, with 55 outlets, while the Pizza Piazza chain was subsequently sold to Passion For Food for £11.25 million and 102 Pizzaland restaurants were converted to Pizza Huts and other Whitbread restaurant brands. The acquired pizza chains were jettisoned to avoid a conflict with Pizza Hut.

In the summer of 1997 Jarvis stepped down as chief executive and was replaced by David Thomas, who had joined Whitbread in 1984 as a regional director of the Inns division. Thomas took over a company that had seen sales and profits rise throughout the 1990s, thanks in large part to Whitbread's increasing emphasis on nonbeer activities.

Failed Allied Domecq Bid in the Late 1990s

By fiscal 1998–99 the evolution of the company away from its roots was increasingly obvious—less than 12 percent of operating profits were generated by the brewing operations that year. The continuing lackluster beer sales led Whitbread to close one of its breweries and to sell another one, leaving it with three breweries capable of producing more than one million barrels a year. Also during the year, the company sold off 253 of its leased pubs, 40 Beefeater outlets, and the Gatehouse Nursery unit. In August 1998 Whitbread merged its wine and alcohol retail outlets—Thresher, Wine Rack, and others—with those of Allied Domecq PLC, forming a 50–50 joint venture called First Quench Retailing Ltd.

At this point, Whitbread's core operations in brewing and pubs were in mature industries with little prospect for future growth. Thomas saw one opportunity in this area—consolidating the group's collection of pubs with those of another company, thereby gaining the cost savings of economies of scale. When Allied Domecq placed its U.K. retailing operations up for sale, including 3,500 pubs and its stakes in soft drink maker Britvic and in First Quench, Thomas aggressively pursued a deal. In May 1999, after lengthy negotiations that eventually turned hostile, Whitbread and Allied reached an agreement on a £2.36 billion offer, later raised to £2.85 billion under pressure from a rival bid by Punch Taverns. In July 1999, the Office of Fair Trading (OFT) referred Whitbread's bid to the Competition Commission, a development that killed the bid because it had been made conditional on OFT approval. Whitbread declined to make an unconditional offer, ending its bid for control of the Allied properties, which were subsequently purchased by Punch Taverns. Whitbread also shelved a planned spinoff of its beer unit, the Whitbread Beer Company. Had its takeover of the Allied pubs gone through, Whitbread would have had to divest its brewery operations to comply with the 1989 beer orders of the MMC.

New Era in the New Millennium, Minus Beer and Pubs

In the wake of this failed bid, Whitbread embarked on a remarkable two-year period of transformation that launched the company into a new era. The company first completed two smaller but telling acquisitions, indicating the future direction. In September 1999 Whitbread spent £78.3 million for Racquets & Healthtrack Group Ltd., cementing its position as the largest operator of health and fitness clubs in the United Kingdom. The six Racquets & Healthtrack clubs were later rebranded under the David Lloyd Leisure name, increasing the size of that chain to 47 outlets and 170,000 members. Then in January 2000 Whitbread took over Swallow Group plc in a £730 million deal. Swallow operated 36 upscale hotels in the United Kingdom; under Whitbread they would be converted to the Marriott brand, nearly doubling the size of that chain from 5,700 rooms to almost 11,000.

Shortly after completion of the Swallow buy, Whitbread made the historic decision to sell off both its brewing and pubs operations. Whitbread Beer Company was the first to go and was purchased by Interbrew S.A. in May 2000 for £400 million. Then in May 2001 the pubs were offloaded to Morgan Grenfell Private Equity, a unit of Deutsche Bank AG, for £1.63 billion. The sale did not include the so-called food-led pubs, or pub restaurants, namely, Brewers Fayre, Brewsters, and Beefeater. Part of the proceeds from the sale of the pubs—£1.1 billion worth—was returned to shareholders at the equivalent of £2.30 per share; most of the remainder went to reduce debt. In between these two transactions, in October 2000, Whitbread also disposed of its 50 percent interest in First Quench. By mid-2001, then, a new Whitbread had emerged, focused on upscale and budget hotels, restaurants, and health and fitness clubs. While this transformation was taking place, a new chairman came on board in June

2000; succeeding Angus was John Banham, who was already serving as chairman of two other U.K. firms: aggregates producer Tarmac plc and retailer Kingfisher plc.

In the months that followed the sale of the pub estate, Whitbread began repositioning its remaining operations to secure the company's future. In August 2001 Whitbread announced that it would spend more than £500 million over the following five years to double the number of David Lloyd Leisure outlets to 100. At the same time the Curzon health club chain, which served the budget end of the market, was slated for divestment to further the company's focus on the upscale market served by the David Lloyd clubs. Curzon was subsequently sold in 2002. The restaurant portfolio was also in need of an overhaul, as several of the Whitbread chains were not performing satisfactorily. In May 2002 Whitbread sold its Pelican and BrightReasons restaurant groups to Tragus Holdings Limited for £25 million in a management-led buyout. Included in the deal were 153 restaurants under the Café Rouge, Bella Pasta, Mamma Amalfi, Abbaye, Leadenhall Wine Bar, and Oriel names. This left Whitbread with its Pizza Hut, Costa Coffee, and T.G.I. Friday's restaurants, in addition to the Brewers Fayre, Brewsters, and Beefeater pub restaurants.

The restaurant sell-off completed, in large part, Whitbread's disposal program, leading the company to focus on organically growing the remaining core. In addition to the planned expansion of David Lloyd Leisure, there were plans to increase the number of Costa Coffee outlets from 300 to 500 by 2004. Although acquisitions could not be entirely ruled out, the company's rather spotty track record in that area made any major deals less likely, particularly given the more uncertain economic conditions of the early 21st century. Following the bold, transformative transactions that severed Whitbread from its long history, it would not be unexpected for the company to settle in for a healing period marked by more routine activities.

Principal Subsidiaries

Whitbread Group PLC; Whitbread Restaurants Holdings GmbH (Germany); Country Club Hotels Ltd.; David Lloyd Leisure Ltd.; Swallow Group Ltd.; Swallow Hotels Ltd.; Whitbread Hotels Ltd.

Principal Competitors

Hilton Group plc; De Vere Group PLC; Six Continents Hotels, Inc.; City Centre Restaurants plc; Thistle Hotels Plc; PizzaExpress PLC; Cannons Group Ltd.

Further Reading

Barrow, Martin, "Brewer to Spend £300m on Retail to Offset Decline," *Times* (London), November 2, 1995, p. 27.
Britton, Noelle, "Whitbread Brews Up a Potent Mix," *Marketing,* December 4, 1986, pp. 26+.
Buckley, Neil, "A New Brew for Whitbread," *Financial Times,* August 12, 1995, p. WFT5.
"A Conundrum That Could Have Whitbread Crying in Its Beer," *Times* (London), May 13, 1992, p. 21.
Craig, Malcolm, "What's Next for Whitbread?," *Leisure and Hospitality Business,* April 5, 2001, p. 10.

Daneshkhu, Scheherazade, "Whitbread to Sell Pelican Restaurants," *Financial Times,* October 15, 2001, p. 30.

Gwyther, Matthew, "Whitbread on the Wagon," *Management Today,* September 2001, pp. 74–75, 77, 79.

Holstein, William J., and Richard A. Melcher, "Whitbread Wakes Up with a Headache," *Business Week,* April 29, 1985, pp. 44 +.

Jones, Adam, "Whitbread Exits Bistros and Pasta Cafes," *Financial Times,* June 1, 2002, p. 12.

"Losing a Beer Belly," *Economist,* August 12, 1995, p. 54.

McLaughlin, John, "Too Close for Comfort: French Marriage a Failure for Whitbread and Pizza Hut," *Restaurant Business,* September 1, 1992, p. 30.

Murray, Alasdair, "Whitbread to Seek Links with Regionals," *Times* (London), August 12, 1996, p. 40.

Parker-Pope, Tara, "Whitbread PLC Expands into Leisure As Traditional Beer Market Contracts," *Wall Street Journal,* August 9, 1995, p. A6.

Ritchie, Berry, *An Uncommon Brewer: The Story of Whitbread, 1742– 1992,* London: James and James, 1992.

Saigol, Lina, "Whitbread Returns £1.1bn to Shareholders," *Financial Times,* March 21, 2001, p. 26.

Saigol, Lina, and John Thornhill, "Future Whitbread Butterfly Emerges from Its Chrysalis," *Financial Times,* October 20, 2000, p. 26.

Simms, Jane, "Doubting Thomas," *Director,* September 2001, pp. 60–64.

Walsh, Dominic, "Fewer Doubts About Thomas," *Leisure and Hospitality Business,* January 10, 2002, p. 8.

Willman, John, "All Eyes Focus on Whitbread's Plans to Rebuild Its Life," *Financial Times,* October 22, 1999, p. 28.

Yates, Andrew, "They're Not Only Here for the Beer," *Independent* (London), May 19, 1999, p. BR3.

—update: David E. Salamie

Wincanton plc

Cale House
Station Road
Wincanton, Somerset BA9 9AD
United Kingdom
Telephone: (+44) 1963-828-282
Fax: (+44) 1963-828-288
Web site: http://www.wincanton.co.uk

Public Company
Incorporated: 2001
Employees: 16,632
Sales: £745 million ($1.06 billion) (2002)
Stock Exchanges: London
Ticker Symbol: WIN
NAIC: 541614 Process, Physical Distribution, and
    Logistics Consulting Services; 488999 All Other
    Support Activities for Transportation

Wincanton plc is one of the United Kingdom's leading logistics companies focused on three core markets: warehousing, fleet management, and supply chain systems. The company's warehousing operations consist of 52 automated and nonautomated chilled and ambient temperature warehouses across the United Kingdom, ranging from 1,500 square meters to 30,000 square meters in size; about half of these warehouses are temperature-controlled facilities, representing nearly 250,000 square meters in the company's total operating capacity of nearly 800,000 square meters. The company's Fleet Management operation oversees a fleet of nearly 4,000 tractors and 5,000 trailers, about 40 percent of which are directly owned by Wincanton. The company, which had long been a milk carrier for the Milk Marketing Board and others, now offers temperature-controlled, fluid, bulk, and dry freight distribution services for customers ranging from Air Products and BP Castrol, to Dairy Crest, Heinz, and Texaco, and many of the United Kingdom's major grocery retail groups. The company's Supply Chain Systems operation offers IT and related services for fleet optimization, warehouse management systems, customer-systems interfaces, and other logistics and warehousing systems.

Wincanton was part of Unigate, renamed Uniq in 2000, before being demerged as an independent, publicly listed company in 2001. Wincanton is headed by Chairman Victor W. Benjamin and, since October 2002, CEO Paul Bateman, formerly of the Tesco supermarket group. Bateman's appointment was seen by many as a signal that Wincanton intends to extend its U.K.-centric operations onto the European mainland.

Unigate Offshoot in the 1920s

Named for its location in the town of Wincanton, well known for its racetrack, Wincanton traces its origins back to the early years of food distribution conglomerate Unigate Plc. When that company, which changed its name to Uniq in 2000 after shedding its dairy business, decided to separate its distribution and logistics operations into two separate, publicly listed entities, Wincanton plc was launched as an independent company with a listing on the London Stock Exchange. Yet Wincanton had long since established a name for itself as one of the United Kingdom's leading logistics companies.

Unigate started operations in the 1880s when brothers Charles and Leonard Gates took over their father's store in Guildford, Surrey, which was originally a grocery store, with strong liquor and beer sales. The Gates brothers added coffee and tea sales before deciding to exit liquor sales altogether—going so far as to pour their existing stock into the street. Instead, the Gates brothers decided to go into the dairy business, adding a milk separator and adopting the name West Surrey Dairy in 1885. That company grew into West Surrey Central Dairy Company, with creameries located throughout England and Ireland by the turn of the century.

Distribution operations—carrying raw milk from the farms to the company's dairies, and from the dairies to its customers—quickly became a part of the company's business. West Surrey began adding other products, such as powdered milk, which led to the creation of its Cow & Gate brand in 1908. After going public in 1917, the company changed its name to Cow & Gate Co. in 1929.

By then, the company's distribution operations had grown to a sufficient scale to create a dedicated distribution subsidiary,

Company Perspectives:

Vision: To be recognised by customers, employees and investors as "best in class," the premier supply chain solutions company for customers, the employer of choice for top industry professionals, the sector preference for investors.

Values: Our core values are: Build and maintain close harmony with our CUSTOMERS. Treat every EMPLOYEE with care, respect and integrity. Recruit the best PEOPLE and develop them to their full potential. Harness the flair of the INDIVIDUAL. Ensure that TEAMWORK thrives. Minimise operational effects upon the COMMUNITY and the environment.

which was launched in Sherborne, Dorset, in 1925. In 1927, that business was moved to one of Cow & Gate's locations in Wincanton, where it became known as Wincanton Transport & Engineering. Wincanton's early mandate was to provide maintenance services for Cow & Gate's dairy operations and its growing distribution fleet. Cow & Gate's continued expansion, especially as the company became a leading producer of infant formulas, led Wincanton to expand its operations to include managing the company's warehouses as well.

The Logistics of Growth in the 1970s

Cow & Gate merged with United Dairies, a leading producer of dairy products in the United Kingdom, to form Unigate Ltd. in 1959. Under Unigate, the Wincanton subsidiary saw its status grow, as it grew into a full-fledged engineering and transportation business responsible not only for supporting Unigate's diversifying operations, but also for developing its own growth outside of Unigate. A major development came with Wincanton's own diversification, as it added a fleet of tanker trucks and began transporting milk for the government-controlled Milk Marketing Board. Those operations led the company into other areas of liquids transport, including fuel transportation. Meanwhile, Unigate's diversification into the retail sector, as it built up a number of retail brands, including the Kibby's supermarket chain, a network of Uni-Wash laundromats, and a chain of clothing shops, boosted Wincanton's own warehousing and distribution operations.

Wincanton began to develop into a full-fledged logistics group in the 1970s, particularly with the addition of temperature-controlled warehousing operations during that decade. By then Wincanton had been split into its two components, Wincanton Engineering Ltd. and Wincanton Transport Ltd. The latter, which took over the distribution fleet, began providing temperature-controlled warehousing for a variety of third-party manufacturers and distribution groups. This activity became one of Wincanton's core specialties, as it developed its expertise in the design and construction of warehouses, the creation of automated warehouse systems, and warehouse management. Wincanton also developed competence in temperature-controlled distribution, forming its Wincanton Chilled Distribution division.

Unigate, which had been developing its own diversified range of businesses—including the Casa Bonita chain of Mexi-

can restaurants in the United States, and poultry processing activities through Turner's Turkeys and JP Wood—contributed to Wincanton's growth through a series of acquisitions in the mid-1980s. In 1985, the company tacked on Arlington Motor Holdings, bought for £10.5 million, and added Colchester Car Auctions the following year, as Wincanton built up the fleet management side of its expanding logistics business.

Unigate added Job's Fast Food Distribution in 1987. In 1988, the company paid £10 million to acquire four new companies—Commercial & Trailer, which specialized in tractor-trailer sales; North Shropshire Motor Auctions; Rydale Truck & Coach; and Southern Bros—enabling Wincanton to increase its purchasing power. By the beginning of the 1990s, Wincanton had positioned itself as one of the United Kingdom's leading fleet management groups.

Independence in the 21st Century

Wincanton boosted its warehousing operations with the acquisition of J. Whittam Ltd. in 1992. Unigate, meanwhile, had begun a major restructuring program—including the sale of the company's liquid milk processing operations—in an effort to concentrate its operations on a more narrowly focused range of activities. As part of that restructuring, which was to continue throughout much of the decade, Wincanton absorbed the Unigate Chilled Distribution division, which included its own warehousing and retail distribution operations, in 1992. The merger doubled Wincanton's size and resulted in the formation of the newly named subsidiary, Wincanton Distribution Services.

By then, the heavily fragmented U.K. logistics sector was undergoing its first consolidation spree, as the British recession deepened, and as the country's supermarket and other retail groups were themselves consolidating their sectors. Wincanton joined the consolidation drive in 1993 when it paid £54 million to acquire a smaller competitor, Glass Glover Plc. That company, based in Rotherham, Doncaster, held a warehouse and distribution portfolio similar to that of Wincanton, with operations supporting a number of the United Kingdom's major supermarket groups. Glass Glover, which had been taken private in a management buyout in 1988 and had been preparing to relist in the early 1990s, filled out Wincanton's geographic spread with complementary operations focused primarily on the North of England and Scotland. The purchase also made Wincanton the United Kingdom's leading provider of distribution services in the supermarket sector.

Wincanton took another step forward in 1994 when it began construction of its first third-party automated warehouse, tapping in to the growing trend for manufacturers to outsource their logistics operations. Wincanton's expertise enabled it to become one of the United Kingdom's leading providers of automated warehousing and related supply chain services, with clients including St. Ivel, Britvic, GlaxoSmithKline, Littlewoods, Nestlé, Mars, and Heinz.

Wincanton continued its growth in 1995, adding the Fern Tankers group to boost its liquids distribution operations. That same year, the company attempted to diversify its business, buying the Guard Defence Security Services group. Yet the continuing consolidation of both the logistics and security

Key Dates:

1882: Gates brothers found the predecessor to Unigate and the company enters the dairy processing industry.

1925: The growth of the dairy distribution business leads to creation of a dedicated dairy plant and fleet maintenance and management division, Wincanton Transport & Engineering.

1950s: Wincanton begins milk distribution operations for the Milk Marketing Board.

1970s: Wincanton splits into two divisions, Wincanton Engineering and Wincanton Transport, and the latter forms the basis of the future Wincanton group.

1986: The company acquires Colchester Car Auctions.

1988: The company acquires Commercial & Trailer, North Shropshire Motor Auctions, Rydale Truck & Coach, and Southern Bros.

1992: The company acquires J. Whittam Ltd.; Wincanton merges with Unigate Chilled Distribution, name changes to Wincanton Distribution Services.

1993: The company acquires Glass Glover Plc for £54 million.

1994: The company begins construction of its first automated warehouse.

1995: The company changes its name to Wincanton Logistics and acquires Fern Tankers.

1998: The company acquires Rokold European Transport Ltd.

2000: Unigate sells off its dairy business and is renamed as Uniq Plc.

2001: Wincanton "demerges" from Uniq as a separate, publicly listed company, Wincanton plc.

2002: Wincanton wins a contract to supply most of Total's fuel tanker transportation in the United Kingdom.

services markets led Unigate to shed Guard Defence just two years later. Nonetheless, in 1995 Wincanton changed its name to emphasize its transformation into a full-fledged logistics group, becoming Wincanton Logistics Ltd.

Unigate, which was in the process of shedding much of its dairy operations, had begun an aggressive acquisition and diversification drive in the late 1990s. Wincanton benefited from Unigate's expansion drive with the addition of chilled foods distribution specialist Rokold European Transport Ltd. in 1998.

The sell-off of the rest of Unigate's dairy operations to Dairy Crest in 2000 set the stage for Wincanton's independence. Following the sale, Unigate changed its name to Uniq—maintaining the "uni" of its former name and adding a "q" for "quality"—and regrouped around two core divisions, Uniq and Wincanton. By the end of that year, Uniq acknowledged

that it intended to demerge its operations, unveiling Wincanton as a separate company.

The demerger took place in 2001, when Wincanton became Wincanton plc, and placed its shares under its own name on the London Stock Exchange. The move offered the perspective of still greater growth for Wincanton—for years the company's reputation had suffered from its position as "just" a part of Unigate. Now under its own name, Wincanton was able to assert its position as one of the United Kingdom's leading supply chain management companies.

The company quickly signed contracts with such major clients as Safeway, Comet, Somerfield, BP, and B&Q, and extended into Ireland with a contract with Superquinn, by mid-2001. The company also was enjoying the widening trend toward outsourcing logistics operations among the United Kingdom's major retail and manufacturing groups. Wincanton's success continued into the following year, as it won the distribution contract for the newly formed First Milk dairy cooperative in August 2002 and, in October 2002, became the primary fuel distributor for Total's U.K. service station operations. Wincanton had a strategic aim to expand onto the European continent, as the trend toward outsourcing there gained momentum. The company's international interests were confirmed by the appointment of former Tesco executive Paul Bateman, who played a role in Tesco's own international expansion drive in the 1990s, as company CEO. Wincanton, with more than 75 years in the business, was poised to expand its operation in an effort to become one of Europe's leading logistics companies.

Principal Subsidiaries

Wincanton Holdings Limited; Wincanton Group Limited; Wincanton Ireland Limited (Republic of Ireland); UDS Properties Limited.

Principal Competitors

Exel Plc; Tibbett and Britten Group PLC; Securicor PLC; TNT UK Ltd.; TDG PLC; GEO Logistics Ltd.; Kuehne and Nagel UK Ltd.; Allport Ltd.

Further Reading

"Delivering Excellence," *Grocer,* June 23, 2001, p. S18.

"Good Progress for Wincanton," *Evening Mail,* June 6, 2002, p. 33.

Gough, Helen, "Wincanton Goes It Alone," *Dairy Industries International,* September 2001, p. 31.

Hailey, Roger, "Tesco's Bateman Takes Over at Wincanton," *Europe Intelligence Wire,* October 10, 2002.

Rowe, Janet, "The Wincanton Way," *Dairy Industries International,* December 1999, p. 45.

Williams, Philip, "Wincanton Upbeat After Demerger," *Birmingham Post,* June 7, 2002, p. 23.

—M.L. Cohen

Womble Carlyle Sandridge & Rice, PLLC

One West Fourth Street
Winston-Salem, North Carolina 27101
U.S.A.
Telephone: (336) 721-3600
Fax: (336) 721-3660
Web site: http://www.wcsr.com

Limited Liability Company
Founded: 1876 as Watson & Glenn
Employees: 1,115
Sales: $174 million (2001 est.)
NAIC: 541110 Offices of Lawyers

Womble Carlyle Sandridge & Rice, PLLC is a full service regional law firm with five offices in North Carolina (Winston-Salem, Raleigh, Durham, Charlotte, and Greensboro) and other offices in Atlanta, Georgia; Greenville, South Carolina; McLean, Virginia; and Washington, D.C. Its lawyers serve a variety of business, governmental, and nonprofit clients in local, regional, national, and international matters. The firm has won recognition for using the latest technology, while at the same time emphasizing its legacy as one of the South's oldest law firms. With long-term clients such as RJR Nabisco and Wachovia Bank, N.A., Womble Carlyle is one of the nation's fastest-growing law firms.

Origins and Early History

The partnership that eventually became known as Womble Carlyle Sandridge & Rice was formed after Major T.J. Brown in 1872 moved his tobacco business to the small town of Winston, North Carolina, and the town gained its first railroad. Five tobacco companies were operating in Winston by 1875, including the R.J. Reynolds Tobacco Company. To take advantage of new opportunities in the rapidly growing town, William Bynum Glenn moved to Winston and teamed up with local lawyer Cyrus Barksdale Watson to form the law firm of Watson & Glenn in 1876.

By 1884 the two founding partners had begun representing the city of Winston, one of the firm's long-term clients. In the

1880s it also began serving Forsyth County (the home of Winston and the nearby smaller town of Salem), Stokes County, Stanly County, and companies such as the Richmond & Danville Railroad, its first railroad client.

In 1885 Watson left the partnership, so William Glenn joined with Robert B. Glenn to form Glenn & Glenn. Like other small firms of the day, the partnership provided general legal services for individuals, businesses, and governments involving wills, real estate, fraud, contracts, and other civic and criminal cases.

By January 1891 the firm was renamed Glenn & Manley, after the death of William Glenn and the recent arrival of Clement Manley. In the early 1890s Manley served local clients in several drawn-out patent cases. Although not a patent specialist, Manley was able to defeat the American Tobacco Company in lawsuits that "gained for the firm its greatest fame," according to firm historian Lynn Roundtree. Meanwhile, the firm started representing insurance companies such as the Home Insurance Company of New Orleans, the New York Bowery Fire Insurance Company, and the Northwestern North Carolina Railroad and its parent corporation, the Southern Railway Company.

The partnership in the late 1890s grew along with the community. By 1896 Forsyth County had 62 tobacco factories, and even representatives of Chinese and Japanese cigarette companies came to Winston to buy the latest technology. In 1896 the partnership recruited William M. Hendren, and the following year it became known as Glenn, Manley & Hendren. The small law firm continued to serve Western Union and the Wachovia National Bank as the new century approached.

The Partnership in the Early 20th Century

The early partners' strong support of the Democratic Party was highlighted in November 1904 when Robert B. Glenn was elected governor of North Carolina. In 1905 the North Carolina Bar Association chose Clement Manley as its seventh president. The firm still represented the R.J. Reynolds Tobacco Company, which had grown by acquiring other local tobacco interests. Other corporate clients included the P.H. Hanes Knitting Company and the Chatham Manufacturing Company.

Company Perspectives:

We will provide value to our clients by combining professional skill, technology, and a thorough understanding of our clients' needs to deliver high quality, cost effective and responsive services. With approximately 450 lawyers among its ranks, Womble Carlyle is one of the largest law firms in the mid-Atlantic and the Southeast, as well as one of the most technologically advanced. Founded in 1876, the Firm celebrated its 125th anniversary in 2001.

After Governor Glenn decided not to run for reelection and in 1909 announced that he would not return to the law firm, the partnership added Bunyan Snipes Womble, who in 1906 had been one of the first five graduates of the Trinity College (later renamed Duke University) School of Law. In addition to serving clients, Womble played a key role in the 1913 consolidation of Winston and Salem into Winston-Salem.

Firm client R.J. Reynolds about this time brought a Barnum & Bailey camel to town and used it as the model for its new best-selling Camel cigarettes. The tobacco company in 1918 made 12 billion cigarettes; many were sent to France for the nation's soldiers in World War I. When R.J. Reynolds died in 1918, partner Clement Manley handled the tobacco tycoon's will and estate proceedings.

In the early 20th century the firm faced difficult challenges due to North Carolina's Jim Crow laws requiring racial segregation. For example, in 1918 William Hendren represented a black man who successfully sued a white man and won damages for his client. That was the same year that a white mob killed five Winston blacks, in spite of Hendren and others, who urged calm.

Firm Chairman John L.W. Garrou in 2001 cited this 1918 case as an example of "how consistently our firm has taken the often unpopular stand, against white supremacy and racism." Of course, in the early 20th century virtually no law firms included black lawyers. Garrou admitted the partnership back then would be considered "patronizing or racist" based on modern standards, but it still "consistently took the side of toleration and against the extreme racial animosity of the day."

The law firm gained new clients during the booming economy of the 1920s. For example, the North Carolina Baptist Hospital and the Security Life and Trust Company soon became major Winston-Salem employers and clients of Manley, Hendren & Womble. Hendren in 1925 was elected president of the North Carolina Bar Association, and Womble began serving terms in the state House of Representatives and Senate.

The firm hired Irving Carlyle in 1923 and William P. Sandridge in 1930 as associates. The partnership did better during the Great Depression than many other law firms, in large part because of the stability of R.J. Reynolds Tobacco Company and other large corporate clients. In addition, by the mid-1930s large corporations such as Standard Oil of New Jersey, Montgomery Ward, Duke Power Company, and American Express had chosen the firm as its local counsel. By the end of the

decade, Manley, Hendren and Womble had four partners and one associate.

In 1940 the firm hired Leon L. Rice, Jr. Only the third tax law specialist in North Carolina, Rice led the firm's tax practice during World War II and afterward. During the war the firm's client R.J. Reynolds Tobacco Company was convicted of violating the Sherman Antitrust Act. In 1942 the partnership changed its name to Womble, Carlyle, Martin & Sandridge.

Post-World War II Practice

As Winston-Salem grew and prospered after World War II, the law firm also expanded. Its service to Wachovia Bank and Trust Company, R.J. Reynolds Tobacco, and the Southern Railway Company provided a steadily growing income in the 1950s. Other clients included insurance companies such as Security Life and Trust Company, the Equitable Life Assurance Society, and the Metropolitan Life Insurance Company. In the late 1950s the firm added Western Electric and the Transcontinental Gas Pipe Line Corporation, while continuing to serve many local and regional clients, whether businesses or individuals.

Leon Rice's tax practice also grew, and in 1957 the American Law Institute of the American Bar Association published Rice's coauthored book, *Basic Pension and Profit-Sharing Plans*. By the end of the 1950s the firm, renamed Womble Carlyle Sandridge & Rice, included ten lawyers and four staff workers.

The firm's attorneys continued to make major contributions outside their law careers. For example, B.S. Womble as the chairman of the Duke University Board of Trustees from 1960 to 1963 ended his opposition to racial integration and thus helped Duke admit its first black students. Meanwhile, the firm's partners led the effort to desegregate the local Forsyth County Bar Association in 1963 and the North Carolina Bar Association a few years later.

Between 1968 and 1971 the firm participated in a massive lawsuit resulting from a midair collision between a Piedmont Aviation 727 and a Cessna 310 that killed all passengers and crew members of both planes. Along with large national law firms, Womble Carlyle represented Aviation Underwriters, which was Piedmont's insurance company. According to firm historian Lynn Roundtree, "This multiparty, multistate litigation brought Womble Carlyle to the forefront among North Carolina law firms involved with aircraft insurance carriers. For the first time in American aviation history, all cases arising out of a major air crash were settled simultaneously. As a result of the Piedmont case, the firm became North Carolina counsel for the major national aircraft insurance carriers and began to handle an increasing volume of aircraft and product-liability litigation. More importantly, the case put Womble Carlyle in the 'major league' of litigation with the large New York and Washington law firms."

In the 1970s the firm followed national trends when it hired its first paralegals and became more specialized. In 1979 it became the first large North Carolina firm to hire an African American lawyer, and two years later it was one of the first in the state to name a woman as partner.

Key Dates:

1876: Cyrus Watson and W.B. Glenn begin the law firm in Winston, North Carolina.

1891: The firm is renamed Glenn & Manley.

1911: Manley, Hendren & Womble becomes the firm's new name.

1940s: The firm's tax and labor practices are started or expanded.

1954: The firm changes its name to Womble Carlyle Sandridge & Rice.

1982: The firm opens its Raleigh office, its first branch outside of Winston-Salem.

1984: The Charlotte office is started.

1993: The Atlanta office is the first opened outside of North Carolina.

1996: John Garrou replaces Murray Greason as the management committee chairman; firm merges with Atlanta business law firm of Parker, Johnson, Cook and Dunlevie.

1997: New offices are opened in Research Triangle Park, North Carolina, and Washington, D.C.

1999: Womble Carlyle opens its Greenville, South Carolina office.

2000: The firm's Ancillary Services Group becomes a separate company called FirmLogic, LP.

2001: The firm publishes its history to celebrate its 125th anniversary.

2002: Womble Carlyle merges with Pepper & Corazzini of Washington, D.C.

In 1982 the firm, with 59 lawyers, began its first branch office, partly in response to Price Waterhouse consultants who had suggested entering new markets. The new Raleigh office opened on June 1, 1982, to focus on public finance, corporate law, securities, commercial real estate, and government relations. It was the first North Carolina law firm to open a branch office.

Two years later Womble Carlyle opened its second branch office in Charlottesville. By the end of the decade the firm included 100 lawyers. Such growth was typical of other law firms in the 1980s as the economy added 20 million new jobs. Many firms prospered during the decade by helping corporate mergers and acquisitions. For example, Womble Carlyle advised Wachovia Bank in its 1985 acquisition of the First Atlanta Corporation and then the creation of First Wachovia Corporation as the new holding company.

Developments in the 1990s and the New Millennium

After suffering from an economic downturn in the early 1990s, business and the legal profession expanded in the rest of the decade. Womble Carlyle participated in this boom by opening its Atlanta office in 1993. By 2002 the Atlanta office's 70 lawyers provided most legal specialties to corporate and other clients. By adding other new offices and completing mergers with smaller firms, Womble Carlyle in 2002 included about 450 lawyers.

To better serve its clients, Womble Carlyle invested heavily in new technology during the 1990s and the new century. It launched its first web site in 1995 and then its updated site in March 2001. Its staff created and supported private web sites for the international network of 158 law firms called Lex Mundi, as well as participants in the Product Liability Advisory Council.

On November 1, 2000, Womble Carlyle spun off its Ancillary Services Group to create FirmLogic, L.P. This new company offered technology support systems, practice management assistance, web development, trial consulting, and other services to law firms and corporate law departments that previously could not afford such benefits. Based in Winston-Salem and with branches in Atlanta, Houston, and Raleigh, FirmLogic by the spring of 2001 employed more than 300 individuals who served more than 2,000 American and European clients. Womble Carlyle in 2002 remained FirmLogic's majority shareholder.

Womble Carlyle included on its web site the following representative clients: Bank of America; Cisco Systems, Inc.; DB Alex, Brown LLC; Remington Arms Corporation; John Hancock Mutual Life Insurance Company; Food Lion; GlaxoSmithKline; Wake Forest University; Meredith College; and Salem College.

The firm in 2000 did quite well financially, with its gross revenues of $164 million earning it the number 89 ranking in the *American Lawyer*'s annual listing of the United States' largest law firms. The firm's revenues increased 27.6 percent from 1999, while its profits per partner increase of 31.7 percent made it the 13th fastest-growing firm in the country. It opened six new offices in the 1990s and early 2000s and more than doubled its number of lawyers during the same period.

In July 2002 the *American Lawyer* published its annual list of the nation's largest law firms. It ranked Womble Carlyle as number 90 based on 2001 gross revenue of $174 million. With 429 lawyers and 149 equity partners, the firm's profits per equity partner of $475,000 ranked it at number 79, down from number 78 in 2000.

While changing rapidly, Womble Carlyle maintained continuity by showcasing its roots. For example, in 2001 the firm marked its 125th anniversary by publishing a hardcover book on its history by Lynn Roundtree, a Chapel Hill historian who also edited *Seeking Liberty and Justice: A History of the North Carolina Bar Association*. Partners who were descendants of the firm's name partners provided additional continuity. Thus Womble Carlyle balanced both the old and new, both its heritage and traditions, with innovative technology and recent rapid growth, to prepare it for future challenges in the 21st century.

Principal Operating Units

Antitrust, Trade Practices and Commerce; Banking, Finance and Property; Bankruptcy and Creditors' Rights; Business Litigation; Corporate and Securities; Employee Benefits; Environmental Law and Toxic Tort Litigation; Government Relations; Health Care; Insurance; Governmental and Tort Litigation; Intellectual Property; International; Labor and Employment; Product Liability Litigation; Tax; Technology and Commerce; Trusts and Estates.

Principal Competitors

Williams & Connolly LLP; Bingham Dana LLP; Mayer, Brown, Rowe & Maw.

Further Reading

Garrou, John L.W., *Womble Carlyle Sandridge & Rice, PLLC: The First 125 Years of a Law Firm,* New York: The Newcomen Society of the United States, 2001.

Roundtree, Lynn Paul, *The Best Is Yet to Be: The First 125 Years of a Law Firm,* Winston-Salem, N.C.: Womble Carlyle Sandridge & Rice, in association with John F. Blair Publisher, 2001.

—David M. Walden

XTO Energy Inc.

810 Houston Street, Suite 2000
Fort Worth, Texas 76102-6298
U.S.A.
Telephone: (817) 870-2800
Fax: (817) 870-1671
Web site: http://www.crosstimbers.com

Public Company
Incorporated: 1990 as Cross Timbers Oil Company
Employees: 742
Sales: $838.7 million (2001)
Stock Exchanges: New York
Ticker Symbol: XTO
NAIC: 211111 Crude Petroleum and Natural Gas
   Extraction

XTO Energy Inc., formerly known as Cross Timbers Oil Company, is a large independent Fort Worth, Texas, oil company that has made its mark by exploiting proved natural gas and oil properties divested by others. The company's principal holdings are located in Alaska, Arkansas, Texas, Kansas, New Mexico, Oklahoma, and Wyoming. In recent years XTO has thrived because of an early decision to focus on natural gas, buying properties at the bottom of the market, thereby achieving a lower cost structure and a competitive edge as the natural gas market has made significant gains. XTO is known for its innovative spirit, from the way it structures its many acquisitions to the way it is able to exploit properties that others had essentially abandoned. The company is also meticulous, conducting a thorough review of each well twice a year.

Working for Southland Royalty First: 1967–85

The predecessor to XTO Energy, Cross Timbers Oil Company, was founded by three friends—Jon Brumley, Bob R. Simpson, and Steve Palko—former executives of Southland Royalty Company who lost their positions following a hostile takeover. The oldest, Brumley, came to Fort Worth-based Southland in 1967 after earning an M.B.A. from the University

of Pennsylvania's Wharton School of Business, starting out as a risk analyst. At that time, Southland was an exploration company, but in 1976, two years after Brumley ascended to the presidency, it became acquisition driven and focused on exploitation efforts. It was in that year that Southland purchased San Juan Basin gas properties, holding a trillion cubic feet of gas reserves, from Aztec Oil & Gas.

Also in 1976 Bob R. Simpson went to work for Southland as a tax manager. Raised in west Texas, the son of a cotton farmer, he grew up enamored with the oil business. Interviewed for a PBS series on small businesses, Simpson recalled how his father "would drive up and down the road, and he would point at pump jacks. And he said, 'Son, I almost bought that land, and if I had, we'd have been wealthy as royalty.' And so, I ended up associating success and prosperity with oil . . . and I liked the smell of the gas tank when we were filling up." Coupled with his desire to become involved in oil was an instinctive entrepreneurial spirit: By the age of four he had an egg route, selling his produce door to door. He was also a gifted student who went to Baylor University on academic scholarships, earning an undergraduate degree in accounting and later an M.B.A. At Southland he quickly established himself as an important part of the team and with Brumley serving as a mentor he rose to the rank of vice-president of finance and corporate development in just three years.

The third cofounder of Cross Timbers was Palko, who supplied the engineering expertise. He was the last of the three men to join Southland. After earning an electrical engineering degree from the University of Texas in 1971, he went to work for Exxon. After several years he grew tired of the big corporation environment and decided to try life at a smaller company. He applied for a job with Southland and in 1982 became manager of reservoir engineering. Two years later he was named vice-president of reservoir engineering.

In 1985 Southland was a successful and stable business when management learned that Burlington Northern Railroad had acquired a significant stake in the company. Burlington soon forced a sale and Southland's management team found itself suddenly out of work. After recovering from the surprise and disorientation of having their professional lives turned upside down, Brumley, Simpson, Palko, and assistant treasurer

Louis G. Baldwin decided to form their own oil and gas business, pursuing the same strategy that worked so well for them at Southland: acquiring underdeveloped properties and exploiting their maximum potential. In 1986 they formed Cross Timbers Oil Company as a partnership. The name was an allusion to the stretch of land between east Texas and west Texas called Cross Timbers, a no-man's land that in the 1800s separated settlers from the plains Indians. Although the founders of the company were well connected in their field and able to quickly raise $20 million in seed money, Cross Timbers remained a shoestring affair for some time. At first it employed just eight people, the office furniture drawn from their own homes, and space was at such a premium that Palko and Simpson had to share desk space with a secretary. During the early lean years, moreover, the founders received no salary.

Operating Strategy Formulated in Early Years

In this formative period for Cross Timbers, management developed an operating strategy. It sought to hire talented personnel at all levels in the company, luring away a number of colleagues at Southland, then created an environment that encouraged innovation. Cross Timbers also decided to pay top dollar for properties with long-lived reserves, and to resist the temptation to sell quality acquisitions if they failed to show immediate results. In identifying acquisition candidates, Palko and his team made a thorough evaluation of the properties to determine upside potential, relying on a wealth of geologic information, including well logs, production histories, and two- or three-dimensional seismic studies. Once a promising property was identified, Simpson stepped in to make the acquisition, often devising a creative approach to financing in order to salvage a deal. Palko then followed the company's established approach to exploiting a new property. In the first stage, productivity of existing wells was increased through relatively simple upgrades, such as lowering system pressures, adding compression, changing line sizes, or installing pump-off controllers. Cross Timbers then sought to "exploit and extend" the property through a number of drilling methods. The final step was for Cross Timbers to drill its own wells on the property, again relying on its staff of skilled engineers to determine choice locations. Knowledge gained from drilling was then used to determine if the company should acquire greater interests in a leased property or acquire nearby property in order to take advantage of a perceived trend. The company also instituted a policy to review each well twice a year, and despite the fact that Cross Timbers operated thousands of wells, it developed a specific plan for each one.

In 1990 Cross Timbers Oil Company was incorporated to act as the managing general partner of the business, which now included six limited partnerships and two corporations. The company was well established and prospering, but after five years the original backers were looking to harvest their investment and the founders wished to continue in business. To satisfy both parties, management in 1991 formed Cross Timbers Royalty Trust, which received a portion of the profits made on the company's properties. Units of the trust were then sold publicly, allowing the original investors to cash in should they desire. Then in 1993 Cross Timbers took a more decisive step by making an initial public offering (IPO) of its stock, allowing investors to sell their shares while at the same time giving the company the flexibility to use stock in future acquisitions. At this point, Cross Timbers had about 40 million barrels of oil reserves and in 1992 generated $92 million in revenues and net income of $7.1 million. After the IPO it had a $200 million market cap, roughly twice the size of Southland when the Cross Timbers founders had been ousted.

Now a public company, Cross Timbers announced that it planned to spend $250 million over the next five years acquiring new properties, targeting those in the $5 million to $50 million price range. The strategy was facilitated by a greater willingness of larger companies to divest non-essential assets. The company's first major deal soon followed its IPO, the $37.1 million purchase of west Texas and southeast New Mexico properties from Atlantic Richfield Co. In less than two years Cross Timbers reached its $250 million goal, capped by the 1995 $123 million acquisition of 375 wells from Santa Fe Minerals located in the Hugoton Field of Kansas and Oklahoma. According to Simpson, this group of properties represented the crown jewels of Cross Timbers' holdings.

In 1996 Brumley decided to step down as chairman of the board in an amicable parting. He indicated that because his day-to-day involvement in the business was no longer necessary he felt he could now leave to pursue other interests. Several months later, in fact, he was asked by T. Boone Pickens and Richard Rainwater to chair Mesa Inc. Simpson replaced Brumley as chair while retaining his post as CEO, and one of his first decisions in his new capacity would have a major impact on the future of Cross Timbers. In 1995 the company's assets were divided half oil and half gas, but Simpson now opted to change that ratio to two-thirds natural gas, which he hoped would generate higher profits, due in large part to the lower costs of handling the commodity compared to oil. In addition, because gas was a closed North American market it was less vulnerable to the actions of OPEC, as well as fast becoming the fuel of choice for electric generation. Simpson's timing proved to be perfect, as Cross Timbers was able to buy a substantial number of properties before the natural gas market began to take off, thereby achieving a lower cost structure to provide a competitive edge and increased profitability.

In 1997 Cross Timbers spent $256 million on acquisitions, primarily gas-producing properties. The most significant was a $195 million purchase of 170,000 acres in the San Juan basin in New Mexico from Amoco Production Co., a deal that epitomized the trend of major oil companies unloading domestic properties in order to focus on international plays that held the potential for blockbuster results. Also in 1997 Cross Timbers spent $39 million to acquire properties in Oklahoma, Kansas, and Texas. With oil prices down, the company on the strength

Key Dates:

1986: Cross Timbers Oil Company is formed as a partnership.
1990: Cross Timbers is incorporated.
1993: Company goes public.
1996: Jon Brumley steps down as chair, replaced by Bob Simpson.
2001: Cross Timbers changes name to XTO Energy Inc.

of its gas operations was able to produce revenues of $198.2 million in 1997, a 24 percent increase over the previous year, and post net income of nearly $24 million.

Growing out of a Slump: 1998–99

Like the rest of the industry, Cross Timbers was tested during the price crash of 1998–99, when oil prices reached their lowest levels since the 1930s. Unlike many of its competitors, however, Cross Timbers had a strong gas business and could better weather the storm. Rather than sell assets and focus on debt reduction, it opted to grow out of the downturn and acquire even more gas properties. During a two-year span, from the end of 1997 to the end of 1999, it spent nearly $1 billion on new properties, most of which were gas assets. Recalling this period, Simpson told the *American Oil & Gas Reporter,* "Wall Street was telling us to pull back, sell properties and reduce debt. But this company is nothing if not opportunity-driven, and opportunity after opportunity kept sticking its head up. We decided to take on more debt, turning our back to (Wall) Street and taking the heat because we knew the next part of the up-and-down price cycle would require us to grow. We absolutely ripped our balance sheet to shreds all through '99. We bought properties with the idea that by the time our competition was back in the 'buy' mode, we would already be done and could tidy up our balance sheet during the up cycle." Simpson even took the unusual step in 1998 of buying stock in energy companies he felt were undervalued as a way to take a position in promising assets. Simpson also displayed his innovative edge by finding a way to salvage major deals that appeared dead. In the summer of 1999 he landed two major acquisitions, paying $235 million to Spring Holding Co. for properties in Arkoma Basin, an area that Cross Timbers has been attracted to for years. A subsequent $231 million purchase of properties in the same area from Ocean Energy Inc. instantly made Cross Timbers the largest producer of gas in Arkansas. In order to pay for these transactions, Simpson essentially fabricated a financial instrument out of whole cloth. He convinced Lehman Brothers Holdings Inc. to provide an equity-based bridge loan, in effect making Lehman a financial partner. It proved to be a smart decision for both parties: Within months Cross Timbers was able to buy out Lehman Brothers' share of the properties. Cross Timbers also defied conventional wisdom in 1999 when it decided to cut its dividend 75 percent, to just a penny a share, in order to address

its high debt. The company lost nearly $71.5 million in 1998, then returned to profitability in 1999, recording net income of $45 million on revenues of $343.2 million.

Not only did a rebounding market, driven by natural gas, allow Cross Timbers to immediately clean up its balance sheet, acquisitions made during the lean months poised the company for spectacular results going forward. In 2000 revenues ballooned to more than $600 million, and net income more than doubled, totaling $115.2 million. As a result, a little more than a year after slashing its dividend, Cross Timbers was able to announce a three-for-two stock split. Moreover, in only a matter of a few years the company went from nowhere to becoming the fourth largest independent owner of domestic natural gas reserves in the country. Results in 2001 were even more spectacular, with revenues improving to $839 million and net income to nearly $250 million.

In 2001 Cross Timbers also elected to change its name, which for years had confused many investors who thought that the company was involved in the timber business. The ticker symbol XTO was adopted and the company now became XTO Energy Inc. It also continued to buy more gas-producing properties, spending $242 million in 2001. With almost all of the new U.S. power plants planning to rely on natural gas, leading to an expected 40 percent increase in demand by 2015, XTO with its considerable gas reserves, as well as demonstrated expertise, was well positioned for many more years of solid growth.

Principal Subsidiaries

Cross Timbers Energy Services, Inc; Cross Timbers Trading Company; Ringwood Gathering Company; Timberland Gathering & Processing Company, Inc.; WTW Properties, Inc.

Principal Competitors

Apache Corporation; BP p.l.c.; Exxon Mobil Corporation.

Further Reading

Beims, Tim, "Natural Gas Reserves Give Cross Timbers the Winning Hand," *American Oil & Gas Reporter,* March 2001.

Bronstad, Amanda, "Acquisitions Bolster XTO to Record Growth," *Business Press,* October 30, 1998, p. 3.

Haines, Leslie, "XTO Energy Matures," *Oil and Gas Investor,* July 2001.

Maxon, Terry, "Texas-Based Cross Timbers Oil Reaps Benefits of Expanded Natural-Gas Activity," *Dallas Morning News,* November 24, 2000.

Rhodes, Anne, "Cross Timbers' Acquisition Strategy Underpins Explosive Rate of Growth," *Oil and Gas Journal,* June 1, 1998, p. 25.

Suggs, Welch, "Cross Timbers Joins the Ranks of Top Independents," *Dallas Business Journal,* October 24, 1997, p. 8.

Willis, Belinda, "Cross Timbers Is 'Long on Opportunity,' Analysts Say," *Business Press,* March 1, 1996, p. 4.

—Ed Dinger

Zomba Records Ltd.

Zomba House
165-167 High Road
London NW10 2SG
United Kingdom
Telephone: 44-20-8459-8899
Fax: 44-20-8451-4158
Web site: http://www.zomba.co.uk

Private Company
Incorporated: 1975
Employees: 1,000
Sales: $1 billion (2001 est.)
NAIC: 512210 Record Production; 512220 Musical
    Recording, Releasing, Promoting, and Distributing;
    512230 Music Publishers; 512240 Sound Recording
    Studios; 532490 Audio Visual Equipment Rental or
    Leasing

Zomba Records Ltd. is the largest independent record company in the world. The firm operates a number of labels, including Jive (one-fifth owned by Bertelsmann Music Group), Volcano, Mojo, Reunion, Essential, and Verity, and also has music publishing, record distribution, equipment rental, recording studio, and artists management interests. Although Zomba's releases range in style from rap to gospel to hard rock, the company is best known for glossy pop hitmakers Britney Spears, the Backstreet Boys, and 'N Sync, all of whom record for Jive. The firm is owned by cofounder Clive Calder, who serves as its chairman and CEO.

Beginnings

Zomba traces its roots to 1971, when aspiring South African musicians Clive Calder and Ralph Simon formed a new business to release records, promote concerts, and publish music. Calder, from Johannesburg, had never attended college, but had played bass guitar in local bands and later worked as a talent scout for music industry giant EMI. Simon, a keyboard player, had become interested in rock music during a year of study in Connecticut,

where he attended concerts at New York's famed Fillmore East. In 1975 the pair moved their base of operations to London, where they renamed the company Zomba, after the capital of the African country of Malawi. According to legend, the members of a tribe there had superior hearing. In 1978 the company expanded its reach to New York City, and three years later Zomba formed a new record label, Jive (named after the African style of music called "township jive"). During this period the company had its first hits with singer Billy Ocean, hard rockers Def Leppard, and early rappers Whodini. Zomba's publishing business also was doing well, signing deals with British punk/new wave stars Elvis Costello and The Boomtown Rats. Another key relationship was developed with South African record producer Robert "Mutt" Lange, who had worked on hits like AC/DC's "Highway to Hell." The input of Calder, who often chose his acts' songs and worked with them in the recording studio, was an important factor in the company's success as well.

During the 1980s the rap-oriented Jive label had hits with acts that included A Tribe Called Quest and DJ Jazzy Jeff and the Fresh Prince, while divisions Zomba Management and Zomba Music Publishing became powerful forces in their respective areas. The decade also saw the firm establish recording studios in the United Kingdom and the United States. A new label, Silvertone, was formed in 1988, and it soon had hits with Stone Roses, a British group, though the act was later lost to Geffen Records. Silvertone focused on rock and blues, working with only a handful of artists including Buddy Guy and John Lee Hooker. At the end of the decade Jive found further success with contemporary rhythm and blues performers Boogie Down Productions and Kool Moe Dee.

Partner's Buyout in 1990

In 1990 Zomba caught the attention of EMI, which made a serious effort to purchase the company. It was ultimately turned down, and Calder subsequently bought out his partner's stake in the firm. Simon later moved to San Francisco to start his own label, Scintilla. By this time Zomba's recordings were being distributed by Bertelsmann Music Group (BMG), which in late 1991 bought a 25 percent stake in the company's music publishing business, expanding on a previous investment. The deal gave

428

Company Perspectives:

Zomba is the largest independent music operation in the world. Jive Records is the flagship label of the Zomba Label Group, which also encompasses the record labels Jive Electro, Silvertone, Verity, Volcano and Reunion, among others. Zomba is home to some of the biggest contemporary pop, R&B, gospel, hip-hop and rock artists in the world, including teen phenomenons Backstreet Boys, Britney Spears, NSYNC and Aaron Carter; Grammy Award winner R. Kelly; hip-hop icon Mystikal; and Volcano's multi-platinum rockers Tool and 311. Jive Records, in particular, is known for consistently breaking the hottest acts. In fact, two-thirds of Jive's artist roster has achieved Gold or Platinum status—a claim no other record label can make.

BMG sub-publishing of Zomba-owned compositions in some foreign markets, as well as part-ownership of Zomba's production arm and its background music catalog. The company's publishing organization was having success at this time with songs featured on Michael Jackson and Bryan Adams releases.

In 1992 Zomba acquired controlling interest in a classical music label, Conifer Records Ltd. Founded in 1977, Conifer was the United Kingdom's largest distributor of classical and spoken word recordings and the owner of six record labels. In 1993 Zomba set up a new film and television music division called Zomba Music Services, which would offer prerecorded music and publishing services for soundtracks. In addition to the company's roster of hit artists and songs, the new operation owned the rights to an extensive collection of specialty recordings that ranged from marching bands to Hungarian folk music. Zomba units Coombe and First Com already offered similar services, but the new division was expected to take a more aggressive approach toward marketing. The year 1993 also saw formation of a joint venture, Portman Music, with Portman Entertainment.

In February 1994 Zomba bought Brentwood Music Group, Inc., a Christian music company. The 14-year-old Brentwood had seven record labels and a publishing division, and distributed its products to more than 40 countries. Jive Records had signed two black gospel acts the year before, and Zomba later launched a gospel label, Verity. At the end of the year the company branched out yet again, this time with a move into Latin music. An estimated $5 million was spent to acquire the catalogs of Grever International S.A. of Mexico City and Golden Sands Enterprises, Inc. of San Antonio, Texas, both of which were owned by the Grever family.

In early 1996 Zomba sold the Conifer operation to BMG, citing the need to focus on its Jive and Silvertone labels, and bought Hilton Sound, a British audio equipment rental company. Hilton was folded into Zomba's previously established Dreamhire, which had offices in the United Kingdom, New York, and Nashville, making the company the world leader in this field. In the summer Zomba bought three-fourths of Windsong Exports and Pinnacle Distribution, a London-based company owned by Steve Mason. The deal also included 80 percent of Rough Trade Records Germany and all of Rough Trade's mid-European opera-

tions, which were later renamed Zomba Distribution. Windsong operated several record labels, and Pinnacle was the largest independent music distributor in the United Kingdom. The year also saw Zomba sign a long-term deal with Britain's Channel Four to supply it with soundtrack music.

BMG Buying into Jive in Late 1996

In the fall of 1996 Zomba sold 20 percent of its record division to BMG Entertainment for an estimated $25 million, further cementing ties between the two companies. The division included Jive and Silvertone as well as the Christian music companies, the Dreamhire equipment rental business, film music operation Segue Music, and the Battery recording studios. The same month Zomba acquired another Christian record label, Reunion Records, from Arista Records Nashville, a BMG company. Reunion was one of the top "contemporary Christian" imprints, with artists such as Michael W. Smith and Kathy Troccolli.

In November Zomba signed an agreement with Virgin Music Group Worldwide for the latter to handle distribution in Latin America, Africa, and some European countries. The move completed a reconfiguration of the company's distribution system that had been underway since a contract with BMG International had lapsed. Zomba now dealt with 13 different companies to distribute its product around the world. The privately held Zomba, which offered little public information about its finances, had estimated revenues of $500 million by this time.

Zomba's Christian music arm expanded again in 1997 with the purchase of Benson Music Group from Music Entertainment Group. The Christian operations were subsequently consolidated into the new Nashville-based Provident Music Group, with Provident Music Distribution created to service the Christian specialty-store market. Distribution to mainstream retailers of Zomba's Christian releases, which included crossover hitmakers Jars of Clay, was handled by BMG. The company also opened a new office and studio in Sweden as part of a joint venture with the Cheiron company during the year.

In the spring of 1998 Zomba bought Volcano, a two-year-old rock record label that had Tool, Matthew Sweet, and the O'Jays under contract. A short time later the company sold half of the label to Q Prime, Inc. Zomba was now enjoying its biggest hits ever with teen-oriented vocal group the Backstreet Boys and former Mouseketeer Britney Spears. Their label, Jive, also had success with harder-edged releases by slain rap star Tupac Shakur.

Further Expansion and Bigger Hits in 1999

In 1999 Zomba continued its expansion, creating the London-based International Record Group and forming new companies in Australia, France, Singapore, and Canada. In July Zomba's Jive label had three of the top five albums in the United States: the Backstreet Boys' *Millennium* (number one), Britney Spears's *Baby One More Time* (number four), and Too $hort's *Can't Stay Away* (number five), making it the top label in the country.

The fall of 1999 saw controversy erupt when Jive Records signed 'N Sync, a teen-pop "boy band" in the mold of the

Backstreet Boys. BMG had released 'N Sync's debut album the previous year and claimed to still have them under contract. BMG and Trans Continental Records, the management company that had groomed both bands, subsequently sued 'N Sync and Jive for $150 million for breach of contract. Soon afterward the Backstreet Boys began to hint that they wanted to leave Jive over concerns that the label could not adequately promote two similar groups. The dispute was settled in December when BMG backed down from its claim to 'N Sync, in exchange for a one-year extension of its profitable contract to distribute Zomba products in the United States.

The year 2000 saw Zomba continue to open regional companies, forming new units in Italy, Spain, Norway, Denmark, New Zealand, Korea, and Japan, making it clear that the music of Britney Spears and the Backstreet Boys was popular internationally, not just with 14-year-old American girls. The firm was now the leading independent record company in the world, fast approaching major label status.

In May 2001 Zomba created Ingenuity Entertainment to offer management services to film music composers, editors, and supervisors. International expansion continued during the year with the creation of Zomba companies in Brazil and Portugal. In August, after lengthy negotiations, Zomba again renewed its distribution deal with BMG for the United States and Canada, and entered into a strategic alliance with BMG's Australian division. The company also settled a copyright-infringement suit against MP3.com, an online music download service, and subsequently signed a contract with the firm to offer Zomba recordings online for a fee. The settlement terms were not disclosed, but were estimated to be in the millions. Zomba, which already had licensed tracks to MusicNet, later agreed to sell its recordings online through Pressplay as well.

In September the Jive label acquired Mojo Records, home to swing band Cherry Poppin' Daddies and ska-punk group

Goldfinger. Later in the year Zomba put its British Battery studios and Dreamhire pro sound rental operations up for sale, due to a lack of recording activity in that country. At the start of November the firm's marketing units were put into high gear when Jive released the latest albums by the Backstreet Boys and Britney Spears. Zomba was now considered the most profitable record company in the world, earning an estimated $300 million in profits on $1 billion in sales. Despite its success, CEO Clive Calder remained little known outside of the industry, refusing interviews and shunning the celebrity status in which industry rivals David Geffen and Clive Davis reveled.

In slightly more than 25 years in existence, Zomba Records Ltd. had grown into the largest independent music company in the world, and also the most profitable. Although it was best known as the home of Britney Spears, the Backstreet Boys, and 'N Sync, the diverse company also found success with its publishing, recording, equipment rental, and soundtrack music businesses. Zomba's growing network of regional marketing companies was bringing it ever closer to the rarefied atmosphere of major label status.

Principal Divisions

Zomba Group of Companies; Zomba Recording Corp.; Zomba Label Group; Zomba Music Publishing; Zomba International Records Group; Provident Music Group; Ingenuity Entertainment.

Principal Competitors

Sony Music Entertainment, Inc.; Universal Music Group; BMG Entertainment; Warner Music Group; EMI Group plc.

Further Reading

Bessman, Jim, "Chicago's Zomba Making Hits with Hula & Fingers," *Billboard,* August 17, 1991, p. 25.
"BMG Entertainment Acquires Share in Zomba Group Record Division," *Billboard,* November 9, 1996, p. 6.
Clark-Meads, Jeff, "Zomba Buys 75% of Windsong/Pinnacle," *Billboard,* July 20, 1996, p. 6.
Darden, Bob, "Zomba Acquires Brentwood Group; Secular Distribution Awaits Christian Indie," *Billboard,* February 19, 1994, p. 10.
Dove, Siri Stavenes, "Zomba Tests Network with Major Releases," *Music & Media,* November 12, 2001, p. 3.
Eade, Catherine, "Jive Is Capitalising on the Growing Interest in R&B in the U.K.," *Music Week,* November 19, 1994, p. 6.
Ferguson, John, "Virgin Deal Completes Zomba's Int'l Network," *Billboard,* November 2, 1996, p. 1.
Furman, Phyllis, "No Jive, He's a Hit at Calling Tunes," *New York Daily News,* July 24, 2000, p. 24.
Kafka, Peter, and Brett Pulley, "Jive Talking," *Forbes,* March 19, 2001, p. 138.
Lichtman, Irv, "Zomba Enters Latin Pub. Field with Grever Purchase," *Billboard,* December 10, 1994, p. 9.
——, "Zomba Pub. Maintains Winning Ways," *Billboard,* November 6, 1999.
Lieberman, Allyson, "BMG Sues 'N Sync for $150M; New Label, Jive, Also Hit in Breach of Contract Claim," *New York Post,* October 14, 1999, p. 39.
——, "He's the Wizard of Jive—'Secretive' Clive Calder Sits on Top of the Music World," *New York Post,* November 19, 2000, p. 54.

Masson, Gordon, "Zomba Opens New Affiliates to Boost Euro Presence," *Billboard,* April 22, 2000, p. 52.

McClure, Steve, and Dominic Pride, "Zomba Expands Internationally," *Billboard,* September 11, 1999, p. 16.

Newman, Melinda, "'N Sync Suits Settled; Zomba, BMG Extend Pact," *Billboard,* January 8, 2000, p. 6.

O'Connor, Ashling, "Survey—Creative Business: Clive Calder," *Financial Times,* February 13, 2001.

Peers, Martin, "Backstreet Boys, 'N Sync Draw Record Labels," *Financial Express,* October 8, 1999.

Price, Deborah Evans, "Zomba Buys Benson Group; Plans Christian Music Umbrella Co.," *Billboard,* March 15, 1997, p. 12.

——, "Zomba Forms Christian Music Umbrella," *Billboard,* June 28, 1997, p. 6.

Pride, Dominic, "The Secret of Jive's Int'l Success," *Billboard,* October 30, 1999, p. 72.

——, "Zomba Ups Global Presence," *Music & Media,* September 11, 1999, p. 1.

Schoepe, Zenon, "Zomba Acquires Hilton Sound," *Billboard,* February 17, 1996, p. 51.

Selvin, Joel, "Major Music Company/Big Leaguers Back," *San Francisco Chronicle,* December 1, 1991, p. 57.

Usborne, David, " 'Howard Hughes' of the Pop World in $3bn Deal," *Independent—London,* December 15, 2001, p. 10.

Verna, Paul, "BMG Buys 25% Interest in Zomba Music," *Billboard,* December 14, 1991, p. 79.

—Frank Uhle

INDEX TO COMPANIES

Index to Companies

Listings in this index are arranged in alphabetical order under the company name. Company names beginning with a letter or proper name such as Eli Lilly & Co. will be found under the first letter of the company name. Definite articles (The, Le, La) are ignored for alphabetical purposes as are forms of incorporation that precede the company name (AB, NV). Company names printed in bold type have full, historical essays on the page numbers appearing in bold. Updates to entries that appeared in earlier volumes are signified by the notation (upd.). Company names in light type are references within an essay to that company, not full historical essays. This index is cumulative with volume numbers printed in bold type.

Biomega Corp., **18** 422
Biomet, Inc., 10 156–58
Bionaire, Inc., **19** 360
BioSensor A.B., **I** 665
Biotechnica International, **I** 286
Bioteknik-Gruppen, **I** 665
Bioter-Biona, S.A., **II** 493
Bioter S.A., **III** 420
Biotherm, **III** 47
Biovail Corporation, 47 54–56
Biralo Pty Ltd., **48** 427
Bird & Sons, **22** 14
Bird Corporation, 19 56–58
Birdair, Inc., **35** 99–100
Birds Eye, **32** 474
Birdsall, Inc., **6** 529, 531
Bireley's, **22** 515
Birfield Ltd., **III** 494
Birkbeck, **10** 6
**Birkenstock Footprint Sandals, Inc., 12
33–35; 42 37–40 (upd.)**
Birmingham & Midland Bank. *See*
Midland Bank plc.
Birmingham Joint Stock Bank, **II** 307
Birmingham Screw Co., **III** 493
Birmingham Slag Company, **7** 572–73,
575
**Birmingham Steel Corporation, 13
97–98; 18** 379–80; **19** 380; **40 70–73
(upd.)**
Birra Moretti, **25** 281–82
Birtman Electric Co., **III** 653; **12** 548
Biscayne Bank. *See* Banco Espírito Santo e
Comercial de Lisboa S.A.
Biscayne Federal Savings and Loan
Association, **11** 481
Biscuiterie Nantaise, **II** 502; **10** 323
Biscuits Belin, **II** 543
Biscuits Delacre, **II** 480; **26** 56
Biscuits Gondolo, **II** 543
Bishop & Babcock Manufacturing Co., **II**
41
Bishop & Co. Savings Bank, **11** 114
Bishop National Bank of Hawaii, **11** 114
Bishopsgate Insurance, **III** 200
BISSELL, Inc., 9 70–72; 30 75–78 (upd.)
Bit Software, Inc., **12** 62
Bits & Pieces, **26** 439
Bitumax Proprietary, **III** 672
Bitumen & Oil Refineries (Australia) Ltd.,
III 672–73
BIW. *See* Bath Iron Works.
BIZ Enterprises, **23** 390
BizBuyer.com, **39** 25
Bizmark, **13** 176
BizMart, **6** 244–45; **8** 404–05
BJ Services Company, 15 534, 536; **25
73–75**
BJ's Pizza & Grill, **44** 85
BJ's Restaurant & Brewhouse, **44** 85
BJ's Wholesale Club, **12** 221; **13** 547–49;
33 198
BJK&E. *See* Bozell Worldwide Inc.
Björknäs Nya Sågverks, **IV** 338
BK Tag, **28** 157
BK Vision AG, **52** 357
BKW, **IV** 229
BL Ltd., **I** 175; **10** 354
BL Systems. *See* AT&T Istel Ltd.
BL Universal PLC, **47** 168
The Black & Decker Corporation, I 667;
III 435–37, 628, 665; **8** 332, 349; **15**
417–18; **16** 384; **17** 215; **20 64–68
(upd.); 22** 334; **43** 101, 289

Black & Veatch LLP, 22 87–90
Black Arrow Leasing, **II** 138; **24** 193
Black Box Corporation, 20 69–71
Black Clawson Company, **24** 478
Black Entertainment Television. *See* BET
Holdings, Inc.
Black Flag Co., **I** 622
Black Hawk Broadcasting Group, **III** 188;
10 29; **38** 17
Black Hills Corporation, 20 72–74
Black Pearl Software, Inc., **39** 396
Black Spread Eagle, **II** 235
Blackburn Group, **III** 508; **24** 85
Blackhawk Holdings, Inc. *See* PW Eagle
Inc.
Blackhorse Agencies, **II** 309; **47** 227
Blackmer Pump Co., **III** 468
Blacks Leisure Group plc, 39 58–60
Blackstone Capital Partners L.P., **V** 223; **6**
378; **17** 366
The Blackstone Group, **II** 434, 444; **IV**
718; **11** 177, 179; **13** 170; **17** 238, 443;
22 404, 416; **26** 408; **37** 309, 311
Blackstone Hotel Acquisition Co., **24** 195
Blaine Construction Company, **8** 546
Blair and Co., **II** 227
Blair Corporation, 25 76–78; 31 53–55
Blair Paving, **III** 674
Blair Radio, **6** 33
Blakiston Co., **IV** 636
Blane Products, **I** 403
Blanes, S.A. de C.V., **34** 197
Blatz Breweries, **I** 254
Blaupunkt-Werke, **I** 192–93
BLC Insurance Co., **III** 330
BLD Europe, **16** 168
Bleichröder, **II** 191
Blendax, **III** 53; **8** 434; **26** 384
Blessings Corp., 14 550; **19 59–61**
Blimpie International, Inc., **15 55–57; 17**
501; **32** 444; bf]XLIX **60–64 (upd.)**
Bliss Manufacturing Co., **17** 234–35
Blitz-Weinhart Brewing, **18** 71–72; **50**
112, 114
Bloch & Guggenheimer, Inc., **40 51–52**
Blochman Lawrence Goldfree, **I** 697
Block Drug Company, Inc., 6 26; **8
62–64; 27 67–70 (upd.)**
Block Financial Corporation, **17** 265; **29**
227
Block Management, **29** 226
Block Medical, Inc., **10** 351
**Blockbuster Entertainment Corporation,
II** 161; **IV** 597; **9 73–75**, 361; **11**
556–58; **12** 43, 515; **13** 494; **18** 64, 66;
19 417; **22** 161–62; **23** 88, 503; **25**
208–10, 222; **26** 409; **28** 296; **29** 504
Blockbuster Inc., 31 56–60 (upd.),
339–40; **50** 61
Blockson Chemical, **I** 380; **13** 379
Bloedel, Stewart & Welch, **IV** 306–07
Blohm & Voss, **I** 74
**Blonder Tongue Laboratories, Inc., 48
52–55**
Bloomberg L.P., 18 24; **21 67–71**
Bloomingdale's Inc., I 90; **III** 63; **IV** 651,
703; **9** 209, 393; **10** 487; **12 36–38**, 307,
403–04; **16** 328; **23** 210; **25** 257; **31** 190
Blount International, Inc., I 563; **12
39–41; 24** 78; **26** 117, 119, 363; **48
56–60 (upd.)**
BLP Group Companies. *See* Boron, LePore
& Associates, Inc.
BLT Ventures, **25** 270

Blue Arrow PLC, **II** 334–35; **9** 327; **30**
300
Blue Bell Creameries L.P., 30 79–81
Blue Bell, Inc., **V** 390–91; **12** 205; **17** 512
Blue Bird Corporation, 35 63–66
Blue Bunny Ice Cream. *See* Wells' Dairy,
Inc.
Blue Byte, **41** 409
Blue Chip Stamps, **III** 213–14; **30** 412
Blue Circle Industries PLC, III 669–71,
702
**Blue Cross and Blue Shield Association,
10 159–61; 14** 84
Blue Cross and Blue Shield Mutual of
Northern Ohio, **12** 176
Blue Cross and Blue Shield of Colorado,
11 175
Blue Cross and Blue Shield of Greater
New York, **III** 245, 246
Blue Cross and Blue Shield of Ohio, **15**
114
Blue Cross Blue Shield of Michigan, **12** 22
Blue Cross of California, **25** 525
Blue Cross of Northeastern New York, **III**
245–46
Blue Diamond Growers, 28 56–58
Blue Dot Services, **37** 280, 283
Blue Funnel Line, **I** 521; **6** 415–17
Blue Line Distributing, **7** 278–79
Blue Metal Industries, **III** 687; **28** 82
Blue Mountain Arts, Inc., IV 621; **29
63–66**
Blue Mountain Springs Ltd., **48** 97
Blue Ribbon Beef Pack, Inc., **II** 515–16
Blue Ribbon Sports. *See* Nike, Inc.
Blue Ridge Grocery Co., **II** 625
Blue Ridge Lumber Ltd., **16** 11
Blue Shield of California, **25** 527
Blue Square Israel Ltd., 41 56–58
Blue Tee Corporation, **23** 34, 36
Blue Water Food Service, **13** 244
Bluebird Inc., **10** 443
Bluffton Grocery Co., **II** 668
Blumberg Communications Inc., **24** 96
Blunt Ellis & Loewi, **III** 270
Blyth and Co., **I** 537; **13** 448, 529
Blyth Eastman Dillon & Company, **II** 445;
22 405–06
Blyth Industries, Inc., 18 67–69
Blyth Merrill Lynch, **II** 448
Blythe Colours BV, **IV** 119
BMC Industries, Inc., 6 275; **17 48–51**
BMC Software Inc., **14** 391
BMG/Music, **IV** 594; **15** 51; **37** 192–93.
See also Bertelsmann Music Group.
BMHC. *See* Building Materials Holding
Corporation.
BMI. *See* Broadcast Music Inc.
BMI Ltd., **III** 673
BMI Systems Inc., **12** 174
BMO Corp., **III** 209
BMO Nesbitt Burns, **46** 55
BMW. *See* Bayerische Motoren Werke.
BNA. *See* Banca Nazionale
dell'Agricoltura *or* Bureau of National
Affairs, Inc.
BNCI. *See* Banque Nationale Pour le
Commerce et l'Industrie.
BNE. *See* Bank of New England Corp.
BNG, Inc., **19** 487
BNP Paribas Group, 36 94–97 (upd.); 42
349
BNS Acquisitions, **26** 247
Boa Shoe Company, **42** 325

The Connell Company, 29 129–31
Conner Corp., 15 327
Conner Peripherals, Inc., 6 230–32; 10
403, 459, 463–64, 519; 11 56, 234; 18
260
Connie Lee. See College Construction
Loan Insurance Assoc.
Connoisseur Communications, 37 104
Connolly Data Systems, 11 66
Connolly Tool and Machine Company, 21
215
Connors Brothers, II 631–32
Connors Steel Co., 15 116
Conoco Inc., I 286, 329, 346, 402–04; II
376; IV 365, 382, 389, 399–402, 413,
429, 454, 476; 6 539; 7 346, 559; 8 152,
154, 556; 11 97, 400; 16 127–32 (upd.);
18 366; 21 29; 26 125, 127; 50 178, 363
Conorada Petroleum Corp., IV 365, 400
Conover Furniture Company, 10 183
ConQuest Telecommunication Services
Inc., 16 319
Conquistador Films, 25 270
Conrad International Hotels, III 91–93
Conrail Inc., 22 167, 376. See also
Consolidated Rail Corporation.
Conran Associates, 17 43
Conrock Co., 19 70
Conseco Inc., 10 246–48; 15 257; 33
108–12 (upd.)
Consgold. See Consolidated Gold Fields of
South Africa Ltd. and Consolidated Gold
Fields PLC.
Conshu Holdings, 24 450
Conso International Corporation, 29
132–34
Consodata S.A., 47 345, 347
Consolidated Aircraft Corporation, 9 16,
497
Consolidated Aluminum Corp., IV 178
Consolidated Asset Management Company,
Inc., 25 204
Consolidated-Bathurst Inc., IV 246–47,
334; 25 11; 26 445
Consolidated Brands Inc., 14 18
Consolidated Cable Utilities, 6 313
Consolidated Cement Corp., III 704
Consolidated Cigar Holdings, Inc., I
452–53; 15 137–38; 27 139–40; 28 247
Consolidated Coal Co., IV 82, 170–71
Consolidated Coin Caterers Corporation, 10
222
Consolidated Controls, I 155
Consolidated Converting Co., 19 109
Consolidated Copper Corp., 13 503
Consolidated Delivery & Logistics, Inc.,
24 125–28
Consolidated Denison Mines Ltd., 8 418
Consolidated Diamond Mines of South-
West Africa Ltd., IV 21, 65–67; 7
122–25; 16 26; 50 31
Consolidated Distillers Ltd., I 263
Consolidated Edison Company of New
York, Inc., I 28; V 586–89; 6 456; 35
479
Consolidated Edison, Inc., 45 116–20
(upd.)
Consolidated Electric & Gas, 6 447; 23 28
Consolidated Electric Power Asia, 38 448
Consolidated Electric Supply Inc., 15 385
Consolidated Electronics Industries Corp.
(Conelco), 13 397–98
Consolidated Foods Corp., II 571–73, 584;
III 480; 12 159, 494; 22 27; 29 132

Consolidated Freightways Corporation,
V 432–34; 6 280, 388; 12 278, 309; 13
19; 14 567; 21 136–39 (upd.); 25
148–50; 48 109–13 (upd.)
Consolidated Gas Company. See Baltimore
Gas and Electric Company.
Consolidated Gold Fields of South Africa
Ltd., IV 94, 96, 118, 565, 566
Consolidated Gold Fields PLC, II 422; III
501, 503; IV 23, 67, 94, 97, 171; 7 125,
209, 387
Consolidated Grocers Corp., II 571
Consolidated Insurances of Australia, III
347
Consolidated International, 50 98
Consolidated Marketing, Inc., IV 282; 9
261
Consolidated Mines Selection Co., IV 20,
23
Consolidated Mining and Smelting Co., IV
75
Consolidated National Life Insurance Co.,
10 246
Consolidated Natural Gas Company, V
590–91; 19 100–02 (upd.)
Consolidated Oatmeal Co., II 558
Consolidated Papers, Inc., 8 123–25; 36
126–30 (upd.)
Consolidated Plantations Berhad, 36
434–35
Consolidated Power & Light Company, 6
580
Consolidated Power & Telephone
Company, 11 342
Consolidated Press Holdings, 8 551; 37
408–09
Consolidated Products, Inc., 14 130–32,
352
Consolidated Rail Corporation, II 449;
V 435–37, 485; 10 44; 12 278; 13 449;
14 324; 29 360; 35 291. See also
Conrail Inc.
Consolidated Rand-Transvaal Mining
Group, IV 90; 22 233
Consolidated Rock Products Co., 19 69
Consolidated Specialty Restaurants, Inc.,
14 131–32
Consolidated Steel, I 558; IV 570; 24 520
Consolidated Stores Corp., 13 543; 29 311;
35 254; 50 98
Consolidated Temperature Controlling Co.,
II 40; 12 246; 50 231
Consolidated Theaters, Inc., 14 87
Consolidated Tire Company, 20 258
Consolidated Trust Inc., 22 540
Consolidated Tyre Services Ltd., IV 241
Consolidated Vultee, II 7, 32
Consolidated Zinc Corp., IV 58–59, 122,
189, 191
Consolidation Coal Co., IV 401; 8 154,
346–47
Consolidation Services, 44 10, 13
Consorcio G Grupo Dina, S.A. de C.V.,
36 131–33
Consortium, 34 373
Consortium de Realisation, 25 329
Consortium De Realization SAS, 23 392
Consoweld Corporation, 8 124
Constar International Inc., 8 562; 13 190;
32 125
Constellation, III 335
Constellation Energy Corporation, 24 29
Constellation Enterprises Inc., 25 46
Constellation Insurance Co., III 191–92

Constinsouza, 25 174
Constitution Insurance Company, 51 143
Construcciones Aeronáuticas SA, I 41–42;
7 9; 12 190; 24 88. See also European
Aeronautic Defence and Space Company
EADS N.V.
Construcciones y Contratas, II 198
Construction DJL Inc., 23 332–33
Construtora Moderna SARL, IV 505
Consul GmbH, 51 58
Consul Restaurant Corp., 13 152
Consumer Access Limited, 24 95
Consumer Products Company, 30 39
Consumer Value Stores, V 136–37; 9 67;
18 199; 24 290
Consumer's Gas Co., I 264
ConsumerNet, 49 422
Consumers Cooperative Association, 7 174.
See also Farmland Industries, Inc.
Consumers Distributing Co. Ltd., II 649,
652–53
Consumers Electric Light and Power, 6
582
The Consumers Gas Company Ltd., 6
476–79; 43 154. See also Enbridge Inc.
Consumers Mutual Gas Light Company.
See Baltimore Gas and Electric
Company.
Consumers Power Co., V 577–79,
593–94; 14 114–15, 133–36
Consumers Public Power District, 29 352
Consumers Union, 26 97–99
Consumers Water Company, 14 137–39;
39 329
Contact Software International Inc., 10 509
Contadina, II 488–89
Container Corporation of America, IV 295,
465; V 147; 7 353; 8 476; 19 225; 26
446
The Container Store, 36 134–36
Container Transport International, III 344
Containers Packaging, IV 249
Contaminant Recovery Systems, Inc., 18
162
CONTAQ Microsystems Inc., 48 127
Conte S.A., 12 262
Contech, 10 493
Contel Corporation, II 117; V 294–98; 6
323; 13 212; 14 259; 15 192; 43 447
Contempo Associates, 14 105; 25 307
Contempo Casuals, Inc. See The Wet Seal,
Inc.
Contemporary Books, 22 522
Content Technologies Inc., 42 24–25
Contex Graphics Systems Inc., 24 428
Contherm Corp., III 420
Conti-Carriers & Terminals Inc., 22 167
Contico International, L.L.C., 51 190
ContiCommodity Services, Inc., 10 250–51
ContiGroup Companies, Inc., 43 119–22
(upd.)
Continental Airlines, Inc., I 96–98, 103,
118, 123–24, 129–30; 6 52, 61, 105,
120–21, 129–30; 12 381; 20 84, 262; 21
140–43 (upd.); 22 80, 220; 25 420, 423;
26 439–40; 34 398; 52 89–94 (upd.)
Continental Aktiengesellschaft, V
240–43, 250–51, 256; 8 212–14; 9 248;
15 355; 19 508
Continental American Life Insurance
Company, 7 102
Continental Assurance Co., III 228–30

Moore-Handley, Inc., IV 345–46; 39 290–92
Moore McCormack Resources Inc., 14 455
Moore Medical Corp., 17 331–33
Moorhouse, II 477
Moran Group Inc., II 682
Moran Health Care Group Ltd., 25 455
MoRan Oil & Gas Co., IV 82–83
Moran Towing Corporation, Inc., 15 301–03
Morana, Inc., 9 290
Moreland and Watson, IV 208
Moretti-Harrah Marble Co., III 691
Morgan & Banks Limited, 30 460
Morgan & Cie International S.A., II 431
Morgan Construction Company, 8 448
Morgan Edwards, II 609
Morgan Engineering Co., 8 545
Morgan Grampian Group, IV 687
Morgan Grenfell Group PLC, II 280, 329, 427–29; IV 21, 712
The Morgan Group, Inc., 46 300–02
Morgan Guaranty International Banking Corp., II 331; 9 124
Morgan Guaranty Trust Co. of New York, I 26; II 208, 254, 262, 329–32, 339, 428, 431, 448; III 80; 10 150
Morgan Guaranty Trust Company, 11 421; 13 49, 448; 14 297; 25 541; 30 261
Morgan, Harjes & Co., II 329
Morgan, J.P. & Co. Inc. See J.P. Morgan & Co. Incorporated.
Morgan, Lewis & Bockius LLP, 29 332–34
Morgan, Lewis, Githens & Ahn, Inc., 6 410
Morgan Mitsubishi Development, IV 714
Morgan Schiff & Co., 29 205
Morgan Stanley Dean Witter & Company, 33 311–14 (upd.); 38 289, 291, 411
Morgan Stanley Group, Inc., I 34; II 211, 330, 403, 406–08, 422, 428, 430–32, 441; IV 295, 447, 714; 9 386; 11 258; 12 529; 16 374–78 (upd.); 18 448–49; 20 60, 363; 22 404, 407; 25 542; 30 353–55; 34 496; 36 153
Morgan Yacht Corp., II 468
Morgan's Brewery, I 287
Mori Bank, II 291
Moria Informatique, 6 229
Morino Associates, 10 394
Morita & Co., II 103
Mormac Marine Group, 15 302
Morning Star Technologies Inc., 24 49
Morning Sun, Inc., 23 66
Morningstar Storage Centers LLC, 52 311
Morris Air, 24 455
Morris Communications Corporation, 36 339–42
Morris Motors, III 256; 7 459; 50 67
Morris Travel Services L.L.C., 26 308–11
Morrison & Co. Ltd., 52 221
Morrison Homes, Inc., 51 138
Morrison Industries Ltd., IV 278; 19 153
Morrison Knudsen Corporation, IV 55; 7 355–58; 11 401, 553; 28 286–90 (upd.); 33 442; 50 36350 363. See also The Washington Companies.
Morrison Machine Products Inc., 25 193
Morrison Restaurants Inc., 11 323–25; 18 464
Morse Chain Co., III 439; 14 63

Morse Equalizing Spring Company, 14 63
Morse Industrial, 14 64
Morse Shoe Inc., 13 359–61
Morss and White, III 643
Morstan Development Co., Inc., II 432
Mortgage & Trust Co., II 251
Mortgage Associates, 9 229
Mortgage Guaranty Insurance Corp. See MGIC Investment Corp.
Mortgage Insurance Co. of Canada, II 222
Mortgage Resources, Inc., 10 91
Morton Foods, Inc., II 502; 10 323; 27 258
Morton International Inc., 9 358–59 (upd.), 500–01; 16 436; 22 505–06; 43 319
Morton Thiokol Inc., I 325, 370–72; 19 508; 28 253–54. See also Thiokol Corporation.
Morton's Restaurant Group, Inc., 28 401; 30 329–31
Mos Magnetics, 18 140
MOS Technology, 7 95
Mosby-Year Book, Inc., IV 678; 17 486
Moseley, Hallgarten, Estabrook, and Weeden, III 389
Mosher Steel Company, 7 540
Mosinee Paper Corporation, 15 304–06
Moskatel's, Inc., 17 321
Mosler Safe Co., III 664–65; 7 144, 146; 22 184
Moss Bros Group plc, 51 252–54
Moss-Rouse Company, 15 412
Mossgas, IV 93
Mossimo, Inc., 27 328–30
Mostek Corp., I 85; II 64; 11 307–08; 13 191; 20 175; 29 323
Mostjet Ltd. See British World Airlines Ltd.
Móstoles Industrial S.A., 26 129
Mostra Importaciones S.A., 34 38, 40
Motel 6 Corporation, 10 13; 13 362–64. See also Accor SA
Mother Karen's, 10 216
Mother's Oats, II 558–59; 12 409
Mothercare Stores, Inc., 16 466
Mothercare UK Ltd., 17 42–43, 334–36
Mothers Against Drunk Driving (MADD), 51 255–58
Mothers Work, Inc., 18 350–52
Motif Inc., 22 288
Motion Designs, 11 486
Motion Factory, Inc., 38 72
Motion Picture Association of America, 37 353–54
Motion Picture Corporation of America, 25 326, 329
Motiva Enterprises LLC, 41 359, 395
MotivePower. See Wabtec Corporation.
The Motley Fool, Inc., 40 329–31
Moto Photo, Inc., 45 282–84
Moto-Truc Co., 13 385
Motor Cargo Industries, Inc., 35 296–99
Motor Club of America Insurance Company, 44 354
Motor Coaches Industries International Inc., 36 132
Motor Haulage Co., IV 181
Motor Parts Industries, Inc., 9 363
Motor Transit Corp., I 448; 10 72
Motor Wheel Corporation, 20 261; 27 202–04
Motorcar Parts & Accessories, Inc., 47 253–55

Motoren-und-Turbinen-Union, I 151; III 563; 9 418; 15 142; 34 128, 131, 133
Motoren-Werke Mannheim AG, III 544
Motorenfabrik Deutz AG, III 541
Motorenfabrik Oberursel, III 541
Motornetic Corp., III 590
Motorola, Inc., I 534; II 5, 34, 44–45, 56, 60–62, 64; III 455; 6 238; 7 119, 494, 533; 8 139; 9 515; 10 87, 365, 367, 431–33; 11 45, 308, 326–29 (upd.), 381–82; 12 136–37, 162; 13 30, 356, 501; 17 33, 193; 18 18, 74, 76, 260, 382; 19 391; 20 8, 439; 21 123; 22 17, 19, 288, 542; 26 431–32; 27 20, 341–42, 344; 33 47–48; 34 296–302 (upd.); 38 188; 43 15; 44 97, 357, 359; 45 346, 348; 47 318, 320, 385; 48 270, 272
Motown Records Company L.P., II 145; 22 194; 23 389, 391; 26 312–14
Moulinex S.A., 22 362–65
Mound Metalcraft. See Tonka Corporation.
Mount. See also Mt.
Mount Hood Credit Life Insurance Agency, 14 529
Mount Isa Mines, IV 61
Mount Vernon Group, 8 14
Mountain Fuel Supply Company. See Questar Corporation.
Mountain Fuel Supply Company, 6 568–69
Mountain Pass Canning Co., 7 429
Mountain Safety Research, 18 445–46
Mountain State Telephone Company, 6 300
Mountain States Mortgage Centers, Inc., 29 335–37
Mountain States Power Company. See PacifiCorp.
Mountain States Telephone & Telegraph Co., V 341; 25 495
Mountain States Wholesale, II 602; 30 25
Mountain Valley Indemnity Co., 44 356
Mountain West Bank, 35 197
Mountleigh PLC, 16 465
Mounts Wire Industries, III 673
Mountsorrel Granite Co., III 734
Mouvement des Caisses Desjardins, 48 288–91
Movado Group, Inc., 28 291–94
Movado-Zenith-Mondia Holding, II 124
Movie Gallery, Inc., 31 339–41
Movie Star Inc., 17 337–39
Movies To Go, Inc., 9 74; 31 57
Movil@ccess, S.A. de C.V., 39 25, 194
Moving Co. Ltd., V 127
The Moving Picture Company, 15 83; 50 124, 126
The Mowry Co., 23 102
MP3.com, 43 109
MPB Corporation, 8 529, 531
MPI. See Michael Page International plc.
MPM, III 735
MPS Group, Inc., 49 264–67
Mr. Bricolage S.A., 37 258–60
Mr. Coffee, Inc., 14 229–31; 15 307–09; 17 215; 27 275; 39 406
Mr. D's Food Centers, 12 112
Mr. Donut, 21 323
Mr. Gasket Inc., 11 84; 15 310–12
Mr. Gatti's, 15 345
Mr. Goodbuys, 13 545
Mr. How, V 191–92
Mr. M Food Stores, 7 373
Mr. Maintenance, 25 15
Mr. Payroll Corp., 20 113

Omega Gas Company, **8** 349
Omega Gold Mines, **IV** 164
Omega Protein Corporation, **25** 546
O'Melveny & Myers, 37 290–93
Omex Corporation, **6** 272
OMI Corporation, **IV** 34; **9** 111–12; **22** 275
Omlon, **II** 75
Ommium Française de Pétroles, **IV** 559
Omnes, **17** 419
Omni Construction Company, Inc., **8** 112–13
Omni Hearing Aid Systems, **I** 667
Omni Hotels Corp., 12 367–69
Omni-Pac, **12** 377
Omni Products International, **II** 420
Omni Services, Inc., **51** 76
Omnibus Corporation, **9** 283
Omnicad Corporation, **48** 75
Omnicare, Inc., 13 150; **49 307–10**
Omnicom Group Inc., I 28–32, 33, 36; **14** 160; **22 394–99 (upd.); 23** 478; **43** 410. *See also* TBWA Worldwide.
Omnipoint Communications Inc., **18** 77
OmniSource Corporation, 14 366–67
OmniTech Consulting Group, **51** 99
Omnitel Pronto Italia SpA, **38** 300
Omron Corporation, 28 331–35 (upd.)
Omron Tateisi Electronics Company, II 75–77; III 549
ÖMV Aktiengesellschaft, IV 234, 454, **485–87**
On Assignment, Inc., 20 400–02
On Command Video Corp., **23** 135
On Cue, **9** 360
On-Line Software International Inc., **6** 225
On-Line Systems. *See* Sierra On-Line Inc.
Onan Corporation, **8** 72
Onbancorp Inc., **11** 110
Once Upon A Child, Inc., **18** 207–8
Oncogen, **III** 18
Ondal Industrietechnik GmbH, **III** 69; **48** 423
Ondulato Imolese, **IV** 296; **19** 226
1-800-FLOWERS, Inc., 26 344–46; 28 137
1-800-Mattress. *See* Dial-A-Mattress Operating Corporation.
One For All, **39** 405
One Hundred Thirtieth National Bank, **II** 291
One Hundredth Bank, **II** 321
One Price Clothing Stores, Inc., 20 403–05
O'Neal, Jones & Feldman Inc., **11** 142
OneBeacon Insurance Group LLC, **48** 431
Oneida Bank & Trust Company, **9** 229
Oneida County Creameries Co., **7** 202
Oneida Gas Company, **9** 554
Oneida Ltd., 7 406–08; 31 352–355 (upd.)
ONEOK Inc., 7 409–12
Onex Corporation, 16 395–97; 22 513; **24** 498; **25** 282; **50** 275
OneZero Media, Inc., **31** 240
Onitsuka Tiger Co., **V** 372; **8** 391; **36** 343–44
Online Distributed Processing Corporation, **6** 201
Online Financial Communication Systems, **11** 112
Only One Dollar, Inc. *See* Dollar Tree Stores, Inc.

Onoda Cement Co., Ltd., I 508; **III 717–19**
Onomichi, **25** 469
OnResponse.com, Inc., **49** 433
Onsale Inc., **31** 177
Onstead Foods, **21** 501
OnTarget Inc., **38** 432
Ontario Hydro Services Company, 6 541–42; 9 461; **32 368–71 (upd.)**
Ontario Power Generation, **49** 65, 67
Ontel Corporation, **6** 201
OnTrak Systems Inc., **31** 301
Oode Casting Iron Works, **III** 551
O'okiep Copper Company, Ltd., **7** 385–86
Opel. *See* Adam Opel AG.
Open Board of Brokers, **9** 369
Open Cellular Systems, Inc., **41** 225–26
Open Market, Inc., **22** 522
OpenTV, Inc., **31** 330–31
Operadora de Bolsa Serfin. *See* Grupo Financiero Serfin, S.A.
Operon Technologies Inc., **39** 335
Opinion Research Corporation, 35 47; **46 318–22**
Opp and Micolas Mills, **15** 247–48
Oppenheimer. *See* Ernest Oppenheimer and Sons.
Oppenheimer & Co., **17** 137; **21** 235; **22** 405; **25** 450
Opryland USA, **11** 152–53; **25** 403; **36** 229
Opsware Inc., 49 311–14
Optel Corp., **17** 331
OPTi Computer, **9** 116
Opti-Ray, Inc., **12** 215
Optical Radiation Corporation, **27** 57
Optilink Corporation, **12** 137
Optima Pharmacy Services, **17** 177
Optimum Financial Services Ltd., **II** 457
Option Care Inc., 48 307–10
Optische Werke G. Rodenstock, 44 319–23
Opto-Electronics Corp., **15** 483
Optronics, Inc., **6** 247; **24** 234
Optus Communications, **25** 102
Optus Vision, **17** 150
Opus Group, 34 321–23
OPW, **III** 467–68
Oracle Corporation, 24 367–71 (upd.); 25 34, 96–97, 499
Oracle Systems Corporation, 6 272–74; 10 361, 363, 505; **11** 78; **13** 483; **14** 16; **15** 492; **18** 541, 543; **19** 310; **21** 86; **22** 154, 293
Orange and Rockland Utilities, Inc., **45** 116, 120
Orange Julius of America, **10** 371, 373; **39** 232, 235
Orange Line Bus Company, **6** 604
Orange PLC, **24** 89; **38** 300
Orb Books. *See* Tom Doherty Associates Inc.
Orbis Entertainment Co., **20** 6
Orbis Graphic Arts. *See* Anaheim Imaging.
Orbital Engine Corporation Ltd., **17** 24
Orbital Sciences Corporation, 22 400–03
Orchard Supply Hardware Stores Corporation, 17 365–67; 25 535
Orcofi, **III** 48
OrderTrust LLP, **26** 440
Ore and Chemical Corp., **IV** 140
Ore-Ida Foods Incorporated, II 508; **11** 172; **12** 531; **13 382–83; 36** 254, 256
Orebehoved Fanerfabrik, **25** 464

Oregon Ale and Beer Company, **18** 72; **50** 112
Oregon Chai, Inc., 49 315–17
Oregon Craft & Floral Supply, **17** 322
Oregon Cutting Systems, **26** 119
Oregon Dental Service Health Plan, Inc., 51 276–78
Oregon Metallurgical Corporation, 20 406–08
Oregon Pacific and Eastern Railway, **13** 100
Oregon Steel Mills, Inc., 14 368–70; 19 380
O'Reilly Automotive, Inc., 26 347–49
Orenda Aerospace, **48** 274
Orford Copper Co., **IV** 110
Organización Soriana, S.A. de C.V., 35 320–22
Organon, **I** 665
Orico Life Insurance Co., **48** 328
Oriel Foods, **II** 609
Orient, **21** 122
Orient Express Hotels Inc., **29** 429–30
Orient Glass, **III** 715
Orient Leasing. *See* Orix Corporation.
Orient Overseas, **18** 254
Oriental Brewery Co., Ltd., **21** 320
Oriental Cotton Trading. *See* Tomen Corporation.
Oriental Land Co., Ltd., **IV** 715
Oriental Precision Company, **13** 213
Oriental Trading Corp., **22** 213
Oriental Yeast Co., **17** 288
Origin Energy Limited, **43** 75. *See also* Boral Limited.
Origin Systems Inc., **10** 285
Origin Technology, **14** 183
Original Arizona Jean Company. *See* J.C. Penney Company, Inc.
Original Cookie Co., **13** 166. *See also* Mrs. Fields' Original Cookies, Inc.
Original Musical Instrument Company (O.M.I.), **16** 239
Original Wassertragers Hummel, **II** 163
Origins Natural Resources Inc., **30** 190
Orinoco Oilfields, Ltd., **IV** 565
Orion, **III** 310
Orion Bank Ltd., **II** 271, 345, 385
Orion Healthcare Ltd., **11** 168
Orion Personal Insurances Ltd., **11** 168
Orion Pictures Corporation, II 147; **6 167–70; 7** 336; **14** 330, 332; **25** 326, 328–29; **31** 100
Orit Corp., **8** 219–20
ORIX Corporation, II 442–43, 259, 348; **44 324–26 (upd.)**
Orkem, **IV** 547, 560; **21** 205
Orkin Pest Control, **11** 431–32, 434
Orkla A/S, 18 394–98; 25 205–07; 36 266
Orlimar Golf Equipment Co., **45** 76
Orm Bergold Chemie, **8** 464
Ormco Corporation, **14** 481
ÖROP, **IV** 485–86
Orowheat Baking Company, **10** 250
La Oroya, **22** 286
ORSCO, Inc., **26** 363
Ortho Diagnostic Systems, Inc., **10** 213; **22** 75
Ortho Pharmaceutical Corporation, **III** 35; **8** 281; **10** 79–80; **30** 59–60
Orthodontic Centers of America, Inc., 35 323–26
Orthopedic Services, Inc., **11** 366

586

Withington Company. *See* Sparton
Corporation.
Wittington Investments Ltd., **13** 51
The Wiz. *See* Cablevision Electronic
Instruments, Inc.
Wizards of the Coast Inc., 24 537–40; 43
229, 233
WizardWorks Group, Inc., **31** 238–39
WLIW-TV. *See* Educational Broadcasting
Corporation.
WLR Foods, Inc., 14 516; **21 534–36; 50**
494
WM Investment Company, **34** 512
**Wm. Morrison Supermarkets PLC, 38
496–98**
Wm. Underwood Company, **40** 53
Wm. Wrigley Jr. Company, 7 594–97
WMC, Limited, 43 469–72
WMS Industries, Inc., III 431; **15
537–39; 41** 215–16
WMX Technologies Inc., 11 435–36; **17
551–54; 26** 409
Woermann and German East African
Lines, **I** 542
Wöhlk, **III** 446
Wolf Furniture Enterprises, **14** 236
Wolfe & Associates, **25** 434
Wolfe Industries, Inc., **22** 255
Wolff Printing Co., **13** 559
**The Wolfgang Puck Food Company,
Inc., 26 534–36**
Wolohan Lumber Co., 19 503–05; 25
535
Wolters Kluwer NV, IV 611; **14 554–56;
31** 389, 394; **33 458–61 (upd.)**
Wolvercote Paper Mill, **IV** 300
Wolverine Die Cast Group, **IV** 165
Wolverine Insurance Co., **26** 487
Wolverine Tube Inc., 23 515–17
Wolverine World Wide Inc., 16 544–47;
17 390; **32** 99; **44** 365
Womack Development Company, **11** 257
**Womble Carlyle Sandridge & Rice,
PLLC, 52 421–24**
Women's Specialty Retailing Group. *See*
Casual Corner Group, Inc.
Women's World, **15** 96
Wometco Coca-Cola Bottling Co., **10** 222
Wometco Coffee Time, **I** 514
Wometco Enterprises, **I** 246, 514
Wonderware Corp., **22** 374
Wong International Holdings, **16** 195
Wood Fiberboard Co., **IV** 358
Wood Gundy, **II** 345; **21** 447
Wood Hall Trust plc, I 438, 592–93; **50**
200
Wood-Metal Industries, Inc. *See* Wood-
Mode, Inc.
Wood-Mode, Inc., 23 518–20
Wood River Oil and Refining Company, **11**
193
Wood Shovel and Tool Company, **9** 71
Wood, Struthers & Winthrop, Inc., **22** 189
Wood Wyant Inc., **30** 496–98
Woodall Industries, **III** 641; **14** 303; **50**
310
Woodard-Walker Lumber Co., **IV** 358
Woodbridge Winery, **50** 388
Woodbury Co., **19** 380
Woodcock, Hess & Co., **9** 370
Woodfab, **IV** 295; **19** 225
Woodhaven Gas Light Co., **6** 455
Woodhill Chemical Sales Company, **8** 333
Woodland Publishing, Inc., **37** 286

Woodlands, **7** 345–46
Woods and Co., **II** 235
Woods Equipment Company, **32** 28
Woodside Travel Trust, **26** 310
Woodville Appliances, Inc., **9** 121
Woodward-Clyde Group Inc., **45** 421
Woodward Corp., **IV** 311; **19** 267
**Woodward Governor Company, 13
565–68; 49 453–57 (upd.)**
Woodworkers Warehouse, **22** 517
Woolco Department Stores, **II** 634; **7** 444;
V 107, 225–26; **14** 294; **22** 242
Woolverton Motors, **I** 183
The Woolwich plc, 30 492–95
Woolworth Corporation, II 414; **6** 344;
V 106–09, **224–27; 8** 509; **14** 293–95;
17 42, 335; **20 528–32 (upd.); 25** 22.
See also Venator Group Inc.
Woolworth Holdings, **II** 139; **V** 108; **19**
123; **24** 194
Woolworth's Ltd., **II** 656. *See also*
Kingfisher plc.
Wooster Preserving Company, **11** 211
Wooster Rubber Co., **III** 613
Worcester City and County Bank, **II** 307
Worcester Gas Light Co., **14** 124
Worcester Wire Works, **13** 369
Word, Inc., **14** 499; **38** 456
Word Processors Personnel Service, **6** 10
WordPerfect Corporation, 6 256; **10** 519,
556–59; 12 335; **25** 300; **41** 281. *See
also* Corel Corporation.
WordStar International, **15** 149; **43** 151.
See also The Learning Company Inc.
Work Wear Corp., **II** 607, **16** 229
**Working Assets Funding Service, 43
473–76**
Working Title Films, **23** 389
Workscape Inc., **42** 430
World Air Network, Ltd., **6** 71
World Airways, **10** 560–62; **28** 404
World Bank Group, 33 462–65
World Book Group. *See* Scott Fetzer
Company.
World Book, Inc., IV 622; **12 554–56**
World Championship Wrestling (WCW),
32 516
World Color Press Inc., 12 557–59; 19
333; **21** 61
World Commerce Corporation, **25** 461
World Communications, Inc., **11** 184
**World Duty Free Americas, Inc., 29
509–12 (upd.)**
World Duty Free plc, **33** 59
World Film Studio, **24** 437
World Financial Network National Bank, **V**
116
World Flight Crew Services, **10** 560
World Foot Locker, **14** 293
**World Fuel Services Corporation, 47
449–51**
World Gift Company, **9** 330
World International Holdings Limited, **12**
368
World Journal Tribune Inc., **IV** 608
World Machinery Company, **45** 170–71
World Online, **48** 398–39
World Poker Tour, LLC, **51** 205, 207
World Publishing Co., **8** 423
World Savings and Loan, **19** 412; **47**
159–60
World Service Life Insurance Company, **27**
47

World Trade Corporation. *See* International
Business Machines Corporation.
World Trans, Inc., **33** 105
World-Wide Shipping Group, **II** 298; **III**
517
**World Wrestling Federation
Entertainment, Inc., 32 514–17**
World Yacht Enterprises, **22** 438
World's Finest Chocolate Inc., 39
422–24
WorldCom, Inc., **14** 330, 332; **18** 33, 164,
166; **29** 227; **38** 269–70, 468; **46** 376.
See also MCI WorldCom, Inc.
WorldCorp, Inc., 10 560–62
WorldGames, **10** 560
WorldMark, The Club, **33** 409
Worlds of Fun, **22** 130
Worlds of Wonder, Inc., **25** 381; **26** 548
Worldview Systems Corporation, **26** 428;
46 434
WorldWay Corporation, **16** 41
Worldwide Fiber Inc., **46** 267
Worldwide Insurance Co., **48** 9
Worldwide Logistics, **17** 505
**Worldwide Restaurant Concepts, Inc.,
47 452–55**
Worldwide Semiconductor Manufacturing
Co., **47** 386
Worldwide Underwriters Insurance Co., **III**
218–19
Wormald International Ltd., **13** 245, 247
Worms et Cie, 27 275–76, **513–15**
Wormser, **III** 760
Worth Corp., **27** 274
Wortham, Gus Sessions, **III** 193; **10** 65
Worthen Banking Corporation, **15** 60
Worthington & Co., **I** 223
Worthington Corp., **I** 142
Worthington Foods, Inc., I 653; **14
557–59; 33** 170
Worthington Industries, Inc., 7 598–600;
8 450; **21 537–40 (upd.)**
Worthington Telephone Company, **6** 312
Woven Belting Co., **8** 13
WPL Holdings, 6 604–06
WPM. *See* Wall Paper Manufacturers.
WPP Group plc, I 21; **6 53–54; 22** 201,
296; **23** 480; **48 440–42 (upd.).** *See also*
Ogilvy Group Inc.
Wrather Corporation, **18** 354
Wrenn Furniture Company, **10** 184
WRG. *See* Wells Rich Greene BDDP.
Wright & Company Realtors, **21** 257
Wright Aeronautical, **9** 16
Wright Airplane Co., **III** 151; **6** 265
Wright and Son, **II** 593
Wright Company, **9** 416
Wright Engine Company, **11** 427
Wright Group, **22** 519, 522
Wright Manufacturing Company, **8** 407
Wright Plastic Products, **17** 310; **24** 160
Wright, Robertson & Co. *See* Fletcher
Challenge Ltd.
Wright Stephenson & Co., **IV** 278
Wrightson Limited, **19** 155
Write Right Manufacturing Co., **IV** 345
WS Atkins Plc, 45 445–47
WSGC Holdings, Inc., **24** 530
WSI. *See* Weather Services International.
WSI Corporation, **10** 88–89
WSM Inc., **11** 152
WSMC. *See* Worldwide Semiconductor
Manufacturing Co.
WSMP, Inc., **29** 202

INDEX TO INDUSTRIES

Index to Industries

Panalpina World Transport (Holding) Ltd., 47
People Express Airlines, Inc., I
Petroleum Helicopters, Inc., 35
Philippine Airlines, Inc., 6; 23 (upd.)
Preussag AG, 42 (upd.)
Qantas Airways Limited, 6; 24 (upd.)
Reno Air Inc., 23
Royal Nepal Airline Corporation, 41
Ryanair Holdings plc, 35
SAA (Pty) Ltd., 28
Sabena S.A./N.V., 33
The SAS Group, 34 (upd.)
Saudi Arabian Airlines, 6; 27 (upd.)
Scandinavian Airlines System, I
Singapore Airlines Ltd., 6; 27 (upd.)
SkyWest, Inc., 25
Société Tunisienne de l'Air-Tunisair, 49
Southwest Airlines Co., 6; 24 (upd.)
Spirit Airlines, Inc., 31
Sun Country Airlines, 30
Swiss Air Transport Company, Ltd., I
Swiss International Air Lines Ltd., 48
TAP—Air Portugal Transportes Aéreos Portugueses S.A., 46
Texas Air Corporation, I
Thai Airways International Public Company Limited, 6; 27 (upd.)
Tower Air, Inc., 28
Trans World Airlines, Inc., I; 12 (upd.); 35 (upd.)
TransBrasil S/A Linhas Aéreas, 31
Transportes Acreos Portugueses, S.A., 6
TV Guide, Inc., 43 (upd.)
UAL Corporation, 34 (upd.)
United Airlines, I; 6 (upd.)
US Airways Group, Inc., 28 (upd.); 52 (upd.)
USAir Group, Inc., I; 6 (upd.)
VARIG S.A. (Viação Aérea Rio-Grandense), 6; 29 (upd.)
WestJet Airlines Ltd., 38

AUTOMOTIVE

AB Volvo, I; 7 (upd.); 26 (upd.)
Adam Opel AG, 7; 21 (upd.)
Aisin Seiki Co., Ltd., 48 (upd.)
Alfa Romeo, 13; 36 (upd.)
Alvis Plc, 47
American Motors Corporation, I
Applied Power Inc., 32 (upd.)
Arvin Industries, Inc., 8
Autocam Corporation, 51
Automobiles Citroen, 7
Automobili Lamborghini Holding S.p.A., 13; 34 (upd.)
AutoNation, Inc., 50
Bajaj Auto Limited, 39
Bayerische Motoren Werke AG, I; 11 (upd.); 38 (upd.)
Bendix Corporation, I
Blue Bird Corporation, 35
Bombardier Inc., 42 (upd.)
Borg-Warner Automotive, Inc., 14; 32 (upd.)
The Budd Company, 8
CARQUEST Corporation, 29
Chrysler Corporation, I; 11 (upd.)
CNH Global N.V., 38 (upd.)
Consorcio G Grupo Dina, S.A. de C.V., 36
CSK Auto Corporation, 38
Cummins Engine Company, Inc., I; 12 (upd.); 40 (upd.)
Custom Chrome, Inc., 16
Daihatsu Motor Company, Ltd., 7; 21 (upd.)
Daimler-Benz A.G., I; 15 (upd.)

DaimlerChrysler AG, 34 (upd.)
Dana Corporation, I; 10 (upd.)
Deere & Company, 42 (upd.)
Delphi Automotive Systems Corporation, 45
Don Massey Cadillac, Inc., 37
Donaldson Company, Inc., 49 (upd.)
Douglas & Lomason Company, 16
Ducati Motor Holding S.p.A., 30
Eaton Corporation, I; 10 (upd.)
Echlin Inc., I; 11 (upd.)
Edelbrock Corporation, 37
Federal-Mogul Corporation, I; 10 (upd.); 26 (upd.)
Ferrari S.p.A., 13; 36 (upd.)
Fiat SpA, I; 11 (upd.); 50 (upd.)
FinishMaster, Inc., 24
Ford Motor Company, I; 11 (upd.); 36 (upd.)
Ford Motor Company, S.A. de C.V., 20
Fruehauf Corporation, I
General Motors Corporation, I; 10 (upd.); 36 (upd.)
Gentex Corporation, 26
Genuine Parts Company, 9; 45 (upd.)
GKN plc, 38 (upd.)
Group 1 Automotive, Inc., 52
Harley-Davidson Inc., 7; 25 (upd.)
Hayes Lemmerz International, Inc., 27
The Hertz Corporation, 33 (upd.)
Hino Motors, Ltd., 7; 21 (upd.)
Holley Performance Products Inc., 52
Hometown Auto Retailers, Inc., 44
Honda Motor Company Limited (Honda Giken Kogyo Kabushiki Kaisha), I; 10 (upd.); 29 (upd.)
Insurance Auto Auctions, Inc., 23
Isuzu Motors, Ltd., 9; 23 (upd.)
Kelsey-Hayes Group of Companies, 7; 27 (upd.)
Kia Motors Corporation, 12; 29 (upd.)
Lear Seating Corporation, 16
Les Schwab Tire Centers, 50
Lithia Motors, Inc., 41
Lotus Cars Ltd., 14
Lund International Holdings, Inc., 40
Mack Trucks, Inc., I; 22 (upd.)
The Major Automotive Companies, Inc., 45
Masland Corporation, 17
Mazda Motor Corporation, 9; 23 (upd.)
Mel Farr Automotive Group, 20
Metso Corporation, 30 (upd.)
Midas International Corporation, 10
Mitsubishi Motors Corporation, 9; 23 (upd.)
Monaco Coach Corporation, 31
Monro Muffler Brake, Inc., 24
National R.V. Holdings, Inc., 32
Navistar International Corporation, I; 10 (upd.)
Nissan Motor Co., Ltd., I; 11 (upd.); 34 (upd.)
O'Reilly Automotive, Inc., 26
Officine Alfieri Maserati S.p.A., 13
Oshkosh Truck Corporation, 7
Paccar Inc., I
PACCAR Inc., 26 (upd.)
Pennzoil Company, 20 (upd.)
Pennzoil-Quaker State Company, 50 (upd.)
Penske Corporation, 19 (upd.)
The Pep Boys—Manny, Moe & Jack, 11; 36 (upd.)
Peugeot S.A., I
Piaggio & C. S.p.A., 20
Porsche AG, 13; 31 (upd.)
PSA Peugeot Citroen S.A., 28 (upd.)
R&B, Inc., 51
Regie Nationale des Usines Renault, I

Renault S.A., 26 (upd.)
Republic Industries, Inc., 26
The Reynolds and Reynolds Company, 50
Robert Bosch GmbH., I; 16 (upd.); 43 (upd.)
RockShox, Inc., 26
Rockwell Automation, 43 (upd.)
Rolls-Royce plc, I; 21 (upd.)
Rover Group Ltd., 7; 21 (upd.)
Saab Automobile AB, 32 (upd.)
Saab-Scania A.B., I; 11 (upd.)
Safelite Glass Corp., 19
Saturn Corporation, 7; 21 (upd.)
Sealed Power Corporation, I
Sheller-Globe Corporation, I
Sixt AG, 39
Skoda Auto a.s., 39
Spartan Motors Inc., 14
SpeeDee Oil Change and Tune-Up, 25
SPX Corporation, 10; 47 (upd.)
Standard Motor Products, Inc., 40
Superior Industries International, Inc., 8
Suzuki Motor Corporation, 9; 23 (upd.)
Sytner Group plc, 45
Tower Automotive, Inc., 24
Toyota Motor Corporation, I; 11 (upd.); 38 (upd.)
TRW Inc., 14 (upd.)
Ugly Duckling Corporation, 22
United Auto Group, Inc., 26
United Technologies Automotive Inc., 15
Valeo, 23
Volkswagen Aktiengesellschaft, I; 11 (upd.); 32 (upd.)
Walker Manufacturing Company, 19
Winnebago Industries Inc., 7; 27 (upd.)
Woodward Governor Company, 49 (upd.)
ZF Friedrichshafen AG, 48
Ziebart International Corporation, 30

BEVERAGES

A & W Brands, Inc., 25
Adolph Coors Company, I; 13 (upd.); 36 (upd.)
Allied Domecq PLC, 29
Allied-Lyons PLC, I
Anchor Brewing Company, 47
Anheuser-Busch Companies, Inc., I; 10 (upd.); 34 (upd.)
Asahi Breweries, Ltd., I; 20 (upd.); 52 (upd.)
Bacardi Limited, 18
Banfi Products Corp., 36
Baron Philippe de Rothschild S.A., 39
Bass PLC, I; 15 (upd.); 38 (upd.)
BBAG Osterreichische Brau-Beteiligungs-AG, 38
Beringer Wine Estates Holdings, Inc., 22
The Boston Beer Company, Inc., 18; 50 (upd.)
Brauerei Beck & Co., 9; 33 (upd.)
Brown-Forman Corporation, I; 10 (upd.); 38 (upd.)
Cadbury Schweppes PLC, 49 (upd.)
Canandaigua Brands, Inc., 34 (upd.)
Canandaigua Wine Company, Inc., 13
Carlsberg A/S, 9; 29 (upd.)
Carlton and United Breweries Ltd., I
Casa Cuervo, S.A. de C.V., 31
Cerveceria Polar, I
The Chalone Wine Group, Ltd., 36
Clearly Canadian Beverage Corporation, 48
Coca Cola Bottling Co. Consolidated, 10
The Coca-Cola Company, I; 10 (upd.); 32 (upd.)
Corby Distilleries Limited, 14
Cott Corporation, 52

ELECTRICAL & ELECTRONICS

ENTERTAINMENT & LEISURE

FINANCIAL SERVICES: NON-BANKS

HEALTH & PERSONAL CARE PRODUCTS

Unitrin Inc., 16
UNUM Corp., 13
UnumProvident Corporation, 52 (upd.)
USAA, 10
USF&G Corporation, III
Victoria Group, 44 (upd.)
VICTORIA Holding AG, III
W.R. Berkley Corp., 15
Washington National Corporation, 12
White Mountains Insurance Group, Ltd., 48
Willis Corroon Group plc, 25
''Winterthur'' Schweizerische
   Versicherungs-Gesellschaft, III
The Yasuda Fire and Marine Insurance
   Company, Limited, III
The Yasuda Mutual Life Insurance
   Company, III; 39 (upd.)
''Zürich'' Versicherungs-Gesellschaft, III

LEGAL SERVICES

Akin, Gump, Strauss, Hauer & Feld,
   L.L.P., 33
American Bar Association, 35
American Lawyer Media Holdings, Inc., 32
Amnesty International, 50
Arnold & Porter, 35
Baker & Hostetler LLP, 40
Baker & McKenzie, 10; 42 (upd.)
Baker and Botts, L.L.P., 28
Bingham Dana LLP, 43
Brobeck, Phleger & Harrison, LLP, 31
Cadwalader, Wickersham & Taft, 32
Chadbourne & Parke, 36
Cleary, Gottlieb, Steen & Hamilton, 35
Clifford Chance LLP, 38
Coudert Brothers, 30
Covington & Burling, 40
Cravath, Swaine & Moore, 43
Davis Polk & Wardwell, 36
Debevoise & Plimpton, 39
Dechert, 43
Dewey Ballantine LLP, 48
Dorsey & Whitney LLP, 47
Fenwick & West LLP, 34
Foley & Lardner, 28
Fried, Frank, Harris, Shriver & Jacobson,
   35
Fulbright & Jaworski L.L.P., 47
Gibson, Dunn & Crutcher LLP, 36
Heller, Ehrman, White & McAuliffe, 41
Hildebrandt International, 29
Hogan & Hartson L.L.P., 44
Holme Roberts & Owen LLP, 28
Hughes Hubbard & Reed LLP, 44
Hunton & Williams, 35
Jones, Day, Reavis & Pogue, 33
Kelley Drye & Warren LLP, 40
King & Spalding, 23
Latham & Watkins, 33
LeBoeuf, Lamb, Greene & MacRae,
   L.L.P., 29
The Legal Aid Society, 48
Mayer, Brown, Rowe & Maw, 47
Milbank, Tweed, Hadley & McCloy, 27
Morgan, Lewis & Bockius LLP, 29
O'Melveny & Myers, 37
Paul, Hastings, Janofsky & Walker LLP,
   27
Paul, Weiss, Rifkind, Wharton & Garrison,
   47
Pepper Hamilton LLP, 43
Pillsbury Madison & Sutro LLP, 29
Pre-Paid Legal Services, Inc., 20
Proskauer Rose LLP, 47
Ropes & Gray, 40
Shearman & Sterling, 32
Sidley Austin Brown & Wood, 40

Simpson Thacher & Bartlett, 39
Skadden, Arps, Slate, Meagher & Flom, 18
Snell & Wilmer L.L.P., 28
Stroock & Stroock & Lavan LLP, 40
Sullivan & Cromwell, 26
Vinson & Elkins L.L.P., 30
Wachtell, Lipton, Rosen & Katz, 47
White & Case LLP, 35
Williams & Connolly LLP, 47
Wilson Sonsini Goodrich & Rosati, 34
Winston & Strawn, 35
Womble Carlyle Sandridge & Rice, PLLC,
   52

MANUFACTURING

A. Schulman, Inc., 49 (upd.)
A.B.Dick Company, 28
A.O. Smith Corporation, 11; 40 (upd.)
A.T. Cross Company, 17; 49 (upd.)
A.W. Faber-Castell
   Unternehmensverwaltung GmbH & Co.,
   51
AAF-McQuay Incorporated, 26
AAON, Inc., 22
AAR Corp., 28
ABC Rail Products Corporation, 18
Abiomed, Inc., 47
ACCO World Corporation, 7; 51 (upd.)
Acme-Cleveland Corp., 13
Acuson Corporation, 36 (upd.)
Adams Golf, Inc., 37
Adolf Würth GmbH & Co. KG, 49
AEP Industries, Inc., 36
Ag-Chem Equipment Company, Inc., 17
AGCO Corp., 13
Aisin Seiki Co., Ltd., III
AK Steel Holding Corporation, 41 (upd.)
Aktiebolaget Electrolux, 22 (upd.)
Aktiebolaget SKF, III; 38 (upd.)
Alamo Group Inc., 32
Alberto-Culver Company, 36 (upd.)
Aldila Inc., 46
Alfa-Laval AB, III
Allen Organ Company, 33
Alliant Techsystems Inc., 8; 30 (upd.)
Allied Healthcare Products, Inc., 24
Allied Products Corporation, 21
Allied Signal Engines, 9
AlliedSignal Inc., 22 (upd.)
Allison Gas Turbine Division, 9
Alltrista Corporation, 30
Alps Electric Co., Ltd., 44 (upd.)
Alvis Plc, 47
Amer Group plc, 41
American Biltrite Inc., 43 (upd.)
American Business Products, Inc., 20
American Cast Iron Pipe Company, 50
American Homestar Corporation, 18; 41
   (upd.)
American Locker Group Incorporated, 34
American Standard Companies Inc., 30
   (upd.)
American Tourister, Inc., 16
American Woodmark Corporation, 31
Ameriwood Industries International Corp.,
   17
AMETEK, Inc., 9
AMF Bowling, Inc., 40
Ampex Corporation, 17
Amway Corporation, 30 (upd.)
Analogic Corporation, 23
Anchor Hocking Glassware, 13
Andersen Corporation, 10
The Andersons, Inc., 31
Andreas Stihl, 16
Andritz AG, 51
Anthem Electronics, Inc., 13

Apasco S.A. de C.V., 51
Applica Incorporated, 43 (upd.)
Applied Films Corporation, 48
Applied Materials, Inc., 10; 46 (upd.)
Applied Micro Circuits Corporation, 38
Applied Power Inc., 9; 32 (upd.)
ARBED S.A., 22 (upd.)
Arctco, Inc., 16
Arctic Cat Inc., 40 (upd.)
Ariens Company, 48
Armor All Products Corp., 16
Armstrong World Industries, Inc., III; 22
   (upd.)
Artesyn Technologies Inc., 46 (upd.)
Asahi Glass Company, Ltd., 48 (upd.)
Ashley Furniture Industries, Inc., 35
ASML Holding N.V., 50
Astronics Corporation, 35
ASV, Inc., 34
Atlas Copco AB, III; 28 (upd.)
Avedis Zildjian Co., 38
Avery Dennison Corporation, 17 (upd.); 49
   (upd.)
Avondale Industries, 7; 41 (upd.)
Badger Meter, Inc., 22
Baker Hughes Incorporated, III
Baldor Electric Company, 21
Baldwin Piano & Organ Company, 18
Baldwin Technology Company, Inc., 25
Balfour Beatty plc, 36 (upd.)
Ballantyne of Omaha, Inc., 27
Ballard Medical Products, 21
Bally Manufacturing Corporation, III
Baltek Corporation, 34
Barmag AG, 39
Barnes Group Inc., 13
Barry Callebaut AG, 29
Bassett Furniture Industries, Inc., 18
Bath Iron Works, 12; 36 (upd.)
Beckman Coulter, Inc., 22
Beckman Instruments, Inc., 14
Becton, Dickinson & Company, 36 (upd.)
Beiersdorf AG, 29
Belden Inc., 19
Bell Sports Corporation, 16; 44 (upd.)
Beloit Corporation, 14
Benjamin Moore & Co., 13; 38 (upd.)
Bernina Holding AG, 47
Berry Plastics Corporation, 21
BIC Corporation, 8; 23 (upd.)
BICC PLC, III
Billabong International Ltd., 44
Binks Sames Corporation, 21
Binney & Smith Inc., 25
Biomet, Inc., 10
BISSELL Inc., 9; 30 (upd.)
The Black & Decker Corporation, III; 20
   (upd.)
Blount International, Inc., 48 (upd.)
Blount, Inc., 12
Blyth Industries, Inc., 18
BMC Industries, Inc., 17
Bodum Design Group AG, 47
Boral Limited, 43 (upd.)
Borden, Inc., 22 (upd.)
Borg-Warner Automotive, Inc., 14
Borg-Warner Corporation, III
Boston Scientific Corporation, 37
The Boyds Collection, Ltd., 29
Brannock Device Company, 48
Brass Eagle Inc., 34
Bridgeport Machines, Inc., 17
Briggs & Stratton Corporation, 8; 27 (upd.)
BRIO AB, 24
British Vita plc, 33 (upd.)
Brother Industries, Ltd., 14
Brown & Sharpe Manufacturing Co., 23
Brown-Forman Corporation, 38 (upd.)

MANUFACTURING (continued)

MATERIALS

MINING & METALS

PERSONAL SERVICES

PETROLEUM

REAL ESTATE

RETAIL & WHOLESALE

TELECOMMUNICATIONS

WASTE SERVICES

GEOGRAPHIC INDEX

Geographic Index

Japan

NOTES ON CONTRIBUTORS

Notes on Contributors

BIANCO, David P. Freelance writer, editor, and publishing consultant.

BISCONTINI, Tracey Vasil. Pennsylvania-based freelance writer, editor, and columnist.

BROWN, Erin. Freelance writer.

BRYNILDSSEN, Shawna. Freelance writer and editor based in Bloomington, Indiana.

COHEN, M. L. Novelist and freelance writer living in Paris.

COVELL, Jeffrey L. Seattle-based freelance writer.

CULLIGAN, Susan B. Minnesota-based freelance writer.

DINGER, Ed. Freelance writer and editor based in Bronx, New York.

HEER-FORSBERG, Mary. Freelance writer in the Minneapolis area.

INGRAM, Frederick C. Utah-based business writer who has contributed to *GSA Business, Appalachian Trailway News,* the *Encyclopedia of Business,* the *Encyclopedia of Global Industries,* the *Encyclopedia of Consumer Brands,* and other regional and trade publications.

LORENZ, Sarah Ruth. Minnesota-based freelance writer.

PEIPPO, Kathleen. Minneapolis-based freelance writer.

RHODES, Nelson. Freelance editor, writer, and consultant in the Chicago area.

ROTHBURD, Carrie. Freelance writer and editor specializing in corporate profiles, academic texts, and academic journal articles.

SALAMIE, David E. Part-owner of InfoWorks Development Group, a reference publication development and editorial services company.

TRADII, Mary. Freelance writer based in Denver, Colorado.

UHLE, Frank. Ann Arbor-based freelance writer; movie projectionist, disc jockey, and staff member of *Psychotronic Video* magazine.

WALDEN, David M. Freelance writer and historian in Salt Lake City; adjunct history instructor at Salt Lake City Community College.

WOODWARD, A. Freelance writer.